ROCK & ROLL REFERENCE SERIES

TOM SCHULTHEISS, Series Editor

1 ALL TOGETHER NOW
The First Complete
Beatles Discography, 1961-1975
by Harry Castleman & Walter J. Podrazik

2 THE BEATLES AGAIN
[Sequel to **ALL TOGETHER NOW**]
by Harry Castleman & Walter J. Podrazik

3 A DAY IN THE LIFE
The Beatles Day-By-Day, 1960-1970
by Tom Schultheiss

4 THINGS WE SAID TODAY
The Complete Lyrics and a Concordance
to The Beatles' Songs, 1962-1970
by Colin Campbell & Allan Murphy

5 YOU CAN'T DO THAT !
Beatles Bootlegs
& Novelty Records, 1963-1980
by Charles Reinhart

6 SURF'S UP !
The Beach Boys On Record, 1961-1981
by Brad Elliott

7 COLLECTING THE BEATLES
An Introduction & Price Guide
to Fab Four Collectibles, Records
& Memorabilia
by Barbara Fenick

8 JAILHOUSE ROCK
The Bootleg Records
of Elvis Presley, 1970-1983
by Lee Cotten & Howard A. De Witt

9 THE LITERARY LENNON
A Comedy of Letters
*The First Study of All the Major
and Minor Writings of John Lennon*
by Dr. James Sauceda

10 THE END OF THE BEATLES ?
Sequel to *The Beatles Again*
and *All Together Now*
by Harry Castleman & Walter J. Podrazik

11 HERE, THERE & EVERYWHERE
The First International
Beatles Bibliography, 1962-1982
by Carol D. Terry

12 CHUCK BERRY
Rock 'N' Roll Music
Second Edition, Revised
by Howard A. De Witt

13 ALL SHOOK UP
Elvis Day-By-Day, 1954-1977
by Lee Cotten

14 WHO'S NEW WAVE IN MUSIC
An Illustrated Encyclopedia, 1976-1982
by David Bianco

**15 THE ILLUSTRATED DISCOGRAPHY
OF SURF MUSIC, 1961-1965**
Second Edition, Revised
by John Blair

16 COLLECTING THE BEATLES, VOL. 2
An Introduction & Price Guide
to Fab Four Collectibles, Records
& Memorabilia
by Barbara Fenick

17 HEART OF STONE
The Definitive Rolling Stones
Discography, 1962-1983
by Felix Aeppli

18 BEATLEFAN
The Authoritative
Publication of Record
For Fans of the Beatles, Vols. 1 & 2
Reprint Edition, With Additions

ROCK & ROLL REMEMBRANCES SERIES

TOM SCHULTHEISS, Series Editor

1 AS I WRITE THIS LETTER
An American Generation
Remembers The Beatles
by Marc A. Catone

2 THE LONGEST COCKTAIL PARTY
An Insider's Diary of The Beatles
Reprint Edition, With Additions
by Richard DiLello

3 AS TIME GOES BY
Living In The Sixties
Reprint Edition, With Additions
by Derek Taylor

4 A CELLARFUL OF NOISE
Reprint Edition, With Additions
by Brian Epstein

5 THE BEATLES AT THE BEEB
The Story of Their Radio Career, 1962-65
Reprint Edition, With Additions
by Kevin Howlett

6 THE BEATLES READER
A Selection of Contemporary Views,
News & Reviews of The Beatles
In Their Heyday
by Charles P. Neises

7 THE BEATLES DOWN UNDER
Reprint Edition, With Additions
by Glenn A. Baker

Here, there & everywhere

The First International Beatles Bibliography, 1962-1982

Compiled and edited by

Carol D. Terry

pierian press

1985

ISBN 0-87650-163-3
LC 84-61229

PIERIAN PRESS
P.O. Box 1808
Ann Arbor, MI 48106

Contents

Foreword, by Tom Schultheiss vii
Preface ix
   Acknowledgements x
Introduction xi

How to Use This Book xiii
Guidelines for Contributors xix

BIBLIOGRAPHY SECTIONS
   Books 1
   Chapters & Parts of Books 17
   Fan Magazines 27
   Magazine Articles 33
   Newspaper Articles 113
   Periodical Issues 141
   Reviews of Books 145
   Reviews of Films 155
   Reviews of Recordings 161
   Sheet Music Books 171

ADDRESS DIRECTORY 175

INDEXES
   Author Index 179
   Title Index 193
   Subject Index 243

Illustrations   vi, viii, xxii, 8, 16, 26, 32, 46, 59, 72, 86, 98,
   114, 128, 140, 144, 154, 170, 176, 178, 242, 283

Foreword

It is with great pleasure and pride that Pierian Press finally releases Carol Terry's long awaited Beatles bibliography, surely the most ambitious and labor intensive Beatles volume we have ever published. As such, it is the forerunner of what we hope will evolve into a series of bibliographic volumes devoted to rock-and-roll figures — it should be noted that the Press is already committed to just such a volume on the Rolling Stones, *Yesterday's Papers*, by Jessica MacPhail — and, we hope, eventual online access to such databases for rock researchers and fans.

Purchasers of this volume, those with other than an avid interest in the Beatles as well as the millions of fans devoted to the group, will undoubtedly recognize it for what it is, a unique and truly monumental work of reference, and one which has for too long — quite amazingly — needed to be done. Beatle fans, while being in the best position to attest to the book's value, will in all probability also be its most severe critics, and could doubtless produce hundreds and even thousands of articles and news notes not listed here from scrapbooks, attic trunks and closet cubbyholes. Indeed, thousands of other citations were deliberately withheld from inclusion in *Here, There & Everywhere* due to questionable or very incomplete data. The number of possible entries, to anyone familiar with Beatles literature, can easily be estimated to be in the hundreds of thousands.

Despite such potential criticisms and ominous figures, there should be no apologies extended for the "limited" size and scope of this book. With approximately 8000 citations, and three enormous indexes, it is an unprecedented accomplishment in the universe of Beatles publications and, despite last year's publication of Bill Harry's *Paperback Writers*, it remains — in the truest sense — unquestionably *the first* international Beatles bibliography, the subtitle we announced for it several years ago.

Harry's paperback volume, deliberately short on bibliographic details and long on photographs, was accorded the luxury of two subtitles by its publisher: *The History of the Beatles In Print*, and *An Illustrated Bibliography*. It is decidedly more the former than the latter, and serves much more as a discursive survey and readable guide designed for browsing (major sections are not arranged alphabetically, but chronologically). The two volumes are simply not comparable in any critical sense; they exist for different reasons.

Well over three years of work is reflected in the pages which follow. The undertaking has been incredibly formidable, has involved thousands of hours of compilation, data entry, proofreading, corrections, programming, programming disasters, more proofreading, more corrections, subject analysis and assignment, and more corrections. The result is an unparalleled compilation, featuring the most extensive list of books on the Beatles ever assembled, as well as many other hitherto unequaled features.

And it is only the beginning.

Maintained as an ongoing computer database, future expanded editions of this work are planned. Contributions and corrections from all users of this volume, from all areas and in all languages of the world are encouraged, in accordance with the "Guidelines for Contributors" printed herein. This invitation is addressed especially to those who may find "shortcomings" in terms of the amount of information provided in *Here, There & Everywhere*!

Congratulations to Carol Terry for toughing it out through the harrowing, maddening process of bringing this volume to fruition. A magnificent achievement! And one probably deserving of a good rest. But, being the trooper that she is, I'm sure Carol is even now — perhaps in feeble, faltering, and unbelieving intonations — forcing her lips to form the words: "On to the next edition!"

Tom Schultheiss

Preface

Once upon a time this bibliography was a mere personal whim. At first, my simple idea was to find some good articles on the Beatles for a "sort of scrapbook." I envisioned making photocopies of interviews, good pictures, etc., and gathering them into a personal deluxe Beatles memory book.

Although my mother had good-naturedly indulged me with countless magazines years before, most had been long since cut up posthaste for artistic collages, book covers, and so on. A degree of personal financial independence allowed me to start buying books on the Beatles myself, but I was not always pleased with their quality or content. Hence, the idea for my own creation took form.

It wasn't long before I was totally amazed at how many articles there were. I kept thinking that once I had collected just a few more references, I'd go back and look at them all and select the best ones to copy. Soon, however, the challenge of the citation hunter/gatherer role was not just a means to an end, but an end in itself . . . for which there was no end in sight! Selectivity was left behind as the sheer excitement of accumulating hundreds of slips of paper steadily grew.

One day I became aware of the Beatles books published by the Pierian Press — the Castleman/Podrazil discographies, the Campbell/Murphy concordance, and the Schultheiss chronology — and was very impressed. (This was, of course, before they themselves knew they had the makings of an unending "Rock & Roll Reference Series" in their catalog.) At a time when my bookshelf over-runneth with shallow and even sometimes exploitative titles (of which, regrettably, there have recently been many more), here was one publisher producing actual reference books on the Beatles.

Anyway, I couldn't resist writing to Pierian to see if they might be interested in publishing a bibliography. It certainly seemed logical that they might, based on the nature of the works mentioned above. Now that one could find out what the Beatles had recorded and what they said on the recordings, even how often they said it, and when and where they said and did things, one might as well be able to find out what they said in interviews and what others said about them and their work. So, I picked the name Tom Schultheiss out of the introductory matter of one book and wrote.

Sure enough, I heard back straightaway from Himself that indeed they were interested and ready to sign a contract. (Actually, Tom had already thought of doing a bibliography, once had someone at the Press working on one, but hadn't found anyone willing to finish the job.)

Oh, yes! I remember it well. The excitement of being published. The thrill of producing something on the Beatles that would be useful to others, even those born too late to remember them personally. Little did I know then that the expression "publishing lag" was more than just a catchy phrase. Naive as I was, I figured — a bit more work and a little polish and it would be ready to go, right!? But here it is . . . four years later and we're just going to press. Actually, the bulk of my hunter/gatherer work was completed light years ago, but I hadn't anticipated what would be involved in computerizing the database. Since then, many hours of photocopying citations, computer inputing, proofing, deleting duplicates, verifying, proofing, indexing, inputing correctings, proofing, etc., have been lavished on this work to make it as user friendly as possible.

That is the story of how and why this book came to be. I hope it will be interesting and helpful to researchers, collectors, and fans in general. Maybe now I'll get to making that wonderful scrapbook!

CDT

Acknowledgements

To Himself, Tom Schultheiss . . . Thanks for the enthusiastic response to my inquiry and for holding my hand ever since.

To those who've shared magazines or contributed entries . . . Thanks for your interest and help: Gerhard Karl Bohrer, Brian R. Budde, Carl S. Caplan, Barbara Fenick, Arno Guzek, John Landau, Fred Lark, Mike Lefebvre, Grace Meisel, Wally Podrazik, Nancy Schnepp, Peter Schuster, David Schwartz, Pat Simmons, David J. Smith, Donna Ridley Smith, Beverly Trietsch, Mary Jo Truttschel, Keith Vaughan, and Jacques Volcouve. Thanks, too, to Kathy Para at Pierian Press for so ably handling the data entry for most of this book.

To those who've often asked over the years how things were coming, and listened sympathetically when I made small whimpering noises about shuffling through printouts or shared my excitement when things seemed to be moving along . . . Thanks so much for your encouragement.

To my best friends, Imogene and Jeannie . . . Very special thanks for all your love and support.

To the Beatles, collectively and individually . . . Thanks for so many things including the aura, if you will, that would make such a potentially tedious project as this one fun. Thanks for all the untold and continuing hours of listening pleasure. For helping to begin my love of music. For the electric excitement of seeing you twenty years ago, as well as the warm happy feeling I can't help getting when listening to the old recordings today. Thanks for the current and future pleasure of waiting for a new film, record, or just news. My memories of growing up are interwoven with memories of you. I hope you get personal pleasure and satisfaction from knowing how you've enriched the lives of so many. I wish that each of you and yours will always be well, happy, and content.

Introduction

PURPOSE

The raison d'etre of this book is to provide access to information on the Beatles. At the same time, it assumes a certain degree of familiarity with the lives and careers of the Beatles as a group and as individuals (hereafter, we will use "Beatles" to refer to both group and solo contexts for the sake of convenience).

To attempt to make this work into something other than strictly a bibliography would involve the inclusion of much more information already contained in other books (notably, other reference books by Pierian Press!), and so it was decided that it was not within the purview of this work to explain the reasons for the presence of many of the citations.

It may be that you do not know who Stuart Sutcliffe was and why a catalog of his paintings is listed in the Books section; or why reviews of the films "All This And World War II" and "Time Bandits" are included; or what the LP called **The Decca Tapes** is all about; or why fan clubs for Cilla Black or Jane Asher are listed in the Fan Magazines section; or why materials on The Rutles are included. Answers lie within any number of discographies and biographies on the Beatles, and so are not dealt with here.

SCOPE

This work was designed not as a selective bibliography, but rather as a comprehensive enumerative bibliography listing as much as could be gathered with the tools and resources available to the compiler.

Much of what is written about the Beatles is inaccurate — falsehoods at worst, incomplete retellings at best. Of course, much is also interesting, historical, insightful, etc. This tool does not attempt to distinguish which is which. My intention is merely to provide access to as many varied items as possible so that the user may decide on their value or relevance to his or her own information needs.

The basic time span covered by this book is 1962 through 1982. While there are some citations from these two early years, they are few compared to 1964, when items started appearing heavily. Active searching for magazine and newspaper articles for this volume ceased with 1982; however, a number of randomly collected entries beyond this general cutoff date do appear. A concerted effort was made to include new books through the end of 1984, the publication of which is somewhat more easily monitored.

This important section, the Fan Magazines section, and the Address Directory are particularly current in this respect.

INCLUSIVENESS

Basically, this book includes citations culled from available indexes and reference tools, along with others collected and verified first hand. Those in the latter category include newly indexed citations gathered from *Rolling Stone* magazine which, due to its uniqueness and incomplete indexing coverage, was hand-searched issue by issue. We hope very much to have the opportunity to include citations collected through similar searches of periodicals like *Melody Maker* and *New Musical Express* for the next edition of this work, although some coverage of the former title by indexing services is reflected here. Unfortunately, we did not have access to many non-U.S. indexing tools or magazines, so there are not as many foreign citations as we would like to have included. Again, we hope to provide access to materials covered by many of these tools in another edition.

Also included are many valuable but previously unindexed citations — entries purposefully collected from major Beatles magazines like *The Beatles Book*, *Beatlefan*, *Beatles Unlimited*, etc., as well as from important specialized magazines known to frequently carry Beatles articles, such as *Record Collector*. (The importance of these small periodicals, chosen both for their overall quality but also for their inexpensiveness and continued availability, cannot be overemphasized. As repositories of relevant and well done pieces on the Beatles, they are unequaled in the general literature.) Other entries have been discovered in footnotes and bibliographies, publisher catalogs, dealer lists, etc., and through serendipity.

For every citation from an indexed periodical, there are undoubtedly scores of unindexed ones, many from magazines published in the early sixties. We have many hundreds of incomplete citations for such articles, but have decided not to include them in this work. (Oh, for a nickel for every one this compiler cut up or tossed away in her youth!) Many of the periodicals they appear in have by now disappeared from circulation, are in the hands of memorabilia dealers, or are hidden in attics and closets of unknowing owners. To readers who locate any of these, we and other readers would greatly appreciate your sharing them with us. Please see the "Guidelines for Contributors" section for details. This section will also provide instructions on sharing your information on fan clubs and their publications, should you have additional or more recent information than that in Section 3, Fan Magazines.

Hours of proofreading have gone into making this work as error free as possible. Numerical gaps in the list of entries in many sections of the bibliography reflect the fact that we have continued to edit, modify and delete information up to the last possible moment. However, it would be a miracle if no errors existed. If in the course of using this tool you discover an error, either typographical or an actual incorrect entry, please do let us know so that it can be corrected. Thank you.

How to Use This Book

Here, There & Everywhere is divided into fourteen major sections: ten sections with bibliographic entries grouped according to format, an address directory of Beatles fan magazines and organizations, and three index sections (authors, titles, subjects). Although the logical starting place for many searches will be the subject index, the user should become familiar with all the individual sections. For some information needs, going directly to a particular section will prove the most helpful approach.

Each section is arranged alphabetically, letter-by-letter (spaces and marks of punctuation are ignored). In most of the bibliographic sections, entries are ordered according to the author's last name, or by title if there is no author given. (Citations in the reviews sections are grouped under the *title reviewed*.) Personal names beginning with the same word as an "unauthored" title entry precede such title entries. Jointly authored entries (two or more names) follow the sequence of entries by the principal author writing as an individual. Throughout, simple abbreviations are alphabetized as if spelled out, complex abbreviations are filed as spelled (as if they were a word). Names beginning with "Mc" are filed as if spelled "Mac," and are interfiled with other entries actually beginning with "Mac." When in alphabetical proximity, sequences of dates have largely been left in chronological order; isolated dates and other numbers are filed as if spelled out.

Each bibliographic entry (citation) is preceded by a unique alphanumeric code — its individual entry number. The author, title and subject indexes contain references to these entry numbers, not to page numbers. This coded entry number may be thought of as the address in the book of each particular citation. The code consists of two parts — a letter (or letters), followed by a number. The letter(s) identify the section in which the citation can be found. Letter(s) are referred to hereafter as the prefix code. The number indicates where the citation falls within its section numerically.

The following is a list of all the sections, in order, with their prefix codes; this is followed by detailed discussions of each section individually:

Bibliographic Sections	Prefix Codes
BOOKS	B
CHAPTERS & PARTS OF BOOKS	C
FAN MAGAZINES	F
MAGAZINE ARTICLES	M
NEWSPAPER ARTICLES	N
PERIODICAL ISSUES	P
REVIEWS OF BOOKS	RB
REVIEWS OF FILMS	RF
REVIEWS OF RECORDINGS	RR
SHEET MUSIC BOOKS	S

Section 1: BOOKS

This is the most detailed and complete list of books relating to the Beatles ever published. Counting all variations found — original titles, translations, editions, and bindings — over 600 distinct publications devoted entirely or almost entirely to the Beatles (or *by* the Beatles) are listed in this section. No attempt has been made to list the various printings of the same edition of a book unless notable changes were made between such printings. *This all-important section is virtually complete through 1984.*

Editions of the same title are filed chronologically by date. Translations of English language titles are interfiled alphabetically by foreign title under the author's name. Typical citations include: author(s) and/or title; subtitle; edition; place of publication; publisher; year of publication; number of pages; binding — clothbound/hardbound (cl.) or paperback (pa.); presence of illustrations (illus.).

This section also includes some of the more popular lyrics and sheet music books likely to be found in bookstores (as opposed to record stores or music stores) — *The Compleat Beatles*, *Paul McCartney: Composer/Artist*, *The Beatles Illustrated Lyrics* — while most other sheet music books (songbooks) are listed in a section of their own.

It is possible that some periodical issues have inadvertently been included in this section as books, due to an inability to determine first hand the true nature of the publication named.

Also included in this section are such miscellaneous things as dissertations, exhibit catalogs, board games, posters, calendars and card sets.

If interested only in books on one individual, the most efficient method would be to consult the Subject Index, locating all the entry numbers under that person's name preceded by the prefix code for this section.

The prefix code for this section is B . . . for Books.

Section 2: CHAPTERS & PARTS OF BOOKS

This section provides nearly 350 citations to Beatles-related chapters, parts and mentions of the Beatles in books *not entirely devoted to the Beatles*, or in books devoted to the Beatles but containing many separately titled sections or contributions by various authors which leant themselves to further bibliographic analytics. In the latter case, the entire book so analyzed is also included in the Books section as a separate entry.

This section is comprised almost entirely of books handled by the compiler; therefore, the section could be much larger than it is. Though limited, it should be useful because it was compiled on the basis of titles that would be readily available in many public libraries. If you wish to search further than the titles listed here, you may use almost any music reference book and even general encyclopedias.

The prefix code is C . . . for Chapters.

Section 3: FAN MAGAZINES

This is the most comprehensive listing of active and defunct Beatles-related fan magazines (fanzines) ever assembled — 158 in all. Though international in scope, it is largely comprised of fanzines published in the U.S. Included is the most recent and detailed information that could be found: inclusive publication dates; place of publication; publisher/editor (often the same); cessation, absorption and supersession notes, etc. Only regularly published fan magazines are listed; for entire issues of periodicals devoted to the Beatles of other than a regular, fan-oriented nature, see the Periodical Issues section.

This section is arranged by the title of the magazine; names which appear to serve as both the name of the fanzine and the name of the publishing organization or fan club are common. Fan club names distinct from that of the publication itself appear as cross-references within this section, and are also accessible via the Subject Index. The names of the editors mentioned in this section appear in the Author Index.

An Address Directory of all currently active Beatles and Beatles-related fan publications and organizations around the world — some 50 of them — is included in this volume. When writing for subscription information or sample copies, *always include a stamped, self-addressed envelope.*

If interested only in titles associated with one individual, begin your search in the Subject Index.

The prefix code is F . . . for Fan magazine.

Section 4: MAGAZINE ARTICLES

Almost 3800 references to magazine articles are included in this section. This includes indexing of a number of the foremost Beatles fanzines, selected principally for their quality and their continued availability (both current and back issues).

Publications like *Variety* and *Rolling Stone* have been treated as magazines and indexed here, even though published in a tabloid format.

It is possible that some newspaper articles have inadvertently been included in this section due to an inability to determine first hand the true nature of the publication named.

Following the author and/or title, typical citations include: name of the publication; volume and/or issue number(s) (separated by a colon); date of publication (in parentheses); inclusive page numbers (preceded by "p" or "pp"); presence of illustrations (illus.).

General magazine issues which feature cover portraits of the Beatles are entered here by title, followed by date and issue information.

Except for conveniently accessing all magazine articles by a given author, it will be best to search this section through the Subject Index.

The prefix code is M . . . for Magazine.

Section 5: NEWSPAPER ARTICLES

Nearly 1200 newspaper articles are listed in this section, with newspapers defined as publications of a daily nature or those of other frequencies which are generally known as newspapers.

It is possible that some magazine articles have inadvertently been included in this section due to an inability to determine first hand the true nature of the publication named.

Most citations in this section are from several major newspapers: *The Times* (London), the *New York Times*, the *Christian Science Monitor*, the *Wall Street Journal*, the *Los Angeles Times*, etc. Others in smaller papers have been included as encountered, however.

As with magazine articles, typical citations adhere to a certain format: following the author and/or title of the article appears the name of the publication; volume and/or issue number(s) (separated by a colon); date of publication (in parentheses); inclusive page numbers (preceded by "p" or "pp"); and the presence of illustrations (illus.). However, in a sharp departure from magazine articles, *page references* to articles in publications like *The Times*, the *New York Times*, and others are comprised of two elements (and perhaps a colon). The first is the page number, the second is *the column on the page* where the article appears. (Columns 1 through 8 are denoted with the letters "a" through "h" by *The Times* (London); a reference to "14h" therefore means "page 14, column 8").

Also, Sunday sections of the *New York Times* other than the main newspaper sections are often identified by roman numerals which precede the date; thus, "IV (May 3, 1983) 3:4" means "Section 4, page

3, column 4" – perhaps a separate entertainment section or book review section (IV) for that Sunday.

As most authors of newspaper articles are not identified, access to this section is best made through the Title or Subject Index.

The prefix code is N . . . for Newspaper.

Section 6: **PERIODICAL ISSUES**

This section lists over 100 periodical issues of a special, usually one-time nature devoted entirely or almost entirely to the Beatles. Excluded are regularly issued fan-oriented periodicals devoted entirely to the Beatles, which are covered in the Fan Magazines section.

It is possible that a few books have inadvertently been included in this section as periodical issues due to an inability to determine first hand the true nature of the publication named.

Like *Section 2*, this list could be considerably larger had more of these elusive periodicals been available for examination. Many of the incomplete citations withheld from inclusion in this work would fall into this category. This type of publication is primarily of interest to collectors.

The prefix code is P . . . for Periodical.

Sections 7, 8 & 9: **REVIEWS OF . . .**

These three sections contain citations to reviews of books, films, and recordings respectively. Each section is arranged alphabetically by the title of the item reviewed.

. . . BOOKS

Over 650 citations appear in this section.

Reviews of different English language editions of the same book with the same title have been merged in a single list. Reviews of the same book published under different titles appear separately, according to the title used in the review.

Totally different books with identical titles have been differentiated by a parenthetical reference to the author's surname.

. . . FILMS

Some 425 review citations are included.

Feature length, educational and other 8mm and 16mm, and videocassettes are presented in one title sequence, with parenthetical format identifiers for all but the feature films.

. . . RECORDINGS

Close to 600 reviews of albums, EPs, singles, bootlegs, and a few novelty and other Beatles-related recordings are referenced.

Users uncertain of titles presumed to begin with the words "The Beatles" should search instead under the remaining portion of the title.

Reviews of the album variously known as **Hey Jude** and **The Beatles Again** appear under both titles.

Although some magazine or newspaper articles may include reviews, they are not listed here unless they were identified as a review in the indexes consulted or were otherwise known to be a review. Therefore, if you are interested in obtaining all the critical comments on a title, you will want to take note of not only the citations appearing in the review sections, but also any other references identified in the Subject Index (those in other sections). If you want to read only reviews of a title, it should be enough to go directly to the lists in the review section.

The prefix code for *Section 7* is RB . . . Reviews/ Books.

The prefix code for *Section 8* is RF . . . Reviews/ Films.

The prefix code for *Section 9* is RR . . . Reviews/ Recordings.

Section 10: **SHEET MUSIC BOOKS**

This section lists 170 sheet music books (song-books) by title, principally those published in the U.S. and U.K. Only references to anthologies were collected for the present volume; published sheet music for individual songs was not sought out.

Such volumes often carry no publication date, and so this either does not appear or has been subsumed in many cases on the basis of the general appearance of the volume itself.

Editions of sheet music books more likely to be carried in bookstores (rather than in music stores) are listed in the Books section (e.g., *The Compleat Beatles*, *The Beatles Illustrated Lyrics*, *Paul McCartney: Composer/Artist*, etc.).

By using the Subject Index, sheet music books can be approached according to a particular instrumental scoring or arrangement (e.g., flute songbooks, guitar songbooks, piano songbooks, etc.), by specific composer (e.g., Lennon, McCartney, Harrison, Starr, etc.), or by particular album score (**Revolver, Let It Be, Plastic Ono Band, Double Fantasy**, etc.).

The prefix code is S . . . for Sheet music.

Section 11: **ADDRESS DIRECTORY**

This is the most complete international address list of currently active Beatles fanzines, fan clubs and information services available today. All addresses have been verified through personal correspondence; although steps to insure currency have been maintained up to press time (e.g., the address for *Cavern Mecca* was deleted when the publication ceased in December 1984), the fluid nature of fanzine publications may have resulted in some further additions or deletions not reflected in this listing.

The Directory is worldwide in scope, but with heavy U.S. emphasis. Some addresses represent recently formed entities with only a few members or subscribers, but a number of older organizations have hundreds or even thousands of members. A few are surprisingly large (the Japanese *Beatles Cine Club* claims a membership of 50,000). Special mention should be made of *The Beatles Book*, which was the Beatles' official monthly fan club publication begun in the early sixties. All of the original monthly issues were reprinted beginning in the seventies (though some of these are now also out-of-print), and the title has continued beyond the reissues with slick, attractive and all new monthlies. Very useful articles on the Beatles also appear in the same publisher's magazine, *Record Collector*, also fully indexed in this book.

When writing to any of the addresses listed in the Directory for more information or sample issues, *it is imperative that inquiries be accompanied by a stamped, self-addressed envelope or international reply coupon.* Most such publications or clubs are operated on shoestring budgets by as few as one or two persons, and failure to include the means to respond to your inquiry will probably result in no reply at all.

Prices given represent, in most cases, the price in U.S. dollars *for U.S. subscribers.* Inquire about exact rates to fit your geographical location before sending payment. Foreign subscribers or U.S. subscribers who order overseas titles should expect to be charged higher rates or additional postage costs.

Sections 11, 12 & 13: INDEXES

The final three sections of *Here, There & Everywhere* are the index sections: Author Index (over 4800 references), Title Index (over 7100 references), and Subject Index (some 13,500 references). All three continue the letter-by-letter arrangement described above, and all offer running heads at the top of each page which identifies the beginning word of the first and last name, title or subject on the page.

Author Index entries are in sequence by surname. Surnames containing prefixes such as "De," "O'," "Van," or "Von" are filed as single names beginning with the prefixes. Again, names prefixed with "Mc" are interfiled as if spelled "Mac."

Names have generally been recorded as they appear in the various sources used to compile this work. Therefore, the same author may be listed in more than one place if his or her forename was found in varying forms (e.g., B., Bill, and William). The prodigious task of verifying that all forms of a name were in fact referring to the same person, and then collecting all such references under one form, would have added years more to the publication schedule of this work and so was not undertaken.

Using the Subject Index

Approximately one third of this volume is given over to indexes, critical features in any work of such magnitude. The most important index, and the most difficult to compile, has been the Subject Index.

User friendliness was the goal in mind in the creation of this index, which is designed to accomodate very specific interests. If searching for information on a very specific topic, try that topic in the index. Although headings have been arbitrarily created for this work, they are hopefully logical enough to be used easily. If your topic is found, begin by searching the citations recorded under that heading. You may need to go no further.

If your topic is not found or if you need more information, move to a slightly less specific heading or headings, then to an even less specific one, and so on. The broadest headings we have used in the Index are the names of individuals with no further indication of the subject (e.g., Lennon, John). This may seem very general, but it does at least identify the primary subject of an article which otherwise has a very ambiguous or totally nondescriptive title, and which could not be examined first hand. The subject heading "Beatles" by itself would, of course, have been too unwieldy to be very useful, and so has been subdivided into many subheadings. Citations whose subjects were unknown (because we were unable to examine them) or were too broad in nature to be indexed more specifically than by "Beatles" are not represented in the Subject Index.

In using any of the indexes, simply make note of the letter(s) used as the prefix code (which identify the section where the entry can be found), and the number sequence which follows (the address of the entry within each section). Running heads at the top of each of the ten bibliographic sections will help you to quickly locate not only the section, but also the first and last entry on the page. These features will prove especially useful if you are looking for a certain type of source. If searching only for newspaper articles, for example, you need copy down only those entry numbers beginning with the letter 'N'. If you are looking for a certain magazine article, copy only the citations beginning with 'M'. If only reviews, you'll want to record only those preceded by the pertinent review section code, RB, RF or RR.

The following is a list of pointers designed to give users some familiarity with features of the Subject Index. The more intensively you plan to use this index, the more helpful this information will be:

1. "See" references: These cross-references direct you from one subject heading to another "preferred" (for our purposes) heading under which citations have been grouped; examples:
Interviews see names of individuals
Starkey, Richard see Starr, Ringo
The first example directs you to the specific name of an individual, under which "interview" is used as a subheading (e.g., Harrison, George: interview); the

second identifies the preferred name of an individual known by more than one name.

2. "See also" references: These cross-references direct you to *additional* entries pertaining to your subject which are grouped under a different but related subject heading; example:

'Get Back' (LP) see also Let It Be (LP)

You should check under both headings given in a "see also" reference to find the maximum number of entries on your subject. (Such references refer from both headings, one to the other.)

These two types of cross-references have been used whenever it seemed they would be helpful to the user. Occasionally, however, the same entry numbers are listed under more than one heading rather than being cross-referenced. This is especially true where one heading seemed as important or as likely to be checked first as the other.

3. Title formats: Titles of films, songs, magazines, plays, tv or radio shows are within quotation marks in the Subject Index, as they are when referred to in the subject notes which conclude many entries.

Titles of LPs, EPs, and books are in capital letters, as they are in the review sections.

All titles are followed by parenthetical statements which serve to distinguish between different things with the same title; for example: "Help!" (film), HELP! (LP), and "Help!" (song).

4. Subject headings: Headings for this index were designed to reflect the many varied interests and needs of knowledgeable users of this volume, but should nevertheless serve anyone new to the subject in a clear and straightforward fashion. Every attempt has been made at consistency in indexing. If there is any question about what a particular subject heading refers to, a turn back to one of the referenced citations should give a better idea.

(a.) As already indicated, very specific searches are possible which, if they prove unfruitful, can be followed by slightly less specific searches; example:

Lennon, John: remark on popularity of Beatles
    and Jesus – radio ban

This is a very specific heading. A slightly less specific one would be:

Lennon, John: remark on popularity of Beatles
    and Jesus

This second heading refers to entries which may or may not mention a radio ban, but do deal with the same general subject. A much less specific heading would simply be:

Lennon, John

This last type of heading is used only when a more specific heading could not be determined; it serves to prevent the necessity for users of having to scan through the title index or the main sections in search of articles on an individual. Such headings are not cross-referenced elsewhere in the index.

Another example of a more general heading used when specifics are unknown is:

Beatles: 1966

This heading identifies for the user those entries known to deal with the Beatles in 1966 (with no specifics); it does *not* indicate the date of publication of the entry. Again, it serves to at least isolate and alert the user to entries in a general way, though the narrower subject may not have been determined further; conversely, other entries recorded under more specific headings may also deal with the Beatles in 1966, but are not cross-referenced back to the less specific headings.

(b.) Certain types of headings have also been used to group particular topics together when it was thought this might be helpful to the user. An example would be the heading "Legal action: . . .".

All entries under this type of heading deal with actual legal actions as opposed to offering general information; example:

Legal action: John Lennon – deportation

This heading indexes only entries which discuss or report upon specific legal actions involving John Lennon's deportation trial or proceedings. A more general approach to the subject of Lennon's deportation would be:

Lennon, John: deportation

This heading covers not only all the entries listed under the "Legal action:" heading, but also other, more general citations on the subject.

Another example of entries grouped together on the basis of shared characteristics would be the heading:

Beatles: early American press

This refers to citations published in late 1963 or early 1964, and the heading serves to group initial U.S. press reaction together. (These entries may also be accessible through other subject headings.)

5. Unindexed entries: When it was not possible to examine a book or article, or to determine the subject of an entry from the title or by other means, it could not be indexed for the Subject Index. There are relatively few unindexed entries when compared to those which have been indexed. However, in order to fully exploit the bibliography, it is important to keep them in mind. You may still access such entries in several ways:

You may approach them by the author's name, if known, through the Author Index.

You may scan the Title Index for potentially relevant titles, keeping in mind that those which are very vague are more likely to be the ones which are unindexed.

You may also scan through citations in the individual sections of the book, again keeping in mind the limitations of the indexing work which has been done. Titles giving no clue as to their subject, especially those of more obscure publications, have probably not been available for examination and are more likely to be those which are not indexed by subject.

Guidelines for Contributors

When confronting the subject of the Beatles, the temptation for the erstwhile bibliographer — faced with the task of gathering citations for a resource guide on a topic which seems to stretch limitlessly to the horizon (the Beatles are quite literally "here, there and everywhere") — may be to throw up their hands in despair and feverishly exclaim "Selective Bibliography!" This has always seemed to me a bit faint-hearted, and not a little misleading. The premise behind selectivity, so I assume, is to present the best, the most useful, the most accessible, the most valuable — in short, a sampling "selected" from a familiarity with and an exposure to *all* or nearly all of the materials available. But, if sifting through *all* of the citations pertinent to a subject in a field where no comprehensive bibliography exists, why not take the comprehensive approach? In the absence of such an all-encompassing resource, one can only assume a reluctance on the part of the compiler to delve, to search — in other words, to do the *work* — and one comes away holding the "selective" effort in some suspicion as a result.

All of this may serve to partially explain why there has been no major attempt at a formally structured Beatles bibliography before, selective or otherwise: the amount of information is staggering. Most interesting of all to observe will be the reaction of writers and scholars to the availability of this work, insofar as the production of books on the Beatles has already been so prodigious *without* it. What will they be encouraged to publish now that they have easy access to the work of others?

It was with considerations such as these in mind that the goal of this project, once begun so innocently for personal reasons, changed to one of gathering *everything ever printed everywhere* into a comprehensive listing which would identify and make sense of the vast universe of Beatles literature, leaving selectivity to a later date. As time passed, it was recognized that this ambitious idea could not be accomplished alone, as the list of contributors in the acknowledgements of this work testifies.

This section on guidelines is designed to invite many more people to contribute to future editions of this volume, and to thereby make the goal of comprehensiveness even more of a reality. Do you have to be a librarian or bibliographer to contribute? No! Although some professionals may shudder at the prospect of unlettered "mere fans" doing the work of a professional, we have found fans to be among the most enthusiastic, dedicated and — dare I say — fanatical in their devotion to getting *everything*, getting it *right*, and getting it *done*. Professionals who are unfamiliar with their own history will be surprised to learn that the turn of the century forerunners of the commercially produced indexes they rely so heavily upon today were the fruits of just such "cooperative indexing" efforts, and did not spring full-grown from the head of H.W. Wilson (namesake of a leading indexing firm) or other more structured entities.

How can you help? There are many newspapers and periodicals which are not indexed by indexing services, and you can be responsible for going back to 1962 and searching through issues by hand (assuming you have access to them in a library near you, or in a personal collection). There are many music books which have entire chapters or other sections devoted to the Beatles, and these, too, are largely unindexed. You can locate groups of such books in your local library (they are generally all in one place) and peruse them by hand. You may have a personal collection of all sorts of printed materials — even things not presently covered in *Here, There & Everwhere*, such as concert programs or press packages for recordings — which you can dig out of your closet and make a list of for our next edition. Perhaps you have a pile of early "teen" magazines in your attic? Or, perhaps you have an entire back run of an old Beatles fan magazine, and can give us more details — when it began, when it stopped publishing — for our Fan Magazines section? Or, you may have access to a large library which has holdings of newspaper and magazine indexes which we do not have access to, and can search through such indexes for us? What you do will largely be up to you and your motivation for contributing your time. Most importantly, *don't start doing things without contacting us first*, so that your efforts can be coordinated with the work of others, thus avoiding duplication.

We are especially interested in volunteers in the United Kingdom, Europe, and other parts of the world. Individuals with entire collections, random early issues or clippings from British music papers and newspapers could make an especially important contribution. Those in other countries can help in gathering information on books published in their country as well as other materials. There are opportunities for roles as "national editors" for individuals willing to coordinate the activities of others within their own nation or locality.

If you do not wish to spend your time searching or indexing the materials you have available to you but are willing to briefly loan them out for this purpose or allow someone to come and examine them, we would like the opportunity to put another volunteer in touch with you. Let us know what you have, and what you are willing to do.

There are many ways that volunteers can make a meaningful contribution to the next edition of *Here, There & Everywhere*. Write to us and let us know your interests, resources and capabilities. You will be sent very detailed guidelines on the form in which you should make your submissions; do not send anything in before requesting these format instructions. Every individual who makes a significant contribution to our next edition will be acknowledged in the book (sorry, sending in just one magazine clipping to get your name in the book doesn't count). To get involved in this massive data gathering process, please write to: Carol Terry c/o Pierian Press, P.O. Box 1808, Ann Arbor, Michigan 48106 U.S.A.

Thank you!

Here, there & everywhere

The First International Beatles Bibliography, 1962-1982

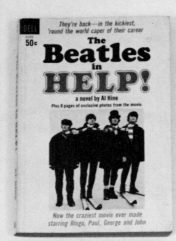

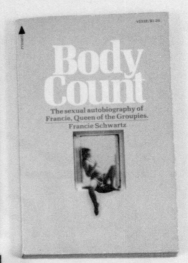

STRAWBERRY FIELDS FOREVER:
JOHN LENNON REMEMBERED

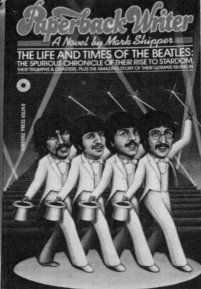

HOW I
WON THE
WAR

A NOVEL BY PATRICK RYAN · NOW A UNITED ARTISTS FILM
STARRING JOHN LENNON AND DIRECTED BY RICHARD LESTER

B 0001 Achard, Maurice. Pour John Lennon.
        Paris, France: Alain Moreau, 1981.
        130pp. pa.
B 0002 Adler, Bill, ed. Dear Beatles. London:
        Blond & Briggs, 1964. 48pp. cl. illus.
        (Fan letters.)
B 0003 Adler, Bill, ed. Dear Beatles. New York:
        Grosset & Dunlap/Wonder, 1966. 48pp. cl.
        illus.
        (Fan letters.)
B 0004 Adler, Bill, ed. Love Letters To The Beatles.
        Don Mills, Ont.: Longmans, 1964. 92pp.
        illus.
        (Fan letters.)
B 0005 Adler, Bill, ed. Love Letters To The Beatles.
        London: Anthony Blond, 1964. 92pp. illus.
        (Fan letters.)
B 0006 Adler, Bill, ed. Love Letters To The Beatles.
        New York: G.P. Putnam's, 1964. 92pp. illus.
        (Fan letters.)
B 0007 Aldridge, Alan, ed. The Beatles Illustrated
        Lyrics. London: Macdonald, 1969. 156pp.
        illus.
B 0008 Aldridge, Alan, ed. The Beatles Illustrated
        Lyrics (1st American ed.). New York:
        Delacorte/Seymour Lawrence, 1969. 156pp.
        cl. and pa. illus.
B 0009 Aldridge, Alan, ed. The Beatles Illustrated
        Lyrics (1st Dell edition). New York: Dell,
        1972. 156pp. cl. and pa. illus.
        (Reprint of the 1969 Delacorte edition.)
B 0010 Aldridge, Alan, ed. The Beatles Illustrated
        Lyrics. New York:
        Delta/Seymour Lawrence Book, 1980.
        156pp. cl. and pa. illus.
B 0011 Aldridge, Alan, ed. The Beatles Illustrated
        Lyrics. London: Macdonald/Futura, 1980.
        156pp. cl. and pa. illus.
B 0012 Aldridge, Alan, ed. The Beatles Illustrated
        Lyrics 2. London: BPC Publishing, 1971.
        128pp. pa. illus.
B 0013 Aldridge, Alan, ed. The Beatles Illustrated
        Lyrics 2 (1st American ed.). New York:
        Delacorte/Seymour Lawrence, 1971. 124pp.
        cl. and pa. illus.
B 0014 Aldridge, Alan, ed. The Beatles Illustrated
        Lyrics 2. London: Macdonald/Futura, 1980.
        126pp. cl. and pa. illus.
B 0015 Aldridge, Alan, ed. The Beatles Illustrated
        Lyrics 2. New York:
        Delta/Seymour Lawrence Book, 1980.
        126pp. cl. and pa. illus.
B 0016 Aldridge, Alan, ed. The Beatles Illustreret
        Sangbog, translated by J. K. Nacht.
        Tampere, Finland:
        Danske Boghandleres Bogimport, 1969.
        158pp. illus.
        (Aldridge's book in Finnish.)
B 0017 Aldridge, Alan, ed. Les Beatles: Chansons
        Illustrees 2, translated by Dominique Pires.
        Paris, France: Albin Michel, 1971.
        138pp. pa. illus.
        (His "Illustrated Lyrics 2" in French.)
B 0018 Aldridge, Alan, ed. Les Beatles; Le Livre-Show
        Illustre Des Chansons Et Ballads, translated
        by Marie-Therese Wasserman. Paris, France:
        A. Michel, 1969. 160pp. pa. illus.
        (French version of Aldridge's "Illustrated
        Lyrics.")
B 0019 Aldridge, Alan, ed. The Beatles Lyrics.
        London: Futura, 1975. 208pp. pa. illus.
B 0020 Aldridge, Alan, ed. The Beatles Lyrics Complete.
        London: Futura, 1974. 192pp. pa. illus.
B 0021 Aldridge, Alan, ed. The Beatles Song Book 1.
        Munich, W.Ger.: Wilhelm Goldmann Verlag,
        1981. 190pp. pa. illus.
        (With 13-page essay on Lennon and The
        Beatles.)
B 0022 Aldridge, Alan, ed. The Beatles Song Book 1.
        Guetersloh, W.Ger.: Bertelsmann, 1981.

B 0022 (cont.) 190pp. pa. illus.
        (Book club reissue of Goldmann Verlag
        edition.)
B 0023 Aldridge, Alan, ed. The Beatles Song Book 2.
        Munich, W.Ger.: Wilhelm Goldmann Verlag,
        1981. 160pp. pa. illus.
        (With Lennon obituary by Andre Heller.)
B 0024 Aldridge, Alan, ed. The Beatles Songbook I (Das
        Farbige Textbuch Der Beatles), translated by
        Peter Zetner. Munich, W. Ger.:
        Deutscher Taschenbuch, 1971. 208pp. pa.
        illus.
        (Lyrics in English and German.)
B 0025 Aldridge, Alan, ed. The Beatles Songbook II.
        Munich, W. Ger.: Deutscher Taschenbuch, 1981.
        180pp. pa. illus.
        (Lyrics in English and German.)
B 0026 Aldridge, Alan, ed. Beatles V Pisnich A V
        Obrazech, translated by Uusi Kivipaino.
        Tampere, Finland: Panton, 1969. 156pp.
        illus.
        ("Illustrated Lyrics" in Finnish.)
B 0027 Aldridge, Alan, ed. Il Libro Delle Canzoni Dei
        Beatles. Milan, Italy: Arnoldo Mondadori,
        1969. illus.
        (His "Illustrated Lyrics" in Italian.)
B 0028 Aldridge, Alan, ed. More Beatles Illustrated
        Lyrics. London: Macdonald, 1971. 128pp.
        illus.
B 0029 Alicio, Stella H. Elvis Presley - The Beatles.
        West Haven, CT: Pendulum Press, 1979.
        64pp. illus.
        (Children's book.)
B 0030 All You Need Is Love, by The Beatles & Die
        Rixdorfer. Munich, W. Ger.: Hanser, 1968.
        64pp.
B 0031 Antoni, Roberto. Il Viaggio Dei Cuori Solitari:
        Un Libro Sui Beatles. Milan, Italy:
        Il Formichiere, 1979. 172pp.
        (Includes discography, pages 121-125.)
B 0032 The Art Of The Beatles. London: Anthony Blond,
        1984. 144pp. cl. illus.
        (Based on Walker Art Gallery (Liverpool)
        catalog.)
B 0033 Bacon, David and Norman Maslov. The Beatles
        England: There Are Places I'll Remember.
        San Francisco, CA: 910 Press, 1982.
        144pp. cl. and pa. illus.
B 0034 Bacon, David and Norman Maslov. The Beatles
        England: There Are Places I'll Remember.
        London: Columbus Books, 1982. 144pp.
        cl. and pa. illus.
B 0035 Bacon, David and Norman Maslov. The Beatles
        England: There Are Places I'll Remember.
        Tokyo: CBS/Sony Publishing Inc., 1982.
        144pp. cl. and pa. illus.
B 0036 Bacon, David and Norman Maslov. The Beatles
        England: There Are Places I'll Remember.
        New York: Quality Paperback Book Club, 1982.
        144pp. pa. illus.
B 0037 Baker, Glenn A. The Beatles Down Under.
        Glebe, NSW, Aust.: Wild and Woolley, 1982.
        128pp. pa. illus.
B 0038 Bakker, Erik M. and Koos Janssen. Dig It (The
        Beatles Bootleg Book, Vol. One).
        Alphen Aan de Rijn, Holland: Rock Book Centre,
        1974. 34pp. pa. illus.
B 0039 The Ballad Of John And Yoko, By The Editors Of
        Rolling Stone. Garden City, NY: Doubleday,
        1982. 318pp. cl. and pa. illus.
B 0040 The Ballad Of John And Yoko, By The Editors Of
        Rolling Stone. London: Michael Joseph, 1982.
        318pp. pa. illus.
B 0041 La Ballade De John & Yoko, translated by Jean
        Bonnefoy and R. Hupp. Paris, France:
        Editions Denoel, 1982. 418pp. pa. illus.
        ("The Ballad Of John And Yoko" in French.)
B 0042 Balladen Om John Och Yoko, translated by
        Christine Douda. Stockholm, Sweden:
        Askild och Karnekull Forlag, 1983.
        376pp. illus.

("The Ballad Of John And Yoko" in Swedish.)

B 0043 Barrow, Tony. P.S. We Love You: The Beatles
        Story 1962/3. London: Daily Mirror, 1982.
        48pp.

B 0044 Beatlemania: The Illustrated Treasury.
        Montreal, Canada:
        F.L.A.I.R. Group (Canada) Ltd., 1984. illus.
        (Boxed trivia board game; 2000+ questions.)

B 0045 Los Beatles (Second ed.). Madrid, Spain:
        Ediciones Jucar, 1975. 233pp. pa.
        (In Spanish.)

B 0046 The Beatles. Haarlem, Holland: De Spaarnestad,
        1964. 70pp.

B 0047 The Beatles. Tokyo: Shinko Music Pub. Co., 1973.
        126pp. pa. illus.
        (In Japanese.)

B 0048 The Beatles. Japan: Eichi Books, 1974.
        208pp. pa. illus.
        (In Japanese.)

B 0049 The Beatles American Discography And Price
        Guide. Phoenix, AZ: O'Sullivan Woodside,
        1977. pa.

B 0050 The Beatles, By Royal Command: Their Own Story
        Of The Most Fabulous Night Of Their Career.
        London: Daily Mirror Newspapers, 1963.
        30pp. pa. illus.

B 0051 Beatles Catalog. Japan: 1977. 220pp. pa. illus.
        (In Japanese.)

B 0052 Beatles Catalog. Japan: 1981. 220pp. pa. illus.
        (In Japanese. Minor revisions to 1977
        edition.)

B 0053 The Beatles Collection. Liverpool, Eng.:
        City Of Liverpool Public Relations Office, 1974.
        (Album-size souvenir packet.)

B 0054 The Beatles Diary. Glasgow, Scotland:
        Beat Productions, 1965. 132pp. pa. illus.
        (Events from 1965, with brief biographies.)

B 0055 Beatles Discographie, presented by Simon's
        Laden. Hamburg, W. Ger.: Tutor, 1976.
        20pp.

B 0056 The Beatles For The Record: The Story Of The
        Beatles In Words And Pictures.
        Knutsford, Eng.: Stafford Pemberton, 1981.
        96pp. pa. illus.

B 0057 The Beatles For The Record: The Story Of The
        Beatles In Words And Pictures.
        Don Mills, Ont.: Totem Books, 1982.
        96pp. pa. illus.

B 0058 The Beatles: It Was Twenty Years Ago ....
        London: Michael Press, 1984. 120pp. pa.
        illus.
        (Newspaper clippings, 1964-1966.)

B 0059 The Beatles Lyrics. London:
        Futura Publictaions Ltd., 1979. 220pp. pa.
        illus.

B 0060 The Beatles Lyrics Illustrated, introduction by
        Richard Brautigan. New York: Dell, 1975.
        208pp. pa. illus.

B 0061 Beatles No Kisenki, compiled by Editors of
        Music Life. Tokyo: Shinko Music, 1972.
        480pp. pa. illus.
        (Stories, interviews and photos.)

B 0062 The Beatles Official Coloring Book.
        n.p.(U.K.): Peerless Manufacturing/NEMS,
        1964. 128pp.

B 0063 The Beatles Press Book. London:
        Apple Press Office, 1969. 32pp. pa. illus.

B 0064 The Beatles: Starring In "A Hard Day's Night".
        Manchester, Eng.: World Distributors, 1964.
        34pp. illus.

B 0065 The Beatles: The Real Story. New York:
        Berkley Medallion Books, 1968. 224pp. pa.
        illus.

B 0066 The Beatles - 24 Posters. Guildford,Surrey,Eng:
        Colour Library Books Ltd., 1983. 24pp. pa.
        illus.
        (Tear-out poster-size photos.)

B 0067 The Beatles Up To Date. New York:
        Lancer Books, Inc., 1964. 128pp. pa. illus.

B 0069 Beckley, Timothy Green. Lennon Up Close &
        Personal. New York: Sunshine Publications,
        1980. 160pp. pa. illus.

B 0070 Beckley, Timothy Green. Lennon: What Happened!.
        New York: Sunshine Publications, 1980.
        160pp. pa. illus.

B 0071 Beckmann, Dieter and Klaus Martens. Star Club.
        Reinbek, W.Ger.: Rowohlt Taschenbuch, 1980.
        270pp. pa. illus.

B 0072 Bedford, Carol. Waiting For The Beatles: An
        Apple Scruff's Story. Poole, Dorset:
        Blandford Press, 1984. 296pp. cl. and pa.
        illus.
        (Memories of the "Apple Scruffs" fan
        group.)

B 0073 Best, Pete. Beatle! The Pete Best Story. London:
        Plexus Publishing, 1985. 192pp. pa. illus.

B 0074 Big Oltre La Leggenda: John Lennon, Bob Marley,
        Beatles. Italy: Publiflash, 1981. 62pp. pa.
        illus.

B 0075 Blake, John. All You Needed Was Love; The
        Beatles After The Beatles.
        Feltham,Middx.,Eng.: Hamlyn, 1981.
        228pp. illus.

B 0076 Blake, John. All You Needed Was Love; The
        Beatles After The Beatles. New York:
        Putnam's/Perigee Books, 1981. 288pp.
        cl. and pa. illus.

B 0077 Blessing, Adam. Out Of The Mouths Of Beatles.
        New York: Dell, 1964. 62pp. pa. illus.

B 0078 Bourre, Jean-Paul. John Lennon - Le Beatle
        Assassine. Paris, France:
        Nouvelles Editions Encre, 1983. 230pp. pa.
        illus.
        (In French.)

B 0079 Bow, Dennis. Die Beatles Kommen (Fahrplan Einer
        Weltsensation). Munich, W. Ger.:
        Lichtenberg Verlag, 1964. 164pp. pa. illus.

B 0080 Braun, Michael. Love Me Do; The Beatles'
        Progress. Harmondsworth, Eng.:
        Penguin Books, 1964. 142pp. pa. illus.

B 0081 Braun, Michael. Love Me Do: The Beatles'
        Progress. Harmondsworth, Eng.:
        Penguin Books, 1977. 142pp. cl. and pa.
        illus.
        (Originally published 1964.)

B 0082 Braun, Michael. Love Me Do: The Beatles'
        Progress. Malta:
        Melita Music/Interprint Ltd., 1977.
        176pp. pa. illus.

B 0083 Breuer, Rainer and Alain Alcot. Imagine John
        Lennon 1. Trier, France: Editions Treves,
        1981. 84pp. pa.
        (Lyrics analysis, with discography.)

B 0084 Brousseau, Serge. La Prodigieuse Carriere Des
        Beatles: Leur Jeunesse, Leur Popularite,
        Leur Vie Amoureuse. Montreal, Canada:
        Editions des Succes Populaires, 1964.
        34pp. illus.

B 0085 Brown, Peter and Steven Gaines. The Love You
        Make: An Insider's Story Of The Beatles.
        New York: McGraw-Hill Book Co., 1983.
        496pp. cl. illus.

B 0086 Brown, Peter and Steven Gaines. The Love You
        Make: An Insider's Story Of The Beatles.
        New York: New Amer. Library/Signet, 1984.
        432pp. pa. illus.

B 0087 Brown, Peter and Steven Gaines. The Love You
        Make: An Insider's Story Of The Beatles.
        London: Pan Books Ltd., 1984. 432pp. pa.
        illus.

B 0088 Brown, Peter and Steven Gaines. Yesterday - Les
        Beatles: Voyage Intime Dans Une Legende,
        translated by Christiane Ramasseul.
        Paris, France: Robert Laffont, 1984.
        434pp. pa. illus.
        ("The Love You Make" in French.)

B 0089 Burke, John. The Beatles In A Hard Day's Night.
        New York: Dell Publishing Co., 1964.

156pp. pa. illus.
(Novelization of Alun Owen's screenplay.)

B 0090 Burke, John. A Hard Day's Night. London:
Pan Books Ltd., 1964. 130pp. pa. illus.
(Novelization of Alun Owen's screenplay.)

B 0091 Burke, John. A Hard Day's Night. Malta:
Melita Music/Interprint Ltd., 1977.
130pp. pa. illus.
(Novelization of Alun Owen's screenplay.)

B 0092 Burt, Robert, comp. The Beatles: The Fabulous
Story Of John, Paul, George And Ringo.
London: Octopus, 1975. 92pp. illus.

B 0093 Burt, Robert, comp. and Jeremy Pascall. The
Beatles: The Fab Four Who Dominated Pop
Music For A Decade. Rev. ed. London:
Treasure Press, 1983. 92pp. cl. illus.
(Reworking of Burt's 1975 book.)

B 0094 Campbell, Colin and Allan Murphy. Things We
Said Today; The Complete Lyrics And A
Concordance To The Beatles' Songs, 1962-1970.
Ann Arbor, MI: Pierian Press, 1980.
388pp. cl.
(The lyrics as sung on recordings, with
word index.)

B 0095 Capisani, Alberino Daniele. Paul McCartney:
Canzonie Musica. Rome, Italy: Lato Side,
1981. 122pp. pa. illus.
(In Italian.)

B 0096 Carpozi, George, Jr. John Lennon: Death Of A
Dream. New York: Manor Books, 1980.
254pp. pa. illus.

B 0097 Carpozi, George, Jr. John Lennon No Reply.
Japan: 1980. 252pp. pa. illus.
(Japanese version of "Death Of A Dream.")

B 0098 Carr, Roy and Tony Tyler. The Beatles,
translated by L. Soum and J-M Denis.
Paris, France: Editions Delville, 1976.
130pp. pa. illus.
(The "Illustrated Record" in French.)

B 0099 Carr, Roy and Tony Tyler. The Beatles (Second
edition), translated by Marie Odile Duclous.
Paris, France: Editions Delville, 1984.
140pp. pa. illus.
(The "Illustrated Record" in French.)

B 0100 Carr, Roy and Tony Tyler. The Beatles; An
Illustrated Record. London:
New English Library, 1975. 128pp.
cl. and pa. illus.

B 0101 Carr, Roy and Tony Tyler. The Beatles; An
Illustrated Record. New York: Harmony Books,
1975. 128pp. cl. and pa. illus.

B 0102 Carr, Roy and Tony Tyler. The Beatles; An
Illustrated Record, rev. ed. London:
New English Library, 1978. 128pp.
cl. and pa. illus.

B 0103 Carr, Roy and Tony Tyler. The Beatles; An
Illustrated Record, rev. ed. New York:
Harmony Books, 1978. 128pp. cl. and pa.
illus.

B 0104 Carr, Roy and Tony Tyler. The Beatles: An
Illustrated Record (2d rev. ed.). London:
New English Library, 1981. 136pp. pa. illus.

B 0105 Carr, Roy and Tony Tyler. The Beatles: An
Illustrated Record (2d rev. ed.). New York:
Harmony Books, 1981. 136pp. pa. illus.

B 0106 Carr, Roy and Tony Tyler. The Beatles - Eine
Illustrierte Dokumentation, translated by
Teja Schwaner and F. Ch. Winkelmann.
Dreieich, W. Ger.: Abi Melzer Produktions,
1977. 128pp. illus.
(Translation of their "Illustrated
Record.")

B 0107 Carr, Roy and Tony Tyler. I Favolosi Beatles,
translated by Massimo Villa. Milan, Italy:
Sonzogno, 1980. 128pp. cl. illus.
(Italian "Illustrated Record.")

B 0108 Castleman, Harry and Walter J. Podrazik. All
Together Now; The First Complete Beatles
Discography, 1961-1975. Ann Arbor, MI:
Pierian Press, 1975. 388pp. cl. illus.

(Only about 800 bound copies with 1975
imprint.)

B 0109 Castleman, Harry and Walter J. Podrazik. All
Together Now; The First Complete Beatles
Discography, 1961-1975. Ann Arbor, MI:
Pierian Press, 1976. 388pp. cl. illus.
(Includes minor corrections to 1975
printing.)

B 0110 Castleman, Harry and Walter J. Podrazik. All
Together Now; The First Complete Beatles
Discography, 1961-1975. New York:
Ballantine Books, 1976. 388pp. pa. illus.
(Originally published by Pierian Press.)

B 0111 Castleman, Harry and Walter J. Podrazik. The
Beatles Again. Ann Arbor, MI: Pierian Press,
1977. 282pp. cl. illus.
(Sequel to "All Together Now.")

B 0112 Castleman, Harry and Walter J. Podrazik. The
End Of The Beatles? Ann Arbor, MI:
Pierian Press, 1985. 576pp. cl. illus.
(Sequel to "The Beatles Again.")

B 0113 A Catalogue Of Compositions By John Lennon &
Paul McCartney: Recorded By The Beatles And
Other World Famous Artistes. London:
Northern Songs Ltd., n.d. 56pp. pa.
(Surveys cover versions through "Sgt.
Pepper" LP.)

B 0114 Catone, Marc A. As I Write This Letter: An
American Generation Remembers The Beatles.
Ann Arbor, MI: Greenfield Books/Pierian,
1982. 286pp. cl. illus.
(Fan letters and drawings reveal Beatles'
influence.)

B 0115 Cepican, Bob and Walleed Ali. Yesterday ...
Came Suddenly: The Definitive History Of The
Beatles. New York: Arbor House, 1984. 320pp. cl.
illus.
(Announced, but publication not confirmed.)

B 0116 Cerf, Christopher, ed. Help! The Beatles.
New York: Random House, 1965. 28pp. cl.
illus.

B 0117 Cerna, Miroslava and Jiri Cerny. Poplach Kolem
Beatles, Liverpoolskych Zpevaku, Notovych
Analfabetu, Hudbeniku & Autoru ...
Bratislava, Czech.: Panton, 1965. 152pp. illus.

B 0118 Cernia, D. and C. West. John Lennon: La Storia
Di Un Mito Che Non Muore. Italy: Editnova,
1981. 144pp. cl. illus.

B 0119 Ciccaleni, Raffaele. The Beatles. Rome, Italy:
Lato Side, 1981. 156pp. pa. illus.
(In Italian.)

B 0120 Cillero, Antonio. Beatles 2. Madrid, Spain:
Ediciones Jucar, 1976. 220pp. pa. illus.

B 0121 Coleman, Ray. John Winston Lennon (1940-1966).
London: Sidgwick & Jackson, 1984. illus.
(Volume I of Coleman's biography.)

B 0122 Coleman, Ray. John Ono Lennon (1967-1980).
London: Sidgwick & Jackson, 1984. illus.
(Volume II of Coleman's biography.)

B 0123 The Compleat Beatles, Volume One; Music
Arranged and Edited by Milton Okun.
New York: Delilah/ATV/Bantam, 1981.
512pp. pa. illus.

B 0124 The Compleat Beatles, Volume Two; Music
Arranged and Edited by Milton Okun.
New York: Delilah/ATV/Bantam, 1981.
510pp. pa. illus.

B 0125 The Complete Beatles Lyrics. London:
Omnibus Press, 1982. 224pp. pa. illus.

B 0126 Condon, Richard. A Talent For Loving.
New York: Crest Books, 1962. 256pp. pa.
illus.
(Proposed basis for Beatles movie.)

B 0127 Connolly, Ray. John Lennon 1940-1980, A
Biography. London: Fontana, 1981. 192pp. pa.
illus.

B 0128 Cooper, R. M. Beatlemania; An Adolescent
Contraculture. Montreal, Canada:
McGill University, 1968. 124pp. illus.
(Master's dissertation.)

B 0129 Corbin, Carole Lynn. John Lennon. New York:

Franklin Watts, 1982. 120pp.

B 0130 Cott, Jonathan and David Dalton. The Beatles
       Get Back. London: Apple Publishing, 1969.
       158pp. cl. and pa. illus.
       (Includes photos by Ethan Russell.)

B 0131 Cowan, Philip. Behind The Beatles Songs.
       London: Polytantric Press, 1978. 64pp. pa.
       illus.

B 0132 Cowan, Philip. Behind The Beatles Songs.
       Japan: Toshiba Emi Music, 1980. 254pp. pa.
       illus.
       (In Japanese.)

B 0133 Cowan, Philip. Nantatte Beatles, translated by
       K. Ishizaka. Tokyo: Shinko Music, 1980.
       256pp. pa. illus.
       (Japanese transl. of "Behind The Beatles
       Songs.")

B 0134 Cox, Perry and Joe Lindsay. The Complete
       Beatles U.S. Record Price Guide - First
       Edition. Phoenix, AZ: O'Sullivan Woodside,
       1983. 184pp. pa. illus.
       (Limited edition of 4800 copies.)

B 0135 Dain, J., ed. The Beatles Book Christmas
       Special. n.p.(U.K.): Surridge Dawson, 1965.
       64pp. pa. illus.

B 0136 Davies, Hunter. Alles Was Du Brauchst Ist Liebe.
       Guetersloh, W.Ger.: Bertelsmann, 1968.
       336pp. cl. illus.
       ("The Authorized Biography," in German.)

B 0137 Davies, Hunter. Alles Was Du Brauchst Ist Liebe.
       Munich, W. Ger.: Droemer Knaur, 1970.
       360pp. pa. illus.
       ("The Authorized Biography," in German.)

B 0138 Davies, Hunter. De Beatles; Geautoriseerde
       Biografie, translated by Jan Donkers and
       Theo Capel. Utrecht, Holland:
       A.W. Bruna & Zoon, 1968. 364pp. illus.
       (Davies' biography in Dutch.)

B 0139 Davies, Hunter. I Beatles. Milan, Italy:
       Longanesi, 1968. illus.
       (The authorized biography in Italian.)

B 0140 Davies, Hunter. Les Beatles, translated by
       Delia Chopin. Montreal, Canada:
       Presses de la Cite, 1976. 420pp. pa.
       (The 1968 French edition with new
       discography, etc.)

B 0141 Davies, Hunter. Les Beatles; Leur Biographie
       Officielle, translated by Delia Chopin.
       Paris, France: Solar, 1968. 344pp. cl.
       illus.
       (The authorized biography in French.)

B 0142 Davies, Hunter. Los Beatles. Barcelona, Spain:
       Biblioteca Universal Caralt, 1977.
       444pp. pa. illus.
       (His biography in Spanish.)

B 0143 Davies, Hunter. The Beatles (Revised edition).
       New York: McGraw-Hill, 1978. 382pp. cl.
       illus.
       (Revision of the 1968 edition.)

B 0144 Davies, Hunter. The Beatles; The Authorized
       Biography. London: Heinemann, 1968.
       374pp. illus.

B 0145 Davies, Hunter. The Beatles; The Authorized
       Biography. New York: McGraw-Hill, 1968.
       358pp. cl. illus.

B 0146 Davies, Hunter. The Beatles: The Authorized
       Biography. Tokyo: Soshisha, 1969. 392pp. pa.
       illus.
       (In Japanese.)

B 0147 Davies, Hunter. The Beatles; The Authorized
       Biography. New York: Dell, 1969. 374pp. pa.
       illus.
       (Reprint of 1968 ed.)

B 0148 Davies, Hunter. The Beatles; The Authorized
       Biography (New edition). London: Mayflower,
       1969. 384pp. pa. illus.

B 0149 Davies, Hunter. The Beatles; The Authorized
       Biography (Revised edition). London:
       Heinemann, 1978. 374pp. cl. illus.

B 0150 Davies, Hunter. The Beatles; The Authorized

Biography (New edition). London:
Mayflower/Granada, 1978. 400pp. pa. illus.

B 0151 Davies, Hunter. Die Geschichte Der Beatles.
       Munich, W. Ger.: Droemer Knaur, 1968. illus.
       ("The Authorized Biography" in German.)

B 0152 Davies, Hunter. Die Geschichte Der Beatles.
       Munich, W. Ger.: Droemer Knaur, 1978.
       366pp. pa. illus.
       ("The Authorized Biography, revised," in
       German.)

B 0153 Davis, Edward E., comp. The Beatles Book.
       New York: Cowles Education Corp, 1968.
       222pp.
       (Collection of essays.)

B 0154 De Blasio, Edward. All About The Beatles.
       New York: Macfadden-Bartell, 1964.
       104pp. pa. illus.

B 0155 Del Buono, Robert and Cindy Del Buono. The
       Beatles: A Collection. Philadelphia, PA:
       Robcin Associates, 1982. 128pp. pa. illus.

B 0156 Dewes, Klaus and Rudi Oertel. Paul McCartney
       Und The Wings. Bergisch Gladbach, W. Ger.:
       Gustav Lubbe, 1980. 220pp. pa. illus.
       (Includes discography.)

B 0157 Diettrich, Eva. Tendenzen Der Pop-Musik:
       Dargestellt Am Beispiel Der Beatles.
       Wien, Austria: Wien University, 1977.
       114pp.
       (Ph.D. dissertation; passim.)

B 0158 Diettrich, Eva. Tendenzen Der Pop-Musik:
       Dargestellt Am Beispiel Der Beatles.
       Tutzing,W.Ger.: Schneider, 1979. 88pp.
       (Passim.)

B 0159 Di Franco, J. Philip. The Beatles In Richard
       Lester's A Hard Day's Night; A Complete
       Pictorial Record Of The Movie.
       Harmondsworth, Eng.: Penguin, 1977.
       298pp. illus.
       (Reprints the Chelsea House edition of
       1970.)

B 0160 Di Franco, J. Philip. The Beatles In Richard
       Lester's A Hard Day's Night: A Complete
       Pictorial Record Of The Movie. New York:
       Chelsea House, 1977. 314pp. cl. illus.

B 0161 Di Franco, J. Philip. The Beatles In Richard
       Lester's A Hard Day's Night: A Complete
       Pictorial Record Of The Movie. New York:
       Penguin Books, 1978. 314pp. pa. illus.

B 0162 Di Franco, J. Philip. A Hard Day's Night, With
       The Beatles; A Director's Handbook.
       New York: Chelsea House, 1970. 298pp. illus.

B 0163 DiLello, Richard. The Longest Cocktail Party;
       An Insider's Diary Of The Beatles, Their
       Million-Dollar Apple Empire, And Its Wild
       Rise And Fall. Chicago: Playboy Press, 1972.
       326pp. cl. illus.

B 0164 Di Lello, Richard. The Longest Cocktail Party:
       An Insider's Diary Of The Beatles, Their
       Million-Dollar Apple Empire, And Its Wild
       Rise And Fall. London: Charisma Books, 1973.
       336pp. pa. illus.

B 0165 DiLello, Richard. The Longest Cocktail Party:
       An Insider's Diary Of The Beatles, Their
       Million-Dollar Apple Empire, And Its Wild
       Rise And Fall. New York: Playboy Paperbacks,
       1981. 296pp. pa. illus.

B 0166 Di Lello, Richard. The Longest Cocktail Party:
       An Insider's Diary Of The Beatles, Their
       Million-Dollar Apple Empire, And Its Wild
       Rise And Fall. Ann Arbor, MI: Pierian Press,
       1983. 352pp. cl. illus.
       (Playboy edition reprint, with new index.)

B 0167 Dister, Alain. Les Beatles. Paris,France:
       Albin Michel, 1972. 188pp. pa. illus.
       (In French;discography, filmography,
       bibliography.)

B 0168 Dister, Alain. Les Beatles (New edition).
       Paris: Albin Michel, 1975. 188pp. pa. illus.
       (In French;discography, filmography,
       bibliography.)

B 0169 Dister, Alain. Les Beatles (New edition).
Paris: Albin Michel, 1978. 190pp. illus.
(In French.)

B 0170 Doney, Malcolm. Lennon And McCartney.
New York: Hippocrene Books, 1981. 128pp. cl.
illus.

B 0171 Doney, Malcolm. Lennon And McCartney. London:
Midas Books, 1981. 128pp. cl. illus.

B 0172 Doney, Malcolm. Lennon And McCartney. London:
Omnibus Press, 1983. 128pp. cl. illus.

B 0173 Doney, Malcolm. Lennon/McCartney.
Cologne, W. Ger.: Amsco Publications, 1981.
96pp. illus.
(German translation of his book.)

B 0174 Edwards, Henry. Sgt. Pepper's Lonely Hearts
Club Band. New York: Pocket Books, 1978.
(Fiction.)

B 0175 Edwards, Henry. Sgt. Pepper's Lonely Hearts
Club Band. London: Star Books, 1979.
(Fiction.)

B 0176 Ehrhardt, Christiane. Die Beatles: Fabelwesen
Unserer Zeit?. Diessen, W. Ger.:
W. Frhr. v. Tucker, 1965. 160pp.

B 0177 "Eight Days A Week" Beatles Song Calendar 1983.
San Rafael, CA: Lyric Art Productions, 1982.
24pp. pa.
(Wall calendar.)

B 0178 Epstein, Brian. A Cellarful Of Noise. London:
Souvenir, 1964. 132pp. cl. illus.

B 0179 Epstein, Brian. A Cellarful Of Noise. London:
New English Library/4-Square, 1964.
132pp. pa. illus.

B 0180 Epstein, Brian. A Cellarful Of Noise.
Garden City, NY: Doubleday, 1964. 128pp. cl.
illus.

B 0181 Epstein, Brian. A Cellarful Of Noise.
Adelaide, Aus.: Rigby Ltd., 1964. 120pp.
illus.

B 0182 Epstein, Brian. A Cellarful Of Noise.
New York: Pyramid Books, 1965. pa. illus.

B 0183 Epstein, Brian. A Cellarful Of Noise. Tokyo:
Shinshokan, 1972. 256pp. cl. illus.
(In Japanese.)

B 0184 Epstein, Brian. A Cellarful Of Noise. London:
New English Library, 1981. 110pp. pa. illus.

B 0185 Epstein, Brian. A Cellarful Of Noise.
Ann Arbor, MI: Pierian Press, 1984.
142pp. cl. illus.
(Reprints Souvenir edition, with new
index.)

B 0186 Evans, Mike. The Art Of The Beatles.
Liverpool, Eng.: Merseyside County Council,
1984. 80pp. pa. illus.

B 0187 Evans, Mike. Nothing To Get Hung About: A Short
History Of The Beatles. Liverpool, Eng.:
Liverpool Public Relations Office, 1974.
30pp. pa. illus.

B 0188 Evans, Mike and Ron Jones. In The Footsteps Of
The Beatles. Liverpool, Eng.:
Merseyside County Council, 1981. 72pp. pa.

B 0189 Fast, Julius. The Beatles; The Real Story.
New York: Putnam's, 1968. 252pp. cl. illus.

B 0190 Fast, Julius. The Beatles; The Real Story.
New York: Berkeley Medalion, 1968.
252pp. pa. illus.

B 0191 Fawcett, Anthony. John Lennon, translated by D.
Eguchi, J. Harrison, and H. Sawa. Tokyo:
Shinko Music, 1978. 336pp. pa. illus.
(Japanese translation of "One Day At A
Time.")

B 0192 Fawcett, Anthony. John Lennon (Beatle,
Kunstler, Provokateur), translated by
Hannelore Zander. Bergisch Gladbach, W.Ger.:
Gustav Lubbe, 1979. 270pp. pa. illus.
("One Day At A Time," 4th ed. rev., in
German.)

B 0193 Fawcett, Anthony. John Lennon: One Day At A
Time; A Personal Biography Of The Seventies.
New York: Grove Press, 1976. 192pp.
cl. and pa. illus.

B 0194 Fawcett, Anthony. John Lennon: One Day At A
Time: A Personal Biography Of The Seventies.
London: New English Library, 1977.
192pp. cl. and pa. illus.

B 0195 Fawcett, Anthony. John Lennon: One Day At A
Time (Revised edition.). New York:
Grove Press, 1980. 192pp. pa. illus.
(Revised edition.)

B 0196 Fenick, Barbara. Collecting The Beatles: An
Introduction & Price Guide To Fab Four
Collectibles, Records, & Memorabilia.
Ann Arbor, MI: Pierian Press, 1982.
292pp. cl. illus.

B 0197 Fenick, Barbara. Collecting The Beatles: An
Introduction & Price Guide To Fab Four
Collectibles, Records, & Memorabilia.
Chicago,IL: Contemporary Books, 1984.
292pp. pa. illus.

B 0198 Foreman, J.B. The Beatles Quiz Book. London:
William Collins Sons, 1964. 36pp. pa. illus.

B 0199 Ein Fotorama Uber Die Beatles.
Hamburg, W. Ger.: Neuer Tesloff, 1963.
illus.
(Twelve photocards with captions, 3 1/2 x
5".)

B 0200 Freeman, Robert. Yesterday: Photographs Of The
Beatles. London: Weidenfeld & Nicholson,
1983. 96pp. cl. illus.
(Eighty pages of Freeman's photos.)

B 0201 Freeman, Robert. Yesterday - The Beatles
1963-1965. New York:
Holt, Rinehart, Winston, 1983. 96pp. cl.
illus.
(Eighty pages of Freeman's photos.)

B 0202 Friede, Goldie, Robin Titone and Sue Weiner.
The Beatles A To Z. New York: Methuen, Inc.,
1980. 248pp. pa. illus.

B 0203 Friede, Goldie, Robin Titone and Sue Weiner.
The Beatles A To Z. London: Eyre Methuen,
1980. 248pp. pa. illus.

B 0204 Friedman, Rick. The Beatles' Press Conference.
New York: Simon and Schuster, 1967. pa.

B 0205 Friedman, Rick, comp. The Beatles; Words
Without Music. New York:
Grosset & Dunlap/Workman, 1968. 80pp. pa.
illus.

B 0206 Gabor, Koltay. John Lennon 1940-1980.
Budapest, Hungary: Zenemuekiado, 1981.
184pp. illus.
(In Hungarian.)

B 0207 Gambaccini, Paul. Paul McCartney. Tokyo:
Shinko Music, 1977. 224pp. pa. illus.
(Japanese edition of "In His Own Words.")

B 0208 Gambaccini, Paul. Paul McCartney In His Own
Words. New York: Flash Books, 1976.
112pp. pa. illus.

B 0209 Gambaccini, Paul. Paul McCartney In His Own
Words. London: Omnibus, 1976. 112pp. pa.
illus.

B 0210 Gambaccini, Paul. Paul McCartney In His Own
Words. New York: Delilah/Putnam's, 1983.
112pp. pa. illus.

B 0211 Garbarini, Vic, Brian Cullman and Barbara
Graustark. Strawberry Fields Forever: John
Lennon Remembered. Tokyo: Kawade, 1981.
256pp. cl.
(In Japanese.)

B 0212 Garbarini, Vic, Brian Cullman and Barbara
Graustark. Strawberry Fields Forever; John
Lennon Remembered. New York: Bantam, 1980.
178pp. pa. illus.

B 0213 Gelly, David. Facts About A Rock Group,
Featuring Wings. New York: Harmony Books,
1977. 64pp. illus.

B 0214 Gelly, David. Featuring Paul McCartney And
Wings: Facts About A Pop Group. London:
G. Whizzard/Deutsch, 1976. 64pp. cl. illus.

B 0215 Gelly, David. Wie Eine Pop-Gruppe Arbeitet.
Hamburg, W.Ger.: Tessloff Verlag, 1978.
62pp. cl. illus.

(German version of his "Facts About A Pop
    Group.")
B 0216 Gelly, David. Wings, translated by M. Saito.
    Tokyo: Shinko Music, 1977. 56pp. pa. illus.
    (Translation of "The Facts About A Rock
    Group.")
B 0217 Geppert, Georg. Songs Der Beatles. Texte Und
    Interpretationen. 2d ed. Munich, W. Ger.:
    Kosel, 1968. 110pp. pa.
    ("Songs of The Beatles. Text and
    Interpretation.")
B 0218 Goodgold, Edwin and Dan Carlinsky. The Complete
    Beatles Quiz Book. New York: Warner Books,
    1975. 128pp. pa. illus.
B 0219 Goodgold, Edwin and Dan Carlinsky. The Complete
    Beatles Quiz Book. New York:
    Bell Publishing, 1982. 128pp. cl. illus.
B 0220 Grasso, Rosario. The Beatles In Italy 1963-80.
    Catania, Italy: Edizioni Dafni, 1980.
    320pp. pa. illus.
    (Includes complete Italian discographies.)
B 0221 Green, John. Dakota Days: The Untold Story Of
    John Lennon's Final Years. New York:
    St. Martin's Press, 1983. 272pp. pa. illus.
    (John Lennon and Yoko Ono.)
B 0222 Green, John. Dakota Days: The Untold Story Of
    John Lennon's Final Years. London:
    W. H. Allen/Comet, 1984. 272pp. pa. illus.
    (John Lennon and Yoko Ono.)
B 0223 Griffin, Alistair. On The Scene At The Cavern.
    London: Hamish Hamilton, 1964. pa. illus.
    (Booklet actually written by Tony Barrow.)
B 0224 Griffin, Alistair. On The Scene At The Cavern.
    Morecambe, Eng.: Tony Barrow International,
    1984. 40pp. pa. illus.
    (Reissue of booklet by Tony Barrow.)
B 0225 Grove, Martin A. Beatle Madness. New York:
    Manor Books, 1978. 252pp. pa. illus.
B 0226 Grove, Martin A. Kyojitsu No Setten, translated
    by N. Yoshinari. Tokyo: Shinko Music, 1979.
    320pp. pa. illus.
    (Japanese translation of "Beatle
    Madness.")
B 0227 Grove, Martin A. Paul McCartney - Beatle With
    Wings. New York: Manor Books, 1978.
    254pp. pa. illus.
B 0228 Guzek, Arno. Across The Universe.
    Hvidorre, Denmark: Arno Guzek, 1980.
    28pp. pa.
    (Discography.)
B 0229 Guzek, Arno. The Beatles Discography.
    Hvidorre, Denmark: Arno Guzek, 1976.
    72pp. pa.
    (Discography.)
B 0230 Guzek, Arno and C. Mattoon. Recordings Of John,
    Paul, George & Ringo. Portland, OR:
    Gu-Ma Productions, 1977. 122pp. pa. illus.
    (Revision of his "Beatles Discography,"
    1976.)
B 0231 Hamblett, Charles. Here Are The Beatles.
    London: New English Library/4-Square, 1964.
    128pp. pa. illus.
B 0232 Hamilton, Alan. Paul McCartney. London:
    Hamish Hamilton, 1983. 60pp. illus.
    (Biographic profile for juvenile readers.)
B 0233 Hamlin, Bruce. The Beatles Records In Australia.
    Australia: Bruce Hamlin, 1981. 128pp. pa.
    illus.
    (Photocopied typed text, hand-bound by
    author.)
B 0234 Hands Across The Water - Wings Tour U.S.A.,
    photographs by Hipgnosis.
    Limpsfield,Surrey,Eng.:
    Paper Tiger/Dragon's World, 1978. 156pp. pa.
    illus.
B 0235 Hands Across The Water - Wings Tour U.S.A.,
    photographs by Hipgnosis. Danbury, NH:
    Reed Books/Addison House, 1978. 156pp. pa.
    illus.
B 0236 Hansen, Jeppe. Beatles - Diskografi, 1961-1972.

Slagelse, Denmark:
    Slagelse Central-Bibliotek, 1973. 34pp.
B 0237 Hardy, Phil. The Beatles. New York: Macmillan,
    1972. illus.
B 0238 Harrison, George. I Me Mine.
    Guildford,Surrey,Eng: Genesis Publications,
    1980. 400pp. cl. illus.
    (Leather-bound limited edition.)
B 0239 Harrison, George. I Me Mine. New York:
    Simon and Schuster, 1981. 400pp. cl. illus.
B 0240 Harrison, George. I Me Mine. London:
    W.H. Allen, 1981. 400pp. cl. illus.
B 0241 Harry, Bill. Beatlemania: An Illustrated
    Filmography. London: Virgin Books, 1984.
    192pp. pa. illus.
    (The Beatles in films, videos and on TV.)
B 0242 Harry, Bill. The Beatles. Liverpool, Eng.:
    Beatles City Ltd., 1984. 28pp. pa. illus.
    (History by Harry within "Beatles City"
    catalog.)
B 0243 Harry, Bill. The Beatles Who's Who. New York:
    Delilah Books, 1982. 192pp. pa. illus.
B 0244 Harry, Bill. The Beatles Who's Who. London:
    Aurum Press, 1983. 192pp. pa. illus.
B 0245 Harry, Bill. The Book Of Lennon: The Complete
    Lennon Sourcebook. London: Aurum Press, 1984.
    224pp. pa. illus.
    (By Lennon's former classmate and
    publisher.)
B 0246 Harry, Bill. The Book Of Lennon: The Complete
    Lennon Sourcebook. New York:
    Delilah Communications, 1984. 224pp. pa.
    illus.
    (By Lennon's former classmate and
    publisher.)
B 0247 Harry, Bill. Mersey Beat: The Beginnings Of The
    Beatles. London: Omnibus Press, 1977.
    96pp. pa. illus.
B 0248 Harry, Bill. Mersey Beat: The Beginnings Of The
    Beatles. New York: Quick Fox, 1977.
    96pp. pa. illus.
B 0249 Harry, Bill. Paperback Writers: An Illustrated
    Bibliography. London: Virgin Books, 1984.
    192pp. pa. illus.
    (Title page: "The History Of The Beatles
    In Print.")
B 0250 Hemenway, Robert. The Girl Who Sang With The
    Beatles And Other Stories. New York: Knopf,
    1970. 210pp. cl.
B 0251 Hemenway, Robert. The Girl Who Sang With The
    Beatles And Other Stories. London:
    Macdonald & Co., 1970. 210pp. cl.
B 0252 Hine, Al. The Beatles In Help!. London:
    Mayflower/Dell Books Ltd., 1965. 166pp. pa.
    illus.
    (Novelization of screenplay.)
B 0253 Hine, Al. The Beatles In Help!. New York: Dell,
    1965. 166pp.
B 0254 Hine, Al. Help! Red De Beatles! Translated by
    P. A. Zandstra. The Hague, Holland:
    Nederlandse Boekenclub, 1966. 240pp. illus.
B 0255 Hoffman, Dezo. The Beatle Book. New York:
    Lancer Books, 1964. 128pp. pa. illus.
B 0256 Hoffman, Dezo. The Beatles. Tokyo:
    Shinko Music Pub. Co. Ltd., 1976. 128pp. pa.
    illus.
    (In Japanese; primarily exclusive photos.)
B 0257 Hoffman, Dezo. The Beatles Conquer America: The
    Photographic Record Of Their First Tour.
    London: Virgin Books, 1984. 160pp. pa.
    illus.
    (Beatles' first U.S. visit; 300 photos.)
B 0258 Hoffman, Dezo. The Beatles: Dezo Hoffman.
    Tokyo: Shinko Music Pub. Co. Ltd., 1975. pa.
    illus.
    (In Japanese.)
B 0259 Homenaje A John Lennon. Madrid, Spain:
    Ediciones de la Banda de Moebi, 1981.
    64pp. illus.
B 0260 Hommage An John Lennon. Deizisau, W.Ger.:

Schreiber & Leser, 1981. 104pp. pa. illus.
("L'Hommage De La Bande Dessinee" in
German.)

B 0261 L'Hommage De La Bande Dessinee - (A Suivre)
Special John Lennon. Paris, France:
Casterman, 1981. 104pp. cl. and pa. illus.
(Translated into "Hommage An John Lennon.")

B 0262 Horn, Martin E. The Music Of The Beatles.
Bound Brook,NJ: Big Eye Publications, 1984.
112pp. pa. illus.
(In-depth reviews of Beatles' recordings.)

B 0263 House, Jack, comp. The Beatles Quiz Book.
London: William Collins & Sons, Ltd., 1964.
32pp. pa. illus.

B 0264 House, Jack, comp. The Beatles Quiz Book.
New York: Collins, 1964. 32pp. pa. illus.

B 0265 Howlett, Kevin. The Beatles At The Beeb; The
Story Of Their Radio Career, 1962-1965.
London: British Broadcasting Corp., 1982.
128pp. pa. illus.

B 0266 Howlett, Kevin. The Beatles At The Beeb: The
Story Of Their Radio Career, 1962-65.
Ann Arbor, MI: Pierian Press, 1983.
138pp. cl. illus.
(Reprints 1982 BBC edition, with new
index.)

B 0267 Humphrey-Smith, Cecil and et al. Up The
Beatles' Family Tree. Canterbury, Eng.:
Achievements Ltd., 1966. 12pp. pa. illus.
(Genealogy.)

B 0268 Huyette, Marcia. John Lennon: A Real Live
Fairytale. Cornish, NH: Hidden Studio, 1982.
64pp.

B 0269 Insolera, Manuel. Paul McCartney. Rome, Italy:
Arcana Editrice, 1979. 176pp. pa. illus.
(In Italian.)

B 0270 Janos, Sebok. A Beatlestol Az Uj Hullamig.
Budapest, Hungary: Zenemukiado, 1981.
364pp. pa. illus.

B 0271 Jasper, Tony. Paul McCartney And Wings.
London: Octopus, 1977. 94pp. illus.

B 0272 Jasper, Tony. Paul McCartney And Wings.
Secaucus, NJ: Chartwell Books, 1977.
94pp. cl. illus.

B 0273 John Lennon. Hastings,Sussex,Eng.:
SB Publishing & Promotions, 1980. 16pp.
illus.
(Fold-out poster.)

B 0274 John Lennon - A Family Album. Photographs by
Nishi F. Saimaru. Tokyo: FLY Communications,
1982. 126pp. pa. illus.

B 0275 John Lennon: A Man Who Cared: The Fabulous
Story Of John Lennon And The Beatles.
Ridgefield, CT: Paradise Press Inc., 1980.
82pp. pa. illus.

B 0276 John Lennon Canzonie Musica. Rome, Italy:
Lato Side Editori, 1981. 140pp. pa. illus.
(In Italian.)

B 0277 John Lennon: Im Spiegel Der Weltpresse, edited
by Thomas Schmid. Zurich, Switz.:
Schweiz. und Internationaler/Argus der Presse,
1981. 96pp. pa. illus.
(News clippings, primarily in German.)

B 0278 John Lennon Last Message. Japan: 1981.
216pp. cl. illus.
(In Japanese.)

B 0279 John Ono Lennon 1940-1980. Japan: 1981.
212pp. pa. illus.
(In Japanese.)

B 0280 Jurgs, Michael, Hans Heinrich Ziemann and D.
Meyer. Das Album Der Beatles.
Hamburg, W. Ger.:
Stern-Bucher/Gruner & Jahr, 1981. 384pp. cl.
illus.
(Includes German discography, pages
371-382.)

B 0281 Keenan, Deborah. On Stage: The Beatles.
Mankato, MN: Creative Education Society,
1976. 46pp. cl.
(Children's book.)

B 0282 Keenan, Deborah. On Stage With The Beatles.
Mankato, MN: Creative Education, 1975.
cl. and pa.
(Children's book.)

B 0283 Keppel, Karin. John Lennon Hat Mir Das Rauchen
Verboten (John Lennon Forbade Me To Smoke).
Reinbek, W. Ger.: Rowohlt Taschenbuch, 1982.
222pp.
(Fiction.)

B 0284 Koluda, Shilow. Paul McCartney & Wings.
Tokyo, Japan: Nichion, 1978. 200pp. pa.
illus.
(In Japanese.)

B 0285 Kramer, Howard. The Beatles Labels. n.p.:
Howard Kramer, 1984. 14pp. pa. illus.
(Self-published survey of record labels up
to 1971.)

B 0286 Kreimer, Juan Carlos. Beatles & Co.
Buenos Aires, Arg.: Editorial Galerna, 1968.
72pp. pa. illus.

B 0287 Lapidos, Mark and Carol Lapidos. A Loving
Tribute To John Lennon. Westwood, NJ:
Mark Lapidos Prodns., 1981. 40pp.
(Distributed free at "Beatlefest '81.")

B 0288 Larkin, Rochelle. The Beatles: Yesterday ...
Today ... Tomorrow. New York:
Scholastic Book Services, 1974. 108pp. pa.
(Young adult book.)

B 0289 Larkin, Rochelle. The Beatles: Yesterday ...
Today ... Tomorrow. New York:
Scholastic Book Services, 1977. 108pp. pa.
illus.
(First issued 1974; reissued again in
1981.)

B 0290 Larkin, Rochelle. The Beatles: Yesterday ...
Today ... Tomorrow. London:
Scholastic Book Services, 1977. 108pp. pa.
illus.
(Originally published 1974.)

B 0291 Larkin, Rochelle. The Beatles: Yesterday ...
Today ... Tomorrow. Malta:
Melita Music/Interprint Ltd., 1977.
108pp. pa. illus.
(Originally published 1974.)

B 0292 Leach, Sam, comp. Die Beatles In America.
Hamburg, W. Ger.: Neuer Tessloff-Verlag,
1964. n.p. illus.

B 0293 Leach, Sam, comp. Follow The Merseybeat Road!
Liverpool, Eng.: Eden Publications, 1983.
32pp. pa. illus.
(Photo survey of Beatles' early years.)

B 0294 Leaf, Earl. The Original Beatles Book:
Delicious Insanity, Where Will It End?
Los Angeles: Petersen, 1964. n.p. illus.

B 0295 Leblanc, Jacques. Lennon/McCartney.
Paris, France: Jacques Grancher/Best, 1981.
130pp. pa. illus.

B 0296 Leigh, Spencer. Let's Go Down The Cavern.
Liverpool, Eng.: Royal Life Insurance, 1983.
30pp. illus.

B 0297 Leigh, Spencer. Let's Go Down The Cavern: The
Story Of Liverpool's Merseybeat. London:
Vermillion Books, 1984. illus.
(Larger version of the 1983 work.)

B 0298 Lennon, Cynthia. Sugao No John Lennon,
translated by D. Eguchi and C. Mizuno.
Tokyo: Shinko Music, 1979. 296pp. pa. illus.
(Japanese translation of "A Twist Of
Lennon.")

B 0299 Lennon, Cynthia. A Twist Of Lennon. London:
Star Books/W.H. Allen, 1978. 182pp. pa.
illus.

B 0300 Lennon, Cynthia. A Twist Of Lennon. New York:
Avon Books, 1980. 198pp. pa. illus.

B 0301 Lennon, John. Bag One; A Suite Of Lithographs.
New York: Lee Nordness Galleries, 1970.
24pp. pa. illus.
(Exhibit catalog; unpaged.)

B 0302 Lennon, John. Bag One Exhibition Catalog.
Rome, Italy: Galleria "Ponte Sisto", 1971.

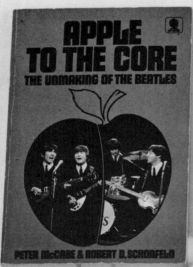

APPLE
TO THE CORE
THE UNMAKING OF THE BEATLES

PETER McCABE & ROBERT D. SCHONFELD

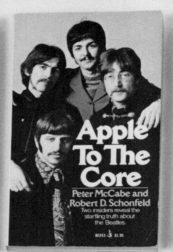

Apple
To The
Core

Peter McCabe and
Robert D. Schonfeld
Two insiders reveal the
startling truth about
the Beatles.

The Unmaking of the Beatles

APPLE
TO THE CORE

The truth
that's never
been told
before about
the breakup
of the
Beatles!

PETER McCABE and
ROBERT D. SCHONFELD

THE
JOHN
LENNON
STORY
GEORGE TREMLETT

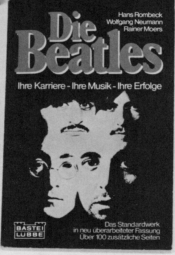

Hans Rombeck
Wolfgang Neumann
Rainer Moers

Die
Beatles

Ihre Karriere · Ihre Musik · Ihre Erfolge

BASTEI
LÜBBE

Das Standardwerk
in neu überarbeiteter Fassung
Über 100 zusätzliche Seiten

CYNTHIA
LENNON
A Twist of
Lennon

HER FIRST-HAND
STORY OF THAT
INCREDIBLE
PHENOMENON—
THE BEATLES

60p

Love Letters
to the BEATLES

selected by Bill Adler · drawings by Osborn

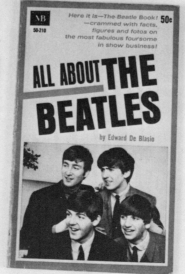

MB
50-210

Here it is—The Beatle Book!
—crammed with facts,
figures and fotos on
the most fabulous foursome
in show business!

50c

ALL ABOUT THE
BEATLES

by Edward De Blasio

445-06191-125

$1.25

THE FAMOUS ROLLING STONE INTERVIEWS
—PLUS 59 RARE PHOTOGRAPHS

LENNON
REMEMBERS

     24pp. pa. illus.
     (In Italian; only 500 copies printed.)

B 0303 Lennon, John. En Flagrant Delire, translated by
     Rachel Mizrahi and Christiane Rochefort.
     Paris: Robert Laffont, 1965. 92pp. cl.
     illus.
     (In French; reprinted 1981 with different
     cover.)

B 0304 Lennon, John. En Flagrant Delire, translation
     by Christiane Rochefort and Rachel Mizrahi.
     New York: Simon and Schuster, 1965.
     84pp. illus.
     (French translation of "In His Own Write.")

B 0305 Lennon, John. In His Own Write; and, A Spaniard
     In The Works. New York:
     New Amer. Library/Signet, 1967. 176pp. pa.
     illus.

B 0306 Lennon, John. In His Own Write & A Spaniard In
     The Works. New York:
     New Amer. Library/Signet, 1981. 176pp. pa.
     illus.

B 0307 Lennon, John. In Seiner Eigenen Schreibe,
     translated by Helmut Kossodo and Wolf D.
     Rogosky. Reinbek, W. Ger.:
     Rowohlt Taschenbuch, 1981. 172pp. pa. illus.
     ("In His Own Write," in German.)

B 0308 Lennon, John. In Seiner Eigenen Schreibe,
     translated by Helmut Kossodo and Wolf D.
     Rogosky. Hamburg, W. Ger.:
     Helmut Kossodo Verlag, 1981. 110pp. pa.
     illus.
     ("In His Own Write," in German.)

B 0309 Lennon, John. In Seiner Eigenen Schreibe/Ein
     Spanier Macht Noch Keinen Sommer.
     Frankfurt, W. Ger.: 2001 Verlag, 1974.
     238pp. pa. illus.
     (Lennon's two books, in German.)

B 0310 Lennon, John. The John Lennon Diary 1969.
     n.p.: tobe corporation, 1982.

B 0311 Lennon, John. John Lennon En Su Tinta.
     Buenos Aires, Arg.: Editorial Bocarte, 1968.
     104pp. pa. illus.
     ("In His Own Write" in Spanish.)

B 0312 Lennon, John. John Lennon In His Own Write.
     London: Jonathan Cape, 1964. 80pp. illus.

B 0313 Lennon, John. John Lennon In His Own Write.
     New York: Simon and Schuster, 1964.
     80pp. cl. illus.

B 0314 Lennon, John. John Lennon: In His Own Write.
     Tokyo: Shobun-sha Publisher, 1975.
     88pp. cl. illus.
     (In Japanese.)

B 0315 Lennon, John. John Lennon In His Own Write.
     Harmondsworth, Eng.: Penguin Books, 1980.
     80pp. pa. illus.

B 0316 Lennon, John. John Lennon In Seiner Eigenen
     Schreibe. Hamburg, W.Ger.: Rororo Panther,
     1981. 172pp. pa. illus.
     ("In His Own Write" in German.)

B 0317 Lennon, John. John Lennon Pa Eget Satt.
     n.p.(U.K.): The Chaucer Press, 1981.
     80pp. pa. illus.
     ("In His Own Write" in Swedish.)

B 0318 Lennon, John. John Lennon Pa Eget Satt,
     translation by Peter Curman and Ingemar
     Lindahl. Stockholm, Sweden:
     Wahlstrom och Widstrand, 1965. 80pp. illus.
     (Swedish translation of "In His Own
     Write.")

B 0319 Lennon, John. John Lennonsense. Tokyo, Japan:
     Shobun-sha, 1975. 86pp. pa. illus.
     (Japanese version of "In His Own Write.")

B 0320 Lennon, John. The Lennon Play: In His Own
     Write, by John Lennon, Adrienne Kennedy and
     Victor Spinetti. London: Cape, 1968.
     36pp. illus.

B 0321 Lennon, John. The Lennon Play: In His Own
     Write, by John Lennon, Adrienne Kennedy and
     Victor Spinetti. New York:
     Simon and Schuster, 1969. 36pp. illus.

B 0322 Lennon, John. The Penguin John Lennon.
     Harmondsworth, Eng.: Penguin, 1966.
     158pp. pa. illus.

B 0323 Lennon, John. The Penguin John Lennon.
     Harmondsworth, Eng.: Penguin, 1969.
     160pp. pa. illus.
     (New Illustrations.)

B 0324 Lennon, John. The Penguin John Lennon.
     Melbourne, Aus.: Penguin Books, 1980.
     158pp. pa. illus.
     (Lennon's two books.)

B 0325 Lennon, John. A Spaniard In The Works. London:
     Jonathan Cape, 1965. 90pp. illus.

B 0326 Lennon, John. A Spaniard In The Works.
     New York: Simon and Schuster, 1965.
     96pp. cl. illus.

B 0327 Lennon, John. A Spaniard In The Works: His
     Second Book. Harmondsworth, Eng.:
     Penguin Books, 1980. 94pp. pa. illus.

B 0328 Lennon, John. Ein Spanier Macht Noch Keinen
     Sommer. Hamburg, W. Ger.:
     Helmut Kossodo Verlag, 1981. 128pp. pa.
     illus.
     ("A Spaniard In The Works" in German.)

B 0329 Lennon, John. Vivendo Cantando, translated by
     Adriana Pellegrini. Milan, Italy: Longanesi,
     1964. 78pp. illus.
     ("In His Own Write" in Italian.)

B 0330 Lennon, John. The Writings Of John Lennon (In
     His Own Write & A Spaniard In The Works).
     New York: Simon & Schuster, 1981. 176pp.
     cl. and pa. illus.

B 0331 Lennon: An Appreciation. London: Choice, 1980.
     16pp. illus.
     (Fold-out poster.)

B 0332 Lennon 1981 Color Calendar. New York:
     Sunshine Publications, 1980. 36pp. illus.

B 0333 Beatles A - Z. n.p.(UK): John Neville Leppert,
     1976. pa.
     (Self-produced discography.)

B 0334 Leukefeld, Peter. John Lennon - In Memoriam.
     Munich, W. Ger.: Wilhelm Heyne, 1981.
     190pp. pa. illus.

B 0335 Long, Jeff, ed. Lennon '69: Search For
     Liberation. Los Angeles:
     Bhaktivedanta Book Trust, 1981. 66pp. pa.
     (Transcript of interview.)

B 0336 Loucks, Kathleen A. The Beatles: A Bibliography.
     Kent,OH: Kent State Univeristy, 1974.
     106pp.
     (Master's dissertation.)

B 0337 Luqui, Joaquin. Los Beatles Que Amo.
     Madrid, Spain: Nuevos Ediciones, 1977.
     (Includes discography, pages 173-186.)

B 0338 McCabe, Peter and Robert Schonfeld. Apple To
     The Core: The Unmaking Of The Beatles.
     London: Martin Brian and O'Keefe, 1972.
     210pp. cl. and pa.

B 0339 McCabe, Peter and Robert Schonfeld. Apple To
     The Core: The Unmaking Of The Beatles.
     New York: Pocket Books/Simon & Schuster,
     1972. 200pp. illus.

B 0340 McCabe, Peter and Robert D. Schonfeld. Apple To
     The Core: The Unmaking Of The Beatles.
     London: Sphere Books Ltd., 1973. 210pp. pa.
     illus.

B 0341 McCabe, Peter and Robert D. Schonfeld. Apple To
     The Core: The Unmaking Of The Beatles.
     Tokyo: Soshisha, 1973. 362pp. cl. illus.
     (In Japanese.)

B 0342 McCabe, Peter and Robert D. Schonfeld. Apple To
     The Core: The Unmaking Of The Beatles.
     Malta: Melita Music/Interprint Ltd., 1977.
     210pp. pa. illus.

B 0343 McCabe, Peter and Robert D. Schonfeld. John
     Lennon: For The Record. London:
     Bantam Books, 1984. 120pp. pa. illus.
     (Background interview to "Apple To The
     Core.")

B 0344 McCartney, Linda. Linda's Calendar 1982.

London: MPL Communications, 1981. illus.
(Wall calendar.)

B 0345 McCartney, Linda. Linda's Pictures. New York:
Alfred A. Knopf, Inc., 1976. 170pp.
cl. and pa. illus.

B 0346 McCartney, Linda. Linda's Pictures. New York:
Ballantine Books, 1976. 170pp. pa. illus.

B 0347 McCartney, Linda. Linda's Pix For '76. London:
MPL Communications, 1976. illus.

B 0348 McCartney, Linda. Linda's Plates For '78.
London: MPL Communications, 1978. illus.

B 0349 McCartney, Linda. Linda's Signs For '79.
London: MPL Communications, 1979. illus.

B 0350 McCartney, Linda. Matey For Eighty. London:
MPL Communications, 1980. 120pp. pa. illus.

B 0351 McCartney, Linda. Nashville Diary. London:
MPL Communications, 1975. illus.

B 0352 McCartney, Linda. Photographs. New York:
MPL Communications Ltd., 1982. 134pp.
cl. and pa. illus.

B 0353 McCartney, Linda. (Picture Calendar For 1977).
London: MPL Communications, 1977. illus.

B 0354 McCartney, Paul. Paul McCartney Composer/Artist.
London: Pavilion Books Limited, 1981.
272pp. cl. and pa. illus.
(Drawings and sheet music.)

B 0355 McCartney, Paul. Paul McCartney Composer/Artist.
New York: Simon and Schuster, 1981.
272pp. cl. and pa. illus.
(Drawings and sheet music.)

B 0356 McCartney, Peter Michael. The Macs: Mike
McCartney's Family Album. New York:
Delilah Books/Putnam's, 1981. 192pp. pa.
illus.

B 0357 McCartney, Peter Michael. Thank U Very Much:
Mike McCartney's Family Album. London:
Arthur Baker/Weidenfeld, 1981. 192pp. cl.
illus.

B 0358 McCartney, Peter Michael. Thank U Very Much:
Mike McCartney's Family Album. London:
Granada Pub. Limited, 1982. 192pp. pa.
illus.

B 0359 McCartney, Peter Michael. Thank U Very Much:
Mike McCartney's Family Album.
Liverpool, Eng.: Here And Now Publishing,
1984. 192pp. pa. illus.
(International Garden Festival special
edition.)

B 0360 McGeary, Mitchell. The Beatles Complete
Discography. 5th rev. ed. Olympia, WA:
McGeary, 197?. 18pp. illus.

B 0361 McGeary, Mitchell. The Beatles Complete
Discography. 7th ed. Olympia, WA: McGeary,
1975. 18pp. illus.

B 0362 McGeary, Mitchell. The Beatles Discography. 8th
ed. Olympia, WA: McGeary, 1975. 28pp. illus.

B 0363 McGeary, Mitchell. The Beatles Discography. 9th
ed. Lacey, Wa: Ticket To Ryde Ltd., 1976.
34pp. illus.

B 0364 McGeary, Mitchell and William McCoy. Every
Little Thing: The Beatles On Record.
Lacey, WA: Ticket to Ryde, Ltd., 1979.
12pp. pa. illus.

B 0365 Magical Mystery Tour. London:
Hansen Publications, 1967. 36pp. illus.
(Sheet music-in-folio.)

B 0366 Malms, Jochen. Paul McCartney & Wings, edited
by Thomas Jeier. Munich, W. Ger.:
Wilhelm Heyne, 1981. 160pp. pa. illus.

B 0367 Marchbank, Pearce, ed. With The Beatles: The
Historic Photographs Of Dezo Hoffman.
London: Omnibus, 1982. 126pp. pa. illus.

B 0368 Marchbank, Pearce, ed. With The Beatles: The
Historic Photographs Of Dezo Hoffman.
New York: Putnam, 1983. 112pp. pa. illus.

B 0369 Marchbank, Pearce, ed. With The Beatles: The
Historic Photographs Of Dezo Hoffman.
Sydney, Australia: Omnibus, 1983. pa. illus.

B 0370 Martin, George and Jeremy Hornsby. All You Need
Is Ears. London: MacMillan, 1979. 286pp.

illus.

B 0371 Martin, George and Jeremy Hornsby. All You Need
Is Ears. New York: St. Martin's Press, 1979.
286pp. cl. and pa. illus.

B 0372 Martins, Tdeu Gonzaga. John Lennon.
Porto Alegre,Brazil: Sintese, 1981.
128pp. pa. illus.

B 0373 Matahira, Toru. Beatles Movie Catalog. Japan:
1979. 256pp. pa. illus.
(Japanese text, with photos from Beatles
films.)

B 0374 Maugham, Patrick. The Beatles. London: Pyx,
1963. 32pp. pa. illus.

B 0375 Meenach, Thomas J., III. The Apple Family Tree
House: A Record Discography. Spokane, WA:
Beatles for Sale, U.S.A., 1976. 38pp. pa.
illus.

B 0376 Mellers, Wilfred. The Music Of The Beatles:
Twilight Of The Gods. New York:
Schirmer Books/Macmillan, 1975. 216pp. pa.
illus.

B 0377 Mellers, Wilfred. Twilight Of The Gods: The
Beatles In Retrospect. London:
Faber & Faber, 1973. 216pp. illus.

B 0378 Mellers, Wilfred. Twilight Of The Gods: The
Music Of The Beatles. New York: Viking, 1974.
216pp. pa. illus.

B 0379 Mendelsohn, John. Paul McCartney; A Biography
In Words & Pictures. New York:
Sire Books/Chappell Music, 1977. 56pp.
illus.

B 0380 Mesalles, Jordi. Els "Beatles" Contra Els
"Rolling Stones". Barcelona, Spain:
Edicions 62, 1981. illus.
(In Spanish.)

B 0381 Michaels, Ross. George Harrison: Yesterday And
Today. London: Music Sales, 1977. 96pp. pa.
illus.

B 0382 Michaels, Ross. George Harrison: Yesterday And
Today. New York: Flash Books, 1977.
96pp. pa. illus.

B 0383 Miles, Barry, comp. The Beatles In Their Own
Words, ed. by Pearce Marchbank. New York:
Quick Fox, 1978. 128pp. pa. illus.

B 0384 Miles, Barry, comp. The Beatles In Their Own
Words, edited by Pearce Marchbank. London:
Omnibus/Music Sales, 1979. 128pp. pa. illus.

B 0385 Miles, Barry, comp. The Beatles In Their Own
Words, edited by Pearce Marchbank. London:
W.H. Allen, 1981. 128pp. cl. illus.

B 0386 Miles, Barry, comp. Die Beatles - Wie Sie Sich
Selbt Sehen, edited by Pearce Marchbank.
Bergisch Gladbach, W.Ger.: Gustav Lubbe, 1981.
208pp. pa. illus.
("Beatles In Their Own Words," in German.)

B 0387 Miles, Barry, comp. John Lennon Goroku,
translated by H. Kobayashi. Tokyo:
Shinko Music, 1981. 128pp. pa. illus.
("John Lennon In His Own Words" in
Japanese.)

B 0388 Miles, Barry, comp. John Lennon In His Own
Words. London: Omnibus Press, 1980.
128pp. pa. illus.

B 0389 Miles, Barry, comp. John Lennon In His Own
Words. New York: Quick Fox, 1981. 128pp. pa.
illus.

B 0390 Miles, Barry, comp. John Lennon In His Own
Words. London: W.H. Allen, 1981. 128pp. cl.
illus.

B 0391 Miles, Barry, comp. John Lennon Par Liu-Meme.
Paris, France: Music Geant, 1981. 128pp. pa.
illus.
("John Lennon In His Own Words" in French.)

B 0392 Miles, Barry, comp. John Lennon Wie Er Sich
Selbst Sah, translated by Michael Kubiak.
Bergisch Gladbach, W.Ger.:Bastei-Wilhelm Luebb
1981. 218pp. pa. illus.
("John Lennon In His Own Words" in German.)

B 0394 Minoff, Lee and et al. The Beatles In "Yellow
        Submarine", Starring Sergeant Pepper's
        Lonely Hearts Club Band. London:
        New English Library, 1968. 128pp. illus.
B 0395 My Beatles. Japan: 1981. 300pp. pa. illus.
        (In Japanese.)
B 0396 Naha, Ed., ed. John Lennon And The Beatles
        Forever. New York: Tower Books, 1981.
        166pp. pa.
        (Copyrighted 1978.)
B 0397 Naha, Ed., ed. John Lennon 1940-1980: L'Homme,
        Sa Musique, La Tragedie. Montreal, Canada:
        Editions Select, 1981. 202pp. pa. illus.
        ("John Lennon And The Beatles Forever" in
        French.)
B 0398 Naha, Ed., ed. John Lennon 1940-1980,
        translated by Carla Wiberg.
        Stockholm, Sweden: B. Wahlstroms, 1981.
        120pp. pa.
        ("John Lennon And The Beatles Forever" in
        Swedish.)
B 0399 Nakano, O. Beatles Phenomenon. Tokyo:
        Kinokuniya Books, 1978. 196pp. pa. illus.
        (In Japanese.)
B 0400 Neises, Charles P., ed. The Beatles Reader; A
        Selecton Of Contemporary Views, News And
        Reviews Of The Beatles In Their Heyday.
        Ann Arbor, MI: Pierian Press, 1984.
        226pp. cl.
        (Collection of articles and essays.)
B 0401 News Collection Japan 1980. Japan: Yajirobe,
        1980. pa.
        (News clippings on McCartney's abortive
        tour.)
B 0402 Nibbervoll, Ed and Evan Thorburn. 1000 Beatle
        Facts (And A Little Bit Of Hearsay).
        Sydney, Australia: J. Albert & Son, 1977.
        72pp. pa. illus.
B 0403 Niedergesass, Siegfried. Die Beatles.
        Hamburg, W. Ger.: Cecilie Dressler Verlag,
        1976. 168pp. illus.
B 0404 Noebel, David A. The Beatles: A Study In Drugs,
        Sex And Revolution. Tulsa, OK:
        Christian Crusade Publications, 1969.
        64pp. pa. illus.
B 0405 Noebel, David A. Communism, Hypnotism, And The
        Beatles. Manitou Springs, CO:
        Summit Ministries, 1965. pa.
B 0406 Noebel, David A. The Legacy Of John Lennon:
        Charming Or Harming A Generation?.
        Manitou Springs, CO: Summit Ministries, 1982.
        140pp. pa. illus.
B 0407 Noebel, David A. The Legacy Of John Lennon:
        Charming Or Harming A Generation.
        Nashville, TN: Thomas Nelson, 1982.
        164pp. cl. and pa. illus.
B 0408 Norman, Philip. Shout!. London:
        Corgi/Transworld, 1982. 434pp. pa. illus.
B 0409 Norman, Philip. Shout! Die Wahre Geschichte Der
        Beatles, translated by Hermann Voelkel and
        Barbara Scheibe. Munich, W.Ger.:
        Wilhelm Goldmann, 1982. 300pp. cl. and pa.
        illus.
        (Translation, with discography by Rainer
        Moers.)
B 0410 Norman, Philip. Shout! The Beatles In Their
        Generation. New York: Simon and Schuster,
        1981. 414pp. cl. and pa. illus.
B 0411 Norman, Philip. Shout! The Beatles In Their
        Generation. New York: Warner Books, 1982.
        558pp. pa. illus.
B 0412 Norman, Philip. Shout! The True Story Of The
        Beatles. London: Elm Tree/Hamish Hamilton,
        1981. 400pp. pa. illus.
B 0413 Ocean, Humphrey. The Ocean View: Paintings And
        Drawings Of Wings American Tour April To
        June 1976. London: MPL Communications, 1982.
        70pp. cl. illus.

B 0414 Official Beatles' Fan Club "Book, 1970".
        New York: The Official Beatles Fan Club,
        1970. n.p. pa. illus.
B 0415 Official Beatles Fan Club "Book", 1971.
        New York: Official Beatles Fan Club/Apple
        Music Inc., 1971. n.p. pa. illus.
B 0416 O'Grady, Terence J. The Beatles: A Musical
        Evolution. Boston,MA: Twayne, 1983.
        232pp.
B 0417 O'Grady, Terence J. The Music Of The Beatles
        From 1962 To "Sergeant Pepper's Lonely
        Hearts Club Band". Madison, WI:
        University of Wisconsin, 1975.
        (Ph.D. dissertation.)
B 0418 Ono, Yoko. Grapefruit. Bellport, NY:
        Wunternaum, 1964. n.p.
        (Limited edition of 500 copies.)
B 0419 Ono, Yoko. Grapefruit. Tokyo: Wunternaum, 1964.
        n.p.
        (In Japanese; limited edition of 500
        copies.)
B 0420 Ono, Yoko. Grapefruit. New York:
        Simon and Schuster, 1970. 288pp. cl. illus.
B 0421 Ono, Yoko. Grapefruit. New York: Touchtone,
        1970. 288pp. pa. illus.
B 0422 Ono, Yoko. Grapefruit. London:
        Peter Owen Limited, 1970. 288pp. cl. illus.
B 0423 Ono, Yoko. Grapefruit. Frankfurt, W.Ger.:
        Baermeier & Nikel, 1970. illus.
B 0424 Ono, Yoko. Grapefruit. London: Sphere Books,
        1971. 288pp. pa. illus.
B 0425 Ono, Yoko. John Lennon: Summer Of 1980.
        New York: Perigee, 1983. 112pp. pa. illus.
        (Photos by eight photographers.)
B 0426 Ono, Yoko. John Lennon: Summer Of 1980.
        London: Chatto and Windus, 1984. 112pp. pa.
        illus.
        (The 78 photos in the U.S. edition, plus a
        poster.)
B 0427 Ono, Yoko. Pomelo; Un Libro de Instructiones de
        Yoko Ono. Buenos Aires, Arg.:
        Ediciones de la Flor, 1970. 288pp. pa.
        illus.
        (Translation of "Grapefruit.")
B 0428 Ono, Yoko. This Is Not Here. Syracuse, NY:
        Everson Museum, 1971. 18pp. illus.
        (Exhibit catalog.)
B 0429 Ono, Yoko. Yoko At Indica: Unfinished Paintings
        And Objects By Yoko Ono, November 1966.
        London: Indica Gallery, 1966. 48pp. illus.
        (Exhibit catalog.)
B 0430 Orton, Joe. Up Against It: A Screenplay For The
        Beatles. London: Eyre Methuen, 1979.
        88pp. pa.
B 0431 Orton, Joe. Up Against It: A Screenplay For The
        Beatles. New York: Grove Press, 1979.
        88pp. pa.
B 0432 Pang, May and Henry Edwards. Geliebter John,
        translated by Sylvia Madsack and Hartmut
        Zahn. Munich, W.Ger.: Wilhelm Heyne Verlag,
        1983. 396pp. pa. illus.
        ("Loving John" in German.)
B 0433 Pang, May and Henry Edwards. Loving John.
        London: Corgi Books, 1983. 342pp. pa. illus.
B 0434 Pang, May and Henry Edwards. Loving John: The
        Untold Story. New York: Warner Books, 1983.
        336pp. pa. illus.
B 0435 Parkinson, Norman. The Beatle Book. London:
        Hutchinson, 1964. 32pp. pa. illus.
B 0436 Parkinson, Norman. The Beatle Book. Malta:
        Melita Music/Interprint Ltd., 1977.
        36pp. pa. illus.
B 0437 Pascall, Jeremy. Die Beatles Story.
        Grosshesselohe, W.Ger.: Phoebus/RV-Officin,
        197?. 64pp. pa. illus.
        ("The Beatles Story" in German
        translation.)
B 0438 Pascall, Jeremy. The Beatles Story: Story Of
        Pop Special. London: Phoebus Publishing Co.,

1974. 64pp. pa. illus.

B 0439 Pascall, Jeremy. Historien Om Beatles,
       translated by Peter Caracalla.
       Copenhagen, Denmark: Palle Fogtdal A/S, 1976.
       64pp. pa. illus.
       ("The Beatles Story" in Danish
       translation.)

B 0440 Pascall, Jeremy. Paul McCartney & Wings.
       Feltham,Middx.,Eng.: Hamlyn, 1977.
       96pp. illus.

B 0441 Pascall, Jeremy. Paul McCartney & Wings.
       London: Phoebus, 1977. 96pp. illus.

B 0442 Pascall, Jeremy. Paul McCartney & Wings.
       Secaucus, NJ: Chartwell Books, 1977.
       96pp. cl. illus.

B 0443 Pascall, Jeremy. La Storia Dei Beatles.
       Milan, Italy: Edizione A.I.D., 1977.
       66pp. pa. illus.
       ("The Beatles Story"; Italian discography
       added.)

B 0444 Pascall, Jeremy. Story Of Rock - The Beatles.
       New York: Phoebus Publishing Co., 1973.
       64pp. cl. illus.

B 0445 Pascall, Jeremy and Robert Burt. The Beatles.
       London: Octopus, 1975. 92pp. cl. illus.

B 0446 Pastonesi, Marco. Beatles. Milan, Italy:
       Gammalibri, 1980. 168pp. pa. illus.
       (Includes discography, pages 153-164.)

B 0447 Pawlicki, Michael J. Contemporary Attitudes
       Towards The Music Of The Beatles.
       Los Angeles: Univeristy of California, 1969.
       154pp.
       (Dissertation, with bibliography and
       discography.)

B 0448 Peebles, Andy. All That John Lennon 1940-1980:
       You Said Good-bye But We Say Hello,
       translated by Ikezawa Natuki. Tokyo:
       Chuokoron-sha, 1981. 346pp. pa. illus.
       ("The Lennon Tapes" in Japanese.)

B 0449 Peebles, Andy. John Lennon La Ultima
       Conversacion. Madrid, Spain:
       Ultramar Editores, 1981. 152pp. pa. illus.
       ("The Lennon Tapes" in Spanish.)

B 0450 Peebles, Andy. The Last Lennon Tapes: John
       Lennon And Yoko Ono Talk To Andy Peebles,
       December 6, 1980. New York:
       Dell/Fred Jordan, 1983. 180pp. pa. illus.

B 0451 Peebles, Andy. Last Message. Tokyo, Japan:
       Kodan-sha, 1981. 214pp. illus.
       ("The Lennon Tapes" in Japanese.)

B 0452 Peebles, Andy. The Lennon Tapes; John Lennon
       And Yoko Ono In Conversation With Andy
       Peebles, 6 December 1980. London:
       BBC Publications, 1981. 96pp. pa. illus.

B 0453 Peebles, Andy. Lennon Uber Lennon - Leben In
       Amerika, translation by Wolfgang Doebeling.
       Hamburg, W. Ger.: Rowohlt Taschenbuch, 1981.
       140pp. pa. illus.
       ("The Lennon Tapes" in German.)

B 0454 Peebles, Andy. Lennon Uber Lennon - Leben In
       Amerika. Hamburg, W. Ger.:
       Rowohlt Taschenbuch, 1981. 140pp. pa. illus.
       ("The Lennon Tapes" in German.)

B 0455 Philbin, Marianne. Give Peace A Chance: Music
       And The Struggle For Peace. Chicago, IL:
       Chicago Review Press, 1983. 128pp. pa.
       illus.
       (Sections on John Lennon.)

B 0456 Photo Gallery - Rock Fun - Wings. Tokyo:
       Rock Fun, 1977. 96pp. pa. illus.

B 0457 The Pierian Press 'Day In The Life' Fab Four
       Twenty-Year Calendar For 1983, with text by
       Tom Schultheiss and drawings by Susan K.
       Park. Ann Arbor, MI: Pierian Press, 1982.
       24pp. pa. illus.
       (Wall calendar with 1963 daily events.)

B 0458 The Pierian Press Day In The Life Fab Four
       Twenty-Year Calendar For 1984, with text by
       Tom Schultheiss and drawings by Susan K.
       Park. Ann Arbor, MI: Pierian Press, 1984.

24pp. pa. illus.
       (Wall calendar with 1964 events.)

B 0459 The Pierian Press Day In The Life Fab Four
       Twenty-Year Calendar For 1985, with text by
       Tom Schultheiss and drawings by Susan K.
       Park. Ann Arbor, MI: Pierian Press, 1984.
       24pp. pa. illus.
       (Wall calendar with 1965 events.)

B 0460 Pirmantgen, Patricia. The Beatles.
       Mankato, MN: Creative Education, 1974.
       32pp. cl. and pa. illus.
       (Children's book.)

B 0461 Pirmantgen, Patricia. The Beatles.
       Mankato, MN: Creative Educational Society/
       Children's Press, 1975. 32pp. illus.
       (Children's book.)

B 0462 Porter, Stephen C. Rhythm And Harmony In The
       Music Of The Beatles. New York:
       City University of New York, 1979.
       (Ph.D. dissertation.)

B 0463 Presler, Ales. Beatles Se Stejne Rozpadli.
       Prague, Czech.: Mlada fronta, 1982. illus.
       (In Czechoslovakian.)

B 0464 Pro Art Staff. Das Phanomen Beatles. Germany:
       Pro Art, 1975. 28pp. pa. illus.
       (Catalog of exhibit shown in German
       savings banks.)

B 0465 Reinhart, Charles F. Beatles Novelty
       Discography. Lancaster, PA:
       Charles F. Reinhart, Jr., 1977. 24pp. pa.
       illus.

B 0466 Reinhart, Charles F. You Can't Do That! Beatles
       Bootlegs & Novelty Records (Includes John
       Lennon Tribute Records). Chicago, IL:
       Contemporary Books, 1984. 464pp. pa. illus.
       (Reprints the Pierian edition, with added
       appendix.)

B 0467 Reinhart, Charles F. You Can't Do That! Beatles
       Bootlegs & Novelty Records, 1963-80.
       Ann Arbor, MI: Pierian Press, 1981.
       412pp. cl. illus.

B 0468 Rombeck, Hans and Wolfgang Neumann. Die Beatles
       (Ihre Karriere, Ihre Musik, Ihre Erfolge).
       Bergisch Gladbach, W.Ger.: Gustav Lubbe, 1977.
       238pp. pa. illus.

B 0469 Rombeck, Hans, Wolfgang Neumann and Rainer
       Moers. Die Beatles (Ihre Karriere, Ihre
       Musik, Ihre Erfolge). Bergisch Gladbach, W.Ger.:
       Gustav Lubbe, 1981. 254pp. pa. illus.
       (Revised and updated edition.)

B 0470 Rosenbaum, Helen. The Beatles Trivia Quiz Book.
       New York: New American Library/Signet, 1978.
       162pp. pa. illus.

B 0471 Russell, Jeff. The Beatles Album File And
       Complete Discography. Poole,Dorset,Eng.:
       Blandford Books, 1982. 256pp. cl. and pa.
       illus.

B 0472 Russell, Jeff. The Beatles On Record: A
       Listener's Guide. New York:
       Charles Scribner's Sons, 1982. 224pp.
       cl. and pa. illus.

B 0473 Ryan, David Stuart. John Lennon's Secret.
       London: Kozmik Press Centre, 1982.
       256pp. cl. and pa. illus.

B 0474 Ryan, Patrick. How I Won The War; Lieutenant
       Ernest Goodbody As Told To Patrick Ryan.
       New York: Ballantine Books, 1967. 256pp. pa.
       (Fiction; source of the Lennon film.)

B 0475 Saimaru, Nishi F. John Lennon: A Family Album.
       Tokyo: Kadokawa Shoten, 1982. 128pp. pa.
       illus.

B 0476 Sarino, C.E. La Storia Dei Beatles.
       Milan, Italy: AID, 1977. cl.
       (In Italian.)

B 0477 Saroyan, Aram. The Beatles. n.p.:
       Barn Dream Press, 1971.
       (Four pages, each with a Beatle's name on
       it.)

B 0478 Sauceda, James. The Literary Lennon: A Comedy
       Of Letters. Ann Arbor, MI: Pierian Press,

1983. 226pp. cl.
(Analysis of Lennon's prose.)

B 0479 Scaduto, Anthony. The Beatles. New York:
New Amer. Library/Signet, 1968. 158pp.
cl. and pa. illus.

B 0480 Schaffner, Nicholas. The Beatles Forever.
Harrisburg, PA: Cameron House/Stackpole,
1977. 222pp. cl. illus.

B 0481 Schaffner, Nicholas. The Beatles Forever.
New York: McGraw-Hill, 1978. 222pp. pa.
illus.

B 0482 Schaffner, Nicholas. The Boys From Liverpool;
John, Paul, George, Ringo. New York:
Methuen, 1980. 184pp. cl. illus.

B 0483 Schaumburg, Ron. Growing Up With The Beatles.
New York: Pyramid/Harcourt Brace, 1976.
160pp. illus.

B 0484 Schaumburg, Ron. Growing Up With The Beatles.
New York: Perigee Books, 1980. 160pp. pa.
illus.

B 0485 Schaumburg, Ron. Growing Up With The Beatles.
Tokyo: Shinko Music, 1981. 160pp. pa. illus.
(Japanese edition.)

B 0486 Schroeder, Michael, editor. ...It Was Twenty
Years Ago Today...Die Beatles Und Die
60ziger Jahre. Berlin, W.Ger.:
Froelich & Kaufmann, 1982. 304pp. illus.
(The Beatles and sixties politics.)

B 0487 Schultheiss, Tom. The Beatles: A Day In The
Life; The Day-By-Day Diary, 1960-1970.
London: Omnibus Press, 1981. 336pp. pa.
illus.
(Originally published by Pierian Press,
1980.)

B 0488 Schultheiss, Tom. The Beatles: A Day In The
Life; The Day-By-Day Diary, 1960-1970.
New York: Quick Fox, 1981. 336pp. pa. illus.
(Originally published by Pierian Press,
1980.)

B 0489 Schultheiss, Tom. The Beatles: A Day In The
Life; The Day-By-Day Diary, 1960-1970.
New York: Perigee/Putnam's, 1982. 336pp. pa.
illus.
(Reprints the Quick Fox edition.)

B 0490 Schultheiss, Tom. A Day In The Life; The
Beatles Day-By-Day, 1960-1970.
Ann Arbor, MI: Pierian Press, 1980.
336pp. cl. illus.

B 0491 Schworck, Ernest E. John Lennon 1940-1980:
Front Page News Book. La Habra, CA: ESE
California, 1981. 90pp. cl. and pa. illus.

B 0492 Seloron, Francoise. Les Beatles.
Paris, France: Nouvelles Editions Polaires,
1972. 132pp. pa. illus.
(Includes discography, pages 121-129.)

B 0493 Seloron, Francoise. Les Beatles. Paris:
Editions Chiron, 1974. 140pp. pa. illus.

B 0494 Sheff, David. Les Beatles, Yoko Ono Et Moi,
translated by Francesca Dandolo.
Paris, France: Editions Generique, 1982.
182pp. pa. illus.
(The "Playboy Interviews" in French.)

B 0495 Sheff, David. John Lennon Playboy Interview.
Tokyo: Shueisha Publishing Co., 1981.
192pp. cl. illus.
(In Japanese.)

B 0496 Sheff, David. The Playboy Interviews With John
Lennon & Yoko Ono. New York: Playboy Press,
1981. 194pp. cl. illus.

B 0497 Sheff, David. The Playboy Interviews With John
Lennon & Yoko Ono. New York: Berkley Books,
1982. 238pp. pa. illus.

B 0498 Sheff, David. The Playboy Interviews With John
Lennon & Yoko Ono. Sevenoaks,Kent,Eng.:
New English Library, 1982. 194pp. pa. illus.

B 0499 Shepherd, Billy. The Beatles, translated by J.
Frejlev. Odense, Denmark:
Skandinavisk Bogforlag, 1964. 224pp. illus.
(Danish translation of "True Story Of The
Beatles.")

B 0500 Shepherd, Billy. The True Story Of The Beatles.
London: Beat Publications Ltd., 1964.
224pp. pa. illus.

B 0501 Shepherd, Billy. The True Story Of The Beatles.
New York: Bantam Books, 1964. 224pp.
cl. and pa. illus.

B 0502 Shepherd, Billy. Die Wahre Geschichte Der
Beatles, translated by Emile Gatta.
Munich, W. Ger.: Paul List Verlag, 1964.
190pp. cl. illus.
("True Story of The Beatles," in German.)

B 0503 Shepherd, Billy. Wij Zijn De Beatles,
translated by Ton Stam. Utrecht, Holland:
Het Spectrum, 1964. 190pp. cl. illus.
("True Story Of The Beatles," in Dutch.)

B 0504 Shipper, Mark. Eh?, translated by Y. Yamamoto.
Tokyo: Shinko Music, 1979. 400pp. pa. illus.
(Japanese translation of "Paperback
Writer.")

B 0505 Shipper, Mark. Paperback Writer; The Life And
Times Of The Beatles. New York:
Fred Jordan Books/Sunridge, 1978. 254pp.
illus.
(Fiction.)

B 0506 Shipper, Mark. Paperback Writer; The Life And
Times Of The Beatles. London:
New English Library, 1978. 254pp. pa. illus.
(Fiction.)

B 0507 Shipper, Mark. Paperback Writer: The Life And
Times Of The Beatles. New York: Ace Books,
1980. 254pp. pa. illus.
(Fiction.)

B 0508 Shotton, Pete and Nicholas Schaffner. The
Beatles, John Lennon And Me. New York:
Stein & Day, 1984. 400pp. pa. illus.
(Retitled reprint of "John Lennon: In My
Life.")

B 0509 Shotton, Pete and Nicholas Schaffner. John
Lennon: In My Life. New York: Stein & Day,
1983. 192pp. cl. and pa. illus.

B 0510 Sierra i Fabra, Jordi. Beatles, Musicos Del
Siglo XX. 1st ed. Barcelona, Spain:
Musica de Nuestro Tiempo, 1976. 166pp.
illus.
(Includes discography, pages 148-156.)

B 0511 Sierra i Fabra, Jordi. John Lennon.
Barcelona, Spain: Teorema, 1981. 204pp.
illus.
(In Spanish.)

B 0512 Sierra i Fabra, Jordi. John Lennon: El Genio
Beatle. Barcelona, Spain:
Musica De Nuestro Tiempo, 1978. 150pp. pa.
illus.
(In Spanish.)

B 0513 Simms, Alastair. Los Beatles.
Buenos Aires, Arg.:
Ediciones Technical Press, 1976. 96pp. pa.
illus.
(In Spanish.)

B 0514 Smith, Larry Richard. The Beatles As Act: A
Study Of Control In A Musical Group.
Urbana, IL: University of Illinois, 1970.
116pp.
(Doctoral dissertation.)

B 0515 Snell, Conrad. John Lennon 4 Ever. New York:
Crown/Summit Books, 1981. 140pp. pa. illus.

B 0516 Soffritti, Daniele. I Beatles Dal Mito Alla
Storia: La Prima Biografia Storico-Critica
Del Piu Celebre Gruppo Di Tutti I Tempi.
Rome, Italy: Savelli Editori, 1980.
172pp. pa. illus.

B 0517 Il Sottomarino Gallo. Milan, Italy:
Arnoldo Mondadori Editore, 1969. illus.
("The Yellow Submarine.")

B 0518 Speciaal Album. The Hague, Holland:
Wereldkroniek, 1964. 66pp.

B 0519 A Special Tribute To John Lennon.
Liverpool, Eng.: Liverpool Echo, 1984.
48pp. illus.
("Echo" newspaper articles reproduced.)

B 0520 Spence, Helen. The Beatles. New York:
       Crescent Books, 1981. 96pp. cl. illus.
B 0521 Spence, Helen. The Beatles Forever.
       Guildford,Surrey,Eng: Colour Library Int'l,
       1981. 96pp. cl. and pa. illus.
B 0522 Spencer, William F. Das War John Lennon - Alles
       Uber Ihn Und Die Beatles. Munich, W. Ger.:
       Moewig, 1980. 168pp. pa. illus.
B 0523 Stannard, Neville G. The Long & Winding Road: A
       History Of The Beatles On Record. London:
       Virgin Books Ltd., 1982. 240pp. pa. illus.
B 0524 Stannard, Neville G. The Long & Winding Road: A
       History Of The Beatles On Record. Revised
       ed. London: Virgin Books, 1983. 240pp. pa.
       illus.
B 0525 Stannard, Neville G. The Long & Winding Road: A
       History Of The Beatles On Record. New York:
       Avon Books, 1984. 240pp. pa. illus.
B 0526 Stannard, Neville G. and John Tobler. Working
       Class Heroes: The History Of The Beatles'
       Solo Recordings. London: Virgin Books, 1983.
       240pp. pa. illus.
B 0527 Stein, Shifra, comp. The Good Life; Personal
       Expressions Of Happiness By Paul McCartney.
       Kansas City, MO: Hallmark Cards, 1973.
       62pp.
B 0528 Stetzer, Charles W. Four Aspects Of The Music
       Of The Beatles: Instrumentation, Harmony,
       Form, And Album Unity. Rochester,NY:
       University of Rochester, 1976. 158pp.
          (Master's dissertation, Eastman School of
          Music.)
B 0529 Stigwood, Robert and Dee Anthony. The Official
       Sgt. Pepper's Lonely Hearts Club Band
       Scrapbook: The Making Of The Hit Movie
       Musical. New York: Wallaby/Pocket Books,
       1978. 80pp. pa. illus.
B 0530 Stokes, Geoffrey. The Beatles. New York:
       Times Books/Rolling Stone, 1981. 246pp.
       cl. and pa. illus.
B 0531 Stokes, Geoffrey. The Beatles. London:
       W.H. Allen, 1981. 246pp. cl. illus.
B 0532 Stokes, Geoffrey. The Beatles. London: Omnibus,
       1981. 246pp. pa. illus.
B 0533 Stokes, Geoffrey. The Beatles. Tokyo: Soshisha,
       1981. 268pp. pa. illus.
          (In Japanese.)
B 0534 Sullivan, Bob. The Great Beatle Rip Off.
       Providence, RI: Beatle Collectors Club
       of America, 1977.
B 0535 Sutcliffe, Stuart. Stuart Sutcliffe.
       Liverpool, Eng.: Walker Art Gallery, 1964.
       12pp.
B 0536 Sutton, Margaret. We Love You Beatles.
       Garden City, NY: Doubleday, 1971. 48pp. cl.
       illus.
          (Children's book.)
B 0537 Swenson, John. The Beatles Yesterday & Today.
       New York: Zebra Books, 1977. 160pp. pa.
       illus.
B 0538 Swenson, John. The Beatles Yesterday & Today!.
       Tokyo: Seinen Syokan, 1977. 200pp. pa.
       illus.
          (In Japanese.)
B 0539 Swenson, John. The John Lennon Story.
       New York: Leisure Books, 1981. 224pp. pa.
       illus.
B 0540 Tabatch, Warren. John Lennon: A Personal
       Pictorial Diary. New York: Sportomatic Ltd.,
       1981. 110pp. pa. illus.
B 0541 Tachikawa, N. Kaiketsu Beatles No Densetsu.
       Tokyo: Shinko Music, 1975. 416pp. pa. illus.
          (Japanese reference book with discography.)
B 0542 Taylor, Derek. As Time Goes By: Living In The
       Sixties. London: Davis-Poynter Limited, 1973.
       160pp. cl. illus.
B 0543 Taylor, Derek. As Time Goes By: Living In The
       Sixties. San Francisco, CA: Straight Arrow,
       1973. 224pp. pa. illus.
B 0544 Taylor, Derek. As Time Goes By: Living In The

Sixties. London: Abacus/Sphere Books, 1974.
       194pp. pa. illus.
B 0545 Taylor, Derek. As Time Goes By: Living In The
       Sixties. Ann Arbor, MI: Pierian Press, 1983.
       236pp. pa. illus.
          (Reprints Straight Arrow edition, with new
          index.)
B 0546 Taylor, Derek. Fifty Years Adrift (In An
       Open-Necked Shirt). Guilford, Surrey:
       Genesis Publications, 1985. 552pp. cl. illus.
          (Leather-bound limited edition of 2000
          copies.)
B 0547 Terry, Carol D. Here, There & Everywhere: The
       First International Beatles Bibliography,
       1962-1982. Ann Arbor, MI: Pierian Press,
       1985. 256pp. cl. illus.
          (Computerized bibliography of some 8000
          entries.)
B 0548 Tobler, John. The Beatles. London: W.H. Smith,
       1984. 192pp. cl. illus.
B 0549 Tobler, John. The Beatles. New York:
       Exeter Books, 1984. 192pp. cl. illus.
B 0550 Tremlett, George. The John Lennon Story.
       London: Futura, 1976. 160pp. pa. illus.
B 0551 Tremlett, George. The Paul McCartney Story.
       London: Futura, 1975. 192pp. pa. illus.
B 0552 Tremlett, George. The Paul McCartney Story.
       New York: Popular Library, 1977. 192pp.
       illus.
B 0553 Tremlett, George. The Paul McCartney Story, New
       ed. London: White Lion, 1976. 192pp. illus.
B 0554 A Tribute To John Lennon 1940-1980, edited by
       Lyn Belanger, Michael Brecher, Jo Kearns,
       Nicolas Lock and Mike Shatzkin. London:
       Proteus Books, 1981. 96pp. cl. illus.
          (Reprints some 40 eulogies.)
B 0555 26 Days That Rocked The World!. Los Angeles:
       O'Brien Publishing Co., 1978. 64pp. pa.
       illus.
          (Reprints of newspaper stories.)
B 0556 Ungvari, Tamas. Beatles Biblia; A Negy Apostol
       Mitosza. Budapest, Hungary: Gondolat, 1969.
       308pp. illus.
          (Includes discography, pages 300-305.)
B 0557 Ungvari, Tamas. Beatles Biblia; A Negy Apostol
       Mitosza. Budapest, Hungary: Zenemuekiado,
       1982. 352pp. illus.
          (Updates the 1969 edition.)
B 0558 Van de Bunt, Jan and et al. Beatles: Concert-ed
       Efforts. Alphen Aan de Rijn, Holland:
       Beatles Unlimited, 1979. 108pp. pa. illus.
          (Concert schedules and venues.)
B 0559 Van der Meijden, Henk and Jan Langereis. Yeah,
       Yeah, Yeah, Zo Zijn De Beatles!.
       Amsterdam, Holland: Strengholt, 1964.
       160pp. illus.
          (Includes discography, pages 159-160.)
B 0560 Van Driver, Lavinia. The 1976 George Harrison
       Interview. Hertogenbosch, Holland:
       Donkey Productions, 1984. 28pp. pa. illus.
          (Ann Nightingale BBC Radio interview
          transcribed.)
B 0561 Van Driver, Lavinia. The 1975 John Lennon
       Interview. Hertogenbosch, Holland:
       Donkey Productions, 1982. 16pp. pa. illus.
          (Transcription of an interview with Bob
          Harris.)
B 0562 Van Fulpen, Har. The Beatles: An Illustrated
       Diary. London: Plexus Publishing, 1983.
       176pp. pa. illus.
          (English translation of "Beatles Dagboek.")
B 0563 Van Fulpen, Har. Beatles Dagboek.
       Amsterdam, Holland: Loeb Uitgevers, 1982.
       192pp. pa. illus.
          (Chronology and articles; in Dutch.)
B 0564 Van Fulpen, Har. John Lennon 1940-1980,
       translated by Ruud't Hoen. Paris, France:
       Artefact, 1980. 82pp. pa. illus.
          (In French; with chronology and
          discography.)

B 0565 Van Fulpen, Har. Souvenirs Des Beatles,
        translated by Agnes Groleau and Alberto
        Rodrigues. Enghien, France: Artefact, 1983.
        186pp. pa. illus.
        (French translation of "Beatles Dagboek.)
B 0566 Van Haarlem, Rene and Evert Vermeer. Lots Of
        Liverpool. Alphen Aan de Rijn, Holland:
        Beatles Unlimited, 1982. 54pp. pa.
        (Beatles-related sights and stories.)
B 0567 Vollmer, Jurgen. Rock 'N' Roll Times.
        Paris, France: Edition De Nesle, 1981.
        102pp. pa. illus.
        (Layout differs from the English language
        edition.)
B 0568 Vollmer, Jurgen. Rock 'N' Roll Times: The Style
        And Spirit Of The Early Beatles And Their
        First Fans. New York: Google Plex Books,
        1981. 108pp. pa. illus.
B 0569 Wallgren, Mark. The Beatles On Record.
        New York: Fireside, 1982. 336pp. pa. illus.
B 0570 Weidmann, Gerhard. Beatles Forever.
        Solingen, W.Ger.: Aktuell Verlag, 1972.
        80pp. pa. illus.
B 0571 Wenner, Jann. John Lennon Erinnert Sich.
        Hamburg, W. Ger.: Publication Release, 1973.
        122pp. pa. illus.
        ("Lennon Remembers," in German.)
B 0572 Wenner, Jann. John Lennon Erinnert Sich ("Der
        Traum Ist Aus, Baby!"). Hamburg, W. Ger.:
        Release, 1980. 126pp. pa. illus.
        ("Lennon Remembers," in German; new
        "Foreword.")
B 0573 Wenner, Jann. Lennon Recuerda. Madrid, Spain:
        Ayuso/Akal Editores, 1975. 120pp. pa. illus.
        ("Lennon Remembers" in Spanish.)
B 0574 Wenner, Jann. Lennon Remembers.
        Harmondsworth, Eng.: Penguin Books Ltd.,
        1972. 188pp. pa. illus.
B 0575 Wenner, Jann. Lennon Remembers. Tokyo:
        Soshisha Ltd., 1972. 336pp. cl. illus.
        (In Japanese.)
B 0576 Wenner, Jann. Lennon Remembers.
        Melbourne,Aust.: Penguin Books, 1980.
        188pp. pa. illus.
        (1980 reprint.)
B 0577 Wenner, Jann. Lennon Remembers. New ed.
        Harmondsworth, Eng.: Penguin, 1973.
        192pp. pa. illus.
B 0578 Wenner, Jann. Lennon Remembers: The Frankest
        Beatle Reveals All. London:
        Talmy, Franklin Limited, 1972. 192pp. cl.
        illus.
B 0579 Wenner, Jann. Lennon Remembers: The Rolling
        Stone Interviews. San Francisco, CA:
        Straight Arrow Books, 1971. 192pp. cl.
        illus.
B 0580 Wenner, Jann. Lennon Remembers: The Rolling
        Stone Interviews. New York: Popular Library,
        1971. 192pp. pa. illus.
B 0581 Wenner, Jann. Lennon Uber Lennon - Abschied Von
        Den Beatles, translated by Niko Hansen.
        Reinbek, W. Ger.: Rowohlt Taschenbuch, 1981.
        220pp. pa. illus.
        ("Lennon Remembers," in German.)
B 0582 Wiener, Jon. Come Together: John Lennon In His
        Time. New York: Random House, 1984.
        380pp. cl. and pa. illus.
        (Includes a review of Lennon's FBI files.)
B 0583 Wilk, Max, ed. Les Beatles Dans Le Sous-Marin
        Jaune, translated by France-Marie Watkins.
        Paris, France: Julliard, 1968. 64pp. cl.
        illus.

("Yellow Submarine" in French.)
B 0584 Wilk, Max, ed. Yellow Submarine; This Voyage
        Chartered By Max Wilk. London:
        New English Library/4-Square, 1968.
        160pp. pa. illus.
B 0585 Wilk, Max, ed. Yellow Submarine; This Voyage
        Chartered By Max Wilk. New York:
        New Amer. Library/Signet, 1968. 128pp. cl.
        illus.
B 0586 Williams, Allan and William Marshall. Die Echte
        Beatles Story. Bussum, Holland: Centripress,
        197?. illus.
        ("The Man Who Gave The Beatles Away" in
        Dutch.)
B 0587 Williams, Allan and William Marshall. The Man
        Who Gave The Beatles Away. London:
        Elm Tree/Hamilton, 1975. 236pp. cl. illus.
B 0588 Williams, Allan and William Marshall. The Man
        Who Gave The Beatles Away. New York:
        Macmillan, 1975. 216pp. cl. illus.
B 0589 Williams, Allan and William Marshall. The Man
        Who Gave The Beatles Away. London:
        Coronet/Hodder & Stoughton, 1976. 238pp. pa.
        illus.
B 0590 Williams, Allan and William Marshall. The Man
        Who Gave The Beatles Away. Tokyo: Soshisha,
        1976. 370pp. cl. illus.
        (In Japanese.)
B 0591 Williams, Allan and William Marshall. The Man
        Who Gave The Beatles Away. New York:
        Ballantine Books, 1977. 236pp. pa. illus.
B 0592 Wings. London: MPL Communications, Inc., 1976.
        14pp. illus.
        (World tour booklet.)
B 0593 Wings. Tokyo, Japan: Rock Fun, 1977. illus.
        (Photo book, with discography and
        chronology.)
B 0594 Wings Fun Club Lyric Book. London:
        MPL Communications, Inc., 1976. 16pp.
        (Lyrics for "At The Speed Of Sound" LP.)
B 0595 Wings Japan Tour 1980. Japan: Udo Artists Inc.,
        1980. 48pp. pa. illus.
        (Tour book for McCartney's abortive Japan
        tour.)
B 0596 Wlaschek, Mathias and Wilfred Pelz. The Beatles
        - Here, There (And Everywhere?).
        Cologne, W.Ger.: Modern Music, 1984.
        1983pp. pa. illus.
        (Discographies (5000+ records) for 50+
        nations.)
B 0597 Woffinden, Bob. The Beatles Apart. London:
        Proteus Books, 1981. 144pp. pa. illus.
B 0598 Wootton, Richard. John Lennon: An Illustrated
        Biography. London: Hodder & Stoughton, 1984.
        128pp. cl. and pa. illus.
        (Children's book.)
B 0599 Yellow Submarine Gift Book. Manchester, Eng.:
        World Distributors Ltd., 1968. cl.
B 0600 Young, Paul. The Lennon Factor. New York:
        Stein and Day, 1972. 120pp. cl. illus.
B 0601 Zanderbergen, George. The Beatles.
        Mankato, MN: Crestwood House, 1976.
        48pp. illus.
        (Children's book.)
B 0602 Zanderbergen, George. The Beatles (Second ed.).
        Mankato, MN: Crestwood House, 1978.
        48pp. cl. illus.
B 0603 Zeisberg, Bernd. Turn Me On Dead Man.
        West Germany: Bernd Zeisberg, 1981.
        52pp. pa. illus.
        ("Paul-Is-Dead" rumors; only 50 copies
        printed.)

C 0001 Acker, Steve. "John Ono Lennon: 1940-1980." in
A Tribute To John Lennon 1940-1980. London:
Proteus, 1981.
(Eulogy; page 45.)

C 0002 Adler, Renata. "The Beatles: A Good
Non-Literary Education Under Forty." in her
A Year In The Dark; Journal Of A Film
Critic. New York: Random House, 1969.
(On film "Yellow Submarine.")

C 0003 Aguilar, Art. "The Walrus Was John." in A
Tribute To John Lennon 1940-1980. London:
Proteus, 1981.
(Eulogy; pages 70-72.)

C 0004 Aldridge, Alan. "Beatles Not All That Turned
On." in The Age Of Rock, ed. by Jonathan
Eisen. New York: Random House, 1969. illus.
(Pages 138-146; interview with Paul
McCartney.)

C 0005 "Another Random Note." in The Rolling Stone
Rock 'N' Roll Reader, ed. by Ben
Fong-Torres. New York: Bantam, 1974.
(Pages 30-31.)

C 0006 "Apple Closed; Beatles Give It Away." in The
Rolling Stone Rock 'N' Roll Reader, ed. by
Ben Fong-Torres. New York: Bantam, 1974.
(Pages 26-27.)

C 0007 Arnold, Roxane. "John Lennon And The FBI." in
Give Peace A Chance, ed. by Marianne
Philbin. Chicago, IL: Chicago Review Press,
1983. illus.
(Pages 31-43;from "Los Angeles Times," Mar.
22, 1983.)

C 0008 Aronowitz, Alfred G. "Music's Gold Bugs: The
Beatles." in The New Sound - Yes!, ed. by
Ira Peck. New York: Four Winds Press, 1966.
illus.
(Pages 45-61; The Beatles circa 1964.)

C 0009 Ashton, Bill. "Lennon On Record: Two Decades Of
Pop Genius." in A Tribute To John Lennon
1940-1980. London: Proteus, 1981.
(Eulogy; page 60.)

C 0010 Baacke, Dieter. Beat - Die Sprachlose
Opposition. Munich, W. Ger.: Juventa, 1968.
("Rock - The Speechless Opposition";
passim.)

C 0011 "Bachelor Paul." in Mersey Beat, ed. by Bill
Harry. London: Omnibus, 1977.
(Page 70.)

C 0012 Barnes, Clive. "Intellectual Lennon: Social
Revolutionary." in A Tribute To John Lennon
1940-1980. London: Proteus, 1981.
(Eulogy; page 33.)

C 0013 Batz, Bob, Jr. "Lennon Death Puts Cloud Over
Youth." in A Tribute To John Lennon
1940-1980. London: Proteus, 1981.
(Eulogy from "Dayton Daily News"; page 46.)

C 0014 Beart, Guy. Couleurs Et Coleres Du Temps:
L'Integrale Des Poemes Et Chansons. Paris:
Seghers, 1976.
(Beatles discography, pages 269-270.)

C 0015 Beat Book One. London:
D. C. Thomson & Co., Ltd., 1963.
(Contains early mention of beat group The
Beatles.)

C 0016 "Beatcomber In Book Form." in Mersey Beat, ed.
by Bill Harry. London: Omnibus, 1977. illus.
(On "In His Own Write"; page 70.)

C 0017 "Beatle Buys ...." in Mersey Beat, ed. by Bill
Harry. London: Omnibus, 1977.
(Beatles merchandise; page 73.)

C 0018 "A Beatle Named George." in Mersey Beat, ed. by
Bill Harry. London: Omnibus, 1977. illus.
(Young George; page 89-90.)

C 0019 "A Beatle Named Ringo." in Mersey Beat, ed. by
Bill Harry. London: Omnibus, 1977. illus.
(Ringo's mother interviewed; page 92.)

C 0020 "Beatle News." in Mersey Beat, ed. by Bill
Harry. London: Omnibus, 1977. illus.
(Page 83.)

C 0021 "Beatles." in Mersey Beat, ed. by Bill Harry.

London: Omnibus, 1977. illus.
(Front cover earliest-ever photo; page 69.)

C 0022 "The Beatles." in Catalogue Of Rock & Roll
Memorabilia, 1956-1983 (Twistin'). London:
Sotheby Parke Bernet, 1983. illus.
(Beatles memorabilia for sale, lots
134-477.)

C 0023 "The Beatles." in Mersey Beat, ed. by Bill
Harry. London: Omnibus, 1977.
(Return from Hamburg; page 48.)

C 0024 "The Beatles." in Mersey Beat, ed. by Bill
Harry. London: Omnibus, 1977. illus.
(Beatles' Christmas show; page 65.)

C 0025 "The Beatles." in Rock 'N' Roll And Advertising
Art (Boogie). London: Sotheby Parke Bernet,
1981.
(Auction catalog of Beatles memorabilia.)

C 0026 "The Beatles." in Rock & Roll Memorabilia
(Jive). London: Sotheby Parke Bernet, 1982.
(Beatles memorabilia, lots 81-293.)

C 0027 "The Beatles." in The Illustrated Encyclopedia
Of Rock. New York: Harmony Books/Crown, 1977.
illus.
(Pages 24-27.)

C 0028 "The Beatles As Merchandise: A List Of Licensed
Manufacturers & Their Products." in
Collecting The Beatles, by Barbara Fenick.
Ann Arbor, MI: Pierian Press, 1982.
(Reprints an early document; pages
225-232.)

C 0029 "The Beatles At No. 3." in Mersey Beat, ed. by
Bill Harry. London: Omnibus, 1977. illus.
("Love Me Do"; page 46.)

C 0030 "Beatles Back Home." in Mersey Beat, ed. by
Bill Harry. London: Omnibus, 1977. illus.
(Photos; page 57.)

C 0031 "Beatles Change Drummer!" in Mersey Beat, ed.
by Bill Harry. London: Omnibus, 1977. illus.
(Ringo in, Pete Best out, page 36.)

C 0032 "The Beatles' First Sitting." in Mersey Beat,
ed. by Bill Harry. London: Omnibus, 1977.
illus.
(Beatles' first-ever group photos; page
67.)

C 0033 "Beatles Head Merseyside Tops." in Mersey Beat,
ed. by Bill Harry. London: Omnibus, 1977.
illus.
("Love Me Do" released; page 43.)

C 0034 "The Beatles In Action ...." in Mersey Beat,
ed. by Bill Harry. London: Omnibus, 1977.
illus.
(Tower Ballroom concert photo; page 25.)

C 0035 "The Beatles In The States." in Mersey Beat,
ed. by Bill Harry. London: Omnibus, 1977.
(Page 73.)

C 0036 "Beatles News: A Mixed Bag Of Apples & Acorns."
in The Rolling Stone Rock 'N' Roll Reader,
ed. by Ben Fong-Torres. New York: Bantam,
1974.
(Pages 31-34.)

C 0037 "Beatles No. 1 Again." in Mersey Beat, ed. by
Bill Harry. London: Omnibus, 1977. illus.
("Please Please Me"; page 51.)

C 0038 "The Beatles On The Block." in Collecting The
Beatles, by Barbara Fenick. Ann Arbor, MI:
Pierian Press, 1982. illus.
(Sales at Sotheby's, London; pages
233-268.)

C 0039 "The Beatles Open A Boutique: Apple." in The
Rolling Stone Rock 'N' Roll Reader, ed. by
Ben Fong-Torres. New York: Bantam, 1974.
(Pages 16-17.)

C 0040 "Beatles Record." in Mersey Beat, ed. by Bill
Harry. London: Omnibus, 1977.
(Fan letters; page 50.)

C 0041 "Beatles Sign Recording Contract!" in Mersey
Beat, ed. by Bill Harry. London: Omnibus,
1977. illus.
(With Polydor in Germany; page 18.)

C 0042 "Beatles Splitting? Maybe, Says John." in The

Rolling Stone Rock 'N' Roll Reader, ed. by
Ben Fong-Torres. New York: Bantam, 1974.
(Pages 45-49.)

C 0043 "Beatles Star In Big Saturday Spectacular." in
Mersey Beat, ed. by Bill Harry. London:
Omnibus, 1977.
(Majestic Ballroom, Birkenhead; page 35.)

C 0044 "Beatles - Successful." in Mersey Beat, ed. by
Bill Harry. London: Omnibus, 1977.
(Beatles leave for Hamburg; page 29.)

C 0045 "Beatles Top Poll!" in Mersey Beat, ed. by Bill
Harry. London: Omnibus, 1977. illus.
(Mersey Beat poll; page 27.)

C 0046 "Beatles Triumphant Return Home." in Mersey
Beat, ed. by Bill Harry. London: Omnibus,
1977. illus.
(Return to Liverpool; page 81.)

C 0047 "Beatles Visit Widnes." in Mersey Beat, ed. by
Bill Harry. London: Omnibus, 1977.
(Sign autographs in record shop; page 41.)

C 0048 Belz, Carl. "Rock And Fine Art." in The Beatles
Reader, ed. by Charles P. Neises.
Ann Arbor, MI: Pierian Press, 1984.
(Pages 65-71.)

C 0049 Belz, Carl. Rock E No Shiten (The Story Of
Rock), trans. by Toyo Nakamura and Toru
Mitsui. Tokyo: Ongaku n Tomo, 1972.
362pp.
(Passim.)

C 0050 Belz, Carl. The Story Of Rock. New York:
Oxford University Press, 1969. 256pp. illus.
(Passim.)

C 0051 Berger, Joseph. "Fans Grieve For Lennon At
Vigils." in A Tribute To John Lennon
1940-1980. London: Proteus, 1981.
(Eulogy; pages 89-91.)

C 0052 Bernstein, Sid. "The Beatles Take New York." in
The Sixties, edited by Lynda R. Obst.
New York: Random House/Rolling Stone, 1977.
illus.
(Pages 111-119.)

C 0053 Best, Pete. "My Beatle Days." in Mersey Beat,
ed. by Bill Harry. London: Omnibus, 1977.
illus.
(Page 57.)

C 0054 "Big 'Beatles' Controversy." in Mersey Beat, ed.
by Bill Harry. London: Omnibus, 1977. illus.
(Fan letters; page 58-59.)

C 0055 "Biography - George Harrison." in Current
Biography Yearbook. New York:
H.W. Wilson Co., 1967. illus.
(Pages 157-159.)

C 0056 "Biography - John Lennon." in Current Biography
Yearbook. New York: H.W. Wilson Co., 1965.
illus.
(Pages 255-257.)

C 0057 "Biography - Paul McCartney." in Current
Biography Yearbook. New York:
H.W. Wilson Co., 1967. illus.
(Pages 251-253.)

C 0058 "Biography - Ringo Starr." in Current Biography
Yearbook. New York: H.W. Wilson Co., 1965.
illus.
(Pages 404-407.)

C 0059 "Biography - Yoko Ono." in Current Biography
Yearbook. New York: H.W. Wilson Co., 1973.
illus.
(Pages 335-338.)

C 0060 Birmingham, Stephen. Life At The Dakota: New
York's Most Unusual Address. New York:
Random House, 1979. 268pp. cl. illus.
(Including the Lennons.)

C 0061 Bliss, James, Joseph Morella and Ann Novotny.
The Left-Handers' Handbook. New York:
A&W Publishers, 1980. 160pp. pa. illus.
(McCartney and Starr as "lefties.")

C 0062 Bontinck, Irmgard, ed. New Patterns Of Musical
Behavior In The Young Generation In
Industrial Societies. Vienna, Austria:
Universal Edition, 1974. 240pp. pa.

(Papers of the 1972 Symposium; passim.)

C 0063 Bowman, David. "Scenarios For The Revolution In
Pepperland." in The Beatles Reader, ed. by
Charles P. Neises. Ann Arbor, MI:
Pierian Press, 1984.
(Pages 167-175.)

C 0064 Boyd, Denny. "This Is All About The John Lennon
I Lost." in A Tribute To John Lennon
1940-1980. London: Proteus, 1981.
(Eulogy; pages 9-11.)

C 0065 Brauer, Ralph. "Iconic Modes: The Beatles." in
Icons Of America. Bowling Green, OH:
Bowling Green Univ. Press, 1978.
(Pages 112-123.)

C 0066 Brauer, Ralph. "Iconic Modes: The Beatles." in
The Beatles Reader, ed. by Charles P.
Neises. Ann Arbor, MI: Pierian Press, 1984.
(Pages 141-150.)

C 0067 Buckley, William F., Jr. "The Beatles And The
Guru." in The Beatles Reader, ed. by Charles
P. Neises. Ann Arbor, MI: Pierian Press,
1984.
(Pages 23-24.)

C 0068 Buckley, William F., Jr. "The Right Beat?" in
The Beatles Book, ed. by Edward E. Davis.
New York: Cowles Education Corp., 1968.
(Pages 38-43.)

C 0069 Campbell, Colin and Allan Murphy. "From Romance
To Romanticism; Analysing The Beatles
Lyrics." in Things We Said Today.
Ann Arbor, MI: Pierian Press, 1980.
(Pages xxi-xxxi.)

C 0070 "Can You Recognise John Lennon?" in Mersey
Beat, ed. by Bill Harry. London: Omnibus,
1977. illus.
(Early "Quarrymen" photo; page 77.)

C 0071 Carter, Al. "A Lot Of People Were Crying." in A
Tribute To John Lennon 1940-1980. London:
Proteus, 1981.
(Eulogy; pages 37-38.)

C 0072 Carter, Jimmy. (Untitled) in A Tribute To John
Lennon 1940-1980. London: Proteus, 1981.
(Eulogy; page 24.)

C 0073 Casey, Howie. "The Silver Beatles." in Mersey
Beat, ed. by Bill Harry. London: Omnibus,
1977. illus.
(The Beatles in Hamburg; page 52.)

C 0074 Castleman, Harry and Walter J. Podrazik.
Watching TV: Four Decades Of American
Television. New York: McGraw-Hill, 1982.
illus.
("The Ed Sullivan Show" debut, pages
167-168.)

C 0075 Chapple, Steve and Reebee Garofalo. Rock 'N'
Roll Is Here To Pay. Chicago: Nelson-Hall,
1977.
(Pages 69-71, 277-278, and passim.)

C 0076 Chasins, Abram. "High Brows Vs. No Brows." in
The Beatles Reader, ed. by Charles P.
Neises. Ann Arbor, MI: Pierian Press, 1984.
(Pages 91-95.)

C 0077 Christian, Russ. "Lennon Remembered For More
Than Music." in A Tribute To John Lennon
1940-1980. London: Proteus, 1981.
(Eulogy; page 24.)

C 0078 "Classified Adverts." in Mersey Beat, ed. by
Bill Harry. London: Omnibus, 1977.
(Ads placed by The Beatles; page 26.)

C 0079 Cocks, Jay. "The Last Day In The Life." in A
Tribute To John Lennon 1940-1980. London:
Proteus, 1981.
(Eulogy; page 61.)

C 0080 Cohn, Nik. "The Beatles." in Rock; From The
Beginning. New York: Stein & Day, 1969.
illus.
(Pages 147-164; career survey.)

C 0081 Cohn, Nik and Guy Peelaert. Rock Dreams (Rock
'N' Roll For Your Ears!). Munich, W. Ger.:
Rogner & Bernhard, 1982. illus.
(Passim.)

C 0082 Connolly, Ray. "The Surreal Genius Of Rock." in
A Tribute To John Lennon 1940-1980. London:
Proteus, 1981.
(Eulogy; pages 48-50.)

C 0083 Cott, Jonathan. "A Hard Day's Knights." in The
Young American Writers, ed. by Richard
Kostelanetz. New York: Funk and Wagnalls,
1967.
(Pages 83-90.)

C 0084 Cott, Jonathan. "A Hard Day's Knights." in The
Beatles Reader, ed. by Charles P. Neises.
Ann Arbor, MI: Pierian Press, 1984.
(Pages 157-163.)

C 0085 Cott, Jonathan. He Dreams What Is Going On
Inside His Head: Ten Years Of Writing.
San Francisco, CA: Straight Arrow Books,
1973. 352pp. pa. illus.
(Chapter on John Lennon.)

C 0086 Cott, Jonathan. "John Lennon." in The Rolling
Stone Interviews, comp. by the editors of
Rolling Stone. New York: Paperback Library,
1971. illus.
(Pages 188-205; from November 1968 issue
of RS.)

C 0087 Cott, Jonathan. "Mystery Tour Shot Down." in
The Rolling Stone Rock 'N' Roll Reader, ed.
by Ben Fong-Torres. New York: Bantam, 1974.
(Pages 24-26.)

C 0088 Cott, Jonathan and David Dalton. "Let It Be."
in The Rolling Stone Rock 'N' Roll Reader,
ed. by Ben Fong-Torres. New York: Bantam,
1974.
(Pages 59-71.)

C 0089 "A Country House For Paul." in Mersey Beat, ed.
by Bill Harry. London: Omnibus, 1977. illus.
(Page 88.)

C 0090 "The Daily Howl." in Mersey Beat, ed. by Bill
Harry. London: Omnibus, 1977.
(Lennon's early notebook; page 77.)

C 0091 Davies, Hunter. "Twist And Shout: The Early
Days And The Beatles Years." in John Lennon:
The Life And Legend. Melbourne, Aust.:
Newspress/Age Publications, 1981.
(Pages 16-21,24-27.)

C 0092 Davis, Edward E. "On With The Show, Good Health
To You." in his The Beatles Book. New York:
Cowles Education Corp., 1968.
(Pages 162-175.)

C 0093 Denisoff, R. Serge. Solid Gold: The Popular
Record Industry. New Brunswick, NJ:
Transaction Books, 1975.
(Pages 24-25, 243-244, and passim.)

C 0094 Dickerson, Robert B., Jr. "John Lennon." in his
Final Placement. Algonac, MI:
Reference Publications, 1982.
(Pages 145-46 on Lennon's death and
burial.)

C 0095 "Discography." in The Beatles Book, ed. by
Edward E. Davis. New York:
Cowles Education Corp., 1968.
(Pages 202-213.)

C 0096 "Dream Is Ended." in A Tribute To John Lennon
1940-1980. London: Proteus, 1981.
(Eulogy; page 68.)

C 0097 "The Dream Is Over." in John Lennon: The Life
And Legend. Melbourne, Aust.:
Newspress/Age Publications, 1981.
(Eulogy; pages 4-5.)

C 0098 Dyer, Richard. "Within His Music." in A Tribute
To John Lennon 1940-1980. London: Proteus,
1981.
(Eulogy; pages 25-30.)

C 0099 "Editorial." in Mersey Beat, ed. by Bill Harry.
London: Omnibus, 1977.
(No Beatles decline seen; page 87.)

C 0100 Epstein, Brian. "Record Releases." in Mersey
Beat, ed. by Bill Harry. London: Omnibus,
1977.
(Record reviews; page 22.)

C 0101 Epstein, Brian. "Record Releases." in Mersey

C 0101   Beat, ed. by Bill Harry. London: Omnibus,
1977.
(Record reviews; page 23.)

C 0102 Epstein, Brian. "Stop The World." in Mersey
Beat, ed. by Bill Harry. London: Omnibus,
1977.
(Record reviews; page 19.)

C 0103 Epstein, Brian. "U.S. Tour." in Mersey Beat,
ed. by Bill Harry. London: Omnibus, 1977.
illus.
(Page 94.)

C 0104 Ewen, David. All The Years Of American Popular
Music. Englewood Cliffs,NJ: Prentice-Hall,
1977.
(Pages 612-617 and passim.)

C 0105 Fawcett, Anthony. "The Beatles In Four Part
Disharmony." in The Sixties, edited by Lynda
R. Obst. New York:
Random House/Rolling Stone, 1977.
(Pages 312-313; breakup of Apple and The
Beatles.)

C 0106 Fischer, Stuart. "The Beatles." in his Kids'
TV: The First 25 Years. New York:
Facts On File, 1983. illus.
(Pages 163-64 on the cartoon series.)

C 0107 Fleischer, Leonore. "Down The Rabbit Hole." in
The Beatles Book, ed. by Edward E. Davis.
New York: Cowles Education Corp., 1968.
(Pages 176-186.)

C 0108 Freudenberger, Herbert J. "All The Lonely
People, Where Do They All Come From?" in The
Beatles Book, ed. by Edward E. Davis.
New York: Cowles Education Corp., 1968.
(Pages 146-161.)

C 0109 Frith, Simon. Sound Effects: Youth, Leisure,
And The Politics Of Rock 'N' Roll.
New York: Pantheon Books, 1981.
(Passim.)

C 0110 "From The Family Album." in Mersey Beat, ed. by
Bill Harry. London: Omnibus, 1977. illus.
(Childhood photos of George; page 89.)

C 0111 "From The Family Album." in Mersey Beat, ed. by
Bill Harry. London: Omnibus, 1977. illus.
(Childhood photos of Ringo; page 93.)

C 0112 Frost, David. "John's Gospel." in The Beatles
Reader, ed. by Charles P. Neises.
Ann Arbor, MI: Pierian Press, 1984.
(Pages 17-19.)

C 0113 Gabree, John. "The Beatles In Perspective." in
The Beatles Reader, ed. by Charles P.
Neises. Ann Arbor, MI: Pierian Press, 1984.
(Pages 131-138.)

C 0114 Gambaccini, Paul. "Thank You Very Much And I
Hope I've Passed The Audition: A John Lennon
Top 20." in John Lennon: The Life And
Legend. Melbourne, Aust.:
Newspress/Age Publications, 1981.
(Pages 58-59.)

C 0115 "George Harrison." in Mersey Beat, ed. by Bill
Harry. London: Omnibus, 1977. illus.
(Page 92.)

C 0116 "George Harrison." in The Book Of People, by
Christopher P. Andersen. New York:
G. P. Putnam's, 1981.
(Page 192; capsule biography.)

C 0117 Gerry And The Pacemakers. "Congratulations,
'Beatles'!" in Mersey Beat, ed. by Bill
Harry. London: Omnibus, 1977.
("Love Me Do" success; page 48.)

C 0118 "The Ghost Of Ringo Haunts This Group." in
Mersey Beat, ed. by Bill Harry. London:
Omnibus, 1977. illus.
(Rory Storm & The Hurricanes; page 66.)

C 0119 Gleason, Ralph J. "Like A Rolling Stone." in
The American Experience: A Radical Reader,
ed. by Harold Jaffe and John Tyfell.
New York: Harper & Row, 1970.
(Pages 333-345; passim.)

C 0120 Gleason, Ralph J. "Like A Rolling Stone." in
The Beatles Book, ed. by Edward E. Davis.

New York: Cowles Education Corp., 1968.
(Pages 187-201.)

C 0121 Goldman, Albert. "The Beatles' Abbey Road." in
his Freakshow. New York: Atheneum, 1971.
illus.
(Pages 130-132.)

C 0122 Goldman, Albert. "The Beatles Decide To Let It
Be - Apart." in his Freakshow. New York:
Atheneum, 1971. illus.
(Pages 154-156; Beatles break-up analyzed.)

C 0123 Goldmann, Frank. Chatterbox - Preiskatalog Fur
Schallplatten, 1954-81.
Eberdingen-Hochdorf,W.Ger.:F.M. Goldmann,1982.
(Price guide to recordings, including
Beatles.)

C 0124 Goldmann, Frank and Klaus Hiltscher. Gimmix
Book Of Records. Zurich, Switzerland:
Edition Olms, 1981. cl. illus.
(Pages 61-63,65,91,99-100,113,121.)

C 0125 Goldstein, Al and Jim Buckley. The Screw
Reader. New York: Lyle Stuart, Inc., 1971.
180pp. cl. illus.
(Includes interview with the Lennons.)

C 0126 Goldstein, Richard. "Are The Beatles Waning?"
in The Beatles Book, ed. by Edward E. Davis.
New York: Cowles Education Corp., 1968.
(Pages 128-135.)

C 0127 Goldstein, Richard, ed. Poetry Of Rock.
New York: Bantam, 1969. illus.
(Section Two treats song "In My Life.")

C 0128 "Goodbye Stu!" in Mersey Beat, ed. by Bill
Harry. London: Omnibus, 1977.
(News of Stu Sutcliffe's death; page 32.)

C 0129 Goodman, Ellen. "The Promise Is Gone." in A
Tribute To John Lennon 1940-1980. London:
Proteus, 1981.
(Eulogy; pages 58-60.)

C 0130 Gray, Andy. Great Pop Stars. England:
Hamlyn Pub. Group Limited, 1973. 160pp. cl.
illus.
(Passim.)

C 0131 "Great News Of 'The Beatles'." in Mersey Beat,
ed. by Bill Harry. London: Omnibus, 1977.
illus.
(Sign with EMI; page 33.)

C 0132 Hall, Les. "Scene & Heard." in Mersey Beat, ed.
by Bill Harry. London: Omnibus, 1977. illus.
(George Harrison interview, page 83.)

C 0133 Hall, Les. "Scene & Heard." in Mersey Beat, ed.
by Bill Harry. London: Omnibus, 1977. illus.
(Harrison's mother interviewed; page 90.)

C 0134 Harris, Martha S. "Minstrel Extraordinaire." in
A Tribute To John Lennon 1940-1980. London:
Proteus, 1981.
(Eulogy; page 83.)

C 0135 Harry, Bill. "Transatlantic Call." in Mersey
Beat, ed. by Bill Harry. London: Omnibus,
1977.
(Beatles in the U.S., 1964; page 91.)

C 0136 Harry, Bill. "With George." in Mersey Beat, ed.
by Bill Harry. London: Omnibus, 1977. illus.
(Page 73.)

C 0137 Hentoff, Nat. "I Read The News Today, Oh Boy."
in The Beatles Book, ed. by Edward E. Davis.
New York: Cowles Education Corp., 1968.
(Pages 32-37.)

C 0138 Hershow, Sheila. "Writing The Score For A
Generation." in A Tribute To John Lennon
1940-1980. London: Proteus, 1981.
(Eulogy; pages 82-83.)

C 0139 Hilburn, Robert. "John Lennon: No Secret
Interior, Just Integrity." in A Tribute To
John Lennon 1940-1980. London: Proteus, 1981.
(Eulogy; page 35.)

C 0140 Hipgnosis and Roger Dean. Album Cover Album,
translated by Arthur Kalkbrenner.
Zurich, Switzerland: Edition Olms, 1980. cl.
illus.
(Passim.)

C 0141 Hoffman, Frank. "The Beatles." in The

Literature Of Rock, 1954-1968.
Metuchen, NJ: Scarecrow, 1981.
(With bibliography.)

C 0142 Holroyd, Stephen. "The Second Golden Age Of
Pop." in The Beatles Reader, ed. by Charles
P. Neises. Ann Arbor, MI: Pierian Press,
1984.
(Pages 99-103.)

C 0143 Hopkins, Jerry. Elvis: A Biography. New York:
Simon & Schuster, 1971.
(Beatles mentioned, passim.)

C 0144 Hopkins, Jerry. Elvis: The Final Years.
New York: St. Martin's, 1980.
(Beatles mentioned on pages 14,56,95,175.)

C 0145 Hopkins, Jerry. "England's Challenge: Beatles
Rule!" in The Rock Story. New York: Signet,
1970. illus.
(Pages 67-77; Beatles reception in U.S.)

C 0146 Huntington, Robert L., Jr. "Lost: Another Great
Spirit." in A Tribute To John Lennon
1940-1980. London: Proteus, 1981.
(Eulogy; pages 54-55.)

C 0147 "In My Life ... A Personal File." in John
Lennon: The Life And Legend.
Melbourne, Aust.:
Newspress/Age Publications, 1981.
(Lennon memorabilia photos, pages 28-47.)

C 0148 Jahn, Mike. Rock From Elvis Presley To The
Rolling Stones. New York:
Quadrangle/Times Books, 1973.
(Passim.)

C 0149 Jasper, Tony. "Beatles All The Way." in
Understanding Pop. London: SCM Press, 1972.
illus.
(Pages 152-158; career survey.)

C 0150 Jasper, Tony. "New Words For A New Age." in
Understanding Pop. London: SCM Press, 1972.
illus.
(Pages 74-82; evolution of Beatles'
lyrics.)

C 0151 Javna, John and Gordon Javna. 60s!. New York:
St. Martin's Press, 1983. pa. illus.
(Contains a section on The Beatles.)

C 0152 "John Acquires Stuart's Painting." in Mersey
Beat, ed. by Bill Harry. London: Omnibus,
1977.
(Page 96.)

C 0153 "John And Yoko: Busted And Naked." in The
Rolling Stone Rock 'N' Roll Reader, ed. by
Ben Fong-Torres. New York: Bantam, 1974.
(Pages 28-30.)

C 0154 "John Lennon." in A Tribute To John Lennon
1940-1980. London: Proteus, 1981.
(Eulogy; pages 44-45.)

C 0155 "John Lennon." in Mersey Beat, ed. by Bill
Harry. London: Omnibus, 1977.
(Page 64.)

C 0156 "John Lennon." in The Music Makers. New York:
Harry N. Abrams, 1979. illus.
(Pages 236-37; brief biography and group
photo.)

C 0157 "John Lennon - In His Own Write." in Mersey
Beat, ed. by Bill Harry. London: Omnibus,
1977. illus.
(On Lennon's new book; page 78.)

C 0158 "John Lennon (1940-1980). Mutmassungen Uber
Einen Egomaniac." in Rock Session 5, edited
by Walter Hartmann, et al.
Reinbeck, W. Ger.: Rowohlt Taschenbuch, 1981.
pa. illus.
(Pages 4-12.)

C 0159 "John Lennon's Death." in A Tribute To John
Lennon 1940-1980. London: Proteus, 1981.
(Eulogy; page 46.)

C 0160 "John Lennon's Dream Is Over." in A Tribute To
John Lennon 1940-1980. London: Proteus, 1981.
(Eulogy; pages 67-68.)

C 0161 Johnson, Timothy W. "A Hard Day's Night." in
Magill's Survey Of Cinema, Volume 2, ed. by
Frank N. Magill. Englewood Cliffs,NJ:

Salem Press, 1980.
(Critique of the Beatles' film.)

C 0162 Jones, George. "Special 'Mersey Beat' Visit To The Beatles Film Set." in Mersey Beat, ed. by Bill Harry. London: Omnibus, 1977. illus.
("A Hard Day's Night"; page 80.)

C 0163 Jones, Peter. "UK Colleagues Generous With Their Tributes." in A Tribute To John Lennon 1940-1980. London: Proteus, 1981.
(Eulogy; partial reprint from "Billboard"; page 56.)

C 0164 Joyce, Fay S. "Starting Over: Life Without John Lennon." in A Tribute To John Lennon 1940-1980. London: Proteus, 1981.
(Eulogy; pages 75-77.)

C 0165 Kael, Pauline. "Metamorphosis Of The Beatles." in her Going Steady. Boston: Little, Brown & Co., 1970.
(On film "Yellow Submarine.")

C 0166 Kauffmann, Stanley. "Yellow Submarine." in his Figures Of Light; Film Criticism And Comment. New York: Harper & Row, 1971.
(Pages 117-118.)

C 0167 Kaufman, Murray. Murray The K Tells It Like It Is, Baby. New York: Holt, Rinehart & Winston, 1966. cl.
(Includes this DJ's Beatles experience.)

C 0168 Keesee, Allen. "Indian Influence On The Beatles." in The Beatles Book, ed. by Edward E. Davis. New York: Cowles Education Corp., 1968.
(Pages 86-98.)

C 0169 Kempton, Murray. "The Beatles." in The Age Of Rock, ed. by Jonathan Eisen. New York: Random House, 1969.
(Pages 147-148.)

C 0170 Keylin, Arleen and Laurie Barnett. The Sixties; As Reported By The New York Times. New York: Arno Press Inc., 1980. 256pp. cl. illus.
(Reprints newspaper headlines; some Beatles.)

C 0171 Kloman, William. "The Maharishi Meets The Press." in The Rolling Stone Rock 'N' Roll Reader, ed. by Ben Fong-Torres. New York: Bantam, 1974.
(Pages 20-24.)

C 0172 Kopkind, Andrew. "Lennon Without Tears." in A Tribute To John Lennon 1940-1980. London: Proteus, 1981.
(Eulogy; page 63-66.)

C 0173 Kornheiser, Tony and Tom Zito. "Lennon: Always Up Front." in A Tribute To John Lennon 1940-1980. London: Proteus, 1981.
(Eulogy; pages 32-33.)

C 0174 Kramer, Marcus, Rabbi. "Everyone Should Speak Lennon's Language." in A Tribute To John Lennon 1940-1980. London: Proteus, 1981.
(Eulogy; pages 34-35.)

C 0175 "The Lads From Liverpool." in Mersey Beat, ed. by Bill Harry. London: Omnibus, 1977. illus.
(Photos; page 61.)

C 0176 Laing, Dave. Sound Of Our Time. Chicago: Quadrangle, 1970. 138pp. illus.
(The Beatles are discussed in section three.)

C 0177 "Last Beatles Show." in Mersey Beat, ed. by Bill Harry. London: Omnibus, 1977. illus.
(Concert fans unable to hear show; page 65.)

C 0178 Lawrence, J. "Explicating The Beatles." in The Age Of Rock 2, ed. by Jonathan Eisen. New York: Vintage Books, 1970.
(Pages 173-179.)

C 0179 Lazar, Jerry. "Magical History Tour." in The Beatles Reader, ed. by Charles P. Neises. Ann Arbor, MI: Pierian Press, 1984.
(Pages 195-198.)

C 0180 Leary, Timothy. "Thank God For The Beatles." in The Beatles Book, ed. by Edward E. Davis.

New York: Cowles Education Corp., 1968.
(Pages 44-55.)

C 0181 Lee, Al. "The Poetics Of The Beatles." in The Beatles Book, ed. by Edward E. Davis. New York: Cowles Education Corp., 1968.
(Pages 99-127.)

C 0182 Lee, Edward. Music Of The People - From Beowulf To The Beatles. London: Barrie & Jenkins, 1970. 274pp. illus.
(Passim.)

C 0183 "Legacy Of Lennon." in A Tribute To John Lennon 1940-1980. London: Proteus, 1981.
(Eulogy; pages 20-21.)

C 0184 Lennon, John. "Around And About, By Beatcomber." in Mersey Beat, ed. by Bill Harry. London: Omnibus, 1977.
(Lennon's occasional column, page 23.)

C 0185 Lennon, John. "Being A Short Diversion On The Dubious Origins Of Beatles." in Mersey Beat, ed. by Bill Harry. London: Omnibus, 1977.
(Page 17.)

C 0186 Lennon, John. "Classified Ads." in Mersey Beat, ed. by Bill Harry. London: Omnibus, 1977.
(Five Lennon "ads," page 20.)

C 0187 Lennon, John. "The Land Of The Lunapots." in Mersey Beat, ed. by Bill Harry. London: Omnibus, 1977.
(Poem; page 76.)

C 0188 Lennon, John. "A Message To Merseyside." in Mersey Beat, ed. by Bill Harry. London: Omnibus, 1977.
(Page 53.)

C 0189 Lennon, John. "On Safairy With Whide Hunter, By Beatcomber." in Mersey Beat, ed. by Bill Harry. London: Omnibus, 1977.
(Fiction; page 38.)

C 0190 Lennon, John. "Small Sam, By Beatcomber." in Mersey Beat, ed. by Bill Harry. London: Omnibus, 1977.
(Fiction; page 36.)

C 0191 Lennon, John. "The Tales Of Hermit Fred." in Mersey Beat, ed. by Bill Harry. London: Omnibus, 1977.
(Poem; page 76.)

C 0192 Lewisohn, Mark. "Some Days In The Life." in John Lennon: The Life And Legend. Melbourne, Aust.: Newspress/Age Publications, 1981.
(Chronology, pages 60-61.)

C 0193 Lichter, Paul. The Boy Who Dared To Rock: The Definitive Elvis. New York: Doubleday, 1978.
(Beatles mentioned pages 61,62,64,80,110.)

C 0194 Lydon, Susan. "New Things For Beatles: Magical Mystery Tour." in The Rolling Stone Rock 'N' Roll Reader, ed. by Ben Fong-Torres. New York: Bantam, 1974.
(Pages 17-20.)

C 0195 McCartney, Paul. "Beatles Record At E.M.I." in Mersey Beat, ed. by Bill Harry. London: Omnibus, 1977.
(Page 39.)

C 0196 McCartney, Paul. "Hamburg." in Mersey Beat, ed. by Bill Harry. London: Omnibus, 1977. illus.
(Beatles history; page 40.)

C 0197 McCartney, Paul. "A Little Bare." in Mersey Beat, ed. by Bill Harry. London: Omnibus, 1977. illus.
(Beatles' history; page 38.)

C 0198 McCartney, Paul. "Mama's Little Girl." in Sisters Under The Skin, by Norman Parkinson. New York: St. Martin's, 1979. illus.
(Handwritten lyrics, page 52 from title page.)

C 0199 "McCartney, Solo, Clearing Up A Few Things." in The Rolling Stone Rock 'N' Roll Reader, ed. by Ben Fong-Torres. New York: Bantam, 1974.
(Pages 49-54.)

C 0200 McGregor, Craig. "The Beatles' Betrayal." in Up Against The Wall, America. Sydney, Australia: Angus & Robertson, 1973.

illus.
(Pages 62-63.)

C 0201 "The Man Who Discovered The Beatles." in Mersey
Beat, ed. by Bill Harry. London: Omnibus,
1977. illus.
(Promoter Brian Kelly; page 52.)

C 0202 Marchbank, Pearce and Miles. The Illustrated
Rock Almanac. New York:
Paddington Press, ltd., 1977. 191pp. pa.
illus.
(Beatles mentioned throughout.)

C 0203 Marcus, Greil. "The Beatles." in The Rolling
Stone Illustrated History Of Rock & Roll,
ed. by Jim Miller. Rev.ed. New York:
Random House/Rolling Stone, 1980. illus.
(Pages 177-189.)

C 0204 Marcus, Greil. Mystery Train: Images Of America
In Rock 'N' Roll Music. New York:
E.P. Dutton & Co., 1975.
(Passim.)

C 0205 Martin, George. Making Music. New York: Quill,
1983. 352pp. pa. illus.
(Includes McCartney interviews.)

C 0206 Martynova, A. "Beatles As Cinderella: A Soviet
Fairy Tale." in The Age Of Rock 2, ed. by
Jonathan Eisen. New York: Vintage Books,
1970.
(Pages 214-218; Beatles' fairy tale rise
to stardom.)

C 0207 May, Chris and Tim Phillips. British Beat.
London: Sociopack Publications Ltd., n.d.
104pp. pa. illus.
(Beatles discussed.)

C 0208 Melly, George. "John Lennon." in A Tribute To
John Lennon 1940-1980. London: Proteus, 1981.
(Eulogy; pages 39-42.)

C 0209 "The Mersey Sound." in Mersey Beat, ed. by Bill
Harry. London: Omnibus, 1977. illus.
(B.B.C. documentary; page 60.)

C 0210 Middleton, Richard. Pop Music And The Blues: A
Study Of The Relationship And Its
Signifcance. London: Victor Gollancz Ltd.,
1972.
(Pages 167-174, 182-184, 232-235, 242-247
& passim.)

C 0211 "M.J.Q. Dig The Beatles." in Mersey Beat, ed.
by Bill Harry. London: Omnibus, 1977. illus.
(Modern Jazz Quartet; page 80.)

C 0212 Moon, Lilith. "Beatlemaniacs Never Die (But
They Sure Get Carried Away)." in The Beatles
Reader, ed. by Charles P. Neises.
Ann Arbor, MI: Pierian Press, 1984.
(Pages 183-185.)

C 0213 "Moving On." in Mersey Beat, ed. by Bill Harry.
London: Omnibus, 1977.
(U.S. reaction to Beatles; page 70.)

C 0214 Murray, John. "John Lennon's Music Will Never
Die." in A Tribute To John Lennon 1940-1980.
London: Proteus, 1981.
(Eulogy; pages 55-56.)

C 0215 "Music And Entertainment." in Catalogue Of
Autograph Letters, Literary Manuscripts And
Historical Documents (Trinket). London:
Sotheby Parke Bernet, 1980.
(Beatles memorabilia for sale, lots
153-157.)

C 0216 "Musicians On Peace." in Give Peace A Chance,
ed. by Marianne Philbin. Chicago, IL:
Chicago Review Press, 1983. illus.
(Photos of Lennon memorabilia after page
58.)

C 0217 Napier-Bell, Simon. You Don't Have To Say You
Love Me. London: New English Library, 1982.
pa.
(John Lennon and Brian Epstein's
relationship.)

C 0218 Neal, Larry. "A Different Bag." in The Beatles
Book, ed. by Edward E. Davis. New York:
Cowles Education Corp., 1968.
(Pages 136-145.)

C 0219 "The Nearness Of You." in Mersey Beat, ed. by
Bill Harry. London: Omnibus, 1977. illus.
(On Pete Best; page 46.)

C 0220 Neises, Charles P. "Booting The Beatles." in
his The Beatles Reader. Ann Arbor, MI:
Pierian Press, 1984.
(Pages 189-192.)

C 0221 "New Beatles Book." in Mersey Beat, ed. by Bill
Harry. London: Omnibus, 1977. illus.
(Shepherd's "True Story"; page 79.)

C 0222 "New Beatles Film." in Mersey Beat, ed. by Bill
Harry. London: Omnibus, 1977.
(George Harrison interviewed; page 87.)

C 0223 "News From Germany." in Mersey Beat, ed. by
Bill Harry. London: Omnibus, 1977. illus.
(Beatles at the Star Club; page 32.)

C 0224 "No Book For John This Year." in Mersey Beat,
ed. by Bill Harry. London: Omnibus, 1977.
(No follow-up to "In His Own Write"; page
87.)

C 0225 Norman, Philip. The Road Goes On Forever.
New York: Fireside, 1982. pa.
(Includes three Beatles-related sections.)

C 0226 O'Donnell, Jim. The Rock Book. New York:
Pinnacle Books, 1975. 278pp. pa. illus.
(Includes Beatles.)

C 0227 O'Grady, Terence J. "The Ballad Style In The
Early Music Of The Beatles." in The Beatles
Reader, ed. by Charles P. Neises.
Ann Arbor, MI: Pierian Press, 1984.
(Pages 79-88.)

C 0228 O'Grady, Terence J. "'Rubber Soul' And The
Social Dance Tradition." in The Beatles
Reader, ed. by Charles P. Neises.
Ann Arbor, MI: Pierian Press, 1984.
(Pages 47-55.)

C 0229 Ono, Yoko. "Surrender To Peace." in Give Peace
A Chance, ed. by Marianne Philbin.
Chicago, IL: Chicago Review Press, 1983.
illus.
(Pages 27-30; from "New York Times," Jan.
24, 1983.)

C 0230 Osborne, Jerry and Bruce Hamilton. A Guide To
Record Collection. Phoenix, AZ: O'Sullivan,
1979. 160pp. pa. illus.
(Record price lists, including Beatles.)

C 0231 "The Other Beatle." in Mersey Beat, ed. by Bill
Harry. London: Omnibus, 1977. illus.
(Pete Best; page 55.)

C 0232 Packard, Vance. "Building The Beatle Image." in
The Beatles Reader, ed. by Charles P.
Neises. Ann Arbor, MI: Pierian Press, 1984.
(Pages 11-13.)

C 0233 Palmer, Tony. "Mighty Goods: The Beatles." in
All You Need Is Love. New York: Grossman,
1976. cl. illus.
(Pages 230-251; career survey.)

C 0234 Palmer, Tony. "Mighty Goods: The Beatles." in
All You Need Is Love. New York:
Penguin Books, 1977. pa. illus.
(Pages 230-251; career survey.)

C 0235 Palmer, Tony. "Orchideen Aus Hawai (Die
Beatles)." in All You Need Is Love, edited
by Paul Medlicott. Munich, W. Ger.:
Droemer Knaur, 1977. cl. illus.
(Pages 254-275; German translation of his
book.)

C 0236 "Paul McCartney." in Mersey Beat, ed. by Bill
Harry. London: Omnibus, 1977. illus.
(Page 63.)

C 0237 "Paul McCartney." in The Book Of People, by
Christopher P. Andersen. New York:
G. P. Putnam's, 1981.
(Page 259; capsule biography.)

C 0238 Peellaert, Guy and Nik Cohn. Rock Dreams.
New York: Popular Library, 1973. 176pp. pa.
illus.
(Beatles discussed.)

C 0239 "Pete Best With All-Stars." in Mersey Beat, ed.
by Bill Harry. London: Omnibus, 1977.

(Joins Lee Curtis & The All-Stars; page 36.)

C 0240 "Pete In States." in Mersey Beat, ed. by Bill Harry. London: Omnibus, 1977. illus.
(Pete Best; page 79.)

C 0241 Peyser, Joan. "The Music Of Sound Or, The Beatles And The Beatless." in The Age Of Rock, ed. by Jonathan Eisen. New York: Random House, 1969. illus.
(Pages 126-137.)

C 0242 Pichaske, David R. A Generation In Motion: Popular Music And Culture In The Sixties. New York: Schirmer/Macmillan, 1979.
(Pages 186-189 and passim.)

C 0243 Pichaske, David R. "Sustained Performances: Sgt. Pepper's Lonely Hearts Club Band." in The Beatles Reader, ed. by Charles P. Neises. Ann Arbor, MI: Pierian Press, 1984.
(Pages 59-62.)

C 0244 Plaumann, Klaus. "Die Giganten." in The Beatage (Die Fruhen Tage Des Rock In Deutschland Und Gross Britannien). Frankfurt, W. Ger.: 2001, 1978. cl. and pa. illus.
(Pages 210-262.)

C 0245 Podell, Janet. "John Lennon." in The Annual Obituary 1980, ed. by Roland Turner. London: Macmillan Press, 1981.
(Pages 761-766; book is also dedicated to John.)

C 0246 Podell, Janet. "John Lennon." in The Annual Obituary 1980, ed. by Roland Turner. New York: St. Martin's, 1981.
(Pages 761-766; book is also dedicated to John.)

C 0247 Podrazik, Wally. "Foreword." in You Can't Do That! by Charles Reinhart. Ann Arbor, MI: Pierian Press, 1982.
(Pages xiii-xiv.)

C 0248 Podrazik, Wally. "Foreword To The 1983 Edition." in The Longest Cocktail Party, by Richard Di Lello. Ann Arbor, MI: Pierian Press, 1983.
(Page xiii.)

C 0249 Poirier, Richard. "Learning From The Beatles." in The Age Of Rock, ed. by Jonathan Eisen. New York: Random House, 1969. illus.
(Pages 160-179; 1967 musical period.)

C 0250 Poirier, Richard. "Learning From The Beatles." in The Beatles Book, ed. by Edward E. Davis. New York: Cowles Education Corp., 1968.
(Pages 12-31.)

C 0251 Poirier, Richard. "Learning From The Beatles." in The Beatles Reader, ed. by Charles P. Neises. Ann Arbor, MI: Pierian Press, 1984.
(Pages 107-128.)

C 0252 Poirier, Richard. "Learning From The Beatles." in his The Performing Self. New York: Oxford University Press, 1971.
(Pages 112-140.)

C 0253 Pollock, Bruce. When Rock Was Young: A Nostalgic Review Of The Top 40 Era. New York: Holt, Rinehart & Winston, 1981. pa.
(Passim.)

C 0254 Pollock, Bruce and John Wagman. The Face Of Rock & Roll: Images Of A Generation. New York: Holt, Rinehart & Winston, 1978. pa. illus.
(Pages 96-101 and passim.)

C 0255 "Popular Entertainment." in Catalogue Of Autograph Letters, Literary Manuscripts And Historical Documents (Ampersand). London: Sotheby Parke Bernet, 1981.
(Beatles memorabilia for sale, lots 270-274, 292.)

C 0256 "Popular Entertainment." in Catalogue Of Autograph Letters, Literary Manuscripts And Historical Documents (Sprint). London: Sotheby Parke Bernet, 1981.
(Beatles memorabilia for sale, lots

170-177.)

C 0257 "Popular Entertainment And Ballet." in The Collection Of Autograph Letters, Historical Documents And .... (Rawlins). London: Sotheby Parke Bernet, 1980.
(Beatles memorabilia for sale, lots 912-914.)

C 0258 "Popular Entertainment And Cinema." in Catalogue Of Autograph Letters, Literary Manuscripts And Historical Documents (Iago). London: Sotheby Parke Bernet, 1980.
(Beatles memorabilia for sale, lots 351-371.)

C 0259 "The Press Conference: John Lennon And Yoko Ono Talk About Peace." in Give Peace A Chance, ed. by Marianne Philbin. Chicago, IL: Chicago Review Press, 1983. illus.
(Pages 19-25; from "Rolling Stone," 1970.)

C 0260 "A Random Note." in The Rolling Stone Rock 'N' Roll Reader, ed. by Ben Fong-Torres. New York: Bantam, 1974.
(Pages 27-28.)

C 0261 "Readers' Letters." in Mersey Beat, ed. by Bill Harry. London: Omnibus, 1977. illus.
(Beatles' first fan mail; page 20.)

C 0262 Rimler, Walter. "George Harrison: Fall From Grace." in his Not Fade Away. Ann Arbor, MI: Pierian Press, 1984. illus.
(Pages 153-161; Harrison as composer.)

C 0263 Rimler, Walter. "John Lennon: The Great Swan Of Liverpool." in his Not Fade Away. Ann Arbor, MI: Pierian Press, 1984. illus.
(Pages 135-143; Lennon as composer.)

C 0264 Rimler, Walter. "Partnerships." in his Not Fade Away. Ann Arbor, MI: Pierian Press, 1984. illus.
(Pages 31-37 on The Beatles.)

C 0265 Rimler, Walter. "Paul McCartney: Keeper Of The Flame." in his Not Fade Away. Ann Arbor, MI: Pierian Press, 1984. illus.
(Pages 143-153; McCartney as composer.)

C 0266 "Ringo." in Mersey Beat, ed. by Bill Harry. London: Omnibus, 1977.
(Photo; page 54.)

C 0267 "Ringo." in Mersey Beat, ed. by Bill Harry. London: Omnibus, 1977. illus.
(Page 71.)

C 0268 "Ringo & Steptoe." in Mersey Beat, ed. by Bill Harry. London: Omnibus, 1977. illus.
(Ringo meets Wilfred Brambell; page 84.)

C 0269 "Ringo For 'Juke Box Jury'." in Mersey Beat, ed. by Bill Harry. London: Omnibus, 1977. illus.
(Page 86.)

C 0270 "Ringo Produces Book Of Photographs." in Mersey Beat, ed. by Bill Harry. London: Omnibus, 1977. illus.
(To be published in U.S.; page 88.)

C 0271 "Ringo Starr (Richard Starkey)." in The Book Of People, by Christopher P. Anderson. New York: G. P. Putnam's, 1981.
(Pages 372-373; capsule biography.)

C 0272 Roberts, Richard. "'Yesterday' Mourning Before Sunrise." in A Tribute To John Lennon 1940-1980. London: Proteus, 1981.
(Eulogy; pages 12-13.)

C 0273 "Rock And Roll Memorabilia." in Collectors' Carrousel (4907Y). New York: Sotheby Parke Bernet, 1982.
(Beatles memorabilia, lots 223-263.)

C 0274 Rooney, Andy. "Why Some Wept For John Lennon." in A Tribute To John Lennon 1940-1980. London: Proteus, 1981.
(Eulogy; pages 85-86.)

C 0275 Rorem, Ned. "The Music Of The Beatles." in The Age Of Rock, ed. by Jonathan Eisen. New York: Random House, 1969. illus.
(Pages 149-159; analysis of Beatles' music.)

C 0276 Rorem, Ned. "Why The Beatles Are Good." in The

Beatles Book, ed. by Edward E. Davis.
New York: Cowles Education Corp., 1968.
(Pages 1-11.)

C 0277 Rosten, Leo, ed. The Look Book. New York:
Harry N. Abrams Inc., 1975.
(Full page Richard Avedon photos, pp.
274-279.)

C 0278 Rowlands, John. Spotlight Heroes: Two Decades
Of Rock And Roll Superstars As Seen Through
The Camera Of John Rowlands. New York:
McGraw-Hill, 1981. pa.
(Photos: pages 4,5,17,57,68,69.)

C 0279 Roxon, Lillian. Lillian Roxon's Rock
Encyclopedia. 2d ed. New York:
Grosset & Dunlap, 1971. pa.
(Pages 30-38.)

C 0280 Saleh, Dennis. Rock Art: Fifty-Two Record Album
Covers. n.p.: Comma Books, 1977. 136pp. pa.
illus.
(Includes Beatles' LP covers.)

C 0281 Sarris, Andrew. "A Hard Day's Night." in his
Confessions Of A Cultist: On Cinema,
1955-69. New York: Simon & Schuster, 1970.
(Pages 160-163 on the film "A Hard Day's
Night.")

C 0282 Satkin, Marc. The Official Rock And Roll Trivia
Quiz Book. New York: Signet Books, 1977.
158pp. pa. illus.
(Includes Beatles.)

C 0283 Schafer, William J. "Concepts And Concept
Albums." in Rock Music. Minneapolis:
Augsburg Publishing House, 1972. illus.
(Pages 103-123; treats "Sgt. Pepper" LP.)

C 0284 Schafer, William J. "Part 1: Rock Beginnings."
in Rock Music. Minneapolis:
Augsburg Publishing House, 1972. illus.
(Pages 13-46; discussion and Beatles
discography.)

C 0285 Schafer, William J. "We All Live In A Yellow
Submarine." in Rock Music. Minneapolis:
Augsburg Publishing House, 1972. illus.
(Pages 34-44; post-1965 musical period.)

C 0286 Schaffner, Nicholas. "The Beatles." in The
British Invasion. New York: McGraw-Hill,
1982.
(Pages 13-53; and passim.)

C 0287 Schaffner, Nicholas and Elizabeth Schaffner.
"The Beatles." in 505 Rock 'N' Roll
Questions Your Friends Can't Answer.
New York: Walker, 198.
(Pages 29-43; trivia questions and
answers.)

C 0288 Schmidt-Joos, Siegfried and B. Graves. Rock
Lexikon. Hamburg, W. Ger.:
Rowohlt Taschenbuch, 1979. pa.
(Contains two-page Beatle biographies.)

C 0289 Schultheiss, Tom. "Foreword." in As I Write
This Letter, by Marc A. Catone.
Ann Arbor, MI: Greenfield Books/Pierian,
1982.
(Pages xi-xii.)

C 0290 Schultheiss, Tom. "Foreword." in The Literary
Lennon: A Comedy Of Letters, by James
Sauceda. Ann Arbor, MI: Pierian Press, 1983.
(Pages ix-x.)

C 0291 Schwartz, Francie. Body Count. San Francisco:
Straight Arrow/Quick Fox, 1972.
(Section on her relationship with Paul
McCartney.)

C 0292 "Seaside Rock - The Beatles." in Mersey Beat,
ed. by Bill Harry. London: Omnibus, 1977.
illus.
(Photo; page 42.)

C 0293 Shankar, Ravi. My Music, My Life. New York:
Simon and Schuster, 1968. 160pp. cl. illus.
(George Harrison discussed.)

C 0294 Shapiro, Nat. "Popular Music, 1960-1964." in
Popular Music, Vol. 3:1960-1964, ed. by Nat
Shapiro. New York: Adrian Press, 1967.
(Pages 1-6 and passim.)

C 0295 Shapiro, Nat. "Popular Music, 1965-1969." in
Popular Music, Vol. 6: 1965-1969, ed. by Nat
Shapiro. New York: Adrian Press, 1973.
(Pages 1-8 and passim.)

C 0296 Sheff, David. "John Lennon And Yoko Ono." in
The Playboy Interview, ed. by G. Barry
Golson. New York: Playboy, 1981. cl.
("Playboy" interview published January 1981.)

C 0297 Short, Don. "The Lighter Side Of John Lennon."
in A Tribute To John Lennon 1940-1980.
London: Proteus, 1981.
(Eulogy; page 30.)

C 0298 Silver, Caroline. The Pop Makers. New York:
Scholastic Book Services, 1966. 127pp. pa.
illus.
(Covers Beatles.)

C 0299 Simon, George T. Best Of The Music Makers.
New York: Doubleday, 1979.
(The Beatles, pages 50-54.)

C 0300 Simon, John Ivan. "Let It Be." in his Movies
Into Film; Film Criticism, 1967-1970.
New York: Dial, 1971.
(Pages 127-129.)

C 0301 Smith, Alan. "At A Recording Session With The
Beatles." in Mersey Beat, ed. by Bill Harry.
London: Omnibus, 1977. illus.
(Page 49.)

C 0302 Smith, Alan. "The Beatles." in Mersey Beat, ed.
by Bill Harry. London: Omnibus, 1977.
(Page 44.)

C 0303 Smith, Alan. "London Beat." in Mersey Beat, ed.
by Bill Harry. London: Omnibus, 1977.
(On The Beatles' future; page 47.)

C 0304 Smith, Sharon. Women Who Make Movies.
New York: Hopkinson and Blake, 1975.
(Yoko Ono, pages 194-195.)

C 0305 Snyder, Patrick. "People And Things That Went
Before." in The Beatles Reader, ed. by
Charles P. Neises. Ann Arbor, MI:
Pierian Press, 1984.
(Pages 201-212.)

C 0306 "Social History, Entertainment, Sport, Etc." in
Catalogue Of Autograph Letters, Literary
Manuscripts And Historical Documents (Cat).
London: Sotheby Parke Bernet, 1979.
(Beatles memorabilia for sale, lots
196-197.)

C 0307 Southhall, Brian. Abbey Road: The Story Of The
World's Most Famous Recording Studios.
Cambridge, Eng.: Patrick Stephens Limited,
1982. 218pp. cl. illus.
(Foreword by Paul McCartney.)

C 0308 Stafford, Peter. "I'd Love ... To Tur .. r .. r
.. n You On." in The Beatles Book, ed. by
Edward E. Davis. New York:
Cowles Education Corp., 1968.
(Pages 56-85.)

C 0309 Stambler, Irwin. "The Beatles." in Encyclopedia
Of Pop, Rock And Soul. New York:
St. Martin's, 1974. illus.
(Pages 44-47; biographical surveys.)

C 0310 Stanley, Hiram. "Hiram's Report." in The
Beatles Reader, ed. by Charles P. Neises.
Ann Arbor, MI: Pierian Press, 1984.
(On February 1964 visit; pages 5-8.)

C 0311 "Star Drummer!" in Mersey Beat, ed. by Bill
Harry. London: Omnibus, 1977. illus.
(Ringo Starr; page 38.)

C 0312 Starrett, Ian. "The Beatles In Ireland." in
Mersey Beat, ed. by Bill Harry. London:
Omnibus, 1977.
(Northern Ireland concerts; page 91.)

C 0313 "Strawberry Fields Forever." in A Tribute To
John Lennon 1940-1980. London: Proteus, 1981.
(Eulogy; pages 72-73.)

C 0314 Suczek, Barbara. "The Curious Case Of The
'Death' Of Paul McCartney." in The Beatles
Reader, ed. by Charles P. Neises.
Ann Arbor, MI: Pierian Press, 1984.
(Pages 27-39.)

C 0315 Sutcliffe, Phil. "How John Was Overwhelmed By Life And Death." in A Tribute To John Lennon 1940-1980. London: Proteus, 1981.
(Eulogy; pages 15-18.)

C 0316 "The Talk Of The Town." in A Tribute To John Lennon 1940-1980. London: Proteus, 1981.
(Eulogy; page 75.)

C 0317 Taupin, Bernie. The One Who Writes The Words For Elton John. New York: Knopf, 1976. pa. illus.
(Lennon montage for "Bennie & The Jets," page 110.)

C 0318 Taupin, Bernie. The One Who Writes The Words For Elton John. New York: Knopf, 1976. pa. illus.
(Ringo Starr drawing for "Snookeroo," page 144.)

C 0319 Taylor, Leon. "They Loved Him, Yeah, Yeah, Yeah." in A Tribute To John Lennon 1940-1980. London: Proteus, 1981.
(Eulogy ;page 23.)

C 0320 Tennis, Craig. Johnny Tonight!. New York: Pocket Books, 1980.
(Pages 158-160;John and Paul on "Tonight.")

C 0321 Tobler, John and Pete Frame. Rock 'N' Roll: The First 25 Years. New York: Exeter Books, 1980. 252pp. cl. illus.
(Passim.)

C 0322 Tobler, John and Stuart Grundy. "Chris Thomas." in their The Record Producers. New York: St. Martin's Press, 1982.
(Pages 227-229 on The Beatles.)

C 0323 Tobler, John and Stuart Grundy. "George Martin." in their The Record Producers. New York: St. Martin's Press, 1982.
(Pages 111-117 and passim on The Beatles.)

C 0324 Tobler, John and Stuart Grundy. "Phil Spector." in their The Record Producers. New York: St. Martin's Press, 1982.
(Pages 52-53 and passim on The Beatles.)

C 0325 25 Years Of Rock & Roll. Tulsa,OK: Harrison House, 1979. 96pp. cl. illus.
(Chapter on The Beatles.)

C 0326 "A Unique Reception." in Mersey Beat, ed. by Bill Harry. London: Omnibus, 1977.
(Return from Hamburg; page 50.)

C 0327 Virginia. "Mersey Roundabout." in Mersey Beat, ed. by Bill Harry. London: Omnibus, 1977.
(Beatles fan club formed; page 21.)

C 0328 Walters, Lu. "Ringo." in Mersey Beat, ed. by Bill Harry. London: Omnibus, 1977. illus.
(Page 53.)

C 0329 Watts, Michael. "Some Time In New York City: Lennon After The Beatles." in John Lennon: The Life And Legend. Melbourne, Aust.: Newspress/Age Publications, 1981.
(Pages 48-55.)

C 0330 "A Wave From Paul." in Mersey Beat, ed. by Bill Harry. London: Omnibus, 1977.
(Photo; page 84.)

C 0331 Wenner, Jann. "The Beatles: On The Occasion Of Their Authorized Biography." in The Rolling Stone Rock 'N' Roll Reader, ed. by Ben Fong-Torres. New York: Bantam, 1974.
(Pages 71-82.)

C 0332 Wenner, Jann. "One Guy Standing There, Shouting 'I'm Leaving'." in The Rolling Stone Rock 'N' Roll Reader, ed. by Ben Fong-Torres. New York: Bantam, 1974.
(Pages 54-59.)

C 0333 Wenner, Jann. "Rock And Roll Music." in The Rolling Stone Rock 'N' Roll Reader, ed. by Ben Fong-Torres. New York: Bantam, 1974.
(Pages 82-86.)

C 0334 Wiener, Jon. "'Give Peace A Chance': An Anthem For The Anti-War Movement." in Give Peace A Chance, ed. by Marianne Philbin. Chicago, IL: Chicago Review Press, 1983. illus.
(Pages 11-17.)

C 0335 Williams, Jean. "Artists Express Love, Respect, Gratefulness For Ex-Beatle." in A Tribute To John Lennon 1940-1980. London: Proteus, 1981.
(Eulogies; pages 21, 51, 66.)

C 0336 Williams, Richard. "Gimme Some Truth: The Thoughts Of John Lennon." in John Lennon: The Life And Legend. Melbourne, Aust.: Newspress/Age Publications, 1981.
(Quotations, pages 56-57.)

C 0337 Williams, Richard. Out Of His Head; The Sound Of Phil Spector. London: Abacus/Sphere Books, 1972.
(Covers Spector's relationship with The Beatles.)

C 0338 Willmott, Nigel. "We've Lost Part Of Ourselves." in A Tribute To John Lennon 1940-1980. London: Proteus, 1981.
(Eulogy; pages 50-51.)

C 0339 "Wings' Story." in Rock Family Trees. New York: Quick Fox, 1979.
(Page 24.)

C 0340 "With Mike And Bern." in Mersey Beat, ed. by Bill Harry. London: Omnibus, 1977.
(Rehearsals at ABC Theatre, Blackpool; page 85.)

C 0341 "Witty John." in Mersey Beat, ed. by Bill Harry. London: Omnibus, 1977. illus.
(Photo; page 53.)

C 0342 Wood, Michael. "Arts In Society: John Lennon's School Days." in The Age Of Rock, ed. by Jonathan Eisen. New York: Random House, 1969. illus.
(Pages 121-125.)

C 0343 Wooler, Bob. "John, Paul, George and Pete ...." in Mersey Beat, ed. by Bill Harry. London: Omnibus, 1977.
(Page 31.)

C 0344 Wooler, Bob. "Well Now - Dig This!" in Mersey Beat, ed. by Bill Harry. London: Omnibus, 1977.
(On Beatles' popularity; page 22.)

C 0345 "Worst Beatle Book Yet?" in Mersey Beat, ed. by Bill Harry. London: Omnibus, 1977.
("Here Come The Beatles"; page 95.)

C 0346 Yates, Paula. Rock Stars In Their Underpants. London: Virgin Books, 1980. 86pp. pa. illus.
(Paul McCartney wearing ladies knickers.)

C 0347 Yorke, Ritchie. "Bedding In For Peace: John And Yoko In Canada." in The Rolling Stone Rock 'N' Roll Reader, ed. by Ben Fong-Torres. New York: Bantam, 1974.
(Pages 34-43.)

C 0348 Yorke, Ritchie. "John, Yoko And Eric Clapton Kick Up Their Blue Suede Shoes." in The Rolling Stone Rock 'N' Roll Reader, ed. by Ben Fong-Torres. New York: Bantam, 1974.
(Pages 43-45.)

C 0349 Zibart, Eve. "The Lennon Sound." in A Tribute To John Lennon 1940-1980. London: Proteus, 1981.
(Eulogy; pages 80-81.)

The Write Thing #42

the Beatles

With A Little Help From My Friends

JANUARY 1984 — ISSUE #45

BEATLEMANIA IS HERE
FOR SOME TIME TO COME!

BEATLES NOW

Beatlefan

beatles unlimited

an independent bimonthly for the fans of john, paul, george and ringo

published in the netherlands

The McCartney Observer

The Harrison Alliance

Videosyncrasy: A Guide to Harrison on Video

YEAH YEAH YEAH

IT WAS 20 YEARS AGO

F 0001 ABBEY ROAD. November 1971 - ?
         Simsboro, LA: Vickie Mikulis/Abbey Road
         Chapter - Apple Tree. illus.
         (Ceased; ongoing as late as January 1972.)
     Abbey Road Chapter - Apple Tree see ABBEY
     ROAD.
F 0002 ABBEY ROAD REVIEW. ? - ?
         Detroit, MI: Jane Tate. illus.
         (Ceased.)
F 0003 ACROSS THE UNIVERSE. ? - ?
         Mesa, AZ: Terri Wood. illus.
         (Ceased;ongoing as late as Vol.2,No.2
         (July 1976).)
F 0004 ALL THINGS MUST PASS. December 1971,
         Vol.1, No.1 - March 1981, Vol.2, No.1.
         Brooklyn, NY: Penguin Records. illus.
         (Ceased; seven issues published.)
F 0005 ALL TOGETHER NOW. February 1976, No.1 - ?
         Palo Alto, CA: Dianne Cuccia. illus.
         (Ceased; was "Get Back"?)
F 0006 ALL TOGETHER NOW. August 1978, No.1 - .
         Escondido, CA: Vlasta Paul. illus.
F 0007 ALMA DE GOMA. ? - ?
         Buenos Aires,Argen.: Horacio
         Dubini/Argentina Beatles Fan Club. illus.
         ("Rubber Soul"; ceased?)
F 0008 THE APPLE. ? - October 1971.
         Simsboro, LA: Vickie Mikulis/Apple Chapter -
         OBFC. illus.
         (Also called "Apple Seed"; became "Abbey
         Road.")
     Apple Chapter - OBFC see THE APPLE.
F 0009 APPLE JuCe. ? - ?
         Rego Park, NY: Judee Gould and Celene
         Steinberg. illus.
         (Ceased; ongoing as late as Fall 1971,
         No.4.)
F 0010 APPLE PRESS. December 1972, No.1 - ?
         Hawthorne, NY: Independent Apple
         Enterprises/Linda Kretschmann. illus.
         (Ceased.)
F 0011 APPLE SCRUFFS INC. ? - ?
         Scotia, NY: Lynn Fischer. illus.
         (Ceased.)
     APPLE SEED see THE APPLE.
F 0012 APPLE'S KIN. January 1982, No.1 - .
         Seattle, WA: Leanne Clarke. illus.
     Apple Tree see ABBEY ROAD; ONO ODYSSEY.
F 0013 AROUND THE BEATLES. ? - late 1968.
         Dearborn, MI: Jeri Bethmann. illus.
         (Merged with "Father Lennon's Many
         Children.")
F 0014 BEAT LAND. ? - ?
         Birmingham, Eng.: West Midland Beatles Fan
         Club. illus.
         (Ceased?)
F 0015 BEATLEADS. September 1983, No.1 - .
         Springfield, IL: Katie Collard. illus.
F 0016 BEATLEFAN. January 1979, Vol.1, No.1 - .
         Decatur, GA: The Goody Press. illus.
F 0017 BEATLE FANS OF THE WORLD UNITE. ? - ?
         illus.
         (Ceased; ongoing as late as September
         1968.)
F 0018 BEATLE FILM SOCIETY OF AMERICA. ? - ?
         Spokane, WA: Beatle Film Society Of America.
         illus.
         (Ceased.)
     Beatle Kingdom Fan Club see LENNON LEAGUE.
F 0019 BEATLE MAGAZINE. May/June 1984, Vol.1,
         No.1 - .
         Churchville, NY: Jim Havalock. illus.
F 0020 BEATLEMANIA. Summer 1982, No.1 - .
         Gera-Luson, E.Ger.: Hartmut Schwarz. illus.
F 0021 BEATLEMANIE. July/August 1977, No.1 - ca.
         May 1980.
         Montreal, Canada: Jean Paul Gobell. illus.
         (Ceased; supplemented by "8 Days A Week
         News.")

F 0022 THE BEATLE PEACE FOLLOWERS. November 1970,
         No.1 - 1973, No.?
         Pittsburgh, PA: Barb Whatmough. illus.
         (Became "The Working Class Hero Club.")
F 0023 BEATLES. ? - ?
         Oneonta, NY: Becky Test. illus.
         (Ceased.)
F 0024 THE BEATLES. February 1969, No.1 - .
         Tokyo, Japan: Beatles Cine Club. illus.
F 0025 BEATLES & WINGS FAN CLUB. ? - ?
         Hernsbach, W.Ger.: Wolfgang Vock. illus.
         (Ceased; ongoing as late as 1980.)
F 0026 BEATLES & WINGS FAN CLUB. ? - ?
         Vancouver, Canada: Linda Matthews. illus.
         (Ceased?)
F 0027 BEATLES APPRECIATION FAN CLUB. ? - ?
         Stafford, England: Beatles Appreciation Fan
         Club. illus.
         (Ceased.)
F 0028 BEATLES APPRECIATION SOCIETY. ? - ?
         Hobart, Australia: Peter Mutton. illus.
         (Ceased.)
F 0029 BEATLES APPRECIATION SOCIETY MAGAZINE. ? -
         November/December 1977, No.4.
         Norwich, England: Beatles Appreciation
         Society. illus.
         (Ceased.)
F 0030 BEATLES BEAT FAN CLUB. early 1982 - ?
         Ripley, MS: Royce Hart. illus.
         (Ceased.)
F 0031 THE BEATLES BEAT DOWNUNDER. 1983, No.1 - .
         Magill, Australia: Graham L. Moyle. illus.
F 0032 THE BEATLES BOOK. Republication began May
         1976, No.1 - .
         London: Beat Publications. illus.
         (First issued Aug. 1963, No.1 - Dec. 1969,
         No.77.)
F 0033 THE BEATLES CAVERN CLUB. ? - 1978.
         Sao Paulo, Brazil: Beatles Cavern Club.
         illus.
         (Ceased; became "Revolution.")
     Beatles Cine Club see THE BEATLES.
F 0034 THE BEATLES CITY MAGAZINE. February 1984,
         No.1 - .
         Liverpool, Eng.: Beatles City Ltd. illus.
F 0035 BEATLES COLLECTOR. August 1979?, No.1 - ?
         Galveston, TX: Phillip LeVrier. illus.
         (Ceased; ongoing as late as No.6, ca.
         Sept.1981.)
     THE BEATLES COLLECTOR see BEATLES COLLECTOR.
F 0036 BEATLES COLLECTORS CLUBS OF AMERICA. ? - ?
         Rhode Island: Bob Sullivan. illus.
         (Ceased.)
F 0037 THE BEATLES CONNECTION. January 1983,
         Vol.1, No.1 - .
         Pinellas Park, FL: Craig R. Still. illus.
F 0038 BEATLES DIGEST. May/June 1975, No.1 - ?
         Pendleton, SC: Kurt Neiburg. illus.
         (Ongoing as late No.3.)
     Beatles Fan Club Of Austria see YESTERDAY.
F 0039 BEATLES FOR SALE. ? - ?
         Spokane, WA: Beatles For Sale. illus.
         (Ceased?)
     The Beatles Information Center see
     BEATLES-NYTT.
F 0040 BEATLES NEWS. January 1973, No.1 - .
         Bochum, W.Ger.: Michael Krieger. illus.
F 0041 BEATLES NEWS BOOK. January 1973, No.1 - .
         Bochum, W.Ger.: Michael Krieger. illus.
F 0042 BEATLES NOW. January/March 1982, No.1 - .
         London: Roger N. Akehurst. illus.
F 0043 BEATLES-NYTT. October 1973, No.1 - .
         Stockholm, Sweden: The Beatles Information
         Center. illus.
F 0044 BEATLES PLAYBACK. 1975, Nos.1 - 3.
         Amsterdam, Holland: Vereiniging Nederlandse
         Beatles Fanclub. illus.
         (Ceased after three issues.)
F 0045 BEATLES REPORT. April 1976, No.1 -

Cologne, W.Ger.: Beatles Information Center
— West Germany. illus.
(An "acoustic magazine" (90-minute
cassettes).)

F 0046 BEATLES RULE. August 1969, No.1 — ?
St. Paul, MN: Barbara Fenick. illus.
(Succeeded "Father Lennon's Many
Children.")

F 0047 THE BEATLES SGT PEPPER'S LONELY HEARTS CLUB
BAND. October/November 1983, No.1 — .
Tampa, FL: Tami Hignite. illus.

F 0048 BEATLES UNLIMITED. December 1974, No.1 — .
Nieuwegein, Holland: Beatles Unlimited.
illus.
(Dutch language counterpart: "Beatles Werk
Group.")

THE BEATLES UNOFFICIAL FAN CLUB MAGAZINE see
REVOLVER.

F 0049 BEATLES VIDEO NEWSLETTER. May/June 1983,
No.1 — .
Springfield, MA: John Dobrydnio and Gloria
Patti. illus.

F 0050 BEATLES VISIE. January 1980, No. — .
Amsterdam, Holland: Vereiniging Nederlandse
Beatles Fanclub. illus.
(Called "Chains," November 1963-February
1970.)

F 0051 BEATLES WERK GROUP. 1973 — ?
Nieuwegein, Holland: Beatles Werk Group.
illus.
(English language counterpart: "Beatles
Unlimited.")

F 0052 THE BEATLES — YESTERDAY AND TODAY.
January/February 1971, No.1 — mid-1976?
Highland Park, IL: Vikki Paradiso. illus.
(Ceased;ongoing as late as Feb./June 1976,
No.9.)

F 0053 BEATLES YESTERDAY & TODAY ORGANIZATION. ? — ?
Gothenburg, Sweden: Beatles Yesterday &
Today Organization. illus.
(Ceased.)

F 0054 BOSS BEATLES FAN CLUB. ? — November/
December 1968.
San Diego, CA: Cindi Gonzalez. illus.
(Ceased.)

BRITISH BEATLES APPRECIATION SOCIETY MAGAZINE
see BEATLES APPRECIATION SOCIETY MAGAZINE.

F 0055 CAVERN MECCA. January 1981, No.1 — December
1984.
Liverpool, Eng.: Jim and Liz Hughes. illus.
(Ceased.)

F 0056 CHAINS. ? — ?
Amsterdam, Holland: Vereiniging Nederlandse
Beatles Fanclub. illus.
(Later became "Beatles Visie.")

F 0057 CILLA BLACK FAN CLUB. ? — ?
Sale,Cheshire,Eng.: Joan Organ. illus.
(Ceased?)

Les Club des 4 de Liverpool see THE FAB FOUR
PUBLICATION.

F 0058 CLUB SANDWICH. February/March 1977, No.1 — .
London, England: Wings Fun Club. illus.
(Formerly "Paul McCartney And Wings Fan
Club.")

Col. Lectiu Beatleman see OB LA DI OB LA
DA.

F 0059 COME TOGETHER. 1979, Vol.1, No.1 — ?
Kettering, England: Carl Dunkley. illus.
(Ceased?; ongoing as late as 1980, Vol.2,
No.7.)

F 0060 DARK HORSE. November/December 1981, No.1 —
June/July 1982, No.4.
West Haven, CT: Joey Chadderton. illus.
(Merged with "Good Day Sunshine," June
1983.)

DIG IT see WITH A LITTLE HELP FROM MY
FRIENDS.

F 0061 8 DAYS A WEEK NEWS. ? — ?
Montreal, Canada: Jean Paul Gobell. illus.

(Ceased?; English supplement to
"Beatlemanie.")

F 0062 ENGLISH BOUND BEATLE FANS CLUB. ? — ?
Flint, MI: Jamie Sim. illus.
(Ceased; ongoing as late as April 1969,
No.7.)

F 0063 EVERY LITTLE THING. ? — ?
Tamworth, Eng.: Every Little Thing. illus.
(Ceased?)

F 0064 THE FAB FOUR PUBLICATION. November 1973,
No.0 — .
Paris, France: Les Club des 4 de Liverpool.
illus.

F 0065 FATHER LENNON'S MANY CHILDREN. October
1967 — January 1969.
St. Paul, MN: Barbara Fenick. illus.
(Absorbed "Around The Beatles";became
"Beatles Rule.")

F 0066 FIVE BITES OF THE APPLE. April/May 1971,
No.1 — December/January/February 1972-73.
Great Neck, NY: Linda Woods/Five Bites
Chapter — OBFC. illus.
(Ceased.)

F 0067 FLORIDA BEATLES FAN CLUB. ? — ?
Pompano Beach, FL: Claudette Cyr/Paul
McCartney Fan Club. illus.
(Ceased; ongoing as late as August 1969.)

F 0068 FROM ME TO YOU. July 1978, No.1 — .
Bad Hersfeld,W.Ger.: Peter Schuster. illus.

F 0069 GEAR BOX. March 1976, No.1 — .
Cleveland, OH: Barb Paulson/Mike McCartney
Fan Club. illus.
(Was "Mike McGear Fan Club.")

F 0070 GEORGE GERNAL. ? — ?
Collegeville, PA: Pat Kinzer/George Harrison
Fan Club — OBFC. illus.
(Annual; ongoing as late as 1967, No.7.)

F 0071 GEORGE HARRISON FAN CLUB. ? — November
1982.
Luton, England: Anne Wallis. illus.
(Ceased.)

George Harrison Fan Club — OBFC see GEORGE
GERNAL; HARRISON HERALD.

F 0072 GET BACK. ? — ?
Oberursel, W. Ger.: Karlheinz Borchert.
illus.
(Ceased;ongoing as late as early 1979.)

F 0073 GET BACK. early 1975 — ?
Palo Alto, CA: Dianne Cuccia and Peggy Evans.
illus.
(Ceased; became "All Together Now"?)

F 0074 GOOD DAY SUNSHINE. early 1979 — December
1980, Year 3, Issue 9.
Rio Grande, PR: Rosita Rodriguez. illus.
(Resumed by Charles Rosenay, January 1981,
No.1.)

F 0075 GOOD DAY SUNSHINE. January/February 1981,
No.1 — .
New Haven, CT: Liverpool Productions. illus.
(Absorbed "Good Day Sunshine" and "Dark
Horse.")

F 0076 THE HARRISON ALLIANCE. May 1972, No.1 — .
Bristol, CT: Patti Murawski. illus.
(Successor to "Indiana OBFC.")

F 0077 HARRISON HERALD. mid-1965 — early 1972.
Collegeville, PA: Pat Kinzer/George Harrison
Fan Club — OBFC. illus.
(Ceased; ongoing as late as December 1971,
No.32.)

Harrison/Lennon Followers — Beatles USA
Ltd. see TRAILS OF GEORGE AND JOHN.

F 0078 HELTER SKELTER. ? — ?
Gloucester, England: Helter Skelter. illus.
(Ceased.)

F 0079 HERE, THERE AND EVERYWHERE. ca. August
1973, No.1 — ?
Boston, MA: Joe Pope/Strawberry Fields
Forever. illus.
(Ceased?; at least four issues published.)

F 0080 HERE, THERE AND EVERYWHERE. ca. 1979 —

February/March/April 1981, Vol.3 No.1 (?).
Tigard, OR: Katie Lieuallen. illus.
(Ceased; merged with "Good Day Sunshine.")

F 0081 IMAGINE. March/April 1978, No.1 – ?
Waterbury, CT: Gorman Bechard, Jr. illus.
(Ceased; ongoing as late as Jul./Aug.
1979, No.9.)

Independent Apple Enterprises see APPLE
PRESS.

F 0082 INDEPENDENT FREE APPLE. ? – ?
Westminster, CA: Independent Free Apple.
illus.
(Ceased.)

F 0083 INDIANA OBFC. 1972 – 1974.
Goshen, IN: Pam Elijah/Indiana Official
Beatles Fan Club. illus.
(Successor to "Harrison Herald.")

Indiana Official Beatles Fan Club see INDIANA
OBFC.

F 0084 THE INNER LIGHT. ca. early 1975 – ?
San Mateo, CA: Rich Friedland. illus.
(Ceased;ongoing as late as Vol.2, No.9,
1976.)

F 0085 INSTANT KARMA. December 1981, No.1 – .
Sault Ste.Marie, MI: Marsha Ewing. illus.

F 0086 IN THE CORE OF THE APPLE. ? – ?
Jackson, OH: Mabel McManis. illus.
(Ceased.)

F 0087 JOHN LENNON CANONIZATION COALITION. June
1980, No.1 – December 1980.
Louisville, KY: Ann Lawter. illus.
(Ceased.)

John Lennon Fan Club see also LENNON LYRICS;
NORWEGIAN WOOD.

F 0088 JOHN LENNON FAN CLUB. ? – ?
Bad Tolz, W. Ger.: Heidi Stempf. illus.
(Ceased.)

F 0089 JOHN LENNON FAN CLUB. ? – ?
Bellington, Eng.: Shirley Mitchell. illus.
(Ceased?)

F 0090 JOHN LENNON FAN CLUB. ? – ?
N. Plainfield, NJ: Barbara Cook. illus.
(Ceased?)

F 0091 KINGDOM BEAT. June 1970 – October 1972.
Philadelphia, PA: Vickie Rhody/Beatle
Kingdom Fan Club. illus.
(Ceased.)

F 0092 LENNON LEAGUE. ca. May 1969, No.1 (one
issue only).
Phoenix, AZ: Kay Wade/Official John Lennon
Chapter (Beatles USA Ltd.). illus.
(Was "Norwegian Wood"; became "Lennon
Listener.")

F 0093 LENNON LISTENER. August 1, 1969, No.2 – ?
Phoenix, AZ: Kay Wade/Official John Lennon
Chapter (Beatles USA Ltd.). illus.
(Ceased; formerly "Lennon League.")

F 0094 LENNON LUCUBRATION. 1973, No.1 – ?
Plainfield, NJ: Barb Clark. illus.
(Ceased; ongoing as late as 1974, No.5.)

F 0095 LENNON LYRICS. 1964 – May/June 1968.
Howell, MI: Judy Johnson/John Lennon Fan
Club. illus.
(Became "Norwegian Wood.")

F 0096 LET IT BE. ? – ?
Chicago, IL: Sharon Uzarewicz. illus.
(Ceased; ongoing as late as 1972.)

F 0097 LETTERS ABROAD. ? – ?
New York, NY: Letters Abroad. illus.
(Ceased?)

F 0098 LIVE. January 1977 – ?
Tijucas, Brazil: Henrique Carballal Alvarez.
illus.
(Ceased?)

F 0099 LUV 'N' STUFF. ? – ?
Chicago, IL: Joanne Maggio/Paul McCartney
Chapter – OBFC. illus.
(Ceased; ongoing as late as April/May
1971.)

F 0100 MACCA. ? – ?

Forest Park, IL: Jamie Louise Alonzo. illus.
(Ceased; ongoing at least January to
October 1978.)

F 0101 McCARTNEY. early 1973 – ?
Plainfield, NJ: Marie Lacey. illus.
(Ceased; title varies: "McCartney Lovers &
Friends"; "McCartney Publications."

F 0102 McCARTNEY. November 1982, No.1 – .
Glasgow, Scotland: Paul McCartney Fan Club
of Scotland. illus.
(Formerly "Ram On.")

F 0103 McCARTNEY FAMILY FAN CLUB. November 1976,
No.1 – ?
San Diego, CA: Ellen Martorana. illus.
(Ceased; ongoing as late as February 1977,
No.2.)

F 0104 McCARTNEY LTD. ? – ?
Indianapolis, IN: Sarah Nolte. illus.
(Ongoing 1972-77 at least;now "McCartney
Observer.")

McCARTNEY LOVERS AND FRIENDS see McCARTNEY.

F 0105 McCARTNEY MANIACS UNLIMITED. ? – ?
Norfolk, VA: Lois Phares. illus.
(Ceased.)

F 0106 THE McCARTNEY OBSERVER. Spring 1977, No.1 – .
La Crosse, KS: Doylene Kindsvater. illus.
(Formerly "McCartney Ltd.")

McCARTNEY PUBLICATIONS see McCARTNEY.

F 0107 McCARTNEY'S GAZETTE. ? – ?
Longuevil, Canada: D. Williamson. illus.
(Ceased.)

F 0108 MACLEN. October 1974, No.1 – ?
West Haven, CT: Margie Paturzo and Ann Bruno.
illus.
(Ceased; ongoing as late as October 1976,
No.15.)

F 0109 MAGICAL MYSTERY TOUR. May 1, 1975, No.1 –
October 1978 (?).
Forest Park, IL: Jamie Louise Alonzo. illus.
(Ceased; ongoing as late as April 1978.)

F 0110 MATERIAL WORLD TIMES. ? – late 1960s.
Oak Park, IL: Ceil Silveri. illus.
(Ceased.)

F 0111 MAXWELL'S SILVER HAMMER. Spring 1980,
Vol.1, No.1 – September 1981.
Larchmont, NY: Allison Villone. illus.
(Ceased; issue No.7 was April 1981.)

F 0112 MEET THE BEATLES AGAIN. ? – ?
St. Petersburg, FL: Meet The Beatles Again.
illus.
(Ceased.)

F 0113 THE MESS. January 1974, No.1 – August
1974, No.4.
Minneapolis, MN: Becki Larter/Barbara Fenick.
illus.
(Formerly "Beatles Rule"; became "The
Write Thing.")

Mike McCartney Fan Club see GEAR BOX.

F 0114 MIKE McGEAR FAN CLUB. mid-1970s – ?
Genoa, IL: Barbara Paulson. illus.
(Now Mike McCartney Fan Club ("Gear Box").)

F 0115 MRS LENNON'S APPLE FARM. January/February
1972 – ?
Santa Monica, CA: Mar Young. illus.
(Ceased; formerly "Ono Odyssey.")

F 0116 MY SWEET LADY JANE. January 1982, No.1 – .
Campbell, CA: Penny Lane. illus.

Nederlandse Beatles Fanclub see NOTA BEATLES.

F 0117 NEW BEATLES FAN CLUB. ? – mid-1970s.
Vienna, VA: Martha Wagar. illus.
(Ceased; ongoing as late as August 1976,
No.11.)

F 0118 NORWEGIAN WOOD. July/August – September/
October 1968.
Highland Park, IL: Vikki Paradiso/John
Lennon Fan Club. illus.
(Formerly "Lennon Lyrics"; became "Lennon
League.")

F 0119 NORWEGIAN WOOD - BEATLES FANKLUBB. March
          27, 1980, No.1 - .
          Gjovik, Norway: Erlend Flaten. illus.
F 0120 NOTA BEATLES. ? - ?
          Amsterdam, Holland: Nederlandse Beatles
          Fanclub. illus.
          (Ceased; ongoing as late as February 1978,
          No.108.)
F 0121 OB LA DI OB LA DA. October 1983, No.1 - .
          Barcelona, Spain: Albert Bel/Col. Lectiu
          Beatleman. illus.
F 0122 OCTOPUS GARDEN CHAPTER. ? - ?
          Gary, IN: Pam Aubuchon/Octopus Garden
          Chapter - OBFC. illus.
          (Ceased.)
F 0123 OFFICIAL BEATLES FAN CLUB. May 1962 -
          1971.
          Liverpool, Eng.: Freda Kelly/Official
          Beatles Fan Club. illus.
          (Ceased.)
        Official Beatles Fan Club (OBFC) see ABBEY
          ROAD; THE APPLE; GEORGE GERNAL; HARRISON
          HERALD; INDIANA OBFC; LUV 'N' STUFF; OCTOPUS
          GARDEN CHAPTER; OFFICIAL YOKO LENNON CHAP-
          TER; ORANGE APPLE JAM CHAPTER.
F 0124 O'NO FOUNDATION. February 1984, Vol. 1,
          No. 1 - .
          Dallas, Texas: Vickie Woods-Lovett. illus.
          (Formerly "Yoko O'no Foundation.")
F 0125 ONO ODYSSEY. ? - November 1971.
          Santa Monica, CA: Mar Young/Official Yoko
          Lennon Chapter - Apple Tree. illus.
          (Became "Mrs. Lennon's Apple Farm.")
F 0126 ORANGE APPLE JAM CHAPTER. ? - ?
          Pompano Beach, FL: Betty Heiser/Orange Apple
          Jam Chapter - OBFC. illus.
          (Ceased.)
F 0127 OUR STARR. November 1973, No.1 - Summer
          1974, No.5.
          Glen Oaks, NY: Laura Rickarby. illus.
          (Ceased; resumed as "Our Starr Monthly.")
F 0128 OUR STARR MONTHLY. October 1974, No.1 -
          early 1976, No.7.
          Gretna, LA: Allen Seal. illus.
          (Ceased; preceded by "Our Starr.")
F 0129 PAPERBACK WRITER INTERNATIONAL BEATLES FAN
          CLUB. ? - ?
          Baldwin, NY: Richard Hoffman. illus.
          (Ceased;ongoing as late as Feb./Mar. 1978,
          No.6.)
F 0130 PAUL McCARTNEY AND WINGS FAN CLUB. August
          1972 - late 1976?
          London, England: Claire. illus.
          (Forerunner of Wings Fun Club's "Club
          Sandwich.")
        Paul McCartney Chapter - OBFC see LUV 'N'
          STUFF.
F 0131 PEOPLE FOR PEACE. December 1980, Vol.1,
          No.1 - .
          New York, NY: Jeannie Roberts. illus.
F 0132 PEPPERLAND. Summer 1973 - ?
          Lake Hiawatha, NJ: John McGann. illus.
          (Ceased.)
F 0133 POTTIE BIRD BEATLE CHAPTER. ? - ?
          Concord, NH: Pottie Bird Beatle Chapter -
          Beatles USA Ltd. illus.
          (Ceased; ongoing as late as April 1970.)
F 0134 RAM ON. 1981 - late 1982.
          Glasgow, Scotland: Paul McCartney Fan Club
          of Scotland. illus.
          (Became "McCartney.")
F 0135 RED ROSE SPEEDWAY. February 1978, Vol.1,
          No.1 - .
          St. Louis, MO: Donna Neal (Lady Madonna).
          illus.
          (Issues on tape cassettes; formerly called
          "Red Rose Speedway Fan Club For The
          Blind And Physically Handicapped.")
        RED ROSE SPEEDWAY FAN CLUB FOR THE BLIND AND
          PHYSICALLY HANDICAPPED see RED ROSE

          SPEEDWAY.
F 0136 REVOLUTION. September/October 1978, No.1 - .
          Sao Paolo, Brazil: Marco Antonio Mallagola.
          illus.
          (Formerly "The Beatles Cavern
          Club.")
F 0137 REVOLUTION PRESS. ? - ?
          Yonkers, NY: Paulie. illus.
          (Ceased; ongoing as late as January 1970.)
F 0138 REVOLVER. January 1983 - ?
          Woking, Surrey,Eng.: Gwyn Jenkins. illus.
          (Was "The Beatles Unofficial Fan Club
          Magazine.")
F 0139 RINGO. 1982 - ?
          Chesham, England: The Ringo Starr Fan Club.
          illus.
          (Ceased?)
        RINGO MAGAZIN see RINGO MAGAZINE.
F 0140 RINGO MAGAZINE. December 1978, No.1 - .
          Hasselroth, W.Ger.: Mo Shears and Sabine
          Dorsam. illus.
          (Was "Ringo Magazin" (Judith Phillip,
          Wurtzburg).)
F 0141 RINGO STARR FAN CLUB. ? - ?
          Chesham, England: Chris Daniels. illus.
          (Ceased.)
        The Ringo Starr Fan Club see RINGO.
F 0142 SGT PEPPER POSTEN. November 1981, No.1 - .
          Oslo, Norway: Askeroi Grei/Sgt. Pepper's
          (Lonely Hearts) Club. illus.
          (Last issue March 1983, No.11/12; more
          planned.)
        Sgt. Pepper's (Lonely Hearts) Club see
          SGT. PEPPER POSTEN.
F 0143 STRAWBERRY FIELDS FOREVER. February 1973,
          No.1 - .
          Boston, MA: Joe Pope. illus.
F 0144 THINGS WE TELL TODAY. November 1977, No.1 - .
          Cologne, W.Ger.: Beatles Information Center
          - West Germany. illus.
F 0145 TOMORROW NEVER KNOWS. January 1983, No. 1 - ?
          Thorpe Bay, Eng.: Simon Wordsworth and Andy
          Hayes. illus.
          (Ceased.)
F 0146 TRAILS OF GEORGE AND JOHN. ? -
          November/December 1971.
          Culver City, CA: Harrison/Lennon Followers -
          Beatles USA Ltd. illus.
          (Ceased.)
        Vereiniging Beatles Nederlandse Fanclub see
          BEATLES PLAYBACK; BEATLES VISIE.
F 0147 WATERFALLS. March 1983, No.1 - .
          Linz, Austria: Karin Gattermayr and Judith
          Phillip. illus.
        West Midlands Fan Club see BEAT LAND.
F 0148 WHAT GOES ON. July 1981, Vol.1, No.1 -
          February 1983, Vol.2, No.7.
          Ridgefield, NJ: PaulVinDon Publishing/Paul
          and Donna Bruker. illus.
          (Ceased.)
F 0149 WINGS FAN CLUB. ? - ?
          Fronderberg, W.Ger.: Stefanie Brummer.
          illus.
          (Ceased.)
        Wings Fun Club see CLUB SANDWICH.
F 0150 WINGS INFO CENTER. ? - ?
          Hattersheim,W.Ger.: Michael Wahle. illus.
          (Ceased?)
F 0151 WITH A LITTLE HELP FROM MY FRIENDS. April
          1972, No.1 - .
          Cleveland, OH: Joy Kilbane and Pat Simmons.
          illus.
          (Formerly "Dig It.")
F 0152 THE WORKING CLASS HERO CLUB. 1974, No.? - .
          Pittsburgh, PA: Barb Whatmough. illus.
          (Formerly "The Beatle Peace Followers.")

F 0153 WORKING CLASS HERO, VOL. I.   Spring 1985,
      Volume 1 - .
      Jefferson City, MO: Patty Owens Rycyk.
      illus.
F 0154 THE WRITE THING.   July 1974, No.5 - .
      Minneapolis, MN: Barbara Fenick. illus.
      (Formerly "The Mess.")
F 0155 YELLOW SUBMARINE.   ? - ?
      Kenmore, NY: Tim Trafalski. illus.
      (Ceased.)

F 0156 YESTERDAY.   January 1981, No.1 - .
      Vienna, Austria: Beatles Fan Club of Austria.
      illus.
F 0157 YESTERDAY FAN CLUB.   ? - ?
      Corona, CA: Bryan Shonyo. illus.
      (Ceased.)
F 0158 YOKO ONLY.   September/October 1983, No.1 - .
      Toms River, NJ: Brian Hendel. illus.
      YOKO O'NO FOUNDATION   see   O'NO FOUNDATION.

M 0001 "A & M Wins Harrison's New Label." Billboard 86
(June 1, 1974) p3+.

M 0002 "Abbey Road Sight And Sound Experience."
The Beatles Book 87 (July 1983) pp42-43.
illus.
(EMI's Abbey Road Studios open to tours,
1983.)

M 0003 Abbott, Mary and Charlene Bass. "A Tribute To
Beatle John." The Beatles Book 57 (April
1968) p8.
(Song.)

M 0004 Abelson, Danny and et al. "Mersey Moptop
Faverave Fabgearbeat." National Lampoon 1:91
(October 1977) pp43-50.

M 0005 "ABKCO, Beatles Widen Battle In US, UK Courts."
Variety 273 (November 28, 1973) p49.

M 0006 "Abkco Profit Clipped By Beatles Breakup:
Rolling Stones Also Sue." Variety 264
(August 25, 1971) p43.

M 0007 "ABKCO Wins Point On Jurisdiction In Suit Vs.
Beatles." Variety 283 (June 16, 1976)
p51.

M 0008 Abrahamsen, Peter. "Til John Lennon."
MM (Copenhagen, Denmark) (December 1980)
p3. illus.
(Poem.)

M 0009 "According To John: Remark About Christianity."
Time 88 (August 12, 1966) p38. illus.
(Lennon's "Jesus" remark.)

M 0010 Ackerman, P. "Beatles Doing Own Things: Paul
Quits." Billboard 82 (April 18, 1970)
p1+.

M 0011 Adams, Mike. "Complete Beatles' U.K. LP
Discography + Values." Record Collector 12
(August 1980) p9.

M 0012 Addison, Richard. "'Eleanor Rigby' And All
That." Music in America 30 (November 1966)
pp293-294.
(On the "Revolver" LP.)

M 0013 "Adult Okay Endangers Beatles?" Variety 235
(August 19, 1964) p3.

M 0014 "Advertisements." Beatles Unlimited
(Regular feature, issues 1-   .)

M 0015 Agustin, Jose. "La Obra Artistica De John
Lennon." Territorios 5 (November 1980)
pp17-20.
(Issue has cover drawing of Lennon.)

M 0016 "Ailes Sur Condres." Rock et Folk (Paris) 147
(April 1979) pp76-85. illus.
(Paul McCartney and Wings.)

M 0017 Akehurst, Roger. "Wednesday 22nd Sept. 1982."
Beatles Now 4 (Autumn 1982) p13. illus.
(McCartney at Abbey Road Studios.)

M 0018 Albright, Thomas. "Visuals: The New Album Art."
Rolling Stone 8 (April 6, 1968) p19+.
(Beatles and others.)

M 0019 Alethes. "Las Canciones De Los Beatles."
Heterofonia 5:25 (1972) pp31-33.

M 0020 Alexander, Shana. "Ringo, Ringo, Let Down Your
Hair!" Life 59 (September 10, 1965)
p28. illus.

M 0021 Alfonso, B. "From The Crow's Nest: A Bio."
Songwriter 6 (January 1981) p8+.
(John Lennon.)

M 0022 "Alien Alias." The Beatles Book 52 (November
1967) pv.
(McCartney's "Apollo C. Vermouth" alias.)

M 0023 Alion, Y. "Beatles Show." Ecran 60 (July 15,
1977) pp6-7.
(Beatles film retrospective held in Paris.)

M 0024 "Allen Klein Co. Won $4,200,000 In Beatles
Case." Variety 285 (January 26, 1977)
p82.

M 0025 "Allen Klein: 'I Cured All Their Problems'."
Rolling Stone 47 (November 29, 1969)
p1+. illus.

M 0026 "Allen Klein Pins Down Beatles For $24 Million
Suit In N.Y. Court." Variety 280 (October
29, 1975) p62.

M 0027 "Allen Klein's Conviction Upheld."
Rolling Stone 310 (February 7, 1980)
p20. illus.

M 0028 "Allen Klein Seen Exciting Beatles Deal."
Variety 255 (July 2, 1969) p51.

M 0029 "All My Own Work." Time 83 (May 1, 1964)
pE7+. illus.
(John Lennon.)

M 0032 Alm, Torbjorn. "Norwegian Wood."
Beatles Unlimited 11 (January 1977)
p22.
(Beatles-related events in Norway in 1976.)

M 0033 Alterman, Loraine. "Elephant's Memory."
Melody Maker 47 (April 15, 1972) p15. illus.

M 0034 Alterman, Loraine. "Ringo's Agenda: Movie,
Music, But No Beatles." Rolling Stone 161
(May 23, 1973) p16. illus.
(No Beatles reunion soon, says Ringo.)

M 0035 Alterman, Loraine. "Yoko: How I Rescued John
From Chauvinism." Melody Maker 48 (September
22, 1973) p13. illus.

M 0036 Altham, Keith. "Off The Road." Hit Parader XXV:2
(October 1966) ppB6-B7. illus.
(Filming the Granada-TV special, Christmas
1965.)

M 0037 Alverson, Charles. "The OBE: Lennon's Soul
Redeemed." Rolling Stone 49 (December 27,
1969) p8. illus.

M 0038 Alverson, Charles. "Ono: More Beatles Than
Plastic." Rolling Stone 50 (January 21, 1970)
p7.

M 0039 Alverson, Charles. "Plastic: Wailing With Mrs.
Lennon." Rolling Stone 51 (February 7, 1970)
p13. illus.

M 0040 "Amateur Tapes Of Beatles Concerts Cue Legal
Queries." Variety 287 (May 11, 1977)
p478.

M 0041 "American Bobbies Bug The Beatles."
Melody Maker 39 (September 12, 1964)
p3. illus.

M 0042 "American Report." The Beatles Book 15
(October 1964) pp25,31.
(August 1964.)

M 0043 "America Picks Our Pops!" Melody Maker 39
(January 25, 1964) p1. illus.

M 0044 "America Woos The Fab Four." Melody Maker 54
(May 26, 1979) p13.

M 0045 Anderson, T. "The Beatles: Bridging The
Cultural Gap." Continuum 5 (Fall 1967)
pp594-597.

M 0046 Anderson, W. "Sic Transit Eleanor Rigby."
Stereo Review 30 (February 1973) p6.

M 0048 " ... And This Week George Reviews The New Pop
Records." Melody Maker 39 (February 1, 1964)
p13. illus.

M 0049 "Another Beatles Christmas Record."
Beatles Unlimited 17 (November 1977)
pp8-9.
(Picture and text of the 1964 fan club
record.)

M 0050 "Anti-Beatles Club." Variety 233 (February 19,
1964) p49.
(St. Mary's Grade School band members,
Bismarck, ND.)

M 0051 "Antoine Pirated Beatles' 'Sub' Paris Court
Rules." Variety (November 11, 1970)
p260.
(Suit regarding "Yellow Submarine.")

M 0052 "Apple." The Beatles Book 57 (April 1968)
pp25,31.
(Network of Apple companies.)

M 0053 "Apple And The Beatles." Rolling Stone 1
(November 9, 1967) p3. illus.

M 0054 "'Apple' Boutique Part Of Mushrooming Empire

Under Beatles Moniker." Variety 249
(December 20, 1967) p50.

M 0055 "Apple Businessmen." The Beatles Book 76
(November 1969) pp24,29.
(Activities at Apple offices.)

M 0056 "Apple Is Closed; Beatles Give It All Away
Free." Rolling Stone 17 (September 14, 1968)
p4.

M 0057 "Apple Mysteries." Record Collector 4
(December 1979) pp22-23.
(Obscure Apple recordings listed.)

M 0058 "Apple On Capitol." Rolling Stone 14 (July 20,
1968) p1.

M 0059 "Apple Opens." The Beatles Book 54 (January
1968) p25.
(Apple Boutique, Baker Street.)

M 0060 "Apple's 'Bangledesh' Raises $4.5 Mil For Kids;
Anyone Else Taking A Bite?" Variety 265
(January 12, 1972) p2.

M 0061 "Apples For The Beatles." Time 92 (September
6, 1968) pp59-60.

M 0062 "Appoint Receiver For The Beatles, Allen Klein
Out." Variety 262 (March 17, 1971)
p61.

M 0063 "Are They More Pop Than Maharishi Now?"
Rolling Stone 12 (June 22, 1968) p18. illus.

M 0064 Aronowitz, Alfred G. "Ballad Of John, Yoko, And
Frank Zappa." Melody Maker 46 (June 19, 1971)
p31. illus.

M 0065 Aronowitz, Alfred G. "The Beatles." Jazz & Pop
8 (April 1969) pp56-57. illus.

M 0066 Aronowitz, Alfred G. "Lennon - Now It's Legs
For Peace." Melody Maker 45 (December 26,
1970) p13. illus.
(Film.)

M 0067 Aronowitz, Alfred G. "The Return Of The
Beatles." Saturday Evening Post 237
(August 8, 1964) pp22-29. illus.

M 0068 Aronowitz, Alfred G. "Two Questions About
Lennon." Rolling Stone 168 (August 29, 1974)
p19. illus.

M 0069 Aronowitz, Alfred G. "Why Is George In New
York?" Rolling Stone 60 (June 11, 1970)
p32+. illus.

M 0070 Aronowitz, Alfred G. "Wisdom Of Their Years."
Life (January 31, 1969) p12.
(On the "White Album.")

M 0071 Aronowitz, Alfred G. "Yeah! Yeah! Yeah! Music's
Gold Bugs: The Beatles."
Saturday Evening Post 237 (March 21, 1964)
pp30-35. illus.

M 0072 Arrington, C. and F. Hauptfuhrer. "Paul Plunges
Into Work, George Stays Cloistered And Yoko
Reaches Out With Two New Songs." People 15
(February 23, 1981) p40+. illus.

M 0073 "Artist's Biographies." Billboard 76 (February
1, 1964) p14. illus.

M 0074 Ashford, Paul. "Paul McCartney: An Exclusive
Interview With The Prince Of Pop."
Int'l Musician & Recording World 5:11
(November 1983) pp22-27. illus.
(Issue has cover photo of Paul.)

M 0075 Ashman, Mike. "Beatles 1963-1973."
Records and Recording 16 (September 1973)
pp24-30. illus.

M 0076 Ashton, John. "Hearing Lennon's Secret
Messages." New Society (December 18/25, 1980)
pp550-551. illus.

M 0077 "As I Write This Letter." Beatles Now
(Regular feature, issue No.7-   , July
1983-   .)

M 0078 "As One Of The Beatles."
High Fidelity/Musical America 14:11
(November 1964) p125.
(John Lennon.)

M 0079 Aspinall, Neil. "Neil's Column."
The Beatles Book
(Occasional feature, issues 33-44,
1966-1967.)

M 0080 Aspinall, Neil. "Those Were The Days."

Beatlefan 2:6 (October 1980) p28.
("The Beatles And Me," 16 Magazine, April
'66.)

M 0081 Aspinall, Neil. "With The Beatles, No. 2: The
First Official Mal Evans Story."
The Beatles Book 46 (May 1967) pp11-12.
(Mal Evans' hiring by The Beatles.)

M 0082 Aspinall, Neil. "With The Beatles, No. 5:
George's California Trip." The Beatles Book 51
(October 1967) pp25-26+.
(August 1967.)

M 0083 "As You Picked 'Em: 'The Beatles 1971-1976'."
Beatlefan 2:6 (October 1980) p13.
(Nominations for fictional Beatles album.)

M 0084 Atlas, J. "Lennon: I Apologize." Melody Maker
49 (April 13, 1974) p14.

M 0085 Atlas, J. "Together Again: John, George, &
Ringo." Melody Maker 48 (March 31, 1973)
pp8-9+. illus.

M 0086 "At Pattie And George's Press Reception."
The Beatles Book 32 (March 1966) pp10-11.
(Photos.)

M 0087 "At The Garden." New Yorker 50 (January 13,
1975) p30.
(George Harrison concert.)

M 0088 Attie and Brown. "John Lennon."
Radical History Review 24 (Fall 1980)
p188.

M 0089 "ATV Leaves Door Open For Beatles." Billboard
81 (October 11, 1969) p82.

M 0090 "ATV Music Put Up For Sale; Ex-Beatle Bids For
Northern." Variety 305 (November 25, 1981)
p2+.

M 0091 "ATV's Stake In Northern Songs Now Tops 50
Percent." Variety 256 (October 8, 1969)
p51.

M 0092 "ATV Wins Cliffhanger vs. Beatles In Fight To
Take Over Northern Songs." Variety 255
(May 21, 1969) p53.

M 0093 Avedon, Richard. "The Beatles, A Color Folio."
Look (January 9, 1968) pp33-41. illus.

M 0094 "Baby Grand Guitar." Art & Artists 6 (January
1972) p29.
(John Lennon; reproduction.)

M 0095 "Back On The Road." Beatlefan 1:4 (June 1979)
pp1,4.
(Paul McCartney and Wings.)

M 0096 "Back To The Egg." Beatlefan 1:4 (June 1979)
pp1,4-5,9.
(Discussion of the album.)

M 0097 Bacon, David and Norman Maslov. "'The Beatles
England'." Beatlefan 4:4 (June 1982)
pp4-5.
(Excerpt from their book.)

M 0098 Bacon, Dorothy. "I Want To Live In Peace."
Life 67 (November 7, 1969) pp105-106. illus.
(Interview with Paul McCartney.)

M 0099 "Badfinger: A Musical Tragedy." Beatlefan 1:5
(August 1979) p11.
(Interview.)

M 0100 "Badfinger: Rising From The Ashes." Beatlefan 1:6
(October 1979) p15.

M 0101 "Bag One: Opening Of The Show Of Erotic
Lithographs At The Nordness Galleries."
New Yorker 46 (February 21, 1970) pp29-30.
(John Lennon.)

M 0102 Bailey, Andrew. "Apple Scruffs Come To Dinner."
Rolling Stone 73 (December 24, 1970)
p14+.

M 0103 Bailey, Andrew. "George Does A Turn For Ravi."
Rolling Stone 69 (October 29, 1970)
p26. illus.

M 0104 Bailey, Andrew. "Paul On Tour; No Wingsmania
Yet." Rolling Stone 116 (August 31, 1972)
p6. illus.

M 0105 Bailey, Andrew and David Hamilton. "George
Harrison: The Niceman Cometh."
Rolling Stone 174 (November 21, 1974)
p11+.
(Harrison's first U.S. tour in eight

years.)
M 0106 "Bailey's Box." Camera 45 (February 1966)
pp34-35. illus.
(John Lennon and Paul McCartney.)
M 0107 Baker, Mark. "Beatles' Memorabilia."
The Beatles Book 70 (February 1982)
ppix-xii.
(Sotheby auction, December 22, 1981.)
M 0108 Baker, Stephen. "EMI: The Unreleased
Recordings." Beatles Now 4 (Autumn 1982)
p6.
M 0109 Baker, Stephen. "The Export Series."
Beatles Now 6 (May 1983) pp14-15. illus.
(EMI export singles and albums.)
M 0110 Baker, Stephen. "Second Great Mersey Beatle
Extravaganza." Beatles Now 4 (Autumn 1982)
pp4-5. illus.
(Liverpool fan convention report.)
M 0111 "Baker Street Battles Beatles." Rolling Stone 5
(February 10, 1968) p8.
M 0112 Bakker, Erik M. "The Beatles: Sweet Apple
Trax." Beatles Unlimited 1 (March 1975)
p7.
(Describes the bootleg LP.)
M 0113 Bakker, Erik M. "Editorial." Beatles Unlimited
(Regular feature, issues 1- .)
M 0114 Bakker, Erik M. "Every Morning Brings A New
Day." Beatles Unlimited 6 (March 1976)
p18.
(Paul McCartney & Wings in Holland, March
1976.)
M 0115 Bakker, Erik M. "I Can't Tell You How I Feel."
Beatles Unlimited 6 (March 1976) p18.
(Paul McCartney & Wings in Holland, March
1976.)
M 0116 Bakker, Erik M. "Ride On My Fast City-Line."
Beatles Unlimited 6 (March 1976) p19.
(Paul McCartney & Wings in Holland, March
1976.)
M 0117 Bakker, Erik M. "Rock 'N Roll Auction 1981."
Beatles Unlimited 40 (1982) pp4-7.
(At London's Sotheby's, December 1981.)
M 0118 Bakker, Erik M. "Wings In Munich."
Beatles Unlimited 9 (September 1976)
p21.
(Concert of September 27, 1976.)
M 0119 Bakker, Erik M. and Henk Hager. "August 1976."
Beatles Unlimited 9 (September 1976)
pp18-19.
(The McCartney's visit Holland, August 19.)
M 0120 Bakker, Erik M., Evert Vermeer and Henk Hager.
"Allan Williams." Beatles Unlimited 9
(September 1976) pp10-11.
(Interview.)
M 0121 Bakshian, Aram, Jr. "Requiem For A Beatle."
American Spectator 14 (February 1981)
pp20-21.
(John Lennon.)
M 0122 "'The Ballad Of John And Yoko'." Rolling Stone
34 (May 31, 1969) p10.
M 0123 Ballister, B. "Who Killed The Toronto Peace
Festival." Rolling Stone 73 (December 24,
1970) pp37-43. illus.
M 0124 Ballon, Ian. "Beatlemania In Canada This
Summer." Beatles Unlimited 10 (November 1976)
p10.
(Resurgence began in February 1976.)
M 0125 Ballon, Ian. "'Beatles In Germany' In Canada,
And Others." Beatles Unlimited 15 (September
1977) pp6-8.
(The Hamburg tapes and other recent
albums.)
M 0126 Ballon, Ian. "Canada Updated."
Beatles Unlimited 18 (January 1978)
p23.
(Beatles events in Canada.)
M 0127 Ballon, Ian. "Canada Updated."
Beatles Unlimited 21 (July 1978) p23.
(Beatles events in Canada.)
M 0128 Ballon, Ian. "Klaatu Update."

Beatles Unlimited 13 (May 1977) pp18-20.
(Facts on the group and LP, "Klaatu.")
M 0129 Ballon, Ian. "Ob La Di, Ob La Da, Life Goes
On." Beatles Unlimited 14 (July 1977)
pp15-19.
(Canadian discography.)
M 0130 Bananas. New York: Scholastic Magazines Inc.,
1976.
(Cover portrait.)
M 0131 "Band On The Bayou: The McCartneys' Cruise
Through New Orleans." Rolling Stone 183
(March 27, 1975) pp10-11. illus.
M 0132 "Band On The Run: Wings Soar Sunward."
Melody Maker 48 (December 1, 1973)
p48.
M 0133 "Bang! Beatles Are Back!" Melody Maker 39
(July 18, 1964) p1+. illus.
M 0134 "Bangla Desh LP: A Federal Case?"
Rolling Stone 108 (May 11, 1972) p10.
M 0135 "Bangladesh: The Film Of The Concert."
Hit Parader 31:98 (September 1972)
pp32-36. illus.
(Cover photo of George.)
M 0136 Bangs, Lester. "Dandelions In Still Air: The
Withering Away Of The Beatles." Creem 7
(June 1975) pp46-47+. illus.
M 0137 Bangs, Lester. "Ex-Beatles Keep Trying."
Stereo Review 34 (March 1975) pp80-81.
(On Harrison's "Dark Horse" LP.)
M 0138 Bangs, Lester. "John Lennon Is Alive And A
Voidoid: A Rock & Roll Fantasy."
Village Voice 26 (July 1, 1981) pp38-39.
illus.
M 0139 Bangs, Lester. "Paul And Linda: 'Alright
Tonight'." Stereo Review 35 (October 1975)
p82.
M 0140 Bangs, Lester. "Paul And Linda McCartney:
Bionic Couple Serves It Your Way." Creem 8:3
(August 1976) pp34-39. illus.
M 0141 "Ban Wings On Radio (In Japan)." Billboard 92
(February 23, 1980) p48.
M 0142 Barackman, Michael. "Beatles' Tapes Unleashed
In UK." Phonograph Record Magazine
(October 1976) p28.
M 0143 Barackman, Michael. "World War II Brought To
You By The Beatles."
Phonograph Record Magazine (October 1976)
pp25-26.
(Film "All This And World War II.")
M 0144 "Barbara Bach & Ringo Are Now Starring In An
Altered State." People 15 (May 11, 1981)
p44. illus.
M 0145 "Bards Of Pop." Newsweek 67 (March 21, 1966)
p102. illus.
M 0146 Barfield, Nic. "Sotheby's Memorabilia Auction."
The Beatles Book 90 (October 1983)
pp42-47.
(Beatles items in Sotheby's sale of Sept.
1, 1983.)
M 0147 Barnard, Stephen. "Getting His Wings."
Let It Rock (March 1974) pp28-29.
(Paul McCartney.)
M 0148 Barnes, Ken. "The Weird World Of Beatle
Novelties." Who Put The Bomp 13 (Spring 1975)
pp13-15.
(Additions in issue nos. 14, 15 & 16.)
M 0149 Barron, F. "New Audience For Beatles Via
Movie." Billboard 88 (March 13, 1976)
p30.
M 0150 Barrow, Tony. "Alistair Taylor Recalls How
Brian Epstein Discovered The Beatles."
The Beatles Book 73 (May 1982) ppiii-viii.
(Interview.)
M 0151 Barrow, Tony. "Back On The Merseyside."
The Beatles Book 82 (February 1983)
pp4-9. illus.
(Barrow's January 1963 visit with Brian
Epstein.)
M 0152 Barrow, Tony. "Beatle At The Back."
Melody Maker 43 (February 24, 1968)

p15. illus.
(Ringo Starr.)

M 0153 Barrow, Tony. "The Beatles And The Press."
The Beatles Book 62 (June 1981) ppiii-vi.

M 0154 Barrow, Tony. "The Beatles' Christmas Fan Club
Discs." The Beatles Book 56 (December 1980)
ppiii-vi.

M 155 Barrow, Tony. "Beatles First Film & Special
Xmas Record." The Beatles Book 92 (December
1983) pp14-19. illus.
(Events of November 1963.)

M 0156 Barrow, Tony. "The Beatles On Holiday."
The Beatles Book 85 (May 1983) pp4-7. illus.
(Events of April 1963.)

M 0157 Barrow, Tony. "Beatles On Tour."
The Beatles Book 83 (March 1983) pp4-10.
illus.
(Helen Shapiro interviewed about the
Beatles.)

M 0158 Barrow, Tony. "The Beatles Record 'Please
Please Me'." The Beatles Book 80 (December
1982) pp4-10.

M 0159 Barrow, Tony. "Beatle Who's Changed The Most."
Melody Maker 43 (February 17, 1968)
p11. illus.
(George Harrison.)

M 0160 Barrow, Tony. "Brian Epstein."
The Beatles Book 93 (January 1984)
pp27-31. illus.
(Interview.)

M 0161 Barrow, Tony. "Brian Epstein, Part Three: The
Philippine Affair." The Beatles Book 60
(April 1981) ppiii-viii.

M 0162 Barrow, Tony. "Brian Epstein, Part Two."
The Beatles Book 59 (March 1981) ppiii-vi.

M 0163 Barrow, Tony. "Brian Epstein: Would The Beatles
Have Succeeded Without Him? Part One."
The Beatles Book 57 (January 1981)
ppvi-xi.

M 0164 Barrow, Tony. "The Cavern." The Beatles Book 72
(April 1982) ppiii-vi.
(Bob Wooler reminisces.)

M 0165 Barrow, Tony. "Everyone Wants To Record A
Lennon & McCartney Song." The Beatles Book 84
(April 1983) pp4-11. illus.

M 0166 Barrow, Tony. "Facts And Shocks."
The Beatles Book 81 (January 1983)
pp4-8. illus.
(Barrow interviews the Beatles, December
1962.)

M 0167 Barrow, Tony. "First Beatles Xmas."
The Beatles Book 93 (January 1984)
pp16-20. illus.
(December 1963.)

M 0168 Barrow, Tony. "The Girls They Like."
The Beatles Book 86 (June 1983) pp4-11.
illus.
(Press interest in Beatles' choice of
women.)

M 0169 Barrow, Tony. "How Beatlemania Really Began!"
The Beatles Book 91 (November 1983)
pp16-20. illus.
(Events of October 1963.)

M 0170 Barrow, Tony. "How I Got Publicity For 'Love Me
Do'." The Beatles Book 79 (November 1982)
pp14-21.

M 0171 Barrow, Tony. "I Introduced The Beatles, Says
David Hamilton." The Beatles Book 89
(September 1983) pp30-35. illus.
(The compere of their August 5, 1963
concert.)

M 0172 Barrow, Tony. "The John Lennon I Knew."
The Beatles Book 58 (February 1981)
ppiii-viii.

M 0173 Barrow, Tony. "'Lennon'." The Beatles Book 68
(December 1981) ppix-xii.
(Musical play premieres in Liverpool.)

M 0174 Barrow, Tony. "Lennon The Outrageous Beatle."
Melody Maker 43 (March 2, 1968) p7. illus.

M 0175 Barrow, Tony. " 'The Love You Make'."

The Beatles Book 89 (September 1983)
pp42-46.
(On Peter Brown's book.)

M 0176 Barrow, Tony. "New Recruits To The Beatles
Empire." The Beatles Book 90 (October 1983)
pp17-21. illus.
(NEMS' expanding staff, September 1963.)

M 0177 Barrow, Tony. "The Official Beatles Fan Club."
The Beatles Book 85 (May 1983) pp15-22.
illus.
(The story of the U.K. fan club.)

M 0178 Barrow, Tony. "Paul - The Cute Beatle Boy."
Melody Maker 43 (February 10, 1968)
p7. illus.

M 0179 Barrow, Tony. "Talking To The Beatles."
The Beatles Book 88 (August 1983) pp4-7.
(John and Paul talk about composing.)

M 0180 Barrow, Tony. "Thank U Very Much By Mike
McCartney: Launch Party." The Beatles Book 69
(January 1982) ppiii-v.
(Launch party to debut McCartney's book.)

M 0181 Barrow, Tony. "Their First Movie."
The Beatles Book 81 (January 1983)
pp30-34. illus.
(Filmed at the Cavern, August 22, 1962.)

M 0182 Barrow, Tony. "Their Manager: Brian Epstein."
The Beatles Book 1 (August 1963) pp18-19.

M 0183 Barrow, Tony. "Their Recording Manager: George
Martin." The Beatles Book 1 (August 1963)
pp22-23.

M 0184 Barrow, Tony. "What A Party!" The Beatles Book 87
(July 1983) pp4-11. illus.
(Paul McCartney's 21st birthday party.)

M 0185 Barrow, Tony. "With A Little Help From Their
Friends." The Beatles Book 66 (October 1981)
ppiii-v.
(NEMS staff members discussed.)

M 0186 Barrow, Tony. "With A Little Help From Their
Friends, Part Two." The Beatles Book 67
(November 1981) ppvi-ix.
(More Beatles' business associates.)

M 0187 Barrow, Tony. "With The Beatles Again!"
The Beatles Book 74 (June 1982) ppiii-vii.
(Alistair Taylor reminisces.)

M 0188 Barry, Art. "Beatles May Come Home."
Beatles Unlimited 27 (July 1979) pp14-16.
(Dick Clark's "Birth Of The Beatles.")

M 0189 Barry, Art. "Birth Of The Beatles."
Beatles Unlimited 29 (November 1979)
pp10-11.
(TV special, November 23, 1979.)

M 0190 Barry, Art. "Good Egg." Beatles Unlimited 27
(July 1979) p22.
(June 11 press party launches "Back To The
Egg.")

M 0191 Barry, Art. "U.S.A. Updated."
Beatles Unlimited 18 (January 1978)
pp19,22.
(Beatles events in the U.S.)

M 0192 Barry, Art. "U.S.A. Updated."
Beatles Unlimited 23 (November 1978)
p6,20.
(Beatles events in the U.S.)

M 0193 Barry, Art. "U.S.A. (West Coast)."
Beatles Unlimited 34 (1981) pp35-36.
(News on U.S. memorial vigils for Lennon.)

M 0194 Barry, Art. "Wings Over California."
Beatles Unlimited 9 (September 1976)
pp12-13.
(San Diego and Los Angeles concerts.)

M 0195 Barry, Art. "Wings Over The World."
Beatles Unlimited 25 (March 1979) p6.
(Paul McCartney TV special, March 16,
1979.)

M 0196 Bartimole, John. "John Lennon (October 9th,
1940-December 8th, 1980)."
Song Hits Magazine 45:181 (March 1981)
p22.

M 0197 Bashe, Philip. "An Expression Of Sorrow; John
Lennon Shot Dead At 40." Circus (January 31,

1981) pp36-39.

M 0198 Batt, Shodhan. "By George, A Beatle Is In India." The Beatles Book 40 (November 1966) pp6-7.

M 0199 Batterson, David. "Lennon As Lenin, Or ... Communistic Cacophony Comments On And By The Christian Crusade's Chief Chronicler: Rev. David A. Noebel." Creem 4 (November 1972) p32+. illus.

M 0200 "Battle Of John And Yoko." Rolling Stone 109 (May 25, 1972) p10.

M 0201 Battock, G. "Last Estate." Gay 2:55 (July 19, 1971) p8.
(John Lennon.)

M 0202 "Beach A Whale For Peace." Rolling Stone 62 (July 9, 1970) p6.
(Lennon and the Toronto Peace Festival.)

M 0203 "Beatarama." Melody Maker 38 (December 21, 1963) p7. illus.

M 0204 "Beat Elite." Melody Maker 40 (September 25, 1965) p9. illus.
(George Harrison.)

M 0205 "Beatle & English News." 16 Magazine 10:9 (February 1969) p64.

M 0206 "Beatle & English News." 16 Magazine 10:12 (May 1969) p27.

M 0207 "Beatle Ballet." Horizon 23 (1980) pp18-19.
("All You Need Is Love.")

M 0208 "Beatle Believers Band Together." Teen 20 (November 1976) p45.

M 0209 "Beatle Bomb." Village Voice (April 20, 1982) p26.
(Jurgen Vollmer's book, "Rock & Roll Times.")

M 0210 "Beatle Bookshelf." Beatlefan 2:5 (August 1980) pp25,30.
(Current Beatles-related publishing activity.)

M 0211 "Beatle Bookshelf." Beatlefan (Regular feature, vln1-   , 1978-   .)

M 0212 "Beatle Booted." Senior Scholastic 102 (May 14, 1973) p22. illus.
(John Lennon.)

M 0213 "Beatle-Browed Israeli Officials Ponder Permit For Britain's Beatles." Variety 234 (March 11, 1964) p2.

M 0214 "Beatle Business; Record Sales." Time 84 (October 2, 1964) p112. illus.

M 0215 "Beatle Cartoon Remembered." Beatlefan 1:3 (April 1979) p4,18.
(Cartoon series episodes.)

M 0216 "Beatledammerung." Time 97 (January 25, 1971) p55. illus.
(John Lennon.)

M 0217 "Beatlefan Letters." Beatlefan (Regular feature, vln2-   , 1979-   .)

M 0218 "Beatlefan Photo Contest." Beatlefan 2:1 (December 1979) p23.
(Winning photos.)

M 0219 "Beatle Fans At NY Commodore For Two Days." Billboard 86 (September 7, 1974) p16.

M 0220 "Beatlefan Trivia Quiz." Beatlefan 3:4 (June 1981) p17.

M 0221 "The Beatlefan Trivia Test." Beatlefan 2:3 (April 1980) p14.

M 0222 "Beatle Feet." The Beatles Book 18 (January 1965) pp12-13.
(Photos.)

M 0223 "Beatlefest." New Yorker 50 (September 23, 1974) p30.

M 0224 "Beatlefest '79 - NYC." Beatles Unlimited 25 (March 1979) p16.
(New York fan convention, February 24-25.)

M 0225 "Beatle Fever Hits Britain." Melody Maker 38 (October 26, 1963) p3. illus.

M 0226 "Beatle Flashes." 16 Magazine 10:7 (December 1968) p6.

M 0227 "Beatle George Harrison In A & M Production Deal." Variety 275 (June 5, 1974) p2.

M 0228 "Beatle George Visits Los Angeles."

Rolling Stone 14 (July 20, 1968) p6.

M 0229 "Beatle Harrison Target Of $10 Mil Pact Suit By A & M." Variety 284 (October 6, 1976) p63.

M 0230 "Beatle In The Raw." Newsweek 72 (November 25, 1968) p102. illus.
(John Lennon.)

M 0231 "Beatle Lennon Gains In Fight To Stay In U.S." Variety 280 (October 8, 1975) p2.

M 0232 "Beatle LP Boycott: Outrageous Price." Rolling Stone 51 (February 7, 1970) p13.

M 0233 "Beatlemania." Newsweek 62 (November 18, 1963) p104. illus.

M 0234 "Beatlemania." Musical Leader 98 (September 1966) p14.

M 0235 "Beatlemania." Beatlefan 1:5 (August 1979) p5,13.
(Origins of the stage show.)

M 0236 "Beatlemania And The Fast Buck: Beatle-Touched Items Sold At Fancy Prices." Christian Century 82 (February 24, 1965) p230.

M 0237 "Beatlemania Doesn't Stop With Disks, Mops Up With Fancy $2 Fan Club Too." Variety 235 (May 27, 1964) p49.

M 0238 "'Beatlemania' Does Solid Job Showing What Era Was Like." Variety 290 (February 15, 1978) p68.
(Stage show.)

M 0239 "Beatlemania Hits Dominion So Hard Even French Canadians Show Interest." Variety 234 (March 11, 1964) p46.

M 0240 "Beatlemania Hits The U.S." Senior Scholastic 84 (February 21, 1964) p21.

M 0241 "Beatlemania's Second Wish." Variety 235 (July 22, 1964) p73.

M 0242 "Beatlemania Still Pulls Fans To Boston Festival; Tokyo Gig Is Featured." Variety 279 (August 6, 1975) p47.

M 0243 "Beatlemania Strikes Again!" Melody Maker 41 (June 18, 1966) p1+.

M 0244 "Beatlemania; The FBI Was Taking Notes." Time 121:14 (April 4, 1983) p31.

M 0245 "Beatlemania: The Most Or The Worst?" Senior Scholastic 86 (February 4, 1965) pp10-11. illus.
(Pro and con discussion.)

M 0246 "Beatlemania Turns To 'Beatle-waneia'." Billboard 78 (September 3, 1966) p12+.

M 0247 "Beatlemania Without Beatles Is Pale Stuff At Let It Be Pic Preem." Variety 259 (May 27, 1970) p18.

M 0248 "Beatle Man; Manager For Beatles." New Yorker 39 (December 28, 1963) pp23-24.
(Brian Epstein.)

M 0249 "Beatle News." The Beatles Book (Regular feature, issues 1-76, Aug.1963-Nov.1969.)

M 0250 "Beatlenews Roundup." Beatlefan (Regular feature, vln1-   , 1978-   .)

M 0251 "Beatle News Sept. '62." The Beatles Book 78 (October 1982) pp11-14.
(Reprints of 1962 news reports.)

M 0252 "Beatle Paul And LSD." Melody Maker 42 (July 1, 1967) p9. illus.

M 0253 "Beatle Pen Pals." The Beatles Book (Regular feature, issues 12-77.)

M 0254 "Beatle Quickies." The Beatles Book 72 (July 1969) p31.
(Current news.)

M 0255 "Beatle Roundup." Newsweek 76 (September 7, 1970) pp85-86. illus.

M 0256 "Beatles." Mersey Beat 3:66 (January 30, 1964) p1.
(Front cover earliest-ever photo.)

M 0257 "Beatles." Melody Maker 40 (August 7, 1965) p3.

M 0258 "Beatles." Rolling Stone 243 (July 14, 1977) p36.

M 0259 "Beatles." Rolling Stone 255 (December 29, 1977)
        p39.
M 0260 "The Beatles." Mersey Beat 3:59 (October 24,
        1963) p1.
        (Cover photo.)
M 0261 "The Beatles." Hit Parader XXV:28 (October 1966)
        ppB1-B16. illus.
        (Sixteen page insert between pages 34 and
        35.)
M 0262 "The Beatles." Life 7:2 (February 1984)
        pp58-67. illus.
        (Twenty-year anniversary features and
        cover portrait.)
M 0263 "Beatles' Abbey Road LP Warms Up Price Wars In
        British Disk Shops." Variety 256 (October
        15, 1969) p57.
M 0264 "Beatles Accept ATV Offer On Their Songs."
        Billboard 81 (December 20, 1969) p8.
M 0265 "Beatles: A Find For England's Balance Of
        Payment." Cash Box 25 (March 7, 1964)
        p53.
M 0266 "Beatles Again Offs Get Back." Rolling Stone 50
        (January 21, 1970) p14.
M 0267 "Beatles Again Top Gold Disk Winners In RIAA
        R66 List; Yanks Bounce Back." Variety 245
        (December 28, 1966) p1+.
M 0268 "'Beatles Again' You Figure It." Rolling Stone 54
        (March 19, 1970) p8.
        ("Beatles Again" album.)
M 0269 "Beatles Almanac." Beatlefan
        (Occasional feature, v2n4-v3n2, 1980-81.)
M 0270 "The Beatles: An Almanac." Beatlefan 2:3
        (April 1980) p19.
M 0271 "The Beatles And The Rolling Stones; Effect On
        Jazz Industry." Music Journal Annual (1965)
        p84.
M 0272 "The Beatles Are Back" Beatlefan 1:6 (October
        1979) pp1,4,15.
        (Premature U.N. reunion concert news.)
M 0273 "Beatles Art Gallery." Beatlefan 2:4 (June 1980)
        p32.
        (Art work.)
M 0274 "Beatles As A World Commodity." Billboard 76
        (December 5, 1964) p3.
M 0275 "The Beatles As Sermon." Variety (August 10,
        1966) p2+.
M 0276 "The Beatles - As You've Never Seen Them
        Before." 16 Magazine 10:8 (January 1969)
        pp40-41.
M 0277 "The Beatles A To Z." Village Voice (January
        24, 1977) p63.
        (Full page WNEW-FM Beatles' marathon ad.)
M 0278 "Beatles At The Cavern In The Early Days."
        Mersey Beat (August 15, 1963) p8.
        (Photograph.)
M 0279 "Beatles, ATV Seen Nearing Harmony." Billboard
        81 (October 18, 1969) p79.
M 0280 "The Beatles Autumn Tour." The Beatles Book 3
        (October 1963) p27.
        (Schedule.)
M 0281 "The Beatles; A Year In The Lives."
        Rolling Stone 385 (December 23, 1982)
        p84. illus.
M 0282 "Beatles Back?" Record Mirror (January 1, 1977)
        p3.
        (Reunion rumors.)
M 0283 "Beatles Back? Producer Says It May Happen."
        Variety 296 (September 26, 1979) p67.
M 0284 "Beatles Bag Two Of EMI's Four Goldisks."
        Variety 234 (March 4, 1964) p56.
M 0285 "Beatles Beating A New Path To Corporate
        Karma." Business Week (May 18, 1968)
        p40. illus.
        (Apple Corps Ltd.)
M 0286 "Beatles Beguile East Coast." Billboard 76
        (February 22, 1964) p1+.
        (U.S. tour.)
M 0287 "Beatles Besieged; Allen Klein To Manage
        Enterprises." Time 93 (May 30, 1969)
        p78. illus.

M 0288 "Beatles Blanket U.S. Charts; 'Love' Vaults
        1,000,000." Variety (April 8, 1964)
        p2+.
M 0289 "Beatles Blast Own Hit Disc!" Melody Maker 38
        (July 22, 1963) p1. illus.
M 0290 "Beatles Boffola In Solo LP Sales." Variety 261
        (December 9, 1970) p1.
M 0291 "Beatles Boffo 250G In Chicago." Variety
        (September 1, 1965) p45.
M 0292 "Beatles Bonanza." Melody Maker 39 (March 28,
        1964) p1. illus.
M 0293 "Beatles' Bonn Tour A Sales Blitzkrieg."
        Billboard 78 (July 9, 1966) p42.
M 0294 "The Beatles Book First Song Pop. Poll."
        The Beatles Book 28 (November 1965)
        p11.
        (Favorite songs poll.)
M 0295 "The Beatles Book Overseas Song Pop Poll."
        The Beatles Book 30 (January 1966)
        p10.
        (Popularity poll.)
M 0296 "Beatles Booming Britains Biscuits Biz Past
        $60-Mil Mark; EMI Shares Soar." Variety 234
        (March 4, 1964) p55.
M 0297 "Beatles Boost EMI Income To New High."
        Billboard 76 (October 10, 1964) p1+.
M 0298 "The Beatles Bootleg Roundup." Beatlefan 3:4
        (June 1981) p3.
        (The 25 "most essential" Beatle bootlegs.)
M 0299 "Beatles Break Bounds Of Pop." Melody Maker 41
        (July 30, 1966) p3. illus.
M 0300 "Beatles Breaking Up: McCartney." Variety 245
        (January 25, 1967) p47.
M 0301 "Beatles Breakup Cues Furor Over A Split
        Copyright." Variety 262 (February 24, 1971)
        p47.
M 0302 "Beatles Broke? McCartney: Aye; Klein Denies
        It." Variety 261 (January 27, 1971)
        p1+.
M 0303 "Beatles Broke, Paul Charges." Rolling Stone 76
        (February 18, 1971) p14.
M 0304 "Beatles Business Booms But Blessings Mixed."
        Billboard 76 (February 29, 1964) p1+.
M 0305 "Beatles Buy Advanced Tape Recorder."
        The Beatles Book 75 (October 1969)
        p31.
        (Sixteen-track installed at Apple.)
M 0306 "Beatles: Cheerful Coherence." Time 94
        (October 3, 1969) p57. illus.
M 0307 "The Beatles' Christmas Album."
        Beatles Unlimited 17 (November 1977)
        p24.
        (On The Beatles' U.S. Christmas album.)
M 0308 "The Beatles Christmas Record."
        Beatles Unlimited 17 (November 1977)
        pp4-7.
        (Picture and text of the 1963 fan club
        record.)
M 0309 "Beatles' City General Manager." Music Week
        (May 29, 1982) p29.
        (Ad invites management applicants for
        research.)
M 0310 "The Beatles Come In Colors." Rolling Stone 3
        (December 14, 1967) p8.
        (Beatles' voice patterns in color
        registers.)
M 0311 "Beatles' Concert On Tape 'N' Toll First Of
        Kind." Variety 234 (March 18, 1964)
        p1+.
M 0312 "Beatles' Copyrights Guarded." Billboard 92
        (August 16, 1980) p36.
M 0313 "Beatles, CSC Slate Studio." Billboard 80
        (December 28, 1968) p1+.
M 0314 "Beatles Curtail 1-Niters For Safety But Will
        Lift Ban For Edinburgh Date." Variety 233
        (December 11, 1963) p1.
M 0315 "Beatles Declare National Apple Week."
        Rolling Stone 15 (August 10, 1968)
        p6.
M 0316 "Beatles Diary." Beatles Now 4 (Autumn 1982)

p3. illus.
(Current news.)

M 0317 "Beatles Diary 1962." The Beatles Book
(Regular feature, issues 78-81, 1982-83.)

M 0318 "Beatles Diary 1963." The Beatles Book
(Regular feature, issues 82-93, 1983-84.)

M 0319 "Beatles' Disk Ban Spreading: Will Sales Hurt?"
Variety 255 (June 4, 1969) p55.
("The Ballad Of John and Yoko.")

M 0320 "Beatles' Disk Sales Exceed 100,000,000."
Variety 237 (February 3, 1965) p49.

M 0321 "Beatles' Dispute Tying Up $9 Million; No
Reunion Seen." Variety 273 (December 12,
1973) p47.

M 0322 "Beatles Documentary Definitive, Detailed."
Billboard 93 (May 9, 1981) p29.
("The Beatles: Days In Their Lives.")

M 0323 "Beatle $." Melody Maker 40 (May 1, 1965)
pp8-9.

M 0324 "Beatles Don't 'Bug' Kenin But He Wants
Anglo-U.S. Tooter Balance Enforced."
Variety 234 (April 15, 1964) p51.

M 0325 "Beatles Draw 'Only' 100G In K.C. Stad.; Tour
Is Over But Malady Lingers On." Variety 236
(September 23, 1964) p85.

M 0326 "Beatles '80: A Diary Of Recent News And
Events." The Beatles Book
(Regular reprint feature, issues 47-56,
1980.)

M 0327 "Beatles End U.S. Tour By Fracturing Frisco,
Total 'Take-Home' At $1 Mil." Variety 240
(September 8, 1965) p51.

M 0328 "Beatles' Epstein Left $638,000." Variety 249
(January 10, 1968) p2.

M 0329 "Beatles Exhibit At Abbey Road." Billboard
(June 25, 1983) p48.

M 0330 "Beatles Ex-Manager Faces Tax Charge Over Promo
Disks." Variety 286 (April 13, 1977)
p61.
(Allen Klein.)

M 0331 "Beatles Farewell." Freedom News 5:4 (April
1971) p37.

M 0332 "Beatles Fight Album Release." Melody Maker 52
(April 9, 1977) p4.
(Star Club tapes.)

M 0333 "Beatles Film Into Commie Markets." Variety 235
(August 12, 1964) p23.
("A Hard Day's Night" in Czechoslovakia.)

M 0334 "Beatles' Film Prod. Offshoot Swings With
Projects; Map Combo's Third Pic." Variety
250 (May 8, 1968) p241+.

M 0335 "Beatles' 5-Year Gross 'Estimated' At Over
$70-Mil." Variety 248 (September 27, 1967)
pp1,60.
(Estimate by Dick James, Northern Songs.)

M 0336 "Beatles Flip Cap's '64 Gross To Alltime High."
Variety 237 (January 13, 1965) p59.

M 0337 "Beatles Fly To Face Knockers." Melody Maker 41
(August 13, 1966) p1+.

M 0338 "Beatles For Sale." The Beatles Book 82
(February 1983) pp38-42. illus.
(Sotheby's December 1982 memorabilia
auction.)

M 0339 "The Beatles Fourth Christmas Record."
Beatles Unlimited 17 (November 1977)
pp13-14.
(Picture and text of the 1966 fan club
record.)

M 0340 "Beatles' Gale Warnings Up; Cities Gird For
Teen Tempest." Variety 236 (August 26, 1964)
p43+.

M 0341 "Beatles Gallery." Beatlefan
(Regular feature, v2n5-v2n6, 1980.)

M 0342 "Beatles Get Back LP Due In July."
Rolling Stone 37 (July 12, 1969) p8. illus.

M 0343 "Beatles Get Back Track By Track."
Rolling Stone 42 (September 20, 1969)
p8. illus.
(On the "Get Back" bootleg LP.)

M 0344 "Beatles Get Ticker Tape Welcome!"

Melody Maker 39 (August 22, 1964) p1. illus.

M 0345 "Beatles' Global Gross: $98-Mil." Variety 246
(May 10, 1967) p2.

M 0346 "Beatles Going Public? Not Yet, Says Epstein."
Billboard 76 (October 31, 1964) p4.

M 0347 "Beatles Grooving 1,000,000-Seller LP In
British Market." Variety 236 (October 14,
1964) p51.

M 0348 "'Beatles Guitar' Man." Beatlefan 1:6
(October 1979) p13.
(Tony Saks and his autographed guitar.)

M 0349 "The Beatles' Hamburg Showcase Folds In Oct."
Variety (October 1, 1969) p61.
(Closing of the Star Club.)

M 0350 "Beatles 'Hearts' Earns Gold Disk." Variety 247
(May 31, 1967) p41.

M 0351 "Beatles Heat Flares In Court." Billboard 76
(January 25, 1964) p1+. illus.

M 0352 "Beatles Hit Charts For Seven!" Melody Maker 38
(December 7, 1963) p1. illus.

M 0353 "Beatles Hit Jackpot; Find Gold 21 In Them Thar
Disks." Billboard 78 (September 24, 1966)
p6.

M 0354 "Beatles' House Guru Conjures Up Spiritual
Bonanza At N.Y. Seance." Variety 249
(January 24, 1968) p2+.

M 0355 "Beatles In America." Melody Maker 39
(February 15, 1964) pp1-4. illus.

M 0356 "Beatles, Inc." Newsweek 71 (May 27, 1968)
p68. illus.

M 0357 "Beatles In Disc Storm (First Record Made In
1961)." Melody Maker 39 (May 30, 1964)
p1.

M 0358 "Beatles - In Germany '66." Beatles Unlimited 5
(January 1976) pp18-21.
(June 1966.)

M 0359 "Beatles In Interview Row." Melody Maker 41
(June 4, 1966) p4.

M 0360 "The Beatles In Scotland." Sixteen Magazine 6:10
(March 1965) pp38-39.

M 0361 "Beatles In The Web." Newsweek 74 (October 20,
1969) pp130-131. illus.

M 0362 "Beatles Is Coming." Newsweek 63 (February 3,
1964) p77.

M 0363 "Beatles Items Generate $$." Billboard 92
(November 1, 1980) p80.

M 0364 "Beatles' 'Jude' Spins 'Em To 16th Goldisk."
Variety 252 (October 2, 1968) p53.

M 0365 "Beatles Kick Off Far West Tour Aug. 19 With
25G Guarantee Vs. 60% Of Gross." Variety 234
(April 22, 1964) p136.

M 0366 "Beatles, Klein Suit Gets Light." Billboard 88
(February 14, 1976) p10+.

M 0367 "Beatles Label To Bow In U.K." Billboard 80
(July 27, 1968) p50.

M 0368 "Beatles Laff All Way To Poor House Over
Apple's Alleged Fiscal Follies." Variety 256
(October 1, 1969) p61.

M 0369 "The Beatles Lead Now." The Beatles Book 58
(May 1968) p25.
(Leaders of popular music.)

M 0370 "Beatles' Lennon, McCartney Top BMI Songwriters
With 10 Tunes In Best 100." Variety
(January 20, 1965) p49.

M 0371 "Beatles Live - At The Cavern!" Melody Maker 56
(April 11, 1981) p4.
(A "lost" LP.)

M 0372 "Beatles Live LP In Works." Rolling Stone 236
(April 7, 1977) p20.
(The Hollywood Bowl album.)

M 0373 "Beatles' Long And Winding Road To Oblivion."
Melody Maker 46 (January 9, 1971) p3.

M 0374 "Beatles Make Counter Bid In Fight Vs. Grade
For Northern Songs Ltd." Variety 254
(April 30, 1969) p57+.

M 0375 "Beatles Management Fees Hikes ABKCO's Sixmonth
Operating Profit To 827G." Variety 259
(May 20, 1970) p47.

M 0376 "Beatles Map 3 London Concerts In Dec. For 1st
Stage Dates In 2 Years." Variety 252

(November 13, 1968) p143.

M 0377 "Beatles May Do Free Concert Tour In U.S.A."
Rolling Stone 23 (December 7, 1968)
p1.

M 0378 "Beatles Mulling Stage Comeback." Variety 252
(October 9, 1968) p1+.

M 0379 "Beatles Nab Another $1-Mil Album Seller."
Variety 234 (April 15, 1964) p47.

M 0380 "Beatles Nabbing 100G For NY 1-Niter on U.S.
Tour: L.A.'s 90G For 2 Nites." Variety 238
(March 17, 1965) p82+.

M 0381 "Beatles, Natch, Cop Ivor Novello Kudo."
Variety 234 (April 1, 1964) p65.

M 0382 "Beatles; Nay, Nay, Nay." Forbes 96 (September
1, 1965) p31.

M 0383 "Beatles' New Revolver LP Explodes Into
Britain's Most 'Covered' Album." Variety 243
(August 3, 1966) p53.

M 0384 "Beatles News Diary." Beatles Now
(Regular feature, issue No.5-   ,Winter
1983-   .)

M 0385 "Beatles News Oct. '62." The Beatles Book 79
(November 1982) pp10-12.
(Press clippings.)

M 0386 "Beatles News Nov. '62." The Beatles Book 80
(December 1982) pp14-19.
(Press clippings.)

M 0387 "Beatles News Dec. '62." The Beatles Book 81
(January 1983) pp10,12. illus.
(Press clippings.)

M 0388 "Beatles News Jan. '63." The Beatles Book 82
(February 1983) pp10-15. illus.
(Press clippings.)

M 0389 "Beatles News Feb. '63." The Beatles Book 83
(March 1983) pp14-21. illus.
(Press clippings.)

M 0390 "Beatles News Mar. '63." The Beatles Book 84
(April 1983) pp14-22. illus.
(Press clippings.)

M 0391 "Beatles News Apr. '63." The Beatles Book 85
(May 1983) pp10-14. illus.
(Press clippings.)

M 0392 "Beatles News May '63." The Beatles Book 86
(June 1983) pp14-21. illus.
(Press clippings.)

M 0393 "Beatles News June '63." The Beatles Book 87
(July 1983) pp14-20. illus.
(Press clippings.)

M 0394 "Beatles News July '63." The Beatles Book 88
(August 1983) pp12-21. illus.
(Press clippings.)

M 0395 "Beatles News Aug. '63." The Beatles Book 89
(September 1983) pp10-16. illus.
(Press clippings.)

M 0396 "Beatles News Sept. '63." The Beatles Book 90
(October 1983) pp10-15. illus.
(Press clippings.)

M 0397 "Beatles News Oct. '63." The Beatles Book 91
(November 1983) pp9-13. illus.
(Press clippings.)

M 0398 "Beatles News Nov. '63." The Beatles Book 92
(December 1983) pp8-13. illus.
(Press clippings.)

M 0399 "Beatles News Dec. '63." The Beatles Book 93
(January 1984) pp9-15. illus.
(Press clippings.)

M 0400 "Beatles' Next LP Due In October."
Rolling Stone 43 (October 4, 1969)
p6.

M 0401 "The Beatles 1968 Christmas Record."
Beatles Unlimited 17 (November 1977)
pp17-19.
(Picture and text of the 1968 fan club
record.)

M 0402 "The Beatles 1963/4 & 1964/5 Christmas Shows."
Beatles Unlimited 16 (November 1977)
pp9-16.

M 0403 "Beatles Nixing All Tour Offers." Variety 257
(December 17, 1969) p55.

M 0404 "Beatles: No Discernible Pattern."

Rolling Stone 32 (May 3, 1969) p10.

M 0405 "Beatles' Northern Songs Hikes Dividend to 36
Percent." Variety 254 (March 5, 1969)
p67.

M 0406 "The Beatles Now." The Beatles Book 8
(December 1976) ppiii-iv.

M 0407 "Beatles Now Legal In South Africa!"
Melody Maker 46 (June 19, 1971) p12.

M 0408 "Beatles Offered $40 Million."
Songwriters Review 31:2 (1976) p1.
(For one concert.)

M 0409 "Beatles OK Maharishi Film." Rolling Stone 2
(November 23, 1967) p6.

M 0410 "Beatle Solo Boom - By George!" Melody Maker 46
(January 30, 1971) p1.

M 0411 "Beatles' 1,000,000 Advance For Latest Single
Gives 'Em Pre-Sale Gold Disk." Variety 233
(December 4, 1963) p1+.
("I Wanna Hold Your Hand.")

M 0412 "Beatles' $1,000,000 U.S. Tour." Variety 235
(August 19, 1964) p47+.

M 0413 "Beatles Only Slightly Boff: Big U.S. Grosses
Though Not SRO." Variety 243 (August 17,
1966) p43+.

M 0414 "Beatles Personal Letters." Sixteen Magazine 6:10
(March 1965) p50.

M 0415 "The Beatles: Planning A $30-Million One-Night
Stand." The Star (March 2, 1976) pp4-5.
(Reunion concert rumors.)

M 0416 "Beatle Split Rumour: Apple Is Alive And
Healthy In The UK." Rolling Stone 27
(February 15, 1969) p4.

M 0417 "Beatles' Press Confab An Experience Midway
Between Nightmare And Art." Variety 239
(August 18, 1965) p41.

M 0418 "Beatles' Pubbery Profit At 1.7 Mil, Topping
Forecast." Variety (September 1, 1965)
p45.
(Northern Songs.)

M 0419 "Beatles Publisher And Beatlemania Producers
Get Court Injunction." Variety 300
(August 6, 1980) p2+.
(Stage show "Beatlemania.")

M 0420 "Beatles Publisher Pursues Pix Using Tunes
Without A License." Variety 295 (May 23,
1979) p81+.

M 0421 "Beatles Puzzle." Beatlefan 2:2 (February 1980)
p17.
(Answer to puzzle in v2n1.)

M 0422 "Beatles' Quickie 2-Wk U.S. Tour Flips Their
Cap L.P. Past 2,000,000 Mark." Variety 234
(February 26, 1964) p65+.

M 0423 "Beatles Rain Check." Variety 283 (June 9, 1976)
p64.

M 0424 "Beatles Reaction Puzzles Even Psychologists."
Science Newsletter 85 (February 29, 1964)
p141.

M 0425 "Beatles' Record-Busting LP May Be All-Time
Biggest." Rolling Stone 24 (December 21,
1968) p1+.
("White Album.")

M 0426 "Beatles Reissues Hurting Sales Of New Talent's
Disks In UK." Variety 282 (April 14, 1976)
p76.

M 0427 "Beatles Reject $1 Mil Offer." Billboard 79
(January 21, 1967) p4.

M 0428 "Beatles Reunion Alot Of Hot Air." Variety 282
(March 17, 1976) p81.

M 0429 "Beatles Reunion Rumor Wrong; Only Paul Plays
At Charity Date." Billboard 92 (January 12,
1980) p43.

M 0430 "Beatles 'Reunited' By Creative Programming."
Billboard 92 (November 29, 1980) p19.

M 0431 "Beatles Run Rampant On Charts, Arrive In U.S.
This Week." Cash Box 25 (February 8, 1964)
p7+.

M 0432 "Beatles' Sales Hit 150,000,000 Disks."
Variety 243 (August 3, 1965) p1.

M 0433 "Beatles Say Yeah To 9-Yr EMI Pact." Variety
245 (February 15, 1967) p43.

M 0434 "Beatles' Score: 80,000,000 Disks." Variety 235
       (August 12, 1964) p1+.
M 0435 "Beatles Scrapbook." Beatlefan
       (Occasional feature, v3n5-   , 1980-   .)
M 0436 "Beatles Secret." The Reporter 30 (February 27,
       1964) p16+.
M 0437 "Beatles' 'Sgt. Pepper' Made Into Multi Media
       Click At Beacon." Variety 277 (November 20,
       1974) p48.
M 0438 "Beatles Set Apple Corps With Capitol."
       Billboard 80 (June 29, 1968) p1+.
M 0439 "Beatles' Set Hot B.O. Pace For UA; Ad Campaign
       Now Aimed At Adults." Variety 236 (August
       26, 1964) p04.
M 0440 "Beatles Set Zapple Tag For New Label Due In
       May." Billboard 81 (April 12, 1969)
       p78.
M 0441 "The Beatles Seventh Christmas Record."
       Beatles Unlimited 17 (November 1977)
       pp20-22.
           (Picture and text of the 1969 fan club
           record.)
M 0442 "Beatles Show On Broadway Has Mania Against
       Critics." Variety 287 (July 27, 1977)
       p2+.
           (Stage show "Beatlemania.")
M 0443 "Beatles Show Set." Billboard 94:11 (March 20,
       1982) p2.
           ("The Beatles At The Beeb" radio special.)
M 0444 "Beatles Single Stirs Storm Anti-Christ?"
       Billboard 81 (June 7, 1969) p4.
M 0445 "Beatles '65' Goes From 98 To No. 1 On BB
       Chart." Billboard 77 (January 16, 1965)
       p4.
M 0446 "Beatles VI World Premiere: KRLA First With
       Beatles' Album." KRLA Beat (Los Angeles)
       (June 9, 1965) p1,11.
           (Album preview.)
M 0447 "Beatles Sold 55,000,000 (I.E., 545,000,000)
       'Units' In 10 Years Making." Variety 268
       (October 18, 1972) p1.
M 0448 "Beatles' Soundtrack A Blockbuster Before Their
       1st Pic's Release." Variety 235 (July 1,
       1964) p1+.
M 0449 "Beatles Splitting? Maybe, Says John,"
       Rolling Stone 50 (January 21, 1970)
       p7. illus.
M 0450 "Beatles' Stage Comeback To Spark First Live
       LP, TV Spec, And Film Documentary." Variety
       253 (January 15, 1969) p2.
M 0451 "Beatles Started The Big Breakthrough."
       Melody Maker 40 (June 26, 1965) ppii-iii.
       illus.
M 0452 "Beatles Statue Fund." Beatles Now 3 (Summer
       1982) p12. illus.
           (Full-page funds solicitation.)
M 0453 "Beatles Still Await Ruling On Royalties."
       Financial Post 63 (April 26, 1969)
       p3.
M 0454 "Beatles Still Clearing Up $ Problems Says
       Apple Manager." Billboard 86 (March 16, 1974)
       p52.
M 0455 "Beatles Still In Stalemate Over How To Split
       Their Partnership Shares." Variety 267
       (May 24, 1972) p51.
M 0456 "Beatles, Stones To Link Up?" Melody Maker 42
       (October 21, 1967) p1.
M 0457 "Beatles' Success In U.S. A Trend For The
       British?" Variety 233 (February 5, 1964)
       p46.
M 0458 "Beatles Swing In Marketplace."
       Printers' Ink (Eastern ed.) (February 21,
       1964) p10+.
M 0459 "The Beatles: 10 Years On, 1964-1974."
       Hit Parader Annual (Winter 1974) pp11-13.
       illus.
M 0460 "Beatles - The DJs Verdict." Melody Maker 38
       (August 24, 1963) pp8-9. illus.
M 0461 "Beatles; The Facts." Melody Maker 45
       (August 15, 1970) p27. illus.

M 0462 "Beatles: The Last Rites." Melody Maker 46
       (February 27, 1971) p17.
M 0463 "The Beatles Third Christmas Record."
       Beatles Unlimited 17 (November 1977)
       pp10-12.
           (Picture and text of the 1965 fan club
           record.)
M 0464 "Beatles' Tifts In Court Still Blazing Wildly."
       Billboard 76 (February 8, 1964) p4.
M 0465 "Beatles To Appear Live And John In The Nude."
       Rolling Stone 21 (November 9, 1968)
       p4.
M 0466 "Beatles To Cut For Apple Label; Stay With
       EMI." Variety 251 (June 26, 1968) p43.
M 0467 "Beatles To Do Three-LP Set?" Rolling Stone 14
       (July 20, 1968) p4.
M 0468 "Beatles Together For Lennon Tribute."
       Rolling Stone 345 (June 11, 1981) p13.
M 0469 "Beatles To Launch A 2d Label, Zapple."
       Variety 254 (April 9, 1969) p65.
M 0470 "Beatles Top English Poll." Rolling Stone 1
       (November 9, 1967) p4.
M 0471 "Beatles Top Poll!" Mersey Beat 1:13 (January
       4, 1962) p1. illus.
           (Mersey Beat poll of readers.)
M 0472 "Beatles Tornado Storms Its Way Eastward."
       Cash Box 25 (August 29, 1964) p6. illus.
           (On The Beatles month-long tour.)
M 0473 "The Beatles' Toronto Take Home Pay: 100G."
       Variety 243 (June 1, 1966) p49.
M 0474 "Beatles To Unite In Monster Rock Fest At
       Monticello, N.Y." Variety 274 (April 24,
       1974) p1.
M 0475 "Beatles 'Tour' No Wow On TV But Disk Triumphs
       In Singles Charts." Variety 249 (January 17,
       1968) p45.
M 0476 "Beatles' 'Tripper' Their 10th No. 1 Hit."
       Variety 241 (December 8, 1965) p55.
M 0477 "Beatles Tuning Up." The Beatles Book 21
       (April 1965) pp20-21.
           (Photos.)
M 0478 "Beatles' TV Spec Draws Critical Rap; Loses
       Ratings, But Will Turn Profit." Variety 249
       (January 10, 1968) p1+.
M 0479 "The Beatles:Twenty Years Ago The Photogenic
       Four Arrived In The U.S., Where Fans Both
       Looked And Listened." People 21:5 (February
       6, 1984) pp65-66+. illus.
M 0480 "Beatles Under The Microscope."
       Music & Video Week (London) (March 20, 1982)
       p13.
M 0481 "Beatles Unlimited 2nd Anniversary."
       Beatles Unlimited 13 (May 1977) p23.
           (Second year of publication celebration.)
M 0482 "Beatles Up EMI Fiscal Profit To Peak
       $16,975,000." Variety 240 (September 29,
       1965) p43.
M 0483 "Beatles Up-To-The-Minute Facts." Tiger Beat 5:2
       (October 1969) p41.
M 0484 "Beatles Up-To-The-Minute Facts." Tiger Beat 5:3
       (November 1969) p33.
M 0485 "Beatles Up-To-The-Minute Facts." Tiger Beat 5:4
       (December 1969) p40.
M 0486 "Beatles USA." Melody Maker 40 (August 28, 1965)
       p7.
M 0487 "Beatles' U.S. Personals May Be Dented By
       Religioso Rhubarb & DJ Blackout." Variety
       243 (August 10, 1966) p2+.
M 0488 "Beatles Video." Beatlefan
       (Regular feature, v3n6-   , 1980-   .)
M 0489 "The Beatles - What The Merseyside Wonders
       Think Of The Latest Batch Of Pop Singles."
       Melody Maker 38 (June 29, 1963) pp8-9.
       illus.
M 0490 "Beatles Will Live Again At Philadelphia
       Festival." Billboard 88 (May 1, 1976)
       p37.
M 0491 "Beatles Will Make $ Million On U.S. Tour,
       Epstein Predicts." Billboard 77 (May 8, 1965)
       p14.

M 0492 "The Beatles, Will They Sing Again For $50
　　　 Million." People 5 (April 5, 1976)
　　　 pp14-19. illus.
M 0493 "Beatles Win 5 Awards For Songs They Write."
　　　 Billboard 76 (April 11, 1964) p4.
M 0494 "Beatles Win New Fan Club - Top British
　　　 Politicos." Variety 234 (February 26, 1964)
　　　 p65.
M 0495 "Beatles Win Over America." Cash Box 25
　　　 (February 22, 1964) p6. illus.
M 0496 "Beatles Win Press Award." Melody Maker 39
　　　 (January 4, 1964) p1. illus.
M 0497 "Beatles' Yogi To Tour U.S. With Beach Boys."
　　　 Variety 250 (March 20, 1968) p1+.
M 0498 "The Beatles: 'You Never Give Me Your Money'."
　　　 Rolling Stone 46 (November 15, 1969)
　　　 p1+. illus.
M 0499 "Beatles Zap USA, Ltd." Rolling Stone 5
　　　 (January 10, 1968) p1,2. illus.
M 0500 "Beats And Beatles." New Statesman 67
　　　 (January 17, 1964) p82.
M 0501 Beatty, J. "'Eleanor Rigby': Structure In The
　　　 Arts." Centerpoint 4:2 (1980) pp14-35. illus.
M 0502 Beaupre, L. "Beatle Bugs Smothers Bros. In
　　　 Comeback Bow; Oust Lennon." Variety 274
　　　 (March 20, 1974) p65.
M 0503 "Beauty And The Beatles." McCall's 92
　　　 (July 1965) pp78-83+.
M 0504 Begley, Geoff. "Wembley 1976."
　　　 Beatles Unlimited 10 (November 1976)
　　　 p19.
　　　 (Wings concert.)
M 0505 Beller, Daniel. "Bob Wooler." Beatles Now 5
　　　 (Winter 1983) pp10-12. illus.
M 0506 Beller, Daniel. "Magical Mystery Tour: The
　　　 Beatles Story On Israeli Radio."
　　　 Beatles Now 5 (Winter 1983) p9. illus.
　　　 (Interview with radio series creator Yoav
　　　 Kuttner.)
M 0507 Beller, Daniel. "A Peace Forest In Israel?"
　　　 Beatles Now 3 (Summer 1982) p13.
M 0508 Beller, Miles. "Meet The Rutles." New West 3
　　　 (March 27, 1978) pp58-59. illus.
　　　 (Rutles parody album of Beatles.)
M 0509 Bender, William. "Letting George Do It." Time 96
　　　 (November 30, 1970) p57. illus.
　　　 (On George Harrison's "All Things Must
　　　 Pass.")
M 0510 Bender, William. "Y'all Come Hear Ringo." Time
　　　 96 (October 26, 1970) p86+. illus.
　　　 (Recording "Beaucoups Of Blues" album.)
M 0511 Benedikt, M. "Yoko Notes." Art & Artists 6
　　　 (January 1972) pp26-29. illus.
M 0512 Benhari. "Baby You're A Rich Man." Good Times 3:42
　　　 (October 23, 1970) p17.
M 0513 Benhari. "Baby You're A Rich Man."
　　　 Other Scenes 5:1 (Spring 1971) p24.
M 0514 Benjamin, Sandy Stert. "Laurence Juber: Winging
　　　 It With Hope." Beatlefan 5:1 (December 1982)
　　　 p9.
　　　 (Interview.)
M 0515 Bennett, Clive. "The Arts; Paul McCartney And
　　　 Wings." Times (October 20, 1976) p11D.
　　　 (Performance discussed.)
M 0516 Bennett, Marty. "Beatles & Stones' Risque LP
　　　 Covers Pose Sales Woes." Variety 252
　　　 (October 16, 1968) p1+.
M 0517 Bennetzen, Jorgen. "Om Og Af Lennon."
　　　 MM (Copenhagen, Denmark) (December 1980)
　　　 p15.
M 0518 Berg, C. "In Praise Of John Lennon."
　　　 Northwest Passage 4:8 (February 1, 1971)
　　　 p21.
M 0519 Berg, David H. "My Turn: The Right To Bear
　　　 Arms." Newsweek (December 29, 1980)
　　　 p8.
　　　 (Death of John Lennon.)
M 0520 Bergenfield, Nathan. "It's All Music." Clavier
　　　 55:6 (September 1976) pp37-40.
M 0521 Berger, Karen. "Paul McCartney: Songs, Success,

And A Solo Career." Accent On Music 7:1
　　　 (September/October 1981) pp8-10. illus.
M 0522 Bergholtz, Artillio. "Latest News On Records
　　　 With Paul, John, George & Ringo."
　　　 Beatles Unlimited
　　　 (Regular feature, issues 18- .)
M 0523 Bergholtz, Artillio. "New Releases."
　　　 Beatles Unlimited
　　　 (Regular feature, issues 18-　, 1978-
　　　 .)
M 0524 Bergholtz, Artillio. "Ring O' Records, Ring O'
　　　 Records." Beatles Unlimited 23 (November
　　　 1978) p19.
　　　 (Conclusion of discography begun issue 20.)
M 0525 Bergholtz, Artillio. "Ring O' Records Special."
　　　 Beatles Unlimited 20 (May 1978) pp13-14.
　　　 (Discography.)
M 0526 Bergholtz, Artillio. "Sweden."
　　　 Beatles Unlimited 34 (1981) pp46-47.
　　　 (Swedish reaction to Lennon's death.)
M 0527 Berkenstadt, James. "Bootlegs Vs. Capitol
　　　 Records: The Continuing Battle Over The
　　　 Beatle Vaults." Goldmine 77 (October 1982)
　　　 p16.
M 0528 Berlin, Alec M. "'82 Touring Guide." Beatlefan
　　　 4:4 (June 1982) pp7-8.
　　　 (Beatle-related Liverpool landmarks.)
M 0529 Berman, L. "Riffs: Yoko Ono's Grief."
　　　 Village Voice 26 (July 29, 1981) p49. illus.
　　　 (On "Season Of Glass" LP.)
M 0530 Besher, Alexander. "Yoko Ono." San Francisco 25:1
　　　 (November 1983) pp58-63. illus.
　　　 (Cover photo of Yoko and Sean.)
M 0531 Bessman, J. "McCartney Denies Guv's Bid To Give
　　　 State 'On Wisconsin' Rights As Memorial To
　　　 John Lennon." Variety 302 (February 18, 1981)
　　　 p2.
M 0532 Best, Pete. "In His Own Words Pete Best Tells
　　　 Of - My Beatle Days." Mersey Beat (August
　　　 15, 1963) p8.
　　　 ("The Beatles Story, Part Ten.")
M 0533 "Best Files $8 Mill Suit." Billboard 77
　　　 (October 9, 1965) p10.
　　　 (Pete Best.)
M 0534 "Best Of The Beatles." Time 86 (December 31,
　　　 1965) p36. illus.
　　　 (Pete Best.)
M 0535 Betrock, Alan. "Beatle-Rock." Jamz 4 (May 1972)
　　　 pp36-42.
　　　 (Additions in issue no. 5, p. 41.)
M 0536 "Beware, The Red Beatles." Newsweek 65
　　　 (February 15, 1965) p89A. illus.
M 0537 Bibey, D. "Beatlefest '83." Beatles Now 7
　　　 (July 1983) pp15,22.
　　　 (Report on New York fan convention, March
　　　 1983.)
M 0538 Biel, D. Michael. "The Real American TV Debut
　　　 Of The Beatles." Goldmine 70 (March 1982)
　　　 p14.
　　　 ("Jack Paar Show," January 3, 1964.)
M 0539 Big Beat And Pop Boys. London:
　　　 City Magazines Ltd., 1964.
　　　 (Beatles cover portrait.)
M 0540 "Big Macca Goes Rhodium." Melody Maker 54
　　　 (November 3, 1979) p10. illus.
　　　 (Paul McCartney.)
M 0541 "Big 7 Gets $6,795 From Lennon." Billboard 88
　　　 (July 24, 1976) p90.
M 0542 Bille, Torben. "I Read The News Today - Eller
　　　 Da John Lennon Igen Blev Godt Stof!"
　　　 MM (Copenhagen, Denmark) (December 1980)
　　　 pp8-9. illus.
M 0543 "Billy Preston Coming." The Beatles Book 73
　　　 (August 1969) p29.
　　　 (Activites at Apple.)
M 0544 "Biography - George Harrison."
　　　 Current Biography Yearbook 27 (November 1966)
　　　 pp23-25. illus.
M 0545 "Biography - John Lennon." Current Biography Yearb
　　　 26 (December 1965) pp19-22. illus.

M 0546 "Biography - Paul McCartney."
Current Biography Yearbook 27 (November
1966) pp32-35. illus.

M 0547 "Biography - Ringo Starr." Current Biography
Yearbook 26 (December 1965) pp38-40. illus.

M 0548 "Biography - Yoko Ono." Current Biography Yearbook
33 (November 1972) pp31-34. illus.

M 0549 "Bios." Cash Box 25 (February 1, 1964)
p16. illus.

M 0550 Bird, Donald A., Stephen Holder and Dianne
Sears. "Walrus Is Greek For Corpse: Rumor
And The Death Of Paul McCartney."
Journal of Popular Culture 10 (Summer 1976)
pp110-121.

M 0551 "Bird On The Wing." Melody Maker 47 (February
26, 1972) p5. illus.

M 0552 Biro, N. "Beatles Law Wrangles Go On In Chicago
& NY." Billboard 76 (February 1, 1964)
p1.

M 0553 "Birth Of The Beatles." Melody Maker 39
(March 28, 1964) pp2-3. illus.

M 0554 "Birth Of The Beatles." Beatlefan 1:5
(August 1979) p1,4.
(Dick Clark's TV special.)

M 0555 "Birth Of The Beatles: A Good Show, But Fab
Four's Help Was Missed." Variety 297
(November 28, 1979) p69.
(Dick Clark's TV special.)

M 0556 Bizot, J.F. "Dossier Pop Music: Les Pop Heureux
Ent Une Histoire." Musique en Jeu 2
(March 1971) pp74-78.

M 0557 Blackburn, Robin and Tariq Ali. "The Dream Is
Over." Space City 3:2 (June 15, 1971)
p10.
(John Lennon.)

M 0558 Blackburn, Robin and Tariq Ali. "Lennon: The
Working-Class Hero Turns Red." Ramparts 10
(July 1971) pp43-49.
(Interview.)

M 0559 Blackburn, Robin and Tariq Ali. "Working Class
Hero!" Liberated Guardian 2:2 (May 20, 1971)
p11.
(John Lennon.)

M 0560 "Black Flag Flies At Beatles' Headquarters."
Variety 260 (August 19, 1970) p50.

M 0561 "Blackpool Pix." The Beatles Book 26 (September
1965) pp8-9.
(Performance photos.)

M 0562 Blake, John. "John & Yoko." Us 5:25 (December
8, 1981) pp70-77.
(Excerpt from his book "All You Needed Was
Love.")

M 0563 "Blind Date." Melody Maker 39 (August 22, 1964)
p13. illus.
(Brian Epstein.)

M 0564 "Blind Date." Melody Maker 39 (December 5, 1964)
pp10-11. illus.
(John Lennon.)

M 0565 "Blind Date." Melody Maker 39 (December 12,
1964) p7+.
(Paul McCartney.)

M 0566 "Blind Date." Melody Maker 39 (December 19,
1964) p9.
(George Harrison.)

M 0567 "Blind Date." Melody Maker 39 (December 26,
1964) p16.
(Ringo Starr.)

M 0568 "Blind Date." Melody Maker 40 (October 2, 1965)
p8.
(Brian Epstein.)

M 0569 "Blind Date." Melody Maker 40 (December 11,
1965) p10.
(John Lennon.)

M 0570 "Blind Date." Melody Maker 40 (December 18,
1965) p9. illus.
(George Harrison.)

M 0571 "Blind Date." Melody Maker 41 (February 19,
1966) p9. illus.
(Paul McCartney.)

M 0572 "Blind Date." Melody Maker 41 (February 26,

1966) p14. illus.
(Ringo Starr.)

M 0573 "Blind Date." Melody Maker 42 (February 25,
1967) p13. illus.
(Paul McCartney.)

M 0574 "Blitz In Britain." Time 107 (May 3, 1976)
p60. illus.

M 0575 "Blue-Chip Beatles." Newsweek 66 (October 4,
1965) p82. illus.
(Northern Songs stock sales.)

M 0576 "Blue Meanie Beatle." Rolling Stone 9
(April 27, 1962) p1+. illus.
(Cover portrait.)

M 0577 "Blue Meanies Attack Beatles." Rolling Stone 31
(April 19, 1969) p8. illus.

M 0578 "Blues For The Beatles; U.S. Tour; Reactions To
Lennon Statement." Newsweek 68 (August 22,
1966) p94. illus.

M 0579 Blumentnal, E. "Proxymania." Village Voice 23
(May 29, 1978) p80.
(Stage show "Beatlemania.")

M 0580 Blyth, Karen. "Letter To George."
The Beatles Book 18 (January 1965) p15.
(Fan letter.)

M 0581 Blyth, Karen. "My Idea Of A Meeting Of The
Beatles Haters Brigade." The Beatles Book 24
(July 1965) p21.

M 0582 "BMI Top Writer Awards To McC, Lennon; SG-Col,
Kirshner As Pubs." Billboard 83 (June 5,
1971) p3+.

M 0583 "Bob, George, John, Phil, Ringo, & Johnny."
Rolling Stone 59 (May 28, 1970) p10. illus.
(Reported Dylan-Harrison recording
session.)

M 0584 "Boiling Beatles Blast Copy Cats."
Melody Maker 38 (August 3, 1963) p1. illus.

M 0585 Bonici, Ray and David Lewin. "Paul McCartney."
Us 5:10 (May 12, 1981) pp24-29. illus.
(Excerpts from "Paul McCartney:
Composer/Artist.")

M 0586 "Book Facts." The Beatles Book 52 (August 1980)
pv.
(Odd mentions of the Beatles in two books.)

M 0587 "Book Reveals Lennon's Wild Side: 'I've Always
Needed A Drug To Survive'."
National Enquirer (December 30, 1980)
pp38-39.
(Miles' book, "Beatles In Their Own
Words.")

M 0588 "Book Review." Beatles Unlimited
(Frequent feature, issues 7-   .)

M 0589 "Book Review." Beatles Now illus.
(Regular feature, issues No.4-5,
Aut.'82-Win.'83.)

M 0590 "Book Section." Beatles Now 2 (Spring 1982)
pp11-12.
(News on future publications.)

M 0591 "Bootleg Releases." Beatles Now
(Regular feature, Nos. 4-6, Aut. 1982-May
1983.)

M 0592 "Born." Newsweek 86 (October 20, 1975)
p63.
(Sean Ono Lennon.)

M 0593 Bowles, Jerry. "The Day America Caught Beatle
Fever." Panorama 1:6 (July 1980) pp68-70.
(Excerpt from his book, "A Thousand Days.")

M 0594 Bowman, David. "Scenarios For The Revolution In
Pepperland." Journal of Popular Film 1:3 (1972)
pp173-184. illus.
(Film "Yellow Submarine.")

M 0595 "Bow-Wow Beatle." Mersey Beat (August 29, 1963)
p9.
(A canine Beatle fan.)

M 0596 Boyer, Peter J. "There Will Always Be The
Beatles." Wisconsin State Journal 5
(May 12, 1977) p1.

M 0597 Braam, Willi. "Germany." Beatles Unlimited 34/35
(1981) pp44-46.
(Reaction to Lennon's death in Germany.)

M 0598 "Brace Yourself, They're Back." Business Week

(September 22, 1964) pp28-29. illus.
M 0599 Bramwell, Tony. "With Paul In Hollywood."
        The Beatles Book 61 (August 1968) pp6-11.
        (June 1968.)

M 0600 Braucourt, G. "Beatles Show." Ecran 35
        (April 1975) pp3-4.
        (Beatles film retrospective held in Paris.)

M 0601 Bream, Jon. "Wings Over America: Big Bird
        Touches Down; The Most Popular Ex-Beatle
        Talks To You." Modern Hi Fi & Music
        (October/November 1976) pp15-19.

M 0602 Brennan, Peter. "$150m Beatles Blitz All Set To
        Blast U.S. Again." The Star 3:20 (May 18,
        1976) p15.

M 0603 Breslin, Rosemary. "Secondhand Fans."
        Rolling Stone 415 (February 16, 1984)
        pp62,64. illus.
        (Eighties' teenagers and The Beatles.)

M 0604 "Brian Epstein, Beatles' 29 Yr. Old Mgr.,
        Turning Impresario And Film Producer."
        Variety 234 (March 25, 1964) p7+.

M 0605 "Brian Epstein In Vic Lewis Merger." Variety
        241 (February 2, 1966) p1.

M 0606 "Brian Epstein's Brother Takes Over As Nems
        Chief; No Deal With Beatles." Variety 248
        (September 6, 1967) p45.

M 0607 "Brian Epstein, 32, Beatles' Mentor, Dies In
        London." Variety 248 (August 3, 1967)
        p50+.

M 0608 Briant, Richard. "A Brief Conversation With
        Mc." Relix (November/December 1976)
        pp26-27.

M 0609 Brien, Alan. "Afterthoughts On The Beatles."
        Mademoiselle 59 (August 1964) p239+.

M 0610 Brien, Alan. "The Beatles." Mademoiselle
        (August 1964) pp346-348.

M 0611 Brinckman, Joe. "The Beatles Early Success Was
        Phony." Music Journal 30 (March 1972)
        p40+.

M 0613 "Britain's Beatles' Sales Top 3,000,000."
        Variety 232 (November 13, 1963) p52.

M 0614 "Britain's Prime Minister Reopens Birthplace Of
        Beatles: Yeah! Yeah! Yeah!" Variety 243
        (August 3, 1966) p56.

M 0615 "Britain's Retaliation For Ten Years Of
        Imported Rock And Roll."
        High Fidelity/Musical America 14:4
        (April 1964) p108.
        (On "Meet The Beatles" album.)

M 0616 "British Bookies Now Quoting Odds On Disk Chart
        Winners; Rate Beatles 6-1." Variety 235
        (August 19, 1964) p1+.

M 0617 "British Exports Booming; Beatles."
        National Review 16 (February 25, 1964)
        p142.

M 0618 "British High Court Winds Beatles' Long
        Partnership." Billboard 87 (January 18, 1975)
        p3+.

M 0619 "British Press Cools Toward Beatles." Variety
        234 (March 18, 1964) p47.

M 0620 "British View Of Beatle Theology." Variety
        (September 7, 1966) p45.
        (Synopsis of David Frost piece from the
        Spectator.)

M 0621 Britt, Stan. "The Beatles: All Things Must
        Pass." Cassettes and Cartridges (June 1975)
        pp97-100.
        (Discography.)

M 0622 Bronson, H. "George Harrison: His Guitar Isn't
        Weeping Anymore." Songwriter Magazine 4
        (June 1979) p23. illus.
        (Interview.)

M 0623 Brookhiser, R. "John Lennon, RIP."
        National Review 32 (December 31, 1980)
        p1555.

M 0624 Brown, G. "McCartney: Life After Death."
        Melody Maker 49 (November 30, 1974)
        pp8-9. illus.

M 0625 Brown, G. "Venetian Blinder." Melody Maker 51

(October 2, 1976) p56+. illus.
        (Paul McCartney.)

M 0626 Brown, G. "Wings." Melody Maker 49 (November
        30, 1974) p29. illus.

M 0627 Brown, Ken. "Those Were The Days." Beatlefan 2:3
        (April 1980) p15.
        (Memories of former Quarrymen member.)

M 0628 Brown, Mick. "Beatles Lose Their Live Album
        Battle." Rolling Stone 239 (May 19, 1977)
        p15.
        (The Star Club tapes.)

M 0629 Brown, Mick. "A Conversation With George
        Harrison." Rolling Stone 289 (April 19, 1979)
        pp71-75.
        (Interview.)

M 0630 Brown, Mick. "Performance: Wings In London."
        Rolling Stone 310 (February 7, 1980)
        p92. illus.
        (Concert of December 5, 1979.)

M 0631 Brown, Peter and Steven Gaines. "The
        Blockbuster Book That Bares The Shocking
        Truth About The Sensational Rock Group."
        National Enquirer (March 29, 1983)
        pp40-42. illus.
        (Excerpt from "The Love You Make.")

M 0632 Brown, Peter and Steven Gaines. "The Sizzling
        New Tell-All Book About The Beatles Secret
        Lives." National Enquirer (March 15, 1983)
        pp48-50. illus.
        (Excerpt from "The Love You Make.")

M 0633 Brownmiller, S. "Yoko & John." Rolling Stone
        335 (January 22, 1981) p25. illus.

M 0634 Bryce, Leslie. "Shooting The Beatles."
        The Beatles Book 14 (September 1964)
        p7,31.
        (Still photographer's experiences.)

M 0635 Buckley, William F., Jr. "The Beatles And The
        Guru." National Review 20 (March 12, 1968)
        p259.

M 0636 Buckley, William F., Jr. "John Lennon's
        Almanac." National Review 23 (April 6, 1971)
        p391.

M 0637 Bundgaard, Peder. "Imagine."
        MM (Copenhagen, Denmark) (December 1980)
        p6. illus.
        (On John Lennon.)

M 0638 Burks, J. "A Pile Of Money On Paul's 'Death'."
        Rolling Stone 47 (November 29, 1969)
        p10+.

M 0639 Burks, John. "Songs And Sounds Of The Sixties."
        American Libraries 3 (February 1972)
        pp123-132. illus.

M 0640 Burnett, Ric. "Meeting The Beatles." Beatlefan
        3:6 (October 1981) p26.
        (May 19, 1976 encounter with Paul
        McCartney.)

M 0641 Burry, Lenny. "Pop Star Blasts The Beatles,
        Stones, Spoonful And More." Teen Screen 8:9
        (September 1966) pp20-22.

M 0642 Burstein, D. "Trying To Make A Sad Song
        Better." MacLean's 95 (December 13, 1982)
        p8+. illus.
        (On John Lennon.)

M 0643 Buskin, Richard. "The Dutch Beatles
        Convention." The Beatles Book 85 (May 1983)
        pp42-46.
        (Fourth annual convention, April 9-10,
        1983.)

M 0644 Buskin, Richard. "Liverpool's Best Group."
        The Beatles Book 78 (October 1982)
        pp5-7.

M 0645 "Buying The Beatles." Time 85 (February 19,
        1965) p94.

M 0646 Byron, S. "John And Yoko Coming Unmoored."
        Village Voice 18 (January 18, 1973)
        p75.
        (On film "Imagine.")

M 0647 Bystrom, John L. "Beatlemania In Stockholm."
        Beatles Unlimited 13 (May 1977) p6.
        (Swedish fan convention, February 12,

1977.)

M 0648 Bystrom, John L. "Sweden Updated."
Beatles Unlimited 20 (May 1978) p21.
(Beatle events in Sweden.)

M 0649 Calnek, N. "Letters To The Recordings Editor."
Saturday Review 52 (February 22, 1969)
p76.
(Reply to E. Sander's "The Beatles," Dec.
28.)

M 0650 Cameron, Gail. "The Cool Brain Behind The
Bonfire." Life 57 (August 28, 1964)
p62+. illus.
(Brian Epstein.)

M 0651 Cameron, Gail. "Disaster? Well, Not Exactly:
There Stood The Beatles." Life 57 (August
28, 1964) pp58A-60+. illus.

M 0652 Cameron, Gail. "Yeah-Yeah-Yeah! Beatlemania
Becomes A Part Of U.S. History." Life 56
(February 21, 1964) pp34-34B. illus.

M 0653 Campbell, Colin and Allan Murphy. "Things We
Said Today." Beatlefan 3:4 (June 1981) pp25-27+.
(Excerpt from their book.)

M 0654 Campbell, Mary. "Partners." Music Journal 34
(September 1976) pp7-14+.
(Paul McCartney.)

M 0655 Camper, Diane, Emily Newhall and Phyllis
Malamud. "Gun Control Hodgepodge." Newsweek
25 (December 22, 1980) p47. illus.

M 0656 "Capitol Plots Promo For Rarities Album
Spotting The Beatles." Billboard 92
(April 12, 1980) p6+.

M 0657 "Capitol Says $6.98 Is A Fair Price."
Rolling Stone 53 (March 7, 1970) p8.
(For Beatles album.)

M 0658 "Capitol Wins First Round In Battle Over
Beatles; Disk Orders Top 1-Mil." Variety 233
(January 22, 1964) p69.

M 0659 "Cap Throws Block Vs. VeeJay's Beatles."
Variety (February 12, 1964) p87.
(Capitol Records fights Vee Jay album.)

M 0660 Carballal, Henrique. "'The Beatles At The
Beeb'." Beatlefan 4:3 (April 1982)
p10.
(Background to the BBC radio special.)

M 0661 Carballal, Henrique. "Collecting." Beatlefan 3:6
(October 1981) pp23,24.
(Brazilian discography.)

M 0662 Cardoso, Bill. "Tom & Dick & Harry & John."
New Times 2 (April 5, 1974) p54+.
(Lennon and Nilsson at the Troubador Club.)

M 0663 Carlinsky, Dan. "Here's Some Trivia To Test
Yourself." Wisconsin State Journal 5
(May 12, 1977) p1.
(Beatles trivia test.)

M 0664 Carlsen, R.W. "Feedback: On The Death Of John
Lennon." International Musician 79
(March 1981) p12.

M 0665 Carr, Roy. "Paul McCartney: Is This Man Guilty
Of Power Pop?" Creem 10 (August 1978)
pp50-53+. illus.
(Interview; reprinted from NME.)

M 0666 Carr, Roy. "They Didn't Have To Be So Nice."
New Musical Express (May 17, 1975)
pp26-27.

M 0667 Carr, Roy and T. Tyler. "An Appreciative Look
At The Beatles." Sound (September 1975)
pp54-57.

M 0668 Carroll, Jon. "John Brower Wants Your Shit."
Rolling Stone 56 (April 16, 1970) p8.
(Toronto Peace Festival.)

M 0669 Carroll, Jon. "Moon To Attend Peace Festival?"
Rolling Stone 53 (March 7, 1970) p10. illus.
(John Lennon.)

M 0670 Carroll, Jon and J. Caulfield. "John Goes One
Way, Toronto The Other." Rolling Stone 55
(April 2, 1970) p10.

M 0671 Carson, T. "Riffs: Paul McCartney Is Afraid Of
The Dark." Village Voice 25 (July 2, 1980)
p45.
(On the "McCartney II" album.)

M 0672 Carter, S. "Folk And The Beatles."
English Dance 26:1 (1963) p3.

M 0673 "Cartoon Quiz." The Beatles Book 56 (March 1968)
p26.
(Bob Gibson caricatures.)

M 0674 Casey, Howie. "Those Were The Days." Beatlefan
2:3 (April 1980) p18.
(Beatles' first trip to Hamburg.)

M 0675 Castleman, Harry and Wally Podrazik. "Case Of
The Belittled Beatles Tapes." Stereo Review
39 (November 1977) p66+.
(The Hamburg tapes.)

M 0676 Catone, Marc A. "As I Write This Letter."
The Alternative Review 1:2 (October 1981)
pp16-19.
(Excerpts from his book.)

M 0677 Catone, Marc A. "As I Write This Letter."
Beatlefan 3:6 (October 1981) pp4-6.
(Excerpts from his book.)

M 0678 "Caught In The Act." Melody Maker 49 (January
12, 1973) p55.

M 0679 "Caught In The Act." Melody Maker 48 (June 2,
1973) p51. illus.
(Paul McCartney.)

M 0680 "Caught In The Act." Melody Maker 49 (November
23, 1974) p50. illus.
(George Harrison.)

M 0681 "Caught In The Act." Melody Maker 49 (November
30, 1974) p26.
(George Harrison.)

M 0682 "Caught In The Act." Melody Maker 49 (December
21, 1974) p41.
(George Harrison.)

M 0683 "Caught In The Act." Melody Maker 51 (February
14, 1976) p27.
(The Beatle's films.)

M 0684 "Caught In The Act." Melody Maker 51 (May 15,
1976) p23.
(Paul McCartney.)

M 0685 "Caught In The Act." Melody Maker 51 (October
30, 1976) p22. illus.
(Paul McCartney.)

M 0686 "Cavalier." Sing Out 16:2 (1966) p53.
(Reprinted from White Rock March '65.)

M 0687 "The Cavern: A Revised Map Of The Cavern As
Described By Allan Williams."
Beatles Unlimited 9 (September 1976)
p11.

M 0688 "Cavern Mecca: Liverpool's Beatle Museum And
Information Centre." Beatles Now 1
(January 1982) p8.

M 0689 "CBS Fund Scholarship In Memory Of Lennon."
Variety 302 (March 18, 1981) p301.

M 0690 Cella, Catherine. "Desert Island Discs."
Beatlefan 4:3 (April 1982) p4,25.
(Paul McCartney's selections.)

M 0691 Cella, Catherine. "Glass Onion." Beatlefan 4:2
(February 1982) p23.
(Stevie Wonder and Paul McCartney.)

M 0692 Chambers, John J. "When I'm 64." Beatles Now 4
(Autumn 1982) p11. illus.
(Interview with Liverpool Beatles fan Bill
Gates.)

M 0693 "Chapman Gets 20-To-Life Term." Billboard 93
(September 5, 1981) p4.

M 0694 "Chapman Is Sentenced." Variety 304 (August 26,
1981) p71.

M 0695 "Chapman Pleads Guilty To Murder." Variety 303
(June 24, 1981) p71.

M 0696 Charlesworth, C. "At Home With The Lennons."
Melody Maker 47 (December 23, 1972)
p39.

M 0697 Charlesworth, C. "Beatles Are Bootlegged
Again!" Melody Maker 46 (May 15, 1971)
p1.

M 0698 Charlesworth, C. "Beatles For Sale."
Melody Maker 49 (September 21, 1974)
p33. illus.

M 0699 Charlesworth, C. "Beatles Get Together."
Melody Maker 49 (February 16, 1974)

p1.

M 0700 Charlesworth, C. "Beatles 10 Years After."
Melody Maker 48 (March 10, 1973) pp26-27.
illus.

M 0701 Charlesworth, C. "But Wings Fly High."
Melody Maker 48 (May 19, 1973) p20. illus.

M 0702 Charlesworth, C. "'Chantez A Bit If You Know
Les Mots'." Melody Maker 47 (July 15, 1972)
pp12-13. illus.

M 0703 Charleswroth, C. "John's No. 1 Dream."
Melody Maker 50 (March 1, 1975) pp8-9.
illus.
(Fighting U.S. deportation.)

M 0704 Charlesworth, C. "Lennon Gets His Ticket To
Ride." Melody Maker 51 (August 7, 1976)
p8. illus.
(Wins right to stay in U.S.)

M 0705 Charlesworth, C. "Lennon Today." Melody Maker
48 (November 3, 1973) pp36-37. illus.
(Interview.)

M 0706 Charlesworth, C. "McCartney." Melody Maker 46
(November 20, 1971) pp32-33. illus.

M 0707 Charlesworth, C. "Mutton Dresses As Ram?"
Melody Maker 46 (May 22, 1971) p11.
("Ram" album.)

M 0708 Charlesworth, C. "Rock On!" Melody Maker 50
(March 8, 1975) pp32-33.
(John Lennon interview.)

M 0709 Charlesworth, C. "Wings Album Preview; Return
Of The McCartney Magic." Melody Maker 46
(November 20, 1971) p33.
("Wild Life" album.)

M 0710 "Charley HIFI." Architectural Design 41
(September 1971) p582. illus.
(Ringo Starr.)

M 0711 "Charlotte Moorman." Flash Art (Italy) 46
(June 1974) pp68-69.
(Moorman's performance of Yoko Ono works.)

M 0712 Charone, Barbara. "Take These Broken Wings And
Learn To Fly; McCartney's Band On The Run."
Crawdaddy 59 (April 1976) pp34-41. illus.

M 0713 Chase-Marshall, Janet. "Game Plan." Viva 5
(January 1978) pp35-36. illus.

M 0714 Chasins, Abram. "High-Brows Vs. No-Brows."
McCall's 92 (September 1965) p42+. illus.

M 0715 "Chevy Chase; We Almost Reunited The Beatles."
Creem 8 (December 1976) p22.

M 0716 Christgau, Robert. "John Lennon, 1940-1980."
Village Voice 25 (December 10, 1980)
p1.
(Obituary.)

M 0717 Christgau, Robert. "Secular Music." Esquire 68
(December 1967) pp283-286.
("Sgt. Pepper" album.)

M 0718 Christgau, Robert. "Symbolic Comrades."
Village Voice 26 (January 14, 1981)
pp31-32.
(On "Double Fantasy" LP.)

M 0719 "Christmas Time Is Here Again."
Beatles Unlimited 17 (November 1977)
pp15-16.
(Picture and text of the 1967 fan club
record.)

M 0720 "Cincinnati Pops Honors Lennon On 4-City Trek."
Billboard 93 (November 28, 1981) p43.

M 0721 "Civil Rights Angles Loom In Beatle Ban."
Variety 243 (August 17, 1966) p1+.

M 0722 Clark, Tom and Clark Coolidge. "Playing Wrong
Notes Seriously." Rolling Stone 79
(April 1, 1971) p44+.
(John Lennon quoted.)

M 0723 "Classified Ads." Beatlefan
(Regular feature, v1n1-   , 1978-   .)

M 0724 "Classified Ads, Pen Pals, Messages etc."
Beatles Now 1 (January 1982) p18.

M 0725 "Classifieds." Beatles Now
(Regular feature, issue No.2-   , Spring
1982-   .)

M 0726 "Clean-Up For Yoko Single." Melody Maker 46
(March 13, 1971) p4.

M 0727 Cleave, Maureen. "John Lennon: A Memoir."
Observer Magazine (January 4, 1981)
pp22-27. illus.

M 0728 "Cleffing Beatles Snag 3 Novellos; Other U.K.
Awards." Variety (July 13, 1966) p36.

M 0729 Clerk, C. "'Beatles' Not For Sale."
Melody Maker 56 (August 1, 1981) p3.
(World's rarest Beatles single.)

M 0730 Cluess, Chris and et al. "Apple Boutique
Near-Giveaway Sale." National Lampoon 1:91
(October 1977) pp63-68.

M 0731 "Coast Dejay Paying Beatles $100,000 Vs. 65% Of
Gate For Aug 28 L. A. Gig." Variety 242
(April 20, 1966) p59.

M 0732 Cocks, Jay. "Before History Took Over." Time 119
(May 31, 1982) p67.
(On radio special "Beatles At The Beeb.")

M 0733 Cocks, Jay. "The Last Day In The Life." Time
116:25 (December 22, 1980) p18+. illus.
(John Lennon.)

M 0734 Cocks, Jay. "Rumination And Ruination." Time
116 (September 15, 1980) p91. illus.
(George Harrison.)

M 0735 Coffin, Patricia. "Art Beat Of The 60s." Look 32
(January 9, 1968) pp32-41. illus.

M 0736 Coffin, Patricia. "The Beatles." Look 32
(January 9, 1968) pp32-41. illus.

M 0737 Cohen, J. L. "Dragonflies, Frogs And The
Beatles." Artnews 79 (1980) pp69-70.
(Interview.)

M 0738 Cohen, Jose. "Did Anybody Happen To Hear The
Beatles In The U.S.?" Variety (September 23,
1964) p85.

M 0739 Cohen, M. "John Lennon's Last."
High Fidelity/Musical America 31 (February
1981) p92. illus.
(On "Double Fantasy" LP.)

M 0740 Cohen, Mitch. "McCartney: The Band On The
Road." Phonograph Record Magazine (May 1976)
p16+.

M 0741 Coleman, Ray. "Are The Beatles Slipping?"
Melody Maker 39 (July 25, 1964) pp8-9.
illus.

M 0742 Coleman, Ray. "A Beatle A Week." Melody Maker
39 (February 8, 1964) p13. illus.
(Ringo Starr.)

M 0743 Coleman, Ray. "Beatle Money." Melody Maker
(May 1, 1965) pp8-9. illus.

M 0744 Coleman, Ray. "Beatles Beware! 120,000 Fans Are
After You." Melody Maker 38 (November 2,
1963) p1. illus.

M 0745 Coleman, Ray. "Beatles Broadcast."
Melody Maker 39 (April 11, 1964) p3. illus.

M 0746 Coleman, Ray. "Beatles Feeling Just Fine."
Melody Maker 39 (November 28, 1964)
p1. illus.

M 0747 Coleman, Ray. "Beatles In A Winter Wonderland."
Melody Maker 40 (March 20, 1965) pp10-11.

M 0748 Coleman, Ray. "Beatles '65." Melody Maker 40
(March 27, 1965) p9. illus.
(Interview with Paul McCartney.)

M 0749 Coleman, Ray. "Beatle Who Plans For The
Future." Melody Maker (February 27, 1965)
pp12-13+. illus.
(Interview with Paul McCartney.)

M 0750 Coleman, Ray. "Beatsville." Melody Maker 38
(November 16, 1963) p8.

M 0751 Coleman, Ray. "Brian Epstein Predicts: I Give
The Beatles Two Or Three Years More At The
Top." Melody Maker 40 (January 16, 1965)
p3+.

M 0752 Coleman, Ray. "Carry On, Screamers!"
Melody Maker 39 (October 10, 1964)
p3.

M 0753 Coleman, Ray. "Charles Mingus Challenges The
Beatles!" Melody Maker 39 (June 20, 1964)
p6.

M 0754 Coleman, Ray. "George Harrison." Melody Maker
39 (March 21, 1964) pp10-11.

M 0755 Coleman, Ray. "Hands Off; They're Trying To

Bash The Beatles." Melody Maker 38
(December 14, 1963) p13. illus.

M 0756 Coleman, Ray. "Here We Go Again!" Melody Maker
40 (February 27, 1965) pp12-13+. illus.

M 0757 Coleman, Ray. "How Long Can They Last?"
Melody Maker 39 (March 14, 1964) p9. illus.

M 0758 Coleman, Ray. "I'd Rather Be An Ex-Beatle Than
An Ex-Nazi!" Melody Maker 50 (September 8,
1975) pp28-30.
(George Harrison.)

M 0759 Coleman, Ray. "It's Like Winning The Pools."
Melody Maker 39 (November 7, 1964)
p7. illus.

M 0760 Coleman, Ray. "I've Come To Terms With My
Nose." Melody Maker 39 (November 14, 1964)
p9. illus.
(Ringo Starr.)

M 0761 Coleman, Ray. "John Lennon's Future."
Melody Maker 40 (February 27, 1965)
p1. illus.

M 0762 Coleman, Ray. "Lennon - A Night In The Life."
Melody Maker 49 (September 14, 1974)
pp14-15. illus.

M 0763 Coleman, Ray. "Lennon Pushing The Pop Song To
Its Limit." Melody Maker 41 (October 1966)
pp8-9. illus.

M 0764 Coleman, Ray. "Life With The Lennons."
Melody Maker 40 (April 10, 1965) p11+.
illus.

M 0765 Coleman, Ray. "1964: The Year Of The Beatles."
Melody Maker 39 (December 19, 1964)
pp2-3+. illus.

M 0766 Coleman, Ray. "Now Acker Says It, Yeah! Yeah!
Yeah!" Melody Maker 38 (November 30, 1963)
p5.

M 0767 Coleman, Ray. "'Please - No More Jelly
Babies!'" Melody Maker 38 (November 9, 1963)
pp8-9. illus.

M 0768 Coleman, Ray. "Sometimes, I Wonder How The Hell
We Keep It Up." Melody Maker 39 (October 24,
1964) pp8-9.

M 0769 Coleman, Ray. "Starr Trek." Melody Maker 51
(October 2, 1976) p17. illus.
(Interview.)

M 0770 Coleman, Ray. "Thanks For The Memory."
Melody Maker 52 (October 22, 1977)
p10. illus.
(First Beatles Liverpool convention.)

M 0771 Coleman, Ray. "This Is Mr. Beat!" Melody Maker
38 (October 12, 1963) pp10-11.
(Brian Epstein.)

M 0772 Coleman, Ray. "Three Likely Reunions And Three
We'd Like To See." Melody Maker 48
(April 14, 1973) p33. illus.

M 0773 Coleman, Ray. "The Ultimate Supergroup."
Melody Maker 46 (August 7, 1971) p22+.
illus.
(On the Bangladesh concert.)

M 0774 Coleman, Ray. "Vive Les Beat-tles!"
Melody Maker 39 (January 25, 1964)
p9. illus.
(Paris concerts.)

M 0775 Coleman, Ray. "Well, Could A Beatle Go Solo?"
Melody Maker 39 (March 7, 1964) pp10-11.
illus.

M 0776 Coleman, Ray. "What Difference Will This Piece
Of Paper Make To The Beatles?" Melody Maker
40 (February 20, 1965) p8.
(Marriage of Ringo Starr.)

M 0777 Coleman, Ray. "When I Get On Stage, I Think:
Good God, They're 16, I'm 24." Melody Maker 40
(April 17, 1965) p7.
(Ringo Starr.)

M 0778 Coleman, Ray. "When The Beatles Came Marching
Home." Melody Maker 39 (July 18, 1964)
p8. illus.

M 0779 Coleman, Ray. "When The Screaming Has To Stop."
Melody Maker 39 (July 11, 1964) pp10-11.
illus.

M 0780 Coleman, Ray. "When We Stop Selling Records,

We'll Probably Pack It In." Melody Maker 39
(October 31, 1964) pp10-11.

M 0781 Coleman, Ray. "Wish Elvis All The Best In
'Aladdin'." Melody Maker 40 (January 16,
1965) p8.

M 0782 Coleman, Ray and C. Charlesworth. "A Strange
Day's Night." Melody Maker 46 (November 13,
1971) p9. illus.

M 0783 Coleman, Ray and C. Roberts. "What Makes The
Beatles B-E-A-T." Melody Maker 38 (August
3, 1963) pp6-7. illus.

M 0784 Coleman, T. "'Go On,' Said The Beatle, 'Ask Yer
Mum'." Saturday Evening Post 242 (January
11, 1969) pp54-55. illus.

M 0785 Coles, R. "On The Death Of John Lennon; Why We
Kill Our Heroes." Mademoiselle 87 (June 1981)
p124+.

M 0786 "Collecting." Beatlefan
(Regular feature, v2n3-   , 1980-   .)

M 0787 "Collecting Beatles' Items: What's Available
And How Much Should You Pay?"
The Beatles Book 21 (January 1978)
ppiii-v.

M 0788 Collingham, Anne and Freda Kelly. "The Official
Beatles Fan Club Newsletter."
The Beatles Book
(Regular feature, issues 1-77.)

M 0789 Collis, John. "Acting Naturally." Let It Rock
(March 1974) p30.
(Ringo Starr.)

M 0790 "Colonial, Toronto." Variety 303 (June 10, 1981)
p70.
("Imagine: A Tribute To John Lennon.")

M 0791 Comden, Betty. "Letter From Liverpool, Almost."
Vogue 146 (December 1, 1965) p120+.

M 0792 "Come Together." Newsweek 81 (March 26, 1973)
pp99-100.

M 0793 "Comments: Let Him Be." Rolling Stone 168
(August 29, 1974) p27.
(John Lennon.)

M 0794 "Committees, Gleason Aid Lennon's Deport
Fight." Billboard 84 (June 10, 1972)
p4.

M 0795 Como, W. "Editor's Log." Dance Magazine 55
(February 1981) p28. illus.

M 0796 "Compile A Beatles LP And Win A Rare Set Of
Albums." The Beatles Book 55 (November 1980)
pix.
(Contest.)

M 0797 "Complete List Of Fan Club Secretaries."
The Beatles Book 43 (February 1967)
p24.

M 0798 "Complete List Of Overseas Fan Clubs."
The Beatles Book 20 (March 1965) p11.

M 0799 "Concert." New Yorker 47 (August 14, 1971)
pp28-30.
(George Harrison.)

M 0800 "Concert Reviews." Variety 273 (January 16,
1974) p76.
(Yoko Ono.)

M 0801 "Concert Reviews." Variety 277 (November 20,
1974) p46.
(George Harrison.)

M 0802 "Concert Reviews." Variety 277 (December 11,
1974) p44.
(George Harrison.)

M 0803 Condon, Richard. "Those Were The Days."
Beatlefan 2:5 (August 1980) pp20-21.
(Reprint of Venture magazine article.)

M 0804 "Confiscate Nude Beatles Poster In Paris;
Merely A Montage, Sez Creator." Variety 252
(November 6, 1968) p49.

M 0805 Connelly, Christopher. "Random Notes; Clapton:
One Of Those Years." Rolling Stone 359
(December 24, 1981) p50. illus.
(George Harrison.)

M 0806 Connelly, Christopher. "Random Notes; Little
Richard: The Peace Of The Rock."
Rolling Stone 359 (December 24, 1981)
p49.

(Paul McCartney.)

M 0807 Connelly, Christopher. "Random Notes; Paul McCartney Gets By - With A Little Help." Rolling Stone 359 (December 24, 1981) p47+. illus.

M 0808 Connelly, Christopher. "Random Notes; Yoko: Tributes And Trials." Rolling Stone 359 (December 24, 1981) p47+. illus.

M 0809 Connelly, Christopher. "Yoko Leaves Geffen; New Album Due." Rolling Stone 382 (November 11, 1982) p43.

M 0810 "Contractual Boobytrap Holds Up Release Of Bangla Desh Benefit LP." Variety 265 (December 1, 1971) p45.

M 0811 Cook, Christopher. "Beatles Cartoon Quiz." Beatlefan 1:6 (October 1979) p18.

M 0812 Cook, Christopher. "Beatles Cartoon Quiz." Beatlefan 2:1 (December 1979) p15. (Answers to questions in vln6.)

M 0813 Cook, Christopher. "The Beatles Cartoons And Me." Beatlefan 3:5 (August 1981) pp4-9. (Synopses of the TV cartoon episodes.)

M 0814 Cook, Christopher. "'She Loves You'." Beatlefan 3:5 (August 1981) pp6-9. (Cartoon.)

M 0815 Cook, Christopher. "Thingumybob." Beatlefan 3:2 (February 1981) p29. (John Lennon's remarks about Jesus.)

M 0816 Cook, Christopher. "Thingumybob." Beatlefan 4:1 (December 1981) p16. ("Paul Is Dead" hoax.)

M 0817 Cook, Christopher. "Title Teasers." Beatlefan 2:3 (April 1980) p15. (Trivia quiz in cartoon form.)

M 0818 Cooke, Deryck. "The Lennon-McCartney Songs." Listener (February 1, 1968) pp157-158.

M 0819 Cooke, Deryck. "The Lennon-McCartney Songs." Performing Right 49 (April 1968) pp14-15.

M 0820 Coppage, N. "The Ex-Beatles - Surmounting The Aftermath." Stereo Review 32 (March 1974) pp88-89. illus.

M 0821 Corliss, Richard. "A Beatle Metaphysic." Commonweal (May 12, 1967) pp234-236.

M 0822 Corliss, Richard. "Pop Music: What's Been Happening." National Reivew 19 (April 4, 1967) pp371-374. (Mid-sixties music, including The Beatles.)

M 0823 Cosell, Howard. "The Lennon-Cosell Tapes." Zoo World (December 5, 1974) pp26-27.

M 0824 Costa, Jean-Charles. "Colossal Event." Senior Scholastic 99 (September 27, 1971) pp32-34. (George Harrison.)

M 0825 Cott, Jonathan. "Children Of Paradise - Back To Where We Once Belonged." Rolling Stone 254 (December 15, 1977) p37+. illus.

M 0826 Cott, Jonathan. "A Conversation." Rolling Stone 335 (January 22, 1981) pp37-39. (John Lennon.)

M 0827 Cott, Jonathan. "The Eggman Wears White." Rolling Stone 17 (September 14, 1968) p1+. illus.

M 0828 Cott, Jonathan. "John Lennon Talks." Vogue 153 (March 1, 1969) pp170-171+. illus. (Interview.)

M 0829 Cott, Jonathan. "A Song For Dreaming." Rolling Stone 216 (July 1, 1976) p20. (Beatles' "Slim Slow Slider.")

M 0830 Cott, Jonathan. "'We Thought People Would Understand'." Rolling Stone 5 (February 10, 1968) p22. illus.

M 0831 Cott, Jonathan. "Yoko Ono And Her Sixteen-Track Voice." Rolling Stone 78 (March 18, 1971) p24+. illus.

M 0832 Cott, Jonathan and D. Dalton. "Daddy Has Gone Away Now: Let It Be." Rolling Stone 62 (July 9, 1970) pp20-23. ("Let It Be" album.)

M 0833 "Court Bars Beatles Video." Billboard

(October 23, 1982) p3,84. ("The Compleat Beatles" video documentary.)

M 0834 "Court OKs Old German Beatles LP." Billboard 89 (April 16, 1977) p3+. (Star Club tapes.)

M 0835 "Court Ruling Due On Harrison Disk Suit Jurisdiction." Variety 270 (March 7, 1973) p61.

M 0836 "Court Stops Sales Of Phony Beatles." Billboard 90 (January 28, 1978) p3+.

M 0837 "Court Tables Decision On Beatles For Week." Billboard 83 (March 20, 1971) p3+.

M 0838 Cowley, S.C. "Newsmakers." Newsweek 88 (July 26, 1976) p56. illus. (Paul McCartney.)

M 0839 Cowley, S.C. "Newsmakers." Newsweek 88 (August 2, 1976) p45. illus. (Ringo Starr.)

M 0840 Cowley, S.C. and S. Gary. "Newsmakers." Newsweek 88 (August 9, 1976) pp44-45. illus. (John Lennon.)

M 0841 Coxe, D. "Back Page: A Few Words About A Working-Class Lad From Liverpool, A Great Capitalist Of Our Time." Canadian Business Magazine 54 (May 1981) p142. illus. (John Lennon.)

M 0842 "Cracks Show In Beatles Toronto Teen Image Despite Group's SRO $150,000." Variety 240 (August 25, 1965) p39+.

M 0843 Crawdaddy. New York: Crawdaddy Publishing Co., Inc., 1973. (June issue; cover portrait.)

M 0844 Creem. Birmingham, MI: Creem Magazine, 1976. (Butcher Cover on cover.)

M 0845 "Creemedia: Endless Rain Meets Paper Cup." Creem 13 (August 1981) p46. illus. (On books "Shout!" and "Strawberry Fields Forever.")

M 0846 Cromelin, Richard. "'I Do Play The Drums': Claims Ex-Fab Four Ex-Mop Top Ringo Starr." Creem 8:5 (October 1976) pp32-34+. illus. (Interview.)

M 0847 Crouse, Timothy. "'Birth Of The Beatles' What It Was Like To Be 15 And Greet The 'Fab Four' On Their First Day In America." TV Guide 27 (November 17, 1979) p49+.

M 0848 Curly, John. "The Beatles: Side One." Beatles Unlimited 8 (July 1976) pp19-20. (Commentary on side one of the "White Album.")

M 0849 Curly, John. "The Beatles: Side Three." Beatles Unlimited 12 (March 1977) pp19-21. (Commentary on side three of the "White Album.")

M 0850 Curly, John. "In Memoriam: Pete Ham Of Badfinger." Beatles Unlimited 2 (June 1975) pp19-22. (Obituary.)

M 0851 Cuscuna, M. "George Martin Looks Back To The Beatles And Forward With Seatrain." Jazz & Pop 10 (August 1971) pp24-27. (Interview.)

M 0852 "Cynthia's Secret - How To Hold Your Guy." Sixteen Magazine 6:10 (March 1965) p16.

M 0853 Dale, C. and P. Gambaccini. "Paul McCartney: Ten Days In The Life; Japan Deports Ex-Beatle After Pot Bust." Rolling Stone 312 (March 6, 1980) p18+. illus. (Interview.)

M 0854 Dallas, Karl. "Bring Back Romance!" Melody Maker 49 (October 26, 1974) p38. (John Lennon.)

M 0855 Dalton, David. "Rock And Roll Circus." Rolling Stone 54 (March 19, 1970) p36. illus. (John Lennon and The Rolling Stones.)

M 0856 Damsker, Matt. "Pre-fab Product Is Filling The

Recession-Racked Rock Bin ... "
Electricity (Philadlephia) 136 (October 7,
1982) p7.
(Record reissues and repackagings.)

M 0857 D'Antonio, Dennis. "Haunted By John Lennon's
Murder ... Frightened Beatle Paul McCartney
Turns His Home Into A Fortress."
National Enquirer 56:33 (March 23, 1982)
p4.

M 0858 "Dark Horse, Pale Rider." Teen 19 (February
1975) p45+. illus.
(George Harrison.)

M 0859 Date Book. New York: Young World Press, 1966.
(George and Pattie Harrison cover
portrait.)

M 0860 Date Book. New York: Young World Press, 1966.
(Paul McCartney cover portrait.)

M 0861 Datene, Olivia Kelly. "A Death In The Family"
Beatlefan 3:1 (December 1980) pp13-14.
(John Lennon.)

M 0862 Datene, Olivia Kelly. "His Ultimate
Contribution." Beatlefan 3:1 (December 1980)
p11.
(Reactions to John Lennon's death.)

M 0863 "Dave Brubeck Credits Beatles With Cracking
Music Barriers." Variety 275 (June 26, 1974)
p60.

M 0864 David, Keith. "Beatles Tour?" Rock (April 1974)
p3.

M 0865 "David Platz To Head Northern Songs If Beatles
Gain Control Of Pub Firm." Variety 254
(May 7, 1969) p243+.

M 0866 Davidson, Bill. "'They'll Still Call Me An
Ex-Beatle When I'm 95.' Ringo Tries His
First TV Special - All By Himself."
TV Guide 26 (April 22, 1978) p14+.

M 0867 Davies, Evan. "Psychological Characteristics Of
Beatle Mania." Journal of the History of Ideas
30:2 (April/June 1969) pp273-280.

M 0868 Davies, Hunter. "Beatles." Life 65 (September
20, 1968) pp60-62+. illus.
(An excerpt from his biography of The
Beatles.)

M 0869 Davies, Hunter. "The Beatles." Life 65
(September 13, 1968) pp86-94+. illus.
(From Davies' book; Beatles cover portrait.)

M 0870 Davies, Hunter. "Encyclo(Beatle)pedia!"
The Beatles Book 59 (June 1968) pp25-27+.
(Extracts from his biography.)

M 0871 Davies, Hunter. "'Paul Started It All'."
The Beatles Book 60 (July 1968) pp11-14.
(Origins of the authorized biography.)

M 0872 Davies, Hunter. "Tragic Childhood Turned Lennon
Into Young Punk And Shoplifter."
National Enquirer (December 30, 1980)
p37.
(Excerpted from his book.)

M 0873 Davis, Rod. "All He Was Saying, Is Give Peace A
Chance." Texas Observer 72 (December 26,
1980) pp2-4.
(John Lennon.)

M 0874 Davis, T.N. "Of Many Things; Beatle John
Lennon's Statement." America 115 (August 20,
1966) p164.

M 0875 Dawbarn, Bob. "Is The Beatles Frenzy Cooling
Down?" Melody Maker 39 (June 6, 1964)
p3.
(Interview with Kenny Lynch.)

M 0876 Dawbarn, Bob. "What Now For The Beatles?"
Melody Maker 41 (November 19, 1966)
pp14-15. illus.

M 0877 Dawbarn, Bob. "Why All The Mystery Over The
Magical Mystery Tour?" Melody Maker 43
(January 6, 1968) p5.

M 0878 Dawbarn, Bob. "Why I Dig The Beatles."
Melody Maker 38 (November 23, 1963)
p5.

M 0879 Dawbarn, Bob. "You Know What I'd Love To Do?
Produce An Album For Elvis?" Melody Maker 43
(September 14, 1968) p5.

(Recording of "Hey Jude.")

M 0880 Dawkins, Tony. "International Beatles
Marathon." Beatles Now 3 (Summer 1982)
pp8-9. illus.
(Third Dutch Beatles Convention,
Amsterdam.)

M 0881 Dawson, David. "Yesterday, Fifteen Years On."
Memphis 6 (August 1981) pp23-33. illus.

M 0882 Dawson, J. "Don't Copy - And Keep It Simple."
Melody Maker 38 (February 23, 1963)
p12. illus.
(Interview.)

M 0883 Dawson, J. "Lennon's Eye View." Melody Maker 40
(November 13, 1965) p3.

M 0884 "Day At Night." Rolling Stone 1 (November 9,
1967) p6.

M 0885 "A Day In The Life." Rolling Stone 359
(December 24, 1981) p124. illus.
(Full-page photo of John Lennon.)

M 0886 "'Dead' Beatle Mania Mounts." Melody Maker 44
(November 22, 1969) p1+. illus.
(McCartney death hoax.)

M 0887 Dean, Johnny. "Backstage With The Beatles."
The Beatles Book 90 (October 1983)
pp4-7. illus.
(Gaumont Cinema concert, Bournemouth,
Sept. 1963.)

M 0888 Dean, Johnny. "Beatles Book Relaunched Oct
1st." Record Collector 38 (October 1982)
p3.
(Resumption of official monthly Beatles
fanzine.)

M 0889 Dean, Johnny. "The Beatles Book: The Only
Complete History Of The World's Most Famous
Group." The Beatles Book 1 (May 1976)
ppiv-vi.

M 0890 Dean, Johnny. "The Beatles' First Single."
The Beatles Book 78 (October 1982)
pp18-21.
("Love Me Do.")

M 0891 Dean, Johnny. "Beatles' U.K. LPs."
Record Collector 12 (August 1980) pp4-8.
illus.
(Complete discography appended.)

M 0892 Dean, Johnny. "Beatles U.K. Singles Valued."
Record Collector 9 (May 1980) pp22-27.
illus.
(Complete discography appended.)

M 0893 Dean, Johnny. "Beatles Values And Collecting
E.P.s." Record Collector 17 (January 1981)
p3.
(General commentary on Beatles
memorabilia.)

M 0894 Dean, Johnny. "Brian Even Considered The
Woolworth's Label." The Beatles Book 79
(November 1982) pp30-33.
(Brian Epstein's search for a record
label.)

M 0895 Dean, Johnny. "Brian Meets George Martin."
The Beatles Book 80 (December 1982)
pp32-35.

M 0896 Dean, Johnny. "Editorial." The Beatles Book
(Regular feature, issues 1-   , 1963-   .)

M 0897 Dean, Johnny. "The Fans Meet The Beatles."
The Beatles Book 93 (January 1984)
pp4-8. illus.
(Wimbledon Fan Club convention, December
1963.)

M 0898 Dean, Johnny. "First Impressions."
The Beatles Book 3 (July 1976) ppiv-vi.

M 0899 Dean, Johnny. "Hats On To Wolverhampton."
The Beatles Book 92 (December 1983)
pp4-7. illus.
(Wolverhampton concert, November 1963.)

M 0900 Dean, Johnny. "How Love Me Do Became A Hit."
The Beatles Book 28 (August 1978) ppiii-iv.

M 0901 Dean, Johnny. "John And Yoko's Toronto
Concert." The Beatles Book 76 (November 1969)
pp9-14.
(Mal Evans reminisces.)

M 0902 Dean, Johnny. "A Note To E.M.I."
Record Collector 32 (April 1982) p3.
(Urges E.M.I. special 20th anniversary
releases.)

M 0903 Dean, Johnny. "Paul Talks About Letters,
Reporters, Films, Songs, People And Things."
The Beatles Book 46 (May 1967) p24.

M 0904 Dean, Johnny. "Recording Their First Album."
The Beatles Book 83 (March 1983) pp26-29.
illus.
(Engineer Norman Smith on "Please Please
Me" LP.)

M 0905 Dean, Johnny. "Reissues Can Never Replace
Originals." Record Collector 22 (June 1981)
p3.
(The surpassing value of earliest Beatles
discs.)

M 0906 Dean, Johnny. "Starting The Beatles Book."
The Beatles Book 88 (August 1983) pp8-10.
(Starting the Beatles' UK fan magazine.)

M 0907 Dean, Johnny. "Their Green Street Flat."
The Beatles Book 91 (November 1983)
pp4-7. illus.
(Beatles' apartment in London, October
1963.)

M 0908 Dean, Johnny. "The Truth About The Beatles'
First Single." The Beatles Book 27
(July 1978) ppiii-v.
(Decca audition and after.)

M 0909 Dean, Johnny. "With The Beatles In
Bournemouth." The Beatles Book 89 (September
1983) pp4-7. illus.
(Discusses the August 1963 concert.)

M 0910 Dean, Johnny and Tony Barrow. "Shout! The True
Story Of The Beatles." The Beatles Book 63
(July 1981) ppiii-vii.
(On Philip Norman's book.)

M 0911 Dean, Johnny and Peter Jones. "Beatle People:
The Most Incredible Following The World Has
Ever Known, Part 1." The Beatles Book 54
(October 1980) ppiii-vii.

M 0912 Dean, Johnny and Peter Jones. "Beatle People:
The Most Incredible Following The World Has
Ever Known." The Beatles Book 55 (November
1980) ppiii-viii.
(Second part; continues from previous
issue.)

M 0913 Deardorff, R. "Ringo Starr: Domesticated
Beatle." Redbook 125 (September 1965)
pp60-61+. illus.

M 0914 "Death At The Dakota." Economist 277 (December
13, 1980) p21. illus.
(John Lennon.)

M 0915 DeBruin, Hans. "All Around The 'Butcher
Cover'." Beatles Unlimited 20 (May 1978)
pp4-6.
(Story of first cover of "Yesterday And
Today.")

M 0916 DeBruin, Hans. "Komm Gib Mir Deine Money: Hot
(Coloured) Record News." Beatles Unlimited 22
(September 1978) p18.
(Proliferation of colored vinyl
repressings.)

M 0917 DeBruin, Hans. "Rutlemania." Beatles Unlimited 19
(March 1978) p17.
(On the Rutles LP.)

M 0918 "A Decade Without The Beatles." Beatlefan 2:4
(June 1980) p9.
(Text of "McCartney" LP "interview" with
Paul.)

M 0919 "Decision Near In Lennon Visa Case."
Rolling Stone 111 (June 22, 1972) p30.

M 0920 "Deep Quotes." Rolling Stone 208 (March 11,
1976) p24.
(Harrison and Lennon on reunion offer.)

M 0921 "Deep Quotes." Rolling Stone 211 (April 22,
1976) p28.
(Lennon remarks on "Two Virgins" LP cover.)

M 0922 DeGiusti, Tony. "End Of An Odyssey."
Oklahoma Observer 13 (January 10, 1981)
p6.
(John Lennon.)

M 0923 Delear, Frank. "Flying With The Beatles."
Yankee 43 (January 1979) p112+.

M 0924 Delmas, D. "Les Beatles." Musica Chaix 120
(March 1964) pp32-33.

M 0925 Deni, Laura. "Paul & Linda McCartney: The Price
They Paid For Happiness." Pageant 32
(October 1976) p4+. illus.

M 0926 Denisoff, R. Serge. "Folk-Rock: Folk Music,
Protest, Or Commercialism?"
Journal of Popular Culture 3:2 (1969) pp214-230.

M 0927 Denning, Chris. "A D.J.'s View Of The Beatles."
The Beatles Book 25 (August 1965) p25.

M 0928 DeRhen, A. "Earth Symphony."
High Fidelity/Musical America 22 (April 1972)
ppMA27-28.
(Yoko Ono.)

M 0929 Detheridge, D. "They Were Right To Use A
Standin Says Paul." Melody Maker 48
(July 14, 1973) p3. illus.

M 0930 Dhondy, Farrukh. "An Open Letter To The
Beatles." Listener 78 (September 7, 1967)
pp298-299.

M 0931 Dieckmann, Eddie. "Indian Rope Trick."
Beatles Unlimited 19 (March 1979) pp18-19.
(On the bootleg album.)

M 0932 Difford, Chris. "To Be As Good." Rolling Stone
415 (February 16, 1984) pp59,61. illus.

M 0933 "Dig It; The Beatles Bootleg Book."
Beatles Unlimited
(Regular feature, issues 1-   , 1975-
.)

M 0935 "Discography." Beatles Unlimited 34/35 (1981) pp14-16.
(John Lennon discography.)

M 0936 "Discography: Lennon's Recording Career
1961-1980." Rolling Stone 335 (January 22,
1981) p68.

M 0937 "Disk Fairy Tale Has Sad Ending As Apple's
'Name' Is Mysteriously Yanked." Variety 257
(December 10, 1969) p60.

M 0938 "Disques Du Mas: Imagine." Jazz Magazine 197
(February 1972) pp36-37.
(On the "Imagine" album.)

M 0939 Dister, Alain. "Biographie Beatles."
Rock & Folk (Paris) 118 (November 1976)
pp76-91. illus.
(Cover portrait.)

M 0940 Dister, Alain. "Pop Stars." Jazz Hot 291
(February 1973) pp28-29.
(Ringo Starr.)

M 0941 "Divorced." Time 106 (July 28, 1975) p44.
(Ringo Starr.)

M 0942 Dockstader, T. "Inside-Out: Electronic Rock."
Electronic Music Reports 5 (January 1968)
pp18-20.

M 0943 Doerfler, Marilyn. "Analyzing The Beatles."
Tiger Beat 4:8 (December 14, 1967)
pp48-49+.

M 0944 "Does Anybody Believe Mahareshi?"
Rolling Stone 3 (December 14, 1967)
p4. illus.
(Movie inspired by Beatles' Indian
interests.)

M 0945 Doggett, Peter. "The Apple Label."
Record Collector 46 (June 1983) pp4-12.
illus.
(Includes listing of U.K. Apple
recordings.)

M 0946 Doggett, Peter. " 'The Beatles At Abbey Road'."
The Beatles Book 88 (August 1983) pp38-41.
(The 1983 EMI Abbey Road Studios tour.)

M 0947 Doggett, Peter. "The Beatles' Decca Tapes."
Record Collector 22 (June 1981) pp4-8.
illus.
(On the Beatles' 1962 Decca audition

tapes.)

M 0948 Doggett, Peter. "The Beatles: Early Years."
Record Collector 25 (September 1981)
pp42-43. illus.
(On the Phoenix Hamburg tapes repackaging.)

M 0949 Doggett, Peter. "The Beatles' E.P.s."
Record Collector 45 (May 1983) pp36-39.
illus.
(Includes complete U.K. EP listing.)

M 0950 Doggett, Peter. "The Beatles In Hamburg."
Record Collector 41 (January 1983)
pp4-11. illus.
(Includes discography of Hamburg
recordings.)

M 0951 Doggett, Peter. "The Beatles Interviews."
The Beatles Book 76 (August 1982) ppxi-xii.
(UK album release.)

M 0952 Doggett, Peter. "The Beatles: The 'Get Back'
Sessions." Record Collector 44 (April 1983)
pp4-11. illus.
(The 1969 Beatles album that never made
it.)

M 0953 Doggett, Peter. "The Beatles Unreleased
Recordings." Record Collector 35 (July 1982)
pp4-12. illus.
(Recordings in EMI's vaults.)

M 0954 Doggett, Peter. "The Complete Silver Beatles."
The Beatles Book 78 (October 1982)
p46.
(On the Audio Fidelity album.)

M 0955 Doggett, Peter. "Double Fantasy."
The Beatles Book 56 (December 1980)
ppix-xii.
(Commentary on the Lennons' new LP.)

M 0956 Doggett, Peter. "Ebony And Ivory."
The Beatles Book 73 (May 1982) ppxi-xii.
(The McCartney/Stevie Wonder single.)

M 0957 Doggett, Peter. "George Harrison's Solo
Rarities." Record Collector 32 (April 1982)
pp4-12. illus.
(Complete discography appended.)

M 0958 Doggett, Peter. "'Hear The Beatles Tell All'."
The Beatles Book 59 (March 1981) ppix-xi.
(U.S. album in first U.K. release.)

M 0959 Doggett, Peter. "John Lennon And Yoko Ono."
Record Collector 42 (February 1983)
pp4-12. illus.
(Includes list of work for others since
1971.)

M 0960 Doggett, Peter. "John Lennon's Live
Recordings." Record Collector 59 (July 1984)
pp3-6. illus.

M 0961 Doggett, Peter. "John Lennon's Solo Rarities."
Record Collector 15 (November 1980)
pp4-10. illus.
(Complete discography appended.)

M 0962 Doggett, Peter. "The McCartney Interview."
The Beatles Book 60 (April 1981) ppxi-xii.
(Comment on the LP.)

M 0963 Doggett, Peter. "New Books About The Beatles."
The Beatles Book 69 (January 1982)
ppxi-xii.
(On the books by John Blake and Bob
Woffinden.)

M 0964 Doggett, Peter. "1983 Beatles Song Poll."
The Beatles Book 86 (June 1983) pp42-46.
(Survey results.)

M 0965 Doggett, Peter. "Paul McCartney's Guest
Appearances." Record Collector 55 (March
1984) pp3-6. illus.
(Chronological discography of work for
others.)

M 0966 Doggett, Peter. "Paul McCartney's Solo
Rarities." Record Collector 19 (March 1981)
pp20-27. illus.
(Complete discography appended.)

M 0967 Doggett, Peter. "Rare Recordings Of Beatle
Songs." Record Collector 29 (January 1982)
pp4-11. illus.
(Songs the Beatles wrote for others to

record.)

M 0968 Doggett, Peter. "'Stop And Smell The Roses'."
The Beatles Book 69 (January 1982)
ppix-x.
(On Ringo's new album.)

M 0969 Doggett, Peter. "Tug Of War." The Beatles Book 74
(June 1982) ppx-xi.
(McCartney's new LP.)

M 0970 Doherty, Andy. "The Collector."
Musician, Player & Listener 31 (March 1981)
pp96,108.
(Collecting Beatles records.)

M 0971 Doherty, H. "Spreading His Wings."
Melody Maker 52 (January 15, 1977)
p35. illus.
(Paul McCartney.)

M 0972 Donald, D.K. "Anatomy Of A Bed In." Montrealer
43 (July/August 1969) p28. illus.
(John Lennon.)

M 0974 "Don't Condemn John, Pleads An American Beatle
Person." The Beatles Book 67 (February 1969)
p25.
(Concerning Lennon's divorce.)

M 0975 Dove, I. "Beatlemania Returns As 'Let It Be'
Clicks." Billboard 82 (June 6, 1970)
p1+.
(The film "Let It Be.")

M 0976 Dove, I. "January 1 - March 31, 1964 - 90 Days
That Shook The Industry." Billboard 81
(December 27, 1969) p126. illus.

M 0977 Dove, I. "Talent In Action." Billboard 84
(September 16, 1972) p13.
(Concert for Willowbrook.)

M 0978 "Do We Still Need The Beatles?" Melody Maker 49
(September 7, 1974) pp28-30. illus.

M 0979 Downing, Dave. "Eastern Promise." Let It Rock
(March 1974) pp29-30.
(George Harrison.)

M 0980 "Down The Up Poll." Time 96 (September 28, 1970)
p51.
(Melody Maker Readers' Poll.)

M 0981 "Down Under Pix." The Beatles Book 13
(August 1964) pp10-11.
(Australia-New Zealand tour pictures.)

M 0982 Drake, David. "Beatlefax And Beatle Fans."
New Society (September 30, 1982) pp533-534.
illus.

M 0983 Drake, Kelley M. "Beatles Puzzle." Beatlefan 2:1
(December 1979) p11.

M 0984 "Drawing A Bead On The Beatles." TV Guide
(July 30, 1966) pp20-21. illus.
(Picture feature.)

M 0985 Dronfield, Kim. " 'Beatle It'." Beatles Now 2
(Spring 1982) p16.
(Crossword puzzle.)

M 0986 Dronfield, Kim. "Beatles Crossword."
Beatles Now 4 (Autumn 1982) p16.
(Crossword puzzle.)

M 0987 "Drug Rap In Tokyo Brings Down Wings And
McCartney." People 13 (February 4, 1980)
p111. illus.

M 0988 Dubey, V.K. and J.P. Sen. "George Harrison In
India." Jazz & Pop (July 1968) pp32-33.
illus.

M 0989 Ducray, Francois. "Les Beatles Au Futur."
Rock & Folk (Paris) (November 1976)
pp100-106. illus.

M 0990 Dupree, Tom. "Dracula Schmacula." Zoo World
(June 6, 1974) p12.
(Ringo Starr.)

M 0991 Duston, A. "Lennon, Ono 45 Controversial."
Billboard 84 (June 17, 1972) p65.
("Woman Is The Nigger of the World.")

M 0992 "Dylan In The Isle Of Wight." The Beatles Book 75
(October 1969) pp21-25.
(Beatles visit Bob Dylan.)

M 0993 "Dylan Record Puts Beatles Up A Tree."

Rolling Stone 7 (March 9, 1968) p19.
(Dylan album jacket has their faces in tree.)

M 0994   Eagleton, Terry. "New Bearings: The Beatles." Blackfriars 45 (April 1964) pp175-178.

M 0995   "East German Commies Surrender To Beatles; Battle Was Lost Anyway." Variety 242 (April 6, 1966) p2.

M 0996   "Editorial." Beatles Now
(Regular feature, issue No.1-   , January 1982-)

M 0997   Edlund, A. "The Beatles." Musikrevy 29:6 (1974) pp371-372. illus.

M 0998   Edlund, A. "Beatles; Eller, The Rise & Fall Of The British Empire." Musikrevy 29:5 (1974) pp290-292. illus.

M 0999   Edwards, Henry. "The Provocative Lennon-Ono Marriage." High Fidelity/Musical America 22 (January 1972) p77. illus.

M 1000   Eger, Joseph. "Ives And Beatles." Music Journal 26 (September 1968) p46+.
(Charles Ives.)

M 1001   "The Eggtual Interview About Paul's LP." Beatles Unlimited 27 (July 1979) pp5-10.
(Text of promotional LP.)

M 1002   Elbert, J. "Growing Up With Lennon." Christian Century 97 (December 24, 1980) pp1260-1261.

M 1003   Eldridge, R. "Remember Back In 1963 When Tommy Topped The Bill Over The Beatles?" Melody Maker 44 (June 14, 1969) p5.

M 1004   Ellerton, J. "The Beatles: A Mandala." Tablet 222 (December 21, 1968) pp1265-1266.

M 1005   Ellis, Francis L. "A Meditation On John Lennon." San Francisco 23 (January 1981) p7.

M 1006   Ellis, Roger. "The Beatles' London Town - A Tour." Beatlefan 2:4 (June 1980) pp10-11.
(Recommended stops for London visitors.)

M 1007   Ellis, Roger. "Meeting The Beatles." Beatlefan 2:2 (February 1980) p10.
(January 24, 1977 meeting with Paul McCartney.)

M 1008   "Elton John Celebrates His Friend John Lennon And Gets A Visit From Yoko & Godson Sean." People 18 (August 23, 1982) pp30-31. illus.

M 1009   "Elvis Presley And John Lennon: The Good Die Young." Personality Parade 2:3 (May 1981) pp24-34.

M 1010   Emerson, Ken. "George." Fusion 72 (March 1972) pp32-34. illus.

M 1011   Emery, John. "Beatles Xmas Show." The Beatles Book 19 (February 1965) pp11-13.
(December 1964-January 1965.)

M 1012   Emery, John. "The Liverpool Fan Club." The Beatles Book 30 (January 1966) pp9-10.

M 1013   Emery, John. "The Liverpool Fan Club, Part 2." The Beatles Book 31 (February 1966) p13.

M 1014   Emery, John. "The Liverpool Fan Club, Part 3." The Beatles Book 32 (March 1966) p13.

M 1015   Emery, John. "The Liverpool Fan Club, Part 4." The Beatles Book 33 (April 1966) pp10-11.

M 1016   "EMI Postpones Plans For TV Beatles Package." Billboard (October 2, 1982) p10.
("Greatest Hits" package.)

M 1017   "The End Of The Performing Beatles." The Beatles Book 76 (November 1969) pp21-22.
(August 29, 1966.)

M 1018   "Endpaper." Rolling Stone 361 (January 21, 1982) p84.
(Open letter from Yoko Ono.)

M 1019   "Engaged." Newsweek 88 (September 20, 1976) p65.
(Ringo Starr.)

M 1020   "England's Wings: Beating The Post-Beatle Stigma." Rolling Stone 199 (November 6, 1975)

p10. illus.

M 1021   Epand, Len. "How Do You Feel About This Undying Interest In The Beatles, Ringo?" Zoo World (September 26, 1974) pp12-14.

M 1022   Epand, Len. "Paul McCartney Stages American Wingding." Circus (August 10, 1976) p42.

M 1023   Epand, Len. "Touring In The Material World." Zoo World (December 5, 1974) p14.
(George Harrison.)

M 1024   Epstein, Brian. "Beatles Drop In - By Helicopter." Melody Maker 39 (September 5, 1964) p3. illus.

M 1025   Epstein, Brian. "Beatles Make History." Melody Maker 39 (August 29, 1964) p1+. illus.

M 1026   "Epstein Denies Any Breakup Of Beatles." Variety 245 (November 23, 1966) p53.

M 1027   "Epstein Diversifies; Becomes A Producer." Billboard 76 (October 31, 1964) p1.

M 1028   "Epstein Is Expanding Empire." Billboard 79 (January 28, 1967) p4.

M 1029   "Epstein Values 1/4 Beatles Slice At $4,000,000." Variety 236 (November 11, 1964) p1+.

M 1030   Eremo, J. "In Memory Of John Lennon." Guitar Player 15 (October 1981) p14+.
(Composition scholarship at Julliard.)

M 1031   Evans, M. "Beatles Backtracks: The Strange Story Of The Hamburg Tapes." Melody Maker 48 (August 4, 1973) p28. illus.

M 1032   Evans, M. "Beatles On Stage!" Melody Maker 49 (July 27, 1974) p36.

M 1033   Evans, M. Stanton. "Lennon And The Gun Controllers." Human Events 41 (January 10, 1981) p7+.

M 1034   Evans, Mal. "'The Beatles Get Back'." The Beatles Book 72 (July 1969) pp22-29.
(On the "Get Back" album.)

M 1035   Evans, Mal. "Beatles In India." The Beatles Book 58 (May 1968) pp6-12.
(In Rishikesh.)

M 1036   Evans, Mal. "Beatles In India, Part 2." The Beatles Book 59 (June 1968) pp6-13.

M 1037   Evans, Mal. "The Eighteenth Single: How The Beatles Recorded Their New Single." The Beatles Book 62 (September 1968) pp6-11.
("Hey Jude/Revolution.")

M 1038   Evans, Mal. "George's U.S. Visit." The Beatles Book 66 (January 1969) pp21-26.
(October-December 1968.)

M 1039   Evans, Mal. "Mal's Diary." The Beatles Book 63 (October 1968) pp11-12.
(Recent recording sessions.)

M 1040   Evans, Mal. "Mal's Diary." The Beatles Book 68 (March 1969) pp7-15.
(Recent events.)

M 1041   Evans, Mal. "Mal's Page." The Beatles Book 42 (January 1967) p26.
(Trip to Nairobi, Kenya, with Paul McCartney.)

M 1042   Evans, Mal. "Recording In India: A Special Report On George's Recent Visit To Bombay." The Beatles Book 56 (March 1968) pp7-10.
(January 1968.)

M 1043   Evans, Mal. "Ringo And George In California." The Beatles Book 61 (August 1968) pp24-26+.
(Early June 1968.)

M 1044   Evans, Mal. "Ringo In Rome: Candy: Filming Report From Italy." The Beatles Book 54 (January 1968) pp12-15.

M 1045   Evans, Mal. "Ringo In Rome: Candy: Filming Report From Italy, Part 2." The Beatles Book 55 (February 1968) pp11-15.

M 1046   Evans, Mal. "Thirty New Beatle Grooves On Double Disc Album." The Beatles Book 64 (November 1968) pp7-15.

(The "White Album.")

M 1047 Evans, Mal. "With The Beatles, No. 3: Paul And Mal In The States." The Beatles Book 48 (July 1967) pp9-10.
(April 1967.)

M 1048 Evans, Mal. "Your Album Queries Answered." The Beatles Book 67 (February 1969) pp7,10-13+.

M 1049 Evans, Mal and Neil Aspinall. "How The Magical E.P.s Were Made." The Beatles Book 54 (January 1968) pp8-11.
(The making of recent recordings.)

M 1050 Evans, Mal and Neil Aspinall. "Magical Mystery Tour." The Beatles Book 52 (November 1967) pp6-13.
(Origins of the film.)

M 1051 Evans, Mal and Neil Aspinall. "Mal And Neil Tell You How 'All You Need Is Love' Was Recorded." The Beatles Book 49 (August 1967) pp9-11.

M 1052 Evans, Mal and Neil Aspinall. "New Single Sessions." The Beatles Book 57 (April 1968) pp11-14.
(Recording "Lady Madonna" and other songs.)

M 1053 Evans, Mal and Neil Aspinall. "Recording With The Beatles Then And Now." Teen Set (Summer 1967) pp36-39.

M 1054 Evans, Mal and Neil Aspinall. "Sgt. Pepper." The Beatles Book 47 (June 1967) pp9-12.
(Recording the album.)

M 1055 Evans, Mal and Neil Aspinall. "With The Beatles, No. 1: Recording - Why It Takes So Long Now." The Beatles Book 45 (April 1967) pp10-13.

M 1056 Evans, Mal and Neil Aspinall. "With The Beatles, No. 4: Our Visit To Greece." The Beatles Book 50 (September 1967) pp12-13.

M 1057 Evans, Peter. "The Breakup Of The Beatles...And The Buildup Of Their Wives." Cosmopolitan 172:2 (February 1972) pp122-125+.

M 1058 Evans, Richard. "Meeting The Beatles." Beatlefan 4:5 (August 1982) p21.
(During filming of "Help!")

M 1059 Everett, Kenny. "Beatles Dinner Party." The Beatles Book 48 (July 1967) p25.
("Sgt. Pepper" pre-release party at Epstein house.)

M 1060 Everett, Kenny. "Less Screaming And Oh For A Proper Meal!" Melody Maker 41 (August 27, 1966) p7.

M 1061 Everett, Kenny. "We Love You - John And God!" Melody Maker 41 (August 20, 1966) p14+.

M 1062 Everett, T. "Beatles: Let It Be." Daily Planet 1:16 (June 22, 1970) p17.

M 1063 Everett, T. "Loud Music." Daily Planet 1:13 (May 11, 1970) p9.

M 1064 "Everywhere's Somewhere." New Yorker 47 (January 8, 1972) pp28-29.
(Interview with John Lennon.)

M 1065 "Ex-Beatle Best Wins Playboy Libel Suit." Rolling Stone 20 (October 26, 1968) p4. illus.

M 1066 "Ex-Beatle Drummer Files $8 Mil Libel Suit Vs. Former Mates, 'Playboy' Mag." Variety 240 (October 6, 1965) p55.
(Pete Best.)

M 1068 "Ex-Beatle Hit By A & M's Suit." Billboard 88 (October 9, 1976) p14.
(George Harrison.)

M 1069 "Ex-Beatle Paul McCartney Writes To The Melody Maker With The Last Word On A Well Worn Subject." Melody Maker 45 (August 29, 1970) p29.

M 1070 Eye. New York: The Hearst Corp., 1968.
(Cover portrait of John Lennon.)

M 1071 "An Eye For The Opportune Moment." People 18 (September 20, 1982) pp100-100+. illus.
(Photos by Linda McCartney.)

M 1072 "Eyes Of The Beatles." Vogue 152 (December 1968) pp198-201. illus.

M 1073 "Fab? Chaos; The TV Film, Magical Mystery Tour." Time 91 (January 5, 1968) pp60-61. illus.

M 1074 "Fab Four Single!" Melody Maker 56 (September 26, 1981) p5.
(Unreleased 1963 song "Leave My Kitten Alone.")

M 1075 "Fab Macca: The Truth." Melody Maker 54 (December 1, 1979) p10. illus.
(Interview with Paul McCartney.)

M 1076 Facconi, Renato. "The Italian Discography." Beatles Unlimited 21 (July 1978) pp4-8.

M 1077 "The Faces Of John." The Beatles Book 19 (February 1965) pp20-21.
(Photo essay/commentary.)

M 1078 "The Faces Of Paul." The Beatles Book 18 (January 1965) p15.
(Photo essay/commentary.)

M 1079 "The Faces Of Ringo." The Beatles Book 20 (March 1965) pp20-21.
(Photo essay/commentary.)

M 1080 Fager, Charles E. "Apple Corps Four." Christian Century 86 (March 19, 1969) pp386-388.

M 1081 Fager, Charles E. "Be Grateful, Parents!" Christian Century 86 (January 15, 1969) p92. illus.

M 1082 Faggen, G. "Beatles New U.S. Wave Causes Hardly A Splash." Billboard 76 (November 28, 1964) p24.

M 1083 Faggen, G. "Beatles: Plague Or Boon For Radio?" Billboard 76 (October 10, 1964) p16+. illus.

M 1084 Falchetta, Peter. "Now They're A Lot Richer, Some Are Sadder, All Wiser." Biography News 2 (March 1975) p375. illus.

M 1085 Falloon, Val. "Wings Keep It In The Family." Record World (June 1979) p6,18.
(Recent group activities.)

M 1086 Fallowell, Duncan. "Gimme Some Truth." Sounds 2 (1981) pp48-51. illus.

M 1087 "Fan Fest Update." Beatlefan
(Regular feature, v1n2-   , 1979-   .)

M 1088 "FanScene." Beatlefan
(Regular feature, v3n1-   , 1980-   .)

M 1089 Farber, Jim. "John Lennon And Yoko Ono - Double Fantasy (Geffen)." Circus (January 31, 1981) pp57,59.

M 1090 Farrell, Bobby. "Rarest Rock Show Of All." Life 71 (April 13, 1971) pp20-23. illus.
(George Harrison concert.)

M 1091 Fawcett, Anthony. "The Day John Lennon Stopped Believing In Beatles." Crawdaddy 67 (December 1976) pp32-36. illus.
(Excerpts "John Lennon: One Day At A Time.")

M 1092 Feder, Sue. "The Beatles At Shea Stadium." Beatlefan 3:5 (August 1981) pp18-19.
(Eyewitness account.)

M 1093 "Federal Court Upholds Its Jurisdiction In Copyright Case Involving Lennons." Variety 270 (April 18, 1973) p61.

M 1094 "Feedback." Beatles Unlimited
(Occasional feature, issues 3,4,7.)

M 1095 Feldman, Leslie. "Beatles: Free At Last?" Zoo World (April 11, 1974) p13.

M 1096 Feldman, P. "S. African Broadcastmen Lift 4-Year Record Ban On Beatles." Billboard 83 (March 27, 1971) p53.

M 1097 Feller, Benoit. "Disques Beatles." Rock & Folk (Paris) 118 (November 1976) pp68-75. illus.

M 1098 Fenick, Barbara. "Beatlefest '80." Record Collector 13 (September 1980) pp33-36. illus.
(Memorabilia on sale at 6th New York convention.)

M 1099 Fenick, Barbara. "'Collecting The Beatles'."
Beatlefan 4:5 (August 1982) pp8-9.
(Excerpt from her book.)

M 1100 Fenick, Barbara. "U.S. Beatles Memorabilia: A
Dealer's Eye View Of The Stateside Scene."
Record Collector 7 (March 1980) pp18-24.
illus.

M 1101 Fenick, Barbara. "Where To Look For Beatles
Memorabilia." Record Collector 8 (April 1980)
pp5-8. illus.

M 1102 Fenton, D. "Why Won't Yoko Release Ten For
Two." Ann Arbor Sun 2:9 (May 3, 1974)
p9.

M 1103 Fenton, D. "Why Won't Yoko Release Ten For
Two." Win 10:27 (July 25, 1974) p17.

M 1104 Ferris, T. "Nobody Loves A Beatle Hoaxer."
Rolling Stone 112 (July 6, 1972) p12.

M 1105 Ferris, T. "NY Benefit Nets A Quarter Million."
Rolling Stone 118 (September 28, 1972)
p6.

M 1106 "Fifth Beatles Record." The Beatles Book 72
(July 1969) p31.
(Billy Preston's Apple recordings.)

M 1107 "Fight For A Nation's Fans." Melody Maker 39
(September 26, 1964) pp8-9.
(British tour map.)

M 1108 "Film Fox." Creem 11 (June 1979) p48.
(McCartney making a film.)

M 1109 "Film Fox." Creem 11 (September 1979)
p51.
(Dick Clark's "Birth Of The Beatles.")

M 1110 "Film Fox." Creem 11 (May 1980) p47.
(The Lennons buy Palm Springs mansion.)

M 1111 "Film Fox." Creem 13 (June 1981) p39. illus.
(Ringo Starr in "Caveman.")

M 1112 "Filming Pix." The Beatles Book 22 (May 1965)
pp20-21.
(Photos from "Help!" filming.)

M 1113 "Films." Beatles Unlimited 34/35 (1981) pp22-23.
(John Lennon's film roles.)

M 1114 "Final Bar: John Lennon Obituary." Down Beat
48 (February 1981) p13.

M 1115 "The Final Interview." Beatlefan 3:2 (February
1981) pp4-8.
(First of six parts;Lennon RKO Radio
interview.)

M 1116 "Fine John Lennon $360 For Reefers." Variety
(December 4, 1968) p2.

M 1117 Finley, Michael. "Thingumybob: Dream Of The
13th Beatle." Beatlefan 3:3 (April 1981)
p3.
(Reactions to John Lennon's death.)

M 1118 "First 'Beatles' Disc For Sale?" Rolling Stone
351 (September 3, 1981) p36.

M 1119 "First Cream For Beatles Film May Net UA
$500,000." Variety 235 (July 15, 1964)
p1+.

M 1120 "First Full-Length Biography Of The Beatles."
The Beatles Book 58 (May 1968) pp13-14.
(Hunter Davies' biography.)

M 1121 "First Lennon Single In Five Years Due."
Billboard 92 (October 11, 1980) p6.
("(Just Like) Starting Over.")

M 1122 "First Live Performances For Over 2 Years."
The Beatles Book 65 (December 1968)
pp21-22.
(Plans for a series of live shows.)

M 1123 "The First Time." Rolling Stone 258 (February
9, 1978) p54+.
(Paul McCartney.)

M 1124 Fishel, J. "Wings Tour Report; Paul McCartney
Group Lays NY Out Cold With Blazing
Performance." Billboard 88 (June 5, 1976)
pp36-37. illus.

M 1125 Fisher, Christine. "Wings In Australia."
Beatles Unlimited 5 (January 1976)
pp5-8.
(November 1975.)

M 1126 "557 Abkco Net May Be Bopped By Beatles'
Breakup." Variety 263 (May 26, 1971)

p43.

M 1127 Flake, Carol. "Message From The Eggman."
Village Voice 24 (September 3, 1979)
p66.
(On the "Back To The Egg" album.)

M 1128 Flanagan, Coleen. "Too Biased Against Paul"
The Beatles Book 65 (September 1981)
(On Philip Norman's book, "Shout!")

M 1129 Flans, Robyn. "Ringo." Modern Drummer 5:9
(December 1981) pp10-13+. illus.
(Cover photo of Ringo.)

M 1130 Flattery, Paul. "Paul's Brother: 'I'm
Adequate'." Rolling Stone 168 (August 29,
1974) p26.
(Mike "McGear" McCartney.)

M 1131 Flippo, Chet. "Ex-Beatles Manager Allen Klein
Indicted." Rolling Stone 239 (May 19, 1977)
p14.

M 1132 Flippo, Chet. "For The Record." Rolling Stone
335 (January 22, 1981) p18+. illus.
(John Lennon.)

M 1133 Flippo, Chet. "Grammys: Hard Rock's Soft
Underbelly." Rolling Stone 184 (April 10,
1975) p15. illus.
(John Lennon.)

M 1134 Flippo, Chet. "Imagine: John Lennon Legal."
Rolling Stone 212 (September 9, 1976)
p14.
(Resident status granted.)

M 1135 Flippo, Chet. "Lennon In Court Again: $42
Million Of Old Gold." Rolling Stone 110
(April 8, 1976) p12+. illus.

M 1136 Flippo, Chet. "Lennon's Lawsuit: Memo From
Thurmond." Rolling Stone 192 (July 31, 1975)
p16. illus.
(Thurmond memo to John Mitchell.)

M 1137 Flippo, Chet. "The Private Years."
Rolling Stone 380 (October 14, 1982)
pp38-46. illus.
(Excerpt from book "The Ballad Of John And
Yoko.")

M 1138 Flippo, Chet. "Radio: Tribal Drum."
Rolling Stone 335 (January 22, 1981)
p19.
(John Lennon.)

M 1139 Flippo, Chet. "'Sgt. Pepper' On Broadway."
Rolling Stone 175 (December 5, 1974)
p10.

M 1140 Flower, J.A. "Beatlemania: The Virus Of '64."
Music Journal Annual (1964) p66+.

M 1141 "Following The Beatles." The Beatles Book 12
(July 1964) pp21-25.
(World tour.)

M 1142 Fong-Torres, Ben. "Beatles Talk: Let George Do
It." Rolling Stone 158 (April 11, 1974)
p13.
(Reunion and tour rumors.)

M 1143 Fong-Torres, Ben. "Behind The $230-Million
Offer." Rolling Stone 225 (November 4, 1976)
p12+. illus.
(For Beatles reunion.)

M 1144 Fong-Torres, Ben. "Christ, They Know It Ain't
Easy." Rolling Stone 38 (July 26, 1969)
p8.

M 1145 Fong-Torres, Ben. "Did Allen Klein Take Bangla
Desh Money?" Rolling Stone 105 (March 30,
1972) p1+.

M 1146 Fong-Torres, Ben. "The Greatest Hits Of 1989."
Rolling Stone 316 (May 1, 1980) p14.
(Future albums by The Beatles.)

M 1147 Fong-Torres, Ben. "'Heroes Of Rock 'N' Roll'
Airs." Rolling Stone 285 (February 22, 1979)
p22. illus.
(TV special featuring The Beatles.)

M 1148 Fong-Torres, Ben. "Lennon's Song: The Man Can't
F--k Our Music." Rolling Stone 76 (February
18, 1971) p1+.
(Working Class Hero.)

M 1149 Fong-Torres, Ben. "Lumbering In The Material
World." Rolling Stone 176 (December 19, 1974)

pp52-54+. illus.
(Harrison's 1974 U.S. tour.)

M 1150 Fong-Torres, Ben. "Paul McCartney Reflects On The Loss Of A Friend: What I Should Have Said." Parade Magazine (June 26, 1983) p16.
(On John Lennon.)

M 1151 Fong-Torres, Ben. "Ringo Starr Was In The Crowd; John And Yoko Stayed In Bed." Rolling Stone 218 (July 29, 1976) p9. illus.
(McCartney/Wings concert.)

M 1152 Fong-Torres, Ben. "'Sgt. Pepper' Returns." Rolling Stone 277 (November 2, 1978) p35.
("Sgt. Pepper" film soundtrack.)

M 1153 Fong-Torres, Ben. "A Terrible Example For Youth." American Musical Digest 1 (December 1969) p18.
(Excerpt from Rolling Stone Nov. 29, 1969.)

M 1154 Fong-Torres, Ben. "That's The Way He Planned It." Rolling Stone 91 (September 16, 1971) p10.
(George Harrison and Billy Preston.)

M 1155 Fong-Torres, Ben. "Wings Tour Ends: Up, Up And Away." Rolling Stone 218 (July 29, 1976) p9+. illus.

M 1156 Fong-Torres, Ben. "Yesterday, Today, & Paul." Rolling Stone 215 (June 17, 1976) pp38-43+. illus.
(Interview.)

M 1157 Fonvielle, Chris. "Songs They Never Sang." Who Put The Bomp 14 (Fall 1975) p21.
(Discography; additions in No. 15, page 44.)

M 1158 "Forget Reunion Of Beatles: McCartney." Variety 284 (October 6, 1976) p64.

M 1159 "A Fortune For A Song." People 16:3 (July 20, 1981) p88.
(Quarrymen's 1958 recording offered at auction.)

M 1160 Fotheringham, Allan. "Beatle Menace: How To Preserve Public Safety When Four Kids From Liverpool Visit Canada." MacLean's Magazine 77 (September 19, 1964) pp1-2. illus.

M 1161 Foti, Laura. "'Compleat Beatles' Push Is On; Extensive Cross-Merchandising Campaign Launched." Billboard (November 20, 1982) p29.
(MGM/United Artists video.)

M 1162 "Four Cats On A London Roof." TV Guide (April 19, 1969) pp14-15. illus.
(Picture feature.)

M 1163 "Four Charities Share 250G Take From John-Yoko's Benefit At Garden, N.Y." Variety 269 (December 20, 1972) p49.

M 1164 "4 Individual Beatles Score On Hot 100 For First Time." Billboard 86 (December 21, 1974) p1.

M 1165 "Four Little Beatles And How They Grew." Reader's Digest 91 (December 1967) pp229-230+.
(Abridged from Time.)

M 1166 Fox, H. "Middle East's Music Playing Hot Chart Role." Billboard 78 (November 19, 1966) p1+.

M 1167 "Framing The Beatles." Newsweek 72 (August 19, 1968) p89. illus.

M 1168 "Frankfurt Combo Puts Sauerkraut On Revival Of Beatles." Variety 286 (March 23, 1977) p75.

M 1169 Freed, Richard. "B Is For Beatles And Baroque; Concerning Baroque Beatles Book." Saturday Review 48 (December 25, 1965) p57+. illus.

M 1170 Freedland, N. "Beatles Tunes Employed Well On 'War' Soundtrack." Billboard 88 (November 27, 1976) p38+.
("All This And World War II" album.)

M 1171 Freedland, N. "Harrison, A & M Ties Open New Avenues For Beatles." Billboard 86

(June 8, 1974) p1+.

M 1172 Freeman, Clive. "A German Teenager Asks Paul McCartney To Send All His Loving - And Lots Of Money." People 18:6 (August 9, 1982) pp24-25. illus.
(Paternity suit for $3 million.)

M 1173 "Freezing Hot Mal." The Beatles Book 22 (May 1965) p28.
(Photo: Mal Evans in "Help.")

M 1174 Freilich, Leon. "John's Psychic Secret." Star 9:2 (January 13, 1981) pp20-21. illus.
(Felt he would survive nuclear war in Atlantis.)

M 1175 Fremont-Smith, Eliot. "Death In The Family." Village Voice 25 (December 17, 1980) p61.

M 1176 Fricke, David. "Beatles BBC Tapes." Musician, Player & Listener 45 (July 1982) pp64,70+.

M 1177 Fricke, David. "Geffen Nets Lennon For Album Package." Melody Maker 55 (October 11, 1980) p6.

M 1178 Fricke, David. "George Harrison: Re-Meet The Beatle." Circus 219 (April 17, 1979) pp34-36.

M 1179 Fricke, David. "Yoko Sued Over Copyright Claim." Melody Maker 56 (July 18, 1981) p3.
("I'm Your Angel.")

M 1180 Friede, Goldie, Robin Titone and Sue Weiner. "'The Beatles A-Z'." Beatlefan 2:6 (October 1980) pp10-12.
(Excerpts from their book.)

M 1181 Friend, David. "Beatle Quiz." National Lampoon 1:91 (October 1977) p12.

M 1182 Friis-Mikkelsen, Jarl and John David Heilbrunn. "Livet Er Det Der Sker." MM (Copenhagen, Denmark) (December 1980) p12.
(Obituary.)

M 1183 "Frisco Fans Fierce Devotion Startles More Than Beatles' SRO 49G Take." Variety 236 (August 26, 1964) p43+.

M 1184 Frith, Simon. "About A Lucky Band Who Made The Grade." New Society (March 26, 1981) pp554-555. illus.

M 1185 Frith, Simon. "Mug Of Kintyre." Creem 9 (April 1978) p32. illus.
(Paul McCartney.)

M 1186 Frith, Simon. "The Walrus Was Ringo." Creem 8 (July 1976) p39. illus.

M 1187 Fritts, Tom. "August 1964 Revisited." Beatlefan 1:5 (August 1979) p12.
(Fictional Hollywood Bowl account.)

M 1188 "From Minerva House." Musical Opinion 87 (March 1964) pp325-326.

M 1189 "From The Editor." Rolling Stone 23 (December 7, 1968) p4. illus.
(Regarding the Lennons' nude pictures.)

M 1190 "From Then To You." Beatles Unlimited 17 (November 1977) p23.
(On The Beatles' UK Christmas LP.)

M 1191 Frost, David. "John's Gospel." Spectator (August 12, 1966) pp198-199.

M 1192 Fujita, Shig. "Toshiba-EMI Sets Beatles Promo." Billboard 94:11 (May 20, 1982) p64.
(To celebrate groups formation 20 years ago.)

M 1193 Fulford, R. "Tribal Gods." Saturday Night 96 (March 1981) pp5-6. illus.
(John Lennon.)

M 1194 Fuller, John G. "Trade Winds; Phenomenal Success." Saturday Review 48 (September 18, 1965) p14+. illus.

M 1195 "Full Report On Wings World Tour And New LP Tracks." The Beatles Book 10 (February 1977) ppiii-iv+.

M 1196 Fulper-Smith, Shawn. "'Beatlemania' On Tour." Beatlefan 3:2 (February 1981) p11.
(Stage show.)

M 1197 Fulper-Smith, Shawn. "Collecting." Beatlefan 3:5
(August 1981) p28.
(Release history of Beatles' Hamburg
recordings.)

M 1198 Fulper-Smith, Shawn. "Collecting." Beatlefan 3:6
(October 1981) p23.
(Hamburg recordings release history, part
two.)

M 1199 Fulper-Smith, Shawn. "A Conversation With Allan
Williams." Beatlefan 4:3 (April 1982)
pp18-19.
(Interview.)

M 1200 Fulper-Smith, Shawn. "The Dream Is Not Over."
Beatlefan 3:1 (December 1980) pp10-11.
(Reactions to John Lennon's death.)

M 1201 Fulper-Smith, Shawn. "Fan Fest Update."
Beatlefan 2:6 (October 1980) p21.
(New England Beatles convention, October
10-12.)

M 1202 Fulper-Smith, Shawn. "Fan Fest Update."
Beatlefan 3:1 (December 1980) p7.
(Boston Beatles Convention, early December
1980.)

M 1203 Fulper-Smith, Shawn. "Fan Fest Update."
Beatlefan 4:1 (December 1981) p14.
(Conventions in New London(CT) and Boston.)

M 1204 Fulper-Smith, Shawn. "Following The Beatles'
Trail." Beatlefan 2:6 (October 1980)
pp4-7.
(Beatles-related sites and people in
Liverpool.)

M 1205 Fulper-Smith, Shawn and Marilyn Fulper-Smith.
"Cavern Mecca: The Battle Goes On."
Beatlefan 4:2 (February 1982) p10.
(Mecca's plans for a Beatles museum.)

M 1206 Fulper-Smith, Shawn and Marilyn Fulper-Smith.
(Untitled.) Beatlefan 4:1 (December 1981)
p16.
(Interview with Victor Spinetti.)

M 1207 "Fund Lennon Scholarship." Billboard 98
(March 14, 1981) p3+.

M 1208 "15 Jahre Beatles."
Musik Joker (Hamburg, W. Ger.) (October 1977)
illus.
(Special Beatles section, 32 pages.)

M 1209 "Funny Songs, Protest Songs, Song Songs."
Hit Parader XXV:28 (October 1966) pB9.
(Paul McCartney interviewed.)

M 1210 Gabree, John. "Beatles In Perspective."
Down Beat 34 (November 16, 1967) pp20-22.
illus.

M 1211 Gabree, John. "Beatles' Ninety-Minute Bore, And
The Rolling Stones' Beggars Banquet."
High Fidelity/Musical America 19 (March 1969)
pp84-85.
(On the "White Album.")

M 1212 Gabree, John. "The Heaviest Beatle Of Them
All." High Fidelity/Musical America 21
(March 1971) pp70-71. illus.
(John Lennon and George Harrison.)

M 1213 Gabree, John. "Looking Past The Beatles."
High Fidelity/Musical America 20 (April 1970)
pp83-84.

M 1214 Gaines, James R. "Descent Into Madness."
People 15:24 (June 21, 1981) p69+. illus.
(Pages 69-71,75-76,79.)

M 1215 Gallagher, D. "Paul McCartney: Growing Up, Up,
And Away From The Beatles." Redbook 143
(September 1974) pp78-79. illus.
(Interview.)

M 1216 Gambaccini, Paul. "British Rockers Unite In
Concerts For Kampuchea." Rolling Stone 311
(February 21, 1980) pp17-18. illus.
(Reunion rumor.)

M 1217 Gambaccini, Paul. "A Conversation With Paul
McCartney." Rolling Stone 295 (July 12, 1979)
pp39-46. illus.
(Interview.)

M 1218 Gambaccini, Paul. "Dawn Of The Age Of Venus &
Mars: McCartneys Wings Take To The Stars."
Rolling Stone 191 (July 17, 1975) p9+.
illus.

M 1219 Gambaccini, Paul. "Harrison's 'Extra Texture':
Read All About It." Rolling Stone 198
(October 23, 1975) p15. illus.

M 1220 Gambaccini, Paul. "Historic Cavern Club Given
3-Month Reprieve." Rolling Stone 131
(March 29, 1973) p22.

M 1221 Gambaccini, Paul. "McCartney & Wings At Sea."
Rolling Stone 249 (October 6, 1977)
pp11-12+. illus.
(Interview.)

M 1222 Gambaccini, Paul. "McCartneys Meet Press:
Starting All Over Again." Rolling Stone 137
(June 21, 1973) p10+. illus.

M 1223 Gambaccini, Paul. "McCartney, Wings Plan U.S.
Flight." Rolling Stone 211 (April 22, 1976)
p10. illus.
(U.S. tour.)

M 1224 Gambaccini, Paul. "Paul McCartney."
Rolling Stone 153 (January 31, 1974)
p32+.
(Interview.)

M 1225 Gambaccini, Paul. "Paul McCartney's One-Man
Band." Rolling Stone 319 (June 26, 1980)
p11+. illus.

M 1226 Gambaccini, Paul. "Paul Won't Rest His Wings."
Rolling Stone 226 (December 16, 1976)
p15. illus.
(Interview.)

M 1227 Gambaccini, Paul. "Ringo Remembers ... ."
Rolling Stone (November 18, 1976) p15+.
illus.
(Interview.)

M 1228 Gambaccini, Paul. "Rolling Stone Interview:
Paul McCartney." Rolling Stone 153
(January 31, 1974) pp32-34+. illus.

M 1229 Garbarini, Vic. "The Beatles Years - Ringo
Yesterday & Today."
Musician, Player & Listener 40 (February
1982) pp44-53.
(Interview with Ringo Starr.)

M 1230 Garbarini, Vic. "Paul McCartney - Lifting The
Veil On The Beatles."
Musician, Player & Listener 29 (August 1980)
p44+. illus.
(Interview.)

M 1231 Garbarini, Vic and Barbara Graustark. "John
Lennon." Musician, Player & Listener 31
(March 1981) pp56-61+. illus.

M 1232 Garde, M. "Theology Of George Harrison."
Christianity Today 18 (August 16, 1974)
pp16-17. illus.

M 1233 "Gary Fawkes." The Beatles Book 76 (November
1969) p31.
(Mal Evans' son.)

M 1234 Garztecki, Marek. "Wings In Sweden '72."
Beatles Unlimited 12 (March 1977) pp4-7.
(August 7 Stockholm concert, with
interview.)

M 1235 Geddes, A. "Lennon Lament By Parcel Post:
Calgary's Mail Art Show Weeps Weirdly For
John." Alberta Report 9 (January 11, 1982)
pp45-46. illus.

M 1236 Geffen, David. "A Reminiscence." Rolling Stone
335 (January 22, 1981) p59+.

M 1237 "Geffen's Coup: Lennon & Yoko Signed."
Billboard 92 (October 4, 1980) p6.

M 1238 Geldof, R. "Harrison: An Ex-Beatle Limps Back -
Vancouver, Can." Melody Maker 49 (November
9, 1974) p3. illus.

M 1239 "George Harrison Bangla Desh Benefit."
Rolling Stone 90 (September 2, 1971) p1+.
(Cover portrait.)

M 1240 "George Harrison On Abbey Road." Rolling Stone
44 (October 18, 1969) p8. illus.
("Abbey Road" album.)

M 1241 "George Harrison On The Record." Beatlefan 1:3
(April 1979) pp1,9-12.
(Transcript of Los Angeles press

conference.)

M 1242 "George Harrison Writes Film Score." Rolling Stone 6 (February 24, 1968) p6.
("Wonderwall.")

M 1243 "George Introduces Hare Krishna." The Beatles Book 75 (October 1969) pp7-9.
(Radha Krishna Temple members.)

M 1244 "George Martin On The Beatle Days." Rolling Stone 71 (November 26, 1970) p14.

M 1245 "George Records 'Krishna'." The Beatles Book 73 (August 1969) p29.

M 1246 "George's Solo Career." The Beatles Book 5 (September 1976) ppiii-iv.

M 1247 "German Club Where Beatles Began Reopens." Variety 293 (December 27, 1978) p2.
(Star Club.)

M 1248 Gerson, Ben. "George Harrison's Search For Anonymity." Creem 6 (December 1974) pp44-46+. illus.

M 1249 Gerson, Ben. "Harrison Trial: Is "My Sweet Lord" 'So Fine'?" Rolling Stone 210 (April 8, 1976) p12. illus.

M 1250 Gerson, Ben. "Lennon: Together Again." Rolling Stone 174 (November 21, 1974) p72+.
(On the "Walls And Bridges" album.)

M 1251 Gerson, Ben. "Paul." Fusion 72 (March 1972) pp32-34. illus.
(Cover photo.)

M 1252 "'Get Back' LP In December." The Beatles Book 74 (September 1969) p31.

M 1253 "'Get Back' Postponed." The Beatles Book 73 (August 1969) p29.

M 1254 Gitlin, Todd. "John Lennon Speaking." Commonweal 96 (September 22, 1972) pp500-503.

M 1255 Gitlin, Todd. "The Lennon Legacy." Center Magazine 14 (May/June 1981) pp2-4. illus.

M 1256 Giuliano, Geoffrey. "Yoko Ono." Playgirl 11:2 (July 1983) pp38-42+.

M 1257 Giusto-Davis, JoAnn and Wendy Smith. "The Book Trade Reacts To Lennon's Death With Flurry Of Publishing Activity." Publishers Weekly 218:26 (December 26, 1980) p39+.

M 1258 "Glasgow Slaps Ban On Beatles Queues." Variety 234 (April 15, 1964) p49.

M 1259 Glassenberg, Bob. "Harrison & Friends Dish Out Super Concert For Pakistan Aid." Billboard 83 (August 14, 1971) p18.

M 1260 "Glass Onion." Beatlefan (Occasional feature, v3n6-   , 1980-   .)

M 1261 Glazer, Mitchell. "The George Harrison Interview." Crawdaddy (February 1977) p32+.

M 1262 Glazer, Mitchell. "Growing Up At 33 1/3: The George Harrison Interview." Crawdaddy 69 (February 1977) pp32-41. illus.

M 1263 Glazier, Joel. "Beatlefest '78: New York, February 4 & 5, 1978." Beatles Unlimited 19 (March 1978) p20.
(Fan convention.)

M 1264 Glazier, Joel. "Beatlemania." Beatles Unlimited 19 (March 1978) pp8-10.
(Description of the stage show.)

M 1265 Glazier, Joel. "Commentary: Lennon Peace Forest." Beatlefan 4:1 (December 1981) p11.
(Project of the Jewish National Fund, Israel.)

M 1266 Glazier, Joel. "The 8th New York Beatlefest '81." Beatles Unlimited 39 (1981) pp12-13.

M 1267 Glazier, Joel. "John Lennon Peace Forest." Beatles Unlimited 39 (1981) pp20-21.
(Project of Israel's Jewish National Fund.)

M 1268 Glazier, Joel. "The John Lennon Peace Forest." Beatles Now 4 (Autumn 1982) p12.

M 1269 Glazier, Joel. "A Tale Of Two Cities'

Conventions." Beatles Unlimited 31 (March 1980) pp11-12.
(New York Beatlefest.)

M 1270 Glazier, Joel. "Tribute To John Lennon." Beatles Unlimited 40 (1982) pp18-19.
(Cincinatti Pops Orchestra.)

M 1271 Glazier, Joel. "U.S.A. (East Coast)." Beatles Unlimited 34/35 (1981) pp34-35.
(News on U.S. memorial vigils for Lennon.)

M 1272 Gleason, Ralph J. "Beatles Tell It To The Activists." Jazz & Pop 7 (November 1968) p16.

M 1273 Gleason, Ralph J. "Like A Rolling Stone." American Scholar 36:4 (Fall 1967) pp555-563.
(From book "The American Experience.")

M 1274 Gleason, Ralph J. "Like A Rolling Stone." Jazz & Pop 7 (April 1968) p10. illus.
(From book "The American Experience.")

M 1275 Gleason, Ralph J. "Perspectives." Rolling Stone 110 (June 8, 1972) p314.
(The Lennons' deportation fight.)

M 1276 Gleason, Ralph J. "Perspectives: Are We Lost In A New Dark Age." Rolling Stone 48 (December 13, 1969) p21. illus.
(McCartney death hoax.)

M 1277 Gleason, Ralph J. "Perspectives: 'Bangla Desh' - A Unique Film." Rolling Stone 107 (April 27, 1972) p30.

M 1278 Gleason, Ralph J. "Perspectives: Changing With Money Changers." Rolling Stone 6 (February 24, 1968) p9.
(The Beatles and others.)

M 1279 Gleason, Ralph J. "Perspectives: Dealing With Watergate And The Lennon Case." Rolling Stone 134 (May 10, 1973) p7.

M 1280 Gleason, Ralph J. "Perspectives: Fair Play For John And Yoko." Rolling Stone 111 (June 22, 1972) p34.

M 1281 Gleason, Ralph J. "Perspectives: The British Group Syndrome." Rolling Stone 4 (January 20, 1968) p10.
(Beatles and other groups.)

M 1282 The Globe (Volume 27, Number 53. December 30, 1980). illus.
(Eight-page pull-out on John Lennon.)

M 1283 Goddard, Peter. "Beatles Music." Chatelaine 54 (May 1981) p18.

M 1284 Goddard, Peter. "John Lennon Is A Very Practical Man." Sound (February 1974) pp13-15.

M 1285 Godwin, Joscelyn. "Search & Protest In Popular Songs." Golden Blade (Colgate Univ.) 26 (1974) pp96-106.
(Includes Beatles.)

M 1286 Goldberg, Danny. "A New Sound From A New Team: Paul And Linda McCartney." Circus 5:8 (August 1971) pp32-36. illus.
(Cover photo and detachable poster included.)

M 1287 Goldman, Albert. "Beatles Decide To Let It Be, Apart." Life 68 (April 24, 1970) pp38-39. illus.

M 1288 Goldman, Albert. "Beatles In Oil And Water." Vogue 152 (October 1, 1968) p154+.

M 1289 Goldman, Julia. "The Two Women Who Broke Up The Beatles." McCall's 98 (July 1971) pp72-73+. illus.

M 1290 Goldsmith, Marianne. "Meeting The Beatles." Beatlefan 4:4 (June 1982) p16.
(In the early sixties.)

M 1291 Goldstein, Richard. "Canada, Peacemaker To The World." Village Voice 15:10 (March 5, 1970) p1.
(John Lennon.)

M 1292 Goldstein, Richard. "Culture Shock: The Great White Lie; How Broadway Show Evades The Press." Village Voice 22 (October 3, 1977) p49.
(Stage show "Beatlemania.")

M 1293 Goldstein, Richard. "McCartney: He Coulda Been

JOHN LE
WORKING CLASS HERO
8 F.
salut!
NUMERO SPECIAL
JOH
LENN
LE FIGARO
Nº 99 - FIGARO DU 13 AU 19 DÉCEMBRE 1980
EDITION INTERNATIONALE - 6 F.
MAGAZI
ADIEU AUX ANNEES 60
Document
Pologne
Afghanistan
3/80
DM 4,50
Luxemburg: lfr. 81,– Österreich: S
Star Club
THE BEATL
Das Superheft zur Supergruppe
OHN
ENNON
THE LIFE & LEGEND
LA MORT DES BEATLES
John Lennon assass
Son histoire. Ses amours
Yoko. Son univ
Ses dernières ph
Cr$ 100,00
apresenta
HN LENNON
IBUTO A UM MITO
JOHN LENNON
GIVE PEACE A CHANCE
EDITION SPECIALE
JOHN LENNON
orial Tribute
70p

A Contender." Village Voice 21 (May 31, 1976) p144+.

M 1294 Goldstein, Richard. "New Culture." Vogue 156 (August 1, 1970) p99+.

M 1295 Goldstein, T. "London Town: So What's Wrong With Silly Love Songs?" High Fidelity/Musical America 28 (July 1978) p120. illus.
(On the "London Town" album.)

M 1296 Goodfriend, J. "Beatles Transmogrified Again: A Two-Piano Concerto For Our Time." Stereo Review 45 (September 1980) p75. illus.
(On the "Beatles Concerto" album.)

M 1297 "Good Lord, It's The Same Old Song." Melody Maker 51 (September 18, 1976) p30.
(George Harrison.)

M 1298 Goodman, Hal. "Not Enough Help From My Friends." Psychology Today (April 1983) p25. illus.
(On Lennon/McCartney as songwriters.)

M 1299 Goodman, J. "End Of Metaphor." New Leader 52 (December 22, 1969) pp26-27.

M 1300 Goodman, J. "Music As Child's Play." New Leader 61 (January 29, 1968) pp30-31.

M 1301 Goodman, Pete. "Norman Smith Continues Talking About Balancing The Beatles." The Beatles Book 23 (June 1965) pp13-15.
(Beatles' recording engineer.)

M 1302 Goodman, Rachel. "The Day The King Of Swing Met The Beatles." Esquire 64 (July 1965) pp52-53+. illus.
(The Beatles meet Benny Goodman.)

M 1303 Goodwin, M. "Let It Be." Rolling Stone 61 (June 25, 1970) p52.
(Film.)

M 1304 Gordon, A.M. "Lennon's Leaping Whimsy." Jazz & Pop 8 (March 1969) p45.

M 1305 Gordon, A.M. "Media Masters Meet The Carnal Saints, Or Frankenstein Meets The Wolfman." Jazz & Pop 8 (March 1969) pp41-42.

M 1306 Gordon, Roxy. "Beatlemania." Rolling Stone 142 (August 30, 1973) p76.

M 1307 Gould, H. "Up From Liverpool." Commentary 47 (April 1969) pp79-83.

M 1308 Gracen, Jorie. "Meeting The Beatles." Beatlefan 2:5 (August 1980) p18.
(An encounter in Chicago with Paul McCartney.)

M 1309 "Grand Jury Indicts Allen Klein." Billboard 89 (April 16, 1977) p6.

M 1310 Grant, Suzie. "Interview With Paul." The Beatles Book 51 (July 1980) ppvii-viii.
(On his "McCartney II" LP.)

M 1311 Graustark, Barbara. "Beatles: It's All Over - Official." Melody Maker 55 (September 27, 1980) p9.
(Excerpt from "Newsweek" interview.)

M 1312 Graustark, Barbara. "Ex-Beatle Starting Over." Newsweek 96 (December 22, 1980) pp45-46. illus.
(John Lennon; includes cover portrait.)

M 1313 Graustark, Barbara. "The Last Ballad Of John & Yoko." People 21 (February 20, 1984) pp54-56+. illus.

M 1314 Graustark, Barbara. "Life With And Without Lennon: An Intimate Interview With Yoko Ono." Ladies' Home Journal C:3 (March 1983) pp118-120+. illus.

M 1315 Graustark, Barbara. "Newsmakers." Newsweek 94 (November 5, 1979) p59.
(Paul McCartney.)

M 1316 Graustark, Barbara. "Real John Lennon." Newsweek 96 (September 29, 1980) pp76-77. illus.
(Interview.)

M 1317 Graustark, Barbara. "Sean Lennon: The Wit And Soul Of A Beatle In The Body Of An 8 Year Old." People 21 (February 20, 1984) illus.

M 1318 Graustark, Barbara. "Yoko: An Intimate Conversation." Rolling Stone 353 (October 1, 1981) pp13-18+. illus.

M 1319 Gray, M. "Whisperings." Crawdaddy 11 (May 14, 1972) p3.
(Paul McCartney.)

M 1320 "Great British Achievements: The Beatles Conquer The World - 1960's." TV Times (London) (September 8, 1977) pp42-43.
(Silver Jubilee painting by Maurice Cockrill.)

M 1321 "Great News Of 'The Beatles'." Mersey Beat 1:23 (May 31, 1962) p1. illus.
(Epstein secures EMI contract.)

M 1322 Green, Ann. "My Point Of View." The Beatles Book 48 (July 1967) p13.
(A fan on her favorite group.)

M 1323 Green, Timothy. "Here Come Those Beatles." Life 56 (January 31, 1964) pp24-31. illus.
(Beatlemania.)

M 1324 Greenfield, J. "All Our Troubles Seemed So Far Away." Biography News 2 (March 1975) pp373-374. illus.

M 1325 Greenfield, Meg. "Thinking About John Lennon." Newsweek 96 (December 29, 1980) p68. illus.
(Reflections on the sixties generation.)

M 1326 Grein, Paul. "Chartbeat." Billboard 94:13 (April 3, 1982) p7.
(Chart-topping history by Beatles 18 years ago.)

M 1327 Grein, Paul. "Chartbeat: Beatles Crawl Over Chart." Billboard 93 (May 23, 1981) p6.

M 1328 Grein, Paul. "Dealers Gang New Four-Color Beatles Posters." Billboard 94:13 (April 3, 1982) pp20-21.
(Four posters to promote "Reel Music" LP.)

M 1329 Grein, Paul. "Hands Across The Water; Columbia's Singles Sweep." Billboard (May 15, 1982) p6,76.
(On the success of "Ebony & Ivory.")

M 1330 Grein, Paul. "Paul Mauls Debut Rivals; Stevie Sets Career Record." Billboard 94:14 (April 10, 1982) p6.
("Ebony & Ivory" debuts at 29.)

M 1331 Grevatt, R. "Beatle Mobs Move In And It Is Panicsville." Melody Maker 39 (September 5, 1964) p4.

M 1332 Grevatt, R. "Beatles Are Back With A Bang!" Melody Maker 39 (September 19, 1964) p11.

M 1333 Grevatt, R. "Radio Stations Ignore Ban On Beatle Records." Melody Maker 41 (August 20, 1966) p19.

M 1334 Grevatt, R. "Red Nose Folk Of Showbiz." Melody Maker 41 (September 3, 1966) p3.

M 1335 Groessel, Hans. "Die Beat-Musik; Versuch Einer Analyse." Neue Sammlung 7 (1967)
(Analyses of "Help!" and "Michelle.")

M 1336 Groessel, Hans. "Die Beat-Musik; Versuch Einer Analyse." Das Orchester 17 (December 1969) pp526-530.
(Analyses of "Help!" and "Michelle.")

M 1337 Gross, Leonard. "John Lennon: Beatle On His Own." Look 30 (December 13, 1966) pp58-60+. illus.

M 1338 Grossman, Jay. "Secret Goodies In 'You're Sixteen'." Rolling Stone 156 (March 14, 1974) p24.
(On the "Ringo" album.)

M 1339 "Group After Beatles Fans." Billboard 88 (September 4, 1976) p36.

M 1340 Grunfeld, Frederick V. "Polyphony And A New Vocal Quartet." Horizon 10 (Spring 1968) pp56-59. illus.
("Sgt. Pepper" and "Magical Mystery Tour" LPs.)

M 1341 Grunnet, Per. "The Beatles/John Lennon
        Chronology." MM (Copenhagen, Denmark)
        (December 1980) p4. illus.
M 1342 Grunnet, Per. "John Lennon - Kaerlighed Og
        Energi." MM (Copenhagen, Denmark) (December
        1980) p5. illus.
M 1343 "Guest Appearances." Beatles Unlimited 34/35
        (1981) pp26-27.
        (John Lennon's guest recording
        appearances.)
M 1344 Guild, Hazel. "Beatles Help Spin West German
        Disk Biz To $86-Mil Profit In M65." Variety
        242 (April 13, 1966) p57.
M 1345 Guild, Hazel. "German Police In Summit
        Conference On Strategy To Control Beatle
        Mobs." Variety 243 (June 1, 1966) p41.
M 1346 Guild, Hazel. "Rock 'N' Roll Is Hell As
        Beatlemania Cuts Swath Thru Germany."
        243 Variety (July 13, 1966) p39+.
M 1347 Guzek, Arno. "Denmark." Beatles Unlimited
        34/35 (1981) pp37-38.
        (Danish reactions to John Lennon's death.)
M 1348 Guzek, Arno. "Komplet Engelsk Diskografi."
        MM (Copenhagen, Denmark) (December 1980)
        pp13-14. illus.
        (Discography.)
M 1349 Guzek, Arno. "World A-Z Discography."
        Beatles Now
        (Regular feature, Nos. 1-2, January-Spring
        1982.)
M 1350 Hadju, David. "John Lennon's Video Legacy."
        Video Review 1:11 (February 1981) pp90-91.
M 1351 Hager, Henk. "And When I Go Away."
        Beatles Unlimited 6 (March 1976) p12.
        (Paul McCartney & Wings in Holland, March
        1976.)
M 1352 Hager, Henk. "The Apple Story, 1968-1973: Part
        One." Beatles Unlimited 1 (March 1975)
        pp20-22.
M 1353 Hager, Henk. "The Apple Story, 1968-73: Part
        Two." Beatles Unlimited 2 (June 1975)
        pp6-10.
M 1354 Hager, Henk. "The Apple Story, 1968-1973: Part
        Three." Beatles Unlimited 3 (August 1975)
        pp7-11.
M 1355 Hager, Henk. "The Apple Story, 1968-73: Part
        Four." Beatles Unlimited 4 (November 1975)
        pp18-21.
M 1356 Hager, Henk. "Band On The Run."
        Beatles Unlimited 6 (March 1976) p6.
        (Paul McCartney & Wings in Holland, March
        1976.)
M 1357 Hager, Henk. "The Beatles Amps."
        Beatles Unlimited 7 (May 1976) pp4-6.
        (Photo survey of stage amplifiers.)
M 1358 Hager, Henk. "The Beatles & The New Wave."
        Beatles Unlimited 21 (July 1978) pp18-20.
        (New Wave group influenced by The Four.)
M 1359 Hager, Henk. "Beatles Unlimited First
        Anniversary." Beatles Unlimited 7 (May 1976)
        p3.
        (Publishing one year.)
M 1360 Hager, Henk. "The Cavern." Beatles Unlimited 5
        (January 1976) pp10-13.
        (History and description of the Cavern
        club.)
M 1361 Hager, Henk. "Deccas Come And Deccas Go(ne)."
        Beatles Unlimited 28 (September 1979)
        pp20-22.
        (On "The Decca Tapes" bootleg LP.)
M 1362 Hager, Henk. "The First British Beatles
        Convention." Beatles Unlimited 9 (September
        1976) pp8-9.
        (Norwich, England, August 28, 1976.)
M 1363 Hager, Henk. "George Harrison: Live In The
        Material World." Beatles Unlimited 1
        (March 1975) pp8-10.
        ("Let's Hear One For Lord Buddah" bootleg
        LP.)
M 1364 Hager, Henk. "George Harrison's George

Harrison." Beatles Unlimited 24 (January
        1979) pp4-5.
        (On the George Harrison LP.)
M 1365 Hager, Henk. "George Harrison's Guitars."
        Beatles Unlimited 2 (June 1975) pp11-14.
        (Photo survey of Harrison's guitars.)
M 1366 Hager, Henk. "How I Won The War."
        Beatles Unlimited 3 (August 1975) pp3-6.
        (On Lennon's film role.)
M 1367 Hager, Henk. "I Am Your Singer."
        Beatles Unlimited 6 (March 1976) p7.
        (Paul McCartney & Wings in Holland, March
        1976.)
M 1368 Hager, Henk. "I Feel Like Letting Go."
        Beatles Unlimited 6 (March 1976) pp7-8.
        (Paul McCartney & Wings in Holland, March
        1976.)
M 1369 Hager, Henk. "If I Ever Get Out Of Here."
        Beatles Unlimited 6 (March 1976) pp10-11.
        (Paul McCartney & Wings in Holland, March
        1976.)
M 1370 Hager, Henk. "I'll Be Waiting For You Baby."
        Beatles Unlimited 6 (March 1976) pp9-10.
        (Paul McCartney & Wings in Holland, March
        1976.)
M 1371 Hager, Henk. "In Memoriam: Jimmy McCulloch."
        Beatles Unlimited 28 (September 1979)
        p4.
        (Obituary.)
M 1372 Hager, Henk. "John Lennon's Guitars."
        Beatles Unlimited 10 (November 1976)
        pp12-16.
        (Photo survey.)
M 1373 Hager, Henk. "Mag Review: Harrison Alliance."
        Beatles Unlimited 10 (November 1976)
        p11.
        (Review of the U.S. fanzine.)
M 1374 Hager, Henk. "Norwich Revisited."
        Beatles Unlimited 10 (November 1976)
        pp20-21.
        (Photos of the Norwich fan convention,
        August '76.)
M 1375 Hager, Henk. "Ringo: Drums." Beatles Unlimited 8
        (July 1976) pp16-18.
        (Photo survey of drum kits.)
M 1376 Hager, Henk. "Ringo 1964." Beatles Unlimited 4
        (November 1975) pp21-22.
M 1377 Hager, Henk. "Ring O' Records."
        Beatles Unlimited 20 (May 1978) pp11-13.
        (Story of Ringo Starr's record company.)
M 1378 Hager, Henk. "Sitting In The Stand Of The
        Sports Arena." Beatles Unlimited 6
        (March 1976) pp12-17.
        (Paul McCartney & Wings in Holland, March
        1976.)
M 1379 Hager, Henk. "Standing In The Hall."
        Beatles Unlimited 6 (March 1976) p4.
        (Paul McCartney & Wings in Holland, March
        1976.)
M 1380 Hager, Henk. "That I Would Be Around To See It
        All Come True." Beatles Unlimited 6
        (March 1976) pp4-5.
M 1381 Hager, Henk. "Who's That Coming Round The
        Corner." Beatles Unlimited 6 (March 1976)
        pp8-9.
        (Paul McCartney & Wings in Holland, March
        1976.)
M 1382 Hager, Henk. "Who Will Get His Wings?"
        Beatles Unlimited 18 (January 1978)
        pp20-21.
        (Candidates for Wings' lead guitar slot.)
M 1383 Hager, Henk. "Wings Stage Equipment."
        Beatles Unlimited 6 (March 1976) pp20-22.
M 1384 Hager, Henk. "Wino Junko Can't Say No."
        Beatles Unlimited 6 (March 1976) p9.
        (Paul McCartney & Wings in Holland, March
        1976.)
M 1385 Hager, Hetty, trans. "Lucky Luxy & Lovely
        Linda." Beatles Unlimited 6 (March 1976)
        pp26-31.

(Tony Prince interviews Linda McCartney.)

M 1386 Hall, Claude. "Beatle Mania To Dominate Philadelphia." Billboard 88 (January 24, 1976) p88+.
(Beatlefest '76.)

M 1387 Hall, Claude. "Beatlemonium At Stadium - Youngsters Get Carried Away." Billboard 77 (August 28, 1965) p16. illus.
(Shea Stadium, August 15, 1965.)

M 1388 Hall, Claude. "Bootleg Beatles A Threat." Billboard 89 (May 7, 1977) p3.

M 1389 Hall, Claude. "Will The Real ... Acts Imitating Beatles, Elvis Are Proliferating." Billboard 6 (February 21, 1976)

M 1390 Hall, D. "Beatles U.N. Concert? 3 Reportedly Say 'Let's Go'." Billboard 91 (September 29, 1979) p3.

M 1391 Hallberg, Carl. "Live Beatles On Tape." Beatles Unlimited 2 (June 1975) pp4-5.
(Lists live concerts known to be recorded.)

M 1392 "A Hamburg Survivor." Beatlefan 1:4 (June 1979) pp10,22.
(Tony Sheridan interview, Part Two.)

M 1393 "The Hamburg Tapes." The Beatles Book 15 (July 1977) ppiii-iv.

M 1394 Hamill, Pete. "The Death And Life Of John Lennon." New York 13:50 (December 22, 1980) pp38-50. illus.

M 1395 Hamill, Pete. "Long Night's Journey Into Day: A Conversation With John Lennon." Rolling Stone 188 (June 5, 1975) pp46-48+. illus.
(Interview.)

M 1396 Hamilton, David. "A $50 Million Day's Night." Rolling Stone 172 (October 24, 1974) p45+. illus.
(For a Beatles reunion.)

M 1397 Hamilton, J. "Ringo Goes Single." Look 34 (February 10, 1970) pp40-44. illus.

M 1398 Hamlin, Bruce. "The Beatles Australian Singles." Beatles Unlimited 45 (1982) p17.
(Pending release of Australian boxed set.)

M 1399 Hammer, Joshua. "The Maharishi Wants Everybody To Levitate For Peace, But Some Iowans Are Hopping Mad." People 21:5 (February 6, 1984) pp48-49+. illus.
(The Maharishi and his University, Fairfield, Iowa.)

M 1400 Hannah, Dorene. "How Different From The Cavern Days." The Beatles Book 8 (March 1964) pp6-7.

M 1401 Harding, Helen. "I Am A Beatle Person." The Beatles Book 4 (November 1963) p20.

M 1402 Haring, Hermann. "War Is Over - If You Want It John Lennon." Musik Express (Hamburg,W.Ger.) (February 1981) pp8-11-64+. illus.

M 1403 Harris, B. "Beatles Nobody Got To Hear." Broadside & The Free Press 9:14 (August 26, 1970) p12.

M 1404 Harris, B. and S. Harris. "Hot As Sun: The Beatles Album No One Will Ever Hear." Rolling Stone 66 (September 17, 1970) pp26-27. illus.
(Reprinted from "Touch.")

M 1405 Harris, Bruce. "In Defense Of Paul McCartney." Words & Music 2:3 (June 1972) pp16-23.

M 1406 Harrison, E. "Industry Reacts To A & M - Harrison Suit." Billboard 88 (December 18, 1976) p4.

M 1407 Harrison, E. "L.A. 'Beatlemania' Top Entertainment." Billboard 90 (February 11, 1978) p34.

M 1408 Harrison, George. "No Private Life - But We Love It!" Mersey Beat (August 29, 1963) p9.
("The Beatles Story, Part Eleven.")

M 1409 Harrison, George. "We're Just People." Hit Parader XXV:28 (October 1966) illus.

(George talks on fame and fortune.)

M 1410 Harrison, T. "Looking A Dark Horse In The Mouth: George Harrison." Beetle 6 (March 1975) pp40-47. illus.
(Press conference transcript, pp. 45-47.)

M 1411 "Harrison And The Slow Death Mystery." Melody Maker 45 (October 24, 1970) p8. illus.

M 1412 "Harrison Billed $587,000 In 'My Sweet Lord' Case; Allen Klein To Collect." Variety 302 (March 4, 1981) p2.

M 1413 "Harrison In Big Bootleg War." Melody Maker 46 (October 9, 1971) p1.

M 1414 "Harrison Launches Own Label." Melody Maker 49 (May 25, 1974) p4.

M 1416 "Harrison Song In Dispute." Billboard 83 (March 6, 1971) p54.
("My Sweet Lord.")

M 1417 "Harrison's TV Blast Brings Menon Reply." Billboard 83 (December 4, 1971) p4.

M 1418 "Harrison Suit Wins 1st Round." Billboard 85 (May 3, 1973) p3.

M 1419 "Harrison Switches Labels." Melody Maker 51 (November 6, 1976) p4.
(Moves from A&M to Warner Brothers.)

M 1420 "Harrison Tour Set: They're All Hustling Him." Rolling Stone 159 (April 25, 1974) p13.

M 1421 "Harrison Will Play 50 Dates." Billboard 86 (September 28, 1974) p14. illus.

M 1422 "Harrison Wraps 27-City Tour At Garden, N.H.; Ex-Beatle Fizzles." Variety 277 (December 25, 1974) p34.

M 1423 Harry, Bill. "Alvin Stardust Recalls The Day Ringo Almost Drowned." The Beatles Book 61 (May 1981) ppvi-viii.
(Anecdotes from Tremlett's book, "Alvin Stardust.")

M 1424 Harry, Bill. "Beatle Books." The Beatles Book 84 (April 1983) pp40-44. illus.
(A look back at early Beatles books; Part I.)

M 1425 Harry, Bill. "The Beatle Detective." Beatles Now
(Regular feature, issue No.3-   , Summer 1982-   .)

M 1426 Harry, Bill. "The Beatles At The Star Club." The Beatles Book 81 (January 1983) pp14-15+. illus.

M 1427 Harry, Bill. "Beatles Films." The Beatles Book 49 (May 1980) pix.

M 1428 Harry, Bill. "Beatles Hits By Others." The Beatles Book 51 (July 1980) pix.
(Cover versions of Beatles' tunes.)

M 1429 Harry, Bill. "The Beatles' Liverpool: A Guide To The Places Associated With John, Paul, George And Ringo." The Beatles Book 40 (August 1979) ppiii-v.

M 1430 Harry, Bill. "The Beatles' Liverpool Days." The Beatles Book 29 (September 1978) ppiii-v.

M 1431 Harry, Bill. "The Beatles' Liverpool Days, Part Two." The Beatles Book 30 (October 1978) ppiii-v.

M 1432 Harry, Bill. "The Beatles' London; Part One: The Beatles' Radio, TV, Stage And Recording Venues." Record Collector 5 (January 1980) pp10-12.

M 1433 Harry, Bill. "The Beatles' London; Part Two: Their Offices, Homes And Haunts In The Capital." Record Collector 6 (February 1980) pp7-9.

M 1434 Harry, Bill. "Beatles' Novelties And Oddities." The Beatles Book 72 (April 1982) ppx-xi.
(Bootleg and novelty records.)

M 1435 Harry, Bill. "Beatles' Tributes, Spoofs &

Novelty Discs." The Beatles Book 61
(May 1981) ppxi-xii.
M 1436 Harry, Bill. "Beatles Win Again!"
The Beatles Book 82 (February 1983)
pp18-21. illus.
(1962 Mersey Beat poll.)
M 1437 Harry, Bill. "Bert Kaempfert: The Man Who Gave
Brian Epstein The Beatles."
The Beatles Book 52 (September 1980)
ppix-x.
M 1438 Harry, Bill. "Bill Harry's Detective Column."
Beatles Now 5 (Winter 1983) p5.
M 1439 Harry, Bill. "Billy J. Kramer - The 'J' Was For
Julian." The Beatles Book 88 (August 1983)
pp33-37. illus.
(Kramer recalls the early Beatles.)
M 1440 Harry, Bill. "'Caveman'." The Beatles Book 64
(August 1981) ppix-xi.
(Film starring Ringo Starr.)
M 1441 Harry, Bill. "Collector's Books."
The Beatles Book 54 (October 1980)
pviii.
(Describes "The Longest Cocktail Party.")
M 1442 Harry, Bill. "A Death In The Family."
Beatlefan 3:1 (December 1980) pp18,20.
(John Lennon.)
M 1443 Harry, Bill. "FanScene." Beatlefan 4:2
(February 1982) p3,20.
(Photo captions to Harry's book, "Mersey
Beat.")
M 1444 Harry, Bill. "Gambier Terrace." Beatles Now 6
(May 1983) pp8-9. illus.
(Early John Lennon apartment in Liverpool.)
M 1445 Harry, Bill. "'In Town Where I Was Born'."
Beatlefan 2:5 (August 1980) p16.
(The battle over a Beatles' statue in
Liverpool.)
M 1446 Harry, Bill. "London Beatles Museum Update."
Beatlefan 2:6 (October 1980) pp8-9.
(London's Victoria and Albert Museum.)
M 1447 Harry, Bill. "The Long And Winding Road."
The Beatles Book 77 (September 1982)
ppix-xii.
(Neville Stannard's book.)
M 1448 Harry, Bill. "'Love Me Do'," Beatlefan 4:6
(October 1982) pp4-5.
(Former "Mersey Beat" editor looks back.)
M 1449 Harry, Bill. "Oddities." The Beatles Book 49
(May 1980) px.
(Fiction about The Beatles.)
M 1450 Harry, Bill. "Oooops!" The Beatles Book 49
(May 1980) px.
(Published errors on The Beatles.)
M 1451 Harry, Bill. "Over The Water."
The Beatles Book 80 (December 1982)
pp21-23.
(Concerts across the Mersey river, Nov.
1962.)
M 1452 Harry, Bill. "'Paul McCartney:
Composer/Artist'." The Beatles Book 67
(November 1981) ppiii-v.
(On McCartney's book.)
M 1453 Harry, Bill. "Question Time." The Beatles Book 50
(June 1980) pvii.
(Trivia quiz.)
M 1454 Harry, Bill. "Quiz." The Beatles Book 49
(May 1980) pix.
M 1455 Harry, Bill. "Shout! The True Story Of The
Beatles." The Beatles Book 61 (May 1981)
ppiii-v.
(On Philip Norman's biography.)
M 1456 Harry, Bill. "Stu Sutcliffe: Would He Have
Changed The Beatles Had He Lived?"
Record Collector 1 (September 1979)
pp6-8.
M 1457 Harry, Bill. "The Unique Humour Of The
Beatles." The Beatles Book 33 (January 1979)
ppiii-v.
M 1458 Harry, Bill. "What The Beatles Didn't Mean To
Say." The Beatles Book 38 (June 1979)

ppiii-v.
(Controversial lyrics explained.)
M 1459 Harry, Bill. "Where They Lived And Played."
The Beatles Book 75 (July 1982) ppiii-vi.
(Liverpool today.)
M 1460 Harry, Bill. "With A Little Help ... "
The Beatles Book 49 (May 1980) px.
(The Fourmost and The Beatles.)
M 1461 Harry, Bill and Tony Barrow. "The Truth About
The Decca Audition." The Beatles Book 71
(March 1982) ppiii-viii.
M 1462 Hart, Bob. "Beatle Hits: It's 'Yesterday' Again
In Britain." Rolling Stone 214 (June 3, 1976)
p12.
(23 old Beatles songs in Top 100.)
M 1463 Haviv, Mitch. "Cynthia Lennon Twist Framed."
Beatlefan 3:6 (October 1981) p14.
(First U.S. art exhibit, Long Island, NY.)
M 1464 Haviv, Mitch. "'Rockshow': A Review."
Beatlefan 3:2 (February 1981) p17.
(Paul McCartney and Wings concert film.)
M 1465 Hayles, David. "Beatles' Memorabilia: Fan Club
Material, Tour Programmes, Posters,
Magazines, Etc." Record Collector 25
(September 1981) pp4-11. illus.
M 1466 Hayles, David. "Beatles' U.K. Books &
Magazines." Record Collector 17 (January
1981) pp28-33. illus.
(Collectible publications from the early
years.)
M 1467 "Hear That Big Sound." Life 58 (May 21, 1965)
pp90-94+. illus.
(With report by T. Thompson.)
M 1468 "A Heart To Heart Talk With Paul McCartney."
Sixteen Magazine 6:10 (March 1965)
pp22-23.
M 1469 Heckman, Donald. "In The Pop Bag."
American Record Guide (October 1967)
pp168-169. illus.
(On the "Sgt. Pepper" LP.)
M 1470 Hedgepeth, William. "Yellow Submarine." Look 32
(July 23, 1968) pp37-41+. illus.
M 1471 Heenan, Edward F. "Religious Rock: What Is It
Saying." Popular Music & Society 2:4 (1973)
pp311-320.
M 1472 "Hello, Goodbye, Hello" Time 95 (April 20, 1970)
p57. illus.
(Paul McCartney.)
M 1473 "Help! Four Beatles Surrounded By Reunion
Rumors." Variety 270 (April 18, 1973)
p61.
M 1474 Hendra, Tony and Peter Kleinman. "He Blew His
Mind Out In A Car; The True Story Of Paul
McCartney's Death." National Lampoon 1:91
(October 1977) pp77-79.
M 1475 Heneghan, Christy. "The Making Of 'A Hard Day's
Night': Part 1." Beatles Unlimited 8
(July 1976) pp4-6.
(Shooting The Beatles' first film.)
M 1476 Heneghan, Christy. "The Making Of 'A Hard Day's
Night': Part 2." Beatles Unlimited 10
(November 1976) pp4-6.
(Beatles' first film.)
M 1477 Hennessey, H. "Crosby's Co. Faces The Naked
Truth - Bows Nude LP In U.S." Billboard 80
(November 9, 1968) p1+.
("Two Virgins" LP.)
M 1478 Hennessey, M. "Beatles In Europe."
Melody Maker 40 (June 26, 1965) p3. illus.
M 1479 Hennessey, M. "Copyright Error Will Cost EMI
$$; No Royalties Ever Paid On Song In 1964
Beatles Album." Billboard 89 (July 16, 1977)
p6.
M 1480 Hennessey, M. "The Epstein Interviews."
Melody Maker 42 (August 19, 1967) p14.
M 1481 Hennessey, M. "French 'Oo-la-la' The Beatles."
Billboard 77 (July 3, 1965) p18.
M 1482 Hennessey, M. "Love From The Beatles."
Melody Maker 42 (July 22, 1967) p5.
(Interview with Brian Epstein.)

M 1483 Hennessey, M. "'Stars' Story: Inspired By
     Pirate Album." Billboard 93 (August 15, 1981)
     p14+.

M 1484 Henshaw, L. "After The Stones And The Beatles,
     Will Allen Klein Take On The Chancellor?"
     Melody Maker 44 (July 19, 1969) p7.

M 1485 Henshaw, L. "Censored." Melody Maker 47
     (March 11, 1972) pp24-25. illus.
     (On "Give Ireland Back To The Irish.")

M 1486 Henshaw, L. "10 Million Pounds Worth Of Beatles
     Songs." Melody Maker 44 (May 10, 1969)
     p19.

M 1487 Herbeck, R. "Beatles Get No $ From
     'Beatlemania'." Billboard 90 (March 25, 1978)
     p114.

M 1488 Herbeck, R. "Ringo Parodies Twain In Uniquely
     Visual Video Bow." Billboard 90 (April 29,
     1978) p36.

M 1489 Herbeck, R. "Ringo Starr's TV Special Truly
     Special Event." Billboard 90 (March 18, 1978)
     p20. illus.

M 1490 "Here Are The Runners-Up In Our Draw A Beatle
     Competition." The Beatles Book 44 (March
     1967) pp12-13.

M 1493 Hertzberg, H. "Reporter At Large: Poetic
     Larks Bid Bald Eagle Welcome Swan Of
     Liverpool." New Yorker 48 (December 9,
     1972) pp138-152+.
     (John Lennon.)

M 1494 Heyn, Dalma. "The Alarmingly Normal
     McCartneys." McCall's III:II (August 1984)
     pp94-95+. illus.
     (Paul and Linda today.)

M 1495 Hicks, Jim. "Is That You In There, Ringo?"
     Life 66 (June 13, 1969) illus.

M 1496 High Times. Farmingdale, NY: Trans-High Corp.,
     1979.
     (Cover portrait.)

M 1497 "Hightower Heads John, Yoko Anti-Deport Drive."
     Variety 269 (December 6, 1972) p55.

M 1498 Hill, Ronald. "Rattle Of A Simple Girl."
     Theatre World 59 (October 1963) p16. illus.
     (Fairfield Hall concert, Croyden.)

M 1499 Hill, S. "A Miraculous Simplicity."
     Melody Maker 55 (June 14, 1980) p9. illus.
     (Paul McCartney interview.)

M 1500 Hines, Iain. "The Beatles Hamburg Days: An
     Eye-Witness Account." The Beatles Book 12
     (April 1977) ppiii-vi.

M 1501 Hines, Iain. "The Beatles Hamburg Days: An
     Eye-Witness Account, Part 2."
     The Beatles Book 13 (May 1977) ppiii-v.

M 1502 Hines, Iain. "The Beatles Hamburg Days: An
     Eye-Witness Account, Part 3."
     The Beatles Book 14 (June 1977) ppiii-iv.

M 1503 Hines, Iain. "Hamburg Souvenirs."
     The Beatles Book 20 (December 1977)
     pv.
     (Memorabilia.)

M 1504 Hines, Iain. "Hamburg: The City Where The
     Beatles Developed Their Original Sound."
     The Beatles Book 16 (August 1977) ppiii-iv.

M 1505 Hines, Iain. "The Story Behind The Hamburg
     Tapes." The Beatles Book 17 (December 1977)
     ppiii-vi.

M 1506 Hines, Iain. "Their First Visit To Hamburg,
     Part One." The Beatles Book 36 (July 1966)
     p8.

M 1507 Hines, Iain. "Their First Visit To Hamburg,
     Part Two." The Beatles Book 37 (August 1966)
     p11.

M 1508 Hines, Iain. "Their First Visit To Hamburg,
     Final Part." The Beatles Book 38 (September
     1966) p8,31.

M 1509 Hines, Iain. "The Truth About Those Early

Beatles Recordings." The Beatles Book 7
     (November 1976) ppiii-v.

M 1510 Hinton, B. "All Grown Up: Revolver."
     Melody Maker 56 (March 28, 1981) p15. illus.

M 1511 Hirshfeld. "Caricature." Show 4:5 (May 1964)
     p88.
     (Beatles caricature.)

M 1512 "Hirsute Trio." The Beatles Book 75 (October
     1969) p31.
     (Hair and moustache news.)

M 1513 "A Historical Premiere." The Beatles Book 54
     (October 1980) pviii.
     (Premiere of "The Yellow Submarine" film.)

M 1514 "Historic Beatles-Elvis Meeting." Melody Maker
     40 (September 4, 1965) p5.

M 1515 Hoare, Ian. "All Shine On." Let It Rock
     (March 1974) p28+.
     (John Lennon.)

M 1516 Hochadel, Richard M. "A Magical Mystery Tour:
     Collecting Beatles Telecasts, Part 1."
     Goldmine 91 (December 1983) pp40-41+. illus.

M 1517 Hochadel, Richard M. "Yellow Matter Custard:
     Collecting Beatles Broadcasts." Goldmine 77
     (October 1982) pp10-15.

M 1518 Hodenfield, Chris. "George Martin Recalls The
     Boys In The Band." Rolling Stone 217
     (July 15, 1976) p9+. illus.

M 1519 Hodenfield, J. "Delaney & Bonnie's Super
     Times." Rolling Stone 50 (January 21, 1970)
     p8.
     (George Harrison.)

M 1520 Hodenfield, J. "'Ethel? It's Me, Yeah,
     Doreen'." Rolling Stone 60 (June 11, 1970)
     p30.

M 1521 Hoffmann, R. "Der Rest Ist Singsang-Ein
     Ex-Beatle Auf Tournee." Neue Musikzeitung 21
     (August/September 1972) p10. illus.
     (Paul McCartney.)

M 1522 Holbrook, David. "Jerry Baby's."
     Music In Education 28:310 (1964) pp261-264. il

M 1523 Holden, Stephen. "Lennon's Music: A Range Of
     Genius." Rolling Stone 335 (January 22, 1981)
     p64+. illus.

M 1524 Holden, Stephen. "Look Back With Longing."
     Rolling Stone 359 (December 24, 1981)
     p11+.
     (John Lennon.)

M 1525 Holden, Stephen. "On The Wings Of Silly Love
     Songs." Rolling Stone 213 (May 20, 1976)
     p67+.
     (On "Wings At The Speed Of Sound.")

M 1526 Holden, Stephen. "'Que Pasa, New York?' Indeed,
     What Do You Say About Suicide?"
     Rolling Stone 113 (July 20, 1972) p48.
     (On "Some Time In New York City.")

M 1527 Holden, Stephen. "Yoko Ono: In Her Own Write."
     Rolling Stone 347 (July 9, 1981) p55+.
     illus.
     (On the "Season Of Glass" album.)

M 1528 "Hold Out." Design 275 (November 1971)
     p77. illus.
     (Ringo Starr.)

M 1529 "Holiday Snaps August 1963." The Beatles Book 91
     (November 1983) pp24-25. illus.
     (The Beatles vacation in Jersey.)

M 1530 Hollingworth, R. "American Music Scene."
     Melody Maker 47 (August 26, 1972) p8. illus.

M 1531 Hollingworth, R. "John Comes Together - And
     How!" Melody Maker 47 (September 16, 1972)
     p28. illus.

M 1532 Hollingworth, R. "Just Imagine." Melody Maker
     46 (September 4, 1971) p29.
     ("Imagine" album.)

M 1533 Hollingworth, R. "People's Album."
     Melody Maker 47 (June 10, 1972) p9.
     ("Some Time In New York City.")

M 1534 Hollingworth, R. "Save Our Lennons Campaign."
     Melody Maker 47 (June 17, 1972) p6. illus.

M 1535 "Hollywood Bowl." The Beatles Book 15
     (July 1977) pv.

M 1536 Holmstrom, John. "Beat Show." New Statesman 67
        (May 15, 1964) pp783-784.
M 1537 Holyroyd, S. "Second Golden Age Of Pop."
        Melody Maker 41 (October 1966) pp11-13.
        illus.
        (Beatles' songs are evaluated.)
M 1538 Hopkins, Jerry. "Genitalia Slips Quietly Under
        The Counter." Rolling Stone 28 (March 1,
        1969) p6+. illus.
        (John Lennon and Yoko Ono.)
M 1539 Hopkins, Jerry. "James Taylor On Apple: 'The
        Same Old Craperoo'." Rolling Stone 40
        (August 23, 1969) p1+. illus.
M 1540 Hopkins, Jerry. "Lester Since 'A Hard Day's
        Night'." Rolling Stone 106 (April 13, 1974)
        p20.
        (Richard Lester.)
M 1541 Hopkins, Jerry. "Rock & Roll Memorabilia Goes
        Boom." Rolling Stone 231 (January 27, 1977)
        p20+. illus.
M 1542 Hopkins, Jerry. "The Trouble With The Beatles."
        Rolling Stone 62 (July 9, 1970) p12.
M 1543 Horide, Rosie. "'Back To The Egg': Wings' New
        Album Is A Search For Simpler Things."
        The Beatles Book 39 (July 1979) ppiii-v.
M 1544 Horide, Rosie. "'London Town': The Story Behind
        Paul's Latest Album." The Beatles Book 23
        (March 1978) ppiii-v.
M 1545 Horide, Rosie. "The Rutles." The Beatles Book 25
        (May 1978) ppiii-v.
        (On The Beatles parody group.)
M 1546 Horide, Rosie. "Will The Beatles Re-Form?"
        The Beatles Book 24 (April 1978) ppiii-v.
M 1547 Horowitz, I. "Beatles 'Reunited' On 500,000
        Cutout Disks." Billboard 88 (November 6,
        1976) p1+.
        ("Let It Be" album.)
M 1548 Horwood, W. "On Stage."
        Crescendo International 13 (February 1975)
        p4.
M 1549 Hotchkins, A. Bear. "Sugarwater McCartney."
        Willamette Bridge 4:25 (June 24, 1971)
        p19.
M 1550 Houston, B. and C. Roberts. "Beatletalk."
        Melody Maker 39 (May 16, 1964) pp8-9. illus.
M 1551 Howard, Tony. "Beatles In Austria: Dangerous
        Filming In Austrian Alps."
        KRLA Beat (Los Angeles) (June 9, 1965)
        p5,10.
        (Filming Of "Help.")
M 1552 Howes, H.C. "Mik, The Singing Dancing
        Greenlanders." Beaver 295 (Fall 1964)
        pp22-25. illus.
M 1553 "Howling, Not Booing, Says John."
        The Beatles Book 75 (October 1969)
        p31.
        (Toronto concert, September 13-14.)
M 1554 "How One Man Sold The Beatles To America: John
        Lennon - The Inside Story Of His Incredible
        Life." The Star 7:53 (December 30, 1980)
        pp46-47.
M 1556 "How Was The New Album Cover Taken?"
        The Beatles Book 47 (June 1967) p25.
        (Making the jacket of the "Sgt. Pepper"
        LP.)
M 1557 Hughes, D. "Blinkin' Beatles Triumphant Tour."
        Melody Maker 39 (July 4, 1964) p6. illus.
        (Australian tour.)
M 1558 Hughes, D. "Roll Over Australia!" Melody Maker
        39 (June 27, 1964) pp8-9.
M 1559 Hughes, D. "Wet And Wonderful!" Melody Maker 39
        (June 20, 1964) p10. illus.
        (Australian tour.)
M 1560 Hughes, John. "The Fab Four! Adventures In
        Hamburg." National Lampoon 1:91 (October
        1977) pp53-56.
M 1561 Hughes, Liz and Jim Hughes. "Letter To The

Editor." Beatles Unlimited 32 (May 1980)
        p12.
        (Appeal to establish a Liverpool Beatles
        museum.)
M 1562 Hume, P. "The Beatles Forever." Critic 26
        (April/May 1968) pp24-29. illus.
M 1563 Hunger, Julie. "A Chance In A Million."
        The Beatles Book 48 (July 1967) p13.
        (Fan account of watching McCartney's
        house.)
M 1564 "Hungry Beatles Form Apple In Bid For Slice Of
        Trades' Pie." Billboard 80 (May 25, 1968)
        p6.
M 1565 Hunt, Albert. "How Subversive Are The Beatles?"
        Views 5 (Summer 1964) pp55-59.
M 1566 Hunter, George. "Wife Was Planning To Divorce
        John Lennon When He Was Shot."
        National Enquirer 56:37 (April 20, 1982)
        p21.
M 1567 Hunter, N. "Epstein: Restless Empire Builder."
        Billboard 79 (September 9, 1967) p6+.
M 1568 Hutchins, C. "And Here Come The Beatles For One
        More Time (Britain's Biggest-Ever Selling
        Single)." Billboard 76 (February 8, 1964)
        p4+.
M 1569 Hutchins, Chris. "Beatles' Shock Tactics With
        Girls." Globe 28:3 (January 20, 1981)
        pp3-4.
M 1570 Hutchins, Chris. "Elvis Presley." Hit Parader
        XXV:28 (October 1966) pB14. illus.
        (Four hour Bel Air visit, August 27, 1965.)
M 1571 Hutchins, Chris. "The Historic 1965 U.S. Tour."
        Hit Parader XXV:28 (October 1966) ppB2-B3.
        illus.
        (First four tour days in New York City.)
M 1572 Hutchins, Chris. "My Death - By John Lennon."
        Globe 28:2 (January 13, 1981) pp3-4.
M 1573 Hutton, J. "Beatle Listen-In." Melody Maker 42
        (May 27, 1967) p5. illus.
M 1574 Hutton, J. "Beatlemania." Melody Maker 39
        (February 22, 1964) pp10-11. illus.
        (U.S. Tour.)
M 1575 Hutton, J. "Protest Palls - Says Paul."
        Melody Maker 40 (October 2, 1965) p1. illus.
M 1576 Hutton, Jack and Nick James. "Rolling Stone
        Interview: Ringo Starr And George Harrison."
        Rolling Stone 5 (February 10, 1968)
        pp12-13. illus.
        (First published in Melody Maker.)
M 1577 "I Don't Believe In Beatles."
        Willamette Bridge 4:7 (February 18, 1971)
        p9.
M 1578 "'I Don't Like Anything Different Or Unusual'
        Says John." The Beatles Book 38 (September
        1966) pp11-12.
M 1579 Iino, Satoshi. "Ringo On TV Commercial Showing
        How Simple Life Is." Beatles Unlimited 15
        (September 1977) p19.
        (Ringo Starr in Japanese clothing
        commercials.)
M 1580 "I'm A Loser - And I've Lost Someone Who's Near
        To Me." Beatles Unlimited 33 (July 1980)
        p3.
        (Lennon obituary.)
M 1581 "'I'm A Walrus' With Just A Little Lear."
        Rolling Stone 3 (December 14, 1967)
        p21. illus.
M 1582 "In Memoriam ... " Beatlefan 3:1 (December 1980)
        p3.
        (John Lennon eulogy.)
M 1583 "In Memoriam: Mal Evans." Beatles Unlimited 5
        (January 1976) pp3-4.
        (Obituary.)
M 1584 "In Memory Of The Cavern." The Beatles Book 16
        (August 1977) pv.
        (Cavern club.)
M 1585 "In Praise Of John Lennon: The Liverpool Lad As
        Musician, Husband, Father, And Man." People
        14:25 (December 22, 1980) pp26-36.
M 1586 "Inscrutable Orientals Flip Lids Over Beatles

During Tokyo Stand." Variety 243 (July 6,
1966) p39.

M 1587 "Inside Wings: An Interview With Ex-Drummer Joe
English." Beatlefan 1:1 (December 1978)
p1,3.

M 1588 "In The Beatles Song Writing Factory."
Melody Maker 41 (July 16, 1966) p10. illus.

M 1589 Iozzia, B. "2 Beatles Raise 250G For Refugees
Of E. Pakistan In Historic N.Y. Benefit."
Variety 263 (August 4, 1971) p43+.

M 1590 "Irate AFM Flips Lid Over Invasion Of 'Rocking
Redcoats' Sans Culture." Variety 234
(March 25, 1964) p49.

M 1591 "Irate Beatles To Fight ATV's Move To Win
Control Of Northern Songs." Variety 254
(April 16, 1969) p55.

M 1592 "I Read The News Today, Oh Boy." Time 117
(January 12, 1981) p57. illus.
(John Lennon.)

M 1593 "I Read The News Today Oh Boy .... "
Beatles Unlimited
(Regular feature, issues 1- .)

M 1594 Ireland, William. "Another Lennon." Us 5:8
(April 14, 1981) pp24-29. illus.
(Julian Lennon.)

M 1595 Irwin, C. "Cruising With Macca." Melody Maker
53 (April 1, 1978) pp26-27. illus.

M 1596 Irwin, C. "Harrison's Dark Horses."
Melody Maker 49 (August 31, 1974) p15.

M 1597 "I Saw Pinetop Spit Blood." Rolling Stone 54
(February 19, 1970) p10.
(Beatles and the Manson killings.)

M 1598 "Is Beatlemania Dead? North American Tour."
Time 88 (September 2, 1966) p38. illus.

M 1599 "Is Klaatu Band The Beatles?" Billboard 89
(March 26, 1977) p20.

M 1600 "Is Klaatu Spelled Backwards Really Mop Top
Four?" Variety 286 (April 6, 1977)
p110.

M 1601 "Israel Gets First Single In Five Years."
Billboard (Decembe 18, 1982) p9.
(Jackson/McCartney "This Girl Is Mine.")

M 1602 "It Happened In 1967." Rolling Stone 6
(February 24, 1968) pp12-13.

M 1603 "It Happened In 1968." Rolling Stone 26
(February 1, 1969) p15.
(Beatles take song and album of the year.)

M 1604 "It Happened In 1968." Rolling Stone 26
(February 1, 1969) p15.
(Cookie Crumbles Award: Pete Best.)

M 1605 "It Happened In 1968." Rolling Stone 26
(February 1, 1969) p19.
(Paul McCartney on conditions in India.)

M 1606 "It Happened In 1968." Rolling Stone 26
(February 1, 1969) p19.
(What The Beatles did in 1968.)

M 1607 "It Happened In 1969." Rolling Stone 51
(February 7, 1970) p27.
(McCartney death hoax.)

M 1608 "It Happened In 1969." Rolling Stone 51
(February 7, 1970) p26.
(The Beatles Memorial Award: Ringo Starr.)

M 1609 "It Happened In 1969." Rolling Stone 51
(February 7, 1970) p28. illus.
(Best Record Jacket Design: Plastic Ono
Band.)

M 1610 "It Happened In 1970." Rolling Stone 75
(February 4, 1971) p46.
(Shitkicker of The Year: Ringo Starr.)

M 1611 "It Happened In 1970." Rolling Stone 75
(February 4, 1971) p46.
(Spirit In The Sky Award: George Harrison.)

M 1612 "It Happened In 1970." Rolling Stone 75
(February 4, 1971) p46.
(Screaming Yellow Zonker: Yoko Ono.)

M 1613 "It Happened In 1970." Rolling Stone 75
(February 4, 1971) p47.
(Highway 61 Award: John Lennon/Ono Band.)

M 1614 "'It's All A Fantasy, Putting The Beatles Back
Together'." Melody Maker 49 (November 2,

1974) p13. illus.
(George Harrison interview.)

M 1615 "It's Easy If You Try." Canadian Dimension 15
(June 1981) pp50-53. illus.
(John Lennon.)

M 1616 "'I've Thrown Away 30 Songs' Says George."
The Beatles Book 39 (October 1966)
pp6-8.

M 1617 Ivins, Molly. "Lennon And Gun Laws."
Texas Observer 73 (February 27, 1981)
p24.

M 1618 "I Wanna Hold Your Hand ... Again." Time 110
(August 8, 1977) pp54-55. illus.
("Beatlemania" stage play.)

M 1619 "I Wanna Hold Your Stock." Newsweek 65
(March 1, 1965) pp70-71.
(Northern Songs.)

M 1620 "I Want To Write Songs For Revolution." Augur 2:1
(June 1971) p8.

M 1621 Jack, Alex. "The John Lennon Memorial Peace
Contest." East West Journal 11:6 (June 1981)
pp42-45.

M 1622 Jackson, Jeffrey M. and Vernon R. Padgett.
"With A Little Help From My Friend: Social
Loafing And The Lennon-McCartney Songs."
Personality and Social Psychology Bulletin
8:4 (December 1982) pp672-677.

M 1623 Jacobson, B. "By An Unknown Master - The
Baroque Beatles Book."
High Fidelity/Musical America 16 (February
1966) p67.
(On the "Baroque Beatles Book" album.)

M 1624 Jacopetti, R. "Lennon And Primal Scream:
Janov." St. Louis Outlaw 2:1 (April 14, 1971)
p4.

M 1625 Jahn, Mike. "After Sgt. Pepper; Magical Mystery
Tour Album." Saturday Review 50 (December
30, 1967) p55.

M 1626 Jahn, Mike. "Berryized Beatles, Beatlized
Monkees, Unmonkeed Dolenz, Jones."
High Fidelity/Musical America 26 (October
1976) pp96-97. illus.
("Rock 'N' Roll Music" album.)

M 1627 Jahr, C. "'Beatlemania' Is A Scrapbook Of Soggy
Standards." Rolling Stone 243 (July 14, 1977)
p30.
(Stageshow.)

M 1628 James, Clive. "A Cavern In Arcadia." Cream 17
(October 1972) pp24-26+.

M 1629 James, Frederick. "American Tour Report."
The Beatles Book 27 (October 1965)
pp11-15+.
(August 1965.)

M 1630 James, Frederick. "At London's Finsbury Park
Astoria ... Their Spectacular Christmas
Show." The Beatles Book 7 (February 1964)
pp25-27.
(December 1963-January 1964.)

M 1631 James, Frederick. "Beatles Have A Ball In Fancy
Dress." The Beatles Book 55 (February 1968)
pp6-9.
(December 21 "M.M.T." cast party.)

M 1632 James, Frederick. "Beatles Now!"
The Beatles Book 71 (June 1979) p31.
(Current news.)

M 1633 James, Frederick. "Beatles Talk."
The Beatles Book
(Regular feature, issues 19-26 & 29-44,
1965-1967.)

M 1634 James, Frederick. "Behind The Headlines."
The Beatles Book 30 (January 1966)
pp13-14.
(December tour of U.K.)

M 1635 James, Frederick. "The Fifth Beatle Gets
Married." The Beatles Book 63 (October 1968)
pp6-9.
(Neil Aspinall weds Suzy Ornstein.)

M 1636 James, Frederick. "George Speaking."
The Beatles Book 16 (November 1964)
p7,9.

(Interview.)

M 1637 James, Frederick. "How I Won The War."
         The Beatles Book 50 (September 1967)
         pp8-11.
         (John Lennon's film role.)

M 1638 James, Frederick. "In The Studio."
         The Beatles Book 74 (September 1969)
         pp8-13.
         (Recording "Abbey Road" album.)

M 1639 James, Frederick. "Is Sgt. Pepper Too Advanced
         For The Average Pop Fan To Appreciate?"
         The Beatles Book 49 (August 1967) pp24-27.

M 1640 James, Frederick. "John And Yoko Talk About Art
         And Vibrations." The Beatles Book 63
         (October 1968) pp23-24+.

M 1641 James, Frederick. "John Speaking."
         The Beatles Book 15 (October 1964)
         p7,9.
         (Interview.)

M 1642 James, Frederick. "Lennon & McCartney
         (Songwriters) Ltd." The Beatles Book 2
         (September 1963) p20.

M 1643 James, Frederick. "The Mystery Partly
         Explained." The Beatles Book 52 (November
         1967) p14.
         ("Magical Mystery Tour" TV film.)

M 1644 James, Frederick. "New Year's Day: A Date To
         Remember Each Year For The Beatles."
         The Beatles Book 66 (January 1969)
         pp9-11.
         (Anniversary of the Decca audition.)

M 1645 James, Frederick. "Paul Speaking."
         The Beatles Book 13 (August 1964) p7,9.
         (Interview.)

M 1646 James, Frederick. "A Return Visit."
         The Beatles Book 67 (February 1969)
         pp21-22.
         (Visit to fan club headquarters,
         Liverpool.)

M 1647 James, Frederick. "Revolution Report: How The
         Beatles Recorded Their New Single."
         The Beatles Book 60 (July 1968) pp6-8.

M 1648 James, Frederick. "Ringo Speaking."
         The Beatles Book 14 (September 1964)
         pp11-13.
         (Interview.)

M 1649 James, Frederick. "Rumour-Bustin' Report."
         The Beatles Book 6 (January 1964) p25.

M 1650 James, Frederick. "Rumour-Bustin' Report No.
         2." The Beatles Book 15 (October 1964)
         p22.

M 1651 James, Frederick. "So Many Are McCartney's
         Ideas" The Beatles Book 71 (June 1969)
         p23.

M 1652 James, Frederick. "Some Beatle Singles Are No
         Longer Obtainable." The Beatles Book 56
         (March 1968) p13.

M 1653 James, Frederick. "Their Fan Club Secretaries:
         Anne Collingham & Bettina Rose."
         The Beatles Book 5 (December 1963)
         pp22-23.

M 1654 James, Frederick. "Their Road Manager: Neil
         Aspinall." The Beatles Book 3 (October 1963)
         pp20-21.

M 1655 James, Frederick. "Tracks You've Never Heard."
         The Beatles Book 64 (November 1968)
         pp21-24.

M 1656 James, Frederick. "Two Portraits Of George."
         The Beatles Book 68 (March 1969) pp21-22.

M 1657 James, Frederick. "Two Portraits Of John."
         The Beatles Book 70 (May 1969) pp20-23.

M 1658 James, Frederick. "Two Portraits Of Ringo."
         The Beatles Book 69 (April 1969) pp20-22.

M 1659 James, Frederick. "What You Would Like The Boys
         To Do In '69." The Beatles Book 65
         (December 1968) pp7-10.
         (Fans' wishes for the group.)

M 1660 James, Frederick. "Why Did They Grow
         Moustaches?" The Beatles Book 46 (May 1967)
         p7,31.

M 1661 James, Frederick. "Why Haven't The Beatles
         Fixed Another Concert Tour?"
         The Beatles Book 45 (April 1967) p6.

M 1662 James, Frederick. "Why The Beatles?"
         The Beatles Book 8 (March 1964) p27.

M 1663 James, Frederick. "World's First In-Depth
         Preview Of The Beatles' 'Get Back' LP
         Recordings." The Beatles Book 73 (August
         1969) pp7-15.

M 1664 James, Frederick. "The Writing On The Wall."
         The Beatles Book 21 (April 1965) p6,31.
         (On The Beatles' fan club.)

M 1665 James, Nick. "London: Beatles Clip Banned."
         Rolling Stone 4 (January 20, 1968)
         p22.
         ("Hello/Goodbye" film short not shown in
         U.S.)

M 1666 James, Nick. "London: Traffic Moves, Cream In
         Gear." Rolling Stone 3 (December 14, 1967)
         p23.
         (Paul McCartney is in Nice.)

M 1667 James, Nick. "Rolling Stone Interview: George
         Harrison." Rolling Stone 6 (February 24,
         1968) p16. illus.
         (Continued from Feb. 10 issue.)

M 1668 Janov, Arthur and Jacopetti. "Lennon And Primal
         Scream." St. Louis Outlaw 2:1 (April 14,
         1971) p4.

M 1669 Janssen, Koos. "Abbey Road." Beatles Unlimited 1
         (March 1975) pp3-6.
         (Discussion of the LP.)

M 1670 Jay, S.M. "Beatles' Poetry: A Rock Literature."
         Record (December 1968) pp262-267.

M 1671 Jerome, Jim. "The Lord Must Want The Beatles To
         Fly Again: He Gave The McCartneys Wings."
         People 5 (June 7, 1976) pp35-38. illus.

M 1672 "Jimmy McCulloch." Record Collector 3
         (November 1979) p19.
         (Obituary.)

M 1673 Jobes, William. "Lennon: The Artist, The
         Beatle." Biography News 2 (March 1975)
         pp375-376.
         (Interview.)

M 1674 Joe, R. "ABKCO Wins One, Loses One In Beatles
         Litigation." Billboard 88 (June 19, 1976)
         p4.

M 1675 Joe, R. "N.Y. Judge Rules N.Y. A Fine Place For
         Beatles Suits." Billboard 87 (November 1,
         1975) p12.

M 1676 "Joe Jones." Flash Art (Italy) 54 (May 1975)
         pp30-31.
         (Includes Yoko Ono note;text of her record
         "Fly.")

M 1677 "John and George Get Their U.S. Visas."
         Rolling Stone 58 (May 14, 1970) p8. illus.

M 1678 "John And Ono Pitching Pacifism In Times Sq."
         Variety 257 (December 17, 1969) p53.

M 1679 "John And Yoko Arrival In Toronto To Push Peace
         Stirs Unpeaceful Aura." Variety (December
         24, 1969) p2+.

M 1681 "John And Yoko Disavow Toronto." Jazz & Pop 9
         (June 1970) pp8-9.

M 1682 "John And Yoko Disgusted."
         Georgia Straight Augur 1:12 (April 14, 1970)
         p10.

M 1683 "John & Yoko Fight Deportation Decision;
         Hardhats Join Appeal." Rolling Stone 133
         (April 26, 1973) p10. illus.

M 1684 "John And Yoko In Newark, New Jersey."
         Rolling Stone 26 (February 1, 1969)
         p12.

M 1685 "John And Yoko On A Peace Cruise."
         Rolling Stone 42 (September 20, 1969)
         p8.

M 1686 "John And Yoko On The Town." Rolling Stone 86
         (July 8, 1971) p10. illus.

M 1688 "John And Yoko Quit Toronto Festival."
        Kaleidoscope-Madison 2:9 (May 5, 1970)
        p3.
M 1689 "John And Yoko's Christmas Gifts."
        Rolling Stone 50 (January 21, 1970)
        p6.
M 1690 "John And Yoko's First Song." The Beatles Book 72
        (July 1969) p31.
        ("Give Peace A Chance.")
M 1691 "John And Yoko Slapped Hard." Rolling Stone 29
        (March 15, 1969) p12.
        ("Two Virgins" album.)
M 1692 "John & Yoko's New Idea: Pop Combo With
        Chimps." Variet 258 (April 8, 1970)
        p107.
M 1693 "John At Home." The Beatles Book 51 (October
        1967) pp8-11.
M 1694 "John At Home, Part Two." The Beatles Book 52
        (November 1967) pp13-14.
M 1695 "John Lennon." The Beatles Book 57 (January
        1981) ppiii-v.
        (Eulogies.)
M 1696 "John Lennon." Oui 9 (January 1980) p23. illus.
        (Interview.)
M 1697 "John Lennon." Radical History Review 24:188
        (Fall 1980)
M 1698 "John Lennon: A Celebration." Us 5:25
        (December 8, 1981) p49.
        (Advertisement for a 3-hour radio special.)
M 1699 "John Lennon And Yoko Ono: Our Films."
        Filmmakers Newsletter 1:8 (June 1973)
        pp25-27. illus.
        (Interview; special attention to
        "Imagine.")
M 1700 "John Lennon/Bag One." Rolling Stone 62
        (July 9, 1970) p37. illus.
        (Advertisement for lithographs.)
M 1701 "John Lennon/Beatles Discography."
        Schwann-2 Record & Tape Guide 34 (Spring
        1981) pp4-5.
M 1702 "John Lennon Finds Worm In Beatles' Apple."
        Variety 256 (September 24, 1969) p55.
M 1703 "John Lennon Get Cheesed Off." Rolling Stone 53
        (March 7, 1970) p12.
        (Lennon's hair cut.)
M 1704 "John Lennon Had Life After Death Pact With
        Yoko." The Star 7:53 (December 30, 1980)
        p11.
M 1705 "John Lennon: His Final Words On Beatle Music."
        Playboy 28 (April 1981) p179+. illus.
M 1706 "The John Lennon Horoscope." Beatles Unlimited 2
        (June 1975) pp16-17.
M 1707 "John Lennon: Ineligible Alien."
        Rolling Stone 33 (May 17, 1969) p8.
M 1708 "John Lennon Key To Beatles' Future As Group
        Loses Their Togetherness." Variety 258
        (February 18, 1970) p57.
M 1709 "John Lennon (1940-1980)." Rolling Stone 335
        (January 22, 1981) p42+. illus.
        (Chronology.)
M 1710 "John Lennon Remembered, Oct. 9, 1940 - Dec. 8,
        1980." International Musician 79 (January
        1981) p6. illus.
M 1711 "John Lennon Reviews This Week's New Pop
        Records." Melody Maker 39 (January 18, 1964)
        p9. illus.
M 1712 "John Lennon, R.I.P." Music Trades 128
        (December 1980) p10.
M 1713 "John Lennon's Bag." Jazz & Pop 9 (May 1970)
        p10.
        (Lennon's lithographs.)
M 1714 "John Lennon Seen A Winner But Must Pay 7G To
        Big 7." Variety 283 (July 21, 1976)
        p54.
M 1715 "John Lennon's TV Documentary Vs. Capital
        Punishment." Variety (December 17, 1969)
        p38.
M 1716 "John Lennon: The Untold Story."
        National Enquirer (December 30, 1980)

        p36.
M 1717 "John Lennon: Written In The Stars."
        TAT Journal 11 (1981) pp116-122. illus.
        (Astrological transits and his death;
        cover photo.)
M 1718 "John Ono-Lennon." Rolling Stone 337 (February
        19, 1981) p6.
        (Letters to editor.)
M 1719 "John, Paul, George, & Ringo . . . And Bert."
        Variety 276 (August 21, 1974) p58.
        (Stage show.)
M 1720 "John's Last Testament." Melody Maker 56
        (March 7, 1981) p5.
M 1721 "John's Legal Case: Few Options Left."
        Rolling Stone 168 (August 29, 1974)
        p19+.
        (Deportation pending.)
M 1723 Johnson, B.D. "The Boys In The BBC Band."
        MacLean's 95 (April 12, 1982) p66. illus.
        (Radio program "The Beatles At The Beeb.")
M 1724 Johnson, Paul. "The Menace Of Beatlism."
        New Statesman 67 (February 28, 1964)
        pp326-327.
M 1725 Johnson, Rick. "A Case Of Jello Venom." Creem
        10 (June 1978) pp55-56. illus.
M 1726 Johnson, Rick. "Wimp Rock Will Never Die."
        Creem 12 (December 1980) illus.
        (Paul McCartney.)
M 1727 "Johnyoko Drive." Rolling Stone 112 (July 6,
        1972) p8.
M 1728 "John/Yoko Lie Low Until The Baby Comes."
        Rolling Stone 57 (April 30, 1970) p12.
M 1729 Jolidon, Laurence. "Anyone Here Seen America."
        Texas Observer 72 (December 26, 1980)
        p5+.
        (John Lennon.)
M 1731 Jones, J. "Hottest McCartneys These Days Don't
        Go For A Song - Linda's Prints Fetch
        $1,000." People 9 (January 30, 1978)
        pp70-71. illus.
M 1732 Jones, N. "Beatle George And Where He's At."
        Melody Maker 42 (December 16, 1967)
        pp8-9. illus.
M 1733 Jones, N. "People Put You On A Pedestal And
        Really Believe You're Different."
        Melody Maker 42 (December 30, 1967)
        p9. illus.
M 1734 Jones, Nick. "London: Beatle Magic, UFO
        (R.I.P.), And Nice Nice." Rolling Stone 2
        (November 23, 1967) p19.
M 1735 Jones, P. "The Beatles' Best Back As Film
        Aide." Billboard 91 (July 28, 1979)
        p40.
        (Pete Best.)
M 1736 Jones, P. "British Invasion." Billboard 88
        (July 4, 1976) p42+. illus.
M 1737 Jones, P. "Ringo Starts Label; No Reunion
        Possible." Billboard 87 (May 3, 1975)
        p3+.
M 1738 Jones, Peter. "April 1963: The Start Of A
        Legend." The Beatles Book 37 (May 1979)
        ppiii-v.
        (Beatles' money earning begins in earnest.)
M 1739 Jones, Peter. "The Beatles' Christmas Concert."
        The Beatles Book 32 (December 1978)
        ppiii-v.
        (December 1963 concert.)
M 1740 Jones, Peter. "The Beatles' Early Tours."
        The Beatles Book 49 (May 1980) ppiii-vii.
M 1741 Jones, Peter. "Beatles Facts: Sorting Out The
        Truth From Fiction." Record Collector 10
        (June 1980) pp18-21. illus.
        (Problems of Beatle biography.)
M 1742 Jones, Peter. "The Beatles' Incredible 1963

Stage Shows." The Beatles Book 52 (November
    1967) ppiii-viii.
        (Especially Southend Odeon, Dec. 9, 1963.)
M 1743 Jones, Peter. "Buddy Holly's Rare Misses."
    Record Collector 3 (November 1979)
    p5.
        (Paul McCartney's interest in Holly.)
M 1744 Jones, Peter. "An Early Interview With The
    Beatles." The Beatles Book 50 (June 1980)
    ppIII-VI.
        (August 1963.)
M 1745 Jones, Peter. "How The Beatles Sold 'Sgt.
    Pepper'." Record Collector 2 (October 1979)
    pp6-8.
M 1746 Jones, Peter. "John In His Own Quotes."
    The Beatles Book 68 (December 1981)
    ppIII-VI.
        (Memorable Lennonisms.)
M 1747 Jones, Peter. "Northern Songs Ltd. For Beatle
    Songs Unlimited." The Beatles Book 21
    (April 1965) pp9-13.
        (On Dick James.)
M 1748 Jones, Peter. "The People Behind The Beatles."
    The Beatles Book 52 (August 1980) ppiii-x.
        (Brian Epstein, Tony Barrow, George
        Martin, etc.)
M 1749 Jones, Peter. "'Please Please Me': The Single
    That Almost Wasn't Made" The Beatles Book 35
    (March 1979) ppiii-v.
M 1750 Jones, Peter. "UK Colleagues Generous With
    Their Tributes." Billboard (December 20,
    1980)
        (Eulogy.)
M 1751 "Judge Denies Motion For New 'Sweet Lord'
    Trial." Billboard 94 (January 30, 1982)
    p54.
M 1752 "Julian Lennon Visits Yoko." Rolling Stone 380
    (October 14, 1982) p50.
        (At New York's Hit Factory studios.)
M 1753 Jullian, Marcel. "Il Y Avait Kennedy, De
    Gaulle, Les Beatles." Le Figaro Magazine 99
    (December 13, 1980) pp76-81.
M 1754 Jurgs, Michael. "Der Tod Des Beatle (Die
    Beatles Story)." Stern (Hamburg, W. Ger.) 52
    (December 1982) pp8-18-128+. illus.
M 1755 "Just Before The End." Life 4:2 (February 1981)
    p74. illus.
        (John Lennon.)
M 1756 Kahn, H. "Beatles To The Rescue As Fans Take
    The Plunge (Amsterdam)." Melody Maker 39
    (June 20, 1964) p4.
M 1757 Kaminsky, Peter. "(Blind Lemon Preston)": Black
    Troubadour; A Credit To His Race."
    National Lampoon 1:91 (October 1977)
    pp74-75.
M 1758 Kane, Art. "Photographic Impressions Of Beatle
    Songs." Life 65 (September 20, 1968)
    pp63-71.
M 1759 Kanze, Peter. "The Beatles And New York Radio."
    Goldmine 70 (March 1982) pp11-12.
M 1760 Kaplan, Lisa Faye. "Talking With Ringo Starr."
    Redbook 157:1 (May 1981) pp14,16. illus.
M 1761 "Karma Submits Plan On Toronto Peacefest."
    Billboard 82 (March 14, 1970) p4.
M 1762 Katz, Gregory. "Inside The Dakota."
    Rolling Stone 335 (January 22, 1981)
    p17+. illus.
M 1763 Kaylan, Melik. "Law And Disorder."
    Village Voice 26 (January 28, 1981)
    p34.
        (John Lennon.)
M 1764 Kelly, Freda. "Four Points Of View: The Magical
    Mystery Tour." The Beatles Book 52
    (November 1967) pp6-11.
        (Four fans discuss the filming of "M.M.T.")
M 1765 Kelly, Sean. "The Second Coming Of The
    Beatles." National Lampoon 1:91 (October
    1977) pp80-81.
M 1766 Kemper, P. "John Lennon: Zum Verlust Einer
    Symbolfigur." HiFi Stereophonie 20

(March 1981) p250. illus.
M 1767 Kempton, M. "Mark Chapman's Family."
    New York Review of Books 28 (October 22,
    1981) p28.
        (John Lennon.)
M 1768 Kennely, Patricia. "An Apple A Day."
    Jazz & Pop 7 (July 1968) p30.
        (Apple Corps Ltd.)
M 1769 Kennely, Patricia. "Green Apples." Jazz & Pop 7
    (November 1968) pp30-31.
M 1770 "A Kicker Of A Flicker Laid Way Down South
    Where The West Begins, Starring Ringo, The
    Fastest Shot In Liddypool, And The Three
    Other Ornery Blokes." Sixteen Magazine 6:10
    (March 1965) pp6-9.
M 1771 "Kid's New Macabre Game: Is Paul McCartney
    Dead?" Variety 256 (October 22, 1969)
    p67.
M 1772 "Kids 'Won't Speak To Me' So Grandmas Get Up
    $50 For Beatles CP Benefit." Variety 236
    (September 9, 1964) p1+.
M 1773 Kiley, P. "Fab Macca Waives The Rules."
    Melody Maker 54 (December 8, 1979)
    p12. illus.
        (Paul McCartney.)
M 1774 Kilmartin, Terry. "A Beatles Report From
    Australia." The Beatles Book 56 (March 1968)
    p10.
        (Record chart activity.)
M 1775 King, Bill. "A Chat With Derek Taylor."
    Beatlefan 4:6 (October 1982) pp9-10,29.
        (Interview.)
M 1776 King, Bill. "A Conversation With May Pang."
    Beatlefan 5:1 (December 1982) pp7-8.
        (Interview.)
M 1777 King, Bill. "The Family Way, Part II: The
    Cynthia Lennon Interview." Beatlefan 4:3
    (April 1982) pp5-6.
M 1778 King, Bill. "The Family Way: The Cynthia Lennon
    Interview." Beatlefan 4:2 (February 1982)
    pp4-6.
        (Part One; interviewed in Atlanta,
        December 1981.)
M 1779 King, Bill. "The Family Way: The Mike McCartney
    Interview." Beatlefan 4:2 (February 1982)
    pp7-8.
        (Part One; interviewed in December 1981.)
M 1780 King, Bill. "Jurgen Vollmer Interview, Part
    II." Beatlefan 4:6 (October 1982) p6.
M 1781 King, Bill. "The Mike McCartney Interview."
    Beatlefan 4:3 (April 1982) pp7-8.
        (Second installment.)
M 1782 King, Mollie Parry. "Lennon Remembered."
    Beatlefan 3:1 (December 1980) pp22-23.
        (Eulogy.)
M 1783 King, Mollie Parry. "Let Him Go Nameless."
    Beatlefan 3:2 (February 1981) p12.
        (Mark David Chapman.)
M 1784 King, Timothy. "A Decade Without The Beatles."
    Beatlefan 2:4 (June 1980) pp6-7.
        (Fans discuss a possible reunion.)
M 1785 King, William P. "The Beatles Rarities."
    Beatlefan 2:3 (April 1980) pp1,4,6.
        (Background on the album.)
M 1786 King, William P. "Fan Fest Update." Beatlefan 2:5
    (August 1980) pp14,18.
        (Chicago fan convention, August 8-9, 1980.)
M 1787 King, William P. "15 Years Of Beatlemania! Has
    It Really Been That Long?" Beatlefan 1:2
    (February 1979) p1,3.
M 1788 King, William P. "'Instant Memories' Flooding
    Market." Beatlefan 3:2 (February 1981)
    pp16-17.
        (Books and magazines following Lennon's
        death.)
M 1789 King, William P. "A Letter From The Publisher
    ... " Beatlefan 3:2 (February 1981)
    p3.
        (Editorial.)
M 1790 King, William P. "A Letter From The Publisher

... " Beatlefan 3:6 (October 1981)
p29.
(Editorial.)

M 1791 King, William P. "We Loved To Turn Them On: A
Complete Beatles U.S. TV Chronology."
Beatlefan 4:1 (December 1981) pp4-6.

M 1792 King, William P. and Timothy P. King. "Fan Fest
Update." Beatlefan 1:5 (August 1979)
p10.
(Chicago "Beatlefest" fan convention.)

M 1793 King, William P. and Timothy P. King. "Fan Fest
Update." Beatlefan (April 1980) p12.
(New York Beatlefest, March 28-30, 1980.)

M 1794 "King And The Beatles Make A Cartoon Movie."
Editor and Publisher 101 (August 10, 1968)
p59.
("Yellow Submarine.")

M 1795 Kinnersley, Simon. "Son Of A ... " Beatlefan 2:5
(August 1980) p23.
(Interviews with Julian Lennon & Zak
Starkey.)

M 1796 Kirb. "The Beatles Story As A Book Of Facts."
Variety 283 (May 12, 1976) p450.

M 1797 Kirby, F. "The Beatles Have Gone, But
International Music Hasn't Been The Same
Since British Wave Hit In Early 60's."
Variety 293 (January 3, 1979) p167+.

M 1798 Kirk, D. "Why Japan Fears Paul McCartney."
New Statesman 99 (January 25, 1980)
p110.

M 1799 Kirkeby, M. "Geffen Records Signs Lennons,
Elton John." Rolling Stone 330 (November 13,
1980) p36.

M 1800 Kirmser, Earl. "Ferry Back Across The Mersey."
Rolling Stone 105 (March 30, 1972)
p12+. illus.
(The Cavern Club.)

M 1801 Kirsch, B. "Yoko Promos Real 'Top 40' Solo
Album." Billboard 85 (September 29, 1973)
p20.

M 1802 "Kirshner Entertainment Links With Britain's
ATV To Form Major Pub." Variety 260
(August 19, 1970) p47.

M 1803 Kittleson, B. "Beatles Giving Trade A Solid
Bite." Billboard 76 (January 25, 1964)
p4.

M 1804 "Klein, Beatles' Business Agreement Is Spelled
Out." Billboard 81 (May 31, 1969) p94.

M 1805 "Klein Claim Act Against Beatles Gets
Dismissed." Billboard 86 (November 1974)
p3.

M 1806 "Klein Explains Apple's Stand." Billboard 83
(December 4, 1971) p4+.
("Concert for Bangla Desh" LP.)

M 1807 "Klein: It's John's Peace Festival."
Rolling Stone 54 (March 19, 1970) p8.

M 1808 "Klein Refutes McCartney On Beatles' State Of
$$ Union." Billboard 83 (January 30, 1971)
p3.

M 1809 "Klein's Abkco Industries To Take Over Beatles'
Apple Corps." Variety 266 (February 23, 1972)
p57.

M 1810 "Klein Swings First Deal For Beatles In
Settling Assets Row With Triumph." Variety
255 (July 16, 1969) p55.

M 1811 "Klein, Three Beatles In Split." Billboard 85
(April 14, 1973) p44+.

M 1812 "Klein Vs. Lennon Suit Stays In NY." Variety
275 (July 24, 1974) p51.

M 1813 Knight, M.E. and E.G. Katzenstein. "Letters To
The Recordings Editor." Saturday Review 52
(March 29, 1969) p60.
(Reply to E. Sander's "The Beatles," Dec.
28.)

M 1814 Knobler, P. "Editorial." Crawdaddy 75
(August 1977) p5. illus.
(Beatles' continuing popularity.)

M 1815 Knowles, Timothy. "The Fire And The Wheel: John
Lennon And Paul McCartney In Perspective."
Beatles Now 5 (Winter 1983) pp14-15. illus.

M 1816 Kofsky, Frank. "Rolling Stones, Their Satanic
Majesties Request." Jazz & Pop 7 (April 1968)
pp12-15.

M 1817 Kofsky, Frank. "The Scene." Jazz & Pop 7
(February 1968) pp32-33. illus.

M 1818 Kohlmann, W. "Schueler Des 5. Und 6.
Schulijahrs Analysieren Beatlessongs."
Musik Und Bildung 12 (May 1980) pp320-322.
illus.

M 1819 Kohn, Howard. "National Rifle Association."
Rolling Stone 343 (May 14, 1981)
illus. (Cover +.)

M 1820 Kolanjian, Steve. "The Beatles: Part One - On
Disc." Aware 7 (Spring 1981) pp3-20.
(Discography.)

M 1821 Kolanjian, Steve and Mike Rapsis. "The Beatles:
Part One - On Disc." Aware 8 (Winter 1981)
pp3-6.
(Discography continued.)

M 1822 Kooistra, Ger. "John Lennon's Death - An
Astrological View." Beatles Unlimited 34/35 (1
pp12-13.

M 1823 Koolmees, Andre. "Beatles Marathon."
Beatles Unlimited 41 (1982) pp4-6.
(Amsterdam Beatles convention, April 1982.)

M 1824 Kopkind, A. "I Wanna Hold Your Head: John
Lennon After The Fall." Ramparts 9
(April 1971) pp18-19+.

M 1825 Kordosh, J. "John Lennon 1940-1980; Nothing To
Do To Save His Life." Creem 12 (March 1981)
pp2-3. illus.

M 1826 Kozak, Roman. "ABKCO Gets $5 Mil; Pays
$800,000." Billboard 89 (January 22, 1977)
p124.

M 1827 Kozak, Roman. "May Pang Looks Back At 'Loving
John' Days." Billboard (September 3, 1983)
p39.

M 1828 Kozak, Roman. "No Opening, But Beatles Show
Big." Billboard 89 (October 29, 1977)
p42.
(Stage show "Beatlemania.")

M 1829 Kozak, Roman. "Rock 'N' Rolling: Apple Corp.
Losing Apple As Partner." Billboard 92
(June 7, 1980) p52.

M 1830 Kozak, Roman and E. Krentzel. "Rock 'N'
Rolling's McCartney's Arrest Cancels Japan
Tour." Billboard 92 (January 26, 1980)
p14. illus.

M 1831 Kozak, Roman. "Rock 'N' Rolling: McCartney's
Jailing Concludes In Japan." Billboard 92
(February 2, 1980) p55.

M 1832 Kozak, Roman. "Rock 'N' Rolling: Year One Band
Pays Tribute To Lennon." Billboard 93
(February 21, 1981) p37. illus.

M 1833 Kraai, Lila. "Beatlefest '82." Goldmine 77
(October 1982) p9.
(Los Angeles convention, July 9-11.)

M 1834 "Kremlin Is Going Dada Over Beatles." Variety
283 (July 7, 1976) p1.

M 1835 Kroll, Jack. "Beatles Vs. Stones; Rolling
Stones As Rivals." Newsweek 71 (January 1,
1968) pp62-63. illus.

M 1836 Kroll, Jack. "It's Getting Better." Newsweek 69
(June 26, 1967) p70. illus.

M 1837 Kroll, Jack. "Strawberry Fields Forever."
Newsweek 96 (December 22, 1980) pp41-44.
illus.

M 1838 Kubernik, H. "I'm Touring Soon, Says Harrison."
Melody Maker 51 (November 27, 1976)
p57. illus.
(Interview.)

M 1839 Kurtz, Irma. "In The Bag: Yoko Ono." Nova
(March 1969) pp52-57. illus.

M 1840 "'Kyoko, If You're Listening'." Rolling Stone
93 (October 14, 1971) p8. illus.

M 1841 Lacefield, P. "John Lennon." Win Magazine 17
(February 1, 1981) p20.

M 1842 Lachman, Charles. "Beatlemania Is Reborn In
Wake Of Tragedy." The Globe 27:53 (December
30, 1980) p22.

M 1843 Lachman, Charles. "He Was Always Fascinated By
         The Beyond." The Globe 27:53 (December 30,
         1980) p23.
         (John Lennon.)

M 1844 Lachman, Charles. "Lennon: The Beatle Who Lived
         - And Died - Outrageously." The Globe 27:53
         (December 30, 1980) pp22-23. illus.

M 1845 Lachman, Charles. "1980 Took Its Toll Of
         Superstars." The Globe 27:53 (December 30,
         1980) p27.
         (John Lennon.)

M 1846 Lachman, Charles. "They Rose From The Cellar To
         Conquer The World." The Globe 27:53
         (December 30, 1980) pp26-27.

M 1847 Lachman, Charles. "Trail Of Death - Where It
         Started." The Globe 27:53 (December 30, 1980)
         p23.
         (John Lennon.)

M 1848 "Lady Madonna." Rolling Stone 10 (May 11, 1968) p8.

M 1849 Lahr, John. "The Beatles Considered."
         New Republic 185 (December 2, 1981)
         pp19-23. illus.
         (Cover portrait.)

M 1850 Laing, R. D. "They Sought Without Finding."
         Rolling Stone 415 (February 16, 1984) p67.
         illus.

M 1851 Lake, S. "Ringo's Three Chord Trick."
         Melody Maker 50 (April 12, 1975) p8. illus.

M 1852 Lamskin, B. "Got To Be Good Lookin'." Harry 2:19
         (August 30, 1971) p12.

M 1853 Landau, Jon. "Harrison: All Things Must Pass."
         Phoenix 2:49 (December 15, 1970) p13.

M 1854 Landau, Jon. "Lennon Gets Lost In His Rock &
         Roll." Rolling Stone 187 (May 22, 1975)
         p66.
         (On the "Rock 'N' Roll" LP.)

M 1855 Landau, Jon. "McCartney Takes A Stand."
         Rolling Stone 153 (January 31, 1974)
         p48+.
         ("Band On The Run" album.)

M 1856 Landau, Jon. "Rock 'N' Roll Music."
         Rolling Stone 80 (April 15, 1971) p27.
         (Grammy awards.)

M 1857 Landau, Jon. "Rock: Paul Plus Linda." Phoenix 3:21
         (May 25, 1971) p16.

M 1858 Landau, Jon. "Top Twenty: 'The Times, They Are
         A-Middlin'." Rolling Stone 162 (June 6, 1974)
         p66+. illus.
         (On "Band On The Run" LP.)

M 1859 Langone, John. "The Lennon Syndrome." Discover
         2:2 (February 1981) pp72-73+. illus.
         (Obituary.)

M 1860 Lapidos, Mark. "Confessions Of A Beatlefan."
         Beatlefan 2:2 (February 1980) p9.
         (Origins of "Beatlefest" fan conventions.)

M 1861 Lark, Fred. "Beginner's Guide To Imports."
         Beatlefan 4:3 (April 1982) pp20,25.
         (Foreign Beatle record picks.)

M 1862 Lark, Fred. "The Case For An LP Of Unreleased
         Material." Beatlefan 3:5 (August 1981)
         p24.
         (Commentary and list of unreleased tracks.)

M 1863 Lark, Fred. "Collecting." Beatlefan 2:3
         (April 1980) pp10,24.
         (Collecting memorabilia.)

M 1864 Lark, Fred. "A Collector's Proposal."
         Beatlefan 1:6 (October 1979) p5.
         (Re-release of repackaged singles.)

M 1865 Lark, Fred. "A Decade Without The Beatles."
         Beatlefan 2:4 (June 1980) pp8-9.
         (Imaginary Beatles' singles, 1970-76.)

M 1866 Lark, Fred. "Thingumybob." Beatlefan 4:2
         (February 1982) p25.
         (EMI/Capitol repackagings of Beatles'
         material.)

M 1867 Lark, Fred. "Why Not The Real Thing."
         Beatlefan 2:6 (October 1980) p14.
         (Comments on Beatles "Rarities" LP.)

M 1868 "Last Minute Flashes." Sixteen Magazine 6:10
         (March 1965) p54.

M 1869 "Late News." Beatles Now 4 (Autumn 1982)
         p21.

M 1870 "The Latest Teen Talk From Coast To Coast."
         Sixteen Magazine 6:10 (March 1965)
         pp32-33.

M 1871 Laurence, P. "I Was A Very Nervous Character:
         An Interview With George Martin About
         Producing The Beatles And Other Things."
         Audio 62 (May 1978) pp46-48+.

M 1872 Lawter, Ann. "Meeting The Beatles." Beatlefan 2:4
         (June 1980) p14.
         (An encounter with John Lennon.)

M 1873 Lawter, Ann. "Remember ... " Beatlefan 3:1
         (December 1980) pp8-9.
         (Reactions to John Lennon's death.)

M 1874 "Lawyers Say Klein Made Beatles' $ Soar."
         Billboard 83 (March 6, 1971) p4.

M 1875 Lazar, Jerry. "Magical History Tour."
         New Times 10:6 (March 20, 1978) p72+. illus.
         (The state of Beatles collecting.)

M 1876 "LBJ Ignored As NY Crowds Chase Beatles."
         Billboard 76 (February 15, 1964) p8.

M 1877 Ledbetter, Les. "Paul And Linda On The Run In
         New York." Crawdaddy (April 1974) p58+.
         illus.

M 1878 Lee, Krista. "Expert Says He Has Proved - And
         Thousands Believe - Paul McCartney Is Dead."
         Globe 28:46 (November 17, 1981) p3.
         (Joel Glazier.)

M 1879 Lee, Ron. "John Lennon Describes Own Death: A
         Seance With Beatle's Spirit."
         National Examiner 18:3 (January 20, 1981)
         pp20-21.

M 1880 Leenheer, Franck. "The Australian Discography."
         Beatles Unlimited 26 (May 1979) pp4-8.

M 1881 Leenheer, Franck. "The Dutch Discography."
         Beatles Unlimited 15 (September 1977)
         pp11-17.

M 1882 Leenheer, Franck. "The Dutch Discography, Part
         Two." Beatles Unlimited 20 (May 1978)
         p7.

M 1883 Leenheer, Franck. "The French Discography."
         Beatles Unlimited 28 (September 1979)
         pp8-15.

M 1884 Leenheer, Franck. "Komm Gib Mir Deine Money."
         Beatles Unlimited 18 (January 1978)
         pp10-11+.
         (Bootleg Beatles singles: Deccagone, Pye,
         etc.)

M 1885 Leenheer, Franck. "Komm Gib Mir Deine Money."
         Beatles Unlimited 22 (September 1978)
         pp8-10.
         (Counterfeit Beatles records.)

M 1886 Leenheer, Franck. "Komm Gib Mir Deine Money."
         Beatles Unlimited 25 (March 1979) p22.
         (More counterfeit Beatles' discs.)

M 1887 Leenheer, Franck. "Mike McGear: 'Not Just A
         Brother ....'." Beatles Unlimited 39 (1981)
         pp4-8.
         (Interview.)

M 1888 Leenheer, Franck. "'Not Just A Brother ....'."
         Beatles Unlimited 39 (1981) pp4-8.
         (Interview with Mike McGear.)

M 1889 Lees, Gene. "Beatles, Op. 15; Sgt. Pepper's
         Lonely Hearts Club Band."
         High Fidelity/Musical America 17 (August
         1967) p94. illus.
         (On the "Sgt. Pepper" album.)

M 1890 "Legalmania Over Beatlemania." Cash Box 25
         (January 25, 1964) p7.

M 1891 Lemon, Richard. "George, Paul, Ringo, And John;
         The Beatles In The United States." Newsweek
         63 (February 24, 1964) pp54-57. illus.

M 1892 Lennon, John. "Beatalic Graphospasms."
         Saturday Evening Post 237 (March 21, 1964)
         pp40-42.
         (Poetry and prose by Lennon.)

(Singer(s) and composer(s) of Beatles
songs.)

M 1893 Lennon, John. "Beautiful Boy (Darling Boy)."
         Omni Magazine 3:11 (August 1981) p39.
         (Quotation.)
M 1894 Lennon, John. "'Have We All Forgotten What
         Vibes Are?'." Rolling Stone 56 (April 16,
         1970) p1+. illus.
         (Toronto Peace Festival.)
M 1895 Lennon, John. "I Sat Belonely Down A Tree."
         Genesis West 6 (Winter/Spring 1964) p150. illus.
         (Poem and drawing.)
M 1896 Lennon, John. "John's Letter To Paul."
         Melody Maker 46 (December 4, 1971)
         p9. illus.
         (Reply to McCartney's Melody Maker
         interview.)
M 1897 Lennon, John. "Lennon Larfs." Us 5:6 (March 17,
         1981) p32+. illus.
         (Excerpts from John Lennon's two books.)
M 1898 Lennon, John. "My Fat Budgie." Show (December
         1964) pp26-27.
         (Poem.)
M 1899 Lennon, John. "Super Star Comin' Home."
         Rising Up Angry 3:1 (1971) p4.
M 1900 Lennon, John. "Toy Boy." McCall's 93 (December
         1965) p68. illus.
         (Poem.)
M 1901 Lennon, John. "Working Class Hero." Seed 7:2
         (June 29, 1971) pp22-23.
         (Lyrics.)
M 1902 Lennon, John and Yoko Ono. "A Love Letter From
         John And Yoko To People Who Ask Us What,
         When, And Why." Beatlefan 1:4 (June 1979)
         p16.
         (Reprint of the newspaper item.)
M 1903 "Lennon & Fonda Sue U.S. & Nixon."
         Rolling Stone 148 (November 22, 1973)
         p15.
M 1904 "Lennon And McCartney Grab Three Songwriting
         Awards In Britain." Billboard 78 (July 23,
         1966) p46.
M 1905 "Lennon And Ono Spread Peace In Surprise Gig At
         Toronto R & R Bash." Variety (September 17,
         1969) p47.
M 1906 "Lennon Buys Irish Isle As A Hippie Haven But
         Natives Wave Shillelaghs." Variety 257
         (January 14, 1970) p1+.
M 1907 "Lennon Case – A Lemon." Billboard 86
         (December 28, 1974) p6.
M 1908 "Lennon Cuts Single During 'Bed-in'."
         Billboard 81 (June 21, 1969) p92.
M 1909 "Lennon Had Mystical Visions Of His Shooting
         Death." National Enquirer (December 30, 1980)
         p38.
M 1910 "Lennon Has A Legacy." The Nation 31 (December
         20, 1980) p657.
M 1911 "Lennon Heads Charity Concert For Retarded."
         Billboard 84 (August 26, 1972) p6.
M 1912 "Lennon Ignored Seer's Warning." The Globe 27:53
         (December 30, 1980) p28.
M 1913 "Lennon In 4-Letter Word Row." Melody Maker 45
         (December 12, 1970) p1+.
         (Working Class Hero.)
M 1914 "Lennon Interview/The Acid Dream Is Over."
         Willamette Bridge 4:22 (June 3, 1971)
         p7.
         (Interview from underground paper "Red
         Mole.")
M 1915 "The Lennon Issue & Its Cover." Rolling Stone
         338 (March 5, 1981) p6,7.
         (Letters to "Rolling Stone" on its Lennon
         cover.)
M 1916 "Lennon Loses A Court Round." Billboard 88
         (May 1, 1976) p10+.
M 1917 "Lennon-McCartney Songalog: Who Wrote What."
         Hit Parader (April 1972) pp15-17+.
M 1918 "Lennon, McCartney Win Five Novello Awards As
         Composers." Billboard 77 (July 31, 1965)
         p21.
M 1919 "Lennon, Ono Suit Denied." Billboard 85
         (May 12, 1973) p6.

M 1920 "Lennon Recording At New York Studio." Variety
         300 (August 20, 1980) p1+.
         (After five year hiatus.)
M 1921 "Lennon Remembered." Beatlefan 5:1 (December
         1982) p10.
         (Fan letters.)
M 1922 "Lennon Remembers." Rolling Stone 335
         (January 22, 1981) p40+. illus.
         (Excerpt from the interview with Jann
         Wenner.)
M 1923 "Lennon Returns M.B.E." Variety (November 26,
         1969) p2.
M 1924 "Lennon's Appeal." Crawdaddy 25 (June 1973)
         p23. illus.
M 1925 "Lennon's Christmas: TV, Movie, No Records."
         Rolling Stone 125 (January 4, 1973)
         p12.
M 1926 "Lennons In Greece." The Beatles Book 73
         (August 1969) p29.
M 1927 "Lennon's Nude 'Virgins' Too 'Controversial'
         For A Big Mpls. Disc Distributor." Variety
         (January 22, 1969) p47.
         ("Two Virgins" album.)
M 1928 "Lennons: On TV & Vibing McCartneys."
         Rolling Stone 103 (March 2, 1972) p28.
         illus.
M 1929 "Lennons Quit In Toronto Fest Tiff." Billboard
         82 (March 21, 1970) p3.
M 1930 "Lennons Quit Toronto Peace Festival, Claim
         Producers Balked At Free Admission."
         Variety (March 18, 1970) p58.
M 1931 "Lennon Stops Levy In Second Round."
         Rolling Stone 241 (June 16, 1977) p14.
         (Roulette Records to pay John Lennon.)
M 1932 "Lennon Sues Mitchell; Sez Move To Oust Him Was
         A Nixon Conspiracy." Variety 279 (June 18,
         1975) p1+.
M 1933 "The Lennon Tapes: John Lennon, Yoko Ono, Andy
         Peebles." Listener 105 (January 5, 1981)
         pp101-103. illus.
         (Interview, Part 1.)
M 1934 "The Lennon Tapes: John Lennon, Yoko Ono, Andy
         Peebles." Listener 105 (January 29, 1981)
         pp141-142. illus.
         (Interview, Part 2.)
M 1935 "The Lennon Tapes: John Lennon, Yoko Ono, Andy
         Peebles." Listener 105 (February 5, 1981)
         p172.
         (Interview, Part 3.)
M 1936 "Lennon: The Final Interview II." Beatlefan 3:3
         (April 1981) pp7-9+.
         (Part two; Lennon's RKO radio interview.)
M 1937 "Lennon: The Final Interview III." Beatlefan 3:4
         (June 1981) pp6-7,24.
         (Part three; Lennon's RKO radio interview.)
M 1938 "Lennon: The Final Interview IV." Beatlefan 3:5
         (August 1981) pp14,16.
         (Part four; Lennon's RKO radio interview.)
M 1939 "Lennon: The Final Interview V." Beatlefan 3:6
         (October 1981) pp8-9.
         (Part five; Lennon's RKO radio interview.)
M 1940 "Lennon: The Final Interview VI." Beatlefan 4:1
         (December 1981) pp8-9.
         (Part six; Lennon's RKO radio interview.)
M 1941 "Lennon To Star In 90-Minute Smile Pic."
         Variety 251 (July 31, 1968) p1.
M 1942 "Lennon Tribute Planned For Dec. At N.Y. Music
         Hall." Variety 303 (June 24, 1981)
         p1+.
M 1943 "Lennon Vs. McCartney V. Harrison V. Starr."
         Let It Rock (March 1974) pp26-30+.
M 1944 "Lennon Wins U.S. Stay." Variety 283 (August
         4, 1976) p50.
M 1945 "Lennon-Yoko Protest Deportation Order."
         Variety 266 (May 3, 1972) p239.
M 1946 "Less Than A Month Old, The Beatles' Apple
         Label Harvests Big Sales Crop." Variety 252
         (September 25, 1968) p59.
M 1947 Lester, Beth. "Paul's Party." Let It Rock
         (July 1973) pp9-10.

M 1948 "Let It Be." Kaleidoscope-Madison 2:12
        (June 17, 1970) p15.
M 1949 "Let It Be." Seed 5:7 (1970) p14.
M 1950 "Letters." Beatles Now 2 (Spring 1982)
        p10.
M 1951 "Letters." Rolling Stone 25 (January 4, 1969)
        p3.
        (On the Lennons' nude pictures.)
M 1952 "Letters." Rolling Stone 241 (June 16, 1977)
        p14.
        (John Lennon.)
M 1953 "Letters." Rolling Stone 309 (January 24, 1980)
        p8.
        (Beatles statue in Liverpool.)
M 1954 "Letters From Beatles People."
        The Beatles Book
        (Regular feature, issues 1- , 1963-   .)
M 1955 "Letters; John And Yoko." Rolling Stone 383
        (November 25, 1982) p6.
M 1956 "Letter To The Editor." Rolling Stone 244
        (July 28, 1977) p9.
M 1957 "Letters To The Editor." Rolling Stone 350
        (August 20, 1981) p7.
        (On Yoko's "Season Of Glass" LP.)
M 1958 Levine, Faye. "A Beatlological Puzzle." Fusion 72
        (March 1972) p64. illus.
        (Crossword puzzle.)
M 1959 Levine, Faye. "Music: Words And Music By Yoko
        Ono." Ms. 2:4 (October 1973) pp34-37.
M 1960 Levy, Alan. "What Every Woman Should Know About
        The Beatles." Good Housekeeping 161
        (July 1965) p12+. illus.
        (Interview: "Help!" filming in Nassau.)
M 1961 "Levy Loses Lennon Suit." Billboard 88
        (April 24, 1976) p4.
        ("Roots" LP.)
M 1962 Lewis, George H. "The Pop Artist And His
        Product: Mixed Up Confusion."
        Journal of Popular Culture 4:2 (1970) pp327-338.
        (Myths about The Beatles and others.)
M 1963 Lewis, J. "Clipping Of McCartney's Wings."
        Far Eastern Economic Review 107 (February 1,
        1980) p10.
M 1964 Lewis, Kathy. "The Beatles In 1961."
        The Beatles Book 28 (November 1965)
        p9.
M 1965 Lewis, V. "Showbiz Has Lost A Nemperor."
        Melody Maker 42 (September 9, 1967)
        p6.
        (Brian Epstein.)
M 1966 Lewisohn, Mark. "Ask Mark: Mark Lewisohn's
        Letters Page." Beatles Now 8 (October 1983)
        p16.
M 1967 Lewisohn, Mark. "The Beatles' Christmas
        Records." Record Collector 4 (December 1979)
        pp12-13.
M 1968 Lewisohn, Mark. "'The Beatles: Early Years'."
        The Beatles Book 65 (September 1981)
        ppvi-vii.
        (Repackaging of the Hamburg tapes LP.)
M 1969 Lewisohn, Mark. "Beatles '79: A Diary Of Recent
        News And Events." Record Collector
        (Regular reprint feature, issues 3-4,
        1979.)
M 1970 Lewisohn, Mark. "Beatles '80: A Diary Of Recent
        News And Events." Record Collector
        (Regular reprint feature, issues 5-6,
        1980.)
M 1971 Lewisohn, Mark. "Beatles '81: A Diary Of Recent
        News And Events." The Beatles Book
        (Regular reprint feature, issues 58-68,
        1981.)
M 1972 Lewisohn, Mark. "Beatles '82: A Diary Of Recent
        News And Events." The Beatles Book
        (Regular reprint feature, issues 69-79,
        1982.)
M 1973 Lewisohn, Mark. "Beatles '83: A Diary Of Recent
        News And Events." The Beatles Book
        (Regular feature, issues 80-92, 1983.)
M 1974 Lewisohn, Mark. "The Beatles' U.K. T.V.

Appearances." The Beatles Book 50 (June 1980)
        ppix-xi.
M 1975 Lewisohn, Mark. "A Complete Catalogue Of The
        Beatles' U.K. Radio Broadcasts."
        The Beatles Book 47 (March 1980) ppiii-x.
M 1976 Lewisohn, Mark. "A Complete Catalogue Of The
        Beatles' U.K. Radio Broadcasts, Part Two."
        The Beatles Book 48 (April 1980) ppiii-x.
M 1977 Lewisohn, Mark. "The Concert For The People Of
        Kampuchea." Beatles Unlimited 31 (March 1979)
        pp16-17.
        (Hammersmith Odeon, December 29, 1979.)
M 1978 Lewisohn, Mark. "'George Harrison': The Album
        Reviewed." The Beatles Book 36 (April 1979)
        ppiii-v.
M 1979 Lewisohn, Mark. "Getting Up To Date On John,
        George & Ringo." The Beatles Book 22
        (February 1978) ppiii-v.
M 1980 Lewisohn, Mark. "'I Wanna Hold Your Hand'
        Reviewed." The Beatles Book 28 (August 1978)
        pv.
        (Motion picture.)
M 1981 Lewisohn, Mark. "'London Town': The Fax Behind
        The Trax!" The Beatles Book 26 (June 1978)
        ppiii-v.
M 1982 Lewisohn, Mark. "McCartney II."
        The Beatles Book 51 (July 1980) ppiii-iv.
        (Comments on the new LP.)
M 1983 Lewisohn, Mark. "My Beatles Collection."
        Record Collector 3 (November 1979)
        pp14-16.
        (Memorabilia.)
M 1984 Lewisohn, Mark. "The 'Rockshow' Premiere."
        The Beatles Book 63 (July 1981) ppix-x.
        (London film premiere in April.)
M 1985 Lewisohn, Mark. "Take It Away."
        The Beatles Book 76 (August 1982) ppiii-viii.
        (Filming promo video for the single.)
M 1986 Lewisohn, Mark. "A Tale Of Two Conventions."
        The Beatles Book 64 (August 1981) ppiii-vi.
        (Fan gatherings in New York and Leiden,
        Holland.)
M 1987 Lewisohn, Mark. "A Visit To The Record Plant
        And The Hit Factory." The Beatles Book 65
        (September 1981) ppiii-v.
        (Studios used by John Lennon in New York.)
M 1988 Lichtman, I. "ABKCO Collects, But No 'So Fine'
        Profit." Billboard 93 (March 7, 1981)
        p3+.
M 1989 Lichtman, I. "ATV Music Charges Beatles
        Infringement." Billboard (August 27, 1983)
        p30.
        (Sesame Street Record's "Born To Add" LP.)
M 1990 Lichtman, I. "Northern Songs Widening Videotape
        C'right Defense." Billboard 93 (February 7,
        1981) p1+.
M 1991 Lichtman, I. "Publisher In Action Over
        Videotapes." Billboard 92 (March 22, 1980)
        p1+.
M 1992 Lichtman, I. "Video Settlement To Beatles
        Publisher." Billboard 92 (July 26, 1980)
        p1+.
M 1993 Lichtman, I. "We Polish Old Silver - Eastman."
        Billboard 91 (July 7, 1979) p12.
M 1994 Liembacher, E. "Fab Four." Helix 2:17
        (May 23, 1970) p18.
M 1995 Life. Volume 7, Number 2. February 1984.
        New York: Time Inc., 1984. illus.
        (Beatles cover portrait; 20th anniversary
        issue.)
M 1996 "Lift Ban On Beatles Video." Billboard
        (November 6, 1982) p3.
        (MGM can distribute "The Compleat
        Beatles.")
M 1997 "The Lighter Side."
        High Fidelity/Musical America (November 1964)
        p125. illus.
        (On the Beatles' albums to date.)
M 1998 "Linda Eastman (The Mrs.) In McCartney's
        Group." Variety 263 (August 11, 1971)

p51.

M 1999 "Linda McCartney's New Flair For Songwriting
       Awes British Pub Exec." Variety 262
       (March 24, 1971) p75.

M 2000 "Linda's Paul." Us 6:8 (April 13, 1982)
       pp18-19.
           (Photos; new McCartney album and book
           news.)

M 2001 "Linda: Wife On The Run." Rock (January 1975)
       pp17-18.

M 2002 Lippincott, P. "Music." Senior Scholastic 109
       (September 9, 1976) p28. illus.

M 2003 "Liquidate Beatles' Apple Corps Firm." Variety
       278 (May 7, 1975) p2+.

M 2004 "List Of Area Secretaries In The U.K."
       The Beatles Book 23 (June 1965) p5.
           (Beatles' fan club.)

M 2005 "Little Richard Collects." Rolling Stone 246
       (August 25, 1977) p16.
           (Black music royalties from The Beatles.)

M 2006 "Live Appearances." Beatles Unlimited 34/35 (1981)
       pp24-25.
           (John Lennon's live appearances.)

M 2007 "Liverpool Beat Has Its Alger Story: Brian
       Epstein Who Found The Beatles." Variety 232
       (September 18, 1963) p59.

M 2008 "Liverpool's Magical Mystery Store."
       Record Collector 3 (November 1979)
       pp24-25.
           (London memorabilia store.)

M 2009 "Liverpool Solons Reject Bid For Beatles
       Statues." Billboard 88 (November 12, 1977)
       p94.

M 2010 Livingston, A.W. "Commentary: Lennon Helped
       Pave The Way." Billboard 93 (January 10,
       1981) p16.

M 2011 Livingston, A.W. and R. Tepper. "Alan
       Livingston, Capitol's Former President When
       The Beatles Came Calling, Recalls 'British
       Invasion'." Billboard 86 (May 4, 1974)
       p18+. illus.

M 2012 Livingston, G. "'Surrey Sound' Has Thin B.O.
       Fringe As Beatles Top Minets In Hub
       'Contest'." Variety 236 (September 16, 1964)
       p51.

M 2013 Lloyd, Valerie. "My Meetles With The Beatles."
       The Beatles Book 16 (November 1964)
       p15.
           (Contest winner meets the group.)

M 2014 "Local Psychic Presents Fascinating Transcript
       Of Her Experience - A Message From John
       Lennon." Lifestyle 13:11 (February 1981)
       pp5,24.

M 2015 Loder, Kurt. "It's Alright." Rolling Stone 387
       (January 20, 1983) pp51-52. illus.
           (On Yoko Ono.)

M 2016 Loder, Kurt. "The Last Session." Rolling Stone
       335 (January 22, 1981) p67. illus.

M 2017 Loder, Kurt. "Lennon Update." Rolling Stone 336
       (February 5, 1981) p11+. illus.

M 2018 Loder, Kurt. "Yoko Ono: 'Still In A State Of
       Shock'." Rolling Stone 387 (January 20, 1983)
       pp42-43. illus.

M 2019 "London 'Beatlemania' Set, But Suit Looms."
       Variety 296 (October 10, 1979) p2+.
           (Stage play "Beatlemania.")

M 2020 "London Court Ends Beatles Partnership; Apple
       Continues." Variety 277 (January 15, 1975)
       p76.

M 2021 "London Notes." Rolling Stone 71 (November 26,
       1970) p21.
           (George Harrison alias: George O'Hara
           Smith.)

M 2022 "London Notes." Rolling Stone 73 (December 24,
       1970) p16.
           (London play based on "Eleanor Rigby.")

M 2023 "London Notes." Rolling Stone 74 (January 21,
       1971) p18.
           (Lennon/McCartney Northern Songs battle.)

M 2024 "London Notes." Rolling Stone 75 (February 4,

1971) p10.
           (Shirley Bassey gripes about George
           Harrison.)

M 2025 "London Notes." Rolling Stone 77 (March 4, 1971)
       p14.
           (George Harrison in court on driving
           charge.)

M 2026 "London Notes." Rolling Stone 85 (June 24, 1971)
       p22.
           (George Harrison wins "Record Mirror" poll.)

M 2027 "London Notes." Rolling Stone 87 (July 22, 1971)
       p14.
           (Ringo Starr records with B. B. King.)

M 2028 "London Notes." Rolling Stone 92 (September 30,
       1971) p4.
           (Promoters seek Harrison for Bangla Desh
           Two.)

M 2029 "London Notes." Rolling Stone 93 (October 14,
       1971) p4.
           (Capitol executive reviews pending LPs.)

M 2030 "London Notes." Rolling Stone 95 (November 8,
       1971) p26.
           (McCartney's celebration ball for new LP.)

M 2031 "London Notes." Rolling Stone 105 (March 30,
       1972) p10.
           (BBC prepares 12-hour Beatles documentary.)

M 2032 "London Notes." Rolling Stone 108 (May 11, 1972)
       p12.
           (McCartney's "Mary Had A Little Lamb.")

M 2033 "London Notes." Rolling Stone 108 (May 11, 1972)
       p12.
           (Beatles fan club folds.)

M 2034 "London Notes." Rolling Stone 109 (May 25, 1972)
       p24.
           (Five of ten top U.K. LPs for decade:
           Beatles.)

M 2035 "London Notes." Rolling Stone 110 (June 8, 1972)
       p14.
           (Ringo Starr interview quoted.)

M 2036 "Lonely Hearts Club Band." Melody Maker 49
       (August 24, 1974) p7. illus.

M 2037 "Looks As If Those Wedding Bells Have Broken Up
       That Beatles Gang." Variety 258 (April 15,
       1970) p2.

M 2038 "Looneytunes: Preserving The Beatles Fantasy."
       Creem 6 (April 1975) p49+. illus.

M 2039 Loose, Bill. "My Carnival." Beatles Unlimited 28
       (September 1979) pp4-6.
           (Commentary and musical transcription of
           the song.)

M 2040 Loose, Bill. "Report On The Beatlefest '76, Los
       Angeles." Beatles Unlimited 11 (January 1977)
       p15.
           (Beatles fan convention.)

M 2041 "'Lost' Beatles Songs Unearthed By BBC."
       Billboard 94:11 (March 20, 1982) p2.
           (A dozen songs found in BBC archives.)

M 2042 "Lost Troubadour." Economist 277 (December 13,
       1980) p16. illus.
           (John Lennon.)

M 2043 Loupien, S. "Heures Et Humeurs D'un Amateur: Un
       Mois A Paris." Jazz Magazine 294 (February
       1981) p38.
           (On John Lennon.)

M 2044 "'Love Me Do' Due From Capitol." Billboard
       (November 13, 1982) p3.
           (Capitol in U.S. re-release of single.)

M 2045 "'Love Me Do': Peter Jones Tells The Full Story
       Behind The Beatles' First Hit."
       The Beatles Book 34 (February 1979)
       ppiii-v.

M 2046 Luce, P.A. "Great Rock Conspiracy."
       National Review 21 (September 23, 1969)
       p959+.

M 2047 Lydon, S. "Would You Want Your Sister To Marry
       A Beatle?" Ramparts 7 (November 30, 1968)
       pp65-66+.

M 2048 Lynch, Kenny. "Is The Beatles Frenzy Cooling
       Down?" Melody Maker 39 (June 6, 1964)
       p3.

(Interview.)

M 2049 Lyon, George W. "More On Beatles Textual Problems." Journal of Popular Culture 4:2 (Fall 1970) pp549-552.
(Reply to G. Marshall's 1969 article.)

M 2050 Macaire, A. "Un Soiree En Marge." Attitudes International 24 (June 1975) pp55-56.
(Yoko Ono works in Belgian exhibit, May 23, 1975.)

M 2051 McAllister, William. "One Pair Of Eyes." The Beatles Book 73 (August 1969) p31.
(Beatles' influence on music.)

M 2052 McBride, Jim and Larry Williams. "Yeah, Yeah, Yeah." Rolling Stone 415 (February 16, 1984) p31+. illus.
(Twelve memoirs of the Beatles in the sixties.)

M 2053 McCaffrey, Laurie. "A Lucky Liverpool Lady." The Beatles Book 87 (July 1983) pp34-38. illus.
(Former NEMS worker recalls 1963 events.)

M 2054 McCarry, Charles. "John Rennon's Excrusive Gloupie." Esquire 74 (December 1970) pp204-205+. illus.

M 2055 McCartney, Linda. (Untitled.) Creative Camera 178 (April 1979) p137. illus.
(Photo of husband Paul McCartney.)

M 2056 "McCartney & Wings To Tour G. Britain." Rolling Stone 126 (January 18, 1973) p10.

M 2057 "McCartney Breaks The Vinyl Curtain." Billboard 88 (August 28, 1976) p6+.
("Band On The Run" released in Russia.)

M 2058 "McCartney Comes Back." Time 107 (May 31, 1976) pp40-44. illus.
(Cover portrait.)

M 2059 "McCartney 'Death' Gets 'Disc Coverage' Dearth." Billboard 81 (November 8, 1969) p3.

M 2060 "McCartney Denies Beatles' Reunion." Variety 274 (May 8, 1974) p273.

M 2061 "McCartney Disk Bid Is Rejected By 'Quarryman'." Billboard 93 (August 1, 1981) p60.
("That'll Be The Day - In Spite Of All The Danger.")

M 2062 "The McCartney Empire." Beatlefan 2:1 (December 1979) pp10,21.
(McCartney's music publishing holdings.)

M 2063 "McCartney Gets Political." Rolling Stone (November 25, 1982) p37.
(Protests Thatcher health worker policies.)

M 2064 "The McCartney Interview." Beatlefan 2:5 (August 1980) pp12-14.
(From the CBS album with Vic Garbarini.)

M 2065 "McCartney Interview." Beatlefan 2:6 (October 1980) pp24-25.
(From CBS LP with Vic Garbarini, Pt. II.)

M 2066 "The McCartney Interview." Beatlefan 3:2 (February 1981) pp18-19.
(From the CBS LP with Vic Garbarini, Pt. III.)

M 2067 "McCartney Is Home From Visit To Tokyo." Variety 297 (January 30, 1980) p79.

M 2068 "McCartney Is Most Honored." Billboard 91 (October 6, 1979) p64.
("Guinness Book Of World Records.")

M 2069 "McCartney, Martin Tie." Billboard 84 (December 2, 1972) p57.

M 2070 "McCartney On His Own." Saturday Review 53 (May 30, 1970) pp53-54. illus.

M 2071 "McCartney Pens Tune For 007." Rolling Stone 132 (April 12, 1973) p20.
("Live And Let Die.")

M 2072 "McCartney Plays South Of France." Rolling Stone 115 (August 17, 1972) p8.

M 2073 "McCartney Raps Stigwood 'Pepper' As 'Unauthorized'." Variety 271 (August 1, 1973) p39.

M 2074 "McCartney Says He 'Doesn't Trust Klein'; Rebuttal." Variety 262 (February 24, 1971) p47.

M 2075 "McCartneys Back With A Whole Pack Of Geeks." Creem 8 (July 1976) pp60-61. illus.

M 2076 "McCartney Sues Beatles & Co." Rolling Stone 75 (February 4, 1971) p10.

M 2077 "McCartney Sues To Annul Beatles' Apple Corps Tie." Variety 261 (January 13, 1971) p55.

M 2078 "McCartney The Family Favourite." Melody Maker 48 (April 28, 1973) p3. illus.

M 2079 "McCartney To Change Labels." Beatlefan 1:1 (December 1978) p2.

M 2080 "McCartney: Tour And LP News." Beatlefan 1:3 (April 1979) p2.
("Back To The Egg" album.)

M 2081 "McCartney Tour Of US Bowing In Ft. Worth May 3." Variety 282 (April 14, 1976) p73.

M 2082 "McCartney Writing Movie." Billboard 92 (November 22, 1980) p63.
(Based on "Rupert The Bear" comics.)

M 2083 McCormack, Ed. "Elephant's Memory Without The Plastic." Rolling Stone 116 (August 31, 1972)
(Mentions the Lennons.)

M 2084 McCracken, Melinda. "Rock And Roll Revival Surprise: John & Yoko." Rolling Stone 44 (October 18, 1969) p1+.
(Cover portrait.)

M 2085 McCullaugh, J. "Capitol Releases $132.98 Beatles Set." Billboard 90 (November 11, 1978) p8.
("Beatles Gift Box.")

M 2086 McCullaugh, J. "Cap Plans To Issue Beatles Rarities LP." Billboard 91 (September 1, 1979) p3.

M 2087 McDonagh, Des. "News From The U.K." Beatles Unlimited
(Regular feature, issues 8-21.)

M 2088 McDonough, J. "Alexander And Solberg Buy Beatles Console." Billboard 94 (January 30, 1982) p51.
(EMI Redd 37 which recorded almost all their albums.)

M 2089 "McGear: Brother On The Run." Beatles Unlimited 1 (March 1975) pp12-13.
(Review of the "McGear" album.)

M 2090 McGhee, Raymond. "The Early Years." The Beatles Book 5 (December 1963) p27.

M 2091 McGrath, R. "The Basic Repertoire." Georgia Straight 5:52 (March 10, 1971) p19.
(John Lennon.)

M 2092 McKie, Fred. "Those Were The Days: The Concert For Bangla Desh Remembered." Beatlefan 3:5 (August 1981) pp18-19.
(Eyewitness account.)

M 2093 Mackie, Rob. "Ringo: Mr. Nice Guy Comes Into His Own." Rock (March 25, 1974) p12.

M 2094 McNeill, D. "Report On The State Of The Beatles." Crawdaddy 11 (September 1967) pp6-9+. illus.

M 2095 "Mad For John Lennon's Face: Chi Fest Shows Solid 52-Minute 'Closeup'." Variety (November 20, 1968) p1+.
(Films "Two Virgins" and "No. 5.")

M 2096 Mad. Volume 1, No. 121. New York: E. C. Publications Inc., 1968.
(Cover: Alfred E. Neuman as the Maharishi.)

M 2097 "Magical Mystery Non-Benefit." Rolling Stone 34 (May 31, 1969) p12.

M 2099 "Magical Mystery Tour Group." Rolling Stone 4 (January 20, 1968) p2. illus.

M 2100 "Mag Review: Beatles Appreciation Society Bulletin." Beatles Unlimited 7 (May 1976) p19.

(Review of the Australian fanzine.)

M 2101 "Mag Review: Our Starr Monthly."
Beatles Unlimited 3 (August 1975) p14.
(Reviews the Beatles fanzine "Our Starr Monthly.")

M 2102 "Mag Review: The Fab Four Publication."
Beatles Unlimited 4 (November 1975) p11.
(Review of the French fanzine.)

M 2103 "Mag Review: The Write Thing."
Beatles Unlimited 2 (June 1975) p18.
(Review of the Beatles fanzine "The Write Thing.")

M 2104 "Mag Review: With A Little Help From My Friends." Beatles Unlimited 5 (January 1976) p17.
(Review of the American fanzine.)

M 2105 Maher, J. "Beatles Are Enshrined In Mme. Tussaud's Waxworks." Billboard 76 (March 28, 1964) p1+.

M 2106 Maher, J. "Beatles Begin New British Art Push." Billboard 76 (February 15, 1964) p4.

M 2107 Maher, J. "Nobody Loves The Beatles 'Cept Mother, Capitol, Etc." Billboard 76 (March 14, 1964) p3.

M 2108 Maher, J. and T. Noonan. "Chart Crawls With Beatles." Billboard 76 (April 4, 1964) p1+.

M 2109 "Mal Evans: The Beatles Equipment Road Manager." The Beatles Book 18 (January 1965) p9,11.

M 2110 Malone, Pat. "Enter Yoko & Exit Battling Beatles." Star 9:2 (January 13, 1981) pp28-29.

M 2111 "Manitoba Premier To Lennon & Yoko: 'Bring Your Peace Movement'." Variety 257 (December 31, 1969) p2.

M 2112 Manley, Colin. "George Harrison: Record Producer!" The Beatles Book 56 (March 1968) p24.

M 2113 "Mannerist Phase; New Album Of Recordings." Time 92 (December 6, 1968) p53. illus.

M 2114 Manoeuvre, Phillippe. "Starr! Starr!" Rock & Folk (Paris) 118 (November 1976) pp60-67. illus.
(Interview in French.)

M 2115 Marcus, G. H. "These Catalogues Don't Stand On Shelves." Museum News 54:5 (January 1975) pp25-29. illus.
(Mentions Yoko Ono's unfinished works.)

M 2116 Marcus, Greil. "The Band's Last Waltz." Rolling Stone 229 (December 30, 1976) p38. illus.

M 2117 Marcus, Greil. "Beatle Data: They Should've Known Better." Village Voice 22:24 (June 13, 1977) pp36-37+. illus.

M 2118 Marcus, Greil. "John Lennon." New West 6 (January 1981) p128. illus.

M 2119 Marcus, Greil. "Life And Life Only." Rolling Stone 335 (January 22, 1981) pp26-27. illus.
(John Lennon.)

M 2120 Marcus, Greil. "Recollections Of An Amnesiac." Creem 7:1 (June 1975) p69.
(On Lennon's "Rock 'N' Roll" album.)

M 2121 Marcus, Greil. "Refried Beatles." Rolling Stone 217 (July 17, 1976) pp46-47+. illus.
("Rock And Roll Music" album.)

M 2122 Mariager, Ann. "Lennon: Enhver Kvindes Drom." MM (Copenhagen, Denmark) (December 1980) pp10-11. illus.

M 2123 Marsh, Dave. "Another Open Letter To John Lennon." Rolling Stone 298 (August 23, 1979) p28. illus.

M 2124 Marsh, Dave. "The Beatles: Grating Expectations." Rolling Stone 233 (February 24, 1977) p25. illus.
(Reunion rumors.)

M 2125 Marsh, Dave. "Ghoulish Beatlemania."
Rolling Stone 335 (January 22, 1981) pp28-29. illus.

M 2126 Marsh, Dave. "McCartney: Rock & Roll On A Wing & A Prayer." Rolling Stone 216 (July 1, 1976) p102. illus.
(May 14th Philadelphia concert.)

M 2127 Marsh, Dave. "An Open Letter To John Lennon." Rolling Stone 251 (November 3, 1977) p50. illus.

M 2128 Marsh, Dave. "Sue You, Sue Me Blues." Rolling Stone 215 (June 17, 1976) p22.
(Litigation against John Lennon.)

M 2129 Marsh, Dave and Kevin Stein. "Music Appreciation: A Crash Course." Rolling Stone 353 (October 1, 1981) p48. illus.

M 2130 Marshall, Geoffrey. "Taking The Beatles Seriously: Problems Of Text." Journal of Popular Culture 3:1 (1969) pp28-34.

M 2131 Martin, Bernice. "Not Marx But Lennon." Encounter 56 (June 1981) pp49-51. illus.

M 2132 Martin, Brendan. "'Somewhere In England'." The Beatles Book 63 (July 1981) pxi.
(Review of George Harrison's LP.)

M 2133 Martin, G. "Commentary: His Gift - More Than Music." Billboard 93 (January 24, 1981) p16.
(John Lennon.)

M 2134 Martin, Tom P. "Glass Onion." Beatlefan 3:6 (October 1981) p28.
(Listener's guide to Beatles' Decca audition.)

M 2135 Martynova, A. "Beatles As Cinderella: A Soviet Fairy Tale." Rolling Stone 27 (February 15, 1969) p1+.
(Translated from "Sovetskaya Kultura.")

M 2136 "Mary Baker Asks Account Of Beatles' Promotional Funds." Advertising Age 35 (December 14, 1964) p98.

M 2137 Maslin, Janet. "Paul And Carly: Family Affairs." Rolling Stone 267 (June 15, 1978) p89+. illus.

M 2138 Maslin, Janet. "Ringo And Harry - Harry And Ringo." New Times 2 (May 31, 1974) p61+.
(Ringo Starr and Harry Nilsson.)

M 2139 "Masque Los Beatles." Buenos Aires Musical 334 (October 16, 1965) p6.

M 2140 "Matched Pair Of Gunmen." Time 118 (September 7, 1981) p14. illus.
(John Lennon.)

M 2141 Mathews, Tom, et al. "Lennon Alter Ego." Newsweek 96 (December 22, 1980) p34+ illus.
(Cover portrait.)

M 2142 Mautner, Sue. "The Invasion Of A Stately Home." The Beatles Book 36 (July 1966) pp10-11.
(The Beatles visit Chiswick House.)

M 2143 Mayer, Allan, Susan Agrest and Jacob Young. "Death Of A Beatle." Newsweek 96 (December 22, 1980) p31+. illus.
(Cover portrait.)

M 2144 Mayer, Ira. "Live Beatles Tape From Dec., 1962 To Be Made Available Worldwide." Record World (December 4, 1976) p3,22.
(The Hamburg tapes.)

M 2145 Mayo, Anna. "Druidmania." Village Voice 26 (January 14, 1981) p14. illus.
(John Lennon.)

M 2146 "M.B.E." Beatles Unlimited 1 (March 1975) pp16-17.
(Highlights of the Beatles' M.B.E. award.)

M 2147 "The M.B.E. Controversy." The Beatles Book 50 (June 1980) pvii.

M 2148 "Meditation ... " The Beatles Book 52 (November 1967) pp25-26.
(Lennon, Harrison on Transcendental Meditation.)

M 2149 "Meeting The Beatles." Beatlefan
(Occasional feature, v2n2- , 1980- .)

M 2150 "Meet The Staff." Beatles Unlimited 16 (November 1977) pp5-7.
(Staff of "Beatles Unlimited.")

M 2151 Meisel, Perry. "Beatlemania." Village Voice 22:24
        (June 13, 1977) p36.
M 2152 Meisel, Perry. "Sgt. Pepper's Odyssey: A
        Preview Of The Movie 'Yellow Submarine'."
        Yale Literary Magazine (March 1968)
M 2153 Mekas, Jonas. "Apotheosis, Legs And Rape By
        Lennon And Ono." Village Voice 16:1
        (January 7, 1971) p51.
        (Film commentary.)
M 2154 Melhuish, Martin. "Strawberry Fields Forever."
        Modern Hi Fi Stereo Guide (December 1973)
        pp87-88.
M 2155 Mellers, Wilfred. "Imagine."
        Music and Musicians 30 (January 1972)
        pp30-32. illus.
        (John Lennon.)
M 2156 Mellers, Wilfred. "Pop, Ritual, & Commitment."
        Music Teacher & Piano Student 53 (January
        1974) pp10-11.
        (Part one.)
M 2157 Mellers, Wilfred. "Pop, Ritual, & Commitment."
        Music Teacher & Piano Student 53 (February
        1974) pp9-10.
        (Part two.)
M 2158 Mellers, Wilfred. "Pop, Ritual, & Commitment."
        Music Teacher & Piano Student 53 (March 1974)
        pp10-11.
        (Part three.)
M 2159 Melly, George. "John Lennon." Punch (December
        12, 1980)
        (Eulogy.)
M 2160 Meltzer, M. "Mm Hmm." Crawdaddy 13 (February
        1968) p24.
M 2161 Meltzer, R. "The Aesthetics Of Rock."
        Crawdaddy 8 (March 1967) pp11-14+.
        (Part of his "A Sequel: Tomorrow's Not
        Today.")
M 2162 Meltzer, R. "Hate Mail Makes The World Go
        'Round." Coast 18 (February 1977) pp46-47.
        illus.
        (Paul McCartney.)
M 2163 Meltzer, R. "Riffs: Rutles Give Us Back Our
        Birth Right (Kinda)." Village Voice 23
        (March 27, 1978) p50.
        (Rutles album.)
M 2164 "Memorabilia Auction." Record Collector 16
        (December 1980) pp35-39. illus.
        (Beatles items offered at Sotheby auction.)
M 2165 "Memories That Stop Cynthia From Finding New
        Love." Star 8:49 (December 8, 1981)
        p25. illus.
M 2166 Mendelsohn, John. "Beatlemania's Boys In The
        Band." Rolling Stone 265 (May 18, 1978)
        p11+. illus.
        (Stage show.)
M 2167 Men's Wear. New York:
        Fairchild Publications Inc., 1975.
        (Cover portrait.)
M 2168 "Merchandiser Calmly Awaits Beatles Return;
        Mrs. Baker Revamps Old Lines, Readies New."
        Advertising Age 35 (June 15, 1964)
        p3+.
M 2169 Meredith, June. "Ready For Les Beatles."
        The Beatles Book 7 (February 1964)
        pp6-7.
        (Paris, January 1964.)
M 2170 Merritt, Jay. "Former Beatles Manager Klein
        Back In Court." Rolling Stone 290 (May 3,
        1979) p13. illus.
M 2171 "The Mersey Sound." Mersey Beat (October 24,
        1963) p7.
        (On the 30-minute BBC documentary.)
M 2172 Meryman, Richard. "'I Felt The Split Was
        Coming'." Life 70 (April 16, 1971)
        pp52-54+. illus.
        (Paul McCartney; cover portrait.)

M 2174 "The Messengers." Time (September 22, 1967)
        pp60-68.
        (The Beatles as harbingers of a music
        revolution.)
M 2175 Metz, Piotr. "The First Polish Beatles
        Gathering." Beatles Unlimited 10 (November
        1976) p7.
        (Cracow, October 16, 1976.)
M 2176 Metz, Piotr. "Poland." Beatles Unlimited 34/35
        (1981) pp38-40.
        (Polish reactions to Lennon's death.)
M 2177 Metz, Piotr. "Poland Updated."
        Beatles Unlimited 23 (November 1978)
        pp19-20.
        (Beatles-related events in Poland.)
M 2178 Metz, Piotr. "Tracking The Hits: Rozglosnia
        Harcerska, Poland." Beatles Unlimited 14
        (July 1977) pp7-9.
        (Beatles' singles charted on Polish radio.)
M 2179 Metz, Piotr. "Yoko: 1981 In Budapest."
        Beatles Unlimited 42 (1982) p20.
        (Visits Hungary as "Mrs. Schuster.")
M 2180 Mewborn, Brant. "Beyond Beatlemania."
        Rolling Stone 415 (February 16, 1984)
        pp70-71+. illus.
M 2181 Mewborn, Brant. "Pop Phenomena." After Dark 13
        (February 1981) pp14-15. illus.
        (John Lennon.)
M 2182 Mewborn, Brant. "Ringo In The Afternoon."
        Rolling Stone 342 (April 30, 1981)
        p28+. illus.
M 2183 Mewborn, Brant. "Rock's Own Rock On."
        After Dark 9:5 (September 1976) pp52-57.
        illus.
        (Paul McCartney.)
M 2184 Meyer, F. "McCartneys Buy E. H. Morris Music;
        To Be MPL Subsid." Variety 233 (June 30,
        1976) p1+.
M 2185 Meyer, F. "Paul McCartney In CBS Deal For
        U.S.-Can., EMI For Overseas." Variety 293
        (December 6, 1978) p77.
M 2186 Michaels, Leonard. "The Violent Giants."
        Rolling Stone 415 (February 16, 1984)
        p68. illus.
M 2187 Michelini, Chuck. "Blazing Battles Rock
        Marriage Of Ex-Beatle Ringo."
        National Enquirer 56:33 (March 23, 1982)
        p51.
M 2188 Mike. "Johnny Be Good." Willamette Bridge 4:7
        (February 18, 1971) p8.
        (John Lennon.)
M 2189 "Mike McGear's Wedding." The Beatles Book 60
        (July 1968) pp26-27.
        (Photos.)
M 2190 Miller, Chris. "Beat The Meatles."
        National Lampoon 1:91 (October 1977)
        p40+.
M 2191 Miller, Edwin. "Bit By The Beatles." Seventeen 23
        (March 1964) pp82-83. illus.
M 2192 Miller, Edwin. "On The Scene With The Beatles."
        Seventeen 24 (August 1965) pp230-231+.
        illus.
M 2193 Miller, Edwin. "What Are The Beatles Really
        Like?" Seventeen 23 (August 1964) pp236-237+.
        illus.
M 2194 Miller, Jan. "Dark Horse: Transcendental
        Mediocrity." Rolling Stone 180 (February 13,
        1975) p75+.
        (On the "Dark Horse" LP.)
M 2195 Miller, Jim. "Melancholy Masterpiece."
        Newsweek 99 (May 3, 1982) p74.
        (On the "Tug Of War" LP.)
M 2196 Miller, Jim. "Paul McCartney Looks Back."
        Newsweek 99 (May 3, 1982) pp73-74.
        (Interview.)
M 2197 Miller, John J. "At Last! The Beatles Talk
        About Sex, Drugs, Their Women...And Each
        Other!" Motion Picture 64:770 (April 1975)
        pp4-5+.
M 2198 "Millionaire Who Feared Loneliness."

Melody Maker 42 (September 2, 1967)
p4. illus.
(Brian Epstein.)

M 2199 "Million Dollar Offer For Beatles."
Melody Maker 44 (December 13, 1969)
p1.

M 2200 Mintz, Elliot. "The Private Life Of Paul And
Linda McCartney." Us 1:24 (March 21, 1978)
pp48-51. illus.

M 2201 Mintz, Elliot. "Ringo Starr." Viva 5 (February
1978) p44+. illus.
(Interview.)

M 2202 "Mrs. Baker Will Hol' Beatles' Han',
Merchandising-wise." Advertising Age
(February 17, 1964) p1+.

M 2203 "Mrs. Paul McCartney." Vogue 153 (May 1969)
pp152-153. illus.

M 2204 Mitchell, Steve. "Making 'I Wanna Hold Your
Hand'." Filmmakers Newsletter 11:9
(June 1978) pp17-22.
(About the 1978 film by Universal
Pictures.)

M 2205 Mitz, R. "Paul: Live And Flying."
Stereo Review 38 (March 1977) p101. illus.

M 2206 Mitz, R. "Pop Rotogravure." Stereo Review 40
(March 1978) p100. illus.
(Paul McCartney.)

M 2207 "Mix-Master To The Beatles." Time 89 (June 16,
1967) p67. illus.
(George Martin.)

M 2208 Moger, E.S. "Meeting The Beatles." Beatlefan 5:1
(December 1982) p16.
(Fan meets Lennon in Dec. 1971.)

M 2209 "Money And Music." Hit Parader XXV:28
(October 1966) ppB15-B16. illus.
(John Lennon interview.)

M 2210 "Monkees Versus Beatles; Melody Maker Opinion
Poll." Melody Maker 42 (March 25, 1967)
pp10-11. illus.

M 2211 "Monogamy And Music: Life Around The Hearth For
Paul And Linda." People 3 (April 21, 1975)
pp21-25. illus.

M 2212 Montague, Susan. "Why Kids Love Lennon."
Oklahoma Observer 13 (January 10, 1981)
p6.

M 2213 "Moog." The Beatles Book 74 (September 1969)
p31.
(Harrison's moog synthesizer.)

M 2214 Moon, L. "Beatlemaniacs Never Die (But They
Sure Get Carried Away)." Creem 6 (November
1974) pp54-55. illus.

M 2215 "Mopheads, M.B.E." Newsweek 65 (June 28, 1965)
p38. illus.

M 2216 Morales, Aldo. "'Lennon'." Beatlefan 4:6
(October 1982) p24.
(On the off-Broadway play.)

M 2217 "More Recent Letters From Beatle People."
The Beatles Book
(Regular reprint feature, issues 3-40,
47-77.)

M 2218 Morgan, K. "Quebec's Subculture: Gilding The
Beatles." MacLean's 78 (October 2, 1965)
p51.

M 2219 Morgan, Terry. "The Cavern." The Beatles Book 11
(March 1977) ppiii-iv.

M 2220 Morgenstern, J. "Swan Songs." Newsweek 75
(June 8, 1970) pp93-94.

M 2221 Morris, J. "Monarchs Of The Beatle Empire."
Saturday Evening Post 239 (August 27, 1966)
pp22-27. illus.

M 2222 Morris, Jan. "Britain's Finest Hour."
Rolling Stone 335 (January 22, 1981)
p22. illus.
(John Lennon.)

M 2223 Moss, F. "Abbey Road - Nowhere Man."
Dock of the Bay 1:13 (October 28, 1969)
(On the "Abbey Road" album.)

M 2224 Moss, F. "Beatles - Abbey Road." Space City 1:10
(November 22, 1969)
(On the "Abbey Road" album.)

M 2225 "Most Difficult Film The Beatles Never Made."
Melody Maker 41 (May 7, 1966) p3. illus.

M 2226 "The Most Fantastic Game Of Billiard's Ever."
The Beatles Book 31 (February 1966)
pp26-27.
(Photos.)

M 2227 "Motion Pictures: Coming Attractions."
Rolling Stone 290 (May 3, 1979) p41.
(McCartney's "Band On The Run" film.)

M 2228 "Motion Pictures: Coming Attractions."
Rolling Stone 290 (May 3, 1979) p41.
(George Harrison helps finance "Life Of
Brian.")

M 2229 Moyle, Graham. "Somewhere In Australia."
Beatles Unlimited 45 (1982) pp12-13. illus.
(George Harrsion "down under.")

M 2230 "Much Travelled Mary." The Beatles Book 76
(November 1969) p31.
(McCartneys search for country home.)

M 2231 Mudge, Roberta Ann. "Liszt, Chopin, Wordsworth
And The Beatles." Music Journal 29
(April 1971) pp35-36.

M 2232 Mudge, Roberta Ann. "Student Speaks; Knights Of
A Hard Day." Music Journal 26 (March 1968)
p70+. illus.

M 2233 Mulholland, Peter. "Early Apple Recordings."
Record Collector 11 (July 1980) pp19-22.
illus.
(Complete listing.)

M 2234 Muller, Herve. "Les Beatles Apres."
Rock & Folk (Paris) 118 (November 1976)
pp92-99. illus.

M 2235 Mulligan, Brian. "Beatles' Apple In Aug. Bow."
Variety 251 (July 24, 1968) pp45-46.

M 2236 Mulligan, Brian. "Beatles' Multi Music Fronts;
From U.S. Rights To ATV Stock Buy." Variety
254 (April 9, 1969) p65+.

M 2237 Mulligan, Brian. "Beatles' Sales Equal 206-Mil
Singles; Nix Concerts For Other Show Biz
Roles." Variety 248 (October 11, 1967)
p89.

M 2238 Mulligan, Brian. "Beatles' Sales: 545 Mil
Units." Billboard 84 (October 21, 1972)
p1+.

M 2239 Mulligan, Brian. "EMI, Beatles To Renew Pact."
Billboard 81 (September 20, 1969) p1+.

M 2240 Mulligan, Brian. "EMI Spurns Nude Lennon And
Yoko On '2 Virgins' LP." Variety 252
(October 23, 1968) p1+.

M 2241 Mulligan, Brian. "End To Beatles' Legal Hassle
Due Soon." Billboard 86 (December 21, 1974)
p3. illus.

M 2242 Munro, Michael. "A Million Heard The Tragedy
Predicted." Star 9:2 (January 13, 1981)
p21. illus.
(Psychic Alexander Tanous predicted
Lennon's death.)

M 2243 Murray, Charles. "Raps Of Wacky Macca."
New Musical Express (July 26, 1975)
pp20-23+.
(Paul McCartney.)

M 2244 Murray, Charles. "Silly Charlie And The Not-So
Red-Hot 'Pepper'." New Musical Express
(May 25, 1974) p19.

M 2245 Musel, B. "Lennon And McCartney." BMI
(June 1966) p9. illus.

M 2246 Musel, R. "Back To Blighty With The Beatles."
TV Guide 12 (April 18, 1964) pp10-12.

M 2247 "Musical Revue Salutes Lennon." Variety 303
(May 13, 1981) p4+.
("Imagine: A Tribute To John Lennon.")

M 2248 "Musical Satire From Vanguard And Electra."
American Record Guide 32 (February 1966)
pp508-510.
(On "The Baroque Beatles Book" LP.)

M 2249 Music Business. New York: Music Business Inc.,
1965.
(Dec. 31, 1964-Jan. 9, 1965 issue; Beatles
cover.)

M 2250 Mutton, Peter. "A Graphic History."

Beatles Unlimited 8 (July 1976) pp11-15.
    (Beatles' musical group family trees.)
M 2251 "Mystery Develops Over Beatles Live Concert."
    Melody Maker 43 (November 12, 1968)
    p5.
M 2252 "Mystery Tour." Rolling Stone 1 (November 9,
    1967) p4+.
M 2253 "Mystery Tour Making Local Stops Soon."
    Rolling Stone 8 (April 6, 1968) p4.
M 2254 N., A. "The Ballad Of Paul And Tokyo."
    Beatlefan 2:3 (April 1980) p22.
    (Song parody.)
M 2255 "Nab Lennon, Yoko On London Drug Charge."
    Variety (October 23, 1968) p47.
M 2256 Nadel, M. "Thirty Years After." Jazz & Pop 10
    (April 1971) p15. illus.
    (Paul McCartney and John Lennon.)
M 2257 Narducy, R.D. "The Films Of The Beatles: A
    Study In Star Images."
    Dissertation Abstracts 42 (March 1982)
    p3793.
M 2258 "Nay, Nay, Nay." Forbes (September 1, 1965)
    p31. illus.
    (Northern Songs stock sales.)
M 2259 Neapolitan, Jerry. "Feedback." Beatlefan 4:2
    (February 1982) p25.
    (McCartney as musical leader of The
    Beatles.)
M 2260 Neary, John. "Magical McCartney Mystery." Life 67
    (November 7, 1969) pp103-105. illus.
    (Cover portrait.)
M 2261 Neary, T. "Dick James, Global Publisher."
    Songwriters Review 29:1 (1974) p5.
M 2262 Nelson, Milo. "Letter From New York."
    Wilson Library Bulletin 55:6 (February 1981)
    p404.
    (John Lennon's death.)
M 2263 Nelson, Paul. "'Sgt. Pepper' Gets Busted."
    Rolling Stone 275 (October 5, 1978) p71.
    (Soundtrack LP.)
M 2264 Nelson, Paul. "The Strange Case Of John
    Lennon." Circus (March 2, 1976) p11.
M 2265 Nelson, Paul. "'Venus And Mars': Wings'
    Non-Stellar Flight." Rolling Stone 192
    (July 31, 1975) pp52,55.
    (On the "Venus And Mars" album.)
M 2266 "New Acts." Variety 272 (October 31, 1973)
    p54.
    (Yoko Ono.)
M 2267 "New Album In August." The Beatles Book 72
    (July 1969) p31.
    ("Get Back" LP.)
M 2268 "New Album Out This Month." The Beatles Book 74
    (September 1969) p31.
    ("Abbey Road.")
M 2269 "New Albums From Paul & Wings And George
    Harrison." The Beatles Book 9 (January 1977)
    ppiii-iv.
M 2270 "'New Beatle' Klaus Goes Into Hiding."
    Melody Maker 46 (March 27, 1971) p1.
    (Klaus Voorman.)
M 2271 "The New Beatles Book." The Beatles Book 77
    (September 1982) ppiii-v.
    (Plans to resume publication.)
M 2272 "New Beatles Bootlegs." Melody Maker 46
    (February 27, 1971) p5.
M 2273 "New Beatles Double Album Due On November 16."
    Rolling Stone 20 (October 26, 1968)
    p4. illus.
M 2274 "New Beatles Film: 'Let It Be'." Rolling Stone
    47 (November 29, 1969) p6+.
M 2275 "New Beatles: Happiness Is A Warm Gun."
    Rolling Stone 22 (November 23, 1968)
    p8.
M 2277 "New Book News." Beatlefan 3:3 (April 1981)
    p29.
    (Publishing news.)
M 2278 "New Directions For Beatle Business."

Rolling Stone 7 (March 9, 1968) p8.
M 2279 "New Lennons LP." Rolling Stone 127 (February
    1, 1973) p16.
    ("Approximately Infinite Universe.")
M 2280 "New Madness; Rhythm-And-Blues Quartet Called
    The Beatles." Time 82 (November 15, 1963)
    p63. illus.
M 2281 Newman, P.C. "'Restless Spirits Depart, Still
    We're Deep In Each Other's Heart'."
    MacLean's 93 (December 22, 1980) p3. illus.
    (Editorial.)
M 2282 "New Plastic Ono Single." The Beatles Book 73
    (August 1969) p29.
    ("Rock Peace.")
M 2283 "News." Beatles Now
    (Regular feature, Nos.1-2, January-Spring
    1982.)
M 2284 "Newsmakers." Newsweek 68 (September 19, 1966)
    p65. illus.
    (John Lennon.)
M 2285 "Newsmakers." Newsweek 74 (November 3, 1969)
    p62.
    (Paul McCartney.)
M 2286 "Newsmakers." Senior Scholastic (November 10,
    1969) p15.
    (On the McCartney death hoax.)
M 2287 "Newsmakers." Senior Scholastic 95 (November
    10, 1970) p15. illus.
    (Paul McCartney.)
M 2288 "Newsmakers." Newsweek 81 (April 2, 1973)
    p44. illus.
    (John Lennon.)
M 2289 "Newsmakers." Newsweek 84 (November 25, 1974)
    p62. illus.
    (George Harrison.)
M 2290 "New Thing For Beatles: Magical Mystery Tour."
    Rolling Stone 3 (December 14, 1967)
    p1+. illus.
M 2291 Newton, F. "Beatles And Before." New Statesman 66
    (November 8, 1963) p673.
M 2292 "New West Intelligence." New West 2 (January
    31, 1977) p66.
    (John Lennon.)
M 2293 "New York." Rolling Stone 70 (November 12, 1970)
    p8. illus.
    (Paul McCartney.)
M 2294 "NY Hotels Duck Housing Beatles." Variety 235
    (July 1, 1964) p1+.
M 2296 "NY Times Ad Used For Bernstein Beatles
    Appeal." Billboard 88 (October 9, 1976)
    p10.
    (Reunion appeal.)
M 2297 New York Times Magazine. New York:
    New York Times, 1975.
    (Beatles cover portrait.)
M 2298 "Next Beatles Trip August 18." Billboard 76
    (March 28, 1964) p28.
M 2299 Ney, Jutta. "Rock And Roll Revival."
    Jazz & Pop 9 (January 1970) pp61-62.
M 2300 Ney, Jutta. "'War Is Over' If You Want It;
    Happy Christmas From John & Yoko."
    Jazz & Pop 9 (March 1970) pp31-33. illus.
M 2301 "1977 Rolling Stone Critics' Awards."
    Rolling Stone 255 (December 29, 1977)
    p16.
    (Klaatu rumor: Hype of the Year.)
M 2302 "1964; Gerry And The Pacemakers."
    Rolling Stone 381 (October 28, 1982)
    p84.
    (Also discusses The Beatles.)
M 2303 "1962 - The Beatles Year Of Achievement."
    Mersey Beat (December 13, 1962) p14. illus.
    (Full-page review of 1962 events.)
M 2304 "Ninth Beatles Book Competition Results."
    The Beatles Book 43 (February 1967)
    pp12-13.
    (Winners of "Draw A Beatle" contest.)
M 2305 "No Beatles Appeal - McCartney Leaving."

Melody Maker 46 (May 1, 1971) p4.

M 2306 "No Decision On New Single." The Beatles Book 75
(October 1969) p31.
(Recording activities.)

M 2307 "No Freezing On Beatles' Royalties."
Melody Maker 44 (April 12, 1969) p2.

M 2308 Norgaard, P. "Komponisten Paul McCartney."
Dansk Musiktidsskrift 41 (1966) pp108-109.

M 2309 Norman, Philip. "Shout." Us 5:9 (April 28, 1981)
pp45-52. illus.
(Excerpts from his book.)

M 2310 Norman, Philip. "Talk With Yoko."
New York Magazine 14 (May 25, 1981)
pp32-33+. illus.
(Interview.)

M 2311 "Norman Smith Talks About Balancing The
Beatles." The Beatles Book 22 (May 1965)
pp11-13.
(Beatles' recording engineer.)

M 2312 Norris, Bob. "All Over The World."
The Beatles Book 22 (May 1965) p5.
(On Shepherd's "True Story Of The
Beatles.")

M 2313 North, Garrett. "The Richard Starkey Story."
Teen Screen (September 1966) pp24-25.

M 2314 North, P. "Pete Drake & The Steel Beatle."
Rolling Stone 63 (July 23, 1970) p6. illus.
(George Harrison.)

M 2315 North, P. "Ringo & Friends In Country Country."
Rolling Stone 64 (August 6, 1970) pp6-7.
illus.

M 2316 "Northern Songs Battle Over But Malady
Lingers." Variety 256 (October 22, 1969)
p55.

M 2317 "Northern Songs Buying 2 Beatles' Lenmac Firm
In $1,022,000 Cash Deal." Variety (April 13,
1966) p1.

M 2318 "Northern Songs' 'Takeover' Fight Now 3-Way
Battle." Variety 254 (May 7, 1969)
p243.

M 2319 "Notes And Comment." New Yorker 47 (February
5, 1972) pp25-27.
(George Harrison.)

M 2320 "Notes And Comment: More Popular, Or More
Famous, Than Jesus." New Yorker 42
(August 27, 1966) pp21-22.

M 2322 "Now Its 25 Million Pounds For Beatles."
Melody Maker 51 (March 20, 1976) p5.
(Reunion offer.)

M 2323 "Now - 'Live Peace From Toronto'."
Melody Maker 44 (December 6, 1969)
pp20-21. illus.

M 2324 "Now They're A Lot Richer, Some Are Sadder, All
Wiser." Biography News 2 (March 1975)
p375. illus.

M 2325 "Now We Know How Many Holes It Takes To Fill
The Albert Hall." Rolling Stone 338
(March 5, 1981) p16+.
(Ken Kesey on the passing of John Lennon.)

M 2326 Nusser, D. "'Beatlemania' Tees Four Rock
Spinoffs." Billboard 90 (December 2, 1978)
p98.
("Beatlemania" stage show.,)

M 2327 Nusser, D. "Beatles Era Revival Idea Behind $1
Mil N.Y. Show." Billboard 89 (April 16, 1977)
p10+.
(Stage show "Beatlemania.")

M 2328 Nusser, R. "Beatles Magical Mystery Tour."
After Dark 10 (September 1968) p5,15. illus.

M 2329 Nylen, L. "Beatles: En Drom Om Frihet."
Dansk Musiktidsskrift 41:4 (1966) pp104-107.

M 2330 "Obituary." National Review 32 (December 31,
1980) p1555.

M 2331 "Obituary." Current Biography 42 (February 1981)
p47.
(John Lennon.)

M 2332 "Obituary." Downbeat 48 (February 1981)

p13.

M 2333 "Obituary." Guitar Player 15 (February 1981)
p134.
(John Lennon.)

M 2334 Ochs, E. "Tomorrow." Billboard 81 (October 4,
1969) p26.
(John Lennon.)

M 2335 Ochs, E. "Tomorrow." Billboard 82 (March 28,
1970) p10.
(Paul McCartney.)

M 2336 "Odd Info!" The Beatles Book 52 (August 1980)
pviii.
(U.S. town renames local disco The Cavern.)

M 2337 "Official Overseas Beatles Fan Clubs."
The Beatles Book 24 (July 1965) p8.
(Address list.)

M 2338 "Official Up-To-Date List Of Fan Club
Secretaries." The Beatles Book 73 (August
1969) p24.
(U.K. and the world; excludes U.S.A.)

M 2339 "Of Rumor, Myth, And A Beatle." Time 94
(October 31, 1969) p41. illus.
(Paul McCartney.)

M 2340 O'Grady, Terence J. "The Ballad Style In The
Early Music Of The Beatles."
College Music Symposium 19:1 (1979) pp221-230.
illus.

M 2341 O'Grady, Terence J. "Music Of The Beatles From
1962 To Sgt. Pepper's Lonely Hearts Club
Band." Dissertation Abstracts 36 (March 1976)
pp5629A-5630A.
(Abstract of two volume dissertation.)

M 2342 O'Grady, Terence J. "'Rubber Soul' And The
Social Dance Tradition." Ethnomusicology 23:1
(1979) pp87-94.

M 2343 O'Hara, J.D. "Talking Through Their Heads."
New Republic 166 (May 20, 1972) pp30-31.
(John Lennon.)

M 2344 "OK 1st Beatles Cut On Non-EMI Label."
Billboard 90 (March 4, 1978) p60.

M 2345 "Old Bowl Concerts By Beatles Due." Billboard
89 (April 23, 1977) p4+.
(Hollywood Bowl album.)

M 2346 "The Old Team Again." The Beatles Book 74
(September 1969) p31.
(George Martin helps with "Abbey Road.")

M 2347 O'Mahony, Sean. "The End Of An Era."
The Beatles Book 77 (December 1969)
pp8-15.
("Beatles Book" ceases publication.)

M 2348 "On Bass Guitar: Paul McCartney."
The Beatles Book 1 (August 1963) pp10-11.

M 2349 "On Drums: Ringo Starr." The Beatles Book 1
(August 1963) pp12-13.

M 2350 "One And One And One Is Three." Rolling Stone
46 (November 15, 1969) p6. illus.
(McCartney death hoax.)

M 2351 "One Beatles Pic His, Second Later; Shenson's
Unique Reversion Of 'Durable Legend'
Features." Variety 300 (September 3, 1980)
p7+.

M 2352 O'Neil, Tom. "Tom O'Neil Remembers Lennon."
Dixie Flyer (January 1981) p9.

M 2353 O'Neill, Lou, Jr. "Back Pages." Circus
(January 31, 1981) p66.

M 2354 O'Neill, Lou, Jr. "Good Morning America."
Beatlefan 4:1 (December 1981) p12.
(George Harrison interview, Oct. 20, 1981.)

M 2355 O'Neill, Lou, Jr. "Meeting The Beatles."
Beatlefan 3:2 (February 1981) p26.
(Reprinted from "Circus Rock Immortals 1.")

M 2356 "1 Million Pounds For Beatles New LP."
Melody Maker 43 (November 30, 1968)
p1.

M 2357 "On Lead Guitar: George Harrison."
The Beatles Book 1 (August 1963) pp6-7.

M 2358 "Only One Beatle Manages To Crack Iron
Curtain." Variety 284 (August 18, 1976)
p1+.
("Band On The Run" album.)

M 2359 Ono, Yoko. "In Gratitude." Beatlefan 3:2
(February 1981) p32.
(Her thanks for public's condolences.)

M 2360 Ono, Yoko. "Yoko Ono On Yoko Ono."
Film Culture 48:49 (Winter/Spring 1970) pp32-33.
(Discusses "Film No. 4," "Film No. 5," and
"Rape.")

M 2361 Ono, Yoko. "Yoko Talks About It."
Rolling Stone 24 (December 21, 1968)
p15+. illus.
("Two Virgins" film.)

M 2362 "Ono Band Shelve Plans To Issue Old Beatles
Disc." Melody Maker 44 (December 6, 1969)
p4.

M 2363 "Ono, Geffen, WB Sued For Copyright Violation."
Variety 303 (June 24, 1981) p76.
("I'm Your Angel.")

M 2364 "On Rhythm Guitar: John Lennon."
The Beatles Book 1 (August 1963) pp8-9.

M 2365 "On Stage Pix." The Beatles Book 17 (December
1964) pp10-11.
(Performance photos.)

M 2366 "On Tour With The Beatles." Melody Maker 39
(October 17, 1964) pp8-9. illus.

M 2367 "Order Ex-Beatle To Exit U.S." Variety 275
(July 24, 1974) p2+.
(John Lennon.)

M 2368 Ornelas, Rudy. "Beatle Picture Discs."
Beatlefan 3:2 (February 1981) p10.
(Collecting tips.)

M 2369 Ornelas, Rudy. "Fan Fest Update." Beatlefan 3:3
(April 1981) p14.
(Los Angeles Beatles convention, March
14-15.)

M 2370 Ornelas, Rudy and Lou O'Neill. "Fan Fest
Update." Beatlefan 4:1 (December 1981)
p14.
(Los Angeles Beatlefest, November 28-29,
1981.)

M 2371 Orth, M. "Paul Soars." Newsweek 87 (May 17,
1976) p100. illus.

M 2372 Orth, M. "Ringo's Back." Newsweek 82 (October
29, 1973) pp113-114. illus.

M 2373 Osbourne, Christine A. "George Harrison's Hand
Read By Romany Clairvoyant, Eva Petulengro."
The Beatles Book 18 (January 1965)
p7.
(Palm reading.)

M 2374 Osmundsen, J.A. "Science Looks At Beatlemania."
Science Digest 55 (May 1964) pp24-26. illus.

M 2375 "Other Noises, Other Notes." Time 89 (March 3,
1967) p63. illus.

M 2376 Otis. "Let It Be." News From Nowhere 2:10
(July 1970) p10.

M 2377 O'Toole, L. "Legacy Of Lennon." MacLean's 93:3
(December 22, 1980) pp36-38+. illus.
(With editorial comment by P. C. Newman.)

M 2378 "Our American Scrapbook." Life 57 (October 23,
1964) pp105-107. illus.

M 2379 "Our Back Pages: Apple And The Beatles."
Rolling Stone 123 (December 7, 1972)
p26. illus.
(Reprint from first issue.)

M 2380 "Our Back Pages: Mystery Tour." Rolling Stone
123 (December 7, 1972) p26.
(Reprint from first issue.)

M 2381 Our Society Editor. "All The Way In St.
Tropez." Rolling Stone 84 (June 10, 1971)
p1.
(McCartney and Starr at Mick Jagger
wedding.)

M 2382 Ovens, D. "Superstar Show Makes 'Superb' Bangla
Set." Billboard 83 (December 18, 1971)
p3.

M 2383 Overy, P. "London: Yoko Ono's Film 'Number
Four'." Artscanada 24 (June/July 1967) p10.

M 2384 Overy, P. "Unfinished Paintings And Objects At
The Indica Gallery." Artscanada 24
(January 1967) p7. illus.
(Yoko Ono.)

M 2385 Packard, Vance. "Building The Beatle Image."
Saturday Evening Post 237 (March 21, 1964)
p36. illus.

M 2386 Palmer, P. "Beatles Pub Firm Alleges $12
Million Underpayment." Billboard 82
(December 19, 1970) p3+.

M 2387 Palmer, Raymond. "Danger, Beatles At Work."
Saturday Review 51 (October 12, 1968)
pp64-65. illus.

M 2388 Palmer, Robert. "John Lennon: Guiding Force In
Music And Culture Of The 60's."
New York Times Biography Service 11 (December
1980) pp1753-1754. illus.

M 2389 Palmer, Robert. "John Lennon: Must An Artist
Self-Destruct?"
New York Times Biography Service 11 (November
1980) pp1565-1567. illus.

M 2390 Palmer, Robert. "Starting Over." Penthouse 12
(March 1981) pp55-56. illus.
(Interview with John Lennon.)

M 2391 Pannebakker, Frits. "Beatles Return To Their
Home - Liverpool." Beatles Unlimited 1
(March 1975) pp14-15.
(Return from first U.S. visit.)

M 2392 "The Paperback Writer Session."
The Beatles Book 35 (June 1966) pp6-11.
(Recording session.)

M 2393 Parry-King, Jonathan. "Fan Fest Update."
Beatlefan 1:3 (April 1979) p20.
("Beatlefest '79," New York City.)

M 2394 Partridge, R. "Harrison - Dark Horse In
Cannes." Melody Maker 51 (February 7, 1976)
p10.
(The MIDEM music festival.)

M 2395 Patton, Phil. "Strawberry Fields Forever."
New Times 3 (October 4, 1974) p43.

M 2396 Patyna, Joanna. "John Lennon's Shocking Secret
Life." Star 8:49 (December 8, 1981)
pp23,26. illus.

M 2397 "Paul." The Beatles Book 19 (November 1977)
ppiii-v.

M 2398 "Paul And Linda At Corfu." The Beatles Book 72
(July 1969) p31.
(Greek island vacation.)

M 2399 "Paul And Ringo On Film." Rolling Stone 371
(June 10, 1982) p32.
(In "The Cooler," an 11-minute film.)

M 2400 "Paul, Beatles' Battles Behind Him, In Control
As Biz, Band Blossom." Variety 297
(January 9, 1980) p188.
(Interview.)

M 2401 "The Paul LP You'll Never See." Melody Maker 46
(May 29, 1971) p3. illus.

M 2402 "Paul McCartney." Chatelaine 54 (September 1981)
p17. illus.

M 2403 "Paul McCartney And How He Created Wings."
The Beatles Book 2 (June 1976) ppiv-vii.

M 2404 "Paul McCartney At 40." Chatelaine 55
(August 1982) p10. illus.
(On "The Tug Of War" LP.)

M 2405 "Paul McCartney Busted In Tokyo."
Rolling Stone 311 (February 21, 1980)
p14. illus.
(Japan tour.)

M 2406 "Paul McCartney Forms A Band." Rolling Stone 90
(September 2, 1971) p12.

M 2407 "Paul McCartney: From The Beginning." Teen 22
(September 1978) p39. illus.

M 2408 "Paul McCartney On Paul McCartney."
Rolling Stone 58 (May 14, 1970) p8.
(Self-interview accompanies U.K. album.)

M 2409 "Paul McCartney Paces Fund Drive (UNESCO Week
For Venice)." Variety 284 (October 6, 1976)
p64.

M 2410 "Paul McCartney Reviews The New Pop Records."
Melody Maker 39 (January 25, 1964)
p5. illus.

M 2411 "Paul McCartney's Guitars." Beatles Unlimited 4
(November 1975) pp14-17.
(Photo survey.)

M 2412 "Paul McCartney's LSD Tell-All Stirs Brouhaha."
        Variety (June 28, 1967) p1+.
M 2413 "Paul McCartney - So Entstand Die Neue LP."
        Musik Joker (Hamburg) (April 1979)
        pp4-9. illus.
M 2414 "Paul McCartney Throws Swank Party."
        Rolling Stone 97 (December 9, 1971)
        p24. illus.
M 2415 "Paul McCartney Throws 2 Curves."
        Rolling Stone 105 (March 30, 1972)
        p14.
        ("Give Ireland Back To The Irish.")
M 2416 "Paul: Money Can't Buy Him Love." Hullabaloo 1:1
        (October 1966) pp32-33. illus.
        (Issue includes photos of George, Paul and
        John.)
M 2417 "Paul's At Work." Rolling Stone 77 (March 4,
        1971) p10.
M 2418 "Paul's Brother, M. McCartney." Trouser Press 8
        (February 1982) pp21-24. illus.
        (Excerpts from "The Macs.")
M 2419 "Paul's Kid Brother Mike." Teen 19 (January
        1975) p46. illus.
M 2420 "Paul's TV Statement." The Beatles Book 48
        (July 1967) p12.
        (On his use of LSD.)
M 2421 "Peace Anthem." Newsweek 74 (December 1, 1969)
        p2.
        (John Lennon.)
M 2422 Peacock, Steve. "John: Getting Back To The
        Roots (Maybe Not His, But Nevertheless
        Roots)." Rock (March 15, 1974) pp13-14.
M 2423 Pearlman, S. "Saucer Lands In Virginia."
        Crawdaddy 11 (September/October 1967) p24.
M 2424 Pearson, S. "Paul's Shout Up At Shipley."
        Melody Maker 43 (July 13, 1968) p10. illus.
M 2425 Peebles, Andy. "The Lennon Tapes." Listener 105
        (January 22, 1981) pp101-103. illus.
        (Interview with the Lennons, Part One.)
M 2426 Peebles, Andy. "The Lennon Tapes: 'I Can Go
        Right Out Of This Door Now And Go In A
        Restaurant'." Listener 105 (February 5, 1981)
        p172.
        (Interview with the Lennons, Part Three.)
M 2427 Peebles, Andy. "The Lennon Tapes: 'The Rock
        Stars Were Commenting On What I Was Not
        Doing'." Listener 105 (January 29, 1981)
        pp141-142. illus.
        (Interview with the Lennons, Part Two.)
M 2428 Peel, D. "Punks In Leathers From Liverpool."
        Yipster Times 4:7 (October 1976) p21.
M 2429 Peel, Mark. "McCartney And Friends."
        Stereo Review (June 1982) p76.
        (On the "Tug Of War" LP.)
M 2430 Peerdeman, Hillebrand. "Dig It Plus."
        Beatles Unlimited 8 (July 1976) p23.
        (Supplements to regular "Dig It" bootlegs
        feature.)
M 2431 Pekar, H. "From Rock To ???" Down Beat 35
        (May 2, 1968) p21+.
M 2432 "Pen Pals." Beatlefan
        (Regular feature, vln2-   , 1979-   .)
M 2433 "People." Time 88 (September 16, 1966)
        p53. illus.
        (John Lennon.)
M 2434 "People." Time 97 (January 18, 1971) p34.
        illus.
        (Excerpts from Lennon's "Rolling Stone"
        interview.)
M 2435 "People." Time 100 (September 11, 1972)
        p37. illus.
        (John Lennon.)
M 2436 "People." Time 101 (April 2, 1973) p44. illus.
        (John Lennon.)
M 2437 "People." Time 103 (March 25, 1974) p50. illus.
        (John Lennon.)
M 2438 "People." Time 104 (November 11, 1974)
        p51. illus.
        (John Lennon.)
M 2439 "People." Time 105 (January 13, 1975)

p37. illus.
        (John Lennon.)
M 2440 "People." Time 105 (March 17, 1975) p49. illus.
        (John Lennon.)
M 2441 "People." Time (April 19, 1982) p57.
        (The McCartneys meet Yoko Ono in New York.)
M 2442 "People." Time 108 (August 2, 1976) p34. illus.
        (Ringo Starr.)
M 2443 "People." Time 108 (August 9, 1976) p31. illus.
        (John Lennon.)
M 2444 "People." Time 113 (June 11, 1979) p81.
        (John Lennon.)
M 2445 "People." Time 108 (December 6, 1976)
        p81. illus.
        (Linda McCartney.)
M 2446 "People." Time 106 (October 20, 1975)
        p58. illus.
        (John Lennon.)
M 2447 "People." Time (June 7, 1982) p69.
        (On the featurette "The Cooler.")
M 2448 "People Are Talking About The Beatles, Four
        Parody Singers, Now The Passion Of British
        Young." Vogue 143 (January 1, 1964)
        pp100-101. illus.
M 2449 People Weekly - The Beatles: Will They Sing
        Again For $50 Million. Chicago, IL:
        Time, Inc., 1976.
        (Cover portrait.)
M 2450 "Peregrine Worsthorne Discusses The Beatles &
        Mysticism." The National Observer (September
        18, 1967) p12.
M 2451 "Performance." Rolling Stone 137 (June 21, 1973)
        p14.
        (Paul McCartney.)
M 2452 "Performance." Rolling Stone 216 (July 1, 1976)
        p102. illus.
        (Paul McCartney.)
M 2453 "Performance." Rolling Stone 310 (February 7,
        1980) p92. illus.
        (Paul McCartney.)
M 2454 Perry S. "Linda McCartney Animated Short At
        Fest: Firm Eyes Full-Lengther." Variety 299
        (May 14, 1980) p23.
        (The film "Seaside Woman.")
M 2455 "Personal Ads." The Beatles Book
        (Regular reprint feature, issues 6-40, 47-
        .)
M 2456 "Personal Ads." Record Collector
        (Regular feature, issues 1-6, 1979-1980.)
M 2458 "Personal Requests." The Beatles Book 32
        (March 1966) p8.
        (Fan requests.)
M 2459 "Pete Best At The Star Club." Mersey Beat
        (August 15, 1963) p8.
        (Photograph.)
M 2460 "Pete Best On The 'New' Beatles LP."
        Rolling Stone 371 (June 10, 1982) p35.
        (As Dreamers Do.)
M 2461 "Peter Jones Tells The Truth About The Beatles'
        First Ever Interview By A National Pop Paper
        In August 1962." The Beatles Book 31
        (November 1978) ppiii-v.
M 2462 Peterson, Craig. "Another Beatle Tragedy On The
        Way." The Globe 27:53 (December 30, 1980)
        p28. illus.
        (Psychic Gloria James predicted Lennon's
        death.)
M 2463 Phast Phreddie. "The Aesthetics Of Psychedelic
        Music." Bomp 19 (October/November 1978) p34. illus.
        (The Beatles' studio work.)
M 2464 Phillips, Steve. "Beatle News Round-Up."
        Beatles Now 3 (Summer 1982) p2.
M 2465 Phillips, Steve. "Beatles Bootleg Albums: A
        Rip-Off Or A Boon?" Beatles Now 5 (Winter
        1983) p21.
M 2466 Phillips, Steve. "A Beatle's Gig At The

Cavern." The Beatles Book 79 (November 1982)
pp4-9.
(October 1962.)

M 2467 Phillips, Steve. "A Cellar Full Of Joys."
Beatlefan 2:5 (August 1980) p17.
(Magical Mystery Store, Liverpool shrine.)

M 2468 Phillips, Steven. "A Decade Without The
Beatles." Beatlefan 2:4 (June 1980)
p7.
(Why The Beatles' legend persists.)

M 2469 Phillips, Steve. "Epstein." Beatles Now 4
(Autumn 1982) pp14-15. illus.
(Brian Epstein.)

M 2470 Phillips, Steve. "Fab Four Facts." Beatles Now
(Regular feature, issue No,8- , October
1983- .)

M 2471 Phillips, Steve. "Fan Fest Update." Beatlefan 2:4
(June 1980) pp11,28.
(Sheffield, England, May 31, 1980.)

M 2472 Phillips, Steve. "Fans Gather In Liverpool."
Beatlefan 3:6 (October 1981) p18.
(First annual Mersey Beatle Extravaganza.)

M 2473 Phillips, Steve. "Imagine ... Lennon Was A
Monster, It's Easy (And Profitable) If You
Try!" Beatles Now 8 (October 1983)
p19.

M 2474 Phillips, Steve. "'I Was Shivering Inside ...'"
Beatlefan 3:2 (February 1981) p17.
(Reactions to Lennon's death.)

M 2475 Phillips, Steve. "John Lennon: The Very Last
Interview." Beatles Now 8 (October 1983)
pp6-7,15. illus.
(RKO radio interview.)

M 2476 Phillips, Steve. "Latest Dispatch From
Liverpool." Beatlefan 2:6 (October 1980)
p8.
("Beatles Information Centre" and museum.)

M 2477 Phillips, Steve. "'Love Me Do'." Beatlefan 4:6
(October 1982) p5.
(A fan looks back twenty years.)

M 2478 Phillips, Steve. "'Rarities': Another Look."
Beatlefan 2:6 (October 1980) p14.
(Nominations for another rarities album.)

M 2479 Phillips, Steve. "A Scouser's View Of The
'Pool." Beatlefan 2:6 (October 1980)
p7.
(Liverpool yesterday and today.)

M 2480 Phillips, Steve. "Thingumybob." Beatlefan 3:1
(December 1980) p26.
(Commentary on Paul McCartney's career.)

M 2481 Phillips, Steve. "Thingumybob." Beatlefan 3:5
(August 1981) p27.
(Murdered Lennon an FBI/CIA plot victim?)

M 2482 Phillips, Steve. "Wrack My Brain: To Be A
Paperback Writer." Beatles Now 2 (Spring
1982) pp13-14.
(A fan's attempt to write a book on Ringo.)

M 2483 Phillips, Steve and Bill King. "Those Were The
Days." Beatlefan 3:3 (April 1981) p14.
(The Beatles meet Elvis Presley.)

M 2484 Phillips, Tom. "The Album As Art Form: One Year
After Sgt. Pepper." Jazz & Pop 7 (May 1968)
pp35-36. illus.

M 2486 (Photo Of Yoko Ono.) Rolling Stone 387
(January 20, 1983) p5. illus.

M 2487 "Pieces And Comment." Arts Reporting Service 2
(October 18, 1971) pp1-2.
(Report of interview with John and Yoko.)

M 2488 Piercey, Nick. "The Beatles And E.M.I. Records."
Record Collector 50 (October 1983)
pp3-7. illus.
(Mike Heatley on EMI unreleased tracks.)

M 2489 Piercey, Nick. "The Beatles: The Alternate
Takes." Record Collector 38 (October 1982)
pp4-10. illus.
(Different mixes on available recordings.)

M 2490 Pitman, J. "Beatle Image Crisis Again - Is It

Pursuit Of Buck Or Art." Variety 255
(May 28, 1969) p57+.

M 2491 Pitman, J. "Beatles Reunion In Wings; Quartet
Near Settlement." Variety 274 (March 20,
1974) p1+.

M 2492 "A Place In The Sun Was His Very Favorite Spot
On Earth." The Star 7:53 (December 30, 1980)
pp10-11.
(John Lennon.)

M 2493 Planchart, Alejandro E. "Musical Landscape Of
The Beatles." Yale Literary Magazine 136
(March 1968) pp36-40.

M 2494 "Playboy Interview: The Beatles." Playboy 12
(February 1965) p51+.

M 2495 Pleasants, Henry. "The Fifth Beatle; 'A Little
Help From A Friend'." Stereo Review 26:2
(February 1971) p50+. illus.
(Interview with George Martin.)

M 2496 Pleasants, Henry. "Taking The Beatles
Seriously." Stereo Review (November 1967)
pp52,54. illus.
(Music critics' recent comments on The
Beatles.)

M 2497 "Please Please Me Press Release."
The Beatles Book 83 (March 1983) pp30,33.
illus.
(Copy of the actual album press release.)

M 2498 Plummer, M. "Paul McCartney And Wings Talk."
Melody Maker 47 (December 2, 1972)
p10+. illus.

M 2499 Plummer, M. "Wings: Melody Maker Band
Breakdown." Melody Maker 48 (April 21, 1973)
pp18-19. illus.

M 2500 Podrazik, Wally. "And Yet Another Decca Tapes
Release ..." Beatlefan 4:5 (August 1982)
pp22-23.
(By Audio Fidelity Enterprises.)

M 2501 Podrazik, Wally. "The Beatles Rarities."
Beatlefan 2:3 (April 1980) pp4-5.
(Background on the album.)

M 2502 Podrazik, Wally. "'Love Me Do'." Beatlefan 4:6
(October 1982) p5.
(A fan looks back twenty years.)

M 2503 Podrazik, Wally. "Mystery Of The Missing
Beatles Song." Beatlefan 3:3 (April 1981)
p27.
("You Can't Say I Never Told You.")

M 2504 Podrazik, Wally. "Remembrance Of Lennon Past."
Beatlefan 3:1 (December 1980) p23.
(Eulogy.)

M 2505 Podrazik, Wally. "'Sgt. Pepper' - A Look Back."
Beatlefan 4:4 (June 1982) p13.
(Album retrospective.)

M 2506 Podrazik, Wally. "Tales Of Hearsay And
Undisputed Truth For Beatle Watchers."
Beatlefan 2:1 (December 1979) p18.
(Origins of the book "A Day In The Life.")

M 2507 Poirier, R. "Learning From The Beatles."
Partisan Review 34 (Fall 1967) pp526-546.

M 2508 "'Political Censorship'; Now - New BBC Irish
Ban." Melody Maker 47 (February 26, 1972)
p14.
("Give Ireland Back To The Irish.")

M 2509 Polskin, Howard. "How TV Reported The John
Lennon Tragedy." TV Guide 29 (November 21,
1981) pp2-4+. illus.

M 2510 Pond, Steve. "David Geffen Boycotts
'Billboard'." Rolling Stone 338 (March 5,
1981) p16.

M 2511 Pope, Michael E. "And What Have You Done?"
Beatles Unlimited 16 (November 1977)
pp17-20.
(The recording of Lennon's "Happy
Christmas.")

M 2512 Pope, Michael E. "Beatlemania: The London Stage
Show." Beatles Unlimited 31 (March 1979)
pp12-13.

M 2513 Pope, Michael E. "Blindman." Beatles Unlimited 24
(January 1979) pp6-8.
(Ringo Starr's film role.)

M 2514 Pope, Michael E. "Candy." Beatles Unlimited 21
        (July 1978) pp12-15.
          (The film with Ringo Starr.)
M 2515 Pope, Michael E. "Interesting Facts."
        Beatles Unlimited
          (Regular feature, issues 22- .)
M 2516 Pope, Michael E. "Just Call It 'Winter Music'."
        Beatles Unlimited 16 (November 1977)
        pp22-23.
          (On Phil Spector's Christmas Album.)
M 2517 Pope, Michael E. "The Magic Christian."
        Beatles Unlimited 23 (November 1978)
        pp4-6,20.
          (Ringo Starr's film role.)
M 2518 Pope, Michael E. "Money Don't Buy Everything,
        It's True." Beatles Unlimited 18 (January
        1978) pp12-14.
          (The sale of Northern Songs.)
M 2519 Pope, Michael E. "Money Don't Buy Everything,
        It's True: Part Two." Beatles Unlimited 19
        (March 1978) pp4-6.
          (The sale of Northern Songs.)
M 2520 Pope, Michael E. "Money Don't Buy Everything,
        It's True: Part Three." Beatles Unlimited 20
        (May 1978) pp16-19.
          (The sale of Northern Songs.)
M 2521 Pope, Michael E. "Phil Spector."
        Beatles Unlimited 25 (March 1979) pp19-22.
          (Career and discography.)
M 2522 Pope, Michael E. "Reflections On The Death Of
        The Walrus." Beatles Unlimited 34/35 (1981) p41.
          (Eulogy.)
M 2523 Pope, Michael E. "United Kingdom."
        Beatles Unlimited 34/35 (1981) pp40-41.
          (Reactions to Lennon's death in England.)
M 2524 Pope, Michael E. "What A Bastard The World Is."
        Beatles Unlimited 33 (July 1980) pp20-21.
          (On the availability of group and solo
          recordings.)
M 2525 Pope, Michael E. "Where Has All The Beatlemania
        Gone?" Beatles Unlimited 45 (1982) p8.
          (On today's fans.)
M 2526 "Pop Report." Melody Maker 48 (June 9, 1973)
        pp36-37. illus.
          (George Harrison; John Lennon.)
M 2527 "Pop Think In." Melody Maker 40 (December 25,
        1965) p7. illus.
          (Brian Epstein.)
M 2528 "Pop Think In." Melody Maker 41 (January 1,
        1966) p3. illus.
          (Paul McCartney.)
M 2529 "Pop Think In." Melody Maker 41 (January 8,
        1966) p7. illus.
          (Ringo Starr.)
M 2530 "Pop Think In." Melody Maker (January 15, 1966)
        p7. illus.
          (John Lennon.)
M 2531 "Pop Think In." Melody Maker 41 (January 30,
        1966) p7. illus.
          (John Lennon.)
M 2532 "Pop Think In." Melody Maker (July 30, 1966)
        p7. illus.
          (John Lennon.)
M 2533 Porter, Eddie. "City Of Liverpool Beatle Street
        Campaign." Beatles Now 3 (Summer 1982)
        p4. illus.
          (Four Liverpool streets named for Beatles.)
M 2534 Porter, S.C. "Rhythm & Harmony In The Music Of
        The Beatles." Dissertation Abstracts 40
        (August 1979) p532A.
          (Abstract of Porter's dissertation.)
M 2535 "A Portfolio." Rolling Stone 335 (January 22,
        1981) p32+. illus.
          (Photo of John Lennon by Annie Leibovitz.)
M 2536 "Portrait." Chatelaine 42 (February 1969)
        p6. illus.
          (Paul McCartney.)
M 2537 "Portrait." Chatelaine 42 (February 1969)
        p6. illus.
          (Ringo Starr.)

M 2538 "Portrait." Chatelaine 42 (February 1969)
        p6. illus.
          (George Harrison)
M 2539 "Portrait." Chatelaine 42 (February 1969)
        p6. illus.
          (John Lennon.)
M 2540 "Portrait." Chatelaine 45 (July 1972)
        p34. illus.
          (Lennon and McCartney.)
M 2541 "Portrait." Financial Post 74 (December 22,
        1980) p7. illus.
          (John Lennon.)
M 2542 "Portrait." Heritage Canada 4 (June 1978)
        p7.
          (Paul McCartney.)
M 2543 "Portrait." MacLean's 81 (June 1968) p2L
        illus.
          (Ringo Starr.)
M 2544 "Portrait." MacLean's 81 (June 1968) p28.
        illus.
          (John Lennon.)
M 2545 "Portrait." MacLean's 89 (August 1976)
        p53.
          (John Lennon, Paul McCartney, Ringo Starr.)
M 2546 "Portrait." MacLean's 92 (November 5, 1979)
        p40. illus.
          (Paul McCartney.)
M 2547 "Portrait." MacLean's 93 (July 21, 1980)
        p39.
          (George Harrison.)
M 2548 "Portrait." Toronto Life (November 1981)
        p60.
          (Paul McCartney.)
M 2549 "Portrait." Weekend Magazine 27 (October 15,
        1977) p22.
          (Paul McCartney.)
M 2550 "Potential $4 Million Box Office For Beatles On
        Closed Circuit TV." Broadcasting (February
        24, 1964) pp84-85.
M 2551 Pountney, Kate. "Beatle Crush." Guardian
        (November 6, 1963) p7.
M 2552 Powditch, Keith. "Double Album Alphabet."
        The Beatles Book 67 (February 1969)
        p25.
          (Poem based on "White Album" songs.)
M 2553 "Presenting A Concert Of Recently Discovered
        Works By P.D.Q. Bach And 'The Baroque
        Beatles Book'." American Record Guide
        (February 1966) pp508-510.
          (Joshua Rifkin's "Baroque Beatles Book".)
M 2554 "Preserving The Beatles Fantasy." Creem 6
        (April 1975) p49+.
M 2555 "Pretty Penny Lane." Economist 284 (August 21,
        1982) p25. illus.
M 2556 Price, Richard. "It's Never Too Late."
        Rolling Stone 415 (February 16, 1984)
        pp74,76.
          (Personal memoirs.)
M 2557 "Priests Burn Beatles Disks In Mexico; See
        Sharp Slump In Sales." Variety 244
        (August 31, 1966) p1+.
M 2558 "Producer George." The Beatles Book 76
        (November 1969) p31.
          (Harrison's recording activities.)
M 2559 "The Program." Performing Arts (San Francisco)
        12:12 (December 1978)
          (Four-page program for "Beatlemania" stage
          play.)
M 2560 "Programmer's Artist Popularity Poll."
        Billboard 87 (August 16, 1975) p22+. illus.
M 2561 "Promoter Fears About Economics Of The
        Beatles." Variety (February 12, 1964)
        p1+.
M 2562 "Promoter Offers Beatles $30 Million For
        Closed-Circuit TV Concert." Variety 281
        (January 28, 1976) p62.
M 2563 "Prophets." MacLean's 82 (December 1969)
        p7. illus.
M 2564 "Publishers Notes." Beatlefan 4:3 (April 1982)

Santana Surfaces • A Special Report: College
Yok
An Intimate Conversation
Photographs by Annie Leibovitz
By Barbara Graustark
How the Dylan Tour Began
Rolling Stone
Greil Marcus Reviews, George Martin Remembers THE BEATLES
And You Know That Can't Be Bad
YEAH! YEAH! YEAH!
JERRY BROWN: THE PRINCE OF THE WEST
By Joe Klein
The Post-Prime-Time Follies of NBC's SATURDAY NIGHT
Rolling Stones To Tour U.S.A. In April 1969
Ramblin' Notes on the New Beatles Album, With Photos From the Record Sessions
John on Macrobiotics; Yoko Ono on Her Films
Doors' 'Riot' In Phoenix
Plus: Lou Adler Richard Brautigan Edward Kienholz

p3.

M 2565 "Publishers Sue Spinoff Of 'Beatlemania' For
        Infringement ('Beatlefever')." Variety 295
        (May 9, 1979) p533.
M 2566 Pules, H. "George In Hippyland." Melody Maker 42
        (August 19, 1967) p11. illus.
M 2567 Pullen, Rob. "After All Those Years - 'All
        Those Years Ago'." Beatles Unlimited 36
        (June 1981) pp6-7.
        (On the new Harrison single.)
M 2568 Pye, I. "The Erratic, Tormented Genius Of John
        Ono Lennon." Melody Maker 55 (November 8,
        1980) p27. illus.
M 2569 "Queen Elizabeth 2nd Awards Medals To Beatles."
        The National Observer (June 21, 1965)
        p14.
        (M.B.E.)
M 2570 "Queen's Award To Beatles Causing Bit Of
        Ruckus." Billboard 77 (June 26, 1965)
        p3.
M 2571 Quesada, Carmen. (Photos Of John Lennon.)
        New York Arts Journal 15 (September 1979)
        p13. illus.
M 2572 Quigly, Isabel. "The Beatles: A Hard Day's
        Night." Spectator (July 10, 1964) p47.
M 2573 Quinones, Mario. "Beatle Boots."
        Trans-Oceanic Trouser Press 1 (March 1974)
        pp13-16.
        (Discography.)
M 2574 "Quotes Quiz." The Beatles Book 64 (August 1981)
        pvi.
        (Trivia quiz.)
M 2575 "R. Meltzer Interviewed." Crawdaddy 14
        (March/April 1968) pp12-13.
M 2576 Rabe, F. and B. Sundin. "Synpunkter Paa Pop."
        Nutida Musik 9:5/6 (1965/66)
        pp45-48. illus.
M 2577 Rabinowtiz, D. "John Lennon's Mourners."
        Commentary 71 (February 1981) pp58-61.
M 2578 "Radio - Featured Programming." Billboard
        (June 25, 1983) p25.
        (Ringo's "Yellow Submarine" radio special.)
M 2579 Ragan, David. "Death Of A Beatle." The Globe 27:53
        (December 30, 1980) p21. illus.
        (John Lennon.)
M 2580 Raman, A.S. "Ravi Shankar At Home & Abroad."
        Saturday Review 53 (October 10, 1970)
        p47.
        (George Harrison.)
M 2581 Ramparts, Volume 6, No. 3. San Francisco, CA:
        Ramparts Magazine, 1967.
        (John Lennon cover portrait.)
M 2582 "Random Notes." Rolling Stone 17 (September 14,
        1968) p6.
        (New Apple singles anticipated.)
M 2584 "Random Notes." Rolling Stone 18 (September 28,
        1968) p6.
        (Publishers battle over Beatles'
        biography.)
M 2585 "Random Notes." Rolling Stone 18 (September 28,
        1968) p6.
        (McCartney's comments on conditions in
        India.)
M 2586 "Random Notes." Rolling Stone 22 (November 23,
        1968) p6.
        (Paul McCartney composing new song.)
M 2587 "Random Notes." Rolling Stone 25 (January 4,
        1969) p6.
        (John Lennon arrested.)
M 2588 "Random Notes." Rolling Stone 25 (January 4,
        1969) p6+.
        (Beatles have more songs ready.)
M 2589 "Random Notes." Rolling Stone 25 (January 4,
        1969) p25.
        (Vox cancels RS due to nude Lennon photos.)
M 2590 "Random Notes." Rolling Stone 28 (March 1, 1969)
        p6.

        (George Harrison meets Tiny Tim.)
M 2591 "Random Notes." Rolling Stone 29 (March 15,
        1969) p10.
        (John Lennon/Rolling Stones TV special.)
M 2592 "Random Notes." Rolling Stone 29 (March 15,
        1969) p10.
        (Linda Eastman confirms McCartney rumors.)
M 2593 "Random Notes." Rolling Stone 29 (March 15,
        1969) p10.
        ("Let It Be" filming.)
M 2594 "Random Notes." Rolling Stone 30 (April 5, 1969)
        p4.
        (George Harrison on new Clapton/Cream
        album.)
M 2595 "Random Notes." Rolling Stone 30 (April 5, 1969)
        p4.
        (Ringo in "Magic Christian.")
M 2596 "Random Notes." Rolling Stone 32 (May 3, 1969)
        p4.
        (John Lennon talks about his "bed-in".)
M 2597 "Random Notes." Rolling Stone 34 (May 31, 1969)
        p4.
        (Joe Cocker to record George Harrison
        song.)
M 2598 "Random Notes." Rolling Stone 35 (June 14, 1969)
        p4.
        (Ringo Starr in "Magic Christian.")
M 2599 "Random Notes." Rolling Stone 41 (September 6,
        1969) p4.
        (New Beatles album expected.)
M 2600 "Random Notes." Rolling Stone 43 (October 4,
        1969) p4.
        (Mary McCartney born.)
M 2601 "Random Notes." Rolling Stone 43 (October 4,
        1969) p4.
        (Beatles will guest on TV show.)
M 2602 "Random Notes." Rolling Stone 44 (October 18,
        1969) p4.
        (Unreleased Beatles LP already on air.)
M 2603 "Random Notes." Rolling Stone 46 (November 15,
        1969) p4.
        (McCartney produces Mary Hopkin.)
M 2604 "Random Notes." Rolling Stone 46 (November 15,
        1969) p4.
        (Star Club closing in Germany.)
M 2605 "Random Notes." Rolling Stone 46 (November 15,
        1969) p4.
        (Plastic Ono Band cuts single.)
M 2606 "Random Notes." Rolling Stone 47 (November 29,
        1969) p4.
        (Harrison/Lennon may join Delaney & Bonnie
        tour.)
M 2607 "Random Notes." Rolling Stone 47 (November 29,
        1969) p4.
        (Aretha Franklin to record "Let It Be.")
M 2608 "Random Notes." Rolling Stone 47 (November 29,
        1969) p4.
        (Yoko Ono has miscarriage.)
M 2609 "Random Notes." Rolling Stone 48 (December 13,
        1969) p4.
        (Beatles' lyrics book a good Xmas gift.)
M 2610 "Random Notes." Rolling Stone 49 (December 27,
        1969) p3.
        (Mick Jagger comments on Beatles.)
M 2611 "Random Notes." Rolling Stone 49 (December 27,
        1969) p3.
        (Ringo Starr recording oldies LP.)
M 2612 "Random Notes." Rolling Stone 50 (January 21,
        1970) p4.
        (The Beatles' activities; Allen Klein.)
M 2613 "Random Notes." Rolling Stone 50 (January 21,
        1970) p4.
        (Cynthia Lennon to remarry.)
M 2614 "Random Notes." Rolling Stone 51 (February 7,
        1970) p4.
        (Planned Polydor LP angers Lennon.)
M 2615 "Random Notes." Rolling Stone 51 (February 7,
        1970) p4.
        ("Let It Be" single expected.)
M 2616 "Random Notes." Rolling Stone 52 (February 21,

1970) p4.
(Apple staffers sign "No leaks" agreement.)
M 2617 "Random Notes." Rolling Stone 52 (February 21, 1970) p4.
(Ringo Starr to appear on "Laugh In.")
M 2618 "Random Notes." Rolling Stone 53 (March 7, 1970) p4.
(Lennon's coat made from human hair.)
M 2619 "Random Notes." Rolling Stone 53 (March 7, 1970) p4.
(Phil Spector to produce Plastic Ono Band 45.)
M 2620 "Random Notes." Rolling Stone 54 (March 19, 1970) p4.
(Lennon lithograph show in New York.)
M 2621 "Random Notes." Rolling Stone 54 (March 19, 1970) p4.
("Give Peace A Chance" film finished.)
M 2622 "Random Notes." Rolling Stone 54 (March 19, 1970) p4.
("Come Together" lyric from Chuck Berry song.)
M 2623 "Random Notes." Rolling Stone 54 (March 19, 1970) p4.
(ATV pursues remaining Northern stock owners.)
M 2624 "Random Notes." Rolling Stone 55 (April 2, 1970) p4.
("Let It Be" and other film clips pending.)
M 2625 "Random Notes." Rolling Stone 56 (April 16, 1970) p6.
(Beatles' reactions to their M.B.E.s.)
M 2626 "Random Notes." Rolling Stone 56 (April 16, 1970) p6.
(Ringo Starr's new album completed.)
M 2627 "Random Notes." Rolling Stone 57 (April 30, 1970) p6.
(John and pregnant Yoko sell Surrey mansion.)
M 2628 "Random Notes." Rolling Stone 59 (May 28, 1970) p6.
(Beatles win in "Reader's Digest" poll.)
M 2629 "Random Notes." Rolling Stone 60 (June 11, 1970) p4.
(The Lennons and two chimps on radio.)
M 2630 "Random Notes." Rolling Stone 61 (June 25, 1970) p6.
(The Lennons in Los Angeles.)
M 2631 "Random Notes." Rolling Stone 61 (June 25, 1970) p6.
("Let It Be" film in London premiere.)
M 2632 "Random Notes." Rolling Stone 62 (July 9, 1970) p4.
(Three hour version of "Hey Jude.")
M 2633 "Random Notes." Rolling Stone 65 (September 3, 1970) p4.
(Apple office closing down.)
M 2634 "Random Notes." Rolling Stone 65 (September 3, 1970) p4.
(Harrison at bedside of dying mom.)
M 2635 "Random Notes." Rolling Stone 67 (October 1, 1970) p4.
(All Time Beatles Hit Parade.)
M 2636 "Random Notes." Rolling Stone 67 (October 1, 1970) p4.
(Leon Russell to record George Harrison songs.)
M 2637 "Random Notes." Rolling Stone 68 (October 15, 1970) p4.
(Beatles Number 2 in "Melody Maker" poll.)
M 2638 "Random Notes." Rolling Stone 72 (December 2, 1970) p4.
(Rumored Harrison/McCartney tiff in New York.)
M 2639 "Random Notes." Rolling Stone 72 (December 2, 1970) p4.
(Rumored McCartney show at Boston College.)
M 2640 "Random Notes." Rolling Stone 72 (December 2, 1970) p4.
(Ringo Starr's third child expected.)

M 2641 "Random Notes." Rolling Stone 73 (December 24, 1970) p4.
(Allen Klein reports Beatles get together.)
M 2642 "Random Notes." Rolling Stone 74 (January 21, 1971) p18.
(Boston College invites McCartney concert.)
M 2643 "Random Notes." Rolling Stone 75 (February 4, 1971) p4.
(No Harrison song on Leon Russell LP.)
M 2644 "Random Notes." Rolling Stone 76 (February 18, 1971) p4.
(John Lennon in Dylan TV film.)
M 2645 "Random Notes." Rolling Stone 76 (February 18, 1971) p4.
(Derek Taylor with Warner Records.)
M 2646 "Random Notes." Rolling Stone 76 (February 18, 1971) p4.
(Hyperactive kids calmed by Beatles music.)
M 2647 "Random Notes." Rolling Stone 78 (March 18, 1971) p4.
(New McCartney record and TV special.)
M 2648 "Random Notes." Rolling Stone 79 (April 1, 1971) p4.
(South Africa lifts ban on Beatles.)
M 2649 "Random Notes." Rolling Stone 80 (April 15, 1971) p4.
(Paul McCartney's activities.)
M 2650 "Random Notes." Rolling Stone 81 (April 29, 1971) p4.
(Lennon and "Working Class Hero.")
M 2651 "Random Notes." Rolling Stone 81 (April 29, 1971) p4.
(Lyrics for "Open Your Box" controversial.)
M 2652 "Random Notes." Rolling Stone 81 (April 29, 1971) p4.
(McCartney scrap with Grammy photographer.)
M 2653 "Random Notes." Rolling Stone 82 (May 13, 1971) p4.
(Ronnie Spector recorded Harrison tune.)
M 2654 "Random Notes." Rolling Stone 82 (May 13, 1971) p4.
(Rumored McCartney/A&M Records contract.)
M 2655 "Random Notes." Rolling Stone 82 (May 13, 1971) p4.
(Comment on Harrison LP cover.)
M 2656 "Random Notes." Rolling Stone 84 (June 10, 1971) p4.
(News of thirty unreleased Beatles songs.)
M 2657 "Random Notes." Rolling Stone 85 (June 24, 1971) p4.
(McCartneys hire Linda's old friend.)
M 2658 "Random Notes." Rolling Stone 85 (June 24, 1971) p4.
(Ringo Starr film, "Blindman.")
M 2659 "Random Notes." Rolling Stone 86 (July 8, 1971) p4.
(B. B. King to record with Ringo Starr.)
M 2660 "Random Notes." Rolling Stone 87 (July 22, 1971) p4.
(Hippie commune on Lennon's Irish island.)
M 2661 "Random Notes." Rolling Stone 87 (July 22, 1971) p4.
(Johnny Rivers' film with Harrison, Lennon.)
M 2662 "Random Notes." Rolling Stone 88 (August 5, 1971) p4.
(Harrison plans concert for Bangla Desh.)
M 2663 "Random Notes." Rolling Stone 88 (August 5, 1971) p4.
(The Lennons and the "Oz Magazine" trial.)
M 2664 "Random Notes." Rolling Stone 89 (August 19, 1971) p4.
(New Harrison and Billy Preston LP.)
M 2665 "Random Notes." Rolling Stone 89 (August 19, 1971) p4.
(John Lennon records LP; Harrison consults.)
M 2666 "Random Notes." Rolling Stone 89 (August 19, 1971) p4.
(Capitol to release "Hollywood Bowl" LP.)

MAGAZINE ARTICLES

M 2667 "Random Notes." Rolling Stone 89 (August 19, 1971) p4.
  (Bangla Desh concert recorded by Capitol.)
M 2668 "Random Notes." Rolling Stone 90 (September 2, 1971) p4.
  (Lennon writes Rolling Stone note on his LP.)
M 2669 "Random Notes." Rolling Stone 90 (September 2, 1971) p4.
  (Allen Klein also in film "Blindman.")
M 2670 "Random Notes." Rolling Stone 90 (September 2, 1971) p4.
  (Blood, Sweat & Tears ask McCartney to produce.)
M 2671 "Random Notes." Rolling Stone 91 (September 16, 1971) p4.
  (Harrison works on Bangla Desh LP.)
M 2672 "Random Notes." Rolling Stone 91 (September 16, 1971) p4.
  (George Harrison gives Jesse Davis two songs.)
M 2673 "Random Notes." Rolling Stone 91 (September 16, 1971) p4.
  (Postcard from the Lennons.)
M 2674 "Random Notes." Rolling Stone 91 (September 16, 1971) p4.
  (Allen Klein asks Lennon/Harrison/Starr concert.)
M 2675 "Random Notes." Rolling Stone 93 (October 14, 1971) p4.
  (Track lineup for Yoko Ono LP announced.)
M 2676 "Random Notes." Rolling Stone 93 (October 14, 1971) p4.
  (First solo Beatles songbook string album.)
M 2677 "Random Notes." Rolling Stone 93 (October 14, 1971) p4.
  (Stella McCartney born.)
M 2678 "Random Notes." Rolling Stone 93 (October 14, 1971) p4.
  (Harrison's Bangla Desh records in offing.)
M 2679 "Random Notes." Rolling Stone 94 (October 28, 1971) p4.
  (McCartney and Harrison LPs soon.)
M 2680 "Random Notes." Rolling Stone 94 (October 28, 1971) p4.
  (McCartney's new band: Wings.)
M 2681 "Random Notes." Rolling Stone 94 (October 28, 1971) p4.
  (George Martin finds "new" Lennon/McCartney.)
M 2682 "Random Notes." Rolling Stone 95 (November 11, 1971) p4.
  (Lennon/Harrison/Dylan jam session scrubbed.)
M 2683 "Random Notes." Rolling Stone 96 (November 25, 1971) p4.
  (The Lennons to form new band.)
M 2684 "Random Notes." Rolling Stone 96 (November 25, 1971) p4.
  (Ringo Starr in early band with Roy Young.)
M 2685 "Random Notes." Rolling Stone 96 (November 25, 1971) p4.
  (Harrison urges McCartney: use Apple studios.)
M 2686 "Random Notes." Rolling Stone 96 (November 25, 1971) p4.
  (New McCartney LP coming soon.)
M 2687 "Random Notes." Rolling Stone 96 (November 25, 1971) p4.
  (Klaus Voorman signs as producer with Apple.)
M 2688 "Random Notes." Rolling Stone 96 (November 25, 1971) p4.
  (Ringo Starr filming "200 Motels.")
M 2689 "Random Notes." Rolling Stone 97 (December 9, 1971) p4.
  (McCartney LP delayed.)
M 2690 "Random Notes." Rolling Stone 97 (December 9, 1971) p4.
  (Rumored Lennon show at Troubadour Club.)

M 2691 "Random Notes." Rolling Stone 97 (December 9, 1971) p4.
  (Harrison, Ravi Shankar to meet Dick Cavett.)
M 2692 "Random Notes." Rolling Stone 97 (December 9, 1971) p4.
  (Ringo Starr in film "Blindman.")
M 2693 "Random Notes." Rolling Stone 97 (December 9, 1971) p4.
  (Harrison's Bangla Desh LP delayed.)
M 2694 "Random Notes." Rolling Stone 98 (December 23, 1971) p4.
  (Lennon records LP, new Christmas single.)
M 2695 "Random Notes." Rolling Stone 98 (December 23, 1971) p4.
  (Harrison critiques Capitol on Bangla Desh delay.)
M 2696 "Random Notes." Rolling Stone 99 (January 6, 1972) p4.
  (Lennons involved in pro-IRA film.)
M 2697 "Random Notes." Rolling Stone 100 (January 20, 1972) p4.
  (Harrison and Starr on Bobby Keyes LP.)
M 2698 "Random Notes." Rolling Stone 100 (January 20, 1972) p4.
  (Starr plays drums on Bobby Hatfield LP.)
M 2699 "Random Notes." Rolling Stone 100 (January 20, 1972) p4.
  (The Lennons serenade U.N. chief, U Thant.)
M 2700 "Random Notes." Rolling Stone 101 (February 3, 1972) p4.
  (McCartney interview and Lennon's response.)
M 2701 "Random Notes." Rolling Stone 102 (February 17, 1972) p4.
  (George Harrison at Jerry Garcia concert.)
M 2702 "Random Notes." Rolling Stone 102 (February 17, 1972) p4.
  (Lennon invites Harrison to concert film screening.)
M 2703 "Random Notes." Rolling Stone 103 (March 2, 1972) p4.
  (Bob Dylan at Harrison's Bangla Desh concert.)
M 2704 "Random Notes." Rolling Stone 103 (March 2, 1972) p4.
  (Henry McCullough to join Wings.)
M 2705 "Random Notes." Rolling Stone 104 (March 16, 1972) p4.
  (McCartney/Wings in surprise U.K. concerts.)
M 2706 "Random Notes." Rolling Stone 104 (March 16, 1972) p4.
  (Starr on new Billy Preston/Peter Frampton LP.)
M 2707 "Random Notes." Rolling Stone 105 (March 30, 1972) p4.
  (The Harrisons are injured in car accident.)
M 2708 "Random Notes." Rolling Stone 106 (April 13, 1972) p4.
  (Deportation case keeps Lennon from Grammy Awards.)
M 2709 "Random Notes." Rolling Stone 107 (April 27, 1972) p4.
  ("Concert For Bangladesh" film premiere.)
M 2710 "Random Notes." Rolling Stone 107 (April 27, 1972) p4.
  (Ringo Starr on Nilsson LP cut in London.)
M 2711 "Random Notes." Rolling Stone 107 (April 27, 1972) p4.
  (Starr directs T-Rex film documentary.)
M 2712 "Random Notes." Rolling Stone 109 (May 25, 1972) p4.
  (No impropriety found in Bangla Desh probe.)
M 2713 "Random Notes." Rolling Stone 110 (June 8, 1972) p4.
  (The Lennons fight deportation.)
M 2714 "Random Notes." Rolling Stone 112 (July 6, 1972)

p4.
      (Lennon on Elephant's Memory LP.)
M 2715 "Random Notes." Rolling Stone 112 (July 6, 1972)
      p4.
      (New Lennon LP: "Some Time In New York
      City.")
M 2716 "Random Notes." Rolling Stone 112 (July 6, 1972)
      p4.
      (McCartney/Wings plan European tour.)
M 2717 "Random Notes." Rolling Stone 114 (August 3,
      1972) p4.
      (McCartney sought for "little prince" film
      role.)
M 2718 "Random Notes." Rolling Stone 116 (August 31,
      1972) p4.
      (Ringo Starr's recent film roles.)
M 2719 "Random Notes." Rolling Stone 117 (September
      14, 1972) p4.
      (Lennon to play at New York benefit.)
M 2720 "Random Notes." Rolling Stone 118 (September
      28, 1972) p4.
      (McCartney videotapes "Mary Had A Little
      Lamb.")
M 2721 "Random Notes." Rolling Stone 118 (September
      28, 1972) p4.
      (Ringo Starr's furniture design company.)
M 2722 "Random Notes." Rolling Stone 120 (October 26,
      1972) p4.
      (The Lennons plan six-LP live music set.)
M 2723 "Random Notes." Rolling Stone 120 (October 26,
      1972) p4.
      ("Abbey Road" LP in "Cosmopolitan"'s love
      guide.)
M 2724 "Random Notes." Rolling Stone 120 (October 26,
      1972) p4.
      (The Lennons attend Elephant's Memory
      concert.)
M 2725 "Random Notes." Rolling Stone 122 (November 23,
      1972) p6.
      (The McCartneys sing on Carly Simon LP.)
M 2726 "Random Notes." Rolling Stone 123 (December 7,
      1972) p7.
      (The McCartneys record "Live And Let Die.")
M 2727 "Random Notes." Rolling Stone 125 (January 4,
      1973) p5.
      (Rory Storm found dead.)
M 2728 "Random Notes." Rolling Stone 125 (January 4,
      1973) p5.
      (Lennon tops poll as singers' favorite
      singer.)
M 2729 "Random Notes." Rolling Stone 125 (January 4,
      1973) p5.
      (Wings' "Hi Hi Hi" banned by BBC.)
M 2730 "Random Notes." Rolling Stone 125 (January 4,
      1973) p5.
      (Harrison works on own and Cilla Black
      LPs.)
M 2731 "Random Notes." Rolling Stone 128 (February 15,
      1973) p5.
      (Capitol to release 4 LP set - Red, Blue
      albums.)
M 2732 "Random Notes." Rolling Stone 128 (February 15,
      1973) p5.
      (The Lennons sue Northern, Maclen Music.)
M 2733 "Random Notes." Rolling Stone 129 (March 1,
      1973) p3.
      (New Harrison, Wings LPs due soon.)
M 2734 "Random Notes." Rolling Stone 130 (March 15,
      1973) p3.
      (The Lennons buy cards in drugstore.)
M 2735 "Random Notes." Rolling Stone 131 (March 29,
      1973) p3.
      (Harrison sues over bootleg LP.)
M 2736 "Random Notes." Rolling Stone 131 (March 29,
      1973) p3.
      (Lennon rumored to want McCartney reunion.)
M 2737 "Random Notes." Rolling Stone 132 (April 12,
      1973) p5.
      (Harrison, Lennon attend Starr studio
      sessions.)

M 2738 "Random Notes." Rolling Stone 132 (April 12,
      1973) p5.
      (McCartney works on London TV special.)
M 2739 "Random Notes." Rolling Stone 133 (April 26,
      1973) p5.
      (Lennon, Harrison, Starr jam with Dr.
      John.)
M 2740 "Random Notes." Rolling Stone 134 (May 10, 1973)
      p5.
      (Harrison, Starr, Lennon at Streisand
      party.)
M 2741 "Random Notes." Rolling Stone 134 (May 10, 1973)
      p5.
      (Ringo Starr: no reunion plans.)
M 2742 "Random Notes." Rolling Stone 134 (May 10, 1973)
      p5.
      (Lennon writes "Newsweek" on reunion rumors.)
M 2743 "Random Notes." Rolling Stone 135 (May 24, 1973)
      p5.
      (McCartney's newest: "Red Rose Speedway.")
M 2744 "Random Notes." Rolling Stone 135 (May 24, 1973)
      p5.
      (McCartney on new Ringo Starr LP.)
M 2745 "Random Notes." Rolling Stone 135 (May 24, 1973)
      p5.
      (Harrison, Voorman on Cheech and Chong
      LP.)
M 2746 "Random Notes." Rolling Stone 136 (June 7, 1973)
      p5.
      (Harrison's "Material World" LP features
      Starr.)
M 2747 "Random Notes." Rolling Stone 137 (June 21,
      1973) p5.
      (Harrison at Dave Mason, Andy Williams
      session.)
M 2748 "Random Notes." Rolling Stone 138 (July 5, 1973)
      p5.
      (The Harrisons attend a party.)
M 2749 "Random Notes." Rolling Stone 138 (July 5, 1973)
      p5.
      (George Harrison at Led Zeppelin concert.)
M 2750 "Random Notes." Rolling Stone 139 (July 19,
      1973) p5.
      (Lennon denies Beatles reunion.)
M 2751 "Random Notes." Rolling Stone 140 (August 2,
      1973) p5.
      (Beatles on Geraldo Rivera TV special.)
M 2752 "Random Notes." Rolling Stone 140 (August 2,
      1973) p5.
      (Harrison at New York dinner; possible
      tour.)
M 2753 "Random Notes." Rolling Stone 140 (August 2,
      1973) p5.
      (Yoko Ono recording new LP.)
M 2754 "Random Notes." Rolling Stone 141 (August 16,
      1973) p5.
      (Harrison writes two songs for Martha
      Reeves.)
M 2755 "Random Notes." Rolling Stone 141 (August 16,
      1973) p5.
      (McCartney to do TV's "Zoo Gang" theme.)
M 2756 "Random Notes." Rolling Stone 141 (August 16,
      1973) p5.
      (Star Club tapes discovered.)
M 2757 "Random Notes." Rolling Stone 142 (August 30,
      1973) p32.
      (McCartney to oppose "Sgt. Pepper" film.)
M 2758 "Random Notes." Rolling Stone 143 (September
      13, 1973) p30.
      (Lennon to sell Tittenhurst Park home.)
M 2759 "Random Notes." Rolling Stone 145 (October 11,
      1973) p24.
      (Lennon mixing new LP.)
M 2760 "Random Notes." Rolling Stone 145 (October 11,
      1973) p24.
      (Wings records in Africa.)
M 2761 "Random Notes." Rolling Stone 146 (October 25,
      1973) p26.
      (McCartney returns from Africa.)
M 2762 "Random Notes." Rolling Stone 146 (October 25,

1973) p26.
     (Harrison on new Alvin Lee LP.)
M 2763 "Random Notes." Rolling Stone 147 (November 8,
     1973) p32.
     (Lennon works on "Mind Games" LP.)
M 2764 "Random Notes." Rolling Stone 147 (November 8,
     1973) p32.
     (Ringo Starr's new movie: "Stardust.")
M 2765 "Random Notes." Rolling Stone 148 (November 22,
     1973) p32.
     (The Lennons at the Roxy and After Dark.)
M 2766 "Random Notes." Rolling Stone 150 (December 20,
     1973) p28.
     (Lennon cuts hair; rumored split with
     Yoko.)
M 2767 "Random Notes." Rolling Stone 151 (January 3,
     1974) p26. illus.
     (Lennon, Dr. John at L.A. Troubadour.)
M 2768 "Random Notes." Rolling Stone 152 (January 17,
     1974) p22.
     (Starr and Lennon on reunion rumors.)
M 2769 "Random Notes." Rolling Stone 152 (January 17,
     1974) p22.
     (Pattie Harrison with Ron Wood.)
M 2770 "Random Notes." Rolling Stone 152 (January 17,
     1974) p22.
     (McCartney's "Band On The Run" LP.)
M 2771 "Random Notes." Rolling Stone 157 (March 28,
     1974) p28.
     (Yoko Ono: overwork, anemia, low blood
     pressure.)
M 2772 "Random Notes." Rolling Stone 158 (April 11,
     1974) p28. illus.
     (Lennon, Starr, Mal Evans at birthday
     party.)
M 2774 "Random Notes." Rolling Stone 158 (April 11,
     1974) p28.
     (McCartney's "Jet" named after puppy.)
M 2775 "Random Notes." Rolling Stone 158 (April 11,
     1974) p28. illus.
     (Lennon, Starr play at "Jim Keltner Fan
     Club.")
M 2776 "Random Notes." Rolling Stone 159 (April 25,
     1974) p28.
     (Lennon at "Jim Keltner Fan Club" jam.)
M 2777 "Random Notes." Rolling Stone 159 (April 25,
     1974) p28.
     (McCartney's efforts to fill Wings' slots.)
M 2778 "Random Notes." Rolling Stone 160 (May 9, 1974)
     p30.
     (Lennon, McCartney, Starr at Nilsson
     sessions.)
M 2779 "Random Notes." Rolling Stone 160 (May 9, 1974)
     p30.
     (Beatles reunion rumors continue.)
M 2780 "Random Notes." Rolling Stone 162 (June 6, 1974)
     p28. illus.
     ("Band On The Run" goes platinum.)
M 2781 "Random Notes." Rolling Stone 163 (June 20,
     1974) p34.
     (Ringo Starr discusses reunion rumors.)
M 2782 "Random Notes." Rolling Stone 163 (June 20,
     1974) p34.
     (Harrison: new LP, new label-Dark Horse.)
M 2783 "Random Notes." Rolling Stone 164 (July 4, 1974)
     p32.
     (Yoko Ono at James Taylor party.)
M 2784 "Random Notes." Rolling Stone 165 (July 18,
     1974) p28. illus.
     (Ringo Starr loses London Playboy Club
     card.)
M 2785 "Random Notes." Rolling Stone 165 (July 18,
     1974) p28.
     (Lennon records Mick Jagger single.)
M 2786 "Random Notes." Rolling Stone 165 (July 18,
     1974) p28. illus.

     (McCartney gives song to Peggy Lee.)
M 2787 "Random Notes." Rolling Stone 167 (August 15,
     1974) p26.
     (Harrison tour of U.K. and U.S. set.)
M 2788 "Random Notes." Rolling Stone 167 (August 15,
     1974) p26.
     (Lennon mixes album in New York.)
M 2789 "Random Notes." Rolling Stone 168 (August 29,
     1974) p32.
     (Next Starr LP to have Lennon tune.)
M 2790 "Random Notes." Rolling Stone 167 (September
     12, 1974) p30.
     (Lennon to attend Elton John session.)
M 2791 "Random Notes." Rolling Stone 169 (September
     12, 1974) p30.
     (McCartney cuts LP tracks in Nashville.)
M 2792 "Random Notes." Rolling Stone 170 (September
     26, 1974) p22.
     (Boston Beatles convention.)
M 2793 "Random Notes." Rolling Stone 171 (October 10,
     1974) p26.
     (Yoko Ono concerts in Japan.)
M 2794 "Random Notes." Rolling Stone 171 (October 10,
     1974) p26.
     ("Ringo's Night Out" film details.)
M 2795 "Random Notes." Rolling Stone 171 (October 10,
     1974) p26.
     (Lennon's "Walls And Bridges" to debut
     soon.)
M 2796 "Random Notes." Rolling Stone 171 (October 10,
     1974) p26.
     (Harrison tour details.)
M 2797 "Random Notes." Rolling Stone 172 (October 24,
     1974) p28.
     (Harrison: splits with Pattie; Indian
     music fete.)
M 2798 "Random Notes." Rolling Stone 173 (November 7,
     1974) p22.
     (Harrison's donations to charity.)
M 2799 "Random Notes." Rolling Stone 174 (November 21,
     1974) p26. illus.
     (Lennon in Howard Cosell interview.)
M 2800 "Random Notes." Rolling Stone 174 (November 21,
     1974) p26.
     (McCartney records secret Christmas LP.)
M 2801 "Random Notes." Rolling Stone 175 (December 5,
     1974) p26.
     (Fab Four solo activities.)
M 2802 "Random Notes." Rolling Stone 175 (December 5,
     1974) p26.
     (George Harrison press conference.)
M 2804 "Random Notes." Rolling Stone 176 (December 19,
     1974) p22.
     (McCartney in rumored McDonald's
     commercials.)
M 2805 "Random Notes." Rolling Stone 176 (December 19,
     1974) p22.
     (Lennon on Elton John single:"Lucy ...".)
M 2806 "Random Notes." Rolling Stone 180 (January 13,
     1975) p20. illus.
     (Yoko Ono at Poetry Project in New York.)
M 2807 "Random Notes." Rolling Stone 178 (January 16,
     1975) p20. illus.
     (Harrison concert in Boston.)
M 2808 "Random Notes." Rolling Stone 179 (January 30,
     1975) p22.
     (Peter Sellers, Olivia Arias on Dark
     Horse.)
M 2809 "Random Notes." Rolling Stone 179 (January 30,
     1975) p22.
     (Lennon continues deportation battle.)
M 2810 "Random Notes." Rolling Stone 180 (February 13,
     1975) p20.
     (Recent Fab Four activities.)
M 2811 "Random Notes." Rolling Stone 182 (March 13,
     1975) p20.
     (The McCartneys in New Orleans.)

MAGAZINE ARTICLES

M 2812 "Random Notes." Rolling Stone 183 (March 27, 1975) p20.
 (Ringo Starr in "Lisztomania.")
M 2813 "Random Notes." Rolling Stone 183 (March 27, 1975) p20.
 (John Lennon reunited with Yoko.)
M 2814 "Random Notes." Rolling Stone 184 (April 10, 1975) p24.
 (Two John Lennon cuts on David Bowie LP.)
M 2815 "Random Notes." Rolling Stone 184 (April 10, 1975) p24.
 (The McCartneys attend party for Rod Stewart.)
M 2816 "Random Notes." Rolling Stone 185 (April 24, 1975) p22. illus.
 (The McCartneys attend "Tommy" premiere.)
M 2817 "Random Notes." Rolling Stone 186 (May 8, 1975) p26. illus.
 (Harrison attends a McCartney party.)
M 2818 "Random Notes." Rolling Stone 187 (May 22, 1975) p26.
 (Linda McCartney drug arrest.)
M 2819 "Random Notes." Rolling Stone 189 (June 19, 1975) p26.
 (Harrison records, possibly makes tour film.)
M 2820 "Random Notes." Rolling Stone 189 (June 19, 1975) p26.
 (McCartney planning a U.S. tour.)
M 2821 "Random Notes." Rolling Stone 192 (July 31, 1975) p24.
 (Wings' Scotland rehearsal a tour prelude.)
M 2822 "Random Notes." Rolling Stone 193 (August 14, 1975) p20.
 (New McCartney song features Dave Mason.)
M 2823 "Random Notes." Rolling Stone 194 (August 28, 1975) p20.
 (Ringo Starr's 35th birthday party.)
M 2824 "Random Notes." Rolling Stone 194 (August 28, 1975) p20.
 (Harrison, Starr attend Bob Marley concert.)
M 2825 "Random Notes." Rolling Stone 195 (September 11, 1975) p21.
 (No McCartney/Wings U.S. tour expected.)
M 2826 "Random Notes." Rolling Stone 196 (September 25, 1975) p24.
 (Ringo Starr attends party for Dr. John.)
M 2827 "Random Notes." Rolling Stone 197 (October 9, 1975) p24.
 (George Harrison's "Extra Texture" LP.)
M 2828 "Random Notes." Rolling Stone 198 (October 23, 1975) p31. illus.
 (Lennon's deportation gets low INS priority.)
M 2829 "Random Notes." Rolling Stone 201 (December 4, 1975) p24.
 (McCartney late for plane departure.)
M 2830 "Random Notes." Rolling Stone 204 (January 15, 1976) p22.
 (Paul McCartney vacations in Hawaii.)
M 2831 "Random Notes." Rolling Stone 206 (February 12, 1976) p22.
 (No government appeal in Lennon case.)
M 2832 "Random Notes." Rolling Stone 207 (February 26, 1976) p26.
 (Disguised McCartneys plot tour in California.)
M 2833 "Random Notes." Rolling Stone 209 (March 25, 1976) p26.
 (No Harrison/Lennon reunion discussions.)
M 2834 "Random Notes." Rolling Stone 209 (March 25, 1976) p26.
 (Starr at David Bowie post-concert party.)
M 2835 "Random Notes." Rolling Stone 210 (April 8, 1976) p30.
 (Ringo Starr at party with Keith Moon.)
M 2836 "Random Notes." Rolling Stone 212 (May 6, 1976) p24.
 (Wings' tour delayed: McCulloch's finger.)

M 2837 "Random Notes." Rolling Stone 213 (May 20, 1976) p30.
 (McCartney concert tickets in Canada.)
M 2838 "Random Notes." Rolling Stone 216 (July 1, 1976) p22.
 (Lennon: 2 McCartney show seats - for babysitter.)
M 2839 "Random Notes." Rolling Stone 216 (July 1, 1976) p22.
 (Harrison LP and tour rumored.)
M 2840 "Random Notes." Rolling Stone 217 (July 15, 1976) p28.
 (Lennon, Clapton on new Starr album.)
M 2841 "Random Notes." Rolling Stone 220 (August 26, 1976) p28. illus.
 (Ringo Starr shaves head in Monaco.)
M 2842 "Random Notes." Rolling Stone 222 (September 23, 1976) p23.
 ("Band On The Run" first Russian rock album.)
M 2843 "Random Notes." Rolling Stone 222 (September 23, 1976) p20.
 (Ringo Starr attends birthday party.)
M 2844 "Random Notes." Rolling Stone 223 (October 7, 1976) p30.
 (McCartney prepares live tour LP.)
M 2845 "Random Notes." Rolling Stone 224 (October 21, 1976) p49.
 (Bob Dylan comments on The Beatles.)
M 2846 "Random Notes." Rolling Stone 224 (October 21, 1976) p46. illus.
 (Harrison guilty in "My Sweet Lord" case.)
M 2847 "Random Notes." Rolling Stone 225 (November 4, 1976) p29.
 (Harrison, A & M Records in legal dispute.)
M 2848 "Random Notes." Rolling Stone 225 (November 4, 1976) p27. illus.
 (McCartney/Wings Venice benefit concert.)
M 2849 "Random Notes." Rolling Stone 226 (November 18, 1976) p38.
 (Starr sends poet to Lennon birthday.)
M 2850 "Random Notes." Rolling Stone 226 (December 2, 1976) p34.
 (Harrison's Dark Horse label to Warner Bros.)
M 2851 "Random Notes." Rolling Stone 229 (December 30, 1976) p29.
 (Lennon unlikely to sign with Capitol.)
M 2852 "Random Notes." Rolling Stone 229 (December 30, 1976) p29.
 (Wings to visit Russia.)
M 2853 "Random Notes." Rolling Stone 230 (January 13, 1977) p22.
 (Ringo Starr on "pinching" songs.)
M 2854 "Random Notes." Rolling Stone 231 (January 27, 1977) p36. illus.
 (Allen Klein, John and Yoko.)
M 2855 "Random Notes." Rolling Stone 232 (February 10, 1977) p26. illus.
 (Settlement between Beatles and Abkco.)
M 2856 "Random Notes." Rolling Stone 233 (February 24, 1977) p30. illus.
 (John Lennon and Yoko Ono.)
M 2858 "Random Notes." Rolling Stone 235 (March 24, 1977) p24. illus.
 (Paul McCartney won't be in "Sgt. Pepper" film.)
M 2859 "Random Notes." Rolling Stone 237 (April 21, 1977) p43. illus.
 (Hollywood Bowl album; Klaatu rumor.)
M 2860 "Random Notes." Rolling Stone 238 (May 5, 1977) p37.
 (Paul McCartney as editor of own fanzine.)
M 2861 "Random Notes." Rolling Stone 239 (May 19, 1977) p39.
 (George Harrison at Long Beach Grand Prix.)
M 2862 "Random Notes." Rolling Stone 240 (June 2, 1977)

p37.
(Denny Laine and McCartney record in Scotland.)
M 2863 "Random Notes." Rolling Stone 243 (July 14, 1977) p36.
(Abbey Road street sign repeatedly stolen.)
M 2864 "Random Notes." Rolling Stone 244 (July 28, 1977) p41. illus.
(John Lennon in Japan.)
M 2865 "Random Notes." Rolling Stone 249 (October 6, 1977) p37.
("Beatles 4 Ever" film being made.)
M 2866 "Random Notes." Rolling Stone 249 (October 6, 1977) p34.
(Frank Sinatra on The Beatles.)
M 2867 "Random Notes." Rolling Stone 251 (November 3, 1977) p59.
(McCartney's "Buddy Holly Week" hosts Crickets.)
M 2868 "Random Notes." Rolling Stone 251 (November 3, 1977) p56. illus.
(McCartneys welcome first boy child.)
M 2869 "Random Notes." Rolling Stone 253 (December 1, 1977) p32+. illus.
(The Lennons return from Japan.)
M 2870 "Random Notes." Rolling Stone 255 (December 29, 1977) p39.
(Beatles statue in Liverpool.)
M 2871 "Random Notes." Rolling Stone 258 (February 9, 1978) pp21-22.
("Sgt. Pepper" film; no Beatles attend.)
M 2872 "Random Notes." Rolling Stone 260 (March 9, 1978) p38.
(The Lennons buy cows for their farm.)
M 2873 "Random Notes." Rolling Stone 262 (April 6, 1978) p31.
(George Harrison in Maui.)
M 2874 "Random Notes." Rolling Stone 266 (June 1, 1978) p37.
(John Lennon's film role in "Street Messiah.")
M 2875 "Random Notes." Rolling Stone 271 (August 10, 1978) p32.
(Cynthia Lennon's book not halted by John.)
M 2876 "Random Notes." Rolling Stone 273 (September 7, 1978) p24.
(McCartney comments on "Sgt. Pepper" film.)
M 2877 "Random Notes." Rolling Stone 274 (September 21, 1978) p33.
(George Harrison's new album, and new baby.)
M 2878 "Random Notes." Rolling Stone 275 (October 5, 1978) p49. illus.
(Harrison: son born; backs Monty Python film.)
M 2879 "Random Notes." Rolling Stone 276 (October 19, 1978) p47.
(Pope John Paul I comments on The Beatles.)
M 2880 "Random Notes." Rolling Stone 277 (November 2, 1978) p41.
(George Harrison finances Monty Python film.)
M 2881 "Random Notes." Rolling Stone 277 (November 2, 1978) p41.
(Paul McCartney leaves Capitol.)
M 2882 "Random Notes." Rolling Stone 277 (November 2, 1978) p41.
(George Harrison's book, "I Me Mine," to appear.)
M 2883 "Random Notes." Rolling Stone 278 (November 16, 1978) p52.
(Beatles boxed set from Capitol.)
M 2884 "Random Notes." Rolling Stone 278 (November 16, 1978) p52.
(Paul McCartney's recording activities.)
M 2885 "Random Notes." Rolling Stone 280 (December 14, 1978) p51.
(Beatles' boxed set and McCartney hits.)
M 2886 "Random Notes." Rolling Stone 250 (December 14, 1978) p53.

(George Harrison visits "Life of Brian" set.)
M 2887 "Random Notes." Rolling Stone 283 (January 25, 1979) p41.
(Paul McCartney to sign with CBS Records.)
M 2888 "Random Notes." Rolling Stone 284 (February 8, 1979) p32.
(McCartney builds mobile recording studio.)
M 2889 "Random Notes." Rolling Stone 286 (March 8, 1979) p33.
(The Lennons purchase dairy cows.)
M 2890 "Random Notes." Rolling Stone 288 (April 3, 1979) p46.
(McCartney tune in "Rock 'N' Roll High" film.)
M 2891 "Random Notes." Rolling Stone 288 (April 5, 1979) p46.
(Fab Four solo activities.)
M 2892 "Random Notes." Rolling Stone 290 (May 3, 1979) p46.
(Pattie Harrison marries Eric Clapton.)
M 2893 "Random Notes." Rolling Stone 294 (June 28, 1979) p47.
(John Lennon to record again.)
M 2894 "Random Notes." Rolling Stone 294 (June 28, 1979) p47.
(Three Beatles at Eric Clapton wedding.)
M 2895 "Random Notes." Rolling Stone 295 (July 12, 1979) p34.
(The Lennons' "New York Times" ad.)
M 2896 "Random Notes." Rolling Stone 297 (August 9, 1979) p35.
(McCartney's music copyright empire.)
M 2897 "Random Notes." Rolling Stone 302 (October 18, 1979) p48.
(Sid Bernstein seeks Beatles reunion benefit.)
M 2898 "Random Notes." Rolling Stone 303 (November 1, 1979) p35.
(No Beatles reunion for U.N. benefit.)
M 2899 "Random Notes." Rolling Stone 304 (November 15, 1979) p39.
(Beatles reunion for U.N. benefit?)
M 2901 "Random Notes." Rolling Stone 304 (November 15, 1979) p39.
(Apple sues "Beatlemania" stage show.)
M 2902 "Random Notes." Rolling Stone 306 (December 13, 1979) p55.
(George Martin's autobiography.)
M 2903 "Random Notes." Rolling Stone 306 (December 13, 1979) p53.
(John Lennon to begin recording.)
M 2904 "Random Notes." Rolling Stone 309 (January 24, 1980) p34. illus.
(Paul McCartney concert at his Liverpool school.)
M 2905 "Random Notes." Rolling Stone 311 (February 21, 1980) p38.
(Ringo Starr's movie, "Caveman.")
M 2906 "Random Notes." Rolling Stone 312 (March 6, 1980) p40.
(George Martin: no credit for "Let It Be" work.)
M 2907 "Random Notes." Rolling Stone 313 (March 20, 1980) p38.
(Pianist comments on role in Lennon album.)
M 2908 "Random Notes." Rolling Stone 314 (April 3, 1980) p43.
(Aftermath of McCartney's arrest in Japan.)
M 2909 "Random Notes." Rolling Stone 314 (April 3, 1980) p42.
(Capitol to release "Rarities" album.)
M 2910 "Random Notes." Rolling Stone 315 (April 17, 1980) p34. illus.
(The Lennons buy a Florida home.)
M 2911 "Random Notes." Rolling Stone 316 (May 1, 1980) p37. illus.

(Paul McCartney records "McCartney II" album.)

M 2912 "Random Notes." Rolling Stone 319 (June 12, 1980) p26. illus.
(McCartney's new single, album and film.)

M 2913 "Random Notes." Rolling Stone 320 (June 26, 1980) p32.
(Ringo Starr in car crash.)

M 2914 "Random Notes." Rolling Stone 321 (July 10, 1980) p31.
("Seaside Woman" wins film award.)

M 2915 "Random Notes." Rolling Stone 326 (September 18, 1980) p31. illus.
(Lennon recording again.)

M 2916 "Random Notes." Rolling Stone 328 (October 16, 1980) p42. illus.
("Double Fantasy" recording completed.)

M 2917 "Random Notes." Rolling Stone 331 (November 27, 1980) p45.
(Ringo Starr.)

M 2918 "Random Notes." Rolling Stone 337 (February 19, 1981) p38.
(Song dedicated to John Lennon.)

M 2919 "Random Notes." Rolling Stone 339 (March 19, 1981) p36.
(Rumors about new McCartney album.)

M 2920 "Random Notes." Rolling Stone 340 (April 2, 1981) p36.
(On McCartney's Montserrat recording sessions.)

M 2921 "Random Notes." Rolling Stone 341 (April 16, 1981) p36.
(On McCartney's Montserrat album sessions.)

M 2922 "Random Notes." Rolling Stone 342 (April 30, 1981) p32.
(Yoko Ono ready to produce next LP.)

M 2923 "Random Notes." Rolling Stone 342 (April 30, 1981) p32.
(Harrison's "My Sweet Lord" case.)

M 2924 "Random Notes." Rolling Stone 343 (May 14, 1981) p41. illus.
(On Yoko's film, "Walking On Thin Ice.")

M 2925 "Random Notes." Rolling Stone 347 (July 9, 1981) p40.
(Yoko Ono accepts award for John Lennon.)

M 2926 "Random Notes." Rolling Stone 348 (July 23, 1981) p29.
(Paul McCartney's new album forthcoming.)

M 2927 "Random Notes." Rolling Stone 348 (July 23, 1981) p29.
(Ringo Starr plays drums on new Dylan single.)

M 2928 "Random Notes." Rolling Stone 350 (August 20, 1981) p29. illus.
(Photo of George Harrison, Dylan and Clapton.)

M 2929 "Random Notes." Rolling Stone 350 (August 20, 1981) p32.
(Simon & Schuster to publish "I Me Mine.")

M 2930 "Random Notes." Rolling Stone 326 (September 18, 1981) p31. illus.
(John and Yoko's pending album, "Double Fantasy.")

M 2931 "Random Notes." Rolling Stone 353 (October 1, 1981) p71. illus.
(Autograph hunters succeed with Paul and Yoko.)

M 2932 "Random Notes." Rolling Stone 353 (October 1, 1981) p79. illus.
(Paul McCartney's new album.)

M 2933 "Random Notes." Rolling Stone 353 (October 1, 1981) p78.
(Ringo Starr's new album.)

M 2934 "Random Notes." Rolling Stone 361 (January 21, 1982) p27.
(Yoko/McCartney seek Northern Songs purchase.)

M 2935 "Random Notes." Rolling Stone 361 (January 21, 1982) p27. illus.
(Activities a year after Lennon's death.)

M 2936 "Random Notes." Rolling Stone 362 (February 4, 1982) p24.
(Beatles items sold at auction.)

M 2937 "Random Notes." Rolling Stone 362 (February 4, 1982) p24. illus.
(Julian Lennon in a skit in Soho club.)

M 2938 "Random Notes." Rolling Stone 363 (February 18, 1982) p31.
(Rumored McCartney-sponsored Beatles museum.)

M 2939 "Random Notes." Rolling Stone 363 (February 18, 1982) p31.
(Capitol plans Beatles film soundtrack LP.)

M 2940 "Random Notes." Rolling Stone 364 (March 4, 1982) p33.
(McCartney's new LP: "Tug Of War.")

M 2941 "Random Notes." Rolling Stone 382 (November 11, 1982) p30. illus.
(The McCartneys' Abbey Road studio party.)

M 2942 "Random Notes." Rolling Stone 387 (January 20, 1983) p29.
(Linda McCartney's solo debut being produced.)

M 2943 "Random Notes: Beatles Plus Disco Equals 'Stars On'." Rolling Stone 348 (July 23, 1981) p29.
(On the album "Stars On Long Play.")

M 2944 "Random Notes: McCartney Gets Political." Rolling Stone 383 (November 25, 1982) p37.

M 2945 "Random Notes 1979." Rolling Stone 307 (December 27, 1979) pp93-94.
(The year's events, including Beatles.)

M 2946 "Random Notes: Ringo Ailing, Julian Hunting." Rolling Stone 394 (April 28, 1983) p54. illus.
(Julian Lennon has new band, Quasar.)

M 2947 "Random Notes: Ringo Ailing, Julian Hunting." Rolling Stone 394 (April 28, 1983) p54. illus.
(Ringo in hospital with undisclosed ailment.)

M 2948 "Random Notes: Ringo Ailing, Julian Hunting." Rolling Stone 394 (April 28, 1983) p54. illus.
(Paul's film "Give My Regards To Broad Street.")

M 2949 "Random Notes: Ringo's Heir." Rolling Stone 384 (December 9, 1982) p40.
(Zak Starkey.)

M 2950 "Random Notes: 'Why Yoko Made Label Switch'." Rolling Stone 383 (November 25, 1982) p34.
(From Geffen Records to Polygram.)

M 2951 "Rarest Rock Show Of All." Life 71 (August 13, 1971) pp20-23. illus.
(George Harrison.)

M 2952 Rave. n.p.: Rave Magazine, 1967.
(George and Pattie Harrison cover portrait.)

M 2953 Raye, S. "Barbara Bach Keeps Him Going, Says Ringo Starr, Still Banging The Drum Slowly For John." People 15 (February 23, 1981) pp32-34+. illus.

M 2954 Read, Lorna. "Beatlemania: A Review." Record Collector 4 (December 1979) pp17-18.
(Stage show.)

M 2955 Read, Lorna. "Book Review." The Beatles Book 69 (January 1982) ppv-vi.
(On the book "Thank U Very Much.")

M 2956 Read, Lorna. "Mike McCartney Interviewed." The Beatles Book 70 (February 1982) ppiii-vi.

M 2957 Read, Lorna. "Pop Memorabilia Under The Hammer!" Record Collector 30 (February 1982) pp15-18. illus.
(Sotheby's Dec. 23, 1981 memorabilia auction.)

M 2958 "Readables, Listenables, Disables And Other

Ables." Beatles Unlimited
(Occasional feature, issues 23,25.)

M 2959 "Readers And Critics Poll - 1981."
Rolling Stone 364 (March 4, 1982) p36.
(John Lennon nominated Artist of The Year.)

M 2960 "Readers' Poll Results." Creem 12 (March 1981)
p47. illus.
(John Lennon and Yoko Ono.)

M 2962 "Recording Pix." The Beatles Book 15 (October
1964) pp10-11.
(Recording session photos.)

M 2963 "Record Notes." Rolling Stone 58 (May 14, 1970)
p58.
(George Harrison and Ringo Starr.)

M 2964 "Record Notes." Rolling Stone 59 (May 28, 1970)
p52.
(Fake Lennon single appears on radio.)

M 2965 "Record Notes." Rolling Stone 62 (July 9, 1970)
p44.
(Steve Stills is living in Ringo Starr's
house.)

M 2966 "Record Reviews." Beatlefan
(Regular feature, vln1-   , 1978-   .)

M 2967 "Record Reviews (Bootlegs)." Beatles Now illus.
(Regular feature, Nos.1-3, January-Summer
1982.)

M 2968 "Redefining Beatlemania: A Compulsion To Sound
Off On All Sensitive Issues." Variety 244
(August 24, 1966) p51+.

M 2969 Red Mole. "John And Yoko." Seed 7:2 (June 29,
1971) p22.
(Excerpt of interview in "Red Mole.")

M 2971 Redmond, Tim, Alan Kay and Bruce Dancis.
"Inside John Lennon's FBI File."
Michigan Voice 7:2 (May 1983) pp12-14.

M 2972 Redshaw, David. "Barham's Bandi." Let It Rock
(August 1973) p7.
(George Harrison.)

M 2973 Regan, T. "McCartney Conglomerate."
Songwriters Review 34:5 (1979) p3. illus.

M 2974 Reichardt, J. "Art Is Big, Round, And Good."
Studio 174 (September 1967) p81. illus.
(Yoko Ono.)

M 2975 Reilly, Peter. "The Coup That Failed."
Stereo Review 24 (June 1970) p102. illus.
(Ed Sullivan's "Tribute to The Beatles.")

M 2976 Reinhart, Charles. "Collecting." Beatlefan 4:1
(December 1981) p7.
(The writing of the book "You Can't Do
That.")

M 2977 Reinhart, Charles. "John Lennon Tribute
Records." Goldmine 70 (March 1982)
pp15-16.

M 2978 Reinhart, Charles. "Lennon Tributes On Record."
Beatlefan 3:6 (October 1981) p10.
(Posthumous John Lennon tributes on
record.)

M 2979 Reinhart, Charles. "Mop Top Mania Lives ..."
Goldmine (November 1982) p189.

M 2980 Reinhart, Charles. "Sgt. Pepper's Lonely Hearts
Club Fans!" Goldmine 84 (May 1983)
p179.
(Recent Beatles book and record
production.)

M 2981 Reizalg, Leoj. "Magical Mystery Tour '76."
Beatles Unlimited 10 (November 1976)
p18.
(Third annual fan convention, Boston, July
1976.)

M 2982 "Religioso Slants In Beatles Rebellion?"
Variety 234 (March 4, 1964) p55.

M 2983 "Remember Beatlemania?" Beatlefan 1:1
(December 1978) p9.

(Solicitation for first-hand accounts.)

M 2984 "Remembering .... " Beatlefan 1:2 (February
1979) pp4-5,7.
(Letters; fans recall sixties Beatlemania.)

M 2985 "Remembering 'Sgt. Pepper'." Beatlefan 1:4
(June 1979) p9.
(Reprint of 1967 article.)

M 2986 "Remember Those Cartoons?" Beatlefan 1:2
(February 1979) p14.
(List of cartoon series episodes.)

M 2987 Remmerswaal, Jos. "The Clive Epstein
Interview." Beatles Unlimited 24 (January
1979) pp12-18.
(Clive Epstein discusses his brother,
Brian.)

M 2988 Remmerswaal, Jos. "Here, There And Everywhere."
Beatles Unlimited 10 (November 1976)
p9.
(Different versions of Beatles' songs.)

M 2989 Remmerswaal, Jos. "Here, There And Everywhere:
Part Two." Beatles Unlimited 11 (January
1977) p16.
(Different versions of Beatles' songs.)

M 2990 Remmerswaal, Jos. "Here, There And Everywhere,
Part Three." Beatles Unlimited 12 (March
1977) pp17-18.
(Different versions of Beatles' songs.)

M 2991 Remmerswaal, Jos. "Here, There And Everywhere:
Part Four." Beatles Unlimited 14 (July 1977)
p6.
(Different versions of Beatles' songs.)

M 2992 Remmerswaal, Jos. "Here, There And Everywhere,
Part Five." Beatles Unlimited 15 (September
1977) pp20-21.
(Different versions of Beatles' songs.)

M 2993 Remmerswaal, Jos. "Here, There And Everywhere,
Part Six." Beatles Unlimited 18 (January
1978) pp15-16.
(Different versions of Beatles' songs.)

M 2994 Remmerswaal, Jos. "Here, There And Everywhere:
Part Seven." Beatles Unlimited 20 (May 1978)
p15.
(Different versions of Beatles' songs.)

M 2995 Remmerswaal, Jos. "Here, There And Everywhere:
Part Eight." Beatles Unlimited 23 (November
1978) p22.
(Different versions of Beatles' songs.)

M 2996 Remmerswaal, Jos. "Interview: Laurence Juber."
Beatles Unlimited 45 (1982) pp18-21. illus.
(Ex-Wings guitarist.)

M 2997 Remmerswaal, Jos. "Komm Gib Mir Deine Money."
Beatles Unlimited 28 (September 1979)
pp18-20.
(The Deccagone bootleg singles.)

M 2998 Remmerswaal, Jos. "Liverpool Beatles Convention
'81." Beatles Unlimited 38 (September 1981)
pp18-19.
(August 29, 1981.)

M 2999 Remmerswaal, Jos. "L.A. 6th Annual Official
Beatles Fan Convention." Beatles Unlimited 42
(1982) p19.

M 3000 Remmerswaal, Jos. "Paul About 'London Town'."
Beatles Unlimited 19 (March 1978) p7.
(McCartney interview excerpts on the new
LP.)

M 3001 Remmerswaal, Jos. "When Two Great Saints Meet."
Beatles Unlimited 34/35 (1981) pp31-33.
(First meeting of John and Yoko.)

M 3002 Remmerswaal, Jos and Ian Ballon. "Suzy And The
Red Stripes." Beatles Unlimited 15
(September 1977) p5.
(On the single by Linda McCartney.)

M 3003 Renard, Gail and Thomas Schnurmacher. "Eight
Days In Montreal With John And Yoko."
The Beatles Book 74 (September 1969)
pp23-24.
(Queen Elizabeth Hotel bed-in.)

M 3004 Repka, C. "Resurrecting The Beatles: Star-Club
To Stereo; Phonograph Record Made From Tape
Of 1962 Hamburg Performance."

High Fidelity/Musical America 27 (August 1977) pp101-103. illus.

M 3005 "Report From Granada's Manchester TV Studios Where The Stars Gathered To Honour The Song Writing Of John And Paul." The Beatles Book 29 (December 1965) pp8-11.
(Filming TV special.)

M 3006 "Results Of The June Song Poll Competition." The Beatles Book 18 (October 1977) pv.
(Most popular Beatles' tunes.)

M 3007 "Reviews." The Beatles Book
(Regular feature, issue 79- , 1982-   .)

M 3008 "Revolutionary Number 9." Kaleidoscope-Madison 2:20 (September 30, 1970) p9.

M 3009 "Revolution: The Dear John Letters." Rolling Stone 32 (May 3, 1969) p22.
(Letters from and to John Lennon.)

M 3010 "RIAA Gold Disk Awards Point Up Beatles' Boff Biz." Variety 237 (February 10, 1965) p55.

M 3011 Richard, Raymond. "A Beatles Reunion? Would You Like To Go Back To School Again?" Beatles Unlimited 11 (January 1977) pp4-8.
(Interview with George Harrison.)

M 3012 Richard, Raymond. "Paul Murphy On: The Beatles Live At The Star Club." Beatles Unlimited 13 (May 1977) pp7-14.
(Producer of Hamburg tapes LP interviewed.)

M 3013 Ridgeway, James. "Feeling Of Youth: Beatles." New Republic 150 (February 22, 1964) p6.
(Beatles' Washington, DC, press conference.)

M 3014 Riesman, D. "What The Beatles Prove About Teenagers." U.S. News & World Report 56 (February 24, 1964) p88. illus.
(Interview.)

M 3015 "Ringo!?!" Rolling Stone 1 (November 9, 1967) p6.

M 3016 "Ringo Acts Naturally For TV Special." Rolling Stone 262 (April 6, 1978) p13. illus.

M 3017 "Ringo & £$." Beatles Unlimited 7 (May 1976) pp16-17.
(Ringo Starr signs recording contract.)

M 3018 "Ringo: A Space Odyssey." Melody Maker 49 (November 23, 1974) p47. illus.

M 3019 "Ringo A Star." Rolling Stone 22 (November 23, 1968) p4.
("Magic Christian" film.)

M 3020 "Ringo Caught On Pool Table." Rolling Stone 11 (May 25, 1968) p4. illus.
(The film "Candy.")

M 3021 "Ringocyclistics." The Beatles Book 36 (July 1966) pp6-7.
(Photos.)

M 3022 "Ringo, His Tax Exile, His New Fiancee, His Rap On A Beatle Reunion." People 7 (January 17, 1977) pp41-47. illus.

M 3023 "Ringo Loves Her - Yeah! Yeah! Yeah!" Life 4:6 (June 1981) p137+. illus.

M 3024 "Ringo On Drums, Drugs, And The Maharishi." Melody Maker 41 (December 2, 1966) pp14-15. illus.
(Interview.)

M 3025 "Ringo's Latest Discs." Design 271 (July 1971) p92. illus.

M 3026 "Ringo's New Album: A Track By Track Review." The Beatles Book 20 (December 1977) ppiii-iv.
("Ringo The 4th.")

M 3027 "Ringo Stands Up The Queen." Rolling Stone 11 (May 25, 1968) p4.

M 3028 "Ringo Starrs Again." The Beatles Book 6 (October 1976) ppiii-v.

M 3029 "Ringo Starr Talks Naturally." Rolling Stone 152 (January 17, 1974) p10+.
(Interview.)

M 3030 "Ringo Stars In New Rock Film." Melody Maker 47 (October 28, 1972) p5.

M 3031 "Ringo Starts Label." Melody Maker 49 (September 28, 1974) p55. illus.

M 3032 "Ringo's Wedding." The Beatles Book 62 (June 1981) ppx-xi.
(To Barbara Bach.)

M 3033 "Ringo Taps The Press." Teen 19 (February 1975) p44+. illus.

M 3034 "Ringo: What Will He Do Next?" The Beatles Book 57 (April 1968) p7.

M 3035 Rinzler, A. "No Soul In Beatlesville." Nation 198 (March 2, 1964) p221.

M 3036 Robbins, Ira and Scott Isler. "The Rutles: All You Need Is Cash." Trouser Press 5:5 (June 1978) pp10-11. illus.
(The Rutles album story.)

M 3037 Roberts, C. "The Beat Boys." Melody Maker 38 (March 23, 1963) pp8-9. illus.

M 3038 Roberts, C. "Beatles In Person." Meldoy Maker 38 (September 14, 1963) p9. illus.

M 3039 Roberts, C. "How To Write A Hit! Interview With John Lennon And Paul McCartney." Melody Maker 39 (February 1, 1964) p11. illus.

M 3040 Roberts, C. "John Lennon." Melody Maker 39 (April 4, 1964) pp2-3.

M 3041 Roberts, C. "The Night A Mouse Took The Mickey Out Of The Beatles." Melody Maker 38 (September 28, 1963) pp12-13.

M 3042 Roberts, C. "What Next For The Beatles?" Melody Maker 39 (August 15, 1964) p3. illus.

M 3043 Roberts, John. "Meeting The Beatles." Beatlefan 4:2 (February 1982) p18.
(Personal encounters in Los Angeles.)

M 3044 Robins, Wayne. "Keeping The Beatles Legend Alive." Nostalgia World 22 (July 1983) pp14-15.

M 3045 Robinson, Lisa. "The Hit Parader Interview: John Lennon." Hit Parader 34:128 (March 1975) pp36-41. illus.
(Cover photo.)

M 3046 Robinson, Lisa. "If We Ever Did Anything Together ... ." New Musical Express (October 12, 1974) pp5-6.
(John Lennon.)

M 3047 Robinson, Lisa. "Lennon." New Musical Express (March 8, 1975) pp24-26.

M 3048 Robinson, Richard. "Paul McCartney: 'We're Coming To Rock'." Hit Parader Annual (Winter 1974) pp26-27.

M 3049 Rock, John J. "The Beatles Again." Rolling Stone 12 (June 22, 1968) p8.

M 3050 Rock, John J. "Bits Of The Beatles." Rolling Stone 9 (April 27, 1968) p8.

M 3051 Rock, John J. "Changes For The Record." Rolling Stone 15 (August 10, 1968) p8.
(John and Cynthia Lennon separate.)

M 3052 Rock, John J. "Here's Some Things To Tell Your Uncle." Rolling Stone 13 (July 6, 1968) p8.
(Jenny Boyd arrested.)

M 3053 Rock & Folk (No.118, November 1976). Paris, France: Editions du Kiosque, 1976. illus.
(Special Beatles tenth anniversary issue.)

M 3054 "Rock-A-Rama: John Lennon - Rock 'N' Roll." Creem 7:1 (June 1975) p70.
(On Lennon's "Rock 'N' Roll" album.)

M 3055 "Rockers Roll In Auction Bucks." Village Voice (January 5, 1982) pp14-15.
(December Beatles auction at Sotheby's.)

M 3056 "Rock 'N' Roll News." Creem 4 (November 1972) p19. illus.
(The Lennons might move to San Francisco.)

M 3057 "Rock 'N' Roll News." Creem 4 (November 1972) p20.
(Harrison working on new LP.)

M 3058 "Rock 'N' Roll News." Creem 4 (November 1972)

p20. illus.
(Ringo Starr in film "Count Down.")

M 3059 "Rock 'N' Roll News." Creem 4 (November 1972)
p20.
(McCartney making new LP.)

M 3060 "Rock 'N' Roll News." Creem 4 (February 1973)
p15.
(Ringo wants Cheech and Chong for movie.)

M 3061 "Rock 'N' Roll News." Creem 4 (March 1973)
p14.
(Ringo Starr's comments on musicians.)

M 3062 "Rock 'N' Roll News." Creem 4 (April 1973)
p16.
(Capitol plans "Best of Beatles" LP.)

M 3063 "Rock 'N' Roll News." Creem 5 (June 1973)
p15. illus.
(Three Beatles work on Ringo's LP.)

M 3064 "Rock 'N' Roll News." Creem 5:5 (October 1973)
p20.
(Wings to record LP in Lagos, Nigeria.)

M 3065 "Rock 'N' Roll News." Creem 5 (January 1974)
p16.
(Lennon's piano auctioned off.)

M 3066 "Rock 'N' Roll News." Creem 5 (January 1974)
p16.
(Alvin Lee won't record Harrison song.)

M 3067 "Rock 'N' Roll News." Creem 5 (February 1974)
p17. illus.
(Ringo to help on David Cassidy LP.)

M 3068 "Rock 'N' Roll News." Creem 5 (March 1974)
p15.
(Lennon to record oldies LP.)

M 3069 "Rock 'N' Roll News." Creem 5 (March 1974)
p15.
(McCartney praises The Osmonds.)

M 3070 "Rock 'N' Roll News." Creem 5 (May 1974)
p16. illus.
(Paul McCartney not liked in Nigeria.)

M 3071 "Rock 'N' Roll News." Creem 6 (June 1974)
p16.
(Lennon drunk at airport.)

M 3072 "Rock 'N' Roll News." Creem 6 (August 1974)
p15. illus.
(McCartney produces Mike McGear LP.)

M 3073 "Rock 'N' Roll News." Creem 6 (September 1974)
p15.
(Latest news about all four.)

M 3074 "Rock 'N' Roll News." Creem 6:5 (October 1974)
pp15-16. illus.
(John Lennon's legal and marital problems.)

M 3075 "Rock 'N' Roll News." Creem 6:5 (October 1974)
pp15-16.
(George Harrison's U.S. tour.)

M 3076 "Rock 'N' Roll News." Creem 6 (January 1975)
p17.
(Ticket sales for Harrison tour.)

M 3077 "Rock 'N' Roll News." Creem 6 (February 1975)
p15.
(Beatle music repels sharks.)

M 3078 "Rock 'N' Roll News." Creem 6 (February 1975)
p16. illus.
(Harrison may produce Sinatra LP.)

M 3079 "Rock 'N' Roll News." Creem 6 (March 1975)
p15. illus.
(Wings on tour.)

M 3080 "Rock 'N' Roll News." Creem 7:1 (June 1975)
p16.
(John Lennon's "Rock 'N' Roll" LP cover
picture.)

M 3081 "Rock 'N' Roll News." Creem 7:1 (June 1975)
p16.
(Ringo as an actor.)

M 3082 "Rock 'N' Roll News." Creem 10 (May 1979)
p16.
(Ringo Starr at driving school.)

M 3083 "Rock 'N' Roll News." Creem 11 (July 1979)
p15.
(Ringo Starr has surgery.)

M 3084 "Rock 'N' Roll News." Creem 11 (September 1979)
p15. illus.

(McCartney party at Apple Studio.)

M 3085 "Rock 'N' Roll News." Creem 12 (October 1980)
p14.
(John and Yoko in Bermuda; Paul's music.)

M 3086 "Rock 'N' Roll News." Creem 12 (October 1980)
p14.
(Harrison's "I Me Mine" book.)

M 3087 "Rock 'N' Roll News." Creem 12 (December 1980)
p13. illus.
(The Lennons' "Double Fantasy" LP.)

M 3088 "Rock 'N' Roll News." Creem 13 (June 1981)
p13.
(Harrison's plagiarism suit.)

M 3089 "Rock 'N' Roll News." Creem 13 (June 1981)
p14.
(McCartney's new album.)

M 3090 Rockwell, J. "Impassioned Chief Of A
Generation's Idols."
New York Times Biography Service 11 (December
1980) pp1754-1755.
(John Lennon.)

M 3091 "Rod McKuen Says Beatles Saved Folk Music
Folk." Billboard 76 (April 25, 1964)
p12.

M 3092 Rodriguez, J. "Culture Heroes." The Montrealer
43:6 (March 1969) pp38-39.

M 3093 Roeder, B. "Newsmakers." Newsweek 85 (March 17,
1975) pp54-55. illus.
(John Lennon.)

M 3094 Roeder, B. "Newsmakers." Newsweek 85 (October
6, 1975) p59.
(Yoko Ono.)

M 3095 Roeder, B. "Newsmakers." Newsweek 106
(October 20, 1975) p58. illus.
(John Lennon.)

M 3096 Rogers, L. "Lennon: Beatles Could Get Together
Again." Songwriters Review 29:2 (April/May 1974)
p9.

M 3097 Rollin, Betty. "Top Pay Merger: Lennon Ono
Inc." Look 33 (March 18, 1969) pp36-42.
illus.
(Includes cover photo.)

M 3098 "Rolling Stone Interview: John Lennon."
Rolling Stone 22 (November 23, 1968)
p11+. illus.

M 3099 "Rolling Stone Music Awards For 1975."
Rolling Stone 206 (February 12, 1976)
p12+. illus.
(John Lennon.)

M 3100 "Rolling Stone 1979 Readers' Poll."
Rolling Stone 310 (February 7, 1980) p10.
(Paul McCartney: a songwriter of the year.)

M 3101 "The Rolling Stone Red Suspenders Awards;
Critics Choice." Rolling Stone 232
(February 10, 1977) p15. illus.
(Missing in Action Award: Ringo Starr's
hair.)

M 3102 "The Rolling Stone Red Suspenders Awards;
Critics Choice." Rolling Stone 232
(February 10, 1977) p14. illus.
(Paul McCartney: Artist of the Year.)

M 3103 "Rolling Stone Red Suspenders Awards; Readers'
Poll." Rolling Stone 232 (February 10, 1977)
p16.
(Paul McCartney wins two awards.)

M 3104 Rorem, Ned. "America And The Beatles."
London Magazine 7 (February 1968) pp54-64.

M 3105 Rorem, Ned. "Music Of The Beatles."
Music Educator's Journal 55 (December 1968)
pp33-34+. illus.

M 3106 Rorem, Ned. "The Music Of The Beatles."
New York Review Of Books (January 18, 1968)
pp23-27.

M 3107 Rose, Frank. "George Harrison." Circus
(January 20, 1976) pp30-32.

M 3108 Rose, Frank. "Meet The Maniacs." Zoo World
(September 26, 1974) pp18-19.

M 3109 Rosen, Steve. "Another Day In The Life." Creem 6
(June 1974) p18+. illus.
(John Lennon.)

LOOK

35 CENTS · DECEMBER 13, 1966

SIGMUND FR[...]
'A controversial unpub[...]
analysis of Woodrow W[...]

THE POPE'S UNSOLVABLE PRO[...]

Why Paul VI cannot cha[...]
Catholic teaching on birt[...]

JOHN LENNON,
a shorn BEATLE
tries it
on his own

POST

The Saturday Evening Post · May 4, [...]

35c

Here's the scene:
THE BEATLES
MIA FARROW
and a Post reporter
all gather in India
to meditate
with
THE MAHARISHI
MAHESH YOGI

No. 1 ACME

BEATLE[...]
'ROUND THE WORLD

50c

DELL
GIANT
25c

THE **BEATLES**

THE ORIGINAL

BEATLES BOOK·TWO

50c

ALL NEW!
100
EXCLUSIVE PHOTOS

BEATLE ROMANCES: THE GIRLS IN THEIR LIVES

M 3110 Rosenberg, Neil V. "Taking Popular Culture
       Seriously: The Beatles."
       Journal of Popular Culture 4:1 (1970) pp53-56.
       (Reply to G. Marshall's 1969 article.)
M 3111 Ross, D. "The Real Truth About The Beatles."
       Young Judean (June 1964) p20.
M 3112 Rossi, Gloria. "Meeting The Beatles."
       Beatlefan 4:3 (April 1982) p22.
       (London encounters with Paul McCartney.)
M 3113 Rossmann, A. "Die Beatles Als Musical-Stars -
       Der Neue Hit In London." Neue Musikzeitung
       24:2 (1975) p5. illus.
M 3114 Roth, M. "Beatles' Tour Spawns The Stripling
       Set; Chi's Newest, Hottest Pop Concert Mkt."
       Variety 236 (October 7, 1964) p47.
M 3115 Rowe, Graham. "George Harrison And John
       Lennon." Sixteen Magazine 6:10 (March 1965)
       pp46-49.
M 3116 Rowland, Edna. "John Lennon: Hello, Goodbye!"
       Horoscope 47:7 (July 1981) pp15-18.
       (Astrological analysis of Lennon's death.)
M 3117 Rowland, Mark. "John And Yoko: The Long &
       Winding Road." Playgirl 8:10 (March 1981)
       pp21-22. illus.
       (Includes post-Beatles discography.)
M 3118 Rowland, Mark. "Paul!" Playgirl (June 1982)
       pp39-42.
       (Paul McCartney profile and cover photo.)
M 3119 Ruffer, Gerhard. "The German Scene."
       Beatles Unlimited 14 (July 1977) pp19-21.
       (Beatles-related events in Germany,
       1976-77.)
M 3120 Ruffer, Gerhard. "Germany Updated."
       Beatles Unlimited 20 (May 1978) p10.
       (Beatles events in Germany, May '77-Feb.
       '78.)
M 3121 "Rumor Mill." Rolling Stone 130 (March 15, 1973)
       p18.
       (John Lennon; Paul McCartney.)
M 3122 "Rumors Of McCartney's Death Put Beaucoup Life
       Into 'Abbey Road' Sales." Variety (November
       5, 1969) p52.
M 3123 "Rutlemania Hits TV: 'All You Need Is Cash'."
       Rolling Stone 261 (March 23, 1978)
       p18. illus.
M 3124 "Rutles Forever" Beatlefan 1:1 (December 1978)
       p4.
       (TV special.)
M 3125 S., L.N. "Capitol's Rip Off." St. Louis Outlaw
       2:13 (December 24, 1971) p16.
M 3126 Saal, Hubert. "Beatles Minus One." Newsweek 75
       (April 20, 1970) p95. illus.
M 3127 Saal, Hubert. "Confessions Of A Beatle."
       Newsweek 77 (January 18, 1971) pp50-51.
       illus.
       (John Lennon.)
M 3128 Saal, J. "Double Beatle." Newsweek 72
       (December 9, 1968) p109.
M 3129 Sacks, Elizabeth. "At The Premiere."
       The Beatles Book 26 (September 1965)
       p27.
       (Of "Help!")
M 3130 Sacks, Elizabeth. "I Visited The Beatles On The
       Set." The Beatles Book 11 (June 1964)
       pp6-10.
       ("A Hard Day's Night".)
M 3131 Sacks, Leo. "WBCN-FM In Lennon Drive."
       Billboard 94:14 (April 10, 1982) p40.
       (Boston station petition to set "Peace
       Day.")
M 3132 Sakamoto, J. "And The Beat Goes On." MacLean's
       90 (August 8, 1977) pp62-63. illus.
M 3133 Salzman, E. "Nine Ways Of Looking At The
       Beatles, 1963-73." Stereo Review 30
       (February 1973) pp56-63. illus.
       (Cover portrait.)
M 3134 Sander, Ellen. "Beatles: Plain White Wrapper."
       Saturday Review 51 (December 28, 1968) p58.
M 3135 Sander, Ellen. "John And Yoko Ono Lennon: Give
       Peace A Chance." Saturday Reveiw 54

M 3136 (June 28, 1969) pp46-47. illus.
M 3136 Sander, Ellen. "McCartney On His Own."
       Saturday Review 53 (May 30, 1970) pp53-54.
       illus.
       ("McCartney" album.)
M 3137 Sander, Ellen. "The Pantheon." Saturday Review
       51 (October 26, 1968) pp80-81. illus.
M 3138 Sander, Ellen. "Pop In Perspective: A Profile."
       Saturday Review 51 (October 26, 1968)
       pp80-81.
       (Discography, including Beatles.)
M 3139 Sander, Ellen. "Rolling Stones; Beggars'
       Triumph." Saturday Review 52 (January 25,
       1969) p48.
M 3140 Sanders, Richard. "A Starr For Ringo." Us 5:9
       (April 28, 1981) p40+. illus.
M 3141 Sandner, Wolfgang. "Beziehungen Zwischen Pop
       Art Und Pop Music." Hi Fi Stereophonie 19
       (June 1980) pp683-684. illus.
M 3142 Sandner, Wolfgang. "Musik Im Maxilook:
       Nostalgie In Der Rockmusik."
       Hi Fi Stereophonie 14:1 (1975) pp24-28.
       (Includes Beatles.)
M 3143 Santiago, L.P. "The Lyrical Expression Of
       Adolescent Conflict In The Beatles Songs."
       Adolescence 4:14 (1969) pp199-210.
M 3144 Saturday Evening Post. No. 11.
       Philadelphia, PA: Curtis Publishing Co.,
       1964.
       (March 21 issue; cover portrait.)
M 3145 Saturday Evening Post. No. 28.
       Philadelphia, PA: Curtis Publishing Co.,
       1964.
       (August 15 issue; cover portrait.)
M 3146 Saylon, B. "Looking Backwards: Reflections On
       Nostalgia In The Musical Avant-Garde."
       Centerpoint 1:3 (1975) pp5-6.
M 3147 Schade, H. "Verwelktes Kleeblatt; Die Beatles
       Retrospektive Und Ausblick."
       Hi Fi Stereophonie 10 (August 1971)
       p628+. illus.
M 3148 Schaefer, Oda. "Beatlemania." Melos 31
       (November 1964) pp333-341. illus.
M 3149 Schaffner, Nicholas. "Every Little Thing: The
       Story Behind 'Rarities,' The 'New' Beatles
       LP." Trouser Press 7:5 (June 1980)
       pp14-18.
       (Cover photo of The Beatles.)
M 3150 Schaffner, Nicholas. "'Love Me Do'." Beatlefan
       4:6 (October 1982) p5,18.
       (A fan looks back twenty years.)
M 3151 Schaffner, Nicholas. "Remember ... " Beatlefan 3:1
       (December 1980) p8.
       (Reactions to Lennon's death.)
M 3152 Schaffner, Nicholas. "Some Outtakes From
       Beatles History." Beatlefan 3:2 (February
       1981) p9.
       (Little known facts.)
M 3153 Schaffner, Nicholas. "Town That Gave The
       Beatles Away." Beatlefan 2:6 (October 1980)
       pp7-8.
       (Liverpool in 1980.)
M 3154 Schaffner, Nicholas. "Writing A Book About The
       Beatles." Beatlefan 2:1 (December 1979)
       p5,12.
       (Author of "The Beatles Forever.")
M 3155 Schecter, Jerrold. "Beatles Under Wraps In
       Tokyo 'Beetorusi' In Tokyo." Life 61
       (July 15, 1966) pp72-74. illus.
M 3156 Schickel, Richard. "Say Blah-Blah Spaniel."
       Nation (August 8, 1965)
       (On "A Spaniard In The Works.")
M 3157 Schickele, Peter. "About The Awful." Nation
       (June 8, 1964) pp588-589.
       (Commentary on "In His Own Write.")
M 3158 Schiefman, Emma. "The Beatles? Yeah! Yeah!
       Yeah!" The Reading Teacher 19 (October 1965)
       pp31-34.
M 3159 Schindler, Walter. "Die 'Beatlemanie' - Ein
       Ausdruck Unserer Zeit." Praxis der Kinder-
       psychologie Und Kinderpsychiatrie 15 (November
       1966) pp303-307.

("Beatlemania - An Expression Of Our
      Time.")
M 3160 Schnlon, P. "Two Rookies Make Their Beatles
      Movie." Rolling Stone 266 (June 1, 1978)
      p8+. illus.
      ("I Wanna Hold Your Hand.")
M 3161 Schoenfeld, Herm. "Beatles Batter All B.O.
      Records; Parlay N.Y. Fan Hysteria Into
      $150,000 Gross." Variety 236 (September 2,
      1964) p41+.
M 3162 Schoenfeld, Herm. "Beatles Buzzing Like
      Business Bees 'Round Blossoming Apple Corps
      Deals." Variety 250 (May 15, 1968)
      p59+.
M 3163 Schoenfeld, Herm. "Beatles' $304,000 At Shea
      Ballpark All-Time Record 1-Nite Show Biz
      B.O." Variety 239 (August 18, 1965)
      p2+.
M 3164 Schoenfeld, Herm. "Britannia Rules Airwaves;
      Beatles Stir Home Carbons." Variety 233
      (February 12, 1964) p63.
M 3165 Schoenfeld, Herm. "N.Y. Promoter Just About
      Breaks Even On The Beatles' $295,000
      One-Nighter." Variety 244 (August 31, 1966)
      pp41-42.
M 3166 Schoenfeld, Herm. "6,000 Beatle Buffs Flip
      Their Wigs In 2-Show Carnegie Hall Blowout."
      Variety 233 (February 19, 1964) p49+.
M 3167 Schoenfeld, Herm. "'Victory Thru Hair Power'."
      Variety 237 (December 30, 1964) p37+.
M 3169 Schuler, M. "Rockmusik Und Kunstmusik Der
      Vergangenheit-Ein Analytischer Versuch."
      Archiv fur Musikwissenschaft 35:2 (1978)
      pp135-150. illus.
M 3170 Schultheiss, Tom. "Beatle Books: A
      Discriminating Guide."
      Wilson Library Bulletin 55:6 (February 1981)
      pp434-439.
M 3171 Schultheiss, Tom. "Beatle Bookshelf."
      Beatlefan 2:4 (June 1980) p24.
      (Reply to a review of his book.)
M 3172 Schultheiss, Tom. "Building A Beatles Library."
      Beatlefan 3:4 (June 1981) pp4-5,24.
      (Recommended book titles, plus a
      bibliography.)
M 3173 Schwartz, Al. "Lennon Vs. The Fools On The
      Hill." Zoo World (November 7, 1974)
      p14.
M 3174 Schwartz, David. "The Beatlefan Survey."
      Beatlefan 4:2 (February 1982) p19.
      (Questionnaire.)
M 3175 Schwartz, David. "Collecting." Beatlefan 4:2
      (February 1982) pp22,26.
      (Survey of twelve inch Beatle-related
      discs.)
M 3176 Schwartz, David. "Collecting." Beatlefan 4:3
      (April 1982) p20.
      (Beatles recordings; first part.)
M 3177 Schwartz, David. "Collecting." Beatlefan 4:4
      (June 1982) p14.
      (Beatles recordings; second part.)
M 3178 Schwartz, David. "'Love Me Do'." Beatlefan 4:6
      (October 1982) p4.
      (A fan looks back twenty years.)
M 3179 Schwartz, David. "Original Master Beatle
      Recordings." Beatlefan 4:6 (October 1982)
      p8.
M 3180 Schwartz, David. "'Sgt. Pepper' - A Look Back."
      Beatlefan 4:4 (June 1982) pp12-13.
      (Album retrospective.)
M 3181 Schwartz, David. "Survey Results." Beatlefan 4:5
      (August 1982) p19.
      (Fan survey.)
M 3182 Schwartz, David. "Survey Results II."
      Beatlefan 4:6 (October 1982) p14.
      (Fan's favorite choices.)
M 3183 Schwartz, David. "Survey Results III."

Beatlefan 5:1 (December 1982) p13.
      (Fan single and LP favorites.)
M 3184 Schwartz, David and William P. King. "Glass
      Onion." Beatlefan 5:1 (December 1982)
      pp15,26. illus.
      (On Pete Best.)
M 3185 Schwartz, David, Charles Reinhart and Rudy
      Ornelas. "Beatles Picture Discs." Beatlefan
      3:3 (April 1981) p17.
      (Part two; collecting tips.)
M 3186 Schwartz, Francie. "Memories Of An Apple Girl."
      Rolling Stone 46 (November 15, 1969)
      pp23-26. illus.
M 3187 "Scoop." Village Voice 21 (March 8, 1976)
      p20.
      (John Lennon.)
M 3188 "Scoop." Village Voice 21 (June 7, 1976)
      p85.
M 3189 Scoppa, Bud. "Beatles Apart."
      Senior Scholastic 100 (June 31, 1972)
      p28. illus.
M 3190 Scoppa, Bud. "Beatles To Remember, Beatles To
      Forget." Senior Scholastic 98 (March 29,
      1971) p29+.
M 3191 "Scot Teens Who Queued 60 Hrs. For The Beatles
      Were Show Themselves." Variety 234
      (April 15, 1964) p50.
M 3192 Scott, Norman. "'My First Encounter With The
      Beatles'." Beatles Now 2 (Spring 1982)
      pp8-9. illus.
      (Scott was an East London disc jockey in
      early 1963.)
M 3193 Scully, M.G. "John Lennon: The Whole Boat Was
      Moving." Chronicle of Higher Education 21
      (December 15, 1980) p4. illus.
M 3194 Seal, Lou. "George Harrison Discovers The
      Pleasure Of Home, Maui, The Recording Studio
      And Formula One Racing." Wax 4:2 (February
      9, 1979) pp4-8. illus.
M 3195 Search, G. "Ringo Starr Talks Naturally."
      Rolling Stone 152 (January 17, 1974)
      p10+. illus.
M 3196 "See Hot Bidding From Labels In Future For Paul
      McCartney's Wings." Variety 265 (November
      24, 1971) p47.
M 3197 "See McCartney Being Bought Out By Other
      Beatles." Variety 262 (May 5, 1971)
      p51.
M 3198 Segal, E. "Through A Phone Darkly Or Ringo
      Agonistes." Yale Literary Magazine
      (March 1968)
      (Ringo Starr.)
M 3199 Segell, M. "Paul McCartney Signs With Columbia
      Records." Rolling Stone 287 (March 22, 1979)
      p11.
M 3200 Sekuler, Eliot. "Ringo's Beatle Bingo." Circus
      (November 10, 1976) pp50-52.
M 3201 Selvin, Joel. "With The Beatles At The Bowl."
      Melody Maker 52 (May 28, 1977) p13. illus.
      (Interview with V. Gilmore.)
M 3202 "Sgt. Pepper; Latest Album." New Yorker 43
      (June 24, 1967) pp22-23.
M 3203 "'Sgt. Pepper's' Beatle Music May 'Pied Piper'
      Rock Fans To Legit." Variety 276 (October
      23, 1974) p93.
M 3204 Serra, Julio F. "George Harrison In Brazil."
      Beatles Unlimited 25 (March 1979) pp12-14.
      (January-February 1979.)
M 3205 Settimo, Franco. "Yes It Is."
      Beatles Unlimited 36 (June 1981) pp11-15.
      (Italian discography.)
M 3206 "Shake." Berkeley Tribe 2:15 (April 17, 1970)
      p22.
M 3208 Shames, Laurence. "John Lennon, Where Are You?"
      Esquire 94 (November 1980) pp31-38+ illus.
      (Cover portrait.)
M 3209 Shapiro, S. "Sgt. Pepper Hits The Road."
      Crawdaddy 45 (February 1975) pp30-31. illus.

M 3210 "Sharing The Grief." Rolling Stone 335
(January 22, 1981) p20+. illus.
(John Lennon.)

M 3211 Shaw, A. "Rhythm & Blues Revival - No White
Gloved, Black Hits." Billboard 81 (August
16, 1969) p53.

M 3212 "Shea Reunion." The Beatles Book 76 (November
1969) p31.
(Fans gather at Shea Stadium.)

M 3213 Shears, Billy. "Beatles Video: 'Interview With
A Legend' John Lennon With Tom Snyder On The
Tomorrow Show." Beatlefan 3:6 (October 1981)
p18.
(NBC-TV show available on videotape.)

M 3214 Sheff, David. "The Eulogies Ended, Yoko Ono
Faces The Pain Of Life Without John."
People 15:1 (January 12, 1981) p28+. illus.

M 3215 Sheff, David. "In Praise Of John Lennon: The
Liverpool Lad As Musician, Husband, Father,
And Man." People 14:25 (December 22, 1980)
p26+. illus.

M 3216 Sheff, David. "John Lennon And Yoko Ono."
Playboy 28:1 (January 1981) p75+. illus.
(Interview.)

M 3217 Sheff, David. "Yoko And Sean: Starting Over."
People 18 (December 13, 1982) pp42-45.
illus.

M 3218 Sheff, David and Victoria Sheff. "The Betrayal
Of John Lennon." Playboy 31:3 (March 1984)
pp84-87+. illus.
(On the recent spate of
"behind-the-scenes" books.)

M 3219 Sheinkopf, Kenneth G. and Mark R. Weintz. "The
Beatles Are Dead! Long Live The Beatles!"
Popular Music & Society 2:4 (1973) pp320-326.
("Paul-Is-Dead" rumor.)

M 3220 Shepherd, Billy. "The Beatles In Paris."
The Beatles Book 8 (March 1964) pp8-15+.
(January 1964.)

M 3221 Shepherd, Billy. "Beatles On Holiday."
The Beatles Book 12 (July 1964) pp7-13.

M 3222 Shepherd, Billy. "'Constantly Changing Through
The Years'." The Beatles Book 70 (May 1979)
pp23-27.
(John Lennon.)

M 3223 Shepherd, Billy. "The Faces Of George."
The Beatles Book 17 (December 1964)
p9.

M 3224 Shepherd, Billy. "Filming With The Boys In 'A
Hard Day's Night'." The Beatles Book 11
(June 1964) pp13-15+.

M 3225 Shepherd, Billy. "Filming With The Boys In
Beatlescope." The Beatles Book 10 (May 1964)
pp12-15+.
("A Hard Day's Night.")

M 3226 Shepherd, Billy. "Film Talk." The Beatles Book 13
(August 1964) pp12-13.
("A Hard Day's Night.")

M 3227 Shepherd, Billy. "The Helpful Beatle."
The Beatles Book 68 (March 1969) pp22-24.
(George Harrison.)

M 3228 Shepherd, Billy. "He's A Sensitive Soul."
The Beatles Book 69 (April 1969) pp22-25.
(Ringo Starr.)

M 3229 Shepherd, Billy. "Shindig - An On-The-Spot
Report." The Beatles Book 16 (November 1964)
p11.
("Shindig" TV show appearance.)

M 3230 Shepherd, Billy. "Ssssssssh ... Beatles
Recording." The Beatles Book 15 (October
1964) pp13-15.
(At Abbey Road studios.)

M 3231 Shepherd, Billy. "A Tale Of Four Beatles, Part
I." The Beatles Book 2 (September 1963)
pp6-13.

M 3232 Shepherd, Billy. "A Tale Of Four Beatles, Part
II." The Beatles Book 3 (October 1963)
pp6-13.

M 3233 Shepherd, Billy. "A Tale Of Four Beatles, Part
III." The Beatles Book 4 (November 1963)

pp6-13.

M 3234 Shepherd, Billy. "A Tale Of Four Beatles, Part
IV." The Beatles Book 5 (December 1963)
pp6-13.

M 3235 Shepherd, Billy. "A Tale Of Four Beatles, Part
V." The Beatles Book 6 (January 1964)
pp8-15.

M 3236 Shepherd, Billy. "A Tale Of Four Beatles, Part
VI." The Beatles Book 7 (February 1964)
pp8-15.

M 3237 Shepherd, Billy. "A Tale Of Four Beatles, Part
VII." The Beatles Book 9 (April 1964)
pp25-27.

M 3238 Shepherd, Billy. "They Had To Change."
The Beatles Book 77 (December 1969)
pp23-24+.

M 3239 Shepherd, Billy. "Very Much A Doer"
The Beatles Book 71 (June 1969) pp21-23.
(Paul McCartney.)

M 3240 Shepherd, Billy and Johnny Dean. "Behind The
Spotlight." The Beatles Book
(Regular feature, issues 13-62, 1964-1968.)

M 3241 Sherman, Pam. "'Lennon'." Beatlefan 4:6
(October 1982) p24.
(On the off-Broadway play.)

M 3242 Sherman, Suzanne K. "'The Yellow Submarine': A
Fable For Our Time."
Journal of Popular Culture 8:3 (Winter 1974)
pp619-623.
(Film.)

M 3243 "Shindig Pix." The Beatles Book 16 (November
1964) pp12-13.
("Shindig" TV show appearance.)

M 3244 "Shindig T.V. Show." Sixteen Magazine 6:10
(March 1965) p40.
(Beatles action photos.)

M 3245 Shipper, M. "Ringo Sets Up Shop: Ring-O
Records." Phonograph Record Magazine
(October 1976) pp32-33.

M 3246 Shneerson, G. "Pop-Muzyka V Deystivii."
Sovetskaya Muzyka 38 (January 1974)
pp90-101. illus.

M 3247 Sholin, David. "John And Yoko On Marriage,
Children And Their Generation." MS. 9
(March 1981) p58+. illus.

M 3248 Sholin, David. "Die Letzte Interview (The Last
Interview)." From Me To You (West Germany)
(February 1982) pp23-50. illus.
(German translation of RKO interview.)

M 3249 Short, D. "55,600 - Beatles Play To World's
Largest Audience In New York." Melody Maker
40 (August 21, 1965) p3. illus.

M 3250 Short, D. "Historic Beatles-Elvis Meeting."
Melody Maker 40 (September 4, 1965)
p5.

M 3251 Short, D. "With The Beatles In India."
Melody Maker 43 (March 9, 1968) pp12-13.

M 3252 "Short Ads." Beatles Unlimited
(Regular feature, issues 37- .)

M 3253 "Should The Beatles Come Together?"
Melody Maker 49 (April 27, 1974) pp38-39.
illus.

M 3254 "'Shout': An Interview With Author Philip
Norman." Beatlefan 3:4 (June 1981)
pp14-15.

M 3255 "'Shout!': An Interview With Author Philip
Norman." Beatlefan 3:5 (August 1981)
pp10-12.
(Part two; began in v3n4.)

M 3256 "Show Out Of Town." Variety 287 (May 18, 1977)
p124.
(Stage show "Beatlemania.")

M 3257 Show, The Magazine Of Film And The Arts.
Hollywood, CA: Show Publications, 1969.
(Issue for January 1970; cover portrait.)

M 3258 Sick - Monster Issue. New York:
Headline Publications Inc., 1964.
(Ringo on cover;spoofs "Hard Day's Night"
film.)

M 3259 Siegel, Joel. "Beatlephilia: Strange Rumbling
       In Pepperland." Rolling Stone 172 (October
       24, 1974) p44+. illus.
       (Beatlefest fan convention.)
M 3260 Siegel, Joel. "Lennon: Back In The U.S.S.A."
       Rolling Stone 171 (October 10, 1974)
       p11. illus.
       (Lennon's deportation fight.)
M 3261 Siegel, Joel. "What They're Saying." Sing Out
       16:6 (1967) p57.
M 3262 Sievert, Bill. "The Beatles Today: Separate
       Roads, Separate Realities."
       Sound: The Sony Guide To Music (September
       1975) pp19-24.
M 3263 Sigerson, Davitt. "Paul Carries That Weight."
       Village Voice (May 11, 1982) p64.
       (On the "Tug Of War" LP.)
M 3264 Silver, C. "Issue/On John Lennon."
       Alternative Media 12 (Spring 1981)
       p9.
M 3265 Simels, Steve. "George Harrison And Other
       Bores." Stereo Review 42 (April 1979)
       p114. illus.
M 3266 Simels, Steve. "John Lennon/Yoko Ono."
       Stereo Review 46 (March 1981) pp102-103.
       illus.
       (On "Double Fantasy" LP.)
M 3267 Simels, Steve. "Rediscovered Historical
       Beatlefacts." Stereo Review 39 (August 1977)
       p88. illus.
       (Release of two live Beatles LPs.)
M 3268 Simels, Steve. "Secondhand Beatles."
       Stereo Review 40 (June 1978) p93.
       (Stage show "Beatlemania" & Rutles TV
       special.)
M 3269 Simels, Steve. "The Surviving Beatle - And
       Others." Stereo Review 37 (August 1976)
       p38. illus.
       (Paul McCartney.)
M 3270 Simels, Steve. "This Month's Big Six."
       Stereo Review 38 (February 1977) p52.
       (George Harrison.)
M 3271 Simmons, Pat. "Aug. 15, 1966: Meeting The
       Beatles." Beatlefan 2:1 (December 1979)
       p8,18.
       (A Cleveland fan on board the group's
       airplane.)
M 3272 Simmons, Pat. "The Beatles' Touring Days."
       Beatlefan 2:5 (August 1980) pp6-9.
       (Beatles' September 15, 1964, Cleveland
       concert.)
M 3273 Simmons, Pat. "Chicago '82: We Ain't Going
       Nowhere ... " Beatles Unlimited 45 (1982)
       pp9-10.
       (Beatles convention.)
M 3274 Simmons, Pat. "Wings Talk." Beatles Unlimited 9
       (September 1976) pp5-6.
       (Memories of Wings' U.S. tour.)
M 3275 Simmons, Pat and Joy Kilbane. "The Dream Is Not
       Over." Beatlefan 3:1 (December 1980)
       p11.
       (Reactions to John Lennon's death.)
M 3276 Simon, J. "Lennon." New York 15 (October 18,
       1982) p88.
M 3277 Simonds, C.H. "Settling Down." National Review
       23 (February 9, 1971) p145.
       (John Lennon.)
M 3278 Sims, J. "Beatles Meet But Not For 'Reunion'."
       Rolling Stone 133 (April 26, 1973)
       p10.
M 3279 "Sinclair Freedom Rally Stars Lennon And Ono."
       Billboard 83 (December 25, 1971) p4.
M 3280 "Singalong A Beatles - Ugh!" Melody Maker 53
       (August 5, 1978) p13.
       (TV documentary.)
M 3281 "Singer Tony Sheridan Sues Over Beatles LPs."
       Billboard 94 (September 25, 1982) p5.
       (His records "fraudulently" ascribed to
       Beatles.)
M 3282 "Singing Beatles Need New Deal On Finance."

Financial Post 63 (April 12, 1969)
       p43.
M 3283 Sippel, J. "A & M / Harrison: Pact That
       Failed." Billboard 88 (December 11, 1976)
       p6+.
M 3284 Sippel, J. "Apple Sues Capitol For $16
       Million." Billboard 91 (June 9, 1979)
       p4.
M 3285 Sippel, J. "Attorneys To Study Capitol's
       Finances In Cetena Complaint." Billboard 87
       (June 28, 1975) p6.
M 3286 Sixteen Magazine Volume 6, No. 2 New York:
       Girlfriend-Boyfriend Corp. 1964
       (John Lennon cartoon cover.)
M 3287 "'62 Beatles Album Due." Billboard 93
       (March 28, 1981) p9.
       ("Dawn Of the Silver Beatles.")
M 3288 Slagt, Jan and Evert Vermeer. "Drive My Car."
       Beatles Unlimited 8 (July 1976) pp7-9.
       (Paul McCartney & Wings in Holland, March
       1976.)
M 3289 Sloman, Larry. "George's Tour Winds Down In New
       York, And Mr. Harrison Goes To Washington."
       Rolling Stone 179 (January 30, 1975)
       p10+. illus.
M 3290 Smith, Alan. "At A Recording Session With The
       Beatles." Mersey Beat (January 3, 1963)
       p4.
       (Recording "Please Please Me.")
M 3291 Smith, Alan. "A British Tour." Hit Parader XXV:2
       (October 1966) ppB12-B13. illus.
       (Beatles' December 1965 U.K. tour.)
M 3292 Smith, Alan. "John And Yoko." Hit Parader 31:91
       (February 1972) pp31-37+. illus.
       (Cover photo of John and Yoko.)
M 3293 Smith, David J. "'Cavern Mecca' Opens In
       Liverpool." Beatlefan 3:2 (February 1981)
       pp11,21.
       (Beatles museum opens January 3, 1981.)
M 3294 Smith, David J. "Eleanor Rigby Comes To Town."
       Beatles Now 5 (Winter 1983) p4. illus.
       ("Eleanor Rigby" sculpture by Tommy
       Steele.)
M 3295 Smith, David J. "From The 'Top Ten' To Number
       17." Beatles Now 4 (Autumn 1982) pp8-9.
       illus.
       (Beatles' post-Hamburg Liverpool days.)
M 3296 Smith, David J. "The George Harrison Hamburg
       Deportation." Beatles Now 1 (January 1982)
       pp6-7. illus.
M 3297 Smith, David J. "In The Beginning/The Early
       Years." Beatles Now 2 (Spring 1982)
       p3. illus.
       (Documentation on the Beatles' Hamburg
       days.)
M 3298 Smith, David J. "There Beneath The Blue
       Suburban Skies: Penny Lane Revisited."
       Beatles Now 3 (Summer 1982) pp10-11. illus.
       (Paul McCartney at brother's wedding, May
       29, 1982.)
M 3299 Smith, David J. "Wings Over Manchester."
       Beatlefan 2:2 (February 1980) p16.
       (Manchester Apollo, November 28, 1979.)
M 3300 Smith, Donna Ridley. "Beatle And Other
       Fanzines." Sipapu 10:2 (July 1979)
       pp12-13.
M 3301 Smith, H. and L. Harlib. "Scenes: All You Need
       Is Cash." Village Voice 22 (October 17, 1977)
       p20.
       (Rutles TV Special.)
M 3302 Smith, H. and L. Harris. "Scenes: Lennon
       Envisioned." Village Voice 26 (March 11,
       1981) p23.
       (1970-71 Greenwich Village period.)
M 3303 Smith, H. and L. Harlib. "Scenes: New Hash On
       'Cash' Flack." Village Voice 23 (March 20,
       1978) p16.
       (Rutles TV Special.)
M 3304 Smith, L.R. "The Beatles As Act: A Study Of
       Control In A Musical Group."

Dissertation Abstracts 31 (March 1971) pp4809A-4810A.
(Abstract of the dissertation.)

M 3305 Smith, M. "Best Songwriters Since Schubert?" Melody Maker 43 (November 30, 1968) p5.

M 3306 Smith, Terry. "With A Little Help From Some Friends, Kevin Howlett Finds A Treasure Of Lost Beatles Music." People 17:16 (April 26, 1982) pp46-47. illus.
(Finds 88 BBC radio broadcasts not on record.)

M 3307 Snidall, Irene. "A Day To Remember." The Beatles Book 14 (September 1964) p15.
(Meeting The Beatles.)

M 3308 Snow, Temperance. "I Am The (Boston) Walrus." Beatles Unlimited 12 (March 1977) pp12-16.
(George Harrison in Boston, September 1975.)

M 3309 Snyder-Scumpy, Patrick. "Beatles Show: The Great White Shuck?" Rolling Stone 207 (February 26, 1976) p12.
(Promotor Bill Sargeant seeks reunion concert.)

M 3310 Snyder-Scumpy, Patrick. "People And Things That Went Before." Crawdaddy 25 (June 1973) p48+.

M 3311 Snyder-Scumpy, Patrick. "Sometime In L.A.; Lennon Plays It As It Lays." Crawdaddy 34 (March 1974) pp46-54. illus.

M 3312 Snyder-Scumpy, Patrick. "They're Gonna Make A Big Star Out Of WWII." Rolling Stone 229 (December 30, 1976) p19. illus.
("All This And World War II" album.)

M 3313 Snyder-Scumpy, Patrick and Dolores Ziebarth. "'6th Beatle' Mal Evans Killed In Los Angeles." Rolling Stone 206 (February 12, 1976) p10. illus.

M 3314 "Social Notes." Rolling Stone 148 (November 22, 1973) p33.
(McCartney writing score for TV special.)

M 3315 "Social Notes." Rolling Stone 150 (December 20, 1973) p30.
(Yoko Ono at Peter Max gallery opening.)

M 3316 Solloway, Larry. "Jaded Miami Beach Takes Beatles In Stride Despite Shrieking Teenagers." Variety 233 (February 19, 1964) p49.

M 3317 "The Solo Lennon." The Beatles Book 4 (August 1976) ppiv-vi.

M 3318 "Solo Single From Ringo?" Melody Maker 45 (February 28, 1970) p1. illus.

M 3319 "Some Interesting Dates From August In Past Years." The Beatles Book 52 (November 1967) pvi.
(Chronology.)

M 3320 "Something To Be." Great Speckled Bird 4:23 (June 7, 1971) p16.
(John Lennon.)

M 3321 "'Something' To Be Released As Single In U.K." The Beatles Book 76 (November 1969) p31.

M 3322 Somma, Robert. "Ringo." Fusion 72 (March 1972) pp32-34. illus.

M 3323 "Song Is Ended. But Beatles Linger On As Advertisers Utilize Tie-In Rights." Advertising Age 36 (September 6, 1965) pp44-46. illus.

M 3324 "Song Of The Month." The Beatles Book (Lyrics; regular feature, issues 34-49, 53.)

M 3325 "Songs From India On New Beatle LP." Rolling Stone 11 (May 25, 1968) p6.

M 3326 "Songwriters John And Paul Earned $4 Mil." Billboard 77 (January 16, 1965) p14.

M 3327 "Sons Of 'Great White Wonder'." Rolling Stone 53 (March 7, 1970) p8.
("Get Back" bootlegs.)

M 3328 Souster, Tim. "The Beatles In Their Prime."

Listener 85 (April 15, 1971) pp465-467. illus.

M 3329 Souster, Tim. "Rock, Beat, Pop Avantgarde." World Of Music 12:2 (1970) pp32-43. illus.

M 3330 "So What Else Is New? The Beatles Spark Coast Riots, Take Home 150G." Variety 240 (September 1, 1965) p45.

M 3331 Sparn, Ed. "On The Road With Paul McCartney." Senior Scholastic 103 (September 27, 1973) p32+. illus.

M 3332 "A Speakeasy Party." The Beatles Book 50 (September 1967) pp24,31.
(The Beatles meet the Monkees at a London club.)

M 3333 "Spector Of The Beatles." Time 95 (May 18, 1970) p64.
(Phil Spector.)

M 3334 "Spector Wows 'Em At Harrison Date." Rolling Stone 62 (July 9, 1970) p18.
(Making of "All Things Must Pass" LP.)

M 3335 Spencer, Graham. "The Beatles Back Home." Mersey Beat (August 15, 1963) p8.
(Photographs taken at Grafton Ballroom.)

M 3336 Spencer, Neil. "Just A Little Light Rocca From Macca." New Musical Express (September 20, 1975) pp5-6.
(Paul McCartney.)

M 3337 Spencer, Scott. "John Lennon." Rolling Stone 335 (January 22, 1981) p13. illus.

M 3338 "Split Of Beatles Clips Capitol Industries Stock." Variety 258 (April 22, 1970) p55.

M 3339 "Spongers Harassed Beatles Before Klein Moved In, Lennon Tells Court." Variety 262 (March 3, 1971) p51+.

M 3340 "Spot The Beatle Contest Photo." Sixteen Magazine 6:10 (March 1965) p41.

M 3341 Springman, Joanne M. "The Beatles: Let It Be." Triangle 75:3 (1981) pp24,25+.
(1980 Musicological Research Contest winner.)

M 3342 Springman, Joanne M. "The Beatles: Minstrels Or Messiahs?" North Dakota Quarterly 49 (1981) pp106-113.

M 3343 Squire, John. "Lennon & The No. 9 Connection." Beatles Now 7 (July 1983) pp8-9,22. illus.
(The number 9 in Lennon's life.)

M 3344 Sshiefman, Emma. "The Beatles? Yeah! Yeah! Yeah!" Reading Teacher 18 (October 1965) pp31-34.

M 3345 Stanley, Hiram. "Hiram And The Animals." The New Yorker (September 12, 1964) pp40-43.
(Hiram switches from The Beatles to The Animals.)

M 3346 Stanley, Hiram. "Hiram's Report." The New Yorker (February 22, 1964) pp21-23.
(On the Beatles' first visit to New York.)

M 3347 Stanley, Hiram. "A Report From Hiram." The New Yorker (August 22, 1964) pp25-27.
(New York premiere of "A Hard Day's Night.")

M 3348 Stanley, Raymond. "Near-Riot Scenes Fail To Bug Beatles' Aussie Tour, But Hong Kong Biz Slow." Variety 235 (June 24, 1964) p58+.

M 3349 Starr, Ringo. "'Among My Souvenirs'." Mersey Beat (August 29, 1963) p9.
(On gifts sent by fans.)

M 3350 "States Go Beatle Crazy." Melody Maker 39 (January 11, 1964) p4.

M 3351 Stavers, Gloria. "Paul McCartney, A Strange And Special Meeting." Celebrity 2:10 (1976) pp59-61.

M 3352 Steele, J. "Tommy, Lennon, Mao, And The Road To Revolution." Melody Maker 51 (August 28, 1976) pp24-25.
(Winning entry in "Student Rock Essay Contest.")

M 3353 Steiger, Brad. "The Beatles And The Voice From Beyond." Strange 1:3 (1971) pp50-53.

M 3354 Stein. "Fuck." Berkley Tribe 2:20 (May 29, 1970) p5.

M 3355 Stein, David Lewis. "Why The Beatles (Remember Them?) Have So Many Friends In Canada." MacLean's 77 (July 4, 1964) pp48-49. illus.

M 3356 Stein, H. "Oh, Grow Up." Esquire 95 (April 1981) pp16-18. illus.
(John Lennon.)

M 3357 Steinem, Gloria. "Those Were The Days." Beatlefan 2:4 (June 1980) pp20-23.
(Reprint of her "Cosmopolitan" article on Lennon.)

M 3358 Steve. "Ono John." Good Times 4:29 (October 1, 1971) p22.

M 3360 "Stigwood, Shaw Exit Nems Enterprises; Beatles Taking Expanded Mgt. Role." Variety 248 (November 8, 1967) p49+.

M 3361 "Stockholder-Fans Snag Beatles' Music Co. Sale." Variety 257 (February 4, 1970) p2.

M 3362 Stokes, Geoffrey. "Beatlemania: I Wanna Hold Your Wallet." The National Village Voice 21:20 (June 7, 1976) pp32-35. illus.

M 3363 Stokes, Geoffrey. "The Beatles; Some Years In The Life." Rolling Stone 333:334 (December 25, 1980) p107+. illus.
(Excerpt from his book.)

M 3364 "Stones' Man For Beatles." Melody Maker 44 (February 8, 1969) p1.

M 3365 "Stones Set Pear A-Rolling." Rolling Stone 35 (June 14, 1969) p6.

M 3366 Storb, L. "Beat: 'Penny Lane' - Modell Einer Analyse." Musik und Bildung 3 (April 1971) pp189-192. illus.

M 3367 "The Street Signs Go Up." Beatles Now 4 (Autumn 1982) p16. illus.
(Liverpool streets named for Beatles.)

M 3368 "Student Editors Vote Beatles Tops." Billboard 91 (May 5, 1979) p44.

M 3369 Suczek, Barbara. "Curious Case Of The 'Death' Of Paul McCartney." Urban Life & Culture 1:1 (April 1972) pp61-76.

M 3370 "Sue Harrison Again To Prove Plagiarism Had Been International." Variety 289 (November 9, 1977) p49+.
("My Sweet Lord" case.)

M 3371 "Sue Me, Sue You Blues: Harrison's Not 'So Fine'." Crawdaddy 60 (May 1976) p26. illus.

M 3372 Sugg, Alfred. "The Beatles And Film Art." Film Heritage 1:4 (Summer 1966) pp3-13.
("A Hard Day's Night" and "Help!")

M 3373 "Suit Says Paul Can't Write Songs With Linda Unless We Publish 'Em." Variety 263 (July 28, 1971) p36.

M 3374 "Surprise U.S. Hit For Paul." Melody Maker 40 (October 9, 1965) p1. illus.

M 3375 Sussman, Al. "Al Sussman Responds To Critics." Beatlefan 3:6 (October 1981) p24.
(Editorial reply.)

M 3376 Sussman, Al. "The Beatles' Touring Days." Beatlefan 2:5 (August 1980) pp1,4-6.
(The Beatles' August 18, 1965, Atlanta concert.)

M 3377 Sussman, Al. "Commentary: Mourning Becomes Celebration." Beatlefan 4:2 (February 1982) p13.
(One year after John Lennon's death.)

M 3378 Sussman, Al. "A Death In The Family." Beatlefan 3:1 (December 1980) pp12-13.
(John Lennon.)

M 3379 Sussman, Al. "A Decade Without The Beatles." Beatlefan 2:4 (June 1980) pp1,4-6.
(Solo careers.)

M 3380 Sussman, Al. "Fan Fest Update." Beatlefan 3:6 (October 1981) p16.
(New York Beatlefest, September 25-27, 1981.)

M 3381 Sussman, Al. "Further Reflections On Dec. 8, 1980." Beatlefan 3:2 (February 1981) p20.
(Death of John Lennon.)

M 3382 Sussman, Al. "Here, There And Everywhere." Beatlefan 3:3 (April 1981) pp4-6.
(Guide to Beatles-like albums by others.)

M 3383 Sussman, Al. "'Lennon'." Beatlefan 4:6 (October 1982) p24.
(On the off-Broadway play.)

M 3384 Sussman, Al. "Lennon Return Prompts Questions." Beatlefan 2:6 (October 1980) pp12-13.
(Lennon's reemergence in 1980.)

M 3385 Sussman, Al. "'Love Me Do'." Beatlefan 4:6 (October 1982) p5.
(A fan looks back twenty years.)

M 3386 Sussman, Al. "An Open Letter To Beatlefans." Beatlefan 2:1 (December 1979) p5,10.
(Urges Beatlefans to also accept new music.)

M 3387 Sussman, Al. "An Open Letter To Beatlefans II." Beatlefan 2:5 (August 1980) p11.
(On totals of Beatles' record sales.)

M 3388 Sussman, Al. "'Sgt. Pepper' - A Look Back." Beatlefan 4:4 (June 1982) p12.
(Album retrospective.)

M 3389 Sussman, Al. "Thingumybob." Beatlefan 3:6 (October 1981) p7,35.
(The future for three of the remaining Beatles.)

M 3390 Sussman, Al and William P. King. "Fan Fest Update." Beatlefan 3:3 (April 1981) pp12,14.
(New Jersey Beatlefest, Februry 1981.)

M 3391 Sussman, Gerald. "Fuck!" National Lampoon 1:91 (October 1977) pp57-59.

M 3392 Sutherland, S. "Beatles At The Hollywood Bowl; Beatles Live! At The Star Club In Hamburg, Germany; 1962." High Fidelity/Musical America 27 (August 1977) p111.

M 3393 Sutherland, S. "Lennon Death Spurs L.A. Handgun Move." Billboard 93 (February 28, 1981) p3+.

M 3394 Sutherland, S. "Ono LP Broadens Base; Apple Massive Promotion." Billboard 85 (February 17, 1973) p14.

M 3395 "Swede Teenagers Brush The Beatles." Variety 235 (August 5, 1964) p43+.

M 3396 "Swedish Narks Flack For Wings." Rolling Stone 117 (September 14, 1972) p12.

M 3397 Swenson, J. "Do You Want To Know A Secret?" Melody Maker 40 (September 1974) pp34-38. illus.

M 3398 Swenson, John. "Cry For A Shadow." Creem 12 (March 1981) p50.
(On "Double Fantasy" LP.)

M 3399 Swenson, John. "The Rock Heard 'Round The World." Rolling Stone 242 (June 30, 1977) p94+. illus.
("Beatles Tapes" and "Beatles Live" albums.)

M 3400 Swenton, Jennie. "Meeting The Beatles." Beatlefan 2:6 (October 1980) p27.
(A 1979 encounter with John Lennon in New York.)

M 3401 "Swinging With The Beatles." Melody Maker 39 (June 20, 1964) p9.

M 3402 Szwed, J.F. "The Joyful Noise." Jazz 6 (July 1967) p29. illus.

M 3403 Szwed, J.F. "On Tour With The Beatles." Jazz & Pop 7 (January 1968) pp14-15. illus.

M 3404 "Take A Good Look At These Album Covers." Melody Maker 53 (March 11, 1978) p31+.
(Rutles TV parody.)

M 3405 "Talent In Action." Billboard 84 (July 29, 1972) p14.

M 3406 "Talent In Action." Billboard 85 (June 23, 1973)
        p20.
        (Yoko Ono.)

M 3407 "Talent In Action." Billboard 86 (November 30,
        1974) p22.
        (George Harrison.)

M 3408 "Talent In Action." Billboard 88 (April 24,
        1976) p27.
        (Paul McCartney.)

M 3409 "Talking With Ringo Starr." Redbook 157
        (May 1981) p14+. illus.
        (Interview by L. F. Kaplan.)

M 3410 Tamarkin, Jeff. "Beatles, Beatles, Beatles."
        Goldmine 77 (October 1982) p5.
        (Recent Beatle news.)

M 3411 Tamarkin, Jeff. "Pete Best - A Beatle Talks."
        Goldmine 77 (October 1982) pp6-8.
        (Interview.)

M 3412 Tame, A. and P. Chippindale. "Wings Fly High."
        Melody Maker 47 (February 19, 1972)
        p18.

M 3413 Tayler, L. "The Beatles Are Dead? Long Live The
        Beatles!" Melody Maker 41 (November 26, 1966)
        p3. illus.

M 3414 Taylor, A.J.W. "Beatlemania - A Study Of
        Adolescent Enthusiasm."
        British Journal of Social and Clinical
        Psychology 5 (1966) pp81-88.

M 3415 Taylor, Derek. "Derek Taylor Makes A Radio
        Teleprinter Call From The QE2."
        The Beatles Book 72 (July 1969) pp9-14.
        (Lennon unable to sail to U.S.)

M 3416 Taylor, Derek. "Derek Taylor's Life With The
        Beatles." KRLA Beat (Los Angeles) (June 9,
        1965) pp2,6.

M 3417 Teen Life. New York: Publication House Inc.,
        1966.
        (Beatles cover portrait.)

M 3418 "Teens Are Listening To ...." Seventeen 23
        (November 1964) p80.
        ("Something New.")

M 3419 Teen Scoop. New York: Maco Publishing Co., 1967.
        (Beatles cover portrait.)

M 3420 Teen Screen. Hollywood, CA:
        Sunset Publications Inc., 1964.
        (Ringo Starr cover portrait.)

M 3421 Teen Screen - Have The Beatles Had It? Hardly,
        Luv!. Hollywood, CA:
        Teen Screen Publications, 1965.
        (Cover portrait.)

M 3422 Teen World - The Beatles - Our "Naughty" Nights.
        New York: Reese Publishing Co. Inc., 1965.
        (Cover portrait.)

M 3423 The Television Years. New York:
        Popular Library Publishers, 1973.
        (Cover portrait.)

M 3424 Telford, Ray. "Paul: With Half Of Wings In A
        Sling He's Still Flying." Rock (March 25,
        1974) pp13-14.

M 3425 Tepper, R. "Children's Records Are Rocking
        More, But The Beat Isn't Affecting Snow
        White." Billboard 85 (July 7, 1973)
        p39+.

M 3426 "Texas Radio Outlets Don't Accept Lennon's
        Apology As Sincere; Ban Still On." Variety
        244 (August 24, 1966) p51.

M 3427 "Thank You Beatles, Says Jerry Lee Lewis."
        The Beatles Book 11 (June 1964) p11.

M 3428 "Their First Major Booking." Mersey Beat
        (August 29, 1963) p9.
        (Photo from the Larry Parnes tour.)

M 3429 "Them." Cash Box 25 (February 22, 1964)
        p3. illus.

M 3430 Theroux, Paul. "Why We Loved The Beatles."
        Rolling Stone 415 (February 16, 1984) p21.
        (Cover portrait.)

M 3431 "They Are Loved." Billboard (October 23, 1982)
        p6.
        (On EMI re-release of "Love Me Do" in U.K.)

M 3432 "They Rose From The Cellar To Conquer The
        World." Globe 27:53 (December 30, 1980)

M 3433 "'They Won't Let Us Join The Golf Club' Says
        Ringo." The Beatles Book 41 (December 1966)
        pp8-10.

M 3434 "Thingumybob." Beatlefan
        (Regular feature, v3n1-   , 1980-   .)

M 3435 "$30 Million For Beatles Reunion Up In Air."
        Variety 282 (March 10, 1976) p61.

M 3436 "This Column Is For People Who Think They Know
        The Answers .... " Beatles Unlimited
        (Occasional feature, issues 5,7,23.)

M 3437 "This Is Not Here." Melody Maker 46 (October
        23, 1971) p9+.

M 3438 "This Month's Beatle Song." The Beatles Book
        (Lyrics; regular feature, issues 1-33,
        1963-1966.)

M 3439 Thomas, Cheryl. "Beatles Crossword Puzzle."
        Beatlefan 1:4 (June 1979) p7.

M 3440 Thomas, Michael. "George Harrison Tells It Like
        It Is." Holiday 43 (February 1968)
        pp111-112+. illus.
        (Interview.)

M 3441 Thompson, Thomas. "Hear That Big Sound." Life 58
        (May 21, 1965) pp90-94. illus.

M 3442 Thompson, Thomas. "The New Far-Out Beatles."
        Life 62 (June 16, 1967) pp100-102+. illus.

M 3443 "Those Were The Days." Beatlefan
        (Regular feature, v1n1-v3n5, 1978-1981.)

M 3444 "Threat Of Filmed 'Beatlemania' Too Much;
        Beatles Now Suing." Variety 296 (October 3,
        1979) p4+.

M 3445 "Three Beatles - Allen Klein Split; Yoko Ono A
        Spaniard In Works?" Variety 270 (April 4,
        1973) p111.

M 3446 "Three Beatles Wax Christmas Solo LPs."
        Variety 261 (November 18, 1970) p69.

M 3447 "Three Cos. Settle Beatles' Pub Suit." Variety
        299 (July 23, 1980) p128.

M 3448 "Three Ex-Beatles File Suit Vs. Klein, ABKCO."
        Billboard 85 (November 24, 1973) p45.

M 3449 "3 Guinness Honors For Paul McCartney."
        Variety 296 (September 26, 1979) p2.

M 3450 "Three New Beatles Albums By Christmas."
        Rolling Stone 71 (November 26, 1970)
        p6. illus.

M 3451 "Through Lennon's Eyes Darkly." Yipster Times 5:3
        (May 1977) p21.

M 3452 Tiegel, E. "Beatleantics Cause Headaches (In
        California)." Billboard 76 (August 29, 1964)
        p3+.

M 3453 Tiegel, E. "British Beatles Hottest Capitol
        Singles Ever" Billboard 76 (January 18, 1964)
        p1+.

M 3454 Tiegel, E. "Salute to Beatles Changes Knott's
        Berry Farm Image." Billboard 92 (February
        9, 1980) p3+.

M 3455 Tiegel, E. and M. Hennessey. "'Blue Power' Hits
        Discs; Apple Forbidden Fruit?" Billboard 80
        (November 16, 1968) p1+.
        ("Two Virgins" LP.)

M 3456 Tiger, Lionel. "Why, It Was Fun!"
        Rolling Stone 415 (February 16, 1984) pp28,93.
        (Cover portrait.)

M 3457 "Tony Barrow Leaves." Rolling Stone 22
        (November 23, 1968) p8.

M 3458 "The Tony Problem." The Beatles Book 74
        (September 1969) p31.
        (Three "Anthony"s work for Lennon.)

M 3459 "Tony Sheridan Remembers Hamburg." Beatlefan 1:3
        (April 1979) pp1,4,17.
        (Interview.)

M 3460 Toohey, J.V. "Beatle Lyrics Can Help
        Adolescents Identify And Understand Their
        Emotional Health Problems."
        Journal of Scholastic Health 40 (June 1970)
        pp295-296.

M 3461 "To Our Readers." Beatlefan 2:2 (February 1980)
        p5.
        (Editorial.)

M 3462 "To Our Readers." Beatlefan 1:6 (October 1979)

pp17-18.
(Editorial.)

M 3463 "To Our Readers." Beatlefan 2:1 (December 1979)
p25.
(Editorial.)

M 3464 "Top Name Shortage Closing Epstein's Pop
Concert Promotions In West End." Variety 235
(June 10, 1964) p58.

M 3465 "Toronto Peace Festival." Spokane National 4:12
(June 25, 1970) pSU7.
(John Lennon.)

M 3466 "Toronto Without Lennon." Melody Maker 45
(April 11, 1970) p2.

M 3467 "Tracking The Hits: Veronica Top 40."
Beatles Unlimited 5 (January 1976)
pp14-16.
(Beatles' singles charted by Dutch radio.)

M 3468 Traiman, S. "Reconstruct Old Beatles Tape;
Hamburg Songs Will Be Issued By Double H
Co." Billboard 88 (December 11, 1976) p8.
(The Star Club tapes.)

M 3469 Treen, Joe. "Justice For A Beatle: The Illegal
Plot To Prosecute And Oust John Lennon."
Rolling Stone 175 (December 5, 1974)
p9. illus.

M 3470 Treen, Joe. "Lennon Can Stay! Deportation Order
Overturned." Rolling Stone 199 (November 6,
1975) p10+.

M 3471 Treen, Joe. "Lennon Wins Right To Quiz Justice
Dept." Rolling Stone 180 (February 13, 1975)
p12. illus.
(Lennon's deportation fight.)

M 3472 Tremlett, George. "Three Screaming, Raving
Years With The Beatles." Music Echo
(October 30, 1965) p3.
(Chronology.)

M 3473 "Tributes To Brian Epstein." The Beatles Book 51
(October 1967) p12.
(Eulogies.)

M 3474 "Triumphant Return!" The Beatles Book 37
(August 1966) pp6-9.
(The Beatles in Germany, June 1966.)

M 3475 "Triumph Investment Trust Buys 70 Percent Of
Nemperor Holdings For $1,632,000." Variety
254 (March 5, 1969) p67.

M 3476 "Trivia Quiz Winners." Beatlefan 3:5 (August
1981) p24.
(Winners and answers to the quiz, v3n4.)

M 3477 "Trivia Quiz Winners & Answers." Beatlefan 4:6
(October 1982) p7.
(Questions in previous issue.)

M 3478 "Trivia Test Winners And Answers" Beatlefan 2:4
(June 1980) pp26-27.
(Answers to the quiz in v2n3.)

M 3479 "Trouble At The Troubadour – Lennon's Hard
Day's Night." Rolling Stone 159 (April 25,
1974) p13. illus.

M 3480 Truttschel, Mary Jo. "'82 Touring Guide."
Beatlefan 4:4 (June 1982) p7.
(Writing of "The Beatles England.")

M 3481 "Try-Out." The Beatles Book 41 (December 1966)
pp12-13.
(Paul McCartney plays the "tubon.")

M 3482 Tuffin, George and Gilbert Goosens. "An
Introduction To The John Lennon Fantasy
Story: Yellow Submarine Revisited."
Beatles Now 2 (Spring 1982) pp12-13.
(A fan's memories of the news of Lennon's
death.)

M 3483 Turner, Steve. "One Pair Of Eyes."
The Beatles Book 75 (October 1969)
pp10,13.
(Influence of The Beatles.)

M 3484 Turner, Steve. "A Play On The Life Of ...."
Rolling Stone 168 (August 29, 1974)
p26.
(Stage show "Beatlemania.")

M 3485 Tusher, W. "George Harrison On Beatles; Plays
Down Reunion Possibilities At Coast Party
Marking Warner Deal." Variety 285 (November

24, 1976) p113.

M 3486 "TV Special & Album: Beatles First Live Concert
In Two Years." Rolling Stone 26 (February
1, 1969) p12.

M 3487 "20th's 'War' Package Dishes Up All That & The
Beatles, Too." Variety 285 (December 1, 1976)
p61.
("All This And World War II" album.)

M 3488 "A Twist Of Fate That Cost His Life." The Star
7:53 (December 30, 1980) p10.
(John Lennon.)

M 3489 "2 Beatles Cop Novello Award For '64 Top Song."
Variety (July 14, 1965) p43.
("Can't Buy Me Love.")

M 3490 "2 Beatles' Copyright Suit Is 'Confusing'."
Billboard 83 (March 20, 1971) p49.

M 3491 "Two Beatles Earned $18 Million In Cleffer
Fees." Variety 269 (January 31, 1973)
p1+.
(John Lennon, Paul McCartney.)

M 3493 Tyler, T. "Beatles Confidential: Twelve Years
Later And You Still Don't Know." Creem 7
(April 1976) pp38-43. illus.
(Pre-1964 chronology.)

M 3494 Tyler, Tony and Roy Carr. "The Beatles."
New Musical Express (March 9, 1974)
pp30-31.
(Discography.)

M 3495 "UA, EMI To Handle Beatles' New LP; Clarify
Act's Status." Billboard 82 (April 25, 1970)
p3.

M 3496 "U.K. High Court OKs Polydor's Rights To Beatle
Talk Tapes." Variety 283 (August 4, 1976)
p43.
("The Beatle Tapes" album.)

M 3497 "U.K. Service Honors Lennon." Billboard 93
(April 11, 1981) p61.
(Angelican Cathedral, Liverpool.)

M 3498 "UK Teeners' $36 Beatle Vacation With Bop &
Board." Variety 233 (November 27, 1963)
p1+.

M 3499 "U.K. T.V. Bids for Beatle Song Co." Billboard
81 (April 12, 1969) p69.

M 3500 "Unbarbershopped Quartet." Time 83 (February
21, 1964) p46+. illus.

M 3501 Uncle Martin. "Dear Paul And Linda." Seed 7:2
(June 29, 1971) p18.

M 3502 "An Uneggspected Television Programme."
Beatles Unlimited 39 (1981) p19.
("Back To The Egg" publicity films.)

M 3503 Unger, C. "John Lennon's Killer: The Nowhere
Man." New York Magazine 14 (June 22, 1981)
pp30-32+. illus.

M 3504 "Unrecognised." The Beatles Book 74 (September
1969) p31.
(George Harrison.)

M 3505 "The Unreleased Albums Of John, Paul, George,
And Ringo." National Lampoon 1:91 (October
1977) pp69-72.

M 3506 "Unreleased Beatles B'cast Tapes To Be Aired On
U.S. Radio." Variety 306 (March 17, 1982)
p151.
("The Beatles at the Beeb.")

M 3507 "Up-To-Date List Of Area Secretaries."
The Beatles Book 54 (January 1968)
p14.
(Fan club secretaries.)

M 3508 "Up To Date List Of Fan Club Secretaries."
The Beatles Book 66 (January 1969)
p14.
(Address list.)

M 3509 "U.S.A. News From Our Correspondent."
Beatles Unlimited 7 (May 1976) pp16-17.
(Wings tour postponed.)

M 3510 "Use Beatles' Disk As Educational Tool In
Germany." Variety 255 (July 16, 1969)
p55.

M 3511 "US Immigration Now Major Barrier To Beatle
         Reunion." Variety 277 (December 25, 1974)
         p33.
M 3512 "U.S. Notes." The Beatles Book 39 (October 1966)
         p12.
         (August 1966 tour.)
M 3513 "U.S. Rocks & Reels From Beatles' Invasion."
         Billboard 76 (February 15, 1964) p1+. illus.
M 3514 "U.S. Teenagers Welcome The Beatles: Capitol
         Single A Smash, Rush LP." Cash Box 25
         (January 18, 1964) p8.
M 3515 "The Utrecht Beatles Convention."
         The Beatles Book 51 (July 1980) ppv-vi.
         (Dutch Beatle fan convention, April 12.)
M 3516 Vance, Joel. "Bangla Desh Love Feast."
         Stereo Review 28 (May 1972) pp66-67.
         (On the "Concert For Bangla Desh" LP.)
M 3517 Vance, Joel. "Ringo Smells The Roses."
         Stereo Review 47 (March 1982) p110. illus.
         (Album "Stop And Smell The Roses.")
M 3518 Vance, Joel. "Rundgren Faces The Beatles."
         Stereo Review 46:4 (April 1981) p86.
         (His LP Beatles Tribute, "Deface The
         Music.")
M 3519 Van De Bunt, Jan. "Israel Updated."
         Beatles Unlimited 20 (May 1978) p21.
         (Beatles events in Israel.)
M 3520 van der Ven, Guus. "The Beatles In Holland."
         Beatles Unlimited 3 (August 1975) pp18-23.
         (Events of June 1964.)
M 3521 Van Estrik, Rob and Henk Hager. "Dylan & The
         Beatles - I Wanna Hold Your Tambourine Man."
         Beatles Unlimited 19 (March 1978) pp12-17.
M 3522 Van Fulpen, Har. "Wings Hammersmith Odeon
         Concert." Beatles Unlimited 4 (November 1975)
         pp5-8.
         (September 18, 1975.)
M 3523 Van Haarlem, Rene. "The Beatles' Radio
         Activities." Beatles Unlimited 41 (1982) pp12-18.
         (Chronology, 1962-1965.)
M 3524 Van Haarlem, Rene. "Home Is Where The Heart Is
         ... " Beatles Unlimited 45 (1982) pp14-15.
         ("2nd Mersey Beatles Extravaganza,"
         Liverpool.)
M 3525 Vermeer, Evert. "And Here They Are, The
         Beatles." Beatles Unlimited 13 (May 1977)
         pp4-5.
         (On the "Hollywood Bowl" album.)
M 3526 Vermeer, Evert. "The Beatles Concert-ed
         Extras." Beatles Unlimited 32 (May 1980)
         pp7-10.
         (Supplements a book on concert dates and
         venues.)
M 3527 Vermeer, Evert. "The Beatles Concert-ed
         Extras." Beatles Unlimited 36 (June 1981)
         pp20-21.
         (Supplements a book on concert dates and
         venues.)
M 3528 Vermeer, Evert. "The Beatles Concert-ed
         Extras." Beatles Unlimited 38 (September
         1981) pp20-21.
         (Supplements a book on concert dates and
         venues.)
M 3529 Vermeer, Evert. "Beatles' Pilot Fish: Billy J.
         Kramer And The Dakotas." Beatles Unlimited 18
         (January 1978) pp4-7.
         (Career and discography.)
M 3530 Vermeer, Evert. "Beatles' Pilot Fish: Cilla
         Black." Beatles Unlimited 22 (September 1978)
         pp12-16.
         (Career and discography.)
M 3531 Vermeer, Evert. "Bert Kaempfert, 1923-1980."
         Beatles Unlimited 32 (May 1980) p14.
         (Obituary.)
M 3532 Vermeer, Evert. "BU's Fifth Anniversary
         Celebration: Still Crazy After All These
         Years." Beatles Unlimited 31 (March 1980)
         pp8-9.
         ("Beatles Unlimited," Dutch fanzine.)
M 3533 Vermeer, Evert. "EMI - You Know My Game, Look

Up The Number." Beatles Unlimited 23
         (November 1978) pp12-14.
         (Release of the boxed "Beatles Collection"
         of LPs.)
M 3534 Vermeer, Evert. "The 5th International Beatles
         Convention." Beatles Unlimited 25 (March
         1979) p16.
         (Holland.)
M 3535 Vermeer, Evert. "The 4 Gotten 4 Most."
         Beatles Unlimited 42 (1982) pp12-15.
         (On The Fourmost.)
M 3536 Vermeer, Evert. "John Lennon - A Portrait Of
         The Artist." Beatles Unlimited 34/35 (1981) pp4-9.
M 3537 Vermeer, Evert. "Maharishi: Who Ishi? Part
         One." Beatles Unlimited 29 (November 1979)
         pp12-15.
         (Maharishi Mahesh Yogi.)
M 3538 Vermeer, Evert. "Maharishi: Who Ishi? Part
         Two." Beatles Unlimited 30 (January 1980)
         pp4-11.
         (The Beatles in Rishikesh, India.)
M 3539 Vermeer, Evert. "McCartney: Make A Daft Noise
         For Christmas?" Beatles Unlimited 29
         (November 1979) pp5-6.
         (McCartney's single, "Wonderful Christmas
         Time.")
M 3540 Vermeer, Evert. "The Netherlands."
         Beatles Unlimited 34/35 (1981) pp41-44.
         (Dutch reaction to Lennon's death.)
M 3541 Vermeer, Evert. "Peter Sellers."
         Beatles Unlimited 33 (July 1980) p22.
         (Obituary.)
M 3542 Vermeer, Evert. "Second Liverpool Beatles
         Convention." Beatles Unlimited 22 (September
         1978) pp20-22.
         (July 15-16, 1978.)
M 3543 Vermeer, Evert. "Tracking The Hits: Billboard
         Hot 100." Beatles Unlimited 3 (August 1975)
         pp12-13+.
         ("Billboard" charting for Beatles' 1964
         singles.)
M 3544 Vermeer, Evert. "Tracking The Hits: Melody
         Maker." Beatles Unlimited 7 (May 1976)
         pp8-12+.
         (Beatles' singles charting.)
M 3545 Vermeer, Evert. "'We Love You - John And God'."
         Beatles Unlimited 11 (January 1977)
         pp11-14.
         (John Lennon's remarks on Jesus and
         Christianity.)
M 3546 Vermeer, Evert and Erik M. Bakker. "Richard Di
         Lello, Or: A House Hippie On Tour."
         Beatles Unlimited 9 (September 1976)
         pp16-17.
         (Interview.)
M 3547 Vermeer, Evert and Erik M. Bakker. "Trip."
         Beatles Unlimited 9 (September 1976)
         p4.
         (BU editors visit the U.S.)
M 3548 Vermeer, Evert and Frans Steensma. "Beatles'
         Pilot Fish: Peter And Gordon."
         Beatles Unlimited 14 (July 1977) pp12-14.
         (Peter Asher & Gordon Waller.)
M 3549 Vero, Diana. "Outspoken But Charming: A
         Personal Look At The Beatles."
         The Beatles Book 17 (December 1964)
         pp13-15.
         (Meeting The Beatles.)
M 3550 Verrill, A. "Lennon Top Draw At Garden, N.Y.,
         Benefit & News Media Helped Too." Variety
         268 (September 6, 1972) p2.
M 3551 Villone, Allison. "Meeting The Beatles."
         Beatlefan 4:1 (December 1981) pp23,26.
         (A July 30, 1980, encounter with the
         Lennons.)
M 3552 "Visiting George." The Beatles Book 42
         (January 1967) pp10-12.
M 3553 "Visiting Paul." The Beatles Book 43 (February
         1967) pp9-10.
M 3554 "Visiting Ringo." The Beatles Book 44

(March 1967) pp8-11.

M 3555 Vitale, Neal. "Paul McCartney & Wings: Keeping
       Us Guessing." Pop Top (July 1975) p1+.
           (Discography.)

M 3556 Voce, S. "Indian Old Rope Trick."
       Jazz Journal International 21 (October 1968)
       pp10-11.

M 3557 Voce, S. "More Mothers."
       Jazz Journal International 21 (November 1968)
       p12.

M 3558 Vogel, Amos. "I Made A Glass Hammer."
       Village Voice 16:25 (June 24, 1971)
       pp65,74.
           (Making of films "Apotheosis" and "Fly.")

M 3559 Vogel, Karsten. "Uden Forbehold."
       MM (Copenhagen, Denmark) (December 1980)
       p7. illus.

M 3560 Vollmer, Jurgen. "The Beatles In Hamburg:
       Jurgen Vollmer Remembers." Beatlefan 4:5
       (August 1982) pp4-7.

M 3561 Von Faber, Karin. "Paul McCartney: Acting His
       Age." Biography News 1 (June 1974)
       pp670-671. illus.

M 3562 Wain, John. "In The Echo Chamber."
       New Republic 153 (August 7, 1965) pp20-22.
           (John Lennon.)

M 3563 Walker, Jeff. "And All They Gotta Do Is Act
       Naturally." Crawdaddy (June 1978) p24+.
       illus.
           (Film "I Wanna Hold Your Hand.")

M 3564 Walker, Sandy. "Music? It's Just Part Of The
       Peace Campaign." Other Scenes 4:5 (May 1970)
       p16.
           (Interview with John Lennon and Yoko Ono.)

M 3565 Wallgren, Mark. "15 'New' Beatles Singles."
       Beatles Now 7 (July 1983) p16. illus.
           (Collectable Record Corp. singles.)

M 3566 Wallgren, Mark. "Not For Sale." Beatles Now 6
       (May 1983) p11. illus.
           ("Tug Of War" 12-inch promo single.)

M 3567 Wallgren, Mark. "Not For Sale." Beatles Now 7
       (July 1983) p5. illus.
           ("Beatles Movie Medley" 12-inch promo
       single.)

M 3568 Wallgren, Mark. "Not For Sale." Beatles Now 8
       (October 1983) pp9-10. illus.
           (Three 1982 Capitol promo flexi-discs.)

M 3569 "The Walrus Remembered." Beatlefan 3:1
       (December 1980) pp4-6,31.
           (A review of media tributes to John
       Lennon.)

M 3570 Walrustitty, Jethro Q. "An Uneggspected
       Television Programme." Beatles Unlimited 39
       (1981) p19.
           (McCartney's "Back To The Egg" video.)

M 3571 Walsh, A. "Are The Beatles Going Backwards?"
       Melody Maker 43 (November 9, 1968)
       p5. illus.

M 3572 Walsh, A. "Beatle Doubletalk." Melody Maker 41
       (July 9, 1966) p3.

M 3573 Walsh, A. "Cover The Beatles - It's Not So Easy
       Now!" Melody Maker 42 (June 17, 1967)
       p9. illus.

M 3574 Walsh, A. "The Danger Facing Pop."
       Melody Maker 42 (May 20, 1967) p3.
           (Lack of contact with fans.)

M 3575 Walsh, A. "Epstein: It's Impossible To Put My
       Feelings Into Words - Cilla." Melody Maker
       42 (September 9, 1967) p6. illus.

M 3576 Walsh, A. "The George Harrison Interview."
       Melody Maker (September 2, 1967) pp8-9.
       illus.
           (First part.)

M 3577 Walsh, A. "The George Harrison Interview."
       Melody Maker (September 9, 1967) pp12-13.
       illus.
           (Second part.)

M 3578 Walsh, A. "George - More To Life Than Being A
       Beatle." Melody Maker 41 (June 25, 1966)
       p3. illus.

M 3579 Walsh, A. "Lack Of Communication, Could That Be
       The Trouble?" Melody Maker 44 (June 14, 1969
       p7. illus.

M 3580 Walsh, R. "No Reply From The Club Where The
       Beat Boom And The Beatles All Began."
       Melody Maker 40 (August 7, 1965) p9.

M 3581 Walsh, A. "Revolution! That's What The Beatles
       Are Planning With This Apple." Melody Maker
       43 (June 1, 1968) p9.

M 3582 Walsh, A. "A Teenage Hampden Roar Proves
       They're Still The Guvnors!" Melody Maker 40
       (December 11, 1965) pp10-11. illus.

M 3583 Walsh, A. "They Love Em - Ja! Ja! Ja!"
       Melody Maker 41 (July 2, 1966) pp8-9. illus.

M 3584 Walsh, A. "We Have A Handful Of Songs And A
       Band Called The Beatles." Melody Maker 43
       (June 8, 1968) p5.

M 3585 Walsh, A. "Why Does Nobody Love The Beatles?"
       Melody Maker 43 (August 17, 1968) p14.

M 3586 Walsh, A. "Will The Real Richard Starkey Please
       Stand Up?" Melody Maker 43 (March 16, 1968)
       pp12-13. illus.
           (Interview.)

M 3587 "Walter Shenson: A Hard Day's Night."
       Beatlefan 3:4 (June 1981) pp8-10.
           (Interview.)

M 3588 "Wanna Quick Disc Hit? Cover A Tune Cleffed By
       Beatles' Lennon, McCartney." Variety
       (February 23, 1966) p1.

M 3589 "Wanted!" Beatlefan 2:2 (February 1980)
       pp1,4-5.
           (Paul McCartney arrested in Japan.)

M 3590 Wasserman, E. "Yoko Ono At Syracuse: 'This Is
       Not Here'." Artforum 10 (January 1972)
       pp69-73. illus.

M 3591 Watkins, Roger. "'Beatlemania' Bites Britain As
       Four From Liverpool Become A Show Biz
       Phenomenon; Press Clips Top Queen's."
       Variety 233 (January 8, 1964) p194.

M 3592 Watkins, Roger. "Beatlemania Revamps Britain
       Disk Biz By Booming Teen-Angled Indie
       Prods." Variety 241 (January 5, 1966)
       p206.

M 3593 Watkins, Roger. "1964: Year Of The Beatles."
       Variety 237 (January 6, 1965) p185+.

M 3594 Watkins, Roger. "Rocking Redcoats Are Coming;
       Beatles Lead Massive Drive." Variety 233
       (February 19, 1964) p1+.

M 3595 Watts, Michael. "Elton - Oh What A Night!"
       Melody Maker 49 (December 7, 1974)
       p54. illus.
           (John Lennon.)

M 3596 Watts, Michael. "George Harrison: Is There Life
       After Enlightenment?" Melody Maker 54
       (March 10, 1979) pp23-24.
           (Interview.)

M 3597 Watts, Michael. "Lady Of Pain." Melody Maker 48
       (January 27, 1973) pp28-29. illus.

M 3598 Watts, Michael. "Lennon." Melody Maker 46
       (October 2, 1971) pp24-25. illus.

M 3599 Watts, Michael. "Lennon's Next Album."
       Melody Maker 46 (July 31, 1971) p5. illus.

M 3600 Watts, Michael. "Lennon Speaks - But Only
       Just!" Melody Maker 52 (October 15, 1977)
       p1.

M 3601 Watts, Michael. "Lennon Visits Pepper."
       Melody Maker 49 (November 30, 1974)
       p18.

M 3602 Watts, Michael. "Lonely Hearts Club Band."
       Melody Maker 49 (August 24, 1974) p7. illus.

M 3603 Watts, Michael. "The New Harrison Album."
       Melody Maker 48 (June 9, 1973) p3. illus.
           ("Living In The Material World.")

M 3604 Watts, Michael. "Orton And The Beatles: Doomed
       Romance." Melody Maker 54 (November 10, 1979)
       p14.
           (Abandoned third film "Up Against It.")

M 3605 Watts, Michael. "Paul's Protest." Melody Maker
       47 (February 12, 1972) p19.
           ("Give Ireland Back To The Irish.")

M 3606 Watts, Michael. "Ringo." Melody Maker 46
(July 24, 1971) pp20-21+. illus.
(Part one.)

M 3607 Watts, Michael. "Ringo." Melody Maker 46
(July 31, 1971) p15+. illus.
(Part two.)

M 3608 Watts, Michael. "Ringo." Melody Maker 46
(August 7, 1971) p11+. illus.
(Part three.)

M 3609 Watts, Michael. "Ringo Gets It Off His Chest."
Circus 6:2 (November 1971) pp8-12. illus.

M 3610 Watts, Michael. "Rock Giants From A-Z: John
Lennon: Pain For Art's Sake." Melody Maker
49 (February 9, 1974) pp23-24. illus.

M 3611 Watts, Michael. "Rock Giants From A-Z: Paul
McCartney: Putting On The Style."
Melody Maker 49 (February 23, 1974)
pp27-28. illus.

M 3612 Watts, Michael. "Some Straight Talking By
Yoko." Melody Maker 48 (July 14, 1973)
p25.

M 3613 Watts, Michael. "Yellow Perils Of Paulie."
Melody Maker 55 (January 26, 1980)
pp8-9. illus.
(Paul McCartney.)

M 3614 Watts, Michael. "Yoko: The Lady's A Winner."
Melody Maker 48 (June 2, 1973) p33. illus.

M 3615 Watts, Michael. "Yoko - The Loneliness Of The
Naked Artist." Melody Maker 48 (January 6,
1973) p23. illus.

M 3616 Watts, Michael and L. Alterman. "Lennon Stays
In The Shadows." Melody Maker 48 (January
6, 1973) p21.

M 3617 Watts, Michael and V. Wickham. "American Music
Scene." Melody Maker 47 (November 25, 1972)
p6. illus.

M 3618 Weaver, N. "Popping Off." After Dark 10
(July 1968) p3,56. illus.

M 3619 Weber, D. " ... And Paul Is On The Road Again."
Newsweek 82 (October 29, 1973) p113.

M 3620 Webster, Alex. "John." Fusion 72 (March 1972)
pp32-34. illus.

M 3621 "'We Can't Please Everyone' Says Paul."
The Beatles Book 40 (November 1966)
p9.

M 3622 "Wedded Bliss: The Erotic Lithographs Of John
Lennon." Avant Garde 11 (March 1972)
pp18-23. illus.
(Lithograph used as cover photo.)

M 3623 "Weingarten Looks At The Bangla Desh Album."
Audio 56 (April 1972) pp66-67.

M 3624 Weinstein, Robert. "The Man Who Really
Discovered The Beatles."
Modern Hi Fi & Music (September 1975)
pp30-38.

M 3625 Welch, Chris. "All Paul." Melody Maker 48
(December 1, 1973) pp48-49+. illus.

M 3626 Welch, Chris. "And In The Evening She's The
Singer In The Band." Melody Maker 50
(September 27, 1975) pp8-9+.
(Interview with Linda McCartney.)

M 3627 Welch, Chris. "Born To Boogie - A Missed
Opportunity." Melody Maker 47 (December 16,
1972) p51.

M 3628 Welch, Chris. "Doomswatch." Melody Maker 45
(May 16, 1970) pp20-21.

M 3629 Welch, Chris. "Fly Away, Paul." Melody Maker 50
(September 20, 1975) pp8-9+. illus.

M 3630 Welch, Chris. "Goodbye To Yesterday."
Melody Maker 52 (November 19, 1977)
pp8-9. illus.
(Paul McCartney interview.)

M 3631 Welch, Chris. "Just An Ordinary Superstar."
Melody Maker 50 (October 4, 1975) p21+.
(Interview with Paul McCartney.)

M 3632 Welch, Chris. "McCartney: Pressure Cooking."
Melody Maker 51 (March 27, 1976) p13.
(Interview about possible Beatles reunion.)

M 3633 Welch, Chris. "Now Let Boring Controversy
Begin!" Melody Maker 42 (June 3, 1967)
p5. illus.
("Sgt. Pepper's Lonely Hearts Club Band.")

M 3634 Welch, Chris and R. Williams. "Powerhouse Of
Pop." Melody Maker 45 (August 8, 1970) p20.
(Ringo Starr and Paul McCartney.)

M 3635 "Welcome Back." The Beatles Book 54 (October
1980) pix.
(About seven "Welcome Back Beatles"
magazines.)

M 3636 Welding, Pete. "I'm Looking Through You."
Down Beat 35 (January 11, 1968) pp18-19.
(Reply to "The Beatles In Perspective" by
J. Gabree.)

M 3637 Wenner, Jann. "Beatles." Rolling Stone 24
(December 21, 1968) pp10-13. illus.

M 3638 Wenner, Jann. "John Lennon." Rolling Stone 74
(January 21, 1971) pp32-42. illus.
(Interview, part one.)

M 3639 Wenner, Jann. "John Lennon." Rolling Stone 75
(February 4, 1971) pp36-43. illus.
(Interview, part two.)

M 3640 Wenner, Jann. "John Lennon In 'How I Won The
War'." Rolling Stone 1 (November 9, 1967)
p16. illus.
(Cover portrait.

M 3641 Wenner, Jann. "Man Of The Year." Rolling Stone
51 (February 7, 1970) pp24-25. illus.
(John Lennon.)

M 3642 Wenner, Jann. "One Guy Standing There, Shouting
'I'm Leaving'." Rolling Stone 58 (May 14,
1970) p1+. illus.

M 3643 Wenner, Jann. "Paul McCartney." Rolling Stone
57 (April 30, 1970) pp28-31. illus.
(Interview.)

M 3644 Werbin. "Rock Reviews." Phoenix 3:1 (January
1971) p14.

M 3645 Werbin, S. "John & Jerry & David & John & Leni
& Yoko." Rolling Stone 102 (February 17, 1972)
p1+. illus.

M 3646 Werbin, S. "Lennons Discuss Deportation, Allen
Klein, Beatles' Reunion." Rolling Stone 134
(May 10, 1973) p10.

M 3647 Werbin, S. "'Trials Of Oz': An Open And Shut
Case." Rolling Stone 127 (February 1, 1973)
p6. illus.

M 3648 Werbin, S. "Yoko Reaches For That Pain."
Rolling Stone 129 (March 1, 1973) p16+.

M 3649 "We're Tops Again." Melody Maker 39 (December
5, 1964) p1.

M 3651 "We Said It - And They Did It!" Melody Maker 40
(June 19, 1965) p7. illus.
(Beatles honored.)

M 3652 West, Jessamyn. "Salvation: From Billy Sunday
To The Beatles." McCall's 103:7 (April 1976)
pp204-281.

M 3653 Westcott, J. "From A Boy's Point Of View."
Seventeen 25 (September 1966) p14. illus.

M 3654 "West Meets East - George Harrison Talks About
Indian Music." Performing Right 47
(April 1967) pp18-19. illus.

M 3655 "We Wanna Rip You Off." Melody Maker 53
(July 15, 1978) p13.
(Film "I Wanna Hold Your Hand.")

M 3656 "'We Were Giving It All Away'." Rolling Stone
53 (March 7, 1970) p8. illus.

M 3657 Weymouth, Lally. "A Question Of Style."
Rolling Stone 245 (August 11, 1977)
p38+.
(Photo of The Beatles from "Vogue.")

M 3658 "What Do They Do?" The Beatles Book 6
(January 1964) pp26-27.
(Before a performance.)

M 3659 "Whatever Happened To .... ?"
The Beatles Book 54 (October 1980)
pvi.
(Tony Bramwell, early Beatles' associate.)

M 3660 "What Happened In America." The Beatles Book 9

(April 1964) pp6-15.
(February 7-21, 1964.)

M 3661 "What Next In '66 For Beatles And Stones?"
Melody Maker 41 (January 8, 1966) pp8-9.
illus.

M 3662 "What's Beatle." Seventeen 23 (August 1964)
p100.

M 3663 "What's Next For The Fonz? A Guide To Survival
For Henry Winkler From Yesterday's Teen
Idols." TV Mirror (November 1976) p16+.
(Includes Beatles' advice on handling
success.)

M 3664 "What The Beatles Have Done To Hair: Teenaged
British Boys." Look 28 (December 29, 1964)
pp58-59. illus.

M 3665 "What The Bloody Hell Is It?" Rolling Stone 3
(December 14, 1967) p2. illus.
(Richard Lester.)

M 3666 "What The Critics Said." The Beatles Book 13
(August 1964) p15.
(On "A Hard Day's Night.")

M 3667 "What They Play - The Beatles." Melody Maker 39
(December 19, 1964) p21.

M 3668 "What They Think Of You." The Beatles Book 10
(May 1964) pp5-9.
(The Beatles on their fans.)

M 3669 "When Did You Switch On?" The Beatles Book 69
(April 1969) pp7-13.
(Why The Beatles remain popular.)

M 3670 "When Did You Switch On?" The Beatles Book 70
(May 1969) pp7-13.
(Brian Epstein discovers The Beatles.)

M 3671 "When We Stop Selling Records, We'll Probably
Pack It In." Melody Maker 39 (October 31,
1964) pp10-11.
(Paul McCartney.)

M 3672 "Where Are All The Beatle Fans." Rolling Stone
11 (May 11, 1968) p15.
(Poem.)

M 3673 Whitall, S. "It's The Quiet Ones You Have To
Watch." Creem 8 (February 1977) p18+. illus.
(George Harrison.)

M 3674 Whitall, S. "The Wives (And Ladies) That Late
They Loved." Creem 7 (April 1976) pp43-44+.
illus.

M 3675 White, A. "The Beatles Rise Again Thanks To
'Pepper' Film." Billboard 90 (August 26,
1978) p3+.
(Bee Gees' film.)

M 3676 White, A. "Polydor Beatles LP Win Release In
London Court." Billboard 88 (August 7, 1976)
p14+.
(The Star Club tapes.)

M 3677 White, A. and B. Mulligan. "A Dead Apple In
London; Label's Staff Gets Pared."
Billboard 87 (May 10, 1975) p4+.

M 3678 White, C. "The Beatles At Bowl? EMI Mulling
Release." Billboard 89 (February 26, 1977)
p4+.
(Hollywood Bowl album.)

M 3679 White, C. "Reissued Beatle Hits Dominate UK
Chart." Billboard 88 (April 14, 1976)
p69.

M 3680 White, C. "See Way Clear For 'New' Beatles
LPs." Billboard 88 (December 25, 1976)
p54.
(Star Club tapes.)

M 3681 White, T. "When Toussaint Goes Marching In;
Riding On The City Of New Orleans."
Crawdaddy 48 (March 1975) p47. illus.

M 3682 White, Timothy. "Clipping Paul McCartney's
Wings." Rolling Stone 298 (August 23, 1979)
p55.
(On "Back To The Egg.")

M 3683 Whitehorne, R. "Beatles, John Lennon And Youth
Rebel." Organizer 7 (January 1981)
p13.

M 3684 Whittingham, Charles A. "Dear LIFE Reader."
Life 7:2 (February 1984) p1.
("Life"'s publisher on the Beatles' first

U.S. visit.)

M 3685 "Whoop-Up For Wigs." Chemical Week (February
29, 1964) p51+. illus.

M 3686 "Why Yoko Will Never Forgive The Surviving
Beatles." Star 8:49 (December 8, 1981)
p24. illus.

M 3687 Wicker, R. "Wicker Basket." Gay 2:50 (May 10,
1971) p4.
(John Lennon.)

M 3688 Wickham, V. "George Hits At Capitol."
Melody Maker 46 (December 4, 1971)
p6. illus.

M 3689 Wickham, V. "Ono Band On Film." Melody Maker 45
(July 18, 1970) p6. illus.

M 3690 Wickham, V. "Playing For Paul." Melody Maker 46
(May 29, 1971) p8.

M 3691 Widener, Alice. "Lennon, Psychedelic Drugs And
Acid Rock." Human Events 41 (January 3, 1981)
p14.

M 3692 "Wie Eine Pop-Gruppe Arbeitet."
Junior Jungend Zeitschrift (Zurich) (April 197
pp1-7. illus.
(Paul McCartney and Wings.)

M 3693 Wiener, Jon. "John Lennon Versus The F.B.I."
New Republic (May 2, 1983) pp19-23.

M 3694 Wiener, T. "The Rise And Fall Of The Rock
Film." American Film 1:2 (November 1975)
pp25-29. illus.
("A Hard Day's Night" and "Help.")

M 3695 Wikler, Elinor. "Everybody Has A Beatle."
Reader's Digest 89 (October 1966) pp72-75.
illus.

M 3696 "Wildcat 'Beatles' Strike." Variety 234 (February
26, 1964) p65.

M 3697 "Wild Fans Of The Beatles A Shocker Even To
Long-Memory Sophisticates." Variety 236
(September 30, 1964) p2.

M 3698 Wilk, Max. "Log Of The Yellow Submarine."
McCall's 95 (August 1968) pp72-75. illus.

M 3699 Williams, B. "Ringo Cuts Country Album In
Nashville, Harrison Next." Billboard 82
(July 11, 1970) p3.

M 3700 Williams, Jean. "Artists Express Love, Respect,
Gratefulness For Ex-Beatle." Billboard 92
(December 20, 1980) p104.
(Eulogies by Frank Sinatra, John Belushi,
etc.)

M 3701 Williams, Jean. "Concert Upset Sees 'Beatles'
Draw Blasted." Billboard 90 (April 1, 1978)
p3+.

M 3702 Williams, Jean. "Halt Showings Of Beatles
Movie." Billboard 91 (June 16, 1979)
p9.

M 3703 Williams, M. "Wings: Taking Off At Last?"
Melody Maker 54 (June 16, 1979) pp20-21.
illus.
(Interview.)

M 3704 Williams, P. "'Sgt. Pepper' As Noise."
Crawdaddy 11 (September/October 1967) p14.

M 3705 Williams, P. "What Goes On?" Crawdaddy 8
(March 1967)

M 3706 Williams, P. "What Goes On?" Crawdaddy 10
(August 1967) pp31-32.

M 3707 Williams, R.H.L. "Background To The Beatles."
Atlantic Advocate 55 (April 1965) pp24-28.
illus.

M 3708 Williams, Richard. "All Our Yesterdays: The
Beatles 1962-70." Melody Maker 48 (April 28,
1973) p22. illus.

M 3709 Williams, Richard. "Beatles R.I.P.; In-Depth
Review Of Beatles New Album." Melody Maker
45 (May 9, 1970) p5.
("Beatles Again" album.)

M 3710 Williams, Richard. "The Beatles Wealth Is A
Myth." Melody Maker 44 (September 20, 1969)
p19. illus.

M 3711 Williams, Richard. "Caught In The Act."
Melody Maker 45 (May 23, 1970) p19. illus.

M 3712 Williams, Richard. "Forget The Beatles, Listen
To George." Melody Maker 45 (December 5,

1970) p8.
("All Things Must Pass" album.)

M 3713 Williams, Richard. "In The Studio With Lennon And Spector." Melody Maker 46 (November 6, 1971) pp26-27. illus.

M 3714 Williams, Richard. "John & Yoko." Melody Maker 44 (December 6, 1969) pp20-21. illus.

M 3715 Williams, Richard. "John And Yoko." Melody Maker 44 (December 13, 1969) p19. illus.

M 3716 Williams, Richard. "John And Yoko." Melody Maker 44 (December 20, 1969) p18. illus.

M 3717 Williams, Richard. "John And Yoko's Wedding Album Issued." Melody Maker 44 (November 15, 1969) p1. illus.

M 3718 Williams, Richard. "John Lennon - Genius Or Just A Bore?" Melody Maker 44 (September 20, 1969) p13. illus.

M 3719 Williams, Richard. "Listen, John, Why Don't We Do It In The Road?" Melody Maker 45 (January 24, 1970) p9. illus.
(Lennon lithographs.)

M 3720 Williams, Richard. "Paul McCartney; The Truth And That Album." Melody Maker 45 (April 18, 1970) p18.

M 3721 Williams, Richard. "Paul Perplex: A British Commentary." Jazz & Pop 9 (March 1970) pp14-18. illus.

M 3722 Williams, Richard. "Produced By George Martin." Melody Maker 46 (August 21, 1971) p18+. illus.

M 3723 Williams, Richard. "Produced By George Martin." Melody Maker 46 (August 28, 1971) p24+. illus.

M 3724 Williams, Richard. "Produced By George Martin." Melody Maker 46 (September 4, 1971) p25+. illus.

M 3726 Williams, Richard. "Ringo And The Nashville Cat." Melody Maker 45 (August 29, 1970) p8. illus.

M 3728 Willis, Ellen. "George And John." New Yorker 47 (February 27, 1971) pp95-97.

M 3729 Willis, Ellen. "Records: Rock, Etc. The Big Ones." New Yorker 44 (February 1, 1969) pp55-56+.

M 3730 Willis, Michael S. "Lo, The Beatles Descend From Sky For Apotheosis In Frisco." Variety 236 (August 26, 1964) p45.

M 3731 Wilmer, Valerie. "George Martin Talks About The Beatles." Hit Parader 27:51 (October 1968) pp38-39+.

M 3732 Winchester, J. "Revolution Is Not All Blood." Broadside & The Free Press 9:15 (September 9, 1970) p7.

M 3733 "Win Cynthia's Own Portrait Of John - Plus Rare Sets Of Beatles Albums." Star 8:49 (December 8, 1981) p26. illus.
(Ten question contest.)

M 3734 "Wings." Melody Maker 47 (February 19, 1972) p1. illus.

M 3735 "Wings: Music For Yesterday - Or Today?" Melody Maker 50 (September 27, 1975) p38.

M 3736 "Wings Over The World." Beatlefan 1:3 (April 1979) p14.
(TV special.)

M 3737 "Wings: Pop Star Of The Month." Song Hits Magazine 40:122 (April 1976) pp8-9.

M 3738 "Wings UK Tour 1975." Beatles Unlimited 4 (November 1975) pp3-4.
(Tour schedule.)

M 3739 Winn, James A. "The Beatles As Artists; A Meditation For December Ninth."

Michigan Quarterly Review 23:1 (Winter 1984) pp1-20.

M 3740 Winnick, Walter. "The Complete Beatles Bootleg Catalogue." Circus (June 17, 1976) pp42-44.

M 3741 Wise, Marsha. "The Beatles Statue Fund." Beatles Unlimited 30 (January 1980) p23.
(Fund appeal to erect Liverpool statue.)

M 3742 "Without The Beatles." Melody Maker 56 (January 10, 1981) p3.
(BBC-1 documentary.)

M 3743 Woffinden, Bob. "And This Is Me Doing My Businessman Bit Back In '75." New Musical Express (April 12, 1975) pp5-6.
(Ringo Starr.)

M 3744 Wohlfert-Wihlborg, L. "From The Sketch Pad Of John Lennon's First Wife, Cynthia, Come Poignant Memories." People 16 (September 21, 1981) pp90-91. illus.

M 3745 Wojcik, U. "A Spawning Run Of Ecological Ideas." Coevolution Quarterly 30 (Summer 1981) p24.

M 3746 Wolcott, J. "Beatle Burlesque: A Little Song, A Little Dance, A Little Seltzer Down Your Pants." Village Voice 23 (March 27, 1978) p1+.
(Rutles TV special.)

M 3747 Wolfe, Tom. "A Highbrow Under All That Hair?" Book Week (May 3, 1963) p4,10.
(Lennon's "In His Own Write.")

M 3748 "A Wonderful Christmastime For Wings Fans." Beatlefan 2:1 (December 1979) pp1,4,25.
(Tour of U.K. announced.)

M 3749 Wondratschek, Wolf. "Hello, Goodbye." Der Spiegel (December 1980) p166.

M 3750 Wood, Michael. "Etc; Four Beatles, Five Stones." Commonweal 89 (December 27, 1968) pp439-440.

M 3751 Wood, Michael. "John Lennon's Schooldays." New Society (June 27, 1968) pp948-949.

M 3752 Wooler, Bob. "Why Are The Beatles So Popular?" Beatlefan 1:2 (February 1979) p20.
(Reprinted from "Mersey Beat.")

M 3753 "Working Class Hero." Liberated Guardian 2:2 (May 20, 1971) p11.

M 3754 "Worm In The Apple." Newsweek 73 (May 12, 1969) p84+. illus.

M 3755 "Writing Beatles Cop Top Novellos; Other Awards." Variety (March 29, 1967) p68.

M 3756 "Writing Songs With A Little Help From His Friends, Ex-Beatle Gets Plagiarism Rap." Music Trades 129 (May 1981) p136.
(George Harrison and "My Sweet Lord.")

M 3757 "Writing With Paul." Songwriter 6 (January 1981) pp14-15+. illus.
(Excerpt from Lennon "Playboy" interview.)

M 3758 "WWII Brought To You By The Beatles." Phonograph Record Magazine (October 1976) pp25-26.

M 3759 "Y'all Come Hear Ringo." Time 96 (October 26, 1970) p86+. illus.
("Beaucoups of Blues" album.)

M 3760 "Yeah, Yeah, Yeah." Newsweek 63 (February 17, 1964) p88. illus.
(The Beatles in New York.)

M 3761 "Yeah! Yeah! Yeah! The History Of The Beatles." Bananas (Scholastic Mag.) 8 (1976) pp4-8.
(Reprinted in early 1981.)

M 3762 "'Yellow Submarine' Premiere." The Beatles Book 62 (September 1968) pp24-26.
(Film premiere, July 17, 1968.)

M 3763 "Yes, I'm Lonely ... " Beatlefan 3:1 (December 1980) pp7-8.
(Three fans react to Lennon's death.)

M 3764 "Yes, I Remember It Well." Rolling Stone 415 (February 16, 1984) pp22,27. illus.
(Celebrities recount their first Beatles

experience;cover portrait.)
M 3765 "Yesterday: A '60s Hit Is The World's Most
        Frequently Recorded Song." People 21:5
        (February 6, 1984) pp70-71. illus.
        (Seventy of over 1000 cover artists are
        pictured.)
M 3766 "Yoko." Rolling Stone 353 (October 1, 1981)
        pp13-18+. illus.
        (Interview.)
M 3767 "Yoko Ono Inks Worldwide Polydor Deal."
        Billboard (October 16, 1982) p3.
        (Long-term recording contract.)
M 3768 "Yoko Ono, Kunstler Parlay Rock & Law For
        Indian Benefit." Variety 273 (January 2,
        1974) p38.
M 3769 "Yoko Ono Releases Single." Rolling Stone 338
        (March 5, 1981) p47.
M 3770 "Yoko Ono's Endless Faces." Rolling Stone 16
        (August 24, 1968) p6.
M 3771 "Yoko Visits Elton's Garden." Rolling Stone 378
        (September 16, 1982) p37.
        (Yoko Ono on stage with Elton John.)
M 3772 Yorke, Ritchie. "The Beatles Again: The Saddest
        True Story." Jazz & Pop 9 (October 1970)
        pp37-38.
M 3773 Yorke, Ritchie. "Boosting Peace: John And Yoko
        In Canada." Rolling Stone 36 (June 28, 1969)
        p1+. illus.
M 3774 Yorke, Ritchie. "CHUM Unveils 15-Hour Beatles
        Documentary." Billboard 82 (December 5, 1970)
        p71.
M 3775 Yorke, Ritchie. "John's ... Lithographs."
        Rolling Stone 52 (February 21, 1970)
        pp6-7. illus.
M 3776 Yorke, Ritchie. "John, Yoko, & Year One."
        Rolling Stone 51 (February 7, 1970)
        pp18-21. illus.
M 3777 Yorke, Ritchie. "John, Yoko, Kyoko Get
        Trimmed." Rolling Stone 52 (February 21,
        1970) p7. illus.
M 3778 Yorke, Ritchie. "Lennon On Toronto: 'Bloody
        Marvelins'." Rolling Stone 44 (October 18,
        1969) p6. illus.
M 3779 Yorke, Ritchie. "A Private Talk With John."
        Rolling Stone 51 (February 7, 1970)
        pp22-23. illus.

M 3780 Yorke, Ritchie. "Ticket To Ride: The Beatles
        Are Through." Jazz & Pop 9 (July 1970)
        pp16-20. illus.
M 3781 Young, Bernice. "The Beatles In New York."
        The Beatles Book 28 (November 1965)
        pp13-14.
        (August 1965.)
M 3782 Young, Charles M. "George Harrison Cranks It Up
        To 33 And 1/3." Rolling Stone 229 (December
        30, 1976) p11+. illus.
        (Interview.)
M 3783 Young, Charles M. "Lennon Stops Levy In Second
        Round." Rolling Stone 241 (June 16, 1977)
        p14.
        (Roulette Records must pay for "Roots" LP.)
M 3784 "'Young George': The Second Article On The
        Beatles' Childhood Days." The Beatles Book 26
        (September 1965) pp11-13+.
M 3785 "'Young John': The First Of A New Series On The
        Beatles' Childhood Days." The Beatles Book 25
        (August 1965) pp11-13.
M 3786 "'Young Paul': The Third Article On The
        Beatles' Childhood Days." The Beatles Book 27
        (October 1965) pp6-9.
M 3787 "'Young Ringo': The Fourth And Last Article On
        The Beatles' Childhood Days."
        The Beatles Book 28 (November 1965)
        pp6-8.
M 3788 "Your Letters Answered." Record Collector
        (Regular feature, issues 1-6, 1979-1980.)
M 3789 Yurchenco, Henrietta. "Those Beatles Again."
        American Record Guide 34 (November 1967)
        p248. illus.
M 3790 Zehr, Martin. "Beatle Beginnings: The Polydor
        Recordings." Goldmine 70 (March 1982)
        pp12-14.
M 3791 Zeilig, Ken. "John And Yoko." The Beatles Book 18
        (October 1977) ppiii-iv.
        (A 1969 interview.)
M 3792 Ziebarth, D. "Whales Benefit Beached."
        Rolling Stone 265 (May 18, 1978) p30.
M 3793 Zimmerman, P.D. "Inside Beatles." Newsweek 72
        (September 30, 1968) p106+. illus.
M 3794 Zodiac. "Planet News" Ann Arbor Sun 2:7
        (April 5, 1974) p12.
        (John Lennon.)

N 0001 Acker, Steve. "John Ono Lennon: 1940-1980."
The Capitol Reporter (December 11, 1980)
(Eulogy.)

N 0002 "Action Dropped Against Beatles." The Times
(June 26, 1969) p3F.
(Clive Epstein drops writ action.)

N 0003 Adams, Val. "Caste Changes Or, The Sad Tale Of
Four Beatles Who Were Not What They
Supposed." New York Times (November 22, 1964)
p13:3.

N 0004 "Advertisement Calls For A Beatles' Concert."
The Times (September 21, 1976) p14C.
(Sid Bernstein appeal.)

N 0005 "Agent Asks 'Come Together'."
Christian Science Monitor 68 (September 24,
1976) p12.

N 0006 Aguilar, Art. "The Walrus Was John."
The East LA Tribune (December 17, 1980)
(Eulogy.)

N 0007 "Ahen - A Secret Weapon."
Christian Science Monitor 56 (February 21,
1964) p1.

N 0008 "Albums Showing A Beatle And Girl In Nude
Seized." New York Times (January 4, 1969)
p22:1.
("Two Virgins" album.)

N 0009 Alden, Robert. "Wild-Eyed Mobs Pursue Beatles."
New York Times (February 13, 1964) p26:1.
illus.

N 0010 "Allen Klein Loses Tax Appeal." New York Times
II (December 18, 1979) p9:3.
(Tax evasion on sale of Beatles records.)

N 0011 "All You Need Is Love."
Christian Science Monitor 60 (January 22,
1968) p13.

N 0012 "Americans Decide The Beatles Are Harmless;
Coast To Coast Audience On Television."
The Times (February 11, 1964) p8F.
(First U.S. visit.)

N 0013 Ames, Lynne. "'Music 152,' Yeah, Yeah, Yeah."
New York Times XXII (October 31, 1982)
p2:1. illus.
(Mercy College's Beatles course.)

N 0014 Antel, Jean. "Beatle On The Battlefront."
New York Times (January 15, 1967) p13:1.
illus.
(Lennon in film "How I Won The War.")

N 0015 "Anti-Beatle Brigade."
Christian Science Monitor 57 (July 28, 1965)
p5.

N 0016 "Apology After Taylor Party." The Times
(February 28, 1972) p4D.
(Ringo Starr attends Liz Taylor birthday
party.)

N 0017 "Apparel Maker Is Enjoined From Using Name
'Beetles'." New York Times (February 18,
1964) p17:1.

N 0018 "Apple And Peel." The Times (June 24, 1968)
p7D.
(David Peel and the "Apple Peel Players.")

N 0019 "Apple For The Beatles." The Times (November
27, 1967) p7A.
(Apple Boutique opening.)

N 0020 "Apple Peel Encore." The Times (September 16,
1968) p7D.
(David Peel and the "Apple Peel Players.")

N 0021 "Archbishop On Beatles' Search." The Times
(September 1, 1967) p3C.
(Canterbury prelate on Beatles' spiritual
search.)

N 0022 "Are They Talented." Christian Science Monitor
56 (August 26, 1964) p15.

N 0023 Armitage, Peter. "Blueprint For A Beatle:
Television Cartoons." Sunday Times Magazine
(March 6, 1966) p21. illus.

N 0024 Arnold, Martin. "4 Beatles And How They Grew;
Moneywise." New York Times (February 17,
1964) p1:4.

N 0025 Arnold, Roxane. "FBI Sought To Arrest Lennon;
Feared Singer Would Embarrass Nixon."

Los Angeles Times (March 22, 1983)
p1+.

N 0026 "Art Gallery Cleared In Lennon Case."
The Times (April 28, 1970) p3F.
(Obscenity charges dismissed.)

N 0027 "The Arts: From Boogie To Bogey." The Times
(December 15, 1972) p13B.
(Ringo Starr in "Born to Boogie" film.)

N 0028 Ashton, Bill. "Lennon On Record: Two Decades Of
Pop Genius." The Miami Herald (December 14,
1980)
(Eulogy.)

N 0029 "ATV Bid Is Extended." The Times (May 3, 1969)
p13A.
(Northern Songs.)

N 0030 "ATV Bids Again." The Times (October 11, 1969)
p14D.
(ATV bid for Northern Songs.)

N 0031 "ATV Meets On Northern Songs Bid." The Times
(May 16, 1969) p34F.

N 0032 "ATV Must Bid Again." The Times (September 22,
1969) p24E.
(Northern Songs.)

N 0033 "ATV Plea To Panel." The Times (September 24,
1969) p19H.
(Northern Songs.)

N 0034 "ATV Reject A Beatles Film." The Times
(March 8, 1968) p2H.
("Lady Madonna" film.)

N 0035 "ATV Sees 11pc Fall In Profits." The Times
(April 12, 1969) p13E.

N 0036 "ATV View On Northern Songs Profit." The Times
(May 13, 1969) p19E.

N 0037 "Audience In Paris Gives The Beatles An
Ovation." New York Times (January 18, 1964)
p14:1.
(Paris concert.)

N 0038 Austin, Anthony. "Soviet Newspapers Comment On
Lennon - Death Attributed To 'Pathological
Violence' In U.S. - Praise Is Lavished On
The Beatles." New York Times (December 14,
1980) p42:1.

N 0039 "The Authenticity And The Integrity Of John
Lennon's Protest." New York Times (December
23, 1980) p14:4.
(Letter.)

N 0040 "Author Returns His Military Medal." The Times
(June 22, 1965) p10G.
(M.B.E. awards returned in protest.)

N 0041 "Award In 'Surprising Country'."
Christian Science Monitor 57 (August 7, 1965)
p4.

N 0042 "'Back Where You Belong'." New York Times IV
(April 8, 1973) p6.
(John Lennon's deportation case.)

N 0043 "Bad Business." Daily News (Philadelphia)
(April 26, 1982) p26.
(McCartney wished reconcilation with
Lennon.)

N 0044 "Baldwin, Piano Maker, Plans To Enter Market
For Electric Guitars." Wall Street Journal
(June 14, 1965) p6:4.
(Cites Beatles popularity as impetus.)

N 0045 Baltake, Joe. "They're Bringing Back The
Night." Daily News (Philadelphia) (February
9, 1982) pp33,37.
("Hard Day's Night" 1981 film re-release.)

N 0046 "Banner Unfurled In House; Peace Demonstrator
Held." New York Times (October 7, 1969)
p10:1.
("Beatle Power" flag flies in U.S.
Congress.)

N 0047 Barnes, Clive. "Intellectual Lennon: Social
Revolutionary." The Chicago Sun-Times
(December 14, 1980)
(Eulogy.)

N 0048 Barnes, Clive. "New York Notebook." The Times
(March 7, 1981) p13D. illus.
(Lennon's reissued U.S. records.)

N 0049 Barnes, Clive. "Teen-Age Craze Inspires

Ballet." New York Times (December 19, 1963)
p41:1.
    (Ballet "Mods & Rockers.")

N 0050 Barnes, Clive. "Theater; Irreverence On London
Stage Work By John Lennon In 'Triple Bill'."
New York Times (July 9, 1968) p30:4.
    (Play "In His Own Write.")

N 0051 Bart, Peter. "Keeper Of The Beatles."
New York Times II (September 5, 1965)
p7:1.
    (Interview with Walter Shenson.)

N 0052 Basler, Barbara. "Court Gets Wrong Criminal
Record In Lennon Slaying." New York Times II
(December 10, 1980) p6:3.
    (Comment by prosecuting attorney.)

N 0053 Batz, Bob, Jr. "Lennon Death Puts Cloud Over
Youth." The Dayton Daily News (December 10,
1980)
    (Eulogy.)

N 0054 "BBC Cancel Film Of Beatles." The Times
(November 24, 1967) p2F.
    ("Sgt. Pepper" film clips.)

N 0055 "B.B.C. Radio Bans Song On Ulster By
McCartney." New York Times (February 11,
1972) p7:1.
    ("Give Ireland Back To The Irish.")

N 0056 "'Beatle' Admits Car Charge." The Times
(January 26, 1971) p2H.
    (George Harrison.)

N 0057 "Beatle Admits He Drove Carelessly." The Times
(September 30, 1969) p2H.
    (Paul McCartney.)

N 0058 "A Beatle And Wife Are Fined $1,200 In
Marijuana Case." New York Times (April 1,
1969) p55:3.
    (George Harrison.)

N 0059 "Beatle And Wife Fined £500." The Times
(April 1, 1969) p3D.
    (George Harrison.)

N 0060 "Beatle And Wife Fly To U.S." The Times
(March 18, 1969) p1H.
    (Paul McCartney.)

N 0061 "Beatle And Wife Questioned." The Times
(April 24, 1971) p4D.
    (The Lennons are detained in Majorca.)

N 0062 "Beatle And Wife Remanded." The Times
(March 19, 1969) p3D.
    (George Harrison's drug charge.)

N 0063 "A Beatle At The National Theatre." The Times
(January 19, 1968) p6E.
    (Stage play "In His Own Write.")

N 0064 "Beatle Back From Meditation." The Times
(March 2, 1968) p1D.
    (Ringo Starr returns from India.)

N 0065 "A Beatle Ballet." The Times (December 6, 1963)
p16G.
    ("Mods and Rockers.")

N 0066 "The Beatle Break." Sunday Times (November 13,
1966) p8.

N 0067 "Beatle Buys Convent." The Times (March 13,
1970) p2A.
    (George Harrison buys Friar Park.)

N 0068 "Beatle Criticized By Dr. Graham." The Times
(June 21, 1967) p2C.
    (Billy Graham on Paul McCartney.)

N 0069 "Beatle Cut." The Times (January 21, 1970)
p5C.
    (John Lennon has his hair cut off.)

N 0070 "Beatle Drops Northern Songs Link." The Times
(November 9, 1968) p11D.
    (George Harrison withdraws from Northern
Songs.)

N 0071 "Beatle Equity." The Times (February 8, 1965)
p14G.
    (Northern Songs.)

N 0072 "Beatlefest In Jersey." New York Times III
(October 29, 1982) p20:3.
    (10th official area Beatlefest.)

N 0073 "Beatle Garden Charge." The Times (September
2, 1970) p4F.

    (Man found on McCartney property.)

N 0074 "Beatle George Marries An Actress."
New York Times (January 22, 1966) p19:2.
illus.
    (George Harrison weds Pattie Boyd.)

N 0075 "Beatle Guitar Plea." The Times (October 12,
1972) p4H.
    (Paul McCartney appeals for stolen guitar.)

N 0076 "Beatle Is Fined $200." New York Times
(January 22, 1969) p52:2.
    (George Harrison assaults photographer.)

N 0077 "Beatle Manager Accused." The Times (April 7,
1977) p9B.
    (Allen Klein's income tax evasion charge.)

N 0078 "Beatlemania." New York Times VI (December 28,
1980) p19.
    (Publishing activity follows Lennon's
death.)

N 0079 "'Beatlemania' Brings Protest." The Times
(February 27, 1964) p7G.
    (Pan American protests London Airport
melee.)

N 0080 "Beatlemania In Texas."
Christian Science Monitor 56 (July 10, 1964)
p12.
    ("Beatlemania" stage play.)

N 0081 "Beatle Memorabilia Selling Big."
Christian Science Monitor 68 (July 8, 1976)
p2.

N 0082 "Beatle Paul To Marry." The Times (March 12,
1969) p3H.
    (Linda Eastman.)

N 0083 "Beatle Plague." Wall Street Journal (March 12,
1964) p1:5.
    (Many Liverpool youths quit jobs for rock
careers.)

N 0084 "The Beatles." Times Literary Supplement
(May 29, 1981) p605A.
    (Letter replies to recent book reviews.)

N 0085 "Beatles And Two M.P.'s Favor Legal Marijuana."
New York Times (July 25, 1967) p30:1.
    (London Times advertisement.)

N 0086 "The Beatles: An Inside Look At The Fab Four."
Florida Times-Union (Jacksonville) (May 21,
1983) ppD-1,D-4.

N 0087 "Beatles Apparently Win Battle Against
Take-Over." Wall Street Journal (May 19,
1969) p10:2.
    (ATV drops offer for Northern.)

N 0088 "Beatles Are Blamed By Agnew." The Times
(September 15, 1970) p1G.
    (Lyrics attacked by U.S. Vice President.)

N 0089 "Beatles Are Booed At Manila Airport."
New York Times (July 6, 1966) p39:4.
    (Beatles leave Philippines for India.)

N 0090 "'The Beatles Are Free Men'." New York Times II
(July 26, 1970) p16:5.
    (Reply to C. McGregor's June 14 piece.)

N 0091 "Beatles Are 'Helpful,' Prince Philip Thinks."
New York Times (February 26, 1964) p5:6.

N 0092 "Beatles Are 'Just Cuddlesome'." The Times
(May 28, 1964) p7C.
    (Psychological explanation of Beatlemania.)

N 0093 "Beatles 'Are Not Breaking Up'." The Times
(November 16, 1966) p21A.
    (Northern Songs meeting.)

N 0094 "The Beatles Are Planning Full-Scale U.S.
Campaign." New York Times (March 14, 1964)
p12:1.
    (Beatles plan second tour of U.S.)

N 0095 "Beatles Arrive In Tokyo." New York Times
(June 29, 1966) p39:2.

N 0096 "Beatles As Healers." The Times (September 2,
1967) p6H.
    (Medical uses of "Sgt. Pepper" album.)

N 0097 "Beatles' Assets 'Not Now In Jeopardy'."
The Times (February 25, 1971) p4E.
    (Law case to dissolve Beatles.)

N 0098 "Beatles Assigned Receiver: End To Partnership
Sought." Wall Street Journal (March 15, 1971)

p18:5.

N 0099 "Beatles Astonished By Queen's Awards; Other
Britons, Too." New York Times (June 13, 1965)
p1:3.
(Britons react to M.B.E. award.)

N 0100 "Beatles Battle Effort To Buy Firm."
Christian Science Monitor 61 (April 15, 1969)
p50.

N 0101 "The Beatles Beat A Retreat From Fans In
Cleveland." New York Times (August 16, 1966)
p35:2.
(Fans damage Cleveland Municipal Stadium.)

N 0102 "Beatles Beats." Wall Street Journal (February
10, 1966) p1:5.
(Beatles' success no threat to older music
stars.)

N 0103 "Beatles 'Believe In Rebirth'." The Times
(September 30, 1967) p7F.
(Harrison and Lennon on David Frost TV
show.)

N 0104 "Beatles' Bid For Firm Fails; Battle Results In
'Mexican Standoff'." Wall Street Journal
(May 20, 1969) p4:4.

N 0105 "Beatles Bourgeois?" Christian Science Monitor
60 (December 7, 1968) p23.

N 0106 "Beatles: Can Muhammad Ali Coax Back?"
Christian Science Monitor 69 (January 27,
1977) p13.

N 0107 "Beatles Case QC Speaks Of Rule Of Democracy."
The Times (March 3, 1971) p4C.
(Law case to dissolve Beatles.)

N 0108 "Beatles' Closing Concert On Coast Attracts
25,000." New York Times (August 31, 1966)
p38:3.
(Final concert in San Francisco.)

N 0109 "Beatles Convention In Boston Attracts Vendors
But Few Mourners." New York Times II
(December 15, 1980) p9:3.
(First Annual Boston Beatles Convention.)

N 0110 "Beatles 'Could Yet Work Things Out
Satisfactorily'." The Times (February 24,
1971) p3A.
(Law case to dissolve Beatles.)

N 0111 "Beatles Cut Short Meditation." The Times
(April 13, 1968) p4C.
(John Lennon and George Harrison leave
India.)

N 0112 "Beatles Decline." The Times (March 5, 1981)
p4F.
(Ex-Beatles won't attend Lennon memorial.)

N 0113 "Beatles Depart For Britain As 4,000 Admirers
Scream." New York Times (February 22, 1964)
p18:5.

N 0114 "Beatles' Driver Fined." The Times (August 23,
1966) p10F.
(Chauffeur fined.)

N 0115 "Beatles' Drummer To Miss Tour." The Times
(June 4, 1964) p8G.
(Ringo Starr ill.)

N 0116 "Beatles End Separation." New York Times
(November 26, 1966) p32:1.
(First recording in three months.)

N 0117 "Beatles Expected For Meditation." The Times
(January 11, 1968) p6C.
(Visit to India.)

N 0118 "Beatles Fan Mail For Col. Wagg." The Times
(July 16, 1965) p6F.
(Letters sent to colonel who returned
M.B.E.)

N 0119 "Beatles Fans Besiege The Palace." The Times
(October 27, 1965) p22. illus.
(M.B.E. investiture, Buckingham Palace.)

N 0120 "Beatles Fans Fight Police At New Zealand
Concert." New York Times (June 24, 1964)
p20:4.
(Wellington, New Zealand.)

N 0121 "Beatles' Fans Urge Wilson To Save Liverpool
Cavern." New York Times (March 6, 1966)
p22:2.
(5000 sign petition to Prime Minister.)

N 0122 "Beatles' Film And Music Company." The Times
(May 16, 1968) p7H.
(Apple Corps, Ltd. inaugurated.)

N 0123 "Beatles Film For Adults Only." The Times
(February 3, 1965) p13A.
("A Hard Day's Night.")

N 0124 "Beatles' First Shop Has Its Swan Song."
New York Times (July 31, 1968) p26:7.
(Apple Boutique closes.)

N 0125 "Beatles Forever."
Times Educational Supplement (May 22, 1981)
p12E.
(Swedish rock group visits schools.)

N 0126 "Beatles For India Next Month." The Times
(September 11, 1967) p2G.
(To visit India.)

N 0127 "Beatles Gambling Lives In Las Vegas."
New York Times (August 21, 1964) p15:2.
(Las Vegas.)

N 0128 "Beatles Gatecrashers Shown Out." The Times
(December 11, 1965) p12G.
(Hammersmith Show, London.)

N 0129 "Beatles Get A Thought Each." The Times
(August 28, 1967) p2D.
(McCartney's statement on drug use.)

N 0130 "Beatles Get Over $800,000 For Interest On
Royalties." New York Times (April 6, 1966)
p34:3.
(Song royalties for Lennon and McCartney.)

N 0131 "Beatles Get Top British Billing."
Christian Science Monitor 55 (December 30,
1963) p4.

N 0132 "Beatles Greeted By Riot At Paris Sports
Palace." New York Times (June 21, 1965)
p17:6.
(Melee follows concert.)

N 0133 "Beatles' Guru Said To Weigh Moving To U.S. For
Privacy." New York Times (February 25, 1968)
p58:3.

N 0134 "The Beatles Had £10,000 A Month, Council
Says." The Times (March 5, 1971) p2C.
(Law case to dissolve Beatles.)

N 0135 "Beatles Have A Hard Day Of Yoga." The Times
(February 19, 1968) p3F.
(George Harrison and John Lennon in India.)

N 0136 "Beatles In Tuxedos For 'Help'."
New York Times (July 30, 1965) p15:7.
("Help!" premiere.)

N 0137 "Beatles Invited To Venice." The Times
(August 10, 1967) p5E.
(Venice Contemporary Music Festival.)

N 0138 "Beatles' Lawyer Scores Manager; Says In
McCartney Hearing Klein 'Cannot Be
Trusted'." New York Times (February 20, 1971)
p14:2.
(Paul McCartney's lawyer denounces Allen
Klein.)

N 0139 "Beatles Leave Friendly India." New York Times
(July 8, 1966) p39:8.
(Enroute to England.)

N 0140 "Beatles' Legal Links Dissolved." The Times
(January 10, 1975) p4G.
(Partnership dissolved.)

N 0141 "Beatles Manager Here To Quell Storm Over
Remark On Jesus." New York Times (August 6,
1966) p13:5.
(Brian Epstein flies to New York.)

N 0142 "Beatles May Agree." The Times (February 26,
1974) p3A.
(On settling partnership dispute.)

N 0143 "Beatles May Play Together." The Times
(September 22, 1979) p1C.
(Rumored concert for boat people.)

N 0144 "Beatles May Play Together Again."
Los Angeles Times IV (May 15, 1973)
p11.
(Paul McCartney.)

N 0145 "Beatles' McCartney Planning To Marry."
New York Times (March 12, 1969) p40:2.

N 0146 "Beatles Men Go Own Way." The Times (October

NEWSPAPER ARTICLES

31, 1967) p24E.
    (NEMS directors to resign.)

N 0147 "Beatles 'Michelle' Gets Prize."
    New York Times (March 27, 1967) p39:1.
      (Ivor Novello award.)

N 0148 "Beatles' Millions." The Times (September 21,
    1967) p1A.
      (Earnings.)

N 0149 "Beatles Miss Aeschylus." The Times (July 24,
    1967) p1D.
      (Blocked by crowds at Delphi, Greece.)

N 0150 "Beatles Mobbed In London." New York Times
    (July 5, 1965) p2:6.
      (Beatles return from Spain.)

N 0151 "Beatles: Multimedia 'Away With Words'."
    Christian Science Monitor 63 (December 4,
    1971) p18.

N 0152 "Beatles Near Stalemate." The Times (May 2,
    1969) p28D.
      (Northern Songs.)

N 0153 "Beatles Not To Teach." The Times (April 16,
    1968) p8E.
      (John Lennon on meditation course.)

N 0154 "Beatles Offered $1 M For A Day." The Times
    (October 4, 1967) p1H.

N 0155 "Beatles On Coast For Tour Of U.S.; 9,000 At
    Airport." New York Times (August 19, 1964)
    p28:3.
      (San Francisco.)

N 0156 "The Beatles On 'Revolution'."
    New York Times Magazine (October 27, 1968)
    p97. illus.
      ("Revolution" single.)

N 0157 "Beatles On The Beat." The Times (November 11,
    1963) p6G.
      (Arrive at Birmingham concerts in police
      van.)

N 0158 "Beatles On World TV." The Times (May 19, 1967)
    p4F.

N 0159 "Beatles' Partnership Is Dissolved By Judge."
    New York Times (January 10, 1975) p23:3.

N 0160 "Beatles Perform In Atlanta." New York Times
    (August 19, 1965) p36:2.
      (Concert in Atlanta, Georgia.)

N 0161 "Beatles Plan Sweeter Tune To Aid In Take-Over
    Battle." Wall Street Journal (April 11, 1969)
    p17:3.
      (Northern stockholders fight ATV bid.)

N 0162 "Beatles' Plea Delay." The Times (June 11, 1969)
    p26E.
      (Royalties claim.)

N 0163 "Beatle Spokesman Calls Rumor Of McCartney's
    Death 'Rubbish'." New York Times (October
    22, 1969) p8:1.

N 0164 "Beatles Preferred By Lady Gaitskell."
    The Times (May 15, 1964) p8E.

N 0165 "Beatles' Record Label Aims At The Campuses."
    New York Times (December 4, 1968) p56:1.
      (Low cost records for college-age buyers.)

N 0166 "Beatles Relics At Rock Auction." The Times
    (October 14, 1970) p1A.
      (Memorabilia.)

N 0167 "Beatles Reply To TV Film Critics; Viewers'
    Debate." The Times (December 28, 1967)
    p2C.
      (On the "Magical Mystery Tour" film.)

N 0168 "Beatles Return." The Times (July 9, 1966)
    p8G.
      (Return to London.)

N 0169 "Beatles' Ringo Wed Quietly In London."
    New York Times (February 12, 1965) p19:1.
      (Ringo Starr weds Maureen Cox.)

N 0170 "Beatles: Ruling Tomorrow." The Times
    (March 11, 1971) p3C.
      (Law case to dissolve Beatles.)

N 0171 "'Beatles Saved From Bankruptcy'." The Times
    (February 23, 1971) p3G.
      (Law case to dissolve Beatles.)

N 0172 "The Beatle's Scrapbook."
    Sunday Times Magazine (September 1, 1968)

pp18-23. illus.

N 0173 "Beatles Seeking A Song Company; $5.1 Million
    Counter Offer Made To Take-Over Bid."
    New York Times (April 26, 1969) p48:5.
      (Bid Against ATV takeover of Northern
      Songs.)

N 0174 "Beatles Seek Injunction." The Times (April 5,
    1977) p4F.
      (To prevent release of old recordings.)

N 0175 "Beatles Sharing In British Lion." The Times
    (March 19, 1964) p5B.
      (Investment in Balcon group.)

N 0176 "Beatles Signed For Film." New York Times
    (February 18, 1964) p28:6.
      (Signed by United Artists.)

N 0177 "Beatles Solvent, Mr. Klein Says." The Times
    (January 21, 1971) p2C.

N 0178 "Beatles' Song Firm Rallies After Fall."
    The Times (August 30, 1967) p15G.
      (NEMS Enterprises and Northern Songs.)

N 0179 "Beatles' Songs Beat Profit Forecast."
    The Times (August 25, 1965) p11E.
      (Northern Songs.)

N 0180 "Beatles' Songs Issue." The Times (February 13,
    1965) p12B.
      (Northern Songs.)

N 0181 "Beatles' Songs Played In Memory Of Lennon."
    New York Times II (December 10, 1980)
    p2:1.

N 0182 "Beatles' Starr Drops From The Guru's Orbit."
    New York Times (March 2, 1968) p11:4.
      (Ringo and Maureen Starr return to
      London.)

N 0183 "Beatles Sue Over Photographs." The Times
    (December 14, 1963) p5E.
      (Libel action.)

N 0184 "Beatles Sue Promoters Of 'Beatlemania'."
    The Times (September 28, 1979) p6G.
      ("Beatlemania" stage show.)

N 0185 "Beatles Suing For Slander And Libel."
    The Times (January 20, 1967) p9A.

N 0186 "Beatles Take EMI Up The Charts." The Times
    (October 18, 1968) p28E.
      (The "White Album.")

N 0187 "Beatles Take To Their Heels."
    Christian Science Monitor 57 (August 2, 1965)
    p4.

N 0188 "Beatles To Appear In Japan." The Times
    (May 5, 1966) p7F.

N 0189 "Beatles To Battle Firm For Northern Songs
    Ltd." Wall Street Journal (April 21, 1969)
    p14:3.

N 0190 "Beatles To Confer On Bid Rebuff." The Times
    (May 21, 1969) p19G.
      (Northern Songs.)

N 0191 "Beatles To Get $150,000 For Kansas City
    Program." New York Times (August 24, 1964)
    p22:1.
      (Kansas City Stadium Sept. 17.)

N 0192 "Beatles To Issue Batch Of Records; They Are
    Chiefly Producers, Singing Only A Single."
    New York Times (August 7, 1968) p37:1.

N 0193 "Beatles To Shun U.S. Because Of Tax Rift."
    New York Times (January 5, 1965) p24:2.

N 0194 "The Beatles To Sue Clothing Firm." The Times
    (January 2, 1964) p5F.

N 0195 "Beatles' Tour Ends In Relative Peace."
    New York Times (September 22, 1964) p44:5.

N 0196 "Beatles' Trip Put On TV." New York Times
    (December 27, 1967) p74:8.
      ("Magical Mystery Tour" film.)

N 0197 "Beatles' TV Film Mystifies British; Movie
    McCartney Directed Brings Protests To
    B.B.C." New York Times (December 28, 1967)
    p63:4.

N 0198 "A Beatle Sues Record Companies."
    New York Times (February 17, 1973) p39:1.
      (Harrison asks $15 million for private
      disc sales.)

N 0199 "Beatles Urge Complete Acceptance." The Times

(April 26, 1969) p14E.
   (Offer for Northern Songs.)
N 0200 "The Beatles Welcome Army Petition." The Times
   (January 25, 1964) p7A.
       (British garrison's invitation to Berlin.)
N 0201 "'Beatles Were Not Manhandled'." The Times
   (February 22, 1964) p8D.
       (U.K. Embassy party in Washington.)
N 0202 "Beatles Will Escape Federal Income Tax On
   Their Earnings In U.S." Wall Street Journal
   (February 19, 1964) p1:5.
N 0203 "The Beatles Will Manage Themselves."
   The Times (August 31, 1967) p1D.
N 0204 "Beatles Will Sell Interest In A Publishing
   Company." New York Times (October 16, 1969)
   p52:2.
       (Sale of Northern Songs to ATV.)
N 0205 "Beatles Woo Shareholders." The Times
   (April 30, 1969) p21D.
       (Northern Songs.)
N 0206 "Beatle Tells Preference For Religions Of
   India." New York Times (December 12, 1966)
   p57:6.
       (BBC interviews George Harrison in Bombay.)
N 0207 "Beatle Thinks Group Will Regain Harmony."
   New York Times (April 29, 1970) p50:1.
       (George Harrison interview.)
N 0208 "Beatle Wife Misses The Train." The Times
   (August 26, 1967) p2C. illus.
       (Cynthia Lennon.)
N 0209 "Beattle (Sic) Concert Sold Out."
   New York Times (May 5, 1964) p46:1.
       (12,000 tickets for Philadelphia concert.)
N 0210 "Before A Mind Collapses." New York Times
   (December 19, 1980) p34:4.
       (Lennon's death and public instruction.)
N 0211 Benjamin, Philip. "Official Says Soviet Is
   Ready To Discuss Visit By The Beatles."
   New York Times (July 18, 1965) p68:1.
       (Minister Furtseva invites visit
       discussion.)
N 0212 Berger, Joseph. "Fans Grieve For Lennon At
   Vigil." Newsday (December 15, 1980)
       (Eulogy.)
N 0213 Bernard, Jami. "Hundreds Ignore Cold To Keep
   Vigil For John." Post (New York) (December
   10, 1980) p5.
N 0214 Bernstein, Sid. "An Appeal To John, Paul,
   George And Ringo." New York Times III
   (September 9, 1979) p8.
       (Urges benefit concert for Viet boat
       people.)
N 0215 "Bid Briefs; Associated Television." The Times
   (December 2, 1969) p25D.
       (ATV pursues remaining Northern shares.)
N 0216 "Bids And Deals; Hemdale And Triumph In £2.3m
   Package." The Times (August 22, 1972)
   p18A.
       (NEMS Enterprises sold.)
N 0217 "Bids And Deals; Northern Songs Buys Lenmac."
   The Times (April 5, 1966) p17C.
N 0218 "Bids, Deals & Mergers; Associates Deals."
   The Times (October 16, 1969) p26H.
       (The Beatles sell Northern to ATV.)
N 0219 "Bids, Deals & Mergers; Associates Deals."
   The Times (December 2, 1969) p25E.
       (S. G. Warburg deals in Northern shares.)
N 0220 "Bids, Deals And Mergers; Nems Goes Into Music
   Publishing." The Times (April 26, 1968)
   p32E.
       (NEMS Publishing formed.)
N 0221 Bird, David. "Lindsay Deplores Action To Deport
   Lennons As A 'Grave Injustice'."
   New York Times (April 29, 1972) p33:4.
   illus.
N 0222 Bird, David and Albin Krebs. "Help, As
   Interpreted By John Lennon And Yoko Ono."
   New York Times III (November 27, 1980)
   p20:1.
       (The Lennons' views on charity.)

N 0223 Bird, Maryann. "Lennon's Memory Is Not For
   Sale, His U.S. Fans Say." New York Times IV
   (January 12, 1981) p9:3. illus.
       (Fans prefer donations to memorabilia.)
N 0224 Bittan, Dave. "Radio Fans Mourn John."
   News (Philadelphia) (December 9, 1980)
   p20.
N 0225 Blackburn, Robin and Tariq Ali. "The Acid Dream
   Is Over." Observer (March 7, 1971)
   p9.
       (Extracts Lennons' interview in paper "Red
       Mole.")
N 0226 "Bomb Fear Over Ex-Beatle Gift." The Times
   (June 11, 1971) p4A.
       (BBC "bomb" really McCartney birthday
       gift.)
N 0227 "Bootleg Recording Subject Of Hearing."
   New York Times (December 14, 1965) p55:4.
       (Includes counterfeiting of Beatles'
       records.)
N 0228 "Boundaries Of Grief." New York Times IV
   (December 21, 1980) p16:4.
       (Lennon's death vs. El Salvador nuns.)
N 0229 Boyd, Cynthia. "Beatlemaniacs: Collectors Still
   Treasure 'Fab Four' Memorabilia."
   St. Paul Dispatch (November 12, 1982)
   pp9A-10A.
N 0230 Boyd, Denny. "This Is All About The John Lennon
   I Lost." The Vancouver Sun (December 11,
   1980)
       (Eulogy.)
N 0231 Brennan, Brian. "A Bookshelf Of Beatles Books."
   The Calgary Herald (January 31, 1981)
   pH19.
N 0232 Brennon, Phil. "John Lennon's Homosexual
   Secret." National Examiner 19:39 (September
   28, 1982) p5.
       (Rumored affair with Brian Epstein.)
N 0233 Brett, Guy. "Letter To John Lennon." The Times
   (July 22, 1968) p5D.
       (John Lennon's exhibit.)
N 0234 "Brian And The Beatles: Murder Plot Is
   Fantasy." Sunday Times (April 19, 1981)
   p19C.
       (Letter from Tony Barrow on "Shout!")
N 0235 "Brian Epstein Death Is Ruled Accidental."
   New York Times (September 9, 1967) p48:7.
N 0236 "Brian Epstein In Merger." The Times (January
   27, 1966) p6G.
       (NEMS merges with Vic Lewis Organ., Ltd.)
N 0237 "Brian Epstein Is Found Dead; News Brings The
   Beatles Back To London." The Times
   (August 28, 1967) p1G. illus.
N 0238 "Brian Epstein, 32, Beatles' Manager; Singing
   Group's Discoverer And Mentor Is Dead."
   New York Times (August 28, 1967) p31:4.
N 0239 "Briefly From The Boardroom; ATV-Northern
   Songs." The Times (December 11, 1969)
   p25H.
N 0240 "Briefly From The Boardroom; Northern Songs."
   The Times (November 1, 1967) p21D.
       (Chairman's statement.)
N 0241 "Briefly From The Boardroom; Northern Songs."
   The Times (November 9, 1968) p12C.
N 0242 "Briefly From The Boardroom; Northern Songs."
   The Times (November 24, 1967) p23E.
       (Chairman's statement.)
N 0243 "Briefs." Wall Street Journal (February 6, 1964)
   p1:5.
       ("Stamp Out Beatles" movement begins in
       Detroit.)
N 0244 "Briefs." Wall Street Journal (February 20,
   1964) p1:5.
       (Beatles wallpaper available in London.)
N 0245 Brigstocke, Hilary. "Lennons In 'Beautiful'
   Talk With Trudeau." The Times (December 24,
   1969) p4B.
       (Canadian Prime Minister.)
N 0246 "British Broadcaster Bids For The Rights To
   Tunes Of Beatles." Wall Street Journal

(March 31, 1969) p9:4.

N 0247 "Britons Given Chance To Buy Beatle Stocks."
New York Times (February 13, 1965) p9:1.
(Northern Songs' public stock offering.)

N 0248 "Britons Resist Closing Of Club."
New York Times (March 1, 1966) p10:6.
(100 fans barricade Cavern Club entrance.)

N 0249 "Broadcast Ban On Beatles Record." The Times
(May 31, 1969) p4D.
(In Australia.)

N 0250 Brophy, Warwick. "ATV Defeat In Bid For
Northern Songs." The Times (May 17, 1969)
p11D.

N 0251 Brophy, Warwick. "Beatles Decide On Terms Of
Northern Songs Counterbid." The Times
(April 19, 1961) p13F.

N 0252 Brophy, Warwick. "Beatles Offer Board Post To
Howard & Windham." The Times (May 15, 1969)
p24C.

N 0253 Buckley, Thomas. "Beatles Prepare For Their
Debut; Police Patrol Their Hotel And Guard
Theater." New York Times (February 9, 1964)
p70:3.
(Beatle rehearsal.)

N 0254 Buckley, Thomas. "'Ringo' TV Special Has 2
Starrs." New York Times III (April 26, 1978)
p23:1.

N 0255 "Bug Japanese." Christian Science Monitor 58
(July 23, 1966) p5.

N 0256 "Business Appointments." The Times (June 6,
1969) p31G.
(Clive Epstein resigns NEMS directorship.)

N 0257 "Business Appointments." The Times (December
5, 1969) p25C.
(NEMS Enterprises.)

N 0258 "Business Appointments." The Times (October 20,
1970) p26G.
(NEMS Enterprises.)

N 0259 "Business Diary; A Beatle In The City."
The Times (July 3, 1968) p27A. illus.
(Paul McCartney lunches at Lazards.)

N 0260 "Business Diary; BPC's Flourishing Beatle
Book." The Times (April 20, 1972) p25A.
(Beat Publication's official Beatles
magazine.)

N 0261 "Business Diary; Nemperor Vic." The Times
(January 25, 1968) p21A.
(NEMS Enterprises.)

N 0262 "Business Diary; Pop Go The Rumours."
The Times (May 7, 1969) p27A.
(Northern Songs.)

N 0263 "Business Expert To Aid Beatles." The Times
(February 4, 1969) p2C.
(Apple Corps.)

N 0264 "Business Link For Pop Groups?" The Times
(October 16, 1967) p19C.
(Possible business projects with Rolling
Stones.)

N 0265 "The Business World; Pop Group Pays More."
The Times (October 12, 1966) p17B.
(Report on Northern Songs.)

N 0266 "By The Financial Editor; Northern Songs
Disappoint." The Times (October 26, 1967)
p24G.
(Company accounts.)

N 0267 "California Teenagers Squeal."
Christian Science Monitor 56 (August 20,
1964) p4.
("Beatlemania" stage play.)

N 0268 Campbell, Mary. "The Songs Of Lennon-McCartney
Kept Beatles Atop Music World."
Inquirer (Philadlephia) (December 9, 1980)
p7A.

N 0269 "Canadian Delay For Lennon." The Times
(May 27, 1969) p4B.
(Detained by Canadian immigration.)

N 0270 "Captain Returning O.B.E. In Protest."
The Times (June 16, 1965) p12C.
(M.B.E. awards returned in protest.)

N 0271 Carlson, Walter. "Advertising: Beatles To Sing
Tunes For Toys." New York Times (June 1,
1965) p58:3. illus.
(A. C. Gilbert & Co. sponsor cartoon show.)

N 0272 Carlton, Bill. "Yet More Beatles."
Inquirer (Philadelphia) (April 11, 1982)
p10L.
("Reel Music" LP and 88 "forgotten" BBC
songs.)

N 0273 Carmody, Deirdre. "Notes On People."
New York Times (July 18, 1975) p18:2.
(Ringo Starr is divorced from wife
Maureen.)

N 0274 Carpenter, J. "Toronto Finale."
Los Angeles Free Press 7:18 (May 1, 1970)
p41.
(John Lennon.)

N 0275 Carpenter, J. "Toronto Peace Festival."
Los Angeles Free Press 7:15 (April 10, 1970)
p4.

N 0276 Carpenter, J. "Yoko-John Shave Heads For
Peace." Los Angeles Free Press 7:4
(January 23, 1970)

N 0277 Carrighan, Sally. "Who's 'Used'?"
New York Times VI (April 19, 1964)
p46.
(Letter/reply to previous letters.)

N 0278 Carroll, Maurice. "Reagan, Visiting New York,
Talks With The Cardinal And Top Blacks."
New York Times II (December 10, 1980)
p8:2.
(Reagan comments on Lennon's murder.)

N 0279 Carter, Al. "A Lot Of People Were Crying."
The Daily Oklahoman (December 11, 1980)
(Eulogy.)

N 0280 Carthew, Anthony. "Shaggy Englishman Story;
British Long-Hairs Rolling Stones And The
Beatles." New York Times Magazine (September
6, 1964) p18+. illus.

N 0281 "Central Park Section To Honor Lennon."
New York Times II (April 17, 1981) p3:6.
("Strawberry Fields" section legislated.)

N 0282 Chapin, Emerson. "Visit From The Beetorusu
Gives Tokyo Police Hard Day's Night."
New York Times (July 1, 1966) p38:2.
(Tokyo concert.)

N 0283 "Chapman Case Judge Refuses To Bar Public."
New York Times II (June 12, 1981) p3:4.
(Public will attend jury selection.)

N 0284 "Chapman Getting No Special Guards."
New York Times II (August 26, 1981) p3:1.
(Imprisonment.)

N 0285 "Chapman Signed As 'John Lennon'."
Bulletin (Philadelphia) (December 10, 1980)
ppA1,A8.

N 0286 Chartres, John. "Lennon Anniversary; Thousands
Gather To Honour Dead Beatle." The Times
(December 9, 1981) p5B. illus.
(Memorial in Liverpool.)

N 0287 Chartres, John. "Merseyside Mourns
Working-Class Hero." The Times (December 10,
1980) p7F. illus.
(John Lennon mourned in Northern England.)

N 0288 "Child To The Paul McCartneys." New York Times
(August 29, 1969) p17:5.
(Mary McCartney born.)

N 0289 "Choice For Northern." The Times (April 25,
1969) p30E.
(Northern Songs.)

N 0290 Christian, Russ. "Lennon Remembered For More
Than His Music." The San Jose Mercury
(December 18, 1980)
(Eulogy.)

N 0291 "City Leaders Urge Strict Gun Control."
New York Times II (December 15, 1980)
p3:2.
(Reagan urged to heed Lennon's death.)

N 0292 Clark, Alfred E. "2,000 Beatle Fans Storm Box
Office Here; It's An Early Augury Of Show In
August At Shea Stadium." New York Times
(May 1, 1966) p80:5. illus.

(Shea Stadium ticket sales.)

N 0293 Cleave, Maureen. "John Lennon: A Memoir."
Observer (January 4, 1981) pp22-27. illus.

N 0294 Cleave, Maureen. "Old Beatles - A Study In
Paradox." New York Times Magazine (July 3,
1966) pp10-11+. illus.

N 0295 "Cleaver On The Beatles." New York Times VI
(September 7, 1969) p144.
(E. Cleaver's book "Soul On Ice.")

N 0296 "Cleveland To Bar Beatles And The Like In
Public Hall." New York Times (November 4,
1964) p46:1.

N 0297 Clifford, M. "Nothing To Kill Or Die For."
Northwest Passage 21 (December 15, 1980)
p5.

N 0298 Cohn, Nik. "Stuart Sutcliff: Tragic Fifth Man."
Observer Colour Supplement (September 8,
1968) pp23-24.

N 0299 Collins, Bill. "Via BBC, Rare Beatles Tunes."
Inquirer (Philadelphia) (May 31, 1982)
p8-D.
(On radio special "Beatles At The Beeb.")

N 0300 "A Comedy Of Letters."
Times Literary Supplement (March 26, 1964)
p250.
(Lennon's "In His Own Write.")

N 0301 "Comment." Christian Science Monitor 57
(March 23, 1965) p15.

N 0302 "Comment: How About Long Hair?"
Christian Science Monitor 57 (April 12, 1965)
p13.

N 0303 "Comment: How About Long Hair?"
Christian Science Monitor 67 (April 24, 1975)
p15.

N 0304 "Comments On Jesus Spurs A Radio Ban Against
The Beatles." New York Times (August 5, 1966)
p20:3.

N 0305 "Company News: Dividends And Profits; Northern
Songs To Pay 40 Per Cent." The Times
(February 22, 1966) p17E.
(Northern Songs dividend.)

N 0306 "Company News; Extra 2 Points By Northern
Songs." The Times (March 1, 1968) p24E.

N 0307 "Company News In Brief; Northern Songs."
The Times (October 22, 1966) p15G.

N 0308 "Company News; Ten Points Extra By Northern
Songs." The Times (February 28, 1969)
p31A.

N 0309 Connolly, Ray. "The Surreal Genius Of Rock."
Liverpool Daily Post (December 10, 1980)
(Eulogy.)

N 0310 "Correction." New York Times (June 20, 1974)
p41:7.
(Lennon denies benefit involvement.)

N 0311 Corry, John. "Park 'Festival' Lends Hand To The
Retarded." New York Times (August 31, 1972)
p27:1.
("One To One" Festival.)

N 0312 "Counting Cost Of Beatles' Visit." The Times
(November 26, 1963) p6D.
(Wolverhampton.)

N 0313 "The Country Awash With Beatles Music."
Bulletin (Philadelphia) (December 9, 1980)
ppA1,A4.
(Due to Lennon's death.)

N 0314 "Course On Beatles And Lennon." New York Times
(February 8, 1981) p22:4.
(University of Delaware course of study.)

N 0315 Critchley, Julian. "After The Beatles - An
Interest In All Things British." The Times
(November 21, 1969) p11E.

N 0316 "Critics Scorn Beatle Film But Audience Enjoys
Itself." New York Times (July 29, 1965)
p19:4.
("Help!")

N 0317 "Crowds Of Lennon Fans Gather Quickly At The
Dakota And Hospital." New York Times II
(December 9, 1980) p7:2.

N 0318 Crowley, Kieran and Philip Messing. "Chapman's
Last Four Days: A Mystery Tour Of The City."

Post (New York) (December 10, 1980)
p2,51.
(Mark Chapman.)

N 0319 Crowther, Bosley. "The Other Cheek To The
Beatles." New York Times II (September 12,
1965) p70.
(Discusses his review of "Help!")

N 0320 "Crusade Against Lennon Memorabilia."
Rochester Patriot 9 (January 16, 1981)
p2.

N 0321 "'Crying At The Chapel' Heads British Hit
Parade, Topping Beatles For First Time In
Three Years." New York Times (June 10, 1965)
p38.

N 0322 Cummings, Judith. "The Lennons On Record."
New York Times II (August 14, 1980) p24:3.
(The Lennons' first recording in 7 years.)

N 0323 Cummings, Judith. "Lennon The Chameleon."
New York Times III (September 22, 1980)
p26:3.
(Lennon disowns his radical '70s' image.)

N 0324 Cummings, Judith. "Some Beatles Fans Undergo A
Bit Of A Setback." New York Times III
(August 11, 1980) p23:5.
(No "Beatles" streets or housing for
Liverpool.)

N 0325 Cummings, Judith and Albin Krebs. "Farmer
Lennon's Cow." New York Times (July 3, 1980)
p16:3.
(Lennon's Holstein cow brings $265,000.)

N 0326 Cummings, Judith and Albin Krebs. "McCartney
Arrested In Japan On Marijuana Charge."
New York Times II (January 17, 1980) p11:3.
illus.

N 0327 "Daddy(?)" Daily News (Philadelphia) (December
13, 1982) p7.
(Bettina Huebers' McCartney paternity
suit.)

N 0328 "Dali Death-Painting May Provide A Clue."
Post (New York) (December 10, 1980)
p3,51.
(Lennon murder.)

N 0329 Dallos, Robert E. "Beatles Strike Serious Note
In Press Talk; Group Opposes The War In
Vietnam As Being 'Wrong'." New York Times
(August 23, 1966) p30:2.
(New York City press conference.)

N 0330 Damsker, Matt. "An Artist With A Thousand
Visions." Bulletin (Philadelphia) (December
10, 1980) ppA1,A9.
(John Lennon.)

N 0331 Dancis, B. "For The Love Of Lennon."
In These Times 5 (December 24, 1980)
p8.

N 0332 "Dark Horse Record Label Discussed."
Los Angeles Times IV (May 28, 1974)
p12.

N 0333 "Daughter For Beatle." The Times (August 29,
1969) p2F.
(Mary McCartney.)

N 0334 Davies, Hunter. "The Beatles In A New
Dimension." Sunday Times (December 24, 1967)
pp41-42.
("The Magical Mystery Tour.")

N 0335 Davies, Hunter. "Paul McCartney: Confessions Of
An Unemployed Beatle."
Sunday Times Magazine (April 4, 1976)
p46+. illus.
(Paul McCartney.)

N 0336 Davies, Ross. "Business Diary: Furore Across
The Mersey." The Times (March 2, 1978)
p21A.
(Beatles statue in Liverpool.)

N 0337 Davies, Ross. "Liverpool's Own." The Times
(September 24, 1981) p19A.
(On Liverpool's "Beatles industry.")

N 0338 Davis, David. "Beatles To Fight £9.5M ATV Bid."
The Times (April 11, 1969) p21F.
(For Northern Songs.)

N 0339 Davis, William. "Market Lessons For Northern

NEWSPAPER ARTICLES

Songs." Guardian (January 6, 1966)
p11.

N 0340 "Dean Backs Lennon Peace Festival." The Times
(March 30, 1981) p3D. illus.
(Liverpool Cathedral service.)

N 0341 De'Ath, Wilfred. "An American Exile." Observer
(December 8, 1974) pp56,58. illus.
(John Lennon.)

N 0342 "Debris Is Hurled At Beatle Concert."
New York Times (August 20, 1966) p11:4.
(Firecrackers, fruit, etc. thrown at
Memphis.)

N 0343 "Decree For Mrs. Lennon." The Times (November
9, 1968) p15G.
(Cynthia Lennon granted "decree nisi.")

N 0344 "Defense Seeks Log Book In Lennon Slaying
Case." New York Times (January 17, 1981)
p27:5.
(Chapman signed as "John Lennon" in book.)

N 0345 "Delay Is Expected In Chapman Trial."
New York Times II (June 1, 1981) p3:6.
(Chapman defense seeks psychiatric tests.)

N 0346 Dempsey, David. "Why The Girls Scream, Weep,
Flip." New York Times Magazine (February 23,
1964) p15+. illus.

N 0347 "Depressed In Atlanta." New York Times II
(December 12, 1980) p4:3.
(Chapman's friends on his mental
condition.)

N 0348 "Despite Rumors Of Split, Beatles Cut A Big
Melon." New York Times (November 16, 1966)
p53:4.
(Northern Songs 1965-66 fiscal report.)

N 0349 "Discord In Manila." Christian Science Monitor
58 (July 13, 1966) p1.

N 0350 "Discs: Hello Paul - Bye-Bye Beatles."
Christian Science Monitor 62 (July 29, 1970)
p8.

N 0351 "Disorder In Rush For Beatles Tickets."
The Times (October 28, 1963) p6D.
(Newcastle-upon-Tyne concerts.)

N 0352 Dove, Ian. "The Pop Life." New York Times
(January 4, 1974) p22:2.
(10th anniversary of first Beatles'
releases.)

N 0353 "Dream Is Ended." The Savannah Morning News
(December 11, 1980)
(Editorial eulogy.)

N 0354 "Drugs Raid On Beatle." The Times (March 13,
1969) p1D.
(George Harrison.)

N 0355 Dullea, Georgia. "When Death Is Sudden."
New York Times II (December 15, 1980)
p16:1. illus.
(Trauma of widow Yoko Ono.)

N 0356 Dyer, Richard. "Within His Music."
The Boston Globe (December 14, 1980)
(Eulogy.)

N 0357 "Each Beatle Carrying $5.5 Million Insurance."
New York Times (August 14, 1965) p11:3.
($22 million insurance for U.S. tour.)

N 0358 Edwards, Adam. "John Lennon's Murderer Gets 20
Years To Life." The Times (August 25, 1981)
p1E.

N 0359 "Eggs Shower The Beatles." New York Times
(June 28, 1964) p59:5.
(Christchurch, New Zealand.)

N 0360 "Eggs Thrown At Beatles." New York Times
(June 29, 1964) p32:8.
(Brisbane, New Zealand.)

N 0361 Emerson, Gloria. "A Beatle Returns Award As A
Protest." New York Times (October 26, 1969)
p2:4. illus.
(Lennon returns his M.B.E.)

N 0362 Emerson, Gloria. "Beatles Tuning In On Fashion
World." New York Times (November 21, 1967)
p40:1. illus.
(Apple Boutique.)

N 0363 "EMI May Ration Beatle Album." The Times
(November 21, 1968) p28F.

(Demand causes rationing of "White Album.")

N 0364 "Epstein Death Accidental; 'Trouble From
Insomnia'." The Times (September 9, 1967)
p3A. illus.

N 0365 "Epstein Inquest Opens Today." The Times
(August 30, 1967) p2F.

N 0366 "Epstein Is Buried; Inquest Continues."
New York Times (August 31, 1967) p33:1.

N 0367 "Epstein Letter." The Times (September 7, 1967)
p1F.
(Epstein inquest.)

N 0368 "Ex-Beatle Harrison To Make U.S. Tour."
Christian Science Monitor 66 (September 30,
1974) p3.

N 0369 "Ex-Beatle McCartney Forms New Pop Group."
New York Times (August 5, 1971) p25:5.

N 0370 "Ex-Beatles Aide Ruled Guilty."
Wall Street Journal (April 27, 1979) p2:4.
(Allen Klein guilty on tax charge.)

N 0371 "Ex-Beatles McCartney, Harrison."
Christian Science Monitor 65 (July 29, 1973)
p12.

N 0372 "Ex-Beatle Wins Court Fight To Stay In U.S."
The Times (October 8, 1975) p8E.
(Court of Appeals reverses Lennon
deportation.)

N 0373 "Eye Funds, McCartney Asks Court."
New York Times (January 20, 1971) p22:4.
(Partnership dissolution.)

N 0374 "Fair Terms For N Songs Investors." The Times
(October 4, 1969) p15H.
(Terms for public shareholders.)

N 0375 "Fans All Over World Honor Lennon."
New York Times II (December 9, 1981) p2:3.

N 0376 Farrell, William E. "Mourners Come And Go To
Sad Tones Of Beatles' Music."
New York Times II (December 10, 1980)
p6:1.
(Outside the Dakota.)

N 0377 "Father Given Custody Of Yoko Ono's Child."
The Times (September 30, 1971) p1E.

N 0378 "FBI Had Lennon Marked For Bust."
Post (New York) (March 22, 1983) p3.

N 0379 Feller, J. "John Lennon." Guardian 33
(February 4, 1981) p22.

N 0380 Fenton, D. "Why Won't Yoko Release Ten For
Two." Ann Arbor Sun (May 3, 1974)

N 0381 Feron, James. "Singing Beatles Prepare For
U.S.; British Performers Leaving Tomorrow
For Tour." New York Times (February 6, 1964)
p36:6.
(Beatles U.S. tour set.)

N 0382 "Festival For Lennon Defended." The Times
(March 27, 1981) p6E.
(Liverpool Cathedral service.)

N 0383 "Film Music Score By George Harrison."
The Times (December 29, 1967) p2H.
(Harrison to write "Wonderwall" score.)

N 0384 "Films By Lennons Shown At Cannes; Beatle
Scampers After His 'Apotheosis' Is
Screened." New York Times (May 17, 1971)
p43:1.
(Filmmakers' Fortnight Festival.)

N 0385 "Film To Be Shown At Cannes Festival."
Los Angeles Times IV (May 9, 1972)
p14.
(George Harrison.)

N 0386 "Final Speeches In Beatles Case." The Times
(March 2, 1971) p5F.
(Law case to dissolve Beatles.)

N 0387 "Finance, Commerce And Industry; Beatles As A
Market Factor." The Times (February 5, 1964)
p16B.
(EMI record sales.)

N 0388 "First Aid For 130 At Beatles Show." The Times
(December 4, 1965) p6G.
(Girls injured during Glasgow show.)

N 0389 Fiske, Edward B. "Yellow Submarine Is Symbol Of
Youth Churches." New York Times (April 20,
1970) p23:1.

N 0390 "A Fitting Memorial For John Lennon."
New York Times (December 26, 1980) p30:4.
(Performing arts high school.)

N 0391 "$587,000 Award Against Beatle." The Times
(February 28, 1981) p6A.
(George Harrison's "My Sweet Lord" case.)

N 0392 Flatley, G. "Ringo Starr Sets Out To Become A
Legend Of The Silver Screen."
New York Times (February 25, 1977) p126.
illus.

N 0393 "Fleetwood Mac Wins Rock Prize."
New York Times (September 21, 1976) p34:1.
(Paul McCartney is best male vocalist.)

N 0394 "Flock Circling Warwick A Harbinger Of
Beatles." New York Times (August 22, 1966)
p41:4.
(Warwick Hotel, New York City.)

N 0395 Ford, Stephen. "Beatles Hoax Lives On Years
Later." Daily Times News (November 5, 1975)
p15.

N 0396 "A Forgotten Legacy Of John Lennon."
New York Times (December 29, 1980) p18:6.
(Letter condemns Lennon tribute.)

N 0397 "Former Beatle Fails To Get Ban On Articles."
The Times (June 17, 1978) p2B.
(Lennon fails to ban articles by Cynthia.)

N 0398 "Former Beatle On Drug Charges." The Times
(December 23, 1972) p2C.
(Paul McCartney accused of growing
marijuana.)

N 0399 "Former Beatles Manager Sues For Libel."
The Times (February 29, 1972) p7C.
(Allen Klein.)

N 0400 "Former Beatle Sued Over Alleged Loan"
The Times (June 29, 1973) p9B.
(John Lennon sued.)

N 0401 "Former Manager Of Beatles Loses High Court
Plea." The Times (October 29, 1974)
p4F.
(Allen Klein.)

N 0402 "Forms Of Adulation." New York Times (December
10, 1980) p30:1.
(Editorial on John Lennon.)

N 0403 "For Service." The Times (June 16, 1965)
p13G.
(Correspondence regarding M.B.E.s.)

N 0404 "40 Beatles Fans Arrested." The Times
(June 28, 1966) p9C.
(Fans riot in Hamburg.)

N 0405 "400 Riot As Beatles Arrive In Miami."
The Times (February 14, 1964) p15D.
(First U.S. visit.)

N 0406 "4 Sought By Defense In Slaying Of Lennon."
New York Times II (February 26, 1981)
p4:3.
(Chapman's lawyer seeks witnesses.)

N 0407 "4,000 Hail Beatles On Arrival In Miami."
New York Times (February 14, 1964) p16:2.

N 0409 Freed, Richard D. "Beatles Stump Music Experts
Looking For Key To Beatlemania."
New York Times (August 13, 1965) p17:1.
(Musicological analysis.)

N 0410 Freed, Richard D. "Beatle Tunes Become Baroque
'N' Roll." New York Times (November 9, 1965)
p50:1.
(Joshua Rifkin's "Baroque Beatles Book.")

N 0411 "Freighter Is Delivered Here To 'Peace Pilot'
From Israel." New York Times (September 9,
1969) p93:5.
(Lennon's Mid-East peace radio platform.)

N 0412 "From Day To Day; Death Threat After Beatles
Incident." The Times (July 11, 1966)
p9C.
(Threaten U.K. Embassy official,
Philippines.)

N 0413 "From Day To Day; Munich Claims Tax On
Beatles." The Times (July 2, 1966)
p8E.
(City authorities claim entertainment tax.)

N 0414 "From The Royal Academy Summer Exhibition."

The Times (May 3, 1968) p16. illus.
(Photo of McCartney portrait by John
Bratby.)

N 0415 "Furor Over Beatles." New York Times IV
(June 20, 1965) p5:3.
(Beatles' M.B.E. controversy.)

N 0416 Gaiter, Dorothy J. "A Psychologist Admits
Perjury On His Degree." New York Times II
(December 16, 1981) p8:4.
(Chapman defense psychologist.)

N 0417 Gale, Glenn and Linda McCartney. "A Life In The
Day Of Linda McCartney."
Sunday Times Magazine (February 3, 1981)
p62.

N 0418 "'A Garden Of Love'."
Daily News (Philadelphia) (April 20, 1982)
p34.
("Strawberry Fields" in New York's Central
Park.)

N 0419 Gardner, Paul. "The Beatles Are At It Again."
New York Times II (November 22, 1964)
p13:1.

N 0420 Gardner, Paul. "The Beatles Invade, Complete
With Long Hair And Screaming Fans; - 3,000
Fans Greet British Beatles." New York Times
(February 8, 1964) p25:4. illus.
(Beatles land at Kennedy airport.)

N 0421 Gardner, Paul. "The British Boys: High-Brows
and No-Brows." New York Times (February 9,
1964) p19:5. illus.
(Comment on U.S. visit.)

N 0422 Geddes-Brown, Leslie. "Time Bandits All
Handmade In Britain." Sunday Times
(June 21, 1981) p39A. illus.
(On the Harrison-produced film.)

N 0423 "George Harrison." The Times (June 10, 1977)
p2A.
(Divorced.)

N 0424 "George Harrison Banned And Fined." The Times
(February 24, 1971) p2H.
(Driver's license suspended.)

N 0425 "George Harrison Guilty Of Plagiarizing,
Subconsciously, A '62 Tune For A '70 Hit."
New York Times (September 8, 1976) p50:1.

N 0426 "George Harrison Married." The Times (January
22, 1966) p6F.

N 0427 "Get Back To Northern Songs." The Times
(April 25, 1969) p31A.

N 0428 Gilbert, Nick. "Paul Joins Battle With ACC For
All His Yesterdays." Sunday Times (August
22, 1982) p38E. illus.
(McCartney/Yoko seek return of song
rights.)

N 0429 Gilroy, Harry. "End Papers." New York Times
(April 24, 1964) p31:4.
(Review of "In His Own Write.")

N 0430 Gilroy, Harry. "Two Biographies Of The Beatles
Rushed Yo Stores; Authorized Version From
McGraw-Hill Challenged By Putnam 'Real
Story'." New York Times (August 17, 1968)
p25:1. illus.
(Books by Hunter Davies and Julius Fast.)

N 0431 "Girl Gets Back Her Passport." The Times
(May 2, 1968) p4H.
(Jenny Boyd charged.)

N 0432 "Girl On Second Drug Charge." The Times
(May 23, 1968) p3D.
(Jenny Boyd.)

N 0433 "Girls In Miami Shriek Welcome To The Beatles."
New York Times (February 17, 1964) p20:8.
("Ed Sullivan Show"; visit to Miami Beach.)

N 0434 Glueck, Grace. "Art By Yoko Ono Shown At Museum
In Syracuse." New York Times II (October 11,
1971) p48:1. illus.

N 0435 Glueck, Grace. "The Art World, A New Year's
Earful." New York Times II (December 26,
1971) p23:5.
(Yoko Ono and others outline new year for
art.)

N 0436 Gold, Anita. "The Fab Four Have Inspired A

Collecting Coterie." Chicago Tribune
(November 28, 1982) pN4.
N 0437 "Good-bye To The 'Now Generation'."
New York Times (January 12, 1971) p35:4.
(Excerpt from Lennon's "Rolling Stone"
interview.)
N 0438 Goodman, Ellen. "The Promise Is Gone."
The Boston Globe (December 13, 1980)
(Eulogy.)
N 0439 Goodman, George, Jr. "100% Attendance Is 'In'
At George Washington." New York Times
(December 1, 1973) p24:4.
(Church choir performance to honor the
Lennons.)
N 0440 Gould, Jack. "Ed Sullivan Devotes Show To Music
By Beatles." New York Times (March 2, 1970)
p75:1.
N 0441 Gould, Jack. "TV: It's The Beatles (Yeah, Yeah,
Yeah)." New York Times (January 4, 1964)
p47.
N 0442 Gould, Jack. "TV: The Beatles And Their
Audience; Quartet Continues to Agitate The
Faithful." New York Times (February 10, 1964)
p53:2. illus.
("Ed Sullivan Show.")
N 0443 "Grammar School Bans Beatle Haircuts."
The Times (November 18, 1963) p6C.
(Clark's Grammar School.)
N 0444 "Grandmother's Comment."
Christian Science Monitor 56 (October 22,
1964) p15.
N 0445 Green, Robert. "Accentuate The Appropriate."
New York Times (September 18, 1977) p1:2.
illus.
(The Beatles' fashions.)
N 0446 "Greenfield Eyes Effect From The Beatles."
Los Angeles Times VI (February 16, 1975)
p1.
N 0447 Greenfield, Jeff. "They Changed Rock, Which
Changed The Culture, Which Changed Us."
New York Times Magazine (February 16, 1975)
pp12-13+. illus.
N 0448 Greenspur, Roger. "The Screen: Films By John
And Yoko At Whitney Museum." New York Times
(March 21, 1972) p36:1.
N 0449 Groom, Avril. "Linda's View From The Inside Of
The Polaroid." Daily Telegraph (February 26,
1982) p17. illus.
N 0450 "Group 'No Longer Thought Of As The Beatles'."
The Times (February 27, 1971) p3A.
(Law case to dissolve Beatles.)
N 0451 Gruson, Sydney. "Beatles Put Off India
Pilgrimage; TV Special Gets Nod Over
Discipleship In Meditation." New York Times
(September 11, 1967) p53:1.
N 0452 "Gun Control." New York Times (July 24, 1981)
p26:3.
(Lennon death alters race procedures.)
N 0453 "Gunfire Kills John Lennon."
Inquirer (Philadelphia) (December 9, 1980)
pp1A,6A.
N 0454 "Guns And Logic." Wall Street Journal
(December 19, 1980) p24:1.
(John Lennon's death.)
N 0455 Haberman, Clyde. "Silent Tribute To Lennon's
Memory Is Observed Throughout The World."
New York Times I (December 15, 1980) p1:1.
illus.
N 0456 Haberman, Clyde and Albin Krebs. "Blue Meanies
No More." New York Times II (October 16,
1979) p9:4.
(Lennons donate $1000 to New York police.)
N 0457 Haberman, Clyde and Albin Krebs. "Ex-Manager Of
Beatles And Rolling Stones Is Sentenced."
New York Times (August 11, 1979) p17:3.
(Tax evasion on sale of Beatles records.)
N 0458 Haberman, Clyde and Albin Krebs. "Harrison, On
Himself." New York Times III (February 12,
1979) pp10-14.
(Interview.)

N 0459 "Haircuts." Christian Science Monitor 56
(November 24, 1964) p19.
N 0460 "Hair-Dos." Christian Science Monitor 56
(November 5, 1964) p15.
N 0461 "Half Lennon Fortune Left To Wife." The Times
(December 11, 1980) p1H.
(Half estate willed to Yoko Ono Lennon.)
N 0462 "A Hard Day's Drive." The Times (June 17, 1966)
p1E.
(Paul McCartney buys Scottish farm.)
N 0463 Harris, Martha S. "Minstrel Extraordinaire."
Cornwall Local (December 10, 1980)
(Editorial eulogy.)
N 0464 "Harrison Benefit For East Pakistanis."
Christian Science Monitor 63 (July 30, 1971)
p13.
N 0465 Hazelhurst, Peter. "Beatles Begin Their Career
As 'Sages'." The Times (February 21, 1968)
p6A.
(Studying meditation.)
N 0466 "Hearing On Term In Lennon Slaying."
New York Times II (August 24, 1981) p3:1.
(Mark Chapman sentencing.)
N 0467 Heckman, Don. "Carole King Wins 4 Grammys As
Record Industry Lists 'Bests'."
New York Times (March 15, 1972) p95:3.
(Beatles win special award.)
N 0468 Heckman, Don. "Lennon Concert Slated Aug. 30 In
All-Day Fete To Aid Retarded."
New York Times (August 17, 1972) p32:2.
("One To One" Festival.)
N 0469 Heilpern, John. "Brian Epstein: Did He Make The
Beatles, Or Did The Beatles Make Him?"
Observer Colour Supplement (September 1,
1968) pp16-17. illus.
N 0470 Henahan, D. "Art Songs, 4 Big Fans And More."
New York Times (January 12, 1972) p34:4.
(Performance of musical works by the
Lennons.)
N 0471 Herman, Robin and Laurie Johnston. "Theft At
The Courthouse." New York Times II
(December 30, 1982) p3:1. illus.
(1975 John/Yoko painting stolen.)
N 0472 "A Hero's Return To Liverpool." The Times
(September 4, 1981) p2F. illus.
(John Lennon statue photo.)
N 0473 Hershow, Sheila. "Writing The Score For A
Generation." The Federal Times (December 29,
1980)
(Eulogy.)
N 0474 "Hiding Justice." New York Times IV p14:1.
(Chapman's guilty plea.)
N 0476 Hilburn, Robert. "The Gossip Hurts, But Ono
Goes On." Inquirer (Philadelphia) (July 13,
1983) p5-E.
("Insider" gossip-books about John Lennon.)
N 0477 Hilburn, Robert. "John Lennon: No Secret
Interior, Just Integrity."
Los Angeles Times (December 14, 1980)
(Eulogy.)
N 0478 Hilburn, Robert. "Lennon Started Singing Again
- For His Wife, His Son, His New Life."
Inquirer (Philadelphia) (December 9, 1980)
p7A.
N 0479 Hilburn, Robert. "Making Up: McCartney Says In
A Song What He Wishes He Had Told Lennon."
Inquirer (Philadelphia) II (April 25, 1982)
p5.
(Interview.)
N 0480 "Hippies To Look Over Island Offered To Them By
A Beatle." New York Times (November 14, 1969)
p2:5.
(John Lennon's Irish island, Dorinish.)
N 0481 Hogan, Randolph. "The Love They Take And Make."
New York Times VII (April 5, 1981)
p9. illus.

N 0482 Holden, Stephen. "Pop: Miss Flack At Tribute To
Lennon." New York Times (December 12, 1981)
p24:3.
(Roberta Flack tribute performance.)

N 0483 "Holds Press Conference To Kick Off Tour."
Los Angeles Times IV (October 25, 1974)
pl.
(George Harrison.)

N 0484 "Home News; Epstein Lawyers Seek Will: Funeral
To Be In Private." The Times (August 29,
1967) p2A.

N 0485 "Home News; Ringo Starr Sued." The Times
(January 9, 1967) pl0B.

N 0486 Honeycutt, K. "The Beatles Are Invading New
York City Again - On Film." New York Times
II (January 1, 1978) pl:3. illus.

N 0487 "Honours." The Times (June 17, 1965) pl3D.
(Correspondence regarding M.B.E.s.)

N 0488 "Honours." The Times (June 18, 1965) pl3F.
(Correspondence regarding M.B.E.s.)

N 0489 "Honours." The Times (June 19, 1965) p9D.
(Correspondence regarding M.B.E.s.)

N 0490 "Hooliganism 'Will Be Stamped Out'; Incidents
During Visit By Beatles." The Times
(October 23, 1964) pl5F.
(Glasgow, Scotland.)

N 0491 "Hotel Near Beatles's Home Rejected."
The Times (March 22, 1971) p2G.
(Hotel near Paul McCartney's home.)

N 0492 "Houston Has Nation's First All-Beatle
Station." Florida Times-Union (Jacksonville)
(June 20, 1983) pC-4.

N 0493 "How About Long Hair?"
Christian Science Monitor 57 (March 5, 1965)
p15.

N 0494 Howard, Philip. "Lennons To Smile For Charity."
The Times (October 25, 1969) p3D.
(Films to be part of world poverty
exhibit.)

N 0496 "How Tin Pan Alley Beat The Beatles."
Sunday Times (June 6, 1982) pl3E. illus.
(Letters.)

N 0497 Hunn, David. "A Gold Mine At The Bottom Of The
Garden." Observer (June 24, 1979) p35.
illus.
(Paul McCartney.)

N 0498 Huntington, Robert L., Jr. "Lost: Another Great
Spirit." The Hartford Courant (December 16,
1980)
(Eulogy.)

N 0499 "In Brief; Beatle Baby." The Times (May 16,
1969) p2H.
(Linda McCartney expecting.)

N 0500 "In Brief; Beatles' Story On Radio." The Times
(October 15, 1971) p2H.
(Documentary slated for Spring 1972.)

N 0501 "In Brief; Climb To See Lennon." The Times
(June 3, 1969) p5H.
(Montreal hotel "lie in" for peace.)

N 0502 "In Brief; Drugs Class Offer." The Times
(April 9, 1975) p7C.
(Linda McCartney not to fight drug charge.)

N 0503 "In Brief; £18m Lennon Lawsuit." The Times
(March 8, 1975) p4E.
(John Lennon sued by music corporation.)

N 0504 "In Brief; Film On Hanratty." The Times
(January 12, 1972) p2H.
(John Lennon and film on Hanratty murder.)

N 0505 "In Brief; Former Beatle Hurt." The Times
(March 1, 1972) p2H.
(George Harrison in car crash.)

N 0506 "In Brief; Hindu Festival Ban Over Beatles."
The Times (March 30, 1968) p4H.
(Harrison and Lennon barred in India.)

N 0507 "In Brief; Japan Bars Ex-Beatle." The Times
(November 12, 1975) p8B.
(Paul McCartney.)

N 0508 "In Brief; Jet Waits For Pop Star." The Times

(October 28, 1975) p4F.
(Waits 45 minutes for Paul McCartney.)

N 0509 "In Brief; Lennon's Warning." The Times
(December 22, 1969) p5D.
(Warns teens against drug taking.)

N 0510 "In Brief; Lennon Tree Destroyed." The Times
(December 19, 1980) p2E.
(Tree in his memory vandalised in Bromley.)

N 0511 "In Brief; McCartney Farm Search." The Times
(September 21, 1972) p2H.
(Marijuana raid.)

N 0512 "In Brief; McCartney Tour." The Times
(February 28, 1973) p3H.
(To tour England.)

N 0513 "In Brief; Mystic Forgives The Beatles."
The Times (May 28, 1968) p5H.
(Statement by the Maharishi.)

N 0514 "In Brief; Pop Record Seized." The Times
(March 7, 1970) p5H.
(In Singapore.)

N 0515 "In Brief; Ringo Crusade." The Times (September
18, 1974) p3H.
(Against drug taking by young people.)

N 0516 "In Brief; Ringo Starr In Crash." The Times
(May 20, 1980) plE.
(Injured in auto accident.)

N 0517 "In Brief; Son For The Lennons." The Times
(October 10, 1975) p9E.
(Sean Lennon.)

N 0518 "In Brief; The Prejudicial Nude." The Times
(January 24, 1976) p4G.
(Mistrial declared in Lennon publishing
case.)

N 0519 "In Brief; £300 Beatle Fund." The Times
(January 5, 1981) p3E.
(Liverpool Council statue fund fizzles.)

N 0520 "In Brief; £2.9m Settlement By Beatles' Firm."
The Times (January 11, 1977) p5A.
(Apple Corps. and Allen Klein settle.)

N 0521 "Income Of The Beatles For 19 Months Under
Klein Management Said To Be Over £9M."
The Times (February 26, 1971) p4E.

N 0522 "In Defence Of The Beatles' Honour; Motion
Tabled By Liverpool M.P.s." The Times
(June 16, 1965) pl2C.

N 0523 "India Police Visit Beatles' Retreat."
The Times (February 23, 1968) p6F.

N 0524 "In Gratitude." New York Times IV (January 18,
1981) p24.
(Open letter from Yoko Ono.)

N 0525 "In Gratitude." Sunday Times (January 18, 1981)
pll.
(Open letter from Yoko Ono.)

N 0526 "Injured In Auto Accident." Los Angeles Times I
(February 29, 1972) pll.
(George Harrison.)

N 0527 "In Perspective." Times Educational Supplement
(January 9, 1981) pl3B.
(John Lennon.)

N 0528 "Inquest Is Ordered In Death Of Manager Of The
Beatles." New York Times (August 30, 1967)
p4:5.

N 0529 "In U.S. Financial Mop Up."
Christian Science Monitor 56 (September 22,
1964) pll.

N 0530 "In Who's Who In America."
Christian Science Monitor 57 (July 7, 1965)
pl.

N 0531 "Irish Song By McCartney Banned By BBC."
The Times (February 11, 1972) p2H.
("Give Ireland Back to the Irish.")

N 0532 "Irked By Award To Beatles Canadian Returns
Medal." New York Times (June 15, 1965)
pl5:1.
(Canadian returns his M.B.E.)

N 0533 "Israel Bars Beatles." New York Times
(March 18, 1964) p47:3.

N 0534 "Italy Loves Them." Christian Science Monitor 58
(July 18, 1966) p4.

N 0535 "'It's A Hard Night,' Says Springsteen."

Inquirer (Philadlephia) (December 10, 1980)
pA14.
(John Lennon's death.)

N 0536 Jacobs, Sanford L. "It Had To Happen: Promoter
Offers Tax Break For Book On John Lennon."
Wall Street Journal (December 17, 1980)
p29:1.

N 0537 "Jakarta To Burn Beatle Music." New York Times
(August 9, 1965) p8:6.
(Independence Day "celebrations" in
Indonesia.)

N 0538 "Japanese Deport McCartney For Having
Marijuana." New York Times (January 26, 1980)
p2:4.

N 0539 "Jean's Rival." Christian Science Monitor 56
(February 15, 1964) p1.

N 0540 "A Jersey Prosecutor Bans Sale Of A Beatles'
Album." New York Times (January 25, 1969)
p24:3.
("Two Virgins" album.)

N 0541 "Jesus Freaks Silence Lennon." Overthrow 3
(January 1981) p1.

N 0542 Jewell, Derek. "How Paul Beat His Tokyo Blues."
Sunday Times (May 18, 1980) p37. illus.

N 0543 "Jimmy McCulloch, Was Guitarist In Paul
McCartney's Wings Band." New York Times IV
(September 28, 1979) p15:1.
(McCulloch found dead in London home.)

N 0544 Jobes, William. "'Political Motive' In Move To
Deport John Lennon." The Times (December 16,
1974) p6C.
(John Lennon's deportation case.)

N 0545 "John And Yoko Sex Seen."
Los Angeles Free Press 7:4 (January 23, 1970)

N 0546 "John Lennon." New York Times (March 24, 1974)
p37:4.
(Still in U.S. after year-old expulsion
order.)

N 0547 "John Lennon." Chicago Tribune (December 10,
1980)
(Editorial eulogy.)

N 0548 "John Lennon." Militant 44 (December 19, 1980)
p2.

N 0549 "John Lennon Appeals." The Times (April 4, 1973)
p8F.
(John Lennon's deportation case.)

N 0550 "John Lennon - A 16 Page Tribute To A Man In
The Life Of Us All."
Inquirer (Philadelphia) (December 10, 1980)
ppG1-G16.

N 0551 "John Lennon Can Stay In U.S." The Times
(July 28, 1976) p6E.
(Deportation case.)

N 0552 "John Lennon Disc 'Plastic Ono Band'."
Christian Science Monitor 63 (March 19, 1971)
p4.

N 0553 "John Lennon Divorced." New York Times
(November 9, 1968) p37:2.

N 0554 "John Lennon; Dominant Role In A Pop Music
Revolution." The Times (December 10, 1980)
p17F. illus.
(Obituary.)

N 0555 "John Lennon Fined £150 On Drug Charge."
The Times (November 29, 1968) p4F.

N 0556 "John Lennon Flies 2,000 Miles To Marry
Quietly." The Times (March 21, 1969)
p5C. illus.

N 0557 "John Lennon: Good Words."
Christian Science Monitor 64 (July 3, 1972)
p17.

N 0558 "John Lennon In Demonstration." The Times
(August 12, 1971) p4B.
(Oz trial and Northern Ireland.)

N 0559 "John Lennon Is Dead, A Man Who Touched Truth."
Inquirer (Philadelphia) (December 10, 1980)
pA16.

N 0560 "John Lennon Is Slain In New York."
News (Philadelphia) (December 9, 1980)
ppA1,A4.

N 0561 "John Lennon Marries Yoko Ono In Gibraltar."

New York Times (March 21, 1969) p40:2.

N 0562 "John Lennon: Must An Artist Self-Destruct?"
New York Times II (November 9, 1981) p1:1.
illus.
(Robert Palmer interview.)

N 0563 "John Lennon Remembered." New York Times
(December 9, 1981) p1:3. illus.
(Illustration.)

N 0564 "The John Lennons Buy Land Upstate And Will
Raise Cattle." New York Times (February 5,
1978) p45:6.

N 0565 "John Lennons Convey Greetings Via Billboards."
New York Times (December 16, 1969) p54:1.
(Xmas billboards in major U.S. cities.)

N 0567 "John Lennon's Death."
Columbus Citizen-Journal (December 11, 1980)
(Editorial eulogy.)

N 0568 "John Lennon's Deportation From U.S. Delayed."
The Times (September 24, 1975) p5F.

N 0569 "John Lennon's Dream Is Over."
Bulletin (Philadelphia) (December 10, 1980)
pB6.
(Editorial eulogy.)

N 0570 "John Lennon Seeks A Visa To Visit U.S. This
Month." New York Times (May 16, 1969)
p41:1.
(Lennon declared inadmissable.)

N 0571 "John Lennon Sends Back His MBE." The Times
(November 26, 1969) p2C.

N 0572 "John Lennon's Journey: Of Triumph And
Tragedy." Post (New York) (December 10, 1980)
p34.

N 0573 "John Lennon Wins 4 Year Battle With U.S.
Immigration." Christian Science Monitor 68
(August 4, 1976) p14.

N 0574 "Johnsons Use Beatles' Suite." New York Times
(October 24, 1966) p14:6.
(President Johnson in Manila, Philippines.)

N 0575 Johnston, Laurie. "Notes On People."
New York Times (March 4, 1975) p30:3.
(Linda McCartney arrested on marijuana
charge.)

N 0576 Johnston, Laurie. "Notes On People."
New York Times (March 7, 1975) p19:3.
(John Lennon comments on his marital
separation.)

N 0577 Johnston, Laurie. "Notes On People."
New York Times (April 9, 1975) p55:2.
(Paul and Linda McCartney.)

N 0578 Johnston, Laurie. "Notes On People."
New York Times (October 10, 1975) p43:5.
(Yoko Ono gives birth to Sean Ono Lennon.)

N 0579 Johnston, Laurie. "Notes On People."
New York Times (November 21, 1975) p48:5.
(Linda McCartney's drug charge dismissed.)

N 0580 Johnston, Laurie. "Notes On People."
New York Times (January 24, 1976) p21:1.
(Big Seven Music Corp. sues the Lennons.)

N 0581 Johnston, Laurie and Albin Krebs. "McCartney On
Top." New York Times II (October 2, 1979)
pp13-2.
(Most honored composer/performer in music.)

N 0582 Johnston, T.H. "Paul Asks High Court: Break Up
The Beatles." Evening News (London)
(December 31, 1971) p1+.

N 0583 Jones, L. "The Dream Is Over."
North American Anarchist 1 (January 1981)
p9.

N 0584 Jones, Tim. "Fight Stops War Satire Film."
The Times (October 24, 1967) p1F.
("How I Won the War.")

N 0585 Joyce, Faye S. "Starting Over: Life Without
John Lennon." St. Petersburg Times
(December 21, 1980)
(Eulogy.)

N 0586 "Judge Refuses 'Freeze' On Beatles' £1M."
The Times (April 2, 1969) p2D.
(Royalties.)

N 0587 "Judgment To Be Given Later In Beatles Case."
The Times (March 6, 1971) p3B.

(Law case to dissolve Beatles.)

N 0588 "Jury In Tate Trial Listen To Beatles Records."
The Times (January 20, 1971) p7D.
(Manson case.)

N 0589 "Just The Usual Din As Beatles Open Tour In
Chicago." New York Times (August 13, 1966)
p10:1.
(Beatles' Chicago concert.)

N 0590 Kantrowitz, Barbara and Jane P. Shoemaker. "Let
It Be: Fans Mourn A Legend Of Rock."
Inquirer (Philadelphia) (December 10, 1980)
ppA1,A13.
(John Lennon.)

N 0591 Kaplan, Morris. "A Beatles Fan, 10, Prompts
Inquiry; Lefkowitz Holds Hearing On
Deceptive Practices In Recording Industry."
New York Times (December 17, 1965) p41:4.

N 0592 Kelly, K. "Legacy Of John Lennon." Guardian 33
(December 31, 1980) p16.

N 0593 Kempton, Murray. "For Innocence: Sudden Death."
Post (New York) (December 10, 1980)
p34.
(John Lennon.)

N 0594 "Killer Stalked Lennon For Days, Got
Autograph." Inquirer (Philadelphia)
(December 10, 1980) ppA1,A14.

N 0595 Klein, Joe. "Cosmic Gumdrops And Musical
Genius." New York Times VII (November 29,
1981) p7.
(On Sheff's "Playboy Interviews.")

N 0596 Klemesrud, Judy. "But His Teeth Are Regular
Pearls." New York Times II (June 1, 1969)
p11:4. illus.
(Interview with Ringo Starr.)

N 0597 Klemesrud, Judy. "Vegetarianism: Growing Way Of
Life, Especially Among The Young."
New York Times (March 21, 1975) p43:1.
(George Harrison as prominent vegetarian.)

N 0598 Kopkind, Andrew. "Lennon Without Tears."
The SoHo News (December 17, 1980)
(Eulogy.)

N 0599 Kornheiser, Toni and Tom Zito. "Lennon: Always
Up Front." The Washington Post (December 10,
1980)
(Eulogy.)

N 0600 Kramer, Marcus, Rabbi. "Everyone Should Speak
Lennon's Language."
The Staten Island Advance (December 19, 1980)
(Eulogy.)

N 0601 Krebs, Albin. "Bride For A Beatle."
New York Times (July 5, 1980) p25:3.
(Ringo Starr to wed Barbara Bach.)

N 0602 Krebs, Albin. "Impending Fatherhood Stays
Lennon Ouster." New York Times (September
24, 1975) p41:1.
(U.S. deportation forestalled by
pregnancy.)

N 0603 Krebs, Albin. "Lennon Is Given 60 Days To
Leave." New York Times (July 18, 1974)
p28:1.

N 0604 Krebs, Albin. "Lennons' Deportation Hearing Is
Delayed." New York Times (May 2, 1972)
p33:1.

N 0605 Krebs, Albin. "Notes On People."
New York Times (April 19, 1972) p42:6.
(The Lennons deportation problems.)

N 0606 Krebs, Albin. "Notes On People."
New York Times (May 10, 1972) p54:4.
(Lennons win another delay in deportation.)

N 0607 Krebs, Albin. "Notes On People."
New York Times (May 13, 1972) p15:6.
(Celebrities testify for the Lennons.)

N 0608 Krebs, Albin. "Notes On People."
New York Times (May 18, 1972) p43:1.
(Beatles agree on partnership money split.)

N 0609 Krebs, Albin. "Notes On People."
New York Times (March 16, 1974) p19:1.
(Lennon's Troubador Club incident
reviewed.)

N 0610 Krebs, Albin. "Notes On People."

New York Times (March 28, 1974) p46:4.
(Lennon's Troubador Club charge dismissed.)

N 0611 Krebs, Albin. "Notes On People."
New York Times (November 2, 1974) p35:5.
(Lennon seeks to question U.S. officials.)

N 0612 Krebs, Albin. "Notes On People."
New York Times (December 14, 1974) p19:3.
(George Harrison at the White House.)

N 0613 Krebs, Albin. "Notes On People."
New York Times (September 16, 1975) p30:3.
(Punitive taxes keep Ringo Starr out of
U.K.)

N 0614 Krebs, Albin. "Notes On People."
New York Times II (June 3, 1977) p2:1.
(Paul McCartney expects birth of fourth
child.)

N 0615 Krebs, Albin. "Notes On People."
New York Times (June 10, 1977) p20:3.
(George Harrison and wife Pattie granted
divorce.)

N 0616 Krebs, Albin. "Notes On People."
New York Times (August 4, 1978) p14:2.
(Son born to George Harrison and Olivia
Arias.)

N 0617 Krebs, Albin and Robert McG., Jr. Thomas. "From
Koch To Lennon: A Posthumous Cultural
Award." New York Times (May 23, 1981)
p15:1. illus.
(Lennon wins New York City culture award.)

N 0618 Krebs, Albin and Robert McG., Jr. Thomas. "Less
Damage." New York Times II (February 27,
1981) p7:4.
(Harrison's "My Sweet Lord" verdict.)

N 0619 Krebs, Albin and Robert McG., Jr. Thomas. "New
Strawberry Fields." New York Times
(August 22, 1981) p48:1. illus.
(Central Park site restored.)

N 0620 "Label Products Rake In Millions."
Christian Science Monitor 56 (July 10, 1964)
p12.

N 0621 Lambert, Tom. "Beatles Phenomenon Explored On
Stage." Los Angeles Times IV (August 23,
1974) p16.
("John, Paul, George, Ringo ... and Burt.")

N 0622 "Landlords Seek Ban On Beatle." The Times
(February 21, 1969) p3G.
(Starr enjoined for Lennon's use of his
residence.)

N 0625 "Latest Wills; John Lennon Leaves £2.5m."
The Times (February 28, 1981) p16E.

N 0626 Lawlor, Julia. "John Lennon Shot To Death."
News (Philadelphia) (December 9, 1980)
p3,20.

N 0627 Leapman, Michael. "Lennon Case Lawyer's Life Is
Threatened." The Times (December 12, 1980)
p6F.
(Chapman's court appointed lawyer.)

N 0628 Leapman, Michael. "Man On Death Charge
'Obsessed By Lennon'." The Times (December
11, 1980) p7D.
(Mark David Chapman.)

N 0629 Leapman, Michael. "Mr. Lindsay Denounces
Attempt To Deport Lennons." The Times
(April 29, 1972) p1B.
(New York City mayor sides with Lennons.)

N 0630 Leapman, Michael. "Two U.S. Unions To Boycott
British Exports." The Times (February 7,
1972) p1D.
(Lennon protests Britain's Irish policy.)

N 0631 Leapman, Michael. "Wave Of Grief Over John
Lennon's Murder; Violent End Of 1960s Hero
Evokes Parallel With The Killing Of
Kennedy." The Times (December 10, 1980)
p1D.

N 0632 Ledbetter, Les. "John Lennon Of Beatles Is
Killed; Suspect Held In Shooting At Dakota."
New York Times (December 9, 1980) p1:2.
illus.

N 0633 Ledbetter, Les. "McCartney, On Visa, Sees
'Loose' Beatles' Reunion." New York Times

(December 26, 1973) p52:1. illus.

N 0634 "Led Zeppelin Supplants Beatles In British
Poll." New York Times (September 16, 1970)
p40:4.
(Led Zeppelin most popular in "Melody Maker"
poll.)

N 0635 Lee, John M. "Multiplying Business Woes Bug The
Beatles." New York Times (April 21, 1969)
p67:7.

N 0636 Lee, John M. "Receiver Named For The Beatles;
McCartney Victor In First Episode In Legal
Contest." New York Times (March 13, 1971)
p36:1.
(Allen Klein ousted as Beatles' manager.)

N 0637 "Legacy Of Lennon." London Daily Express
(December 10, 1980)
(Editorial eulogy.)

N 0638 Lelyveld, Joseph. "Beatles' Guru Is Turning
Them Into Gurus With A Cram Course."
New York Times (February 23, 1968) p13:3.
illus.
(Beatles in Rishikesh, India.)

N 0639 Lelyveld, Joseph. "The Guru: How To Succeed By
Meditating." New York Times IV (March 3,
1968) p1. illus.

N 0640 Lelyveld, Joseph. "Ravi Shankar Gives West A
New Sound That's Old In East."
New York Times (June 20, 1966) p22:6.
(George Harrison studies sitar.)

N 0641 Lelyveld, Joseph. "Wilson Reopens The Cellar
Club Where Beatles Got Their Start."
New York Times (July 24, 1966) p16:3.
(Prime Minister Harold Wilson.)

N 0642 Lennon, John. "The Goon Show Scripts."
New York Times VII (September 30, 1973)
p6.
(Lennon reviews Spike Milligan book.)

N 0643 Lennon, John. "Revolution."
New York Times Magazine (October 27, 1968)
p97.

N 0644 Lennon, John and Yoko Ono. "A Love Letter From
John And Yoko To People Who Ask What, When,
And Why." New York Times IV (May 27, 1979)
p20E.

N 0645 "Lennon And Friend Charged In Possession Of
Marijuana." New York Times (October 19, 1968)
p27:3.
(John Lennon and Yoko Ono.)

N 0646 "Lennon And Yoko Ono Remanded." The Times
(October 21, 1968) p2H.
(Drug charge.)

N 0647 "Lennon Asked To Play Christ." The Times
(December 4, 1969) p1F.
(In pop opera by Andrew Lloyd Webber and
Tim Rice.)

N 0648 "Lennon Book Acquired." New York Times III
(January 29, 1982) p21:4.
(Albert Goldman's pending biography.)

N 0649 "The Lennon Case." New York Times (April 4,
1973) p42:1.
(Lennon's deportation case.)

N 0650 "Lennon Case Accused Alters Plea To Guilty."
The Times (June 23, 1981) p8C.

N 0651 "Lennon Exhibitor Draws Picasso Into His
Defense." New York Times (April 2, 1970)
p45:1.
(Lennon lithographs in London gallery.)

N 0652 "Lennon Fights To Stay." New York Times
(October 21, 1973) p69:3.
(Lennon files suit to secure U.S case
records.)

N 0653 "Lennon Flies A Banner." The Times (December
12, 1969) p2B.
(Unfurls "Britain murdered Hanratty"
banner.)

N 0654 "Lennon Gave An Interview On Final Day."
New York Times II (December 10, 1980)
p6:6.
(RKO General Radio Network interview.)

N 0655 "Lennon Health Centre." The Times (December 24,

1981) p2H.
(Established in Liverpool.)

N 0656 "Lennon Helps Gypsies." The Times (December 1,
1969) p3G.
(Caravan School to be bought for gypsy
children.)

N 0657 "Lennon Interview On Radio Today."
New York Times (December 14, 1980)
pp1-01:2.
(Lennon's last interview.)

N 0658 "Lennon Invitation." The Times (May 28, 1969)
p5E.
(Invites Prime Minister to "lie in" for
peace.)

N 0659 "Lennon Is Guilty In Narcotic Case; Lawyer
Terms Marijuana Part of Past - Fine Is
$360." New York Times (November 29, 1968)
p54:1.
(Convicted in London.)

N 0660 "Lennon Makes Plea At Close Of Hearing."
New York Times (May 18, 1972) p27:8.
(The Lennons' deportation problems.)

N 0661 "A Lennon Memorial." New York Times (December
20, 1980) p24:5.
(Call for 10-minute vigil each Sunday.)

N 0662 "Lennon Murder Charge." The Times (December 24,
1980) p4A.
(Chapman second degree murder charge.)

N 0663 "Lennon Not To Play Christ." The Times
(December 5, 1969) p4F.
(In pop opera by Webber and Rice.)

N 0664 "Lennon Of Beatles Sorry For Making Remark On
Jesus." New York Times (August 12, 1966)
p38:2.

N 0665 "Lennon Offers An Island." The Times (November
14, 1969) p2D.
(To hippy community.)

N 0666 "Lennon On Drug Charge." The Times (October 19,
1968) p1F.

N 0667 Lennon, Peter. "Mersey Beaucoup." Guardian
(January 18, 1964) p5.

N 0668 "Lennon Pictures On Show." The Times (January
23, 1970) p6H.
(Drawings cleared for exhibition in
Detroit.)

N 0669 "Lennon Royalties For Peace." The Times
(January 6, 1970) p1C.
(Song and record royalties to promote
peace.)

N 0670 "The Lennons Applaud The Married State."
The Times (March 22, 1969) p4F.
(John and Yoko.)

N 0671 "Lennons' Final Plea For Residence In U.S."
The Times (July 3, 1972) p5H.
(John Lennon's deportation case.)

N 0672 "Lennons Hurt In Crash." The Times (July 2,
1969) p2C.
(Auto accident in Scotland.)

N 0673 "Lennon's Lithographs Picture His Love Life."
New York Times (January 14, 1970) p42:1.
(Art gallery exhibit and sale.)

N 0674 "Lennons Love U.S." New York Times (March 17,
1972) p47:1. illus.
(U.S. residency problems.)

N 0675 "Lennon Staff Clue In Hampshire Murder
Inquiry." The Times (December 21, 1976)
p3B.
(Lennon staff queried on murder victim.)

N 0676 "Lennon Stay Extended." The Times (March 17,
1972) p7B.
(Can stay in U.S.)

N 0677 "Lennon Sues Government, Alleging Illegal
Wiretaps." New York Times (October 25, 1973)
p53:1.

N 0678 "Lennon Suspect: A Suicide Watch."
Bulletin (Philadelphia) (December 10, 1980)
ppA1,A8.
(Mark Chapman.)

N 0679 "Lennons Win A Skirmish In Battle To Remain In
U.S." New York Times (May 3, 1972) p14:4.

N 0680 "Lennons Win Court Point." The Times (May 3,
       1972) p6G.
            (John Lennon's deportation case.)
N 0681 "Lennon To Make Hanratty Film." The Times
       (December 10, 1969) p1F.
            (Film on the A6 murder.)
N 0682 "Lennon To Pay." The Times (February 12, 1970)
       p2B.
            (To pay fines of S. African rugby team
            protestors.)
N 0683 "Lennon To Sing To Peace." New York Times
       (August 24, 1969) p6:1.
            (Lennons plan Mid-East radio broadcast.)
N 0684 Leo, John. "Educators Urged To Heed Beatles;
       Music's Relevance To U.S. Life Is Tanglewood
       Topic." New York Times (July 25, 1967)
       p29:1.
N 0685 Leonard, John. "'Lennon Energized High Art With
       Pop'." New York Times II (December 14, 1980)
       p1:1. illus.
            (Eulogy.)
N 0686 Lester, Elenore. "Intermedia: Tune In, Turn On
       - And Walk Out?" New York Times VI
       (May 12, 1968) p30. illus.
            (Influence of Beatles and others on new
            art.)
N 0687 Lewis, Anthony. "Lawsuit Spells Breakup For
       Beatles." New York Times (January 1, 1971)
       p18:1. illus.
            (Paul McCartney sues in London court.)
N 0688 Lewis, Anthony. "Queen's Honors List Includes
       The Beatles." New York Times (June 12, 1965)
       p1:8.
            (Queen names Beatles M.B.E. recipients.)
N 0689 Lewis, Frederick. "Britons Succumb To
       Beatlemania." New York Times Magazine
       (December 1, 1963) pp124-126. illus.
N 0690 Lichtenstein, Grace. "40,000 Cheer 2 Beatles In
       Dual Benefit For Pakistanis."
       New York Times (August 2, 1971) p1:1. illus.
            (Concert for Bangladesh.)
N 0691 Lichtenstein, Grace. "If There's Mercy, 'I'd
       Like It, Please'." New York Times IV
       (May 21, 1972) p11:1. illus.
            (More on the Lennons' deportation case.)
N 0692 Lichtenstein, Grace. "U.S. Orders Lennon Out,
       But Yoko May Remain." New York Times
       (March 24, 1973) p20:1. illus.
N 0693 "Life Without Lennon." Sunday Times (May 3,
       1981) p13. illus.
            (Interview with Yoko Ono.)
N 0694 "Linda's Other Love Life." Sunday Times
       (September 26, 1982) p28C. illus.
            (Linda McCartney interview.)
N 0695 Lindsey, Robert. "Shooting Of Reagan Is Leading
       Notables To Increase Security Against
       Assassins." New York Times (May 8, 1981)
       p21:1.
            (Lennon murder sparks more security.)
N 0696 "Lion In The Pop Jungle." New York Times
       (May 21, 1969) p40:1.
            (Beatles name Allen Klein their manager.)
N 0697 "Liverpool Cellar Clubs Rock To Beat Groups;
       Long-Haired Youths With Guitars Take Charge
       As Cult." New York Times (December 26, 1963)
       p34:1. illus.
            (Cavern Club and Beatle craze described.)
N 0698 "Liverpool Council To Honor Beatles."
       Christian Science Monitor 69 (November 18,
       1977) p21.
N 0699 "Liverpool Sound And The London Roar: The
       Beatles At The Royal Variety Performance."
       Illustrated London News 243 (November 16,
       1963) p829. illus.
N 0700 "Liverpool Vigil Today To Mark Lennon Death."
       New York Times III (December 8, 1981)
       p8:5.
N 0701 Lloyd, Eric. "Reading For Pleasure: A Slice Of
       Lennon." Wall Street Journal (June 3, 1964)
       p18:4.

            (Deals with "In His Own Write.")
N 0702 Lloyd, Jack. "There Was A Life After The
       Beatles, But Not What His Fans Expected."
       Inquirer (Philadelphia) (December 10, 1980)
       ppG3,G15.
N 0703 "Local Group." Liverpool Echo (January 13, 1962)
       p18.
            (On the release of "My Bonnie/The Saints.")
N 0704 Loder, Kurt. "Lennon Stands In The Way Of
       Reunion." Daily News (Philadelphia)
       (October 9, 1979)
            (U.N. concert for Indochinese boat people.)
N 0705 "London Day By Day; Shining On." The Times
       (October 23, 1979) p18D.
            (Guinness award to Paul McCartney.)
N 0706 "London In Brief." The Times (September 1, 1970)
       p3A.
            (Trespasser at McCartney home charged.)
N 0707 "London's Beatles." Wall Street Journal
       (December 14, 1967) p1:5.
            (Opening of Apple Boutique.)
N 0708 "Long Hair Discussion."
       Christian Science Monitor 58 (March 31, 1966)
       p23.
N 0709 "Long Hair For Boys."
       Christian Science Monitor 58 (March 1, 1966)
       p15.
N 0710 "Lord Atlee Leaves £6,700." The Times
       (January 6, 1968) p1F.
            (Brian Epstein's estate discussed.)
N 0711 "'Love Beatles'." New York Times VI (March 8,
       1964) p4.
            (Letter/reply to David Dempsey's Feb. 23
            article.)
N 0712 "Love It And Leave It." New York Times
       (May 2, 1972) p42:1.
            (The Lennons' deportation problems.)
N 0713 "L 7 Gets Beatle Brush."
       Christian Science Monitor 56 (January 22,
       1964) p5.
N 0714 Lubasch, Arnold H. "Deportation Of Lennon
       Barred By Court Of Appeals." New York Times
       (October 8, 1975) p42:1.
            (Drug convictions not adequate grounds.)
N 0715 McCartney, Paul and Alan Aldridge. "A Good
       Guru's Guide To The Beatles Sinister
       Songbook." Observer (November 26, 1967)
       pp26-33. illus.
N 0716 "McCartney And Jackson Record With Quincy
       Jones." Daily News (Philadelphia) (May 5,
       1982) p50.
            (Michael Jackson.)
N 0717 "McCartney And Wife Sued On 'Another Day'
       Recording." New York Times (July 23, 1971)
       p15:3.
            (Northern Songs and Maclen Music sue.)
N 0718 "McCartney Asked To Waive 'On, Wisconsin,'
       Royalties." New York Times II (January 21,
       1981) p10:3.
            (State Governor asks song royalty waiver.)
N 0719 "McCartney Calls A Rumor On Marriage Plans 'A
       Joke'." New York Times (August 27, 1966)
       p18:6.
            (Seattle concert.)
N 0720 "McCartney Coast Dates Sell Out Unannounced."
       New York Times (March 26, 1976) p24:1.
            (Two Los Angeles Wings' concerts.)
N 0721 "McCartney Forms New Group."
       Christian Science Monitor 63 (November 10,
       1971) p5.
N 0722 "M'Cartney In Scotland." New York Times
       (October 25, 1969) p16:3. illus.
            (Glasgow visit.)
N 0723 "McCartney Keeping Rights To Wisconsin's State
       Song." New York Times III (February 20, 1981)
       pp24-5.
            (Rejects plea from State Governor.)
N 0724 "McCartney Marries, Teen-Age Fans Weep."
       New York Times (March 13, 1969) p53:1.
            (McCartney weds; Harrison and wife arrested.)

N 0725 "McCartney Memory." Inquirer (Philadelphia)
(April 23, 1982) p2C.
(McCartney wished reconciliation with
Lennon.)

N 0726 "McCartney: Packing Pot Was Stupid."
The Bulletin (Philadelphia) (June 1, 1980)
(Arrested in Japan.)

N 0727 "McCartney Postpones Concert Tour Of U.S."
New York Times (March 29, 1976) p35:4.
(Due to Jimmy McCulloch's fractured
finger.)

N 0728 "McCartney Split With Beatles Denied."
The Times (April 10, 1970) p1G.

N 0729 "McCartney Stays In Detention For Questioning."
The Times (January 19, 1980) p5B.
(Ten day detention in Japan.)

N 0730 "McCartney Tells Why He Left." The Times
(April 11, 1970) p1A.
(Quits Beatles.)

N 0731 "McCartney Tour Off And He Goes Back To Jail."
The Times (January 18, 1980) p9D.
(Detained in Japan.)

N 0732 "McCartney, Wings To Benefit Venice."
New York Times (September 1, 1976) p40:2.
(Venice concert set Sept. 25.)

N 0733 McCormick, L.D. "Filling The World With 'Silly
Love Songs'." Christian Science Monitor 68
(June 3, 1976) p23.
("Wings At The Speed Of Sound" album.)

N 0734 McCoy, Craig R. "400 Gather In Vigil For
Lennon." Bulletin (Philadelphia) (December
10, 1980) pA7.

N 0735 McDowell, Edwin. "Publisher-Agent Dispute Ends
Lennon Book Deal." New York Times (December
26, 1981) p29:1.

N 0736 McEwen, Ritchie. "Lennon In A Sack In
Sacher's." The Times (April 2, 1969)
p6A. illus.
(John Lennon's Vienna press conference.)

N 0737 McFadden, Robert D. "Half-Staff Flags Among
Tributes To John Lennon - World Vigil Set
Tomorrow - Wife In Seclusion."
New York Times (December 13, 1980) p31:6.
illus.

N 0738 McFadden, Robert D. "Legions Of Lennon Admirers
To Join In Tributes Today." New York Times
(December 14, 1980) p43:1.
(Vigils around the world.)

N 0739 McFadden, Robert D. "Lennon's Accused Slayer
Ends 2-Day Hunger Strike At Riker's Island."
New York Times II (December 15, 1980)
p8:3.
(Chapman fears poisoning.)

N 0740 McGregor, Craig. "'So In The End, The Beatles
Have Proved False Prophets'."
New York Times II (June 14, 1970) p13:1.
(Beatles breakup.)

N 0741 McKenzie, M. "Ex-Beatle Harrison's In Town -
With A Difference: He Arrived On Time
Without 'An Entrance'."
Christian Science Monitor 69 (December 6,
1976) p34.

N 0742 "Madison Square Ovation For Two Beatles."
The Times (August 2, 1971) p4A.
(Concert for Bangla Desh.)

N 0743 Maitland, Leslie. "John Lennon Wins His
Residency In U.S." New York Times (July 28,
1976) p16:4. illus.

N 0744 "Makes Queen's List." New York Times (June 12,
1965) p9:2. illus.
(George Harrison.)

N 0745 "Man Accused Of Lennon Killing To Plead
Insanity." The Times (January 7, 1981)
p5A.

N 0746 Mann, William. "The Beatles Revive Hopes Of
Progress In Pop Music." The Times (May 29,
1967) p9.

N 0747 Mann, William. "Paul Goes Solo And Shows
Talent." The Times (April 17, 1970)
p17G. illus.

N 0748 Mann, William. "Strong As Ever; Let It Be."
The Times (May 8, 1970) p9G.
(Beatles' final film.)

N 0749 Mann, William. "Those Inventive Beatles."
The Times (December 5, 1969) p7F.
(On the "Abbey Road" album.)

N 0750 Mann, William. "Without Paul, No Beatles."
The Times (April 11, 1970) p8H.

N 0751 "Manson Wants To Call Beatle." The Times
(October 29, 1970) p7C.
(John Lennon sought as Manson trial
witness.)

N 0752 Marks, J. "No, No, No, Paul McCartney Is Not
Dead." New York Times II (November 2, 1969)
p13:1. illus.

N 0753 Marley, Christopher. "ATV Wins Northern Songs."
The Times (May 20, 1969) p21D.

N 0754 Marling, Susan. "John Lennon Drive Forever."
The Times (August 17, 1982) p8B. illus.
(Housing tract has Beatle street names.)

N 0755 Marshall, Rita. "A Time For Fasting For Biafra
Protestors." The Times (December 27, 1969)
p2B.
(The Lennons' Christmas fast.)

N 0756 Maschler, Tom. "Within Living Memory."
The Times (February 26, 1968) p9G.
(Correspondence.)

N 0757 Maslin, Janet. "Screen: 'Caveman' With Ringo
Starr." New York Times III (April 17, 1981)
p9:3.

N 0758 Mathews, Carol. "235M Estate, & Yoko Gets The
Credit." Post (New York) (December 10, 1980)
p4.
(John Lennon's estate.)

N 0759 Maxwell, Neville. "The Beatles Follow An Old
Pilgrims' Road." The Times (October 14, 1967)
p9G.

N 0760 "Meaning OBE & MBE." Christian Science Monitor 57
(August 19, 1965) p1.

N 0761 Melly, George. "Homage From A Fallen Idol."
Observer Colour Supplement (September 8,
1968) p26+.

N 0762 "A Mercy Plea By John Lennon At U.S. Hearing."
The Times (May 18, 1972) p8E.
(John Lennon's deportation case.)

N 0763 Mills, Nancy. "John, Paul, George, Ringo ...
And Linda." Guardian (December 18, 1974)
p9. illus.

N 0764 Millstein, Ezra. "My Experiment With Truth, Or
- The Search For The Perfect Guru."
New York Times X (April 4, 1971) p1. illus.
(Author's visit to Beatles' guru in India.)

N 0765 "Miss Eleanor Bron In Beatles Film." The Times
(February 9, 1965) p8A.
("Help.")

N 0766 "Mr. Alun Owen's Film Script For Beatles."
The Times (October 31, 1963) p17B.
("A Hard Day's Night.")

N 0767 "Mr. Klein Breaks With The Beatles." The Times
(April 3, 1973) p6H.
(Allen Klein severs ties to Apple.)

N 0768 "Mr. Reagan's Way To Deter Death."
New York Times (December 11, 1980) p34:1.
(Against gun control despite Lennon death.)

N 0769 "Mrs. Lennon Sues For Divorce." The Times
(August 23, 1968) p2H.
(Cynthia Lennon.)

N 0770 Montgomery, Paul L. "The Beatles Bring Shea To
A Wild Pitch Of Hysteria." New York Times
(August 24, 1966) p40:1.
(45,000 attend Shea Stadium concert.)

N 0771 Montgomery, Paul L. "Lennon Murder Suspect
Preparing Insanity Defense." New York Times
II (February 9, 1981) p12:3.
(Chapman undergoing mental tests.)

N 0772 Montgomery, Paul L. "Police Trace Tangled Path
Leading To Lennon's Slaying At The Dakota."
New York Times (December 10, 1980) p1:3.
illus.
(Diagram of Lennon's last movements.)

N 0773 Montgomery, Paul L. "Suspect In Lennon's
       Slaying Is Put Under Suicide Watch."
       New York Times II (December 11, 1980)
       p3:5.
          (Lennon's body is cremated.)
N 0774 Montgomery, Paul L. "Teen-Age Siege Of
       Delmonico's, Beatles' Fortress, Ends 2d
       Day." New York Times (August 30, 1964)
       p95:5.
N 0775 Moorhouse, Geoffrey. "Screaming Money."
       Guardian (April 1, 1964) p9. illus.
N 0776 "More Adventures In Penny Lane." The Times
       (April 29, 1969) p27A.
          (Northern Songs.)
N 0777 "More Protests Over The Beatles." The Times
       (June 22, 1965) p10G.
          (M.B.E. awards returned in protest.)
N 0778 Morrison, Blake. "Sound Of The Sixties."
       Times Literary Supplement (May 15, 1981)
       p547A. illus.
          (Reviews of four Beatle books.)
N 0779 Morse, Steve. "The Beatles: In The Beginning,
       There Was Violence."
       Daily News (Philadelphia) (May 19, 1982)
       p44.
          (On Jurgen Vollmer and Hamburg days.)
N 0780 "MP Suggested Cricket Pitch Demonstrations."
       The Times (August 11, 1972) p3H.
          (John Lennon implicated in Peter Hain
          case.)
N 0781 "Munich Court Says Music."
       Christian Science Monitor 58 (July 19, 1966)
       p2.
N 0782 Murphy, Karen and Ronald Gross. "'All You Need
       Is Love. Love Is All You Need'."
       New York Times (April 13, 1969) p36. illus.
          (Lennon/McCartney lyrics analyzed.)
N 0783 Murray, John. "John Lennon's Music Will Never
       Die." The Denver Post (December 15, 1980)
          (Eulogy.)
N 0784 "Murray Kaufman, Radio's '5th Beatle'."
       Inquirer (Philadelphia) (February 23, 1982)
       p7C.
          (Obituary.)
N 0785 "'Murray The K' Dies Of Cancer."
       Daily News (Philadelphia) (February 22, 1982)
       p44.
          (Obituary.)
N 0786 "Musicke: Olde Mersey; 'Baroque Beatles Book'
       Opened in Concert." New York Times
       (May 16, 1966) p42:1.
          (Concert of Beatles songs in Baroque
          style.)
N 0787 "The Music The Beatles Recorded."
       Inquirer (Philadelphia) (December 10, 1980)
       pG2.
N 0788 Narmetz, Aljean. "Revised 'Heaven's Gate'
       Collapses At Box Office." New York Times III
       (April 28, 1981) p7:6.
          (Small mention of ailing "Caveman"
          showings.)
N 0789 "National's Triple Bill: In His Own Write."
       The Times (June 19, 1968) p11B.
          (Lennon's stage play.)
N 0790 "New Beatles Film." The Times (April 24, 1970)
       p15D.
          ("Let It Be.")
N 0791 "News In Brief; American Tour For Beatles."
       The Times (April 9, 1966) p6F.
N 0792 "News In Brief; Awards To Beatles." The Times
       (July 14, 1965) p5E.
          (Ivor Novello Award.)
N 0793 "News In Brief; Beatle Leaves Hospital."
       The Times (December 11, 1964) p7D.
          (Ringo Starr.)
N 0794 "News In Brief; Beatles Beat." The Times
       (April 29, 1964) p10B.
          (Edinburgh visit.)
N 0795 "News In Brief; Ready For Australia."
       The Times (June 12, 1964) p7A.

N 0796 "A New Slant On Disco And Reggae."
       The Bulletin (Philadelphia) (March 18, 1979)
          (On McCartney's "Goodnight Tonight.")
N 0797 "Newspaper Sued." The Times (June 3, 1972)
       p3A.
          (John Lennon versus "News of the World.")
N 0798 "New View Of Northern Songs." The Times
       (November 6, 1968) p26E.
          (Accounts.)
N 0799 "Next Phase For Northern Songs." The Times
       (May 17, 1969) p12E.
N 0800 Nichols, L. "In And Out Of Books; The Writing
       Beatle." New York Times Book Review
       (April 12, 1964) p8.
          (John Lennon.)
N 0801 "No Beatle Wigs In The Dining Room." The Times
       (February 10, 1964) p8E.
          (First U.S. visit.)
N 0802 "No Guard For The Beatles." The Times
       (June 26, 1964) p6G.
          (Regiment refuses to protect The Beatles.)
N 0803 "No Injunction To Stop Alleged Offence."
       The Times (April 7, 1977) p18F.
          (Release of early recordings not banned.)
N 0804 Norman, Philip. "The Beatle Business."
       Sunday Times Magazine (January 11, 1970)
       p8+. illus.
N 0805 Norman, Philip. "The Beatles: The True Story."
       Sunday Times Magazine (March 29, 1981)
       p24+.
          (Begins four excerpts from "Shout!")
N 0806 Norman, Philip. "The Beatles: The True Story -
       2." Sunday Times Magazine (April 5, 1981)
       p33a. illus.
          (Second excerpt from "Shout!")
N 0807 Norman, Philip. "The Beatles: The True Story -
       3." Sunday Times Magazine (April 12, 1981)
       p55a. illus.
          (Third excerpt from "Shout!")
N 0808 Norman, Philip. "The Beatles: The True Story -
       4." Sunday Times Magazine (April 19, 1981)
       p32a. illus.
          (Final excerpt from "Shout!")
N 0809 Norman, Philip. "I Was Never Lovable, I Was
       Just Lennon." Sunday Times (December 14,
       1980) p33+. illus.
N 0810 Norman, Philip. "Life Without Lennon."
       Sunday Times (May 3, 1981) p13. illus.
          (Interview with Yoko Ono.)
N 0811 Norman, Philip. "Shout! My Quest For The True
       Story Of The Beatles." Sunday Times
       (March 22, 1981) p35A. illus.
N 0812 "Northern Songs: ATV Near Victory." The Times
       (September 20, 1969) p11A.
N 0813 "Northern Songs Director Resigns." The Times
       (August 15, 1970) p16E.
          (Dick James.)
N 0814 "Northern Songs Gets Another Beatle."
       The Times (August 28, 1965) p11F.
N 0815 "Northern Songs Reports Rise In Fiscal '67
       Earnings." Wall Street Journal (October 26,
       1967) p6:2.
          (Earns nearly 1.5 million dollars.)
N 0816 "Northern Songs Talks Continue." The Times
       (September 24, 1969) p22G.
          (Northern Songs.)
N 0817 "Northern Songs 3 1/2 Times Covered."
       The Times (February 20, 1965) p15G.
N 0818 "Noted Musicians To Aid Venice."
       New York Times (September 2, 1976) p25:4.
          (Including Paul McCartney and Wings.)
N 0819 "Notes On People." New York Times (July 28,
       1971) p31:1.
          (Concert for Bangladesh.)
N 0820 "Notes On People." New York Times (September
       10, 1971) p32:6.
          (Lennon in Dick Cavett TV interview.)
N 0821 "Notes On People." New York Times (January 12,
       1972) p33:2.
          (Ringo Starr ill.)

(The Lennons attend murder trial.)

N 0822 "Notes On People." New York Times (March 4,
1972) p21:5.
(Yoko Ono awarded daughter's custody.)

N 0823 "Notes On People." New York Times (September
30, 1972) p29:4.
(Paul McCartney's dog problems.)

N 0824 "Notes On People." New York Times (March 9,
1973) p47:3.
(McCartney fined $240 for growing
marijuana.)

N 0825 "Notes On People." New York Times (April 4,
1973) p39:2.
(Ringo Starr rules out reunion.)

N 0826 "Notes On People." New York Times (November 2,
1973) p37:3.
(Lennon seeks deportation stay.)

N 0827 "Notes On People." New York Times (October 25,
1974) p35:7.
(Harrison announces first tour in 8 years.)

N 0828 "Not Getting Together Despite $50 Million
Offer." Christian Science Monitor 68
(March 31, 1976) p13.

N 0829 "Now In United States."
Christian Science Monitor 56 (February 8,
1964) p15.

N 0830 "Now It's John Ono Lennon." New York Times
(April 23, 1969) p41:4.
(Lennon changes middle name.)

N 0831 "No Wonder The Girls Cry."
Christian Science Monitor 58 (March 26, 1966)
p4.

N 0832 "N Songs Hearing Postponed." The Times
(October 2, 1969) p21D.
(Northern Songs panel hearing.)

N 0833 "Obituary: Mr. Brian Epstein: Record Request
Led Him To Fame With The Beatles."
The Times (August 28, 1967) p8F.

N 0834 "Obscurity At Northern Songs." The Times
(May 3, 1969) p14E.

N 0835 O'Connor, Gillian. "ATV Bids £9.5 M For
Northern Songs." The Times (March 29, 1969)
p13E.

N 0836 O'Connor, John J. "TV: McCartney And His Group
On A.B.C. Tonight; Direct Approach Fits
Former Beatle Best." New York Times
(April 16, 1973) p75:1.

N 0837 "Off-Beat Film On Beatles; London Pavilon: A
Hard Day's Night." The Times (July 7, 1964)
p15E.

N 0838 "Ohio Girls Rush Beatles And Police Interrupt
Show." New York Times (September 16, 1964)
p36:1.
(Cleveland concert.)

N 0839 Oliver, Chris. "Hawaii Gun Store Draws Their
Fury." Post (New York) (December 10, 1980)
p3,51.
(Source of Chapman murder gun.)

N 0840 Oliver, Chris. "Suspect's Dad In Shock - 'He
Loved The Beatles'." Post (New York)
(December 18, 1980) p51.
(Mark Chapman.)

N 0841 "100 Casualities In Beatles Queue." The Times
(November 25, 1963) p14E.
(100 injured buying tickets.)

N 0842 "$150,000 For Book On Beatles." The Times
(February 21, 1968) p1G.
(Hunter Davies' U.S. rights sold.)

N 0843 "100,000 Welcome Beatles Home." The Times
(July 11, 1964) p8G.
(Visit to Liverpool.)

N 0844 "$1 M. Lawsuit In Beatles Firm." The Times
(December 9, 1964) p10E.
(U.S. law suit against Seltaeb.)

N 0845 "$1,000 Lennon Award Established At U.C.L.A."
New York Times III (December 8, 1982)
p29:3.
(Annual graduate research award.)

N 0846 "Open-Air Film Show Rejected." The Times
(September 23, 1969) p5B.

(John Lennon in banned film.)

N 0847 "The Order Of The British Empire; The Prime
Minister's List." The Times (June 12, 1965)
p7D+.
(M.B.E.s.)

N 0848 Osbourn, H.J.I. "What Songs The Beatles Sang."
The Times (December 30, 1963) p9G.
(Letter; reply to Dec. 27 article.)

N 0849 Osmundsen, John A. "4 Beatles And How They
Grew; Peoplewise." New York Times (February
17, 1964) p1:5.

N 0850 "Palace Search For BEM." The Times (November
28, 1969) p1H.
(John Lennon returns M.B.E.)

N 0851 Palmer, Raymond. "How Apple Turned Sour."
Observer (April 6, 1969) p11.

N 0852 Palmer, Robert. "Grammy For Yoko Ono Stirs
Awards Ceremony." New York Times III
(February 25, 1982) p17:5.
("Double Fantasy" LP.)

N 0853 Palmer, Robert. "Lennon Known Both As Author
And Composer." New York Times II (December
9, 1980) p7:6.
(Obituary.)

N 0854 Palmer, Robert. "McCartney's Wings Bring
National Tour To Garden." New York Times
(May 25, 1976) p43:1.

N 0855 Palmer, Robert. "More Lennon In Offing."
New York Times III (June 17, 1981) p25:2.
("Milk And Honey" LP.)

N 0856 Palmer, Robert. "Paul McCartney's Latest Is
Exquisite But Flawed." New York Times II
(April 25, 1982) pp11,19. illus.
("Tug Of War" LP.)

N 0857 Palmer, Robert. "The Real Way To Remember
Lennon." New York Times III (December 9,
1981) p23:1. illus.

N 0858 Palmer, Robert. "Record: Yoko Ono, Solo."
New York Times III (May 20, 1981) p27:5.
("Season Of Glass" LP.)

N 0859 Palmer, Robert. "Two Icons Of Rock Music."
New York Times II (May 31, 1981) p23:1.
illus.

N 0860 Palmer, Robert. "Yoko Ono Asks, 'Was I Supposed
To Avoid The Subject?'" New York Times III
(August 5, 1981) p17:1.
(Interview.)

N 0861 Palmer, Robert. "Yoko Ono On Her Own 'Walking
On Thin Ice'." New York Times III (February
4, 1981) p17:1. illus.

N 0862 Palmer, Tony. "A Is For Apple."
Observer Colour Supplement (September 1,
1968) pp7-13,15. illus.

N 0863 "Panel Discusses ATV's New Move." The Times
(September 23, 1969) p19H.
(Northern Songs.)

N 0864 "Paperback Preview." Sunday Times (March 1,
1981) p43B.
(On Connolly's "John Lennon.")

N 0865 Pard, Richard F. "Stokowski Talks Of Something
Called Beatles; Conductor And Teen-Agers
Hold Dialogue At Carnegie On British
Phenomenon." New York Times (February 15,
1964) p13:5. illus.

N 0866 "Parliament; Beatle Arrest." The Times
(October 25, 1968) p16G.
(John Lennon's drug charge.)

N 0867 "Paterson Submarine Painted Beatle Yellow By
Pranksters." New York Times (February 11,
1969) p63:3.
("Fenian's Ram," world's first sub,
painted yellow.)

N 0868 "Pattern Of Training For Automation; Social
Effects Of Less Work." The Times (June 20,
1964) p6E.
(John Lennon discussed in Parliament.)

N 0869 "Paul McCartney Arrested In Tokyo." The Times
(January 17, 1980) p8F. illus.
(Marijuana possession.)

N 0870 "Paul McCartney Fined For Growing Cannabis."

The Times (March 9, 1973) p6F.
(Marijuana grown on Scottish farm.)

N 0871 "Paul McCartney: New Recording."
Christian Science Monitor 67 (July 17, 1975)
p26.

N 0872 "Paul McCartney Predicts Breakup Of Beatles
Soon." New York Times (January 23, 1967)
p29:1.
(Interview.)

N 0873 "Paul McCartney Punished Enough, Japanese Say."
The Times (January 26, 1980) p5E. illus.
(Deported from Japan.)

N 0874 "Paul McCartney: Tour By Ex-Beatle."
Christian Science Monitor 68 (July 3, 1976)
p23.

N 0875 "Paul: Reunion Ruled Out."
Daily News (Philadelphia) (October 7, 1982)
p40.
(BBC interview.)

N 0876 "Peace And Love." New York Times (December 28,
1971) p28:4.
(Lennons reply to M. T. Cohen Dec. 17
piece.)

N 0877 "Peer To Question Beatles' M.B.E.s." The Times
(June 19, 1965) p6B.

N 0878 "Pennsylvania Move To Ban Beatles." The Times
(August 8, 1966) p6D.
(Religious remark made by John Lennon.)

N 0879 "Penny Lane For A Song." The Times (April 1,
1967) p11A.

N 0880 "Penny Lane For A Song." The Times (April 5,
1967) p13G.
(Reply to April 1 article.)

N 0881 Phillips, McCandlish. "Concentration Of
Squealing Teen-Agers Noted At Hotel;
Phenomenon Traced to English Quartet Called
Beatles." New York Times (August 29, 1964)
p9:1.

N 0882 Phillips, McCandlish. "4 Beatles And How They
Grew; Publicitywise." New York Times
(February 17, 1964) p1:3.

N 0883 Pick, Hella. "Beatle Hysteria Hits U.S."
Guardian (February 8, 1964) p1.

N 0884 "The Pick Of The Year." The Times (February 26,
1982) p5D.
("Double Fantasy" LP.)

N 0885 Pile, Stephen. "For Sale: First Beatles
Record." Sunday Times (July 5, 1981)
p32A.
(McCartney bid rejected.)

N 0886 "Pinning Them Down - If You Can."
Christian Science Monitor 60 (May 20, 1968)
p4.

N 0887 "Plea By Beatles To Stop Records." The Times
(April 6, 1977) p2E.
(Seek ban on release of early recordings.)

N 0888 "Plea By Music Company Fails." The Times
(February 18, 1972) p2D.
(Northern Songs versus Paul McCartney.)

N 0889 "Police Halt Beatles' Show To Avoid Riot In
Australia." New York Times (June 13, 1964)
p14:1.
(Adelaide, Australia; second concert.)

N 0890 "Police Protection For The Beatles." The Times
(November 22, 1963) p15F.
(Police protection in London.)

N 0891 "Police Seize Lennon Prints In Raid."
The Times (January 17, 1970) p3A.
(Lithograph exhibit.)

N 0892 "Police To Study Pills Found In Home Of
Beatles' Mentor." New York Times (August 29,
1967) p5:5.
(Brian Epstein.)

N 0893 Pollack, Lynn. "'Enjoying Beatles'."
New York Times VI (March 15, 1964)
p12.
(Letter/reply to David Dempsey's Feb. 23
article.)

N 0894 "Pop Scene." Christian Science Monitor 60
(December 27, 1968) p15.

N 0895 "'Pot Smoked By Beatles At Palace'." The Times
(March 23, 1970) p1D.
(Lennon's Buckingham Palace visit.)

N 0896 Pountney, Kate. "Beatle Crush." Guardian
(November 6, 1963) p7.

N 0897 "Presley Tops Hit Parade On Beatles' Home
Grounds." New York Times (June 10, 1965)
p38:6.
("Crying in the Chapel" beats out Beatles.)

N 0898 Price, John. "Beatles Apple Sets Legal Poser."
The Times (December 13, 1967) pp22C-22D.
illus.
(Apple Boutique discussed.)

N 0899 "Probe Into Mystery Death Of City Student."
Liverpool Echo (April 14, 1962) p10. illus.
(Stuart Sutcliffe.)

N 0900 Prochman, Bill. "Chapman: Man Who Stopped The
Music." Inquirer (Philadlephia) (December
10, 1980) pA14.

N 0901 "Profit From Beatles." The Times (March 4, 1964)
p5E.
(Airport admission charges for return from
U.S.)

N 0902 "Protest By Councilman Blocks Lennon Tribute."
New York Times II (December 19, 1980)
p2:6.
(Silent tribute by the Council nixed.)

N 0903 "Publishers Sue Lennons For £400,000 Damages."
The Times (January 24, 1973) p10A.
(Northern Songs sues.)

N 0904 "Publishers Sue Mr. McCartney." The Times
(July 26, 1971) p9E.
(Northern Songs sues.)

N 0905 "QC Fears Beatles Cash May Not Meet Tax."
The Times (January 20, 1971) p1H+.

N 0906 "Queen Confers Medals."
Christian Science Monitor 57 (October 27,
1965) p5.
(The Beatles' M.B.E.s.)

N 0907 "Queen's Decoration."
Christian Science Monitor 57 (July 26, 1965)
p13.
(The Beatles' M.B.E.s.)

N 0908 "Quiet Crowd Greets Beatles In Canada."
New York Times (August 23, 1964) p85:8.
(Vancouver, B.C.)

N 0909 Quindlen, Anna. "Imagine All The People
Mourning In The Rain." New York Times II
(December 9, 1981) p2:1. illus.
(Central Park tribute.)

N 0910 Radel, Cliff. "Will You Still Love 'Em When
They're 64?" The Cincinnati Enquirer
(August 26, 1979) pH-7.
(A review of The Beatles' past 15 years.)

N 0911 Radford, Penny. "R & R Steel The Show."
The Times (September 9, 1971) p12A. illus.
(Ringo Starr's designs.)

N 0912 Radford, Penny. "Roundup." The Times (May 6,
1971) p15H. illus.
(Ringo Starr designs "kinetic sculpture.")

N 0913 "Rally For John Lennon On Lenin Hills Upsets
Police." The Times (December 22, 1980)
p4F.
(Soviet police break up Moscow rally.)

N 0914 Ramachandra, C.P. "Top Of The Class - Beatle
George." Observer (February 25, 1968)
p3.

N 0915 "Random Notes From All Over: 'Golden Beatles'."
New York Times (March 2, 1964) p11:1.
(Beatles foreign exchange earnings.)

N 0916 Ranzal, Edward. "Program Sellers For Beatles
Held; 2 Seized By U.S. On Charge Of Being
Bookies Here." New York Times (August 17,
1965) p36:3.
(Beatles' program sellers arrested.)

N 0917 Raymont, Henry. "McGraw-Hill Wins Book On
Beatles; Pays $125,000 To Publish Authorized
Biography." New York Times (February 21,
1968) p44:4.
(Hunter Davies' book.)

N 0918 Raynor, Henry. "Beatles' Anarchic Mystery."
         The Times (December 27, 1967) p11A.
           (On the "Magical Mystery Tour" film.)
N 0919 "Receiver For Beatles Would Be Disaster, QC
         Says." The Times (March 4, 1971) p2D.
           (Law case to dissolve Beatles.)
N 0921 "Record Album Covers." Wall Street Journal
         (July 24, 1969) p1:5.
           (Lennons' "Two Virgins" LP seized in New
           Jersey.)
N 0922 "Records For Christmas."
         Christian Science Monitor 57 (December 4,
         1965) p14.
N 0923 "Red Rap Beatles." Christian Science Monitor 57
         (August 12, 1965) p10.
           (Communist China knocks The Beatles.)
N 0924 Reid, C. "Ravi Shankar And George Beatles."
         New York Times Magazine (May 7, 1967)
         pp28-29+. illus.
N 0925 Reif, Rita. "Auctions." New York Times III
         (December 4, 1981) p24:6.
           (Lennon lithographs to be sold.)
N 0926 Rense, Rip. "'Lost' Beatles Songs Uncovered."
         Los Angeles Herald Examiner (December 10,
         1981) pB1+.
           (Twelve unreleased studio tracks at EMI,
           London.)
N 0927 "Report On Lennon." The Times (February 11,
         1970) p3B.
           (Lithograph report sent to Public
           Prosecutions.)
N 0928 Reusch, V., Mrs. "Beatles Analyzed."
         New York Times VI (April 5, 1964) p10.
           (Letter/reply to letter of March 15.)
N 0929 "Revolution." Wall Street Journal (December 10,
         1980) p30:1.
           (John Lennon obituary.)
N 0930 "Revolutionary Force 9 Recalls Beatles' Song."
         New York Times (March 13, 1970) p26:7.
           ("Revolution 9" source of terrorist group
           name.)
N 0931 Reynolds, Stanley. "Big Time." Guardian
         (June 3, 1963) p10. illus.
N 0932 Rich, Frank. "Growing Up With The Beatles."
         New York Times II (December 14, 1980)
         p30:4.
           (Personal memoir.)
N 0933 Rich, Frank. "Stage: 'Lennon, A Biography,'
         Opens." New York Times III (October 6, 1982)
         p23:3. illus.
           (Theatrical production.)
N 0934 Ricks, Christopher. "Raising The Gaity Of
         Nations." Sunday Times (April 5, 1981)
         p43C. illus.
           (On Philip Norman's "Shout!")
N 0935 "Ringo Starr And Barbara Bach Marry In London."
         New York Times II (April 28, 1981) p8:1.
         illus.
N 0936 "Ringo Starr Decree." The Times (July 18, 1975)
         p3H.
           (Wife Maureen granted divorce.)
N 0937 "Ringo Starr Discusses TV Debut On NBC Special
         'Ringo'." Los Angeles Times II (April 19,
         1978) p5.
N 0938 "Ringo Starr In Hospital." New York Times
         (September 10, 1969) p36:3.
           (Stomach pains.)
N 0939 "Ringo Starr Of Beatles Survives Tonsilectomy."
         New York Times (December 3, 1964) p58:2.
           (Operated on in London.)
N 0940 "Ringo Starr Plays Tennis In South Africa."
         Christian Science Monitor 67 (October 6,
         1975) p10.
N 0941 "Ringo Starr, The Former Beatle, With Barbara
         Bach, ... " The Times (April 28, 1981)
         p2F. illus.

         (Marriage photo.)
N 0942 "Roberta Flack Wins Two Grammies For Her
         Records." New York Times (March 5, 1973)
         p22:1.
           (George Harrison wins award.)
N 0943 Roberts, Richard. "'Yesterday' Mourning Before
         Sunrise." Bulletin (Philadelphia) (December
         10, 1980)
           (Eulogy.)
N 0944 Robinson, David. "Cinema." The Times (July 24,
         1981) p11C. illus.
           (On film "Caveman.")
N 0945 "Rock Age Hero." The Times (October 28, 1981)
         p3E. illus.
           (Bronze Lennon statue in Los Angeles.)
N 0946 Rockwell, John. "For $325, A Chance To Assess
         The Legacy Of The Beatles." New York Times
         II:19 (October 24, 1982) p1,26. illus.
N 0947 Rockwell, John. "4,000 Recall Beatles, Yeah,
         Yeah, Yeah." New York Times (September 8,
         1974)
           (Beatlefest 74.)
N 0948 Rockwell, John. "Harrison, Starr Plan A U.S.
         Tour: Former Beatles Will Play In At Least
         12 Cities In Fall." New York Times
         (March 2, 1974) p22:4.
N 0949 Rockwell, John. "Harrison, Starr Plan A U.S.
         Tour: Former Beatles Will Play In At Least
         12 Cities In Fall." New York Times
         (March 2, 1974) p22:4.
N 0950 Rockwell, John. "How The Electric Guitar Became
         A Way Of Music." New York Times (July 15,
         1974) p33:1.
           (Influence of George Harrison and others.)
N 0951 Rockwell, John. "Leader Of A Rock Group That
         Helped Define A Generation." New York Times
         II (December 9, 1980) p7:2. illus.
           (John Lennon; profile, obituary.)
N 0952 Rockwell, John. "McCartney - The Beatle With
         The Charm Is Back." New York Times II
         (May 16, 1976) p1:1. illus.
           (U.S. tour.)
N 0953 Rockwell, John. "Pop Music: Elton John At The
         Gardens; John Lennon Appears, Singing 3
         Pieces." New York Times (November 30, 1974)
         p20:3. illus.
           (John Lennon sings duos with Elton John.)
N 0954 Rockwell, John. "U.S. Tour Of McCartney And
         Wings Is Off To Triumphal Start In Fort
         Worth." New York Times IV (May 5, 1976)
         p50:3.
N 0955 Rooney, Andy. "Why Some Wept For John Lennon."
         The Chicago Tribune (December 21, 1980)
           (Eulogy.)
N 0956 Rosensohn, Sam and David Seifman. "Beatles And
         Bibles, Drifting And Dope." Post (New York)
         (December 10, 1980) p2.
N 0957 Ross, Evelyn. "All They Need Is Rishikesh."
         Guardian (February 29, 1968) p8.
N 0958 Ruane, Micheal E. and Craig R. McCoy. "'Beatles
         Will Last, They'll Never Die.'"
         Bulletin (Philadelphia) (December 9, 1980)
         pA1.
N 0959 "Rubinstein's Fortissimo, Beats, 'Yeah, Yeah,
         Yeah'." New York Times (June 19, 1964)
         p2:7.
           (Melbourne Beatles fans out-shouted.)
N 0960 "Ruling On Song Theft Hints More Suits."
         Christian Science Monitor 68 (November 18,
         1976) p13.
           ("My Sweet Lord" case.)
N 0961 "Rush For New Issues; Northern Songs Response."
         The Times (February 19, 1965) p19D.
N 0962 Ryan, Desmond. "2 Films Are Inspired By
         Beatles' Music." Inquirer (Philadelphia)
         (October 7, 1977) p15.
           (Films by Robert Stigwood and Steven
           Spielberg.)
N 0963 Ryan, Desmond. "'Hard Day's Night': Even
         Better." Inquirer (Philadelphia) (February

5, 1982) p22.
(On the 1981 film re-release.)

N 0964 "Sales Boost For Lennon Prints." The Times
(January 20, 1970) p3B.
(Sales of lithographs greatly increased.)

N 0965 Scanlon, Karen. "Slaying Stuns Concertgoers."
News (Philadelphia) (December 9, 1980)
p4.
(John Lennon.)

N 0966 Schirmer, Gregory A. "Going For Baroque: Young
Swingers Dig The Old Style Music."
Wall Street Journal (July 29, 1966) p1:4.

N 0967 Schmeider, R. "Heroes." Gay Community News 8
(January 17, 1981) p4.

N 0968 Schmidt, Dana Adams. "John, Paul, Ringo And
George, M.B.E.; Beatles Honored By Queen At
Her 'Keen Pad' As Band Plays 'Humoresque'."
New York Times (October 27, 1965) p49:8.
illus.
(Investiture ceremony, Buckingham Palace.)

N 0970 "School Programs Revised In Greece; Athletics
Made Compulsory - History Is Rewritten."
New York Times (October 12, 1969) p27:1.
(Beatle-style hairdos banned.)

N 0971 Schumach, Murray. "Fans Put On Show To Rival
Beatles'; But TV Rehearsal Goes On Despite
Shrieks Of Crowd." New York Times (August
15, 1965) p82:2.

N 0972 Schumach, Murray. "Shrieks Of 55,000 Accompany
Beatles." New York Times (August 16, 1965)
p29:5. illus.
(Shea Stadium concert.)

N 0973 Schumach, Murray. "Teen-Agers (Mostly Female)
And Police Greet Beatles; British Long-Hairs
In City To Begin 3d Tour Of U.S."
New York Times (August 14, 1965) p11:1.
illus.
(Second formal "tour"; third visit.)

N 0974 "'Screwball' Had No Record."
News (Philadelphia) (December 9, 1980)
p3.
(Mark Chapman.)

N 0975 "Seen But Hardly Heard." The Times (December
27, 1963) p4E.
(Christmas Show.)

N 0976 Selvin, Joel. "The Steady Stream Of Beatles
Songs - On The Pop Scene."
San Francisco Chronicle (June 13, 1976)
p31.

N 0977 "Series Of Concerts To Benefit Victims Of
African Famine." New York Times (June 19,
1974) p37:1.
(John Lennon, Ringo Starr said involved.)

N 0978 Shabecoff, Philip. "Beatles Winning In East
Germany; Group Held 'Okay' In Crisis Over
Cultural Freedom." New York Times (April 17,
1966) p64:3.
(Beatles' become East German folk heroes.)

N 0979 Shabecoff, Philip. "Rising Filipino Terrorism
Is Led By 'Monkees' and Huk 'Beatles'."
New York Times (November 25, 1968) p8:4.
(Philippine Huk insurgents name selves
'Beatles'.)

N 0980 Shakespeare, R.W. "Support Growing For UCS
'Strike Pay' Proposal." The Times (August
13, 1971) p2F.
(John Lennon donates 1000 pounds.)

N 0981 "Shares On The Exchange."
Christian Science Monitor 56 (February 19,
1965) p9B.

N 0982 Shearman, Colin. "Beatlemania: Will EMI Let It
Be?" Guardian (May 2, 1981) p11. illus.

N 0983 "Shell Found At Lennon House." The Times
(May 23, 1970) p3F.
(Incendiary shell.)

N 0984 Shelton, Robert. "The Beatles Will Make The
Scene Here Again, But The Scene Has
Changed." New York Times (August 11, 1965)
p40:1. illus.
(Second U.S. tour scheduled.)

N 0985 Shelton, Robert. "Concentration Of Squealing
Teen-Agers Noted At Hotel; Later, At The
Stadium." New York Times (August 29, 1964)
p9:4.
(Forest Hills Stadium.)

N 0986 Shelton, Robert. "4 Singles Make Up First Crop
Of Beatles' Apple Corps Label."
New York Times (August 27, 1968) p36:1.

N 0987 Shepard, Richard F. "Avant Garde Festival Held
At Armory." New York Times (November 20,
1971) p27:1.
(Eight of the Lennons' works entered.)

N 0988 Shepard, Richard F. "Beatles Broaden Role In
Business; Form Concern For Ventures In Films
And Recordings." New York Times (May 15,
1968) p40:1.
(Lennon/McCartney interviewed.)

N 0990 Shipp, E.R. "Attorney For Lennon Slaying
Suspect Bows Out And Gets Protection."
New York Times (December 12, 1980) p1:5.
illus.
(Defense attorney requests replacement.)

N 0991 Shipp, E.R. "Bargaining In Court."
New York Times II (August 31, 1981) p3:1.
(Chapman trial.)

N 0992 Shipp, E.R. "Chapman Given 20 Years In Lennon's
Slaying." New York Times I (August 25, 1981)
p2:4+. illus.

N 0993 Shipp, E.R. "Chapman, In A Closed Courtroom,
Pleads Guilty To Killing Of Lennon."
New York Times (June 23, 1981) p1:3.

N 0994 Shipp, E.R. "Closed Court In Lennon Case Plea
Termed Unusual." New York Times (June 28,
1981) p40:1.

N 0995 Shipp, E.R. "Expert Witness In Two Trials
Accused Of Lying On Training."
New York Times II (October 7, 1981) p9:1.
(Chapman defense psychologist.)

N 0996 Shipp, E.R. "Jury Choice To Be Difficult For
Lennon Trial Defense." New York Times II
(June 18, 1981) p2:5.
(Chapman jury selection begins.)

N 0997 Shipp, E.R. "Voiding Of Lennon Plea Asked."
New York Times IV (July 10, 1981) p15:1.
(Insanity plea sought.)

N 0998 Short, Dan. "Lennon At Large, Part I: The Wild
Ways Of Joker John." Post (New York)
(December 10, 1980) pp35-37.

N 0999 Short, Don. "Lighter Side Of John Lennon."
Los Angeles Times (December 14, 1980)
(Eulogy.)

N 1000 "Short Takes." Berkeley Barb 30 (April 10, 1980)
p2.
(Paul McCartney.)

N 1001 "Shrieks Drown Beatles At Tribunal Recording."
The Times (December 11, 1963) p6E.
(Leeds.)

N 1002 Shuster, Alvin. "McCartney And Wings Give
Venice Benefit." New York Times (September
27, 1976) p40:1.
(UNESCO concert in St. Marks Square.)

N 1003 Shuster, Alvin. "McCartney Breaks Off With
Beatles." New York Times (April 11, 1970)
p21:2. illus.

N 1004 Shuster, Alvin. "Routine British Day: Mail,
Phone, Bank Strikes." New York Times
(January 31, 1969) p8:4.
(Rooftop concerts.)

N 1005 "Sidelights; Yeah, Yeah, Yeah." New York Times
(February 19, 1965) p48:3.
(Northern Songs' public stock offering.)

N 1006 "Sing A British Tune."
Christian Science Monitor 57 (July 1, 1965)
p1.

N 1007 Sloane, Leonard. "Warner May Bid For Beatles
Ties; Talks Expected On Deal For 15% Of
Northern Songs." New York Times (May 7, 1969)
p59:7.

(Warner Brothers-Seven Arts.)

N 1008 Sloane, Leonard. "Yellow Submarine Art Is The
    Thing Today." New York Times III (August 24,
    1969) p15:3.
       ("Yellow Submarine" art style.)

N 1009 Smith, David. "In Beatles' Wake: Novel Sounds,
    Looks Pay Off For Singers."
    Wall Street Journal (March 5, 1965) p1:4.

N 1010 Snyder, M. "The Beat Goes On And On And On."
    Berkeley Barb 30 (April 10, 1980) p11.

N 1011 "Social News: Beatle Marriage." The Times
    (September 9, 1978) p14A.
       (George Harrison.)

N 1012 "Song Company Of Beatles Resists A Take-Over
    Bid." New York Times (May 17, 1969) p46:3.
       (Northern Songs.)

N 1013 "Songs: ATV New Bid." The Times (October 11,
    1969) p13D.
       (ATV bid for Northern Songs.)

N 1014 "Songs: The Beatles Sell." The Times (October
    16, 1969) p25H.
       (The Beatles sell Northern to ATV.)

N 1015 "Sorrow, Tributes Around The World."
    Inquirer (Philadlephia) (December 10, 1980)
    pA15.
       (John Lennon.)

N 1016 "The Sound Of The Sixties." The Times
    (December 10, 1980) p15A.
       (Editorial on the Beatles.)

N 1017 "S. African Radio Ban On Beatles' Records."
    The Times (August 9, 1966) p6G.
       (John Lennon's religious remark.)

N 1018 "Soviet Critic Asserts The Beatles Are Out Of
    Tune With The Times." New York Times
    (December 4, 1968) p10:4.

N 1019 Standora, Leo. "World-Wide They Sing Slain
    Beatle's Praises." Post (New York)
    (December 10, 1980) p4.
       (John Lennon.)

N 1020 "Starr Stir." The Times (December 9, 1982)
    p3A.
       (Seeks grant to improve mansion.)

N 1021 "The Stars Are Shocked After Murder Of Lennon."
    Bulletin (Philadelphia) (December 10, 1980)
    pA8.

N 1022 Stecklow, Steve. "Springsteen, Audience
    Remember John Lennon."
    Bulletin (Philadelphia) (December 10, 1980)
    pA8.

N 1023 "Steele's Own Tribute To The Beatles."
    The Times (December 4, 1982) p3D. illus.
       (Tommy Steele's "Eleanor Rigby" sculpture.)

N 1024 Stevens, M. "Paul McCartney Tour: Optimism
    Bubbles." Christian Science Monitor 68
    (June 3, 1976) p23. illus.

N 1025 "Stock In Beatle Songs Is Cheaper In London."
    New York Times (August 11, 1966) p35:1.
       (Stock value drops due to Lennon's Jesus
    remark.)

N 1027 Strafford, Peter. "Lawyer Argues Against
    Deporting The Lennons." The Times (May 13,
    1972) p5A.
       (John Lennon's deportation case.)

N 1028 Strafford, Peter. "Mr. Lennon Ordered Out Of
    U.S. In 60 Days." The Times (March 24, 1973)
    p1C.
       (John Lennon's deportation case.)

N 1029 Strauss, Robert. "Lennon's Dream Girl."
    News (Philadelphia) (December 9, 1980)
    p20.

N 1030 Strauss, Robert. "Lennon Was Always The
    Leader." News (Philadelphia) (December 9,
    1980) p4,21.

N 1031 "Strawberry Fields Forever."
    The Worcester Telegram (December 10, 1980)
       (Editorial eulogy.)

N 1032 "Strawberry Fields Forever." New York Times
    (August 28, 1981) p23:4.
       (Yoko's letter on park site.)

N 1033 Strongin, Theodore. "Musicologically . . . ."

New York Times (February 10, 1964) p53:2.
    illus.
       (Comments on their music.)

N 1034 "Stunned Fans Hold Sidewalk Wake."
    News (Philadelphia) (December 9, 1980)
    p5.
       (John Lennon.)

N 1035 "Suit By Former Beatles." The Times (November
    3, 1973) p2D.
       (Beatles sue Allen Klein.)

N 1036 "Summons Over Lennon Prints." The Times
    (February 26, 1970) p2E.

N 1037 "Suspect, 25, Indicted In Murder Of Lennon."
    New York Times II (December 24, 1980)
    p3:1.
       (Chapman gets second degree murder.)

N 1038 Sutcliffe, Phil. "How John Lennon Was
    Overwhelmed By Life And Death."
    Northern Echo (December 10, 1980)
       (Eulogy.)

N 1039 Sutton, Larry. "Suspect Had Told A Devotee To
    Try To Get Autograph Soon."
    Inquirer (Philadelphia) (December 10, 1980)
    pA14.
       (Mark Chapman.)

N 1040 Takiff, Jonathan. "Another Lennon LP!"
    Daily News (Philadelphia) (April 6, 1982)
    p35.
       (Lennon's "Milk And Honey" LP.)

N 1041 Takiff, Jonathan. "Beatles Package Airs In May
    On WMMR." Daily News (Philadelphia)
    (April 6, 1982) p35.
       (BBC's 88 "forgotten" tunes to air in U.S.)

N 1042 Takiff, Jonathan. "Lennon Rocked An Era."
    News (Philadelphia) (December 9, 1980)
    p5+.

N 1043 Talese, Gay. "Beatles And Fans Meet Social Set;
    Chic And Shriek Mingle At Paramount Benefit
    Show." New York Times (September 21, 1964)
    p44:1. illus.
       (Paramount Theatre charity performance.)

N 1044 "Tampa, Florida." The Times (August 12, 1964)
    p7A.
       (First U.S. Tour.)

N 1045 "Tape By Hinckley Is Said To Reveal Obsession
    With Slaying Of Lennon." New York Times
    (May 15, 1981) p19:2.
       (Reagan gunman impelled by Chapman act.)

N 1046 "Tax Offences By Manager Of Beatles."
    The Times (February 20, 1971) p1C.
       (Law case to dissolve Beatles.)

N 1047 Taylor, John Russell. "A British Cartoon Film
    That Should Please Nearly Everyone."
    The Times (July 18, 1968) p7A.
       ("Yellow Submarine.")

N 1048 Taylor, John Russell. "Odeon, Kensington:
    Candy." The Times (February 20, 1969)
    p15G.
       (The film "Candy.")

N 1049 Taylor, John Russell. "Revolution Finds Andy
    Hardy." The Times (May 22, 1970) p7B.
       (On the "Let It Be" album.)

N 1050 Taylor, John Russell. "Rich Man's Plaything."
    The Times III (November 1, 1969) pF-G.
       (On the "Two Virgins" film.)

N 1051 Taylor, Laurie. "Love Me Do." The Times
    (May 7, 1981) p12F.
       (On three new Beatles books.)

N 1052 "Telegrams In Brief." The Times (January 22,
    1964) p10D.
       (British Berlin troops petition Beatles'
    visit.)

N 1053 Tendler, Stewart. "Record Company Signs
    Contract To Issue Album By Former Beatle In
    Russia." The Times (August 12, 1976)
    p1D.
       ("Band On The Run" in Russian release.)

N 1054 "Test Ties - Yeah." Christian Science Monitor
    56 (February 11, 1964) p1.

N 1055 "They Call It Apple Corps."

Christian Science Monitor 60 (October 7, 1968) p6.

N 1056 "The 'Thinking Man's Beatle'."
Bulletin (Philadelphia) (December 9, 1980) pA3.
(John Lennon.)

N 1057 "This Morning, Do Something Nice. Try To Stop World War III." New York Times (October 9, 1969) p39:2.
(Funds sought for Lennon's Mid-East peace ship.)

N 1058 "This Week's List Of Birthdays." Sunday Times (June 14, 1981) p2C. illus.
(McCartney cartoon.)

N 1059 "Three Beatles Abandon Their Appeal."
The Times (April 27, 1971) p5H.
(Law case to dissolve Beatles.)

N 1060 "Three Beatles To Appeal." The Times (March 20, 1971) p4C.
(Law case to dissolve Beatles.)

N 1061 "Tickets For Beatles Go Fast." New York Times (April 23, 1964) p34:4.
(Labor Day Concert, Toronto.)

N 1062 "Ticket To Ride." The Times (May 22, 1982) p5A.
(Liverpool's "Beatles Weekends" tours.)

N 1063 "The Times Diary; Apple First." The Times (August 21, 1970) p8H.
(Recording of Cantata at Islington Church.)

N 1064 "The Times Diary; Beatles' 'Official' Biographer." The Times (February 9, 1968) p8G.
(Hunter Davies' book to appear.)

N 1065 "The Times Diary; Beatle's Scream." The Times (December 18, 1970) p12H.
(John Lennon.)

N 1066 "The Times Diary; Beatle Style." The Times (October 15, 1969) p10F.
(The Beatles' popularity in Russia.)

N 1067 "The Times Diary; Cloudy Skies Over Beatleside." The Times (March 22, 1978) p18D.
(Proposed Liverpool statue.)

N 1068 "The Times Diary; Moving Up." The Times (May 18, 1973) p20D.
(The Lennons move into the Dakota.)

N 1069 "The Times Diary; One Note Rave." The Times (November 14, 1969) p10E.
("Wedding Album" released.)

N 1070 "The Times Diary; Shake Up." The Times (July 1, 1976) p16B.
(Beatles' influence feared in Saudi Arabia.)

N 1071 "The Times Diary; The Beatles Buying A Novel." The Times (April 26, 1968) p10G.
(Apple seeks film rights of novel.)

N 1072 "The Times Diary; The Ono Show." The Times (July 20, 1971) p12F.
(John Lennon comments on Yoko's "Grapefruit" book.)

N 1073 "The Times Diary; Unedited." The Times (November 1, 1969) p6F.
(Press reaction to Lennon film show.)

N 1074 "The Times Diary; Using The Run-Out Grooves." The Times (June 12, 1967) p8G.
("Sgt. Pepper" album.)

N 1075 "The Times Diary; Yeuch!" The Times (October 22, 1969) p10H.
(Rumored death of Paul McCartney.)

N 1076 "To Balk At Bias Bookings."
Christian Science Monitor 56 (July 13, 1964) p2.

N 1077 "To Look For The Beatles, Try 'B' In Who's Who." New York Times (May 19, 1965) p42:2.
(Beatles to be listed in "Who's Who in America.")

N 1078 "Tour By Former Beatle's Group." The Times (July 11, 1972) p6H.
(McCartney and Wings on French tour.)

N 1079 "Touring The Beatles' Liverpool."

New York Times X (April 18, 1982) p3.
(Merseyside County Council's tour.)

N 1080 Towarnicky, Carol. "Lennon .... At 40."
Daily News (Philadelphia) 2 (October 9, 1980) pp29,32.

N 1081 "Transition For ATV." The Times (April 12, 1969) p14D.
(Northern Songs.)

N 1082 "Trashing The Lennon Legend."
Florida Times-Union (Jacksonville) (August 7, 1983) p4.

N 1083 Treaster, Joseph B. "Youths Counsel Troubled Peers; Private Group In New Haven Reaches Counter Culture." New York Times (April 11, 1971) p37:1.
(Youth group "Number Nine" counsels peers.)

N 1084 "Trial Starts Today In Lennon Murder."
New York Times II (June 22, 1981) p3:1.

N 1085 "Trial To Start June 1 In Slaying Of Lennon." New York Times II (May 14, 1981) p10:4.

N 1086 "A Tribute To John Lennon On Anniversary Of His Death." New York Times II (December 9, 1982) p21:4. illus.
(Illustration of Dakota vigil.)

N 1087 "A Tribute To Lennon." New York Times III (December 12, 1980) p29:1.
(Boston Pops at Carnegie Hall, Dec. 13.)

N 1088 "Triumph's Pact With Beatles." The Times (July 10, 1969) p28A.
(Triumph Investment Trust.)

N 1089 "Trouble Seemed So Far Away." The Times (December 8, 1981) p5D. illus.
(First anniversary of Lennon's death.)

N 1090 Trumbull, Robert. "Tokyo Is Girding For The Beatles; Arrival June 30 – 30,000 Tickets Drawn By Lot." New York Times (May 22, 1966) p12:1.
(200,000 apply for 30,000 seats.)

N 1091 "Tunes Bear Basic Beaton Discs."
Christian Science Monitor 58 (August 6, 1966) p6.

N 1092 "12-Medal Man Reacts Sharply To The Beatles." New York Times (June 17, 1965) p3:3.
(Lt. Colonel returns his twelve medals.)

N 1093 "20 Fans Greet Beatles." The Times (June 29, 1966) p8D.
(In Japan.)

N 1094 "Two Beatle Fans Paroled." New York Times (August 26, 1966) p22:8.
(Female fans who threatened hotel leap.)

N 1095 "2 Beatles' Benefits For Pakistanis Are Sold Out." New York Times (July 23, 1971) p15:1.
(36,000 tickets sold.)

N 1096 "Two Beatles Disagree On Shows For Public." New York Times (March 28, 1969) p37:3.
(John Lennon versus Ringo Starr.)

N 1097 "Two Beatles Get More Awards." The Times (March 27, 1968) p14E.

N 1098 "2 Beatles' Home Burglarized." New York Times (April 21, 1964) p41:3.
(Harrison's and Starr's London apartment looted.)

N 1099 "2 Beatles Lose On Visas." New York Times (May 17, 1969) p19:1.
(John Lennon and George Harrison.)

N 1100 "Two Beatles Reunite For Recording Session." New York Times III (February 16, 1981) p13:5.
(Ringo Starr, Paul McCartney in Monserrat.)

N 1101 "Two Beatles Win Song Awards." The Times (March 27, 1967) p10F.

N 1102 "Two British Heroes Protest Award Of Honors To Beatles." New York Times (June 16, 1965) p13:1.
(War heroes protest M.B.E. award.)

N 1103 "250 Calls To Channel 13 Protest Nudity In Movies." New York Times (October 16, 1971) p63:4.
(WNET Free Time "happening" with the Lennons.)

N 1104 "212 Police For Beatles." The Times (December
2, 1963) p7F.
(In Leicester.)

N 1105 "250,000 Australians Jam Beatles' Route."
New York Times (June 15, 1964) p35:7.
(Beatles in Melbourne, Australia.)

N 1106 "2 John Lennon Memorials Draw 4,000 In
Liverpool." New York Times III (March 30,
1981) p20:6.

N 1107 "Two Of Beatles Rock London With An Issue In
Their Music Firm; Shares Valued At $1.3
Million Are Said To Be All Sold Out."
Wall Street Journal (February 18, 1965)
p9:4.
(Northern Songs.)

N 1108 "Two To One Against Beatles." The Times
(June 17, 1965) p6C.
(M.B.E. awards returned in protest.)

N 1109 "2 U.S. Students Held In Spain."
New York Times (July 6, 1965) p5:3.
(Students involved in Barcelona concert
fight.)

N 1110 "Undertaking By Beatle." The Times (March 1,
1969) p2G.
(Ringo Starr.)

N 1111 "Undertakings On Money Owed To Beatles."
The Times (January 27, 1971) p2A.
(Law case to dissolve Beatles.)

N 1112 Unger, A. "Birth Of The Beatles: Little
Insight." Christian Science Monitor 71
(November 21, 1979) p15. illus.

N 1113 "United Artists Schedules Preview Of Beatles
Movie." New York Times (June 16, 1964)
p46:2.

N 1114 "Urgent Checks On New Drug STP." The Times
(July 29, 1967) p1D+.
(McCartney's drug views discussed in
Parliament.)

N 1115 "U.S. And British Taxers Vie To Shear Beatles."
New York Times (January 3, 1965) p84:1.
(U.S. confiscates Beatles' earnings.)

N 1116 "U.S. Ban On Beatles Over Religion." The Times
(August 5, 1966) p8E.
(Religious remark by John Lennon.)

N 1117 "Usual Sound And Fury Confront The Beatles At
London Airport." New York Times (February
23, 1964) p87:4.

N 1118 Van Gelder, L. "Notes On People."
New York Times (July 5, 1972) p53:3.
(Former British Ambassador defends Lennon.)

N 1119 Van Gelder, L. "Notes On People."
New York Times (July 14, 1972) p28:3.
(George Harrison fined $50 for careless
driving.)

N 1120 Van Matre, Lynn. "Yoko & Son."
Daily News (Philadelphia) (December 8, 1982)
(Two years after John Lennon's death.)

N 1121 "Vatican Accepts Lennon's Apology."
New York Times (August 14, 1966) p13:1.

N 1122 Wale, Michael. "The Arts: Paul's Return."
The Times (July 11, 1972) p13D.
(McCartney and Wings on French tour.)

N 1123 Walters, Ray. "Paperback Talk; Beatlemania."
New York Times Book Review 85 (December 28,
1980) pp19-20.
(Book explosion due to Lennon's death.)

N 1124 Wansell, Geoffrey. "Paul McCartney Takes Court
Action To Leave Beatles." The Times
(January 1, 1971) p4B.

N 1125 Wansell, Geoffrey. "Receiver Appointed For The
Beatles." The Times (March 13, 1971)
p2G.
(Law case to dissolve Beatles.)

N 1126 Wardle, Irving. "Beatles: Bridging The Gap."
The Times (October 5, 1968) p22A.
(Reviews Hunter Davies' biography.)

N 1127 Wardle, Irving. "John Lennon Play, 'In His Own
Write,' Is Staged In London."
New York Times (June 20, 1968) p50:5.

N 1128 Wardle, Irving. "Unknown Plays For New

Directors; National Theatre Triple Bill."
The Times (June 19, 1968) p11C.
(Stage play "In His Own Write.")

N 1129 "War Is Over! If You Want It." New York Times
IV (December 21, 1969) p16.
(The Lennons' full page Xmas ad.)

N 1130 Warman, Christopher. "Cheers And Tears As
Beatle Marries." The Times (March 13, 1969)
p10A. illus.
(Paul McCartney weds Linda Eastman.)

N 1131 Warman, Christopher. "Lennon And Picasso Works
Compared." The Times (April 2, 1970)
p4H.

N 1132 "Warner Bros. Subsidiary Mulls Buying Interest
That Beatles Are After."
Wall Street Journal (May 7, 1969) p4:4.
(Atlantic Records considers 15% Northern
buy.)

N 1133 "Warner Joins N Songs Bid." The Times
(May 6, 1969) p28A.
(Warner Bros. - Seven Arts.)

N 1134 Watson, Peter. "All Paul's Work." The Times
(August 25, 1981) p8F. illus.
(Paul's song book drawings.)

N 1135 Watson, Peter. "Lennon's Life." The Times
(November 5, 1981) p12f.
(Notes forthcoming Lennon biography.)

N 1136 Watts, Stephen. "The Beatles' 'A Hard Day's
Night'." New York Times II (April 26, 1964)
p13:1. illus.

N 1137 Watts, Stephen. "Richard Lester's War Movie To
End All War Movies - Maybe." New York Times
II (October 1, 1967) p15:1.
("How I Won The War.")

N 1138 "Wealth Out Of A Texas Oil Barrel." The Times
(September 4, 1982) p4C.
(Yoko Ono among richest people in U.S.)

N 1139 Weberman, A. "John Lennon's Zippie Legacy."
Overthrow 3 (January 1981) p9.

N 1140 Weinraub, Judith. "Linda McCartney's Camera
Solo." New York Times (December 12, 1976)
p86:1. illus.
(Interview with Linda McCartney.)

N 1141 Weinstein, G. "On John Lennon."
Peace Newsletter 4 (January 1981) p27.

N 1142 "Welcome For Beatles." The Times (September 22,
1964) p7B.
(Return to London.)

N 1143 Wells, Jeff and Richard Johnson. "Yoko Asks
Fans To 'Pray For His Soul'."
Post (New York) (December 10, 1980)
p5.

N 1144 "We're Just Us." Christian Science Monitor 58
(December 3, 1966)
(Editorial page.)

N 1145 "What He Meant Was ... ." New York Times
(August 16, 1966) p38:2.
(Editorial on Lennon's controversial
remark.)

N 1146 "What Songs The Beatles Sang ..." The Times
(December 27, 1963) p4F.

N 1147 "Wholesome Nonsense?"
Christian Science Monitor 56 (March 17, 1964)
p15.

N 1148 "Who's Not Who - Beatles." New York Times
(March 8, 1968) p10:1. illus.
(Not listed in Britain's "Who's Who.")

N 1149 "Why They Rock." New York Times VI (March 8,
1964) p4.
(Letter/reply to David Dempsey's Feb. 23
article.)

N 1150 Wicker, Tom. "You, Me And Handguns."
New York Times (December 12, 1980) p35:1.
(Lennon's death and gun control.)

N 1151 William, Davis. "Market Lessons For Northern
Songs." Guardian (January 6, 1966)
p11.

N 1152 Williams, Richard. "Paul McCartney." The Times
(January 4, 1982) p5. illus.

N 1153 Williams, Richard. "Solo Beatles." The Times

(January 23, 1971) p17E.
   (The Lennons' Plastic Ono Band albums.)
N 1154 Williams, Richard. "Solo Beatles." The Times
   (January 23, 1971) p17E.
   (On Harrison's "All Things Must Pass" LP.)
N 1155 "Will Real Beatles Sing Out."
   Christian Science Monitor 64 (January 28,
   1972) p13.
N 1156 Wilson, John S. "2,900-Voice Chorus Joins The
   Beatles." New York Times (February 13, 1964)
   p26:2. illus.
   (Carnegie Hall concert.)
N 1157 "Windfalls At Apple." The Times (July 31, 1968)
   p3D.
   (Apple Boutique closed.)
N 1158 "Wings Tickets Selling Quickly."
   New York Times (April 8, 1976) p42:1. illus.
   (For U.S. tour in May.)
N 1159 "WMCA Bans New Single, 'Ballad,' By Beatle
   Lennon." New York Times (May 24, 1969)
   p70:2.
   ("Ballad of John and Yoko.")
N 1160 "Words For A Beatles Album That Will Never Be."
   New York Times II (February 7, 1971) p15:5.
   illus.
   (Parodies of five Beatles' songs.)
N 1161 "Worldwide Mourning Continues For Lennon."
   Bulletin (Philadelphia) (December 10, 1980)
   pA7.
N 1162 "Writ Against The Beatles." The Times
   (June 24, 1969) p13G.
   (Clive Epstein fights Beatles' claim.)
N 1163 "Writer Presents Different Picture Of Dakota
   Days." Florida Times-Union (Jacksonville)
   (July 1, 1983) pD-16.
N 1164 "Writ Issued On Northern Songs." The Times
   (November 8, 1969) p13F.
   (ATV offer document has writ attached.)
N 1165 "Wrong-handed." Sunday Times (June 28, 1981)
   p21H. illus.
   (Letter on June 14 McCartney cartoon.)
N 1166 "Yoko Donation." The Times (July 13, 1981)
   p6A.

(To violent crime victims in Japan.)
N 1167 "Yoko Ono Asks Mourners To Give To A Foundation
   Lennon Favored." New York Times II
   (December 10, 1980) p7:2.
   (The Spirit Foundation.)
N 1168 "Yoko Ono Loses Baby." New York Times
   (October 17, 1969) p41:1.
   (Miscarriage.)
N 1169 "Yoko Ono Seeks Daughter In U.S." The Times
   (June 2, 1971) p5D.
   (Seeks custody of Kyoko in New York City.)
N 1170 "Yoko Ono's Film Tribute To Lennon On Cable
   TV." New York Times III (June 15, 1981)
   p13:3.
   ("Walking On Thin Ice.")
N 1171 "Yoko Ono's Former Husband Is Jailed."
   The Times (December 23, 1971) p6H.
   (For contempt of court.)
N 1172 "Yoko's Thanks." Inquirer (Philadelphia)
   (April 21, 1982) p2F.
   (For Central Park's "Strawberry Fields"
   garden.)
N 1173 "Yoko To Sue Lord Grade." The Times (November
   26, 1981) p30A.
   (McCartney/Yoko charge breach of trust.)
N 1174 "You Can Bank On Beatles."
   Christian Science Monitor 56 (February 26,
   1964) p1.
N 1175 "Young Lennon Living It Up In London."
   Daily News (Philadelphia) (May 3, 1982)
   p24.
   (Julian Lennon and manager Tariq Siddiqi.)
N 1176 "Youth Shot Near Vigil; Crowd Subdues Suspect."
   New York Times II (December 15, 1980)
   p8:4.
   (Gunplay at Lennon Central Park vigil.)
N 1177 Zeitlin, Kim. "Evidence Of Gaiety."
   New York Times VI (April 19, 1964)
   p46.
N 1178 Zelnick, C.R. "Lennon Fight To Stay In U.S.
   Raises Legal Points."
   Christian Science Monitor 67 (September 8,
   1975) p7.

P 0001 All About The Beatles - No. 1. New York:
YOPU Press, Inc., 1964. illus.

P 0002 Around The World With The Beatles, by George
Harrison. Liverpool: Liverpool Web Ltd.,
1964. 32pp. illus.
(Harrison was a "Liverpool Echo"
columnist.)

P 0003 Beatle Hairdos & Setting Patterns. New York:
Dell Publishing Co., 1964. 50pp. illus.

P 0004 Beatlemania, edited by William T. Anderson.
Derby, CT: Song Hits Magazine, 1978.
70pp. illus.

P 0005 Beatle-Mania, The Authentic Photos. Volume 1,
No. 1. New York: SMP Publishing Ltd., 1964.
illus.

P 0006 Beatle Paul McCartney - His Story By Himself.
London: George Newnes Ltd., 1964. illus.

P 0007 Beatle Ringo Starr - The Story Of A Ring-A-Ding
Star. London: George Newnes Ltd., 1964.
illus.

P 0008 The Beatles. Albany, NY:
Highlights Publications Inc., 1964. illus.

P 0009 The Beatles. London: Pyx Productions, 1963.
32pp. illus.
(Photos by Dezo Hoffman.)

P 0010 The Beatles, ed. by Stephen Kahn. New York:
Beatle Publications, 1964. 66pp. illus.

P 0011 The Beatles (E-Go Collectors Series No. 8),
edited by Ron Haydock. Sherman Oaks, CA:
E-Go Enterprises Inc., 1977. 72pp. illus.

P 0012 The Beatles (Special Collector's Series, Number
6). n.p.: Alan Clark Productions, 1981.
60pp. illus.

P 0013 The Beatles - A Dell Giant - Complete Life
Stories. New York: Dell Publishing Co., 1964.
illus.
(Comic book.)

P 0014 Beatles Anniversary, by Bill Harry. London:
Colourgold Ltd., 1982. 32pp. illus.
(Twentieth anniversary booklet.)

P 0015 The Beatles Are Back, edited by Martin Grove.
New York: Manor Books Inc., 1978. 92pp.
illus.

P 0016 The Beatles Are Here, ed. by Jack J. Podell, et
al. New York: MacFadden-Bartell Corp., 1964.
72pp. illus.

P 0017 Beatles Around The World. London:
Pop Pics Special, 1964. illus.

P 0018 Beatles Around The World - No. 1. New York:
Acme News Co., Inc., 1964. illus.

P 0019 Beatles Around The World - No. 2. New York:
Acme News Co., Inc., 1964. illus.

P 0020 The Beatles At Carnegie Hall. London:
Panther Pictorial, 1964. illus.

P 0021 Beatles Baby Family Album - Beatle Mania
Collectors Item, Volume 1, No. 1. New York:
SMP Publishing Ltd., 1964. illus.

P 0022 The Beatles Book. London:
Periodical Publications, 1963.

P 0023 The Beatles Book Calendar For 1964. London:
Beat Publications, 1963.

P 0024 The Beatles Book - Special Xmas Extra. London:
Beat Publications, 1965. 60pp. illus.

P 0026 The Beatles Color Pin-Up Album. Hollywood, CA:
S.M.H. Publications Inc., 1964. 68pp. illus.

P 0027 The Beatles - Complete Coverage - Exclusive
Photos - The Beatles United States Arrivals
And Appearances. New York:
Beatles Publishing Corp., 1964. illus.

P 0028 The Beatles Complete Life Stories - Special
Edition. Hollywood, CA:
Sunset Publications, Inc., 1964. illus.

P 0029 Beatles - Complete Story From Birth To Now.
New York: Sixteen Magazine, 1965. 72pp.
illus.

P 0030 The Beatles Film. London: George Newnes Ltd.,
1964. 48pp. illus.
("A Hard Day's Night.")

P 0031 The Beatles Forever, edited by Martin Sage.
New York: Lamplight Enterprises, 1973.
76pp. illus.

P 0032 The Beatles Forever, edited by Ed Naha.
New York: O'Quinn Studios, 1978. 76pp.
illus.
(Updates the 1973 ed. by Martin Sage.)

P 0033 The Beatles Forever - Collectors Edition.
New York: Lamplight Enterprises, 1975.
illus.

P 0034 The Beatles In America - Their Own Exclusive
Story And Pictures. London:
The Daily Mirror Newspapers, 1964. illus.
(Photos by Robert Freeman.)

P 0035 The Beatles In Paris. London:
Boyfriend/Photonews, 1964. illus.

P 0036 The Beatles In Sweden. London:
Boyfriend/Photonews, 1963. illus.

P 0037 The Beatles Ltd. London: George Newnes Ltd.,
1964. illus.
(Photos by Robert Freeman)

P 0038 Beatles Make A Movie. New York:
Magnum Publications, 1964. 66pp. illus.
(Beatles cover portrait.)

P 0039 Beatles Movie - The Only Book With The Entire
Story Of "A Hard Days Night". New York:
Boyfriend-Girlfriend Corp., 1964. illus.

P 0040 The Beatles, 1962-1982; Yeah, Yeah, Yeah - The
Beatles 20 Ans, edited by Jacques Volcouve.
Paris: Club des 4 de Liverpool, 1982.
16pp. illus.

P 0041 Beatles On Broadway. Manchester, Eng.:
World Distributors Ltd., 1964. 32pp. illus.
(Compiled by Sam Leach.)

P 0042 Beatles On Broadway. Racine, WI:
Whitman Publishing Co. Ltd., 1964. illus.

P 0043 The Beatles - Personality Annual, Volume 1, No.
1. New York: Country Wide Publications, 1964.
illus.

P 0044 The Beatles - Pictures For Framing. London:
Hutchinson & Co., 1964. illus.

P 0045 The Beatles Punch-Out Portraits.
Manchester, Eng.:
Whitman Publishing Co. Ltd., 1964. illus.

P 0046 Beatles 'Round The World (No. 1, Winter 1964).
New York: Acme News Co., Inc., 1964. illus.

P 0047 The Beatles Scrapbook, by Barry Allen. London:
Giant Step Associates Ltd., 1976. 24pp.
illus.
(Rainbow Giant Special Issue.)

P 0048 The Beatles Starring In A Hard Day's Night.
Manchester, Eng.: World Distributors Ltd.,
1964. illus.

P 0049 The Beatles Story - The Story Of Rock. n.p.:
Paradise Press/Phoebus, 1973. illus.

P 0050 The Beatles Talk. Hollywood, CA:
Deidre Publications Inc., 1964. illus.

P 0051 Beatles - The Fab Four Come Back. New York:
Romance Publishing Corp., 1964. illus.

P 0052 The Beatles - The Greatest! Meet The Dave Clark
Five. New York: Kahn Communications Corp.,
1964. illus.

P 0053 Beatles U.S.A. - Collector's Edition.
New York: Jamie Publications Inc., 1964.
illus.

P 0054 Beatles (U.S.A.) Ltd. New York:
Souvenir Publishing, 1964. illus.
(On U.S. '64 tour.)

P 0055 Beatles (U.S.A.) Ltd. New York:
Souvenir Publishing, 1965. illus.
(On U.S. '65 tour.)

P 0056 Beatles (U.S.A.) Ltd. New York:
Raydell Publishing, 1966. illus.
(On U.S. '66 tour.)

P 0057 Beatles Whole True Story. New York:
Sixteen Magazine, 1966. illus.

P 0058 Beatles - Yesterday And Today, edited by Ron
Mosny. New York: Country Wide Publications,
1975. 72pp. illus.

P 0059 The Best Of The Beatles From Fabulous. London:

Fleetway Publications Ltd., 1964. illus.
(Beatles cover portrait.)

P 0060 Best Of The Beatles - 63 Ways To Meet A Beatle.
New York: MacFadden-Bartell Corp., 1964.
illus.

P 0061 Big Beatle Fun Kit. Hollywood, CA:
Deidre Publications Inc., 1964. illus.

P 0062 Date Book - All About The Beatles. New York:
Young World Press, 1964. illus.

P 0063 Date Book - All About The Beatles - America's
Top DJs Interview The Boys. New York:
Young World Press, 1966. illus.

P 0064 Date Book - Exclusive - Paul Talks About Jane.
New York: Young World Press, 1966. illus.
(Cover portrait.)

P 0065 Dave Clark Five Vs. The Beatles, Volume 1, No.
1. New York: Popular Annual, 1964. illus.

P 0066 Dig - Special Beatles Issue. Hollywood, CA:
Deidre Publications Inc., 1964. 50pp. illus.

P 0067 Elvis Vs. The Beatles, by Albert Hand and Dave
Codwell. New York: Acme News Co., Inc., 1965.
illus.
("Beatles 'Round The World No. 3.")

P 0068 Fab Goes Filming With The Beatles. London:
Fleetway Publications Ltd., 1964. illus.
(Beatles cover portrait.)

P 0069 Fabulous Goes All Beatles. London:
Fleetway Publications Ltd., 1964. illus.
(Beatles cover portrait.)

P 0070 George. Hollywood, CA:
S.M.H. Publications Inc., 1964. 68pp. illus.

P 0071 Gold Key - Beatles Yellow Submarine.
Poughkeepsie, NY:
Western Publishing Co. Inc., 1968. illus.
(Comic book serialization of the movie.)

P 0072 Help. New York: Help! Magazine Inc., 1965.
illus.

P 0073 Histoire Du Rock Les Beatles. n.p.:
Phoebus Publishing Co., 1973. illus.
(In French.)

P 0074 The Inside Story Of The Yellow Submarine. New
York: GO Publishing Co., 1968. illus.

P 0075 John. Hollywood, CA: S.M.H. Publications Inc.,
1964. 68pp. illus.

P 0076 John & Yoko: Their Love Book. New York:
M. F. Enterprises Inc., 1970. 66pp. illus.

P 0077 John Lennon: A Memorial Album. New York:
Friday Publishing Corp., 1981. 98pp. illus.

P 0078 John Lennon: A Personal Pictorial Diary.
New York: Sportomatic Ltd., 1980. 116pp.
illus.

P 0079 John Lennon: A Tribute, No. 1 -
New York: David Zentner Publications, 1980.
84pp. illus.
(Magazine format.)

P 0080 John Lennon: All You Need Is Love. Vol. 1, No.
1 -   . New York: Mar-Jam Publications,
1980. 100pp. illus.
(Magazine format.)

P 0081 John Lennon & The Beatles: A Special Tribute.
New York: Harris Publications, 1980.
66pp. illus.

P 0082 John Lennon/Beatles Memory Book. New York:
Harris Publications, 1981. 68pp. illus.
(Magazine format.)

P 0083 John Lennon - Das War Sein Leben.
Hamburg, W. Ger.: Star Club Verlag, 1982.
90pp. illus.
(Star Club Magazine No. 2/81.)

P 0084 John Lennon: The Legend. Vol. 1, No. 1 -
Ft. Lee, NJ: S. J. Publications, 1981.
68pp. illus.
(Magazine format.)

P 0085 John Lennon: The Life And Legend, by the staff
of the Sunday Times Magazine. Edited by
George Darby and David Robson.
Melbourne, Aus.: Newspress/Age Publications,
1981. 64pp. illus.

P 0086 John Lennon Tribute, by George Carpozi, Jr.
New York: Woodhill Press, 1980. 84pp. illus.

(Magazine format.)

P 0087 John Winston Lennon, 1940-1980.
Copenhagen,Denmark:
Den Selvejende Institution Forlaget
MM, 1980. 16pp. illus.
(Special memorial issue of MM.)

P 0088 Lennon: A Memory. West Hempstead, NY:
ARDA, Inc., 1981. 66pp. illus.

P 0089 Lennon Photo Special. n.p.:
Sunshine Publications, 1980. 96pp. illus.
(Magazine format.)

P 0090 McCartney: Beatle On Wings. New York:
Country Wide Publications, 1976. 98pp.
illus.

P 0091 Meet The Beatles - Photos From Their Personal
Album - A Message To You From The Beatles
Themselves. New York:
MacFadden-Bartell Corp., 1963. illus.

P 0092 Meet The Beatles - Star Special, Number Twelve.
Manchester, Eng.: World Distributors Ltd.,
1963. 40pp. illus.
(Text by Tony Barrow.)

P 0093 National Lampoon. New York:
National Lampoon Magazine, 1977. illus.
(Special Beatles issue, October 1977.)

P 0094 The Official Yellow Submarine Magazine. n.p.:
Pyramid Pubns./King Features, 1968. illus.

P 0095 On The Scene - Exclusive - The Beatles At
Carnegie Hall. London:
Hamilton (Stafford) Co. Ltd., 1964. illus.

P 0097 The Original Beatles Book - Two.
Los Angeles, CA: Petersen Pub. Co., n.d.
illus.

P 0098 Paul. Hollywood, CA: S.M.H. Publications Inc.,
1964. 68pp. illus.

P 0099 Paul McCartney Dead - The Great Hoax, edited by
Florence Brown and Ron Mosny. New York:
Country Wide Publications, 1969. 68pp.
illus.

P 0100 Paul McCartney Dead - The Great Hoax.
New York: Stories, Layouts & Press, 1978.
68pp. illus.

P 0101 Pop Teen, Vol.1, No.1 -   . New York:
Pop Teen Magazine, 1966. 66pp. illus.

P 0102 The Real True Beatles - By Michael Braun, The
Writer Who Knows Them Best. No. 1.
New York: Fawcett Publications, 1964.
96pp. illus.

P 0103 Ringo. Hollywood, CA: S.M.H. Publications Inc.,
1964. 68pp. illus.

P 0104 Ringo's Photo-Album. New York:
Jamie Publications Inc., n.d. 68pp. illus.

P 0105 Rolling Stone. New York:
Straight Arrow Publishers, 1981. 94pp.
illus.
(Special John Lennon issue, January 22,
1981.)

P 0106 Rolling Stone; Special Beatles Anniversary
Issue. New York: Straight Arrow Publishers,
1984. 102pp. illus.
(Issue no. 415, February 16, 1984.)

P 0107 16 Magazine - Beatles - 100 Pix Never Before
Seen (Volume 6, No. 9). New York:
Sixteen Magazine, 1965. illus.

P 0108 16 Magazine Presents: John Lennon and The
Beatles - A Loving Tribute. New York:
Kia-Ora Publications, 1981. 90pp. illus.
(Magazine format.)

P 0109 Star Time Presents The Beatles. New York:
AAA Publishing Co., 1965. illus.

P 0110 Summer Love (Volume 2, No. 47). Derby, CT:
Charlton Comics Group, 1966. illus.
(Comic book with Beatles' theme.)

P 0111 Talking Pictures. Volume 1, No. 1 - Special
Beatles Issue. New York: Herald House, 1964.
illus.

P 0112 Teen Bag's Tribute To John Lennon, No. 1.
New York: Lopez Publications, 1981.

76pp. illus.
        (Magazine format.)
P 0113 Teen Screen Life Story: Ringo. Hollywood, CA:
        SMH Pubns., Inc., 1964. 66pp. illus.
P 0114 Teenset Yellow Submarine Special. Chicago, IL:
        Regensteiner Pub. Enterprises, 1968. illus.
        (Beatles' film characters cover.)
P 0115 Teen Talk - Valuable Collector's Edition On The
        Beatles. New York: Sabre Publishing, 1964.
        66pp. illus.
P 0116 10th Anniversary Collectors Treasure - The
        Beatles - From Beatle Mania To Bangladesh,
        1963-1973. New York: Lamplight Enterprises,
        1972. illus.
        (Cover portrait.)
P 0117 A Tribute To John Lennon & The Beatles.
        New York: Concentric Enterprises, 1980.
        96pp. illus.
P 0118 Welcome Back Beatles, edited by Christopher
        May, written by Howard Blumenthal.
        Englewood Cliffs,NJ:
        Stories, Layouts & Press, 1977. 68pp. illus.
        (August issue.)

P 0119 Welcome Back Beatles, edited by Christopher May.
        Englewood Cliffs,NJ:
        Stories, Layouts & Press, 1977. 68pp. illus.
        (Fall issue.)
P 0120 Welcome Back Beatles, edited by Christopher May.
        Englewood Cliffs,NJ:
        Stories, Layouts & Press, 1977. 68pp. illus.
        (Winter issue.)
P 0121 Welcome Back Beatles, edited by Jeffrey Goodman
        and Kevin Goodman. New York:
        Stories, Layouts & Press, 1978. 68pp. illus.
        (Volume II, No. 4.)
P 0122 Who Will Beat The Beatles - The Mersey Sound
        Hits America. New York: Magnum Publications,
        1964. illus.
P 0123 Wings Pin-Up & Story Poster. London:
        Phoebus Publishing Co., 1977. illus.
        (Fold-out poster magazine.)
P 0124 World Of ... John Lennon And The Beatles.
        New York: Graybar Publishing, 1980.
        86pp. illus.
        (Magazine format.)

PAUL McCARTNEY
IN HIS OWN WORDS

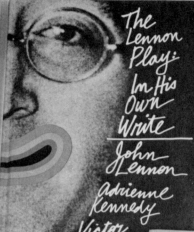

The Lennon Play: In His Own Write
John Lennon
Adrienne Kennedy
Victor...

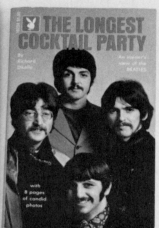

THE LONGEST COCKTAIL PARTY
By Richard DiLello

An insider's view of the BEATLES

with 8 pages of candid photos

THE LENNON TAPES

BBC

LENNON AND McCARTNEY
Malcolm Doney

DIG IT
THE BEATLES BOOTLEG BOOK
VOLUME ONE

John, Paul, George and Ringo sound off about love and war, drugs and God, the Stones, the Maharishi and much more in this cheeky kaleidoscope of quotes and photos

THE Beatles
WORDS WITHOUT MUSIC
Compiled by Rick Friedman
Introduced by Joe O'Brien

In the Footsteps of the Beatles
Mike Evans and Ron Jones

PENNY LANE

"Penny Lane" by the Liverpool artist Maurice Cockrill

A Merseyside County Council Publication

DEREK TAYLOR
As time goes by

ABBEY ROAD
    RB0001   Beatlefan 5:1 (December 1982) p25.

ACROSS THE UNIVERSE
    RB0002   Beatlefan 3:4 (June 1981) p34. Lark, Fred

DAS ALBUM DER BEATLES
    RB0003   Beatles Unlimited 38 (September 1981)
             pp9-10. Braam, Willi

ALL THINGS MUST PASS
    RB0004   AB Bookmans Weekly (March 29, 1971)
             p1046.
    RB0005   Library Journal (May 15, 1971) p1834.

ALL TOGETHER NOW
    RB0006   American Reference Books Annual, Vol.8
             (1977) p469. Loomis, K.C., Jr.
    RB0007   Association For Recorded Sound Col-
             lections. Newsletter. 8:2/3 (1976)
             pp108-112.
    RB0008   Aware 2:4 p21. Kolanjian, Steve
    RB0009   Beatles Unlimited 7 (May 1976) pp14-15.
             Hager, Henk
    RB0010   Book Review Digest (1977) p215.
    RB0011   Cash Box 37:52 (May 15, 1976) p10.
             Fuchs, Stephen
    RB0012   Choice 13:8 (October 1976) p956.
    RB0013   Gramophone 53 (May 1976) p1802.
    RB0014   Illinois Entertainer 2:25 (February 1976)
             p11. Guncheon, Mark
    RB0015   Kliatt Paperback Book Guide 11 (Winter
             1977) p32.
    RB0016   Library Journal 101:19 (November 1, 1976)
             p2284. Fry, Stephen M.
    RB0017   Los Angeles Times (January 8, 1977)
             p10. Hilburn, Robert
    RB0018   Music Educators Journal (March 1976)
             p22.
    RB0019   Reference Services Review 5:1 (January
             1977) p26. Ginsburg, David
    RB0020   Rockingchair 1:5 (August 1977) p8. P.,J.
    RB0021   Rolling Stone (February 24, 1977)
             p25. Marsh, Dave
    RB0022   San Francisco Chronicle (June 13, 1976)
             p31. Selvin, Joel
    RB0023   Seventeen (September 1976) p88.
    RB0024   Variety 283 (May 12, 1976) p450.
    RB0025   Who Put The Bomp 15 (Spring 1976) p25.

ALL YOU NEEDED WAS LOVE
    RB0026   Beatlefan 4:2 (February 1982) pp29-30.
             Hockinson, Mike
    RB0027   Beatlefan 4:2 (February 1982) p30.
             King, William P.
    RB0028   The Beatles Book 69 (January 1982)
             ppxi-xii. Doggett, Peter
    RB0029   Kirkus Reviews 49 (October 1, 1981)
             p1260.
    RB0030   Kliatt Paperback Book Guide 16 (Winter
             1982) p34.
    RB0031   Library Journal 106 (December 15, 1981)
             p2395.
    RB0032   Melody Maker 56 (November 21, 1981)
             p4.
    RB0033   Publishers Weekly 220 (October 23, 1981)
             p60.
    RB0034   Stereo Review 47 (February 1982)
             pp72-73.
    RB0035   Voice of Youth Advocates 5 (August 1982)
             p42.

ALL YOU NEED IS EARS
    RB0036   Beatlefan 2:2 (February 1980) pp1,6-7.
             Ellis, Roger
    RB0037   Beatles Unlimited 36 (June 1961)
             pp7-8. Pope, Michael E.
    RB0038   Billboard 92 (January 5, 1980) p54.
    RB0039   Booklist 76 (February 15, 1980) p806.
    RB0040   Book Review Digest (1980) p809.

    RB0041   Choice 18 (September 1980) p104.
    RB0042   Kirkus Reviews 47 (December 1, 1979)
             p1418.
    RB0043   Library Journal 105 (January 15, 1980)
             p208. Kaye, R.J.
    RB0044   Publishers Weekly 216 (November 26, 1979)
             p45.
    RB0045   Publishers Weekly 221 (June 18, 1982)
             p73.
    RB0046   Times Literary Supplement (September 19,
             1980) p1015.
    RB0047   Wilson Library Bulletin 55 (February 1981)
             p436.

APPLE TO THE CORE
    RB0048   Booklist 69 (September 15, 1972)
             p71.
    RB0049   Books & Bookmen 18 (June 1973) p88.
    RB0050   Guardian Weekly 108 (January 13, 1973)
             p27.
    RB0051   Library Journal 97 (November 15, 1972)
             p3714.
    RB0052   Library Journal 97 (December 15, 1972)
             p4096.
    RB0053   New York Times (August 8, 1972)
             p31.
    RB0054   Popular Music & Society 2:1 pp85-86.
             Denisoff, R. Serge
    RB0055   Publishers Weekly 201 (June 19, 1972)
             p61.
    RB0056   Rolling Stone 122 (November 23, 1972)
    RB0057   Variety 268 (August 16, 1972) p48.

AS I WRITE THIS LETTER
    RB0058   Beatlefan 4:3 (April 1982) p30.
             King, Leslie T.
    RB0059   Beatles Unlimited 42 p17. Vermeer, Evert
    RB0060   The Ithaca Journal (November 16, 1981)
             p9. Scott, Lee
    RB0061   The Post-Standard (Syracuse) (October 25,
             1982) pB1. Goldstein, Marc
    RB0062   Record Collector 38 (October 1982)
             p57.
    RB0063   Stereo Review 47:6 (June 1982) p75.
             Simels, Steve
    RB0064   Trouser Press (January 1983) p31.
             Isler, Scott

AS TIME GOES BY
    RB0065   Creem 5 (January 1974) p60. Edmonds, Ben
    RB0066   Publishers Weekly 204 (October 29, 1973)
             p37.
    RB0067   Punch 265 (August 29, 1973) p284.
    RB0068   Times Literary Supplement (November 15,
             1974) p1290.
    RB0069   Wilson Library Bulletin 55 (February 1981)
             p436.

THE BALLAD OF JOHN AND YOKO
    RB0070   Beatlefan 4:6 (October 1982) p28.
             King, Leslie T.
    RB0071   The Beatles Book 80 (December 1982)
             p47.
    RB0072   Kirkus Reviews 50 (September 1, 1982)
             p1051.
    RB0073   Publishers Weekly 222 (September 17, 1982)
             p112.
    RB0074   Record Collector 40 (December 1982)
             pp62-63.

BEATLE MADNESS
    RB0075   Beatlefan 1:1 (December 1978) p4.
             Budapest, Billy

THE BEATLES (FRIEDMAN)
    RB0076   AB Bookmans Weekly 43 (January 6, 1969)
             p14.

THE BEATLES (HARDY)
    RB0077   Kirkus Reviews 41 (January 1, 1973)

p35.
RB0078   Kirkus Reviews 41 (January 15, 1973)
         p68.
RB0079   Publishers Weekly 203 (January 15, 1973)
         p62.

THE BEATLES (PIRMANTGEN)
RB0080   School Library Journal 22 (September 1975)
         p95.

THE BEATLES (SCADUTO)
RB0081   Commentary 47 (April 1969) p79.

THE BEATLES (SPENCE)
RB0082   Beatlefan 4:2 (February 1982) p29.
         King, Leslie T.

THE BEATLES (STOKES)
RB0083   Beatlefan 3:1 (December 1980) p28.
         King, William P.
RB0084   Beatles Unlimited 37 (July 1981)
         pp18-19. Koolmees, Andre
RB0085   Billboard 93 (January 10, 1981)
         p81.
RB0086   Booklist 77 (January 15, 1981) p662.
         Estes, S.
RB0087   Book Review Digest 77:9 (December 1981)
         p90.
RB0088   Book World 10 (December 7, 1980)
         p8.
RB0089   Kliatt Paperback Book Guide 15 (Spring
         1981) p51.
RB0090   New York Times Book Review 86 (April 5,
         1981) p27.
RB0091   Quill & Quire 47 (March 1981) p62.
RB0092   Times Literary Supplement (May 15, 1981)
         p547a. Morrison, Blake
RB0093   Village Voice 25 (December 17, 1980)
         p61.
RB0094   Wilson Library Bulletin 55 (February 1981)
         p435.

THE BEATLES (ZANDERBERGEN)
RB0095   School Library Journal 23 (March 1977)
         p149.

THE BEATLES: A COLLECTION
RB0096   Beatlefan 4:2 (February 1982) pp30-31.
         Shears, Billy
RB0097   Beatles Now 6 (May 1983) p18. Harry, Bill
RB0098   Beatles Unlimited 41 pp20-21.
         Glazier, Joel

THE BEATLES AGAIN
RB0099   American Reference Books Annual, Vol.10
         (1979) p487. Tudor, Dean.
RB0100   Beatles Unlimited 19 (March 1978)
         pp21-22. Bakker, Erik M.
RB0101   The Calgary Herald (January 31, 1981)
         pH19. Brennan, Brian
RB0102   Choice 15:5 (July 1978) p700.
RB0103   Comic Reader 155 (April 1978) p12.
RB0104   Library Journal 103:7 (April 1, 1978)
         p756. Fry, S.M.
RB0105   Los Angeles Times II:9 (February 18, 1978)
         Hilburn, R.
RB0106   Music Educators Journal 65 (September
         1978) p23.
RB0107   Reference Services Review 6:3 (July 1978)
         p6.
RB0108   Rockingchair 2:3 (March 1978) p6. P., J.

THE BEATLES - A HARD DAY'S NIGHT
RB0109   Beatlefan 1:4 (June 1979) p8.
         King, Leslie

THE BEATLES ALBUM FILE AND COMPLETE DISCOGRAPHY
RB0110   Beatles Now 6 (May 1983) p19.
         Baker, Steve
RB0111   Record Collector 40 (December 1982)

p63.

THE BEATLES: A MUSICAL EVOLUTION
RB0112   Library Journal 108:13 (July 1983)
         p1365. Lutz, Gordon

THE BEATLES: AN ILLUSTRATED RECORD
RB0113   Association For Recorded Sound Col-
         lections. Newsletter. 8:2/3 (1976)
         pp112-113.
RB0114   Beatlefan 3:6 (October 1981) p34.
         Phillips, Steve
RB0115   Booklist 72 (September 1, 1975)
         p10.
RB0116   Kliatt Paperback Book Guide 15 (Spring
         1981) p52.
RB0117   Library Journal 100 (June 1, 1975)
         p50. Smothers, J.
RB0118   New York Times Book Review 86 (April 5,
         1981) p27.
RB0119   School Library Journal 22 (November 1975)
         p97. Minudri, R.
RB0120   School Library Journal 25 (October 1978)
         p167.
RB0121   School Library Journal 26 (August 1980) p39.
RB0122   School Library Journal 27 (August 1981)
         p85.
RB0123   Stereo Review 35 (August 1975) p9.
RB0124   Variety 279 (June 18, 1975) p57.
RB0125   Village Voice 20 (September 1, 1975)
         p44.
RB0126   Wilson Library Bulletin 50 (December 1975)
         p287.
RB0127   Wilson Library Bulletin 55 (February 1981)
         p435.

THE BEATLES APART
RB0128   Beatlefan 4:1 (December 1981) p29.
         Sussman, Al
RB0129   The Beatles Book 69 (January 1982)
         ppxi-xii. Doggett, Peter
RB0130   Melody Maker 56 (November 21, 1981)
         p4.

THE BEATLES: A STUDY IN DRUGS, SEX AND REVOLUTION
RB0131   Popular Music & Society 1:3 pp177-178.
         Rodnitzky, Jerome L.
RB0132   Rolling Stone 92 (September 30, 1971)
         p52.

THE BEATLES A TO Z
RB0133   American Reference Books Annual, Vol.13
         (1982) p525.
RB0134   Beatlefan 3:1 (December 1980) p28.
         Shears, Billy
RB0135   Beatles Unlimited 36 (June 1981)
         pp18-19. Vermeer, Evert
RB0136   Kliatt Paperback Book Guide 15 (Spring
         1981) p52.
RB0137   New York Times Book Review 86 (April 5,
         1981) p27.

THE BEATLES BOOK (DAVIS)
RB0138   Booklist 65 (April 15, 1969) p933.
RB0139   Commentary 47 (April 1969) p79.
RB0140   Jazz & Pop 8 (February 1969) p45.
RB0141   Kirkus Reviews p1140.
RB0142   National Review 21 (April 22, 1969)
         p396.
RB0143   Rolling Stone 28 (March 1, 1969)
         p22.

THE BEATLES - CONCERT-ED EFFORTS
RB0144   Beatlefan 1:5 (August 1979) p18.
         Shears, Billy

BEATLES DAGBOEK
RB0145   Beatlefan 5:6 (October 1983) p21.
         Kozinn, Allan
RB0146   Beatles Unlimited 42 p16. Vermeer, Evert

REVIEWS OF BOOKS

THE BEATLES DISCOGRAPHY
RB0147   Beatlefan 1:4 (June 1979) p22.
         Shears, Billy
RB0148   Beatles Unlimited 8 (July 1976)
         p15. Curly, John

THE BEATLES DOWN UNDER
RB0149   Beatlefan 4:6 (October 1982) p28.
         King, William P.
RB0150   Beatlefan 4:6 (October 1982) p28.
         Rehm, Carl
RB0151   The Beatles Book 75 (July 1982)
         ppx-xi. Doggett, Peter
RB0152   Beatles Unlimited 42 p16. Vermeer, Evert
RB0153   Record Collector 34 (June 1982)
         p41.

THE BEATLES' ENGLAND
RB0154   Beatlefan 4:3 (April 1982) p30.
         King, William P.
RB0155   Booklist 79 (September 1, 1982)
         p23.
RB0156   Record Collector 35 (July 1982)
         p62.

BEATLES FOR CLASSICAL GUITAR
RB0157   Library Journal 100 (July 1975)
         p1327.

THE BEATLES FOREVER (SCHAFFNER)
RB0158   Beatles Unlimited 18 (January 1978)
         pp16-17. Glazier, Joel
RB0159   Best Sellers 38 (April 1978) p15.
         Smith, C.
RB0160   Booklist 74 (February 15, 1978)
         p970. Hunt, C.A.
RB0161   Book Review Digest (1978) p1153.
RB0162   Choice 15 (April 1978) p245.
RB0163   Kirkus Reviews 45 (December 15, 1977)
         p1326.
RB0164   Kliatt Paperback Book Guide 13 (Winter
         1979) p56.
RB0165   Library Journal 102 (December 1, 1977)
         p2435. Freehan, P.G.
RB0166   Publishers Weekly 212 (October 17, 1977)
         p75.
RB0167   School Library Journal 24 (February 1978)
         p71. Jaffe, C.
RB0168   School Library Journal 26 (August 1980)
         p39.
RB0169   Triangle 74 pp1-28.
RB0170   West Coast Review of Books 4 (January
         1978) p43.
RB0171   Wilson Library Bulletin 55 (February 1981)
         p435.

THE BEATLES FOREVER (SPENCE)
RB0172   Record Collector 35 (July 1982)
         p62.

THE BEATLES FOR THE RECORD
RB0173   Beatlefan 4:4 (June 1982) p31.
         Shears, Billy

THE BEATLES ILLUSTRATED LYRICS
RB0174   AB Bookman's Weekly 44 (December 15, 1969)
         p2023.
RB0175   Book Review Digest (1970) p95.
RB0176   Book World 10 (December 21, 1980)
         p12.
RB0177   Library Journal 94 (December 15, 1969)
         p4625. Coats, R.
RB0178   Library Journal 95 (January 15, 1970)
         p161. Nyren, N.S.
RB0179   National Observer 8 (December 15, 1969)
         p17.
RB0180   New Leader 52 (November 10, 1969)
         pp16-17.
RB0181   New Republic 161 (November 8, 1969)
         pp25-26. Whittemore, R.

RB0182   New York Times Book Review (February 15,
         1970) p3.
RB0183   Saturday Review 52 (November 29, 1969)
         p45.
RB0184   The Spectator 223 (December 13, 1969)
         p844.
RB0185   Time 94 (December 5, 1969) p110.
RB0186   Times Literary Supplement (December 11,
         1969) p1433.

THE BEATLES ILLUSTRATED LYRICS - I
RB0187   Beatlefan 3:2 (February 1981) pp28-29.
         King, William P.

THE BEATLES ILLUSTRATED LYRICS - II
RB0188   Beatlefan 3:2 (February 1981) pp28-29.
         King, William P.

THE BEATLES ILLUSTRATED LYRICS 2
RB0189   Library Journal 96 (September 15, 1971)
         p2940.
RB0190   Library Journal 96 (October 1, 1971)
         p3138.
RB0191   Rolling Stone 91 (September 16, 1971)
         p52.

THE BEATLES IN ITALY
RB0192   Beatles Unlimited 38 (September 1981)
         p11. Settimo, Franco

THE BEATLES IN RICHARD LESTER'S "A HARD DAY'S NIGHT"
RB0193   Book World (March 12, 1978) pE6.
RB0194   Kliatt Paperback Book Guide 12 (Fall 1978)
         p53.
RB0195   Library Journal 103 (March 15, 1978)
         p681. Feehan, P.G.
RB0196   Publishers Weekly 212 (November 28, 1977)
         p41.
RB0197   School Library Journal 24 (May 1978)
         p37, 92.

THE BEATLES IN THEIR OWN WORDS
RB0198   Beatlefan 1:3 (April 1979) p8.
         King, William P.
RB0199   Kliatt Paperback Book Guide 13 (Fall 1979)
         p60.
RB0200   Library Journal 104 (May 15, 1979)
         p1143. Feehan, P.G.

THE BEATLES MOVIE CATALOG
RB0201   Beatlefan 2:5 (August 1980) p30.
         Ellis, Roger

THE BEATLES ON RECORD (RUSSELL)
RB0202   Beatles Now 6 (May 1983) p19.
         Baker, Steve

THE BEATLES ON RECORD (WALLGREN)
RB0203   Beatlefan 5:1 (December 1982) p25.
         King, William P.
RB0204   Beatles Now 5 (Winter 1983) p6.
         Baker, Steve

THE BEATLES: THE AUTHORIZED BIOGRAPHY
RB0205   After Dark 10:6, (October 1968)
         pp61-63.
RB0206   Antiquarian Bookman 42 (September 2, 1968)
         p737.
RB0207   Best Sellers 28 (October 1, 1968)
         p266. McGurl, B.J.
RB0208   Booklist 65 (April 1, 1969) p882.
RB0209   Book Review Digest (1968) p311.
RB0210   Book World 2 (September 29, 1968)
         p6. Coleman, J.
RB0211   Book World 3 (July 13, 1969) p17.
RB0212   Book World 3 (December 7, 1969)
         p30.
RB0213   Choice 7 (March 1970) p88.
RB0214   Christian Science Monitor 60 (November
         19, 1968) p1.

RB0215 Commentary 47 (April 1969) p79.
RB0216 Esquire 70 (November 1968) p76.
           Muggeridge, M.
RB0217 Jazz & Pop 7 (November 1968) p49.
RB0218 Kirkus Reviews 36 (July 15, 1968)
           p791.
RB0219 Library Journal 93 (November 1, 1968)
           p4131. Harrison, D.W.
RB0220 Library Journal 93 (November 15, 1968)
           p4429. Clark, C.
RB0221 The Listener 80 (October 3, 1968)
           p447. Mitchell, A.
RB0222 Nation 208 (January 6, 1969) p28.
           Blackburn, S.
RB0223 National Observer 7 (September 16, 1968)
           p19. Walker, J.
RB0224 New Statesman 76 (October 4, 1968)
           p432. French, P.
RB0225 Newsweek 72 (September 30, 1968)
           p106. Zimmerman, P.D.
RB0226 New Yorker 44 (November 9, 1968)
           p239.
RB0227 New York Times Book Review (September 29,
           1968) p7. Peyser, J.
RB0228 The Observer (September 29, 1968)
           p27. Jones, D.A.
RB0229 The Observer (October 12, 1969)
           p38.
RB0230 Publishers Weekly 194 (July 22, 1968)
           p63.
RB0231 Publishers Weekly 195 (May 5, 1969)
           p53.
RB0232 Rolling Stone 20 (October 26, 1968)
           pp15-18.
RB0233 The Times (October 5, 1968) p22A.
           Wardle, Irving
RB0234 Top of the News 25 (January 1969)
           p207.
RB0235 Variety 252 (October 16, 1968) p54.
RB0236 Virginia Quarterly Review 45 (Spring 1969)
           pR62.

THE BEATLES: THE AUTHORIZED BIOGRAPHY - SECOND ED.
RB0237 Beatles Unlimited 21 (July 1978)
           pp9-10. Pope, Michael E.

THE BEATLES: THE REAL STORY
RB0238 Antiquarian Bookman 42 (September 2, 1968)
           p738.
RB0239 Book Review Digest (1968) p412.
RB0240 Book World (September 29, 1968)
           p6. Coleman, J.
RB0241 Christian Science Monitor 60 (November
           19, 1968) p1.
RB0242 Commentary 47 (April 1969) p79.
RB0243 Jazz & Pop 7 (November 1968) p49.
RB0244 Kirkus Reviews 36 (July 15, 1968)
           p793.
RB0245 Library Journal 93 (September 15, 1968)
           p3337. Clark, C.
RB0246 Library Journal 93 (November 1, 1968)
           p4131. Harrison, D.W.
RB0247 National Observer 7 (September 16, 1968)
           p19. Walker, J.
RB0248 Newsweek 72 (September 30, 1968)
           p106. Zimmerman, P.D.
RB0249 New York Times Book Review (September 29,
           1968) p7. Peyser, Joan
RB0250 Publishers Weekly 194 (July 22, 1968)
           p62.

THE BEATLES TRIVIA QUIZ BOOK
RB0251 School Library Journal 25 (March 1979)
           p156.

THE BEATLES - 24 POSTERS
RB0252 Beatlefan 5:6 (October 1983) p21.
           Wallgren, Mark

THE BEATLES WHO'S WHO

RB0253 Beatlefan 4:6 (October 1982) pp28,30.
           Stonehouse, Justin
RB0254 The Beatles Book 79 (November 1982)
           pp46-47.
RB0255 Record Collector 39 (November 1982)
           p59.

THE BEATLES YEARS
RB0256 Books & Bookmen 18 (October 1972)
           p97.
RB0257 New Statesman 84 (November 3, 1972)
           p652.
RB0258 Times Literary Supplement (July 14, 1972)
           p826.

THE BEATLES: YESTERDAY AND TODAY
RB0259 Beatlefan 1:2 (February 1979) p12.
           King, Leslie T.

BEHIND THE BEATLES SONGS
RB0260 Beatlefan 1:6 (October 1979) p18.
           Shears, Billy
RB0261 Beatles Unlimited 23 (November 1978)
           p7. DeBruin, Hans

THE BOYS FROM LIVERPOOL
RB0262 Beatlefan 2:4 (June 1980) p24.
           King, William P.
RB0263 Beatles Unlimited 32 (May 1980)
           p22. Glazier, Joel
RB0264 Booklist 77 (September 1, 1980)
           p48. Williams, D.M.
RB0265 Book Review Digest (1980) p1068.
RB0266 Choice 18 (November 1980) p408.
RB0267 Publishers Weekly 218 (July 18, 1980)
           p61.
RB0268 School Library Journal 27 (October 1980)
           p158. Perry, M.L.
RB0269 Voice of Youth Advocates 3 (October 1980)
           p39. Brown, D.
RB0270 Wilson Library Bulletin 55 (February 1981)
           p435.

THE BRITISH INVASION
RB0271 Beatlefan 4:6 (October 1982) p30.
           Sussman, Al

A CELLARFUL OF NOISE
RB0272 Beatlefan 2:3 (April 1980) p9.
           King, Leslie T.
RB0273 The Beatles Book 71 (March 1982)
           ppx-xii. Doggett, Peter
RB0274 Book Review Digest (1964) p373.
RB0275 Book Week (October 31, 1965) p23.
           Hamill, P.
RB0276 Kirkus Reviews p1034.
RB0277 Library Journal 89 (October 15, 1964)
           p3949. Knapp, M.
RB0278 Library Journal 90 (January 15, 1965) p400.
RB0279 Melody Maker 39 (October 10, 1964)
           pp10-11.
RB0280 Melody Maker 57 (January 2, 1982)
           p30.
RB0281 New Statesman 68 (October 9, 1964)
           p548. Melly, G.
RB0282 New York Review of Books 4 (March 25,
           1965) p10. Jones, D.A.N.
RB0283 Times Literary Supplement (December 10,
           1964) p1122.
RB0284 Wilson Library Bulletin 55 (February 1981)
           p436.

COLLECTING THE BEATLES
RB0285 American Reference Books Annual, Vol.14 (198
           (1983) p447. Grefrath, Richard W.
RB0286 Beatlefan 4:6 (October 1982) p30.
           Schwartz, David
RB0287 Booklist (December 15, 1982) p545.
RB0288 Chicago Tribune 3 (January 7, 1983)
           p10. Gold, Anita

RB0289　City Pages (Minneapolis) (December 1,
　　　　　　1982) p25. Colour, Martian
RB0290　The Dispatch (St. Paul, MN) (November 12,
　　　　　　1982) p9A. Boyd, Cynthia
RB0291　Goldmine 79 (December 1982) p185.
　　　　　　Koenig, John
RB0292　Record Collector 38 (October 1982)
　　　　　　p56.
RB0293　RQ/Reference Quarterly 22:3 (Spring 1983)
　　　　　　p302. Schlachter, Gail
RB0294　Trouser Press (January 1983) p31.
　　　　　　Isler, Scott
RB0295　Wilson Library Bulletin 57:4 (December
　　　　　　1982) p347. Rettig, James

COMMUNISM, HYPNOTISM AND THE BEATLES
RB0296　Books & Bookmen 18 (April 1973)
　　　　　　p66.

THE COMPLEAT BEATLES
RB0297　Audio 66:7 (July 1982) p92.
　　　　　　Tiven, Jon & Sally
RB0298　Beatlefan 3:6 (October 1981) pp32,34.
　　　　　　King, William P.
RB0299　Billboard 93 (October 3, 1981) p32.
RB0300　Book World 11 (December 6, 1981)
　　　　　　p9.

THE COMPLETE BEATLES U.S. RECORD PRICE GUIDE
RB0301　Beatles Now 8 (October 1983) p18.
　　　　　　Baker, Steve

A DAY IN THE LIFE
RB0302　American Reference Books Annual, Vol.12
　　　　　　(1981) p467. Mullins, Melissa D.
RB0303　Aware 7 (Spring 1981) p30.
　　　　　　Kolanjian, Steve
RB0304　Beatlefan 2:3 (April 1980) pp8-9.
　　　　　　Schaffner, Nicholas
RB0305　Beatlefan 2:3 (April 1980) p8.
　　　　　　Shears, Billy
RB0306　Beatles Unlimited 32 (May 1980)
　　　　　　p6. Vermeer, Evert
RB0307　Book Review Digest (1980) p1080.
RB0308　The Calgary Herald (January 31, 1981)
　　　　　　pH19. Brennan, Brian
RB0309　Choice 77 (July 1980) p658.
RB0310　Come Together 2:7 p17.
RB0311　Goldmine (September 1980) p170.
RB0312　Goldmine (April 1983) p198.
RB0313　Library Journal 105 (May 1, 1980)
　　　　　　p1086. Feehan, P.G.
RB0314　Melody Maker (August 15, 1981) p4.
　　　　　　Humphries, Patrick
RB0315　Music & Video Week (London) (March 20,
　　　　　　1982) p13.
RB0316　Music Educators Journal 67 (December 1980)
　　　　　　p74.
RB0317　New York Times (March 14, 1980)
　　　　　　pC12. Rockwell, John
RB0318　Reference Services Review 9:2 (April 1981)
　　　　　　p43. Ginsburg, David
RB0319　School Library Journal 26:9 (May 1980)
　　　　　　p94. Jaffe, C.
RB0320　Sounds (London) (July 12, 1980)
　　　　　　p43. Harry, Bill
RB0321　Village Voice 25 (December 17, 1980)
　　　　　　p61.

EVERY LITTLE THING
RB0322　Beatlefan 2:1 (December 1979) p26.
　　　　　　Shears, Billy
RB0323　Beatles Unlimited 31 (March 1980)
　　　　　　p7. Remmerswaal, Jos

THE FACTS ABOUT A POP GROUP - FEATURING WINGS
RB0324　School Library Journal 24 (January 1978)
　　　　　　p101.
RB0325　Times Literary Supplement (October 22,
　　　　　　1976) p39. Blatchford, R.

FOLLOW THE MERSEYBEAT ROAD
RB0326　Record Collector 57 (May 1984) p40.

GEORGE HARRISON: YESTERDAY AND TODAY
RB0327　Booklist 94 (April 15, 1978) p1311.
　　　　　　Hunt, C.A.
RB0328　Kliatt Paperback Book Guide 12 (Spring
　　　　　　1978) p40.
RB0329　School Library Journal 24 (May 1978)
　　　　　　p92. Jaffe, C.

GRAPEFRUIT
RB0330　Creem 4 (March 1972) p42.
RB0331　The Listener 83 (June 11, 1970)
　　　　　　p792.
RB0332　The Nation 211 (September 7, 1970)
　　　　　　p188.
RB0333　Village Voice 16 (October 7, 1971)
　　　　　　p20.

GROWING UP WITH THE BEATLES
RB0334　Booklist 73 (December 15, 1976)
　　　　　　p585. Hunt, C.A.
RB0335　Kirkus Reviews 44 (September 15, 1976)
　　　　　　p1088.
RB0336　Kliatt Paperback Book Guide 11 (Winter
　　　　　　1977) p34.
RB0337　Library Journal 102 (January 1, 1977)
　　　　　　p112. Gehrman, G.

"HANDS ACROSS THE WATER": WINGS TOUR USA
RB0338　Beatlefan 3:2 (February 1981) p29.
　　　　　　King, Leslie T.
RB0339　Beatles Unlimited 20 (May 1978)
　　　　　　p21. Vermeer, Evert

I ME MINE
RB0340　Beatlefan 2:6 (October 1980) pp19-20.
　　　　　　Schaffner, Nicholas
RB0341　Beatlefan 2:6 (October 1980) p20.
　　　　　　King, William P.
RB0342　Beatlefan 4:1 (December 1981) pp29-30.
　　　　　　Raidonis-Gillis, Laura
RB0343　Beatlefan 4:1 (December 1981) p30.
　　　　　　Lark, Fred
RB0344　The Beatles Book 71 (March 1982)
　　　　　　ppx-xii. Doggett, Peter
RB0345　Beatles Unlimited 33 (July 1980)
　　　　　　pp6-9. Bergholtz, Artillio
RB0346　Billboard 93 (November 28, 1981)
　　　　　　p55.
RB0347　Booklist 78 (November 15, 1981)
　　　　　　p410.
RB0348　Library Journal 107 (January 1, 1982)
　　　　　　p96. Sutton, J.
RB0349　New Republic 185 (December 2, 1981)
　　　　　　p23.
RB0350　The Observer (March 21, 1982) p31.
RB0351　Rolling Stone 326 (September 18, 1980)
　　　　　　p26. Marcus, Greil
RB0352　School Library Journal 28 (January 1982)
　　　　　　p94. Pascal, S.
RB0353　Times Literary Supplement (May 15, 1981)
　　　　　　p547a. Morrison, Blake

IN HIS OWN WRITE
RB0354　Booklist 77 (March 15, 1981) p1004.
RB0355　Book Review Digest (1964) p717.
RB0356　Book Week (May 3, 1963) pp4,10.
　　　　　　Wolfe, Tom
RB0357　Books Today 4 (January 29, 1967)
　　　　　　p11. Petersen, C.
RB0358　The Nation 198 (June 8, 1964) pp588-589.
　　　　　　Schickele, Peter
RB0359　New Statesman 67 (May 1, 1964) p685.
　　　　　　Ricks, Christopher
RB0360　Newsweek 63 (April 27, 1964) p108.
RB0361　New York Times (April 24, 1964) p31:4.
　　　　　　Gilroy, Harry

RB0362   New York Times Book Review 86 (April 5,
         1981) p27.
RB0363   Publishers Weekly 190 (November 28, 1966)
         p65. Fleischer, L.
RB0364   Punch 280 (March 4, 1981) p358.
RB0365   Time (April 27, 1964) ppE7,100.
RB0366   Times Literary Supplement (March 26, 1964)
         p250.
RB0367   Virginia Quarterly Review 40 (Summer 1964)
         pcxxx.
RB0368   Wall Street Journal (June 3, 1964)
         p18:4. Lloyd, Eric.
RB0369   Wilson Library Bulletin 55 (February 1981)
         p435.

IN THE FOOTSTEPS OF THE BEATLES
RB0370   Beatlefan 4:3 (April 1982) p30.
         Fulper-Smith, Shawn
RB0371   Record Collector 35 (July 1982)
         p62.

JOHN LENNON AND THE BEATLES FOREVER
RB0372   Beatles Unlimited 36 (June 1981)
         p18. Vermeer, Evert

JOHN LENNON: DEATH OF A DREAM
RB0373   Beatles Unlimited 36 (June 1981)
         p18. Vermeer, Evert
RB0374   New York Times Book Review 86 (April 5,
         1981) p27.

JOHN LENNON 4 EVER
RB0375   Beatlefan 3:6 (October 1981) pp30-32.
         King, William P.

JOHN LENNON IN HIS OWN WORDS
RB0376   Beatlefan 3:6 (October 1981) p30.
         King, Leslie T.
RB0377   Punch 280 (March 4, 1981) p358.
RB0378   School Library Journal 28 (September 1981)
         p149.
RB0379   Voice of Youth Advocates 4 (October 1981)
         p49.

JOHN LENNON: IN MY LIFE
RB0380   Library Journal 108:19 (November 1, 1983)
         p2086. Feehan, Paul G.

JOHN LENNON 1940-1980 (SCHWORCK)
RB0381   Beatlefan 3:3 (April 1981) p29.
         King, Leslie T.

JOHN LENNON 1940-1980, A BIOGRAPHY
RB0382   Beatlefan 3:6 (October 1981) pp30-32.
         King, William P.
RB0383   British Book News (May 1981) p304.
RB0384   Melody Maker 56 (April 25, 1981)
         p4.
RB0385   The Observer (March 29, 1981) p33.
RB0386   Sunday Times (March 1, 1981) p43b.
RB0387   The Times (May 7, 1981) p12f.
         Taylor, Laurie
RB0388   Times Literary Supplement (May 15, 1981)
         p547a. Morrison, Blake

JOHN LENNON: ONE DAY AT A TIME
RB0389   Billboard 89 (January 22, 1977)
         p68.
RB0390   Booklist 73 (February 15, 1977)
         p874.
RB0391   Book Review Digest (1977) p415.
RB0392   Kliatt Paperback Book Guide 11 (Winter
         1977) p33.
RB0393   New York Review of Books 24 (February 3,
         1977) p31. Miller, M.C.
RB0394   New York Times Book Review (December 12,
         1976) p4. Lyden, M.
RB0395   Rolling Stone (December 16, 1976)
         p103.
RB0396   Wilson Library Bulletin 51 (June 1977)

         p859. McCue, M.
RB0397   Wilson Library Bulletin 55 (February 1981)
         p435.

JOHN LENNON'S SECRET
RB0398   Beatles Now 5 (Winter 1983) p8.
         Glover, David

THE JOHN LENNON STORY
RB0399   Beatlefan 3:6 (October 1981) pp30-32.
         King, William P.

JOHN LENNON SUMMER OF 1980
RB0400   Beatlefan 5:6 (October 1983) p22.
         King, William P.

LENNON AND MCCARTNEY
RB0401   Beatlefan 4:3 (April 1982) p31.
         King, William P.
RB0402   Melody Maker 56 (November 21, 1981)
         p4.

THE LENNON FACTOR
RB0403   AB Bookman's Weekly 50 (July 3, 1972)
         p12.

LENNON REMEMBERS
RB0404   Antioch Review 32 (Spring 1972)
         p243.
RB0405   Atlantic Monthly 228 (November 1971)
         p153. Adams, Phoebe
RB0406   Book Review Digest (1972) p775.
RB0407   Books & Bookmen 18 (December 1972)
         p88.
RB0408   Book World 6 (July 9, 1972) p7.
RB0409   Commonweal 96 (September 22, 1972)
         p500.
RB0410   Guardian Weekly 107 (November 25, 1972)
         p23.
RB0411   Library Journal 96 (November 15, 1971)
         p3917. Storey, E.
RB0412   Library Journal 97 (January 15, 1972)
         p200.
RB0413   New Republic 166 (May 20, 1972)
         p26.
RB0414   New York Times Book Review (February 20,
         1972) p4. O'Hara, J.D.
RB0415   New York Times Book Review 86 (April 5,
         1981) p27.
RB0416   The Observer (October 1, 1972) p41.
RB0417   The Observer (June 3, 1973) p33.
RB0418   Publishers Weekly 200 (September 13, 1971)
         p61.
RB0419   Publishers Weely 201 (May 29, 1972)
         p34.
RB0420   Punch 280 (March 4, 1981) p358.
RB0421   School Library Journal 26 (August 1980)
         p39.
RB0422   Wilson Library Bulletin 55 (February 1981)
         p436.

LENNON '69: SEARCH FOR LIBERATION
RB0423   Beatlefan 3:6 (October 1981) p30.
         King, Leslie T.

THE LENNON TAPES
RB0424   Beatlefan 3:3 (April 1981) pp28-29.
         Shears, Billy
RB0425   Beatles Unlimited 36 (June 1981)
         p18.
RB0426   Melody Maker 56 (April 25, 1981)
         p4.
RB0427   Punch 280 (March 4, 1981) p358.
RB0428   The Times (May 7, 1981) p12f.
         Taylor, Laurie
RB0429   Times Literary Supplement (May 15, 1981)
         p547a. Morrison, Blake

LIFE AT THE DAKOTA
    RB0430 Beatles Unlimited 31 (March 1980)
            pp4-5. Barry, Art

LINDA'S CALENDAR 1982
    RB0431 Beatlefan 4:4 (June 1982) p31.
            King, Leslie T.

LINDA'S PICTURES
    RB0432 Booklist 73 (March 15, 1977) p1065.
    RB0433 Book Review Digest (1977) p839.
    RB0434 Catholic Library World 49 (December 1977)
            p199.
    RB0435 Guardian Weekly 116 (January 23, 1977)
            p22.
    RB0436 Library Journal 102 (January 15, 1977)
            p192. Gehrman, G.
    RB0437 New York Times Book Review (December 12,
            1976) p4. Lyden, M.
    RB0438 School Library Journal 23 (April 1977)
            p83.

LINDA'S SIGNS FOR '79
    RB0439 Beatlefan 1:2 (February 1979) pp13,20.

THE LONG AND WINDING ROAD
    RB0440 Beatlefan 4:5 (August 1982) p26.
            Shears, Billy
    RB0441 The Beatles Book 77 (September 1982)
            ppix-xii. Harry, Bill
    RB0442 Beatles Now 4 (Autumn 1982) p10.
            Phillips, Steve
    RB0443 Record Collector 37 (September 1982)
            pp45-46.

THE LONGEST COCKTAIL PARTY
    RB0444 Book World 6 (November 26, 1972)
            p15.
    RB0445 Kirkus Reviews 40 (September 15, 1972)
            p1124.
    RB0446 Kirkus Reviews 40 (October 15, 1972)
            p1212.
    RB0447 The Observer (December 16, 1973) p32.
    RB0448 Publishers Weekly 202 (September 18, 1972)
            p69.
    RB0449 Publishers Weekly 205 (January 28, 1974)
            p303.
    RB0450 Wilson Library Bulletin 55 (February 1981)
            p436.

LOTS OF LIVERPOOL
    RB0451 Beatlefan 5:1 (December 1982) pp25-26.
            King, Leslie T.

LOVE LETTERS TO THE BEATLES
    RB0452 Book Review Digest (1965) p7.
    RB0453 Christian Science Monitor (July 22, 1964)
            p9. Guidry, F.H.
    RB0454 Harper's 229 (December 1964) p141.
            Lynes, R.
    RB0455 Times Literary Supplement (December 10,
            1964) p1122.

LOVE ME DO - THE BEATLES' PROGRESS
    RB0456 Beatlefan 1:6 (October 1979) p18.
            King, Leslie T.
    RB0457 Times Literary Supplement (December 10,
            1964) p1122.

THE LOVE YOU MAKE
    RB0458 Record Collector 51 (November 1983)
            p40.

LOVING JOHN: THE UNTOLD STORY
    RB0459 Library Journal 108:19 (November 1, 1983)
            p2086. Feehan, Paul G.

THE MACS: MIKE MCCARTNEY'S FAMILY ALBUM
    (see also THANK YOU VERY MUCH)
    RB0460 Beatlefan 4:1 (December 1981) p31.

        King, William P.
    RB0461 Library Journal 106 (November 15, 1981)
            p2239.
    RB0462 Publishers Weekly 220 (October 16, 1981)
            p75.

THE MAN WHO GAVE THE BEATLES AWAY
    RB0463 Kirkus Reviews 43 (April 1, 1975)
            p438.
    RB0464 Library Journal 100 (April 15, 1975)
            p754.
    RB0465 Music Educators Journal 62 (September
            1975) p90.
    RB0466 Popular Music & Society 4:4 p253.
            Dombraski, Jerome K.
    RB0467 Publishers Weekly 207 (March 10, 1975)
            p52.
    RB0468 Rolling Stone (November 17, 1977)
            p101.
    RB0469 Wilson Library Bulletin 55 (February 1981)
            p436.

MATEY FOR EIGHTY
    RB0470 Beatlefan 2:2 (February 1980) p7,9.
            King, Leslie T.

MERSEY BEAT: THE BEGINNINGS OF THE BEATLES
    RB0471 Beatlefan 1:2 (February 1979) p13.
            King, William P.
    RB0472 Beatles Unlimited 20 (May 1978)
            pp8-9. Hager, Henk
    RB0473 Kliatt Paperback Book Guide 13 (Spring
            1979) p33.
    RB0474 Rolling Stone 267 (June 15, 1978)
            p111.
    RB0475 Wilson Library Bulletin 55 (February 1981)
            p436.

THE NEW YORK TIMES GREAT SONGS OF LENNON & MCCARTNEY
    RB0476 Horn Book Magazine 50 (April 1974)
            p174.
    RB0477 Village Voice 19 (March 28, 1974)
            p29.

PAPERBACK WRITER
    RB0478 Booklist 75 (November 1, 1978) p464.
    RB0479 Creem 10 (September 1978) p52.
    RB0480 Library Journal 103 (June 15, 1978)
            p1292. Petticoffer, D.
    RB0481 Los Angeles Times (August 7, 1977)
            p1. Hilburn, Robert
    RB0482 Publishers Weekly 213 (May 1, 1978)
            p82.
    RB0483 Rolling Stone 224 (July 28, 1977)
            p38.
    RB0484 School Library Journal 25 (January 1979)
            p64.
    RB0485 Sewanee Review 86 (October 1978)
            p609. Allen, B.

PAUL MCCARTNEY: A BIOGRAPHY IN WORDS & PICTURES
    RB0486 Beatlefan 1:3 (April 1979) p8.
            King, Leslie T.

PAUL MCCARTNEY & WINGS
    RB0487 Beatlefan 2:1 (December 1979) p26.
            King, Leslie T.

PAUL MCCARTNEY: BEATLE WITH WINGS
    RB0488 Beatlefan 1:1 (December 1978) p4.
            Budapest, Billy

PAUL MCCARTNEY: COMPOSER/ARTIST
    RB0489 Beatlefan 3:4 (June 1981) p28.
            King, Leslie T.
    RB0490 The Beatles Book 67 (November 1981)
            ppiii-vi. Harry, Bill
    RB0491 Library Journal 106 (July 1981)
            p1425.
    RB0492 The Observer (December 6, 1981)

                p29.
RB0493   Oui 10:9 (September 1981) p91.
                Fents, Noah

PAUL MCCARTNEY IN HIS OWN WORDS
RB0494   Booklist 73 (April 15, 1977) p1236.
                Hunt, C.A.
RB0495   Music Educators Journal 63 (April 1977)
                p73.
RB0496   Publishers Weekly 209 (June 28, 1976)
                p97.
RB0497   School Library Journal 23 (April 1977)
                p85.

THE PENGUIN JOHN LENNON
RB0498   The Observer (October 30, 1966)
                p22.

PHOTOGRAPHS
RB0499   Beatlefan 5:1 (December 1982) p25.
                King, Leslie T.

THE PLAYBOY INTERVIEWS WITH JOHN LENNON AND YOKO ONO
RB0500   Beatlefan 4:2 (February 1982) p30.
                King, William P.
RB0501   The Beatles Book 76 (August 1982)
                pxii. Doggett, Peter
RB0502   Booklist 78 (October 15, 1981) p268.
RB0503   Books of the Times 4 (September 1981)
                p418.
RB0504   Choice 19 (September 1981) p68.
RB0505   Kirkus Reviews 49 (October 1, 1981)
                p1281.
RB0506   Library Journal 106 (December 1, 1981)
                p2318.
RB0507   New York Times VII (November 29, 1981)
                p7. Klein, Joe
RB0508   Publishers Weekly 220 (October 16, 1981)
                p65.
RB0509   Record Collector 37 (September 1982)
                p46.

P.S. WE LOVE YOU
RB0510   The Beatles Book 79 (November 1982)
                pp46-47.

ROCK 'N' ROLL TIMES
RB0511   Beatlefan 4:3 (April 1982) p31.
                King, William P.
RB0512   Beatles Now 3 (Summer 1982) p6.
                Smith, David J.
RB0513   Village Voice (April 20, 1982) p26.

SGT. PEPPER'S LONELY HEARTS CLUB BAND
RB0514   Woodwind World-Brass and Percussion
                17 (1978) p19. Musser, W.

SHOUT!
RB0515   Beatlefan 3:3 (April 1981) p28.
                King, William P.
RB0516   The Beatles Book 61 (May 1981) ppiii-v.
                Harry, Bill
RB0517   The Beatles Book 63 (July 1981)
                ppiii-vii. Dean, Johnny & Tony Barrow
RB0518   The Beatles Book 65 (September 1981)
                ppx-xi. Flanagan, Coleen
RB0519   Beatles Unlimited 36 (June 1981)
                p20. Vermeer, Evert
RB0520   Booklist 77 (June 15, 1981) p1328.
                Hooper, W.B.
RB0521   Book Review Digest 77:8 (November 1981)
                p106.
RB0522   Creem 13 (August 1981) p46.
RB0523   Horn Book Magazine 57 (August 1981)
                p462.
RB0524   Kliatt Paperback Book Guide 16 (Spring
                1982) p36.
RB0525   Library Journal 106 (July 1981)
                p1425.
RB0526   The Listener 105 (April 16, 1981)

                p515.
RB0527   Melody Maker 56 (April 25, 1981)
                p4.
RB0528   Newsweek 97 (June 15, 1981) p96.
RB0529   New York Times VII (April 5, 1981)
                p9. Hogan, Randolph
RB0530   The Observer (March 29, 1981) p33.
RB0531   The Observer (July 19, 1981) p29.
RB0532   The Observer (August 15, 1982) p31.
RB0533   Publishers Weekly 219 (February 13, 1981)
                p90.
RB0534   The Spectator 246 (June 13, 1981)
                p23.
RB0535   Sunday Times (April 5, 1981) p43c.
                Ricks, Christopher
RB0536   Time 117 (May 4, 1981) p86.
RB0537   The Times (May 7, 1981) p12f.
                Taylor, Laurie
RB0538   Times Literary Supplement (May 15, 1981)
                p547.

SONGS DER BEATLES: TEXTE UND INTERPRETATIONEN
RB0539   Das Argument 11 pp341-342.
                Heister, Hans-Werner

A SPANIARD IN THE WORKS
RB0540   Atlantic 216 (August 1965) p129.
                Adams, Phoebe
RB0541   Ave Maria 102 (October 16, 1965)
                p27. White, R.
RB0542   Best Sellers 25 (July 15, 1965) p184.
RB0543   Booklist 77 (March 15, 1981) p1004.
RB0544   Book Review Digest (1956) p756.
RB0545   Books Today 4 (January 29, 1967)
                p11. Petersen, C.
RB0546   Book Week (August 8, 1965) p8.
                Schickel, Richard
RB0547   Manchester Guardian 93 (July 22, 1965)
                p11. Johnson, B.S.
RB0548   New Republic 153 (August 7, 1965)
                pp20-22. Wain, John
RB0549   New Statesman 70 (August 13, 1965)
                p222. Hope, Francis
RB0550   New York Herald Tribune (July 6, 1965)
                p17.
RB0551   New York Times (July 1, 1965) p33M.
                Pryce-Jones, A.
RB0552   New York Times Book Review 86 (April 5,
                1981) p27.
RB0553   Publishers Weekly 190 (November 28, 1966)
                p65. Fleischer, Lenore
RB0554   Punch 249 (July 21, 1965) Symons, J.
RB0555   Punch 280 (March 4, 1981) p358.
RB0556   Ramparts 4 (January 1966) p67. Cott, J.
RB0557   Times Literary Supplement (July 29, 1965)
                p658.
RB0558   Virginia Quarterly Review 41 (Autumn 1965)
                pcxlvii.
RB0559   Wall Street Journal (August 8, 1965) p16:6.
RB0560   Wall Street Journal (September 8, 1965)
                p16. Lloyd, Eric
RB0561   Wilson Library Bulletin 55 (February 1981)
                p435.

STRAWBERRY FIELDS FOREVER: JOHN LENNON REMEMBERED
RB0562   Beatlefan 3:2 (February 1981) p28.
                King, William P.
RB0563   Beatles Unlimited 36 (June 1981)
                p18. Vermeer, Evert
RB0564   Booklist 77 (March 15, 1981) p1004.
RB0565   Creem 13 (August 1981) p46.
RB0566   Library Journal 106 (March 1, 1981)
                p560. Sutton, J.
RB0567   New York Times Book Review 86 (April 5,
                1981) p27.

THANK U VERY MUCH
         (see also THE MACS: MIKE MCCARTNEY'S
            FAMILY ALBUM)
RB0568   The Beatles Book 69 (January 1982)

ppv-vi. Read, Lorna
RB0569 The Observer (December 6, 1981)
        p29.

THINGS WE SAID TODAY
RB0570 American Libraries 12:2 (February 1981)
        p102.
RB0571 American Reference Books Annual, Vol.13 (1982)
        p524.
RB0572 Association for Recorded Sound Col-
        lections. Newsletter. 16 (Summer
        1981) p7.
RB0573 Beatlefan 3:2 (February 1981) p28.
        Shears, Billy
RB0574 The Beatles Book 60 (April 1981)
        px. Lewisohn, Mark
RB0575 Beatles Unlimited 36 (June 1981)
        pp19-20. Vermeer, Evert
RB0576 Booklist 78 (December 1, 1981) p517.
RB0577 Book Review Digest 77:7 (October 1981)
        p44.
RB0578 The Calgary Herald (January 31, 1981)
        pH19. Brennan, Brian
RB0579 Choice 18 (May 1981) p1232.
RB0580 Library Journal 106 (February 15, 1981)
        p454. Jewell, Thomas N.
RB0581 Music Educators Journal (May 1981) p23.
RB0582 Record Collector 38 (October 1982)
        p56.
RB0583 Reference Services Review 9:2 (April 1981)
        p44. Ginsburg, David
RB0584 Wilson Library Bulletin 55 (March 1981)
        p539. Bunge, C.

A TRIBUTE TO JOHN LENNON, 1940-1980
RB0585 Beatlefan 4:1 (December 1981) pp30-31.
        King, Leslie T.

26 DAYS THAT ROCKED THE WORLD !
RB0586 Beatlefan 1:5 (August 1979) p18.
        King, Leslie T.

TWILIGHT OF THE GODS
RB0587 Booklist 70 (December 15, 1973)
        p416.
RB0588 Book Review Digest (1974) p815.
RB0589 Book World (July 14, 1974) p2.
RB0590 Choice 11 (November 1974) p1321.
RB0591 Guardian Weekly 109 (December 8, 1973)
        24.
RB0592 Guitar Reviews 2 (December 1973)
        p3.
RB0593 High Fidelity/Musical America 24
        (November 1974) pMA39.
RB0594 Kirkus Reviews 41 (November 1, 1973)
        p1246.
RB0595 Kirkus Reviews 42 (April 1, 1974)
        p405.
RB0596 Library Journal 99 (February 1, 1974)
        p367. Freehan, P. G.
RB0597 The Listener 91 (February 7, 1974)
        p183.
RB0598 Making Music 84 (Spring 1974) p15.
RB0599 Musical Times 118 (July 1977) p563.
RB0600 Music and Letters 55:3 pp337-338.
RB0601 Music and Musicians 22 (April 1974)
        pp36-37.
RB0602 Music Educators Journal 66 (December 1979)
        p94.
RB0603 Music In Education 28:366 p80.
RB0604 Music Journal 32 (September 1974)
        pp22+.
RB0605 Music Review 38:2 pp133-135.
RB0606 Music Teacher and Piano Student 53

(April 1974) p27.
RB0607 New Statesman 86 (November 30, 1973)
        p820. Gelly, D.
RB0608 New York Times 123 (July 4, 1974)
        p17.
RB0609 New York Times VII (September 22, 1974)
        p39. Reynolds, Roger
RB0610 Notes 31:3 p568.
RB0611 The Observer (December 16, 1973)
        p32.
RB0612 Publishers Weekly 204 (November 26, 1973)
        p36.
RB0613 Stereo Review 33 (August 1974) p44.
RB0614 Symphony News 25:5 p25.
RB0615 Times Literary Supplement (April 12, 1974)
        p390.

A TWIST OF LENNON
RB0616 Beatlefan 1:1 (December 1978) p4.
        King, Leslie T.
RB0617 Beatlefan 2:3 (April 1980) p9.
        King, Leslie T.
RB0618 Beatles Unlimited 22 (September 1978)
        p7. McDonagh, Des
RB0619 Melody Maker 53 (July 15, 1978)
        p12.
RB0620 New York Times Book Review 86 (April 5,
        1981) p27.
RB0621 Wilson Library Bulletin 55 (February 1981)
        p436.

UP AGAINST IT - A SCREENPLAY FOR THE BEATLES
RB0622 Beatlefan 3:5 (August 1981) p31.
        King, Leslie T.

WAITING FOR THE BEATLES: AN APPLE SCRUFF'S STORY
RB0623 Record Collector 57 (May 1984) p40.

THE WELL-TEMPERED LENNON-MCCARTNEY
RB0624 Notes 35 p991. Burge, D.

WE LOVE YOU BEATLES
RB0625 Kirkus Reviews 39 (October 1, 1971)
        p1068.
RB0626 Library Journal 97 (February 15, 1972)
        p769.
RB0627 New Yorker 47 (December 4, 1971)
        p190.

WORKING CLASS HEROES
RB0628 Record Collector 50 (October 1983)
        p35.

YESTERDAY - THE BEATLES 1963-1965
RB0629 Beatlefan 5:6 (October 1983) p21.
        Wallgren, Mark

YOU CAN'T DO THAT
RB0630 Aware 8 (Winter 1981) p6. Rapsis, Mike
RB0631 Beatlefan 3:4 (June 1981) pp28,34.
        Shears, Billy
RB0632 The Beatles Book 72 (April 1982)
        ppx-xi. Harry, Bill
RB0633 Beatles Unlimited 38 (September 1981)
        pp7-8. Van Haarlem, Rene
RB0634 Choice (January 1982) p610.
RB0635 Goldmine 62 (July 1981) p144.
RB0636 Hot Wacks Quarterly 9 p27.
RB0637 Music Magazine (Tokyo) (June 1982)
        p157. Mitsui, Toru
RB0638 Record Collector 38 (October 1982)
        p57.
RB0639 Stereo Review (July 1981) p92.
        Simels, Steve

ALL THIS AND WORLD WAR II
    RF0001   After Dark 9:11 (March 1977) p84.
              Stoop, N.M.
    RF0002   Beatles Unlimited 14 (July 1977)
              p5. Koning, Frank
    RF0003   Cue 46:1 (January 8, 1977) p39. Wolf, W.
    RF0004   Film & Broadcasting Review 42:2
              (January 15, 1977) p8.
    RF0005   Mass Media Ministries 12:7 (February 14,
              1977) p7. Schillaci, P.
    RF0006   McCalls 104:6 (March 1977) p80.
              Minton, L.
    RF0007   Monthly Film Bulletin 44:520 (May 1977)
              p91. Meek, S.
    RF0008   New Times 8:2 (January 21, 1977)
              p64. Corliss, R.
    RF0009   Parents Magazine 52:2 (February 1977)
              p14. Ripp, J.
    RF0010   Playboy 24:3 (March 1977) p34.
    RF0011   Time 109:5 (January 31, 1977) p59.
              Porterfield, C.
    RF0012   Variety 285 (November 17, 1976)
              p18.

ALL THOSE YEARS AGO (VIDEO)
    RF0013   Beatlefan 4:1 (December 1981) p23.
              King, William P.

APOTHEOSIS
    RF0014   Village Voice 16:1 (January 7, 1971)
              p51. Mekas, Jonas

BACK TO THE EGG (VIDEO)
    RF0015   Beatles Unlimited 39 (1981) p19.
              Walrustitty, Jethro Q.

BEATLEMANIA - THE MOVIE
    RF0016   Beatlefan 3:6 (October 1981) p12.
              Haviv, Mitch

THE BEATLES IN CONCERT - NO. 1 (SUPER 8MM)
    RF0017   Classic Film Collector 58 (Spring 1978)
              p41. Aben, D.

THE BEATLES IN CONCERT - NO. 2 (SUPER 8MM)
    RF0018   Classic Film Collector 58 (Spring 1978)
              p39. Aben, D.

THE BEATLES INTERVIEW (16MM)
    RF0019   Classic Images 64 (July 1979) p38.
              Aben, D.

THE BEATLES MOVIE MEDLEY (VIDEO)
    RF0020   Beatlefan 5:1 (December 1982) pp19,26.
              King, William P.

THE BIRTH OF THE BEATLES
    RF0021   Beatlefan 1:5 (August 1979) p1,4.
    RF0022   Beatlefan 2:1 (December 1979) p14.
              King, William P.
    RF0023   Beatlefan 2:1 (December 1979) pp14-15.
              Sussman, Al
    RF0024   Beatlefan 2:1 (December 1979) pp15,19.
              Haviv, Mitchell
    RF0025   Beatles Unlimited 29 (November 1979)
              pp10-11. Barry, Art
    RF0026   Creem 11:10 (March 1980) p46. Johnson, R.
    RF0027   Monthly Film Bulletin 47:559 (August 1980)
              p152. Rose, C.

BLINDMAN
    RF0028   Beatles Unlimited 24 (January 1979)
              pp6-8. Pope, Michael E.
    RF0029   Catholic Film Newsletter 37:6 (March 30,
              1972) p32.
    RF0030   Creem 4:2 (July 1972) p51.
    RF0031   Cue 41:15 (April 8, 1972) p6.
    RF0032   Cue 43:9 (March 4, 1974) p34.
    RF0033   Filmfacts 15:12 p275.
    RF0034   Monthly Film Bulletin 41:480 (January

              1974) p4. Milne, T.
    RF0035   Parents Magazine 47:5 (May 1972)
              p16.
    RF0036   Variety 266:9 (April 12, 1972) p16.

BORN TO BOOGIE
    RF0037   Beatles Unlimited 27 (July 1979)
              pp20-21. Pope, Michael E.
    RF0038   Monthly Film Bulletin 40:468 (January
              1973) p5. Dark, C.
    RF0039   Revue Du Cinema/Image Et Son 330
              (July/August 1978) p128. Sauvaget, D.
    RF0040   Revue Du Cinema/Image Et Son 332
              (October 1978) p49. Merigeau, P.
    RF0041   Variety 269:6 (December 20, 1972)
              p18.

BRAVERMAN'S CONDENSED CREAM OF BEATLES
    RF0042   E.F.L.A. Evaluations 8788
    RF0043   Film News 31:4 (October 1974) p9.
    RF0044   Landers Film Reviews 18:7 (March 1974)
              p185.
    RF0045   Media and Methods 10:5 (January 1974)
              p20. Epple, Ron
    RF0046   Media Mix Newsletter 5:4 (February 1974)
              p1.
    RF0047   Previews 3:3 (November 1974) p17.
              Forman, Jack
    RF0048   Probe 6:5 (June 1974) p3.
    RF0049   Sightlines 8:1 (Fall 1974) p22.
    RF0050   Sneak Preview 4:1 (Fall 1974) p9.

CANDY
    RF0051   Beatles Unlimited 21 (July 1978)
              pp12-15. Pope, Michael E.
    RF0052   Cue 43:6 (February 11, 1974) p34.
    RF0053   The Times (February 20, 1969)
              Taylor, John Russell

CAVEMAN
    RF0054   Beatlefan 3:3 (April 1981) p19.
              Harry, Bill
    RF0055   The Beatles Book 64 (August 1981)
              ppix-xi. Harry, Bill
    RF0056   Beatles Unlimited 37 (July 1981)
              p20. Glazier, Joel
    RF0057   Cinefantastique 10:2 (Fall 1980)
              p6. Sammon, P.M.
    RF0058   Cinefantastique 11:2 (Fall 1981)
              p38. Sammon, P.M.
    RF0059   Cinefantastique 11:2 (Fall 1981)
              p52. Counts, K.
    RF0060   Commonweal 108:13 (July 3, 1981)
              p404. Westerbeck, C.L., Jr.
    RF0061   Films In Review 32:6 (June 1981)
              p377. Rogers, T.
    RF0062   Madamoiselle 87:9 (September 1981)
              p56. Rainer, P.
    RF0063   McCalls 108:9 (June 1981) p82. Minton, L.
    RF0064   Monthly Film Bulletin 48:570 (July 1981)
              p133. Auty, M.
    RF0065   New Statesman 102:2627 (July 24, 1981)
              p24. Coleman, J.
    RF0066   New York Times III (April 17, 1981)
              p3. Maslin, Janet
    RF0067   New Yorker 57:13 (May 18, 1981)
              p146. Kael, P.
    RF0068   Playboy 28:7 (July 1981) p44.
              Williamson, B.
    RF0069   Punch 281:7342 (July 29, 1981) p197.
              Powell, D.
    RF0070   Rolling Stone 343 (May 14, 1981)
              p37. Sragow, M.
    RF0071   Time 117:19 (May 11, 1981) p86.
              Corliss, R.
    RF0072   The Times (July 24, 1981) p11c.
              Robinson, David
    RF0073   Variety 302:11 (April 15, 1981)
              p18. Tina
    RF0074   Village Voice 26:16 (April 15, 1981)

p52. Rickey, C.

THE COMPLEAT BEATLES (VIDEO)
RF0075   Beatlefan 5:1 (December 1982) p19.
         Shears, Billy

THE CONCERT FOR BANGLA DESH
RF0076   After Dark 5:1 (May 1972) p70.
RF0077   Catholic Film Newsletter 37:7 (April 15,
         1972) p36.
RF0078   Cosmopolitan 173:1 (July 1972) p14.
RF0079   Creem 4:1 (June 1972) p55.
RF0080   Cue 43:41 (October 28, 1974) p35.
RF0081   Filmfacts 15:6 (1972) p135.
RF0082   Film Information 3:5 (May 1972)
         p3.
RF0083   Films & Filming 19:1 (October 1972)
         p47.
RF0084   Inter/View 22 (June 1972) p47.
RF0085   Life 72:6 (February 18, 1972) p22.
RF0086   Mass Media Ministries 9:2 (May 29, 1972)
         p3.
RF0087   Monthly Film Bulletin 39:462 (July 1972)
         p135.
RF0088   Motion Picture Herald 242:5 (May 1972)
         p611.
RF0089   National Review 24:24 (June 23, 1972)
         p705.
RF0090   New Statesman 84:2159 (August 4, 1972)
         p170.
RF0091   New York 5:14 (April 3, 1972) p59.
RF0092   Parents Magazine 47:5 (May 1972)
         p18.
RF0093   Punch (August 2, 1972) p155.
RF0094   Rolling Stone 107 (April 27, 1972)
         p30. Gleason, Ralph J.
RF0095   Take One 3:5 (May 1971) p27.
RF0096   Time 99:16 (April 17, 1972) p91.

FILM NO. 4
RF0097   Films & Filming 14:1 (October 1967)
         pp24-25. Durgnat, Raymond

FLY
RF0098   Creem 4 (March 1972) p52.
RF0099   Rolling Stone 97 (December 9, 1971)
         p56.

A HARD DAY'S NIGHT
RF0100   AFFS Newsletter (October 1964) pp15-16.
         Stavis, Eugene
RF0101   The Beatles Book 13 (August 1964)
         p15.
RF0102   Cue 43:1 (January 7, 1974) p40.
RF0103   Filmfacts 7 (1964) p196.
RF0104   Film Heritage 1:4 (Summer 1966)
         pp3-13. Sugg, Alfred
RF0105   Film News 32:5 (November 1975) p24.
         Goldstein, R.M.
RF0106   Film Quarterly 18:1 (Fall 1964)
         pp51-54. Seelye, John
RF0107   Films & Filming 10:11 (August 1964)
         p26. Baker, Peter
RF0108   Films in Review 15:8 (October 1964)
         pp503-505. Hagen, Ray
RF0109   Maclean's (September 19, 1964) p68.
         Michener, Wendy
RF0110   Movie 14 (Fall 1965) pp6-11.
         French, Philip
RF0111   New Yorker 40 (August 22, 1964)
         pp25-27.
RF0112   Rolling Stone (December 24, 1982)
         pp372-26. Sragow, M.
RF0113   Sight and Sound 33:4 (Fall 1964)
         pp196-197. Nowell-Smith, Geoffrey
RF0114   Spectator (July 10, 1964) p47.
         Quigly, Isabel
RF0115   Village Voice 9:45 (August 27, 1964)
         p13. Sarris, Andrew

HELP!
RF0116   Cue 43:1 (January 7, 1974) p40.
RF0117   Film Heritage 1:4 (Summer 1966)
         pp3-13. Sugg, Alfred
RF0118   Film Quarterly 19:1 (Fall 1965)
         pp57-58. Sellye, John
RF0119   Films & Filming 12:1 (October 1965)
         p27. Rider, David
RF0120   Films in Review 16:8 (October 1965)
         p513. Wharton, Flavia
RF0121   Movie 14 (Fall 1965) pp6-11.
         French, Philip
RF0122   Sight and Sound 34:4 (Fall 1965)
         pp199-200. Harcourt, Peter
RF0123   Village Voice 10:47 (September 9, 1965)
         p15. Sarris, Andrew

THE HISTORY OF THE BEATLES
RF0124   Beatles Unlimited 21 (July 1978)
         p22. Vermeer, Evert

IMAGINE
RF0125   Films and Filming 19 (September 1973)
         pp65-66. Gow, G.
RF0126   Playboy 20:5 (May 1973) p40.
RF0127   Take One 3 (March/April 1972) pp33-33.
         Boujailly, G.B.
RF0128   Village Voice 18 (January 18, 1973)
         p75. Byron, S.

INTERVIEW WITH A LEGEND
RF0129   Beatlefan 3:6 (October 1981) p18.
         Shears, Billy

I WANNA HOLD YOUR HAND
RF0130   After Dark 11:3 (July 1978) p86.
         Stoop, N.M.
RF0131   Atlantic 242:2 (August 1978) p83.
         Carter, B.
RF0132   The Beatles Book 28 (August 1978)
         pv. Lewisohn, Mark
RF0133   Cosmopolitan 185:1 (July 1978) p16.
         Smith, L.
RF0134   Crawdaddy (June 1978) p24. Walker, J.
RF0135   Creem 10:3 (August 1978) p48.
         Goldstein, T.
RF0136   Cue 47:9 (April 29, 1978) p105. Wolf, W.
RF0137   Film & Broadcasting Review 43:10
         (May 15, 1978) p60.
RF0138   Film Bulletin 47:4/5 (April 1978)
         pB. Toumarkine, D.
RF0139   Film Information 9:5 (May 1978)
         p4. Moss, R.F.
RF0140   Films In Review 29:6 (June 1978)
         p376. Buckley, M.
RF0141   Mass Media Ministries 15:3 (June 12, 1978)
         p7. Schillaci, P.
RF0142   McCalls 105:10 (July 1978) p56.
         Minton, L.
RF0143   Monthly Film Bulletin 45:535 (August 1978)
         p160. Meek, S.
RF0144   New Statesman 95:2467 (June 30, 1978)
         p894. Coleman, J.
RF0145   Newsweek 91:18 (May 1, 1978) p89.
         Ansen, D.
RF0146   New Times 10:10 (May 15, 1978) p81.
         Corliss, R.
RF0147   Parents Magazine 53:6 (June 1978)
         p26. Ripp, J.
RF0148   Rolling Stone 266 (June 1, 1978)
         p8. Scanlon, P.
RF0149   Seventeen 37:7 (July 1978) p61.
         Miller, E.
RF0150   Time 111:19 (May 8, 1978) p70. Rich, F.
RF0151   Variety 290:11 (April 19, 1978)
         p26. Hege.
RF0152   Village Voice 23:18 (May 1, 1978)
         p42. Allen, T.

LET IT BE
RF0153 Catholic Film Newsletter 35:10 (May 30, 1970) p44.
RF0154 Cue (June 6, 1970) p88.
RF0155 Cue 43:1 (January 7, 1974) p40.
RF0156 Cue 43:47 (December 9, 1974) p45.
RF0157 Film Information 1:6 (June 1970) p3.
RF0158 Films In Review 21:7 (August/September 1970) pp439-440. Hart, Henry
RF0159 Rolling Stone 61 (June 25, 1970) p52. Goodwin, M.
RF0160 The Times (May 22, 1970) p7B. Taylor, John Russell
RF0161 Variety 259:1 (May 20, 1970) p15.
RF0162 Village Voice 15:24 (June 11, 1970) p55. Stoller, James

LISZTOMANIA
RF0163 After Dark 8:8 (December 1975) p101. Stoop, N.M.
RF0164 Audience 8:6 (December 1975) p15. Putterman, B.
RF0165 Audience 8:7 (January 1976) p15. Green, L.
RF0166 Audience 8:10 (April 1976) p14. Teegarden, J.
RF0167 Beatles Unlimited 31 (March 1980) pp20-22. Pope, Michael E.
RF0168 Catholic Film Newsletter 40:20 (October 30, 1975) p92.
RF0169 Cue (October 25, 1975) p26. Wolf, W.
RF0170 Essence 6:9 (January 1976) p28. Peterson, M.
RF0171 Film Comment 11:6 (November 1975) p40. Farber, S.
RF0172 Film Information 6:12 (December 1975) p4. Brussat, F.A.
RF0173 Film Quarterly 31:3 (Spring 1978) p55. Care, R.
RF0174 Films & Filming 22:2 (November 1975) p26.
RF0175 Films & Filming 22:4 (January 1976) p31. Elley, D.
RF0176 Listener 94:2433 (November 20, 1975) p696. Millar, G.
RF0177 Mass Media Ministries 12:13 (November 24, 1975) p6. Schillaci, P.
RF0178 McCalls 103:4 (January 1976) p34. Minton, L.
RF0179 Monthly Film Bulletin 42:502 (November 1975) p240. Rayns, T.
RF0180 New Statesman 90:2330 (November 14, 1975) p622. Coleman, J.
RF0181 Newsweek 86:16 (October 20, 1975) p99. Kroll, J.
RF0182 New York 8:43 (October 27, 1975) p76. Simon, J.
RF0183 New Yorker 51:40 (November 24, 1975) p171. Kael, P.
RF0184 Parents Magazine 50:12 (December 1975) p19. Ripp, J.
RF0185 Playboy 23:1 (January 1976) p30.
RF0186 Punch 269:7053 (November 19, 1975) p952. Green, B.
RF0187 Rolling Stone 202 (December 18, 1975) p24. Snyder, Patrick
RF0188 Saturday Review 3:5 (November 29, 1975) p37. Crist, J.
RF0189 Sight & Sound 45:1 (Winter 1975) p66.
RF0190 Take One 4:12 (July 1974) p18. McGilligan, P.
RF0191 Time 106:16 (October 20, 1975) p61. Schickel, R.
RF0192 Variety 280:10 (October 15, 1975) p26. Murf.

LITTLE MALCOLM AND HIS STRUGGLE AGAINST THE EUNUCHS
RF0193 Film 23 (February 1975) p19. Armitage, P.

RF0194 Films & Filming 21:5 (February 1975) p34. Gow, G.
RF0195 Listener 93:2389 (January 9, 1975) p57. Millar, G.
RF0196 Monthly Film Bulletin 42:493 (February 1975) p35. Milne, T.
RF0197 New Statesman 89:2286 (January 10, 1975) p51. Coleman, J.
RF0198 Punch 268:7008 (January 8, 1975) p71. Green, B.
RF0199 Sight & Sound 44:2 (Spring 1975) p132.
RF0200 Variety 275:9 (July 10, 1974) p18.

LIVE AND LET DIE
RF0201 After Dark 6:4 (August 1973) p64.
RF0202 America 129:1 (July 7, 1973) p20.
RF0203 Audience 6:3 (September 1973) p8. Putterman, B.
RF0204 Audience 6:4 (October 1973) p8. Wilson, R.
RF0205 Catholic Film Newsletter 38:13 (July 15, 1973) p65.
RF0206 Christian Century 90:28 (August 1, 1973) p790.
RF0207 Cosmopolitan 175:4 (October 1973) p14. Smith, L.
RF0208 Creem 5:6 (November 1973) p59. Zabowski, B.
RF0209 Cue (June 25, 1973) p6. Mayerson, P.
RF0210 Cue 43:2 (January 14, 1974) p37.
RF0211 Film Information 4:7/8 (July 1973) p4. Coleman, P.
RF0212 Films & Filming 19:12 (September 1973) p54. Gow, G.
RF0213 Films In Review 24:8 (October 1973) p501.
RF0214 McCalls 100:12 (September 1973) p50. Minton, L.
RF0215 MD/Medical News Magazine 17:9 (September 1973) p215.
RF0216 Monthly Film Bulletin 40:475 (August 1973) p172. Strick, P.
RF0217 National Review 25:37 (September 14, 1973) p1002. Brudnoy, D.
RF0218 New Leader 56:15 (July 23, 1973) p24. Simon, J.
RF0219 New Republic 169:4/5 (July 28, 1973) p35. Kauffmann, Stanley
RF0220 New Statesman 86:2207 (July 6, 1973) p30. Coleman, J.
RF0221 New York 6:28 (July 9, 1973) p21. Crist, J.
RF0222 New Yorker (July 9, 1973) p56. Gilliatt, P.
RF0223 Parents Magazine 48:8 (August 1973) p12. Ripp, J.
RF0224 Parents Magazine 49:1 (January 1974) p12. Ripp, J.
RF0225 Playboy 20:10 (October 1973) p34.
RF0226 The Progressive 38:1 (January 1974) p51. Turan, K.
RF0227 PTA Magazine 67:10 (September 1973) p5. Whitehorn, E.
RF0228 Punch 265:6931 (July 11, 1973) p59. Green, B.
RF0229 Senior Scholastic 105:2 (September 26, 1974) p38. Roney, M.
RF0230 Show 3:9 (December 1973) p56.
RF0231 Sight & Sound 42:4 (Fall 1973) p244.
RF0232 Time 102:2 (July 9, 1973) p40. Schickel, R.
RF0233 Variety 271:7 (June 27, 1973) p20.
RF0234 Village Voice 18:38 (September 20, 1973) p65.
RF0235 Vogue 162:3 (September 1973) p100. Drexler, R.
RF0236 World 2:16 (July 31, 1973) p45. Alpert, H.

LOVE ME DO (VIDEO)
    RF0237 Beatlefan 5:1 (December 1982) p26.
         King, William P.

MAGICAL MYSTERY TOUR
    RF0238 Christian Century (March 19, 1969)
         pp386-388. Fager, Charles E.
    RF0239 The Times (December 27, 1967) p11A.
         Raynor, Henry
    RF0240 Village Voice 13:12 (January 4, 1968)
         p23. Marowitz
    RF0241 Village Voice 14:6 (November 21, 1968)
         p55. Stoller, James

MAGICAL MYSTERY TOUR (SUPER 8MM)
    RF0242 Classic Film Collector 61 (Winter 1978)
         p24. Aben, D.

MAGICAL MYSTERY TOUR (VIDEOTAPE)
    RF0243 Village Voice 27:10 (March 9, 1982)
         p57. Aben, D.

THE MAGIC CHRISTIAN
    RF0244 Beatles Unlimited 23 (November 1978)
         pp4-6,20. Pope, Michael E.
    RF0245 Catholic Film Newsletter 35:5 (March 15,
         1970) p21.
    RF0246 Cinema (Winter 1971) p17.
    RF0247 Cue (February 21, 1970) p64.
    RF0248 Film Daily 136:63 (February 20, 1970)
         p5.
    RF0249 Film Information 1:5 (May 1970)
         p5.
    RF0250 Mass Media Ministries 6:24 (April 6, 1970)
         p4.

MONTY PYTHON'S LIFE OF BRIAN
    RF0251 After Dark 12:7 (November 1979)
         p78. Mitchell, M.
    RF0252 America 141:7 (September 22, 1979)
         p135. Blake, R.A.
    RF0253 American Film 5:5 (March 1980) p65.
         Kennedy, H.
    RF0254 Christian Century 96:29 (September 19,
         1979) p899. Wall, J.M.
    RF0255 Cineaste 10:1 (Winter 1979) p68.
         Rubenstein, L.
    RF0256 Cinefantastique 9:1 (Fall 1979)
         p45. Frentzen, J.
    RF0257 Cinema Papers 24 (December 1979)
         p659. Atlman, D.
    RF0258 Commentary 68:6 (December 1979)
         p75. Grenier, R.
    RF0259 Commonweal 106:19 (October 26, 1979)
         p596. Westerbeck, C.L., Jr.
    RF0260 Cosmopolitan 187:5 (November 1979)
         p26. Grenier, R.
    RF0261 Cue 48:18 (September 14, 1979) p10.
         Wolf, W.
    RF0262 Feature (May 1979) p17. Lacayo, R.
    RF0263 Film & Broadcasting Review 44:18
         (September 15, 1979) p97.
    RF0264 Film Bulletin 48:6/7 (September 1979)
         pD. Silk, D.
    RF0265 Films & Filming 26:2 (November 1979)
         p25.
    RF0266 Films In Review 31:1 (January 1980)
         p56. Rogers, T.
    RF0267 Mass Media Ministries 16:7 (September 24,
         1979) p6. Schillaci, P.
    RF0268 McCalls 107:2 (November 1979) p54.
         Minton, L.
    RF0269 Monthly Film Bulletin 46:550 (November
         1979) p229. Jeavons, C.
    RF0270 Nation 229:10 (October 6, 1979)
         p314. Hatch, R.
    RF0271 New Republic 181:12 (September 12, 1979)
         p40. Kauffmann, Stanley
    RF0272 New Statesman 98:2538 (November 9, 1979)
         p737. Coleman, J.

    RF0273 Newsweek 94:10 (September 3, 1979)
         p65. Ansen, D.
    RF0274 New York 12:37 (September 24, 1979)
         p98. Denby, D.
    RF0275 New Yorker 55:28 (August 27, 1979)
         p74. Geng, V.
    RF0276 Parents Magazine 54:11 (November 1979)
         p132. Ripp, J.
    RF0277 Playboy 26:11 (November 1979) p161.
         Potterton, R.
    RF0278 Playboy 26:12 (December 1979) p47.
         Williamson, B.
    RF0279 Punch 275:7208 (November 29, 1978)
         p970. Took, B.
    RF0280 Punch 277:7257 (November 14, 1979)
         p907. Powell, D.
    RF0281 Rolling Stone 302 (October 18, 1979)
         p52. Gambaccini, P.
    RF0282 Seventeen 38:11 (November 1979)
         p67. Miller, E.
    RF0283 Sight & Sound 49:1 (Winter 1979)
         p66.
    RF0284 Time 114:12 (September 17, 1979)
         p101. Schickel, R.
    RF0285 Variety 296:3 (August 22, 1979)
         p30. Cart.
    RF0286 Village Voice 24:35 (August 27, 1979)
         p46. Hoberman, J.

PAPER SHOES
    RF0287 Media Mix Newsletter 5:7 (May 1974)
         p7.

RAGA
    RF0288 Catholic Film Newsletter 36:23 (December
         15, 1971) p121.
    RF0289 Cue (November 27, 1971) p76.
    RF0290 Filmmakers Newsletter 5:9/10 (July 1972)
         p24.
    RF0291 Monthly Film Bulletin 40:475 (August 1973)
         p174. Baxter, J.
    RF0292 New Statesman 87:2246 (April 5, 1974)
         p488. Coleman, J.
    RF0293 Seventeen 3:2 (February 1972) p94.
    RF0294 Variety 265:3 (December 1, 1971)
         p22.

RAPE
    RF0295 The Times (November 1, 1969) ppIII-F.
         Taylor, John Russell
    RF0296 Village Voice 16:1 (January 7, 1971)
         p51. Mekas, Jonas

ROCKSHOW
    RF0297 Beatlefan 3:2 (February 1981) p17.
         Haviv, Mitch
    RF0298 Beatlefan 4:3 (April 1982) p22.
         King, William P.
    RF0299 The Beatles Book 63 (July 1981)
         ppix-x. Lewisohn, Mark

SGT. PEPPER'S LONELY HEARTS CLUB BAND
    RF0300 After Dark 11:4 (August 1978) p56.
         Mewborn, B.
    RF0301 Beatles Unlimited 24 (January 1979)
         p22. De Bruin, Hans
    RF0302 Cosmopolitan 185:4 (October 1978)
         p18. Grenier, R.
    RF0303 Creem 9:11 (April 1978) p50.
    RF0304 Cue 47:13 (June 24, 1978) p12. Davis, D.
    RF0305 Cue 47:16 (August 5, 1978) p17. Wolf, W.
    RF0306 Film & Broadcasting Review 43:17
         (September 1, 1978) p96.
    RF0307 Film Information 9:9 (September 1978)
         p4. Pomeroy, D.
    RF0308 Mass Media Ministries 15:6 (September 11,
         1978) p7. Schillaci, P.
    RF0309 McCalls 106:1 (October 1978) p105.
         Minton, L.
    RF0310 Monthly Film Bulletin 46:541 (February

1979) p32. Brown, G.

RF0311   New Statesman 97:2500 (February 16, 1979)
p228. Hamilton, L.

RF0312   Newsweek 92:5 (July 31, 1978) p42.
Ansen, D.

RF0313   New Times 11:4 (August 21, 1978)
p65. Corliss, R.

RF0314   New York 11:32 (August 7, 1978)
p56. Denby, D.

RF0315   New Yorker 54:24 (July 31, 1978)
p64. Gilliatt, P.

RF0316   Parents Magazine 53:9 (September 1978)
p11. Ripp, J.

RF0317   Playboy 25:11 (November 1978) p42.
Williamson, B.

RF0318   Punch 276:7219 (February 21, 1979)
p323. Took, B.

RF0319   Rolling Stone 263 (April 20, 1978)
p50. Zuckerman, E.

RF0320   Rolling Stone 272 (August 24, 1978)
p16. Young, C.

RF0321   Rolling Stone 275 (October 5, 1978)
p71. Nelson, Paul

RF0322   Seventeen 37:6 (June 1978) p138.
Miller, E.

RF0323   Sight & Sound 48:2 (Spring 1979)
p134.

RF0324   Time 112:5 (July 31, 1978) p86. Skow, J.

RF0325   Variety 291:11 (July 19, 1978) p20. Murf.

RF0326   Village Voice 23:31 (July 31, 1978)
p40. Sarris, A.

SEXTETTE

RF0327   Audience 10:2 (Summer 1978) p39.
Teegarden, J.

RF0328   Cue 48:13 (July 6, 1979) p12. Wolf, W.

RF0329   Film & Broadcasting Review 44:13/14
(July 1, 1979) p77.

RF0330   Film Comment 16:3 (May 1980) p23.
Adair, G.

RF0331   Films In Review 30:7 (August 1979)
p434.

RF0332   Playboy 25:7 (July 1978) p40.
Williamson, B.

RF0333   Variety 290:5 (March 8, 1978) p31. Hege.

RF0334   Village Voice 24:25 (June 18, 1979)
p59.

SON OF DRACULA

RF0335   Beatles Unlimited 28 (September 1979)
pp16-18. Pope, Michael E.

RF0336   Cinefantastique 3:4 (Winter 1974)
p33. Martin, M.

RF0337   Creem 6:3 (August 1974) p62. Edwards, H.

RF0338   Seventeen 33:7 (July 1974) p37.
Miller, E.

TAKE IT AWAY

RF0339   Beatlefan 4:6 (October 1982) p16.
Bearne, David

THAT'LL BE THE DAY

RF0340   Beatles Unlimited 30 (January 1980)
pp14-15. Pope, Michael E.

RF0341   Catholic Film Newsletter 40:1 (January
1975) p2.

RF0342   Cue 44:1 (January 6, 1975) p23.
Mayerson, D.J.

RF0343   Films & Filming 19:10 (July 1973)
p53. Fox, J.

RF0344   Los Angeles Times IV (March 29, 1974)
p15.

RF0345   Los Angeles Times IV (October 30, 1974)
p1.

RF0346   Monthly Film Bulletin 40:472 (May 1973)
p107.

RF0347   New Statesman 85:219 (April 13, 1973)
p562. Coleman, J.

RF0348   New York 8:2 (January 13, 1975)
p61. Crist, J.

RF0349   Seventeen 33:7 (July 1974) p37.
Miller, E.

RF0350   Take One 5:6 (January 1977) p34.
Pollock, D.

RF0351   Time 104:25 (December 16, 1974)
p6. Cocks, J.

RF0352   Variety 273 (November 28, 1973)
pp3-14.

TIME BANDITS

RF0353   Christian Century (January 6, 1982)
p33. Mahan, J.

RF0354   Cineaste 11:4 (1982) p60. Rubenstein, L.

RF0355   Cinefantastique 12:1 (February 1982)
p50. Fox, J.R.

RF0356   Cinemacabre 5 (Fall 1982) p50.
Brodsky, A.

RF0357   Cosmopolitan 192:1 (January 1982)
p14. Flatley, G.

RF0358   Film Bulletin (October 1981) p12.
Silk, D.

RF0359   Film Comment 17:6 (November 1981)
p49. Thompson, A.

RF0360   Film Quarterly 36:1 (Fall 1982)
p41. Gaughn, M.J.

RF0361   McCall's 109:4 (January 1982) p123.
Minton, L.

RF0362   MD/Medical News Magazine 26:1 (January
1982) p270.

RF0363   Monthly Film Bulletin 48:571 (August 1981)
p163. Pym, J.

RF0364   New Republic 185:19 (November 11, 1981)
p25. Kauffmann, Stanley

RF0365   New Republic 185:23 (December 9, 1981)
p20. Kauffmann, Stanley

RF0366   New Statesman 102:2626 (July 17, 1981)
p24. Coleman, J.

RF0367   Newsweek 98:19 (November 9, 1981)
p92. Ansen, D.

RF0368   New York 14:45 (November 16, 1981)
p116. Denby, D.

RF0369   Oui 10:6 (June 1981) p30.

RF0370   Playboy 29:2 (February 1982) p32.
Williamson, B.

RF0371   Punch 281:7341 (July 22, 1981) p152.
Powell, D.

RF0372   Rolling Stone 358 (December 10, 1981)
p61. Sragow, M.

RF0373   Senior Scholastic 114:8 (December 11,
1981) p25. Ronan, M.

RF0374   Seventeen 41:1 (January 1982) p71.
Miller, E.

RF0375   Sight & Sound 50:4 (Fall 1981) p288.

RF0376   Sunday Times (July 26, 1981) p40e.
Brien, Alan

RF0377   Time 118:19 (November 9, 1981) p98.
Corliss, R.

RF0378   Variety 303:12 (July 22, 1981) p18. Pit.

RF0379   Village Voice 26:44 (October 28, 1981)
p52. Rickey, C.

RF0380   Village Voice 26:50 (December 9, 1981)
p78. Byron, S.

RF0381   Village Voice 27:1 (December 30, 1981)
p48. Rickey, C.

TWO HUNDRED MOTELS

RF0382   Beatles Unlimited 26 (May 1979)
p9. Pope, Michael E.

RF0383   Catholic Film Newsletter 36:22 (November
30, 1971) p114.

RF0384   Creem 3:9 (February 1972) p44.

RF0385   Cue (November 20, 1971) p80.

RF0386   Cue 43:18 (May 26, 1974) p34.

RF0387   Film Information 2:12 (December 1971)
p5.

RF0388   Ingenue 14:2 (February 1972) p15.

RF0389   Inter/View 19 (February 1972) p35.

RF0390   Monthly Film Bulletin 39:457 (February
1972) p38.

RF0391   Parents Magazine 47:1 (January 1972)

        p26.
RF0392 Playboy 19:2 (February 1972) p30.
RF0393 Variety 264:12 (November 3, 1971)
        p24.

TWO VIRGINS
RF0394 Film Culture 48 (Winter 1970) pp32-33.
RF0395 The Times (November 1, 1969) ppIII-G.
        Taylor, John Russell

UP YOUR LEGS
RF0396 Village Voice 16:1 (January 7, 1971)
        p51. Mekas, Jonas

YELLOW SUBMARINE
RF0397 Christian Century (March 19, 1969)
        pp386-388. Fager, Charles E.
RF0398 Cue 43:1 (January 7, 1974) p43.
RF0399 Films & Filming 14:12 (September 1968)
        pp46-47. Rider, David
RF0400 Films in Review 19:10 (December 1968)
        pp650-651. Hart, Henry
RF0401 Journal of Popular Film 1:3 (Summer 1972)

        p173.
RF0402 Millimeter 6:2 (February 1978) p14.
        Canemaker, J.
RF0403 Scholastic Teacher (January 1974)
        p29. Maynard, R.A.
RF0404 Sight & Sound 37:4 (Fall 1968) pp204-205.
        Millar, Gavin
RF0405 Take One 1:11 (May/June 1968) p26.
        Armatage, Kay
RF0406 The Times (June 13, 1968) p15.
RF0407 The Times (July 18, 1968) p7A.
        Taylor, John Russell
RF0408 Village Voice 14:5 (November 14, 1968)
        pp45+. Sarris, Andrew
RF0409 Village Voice 14:36 (June 19, 1969)
        p43. Sarris, Andrew
RF0410 Village Voice 14:37 (June 26, 1969)
        pp43+-7. Sarris, Andrew

YELLOW SUBMARINE (16MM)
RF0411 Village Voice 27:52 (December 28, 1982)
        p88. Sarris, Andrew & T. Allen

ABBEY ROAD (LP)
      RR0001   Beatlefan 2:3 (April 1980) p13.
                 Lark, Fred
      RR0002   Beatlefan 3:3 (April 1981) p24.
                 Schwartz, David
      RR0003   Circus (November 1969) p12.
      RR0004   Crawdaddy (March 1976) pp76-82.
      RR0005   Dock of the Bay 1:13 (October 28, 1969)
                 Moss, F.
      RR0006   Down Beat 37 (January 22, 1970)
                 p20. Morgenstern, D.
      RR0007   Leviathan 7 (December 1969) p7.
                 Koonan, K.
      RR0008   Rolling Stone 46 (November 15, 1969)
                 pp32-33. Mendelsohn, John
      RR0009   Rolling Stone 46 (November 15, 1969)
                 p32. Ward, Edmund O.
      RR0010   Saturday Review 52 (October 25, 1969)
                 p69. Sander, Ellen
      RR0011   Seed 4 (1969) pp7+. Eliot
      RR0012   Space City 1:10 (November 22, 1969)
                 Moss, F.
      RR0013   Stereo Review 24 (January 1970)
                 pp85-86.
      RR0014   Time (October 3, 1969) p57.
      RR0015   The Times (December 5, 1969) p7F.
                 Mann, William

AIR TIME (JOHNNY AND THE MOONDOGS SILVER DAYS) (LP)
      RR0016   Beatlefan 4:2 (February 1982) pp27-28.
                 King, William P.

AIRWAVES (LP)
      RR0017   Beatlefan 1:3 (April 1979) p6.
                 King, William P.

ALL THINGS MUST PASS (LP)
      RR0018   Dallas Notes 91 (December 18, 1970)
                 p26. Saunders, M.
      RR0019   Down Beat 38 (February 18, 1971)
                 pp24+.
      RR0020   Jazz & Pop 10 (March 1971) pp42-43.
      RR0021   Melody Maker 45 (December 5, 1970)
                 p8. Williams, R.
      RR0022   New Yorker 47 (February 27, 1971)
                 pp95-97. Willis, E.
      RR0023   Phoenix 2:49 (December 15, 1970)
                 p13. Landau, J.
      RR0024   Rolling Stone 74 (January 21, 1971)
                 p46. Gerson, Ben
      RR0025   Time (November 30, 1970) p57.
                 Bender, William
      RR0026   The Times (January 23, 1971) p17E.
                 Williams, Richard

ALL THIS AND WORLD WAR II (LP)
      RR0027   Crawdaddy (February 1977) p81.
      RR0028   Rolling Stone 231 (January 27, 1977)
                 p68.
      RR0029   Stereo Review 38 (March 1977) p124.

ANGEL BABY/BE MY BABY (45)
      RR0030   Beatlefan 4:5 (August 1982) p25.
                 Reinhart, Charles

APPROXIMATELY INFINITE UNIVERSE (LP)
      RR0031   Circus (May 1973) p50.
      RR0032   Creem 4 (April 1973) p67.
      RR0033   Listening Post 4:4 (April 1973)
                 p9.
      RR0034   Phonograph Record Magazine (April 1973)
                 p25.
      RR0035   Rolling Stone 130 (March 15, 1973)
                 p52.

BACK TO THE EGG (LP)
      RR0036   Beatlefan 1:4 (June 1979) pp1,4-5,9.
      RR0037   The Beatles Book 39 (July 1979)
                 ppiii-v. Horide, Rosie
      RR0038   Beatles Unlimited 26 (May 1979)
                 p10. Hager, Henk
      RR0039   Beatles Unlimited 26 (May 1979)
                 pp11-13. Pullens, Bob
      RR0040   Chicago 28 (September 1979) p108.
      RR0041   Creem 11 (September 1979) p54.
                 Cohen, Mitchell
      RR0042   Los Angeles Times (June 17, 1979)
                 p5.
      RR0043   Rocky Mountain 1 (October 1979)
                 pp88-90.
      RR0044   Rolling Stone 298 (August 23, 1979)
                 p55. White, Timothy
      RR0045   Stereo Review 43:3 (September 1979)
                 p132. Simels, Steve
      RR0046   Village Voice 24 (September 3, 1979)
                 p66. Flake, Carol

BAD BOY (LP)
      RR0047   Beatles Unlimited 20 (May 1978)
                 p20. Smit, Eddy
      RR0048   High Fidelity/Musical America 28
                 (July 1978) pp124-125.
      RR0049   Rolling Stone 269 (July 13, 1978)
                 p52.
      RR0050   Stereo Review 41 (July 1978) pp125+.

BAND ON THE RUN (LP)
      RR0051   Beatlefan 4:2 (February 1982) p27.
                 Schwartz, David
      RR0052   Crawdaddy 34 (March 1974) pp70-71.
      RR0053   Creem 5 (March 1974) p60. Robins, Wayne
      RR0054   Creem 5:11 (April 1974) pp13,52.
                 Christgau, Robert
      RR0055   High Fidelity/Musical America 24
                 (April 1974) p124.
      RR0056   Los Angeles Times (December 16, 1973)
                 p78.
      RR0057   Rolling Stone 153 (January 31, 1974)
                 pp48+. Landau, Jon
      RR0058   Rolling Stone 162 (June 6, 1974)
                 p67.
      RR0059   Stereo Review 32 (March 1974) pp88+.

THE BAROQUE BEATLES BOOK (LP)
      RR0060   American Record Guide 32 (February 1966)
                 pp508-510.
      RR0061   High Fidelity/Musical America 16
                 (February 1966) p67. Jacobson, B.
      RR0062   Saturday Review (December 25, 1965)
                 pp57,61. Freed, Richard D.

THE BEATLE INTERVIEWS (LP)
      RR0063   The Beatles Book 76 (August 1982)
                 ppxi-xii. Doggett, Peter

THE BEATLES (LP)
      RR0064   Beatlefan 4:4 (June 1982) p30.
                 Schwartz, David
      RR0065   Christian Century (March 19, 1969)
                 pp386-388. Fager, Charles E.
      RR0066   Commonweal 89 (December 27, 1968)
                 pp439+. Wood, M.
      RR0067   High Fidelity/Musical America 19
                 (March 1969) pp84-85. Gabree, J.
      RR0068   Life 67 (January 31, 1969) p12.
                 Aronowitz, Alfred G.
      RR0069   Newsweek (December 9, 1968) p109.
                 Saal, Hubert
      RR0070   New Yorker (February 1, 1969) pp55-56+.
                 Willis, Ellen
      RR0071   Rolling Stone (November 23, 1968)
                 p8.
      RR0072   Rolling Stone 24 (December 21, 1968)
                 pp10-13. Wenner, J.
      RR0073   Rolling Stone 24 (December 21, 1968)
                 p11.
      RR0074   Saturday Review 51 (December 28, 1968)
                 p58. Sander, E.
      RR0075   Time (December 6, 1968) p53. Saal, Hubert

THE BEATLES AGAIN (LP)
        (see also HEY JUDE (LP))
    RR0076 Melody Maker 45 (May 9, 1970) p5.
            Williams, R.
    RR0077 Rolling Stone 54 (March 19, 1970) p8.

THE BEATLES AT THE HOLLYWOOD BOWL (LP)
    RR0078 The Beatles Book 15 (July 1977)
            pv.
    RR0079 Beatles Unlimited 13 (May 1977)
            pp4-5. Vermeer, Evert
    RR0080 Christian Science Monitor 69 (June 30,
            1977) p21. Stevens, M.
    RR0081 Crawdaddy 75 (August 1977) pp62-63.
    RR0082 Creem 9 (August 1977) pp60-61.
    RR0083 High Fidelity/Musical America 27
            (August 1977) p111. Sutherland, S.
    RR0084 In These Times 1:37 (August 10, 1977)
            p22. Dancis, B.
    RR0085 Playboy 24 (September 1977) p26.
    RR0086 Rolling Stone 242 (June 30, 1977)
            pp94-97.
    RR0087 Stereo Review 39 (August 1977) p88.
            Simels, S.

THE BEATLES BOX (LP)
    RR0088 Beatlefan 3:6 (October 1981) p27.
            Lark, Fred
    RR0089 Beatles Unlimited 36 (June 1981)
            pp16-17. Pope, Michael E.

THE BEATLES COLLECTION (EPs)
    RR0090 Beatles Unlimited 40 (1982) pp12-13.
            Pope, Michael E.

THE BEATLES COLLECTION (LP)
    RR0091 Beatles Unlimited 23 (November 1978)
            pp12-14. Vermeer, Evert

THE BEATLES CONCERTO (LP)
    RR0092 Stereo Review 45 (September 1980)
            p75. Goodfriend, J.

THE BEATLES INTRODUCE NEW SONGS (LP)
    RR0093 Beatlefan 1:4 (June 1979) p6.
            King, William P.

THE BEATLES INTRODUCE NEW SONGS/SHOUT (45)
    RR0094 Beatlefan 2:1 (December 1979) p9.
            Shears, Billy

THE BEATLES 'LIVE' (LP)
    RR0095 Rolling Stone 62 (July 9, 1970)
            p39. Ward, Ed

THE BEATLES LIVE AT THE STAR CLUB (LP)
    RR0096 Beatles Unlimited 13 (May 1977)
            pp14-15. Hager, Henk
    RR0097 Crawdaddy 75 (August 1977) pp62-63.
    RR0098 Creem 9 (August 1977) pp60-61.
    RR0099 High Fidelity/Musical America 27
            (August 1977) p111. Sutherland, S.
    RR0100 In These Times 1:37 (August 10, 1977)
            p22. Heumann, J.
    RR0101 New York 10 (July 18, 1977) p63.
            Bentkowski, Tom
    RR0102 Playboy 24 (August 1977) p28.
    RR0103 Rolling Stone 242 (June 30, 1977)
            pp94+. Swenson, John
    RR0104 Stereo Review 39 (August 1977) p88.
            Simels, S.

BEATLES MOVIE MEDLEY/FAB FOUR ON FILM (45)
    RR0105 Beatlefan 4:3 (April 1982) pp27-28.
            Shears, Billy
    RR0106 Beatlefan 4:3 (April 1982) p28.
            Fulper-Smith, Shawn

THE BEATLES, 1962-1966 (LP)
    RR0107 Circus (July 1973) p59.

RR0108 Creem 5:2 (July 1973) pp58,71.
RR0109 Listening Post (May/June 1974) p4.
RR0110 Phonograph Record Magazine (July 1973)
        p28.
RR0111 Previews 2:8 (April 1974) p15.

THE BEATLES, 1967-1970 (LP)
    RR0112 Circus (July 1973) p59.
    RR0113 Creem 5:2 (July 1973) pp58,71.
    RR0114 Phonograph Record Magazine (July 1973)
            p28.
    RR0115 Previews 2:8 (April 1974) p15.

BEATLESONGS! (LP)
    RR0116 Beatlefan 4:4 (June 1982) p30.
            Ellis, Roger

THE BEATLES TALK DOWNUNDER (LP)
    RR0117 Beatlefan 4:2 (February 1982) p28.
            Schwartz, David

THE BEATLES TAPES FROM THE DAVID WIGG INTERVIEW (LP)
    RR0118 Rolling Stone 242 (June 30, 1977)
            p94. Swenson, John

BEATLE TALK (LP)
    RR0119 Beatlefan 2:1 (December 1979) p9.
            Lark, Fred

BEAUCOUPS OF BLUES (LP)
    RR0120 Rolling Stone 69 (October 29, 1970)
            p40. Burton, Charles

BEAUTIFUL DREAMER (LP)
    RR0121 Beatlefan 4:5 (August 1982) pp24-25.
            Phillips, Steve
    RR0122 Beatlefan 4:5 (August 1982) p25.
            Carballal, Henrique
    RR0123 Beatlefan 4:5 (August 1982) p25.
            Gumby, D.
    RR0124 Beatlefan 4:5 (August 1982) p25.
            Krider, Bill
    RR0125 Beatles Now 5 (Winter 1983) p18.
            Beller, Daniel

BEHIND CLOSED DOORS (LP)
    RR0126 Beatlefan 3:4 (June 1981) p31.
            Welsh, Michael

THE BEST OF GEORGE HARRISON (LP)
    RR0127 Stereo Review 38 (March 1977) pp96+.

BLAST FROM YOUR PAST (LP)
    RR0128 Billboard 87 (November 29, 1975)
            p60.
    RR0129 Creem 7 (March 1976) p60.
    RR0130 High Fidelity/Musical America 26
            (March 1976) pp106-107.
    RR0131 Stereo Review 36 (April 1976) p92.

BROADCASTS (LP)
    RR0132 Beatlefan 2:5 (August 1980) p26.
            King, William P.
    RR0133 Beatles Now 2 (Spring 1982) p18.

BY GEORGE! (LP)
    RR0134 Beatlefan 4:3 (April 1982) p29.
            King, William P.

BY ROYAL COMMAND (EP)
    RR0135 Beatlefan 1:3 (April 1979) p16.
            Shears, Billy

CASUALTIES (LP)
    RR0136 Beatlefan 3:3 (April 1981) p24.
            Lark, Fred
    RR0137 Beatlefan 3:3 (April 1981) p24.
            Sussman, Al

COLD TURKEY FOR KAMPUCHEA (LP)
    RR0138   Beatlefan 4:2 (February 1982) p27.
                  King, William P.
    RR0139   Beatlefan 4:2 (February 1982) p27.
                  Reinhart, Charles

COME AND GET IT (LP)
    RR0140   Rolling Stone 53 (March 7, 1970)
                  p52. Mendelsohn, John

COME BACK JOHNNY (LP)
    RR0141   Beatlefan 2:3 (April 1980) pp13,23.
                  King, William P.

COMING UP & LUNCH BOX - ODD SOX/COMING UP (45)
    RR0142   Beatlefan 2:3 (April 1980) p7.
                  King, William P.

COMPLAINT TO THE QUEEN (WINGS OVER HOLLAND '72) (LP)
    RR0143   Beatles Now 3 (Summer 1982) p18.

THE COMPLETE SILVER BEATLES (LP)
    RR0144   Beatlefan 4:6 (October 1982) p25.
                  King, William P.
    RR0145   The Beatles Book 78 (October 1982)
                  p46. Doggett, Peter

THE CONCERT FOR BANGLA DESH (LP)
    RR0146   Audio 56 (April 1972) pp66-67.
    RR0147   Billboard (December 18, 1971) p3.
                  Ovens, Don
    RR0148   Crawdaddy 7 (March 19, 1972) p14.
    RR0149   Rolling Stone 101 (February 3, 1972)
                  p42. Landau, Jon
    RR0150   Stereo Review 28 (May 1972) pp66-67.
                  Vance, Joel
    RR0151   Variety 265 (January 12, 1972) pp2+.

CONCERTS FOR THE PEOPLE OF KAMPUCHEA (LP)
    RR0152   Beatlefan 3:3 (April 1981) p24.
                  King, William P.
    RR0153   High Fidelity/Musical America 31:7
                  (July 1981) p76. Cohen, Mitchell
    RR0154   Rolling Stone 348 (July 23, 1981)
                  pp51-52.
    RR0155   Stereo Review 46:7 (July 1981) p101.
                  Simels, Steve

DARK HORSE (LP)
    RR0156   Billboard 86 (December 21, 1974)
                  p63.
    RR0157   Crawdaddy (April 1975) p75.
    RR0158   Creem 6 (March 1975) pp69+. Bangs, Lester
    RR0159   High Fidelity/Musical America 25
                  (April 1975) p101.
    RR0160   Listening Post 6:3 (April 1975)
                  p16. DeFina, D.
    RR0161   Los Angeles Times IV (December 17, 1974)
                  p1.
    RR0162   Los Angeles Times (March 18, 1979)
                  p88.
    RR0163   Melody Maker 49 (December 21, 1974)
                  p36.
    RR0164   New Times 4 (February 7, 1975) p65.
    RR0165   Rolling Stone 180 (February 13, 1975)
                  pp75+. Miller, Jim
    RR0166   Stereo Review 34 (March 1975) pp80-81.
                  Bangs, Lester

THE DECCA TAPES (LP)
    RR0167   Beatlefan 2:2 (February 1980) p20.
                  Shears, Billy
    RR0168   Beatles Unlimited 28 (September 1979)
                  pp20-22. Hager, Henk

DOUBLE FANTASY (LP)
    RR0169   Beatlefan 3:1 (December 1980) p24.
                  King, William P.
    RR0170   Beatlefan 3:1 (December 1980) pp24-25.
                  Schaffner, Nicholas

    RR0171   Beatlefan 3:1 (December 1980) p24.
                  Simmons, Pat
    RR0172   The Beatles Book 56 (December 1980)
                  ppix-xii. Doggett, Peter
    RR0173   Beatles Unlimited 33 (July 1980)
                  pp12-14. Pope, Michael E.
    RR0174   Circus (January 31, 1981) pp36-39.
                  Farber, Jim
    RR0175   Creem 12 (March 1981) p50. Swenson, John
    RR0176   High Fidelity/Musical America 31
                  (February 1981) p92. Cohen, Mitchell
    RR0177   Melody Maker 55 (November 22, 1980)
                  p26.
    RR0178   New York 14 (February 2, 1981) p49.
    RR0179   Stereo Review 46 (March 1981) pp102-103.
                  Simels, Steve
    RR0180   Village Voice 26 (January 14, 1981)
                  pp31-32. Christgau, Robert

DOWN AND OUT? (LP)
    RR0181   Beatlefan 2:4 (June 1980) p13. Lark, Fred
    RR0182   Beatlefan 2:4 (June 1980) p13.
                  Shears, Billy

EARLY YEARS (LP)
    RR0183   The Beatles Book 65 (September 1981)
                  ppvi-vii. Lewisohn, Mark

EBONY AND IVORY/RAINCLOUDS (45)
    RR0184   Beatlefan 4:3 (April 1982) p26.
                  Ellis, Roger
    RR0185   Beatlefan 4:3 (April 1982) p27.
                  King, William P.
    RR0186   The Beatles Book 73 (May 1982) ppxi-xii.
                  Doggett, Peter

ELECTRONIC SOUNDS (LP)
    RR0187   Rolling Stone 39 (August 9, 1964)
                  p37. Ward, Edmund O.

EXTRA TEXTURE (LP)
    RR0188   Beatles Unlimited 4 (November 1975)
                  pp12-13. Hager, Henk
    RR0189   Billboard 87 (October 4, 1975) p64.
    RR0190   Los Angeles Times II (November 15, 1975)
                  p5.
    RR0191   Playboy 23 (February 1976) pp29+.
    RR0192   Rolling Stone 198 (October 23, 1975)
                  p15.
    RR0193   Rolling Stone (November 20, 1975)
                  p75. Marsh, Dave
    RR0194   Stereo Review 36 (February 1976)
                  p81.

FEELING THE SPACE (LP)
    RR0195   Billboard 85 (November 3, 1973)
                  p56.
    RR0196   Crawdaddy 34 (March 1974) p77.
    RR0197   Melody Maker 48 (December 8, 1973)
                  p35.
    RR0198   Rolling Stone 147 (November 8, 1973)
                  p76.
    RR0199   Stereo Review 32 (March 1974) pp88+.

FIRST LIVE RECORDINGS, VOL. I (LP)
    RR0200   Beatlefan 1:4 (June 1979) p6.
                  King, William P.

FIRST LIVE RECORDINGS, VOL. II (LP)
    RR0201   Beatlefan 1:4 (June 1979) p6.
                  King, William P.

FIVE NIGHTS IN A JUDO ARENA (LP)
    RR0202   Beatles Now 5 (Winter 1983) p19.
                  Beller, Daniel

FLY (LP)
    RR0203   Rolling Stone 97 (December 9, 1971)
                  p56. Ferris, Tim
    RR0204   Rolling Stone (January 1972) p77.

Edwards, Henry

FOUR BY THE BEATLES (EP)
    RR0205   Beatlefan 2:4 (June 1980) p14.
             King, William P.

FRANCOIS GLORIEUX PLAYS THE BEATLES, VOL. 2 (LP)
    RR0206   Contemporary Keyboard 6 (July 1980)
             p79.

FROM A WHISPER TO A SHOUT (LP)
    RR0207   Beatles Now 6 (May 1983) p17.
             Phillips, Steve

FROM US TO YOU (LP)
    RR0208   Beatles Now 2 (Spring 1982) p18.

GEORGE HARRISON (LP)
    RR0209   Beatlefan 1:2 (February 1979) pp8-9.
             King, William P.
    RR0210   The Beatles Book 36 (April 1979)
             ppiii-v.
    RR0211   Beatles Unlimited 24 (January 1979)
             pp4-5. Hager, Henk
    RR0212   Feature 95 (April 1979) p68.
    RR0213   High Fidelity/Musical America 29
             (May 1979) pp124-125.
    RR0214   Melody Maker 54 (February 24, 1979)
             p29.
    RR0215   Rolling Stone 289 (April 19, 1979)
             p90.
    RR0216   Stereo Review 42 (April 1979) p114.

GEORGE HARRISON 1974 (LP)
    RR0217   Beatles Unlimited 4 (November 1975)
             p8. Vermeer, Evert

GET BACK (LP)
    RR0218   Rolling Stone 42 (September 20, 1969)
             p8.

THE GIRL IS MINE (45)
    RR0219   Beatlefan 5:1 (December 1982) pp24,26.
             King, William P.

GOLDEN GREATEST HITS (LP)
    RR0220   Beatlefan 2:5 (August 1980) p26.
             Lark, Fred

GONE TROPPO (LP)
    RR0221   Beatlefan 5:1 (December 1982) pp23-24.
             Lark, Fred
    RR0222   Beatlefan 5:1 (December 1982) p23.
             Sussman, Al
    RR0223   Beatlefan 5:1 (December 1982) p24.
             King, William P.
    RR0224   Beatlefan 5:1 (December 1982) p24.
             Podrazik, Wally
    RR0225   The Beatles Book 80 (December 1982)
             pp44,46.
    RR0226   Rolling Stone 389 (February 17, 1983)
             p55. Pond, Steve

GOODNIGHT TONIGHT/DAYTIME NIGHTIME SUFFERING (45)
    RR0227   Beatlefan 1:3 (April 1979) p6,16.
             King, William P.

GOODNIGHT VIENNA (LP)
    RR0228   Billboard 86 (November 23, 1974)
             p80.
    RR0229   Crawdaddy (March 1975) p73.
    RR0230   Creem 6 (February 1975) p67.
             Christgau, Robert
    RR0231   Listening Post 6:3 (April 1975)
             p20. Marshall, David C.
    RR0232   New Times 4 (January 10, 1975) p64.
    RR0233   Rolling Stone 185 (April 24, 1975)
             p62. Nolan, Tom
    RR0234   Stereo Review 34 (March 1975) pp80-81.
             Bangs, Lester

A HARD DAY'S NIGHT (LP)
    RR0235   High Fidelity/Musical America (November
             1964) p125.

A HARD ROAD (LP)
    RR0236   Beatlefan 4:3 (April 1982) p27.
             Reinhart, Charles

HEAR THE BEATLES TELL ALL (LP)
    RR0237   The Beatles Book 59 (March 1981)
             ppix-xi. Doggett, Peter

HER MAJESTY (LP)
    RR0238   Beatlefan 4:2 (February 1982) p28.
             Ellis, Roger

HEY JUDE (LP)
         (see also THE BEATLES AGAIN (LP))
    RR0239   Circus (May 1970) p8.
    RR0240   Melody Maker 54 (May 19, 1979) p35.

HOUND DOG/LONG TALL SALLY (45)
    RR0241   Beatlefan 1:4 (June 1979) p6,9.
             Shears, Billy
    RR0242   Beatlefan 4:5 (August 1982) p25.
             Reinhart, Charles
    RR0243   Beatles Now 1 (January 1982) p13.

IMAGINE (LP)
    RR0244   Creem 3 (December 1971) p48.
    RR0245   Fifth Estate 6:13 (September 29, 1971)
             p14.
    RR0246   Georgia Straight Augur 5:4 (September 24,
             1971) p18. McGrath
    RR0247   High Fidelity/Musical America (January
             1972) p77. Edwards, Henry
    RR0248   Jazz Magazine 197 (February 1972)
             pp36-37.
    RR0249   Melody Maker 46 (September 4, 1971)
             p29. Hollingsworth, R.
    RR0250   Melody Maker 46 (October 9, 1971)
             p21.
    RR0251   Music and Musicians (January 1972)
             pp30-32. Mellers, Wilfred
    RR0252   Rolling Stone 94 (October 28, 1971)
             p48. Gerson, Ben
    RR0253   St. Louis Outlaw 2:10 (October 22, 1971) p7

INDIAN ROPE TRICK (LP)
    RR0254   Beatles Now 6 (May 1983) p17.
             Beller, Daniel
    RR0255   Beatles Unlimited 19 (March 1978)
             pp18-19. Dieckmann, Eddie

INSTANT KARMA (45)
    RR0256   Rolling Stone 56 (April 16, 1970)
             p48. Winner, Langdon

IT'S ALRIGHT (LP)
    RR0257   Beatlefan 5:1 (December 1982) p26.
             King, William P.
    RR0258   Rolling Stone 387 (January 20, 1983)
             pp51-52. Loder, Kurt

JE SUIS LE PLUS MIEUX - THE LAST REUNION (12-INCH
    45)
    RR0259   Beatlefan 4:2 (February 1982) p28.
             Shears, Billy
    RR0260   Beatles Now 2 (Spring 1982) p18.

THE JOHN LENNON COLLECTION (LP)
    RR0261   Beatlefan 5:1 (December 1982) p23.
             King, William P.
    RR0262   The Beatles Book 80 (December 1982)
             pp46-47.

JOHN LENNON/PLASTIC ONO BAND (LP)
    RR0263   Creem 3 (March 1971) p78.
    RR0264   Dallas Notes 91 Saunders, M.

RR0265 Jazz & Pop 10 (March 1971) pp43-44.
       Harris, B.
RR0266 Kudzu 3:5 (March 1971) p6.
RR0267 New Yorker 47 (February 27, 1971)
       pp95-97. Willis, Ellen
RR0268 Rolling Stone 77 (March 4, 1971)
       p49.
RR0269 The Times (January 23, 1971) p17E.
       Williams, Richard

(JUST LIKE) STARTING OVER/KISS KISS KISS (45)
RR0270 Beatlefan 2:6 (October 1980) pp26,29.
       King, William P.

KLAATU (LP)
RR0271 Beatles Unlimited 13 (May 1977)
       pp21-22. Hager, Henk

LET IT BE (LP)
RR0272 Circus (July 1970) p8.
RR0273 Jazz & Pop 9 (September 1970) p54.
       Kennely, P.
RR0274 Jazz & Pop 9 (October 1970) pp37-38.
       Yorke, R.
RR0275 Melody Maker (May 9, 1970) p5.
       Williams, R.
RR0276 Newsweek (June 8, 1970) pp83-84.
RR0277 Rolling Stone 56 (April 16, 1970)
       p48. Winner, Langdon
RR0278 Rolling Stone 60 (June 11, 1970)
       p42. Ward, Edmund O.
RR0279 Rolling Stone (June 25, 1970) p52.
       Goodwin, M.
RR0280 Rolling Stone (July 9, 1970) p39.
       Ward, Edmund O.
RR0281 Time (May 18, 1970) p64.

LET'S HEAR ONE FOR LORD BUDDAH (LP)
RR0282 Beatles Unlimited 1 (March 1975)
       pp8-10. Hager, Henk

LIKE DREAMERS DO (LP)
RR0283 Beatlefan 4:6 (October 1982) p26.
       King, William P.
RR0284 Beatlefan 4:6 (October 1982) p26.
       Schwartz, David

LISTEN TO THIS PICTURE RECORD (LP)
RR0285 Beatles Now 1 (January 1982) p13.

LIVE AND LET DIE (LP)
RR0286 Rolling Stone 132 (April 12, 1973)
       p20.
RR0287 Rolling Stone 150 (December 20, 1973)
       p83.
RR0288 Stereo Review 32 (January 1974)
       p101.

LIVE IN GERMANY (EP)
RR0289 Beatles Now 1 (January 1982) p13.

LIVE PEACE IN TORONTO (LP)
RR0290 Rolling Stone 51 (February 7, 1970)
       p36. Marcus, Greil

LIVERPOOL LIVE (LP)
RR0291 Beatlefan 3:2 (February 1981) p25.
       Shears, Billy

LIVING IN THE MATERIAL WORLD (LP)
RR0292 Crawdaddy 27 (August 1973) p67.
RR0293 Creem 5:5 (October 1973) p17.
RR0294 Los Angeles Times IV (June 5, 1973)
       p8.
RR0295 Melody Maker 48 (June 9, 1973) p3.
       Watts, M.
RR0296 Playboy 20 (October 1973) p44.
RR0297 Previews 2:8 (April 1974) p15.
RR0298 Rolling Stone 139 (July 19, 1973)
       p54. Holden, Stephen

LONDON TOWN (LP)
RR0299 Crawdaddy 85 (June 1978) p69.
RR0300 Creem 10 (July 1978) p59.
RR0301 High Fidelity/Musical America 28
       (July 1978) p120. Goldstein, T.

LOVE SONGS (LP)
RR0302 Stereo Review 40 (March 1978) p102.

MCCARTNEY (LP)
RR0303 Billboard 82 (May 9, 1970) p8. Ochs, Ed
RR0304 Broadside 9:8 (June 16, 1970) p13.
       Murray, T.
RR0305 Circus (July 1970) p8.
RR0306 Jazz & Pop 9 (August 1970) p58.
RR0307 Rolling Stone 58 (May 14, 1970)
       p50. Winner, Langdon
RR0308 Saturday Review 53 (May 30, 1970)
       pp53-54. Sander, Ellen

MCCARTNEY II (LP)
RR0309 Audio 64:8 (August 1980) p64. Tiven, Jon
RR0310 Beatlefan 2:4 (June 1980) pp12-13.
       King, Timothy
RR0311 The Beatles Book 51 (July 1980)
       ppiii-iv. Lewisohn, Mark
RR0312 Beatles Unlimited 32 (May 1980)
       pp4-5. Leenheer, Franck
RR0313 Chicago 29 (September 1980) p142.
RR0314 Rolling Stone 322 (July 24, 1980)
       p54.
RR0315 Stereo Review 45 (September 1980)
       p94. Reilly, P.
RR0316 Stereo Review 45:3 (September 1980)
       p94. Simels, Steve
RR0317 Village Voice 25 (July 2, 1980)
       p45. Carson, T.

*MCGEAR (LP)
RR0318 Beatles Unlimited 1 (March 1975)
       pp12-13.
RR0319 Listening Post 6:5 (June 1975) p7.
       Wilson, David L.
RR0320 Rolling Stone 180 (February 13, 1975)
       p78. Nolan, Tom

MAGICAL MYSTERY TOUR (LP)
RR0321 Beatlefan 3:4 (June 1981) p30.
       Schwartz, David
RR0322 Beatlefan 3:4 (June 1981) p31. Lark, Fred
RR0323 Horizon 10 (Spring 1968) pp56-59.
       Grunfeld, Frederic
RR0324 Jazz & Pop (January 1968) pp14-15.
       Szwed, John F.
RR0325 Newsweek (January 1, 1968) pp62-63.
       Kroll, Jack
RR0326 Saturday Review (December 30, 1967)
       p55. Jahn, Mike
RR0327 Time (January 5, 1968) pp60-61.

MEET THE BEATLES (LP)
RR0328 High Fidelity/Musical America 14:4
       (April 1964) p108.

MIND GAMES (LP)
RR0329 Billboard 85 (November 10, 1973)
       p56.
RR0330 Crawdaddy (February 1974) pp66+.
RR0331 Creem 5 (February 1974) p62.
       Bangs, Lester
RR0332 Creem 5 (March 1974) p13.
       Christgau, Robert
RR0333 High Fidelity/Musical America 24
       (March 1974) p109.
RR0334 Listening Post 5:2 (February 1974)
       p32. Strickland, Geoffrey
RR0335 Los Angeles Times II (October 27, 1973)
       p5.
RR0336 Melody Maker 48 (December 8, 1973)

p35.
RR0337 Previews 2:8 (April 1974) p15.
RR0338 Rolling Stone 151 (January 3, 1974)
        p61.
RR0339 Stereo Review 32 (March 1974) pp88+.

MY SWEET LORD/ISN'T IT A PITY (45)
RR0340 Rolling Stone 73 (December 24, 1970)
        p56. Landau, Jon

NASHVILLE DIARY (EP)
RR0341 Beatlefan 1:6 (October 1979) p8.

(THE NEW) 21 (LP)
RR0342 Beatlefan 1:5 (August 1979) p6.
        King, William P.

NO. 3 ABBEY ROAD NW8 (LP)
RR0343 Beatlefan 1:6 (October 1979) p8.
        King, William P.
RR0344 Beatles Now 1 (January 1982) p12.

ODD SOX (LP)
RR0345 Beatlefan 4:3 (April 1982) pp28-29.
        King, William P.

ORIENTAL NIGHTFISH (LP)
RR0346 Beatlefan 1:5 (August 1979) p6,10.
        King, William P.

PETE BEST: "THE BEATLE THAT TIME FORGOT" (LP)
RR0347 Beatles Now 5 (Winter 1983) p13.
        Beller, Daniel

RAM (LP)
RR0348 Circus (August 1971) p20.
RR0349 Creem 3 (September 1971) p63.
RR0350 Kudzu 3:6 (June 1971) p8. Adcock
RR0351 Melody Maker 46 (May 22, 1971) p11.
        Charlesworth, C.
RR0352 Rock Magazine (July 29, 1971) p27.
        Scoppa, Bud
RR0353 Rolling Stone 86 (July 8, 1971)
        p42. Landau, Jon
RR0354 Seed 7:2 (June 29, 1971) p18.
        Uncle Martin
RR0355 Willamette Bridge 4:25 (June 24, 1971)
        p19. Hotchkins, A. Bear

RARITIES (LP)
RR0356 Beatlefan 1:1 (December 1978) p12.
        Shears, Billy
RR0357 Beatlefan 2:3 (April 1980) pp5-6.
        Sussman, Al
RR0358 Beatlefan 2:6 (October 1980) p14.
        Lark, Fred
RR0359 Stereo Review 45:1 (July 1980) p94.
        Simels, Steve

RECOVERED TRACKS (LP)
RR0360 Beatlefan 3:5 (August 1981) p30.
        Reinhart, Charles

RED ROSE SPEEDWAY (LP)
RR0361 Circus (August 1973) p22.
RR0362 Crawdaddy 26 (July 1973) p78.
RR0363 Creem 5:3 (August 1973) p63.
RR0364 Melody Maker 48 (May 19, 1973) p25.
RR0365 Playboy 20 (September 1973) p42.
RR0366 Previews 2:8 (April 1974) p15.
RR0367 Rolling Stone 138 (July 5, 1973)
        p68. Kaye, Lenny

REEL MUSIC (LP)
RR0368 Beatlefan 4:3 (April 1982) p27.
        Schwartz, David
RR0369 Beatlefan 4:3 (April 1982) p27.
        Sussman, Al
RR0370 Beatles Unlimited 42 (1982) p10.
        Pope, Michael E.

REVOLVER (LP)
RR0371 Melody Maker 56 (March 28, 1981)
        p15. Hinton, B.
RR0372 Music In Education 30:322 (November 1966)
        pp293-294. Addison, R.

RINGO (LP)
RR0373 Billboard 85 (November 3, 1973)
        p56.
RR0374 Crawdaddy 33 (January 1974) pp66-67.
RR0375 High Fidelity/Musical America 24
        (March 1974) p108.
RR0376 Listening Post 5:6 (June 1974) p9.
        Pearson, John
RR0377 Los Angeles Times II (October 27, 1973)
        p5.
RR0378 Los Angeles Times IV (October 30, 1973)
        p8.
RR0379 Phonograph Record Magazine (December 1973)
        p32.
RR0380 Previews 2:8 (April 1974) p15.
RR0381 Rolling Stone 150 (December 20, 1973)
        p73. Gerson, Ben
RR0382 Rolling Stone 156 (March 14, 1974)
        p24. Grossman, Jay
RR0383 Stereo Review 32 (March 1974) pp88+.

RINGO'S ROTOGRAVURE (LP)
RR0384 Crawdaddy (January 1977) p78.
RR0385 Creem 8 (January 1977) p59.
RR0386 Melody Maker 51 (October 23, 1976)
        p27.
RR0387 Rolling Stone 227 (December 2, 1976)
        p96. Altman, Billy
RR0388 Stereo Review 38 (February 1977)
        p102.

RINGO THE 4TH (LP)
RR0389 The Beatles Book 20 (December 1977)
        ppiii-iv.
RR0390 Beatles Unlimited 15 (September 1977)
        p10. Vermeer, Evert
RR0391 Melody Maker 53 (February 11, 1978)
        p20.
RR0392 Rolling Stone 152 (November 17, 1977)
        p252. Holden, Stephen

ROCK 'N' ROLL (LP)
RR0393 Beatles Unlimited 1 (March 1975)
        pp18-19. Hager, Henk
RR0394 Billboard 87 (March 1, 1975) p56.
RR0395 Crawdaddy (July 1975) p74.
RR0396 Creem 7 (June 1975) p69. Marcus, Greil
RR0397 High Fidelity/Musical America 25
        (June 1975) p112.
RR0398 Listening Post 6:5 (June 1975) p6.
        Wilson, David L.
RR0399 Los Angeles Times IV (February 18, 1975)
        p10.
RR0400 Rolling Stone 187 (May 22, 1975)
        p66. Landau, Jon
RR0401 Stereo Review 34 (May 1975) pp75-76.
        Simels, Steve
RR0402 Village Voice 20 (March 10, 1975)
        p101. Marcus, Greil

ROCK 'N' ROLL MUSIC (LP)
RR0403 Family Circle 89 (October 1976)
        pp70+.
RR0404 High Fidelity/Musical America 26
        (October 1976) pp96-97. Jahn, M.
RR0405 Melody Maker 51 (June 26, 1976)
        p22.
RR0406 Rolling Stone 217 (July 17, 1976)
        pp46-47+. Marcus, G.
RR0407 Stereo Review 37 (October 1976)
        p90.

ROCK 'N' ROLL - THE BEATLES & JOHN LENNON (LP)
RR0408   Beatlefan 4:5 (August 1982) p26.
         Lark, Fred

ROUGH NOTES (LP)
RR0409   Beatlefan 3:2 (February 1981) p24.
         Ellis, Roger
RR0410   Beatlefan 3:2 (February 1981) p24.
         Phillips, Steve

ROYAL VARIETY SHOW (EP)
RR0411   Beatles Now 2 (Spring 1982) p18.

THE RUTLES (LP)
RR0412   Beatles Unlimited 19 (March 1978)
         p17. DeBruin, Hans

SEASON OF GLASS (LP)
RR0413   Add Some Music 5:1 (Winter 1982)
         pp32-33. Cunningham, Don
RR0414   Beatlefan 3:4 (June 1981) p30.
         King, William P.
RR0415   High Fidelity/Musical America 31
         (September 1981) p92.
RR0416   Melody Maker 56 (June 13, 1981)
         p22.
RR0417   New York Times III (May 20, 1981)
         p27:5. Palmer, Robert
RR0418   Rolling Stone 347 (July 9, 1981)
         pp55+. Holden, Stephen
RR0419   Stereo Review 46:10 (October 1981)
         p96. Coppage, Noel
RR0420   Village Voice 26 (July 29, 1981)
         p49.

SENTIMENTAL JOURNEY (LP)
RR0421   Circus (July 1970) p8.
RR0422   Jazz & Pop 9 (August 1970) pp59-60.
         Coughlan, J.
RR0423   Rolling Stone 58 (May 14, 1970)
         p56. Marcus, Greil

SGT. PEPPER'S LONELY HEARTS CLUB BAND (LP)
RR0424   American Record Guide 34 (October 1967)
         pp168-169. Heckman, Don
RR0425   Beatlefan 4:1 (December 1981) p28.
         Schwartz, David
RR0426   Esquire 68 (December 1967) pp283-286.
         Christgau, R.
RR0427   High Fidelity/Musical America 17
         (August 1967) p94. Lees, G.
RR0428   Horizon 10 (Spring 1968) pp56-59.
         Grunfeld, Frederic
RR0429   Melody Maker 42 (June 3, 1967) p5.
         Welch, C.
RR0430   Newsweek 69 (June 26, 1967) p70.
         Kroll, Jack
RR0431   New Yorker 43 (June 24, 1967) pp22-23.
RR0432   Saturday Review 50 (August 19, 1967)
         p61. Schrag, P.

SGT. PEPPER'S LONELY HEARTS CLUB BAND (LP-RSO)
RR0433   Beatles Unlimited 22 (September 1978)
         pp4-5. Hager, Henk
RR0434   Rolling Stone 275 (October 5, 1978)
         p71. Nelson, Paul

SHAVED FISH (LP)
RR0435   Beatles Unlimited 4 (November 1975)
         p9.
RR0436   Billboard 87 (November 1, 1975)
         p70.
RR0437   Crawdaddy (March 1976) pp76+.
RR0438   Creem 7 (March 1976) p60.
RR0439   Playboy 23 (March 1976) p32.
RR0440   Rolling Stone 202 (December 18, 1975)
         p68. Marsh, Dave
RR0441   Stereo Review 36 (January 1976)
         pp83+.

SOMETHING NEW (LP)
RR0442   High Fidelity/Musical America (November
         1964) p125.

SOME TIME IN NEW YORK CITY (LP)
RR0443   Christian Science Monitor (August 12,
         1972) p6.
RR0444   Circus (August 1972) p64.
RR0445   Circus (September 1972) p18.
RR0446   Crawdaddy 16 (September 1972) p16.
RR0447   Melody Maker 47 (June 10, 1972)
         p9. Hollingsworth, R.
RR0448   Melody Maker 47 (October 7, 1972)
         p25.
RR0449   Phonograph Record Magazine (August 1972)
         p21.
RR0450   Rolling Stone 112 (July 20, 1972)
         p48. Holden, Stephen

SOMEWHERE IN ENGLAND (LP)
RR0451   Beatlefan 3:4 (June 1981) pp29-30.
         King, William P.
RR0452   Beatlefan 3:4 (June 1981) p30.
         Ellis, Roger
RR0453   Beatlefan 3:4 (June 1981) p30.
         Fulper-Smith, Shawn
RR0454   Beatlefan 3:4 (June 1981) p30.
         Phillips, Steve
RR0455   Beatlefan 3:4 (June 1981) p30.
         Sussman, Al
RR0456   The Beatles Book 63 (July 1981)
         pxi. Martin, Brendan
RR0457   Beatles Unlimited 37 (July 1981)
         pp12-14. Pope, Michael E.
RR0458   Melody Maker 56 (June 6, 1981) p27.
RR0459   New York Times III (May 31, 1981)
         p23:1. Palmer, Robert

SOMEWHERE IN ENGLAND (LP-BOOTLEG)
RR0460   Beatles Now 4 (Autumn 1982) pp19-20.
         Wallgren, Mark

THE SONGS LENNON AND MCCARTNEY GAVE AWAY (LP)
RR0461   Beatlefan 2:2 (February 1980) p19.
         King, William P.

STOP AND SMELL THE ROSES (LP)
RR0462   Beatlefan 4:1 (December 1981) p27.
         King, William P.
RR0463   Beatlefan 4:1 (December 1981) pp27-28.
         Podrazik, Wally
RR0464   The Beatles Book 69 (January 1982)
         ppix-x. Doggett, Peter
RR0465   Rolling Stone 362 (February 4, 1982)
         p55. Schaffner, Nicholas
RR0466   Stereo Review 47 (March 1982) p110.
         Vance, Joel

STRAWBERRY FIELDS FOREVER (LP)
RR0467   Beatlefan 4:6 (October 1982) p26.
         Wallgren, Mark
RR0468   Beatles Now 4 (Autumn 1982) p18.
         Wallgren, Mark

SUITABLE FOR FRAMING (LP)
RR0469   Beatlefan 4:6 (October 1982) p25.
         Wallgren, Mark
RR0470   Beatles Now 4 (Autumn 1982) p19.
         Wallgren, Mark

SWEET APPLE TRAX (LP)
RR0471   Beatles Unlimited 1 (March 1975)
         p7. Bakker, Erik M.

SWEET APPLE TRAX VOL. 3 (LP)
RR0472   Beatlefan 4:5 (August 1982) p24.
         Ellis, Roger
RR0473   Beatlefan 4:5 (August 1982) p24.
         Lark, Fred

TAKE IT AWAY/I'LL GIVE YOU A RING (45)
    RR0474 Beatlefan 4:5 (August 1982) p25.
            King, William P.

33 1/3 (LP)
    RR0475 Beatles Unlimited 11 (January 1977)
            pp18-21. Hager, Henk
    RR0476 Crawdaddy (March 1977) pp65-66.
    RR0477 Creem 8 (March 1977) pp60-61.
    RR0478 High Fidelity/Musical America 27
            (March 1977) p140.
    RR0479 Melody Maker 51 (November 27, 1976)
            p23.
    RR0480 Rolling Stone 230 (January 13, 1977)
            p52.
    RR0481 Stereo Review 38 (March 1977) pp96+.
    RR0482 Village Voice 21 (December 20, 1976)
            pp87-89.

TO KNOW HIM IS TO LOVE HIM/BESAME MUCHO (45)
    RR0483 Beatlefan 1:2 (February 1979) p9.
            Shears, Billy

TONY SHERIDAN AND THE BEATLES (LP)
    RR0484 Beatles Now 5 (Winter 1983) p13.
            Beller, Daniel

TOP OF THE POPS (EP)
    RR0485 Beatles Unlimited 26 (May 1979)
            p14. Forsyth, Ian S.

THE TOY BOY (LIMITED EDITION) (LP)
    RR0486 Beatlefan 4:6 (October 1982) pp25-26.
            Hockinson, Mike

TUG OF WAR (LP)
    RR0487 Beatlefan 4:3 (April 1982) p26.
            King, William P.
    RR0488 Beatlefan 4:4 (June 1982) pp27-28.
            Podrazik, Walter J.
    RR0489 Beatlefan 4:4 (June 1982) p28.
            Schaffner, Nicholas
    RR0490 Beatlefan 4:4 (June 1982) pp29-30.
            Sussman, Al
    RR0491 The Beatles Book 74 (June 1982)
            ppx-xi. Doggett, Peter
    RR0492 Daily News (Philadelphia) (April 30, 1982)
            p62. Aregood, Rich
    RR0493 Newsweek (May 3, 1982) p74. Miller, Jim
    RR0494 New York Times II (April 25, 1982)
            pp11,19. Palmer, Robert
    RR0495 Rolling Stone (May 27, 1982) p52.
            Holden, Stephen
    RR0496 Rolling Stone 385 (December 23, 1982)
            p107.
    RR0497 Stereo Review (June 1982) p76. Peel, Mark
    RR0498 Village Voice (May 11, 1982) p64.
            Sigerson, Davitt

20 GOLDEN HITS (LP)
    RR0499 Beatlefan 2:5 (August 1980) p26.
            Lark, Fred

20 GREATEST HITS (LP)
    RR0500 Beatlefan 5:1 (December 1982) p23.
            Schwartz, David
    RR0501 The Beatles Book 79 (December 1982)
            pp45-46.

20 X 4 (LP)
    RR0502 Beatelfan 1:1 (December 1978) p9.
            King, William P.
    RR0503 Beatles Unlimited 21 (July 1978)
            pp21-23. Dieckmann, Eddie

UNFINISHED MUSIC NO. 1: TWO VIRGINS (LP)
    RR0504 Beatlefan 4:5 (August 1982) p25.
            Reinhart, Charles
    RR0505 Rolling Stone 26 (February 1, 1969)
            p12.

RR0506 Rolling Stone 28 (March 1, 1969)
        p20. Cott, Jonathan

UNFINISHED MUSIC NO. 2: LIFE WITH THE LIONS (LP)
    RR0507 Rolling Stone 39 (August 9, 1969)
            p37. Ward, Edmund O.

VANCOUVER 1964 (LP)
    RR0508 Beatles Now 5 (Winter 1983) p19.
            Beller, Daniel

VEGEMITE (LP)
    RR0509 Beatles Unlimited 40 (1982) pp20-21.
            Vermeer, Evert

VENUS AND MARS (LP)
    RR0510 Beatles Unlimited 2 (June 1975)
            p3.
    RR0511 Crawdaddy 52 (September 1975) pp65-66.
    RR0512 Creem 7 (September 1975) p66.
    RR0513 Los Angeles Times (June 8, 1975)
            p70.
    RR0514 Melody Maker 50 (May 31, 1975) p22.
    RR0515 Rolling Stone 192 (July 31, 1975)
            pp52,55. Nelson, Paul

WALKING ON THIN ICE/IT HAPPENED (45)
    RR0516 Beatlefan 3:2 (February 1981) p24.
            King, William P.

WALLS AND BRIDGES (LP)
    RR0517 Billboard 86 (October 5, 1974) p78.
    RR0518 Crawdaddy 44 (January 1975) pp72-73.
            Snyder-Scumpy, P.
    RR0519 Creem 6 (January 1975) p14.
            Christgau, Robert
    RR0520 Creem 6 (January 1975) p72. Robins, Wayne
    RR0521 Rolling Stone 174 (November 21, 1974)
            pp72+. Gerson, Ben
    RR0522 Stereo Review 34 (March 1975) pp76+.

WATERFALLS/CHECK MY MACHINE (45)
    RR0523 Beatlefan 2:5 (August 1980) p26.
            King, William P.

WHAT A SHAME MARY JANE HAD A PAIN AT THE PARTY (45)
    RR0524 Beatlefan 3:2 (February 1981) p24.
            Lark, Fred

WILD LIFE (LP)
    RR0525 Circus (March 1972) p17.
    RR0526 Creem 4 (March 1972) p47.
    RR0527 Melody Maker 46 (November 20, 1971)
            p33. Charlesworth, C.
    RR0528 Melody Maker 46 (December 11, 1971)
            p14.
    RR0529 Phonograph Record Magazine (January 1972)
            p24.
    RR0530 Rolling Stone 100 (January 20, 1972)
            p48. Mendelsohn, J.
    RR0531 Space City 3:28 (December 23, 1971)
            p9. Lomax
    RR0532 Variety (November 24, 1971) p47.

WINGS AT THE SPEED OF SOUND (LP)
    RR0533 Beatles Unlimited 6 (March 1976)
            pp23-25. Hager, Henk
    RR0534 Billboard 88 (April 17, 1976) p80.
            Kirsch, B.
    RR0535 Christian Science Monitor 68 (June 3,
            1976) p23. McCormick, L.D.
    RR0536 Crawdaddy 61 (June 1976) p65.
    RR0537 Creem 8 (June 1976) p56.
    RR0538 Rolling Stone 213 (May 20, 1976)
            pp67+. Holden, Stephen

WINGS GREATEST (LP)
    RR0539 Beatlefan 1:1 (December 1978) p9.
            King, William P.
    RR0540 Beatles Unlimited 24 (January 1979)

p11. Pope, Michael E.

WINGS OVER AMERICA (LP)
    RR0541 Playboy 24 (April 1977) p24.
    RR0542 Rolling Stone 232 (February 10, 1977)
           p103. Tucker, Ken
    RR0543 Stereo Review 38 (Marcn 1977) p101.

WINGS OVER ATLANTA (LP)
    RR0544 Beatlefan 1:1 (December 1978) p9.
           King, William P.

WOMAN/BEAUTIFUL BOYS (45)
    RR0545 Beatlefan 3:2 (February 1981) p20.
           Lark, Fred

WONDERFUL CHRISTMASTIME/RUDOLPH THE RED-NOSED
  REGGAE (45)
    RR0546 Beatlefan 2:1 (December 1979) p9.
           King, William P.

WONDERWALL MUSIC (LP)

RR0547 Rolling Stone 28 (March 1, 1969)
        p20.

WORKING CLASS HERO (LP)
    RR0548 Beatlefan 3:5 (August 1981) p30.
           Reinhart, Charles
    RR0549 Beatles Now 3 (Summer 1982) p18.

WRACK MY BRAIN/DRUMMING IN MY MADNESS (45)
    RR0550 Beatlefan 3:6 (October 1981) p27.
           King, William P.

YOKO ONO/PLASTIC ONO BAND (LP)
    RR0551 Chinook 3:5 (February 5, 1971) p6.
           Loquidis
    RR0552 The Times (January 23, 1971) p17E.
           Williams, Richard

YOUNGBLOOD (LP)
    RR0553 Beatles Unlimited 22 (September 1978)
           p11. Forsyth, Ian

HELP!
THE BEATLES

Released by United Artists
A Random House Book

THE YELLOW SUBMARINE
GIFT BOOK

WE LOVE YOU BEATLES

Written and Illustrated by MARGARET SUTTON

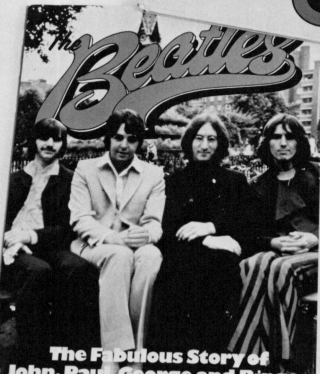

The Beatles
The Fabulous Story of John, Paul, George and Ringo

THE BEATLES ILLUSTRATED Lyrics

Edited by Alan Aldridge

S 0001 All Things Must Pass. New York:
Harrisongs Music/Crown, 1970. 96pp. pa.
(Sheet music-in-folio, with poster-size
photo.)

S 0002 All Things Must Pass. New York:
Hansen Edu. Music & Books, 197?. 96pp. pa.
(Sheet music-in-folio.)

S 0003 The Apple Song Book. New York:
Hansen Edu. Music & Books, 196?. 216pp. pa.
illus.
(Sheet music-in-folio;also other Apple
artists.)

S 0004 The Beatle Beat. New York: Metric Music, 196?.
22pp. pa. illus.
(Sheet music-in-folio.)

S 0005 The Beatle Book Souvenir Song Album Of Recorded
Hits. n.p.: Keys, 196?. 22pp. pa. illus.
(Sheet music-in-folio.)

S 0006 Beatlemania 1963-1966, Vol. I. New York:
Cherry Lane Music. 128pp. pa.
(Sheet music-in-folio; 56 songs for
piano/vocal.)

S 0007 Beatlemania 1967-1970, Vol. II. New York:
Cherry Lane Music. 128pp. pa.
(Sheet music-in-folio; 46 songs for
piano/vocal.)

S 0008 The Beatles. London: Northern Songs Ltd., 1968.
88pp. illus.
(Sheet music-in-folio.)

S 0009 The Beatles: Abbey Road. London: Music Sales.
40pp. pa.
(Sheet music-in-folio.)

S 0010 Beatles/Abbey Road - Matching Music Book.
Miami Beach, FL: Hansen Publications, 1969.
80pp. pa. illus.
(Sheet music-in-folio.)

S 0011 The Beatles: A Hard Day's Night. London:
Music Sales. 40pp. pa.
(Sheet music-in-folio.)

S 0012 The Beatles At The Hollywood Bowl. London:
Music Sales. 32pp. pa.
(Sheet music-in-folio.)

S 0013 The Beatles At The Hollywood Bowl. New York:
Cherry Lane Music. pa.
(Sheet music-in-folio; 13 songs for
piano/vocal.)

S 0014 The Beatles Ballads. London: Music Sales.
56pp. pa.
(Sheet music-in-folio.)

S 0015 The Beatles: Beatles For Sale. London:
Music Sales. 40pp. pa.
(Sheet music-in-folio.)

S 0016 Beatles Best. Milwaukee, WI:
Hal Leonard Publishing, 198?. pa.
(Sheet music-in-folio; easy guitar.)

S 0017 Beatles Best. Milwaukee, WI:
Hal Leonard Publishing, 198?. pa.
(Sheet music-in-folio;19 songs for
portable keyboard.)

S 0018 The Beatles Bumper Songbook. London:
Wise Publications, 1980. 256pp. pa. illus.
(Sheet music-in-folio.)

S 0019 The Beatles: Chord Organ Edition. London:
Music Sales. 186pp. pa. illus.
(Sheet music-in-folio.)

S 0020 The Beatles Classic Guitar Pieces: Tutor, ed.
by Joe Washington. London: Music Sales, 1974.
88pp. pa.
(Sheet music-in-folio.)

S 0021 The Beatles Complete. Miami Beach, FL:
Hansen Publications, 196?. 196pp. pa. illus.
(Sheet music-in-folio.)

S 0022 The Beatles Complete. New York:
Collier-Macmillan, 1972. 220pp. pa. illus.
(Sheet music-in-folio.)

S 0023 The Beatles Complete. New York:
Warner Brothers Pubns., 1976. 480pp. pa.
(Sheet music-in-folio.)

S 0024 Beatles Complete - Easy Guitar, edited by
Milton Okun. Rev. ed. New York:

Cherry Lane Music, 1982. pa.
(Sheet music-in-folio; 160 songs.)

S 0025 The Beatles Complete - For Easy Guitar.
Miami Beach, FL: Hansen Publications, 196?.
208pp. pa. illus.
(Sheet music-in-folio.)

S 0026 The Beatles Complete: For Piano And Guitar, ed.
by Ray Connolly. London: Music Sales, 1971.
220pp. illus.
(Sheet music-in-folio.)

S 0027 The Beatles Complete: Guitar Edition. London:
Music Sales. 208pp. pa. illus.
(Sheet music-in-folio.)

S 0028 The Beatles Complete - Guitar/Vocal, with text
by Ray Connolly. London:
Wise Publications/Music Sales, 1984. illus.
(Sheet music-in-folio; thirty-eight
photos.)

S 0029 The Beatles Complete - Piano/Organ/Vocal, with
text by Ray Connolly. London:
Wise Publications/Music Sales, 1984. illus.
(Sheet music-in-folio; thirty-eight
photos.)

S 0030 The Beatles Complete: Piano Vocal/Easy Organ.
London: Music Sales. 218pp. pa. illus.
(Sheet music-in-folio.)

S 0031 The Beatles Complete Works.
Amsterdam, Holland: Thomas Rap, 1968.
176pp. illus.
(Sheet music-in-folio.)

S 0032 Beatles '80. Tokyo, Japan: Shinko Music, 1980.
240pp. pa.
(Sheet music-in-folio.)

S 0033 The Beatles' Fabulous Favorites. n.p.:
Music Of Today, Inc., 196?. 8pp. pa.
(Sheet music-in-folio (accordian and
guitar).)

S 0034 The Beatles Fantasy. London: Music Sales.
64pp. pa.
(Sheet music-in-folio.)

S 0035 The Beatles For Classical Guitar: Book 1.
London: Music Sales. 88pp. pa.
(Sheet music-in-folio.)

S 0036 The Beatles For Classical Guitar, Book 2.
London: Music Sales. 36pp.
(Sheet music-in-folio.)

S 0037 The Beatles For Classical Guitar/20 Solos,
arranged by Joe Washington. New York:
Music Sales, 1974. 86pp.
(Sheet music-in-folio.)

S 0038 The Beatles Forever, 1964-1969, ed. by 5th
Anniversary Collectors. Miami Beach, FL:
C. H. Hansen, 1969. illus.
(Sheet music-in-folio; five volumes.)

S 0039 The Beatles Greatest Hits For Autoharp.
New York: Cherry Lane Music. pa.
(Sheet music-in-folio; 24 songs.)

S 0040 The Beatles Greatest Hits For Easy Accordian,
edited by Milton Okun. New York:
Cherry Lane Music. pa.
(Sheet music-in-folio; 17 songs.)

S 0041 Beatles Greatest Hits For Flute. New York:
Cherry Lane Music. pa.
(Sheet music-in-folio; 14 songs.)

S 0042 The Beatles Greatest Hits For Guitar, Vol. I.
New York: Cherry Lane Music. pa.
(Sheet music-in-folio; 25 songs.)

S 0043 The Beatles Greatest Hits For Guitar, Vol. II.
New York: Cherry Lane Music. pa.
(Sheet music-in-folio.)

S 0044 Beatles Greatest Hits For Harmonica. New York:
Cherry Lane Music. pa.
(Sheet music-in-folio; 27 songs.)

S 0045 The Beatles Greatest Hits For Recorder.
New York: Cherry Lane Music. pa.
(Sheet music-in-folio; 26 songs.)

S 0046 The Beatles Guitar, edited by Milton Okun.
New York: Cherry Lane Music. pa.
(Sheet music-in-folio.)

S 0047 The Beatles Help!. London: Music Sales.

16pp. pa.
(Sheet music-in-folio.)
S 0048 The Beatles Humour. London: Music Sales.
64pp. pa.
(Sheet music-in-folio.)
S 0049 The Beatles: Let It Be. London: Music Sales.
24pp. pa.
(Sheet music-in-folio.)
S 0050 The Beatles Love Songs. London: Music Sales.
80pp. pa. illus.
(Sheet music-in-folio.)
S 0051 The Beatles: Magical Mystery Tour. London:
Music Sales. 36pp. pa.
(Sheet music-in-folio.)
S 0052 The Beatles 1962-1966. London: Music Sales.
62pp. pa.
(Sheet music-in-folio.)
S 0053 The Beatles 1967-1970. London: Music Sales.
84pp. pa.
(Sheet music-in-folio.)
S 0054 Beatles No.3: Songs By John Lennon & Paul
McCartney, arranged by John Brimhall.
Miami Beach, FL: Hansen Publications, 196?.
18pp. pa.
(Sheet music-in-folio.)
S 0055 The Beatle Sound - For Easy Piano. n.p.:
Shottinger Int'l/Harris Music, 196?.
20pp. pa.
(Sheet music-in-folio.)
S 0056 The Beatles Pop. London: Music Sales.
60pp. pa.
(Sheet music-in-folio,)
S 0057 The Beatles: Revolver. London: Music Sales.
36pp. pa.
(Sheet music-in-folio.)
S 0058 The Beatles Rock 'N' Roll. London: Music Sales.
64pp. pa.
(Sheet music-in-folio.)
S 0059 The Beatles: Rubber Soul. London: Music Sales.
40pp. pa.
(Sheet music-in-folio.)
S 0060 The Beatles: Sgt. Pepper's Lonely Hearts Club
Band. London: Music Sales. 40pp. pa.
(Sheet music-in-folio.)
S 0061 The Beatles '63, ed. by A. Munday. London:
Music Sales, 1974. 100pp. pa.
(Sheet music-in-folio.)
S 0062 The Beatles '64, ed. by A. Munday. London:
Music Sales, 1974. 96pp. pa.
(Sheet music-in-folio.)
S 0063 The Beatles '65, ed. by A. Munday. London:
Music Sales, 1974. 80pp. pa.
(Sheet music-in-folio.)
S 0064 The Beatles '66, ed. by R. Wise. London:
Music Sales, 1974. 28pp. pa.
(Sheet music-in-folio.)
S 0065 The Beatles '67, ed. by R. Wise and P. J. Foss.
London: Music Sales, 1974. 72pp. pa.
(Sheet music-in-folio.)
S 0066 The Beatles '68, ed. by R. Wise and P. J. Foss.
London: Music Sales, 1974. 96pp. pa.
(Sheet music-in-folio.)
S 0067 The Beatles '69, ed. by R. Wise and A. Munday.
London: Music Sales, 1974. 48pp. pa.
(Sheet music-in-folio.)
S 0068 The Beatles '70, ed. by R. Wise. London:
Music Sales, 1974. 88pp. pa.
(Sheet music-in-folio.)
S 0069 Beatles Songs For Easy Piano, arranged by John
Brimhall. New York: Cherry Lane Music. pa.
(Sheet music-in-folio; three volumes.)
S 0070 Beatles Songs For The Recorder, ed. by F. H.
Johnson. London: Music Sales, 1974.
32pp. pa.
(Sheet music-in-folio.)
S 0071 The Beatles, Themes And Variations: Clarinet.
London: Music Sales. 24pp. pa.
(Sheet music-in-folio.)
S 0072 The Beatles, Themes And Variations: Flute.
London: Music Sales. 24pp. pa.

(Sheet music-in-folio.)
S 0073 The Beatles, Themes And Variations: Trumpet.
London: Music Sales. 20pp. pa.
(Sheet music-in-folio.)
S 0074 The Beatles: The Singles Collection, 1962-1970.
London: Music Sales, 1976. 80pp. pa.
(Sheet music-in-folio.)
S 0075 The Beatles To Bacharach: All Organ Edition.
London: Music Sales. 66pp. pa.
(Sheet music-in-folio.)
S 0076 The Beatles To Bacharach: Easy Guitar Edition.
London: Music Sales. 60pp. pa.
(Sheet music-in-folio.)
S 0077 The Beatles: White Album. London: Music Sales.
48pp. pa.
(Sheet music-in-folio.)
S 0078 The Beatles' Years. New York:
Collier-Macmillan, 1972. 196pp. pa.
(Sheet music-in-folio.)
S 0079 The Beatles Years, ed. by Ray Connolly.
London: Music Sales, 1972. 132pp. pa.
(Sheet music-in-folio.)
S 0080 The Beatles: Yellow Submarine.
Miami Beach, FL: Hansen Publications, 1968.
56pp. pa. illus.
(Sheet music-in-folio.)
S 0081 The Best Of The Beatles. Milwaukee, WI:
Hal Leonard Publishing, 198?. 200pp. pa.
(Sheet music-in-folio; easy organ.)
S 0082 A Collection Of Beatles Oldies. London:
Music Sales. 36pp. pa.
(Sheet music-in-folio.)
S 0083 The Concise Beatles Complete. London:
Wise Publications, 1982. 384pp. pa. illus.
(Sheet music-in-folio.)
S 0084 Dark Horse. New York:
Hansen Edu. Music & Books, 1975. 56pp.
(Sheet music-in-folio: George Harrison.)
S 0085 Fingerpicking Lennon & McCartney, by Eric
Schoenberg. New York:
Amsco Music Publishing, 1981. 64pp. pa.
illus.
(Sheet music-in-folio;with cassette tape.)
S 0086 First Book Of Fifty Hit Songs By John Lennon
And Paul McCartney, ed. by P. J. Foss.
London: Music Sales, 1974. 132pp. pa.
(Sheet music-in-folio.)
S 0087 Fourth Book Of Fifty Hit Songs By John Lennon
And Paul McCartney. London: Music Sales,
1974. 172pp. pa.
(Sheet music-in-folio.)
S 0088 George Harrison Anthology. New York:
Warner Bros., 198?. 200pp. pa.
(Sheet music-in-folio; 52 songs,
piano/guitar.)
S 0089 The Golden Beatles. Miami Beach, FL:
Hansen Publications, 196?. 96pp. pa. illus.
(Sheet music-in-folio.)
S 0090 Golden Beatles, Book 1. London: Northern Songs,
1966. 54pp.
(Sheet music-in-folio;lyrics of 50 songs.)
S 0091 Golden Beatles, Book 2. London: Northern Songs,
1966. 54pp. illus.
(Sheet music-in-folio;lyrics of 50 songs.)
S 0092 The Golden Beatles - Vocal. Chicago, IL:
Hansen Publications, 196?. 96pp. pa. illus.
(Sheet music-in-folio.)
S 0093 The Golden Era Of The Beatles. New York:
Hansen Edu. Music & Books, 1972. 156pp. pa.
illus.
(Sheet music-in-folio.)
S 0094 Goodnight Vienna. Miami, FL:
Screen Gems/Columbia, 1975. 72pp. pa.
(Sheet music-in-folio.)
S 0095 Great Songs Of Lennon And McCartney, ed. by
Milton Okun. New York:
Quadrangle/Times Books, 1973. 288pp. pa.
illus.
(Sheet music-in-folio.)
S 0096 Imagine. New York: Maclen Music/ATV-Kirshner,

197?. 40pp. pa.
(Sheet music-in-folio.)

S 0097 It's Easy To Play Beatles. London: Music Sales.
44pp. pa.
(Sheet music-in-folio.)

S 0098 The John Lennon Collection. Milwaukee, WI:
Hal Leonard Publishing, 1983. 64pp. pa.
illus.
(Sheet music-in-folio.)

S 0099 John Lennon: Imagine, ed. by P. J. Foss.
London: Music Sales, 1973. 44pp. pa. illus.

S 0100 John Lennon - Plastic Ono Band. New York:
Maclen Music/Kirshner, 197?. 48pp. pa.

S 0101 John Lennon/Plastic Ono Band: Shaved Fish.
London: Music Sales. 40pp. pa.
(Sheet music-in-folio.)

S 0102 John Lennon: Rock 'N' Roll. New York:
Peer-Southern, 1975.
(Sheet music-in-folio.)

S 0103 John Lennon: Walls And Bridges. London:
Music Sales, 1975. 64pp. pa. illus.
(Sheet music-in-folio.)

S 0104 John Lennon: Walls And Bridges - Listen To This
Song Book. New York: Lennon Music/Big Three,
197. 64pp. illus.
(Sheet music-in-folio.)

S 0105 Eine Kleine Beatlemusik: Piano Solo, arranged
by Harry Wild. London: Northern Songs, 1965.
10pp.
(Sheet music-in-folio.)

S 0106 Eine Kleine Beatlemusik: String Quartet, With
Optional Double Bass, arranged by Harry
Wild. London: Northern Songs, 1965.
(Sheet music-in-folio.)

S 0107 The Latest Beatlebook Of Recorded Hits - For
Guitar, arranged by Duke Miller.
Miami Beach, FL: Hansen Publications, 196?.
32pp. illus.
(Sheet music-in-folio.)

S 0108 Lennon & McCartney/Bacharach & David - The 60s,
edited by Milton Okun. New York:
Cherry Lane Music. 220pp. pa. illus.
(Sheet music-in-folio; 60 songs for
piano/vocal.)

S 0109 Lennon & McCartney 50 Great Songs: All Organ.
London: Music Sales. 128pp. pa.
(Sheet music-in-folio.)

S 0110 Lennon & McCartney 50 Great Songs: Chord Organ.
London: Music Sales. 66pp. pa.
(Sheet music-in-folio.)

S 0111 Lennon & McCartney 50 Great Songs: Easy Big
Note Guitar, ed. by P. J. Foss. London:
Music Sales, 1973. 96pp. pa.
(Sheet music-in-folio.)

S 0112 Lennon & McCartney 50 Great Songs: Easy Big
Note Piano, ed. by P. J. Foss. London:
Music Sales, 1974. 128pp. pa.
(Sheet music-in-folio.)

S 0113 Lennon & McCartney For Clarinet. London:
Music Sales. 64pp. pa.
(Sheet music-in-folio.)

S 0114 Lennon & McCartney For Clarinet, selected and
edited by Leo Alfassy. New York:
Amsco Music Pub. Co., 1976. 64pp.
(Sheet music-in-folio.)

S 0115 Lennon & McCartney For Flute. London:
Music Sales. 64pp. pa.
(Sheet music-in-folio.)

S 0116 Lennon & McCartney For Flute, selected and
edited by Leo Alfassy. New York:
Amsco Music Pub. Co., 1976. 64pp. illus.
(Sheet music-in-folio.)

S 0117 Lennon & McCartney For Recorder, selected and
edited by Ralph Wm. Zeitlin. New York:
Amsco Music, 1975. 80pp. illus.
(Sheet music-in-folio.)

S 0118 Lennon & McCartney For Trumpet. London:
Music Sales. 64pp. pa. illus.

S 0119 Lennon & McCartney For Trumpet, selected and
edited by Leo Alfassy. New York:
Amsco Music, 1976. 64pp. illus.
(Sheet music-in-folio.)

S 0120 The Lennon Collection. Milwaukee, WI:
Hal Leonard Publishing, 198?. pa.
(Sheet music-in-folio; LP songs for
piano/vocal.)

S 0121 Let It Be - The Only Complete Song Album From
The Motion Picture, "Let It Be.". New York:
Hansen Edu. Music & Books, 197?. 64pp.
(Sheet music-in-folio.)

S 0122 Living In The Material World. New York:
Hansen Edu. Music & Books, 1973. 86pp.
(Sheet music-in-folio: George Harrison.)

S 0123 McCartney - Matching Music Book. New York:
McCartney Productions, 197?. 64pp. illus.
(Sheet music-in-folio (piano/vocal).)

S 0124 McCartney II. n.p.: MPL Communications, 197?.
64pp. illus.
(Sheet music-in-folio.)

S 0125 The Music Of Lennon & McCartney; 2d Omnibus Of
Popular Songs. Miami Beach, FL:
Hansen Publications, 1969. 168pp. illus.
(Sheet music-in-folio.)

S 0126 New Songs Of George, Paul & Ringo. New York:
Peer-Southern, 1975. pa.
(Sheet music-in-folio.)

S 0127 The New Songs Of George, Paul & Ringo.
New York: Hansen Edu. Music & Books, 197?.
288pp. pa.
(Sheet music-in-folio.)

S 0128 New Songs Of Paul McCartney. New York:
Peer-Southern, 1975. pa.
(Sheet music-in-folio.)

S 0129 The New Songs Of Paul McCartney. New York:
Hansen Edu. Music & Books, 197?. 112pp. pa.
(Sheet music-in-folio.)

S 0130 Paul McCartney Composer/Artist. Milwaukee, WI:
Hal Leonard Publishing, 198?. cl. and pa. illus
(Sheet music-in-folio; for piano/vocal.)

S 0131 Paul McCartney: McCartney. London: Music Sales.
32pp. pa. illus.
(Sheet music-in-folio.)

S 0132 Paul McCartney: Ram. London: Music Sales.
60pp. pa.
(Sheet music-in-folio.)

S 0133 Paul McCartney: The Best Of McCartney For Easy
Guitar. London: Music Sales. 68pp. pa.
illus.
(Sheet music-in-folio.)

S 0134 Paul McCartney: The Best Of McCartney For Easy
Piano. London: Music Sales. 68pp. pa. illus.
(Sheet music-in-folio.)

S 0135 Paul McCartney: Tug Of War. London:
MPL Communications, 1982. 80pp. pa. illus.
(Sheet music-in-folio.)

S 0136 Pipes Of Peace - Paul McCartney. London:
MPL Communications, 1983. 64pp. pa. illus.
(Sheet music-in-folio.)

S 0137 Pocket Beatles. New York: Cherry Lane Music.
pa. illus.
(Sheet music-in-folio: 120 songs for easy
guitar.)

S 0138 Pocket Beatles Complete, compiled by Pearce
Marchbank and Jane Coke. London:
Wise Pubns./Music Sales, 1979. 384pp. cl.
illus.
(Sheet music-in-folio.)

S 0139 Pocket Beatles Complete, compiled by Pearce
Marchbank and Jane Coke. Frankfurt, W.Ger.:
2001 Verlag, 1979. 384pp. cl. illus.
(Sheet music-in-folio.)

S 0140 Pocket Beatles For Guitar, compiled by Milton
Okun. Greenwich, CT: ATV Music/Cherry Lane,
1980. 256pp. pa.
(Sheet music-in-folio.)

S 0141 Ram. New York: Warner Brothers Music, 1971.
116pp. illus.

    (Sheet music-in-folio.)

S 0142 Rock 'N Roll Music As Recorded By The Beatles.
    New York: Hansen Edu. Music & Books, 1976.
    40pp. pa.
    (Sheet music-in-folio.)

S 0143 Second Book Of Fifty Hit Songs By John Lennon
    And Paul McCartney. London: Music Sales,
    1974. 144pp. pa.
    (Sheet music-in-folio.)

S 0144 The Second Golden Beatles Album.
    Miami Beach, FL: Hansen Publications, 196?.
    104pp. pa. illus.
    (Sheet music-in-folio.)

S 0145 Sgt. Pepper's Lonely Hearts Club Band: The Rock
    Spectacle. New York: Cherry Lane Music.
    80pp. pa.
    (Sheet music-in-folio: 29 songs for
    piano/vocal.)

S 0146 Solo Years. Milwaukee, WI:
    Hal Leonard Publishing, 198?. pa.
    (Sheet music-in-folio: 45 Lennon songs for
    guitar.)

S 0147 The Solo Years. Milwaukee, WI:
    Hal Leonard Publishing, 198?. pa. illus.
    (Sheet music-in-folio: 45 Lennon songs for
    piano.)

S 0148 Some Time In New York City - John & Yoko.
    New York: Maclen Music/ATV-Kirshner, 197?.
    56pp. pa.
    (Sheet music-in-folio.)

S 0149 Songs By George Harrison & Richard Starkey.
    Miami Beach, FL: Hansen Publications, 196?.
    26pp. pa. illus.
    (Sheet music-in-folio.)

S 0150 Songs From Double Fantasy/Season Of Glass.
    Milwaukee, WI: Hal Leonard Publishing, 198?.
    pa. illus.
    (Sheet music-in-folio;album songs for
    piano/vocal.)

S 0151 Songs Of John Lennon. London: Music Sales, 1972.
    84pp. pa.
    (Sheet music-in-folio; 33-page interview
    included.)

S 0152 Songs Of John Lennon. New York:
    Collier-Macmillan, 1972. 88pp. pa. illus.
    (Sheet music-in-folio.)

S 0153 Souvenir Song Album. Amsterdam, Holland:
    Basart, 1964. 18pp. illus.
    (Sheet music-in-folio.)

S 0154 Third Book Of Fifty Hit Songs By John Lennon
    And Paul McCartney. London: Music Sales,
    1974. 150pp. pa.
    (Sheet music-in-folio.)

S 0155 The Third Golden Beatles Album.
    Miami Beach, FL: Hansen Publications, 196?.

    94pp. pa. illus.
    (Sheet music-in-folio
    (piano/vocal);discography.)

S 0156 20 Greatest Hits - The Beatles. New York:
    Cherry Lane Music. pa.
    (Sheet music-in-folio; 20 songs for
    piano/vocal.)

S 0157 Venus And Mars - Piano/Vocal/Guitar Album.
    New York: Hansen Edu. Music & Books, 197?.
    80pp. pa.
    (Sheet music-in-folio.)

S 0158 The Well-Tempered Lennon-McCartney: Seven
    Polyphonic Arrangements For Piano, arranged
    by T. Sivak. New York: Associated, 1978.
    40pp.
    (Sheet music-in-folio.)

S 0159 Wings At The Speed Of Sound. New York:
    Hansen Edu. Music & Books, 197?. 80pp.
    (Sheet music-in-folio.)

S 0160 Wings: Band On The Run. London: Music Sales.
    64pp. pa. illus.
    (Sheet music-in-folio.)

S 0161 Wings Complete. London: Music Sales. 296pp. pa.
    illus.
    (Sheet music-in-folio.)

S 0162 Wings Complete: The Songs Of McCartney And
    Wings. New York: Random House, 1977.
    296pp. pa. illus.
    (Sheet music-in-folio.)

S 0163 Wings Greatest. London: Music Sales. 60pp. pa.
    illus.
    (Sheet music-in-folio.)

S 0164 Wings: London Town. London: Music Sales.
    74pp. pa. illus.
    (Sheet music-in-folio.)

S 0165 Wings Over America. London:
    Music Sales Limited, 1977. 128pp. pa. illus.
    (Sheet music-in-folio.)

S 0166 Wings Over America. New York:
    MPL Communications/Big 3 Music, 1977.
    128pp. pa. illus.
    (Sheet music-in-folio.)

S 0167 Wings: Red Rose Speedway. London: Music Sales.
    64pp. pa. illus.
    (Sheet music-in-folio.)

S 0168 Wings "Wild Life". New York:
    Maclen Music/ATV-Kirshner, 197?. 48pp. pa.
    illus.
    (Sheet music-in-folio.)

S 0169 Wings: Wild Life, ed. by P. J. Foss. London:
    Music Sales, 1973. 44pp. pa. illus.
    (Sheet music-in-folio.)

S 0170 With The Beatles. London: Music Sales/Wise.
    64pp. pa.
    (Sheet music-in-folio.)

ALL TOGETHER NOW
Vlasta Paul, Editor
P.O. Box 271156
Escondido, CA 92027
Quarterly (irregular);
some back issues.
$6.50/yr; sample, $2.00

APPLE'S KIN
Leanne Clarke, Coordinator
c/o 309 16th Street East,
    Apt. 201
Seattle, WA 98112
Nine times/yr;
back issues available.
$4.00/yr

BEATLEADS
Katie Collard, Editor
1751 N. Grand W., Lot #73
Springfield, IL 62702
Six times/yr;
back issues available.
$6.00/yr; sample, $1.00

BEATLEFAN
Bill King, Editor
Goody Press, Inc.
P.O. Box 33515
Decatur, GA 30033
Six times/yr;
most back issues.
$8.00/yr; sample, $2.50

BEATLE MAGAZINE
Jim Havalock, Editor
P.O. Box 29113
River Station
Rochester, NY 14627
Six times/yr;
back issues available.
$12.00/yr; sample, $2.00

BEATLEMANIA
Hartmut Schwarz, Editor
K.-Matthes-Str. 74/162
6502 Gera-Lusan
East Germany
Two times/yr;
most back issues.

THE BEATLES
Kanji Hirota, Editor
Beatles Cine Club
P.O. Box 115
Shibuya Post Office
Tokyo, Japan
Monthly;
back issues available.
4000 yen/yr; sample, 400 yen

THE BEATLES BEAT DOWNUNDER
Graham L. Moyle, Editor
P.O. Box 303
Magill 5072 S.A.
Australia
Four times/yr;
back issues available.
$10.00/yr

THE BEATLES BOOK
Johnny Dean, Editor
Beat Publications
45 St. Mary's Road
Ealing, London W5 5RQ
England
Monthly;
most back issues.
$33.00/yr; sample, $2.50

THE BEATLES CITY MAGAZINE
Ian Wallace, Editor
31 Mathew Street
Liverpool 2, England
Four times/yr;
some back issues.
$8.00/yr

THE BEATLES CONNECTION
Craig R. Still, Editor
P.O. Box 1066
Pinellas Park, FL 33565
Monthly;
back issues available.
$7.00/yr; sample, $1.50

BEATLES DATA RESEARCH
Gerhard Karl Bohrer, Pres.
Steinfelder Strasse 23
D-6748 Bad Bergzabern
West Germany
No publication;
responds to queries.

BEATLES NEWS
Michael Krieger, Editor
P.O. Box 1442
D-4630 Bochum 1
West Germany
Monthly;
some back issues.
$1.00 per issue, plus
postage

BEATLES NEWS BOOK
Michael Krieger, Editor
P.O. Box 1442
D-4630 Bochum 1
West Germany
Six times/yr;
some back issues.
$3.00 per issue, plus
postage

BEATLES NOW
Roger N. Akehurst, Editor
P.O. Box 307
Walthamstow
London E17 4LL
England
Bimonthly;
back issues available.
$12.00/yr; sample, $2.00

BEATLES-NYTT
Artillio Bergholtz, Editor
The Beatles Information Center
P.O. Box 7481
S-10392 Stockholm
Sweden
Bimonthly;
back issues available.
$12.00/yr

THE BEATLES RECORDS
    INFORMATION SERVICE
Bruce Hamlin, Pres.
P.O. Box 6
Dee Why 2099
New South Wales, Australia
No publication;
responds to queries

BEATLES REPORT
Rainer Moers, Editor
Beatles Information Center -
    West Germany
Crackerbox Palace
Im Weidenbruch 4
D-5000 Cologne 80
West Germany
Monthly;
back issues available.
80 DM/yr; sample, 7,50 DM

THE BEATLES SGT. PEPPER'S
    LONELY HEARTS CLUB BAND
Tami Hignite, Editor
508 S. Dakota Ave.
Tampa, FL 33606
Bimonthly;
back issues available.
$8.00/yr; sample, $2.00

BEATLES UNLIMITED
Evert Vermeer, Editor-in-Chief
Postbus 602
3430 AP Nieuwegein
The Netherlands
Bimonthly;
back issues available.
$13.00/yr; sample, $2.00

BEATLES VIDEO NEWSLETTER
John Dobrydnio and
    Gloria Patti, Editors
184 Emerson Street
Springfield, MA 01118
Bimonthly;
some back issues.
$7.00/yr; sample, $1.00

BEATLES VISIE
Bertus Elzenaar, Editor
Vereiniging Nederlandse
    Beatles Fanclub
P.O. Box 1464
1000 BL Amsterdam
The Netherlands
Quarterly;
some back issues.
$8.50/yr; sample, $3.00

BEATLES WERK GROEP
    (later became Dutch version
    of BEATLES UNLIMITED)
Evert Vermeer, Editor-in-Chief
Postbus 602
3430 AP Nieuwegein
The Netherlands
Bimonthly;
some back issues.
$13.00/yr; sample, $2.00

CLUB SANDWICH
Wings Fun Club
P.O. Box 4UP
London W1 4UP
England
Irregular.
$7.50/yr

SPECIAL REPEAT! ALL THE BEST PIX FROM THE FIRST SIX ISSUES..
3/-
The Beatles BOOK
The Beatles MONTHLY BOOK
No. 9
EVERY MONTH
Price ONE SHILLING & SIXPENCE
The Beatles MONTHLY BOOK
No.22
EVERY MONTH
Price ONE SHILLING & SIXPENCE
Price 35p
APPRECIATION SOCIETY MAGAZINE
CONTAINING AN ORIGINAL COLLECTORS COPY OF THE 5th ISSUE OF THE BEATLES FAN CLUB MAGAZINE
EVERY MONTH
Price 40p
The Beatles
APPRECIATION SOCIETY MAGAZINE
CONTAINING AN ORIGINAL COLLECTORS COPY OF THE 9th ISSUE OF THE BEATLES FAN CLUB MAGAZINE
FULL REPORT OF NEW ALBUMS FROM GEORGE HARRISON AND WINGS
EVERY MONTH
The Beatles
APPRECIATION SOCIETY MAGAZINE BOOK
Price 50p
February 1978
CONTAINING AN ORIGINAL COLLECTORS COPY OF THE 22nd ISSUE OF THE BEATLES FAN CLUB MAGAZINE
GETTING UP TO DATE ON JOHN, GEORGE & RINGO
The Beatles MONTHLY BOOK
NOVEMBER
MONTHLY
The Beatles MONTHLY BOOK
OCTOBER 1982
80p
FIRST NEW ISSUE
FREE POSTER OFFER

THE FAB FOUR PUBLICATION
Jacques Volcouve, Editor
Les Club des 4 de Liverpool
43 bis, boulevard Henri IV
75004 Paris, France
Irregular (six times/yr);
back issues available.
150 francs/yr

FROM ME TO YOU
Peter Schuster, Editor
Lappenlied 55
Postfach 555
6430 Bad Hersfeld
West Germany
Irregular;
back issues available.
Inquire about price;
sample, $1.75

GEAR BOX
Barbara Paulson, Editor
The Mike McCartney Fan Club
3621 West 147th Street
Cleveland, OH 44111
Irregular (bimonthly);
no back issues.
$5.00/yr

GOOD DAY SUNSHINE
Charles F. Rosenay, Editor
Liverpool Productions
397 Edgewood Avenue
New Haven, CT 06511
Six times/yr;
back issues available.
$8.00/yr; sample, $1.00

THE HARRISON ALLIANCE
Patti Murawski, Editor
67 Cypress Street
Bristol, CT 06010
Quarterly;
some back issues.
$8.50 for six issues;
sample, $2.00

INSTANT KARMA
Marsha Ewing, Editor
P.O. Box 256
Sault Ste. Marie, MI 49783
Six times/yr;
some back issues.
$10.50/yr

McCARTNEY
David Dunn, Editor
Paul McCartney Fan Club Of
    Scotland
8 Johnson Drive
Cambuslang, Glasgow
Scotland
Irregular (four times/yr);
back issues available.
$4.00/yr; sample, $1.50

THE McCARTNEY OBSERVER
Doylene Kindsvater, Editor
220 East 12th Street
La Crosse, KS 67548
Quarterly;
back issues available.
$6.00/yr plus postage

MY SWEET LADY JANE
Penny Lane, Editor
P.O. Box 1399
Campbell, CA 95008
Four times/yr;
back issues available.
$5.00/yr plus postage

NORWEGIAN WOOD - BEATLES
    FANCLUB
Erlend Flaten, Editor
Storengvegen 14
N-2800 Gjovik
Norway
Six times/yr;
some back issues.
$8.00/yr

OB LA DI OB LA DA
Albert Bel, Pres.
Col. Lectiu Beatleman
Apartado de Correos 27348
08080 Barcelona, Spain
Quarterly (irregular);
some back issues.
$5.00/yr

O'NO FOUNDATION
Vickie Woods-Lovett, Editor
13043 Meandering Way, #269
Dallas, TX 75240
Six times/yr;
back issues available.
$12.50/yr; sample, $1.75

PEOPLE FOR PEACE
Jeannie Roberts, Editor
230 West 101st Street, #324
New York, NY 10025
Bimonthly;
back issues available.
$6.00/yr plus postage;
sample, $1.75

RED ROSE SPEEDWAY
Donna Neal, Editor
1039 A.N. Vandeventer Street
St. Louis, MO 63113
Quarterly;
back issues available.
$6.50/yr; sample, $3.00

"REVOLVER" BEATLE FANZINE
Gwyn Jenkins, Editor
37 Hare Hill Close
Pyrford, Woking
Surrey GU22 8UH
England
Bimonthly;
back issues available.
$10.00/yr; sample, $1.00

RINGO MAGAZINE
Mo Shears and
    Sabine Dorsam, Editors
Starr Struck!
Friedrichstr. 7
6467 Hasselroth 3
West Germany
Quarterly;
back issues available.
$6.00/yr

SGT. PEPPER POSTEN
Askeroi Grei, Editor
Sgt. Pepper's (Lonely Hearts) Club
Postboks 133, Boler
N-0620 Oslo 6
Norway
Irregular;
some back issues.
Inquire about prices.

SGT. PEPPER'S LONELY HEARTS CLUB
Tom McDonald, Pres.
2 Birch Hill Avenue
Wakefield, MA 01880
No publication.

STRAWBERRY FIELDS FOREVER
Joe Pope, Editor
310 Franklin Street, #117
Boston, MA 02110
Irregular;
some back issues.
$10.00 for six issues

THINGS WE TELL TODAY
Rainer Moers, Editor
Beatles Information Center -
    West Germany
Crackerbox Palace
Im Weidenbruch 4
D-5000 Cologne 80
West Germany
Bimonthly;
back issues available.
25 DM/yr; sample, 7,50 DM

WATERFALLS
Karin Gattermayr and
    Judith Philipp, Editors
Keimlgutgasse 1
A-4040 Linz
Austria
Quarterly;
back issues available.
$14.00/yr airmail;
sample, $3.50 airmail

WITH A LITTLE HELP FROM
    MY FRIENDS
Pat Simmons and Joy Kilbane, Eds.
10290 Pleasant Lake, #F21
Cleveland, OH 44130
Quarterly;
no back issues.
$7.00/yr plus postage;
sample, $1.75 plus postage

THE WORKING CLASS HERO
Barb Whatmaugh, Editor
3311 Niagara Street
Pittsburgh, PA 15213
Four times/yr.
$6.50/yr

THE WORKING CLASS HERO, VOL. I
Patty Owens Rycyk, Editor
Star Route Studios
Star Route 2
Jefferson City, MO 65101
Inquire about prices.

THE WRITE THING
Barb Fenick, Editor
P.O. Box 18807
Minneapolis, MN 55418
Quarterly;
back issues available.
$10.00/yr; sample, $2.00

YESTERDAY
Peter Leopold, et al., Eds.
Stock Im Weg 20
1130 Vienna, Austria
Monthly;
back issues available.
$15.00/yr

YOKO ONLY
Brian Hendel, Editor
61 Middle Drive
Toms River, NJ 08753
Six times/yr;
back issues available.
$9.00/yr; sample, $2.00

THE MAN WHO GAVE THE BEATLES AWAY

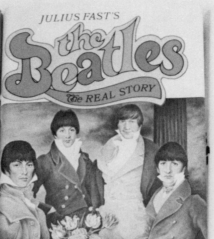

JULIUS FAST'S
the Beatles
The Real Story

THE GIRL WHO SANG WITH THE BEATLES
AND OTHER STORIES BY

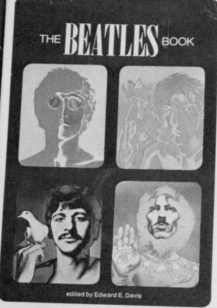

THE **BEATLES** BOOK

edited by Edward E. Davis

The autobiography of the man who discovered the Beatles and other great British artists · Brian Epstein

A Cellarful of Noise

Life at the DAKOTA
STEPHEN BIRMINGHAM

New York's Most Unusual Address

the beatles again!?

Twilight of the Gods
The Music of The Beatles
by Wilfrid Mellers

Abbott, Mary
   M 0003
Abelson, Danny
   M 0004
Aben, D.
   RF0017   RF0018   RF0019
   RF0242   RF0243
Abrahamsen, Peter
   M 0008
Achard, Maurice
   B 0001
Acker, Steve
   C 0001   N 0001
Ackerman, P.
   M 0010
Adair, G.
   RF0330
Adams, Mike
   M 0011
Adams, Phoebe
   RB0405   RB0540
Adams, Val
   N 0003
Adcock
   RR0350
Addison, R.
   RR0372
Addison, Richard
   M 0012
Adler, Bill
   B 0002   B 0003   B 0004
   B 0005   B 0006
Adler, Renata
   C 0002
Agrest, Susan
   M 2143
Aguilar, Art
   C 0003   N 0006
Agustin, Jose
   M 0015
Akehurst, Roger
   F 0042   M 0017
Albright, Thomas
   M 0018
Alcot, Alain
   B 0083
Alden, Robert
   N 0009
Aldridge, Alan
   B 0007   B 0008   B 0009
   B 0010   B 0011   B 0012
   B 0013   B 0014   B 0015
   B 0016   B 0017   B 0018
   B 0019   B 0020   B 0021
   B 0022   B 0023   B 0024
   B 0025   B 0026   B 0027
   B 0028   C 0004   N 0715
Alethes
   M 0019
Alexander, Shana
   M 0020
Alfassy, Leo
   S 0114   S 0116   S 0119
Alfonso, B.
   M 0021
Ali, Tariq
   M 0557   M 0558   M 0559
   N 0225
Ali, Walleed
   B 0115
Alicio, Stella H.
   B 0029
Alion, Y.
   M 0023
Allen, B.
   RB0485
Allen, Barry
   P 0047
Allen, T.
   RF0152   RF0411
Alm, Torbjorn
   M 0032
Alonzo, Jamie Louise
   F 0100   F 0109
Alpert, H.
   RF0236
Alterman, L.
   M 3616
Alterman, Loraine

   M 0033   M 0034   M 0035
Altham, Keith
   M 0036
Altman, Billy
   RR0387
Alvarez, Henrique Carballal
   F 0098
Alverson, Charles
   M 0037   M 0038   M 0039
Ames, Lynne
   N 0013
Anderson, Christopher P.
   C 0116   C 0237   C 0271
Anderson, T.
   M 0045
Anderson, W.
   M 0046
Anderson, William T.
   P 0004
Ansen, D.
   RF0145   RF0273   RF0312
   RF0367
Antel, Jean
   N 0014
Anthony, Dee
   B 0529
Antoni, Roberto
   B 0031
Aregood, Rich
   RR0492
Armatage, Kay
   RF0405
Armitage, P.
   RF0193
Armitage, Peter
   N 0023
Arnold, Martin
   N 0024
Arnold, Roxane
   C 0007   N 0025
Aronowitz, Alfred G.
   C 0008   M 0064   M 0065
   M 0066   M 0067   M 0068
   M 0069   M 0070   M 0071
   RR0068
Arrington, C.
   M 0072
Ashford, Paul
   M 0074
Ashman, Mike
   M 0075
Ashton, Bill
   C 0009   N 0028
Ashton, John
   M 0076
Aspinall, Neil
   M 0079   M 0080   M 0081
   M 0082   M 1049   M 1050
   M 1051   M 1052   M 1053
   M 1054   M 1055   M 1056
Atlas, J.
   M 0084   M 0085
Atlman, D.
   RF0257
Attie
   M 0088
Aubuchon, Pam
   F 0122
Austin, Anthony
   N 0038
Auty, M.
   RF0064
Avedon, Richard
   M 0093
Baacke, Dieter
   C 0010
Bacon, David
   B 0033   B 0034   B 0035
   B 0036   M 0097
Bacon, Dorothy
   M 0098
Bailey, Andrew
   M 0102   M 0103   M 0104
   M 0105
Baker, Glenn A.
   B 0037
Baker, Mark
   M 0107
Baker, Peter

   RF0107
Baker, Stephen
   M 0108   M 0109   M 0110
Baker, Steve
   RB0110   RB0202   RB0204
   RB0301
Bakker, Erik M.
   B 0038   M 0112   M 0113
   M 0114   M 0115   M 0116
   M 0117   M 0118   M 0119
   M 0120   M 3546   M 3547
   RB0100   RR0471
Bakshian, Aram, Jr.
   M 0121
Ballister, B.
   M 0123
Ballon, Ian
   M 0124   M 0125   M 0126
   M 0127   M 0128   M 0129
   M 3002
Baltake, Joe
   N 0045
Bangs, Lester
   M 0136   M 0137   M 0138
   M 0139   M 0140   M 0158
   RR0166   RR0234   RR0331
Barackman, Michael
   M 0142   M 0143
Barfield, Nic
   M 0146
Barnard, Stephen
   M 0147
Barnes, Clive
   C 0012   N 0047   N 0048
   N 0049   N 0050
Barnes, Ken
   M 0148
Barnett, Laurie
   C 0170
Barron, F.
   M 0149
Barrow, Tony
   B 0043   M 0150   M 0151
   M 0152   M 0153   M 0154
   M 0155   M 0156   M 0157
   M 0158   M 0159   M 0160
   M 0161   M 0162   M 0163
   M 0164   M 0165   M 0166
   M 0167   M 0168   M 0169
   M 0170   M 0171   M 0172
   M 0173   M 0174   M 0175
   M 0176   M 0177   M 0178
   M 0179   M 0180   M 0181
   M 0182   M 0183   M 0184
   M 0185   M 0186   M 0187
   M 0910   M 1461   RB0517
Barry, Art
   M 0188   M 0189   M 0190
   M 0191   M 0192   M 0193
   M 0194   M 0195   RB0430
   RF0025
Bart, Peter
   N 0051
Bartimole, John
   M 0196
Bashe, Philip
   M 0197
Basler, Barbara
   N 0052
Bass, Charlene
   M 0003
Batt, Shodhan
   M 0198
Batterson, David
   M 0199
Battock, G.
   M 0201
Batz, Bob, Jr.
   C 0013   N 0053
Baxter, J.
   RF0291
Bearne, David
   RF0339
Beart, Guy
   C 0014
Beatty, J.
   M 0501
Beaupre, L.
   M 0502

Bechard, Gorman
   F 0081
Beckley, Timothy Green
   B 0069   B 0070
Beckmann, Dieter
   B 0071
Bedford, Carol
   B 0072
Begley, Geoff
   M 0504
Bel, Albert
   F 0121
Belanger, Lyn
   B 0554
Beller, Daniel
   M 0505   M 0506   M 0507
   RR0125   RR0202   RR0254
   RR0347   RR0484   RR0508
Beller, Miles
   M 0508
Belz, Carl
   C 0048   C 0049   C 0050
Bender, William
   M 0509   M 0510   RR0025
Benedikt, M.
   M 0511
Benhari
   M 0512   M 0513
Benjamin, Philip
   N 0211
Benjamin, Sandy Stert
   M 0514
Bennett, Clive
   M 0515
Bennett, Marty
   M 0516
Bennetzen, Jorgen
   M 0517
Bentkowski, Tom
   RR0101
Berg, C.
   M 0518
Berg, David H.
   M 0519
Bergenfield, Nathan
   M 0520
Berger, Joseph
   C 0051   N 0212
Berger, Karen
   M 0521
Bergholtz, Artillio
   M 0522   M 0523   M 0524
   M 0525   M 0526   RB0345
Berkenstadt, James
   M 0527
Berlin, Alec M.
   M 0528
Berman, L.
   M 0529
Bernard, Jami
   N 0213
Bernstein, Sid
   C 0052   N 0214
Besher, Alexander
   M 0530
Bessman, J.
   M 0531
Best, Pete
   B 0073   C 0053   M 0532
Bethmann, Jeri
   F 0013
Betrock, Alan
   M 0535
Bibey, D.
   M 0537
Biel, D. Michael
   M 0538
Bille, Torben
   M 0542
Bird, David
   N 0221   N 0222
Bird, Donald A.
   M 0550
Bird, Maryann
   N 0223
Birmingham, Stephen
   C 0060
Biro, N.

M 0552
Bittan, Dave
  N 0224
Bizot, J.F.
  M 0556
Blackburn, Robin
  M 0557 M 0558 M 0559
  N 0225
Blackburn, S.
  RB0222
Blake, John
  B 0075 B 0076 M 0562
Blake, R.A.
  RF0252
Blatchford, R.
  RB0325
Blessing, Adam
  B 0077
Bliss, James
  C 0061
Blumenthal, Howard
  P 0118
Blumentnal, E.
  M 0579
Blyth, Karen
  M 0580 M 0581
Bonici, Ray
  M 0585
Bonnefoy, Jean
  B 0041
Bontinck, Irmgard
  C 0062
Borchert, Karlheinz
  F 0072
Boujailly, G.B.
  RF0127
Bourre, Jean-Paul
  B 0078
Bow, Dennis
  B 0079
Bowles, Jerry
  M 0593
Bowman, David
  C 0063 M 0594
Boyd, Cynthia
  N 0229 RB0290
Boyd, Denny
  C 0064 N 0230
Boyer, Peter J.
  M 0596
Braam, Willi
  M 0597 RB0003
Bramwell, Tony
  M 0599
Braucourt, G.
  M 0600
Brauer, Ralph
  C 0065 C 0066
Braun, Michael
  B 0080 B 0081 B 0082
  P 0102
Brautigan, Richard
  B 0060
Bream, Jon
  M 0601
Brecher, Michael
  B 0554
Brennan, Brian
  N 0231 RB0101 RB0308
  RB0578
Brennan, Peter
  M 0602
Brennon, Phil
  N 0232
Breslin, Rosemary
  M 0603
Brett, Guy
  N 0233
Breuer, Rainer
  B 0083
Briant, Richard
  M 0608
Brien, Alan
  M 0609 M 0610 RF0376
Brigstocke, Hilary
  N 0245
Brimhall, John
  S 0054 S 0069
Brinckman, Joe

M 0611
Britt, Stan
  M 0621
Brodsky, A.
  RF0356
Bronson, H.
  M 0622
Brookhiser, R.
  M 0623
Brophy, Warwick
  N 0250 N 0251 N 0252
Brousseau, Serge
  B 0084
Brown
  M 0088
Brown, D.
  RB0269
Brown, Florence
  P 0099
Brown, G.
  M 0624 M 0625 M 0626
  RF0310
Brown, Ken
  M 0627
Brown, Mick
  M 0628 M 0629 M 0630
Brown, Peter
  B 0085 B 0086 B 0087
  B 0088 M 0631 M 0632
Brownmiller, S.
  M 0633
Brudnoy, D.
  RF0217
Bruker, Donna
  F 0148
Bruker, Paul
  F 0148
Brummer, Stefanie
  F 0149
Bruno, Ann
  F 0108
Brussat, F.A.
  RF0172
Bryce, Leslie
  M 0634
Buckley, Jim
  C 0125
Buckley, M.
  RF0140
Buckley, Thomas
  N 0253 N 0254
Buckley, William F., Jr.
  C 0067 C 0068 M 0635
  M 0636
Budapest, Billy
  RB0075 RB0488
Bundgaard, Peder
  M 0637
Bunge, C.
  RB0584
Burge, D.
  RB0624
Burke, John
  B 0089 B 0090 B 0091
Burks, J.
  M 0638
Burks, John
  M 0639
Burnett, Ric
  M 0640
Burry, Lenny
  M 0641
Burstein, D.
  M 0642
Burt, Robert
  B 0092 B 0093 B 0445
Burton, Charles
  RR0120
Buskin, Richard
  M 0643 M 0644
Byron, S.
  M 0646 RF0128 RF0380
Bystrom, John L.
  M 0647 M 0648
Calnek, N.
  M 0649
Cameron, Gail
  M 0650 M 0651 M 0652
Campbell, Colin

B 0094 C 0069 M 0653
Campbell, Mary
  M 0654 N 0268
Camper, Diane
  M 0655
Canemaker, J.
  RF0402
Capel, Theo
  B 0138
Capisani, Alberino Daniele
  B 0095
Caracalla, Peter
  B 0439
Carballal, Henrique
  M 0660 M 0661 RR0122
Cardoso, Bill
  M 0662
Care, R.
  RF0173
Carlinsky, Dan
  B 0218 B 0219 M 0663
Carlsen, R.W.
  M 0664
Carlson, Walter
  N 0271
Carlton, Bill
  N 0272
Carmody, Deirdre
  N 0273
Carpenter, J.
  N 0274 N 0275 N 0276
Carpozi, George, Jr.
  B 0096 B 0097 P 0086
Carr, Roy
  B 0098 B 0099 B 0100
  B 0101 B 0102 B 0103
  B 0104 B 0105 B 0106
  B 0107 M 0665 M 0666
  M 0667 M 3494
Carrighan, Sally
  N 0277
Carroll, Jon
  M 0668 M 0669 M 0670
Carroll, Maurice
  N 0278
Carson, T.
  M 0671 RR0317
Cart
  RF0285
Carter, Al
  C 0071 N 0279
Carter, B.
  RF0131
Carter, Jimmy
  C 0072
Carter, S.
  M 0672
Carthew, Anthony
  N 0280
Casey, Howie
  C 0073 M 0674
Castleman, Harry
  B 0108 B 0109 B 0110
  B 0111 B 0112 C 0074
  M 0675
Catone, Marc A.
  B 0114 C 0289 M 0676
  M 0677
Caulfield, J.
  M 0670
Cella, Catherine
  M 0690 M 0691
Cepican, Bob
  B 0115
Cerf, Christopher
  B 0116
Cerna, Miroslava
  B 0117
Cernia, D.
  B 0118
Cerny, Jiri
  B 0117
Chadderton, Joey
  F 0060
Chambers, John J.
  M 0692
Chapin, Emerson
  N 0282
Chapple, Steve

C 0075
Charlesworth, C.
  M 0696 M 0697 M 0698
  M 0699 M 0700 M 0701
  M 0702 M 0703 M 0704
  M 0705 M 0706 M 0707
  M 0708 M 0709 M 0782
  RR0351 RR0527
Charone, Barbara
  M 0712
Chartres, John
  N 0286 N 0287
Chase-Marshall, Janet
  M 0713
Chasins, Abram
  C 0076 M 0714
Chippindale, P.
  M 3412
Chopin, Delia
  B 0140 B 0141
Christgau, Robert
  M 0716 M 0717 M 0718
  RR0054 RR0180 RR0230
  RR0332 RR0426 RR0519
Christian, Russ
  C 0077 N 0290
Ciccaleni, Raffaele
  B 0119
Cillero, Antonio
  B 0120
Claire
  F 0130
Clark, Alfred E.
  N 0292
Clark, Barb
  F 0094
Clark, C.
  RB0220 RB0245
Clark, Tom
  M 0722
Clarke, Leanne
  F 0012
Cleave, Maureen
  M 0727 N 0293 N 0294
Clerk, C.
  M 0729
Clifford, M.
  N 0297
Cluess, Chris
  M 0730
Coats, R.
  RB0177
Cocks, J.
  RF0351
Cocks, Jay
  C 0079 M 0732 M 0733
  M 0734
Codwell, Dave
  P 0067
Coffin, Patricia
  M 0735 M 0736
Cohen, J. L.
  M 0737
Cohen, Jose
  M 0738
Cohen, M.
  M 0739
Cohen, Mitch
  M 0740
Cohen, Mitchell
  RR0041 RR0153 RR0176
Cohn, Nik
  C 0080 C 0081 C 0238
  N 0298
Coke, Jane
  S 0138 S 0139
Coleman, J.
  RB0210 RB0240 RF0065
  RF0144 RF0180 RF0197
  RF0220 RF0272 RF0292
  RF0347 RF0366
Coleman, P.
  RF0211
Coleman, Ray
  B 0121 B 0122 M 0741
  M 0742 M 0743 M 0744
  M 0745 M 0746 M 0747
  M 0748 M 0749 M 0750
  M 0751 M 0752 M 0753

M 0754   M 0755   M 0756
M 0757   M 0758   M 0759
M 0760   M 0761   M 0762
M 0763   M 0764   M 0765
M 0766   M 0767   M 0768
M 0769   M 0770   M 0771
M 0772   M 0773   M 0774
M 0775   M 0776   M 0777
M 0778   M 0779   M 0780
M 0781   M 0782   M 0783
Coleman, T.
M 0784
Coles, R.
M 0785
Collard, Katie
F 0015
Collingham, Anne
M 0788
Collins, Bill
N 0299
Collis, John
M 0789
Colour, Martian
RB0289
Comden, Betty
M 0791
Como, W.
M 0795
Condon, Richard
B 0126   M 0803
Connelly, Christopher
M 0805   M 0806   M 0807
M 0808   M 0809
Connolly, Ray
B 0127   C 0082   N 0309
S 0026   S 0028   S 0029
S 0079
Cook, Barbara
F 0090
Cook, Christopher
M 0811   M 0812   M 0813
M 0814   M 0815   M 0816
M 0817
Cooke, Deryck
M 0818   M 0819
Coolidge, Clark
M 0722
Cooper, R. M.
B 0128
Coppage, N.
M 0820
Coppage, Noel
RR0419
Corbin, Carole Lynn
B 0129
Corliss, R.
RF0008   RF0071   RF0146
RF0313   RF0377
Corliss, Richard
M 0821   M 0822
Corry, John
N 0311
Cosell, Howard
M 0823
Costa, Jean-Charles
M 0824
Cott, Jonathan
B 0130   C 0083   C 0084
C 0085   C 0086   C 0087
C 0088   M 0825   M 0826
M 0827   M 0828   M 0829
M 0830   M 0831   M 0832
RB0556   RR0506
Coughlan, J.
RR0422
Counts, K.
RF0059
Cowan, Philip
B 0131   B 0132   B 0133
Cowley, S.C.
M 0838   M 0839   M 0840
Cox, Perry
B 0134
Coxe, D.
M 0841
Crist, J.
B 0188   RF0221   RF0348
Critchley, Julian
N 0315

Cromelin, Richard
M 0846
Crouse, Timothy
M 0847
Crowley, Kieran
N 0318
Crowther, Bosley
N 0319
Cuccia, Dianne
F 0005   F 0073
Cullman, Brian
B 0211   B 0212
Cummings, Judith
N 0322   N 0323   N 0324
N 0325   N 0326
Cunningham, Don
RR0413
Curly, John
M 0848   M 0849   M 0850
RB0148
Curman, Peter
B 0318
Cuscuna, M.
M 0851
Cyr, Claudette
F 0067
Dain, J.
B 0135
Dale, C.
M 0853
Dallas, Karl
M 0854
Dallos, Robert E.
N 0329
Dalton, D.
M 0832
Dalton, David
B 0130   C 0088   M 0855
Damsker, Matt
M 0856   N 0330
Dancis, B.
N 0331   RR0084
Dancis, Bruce
M 2971
Dandolo, Francesca
B 0494
Daniels, Chris
F 0141
D'Antonio, Dennis
M 0857
Darby, George
P 0085
Dark, C.
RF0038
Datene, Olivia Kelly
M 0861   M 0862
David, Keith
M 0864
Davidson, Bill
M 0866
Davies, Evan
M 0867
Davies, Hunter
B 0136   B 0137   B 0138
B 0139   B 0140   B 0141
B 0142   B 0143   B 0144
B 0145   B 0146   B 0147
B 0148   B 0149   B 0150
B 0151   B 0152   C 0091
M 0868   M 0869   M 0870
M 0871   M 0872   N 0334
N 0335
Davies, Ross
N 0336   N 0337
Davis, D.
RF0304
Davis, David
N 0338
Davis, Edward E.
B 0153   C 0068   C 0092
C 0095   C 0107   C 0108
C 0120   C 0126   C 0137
C 0168   C 0180   C 0181
C 0218   C 0250   C 0276
C 0308
Davis, Rod
M 0873
Davis, T.N.
M 0874

Davis, William
N 0339
Dawbarn, Bob
M 0875   M 0876   M 0877
M 0878   M 0879
Dawkins, Tony
M 0880
Dawson, David
M 0881
Dawson, J.
M 0882   M 0883
Dean, Johnny
M 0887   M 0888   M 0889
M 0890   M 0891   M 0892
M 0893   M 0894   M 0895
M 0896   M 0897   M 0898
M 0899   M 0900   M 0901
M 0902   M 0903   M 0904
M 0905   M 0906   M 0907
M 0908   M 0909   M 0910
M 0911   M 0912   M 3240
RB0517
Dean, Roger
C 0140
Deardorff, R.
M 0913
De'Ath, Wilfred
N 0341
De Blasio, Edward
B 0154
DeBruin, Hans
M 0915   M 0916   M 0917
RB0261   RF0301   RR0412
DeFina, D.
RR0160
DeGiusti, Tony
M 0922
Del Buono, Cindy
B 0155
Del Buono, Robert
B 0155
Delear, Frank
M 0923
Delmas, D.
M 0924
Dempsey, David
N 0346
Denby, J.
RF0274   RF0314   RF0368
Deni, Laura
M 0925
Denis, J-M.
B 0098
Denisoff, R. Serge
C 0093   M 0926   RB0054
Denning, Chris
M 0927
DeRhen, A.
M 0928
Detheridge, D.
M 0929
Dewes, Klaus
B 0156
Dhondy, Farrukh
M 0930
Dickerson, Robert B., Jr.
C 0094
Dieckmann, Eddie
M 0931   RR0255   RR0503
Diettrich, Eva
B 0157   B 0158
Difford, Chris
M 0932
Di Franco, J. Philip
B 0159   B 0160   B 0161
B 0162
Di Lello, Richard
B 0163   B 0164   B 0165
B 0166   C 0248
Dister, Alain
B 0167   B 0168   B 0169
M 0939   M 0940
Dobrydino, John
F 0049
Dockstader, T.
M 0942
Doebeling, Wolfgang
B 0453
Doerfler, Marilyn

M 0943
Doggett, Peter
M 0945   M 0946   M 0947
M 0948   M 0949   M 0950
M 0951   M 0952   M 0953
M 0954   M 0955   M 0956
M 0957   M 0958   M 0959
M 0960   M 0961   M 0962
M 0963   M 0964   M 0965
M 0966   M 0967   M 0968
M 0969   RB0028   RB0129
RB0151   RB0273   RB0344
RB0501   RR0063   RR0145
RR0172   RR0186   RR0237
RR0464   RR0491
Doherty, Andy
M 0970
Doherty, H.
M 0971
Dombraski, Jerome K.
RB0466
Donald, D.K.
M 0972
Doney, Malcolm
B 0170   B 0171   B 0172
B 0173
Donkers, Jan
B 0138
Dorsam, Sabine
F 0140
Douda, Christine
B 0042
Dove, I.
M 0975   M 0976   M 0977
Dove, Ian
N 0352
Downing, Dave
M 0979
Drake, David
M 0982
Drake, Kelley M.
M 0983
Drexler, R.
RF0235
Dronfield, Kim
M 0985   M 0986
Dubey, V.K.
M 0988
Dubini, Horacio
F 0007
Duclous, Marie Odile
B 0099
Ducray, Francois
M 0989
Dullea, Georgia
N 0355
Dunkley, Carl
F 0059
Dupree, Tom
M 0990
Durgnat, Raymond
RF0097
Duston, A.
M 0991
Dyer, Richard
C 0098   N 0356
Eagleton, Terry
M 0994
Eastman, Linda   see
        McCartney, Linda
Editors of Music Life
B 0061
Editors of Rolling Stone
B 0039   B 0040
Edlund, A.
M 0997   M 0998
Edmonds, Ben
RB0065
Edwards, Adam
N 0358
Edwards, H.
RF0337
Edwards, Henry
B 0174   B 0175   B 0432
B 0433   B 0434   M 0999
RR0204   RR0247
Eger, Joseph
M 1000

Eguchi, D.
  B 0191   B 0298
Ehrhardt, Christiane
  B 0176
Eisen, Jonathan
  C 0004   C 0169   C 0178
  C 0206   C 0241   C 0249
  C 0275   C 0342
Elbert, J.
  M 1002
Eldridge, R.
  M 1003
Elijah, Pam
  F 0083
Eliot
  RR0011
Ellerton, J.
  M 1004
Elley, D.
  RF0175
Ellis, Francis L.
  M 1005
Ellis, Roger
  M 1006   M 1007   RB0036
  RB0201   RR0116   RR0184
  RR0238   RR0409   RR0452
  RR0472
Emerson, Gloria
  N 0361   N 0362
Emerson, Ken
  M 1010
Emery, John
  M 1011   M 1012   M 1013
  M 1014   M 1015
Epand, Len
  M 1021   M 1022   M 1023
Epple, Ron
  RF0045
Epstein, Brian
  B 0178   B 0179   B 0180
  B 0181   B 0182   B 0183
  B 0184   B 0185   C 0100
  C 0101   C 0102   C 0103
  M 1024   M 1025
Eremo, J.
  M 1030
Estes, S.
  RB0086
Evans, M.
  M 1031   M 1032
Evans, M. Stanton
  M 1033
Evans, Mal
  M 1034   M 1035   M 1036
  M 1037   M 1038   M 1039
  M 1040   M 1041   M 1042
  M 1043   M 1044   M 1045
  M 1046   M 1047   M 1048
  M 1049   M 1050   M 1051
  M 1052   M 1053   M 1054
  M 1055   M 1056
Evans, Mike
  B 0186   B 0187   B 0188
Evans, Peggy
  F 0073
Evans, Peter
  M 1057
Evans, Richard
  M 1058
Everett, Kenny
  M 1059   M 1060   M 1061
Everett, T.
  M 1062   M 1063
Ewen, David
  C 0104
Ewing, Marsha
  F 0085
Facconi, Renato
  M 1076
Fager, Charles E.
  M 1080   M 1081   RF0238
  RF0397   RR0065
Faggen, G.
  M 1082   M 1083
Falchetta, Peter
  M 1084
Falloon, Val
  M 1085
Fallowell, Duncan

  M 1086
Farber, Jim
  M 1089   RR0174
Farber, S.
  RF0171
Farrell, Bobby
  M 1090
Farrell, William E.
  N 0376
Fast, Julius
  B 0189   B 0190
Fawcett, Anthony
  B 0191   B 0192   B 0193
  B 0194   B 0195   C 0105
  M 1091
Feder, Sue
  M 1092
Feehan, Paul G.
  RB0195   RB0200   RB0313
  RB0380   RB0459
Feldman, Leslie
  M 1095
Feldman, P.
  M 1096
Feller, Benoit
  M 1097
Feller, J.
  N 0379
Fenick, Barbara
  B 0196   B 0197   C 0028
  C 0038   F 0046   F 0065
  F 0113   F 0154   M 1098
  M 1099   M 1100   M 1101
Fenton, D.
  M 1102   M 1103   N 0380
Fents, Noah
  RB0493
Feron, James
  N 0381
Ferris, T.
  M 1104   M 1105
Ferris, Tim
  RR0203
5th Anniversary Collectors
  S 0038
Finley, Michael
  M 1117
Fischer, Lynn
  F 0011
Fischer, Stuart
  C 0106
Fishel, J.
  M 1124
Fisher, Christine
  M 1125
Fiske, Edward B.
  N 0389
Flake, Carol
  M 1127   RR0046
Flanagan, Coleen
  M 1128   RB0518
Flans, Robyn
  M 1129
Flaten, Erlend
  F 0119
Flatley, G.
  N 0392   RF0357
Flattery, Paul
  M 1130
Fleischer, Leonore
  C 0107   RB0363   RB0553
Flippo, Chet
  M 1131   M 1132   M 1133
  M 1134   M 1135   M 1136
  M 1137   M 1138   M 1139
Flower, J.A.
  M 1140
Fong-Torres, Ben
  C 0005   C 0006   C 0036
  C 0039   C 0042   C 0087
  C 0088   C 0153   C 0171
  C 0194   C 0199   C 0260
  C 0331   C 0332   C 0333
  C 0347   C 0348   M 1142
  M 1143   M 1144   M 1145
  M 1146   M 1147   M 1148
  M 1149   M 1150   M 1151
  M 1152   M 1153   M 1154
  M 1155   M 1156

Fonvielle, Chris
  M 1157
Ford, Stephen
  N 0395
Foreman, J.B.
  B 0198
Forman, Jack
  RF0047
Forsyth, Ian S.
  RR0485   RR0553
Foss, P. J.
  S 0065   S 0066   S 0086
  S 0099   S 0111   S 0112
  S 0169
Fotheringham, Allan
  M 1160
Foti, Laura
  M 1161
Fox, H.
  M 1166
Fox, J.
  RF0343
Fox, J.R.
  RF0355
Frame, Pete
  C 0321
Freed, Richard
  M 1169
Freed, Richard D.
  N 0409   N 0410   RR0062
Freedland, N.
  M 1170   M 1171
Freehan, P.G.
  RB0165   RB0596
Freeman, Clive
  M 1172
Freeman, Robert
  B 0200   B 0201   P 0034
  P 0037
Freilich, Leon
  M 1174
Frejlev, J.
  B 0499
Fremont-Smith, Eliot
  M 1175
French, P.
  RB0224
French, Philip
  RF0110   RF0121
Frentzen, J.
  RF0256
Freudenberger, Herbert J.
  C 0108
Fricke, David
  M 1176   M 1177   M 1178
  M 1179
Friede, Goldie
  B 0202   B 0203   M 1180
Friedland, Rich
  F 0084
Friedman, Rick
  B 0204   B 0205
Friend, David
  M 1181
Friis-Mikkelsen, Jarl
  M 1182
Frith, Simon
  C 0109   M 1184   M 1185
  M 1186
Fritts, Tom
  M 1187
Frost, David
  C 0112   M 1191
Fry, Stephen M.
  RB0016   RB0104
Fuchs, Stephen
  RB0011
Fujita, Shig
  M 1192
Fulford, R.
  M 1193
Fuller, John G.
  M 1194
Fulper-Smith, Marilyn
  M 1205   M 1206
Fulper-Smith, Shawn
  M 1196   M 1197   M 1198
  M 1199   M 1200   M 1201
  M 1202   M 1203   M 1204

  M 1205   M 1206   RB0370
  RR0106   RR0453
Gabor, Koltay
  B 0206
Gabree, John
  C 0113   M 1210   M 1211
  M 1212   M 1213   RR0067
Gaines, James R.
  M 1214
Gaines, Steven
  B 0085   B 0086   B 0087
  B 0088   M 0631   M 0632
Gaiter, Dorothy J.
  N 0416
Gale, Glenn
  N 0417
Gallagher, D.
  M 1215
Gambaccini, Paul
  B 0207   B 0208   B 0209
  B 0210   C 0114   M 0853
  M 1216   M 1217   M 1218
  M 1219   M 1220   M 1221
  M 1222   M 1223   M 1224
  M 1225   M 1226   M 1227
  M 1228   RF0281
Garbarini, Vic
  B 0211   B 0212   M 1229
  M 1230   M 1231
Garde, M.
  M 1232
Gardner, Paul
  N 0419   N 0420   N 0421
Garofalo, Reebee
  C 0075
Gary, S.
  M 0840
Garztecki, Marek
  M 1234
Gatta, Emile
  B 0502
Gattermayr, Karin
  F 0147
Gaughn, M.J.
  RF0360
Geddes, A.
  M 1235
Geddes-Brown, Leslie
  N 0422
Geffen, David
  M 1236
Gehrman, G.
  RB0337   RB0436
Geldof, R.
  M 1238
Gelly, D.
  RB0607
Gelly, David
  B 0213   B 0214   B 0215
  B 0216
Geng, V.
  RF0275
Geppert, Georg
  B 0217
Gerry And The Pacemakers
  C 0117
Gerson, Ben
  M 1248   M 1249   M 1250
  M 1251   RR0024   RR0252
  RR0381   RR0521
Gilbert, Nick
  N 0428
Gilliatt, P.
  RF0222   RF0315
Gilroy, Harry
  N 0429   N 0430   RB0361
Ginsburg, David
  RB0019   RB0318   RB0583
Gitlin, Todd
  M 1254   M 1255
Giuliano, Geoffrey
  M 1256
Giusto-Davis, JoAnn
  M 1257
Glassenberg, Bob
  M 1259
Glazer, Mitchell
  M 1261   M 1262
Glazier, Joel

M 1263   M 1264   M 1265
M 1266   M 1267   M 1268
M 1269   M 1270   M 1271
RB0098   RB0158   RB0263
RF0056
Gleason, Ralph J.
  C 0119   C 0120   M 1272
  M 1273   M 1274   M 1275
  M 1276   M 1277   M 1278
  M 1279   M 1280   M 1281
  RF0094
Glover, David
  RB0398
Glueck, Grace
  N 0434   N 0435
Gobell, Jean Paul
  F 0021   F 0061
Goddard, Peter
  M 1283   M 1284
Godwin, Joscelyn
  M 1285
Gold, Anita
  N 0436   RB0288
Goldberg, Danny
  M 1286
Goldman, Albert
  C 0121   C 0122   M 1287
  M 1288
Goldman, Julia
  M 1289
Goldmann, Frank
  C 0123   C 0124
Goldsmith, Marianne
  M 1290
Goldstein, Al
  C 0125
Goldstein, Marc
  RB0061
Goldstein, Richard
  C 0126   C 0127   M 1291
  M 1292   M 1293   M 1294
Goldstein, R.M.
  RF0105
Goldstein, T.
  M 1295   RF0135   RR0301
Golson, G. Barry
  C 0296
Gonzalez, Cindi
  F 0054
Goodfriend, J.
  M 1296   RR0092
Goodgold, Edwin
  B 0218   B 0219
Goodman, Ellen
  C 0129   N 0438
Goodman, George, Jr.
  N 0439
Goodman, Hal
  M 1298
Goodman, J.
  M 1299   M 1300
Goodman, Jeffrey
  P 0121
Goodman, Kevin
  P 0121
Goodman, Pete
  M 1301
Goodman, Rachel
  M 1302
Goodwin, M.
  M 1303   RF0159   RR0279
Goosens, Gilbert
  M 3482
Gordon, A.M.
  M 1304   M 1305
Gordon, Roxy
  M 1306
Gould, H.
  M 1307
Gould, Jack
  N 0440   N 0441   N 0442
Gould, Judee
  F 0009
Gow, G.
  RF0125   RF0194   RF0212
Gracen, Jorie
  M 1308
Grant, Suzie
  M 1310

Grasso, Rosario
  B 0220
Graustark, Barbara
  B 0211   B 0212   M 1231
  M 1311   M 1312   M 1313
  M 1314   M 1315   M 1316
  M 1317   M 1318
Graves, B.
  C 0288
Gray, Andy
  C 0130
Gray, M.
  M 1319
Green, Ann
  M 1322
Green, B.
  RF0186   RF0198   RF0228
Green, John
  B 0221   B 0222
Green, L.
  RF0165
Green, Robert
  N 0445
Green, Timothy
  M 1323
Greenfield, J.
  M 1324
Greenfield, Jeff
  N 0447
Greenfield, Meg
  M 1325
Greenspur, Roger
  N 0448
Grefrath, Richard W.
  RB0285
Grei, Askeroi
  F 0142
Grein, Paul
  M 1326   M 1327   M 1328
  M 1329   M 1330
Grenier, R.
  RF0258   RF0260   RF0302
Grevatt, R.
  M 1331   M 1332   M 1333
  M 1334
Griffin, Alistair
  B 0223   B 0224
Groessel, Hans
  M 1335   M 1336
Groleau, Agnes
  B 0565
Groom, Avril
  N 0449
Gross, Leonard
  M 1337
Gross, Ronald
  N 0782
Grossman, Jay
  M 1338   RR0382
Grove, Martin A.
  B 0225   B 0226   B 0227
  P 0015
Grundy, Stuart
  C 0322   C 0323   C 0324
Grunfeld, Frederic
  RR0323   RR0428
Grunfeld, Frederick V.
  M 1340
Grunnet, Per
  M 1341   M 1342
Gruson, Sydney
  N 0451
Guidry, F.H.
  RB0453
Guild, Hazel
  M 1344   M 1345   M 1346
Gumby, D.
  RR0123
Guncheon, Mark
  RB0014
Guzek, Arno
  B 0228   B 0229   B 0230
  M 1347   M 1348   M 1349
Haberman, Clyde
  N 0455   N 0456   N 0457
  N 0458
Hadju, David
  M 1350
Hagen, Ray

RF0108
Hager, Henk
  M 0119   M 0120   M 1351
  M 1352   M 1353   M 1354
  M 1355   M 1356   M 1357
  M 1358   M 1359   M 1360
  M 1361   M 1362   M 1363
  M 1364   M 1365   M 1366
  M 1367   M 1368   M 1369
  M 1370   M 1371   M 1372
  M 1373   M 1374   M 1375
  M 1376   M 1377   M 1378
  M 1379   M 1380   M 1381
  M 1382   M 1383   M 1384
  M 3521   RB0009   RB0472
  RR0038   RR0096   RR0168
  RR0188   RR0211   RR0271
  RR0282   RR0393   RR0433
  RR0475   RR0533
Hager, Hetty
  M 1385
Hall, Claude
  M 1386   M 1387   M 1388
  M 1389
Hall, D.
  M 1390
Hall, Les
  C 0132   C 0133
Hallberg, Carl
  M 1391
Hamblett, Charles
  B 0231
Hamill, P.
  RB0275
Hamill, Pete
  M 1394   M 1395
Hamilton, Alan
  B 0232
Hamilton, Bruce
  C 0230
Hamilton, David
  M 0105   M 1396
Hamilton, J.
  M 1397
Hamilton, L.
  RF0311
Hamlin, Bruce
  B 0233   M 1398
Hammer, Joshua
  M 1399
Hand, Albert
  P 0067
Hannah, Dorene
  M 1400
Hansen, Jeppe
  B 0236
Hansen, Niko
  B 0581
Harcourt, Peter
  RF0122
Harding, Helen
  M 1401
Hardy, Phil
  B 0237
Haring, Hermann
  M 1402
Harlib, L.
  M 3301   M 3303
Harris, B.
  M 1403   M 1404   RR0265
Harris, Bruce
  M 1405
Harris, L.
  M 3302
Harris, Martha S.
  C 0134   N 0463
Harris, S.
  M 1404
Harrison, D.W.
  RB0219   RB0246
Harrison, E.
  M 1406   M 1407
Harrison, George
  B 0238   B 0239   B 0240
  M 1408   M 1409   P 0062
Harrison, J.
  B 0191
Harrison, T.
  M 1410

Harry, Bill
  B 0241   B 0242   B 0243
  B 0244   B 0245   B 0246
  B 0247   B 0248   B 0249
  C 0011   C 0016   C 0017
  C 0018   C 0019   C 0020
  C 0021   C 0023   C 0024
  C 0029   C 0030   C 0031
  C 0032   C 0033   C 0034
  C 0035   C 0037   C 0040
  C 0041   C 0043   C 0044
  C 0045   C 0046   C 0047
  C 0053   C 0054   C 0070
  C 0073   C 0078   C 0089
  C 0090   C 0099   C 0100
  C 0101   C 0102   C 0103
  C 0110   C 0111   C 0115
  C 0117   C 0118   C 0128
  C 0131   C 0132   C 0133
  C 0135   C 0136   C 0152
  C 0155   C 0157   C 0162
  C 0175   C 0177   C 0184
  C 0185   C 0187   C 0188
  C 0189   C 0190   C 0191
  C 0195   C 0196   C 0197
  C 0201   C 0209   C 0211
  C 0213   C 0219   C 0221
  C 0222   C 0223   C 0224
  C 0231   C 0236   C 0239
  C 0240   C 0261   C 0266
  C 0267   C 0268   C 0269
  C 0270   C 0292   C 0301
  C 0302   C 0303   C 0311
  C 0312   C 0326   C 0327
  C 0328   C 0330   C 0340
  C 0341   C 0343   C 0344
  C 0345   M 1423   M 1424
  M 1425   M 1426   M 1427
  M 1428   M 1429   M 1430
  M 1431   M 1432   M 1433
  M 1434   M 1435   M 1436
  M 1437   M 1438   M 1439
  M 1440   M 1441   M 1442
  M 1443   M 1444   M 1445
  M 1446   M 1447   M 1448
  M 1449   M 1450   M 1451
  M 1452   M 1453   M 1454
  M 1455   M 1456   M 1457
  M 1458   M 1459   M 1460
  M 1461   P 0014   RB0097
  RB0320   RB0441   RB0490
  RB0516   RB0632   RF0054
  RF0055
Hart, Bob
  M 1462
Hart, Henry
  RF0158   RF0400
Hart, Royce
  F 0030
Hartmann, Walter
  C 0158
Hatch, R.
  RF0270
Hauptfuhrer, F.
  M 0072
Havalock, Jim
  F 0019
Haviv, Mitchell
  M 1463   M 1464   RF0016
  RF0024   RF0297
Haydock, Ron
  P 0011
Hayes, Andy
  F 0145
Hayles, David
  M 1465   M 1466
Hazelhurst, Peter
  N 0465
Heckman, Don
  N 0467   N 0468   RR0424
Heckman, Donald
  M 1469
Hedgepeth, William
  M 1470
Heenan, Edward F.
  M 1471
Hege
  RF0151   RF0333
Heilbrunn, John David

M 1182
Heilpern, John
N 0469
Heiser, Betty
F 0126
Heister, Hans-Werner
RB0539
Hemenway, Robert
B 0250 B 0251
Henahan, D.
N 0470
Hendel, Brian
F 0158
Hendra, Tony
M 1474
Heneghan, Christy
M 1475 M 1476
Hennessey, H.
M 1477
Hennessey, M.
M 1478 M 1479 M 1480
M 1481 M 1482 M 1483
M 3455
Henshaw, L.
M 1484 M 1485 M 1486
Hentoff, Nat
C 0137
Herbeck, R.
M 1487 M 1488 M 1489
Herman, Robin
N 0471
Hershow, Sheila
C 0138 N 0473
Hertzberg, H.
M 1493
Heumann, J.
RR0100
Heyn, Dalma
M 1494
Hicks, Jim
M 1495
Hignite, Tami
F 0047
Hilburn, Robert
C 0139 N 0476 N 0477
N 0478 N 0479 RB0017
RB0105 RB0481
Hill, Ronald
M 1498
Hill, S.
M 1499
Hiltscher, Klaus
C 0124
Hine, Al
B 0252 B 0253 B 0254
Hines, Iain
M 1500 M 1501 M 1502
M 1503 M 1504 M 1505
M 1506 M 1507 M 1508
M 1509
Hinton, B.
M 1510 RR0371
Hipgnosis
B 0234 B 0235 C 0140
Hirshfeld
M 1511
Hoare, Ian
M 1515
Hoberman, J.
RF0286
Hochadel, Richard M.
M 1516 M 1517
Hockinson, Mike
RB0026 RR0486
Hodenfield, Chris
M 1518
Hodenfield, J.
M 1519 M 1520
Hoen, Ruud't
B 0564
Hoffman, Dezo
B 0255 B 0256 B 0257
B 0258 P 0009
Hoffman, Frank
C 0141
Hoffman, Richard
F 0129
Hoffmann, R.
M 1521

Hogan, Randolph
N 0481 RB0529
Holbrook, David
M 1522
Holden, Stephen
M 1523 M 1524 M 1525
M 1526 M 1527 N 0482
RR0298 RR0392 RR0418
RR0450 RR0495 RR0538
Holder, Stephen
M 0550
Hollingsworth, R.
RR0249 RR0447
Hollingworth, R.
M 1530 M 1531 M 1532
M 1533 M 1534
Holmstrom, John
M 1536
Holroyd, Stephen
C 0142
Holyroyd, S.
M 1537
Honeycutt, K.
N 0486
Hooper, W.B.
RB0520
Hope, Francis
RB0549
Hopkins, Jerry
C 0143 C 0144 C 0145
M 1538 M 1539 M 1540
M 1541 M 1542
Horide, Rosie
M 1543 M 1544 M 1545
M 1546 RR0037
Horn, Martin E.
B 0262
Hornsby, Jeremy
B 0370 B 0371
Horowitz, I.
M 1547
Horwood, W.
M 1548
Hotchkins, A. Bear
M 1549 RR0355
House, Jack
B 0263 B 0264
Houston, B.
M 1550
Howard, Philip
N 0494
Howard, Tony
M 1551
Howes, H.C.
M 1552
Howlett, Kevin
B 0265 B 0266
Hughes, D.
M 1557 M 1558 M 1559
Hughes, Jim
F 0055 M 1561
Hughes, John
M 1560
Hughes, Liz
F 0055 M 1561
Hume, P.
M 1562
Humphrey-Smith, Cecil
B 0267
Humphries, Patrick
RB0314
Hunger, Julie
M 1563
Hunn, David
N 0497
Hunt, Albert
M 1565
Hunt, C.A.
RB0160 RB0327 RB0334
RB0494
Hunter, George
M 1566
Hunter, N.
M 1567
Huntington, Robert L., Jr.
C 0146 N 0498
Hupp, R.
B 0041
Hutchins, C.

M 1568
Hutchins, Chris
M 1569 M 1570 M 1571
M 1572
Hutton, J.
M 1573 M 1574 M 1575
Hutton, Jack
M 1576
Huyette, Marcia
B 0268
Iino, Satoshi
M 1579
Insolera, Manuel
B 0269
Iozzia, B.
M 1589
Ireland, William
M 1594
Irwin, C.
M 1595 M 1596
Ishizaka, K.
B 0133
Isler, Scott
M 3036 RB0064 RB0294
Ivins, Molly
M 1617
Jack, Alex
M 1621
Jackson, Jeffrey M.
M 1622
Jacobs, Sanford L.
N 0536
Jacobson, B.
M 1623 RR0061
Jacopetti
M 1668
Jacopetti, R.
M 1624
Jaffe, C.
RB0167 RB0319 RB0329
Jaffe, Harold
C 0119
Jahn, Mike
C 0148 M 1625 M 1626
RR0326 RR0404
Jahr, C.
M 1627
James, Clive
M 1628
James, Frederick
M 1629 M 1630 M 1631
M 1632 M 1633 M 1634
M 1635 M 1636 M 1637
M 1638 M 1639 M 1640
M 1641 M 1642 M 1643
M 1644 M 1645 M 1646
M 1647 M 1648 M 1649
M 1650 M 1651 M 1652
M 1653 M 1654 M 1655
M 1656 M 1657 M 1658
M 1659 M 1660 M 1661
M 1662 M 1663 M 1664
James, Nick
M 1576 M 1665 M 1666
M 1667
Janos, Sebok
B 0270
Janov, Arthur
M 1668
Janssen, Koos
B 0038 M 1669
Jasper, Tony
B 0271 B 0272 C 0149
C 0150
Javna, Gordon
C 0151
Javna, John
C 0151
Jay, S.M.
M 1670
Jeavons, C.
RF0269
Jeier, Thomas
B 0366
Jenkins, Gwyn
F 0138
Jerome, Jim

M 1671
Jewell, Derek
N 0542
Jewell, Thomas N.
RB0580
Jobes, William
M 1673 N 0544
Joe, R.
M 1674 M 1675
Johnson, B.D.
M 1723
Johnson, B.S.
RB0547
Johnson, F. H.
S 0070
Johnson, Judy
F 0095
Johnson, Paul
M 1724
Johnson, R.
RF0026
Johnson, Richard
N 1143
Johnson, Rick
M 1725 M 1726
Johnson, Timothy W.
C 0161
Johnston, Laurie
N 0471 N 0575 N 0576
N 0577 N 0578 N 0579
N 0580 N 0581
Johnston, T.H.
N 0582
Jolidon, Laurence
M 1729
Jones, D.A.N.
RB0228 RB0282
Jones, George
C 0162
Jones, J.
M 1731
Jones, L.
N 0583
Jones, N.
M 1732 M 1733
Jones, Nick
M 1734
Jones, P.
M 1735 M 1736 M 1737
Jones, Peter
C 0163 M 0911 M 0912
M 1738 M 1739 M 1740
M 1741 M 1742 M 1743
M 1744 M 1745 M 1746
M 1747 M 1748 M 1749
M 1750
Jones, Ron
B 0188
Jones, Tim
N 0584
Joyce, Faye S.
C 0164 N 0585
Jullian, Marcel
M 1753
Jurgs, Michael
B 0280 M 1754
Kael, Pauline
C 0165 RF0067 RF0183
Kahn, H.
M 1756
Kahn, Stephen
P 0010
Kalkbrenner, Arthur
C 0140
Kaminsky, Peter
M 1757
Kane, Art
M 1758
Kantrowitz, Barbara
N 0590
Kanze, Peter
M 1759
Kaplan, Lisa Faye
M 1760
Kaplan, Morris
N 0591
Katz, Gregory

M 1762
Katzenstein, E.G.
  M 1813
Kauffmann, Stanley
  C 0166   RF0219   RF0271
  RF0364   RF0365
Kaufman, Murray
  C 0167
Kay, Alan
  M 2971
Kaye, Lenny
  RR0367
Kaye, R.J.
  RB0043
Kaylan, Melik
  M 1763
Kearns, Jo
  B 0554
Keenan, Deborah
  B 0281   B 0282
Keesee, Allen
  C 0168
Kelly, Freda
  F 0123   M 0788   M 1764
Kelly, K.
  N 0592
Kelly, Sean
  M 1765
Kemper, P.
  M 1766
Kempton, M.
  M 1767
Kempton, Murray
  C 0169   N 0593
Kennedy, Adrienne
  B 0320   B 0321
Kennedy, H.
  RF0253
Kennely, P.
  RR0273
Kennely, Patricia
  M 1768   M 1769
Keppel, Karin
  B 0283
Keylin, Arleen
  C 0170
Kilbane, Joy
  F 0151   M 3257
Kiley, P.
  M 1773
Kilmartin, Terry
  M 1774
Kindsvater, Doylene
  F 0106
King, Bill
  M 1775   M 1776   M 1777
  M 1778   M 1779   M 1780
  M 1781   M 2483
King, Leslie T.
  RB0058   RB0070   RB0082
  RB0109   RB0259   RB0272
  RB0338   RB0376   RB0381
  RB0423   RB0431   RB0451
  RB0456   RB0470   RB0486
  RB0487   RB0489   RB0499
  RB0585   RB0586   RB0616
  RB0617   RB0622
King, Mollie Parry
  M 1782   M 1783
King, Timothy
  M 1784   RR0310
King, Timothy P.
  M 1792   M 1793
King, William P.
  M 1785   M 1786   M 1787
  M 1788   M 1789   M 1790
  M 1791   M 1792   M 1793
  M 3184   M 3390   RB0027
  RB0083   RB0149   RB0154
  RB0187   RB0188   RB0198
  RB0203   RB0262   RB0298
  RB0341   RB0375   RB0382
  RB0399   RB0400   RB0401
  RB0460   RB0471   RB0500
  RB0511   RB0515   RB0562
  RF0013   RF0020   RF0022
  RF0237   RF0298   RR0016
  RR0017   RR0093   RR0132
  RR0134   RR0138   RR0141

RR0142   RR0144   RR0152
RR0169   RR0185   RR0200
RR0201   RR0205   RR0209
RR0219   RR0223   RR0227
RR0257   RR0261   RR0270
RR0283   RR0342   RR0343
RR0345   RR0346   RR0414
RR0451   RR0461   RR0462
RR0474   RR0487   RR0502
RR0516   RR0523   RR0539
RR0544   RR0546   RR0550
Kinnersley, Simon
  M 1795
Kinzer, Pat
  F 0070   F 0077
Kirb
  M 1796
Kirby, F.
  M 1797
Kirk, D.
  M 1798
Kirkeby, M.
  M 1799
Kirmser, Earl
  M 1800
Kirsch, B.
  M 1801   RR0534
Kittleson, B.
  M 1803
Kivipaino, Uusi
  B 0026
Klein, Joe
  N 0595   RB0507
Kleinman, Peter
  M 1474
Klemesrud, Judy
  N 0596   N 0597
Kloman, William
  C 0171
Knapp, M.
  RB0277
Knight, M.E.
  M 1813
Knobler, P.
  M 1814
Knowles, Timothy
  M 1815
Kobayashi, H.
  B 0387
Koenig, John
  RB0291
Kofsky, Frank
  M 1816   M 1817
Kohlmann, W.
  M 1818
Kohn, Howard
  M 1819
Kolanjian, Steve
  M 1820   M 1821   RB0008
  RB0303
Koluda, Shilow
  B 0284
Koning, Frank
  RF0002
Kooistra, Ger
  M 1822
Koolmees, Andre
  M 1823   RB0084
Koonan, K.
  RR0007
Kopkind, Andrew
  C 0172   M 1824   N 0598
Kordosh, J.
  M 1825
Kornheiser, Toni
  N 0599
Kornheiser, Tony
  C 0173
Kossodo, Helmut
  B 0307   B 0308
Kostelanetz, Richard
  C 0083
Kozak, Roman
  M 1826   M 1827   M 1828
  M 1829   M 1830   M 1831
  M 1832
Kozinn, Allan
  RB0145
Kraai, Lila

M 1833
Kramer, Howard
  B 0285
Kramer, Marcus, Rabbi
  C 0174   N 0600
Krebs, Albin
  N 0222   N 0325   N 0326
  N 0456   N 0457   N 0458
  N 0581   N 0601   N 0602
  N 0603   N 0604   N 0605
  N 0606   N 0607   N 0608
  N 0609   N 0610   N 0611
  N 0612   N 0613   N 0614
  N 0615   N 0616   N 0617
  N 0618   N 0619
Kreimer, Juan Carlos
  B 0286
Krentzel, E.
  M 1830
Kretschmann, Linda
  F 0010
Krider, Bill
  RR0124
Krieger, Michael
  F 0040   F 0041
Kroll, Jack
  M 1835   M 1836   M 1837
  RF0181   RR0325   RR0430
Kubernik, H.
  M 1838
Kubiak, Michael
  B 0392
Kurtz, Irma
  M 1839
Lacayo, R.
  RF0262
Lacefield, P.
  M 1841
Lachman, Charles
  M 1842   M 1843   M 1844
  M 1845   M 1846   M 1847
Lacy, Marie
  F 0101
Laden, Simon's
  B 0055
Lahr, John
  M 1849
Laing, Dave
  C 0176
Laing, R. D.
  M 1850
Lake, S.
  M 1851
Lambert, Tom
  N 0621
Lamskin, B.
  M 1852
Landau, Jon
  M 1853   M 1854   M 1855
  M 1856   M 1857   M 1858
  RR0023   RR0057   RR0149
  RR0340   RR0353   RR0400
Lane, Penny
  F 0116
Langereis, Jan
  B 0559
Langone, John
  M 1859
Lapidos, Carol
  B 0287
Lapidos, Mark
  B 0287   M 1860
Lark, Fred
  M 1861   M 1862   M 1863
  M 1864   M 1865   M 1866
  M 1867   RB0002   RB0343
  RR0001   RR0088   RR0119
  RR0136   RR0181   RR0220
  RR0221   RR0322   RR0358
  RR0408   RR0473   RR0499
  RR0524   RR0545
Larkin, Rochelle
  B 0288   B 0289   B 0290
  B 0291
Larter, Becki
  F 0113
Laurence, P.
  M 1871
Lawlor, Julia

N 0626
Lawrence, J.
  C 0178
Lawter, Ann
  F 0087   M 1872   M 1873
Lazar, Jerry
  C 0179   M 1875
Leach, Sam
  B 0292   B 0293   P 0041
Leaf, Earl
  B 0294
Leapman, Michael
  N 0627   N 0628   N 0629
  N 0630   N 0631
Leary, Timothy
  C 0180
Leblanc, Jacques
  B 0295
Ledbetter, Les
  M 1877   N 0632   N 0633
Lee, Al
  C 0181
Lee, Edward
  C 0182
Lee, John M.
  N 0635   N 0636
Lee, Krista
  M 1878
Lee, Ron
  M 1879
Leenheer, Franck
  M 1880   M 1881   M 1882
  M 1883   M 1884   M 1885
  M 1886   M 1887   M 1888
  RR0312
Lees, G.
  RR0427
Lees, Gene
  M 1889
Leigh, Spencer
  B 0296   B 0297
Lelyveld, Joseph
  N 0638   N 0639   N 0640
  N 0641
Lemon, Richard
  M 1891
Lennon, Cynthia
  B 0298   B 0299   B 0300
Lennon, John
  B 0301   B 0302   B 0303
  B 0304   B 0305   B 0306
  B 0307   B 0308   B 0309
  B 0310   B 0311   B 0312
  B 0313   B 0314   B 0315
  B 0316   B 0317   B 0318
  B 0319   B 0320   B 0321
  B 0322   B 0323   B 0324
  B 0325   B 0326   B 0327
  B 0328   B 0329   B 0330
  C 0184   C 0185   C 0186
  C 0187   C 0188   C 0189
  C 0190   C 0191   M 1892
  M 1893   M 1894   M 1895
  M 1896   M 1897   M 1898
  M 1899   M 1900   M 1901
  M 1902   N 0642   N 0643
  N 0644
Lennon, Peter
  N 0667
Lennon, Yoko Ono   see also
  Ono, Yoko
Lennon, Yoko Ono
  M 2359
Leo, John
  N 0684
Leonard, John
  N 0685
Lester, Beth
  M 1947
Lester, Elenore
  N 0686
Leukefeld, Peter
  B 0334
Levine, Faye
  M 1958   M 1959
LeVrier, Phillip
  F 0035
Levy, Alan

M 1960
Lewin, David
  M 0585
Lewis, Anthony
  N 0687   N 0688
Lewis, Frederick
  N 0689
Lewis, George H.
  M 1962
Lewis, J.
  M 1963
Lewis, Kathy
  M 1964
Lewis, V.
  M 1965
Lewisohn, Mark
  C 0192   M 1966   M 1967
  M 1968   M 1969   M 1970
  M 1971   M 1972   M 1973
  M 1974   M 1975   M 1976
  M 1977   M 1978   M 1979
  M 1980   M 1981   M 1982
  M 1983   M 1984   M 1985
  M 1986   M 1987   RB0574
  RF0132   RF0299   RR0183
  RR0311
Lichtenstein, Grace
  N 0690   N 0691   N 0692
Lichter, Paul
  C 0193
Lichtman, I.
  M 1988   M 1989   M 1990
  M 1991   M 1992   M 1993
Liembacher, E.
  M 1994
Lindahl, Ingemar
  M 2318
Lindsay, Joe
  B 0134
Lindsey, Robert
  N 0695
Lippincott, P.
  M 2002
Livingston, A.W.
  M 2010   M 2011
Livingston, G.
  M 2012
Lloyd, Eric
  N 0701   RB0368   RB0560
Lloyd, Jack
  N 0702
Lloyd, Valerie
  M 2013
Lock, Nicolas
  B 0554
Loder, Kurt
  M 2015   M 2016   M 2017
  M 2018   N 0704   RR0258
Lomax
  RR0531
Long, Jeff
  B 0335
Loomis, K.C., Jr.
  RB0006
Loose, Bill
  M 2039   M 2040
Loquidis
  RR0551
Loucks, Kathleen A.
  B 0336
Loupien, S.
  M 2043
Lubasch, Arnold H.
  N 0714
Luce, P.A.
  M 2046
Luqui, Joaquin
  B 0337
Lutz, Gordon
  RB0112
Lyden, M.
  RB0394   RB0437
Lydon, S.
  M 2047
Lydon, Susan
  C 0194
Lynch, Kenny
  M 2048
Lynes, R.

RB0454
Lyon, George W.
  M 2049
Macaire, A.
  M 2050
McAllister, William
  M 2051
McBride, Jim
  M 2052
McCabe, Peter
  B 0338   B 0339   B 0340
  B 0341   B 0342   B 0343
McCaffrey, Laurie
  M 2053
McCarry, Charles
  M 2054
McCartney, Linda
  B 0344   B 0345   B 0346
  B 0347   B 0348   B 0349
  B 0350   B 0351   B 0352
  B 0353   M 2055   N 0417
McCartney, Paul
  B 0354   B 0355   C 0195
  C 0196   C 0197   C 0198
  N 0715
McCartney, Peter Michael
  B 0356   B 0357   B 0358
  B 0359
McCormack, Ed
  M 2083
McCormick, L.D.
  N 0733   RR0535
McCoy, Craig R.
  N 0734   N 0958
McCoy, William
  B 0364
McCracken, Melinda
  M 2084
McCue, M.
  RB0396
McCullaugh, J.
  M 2085   M 2086
McDonagh, Des
  M 2087   RB0618
McDonough, J.
  M 2088
McDowell, Edwin
  N 0735
McEwen, Ritchie
  N 0736
McFadden, Robert D.
  N 0737   N 0738   N 0739
McGeary, Mitchell
  B 0360   B 0361   B 0362
  B 0363   B 0364
McGhee, Raymond
  M 2090
McGilligan, P.
  RF0190
McGrath
  RR0246
McGrath, R.
  M 2091
McGregor, Craig
  C 0200   N 0740
McGurl, B.J.
  RB0207
McKenzie, M.
  N 0741
McKie, Fred
  M 2092
Mackie, Rob
  M 2093
McManis, Mabel
  F 0086
McNeill, D.
  M 2094
Madsack, Sylvia
  B 0432
Maggio, Joanne
  F 0099
Magill, Frank N.
  C 0161
Mahan, J.
  RF0353
Maher, J.
  M 2105   M 2106   M 2107
  M 2108
Maitland, Leslie

N 0743
Malamud, Phyllis
  M 0655
Mallagola, Marco Antonio
  F 0136
Malms, Jochen
  B 0366
Malone, Pat
  M 2110
Manley, Colin
  M 2112
Mann, William
  N 0746   N 0747   N 0748
  N 0749   N 0750   RR0015
Manoeuvre, Phillippe
  M 2114
Marchbank, Pearce
  B 0367   B 0368   B 0369
  B 0383   B 0384   B 0385
  B 0386   C 0202   S 0138
  S 0139
Marcus, G. H.
  M 2115
Marcus, Greil
  C 0203   C 0204   M 2116
  M 2117   M 2118   M 2119
  M 2120   M 2121   RB0351
  RR0290   RR0396   RR0402
  RR0406   RR0423
Mariager, Ann
  M 2122
Marks, J.
  N 0752
Marley, Christopher
  N 0753
Marling, Susan
  N 0754
Marowitz
  RF0240
Marsh, Dave
  M 2123   M 2124   M 2125
  M 2126   M 2127   M 2128
  M 2129   RB0021   RR0193
  RR0440
Marshall, David C.
  RR0231
Marshall, Geoffrey
  M 2130
Marshall, Rita
  N 0755
Marshall, William
  B 0586   B 0587   B 0588
  B 0589   B 0590   B 0591
Martens, Klaus
  B 0071
Martin, Bernice
  M 2131
Martin, Brendan
  M 2132   RR0456
Martin, G.
  M 2133
Martin, George
  B 0370   B 0371   C 0205
Martin, M.
  RF0336
Martin, Tom P.
  M 2134
Martins, Tdeu Gonzaga
  B 0372
Martorana, Ellen
  F 0103
Martynova, A.
  C 0206   M 2135
Maschler, Tom
  N 0756
Maslin, Janet
  M 2137   M 2138   N 0757
  RF0066
Maslov, Norman
  B 0033   B 0034   B 0035
  B 0036   M 0097
Matahira, Toru
  B 0373
Mathews, Carol
  N 0758
Mathews, Tom
  M 2141
Matthews, Linda
  F 0026

Mattoon, C.
  B 0230
Maugham, Patrick
  B 0374
Mautner, Sue
  M 2142
Maxwell, Neville
  N 0759
May, Chris
  C 0207
May, Christopher
  P 0118   P 0119   P 0120
Mayer, Allan
  M 2143
Mayer, Ira
  M 2144
Mayerson, D.J.
  RF0342
Mayerson, P.
  RF0209
Maynard, R.A.
  RF0403
Mayo, Anna
  M 2145
Medlicott, Paul
  C 0235
Meek, S.
  RF0007   RF0143
Meenach, Thomas J., III
  B 0375
Meisel, Perry
  M 2151   M 2152
Mekas, Jonas
  M 2153   RF0014   RF0296
  RF0396
Melhuish, Martin
  M 2154
Mellers, Wilfred
  B 0376   B 0377   B 0378
  M 2155   M 2156   M 2157
  M 2158   RR0251
Melly, George
  C 0208   M 2159   N 0761
  RB0281
Meltzer, M.
  M 2160
Meltzer, R.
  M 2161   M 2162   M 2163
Mendelsohn, John
  B 0379   M 2166   RR0008
  RR0140   RR0530
Meredith, June
  M 2169
Merigeau, P.
  RF0040
Merritt, Jay
  M 2170
Meryman, Richard
  M 2172
Mesalles, Jordi
  B 0380
Messing, Philip
  N 0318
Metz, Piotr
  M 2175   M 2176   M 2177
  M 2178   M 2179
Mewborn, Brant
  M 2180   M 2181   M 2182
  M 2183   RF0300
Meyer, D.
  B 0280
Meyer, F.
  M 2184   M 2185
Michaels, Leonard
  M 2186
Michaels, Ross
  B 0381   B 0382
Michelini, Chuck
  M 2187
Michener, Wendy
  RF0109
Middleton, Richard
  C 0210
Mike
  M 2188
Mikulis, Vickie
  F 0001   F 0008
Miles, Barry
  B 0383   B 0384   B 0385

B 0386   B 0387   B 0388
B 0389   B 0390   B 0391
B 0392   C 0202
Millar, G.
   RF0176   RF0195
Millar, Gavin
   RF0404
Miller, Chris
   M 2190
Miller, Duke
   S 0107
Miller, E.
   RF0149   RF0282   RF0322
   RF0338   RF0349   RF0374
Miller, Edwin
   M 2191   M 2192   M 2193
Miller, Jan
   M 2194
Miller, Jim
   C 0203   M 2195   M 2196
   RR0165   RR0493
Miller, John J.
   M 2197
Miller, M.C.
   RB0393
Mills, Nancy
   N 0763
Millstein, Ezra
   N 0764
Milne, T.
   RF0034   RF0196
Minoff, Lee
   B 0394
Minton, L.
   RF0006   RF0063   RF0142
   RF0178   RF0214   RF0268
   RF0309   RF0361
Mintz, Elliot
   M 2200   M 2201
Minudri, R.
   RB0119
Mitchell, A.
   RB0221
Mitchell, M.
   RF0251
Mitchell, Shirley
   F 0089
Mitchell, Steve
   M 2204
Mitsui, Toru
   C 0049   RB0637
Mitz, R.
   M 2205   M 2206
Mizrahi, Rachel
   B 0303   B 0304
Mizuno, C.
   B 0298
Moers, Rainer
   B 0469
Moger, E.S.
   M 2208
Montague, Susan
   M 2212
Montgomery, Paul L.
   N 0770   N 0771   N 0772
   N 0773   N 0774
Moon, L.
   M 2214
Moon, Lilith
   C 0212
Moorhouse, Geoffrey
   N 0775
Morales, Aldo
   M 2216
Morella, Joseph
   C 0061
Morgan, K.
   M 2218
Morgan, Terry
   M 2219
Morgenstern, D.
   RR0006
Morgenstern, J.
   M 2220
Morris, J.
   M 2221
Morris, Jan
   M 2222
Morrison, Blake

N 0778   RB0092   RB0353
RB0388   RB0429
Morse, Steve
   N 0779
Mosny, Ron
   P 0058   P 0099
Moss, F.
   M 2223   M 2224   RR0005
   RR0012
Moss, R.F.
   RF0139
Moyle, Graham
   M 2229
Moyle, Graham L.
   F 0031
Mudge, Roberta Ann
   M 2231   M 2232
Muggeridge, M.
   RB0216
Mulholland, Peter
   M 2233
Muller, Herve
   M 2234
Mulligan, B.
   M 3677
Mulligan, Brian
   M 2235   M 2236   M 2237
   M 2238   M 2239   M 2240
   M 2241
Mullins, Melissa D.
   RB0302
Munday, A.
   S 0061   S 0062   S 0063
   S 0067
Munro, Michael
   M 2242
Murawski, Patti
   F 0076
Murf
   RF0192   RF0325
Murphy, Allan
   B 0094   C 0069   M 0653
Murphy, Karen
   N 0782
Murray, Charles
   M 2243   M 2244
Murray, John
   C 0214   N 0783
Murray, T.
   RR0304
Musel, B.
   M 2245
Musel, R.
   M 2246
Musser, W.
   RB0514
Mutton, Peter
   F 0028   M 2250
N., A.
   M 2254
Nacht, J.K.
   B 0016
Nadel, M.
   M 2256
Naha, Ed
   B 0396   B 0397   B 0398
   P 0032
Nakamura, Toyo
   C 0049
Nakano, O.
   B 0399
Napier-Bell, Simon
   C 0217
Narducy, R.D.
   M 2257
Narmetz, Aljean
   N 0788
Natuki, Ikezawa
   B 0448
Neal, Donna
   F 0135
Neal, Larry
   C 0218
Neapolitan, Jerry
   M 2259
Neary, John
   M 2260
Neary, T.
   M 2261

Neiburg, Kurt
   F 0038
Neises, Charles P.
   B 0400   C 0048   C 0063
   C 0066   C 0067   C 0076
   C 0084   C 0112   C 0113
   C 0142   C 0179   C 0212
   C 0220   C 0227   C 0228
   C 0232   C 0243   C 0251
   C 0305   C 0310   C 0314
Nelson, Milo
   M 2262
Nelson, Paul
   M 2263   M 2264   M 2265
   RF0321   RR0434   RR0515
Neumann, Wolfgang
   B 0468   B 0469
Newhall, Emily
   M 0655
Newman, P.C.
   M 2281
Newton, F.
   M 2291
Ney, Jutta
   M 2299   M 2300
Nibbervoll, Ed
   B 0402
Nichols, L.
   N 0800
Niedergesass, Siegfried
   B 0403
Noebel, David A.
   B 0404   B 0405   B 0406
   B 0407
Nolan, Tom
   RR0233   RR0320
Nolte, Sarah
   F 0104
Noonan, T.
   M 2108
Norgaard, P.
   M 2308
Norman, Philip
   B 0408   B 0409   B 0410
   B 0411   B 0412   C 0225
   M 2309   M 2310   N 0804
   N 0805   N 0806   N 0807
   N 0808   N 0809   N 0810
   N 0811
Norris, Bob
   M 2312
North, Garrett
   M 2313
North, P.
   M 2314   M 2315
Novotny, Ann
   C 0061
Nowell-Smith, Geoffrey
   RF0113
Nusser, D.
   M 2326   M 2327
Nusser, R.
   M 2328
Nylen, L.
   M 2329
Nyren, N.S.
   RB0178
Obst, Lynda R.
   C 0052   C 0105
Ocean, Humphrey
   B 0413
Ochs, E.
   M 2334   M 2335
Ochs, Ed
   RR0303
O'Connor, Gillian
   N 0835
O'Connor, John J.
   N 0836
O'Donnell, Jim
   C 0226
Oertel, Rudi
   B 0156
O'Grady, Terence J.
   B 0416   B 0417   C 0227
   C 0228   M 2340   M 2341
   M 2342
O'Hara, J.D.
   M 2343   RB0414

Okun, Milton
   B 0123   B 0124   S 0024
   S 0040   S 0046   S 0095
   S 0108   S 0140
Oliver, Chris
   N 0839   N 0840
O'Mahony, Sean
   M 2347
O'Neil, Tom
   M 2352
O'Neill, Lou
   M 2370
O'Neill, Lou, Jr.
   M 2353   M 2354   M 2355
Ono, Yoko
   B 0418   B 0419   B 0420
   B 0421   B 0422   B 0423
   B 0424   B 0425   B 0426
   B 0427   B 0428   B 0429
   C 0229   M 1902   M 2359
   M 2360   M 2361   N 0644
Ono, Yoko see also Lennon,
   Yoko Ono
Organ, Joan
   F 0057
Ornelas, Rudy
   M 2368   M 2369   M 2370
   M 3185
Orth, M.
   M 2371   M 2372
Orton, Joe
   B 0430   B 0431
Osborne, Jerry
   C 0230
Osbourn, H.J.I.
   N 0848
Osbourne, Christine A.
   M 2373
Osmundsen, John A.
   M 2374   N 0849
Otis
   M 2376
O'Toole, L.
   M 2377
Our Society Editor
   M 2381
Ovens, D.
   M 2382
Ovens, Don
   RR0147
Overy, P.
   M 2383   M 2384
P., J.
   RB0020   RB0108
Packard, Vance
   C 0232   M 2385
Padgett, Vernon R.
   M 1622
Palmer, P.
   M 2386
Palmer, Raymond
   M 2387   N 0851
Palmer, Robert
   M 2388   M 2389   M 2390
   N 0852   N 0853   N 0854
   N 0855   N 0856   N 0857
   N 0858   N 0859   N 0860
   N 0861   RR0417   RR0459
   RR0494
Palmer, Tony
   C 0233   C 0234   C 0235
   N 0862
Pang, May
   B 0432   B 0433   B 0434
Pannebakker, Frits
   M 2391
Paradiso, Vikki
   F 0052   F 0118
Pard, Richard F.
   N 0865
Park, Susan
   B 0457   B 0458   B 0459
Parkinson, Norman
   B 0435   B 0436   C 0198
Parry-King, Jonathan
   M 2393
Partridge, R.
   M 2394

Pascal, S.
  RB0352
Pascall, Jeremy
  B 0093 B 0437 B 0438
  B 0439 B 0440 B 0441
  B 0442 B 0443 B 0444
  B 0445
Pastonesi, Marco
  B 0446
Patti, Gloria
  F 0049
Patton, Phil
  M 2395
Paturzo, Margie
  F 0108
Patyna, Joanna
  M 2396
Paul, Vlasta
  F 0006
Paulie
  F 0137
Paulson, Barbara
  F 0069 F 0114
Pawlicki, Michael J.
  B 0447
Peacock, Steve
  M 2422
Pearlman, S.
  M 2423
Pearson, John
  RR0376
Pearson, S.
  M 2424
Peck, Ira
  C 0008
Peebles, Andy
  B 0448 B 0449 B 0450
  B 0451 B 0452 B 0453
  B 0454 M 2425 M 2426
  M 2427
Peel, D.
  M 2428
Peel, Mark
  M 2429 RR0497
Peellaert, Guy
  C 0081 C 0238
Peerdeman, Hillebrand
  M 2430
Pekar, H.
  M 2431
Pelligrini, Adriana
  B 0329
Pelz, Wilfred
  B 0596
Perry, M.L.
  RB0268
Perry S.
  M 2454
Petersen, C.
  RB0357 RB0545
Peterson, Craig
  M 2462
Peterson, M.
  RF0170
Petticoffer, D.
  RB0480
Peyser, Joan
  C 0241 RB0227 RB0249
Phares, Lois
  F 0105
Phast Phreddie
  M 2463
Philbin, Marianne
  B 0455 C 0007 C 0216
  C 0229 C 0259 C 0334
Phillip, Judith
  F 0147
Phillips, McCandlish
  N 0881 N 0882
Phillips, Steve
  M 2464 M 2465 M 2466
  M 2467 M 2469 M 2470
  M 2471 M 2472 M 2473
  M 2474 M 2475 M 2476
  M 2477 M 2478 M 2479
  M 2480 M 2481 M 2482
  M 2483 RB0114 RB0442
  RR0121 RR0207 RR0410
  RR0454

Phillips, Steven
  M 2468
Phillips, Tim
  C 0207
Phillips, Tom
  M 2484
Pichaske, David R.
  C 0242 C 0243
Pick, Hella
  N 0883
Piercey, Nick
  M 2488 M 2489
Pile, Stephen
  N 0885
Pires, Dominique
  B 0017
Pirmantgen, Patricia
  B 0460 B 0461
Pit
  RF0378
Pitman, J.
  M 2490 M 2491
Planchart, Alejandro E.
  M 2493
Plaumann, Klaus
  C 0244
Pleasants, Henry
  M 2495 M 2496
Plummer, M.
  M 2498 M 2499
Podell, Jack J.
  P 0016
Podell, Janet
  C 0245 C 0246
Podrazik, Walter J.
  B 0108 B 0109 B 0110
  B 0111 B 0112 C 0074
  C 0247 C 0248 M 0675
  M 2500 M 2501 M 2502
  M 2503 M 2504 M 2505
  M 2506 RR0224 RR0463
  RR0488
Poirier, Richard
  C 0249 C 0250 C 0251
  C 0252 C 0507
Pollack, Lynn
  N 0893
Pollock, Bruce
  C 0253 C 0254
Pollock, D.
  RF0350
Polskin, Howard
  M 2509
Pomeroy, D.
  RF0307
Pond, Steve
  M 2510 RR0226
Pope, Joe
  F 0079 F 0143
Pope, Michael E.
  M 2511 M 2512 M 2513
  M 2514 M 2515 M 2516
  M 2517 M 2518 M 2519
  M 2520 M 2521 M 2522
  M 2523 M 2524 M 2525
  RB0037 RB0237 RF0028
  RF0037 RF0051 RF0167
  RF0244 RF0335 RF0340
  RF0382 RR0089 RR0090
  RR0173 RR0370 RR0457
  RR0540
Porter, Eddie
  M 2533
Porter, S.C.
  M 2534
Porter, Stephen C.
  B 0462
Porterfield, C.
  RF0011
Potterton, R.
  RF0277
Pountney, Kate
  M 2551 N 0896
Powditch, Keith
  M 2552
Powell, D.
  RF0069 RF0280 RF0371

Presler, Ales
  B 0463
Price, John
  N 0898
Price, Richard
  M 2556
Pro Art Staff
  B 0464
Prochman, Bill
  N 0900
Pryce-Jones, A.
  RB0551
Pules, H.
  M 2566
Pullen, Rob
  M 2567
Pullens, Bob
  RR0039
Putterman, B.
  RF0164 RF0203
Pye, I.
  M 2568
Pym, J.
  RF0363
Quesada, Carmen
  M 2571
Quigly, Isabel
  M 2572 RF0114
Quindlen, Anna
  N 0909
Quinones, Mario
  M 2573
Rabe, F.
  M 2576
Rabinowtiz, D.
  M 2577
Radel, Cliff
  N 0910
Radford, Penny
  N 0911 N 0912
Ragan, David
  M 2579
Raidonis-Gillis, Laura
  RB0342
Rainer, P.
  RF0062
Ramachandra, C.P.
  N 0914
Raman, A.S.
  M 2580
Ramasseul, Christiane
  B 0088
Ranzal, Edward
  N 0916
Rapsis, Mike
  M 1821 RB0630
Raye, S.
  M 2953
Raymont, Henry
  N 0917
Raynor, Henry
  N 0918 RF0239
Rayns, T.
  RF0179
Read, Lorna
  M 2954 M 2955 M 2956
  M 2957 RB0568
Red Mole
  M 2969
Redmond, Tim
  M 2971
Redshaw, David
  M 2972
Regan, T.
  M 2973
Rehm, Carl
  RB0150
Reichardt, J.
  M 2974
Reid, C.
  N 0924
Reif, Rita
  N 0925
Reilly, P.
  RR0315
Reilly, Peter
  M 2975
Reinhart, Charles F.
  B 0465 B 0466 B 0467

C 0247 M 2976 M 2977
M 2978 M 2979 M 2980
M 3185 RR0030 RR0139
RR0236 RR0242 RR0360
RR0504 RR0548
Reizalg, Leoj
  M 2981
Remmerswaal, Jos
  M 2987 M 2988 M 2989
  M 2990 M 2991 M 2992
  M 2993 M 2994 M 2995
  M 2996 M 2997 M 2998
  M 2999 M 3000 M 3001
  M 3002 RB0323
Renard, Gail
  M 3003
Rense, Rip
  N 0926
Repka, C.
  M 3004
Rettig, James
  RB0295
Reusch, V., Mrs.
  N 0928
Reynolds, Roger
  RB0609
Reynolds, Stanley
  N 0931
Rhody, Vickie
  F 0091
Rich, F.
  RF0150
Rich, Frank
  N 0932 N 0933
Richard, Raymond
  M 3011 M 3012
Rickarby, Laura
  F 0127
Rickey, C.
  RF0074 RF0379 RF0381
Ricks, Christopher
  N 0934 RB0359 RB0535
Rider, David
  RF0119 RF0399
Ridgeway, James
  M 3013
Riesman, D.
  M 3014
Rimler, Walter
  C 0262 C 0263 C 0264
  C 0265
Rinzler, A.
  M 3035
Ripp, J.
  RF0009 RF0147 RF0184
  RF0223 RF0224 RF0276
  RF0316
Robbins, Ira
  M 3036
Roberts, C.
  M 0783 M 1550 M 3037
  M 3038 M 3039 M 3040
  M 3041 M 3042
Roberts, Jeannie
  F 0131
Roberts, John
  M 3043
Roberts, Richard
  C 0272 N 0943
Robins, Wayne
  M 3044 RR0053 RR0520
Robinson, David
  N 0944 RF0072
Robinson, Lisa
  M 3045 M 3046 M 3047
Robinson, Richard
  M 3048
Robson, David
  P 0085
Rochefort, Christiane
  B 0303 B 0304
Rock, John J.
  M 3049 M 3050 M 3051
  M 3052
Rockwell, J.
  M 3090
Rockwell, John
  N 0946 N 0947 N 0948
  N 0949 N 0950 N 0951

N 0952   N 0953   N 0954
RB0317
Rodnitzky, Jerome L.
    RB0131
Rodrigues, Alberto
    B 0565
Rodriguez, J.
    M 3092
Rodriguez, Rosita
    F 0074
Roeder, B.
    M 3093   M 3094   M 3095
Rogers, L.
    M 3096
Rogers, T.
    RF0061   RF0266
Rogosky, Wolf D.
    B 0307   B 0308
Rollin, Betty
    M 3097
Rombeck, Hans
    B 0468   B 0469
Ronan, M.
    RF0373
Roney, M.
    RF0229
Rooney, Andy
    C 0274   N 0955
Rorem, Ned
    C 0275   C 0276   M 3104
    M 3105   M 3106
Rose, C.
    RF0027
Rose, Frank
    M 3107   M 3108
Rosen, Steve
    M 3109
Rosenbaum, Helen
    B 0470
Rosenberg, Neil V.
    M 3110
Rosensohn, Sam
    N 0956
Ross, D.
    M 3111
Ross, Evelyn
    N 0957
Rossi, Gloria
    M 3112
Rossmann, A.
    M 3113
Rosten, Leo
    C 0277
Roth, M.
    M 3114
Rowe, Graham
    M 3115
Rowland, Edna
    M 3116
Rowland, Mark
    M 3117   M 3118
Rowlands, John
    C 0278
Roxon, Lillian
    C 0279
Ruane, Micheal E.
    N 0958
Rubenstein, L.
    RF0255   RF0354
Ruffer, Gerhard
    M 3119   M 3120
Russell, Jeff
    B 0471   B 0472
Ryan, David Stuart
    B 0473
Ryan, Desmond
    N 0962   N 0963
Ryan, Patrick
    B 0474
Rycyk, Patty Owens
    F 0153
S., L.N.
    M 3125
Saal, Hubert
    M 3126   M 3127   RR0069
    RR0075
Saal, J.
    M 3128
Sacks, Elizabeth

M 3129   M 3130
Sacks, Leo
    M 3131
Sage, Martin
    P 0031
Saimaru, Nishi F.
    B 0274   B 0475
Saito, M.
    B 0216
Sakamoto, J.
    M 3132
Saleh, Dennis
    C 0280
Salzman, E.
    M 3133
Sammon, P.M.
    RF0057   RF0058
Sander, Ellen
    M 3134   M 3135   M 3136
    M 3137   M 3138   M 3139
    RR0010   RR0074   RR0308
Sanders, Richard
    M 3140
Sandner, Wolfgang
    M 3141   M 3142
Santiago, L.P.
    M 3143
Sarino, C.E.
    B 0476
Saroyan, Aram
    B 0477
Sarris, Andrew
    C 0281   RF0115   RF0123
    RF0326   RF0408   RF0409
    RF0410   RF0411
Satkin, Marc
    C 0282
Sauceda, James
    B 0478   C 0290
Saunders, M.
    RR0018   RR0264
Sauvaget, D.
    RF0039
Sawa, H.
    B 0191
Saylon, B.
    M 3146
Scaduto, Anthony
    B 0479
Scanlon, Karen
    N 0965
Scanlon, P.
    RF0148
Schade, H.
    M 3147
Schaefer, Oda
    M 3148
Schafer, William J.
    C 0283   C 0284   C 0285
Schaffner, Elizabeth
    C 0287
Schaffner, Nicholas
    B 0480   B 0481   B 0482
    B 0508   B 0509   C 0286
    C 0287   M 3149   M 3150
    M 3151   M 3152   M 3153
    M 3154   RB0304   RB0340
    RR0170   RR0465   RR0489
Schaumburg, Ron
    B 0483   B 0484   B 0485
Schecter, Jerrold
    M 3155
Scheibe, Barbara
    B 0409
Schickel, R.
    RF0191   RF0232   RF0284
Schickel, Richard
    M 3156   RB0546
Schickele, Peter
    M 3157   RB0358
Schiefman, Emma
    M 3158
Schillaci, P.
    RF0005   RF0141   RF0177
    RF0267   RF0308
Schindler, Walter
    M 3159
Schirmer, Gregory A.
    N 0966

Schlachter, Gail
    RB0293
Schmeider, R.
    N 0967
Schmid, Thomas
    B 0277
Schmidt, Dana Adams
    N 0968
Schmidt-Joos, Siegfried
    C 0288
Schnlon, P.
    M 3160
Schnurmacher, Thomas
    M 3003
Schoenberg, Eric
    S 0085
Schoenfeld, Herm
    M 3161   M 3162   M 3163
    M 3164   M 3165   M 3166
    M 3167
Schonfeld, Robert
    B 0338   B 0339
Schonfeld, Robert D.
    B 0340   B 0341   B 0342
    B 0343
Schrag, P.
    RR0432
Schroeder, Michael
    B 0486
Schuler, M.
    M 3169
Schultheiss, Tom
    B 0457   B 0458   B 0459
    B 0487   B 0488   B 0489
    B 0490   C 0289   C 0290
    M 3170   M 3171   M 3172
Schumach, Murray
    N 0971   N 0972   N 0973
Schuster, Peter
    F 0068
Schwaner, Teja
    B 0106
Schwartz, Al
    M 3173
Schwartz, David
    M 3174   M 3175   M 3176
    M 3177   M 3178   M 3179
    M 3180   M 3181   M 3182
    M 3183   M 3184   M 3185
    RB0286   RR0002   RR0051
    RR0064   RR0117   RR0284
    RR0321   RR0368   RR0425
    RR0500
Schwartz, Francie
    C 0291   M 3186
Schwarz, Hartmut
    F 0020
Schworck, Ernest E.
    B 0491
Scoppa, Bud
    M 3189   M 3190   RR0352
Scott, Lee
    RB0060
Scott, Norman
    M 3192
Scully, M.G.
    M 3193
Seal, Allen
    F 0128
Seal, Lou
    M 3194
Search, G.
    M 3195
Sears, Dianne
    M 0550
Seelye, John
    RF0106
Segal, E.
    M 3198
Segell, M.
    M 3199
Seifman, David
    N 0956
Sekuler, Eliot
    M 3200
Sellye, John
    RF0118
Seloron, Francoise
    B 0492   B 0493

Selvin, Joel
    M 3201   N 0976   RB0022
Sen, J.P.
    M 0988
Serra, Julio F.
    M 3204
Settimo, Franco
    M 3205   RB0192
Shabecoff, Philip
    N 0978   N 0979
Shakespeare, R.W.
    N 0980
Shames, Laurence
    M 3208
Shankar, Ravi
    C 0293
Shapiro, Nat
    C 0294   C 0295
Shapiro, S.
    M 3209
Shatzkin, Mike
    B 0554
Shaw, A.
    M 3211
Shearman, Colin
    N 0982
Shears, Billy
    M 3213   RB0096   RB0134
    RB0144   RB0147   RB0173
    RB0260   RB0305   RB0322
    RB0424   RB0440   RB0573
    RB0631   RF0075   RF0129
    RR0094   RR0105   RR0135
    RR0167   RR0182   RR0241
    RR0259   RR0291   RR0356
    RR0483
Shears, Mo
    F 0140
Sheff, David
    B 0494   B 0495   B 0496
    B 0497   B 0498   C 0296
    M 3214   M 3215   M 3216
    M 3217   M 3218
Sheff, Victoria
    M 3218
Sheinkopf, Kenneth G.
    M 3219
Shelton, Robert
    N 0984   N 0985   N 0986
Shepard, Richard F.
    N 0987   N 0988
Shepherd, Billy
    B 0499   B 0500   B 0501
    B 0502   B 0503   M 3220
    M 3221   M 3222   M 3223
    M 3224   M 3225   M 3226
    M 3227   M 3228   M 3229
    M 3230   M 3231   M 3232
    M 3233   M 3234   M 3235
    M 3236   M 3237   M 3238
    M 3239   M 3240
Sherman, Pam
    M 3241
Sherman, Suzanne K.
    M 3242
Shipp, E.R.
    N 0990   N 0991   N 0992
    N 0993   N 0994   N 0995
    N 0996   N 0997
Shipper, M.
    M 3245
Shipper, Mark
    B 0504   B 0505   B 0506
    B 0507
Shneerson, G.
    M 3246
Shoemaker, Jane P.
    N 0590
Sholin, David
    M 3247   M 3248
Shonyo, Bryan
    F 0157
Short, D.
    M 3249   M 3250   M 3251
Short, Dan
    N 0998
Short, Don

C 0297   N 0999
Shotton, Pete
   B 0508   B 0509
Shuster, Alvin
   N 1002   N 1003   N 1004
Siegel, Joel
   M 3259   M 3260   M 3261
Sierra i Fabra, Jordi
   B 0510   B 0511   B 0512
Sievert, Bill
   M 3262
Sigerson, Davitt
   M 3263   RR0498
Silk, D.
   RF0264   RF0358
Silver, C.
   M 3264
Silver, Caroline
   C 0298
Silveri, Ceil
   F 0110
Sim, Jamie
   F 0062
Simels, Steve
   M 3265   M 3266   M 3267
   M 3268   M 3269   M 3270
   RB0063   RB0639   RR0045
   RR0087   RR0104   RR0155
   RR0179   RR0316   RR0359
   RR0401
Simmons, Pat
   F 0151   M 3275   M 3271
   M 3272   M 3273   M 3274
   RR0171
Simms, Alastair
   B 0513
Simon, George T.
   C 0299
Simon, J.
   M 3276   RF0182   RF0218
Simon, John Ivan
   C 0300
Simonds, C.H.
   M 3277
Sims, J.
   M 3278
Sippel, J.
   M 3283   M 3284   M 3285
Sivak, T.
   S 0158
Skow, J.
   RF0324
Slagt, Jan
   M 3288
Sloane, Leonard
   N 1007   N 1008
Sloman, Larry
   M 3289
Smit, Eddy
   RR0047
Smith, Alan
   C 0301   C 0302   C 0303
   M 3290   M 3291   M 3292
Smith, C.
   RB0159
Smith, David
   N 1009
Smith, David J.
   M 3293   M 3294   M 3295
   M 3296   M 3297   M 3298
   M 3299   RB0512
Smith, Donna Ridley
   M 3300
Smith, H.
   M 3301   M 3302   M 3303
Smith, L.
   RF0133   RF0207
Smith, Larry Richard
   B 0514
Smith, L.R.
   M 3304
Smith, M.
   M 3305
Smith, Sharon
   C 0304
Smith, Terry

M 3306
Smith, Wendy
   M 1257
Smothers, J.
   RB0117
Snell, Conrad
   B 0515
Snidall, Irene
   M 3307
Snow, Temperance
   M 3308
Snyder, M.
   N 1010
Snyder, Patrick
   C 0305   RF0187
Snyder-Scumpy, Patrick
   M 3309   M 3310   M 3311
   M 3312   M 3313   RR0518
Soffritti, Daniele
   B 0516
Solloway, Larry
   M 3316
Somma, Robert
   M 3322
Soum, L.
   B 0098
Souster, Tim
   M 3328   M 3329
Southhall, Brian
   C 0307
Sparn, Ed
   M 3331
Spence, Helen
   B 0520   B 0521
Spencer, Graham
   M 3335
Spencer, Neil
   M 3336
Spencer, Scott
   M 3337
Spencer, William F.
   B 0522
Spinetti, Victor
   B 0320   B 0321
Springman, Joanne M.
   M 3341   M 3342
Squire, John
   M 3343
Sragow, M.
   RF0070   RF0112   RF0372
Sshiefman, Emma
   M 3344
Stafford, Peter
   C 0308
Stam, Tom
   B 0503
Stambler, Irwin
   C 0309
Standora, Leo
   N 1019
Stanley, Hiram
   C 0310   M 3345   M 3346
   M 3347
Stanley, Raymond
   M 3348
Stannard, Neville G.
   B 0523   B 0524   B 0525
   B 0526
Starr, Ringo
   M 3349
Starrett, Ian
   C 0312
Stavers, Gloria
   M 3351
Stavis, Eugene
   RF0100
Stecklow, Steve
   N 1022
Steele, J.
   M 3352
Steensma, Frans
   M 3548
Steiger, Brad
   M 3353
Stein
   M 3354
Stein, David Lewis
   M 3355
Stein, H.

M 3356
Stein, Kevin
   M 2129
Stein, Shifra
   B 0527
Steinberg, Celene
   F 0009
Steinem, Gloria
   M 3357
Stempf, Heidi
   F 0088
Stetzer, Charles W.
   B 0528
Steve
   M 3358
Stevens, M.
   N 1024   RR0080
Stigwood, Robert
   B 0529
Still, Craig R.
   F 0037
Stokes, Geoffrey
   B 0530   B 0531   B 0532
   B 0533   M 3362   M 3363
Stoller, James
   RF0162   RF0241
Stonehouse, Justin
   RB0253
Stoop, N.M.
   RF0001   RF0130   RF0163
Storb, L.
   M 3366
Storey, E.
   RB0411
Strafford, Peter
   N 1027   N 1028
Strauss, Robert
   N 1029   N 1030
Strick, P.
   RF0216
Strickland, Geoffrey
   RR0334
Strongin, Theodore
   N 1033
Suczek, Barbara
   C 0314   M 3369
Sugg, Alfred
   M 3372   RF0104   RF0117
Sullivan, Bob
   B 0534   F 0036
Sunday Times Magazine
   P 0085
Sundin, B.
   M 2576
Sussman, Al
   M 3375   M 3376   M 3377
   M 3378   M 3379   M 3380
   M 3381   M 3382   M 3383
   M 3384   M 3385   M 3386
   M 3387   M 3388   M 3389
   M 3390   RB0128   RB0271
   RF0023   RR0137   RR0222
   RR0357   RR0369   RR0455
   RR0490
Sussman, Gerald
   M 3391
Sutcliffe, Phil
   C 0315   N 1038
Sutcliffe, Stuart
   B 0535
Sutherland, S.
   M 3392   M 3393   M 3394
   RR0083   RR0099
Sutton, J.
   RB0348   RB0566
Sutton, Larry
   N 1039
Sutton, Margaret
   B 0536
Swenson, J.
   M 3397
Swenson, John
   B 0537   B 0538   B 0539
   M 3398   M 3399   RR0103
   RR0118   RR0175
Swenton, Jennie
   M 3400
Symons, J.
   RB0554

Szwed, John F.
   M 3402   M 3403   RR0324
Tabatch, Warren
   B 0540
Tachikawa, N.
   B 0541
Takiff, Jonathan
   N 1040   N 1041   N 1042
Talese, Gay
   N 1043
Tamarkin, Jeff
   M 3410   M 3411
Tame, A.
   M 3412
Tate, Jane
   F 0002
Taupin, Bernie
   C 0317   C 0318
Tayler, L.
   M 3413
Taylor, A.J.W.
   M 3414
Taylor, Derek
   B 0542   B 0543   B 0544
   B 0545   B 0546   M 3415
   M 3416
Taylor, John Russell
   N 1047   N 1048   N 1049
   N 1050   RF0053   RF0160
   RF0295   RF0395   RF0407
Taylor, Laurie
   N 1051   RB0387   RB0428
   RB0537
Taylor, Leon
   C 0319
Teegarden, J.
   RF0166   RF0327
Telford, Ray
   M 3424
Tendler, Stewart
   N 1053
Tennis, Craig
   C 0320
Tepper, R.
   M 2011   M 3425
Terry, Carol D.
   B 0547
Test, Becky
   F 0023
Theroux, Paul
   M 3430
Thomas, Cheryl
   M 3439
Thomas, Michael
   M 3440
Thomas, Robert McG., Jr.
   N 0617   N 0618   N 0619
Thompson, A.
   RF0359
Thompson, Thomas
   M 3441   M 3442
Thorburn, Evan
   B 0402
Tiegel, E.
   M 3452   M 3453   M 3454
   M 3455
Tiger, Lionel
   M 3456
Tina
   RF0073
Titone, Robin
   B 0202   B 0203   M 1180
Tiven, Jon
   RB0297   RR0309
Tiven, Sally
   RB0297
Tobler, John
   B 0526   B 0548   B 0549
   C 0321   C 0322   C 0323
   C 0324
Toohey, J.V.
   M 3460
Took, B.
   RF0279   RF0318
Toumarkine, D.
   RF0138
Towarnicky, Carol
   N 1080
Trafalski, Tim

F 0155
Traiman, S.
  M 3468
Treaster, Joseph B.
  N 1083
Treen, Joe
  M 3469   M 3470   M 3471
Tremlett, George
  B 0550   B 0551   B 0552
  B 0553   M 3472
Trumbull, Robert
  N 1090
Truttschel, Mary Jo
  M 3480
Tucker, Ken
  RR0542
Tudor, Dean
  RB0099
Tuffin, George
  M 3482
Turan, K.
  RF0226
Turner, Roland
  C 0245   C 0246
Turner, Steve
  M 3483   M 3484
Tusher, W.
  M 3485
Tyfell, John
  C 0119
Tyler, T.
  M 0667   M 3493
Tyler, Tony
  B 0098   B 0099   B 0100
  B 0101   B 0102   B 0103
  B 0104   B 0105   B 0106
  B 0107   M 3494
Uncle Martin
  M 3501   RR0354
Unger, A.
  N 1112
Unger, C.
  M 3503
Ungvari, Tamas
  B 0556   B 0557
Uzarewicz, Sharon
  F 0096
Vance, Joel
  M 3516   M 3517   M 3518
  RR0150   RR0466
Van de Bunt, Jan
  B 0558   M 3519
Van der Meijden, Henk
  B 0559
van der Ven, Guus
  M 3520
Van Driver, Lavinia
  B 0560   B 0561
Van Estrik, Rob
  M 3521
Van Fulpen, Har
  B 0562   B 0563   B 0564
  B 0565   M 3522
Van Gelder, L.
  N 1118   N 1119
Van Haarlem, Rene
  B 0566   M 3523   M 3524
  RB0633
Van Matre, Lynn
  N 1120
Vermeer, Evert
  B 0566   M 0120   M 3288
  M 3525   M 3526   M 3527
  M 3528   M 3529   M 3530
  M 3531   M 3532   M 3533
  M 3534   M 3535   M 3536
  M 3537   M 3538   M 3539
  M 3540   M 3541   M 3542
  M 3543   M 3544   M 3545
  M 3546   M 3547   M 3548
  RB0059   RB0135   RB0146
  RB0152   RB0306   RB0339
  RB0372   RB0373   RB0519
  RB0563   RB0575   RF0124
  RR0079   RR0091   RR0217
  RR0390   RR0509
Vero, Diana
  M 3549

Verrill, A.
  M 3550
Villa, Massimo
  B 0107
Villone, Allison
  F 0111   M 3551
Virginia
  C 0327
Vitale, Neal
  M 3555
Voce, S.
  M 3556   M 3557
Vock, Wolfgang
  F 0025
Voelkel, Hermann
  B 0409
Vogel, Amos
  M 3558
Vogel, Karsten
  M 3559
Volcouve, Jacques
  P 0040
Vollmer, Jurgen
  B 0567   B 0568   M 3560
Von Faber, Karin
  M 3561
Wade, Kay
  F 0092   F 0093
Wagar, Martha
  F 0117
Wagman, John
  C 0254
Wahle, Michael
  F 0150
Wain, John
  M 3562   RB0548
Wale, Michael
  N 1122
Walker, J.
  RB0223   RB0247   RF0134
Walker, Jeff
  M 3563
Walker, Sandy
  M 3564
Wall, J.M.
  RF0254
Wallgren, Mark
  B 0569   M 3565   M 3566
  M 3567   M 3568   RB0252
  RB0629   RR0460   RR0467
  RR0468   RR0469   RR0470
Wallis, Anne
  F 0071
Walrustitty, Jethro Q.
  M 3570   RF0015
Walsh, A.
  M 3571   M 3572   M 3573
  M 3574   M 3575   M 3576
  M 3577   M 3578   M 3579
  M 3581   M 3582   M 3583
  M 3584   M 3585   M 3586
Walsh, R.
  M 3580
Walters, Lu
  C 0328
Walters, Ray
  N 1123
Wansell, Geoffrey
  N 1124   N 1125
Ward, Ed
  RR0095
Ward, Edmund O.
  RR0009   RR0187   RR0278
  RR0202   RR0507
Wardle, Irving
  N 1126   N 1127   N 1128
  RB0233
Warman, Christopher
  N 1130   N 1131
Washington, Joe
  S 0020   S 0037
Wasserman, E.
  M 3590
Wasserman, Marie-Therese
  B 0018
Watkins, France-Marie
  B 0583
Watkins, Roger
  M 3591   M 3592   M 3593

M 3594
Watson, Peter
  N 1134   N 1135
Watts, M.
  RR0295
Watts, Michael
  C 0329   M 3595   M 3596
  M 3597   M 3598   M 3599
  M 3600   M 3601   M 3602
  M 3603   M 3604   M 3605
  M 3606   M 3607   M 3608
  M 3609   M 3610   M 3611
  M 3612   M 3613   M 3614
  M 3615   M 3616   M 3617
Watts, Stephen
  N 1136   N 1137
Weaver, N.
  M 3618
Weber, D.
  M 3619
Weberman, A.
  N 1139
Webster, Alex
  M 3620
Weidmann, Gerhard
  B 0570
Weiner, Sue
  B 0202   B 0203   M 1180
Weinraub, Judith
  N 1140
Weinstein, G.
  N 1141
Weinstein, Robert
  M 3624
Weintz, Mark R.
  M 3219
Welch, C.
  RR0429
Welch, Chris
  M 3625   M 3626   M 3627
  M 3628   M 3629   M 3630
  M 3631   M 3632   M 3633
  M 3634
Welding, Pete
  M 3636
Wells, Jeff
  N 1143
Welsh, Michael
  RR0126
Wenner, Jann
  B 0571   B 0572   B 0573
  B 0574   B 0575   B 0576
  B 0577   B 0578   B 0579
  B 0580   B 0581   C 0331
  C 0332   C 0333   M 3637
  M 3638   M 3639   M 3640
  M 3641   M 3642   M 3643
  RR0072
Werbin
  M 3644
Werbin, S.
  M 3645   M 3646   M 3647
  M 3648
West, C.
  B 0118
West, Jessamyn
  M 3652
Westcott, J.
  M 3653
Westerbeck, C.L., Jr.
  RF0060   RF0259
Weymouth, Lally
  M 3657
Wharton, Flavia
  RF0120
Whatmough, Barb
  F 0022   F 0152
Whitall, S.
  M 3673   M 3674
White, A.
  M 3675   M 3676   M 3677
White, C.
  M 3678   M 3679   M 3680
White, R.
  RB0541
White, T.
  M 3681
White, Timothy
  M 3682   RR0044

Whitehorn, E.
  RF0227
Whitehorne, R.
  M 3683
Whittemore, R.
  RB0181
Whittingham, Charles A.
  M 3684
Wiberg, Carla
  B 0398
Wicker, R.
  M 3687
Wicker, Tom
  N 1150
Wickham, V.
  M 3617   M 3688   M 3689
  M 3690
Widener, Alice
  M 3691
Wiener, Jon
  B 0582   C 0334   M 3693
Wiener, T.
  M 3694
Wikler, Elinor
  M 3695
Wild, Harry
  S 0105   S 0106
Wilk, Max
  B 0583   B 0584   B 0585
  M 3698
William, Davis
  N 1151
Williams, Allan
  B 0586   B 0587   B 0588
  B 0589   B 0590   B 0591
Williams, B.
  M 3699
Williams, D.M.
  RB0264
Williams, Jean
  C 0335   M 3700   M 3701
  M 3702
Williams, Larry
  M 2052
Williams, M.
  M 3703
Williams, P.
  M 3704   M 3705   M 3706
Williams, R.
  M 3634   RR0021   RR0076
  RR0275
Williams, R.H.L.
  M 3707
Williams, Richard
  C 0336   C 0337   M 3708
  M 3709   M 3710   M 3711
  M 3712   M 3713   M 3714
  M 3715   M 3716   M 3717
  M 3718   M 3719   M 3720
  M 3721   M 3722   M 3723
  M 3724   M 3726   N 1152
  N 1153   N 1154   RR0026
  RR0269   RR0552
Williamson, B.
  RF0068   RF0278   RF0317
  RF0332   RF0370
Williamson, D.
  F 0107
Willis, Ellen
  M 3728   M 3729   RR0022
  RR0070   RR0267
Willis, Michael S.
  M 3730
Willmott, Nigel
  C 0338
Wilmer, Valerie
  M 3731
Wilson, David L.
  RR0319   RR0398
Wilson, John S.
  N 1156
Wilson, R.
  RF0204
Winchester, J.
  M 3732
Winkelmann, F.Ch.
  B 0106
Winn, James A.
  M 3739

Winner, Langdon
   RR0256   RR0277   RR0308
Winnick, Walter
   M 3740
Wise, Marsha
   M 3741
Wise, R.
   S 0064   S 0065   S 0066
   S 0067   S 0068
Wlaschek, Mathias
   B 0596
Woffinden, Bob
   B 0597   M 3743
Wohlfert-Wihlborg, L.
   M 3744
Wojcik, U.
   M 3745
Wolcott, J.
   M 3746
Wolf, W.
   RF0003   RF0136   RF0169
   RF0261   RF0305   RF0328
Wolfe, Tom
   M 3747   RB0356
Wondratschek, Wolf
   M 3749
Wood, M.
   RR0066

Wood, Michael
   C 0342   M 3750   M 3751
Wood, Terri
   F 0003
Woods, Linda
   F 0066
Woods-Lovett, Vickie
   F 0124
Wooler, Bob
   C 0343   C 0344   M 3752
Wootton, Richard
   B 0598
Wordsworth, Simon
   F 0145
Yamamoto, Y.
   B 0504
Yates, Paula
   C 0346
Yorke, Ritchie
   C 0347   C 0348   M 3772
   M 3773   M 3774   M 3775
   M 3776   M 3777   M 3778
   M 3779   M 3780   RR0274
Yoshinari, N.
   B 0226
Young, Bernice
   M 3781

Young, C.
   RF0320
Young, Charles M.
   M 3782   M 3783
Young, Jacob
   M 2143
Young, Mar
   F 0115   F 0125
Young, Paul
   B 0600
Yurchenco, Henrietta
   M 3789
Zabowski, B.
   RF0208
Zahn, Hartmut
   B 0432
Zander, Hannelore
   B 0192
Zanderbergen, George
   B 0601   B 0602
Zandstra, P.A.
   B 0254
Zehr, Martin
   M 3790
Zeilig, Ken
   M 3791
Zeisberg, Bernd
   B 0603

Zeitlin, Kim
   N 1177
Zeitlin, Ralph Wm.
   S 0117
Zelnick, C.R.
   N 1178
Zetner, Peter
   B 0024
Zibart, Eve
   C 0349
Ziebarth, D.
   M 3792
Ziebarth, Dolores
   M 3313
Ziemann, Hans Heinrich
   B 0280
Zimmerman, P.D.
   M 3793   RB0225   RB0248
Zito, Tom
   C 0173   N 0599
Zodiac
   M 3794
Zuckerman, E.
   RF0319

"A & M / Harrison: Pact That Failed."
M 3283
"A & M Wins Harrison's New Label."
M 0001
Abbey Road
F 0001
"Abbey Road."
M 1669
"Abbey Road - Nowhere Man."
M 2223
Abbey Road Review
F 0002
"Abbey Road Sight And Sound
Experience."
M 0002
Abbey Road (songbook) see The
Beatles/Abbey Road
Abbey Road: The Story Of The World's
Most Famous Recording Studios
C 0307
"ABKCO, Beatles Widen Battle In US, UK
Courts."
M 0005
"ABKCO Collects, But No 'So Fine'
Profit."
M 1988
"ABKCO Gets $5 Mil; Pays $800,000."
M 1826
"Abkco Profit Clipped By Beatles
Breakup: Rolling Stones Also
Sue."
M 0006
"ABKCO Wins One, Loses One In Beatles
Litigation."
M 1674
"ABKCO Wins Point On Jurisdiction In
Suit Vs. Beatles."
M 0007
"About A Lucky Band Who Made The
Grade."
M 1184
"About The Awful."
M 3157
"Accentuate The Appropriate."
N 0445
"According To John: Remark About
Christianity."
M 0009
"The Acid Dream Is Over."
N 0225
Across The Universe
B 0228 F 0003
"Acting Naturally."
M 0789
"Action Dropped Against Beatles."
N 0002
"Adult Okay Endangers Beatles?"
M 0013
"Advertisement Calls For A Beatles'
Concert."
N 0004
"Advertisements."
M 0014
"Advertising: Beatles To Sing Tunes For
Toys."
N 0271
"The Aesthetics Of Psychedelic Music."
M 2463
"The Aesthetics Of Rock."
M 2161
"After All Those Years - 'All Those
Years Ago'."
M 2567
"After Sgt. Pepper; Magical Mystery
Tour Album."
M 1625
"After The Beatles - An Interest In All
Things British."
N 0315
"After The Stones And The Beatles, Will
Allen Klein Take On The
Chancellor?"
M 1484
"Afterthoughts On The Beatles."
M 0609
"Agent Asks 'Come Together'."
N 0005
The Age Of Rock
C 0004 C 0169 C 0241 C 0249

C 0275 C 0342
The Age Of Rock 2
C 0178 C 0206
"Ahen - A Secret Weapon."
N 0007
"Ailes Sur Condres."
M 0016
"A Is For Apple."
N 0862
"Alan Livingston, Capitol's Former
President When The Beatles Came
Calling, Recalls 'British
Invasion'."
M 2011
"The Alarmingly Normal McCartneys."
M 1494
"The Album As Art Form: One Year After
Sgt. Pepper."
M 2484
Album Cover Album
C 0140
Das Album Der Beatles
B 0280
"Albums Showing A Beatle And Girl In
Nude Seized."
N 0008
"Alexander And Solberg Buy Beatles
Console."
M 2088
"Alien Alias."
M 0022
"Alistair Taylor Recalls How Brian
Epstein Discovered The Beatles."
M 0150
All About The Beatles
B 0154
All About The Beatles - No. 1
P 0001
"Allan Williams."
M 0120
"All Around The 'Butcher Cover'."
M 0915
"Allen Klein Co. Won $4,200,000 In
Beatles Case."
M 0024
"Allen Klein: 'I Cured All Their
Problems'."
M 0025
"Allen Klein Loses Tax Appeal."
N 0010
"Allen Klein Pins Down Beatles For $24
Million Suit In N.Y. Court."
M 0026
"Allen Klein's Conviction Upheld."
M 0027
"Allen Klein Seen Exciting Beatles
Deal."
M 0028
Alles Was Du Brauchst Ist Liebe
B 0136 B 0137
"All Grown Up: Revolver."
M 1510
"All He Was Saying, Is Give Peace A
Chance."
M 0873
"All My Own Work."
M 0029
"All Our Troubles Seemed So Far Away."
M 1324
"All Our Yesterdays: The Beatles
1962-70."
M 3708
"All Over The World."
M 2312
"All Paul."
M 3625
"All Paul's Work."
N 1134
"All Shine On."
M 1515
All That John Lennon 1940-1980: You
Said Good-bye But We Say Hello
B 0448
"All The Lonely People, Where Do They
All Come From?"
C 0108
"All The Way In St. Tropez."
M 2381
All The Years Of American Popular Music

C 0104
"All They Need Is Rishikesh."
N 0957
All Things Must Pass
F 0004 S 0001 S 0002
All Together Now
F 0005 F 0006
All Together Now; The First Complete
Beatles Discography, 1961-1975
B 0108 B 0109 B 0110
All You Needed Was Love; The Beatles
After The Beatles
B 0075 B 0076
All You Need Is Ears
B 0370 B 0371
All You Need Is Love
B 0030 C 0233 C 0234 C 0235
"All You Need Is Love."
N 0011
"'All You Need Is Love. Love Is All You
Need'."
N 0782
Alma De Goma
F 0007
"Al Sussman Responds To Critics."
M 3375
"Alvin Stardust Recalls The Day Ringo
Almost Drowned."
M 1423
"Amateur Tapes Of Beatles Concerts Cue
Legal Queries."
M 0040
"America And The Beatles."
M 3104
"American Bobbies Bug The Beatles."
M 0041
"An American Exile."
N 0341
The American Experience: A Radical
Reader
C 0119
"American Music Scene."
M 1530 M 3617
"American Report."
M 0042
"Americans Decide The Beatles Are
Harmless; Coast To Coast Audience
On Television."
N 0012
"American Tour Report."
M 1629
"America Picks Our Pops!"
M 0043
"America Woos The Fab Four."
M 0044
"'Among My Souvenirs'."
M 3349
"Analyzing The Beatles."
M 0943
"Anatomy Of A Bed In."
M 0972
"And All They Gotta Do Is Act
Naturally."
M 3563
"And Here Come The Beatles For One More
Time (Britain's Biggest-Ever
Selling Single)."
M 1568
"And Here They Are, The Beatles."
M 3525
"And In The Evening She's The Singer In
The Band."
M 3626
" ... And Paul Is On The Road Again."
M 3619
"And The Beat Goes On."
M 3132
"And This Is Me Doing My Businessman
Bit Back In '75."
M 3743
" ... And This Week George Reviews The
New Pop Records."
M 0048
"And What Have You Done?"
M 2511
"And When I Go Away."
M 1351
"And Yet Another Decca Tapes Release
..."

M 2500
The Annual Obituary 1980
    C 0245   C 0246
"Another Beatles Christmas Record."
    M 0049
"Another Beatle Tragedy On The Way."
    M 2462
"Another Day In The Life."
    M 3109
"Another Lennon."
    M 1594
"Another Lennon LP!"
    N 1040
"Another Open Letter To John Lennon."
    M 2123
"Another Random Note."
    C 0005
"Anti-Beatle Brigade."
    N 0015
"Anti-Beatles Club."
    M 0050
"Antoine Pirated Beatles' 'Sub' Paris
    Court Rules."
    M 0051
"Anyone Here Seen America."
    M 1729
"Apology After Taylor Party."
    N 0016
"Apotheosis, Legs And Rape By Lennon
    And Ono."
    M 2153
"Apparel Maker Is Enjoined From Using
    Name 'Beetles'."
    N 0017
"An Appeal To John, Paul, George And
    Ringo."
    N 0214
"Apple."
    M 0052
The Apple
    F 0008
"An Apple A Day."
    M 1768
"Apple And Peel."
    N 0018
"Apple And The Beatles."
    M 0053
"Apple Boutique Near-Giveaway Sale."
    M 0730
"'Apple' Boutique Part Of Mushrooming
    Empire Under Beatles Moniker."
    M 0054
"Apple Businessmen."
    M 0055
"Apple Closed; Beatles Give It Away."
    C 0006
"Apple Corps Four."
    M 1080
The Apple Family Tree House: A Record
    Discography
    B 0375
"Apple For The Beatles."
    N 0019
"Apple Is Closed; Beatles Give It All
    Away Free."
    M 0056
Apple JuCe
    F 0009
"The Apple Label."
    M 0945
"Apple Mysteries."
    M 0057
"Apple On Capitol."
    M 0058
"Apple Opens."
    M 0059
"Apple Peel Encore."
    N 0020
Apple Press
    F 0010
"Apple's 'Bangledesh' Raises $4.5 Mil
    For Kids; Anyone Else Taking A
    Bite?"
    M 0060
"Apple Scruffs Come To Dinner."
    M 0102
Apple Scruffs Inc.
    F 0011
"Apples For The Beatles."

M 0061
Apple's Kin
    F 0012
The Apple Song Book
    S 0003
"The Apple Story, 1968-1973: Part One."
    M 1352
"The Apple Story, 1968-1973: Part
    Three."
    M 1354
"The Apple Story, 1968-73: Part Four."
    M 1355
"The Apple Story, 1968-73: Part Two."
    M 1353
"Apple Sues Capitol For $16 Million."
    M 3284
Apple To The Core: The Unmaking Of The
    Beatles
    B 0338   B 0339   B 0340   B 0341
    B 0342
"Appoint Receiver For The Beatles,
    Allen Klein Out."
    M 0062
"An Appreciative Look At The Beatles."
    M 0667
"April 1963: The Start Of A Legend."
    M 1738
"Archbishop On Beatles' Search."
    N 0021
"Are The Beatles Going Backwards?"
    M 3571
"Are The Beatles Slipping?"
    M 0741
"Are The Beatles Waning?"
    C 0126
"Are They More Pop Than Maharishi Now?"
    M 0063
"Are They Talented."
    N 0022
"Around And About, By Beatcomber."
    C 0184
Around The Beatles
    F 0013
Around The World With The Beatles
    P 0002
"Art Beat Of The 60s."
    M 0735
"Art By Yoko Ono Shown At Museum In
    Syracuse."
    N 0434
"Art Gallery Cleared In Lennon Case."
    N 0026
"Art Is Big, Round, And Good."
    M 2974
"Artist's Biographies."
    M 0073
"Artists Express Love, Respect,
    Gratefulness For Ex-Beatle."
    C 0335   M 3700
"An Artist With A Thousand Visions."
    N 0330
The Art Of The Beatles
    B 0032   B 0186
"The Arts: From Boogie To Bogey."
    N 0027
"Arts In Society: John Lennon's School
    Days."
    C 0342
"Art Songs, 4 Big Fans And More."
    N 0470
"The Arts: Paul McCartney And Wings."
    M 0515
"The Arts: Paul's Return."
    N 1122
"The Art World, A New Year's Earful."
    N 0435
"As I Write This Letter."
    M 0077   M 0676   M 0677
As I Write This Letter: An American
    Generation Remembers The Beatles
    B 0114   C 0289
"Ask Mark: Mark Lewisohn's Letters
    Page."
    M 1966
"As One Of The Beatles."
    M 0078
As Time Goes By: Living In The Sixties
    B 0542   B 0543   B 0544   B 0545
"As You Picked 'Em: 'The Beatles

1971-1976'."
    M 0083
"At A Recording Session With The
    Beatles."
    C 0301   M 3290
"At Home With The Lennons."
    M 0696
"At Last! The Beatles Talk About Sex,
    Drugs, Their Women...And Each
    Other!"
    M 2197
"At London's Finsbury Park Astoria ...
    Their Spectacular Christmas
    Show."
    M 1630
"At Pattie And George's Press
    Reception."
    M 0086
"At The Garden."
    M 0087
"At The Premiere."
    M 3129
"Attorney For Lennon Slaying Suspect
    Bows Out And Gets Protection."
    N 0990
"Attorneys To Study Capitol's Finances
    In Cetena Complaint."
    M 3285
"ATV Bid Is Extended."
    N 0029
"ATV Bids Again."
    N 0030
"ATV Bids £9.5 M For Northern Songs."
    N 0835
"ATV Defeat In Bid For Northern Songs."
    N 0250
"ATV Leaves Door Open For Beatles."
    M 0089
"ATV Meets On Northern Songs Bid."
    N 0031
"ATV Music Charges Beatles
    Infringement."
    M 1989
"ATV Music Put Up For Sale; Ex-Beatle
    Bids For Northern."
    M 0090
"ATV Must Bid Again."
    N 0032
"ATV Plea To Panel."
    N 0033
"ATV Reject A Beatles Film."
    N 0034
"ATV Sees 11pc Fall In Profits."
    N 0035
"ATV's Stake In Northern Songs Now Tops
    50 Percent."
    M 0091
"ATV View On Northern Songs Profit."
    N 0036
"ATV Wins Cliffhanger vs. Beatles In
    Fight To Take Over Northern
    Songs."
    M 0092
"ATV Wins Northern Songs."
    N 0753
"Auctions."
    N 0925
"Audience In Paris Gives The Beatles An
    Ovation."
    N 0037
"Aug. 15, 1966: Meeting The Beatles."
    M 3271
"August 1976."
    M 0119
"August 1964 Revisited."
    M 1187
"The Australian Discography."
    M 1880
"The Authenticity And The Integrity Of
    John Lennon's Protest."
    N 0039
"Author Returns His Military Medal."
    N 0040
"Avant Garde Festival Held At Armory."
    N 0987
"Award In 'Surprising Country'."
    N 0041
"Baby Grand Guitar."
    M 0094

"Baby You're A Rich Man."
   M 0512   M 0513
"Bachelor Paul."
   C 0011
"Background To The Beatles."
   M 3707
"Back On The Merseyside."
   M 0151
"Back On The Road."
   M 0095
"Back Page: A Few Words About A
      Working-Class Lad From Liverpool,
      A Great Capitalist Of Our Time."
   M 0841
"Back Pages."
   M 2353
"Backstage With The Beatles."
   M 0887
"Back To Blighty With The Beatles."
   M 2246
"Back To The Egg."
   M 0096
"'Back To The Egg': Wings' New Album Is
      A Search For Simpler Things."
   M 1543
"'Back Where You Belong'."
   N 0042
"Bad Business."
   N 0043
"Badfinger: A Musical Tragedy."
   M 0099
"Badfinger: Rising From The Ashes."
   M 0100
Bag One; A Suite Of Lithographs
   B 0301
Bag One Exhibition Catalog
   B 0302
"Bag One: Opening Of The Show Of Erotic
      Lithographs At The Nordness
      Galleries."
   M 0101
"Bailey's Box."
   M 0106
"Baker Street Battles Beatles."
   M 0111
"Baldwin, Piano Maker, Plans To Enter
      Market For Electric Guitars."
   N 0044
La Ballade De John & Yoko
   B 0041
Balladen Om John Och Yoko
   B 0042
The Ballad Of John And Yoko
   B 0039   B 0040
"'The Ballad Of John And Yoko'."
   M 0122
"Ballad Of John, Yoko, And Frank
      Zappa."
   M 0064
"The Ballad Of Paul And Tokyo."
   M 2254
"The Ballad Style In The Early Music Of
      The Beatles."
   C 0227   M 2340
Bananas
   M 0130
"Band On The Bayou: The McCartneys'
      Cruise Through New Orleans."
   M 0131
"Band On The Run."
   M 1356
Band On The Run (songbook) see Wings:
      Band On The Run
"Band On The Run: Wings Soar Sunward."
   M 0132
"The Band's Last Waltz."
   M 2116
"Bang! Beatles Are Back!"
   M 0133
"Bangla Desh Love Feast."
   M 3516
"Bangla Desh LP: A Federal Case?"
   M 0134
"Bangladesh: The Film Of The Concert."
   M 0135
"Banner Unfurled In House; Peace
      Demonstrator Held."
   N 0046
"Ban Wings On Radio (In Japan)."

M 0141
"Barbara Bach & Ringo Are Now Starring
      In An Altered State."
   M 0144
"Barbara Bach Keeps Him Going, Says
      Ringo Starr, Still Banging The
      Drum Slowly For John."
   M 2953
"Bards Of Pop."
   M 0145
"Bargaining In Court."
   N 0991
"Barham's Bandi."
   M 2972
"The Basic Repertoire."
   M 2091
"Battle Of John And Yoko."
   M 0200
"BBC Cancel Film Of Beatles."
   N 0054
"B.B.C. Radio Bans Song On Ulster By
      McCartney."
   N 0055
"Beach A Whale For Peace."
   M 0202
The Beatage (Die Fruhen Tage Des Rock
      In Deutschland Und Gross
      britannien)
   C 0244
"Beatalic Graphospasms."
   M 1892
"Beatarama."
   M 0203
Beat Book One
   C 0015
"The Beat Boys."
   M 3037
"Beatcomber In Book Form."
   C 0016
Beat - Die Sprachlose Opposition
   C 0010
"Beat Elite."
   M 0204
"The Beat Goes On And On And On."
   N 1010
Beat Land
   F 0014
Beatle!
   B 0073
"'Beatle' Admits Car Charge."
   N 0056
"Beatle Admits He Drove Carelessly."
   N 0057
Beatleads
   F 0015
"Beatle & English News."
   M 0205   M 0206
"Beatle And Other Fanzines."
   M 3300
"A Beatle And Wife Are Fined $1,200 In
      Marijuana Case."
   N 0058
"Beatle And Wife Fined £500."
   N 0059
"Beatle And Wife Fly To U.S."
   N 0060
"Beatle And Wife Questioned."
   N 0061
"Beatle And Wife Remanded."
   N 0062
"Beatleantics Cause Headaches (In
      California)."
   M 3452
"Beatle At The Back."
   M 0152
"A Beatle At The National Theatre."
   N 0063
"A Beatle A Week."
   M 0742
"Beatle Back From Meditation."
   N 0064
"Beatle Ballet."
   M 0207
"A Beatle Ballet."
   N 0065
The Beatle Beat
   S 0004
"Beatle Beginnings: The Polydor
      Recordings."

M 3790
"Beatle Believers Band Together."
   M 0208
"Beatle Bomb."
   M 0209
The Beatle Book
   B 0255   B 0435   B 0436
"Beatle Books."
   M 1424
"Beatle Books: A Discriminating Guide."
   M 3170
"Beatle Bookshelf."
   M 0210   M 0211   M 3171
The Beatle Book Souvenir Song Album Of
      Recorded Hits
   S 0005
"Beatle Booted."
   M 0212
"Beatle Boots."
   M 2573
"The Beatle Break."
   N 0066
"Beatle-Browed Israeli Officials Ponder
      Permit For Britain's Beatles."
   M 0213
"Beatle Bugs Smothers Bros. In Comeback
      Bow; Oust Lennon."
   M 0502
"Beatle Burlesque: A Little Song, A
      Little Dance, A Little Seltzer
      Down Your Pants."
   M 3746
"The Beatle Business."
   N 0804
"Beatle Business; Record Sales."
   M 0214
"Beatle Buys ...."
   C 0017
"Beatle Buys Convent."
   N 0067
"Beatle Cartoon Remembered."
   M 0215
"Beatle Criticized By Dr. Graham."
   N 0068
"Beatle Crush."
   M 2551   N 0896
"Beatle Cut."
   N 0069
"Beatledammerung."
   M 0216
"Beatle Data: They Should've Known
      Better."
   M 2117
"The Beatle Detective."
   M 1425
"Beatle Doubletalk."
   M 3572
"Beatle Drops Northern Songs Link."
   N 0070
"Beatle Equity."
   N 0071
Beatlefan
   F 0016
"Beatlefan Letters."
   M 0217
"Beatlefan Photo Contest."
   M 0218
"Beatle Fans At NY Commodore For Two
      Days."
   M 0219
Beatle Fans Of The World Unite
   F 0017
"The Beatlefan Survey."
   M 3174
"Beatlefan Trivia Quiz."
   M 0220
"The Beatlefan Trivia Test."
   M 0221
"Beatlefax And Beatle Fans."
   M 0982
"Beatle Feet."
   M 0222
"Beatlefest."
   M 0223
"Beatlefest '80."
   M 1098
"Beatlefest '83."
   M 0537
"Beatlefest '82."

M 1833
"Beatlefest In Jersey."
N 0072
"Beatlefest '78: New York, February 4 &
    5, 1978."
M 1263
"Beatlefest '79 - NYC."
M 0224
"Beatle Fever Hits Britain."
M 0225
Beatle Film Society Of America
F 0018
"Beatle Flashes."
M 0226
"Beatle Garden Charge."
N 0073
"Beatle George And Where He's At."
M 1732
"Beatle George Harrison In A & M
    Production Deal."
M 0227
"Beatle George Marries An Actress."
N 0074
"Beatle George Visits Los Angeles."
M 0228
"Beatle Guitar Plea."
N 0075
Beatle Hairdos & Setting Patterns
P 0003
"Beatle Harrison Target Of $10 Mil Pact
    Suit By A & M."
M 0229
"Beatle Hits: It's 'Yesterday' Again In
    Britain."
M 1462
"Beatle Hysteria Hits U.S."
N 0883
"Beatle Image Crisis Again - Is It
    Pursuit Of Buck Or Art."
M 2490
"Beatle In The Raw."
M 0230
"Beatle Is Fined $200."
N 0076
" 'Beatle It'."
M 0985
"Beatle Lennon Gains In Fight To Stay
    In U.S."
M 0231
"Beatle Listen-In."
M 1573
"Beatle LP Boycott: Outrageous Price."
M 0232
"Beatle Lyrics Can Help Adolescents
    Identify And Understand Their
    Emotional Health Problems."
M 3460
Beatle Madness
B 0225
Beatle Magazine
F 0019
"Beatle Manager Accused."
N 0077
Beatlemania
F 0020   P 0004
"Beatlemania."
    M 0233   M 0234   M 0235   M 1264
    M 1306   M 1574   M 2151   M 3148
    N 0078
Beatlemania; An Adolescent
    Contraculture
    B 0128
"Beatlemania And The Fast Buck:
    Beatle-Touched Items Sold At
    Fancy Prices."
M 0236
Beatlemania: An Illustrated Filmography
    B 0241
"Beatlemania: A Review."
M 2954
"Beatlemania - A Study Of Adolescent
    Enthusiasm."
M 3414
" 'Beatlemania' Bites Britain As Four
    From Liverpool Become A Show Biz
    Phenomenon; Press Clips Top
    Queen's."
M 3591
" 'Beatlemania' Brings Protest."

N 0079
"Beatlemaniacs: Collectors Still
    Treasure 'Fab Four' Memorabilia."
N 0229
"Beatlemaniacs Never Die (But They Sure
    Get Carried Away)."
C 0212   M 2214
"Beatlemania Doesn't Stop With Disks,
    Mops Up With Fancy $2 Fan Club
    Too."
M 0237
" 'Beatlemania' Does Solid Job Showing
    What Era Was Like."
M 0238
"Beatlemania Hits Dominion So Hard Even
    French Canadians Show Interest."
M 0239
"Beatlemania Hits The U.S."
M 0240
"Beatlemania In Canada This Summer."
M 0124
"Beatlemania In Stockholm."
M 0647
"Beatlemania In Texas."
N 0080
" 'Beatlemania' Is A Scrapbook Of Soggy
    Standards."
M 1627
"Beatlemania Is Reborn In Wake Of
    Tragedy."
M 1842
"Beatlemania: I Wanna Hold Your
    Wallet."
M 3362
Beatlemania 1967-1970, Vol. II
    S 0007
Beatlemania 1963-1966, Vol. I
    S 0006
" 'Beatlemania' On Tour."
M 1196
"Beatlemania Returns As 'Let It Be'
    Clicks."
M 0975
"Beatlemania Revamps Britain Disk Biz
    By Booming Teen-Angled Indie
    Prods."
M 3592
"Beatlemania's Boys In The Band."
M 2166
"Beatlemania's Second Wish."
M 0241
"Beatlemania Still Pulls Fans To Boston
    Festival; Tokyo Gig Is Featured."
M 0242
"Beatlemania Strikes Again!"
M 0243
" 'Beatlemania' Tees Four Rock
    Spinoffs."
M 2326
Beatle-Mania, The Authentic Photos.
    Volume 1, No. 1
    P 0005
"Beatlemania; The FBI Was Taking
    Notes."
M 0244
Beatlemania: The Illustrated Treasury
    B 0044
"Beatlemania: The London Stage Show."
M 2512
"Beatlemania: The Most Or The Worst?"
M 0245
"Beatlemania: The Virus Of '64."
M 1140
"Beatle Mania To Dominate
    Philadelphia."
M 1386
"Beatlemania Turns To 'Beatle-waneia'."
M 0246
"Beatlemania: Will EMI Let It Be?"
N 0982
"Beatlemania Without Beatles Is Pale
    Stuff At Let It Be Pic Preem."
M 0247
Beatlemanie
    F 0021
"Die 'Beatlemanie' - Ein Ausdruck
    Unserer Zeit."
M 3159
"Beatle Man; Manager For Beatles."

M 0248
"Beatle Memorabilia Selling Big."
N 0081
"Beatle Menace: How To Preserve Public
    Safety When Four Kids From
    Liverpool Visit Canada."
M 1160
"A Beatle Metaphysic."
M 0821
"Beatle Mobs Move In And ItIs
    Panicsville."
M 1331
"Beatle $."
M 0323
"Beatle Money."
M 0743
"Beatlemonium At Stadium - Youngsters
    Get Carried Away."
M 1387
"A Beatle Named George."
C 0018
"A Beatle Named Ringo."
C 0019
"Beatle News."
C 0020   M 0249
"Beatlenews Roundup."
M 0250
"Beatle News Round-Up."
M 2464
"Beatle News Sept. '62."
M 0251
"Beatle On The Battlefront."
N 0014
"Beatle Paul And LSD."
M 0252
Beatle Paul McCartney - His Story By
    Himself
    P 0006
"Beatle Paul To Marry."
N 0082
The Beatle Peace Followers
    F 0022
"Beatle Pen Pals."
M 0253
"Beatle People: The Most Incredible
    Following The World Has Ever
    Known, Part 1."
M 0911
"Beatle People: The Most Incredible
    Following The World Has Ever
    Known."
M 0912
"Beatlephilia: Strange Rumbling In
    Pepperland."
M 3259
"Beatle Picture Discs."
M 2368
"Beatle Plague."
N 0083
"Beatle Quickies."
M 0254
"Beatle Quiz."
M 1181
"A Beatle Returns Award As A Protest."
N 0361
Beatle Ringo Starr - The Story Of A
    Ring-A-Ding Star
    P 0007
"Beatle-Rock."
M 0535
"Beatle Roundup."
M 0255
Beatles
    B 0446   F 0023
"Beatles."
    C 0021   M 0256   M 0257   M 0258
    M 0259   M 0868   M 3637
Die Beatles
    B 0403
I Beatles
    B 0139
Les Beatles
    B 0140   B 0167   B 0492   B 0493
Les Beatles (New edition)
    B 0168   B 0169
"Les Beatles."
    M 0924
Los Beatles
    B 0142   B 0513

Los Beatles (Second ed.)
  B 0045
The Beatles
  B 0046   B 0047   B 0048   B 0098
  B 0119   B 0237   B 0242   B 0256
  B 0374   B 0445   B 0460   B 0461
  B 0477   B 0479   B 0499   B 0520
  B 0530   B 0531   B 0532   B 0533
  B 0548   B 0549   B 0601   F 0024
  P 0008   P 0009   P 0010   S 0008
The Beatles (Second ed.)
  B 0099   B 0602
"The Beatles."
  C 0022   C 0023   C 0024   C 0025
  C 0026   C 0027   C 0080   C 0106
  C 0141   C 0169   C 0203   C 0286
  C 0287   C 0302   C 0309   C 0065
  M 0260   M 0261   M 0262   M 0610
  M 0736   M 0869   M 0997   M 3494
  N 0084
The Beatles: Abbey Road
  S 0009
"Beatles - Abbey Road."
  M 2224
"The Beatles' Abbey Road."
  C 0121
"Beatles' Abbey Road LP Warms Up Price
    Wars In British Disk Shops."
  M 0263
Beatles/Abbey Road - Matching Music
    Book
  S 0010
The Beatles: A Bibliography
  B 0336
"Beatles Accept ATV Offer On Their
    Songs."
  M 0264
The Beatles: A Collection
  B 0155
"The Beatles, A Color Folio."
  M 0093
The Beatles: A Day In The Life; The
    Day-By-Day Diary, 1960-1970
  B 0487   B 0488   B 0489
The Beatles - A Dell Giant - Complete
    Life Stories
  P 0013
"Beatles: A Find For England's Balance
    Of Payment."
  M 0265
The Beatles Again
  B 0111
"The Beatles Again."
  M 3049
"Beatles Again Offs Get Back."
  M 0266
"The Beatles Again: The Saddest True
    Story."
  M 3772
"Beatles Again Top Gold Disk Winners In
    RIAA R66 List; Yanks Bounce
    Back."
  M 0267
"'Beatles Again' You Figure It."
  M 0268
"The Beatles: A Good Non-Literary
    Education Under Forty."
  C 0002
The Beatles: A Hard Day's Night
  S 0011
"The Beatles: A Hard Day's Night."
  M 2572
"The Beatles' 'A Hard Day's Night'."
  N 1136
The Beatles Album File And Complete
    Discography
  B 0471
"Beatles All The Way."
  C 0149
"The Beatles: All Things Must Pass."
  M 0621
"Beatles Almanac."
  M 0269
"Die Beatles Als Musical-Stars - Der
    Neue Hit In London."
  M 3113
"The Beatles: A Mandala."
  M 1004
The Beatles American Discography And

Price Guide
  B 0049
"The Beatles Amps."
  M 1357
The Beatles: A Musical Evolution
  B 0416
"The Beatles: An Almanac."
  M 0270
"Beatles Analyzed."
  N 0928
"Beatles' Anarchic Mystery."
  N 0918
"Beatles And Before."
  M 2291
"Beatles And Bibles, Drifting And
    Dope."
  N 0956
Beatles & Co
  B 0286
"The Beatles And E.M.I. Records."
  M 2488
"Beatles And Fans Meet Social Set; Chic
    And Shriek Mingle At Paramount
    Benefit Show."
  N 1043
"The Beatles And Film Art."
  M 3372
"The Beatles And New York Radio."
  M 1759
"Beatles & Stones' Risque LP Covers
    Pose Sales Woes."
  M 0516
"The Beatles And The Guru."
  C 0067   M 0635
"The Beatles & The New Wave."
  M 1358
"The Beatles And The Press."
  M 0153
"The Beatles And The Rolling Stones;
    Effect On Jazz Industry."
  M 0271
"The Beatles And The Voice From
    Beyond."
  M 3353
"Beatles And Two M.P.'s Favor Legal
    Marijuana."
  N 0085
Beatles & Wings Fan Club
  F 0025   F 0026
The Beatles: An Illustrated Diary
  B 0562
The Beatles; An Illustrated Record
  B 0100   B 0101
The Beatles; An Illustrated Record,
    rev. ed.
  B 0102   B 0103
The Beatles; An Illustrated Record (2d
    rev. ed.)
  B 0104   B 0105
"The Beatles: An Inside Look At The Fab
    Four."
  N 0086
Beatles Anniversary
  P 0014
The Beatles Apart
  B 0597
"Beatles Apart."
  M 3189
"Beatles Apparently Win Battle Against
    Take-Over."
  N 0087
"Beatles' Apple In Aug. Bow."
  M 2235
"Beatles Apple Sets Legal Poser."
  N 0898
Beatles Appreciation Fan Club
  F 0027
Beatles Appreciation Society
  F 0028
Beatles Appreciation Society Magazine
  F 0029
"Les Beatles Apres."
  M 2234
"The Beatles Are At It Again."
  N 0419
The Beatles Are Back
  P 0015
"The Beatles Are Back"
  M 0272

"Beatles Are Back With A Bang!"
  M 1332
"Beatles Are Blamed By Agnew."
  N 0088
"Beatles Are Booed At Manila Airport."
  N 0089
"Beatles Are Bootlegged Again!"
  M 0697
"The Beatles Are Dead! Long Live The
    Beatles!"
  M 3219
"The Beatles Are Dead? Long Live The
    Beatles!"
  M 3413
"Beatles Are Enshrined In Mme.
    Tussaud's Waxworks."
  M 2105
"'The Beatles Are Free Men'."
  N 0090
"Beatles Are 'Helpful,' Prince Philip
    Thinks."
  N 0091
The Beatles Are Here
  P 0016
"The Beatles Are Invading New York City
    Again - On Film."
  N 0486
"Beatles Are 'Just Cuddlesome'."
  N 0092
"Beatles 'Are Not Breaking Up'."
  N 0093
"The Beatles Are Planning Full-Scale
    U.S. Campaign."
  N 0094
Beatles Around The World
  P 0017
Beatles Around The World - No. 1
  P 0018
Beatles Around The World - No. 2
  P 0019
"Beatles Arrive In Tokyo."
  N 0095
"Beatles Art Gallery."
  M 0273
The Beatles As Act: A Study Of Control
    In A Musical Group
  B 0514
"The Beatles As Act: A Study Of Control
    In A Musical Group."
  M 3304
"The Beatles As Artists; A Meditation
    For December Ninth."
  M 3739
"Beatles As A World Commodity."
  M 0274
"Beatles As Cinderella: A Soviet Fairy
    Tale."
  C 0206   M 2135
"Beatles As Healers."
  N 0096
"The Beatles As Merchandise: A List Of
    Licensed Manufacturers & Their
    Products."
  C 0028
"The Beatles As Sermon."
  M 0275
"Beatles' Assets 'Not Now In
    Jeopardy'."
  N 0097
"Beatles Assigned Receiver; End To
    Partnership Sought."
  N 0098
"Beatles Astonished By Queen's Awards;
    Other Britons, Too."
  N 0099
The Beatles: A Study In Drugs, Sex And
    Revolution
  B 0404
"The Beatles - As You've Never Seen
    Them Before."
  M 0276
" 'The Beatles At Abbey Road'."
  M 0946
"The Beatles At Bowl? EMI Mulling
    Release."
  M 3678
The Beatles At Carnegie Hall
  P 0020
"The Beatles At No. 3."

C 0029
"The Beatles At Shea Stadium."
    M 1092
"'The Beatles At The Beeb'."
    M 0660
The Beatles At The Beeb; The Story Of
    Their Radio Career, 1962-1965
    B 0265   B 0266
"Beatles At The Cavern In The Early
    Days."
    M 0278
The Beatles At The Hollywood Bowl
    S 0012   S 0013
"Beatles At The Hollywood Bowl; Beatles
    Live! At The Star Club In
    Hamburg, Germany; 1962."
    M 3392
"The Beatles At The Star Club."
    M 1426
Beatles A - Z
    B 0333
The Beatles A To Z
    B 0202   B 0203
"'The Beatles A-Z'."
    M 1180
"The Beatles A To Z."
    M 0277
"Beatles, ATV Seen Nearing Harmony."
    M 0279
"Les Beatles Au Futur."
    M 0989
"The Beatles Australian Singles."
    M 1398
"The Beatles Autumn Tour."
    M 0280
"The Beatles; A Year In The Lives."
    M 0281
Beatles Baby Family Album - Beatle
    Mania Collectors Item, Volume 1,
    No. 1
    P 0021
"Beatles Back?"
    M 0282
"Beatles Back Home."
    C 0030
"The Beatles Back Home."
    M 3335
"Beatles Back? Producer Says It May
    Happen."
    M 0283
"Beatles Backtracks: The Strange Story
    Of The Hamburg Tapes."
    M 1031
"Beatles Bag Two Of EMI's Four
    Goldisks."
    M 0284
The Beatles Ballads
    S 0014
"Beatles Batter All B.O. Records;
    Parlay N.Y. Fan Hysteria Into
    $150,000 Gross."
    M 3161
"Beatles Battle Effort To Buy Firm."
    N 0100
"Beatles BBC Tapes."
    M 1176
"The Beatles Beat A Retreat From Fans
    In Cleveland."
    N 0101
The Beatles Beat Downunder
    F 0031
Beatles Beat Fan Club
    F 0030
"Beatles Beating A New Path To
    Corporate Karma."
    M 0285
"Beatles, Beatles, Beatles."
    M 3410
The Beatles: Beatles For Sale
    S 0015
"Beatles Beats."
    N 0102
"Beatles Begin New British Art Push."
    M 2106
"Beatles Begin Their Career As
    'Sages'."
    N 0465
"Beatles Beguile East Coast."
    M 0286

"Beatles 'Believe In Rebirth'."
    N 0103
"Beatles Besieged; Allen Klein To
    Manage Enterprises."
    M 0287
Beatles Best
    S 0016   S 0017
"The Beatles' Best Back As Film Aide."
    M 1735
"The Beatles' Betrayal."
    C 0200
"Beatles Beware! 120,000 Fans Are After
    You."
    M 0744
Beatles Biblia; A Negy Apostol Mitosza
    B 0556   B 0557
"Beatles' Bid For Firm Fails; Battle
    Results In 'Mexican Standoff'."
    N 0104
"Beatles Blanket U.S. Charts; 'Love'
    Vaults 1,000,000."
    M 0288
"Beatles Blast Own Hit Disc!"
    M 0289
"Beatles Boffola In Solo LP Sales."
    M 0290
"Beatles Boffo 250G In Chicago."
    M 0291
"Beatles Bonanza."
    M 0292
"Beatles' Bonn Tour A Sales
    Blitzkrieg."
    M 0293
The Beatles Book
    B 0153   C 0068   C 0092   C 0095
    C 0107   C 0108   C 0120   C 0126
    C 0137   C 0168   C 0180   C 0181
    C 0218   C 0250   C 0276   C 0308
    F 0032   P 0022
The Beatles Book Calendar For 1964
    P 0023
The Beatles Book Christmas Special
    B 0135
"The Beatles Book First Song Pop.
    Poll."
    M 0294
"The Beatles Book Overseas Song Pop
    Poll."
    M 0295
"Beatles Book Relaunched Oct 1st."
    M 0888
The Beatles Book - Special Xmas Extra
    P 0024
"The Beatles Book: The Only Complete
    History Of The World's Most
    Famous Group."
    M 0889
"Beatles Booming Britains Biscuits Biz
    Past $60-Mil Mark; EMI Shares
    Soar."
    M 0296
"Beatles Boost EMI Income To New High."
    M 0297
"Beatles Bootleg Albums: A Rip-Off Or A
    Boon?"
    M 2465
"The Beatles Bootleg Roundup."
    M 0298
"Beatles Bourgeois?"
    N 0105
"Beatles Break Bounds Of Pop."
    M 0299
"Beatles Breaking Up: McCartney."
    M 0300
"Beatles Breakup Cues Furor Over A
    Split Copyright."
    M 0301
"The Beatles: Bridging The Cultural
    Gap."
    M 0045
"Beatles: Bridging The Gap."
    N 1126
"The Beatles Bring Shea To A Wild Pitch
    Of Hysteria."
    N 0770
"Beatles Broadcast."
    M 0745
"Beatles Broaden Role In Business; Form
    Concern For Ventures In Films And

Recordings."
    N 0988
"Beatles Broke? McCartney: Aye; Klein
    Denies It."
    M 0302
"Beatles Broke, Paul Charges."
    M 0303
The Beatles Bumper Songbook
    S 0018
"Beatles Business Booms But Blessings
    Mixed."
    M 0304
"Beatles Buy Advanced Tape Recorder."
    M 0305
"Beatles Buzzing Like Business Bees
    'Round Blossoming Apple Corps
    Deals."
    M 3162
The Beatles, By Royal Command: Their
    Own Story Of The Most Fabulous
    Night Of Their Career
    B 0050
"Beatles: Can Muhammad Ali Coax Back?"
    N 0106
"Beatles Cartoon Quiz."
    M 0811   M 0812
"The Beatles Cartoons And Me."
    M 0813
"Beatles Case QC Speaks Of Rule Of
    Democracy."
    N 0107
Beatles Catalog
    B 0051   B 0052
The Beatles Cavern Club
    F 0033
"Beatles Change Drummer!"
    C 0031
Les Beatles: Chansons Illustrees 2
    B 0017
"Beatles: Cheerful Coherence."
    M 0306
The Beatles: Chord Organ Edition
    S 0019
"The Beatles' Christmas Album."
    M 0307
"The Beatles' Christmas Concert."
    M 1739
"The Beatles' Christmas Fan Club
    Discs."
    M 0154
"The Beatles Christmas Record."
    M 0308
"The Beatles' Christmas Records."
    M 1967
"Beatles' City General Manager."
    M 0309
The Beatles City Magazine
    F 0034
The Beatles Classic Guitar Pieces:
    Tutor
    S 0020
"Beatles' Closing Concert On Coast
    Attracts 25,000."
    N 0108
The Beatles Collection
    B 0053
Beatles Collector
    F 0035
Beatles Collectors Clubs Of America
    F 0036
The Beatles Color Pin-Up Album
    P 0026
"The Beatles Come In Colors."
    M 0310
The Beatles Complete
    S 0021   S 0022   S 0023
The Beatles - Complete Coverage -
    Exclusive Photos - The Beatles
    United States Arrivals And
    Appearances
    P 0027
The Beatles Complete Discography. 5th
    rev. ed.
    B 0360
The Beatles Complete Discography. 7th
    ed.
    B 0361
Beatles Complete - Easy Guitar
    S 0024

The Beatles Complete - For Easy Guitar
   S 0025
The Beatles Complete: For Piano And
   Guitar
   S 0026
The Beatles Complete: Guitar Edition
   S 0027
The Beatles Complete - Guitar/Vocal
   S 0028
The Beatles Complete Life Stories -
   Special Edition
   P 0028
The Beatles Complete -
   Piano/Organ/Vocal
   S 0029
The Beatles Complete: Piano Vocal/Easy
   Organ
   S 0030
Beatles - Complete Story From Birth To
   Now
   P 0029
The Beatles Complete Works
   S 0031
Beatles: Concert-ed Efforts
   B 0558
"The Beatles Concert-ed Extras."
   M 3526   M 3527   M 3528
"Beatles' Concert On Tape 'N' Toll
   First Of Kind."
   M 0311
"Beatles Confidential: Twelve Years
   Later And You Still Don't Know."
   M 3493
The Beatles Connection
   F 0037
The Beatles Conquer America: The
   Photographic Record Of Their
   First Tour
   B 0257
"The Beatles Considered."
   M 1849
Els "Beatles" Contra Els "Rolling
   Stones"
   B 0380
"Beatles Convention In Boston Attracts
   Vendors But Few Mourners."
   N 0109
"Beatles' Copyrights Guarded."
   M 0312
"Beatles 'Could Yet Work Things Out
   Satisfactorily'."
   N 0110
"Beatles Crossword."
   M 0986
"Beatles Crossword Puzzle."
   M 3439
"Beatles, CSC Slate Studio."
   M 0313
"Beatles Curtail 1-Niters For Safety
   But Will Lift Ban For Edinburgh
   Date."
   M 0314
"Beatles Cut Short Meditation."
   N 0111
Beatles Dagboek
   B 0563
I Beatles Dal Mito Alla Storia: La
   Prima Biografia Storico-Critica
   Del Piu Celebre Gruppo Di Tutti I
   Tempi
   B 0516
Les Beatles Dans Le Sous-Marin Jaune
   B 0583
"The Beatles' Decca Tapes."
   M 0947
"Beatles Decide On Terms Of Northern
   Songs Counterbid."
   N 0251
"The Beatles Decide To Let It Be -
   Apart."
   C 0122
"Beatles Decide To Let It Be, Apart."
   M 1287
"Beatles Declare National Apple Week."
   M 0315
"Beatles Decline."
   N 0112
"Beatles Depart For Britain As 4,000
   Admirers Scream."

N 0113
The Beatles: Dezo Hoffman
   B 0258
The Beatles Diary
   B 0054
"Beatles Diary."
   M 0316
"Beatles Diary 1962."
   M 0317
"Beatles Diary 1963."
   M 0318
Beatles Digest
   F 0038
"Beatles Dinner Party."
   M 1059
Beatles Discographie
   B 0055
The Beatles Discography
   B 0229
The Beatles Discography. 8th ed.
   B 0362
The Beatles Discography. 9th ed.
   B 0363
"Beatles' Disk Ban Spreading: Will
   Sales Hurt?"
   M 0319
Beatles - Diskografi, 1961-1972
   B 0236
"Beatles' Disk Sales Exceed
   100,000,000."
   M 0320
"Beatles' Dispute Tying Up $9 Million;
   No Reunion Seen."
   M 0321
"Beatles Documentary Definitive,
   Detailed."
   M 0322
"Beatles Doing Own Things: Paul Quits."
   M 0010
"Beatles Don't 'Bug' Kenin But He Wants
   Anglo-U.S. Tooter Balance
   Enforced."
   M 0324
The Beatles Down Under
   B 0037
"Beatles Draw 'Only' 100G In K.C.
   Stad.; Tour Is Over But Malady
   Lingers On."
   M 0325
"Beatles' Driver Fined."
   N 0114
"Beatles Drop In - By Helicopter."
   M 1024
"Beatles' Drummer To Miss Tour."
   N 0115
"The Beatles Early Success Was Phony."
   M 0611
"The Beatles' Early Tours."
   M 1740
"The Beatles: Early Years."
   M 0948
"'The Beatles: Early Years'."
   M 1968
The Beatles (E-Go Collectors Series No.
   8)
   P 0011
Beatles '80
   S 0032
"Beatles '80: A Diary Of Recent News
   And Events."
   M 0326   M 1970
"Beatles '81: A Diary Of Recent News
   And Events."
   M 1971
"Beatles '83: A Diary Of Recent News
   And Events."
   M 1973
"Beatles '82: A Diary Of Recent News
   And Events."
   M 1972
The Beatles - Eine Illustrierte
   Dokumentation
   B 0106
"Beatles; Eller, The Rise & Fall Of The
   British Empire."
   M 0998
"Beatles: En Drom Om Frihet."
   M 2329
"Beatles End Separation."

N 0116
"Beatles End U.S. Tour By Fracturing
   Frisco, Total 'Take-Home' At $1
   Mil."
   M 0327
"'The Beatles England'."
   M 0097
The Beatles England: There Are Places
   I'll Remember
   B 0033   B 0034   B 0035   B 0036
"The Beatles' E.P.s."
   M 0949
"Beatles' Epstein Left $638,000."
   M 0328
"Beatles Era Revival Idea Behind $1 Mil
   N.Y. Show."
   M 2327
"Beatles Exhibit At Abbey Road."
   M 0329
"Beatles Ex-Manager Faces Tax Charge
   Over Promo Disks."
   M 0330
"Beatles Expected For Meditation."
   N 0117
Die Beatles: Fabelwesen Unserer Zeit?
   B 0176
The Beatles' Fabulous Favorites
   S 0033
"Beatles Facts: Sorting Out The Truth
   From Fiction."
   M 1741
"Beatles Fan Mail For Col. Wagg."
   N 0118
"Beatles Fans Besiege The Palace."
   N 0119
"Beatles Fans Fight Police At New
   Zealand Concert."
   N 0120
"Beatles' Fans Urge Wilson To Save
   Liverpool Cavern."
   N 0121
The Beatles Fantasy
   S 0034
"A Beatles Fan, 10, Prompts Inquiry;
   Lefkowitz Holds Hearing On
   Deceptive Practices In Recording
   Industry."
   N 0591
"Beatles Farewell."
   M 0331
"Beatles Feeling Just Fine."
   M 0746
"Beatles Fight Album Release."
   M 0332
The Beatles Film
   P 0030
"Beatles' Film And Music Company."
   N 0122
"Beatles Film For Adults Only."
   N 0123
"Beatles Film Into Commie Markets."
   M 0333
"Beatles' Film Prod. Offshoot Swings
   With Projects; Map Combo's Third
   Pic."
   M 0334
"Beatles Films."
   M 1427
"Beatles First Film & Special Xmas
   Record."
   M 0155
"Beatles' First Shop Has Its Swan
   Song."
   N 0124
"The Beatles' First Single."
   M 0890
"The Beatles First Sitting."
   C 0032
"Beatles' 5-Year Gross 'Estimated' At
   Over $70-Mil."
   M 0335
"Beatles Flip Cap's '64 Gross To
   Alltime High."
   M 0336
"Beatles Fly To Face Knockers."
   M 0337
"The Beatles Follow An Old Pilgrims'
   Road."
   N 0759

The Beatles For Classical Guitar: Book
  S 0035
The Beatles For Classical Guitar, Book
  S 0036
The Beatles For Classical Guitar/20
  Solos
  S 0037
The Beatles Forever
  B 0480 B 0481 B 0521 B 0570
  P 0031 P 0032
"The Beatles Forever."
  M 1562 N 0125
The Beatles Forever - Collectors
  Edition
  P 0033
The Beatles Forever, 1964-1969
  S 0038
"Beatles For India Next Month."
  N 0126
Beatles For Sale
  F 0039
"Beatles For Sale."
  M 0338 M 0698
Beatles For Sale (songbook) see The
  Beatles/Beatles For Sale
The Beatles For The Record: The Story
  Of The Beatles In Words And
  Pictures
  B 0056 B 0057
"The Beatles Fourth Christmas Record."
  M 0339
"Beatles: Free At Last?"
  M 1095
"Beatles' Gale Warnings Up; Cities Gird
  For Teen Tempest."
  M 0340
"Beatles Gallery."
  M 0341
"Beatles Gambling Lives In Las Vegas."
  N 0127
"Beatles Gatecrashers Shown Out."
  N 0128
De Beatles; Geautoriseerde Biografie
  B 0138
"Beatles Get A Thought Each."
  N 0129
The Beatles Get Back
  B 0130
"'The Beatles Get Back'."
  M 1034
"Beatles Get Back LP Due In July."
  M 0342
"Beatles Get Back Track By Track."
  M 0343
"Beatles Get No $ From 'Beatlemania'."
  M 1487
"Beatles Get Over $800,000 For Interest
  On Royalties."
  N 0130
"Beatles Get Ticker Tape Welcome!"
  M 0344
"Beatles Get Together."
  M 0699
"Beatles Get Top British Billing."
  N 0131
"A Beatle's Gig At The Cavern."
  M 2466
"Beatles Giving Trade A Solid Bite."
  M 1803
"Beatles' Global Gross: $98-Mil."
  M 0345
"Beatles Going Public? Not Yet Says
  Epstein."
  M 0346
"The Beatles: Grating Expectations."
  M 2124
The Beatles Greatest Hits For Autoharp
  S 0039
The Beatles Greatest Hits For Easy
  Accordian
  S 0040
Beatles Greatest Hits For Flute
  S 0041
The Beatles Greatest Hits For Guitar,
  Vol. I
  S 0042
The Beatles Greatest Hits For Guitar,
  Vol. II
  S 0043

Beatles Greatest Hits For Harmonica
  S 0044
The Beatles Greatest Hits For Recorder
  S 0045
"Beatles Greeted By Riot At Paris
  Sports Palace."
  N 0132
"Beatles Grooving 1,000,000-Seller LP
  In British Market."
  M 0347
The Beatles Guitar
  S 0046
"'Beatles Guitar' Man."
  M 0348
"Beatles' Guru Is Turning Them Into
  Gurus With A Cram Course."
  N 0638
"Beatles' Guru Said To Weigh Moving To
  U.S. For Privacy."
  N 0133
"The Beatles Had £10,000 A Month,
  Council Says."
  N 0134
"The Beatles Hamburg Days: An
  Eye-Witness Account."
  M 1500
"The Beatles Hamburg Days: An
  Eye-Witness Account, Part 2."
  M 1501
"The Beatles Hamburg Days: An
  Eye-Witness Account, Part 3."
  M 1502
"The Beatles' Hamburg Showcase Folds In
  Oct."
  M 0349
"Beatles Have A Ball In Fancy Dress."
  M 1631
"Beatles Have A Hard Day Of Yoga."
  N 0135
"The Beatles Have Gone, But
  International Music Hasn't Been
  The Same Since British Wave Hit
  In Early 60's."
  M 1797
"Beatles Head Merseyside Tops."
  C 0033
"Beatles 'Hearts' Earns Gold Disk."
  M 0350
"Beatles Heat Flares In Court."
  M 0351
The Beatles Help!
  S 0047
"Beatles Help Spin West German Disk Biz
  To $86-Mil Profit In M65."
  M 1344
The Beatles - Here, There (And
  Everywhere?)
  B 0596
"Beatles Hit Charts For Seven!"
  M 0352
"Beatles Hit Jackpot; Find Gold 21 In
  Them Thar Disks."
  M 0353
"Beatles Hits By Others."
  M 1428
"Beatles Hits By Others."
  M 1428
"Beatles Hoax Lives On Years Later."
  N 0395
"Beatles' House Guru Conjures Up
  Spiritual Bonanza At N.Y.
  Seance."
  M 0354
The Beatles Humour
  S 0048
Die Beatles (Ihre Karriere, Ihre Musik,
  Ihre Erfolge)
  B 0468 B 0469
The Beatles Illustrated Lyrics
  B 0007 B 0010 B 0011
The Beatles Illustrated Lyrics (1st
  American ed.)
  B 0008
The Beatles Illustrated Lyrics (1st
  Dell edition)
  B 0009
The Beatles Illustrated Lyrics 2
  B 0012 B 0014 B 0015
The Beatles Illustrated Lyrics 2 (1st
  American ed.)
  B 0013

The Beatles Illustreret Sangbog
  B 0016
"The Beatles In Action ...."
  C 0034
The Beatles In A Hard Day's Night
  B 0089
Die Beatles In America
  B 0292
"Beatles In America."
  M 0355
The Beatles In America - Their Own
  Exclusive Story And Pictures
  P 0034
"The Beatles In A New Dimension."
  N 0334
"Beatles In Austria: Dangerous Filming
  In Austrian Alps."
  M 1551
"Beatles In A Winter Wonderland."
  M 0747
"Beatles, Inc."
  M 0356
"The Beatles' Incredible 1963 Stage
  Shows."
  M 1742
"Beatles In Disc Storm (First Record
  Made In 1961)."
  M 0357
"Beatles In Europe."
  M 1478
"The Beatles In Four Part Disharmony."
  C 0105
"'Beatles In Germany' In Canada, And
  Others."
  M 0125
"Beatles - In Germany '66."
  M 0358
"The Beatles In Hamburg."
  M 0950
"The Beatles In Hamburg: Jurgen Vollmer
  Remembers."
  M 3560
The Beatles In Help!
  B 0252 B 0253
"The Beatles In Holland."
  M 3520
"Beatles In India."
  M 1035
"Beatles In India, Part 2."
  M 1036
"Beatles In Interview Row."
  M 0359
"The Beatles In Ireland."
  C 0312
The Beatles In Italy 1963-80
  B 0220
"The Beatles In New York."
  M 3781
"The Beatles In 1961."
  M 1964
"Beatles In Oil And Water."
  M 1288
The Beatles In Paris
  P 0035
"The Beatles In Paris."
  M 3220
"Beatles In Person."
  M 3038
"The Beatles In Perspective."
  C 0113 M 1210
The Beatles In Richard Lester's A Hard
  Day's Night; A Complete Pictorial
  Record Of The Movie
  B 0159 B 0160 B 0161
"The Beatles In Scotland."
  M 0360
The Beatles In Sweden
  P 0036
"The Beatles Interviews."
  M 0951
"The Beatles: In The Beginning, There
  Was Violence."
  N 0779
The Beatles In Their Own Words
  B 0383 B 0384 B 0385
"The Beatles In Their Prime."
  M 3328
"The Beatles In The States."
  C 0035

"Beatles In The Web."
   M 0361
"Beatles In Tuxedos For 'Help'."
   N 0136
"The Beatles Invade, Complete With Long
   Hair And Screaming Fans; - 3,000
   Fans Greet British Beatles."
   N 0420
"Beatles Invited To Venice."
   N 0137
The Beatles In "Yellow Submarine",
   Starring Sergeant Pepper's Lonely
   Hearts Club Band
   B 0394
"Beatles Is Coming."
   M 0362
"Beatles Items Generate $$."
   M 0363
"Beatles: It's All Over - Official."
   M 1311
The Beatles: It Was Twenty Years Ago
   ....
   B 0058
The Beatles, John Lennon And Me
   B 0508
"Beatles, John Lennon And Youth Rebel."
   M 3683
"The Beatles/John Lennon Chronology."
   M 1341
"Beatles' 'Jude' Spins 'Em To 16th
   Goldisk."
   M 0364
"Beatles Kick Off Far West Tour Aug. 19
   With 25G Guarantee Vs. 60% Of
   Gross."
   M 0365
"Beatles, Klein Suit Gets Light."
   M 0366
Die Beatles Kommen (Fahrplan Einer
   Weltsensation)
   B 0079
The Beatles Labels
   B 0285
"Beatles Label To Bow In U.K."
   M 0367
"Beatles Laff All Way To Poor House
   Over Apple's Alleged Fiscal
   Follies."
   M 0368
"Beatles Law Wrangles Go On In Chicago
   & NY."
   M 0552
"Beatles' Lawyer Scores Manager; Says
   In McCartney Hearing Klein
   'Cannot Be Trusted'."
   N 0138
"The Beatles Lead Now."
   M 0369
"Beatles Leave Friendly India."
   M 0139
"Beatles' Legal Links Dissolved."
   N 0140
Les Beatles; Le Livre-Show Illustre Des
   Chansons Et Ballads
   B 0018
"Beatles' Lennon, McCartney Top BMI
   Songwriters With 10 Tunes In Best
   100."
   M 0370
The Beatles: Let It Be
   S 0049
"Beatles: Let It Be."
   M 1062
"The Beatles: Let It Be."
   M 3341
Les Beatles; Leur Biographie Officielle
   B 0141
The Beatles Ltd.
   P 0037
"Beatles Live - At The Cavern!"
   M 0371
"Beatles Live LP In Works."
   M 0372
"The Beatles' Liverpool: A Guide To The
   Places Associated With John,
   Paul, George And Ringo."
   M 1429
"The Beatles' Liverpool Days."
   M 1430

"The Beatles' Liverpool Days, Part
   Two."
   M 1431
"The Beatles' London; Part One: The
   Beatles' Radio, TV, Stage And
   Recording Venues."
   M 1432
"The Beatles' London; Part Two: Their
   Offices, Homes And Haunts In The
   Capital."
   M 1433
"The Beatles' London Town - A Tour."
   M 1006
"Beatles' Long And Winding Road To
   Oblivion."
   M 0373
"Beatles Lose Their Live Album Battle."
   M 0628
The Beatles Love Songs
   S 0050
The Beatles Lyrics
   B 0019   B 0059
The Beatles Lyrics Complete
   B 0020
The Beatles Lyrics Illustrated
   B 0060
"Beatles' McCartney Planning To Marry."
   N 0145
The Beatles: Magical Mystery Tour
   S 0051
"Beatles Magical Mystery Tour."
   M 2328
Beatles Make A Movie
   P 0038
"Beatles Make Counter Bid In Fight Vs.
   Grade For Northern Songs Ltd."
   M 0374
"Beatles Make History."
   M 1025
"Beatles Management Fees Hikes ABKCO's
   Sixmonth Operating Profit To
   827G."
   M 0375
"Beatles Manager Here To Quell Storm
   Over Remark On Jesus."
   N 0141
"Beatles Map 3 London Concerts In Dec.
   For 1st Stage Dates In 2 Years."
   M 0376
"Beatles Marathon."
   M 1823
"Beatles May Agree."
   N 0142
"Beatles May Come Home."
   M 0188
"Beatles May Do Free Concert Tour In
   U.S.A."
   M 0377
"Beatles May Play Together."
   N 0143
"Beatles May Play Together Again."
   N 0144
"Beatles Meet But Not For 'Reunion'."
   M 3278
"Beatles' Memorabilia."
   M 0107
"Beatles' Memorabilia: Fan Club
   Material, Tour Programmes,
   Posters, Magazines, Etc."
   M 1465
"Beatles Men Go Own Way."
   N 0146
"Beatles 'Michelle' Gets Prize."
   N 0147
"Beatles' $1,000,000 U.S. Tour."
   M 0412
"Beatles' Millions."
   N 0148
"The Beatles: Minstrels Or Messiahs?"
   M 3342
"Beatles Minus One."
   M 3126
"Beatles Miss Aeschylus."
   N 0149
"Beatles Mobbed In London."
   N 0150
Beatles Movie - The Only Book With The
   Entire Story Of "A Hard Days
   Night"

   P 0039
Beatles Movie Catalog
   B 0373
"Beatles Mulling Stage Comeback."
   M 0378
"Beatles: Multimedia 'Away With
   Words'."
   N 0151
"Beatles' Multi Music Fronts; From U.S.
   Rights To ATV Stock Buy."
   M 2236
"Beatles Music."
   M 1283
Beatles, Musicos Del Siglo XX. 1st ed.
   B 0510
"Beatles Nab Another $1-Mil Album
   Seller."
   M 0379
"Beatles Nabbing 100G For NY 1-Niter on
   U.S. Tour; L.A.'s 90G For 2
   Nites."
   M 0380
"Beatles, Natch, Cop Ivor Novello
   Kudo."
   M 0381
"Beatles; Nay, Nay, Nay."
   M 0382
"Beatles Near Stalemate."
   N 0152
"Beatles' New Revolver LP Explodes Into
   Britain's Most 'Covered' Album."
   M 0383
Beatles News
   F 0040
"Beatles News: A Mixed Bag Of Apples &
   Acorns."
   C 0036
"Beatles News Apr. '63."
   M 0391
"Beatles News Aug. '63."
   M 0395
Beatles News Book
   F 0041
"Beatles News Dec. '62."
   M 0387
"Beatles News Dec. '63."
   M 0399
"Beatles News Diary."
   M 0384
"Beatles News Feb. '63."
   M 0389
"Beatles News Jan. '63."
   M 0388
"Beatles News July '63."
   M 0394
"Beatles News June '63."
   M 0393
"Beatles News Mar. '63."
   M 0390
"Beatles News May '63."
   M 0392
"Beatles News Nov. '62."
   M 0386
"Beatles News Nov. '63."
   M 0398
"Beatles News Oct. '62."
   M 0385
"Beatles News Oct. '63."
   M 0397
"Beatles News Sept. '63."
   M 0396
"Beatles New U.S. Wave Causes Hardly A
   Splash."
   M 1082
"Beatles' Next LP Due In October."
   M 0400
"The Beatles 1968 Christmas Record."
   M 0401
The Beatles 1967-1970
   S 0053
"The Beatles 1963/4 & 1964/5 Christmas
   Shows."
   M 0402
"Beatles 1963-1973."
   M 0075
The Beatles, 1962-1982; Yeah, Yeah,
   Yeah - The Beatles 20 Ans
   P 0040
The Beatles 1962-1966

S 0052

"Beatles' Ninety-Minute Bore, And The
    Rolling Stones' Beggars Banquet."
M 1211

"Beatles Nixing All Tour Offers."
M 0403

"Beatles Nobody Got To Hear."
M 1403

"Beatles: No Discernible Pattern."
M 0404

Beatles No Kisenki
B 0061

"Beatles' Northern Songs Hikes Dividend
    to 36 Percent."
M 0405

"Beatles Not All That Turned On."
C 0004

"'Beatles' Not For Sale."
M 0729

"Beatles Not To Teach."
N 0153

"Beatles' Novelties And Oddities."
M 1434

Beatles Novelty Discography
B 0465

Beatles Now
F 0042

"Beatles Now!"
M 1632

"The Beatles Now."
M 0406

"Beatles Now Legal In South Africa!"
M 0407

"Beatles No. 1 Again."
C 0037

Beatles No.3: Songs By John Lennon &
    Paul McCartney
S 0054

Beatles-NYTT
F 0043

"Beatles Offer Board Post To Howard &
    Windham."
N 0252

"Beatles Offered $40 Million."
M 0408

"Beatles Offered $1 M For A Day."
N 0154

The Beatles Official Coloring Book
B 0062

"Beatles OK Maharishi Film."
M 0409

"Beatle Solo Boom - By George!"
M 0410

Beatles On Broadway
P 0041   P 0042

"Beatles On Coast For Tour Of U.S.;
    9,000 At Airport."
N 0155

"Beatles' 1,000,000 Advance For Latest
    Single Gives 'Em Pre-Sale Gold
    Disk."
M 0411

"The Beatles On Holiday."
M 0156   M 3221

"Beatles Only Slightly Boff: Big U.S.
    Grosses Though Not SRO."
M 0413

The Beatles On Record
B 0569

The Beatles On Record: A Listener's
    Guide
B 0472

"The Beatles On 'Revolution'."
N 0156

"Beatles On Stage!"
M 1032

"Beatles On The Beat."
N 0157

"The Beatles On The Block."
C 0038

"The Beatles: On The Occasion Of Their
    Authorized Biography."
C 0331

"Beatles On Tour."
M 0157

"Beatles On World TV."
N 0158

"The Beatles Open A Boutique: Apple."
C 0039

"Beatles, Op. 15; Sgt. Pepper's Lonely
    Hearts Club Band."
M 1889

The Beatle Sound - For Easy Piano
S 0055

"Beatles Package Airs In May On WMMR."
N 1041

"Beatles' Partnership Is Dissolved By
    Judge."
N 0159

"The Beatles: Part One - On Disc."
M 1820   M 1821

"Beatles Perform In Atlanta."
N 0160

The Beatles - Personality Annual,
    Volume 1, No. 1
P 0043

"Beatles Personal Letters."
M 0414

Beatles Phenomenon
B 0399

"Beatles Phenomenon Explored On Stage."
N 0621

"Beatles Picture Discs."
M 3185

The Beatles - Pictures For Framing
P 0044

"Beatles' Pilot Fish: Billy J. Kramer
    And The Dakotas."
M 3529

"Beatles' Pilot Fish: Cilla Black."
M 3530

"Beatles' Pilot Fish: Peter And
    Gordon."
M 3548

"Beatles: Plague Or Boon For Radio?"
M 1083

"Beatles: Plain White Wrapper."
M 3134

"The Beatles: Planning A $30-Million
    One-Night Stand."
M 0415

"Beatles Plan Sweeter Tune To Aid In
    Take-Over Battle."
N 0161

Beatles Playback
F 0044

"Beatles' Plea Delay."
N 0162

"Beatle Split Rumour: Apple Is Alive
    And Healthy In The UK."
M 0416

"Beatles' Poetry: A Rock Literature."
M 1670

"Beatle Spokesman Calls Rumor Of
    McCartney's Death 'Rubbish'."
N 0163

The Beatles Pop
S 0056

"Beatles Preferred By Lady Gaitskell."
N 0164

"Beatles Prepare For Their Debut;
    Police Patrol Their Hotel And
    Guard Theater."
N 0253

The Beatles Press Book
B 0063

"Beatles' Press Confab An Experience
    Midway Between Nightmare And
    Art."
M 0417

The Beatles' Press Conference
B 0204

"Beatles' Pubbery Profit At 1.7 Mil,
    Topping Forecast."
M 0418

"Beatles Pub Firm Alleges $12 Million
    Underpayment."
M 2386

"Beatles Publisher And Beatlemania
    Producers Get Court Injunction."
M 0419

"Beatles Publisher Pursues Pix Using
    Tunes Without A License."
M 0420

The Beatles Punch-Out Portraits
P 0045

"Beatles Put Off India Pilgrimage; TV
    Special Gets Nod Over

Discipleship In Meditation."
N 0451

"Beatles Puzzle."
M 0421   M 0983

Los Beatles Que Amo
B 0337

"Beatles' Quickie 2-Wk U.S. Tour Flips
    Their Cap L.P. Past 2,000,000
    Mark."
M 0422

The Beatles Quiz Book
B 0198   B 0263   B 0264

"The Beatles' Radio Activities."
M 3523

"Beatles Rain Check."
M 0423

"The Beatles Rarities."
M 1785   M 2501

"Beatles Reaction Puzzles Even
    Psychologists."
M 0424

The Beatles Reader
B 0400   C 0048   C 0063   C 0066
C 0067   C 0076   C 0084   C 0112
C 0113   C 0142   C 0179   C 0212
C 0220   C 0227   C 0228   C 0232
C 0243   C 0251   C 0305   C 0310
C 0314

"Beatles Record."
C 0040

"Beatles Record At E.M.I."
C 0195

"Beatles' Record-Busting LP May Be
    All-Time Biggest."
M 0425

"Beatles' Record Label Aims At The
    Campuses."
N 0165

"The Beatles Record 'Please Please
    Me'."
M 0158

The Beatles Records In Australia
B 0233

"Beatles Reissues Hurting Sales Of New
    Talent's Disks In UK."
M 0426

"Beatles Reject $1 Mil Offer."
M 0427

"Beatles Relics At Rock Auction."
N 0166

"Beatles Reply To TV Film Critics;
    Viewers' Debate."
N 0167

Beatles Report
F 0045

"A Beatles Report From Australia."
M 1774

"Beatles Return."
N 0168

"Beatles Return To Their Home -
    Liverpool."
M 2391

"Beatles Reunion Alot Of Hot Air."
M 0428

"Beatles Reunion In Wings; Quartet Near
    Settlement."
M 2491

"Beatles Reunion Rumor Wrong; Only Paul
    Plays At Charity Date."
M 0429

"A Beatles Reunion? Would You Like To
    Go Back To School Again?"
M 3011

"Beatles 'Reunited' By Creative
    Programming."
M 0430

"Beatles 'Reunited' On 500,000 Cutout
    Disks."
M 1547

The Beatles (Revised edition)
B 0143

"The Beatles Revive Hopes Of Progress
    In Pop Music."
N 0746

The Beatles: Revolver
S 0057

"Beatles' Ringo Wed Quietly In London."
N 0169

"Beatles R.I.P.; In-Depth Review Of

Beatles New Album."
M 3709
"The Beatles Rise Again Thanks To
    'Pepper' Film."
M 3675
The Beatles Rock 'N' Roll
S 0058
Beatles 'Round The World (No. 1, Winter
    1964)
P 0046
The Beatles: Rubber Soul
S 0059
Beatles Rule
F 0046
"Beatles: Ruling Tomorrow."
N 0170
"Beatles Run Rampant On Charts, Arrive
    In U.S. This Week."
M 0431
"Beatles' Sales Equal 206-Mil Singles;
    Nix Concerts For Other Show Biz
    Roles."
M 2237
"Beatles' Sales: 545 Mil Units."
M 2238
"Beatles' Sales Hit 150,000,000 Disks."
M 0432
"'Beatles Saved From Bankruptcy'."
N 0171
"Beatles Say Yeah To 9-Yr EMI Pact."
M 0433
"Beatles' Score: 80,000,000 Disks."
M 0434
The Beatles Scrapbook
P 0047
"The Beatles Scrapbook."
M 0435
"The Beatle's Scrapbook."
N 0172
"Beatles Secret."
M 0436
"Beatles Seeking A Song Company; $5.1
    Million Counter Offer Made To
    Take-Over Bid."
N 0173
"Beatles Seek Injunction."
N 0174
"Beatles' 'Sgt. Pepper' Made Into Multi
    Media Click At Beacon."
M 0437
The Beatles Sgt. Pepper's Lonely Hearts
    Club Band
F 0047
The Beatles: Sgt. Pepper's Lonely
    Hearts Club Band
S 0060
Beatles Se Stejne Rozpadli
B 0463
"Beatles Set Apple Corps With Capitol."
M 0438
"Beatles' Set Hot B.O. Pace For UA; Ad
    Campaign Now Aimed At Adults."
M 0439
"Beatles Set Zapple Tag For New Label
    Due In May."
M 0440
"The Beatles Seventh Christmas Record."
M 0441
The Beatles '70
S 0068
"Beatles '79: A Diary Of Recent News
    And Events."
M 1969
"Beatles Sharing In British Lion."
N 0175
"Beatles' Shock Tactics With Girls."
M 1569
"Beatles Show"
M 0023 M 0600
"Beatles Show On Broadway Has Mania
    Against Critics."
M 0442
"Beatles Show Set."
M 0443
"Beatles Show: The Great White Shuck?"
M 3309
"The Beatles: Side One."
M 0848
"The Beatles: Side Three."

M 0849
"Beatles Signed For Film."
N 0176
"Beatles Sign Recording Contract!"
C 0041
"Beatles Single Stirs Storm
    Anti-Christ?"
M 0444
"Beatles VI World Premiere: KRLA First
    With Beatles' Album."
M 0446
The Beatles '68
S 0066
"Beatles '65."
M 0748
The Beatles '65
S 0063
"Beatles '65' Goes From 98 To No. 1 On
    BB Chart."
M 0445
The Beatles '64
S 0062
The Beatles '69
S 0067
The Beatles '67
S 0065
The Beatles '66
S 0064
The Beatles '63
S 0061
"Beatles Sold 55,000,000 (I.E.,
    545,000,000) 'Units' In 10 Years
    Making."
M 0447
"Beatles Solvent, Mr. Klein Says."
N 0177
"The Beatles; Some Years In The Life."
M 3363
The Beatles Song Book 1
B 0021 B 0022
The Beatles Song Book 2
B 0023
The Beatles Songbook I (Das Farbige
    Textbuch Der Beatles)
B 0024
The Beatles Songbook II
B 0025
"Beatles' Song Firm Rallies After
    Fall."
N 0178
"Beatles' Songs Beat Profit Forecast."
N 0179
Beatles Songs For Easy Piano
S 0069
Beatles Songs For The Recorder
S 0070
"Beatles' Songs Issue."
N 0180
"Beatles' Songs Played In Memory Of
    Lennon."
N 0181
"Beatles' Soundtrack A Blockbuster
    Before Their 1st Pic's Release."
M 0448
The Beatles (Special Collector's
    Series, Number 6)
P 0012
"Beatles Splitting? Maybe, Says John."
C 0042 M 0449
"Beatles' Stage Comeback To Spark First
    Live LP, TV Spec, And Film
    Documentary."
M 0450
"Beatles Star In Big Saturday
    Spectacular."
C 0043
"Beatles' Starr Drops From The Guru's
    Orbit."
N 0182
The Beatles: Starring In "A Hard Day's
    Night"
B 0064
The Beatles Starring In A Hard Day's
    Night
P 0048
"Beatles Started The Big Breakthrough."
M 0451
"The Beatles Statue Fund."
M 0452 M 3741

"Beatles Still Await Ruling On
    Royalties."
M 0453
"Beatles Still Clearing Up $ Problems
    Says Apple Manager."
M 0454
"Beatles Still In Stalemate Over How To
    Split Their Partnership Shares."
M 0455
"Beatles, Stones To Link Up?"
M 0456
Die Beatles Story
B 0437
"The Beatles Story As A Book Of Facts."
M 1796
The Beatles Story: Story Of Pop Special
B 0438
The Beatles Story - The Story Of Rock
P 0049
"Beatles Strike Serious Note In Press
    Talk; Group Opposes The War In
    Vietnam As Being 'Wrong'."
N 0329
"Beatles Stump Music Experts Looking
    For Key To Beatlemania."
N 0409
"Beatles - Successful."
C 0044
"Beatles' Success In U.S. A Trend For
    The British?"
M 0457
"Beatles Sue Over Photographs."
N 0183
"Beatles Sue Promoters Of
    'Beatlemania'."
N 0184
"Beatles Suing For Slander And Libel."
N 0185
"The Beatles: Sweet Apple Trax."
M 0112
"Beatles Swing In Marketplace."
M 0458
"Beatles Take EMI Up The Charts."
N 0186
"The Beatles Take New York."
C 0052
"Beatles Take To Their Heels."
N 0187
"Beatles Talk."
M 1633
The Beatles Talk
P 0050
"Beatles Talk: Let George Do It."
M 1142
"Beatles' Tapes Unleashed In UK."
M 0142
"Beatles Tell It To The Activists."
M 1272
"Beatles 10 Years After."
M 0700
"The Beatles: 10 Years On, 1964-1974."
M 0459
"The Beatles: The Alternate Takes."
M 2489
The Beatles; The Authorized Biography
B 0144 B 0145 B 0146 B 0147
The Beatles: The Authorized Biography
    (New edition)
B 0148 B 0150
The Beatles: The Authorized Biography
    (Revised edition)
B 0149
"Beatles - The DJs Verdict."
M 0460
Beatles - The Fab Four Come Back
P 0051
The Beatles: The Fab Four Who Dominated
    Pop Music For A Decade. Rev. ed.
B 0093
The Beatles: The Fabulous Story Of
    John, Paul, George And Ringo
B 0092
"Beatles; The Facts."
M 0461
"The Beatles: The 'Get Back' Sessions."
M 0952
The Beatles - The Greatest! Meet The
    Dave Clark Five
P 0052

"Beatles: The Last Rites."
M 0462
The Beatles, Themes And Variations:
   Clarinet
S 0071
The Beatles, Themes And Variations:
   Flute
S 0072
The Beatles, Themes And Variations:
   Trumpet
S 0073
The Beatles; The Real Story
B 0065   B 0189   B 0190
The Beatles: The Singles Collection,
   1962-1970
S 0074
"The Beatles: The True Story."
N 0805
"The Beatles: The True Story - 2."
N 0806
"The Beatles: The True Story - 3."
N 0807
"The Beatles: The True Story - 4."
N 0808
"The Beatles Third Christmas Record."
M 0463
"Beatles' $304,000 At Shea Ballpark
   All-Time Record 1-Nite Show Biz
   B.O."
M 3163
"Beatles' Tifts In Court Still Blazing
   Wildly."
M 0464
"Beatles To Appear In Japan."
N 0188
"Beatles To Appear Live And John In The
   Nude."
M 0465
The Beatles To Bacharach: All Organ
   Edition
S 0075
The Beatles To Bacharach: Easy Guitar
   Edition
S 0076
"Beatles To Battle Firm For Northern
   Songs Ltd."
N 0189
"Beatles To Confer On Bid Rebuff."
N 0190
"Beatles To Cut For Apple Label; Stay
   With EMI."
M 0466
"The Beatles Today: Separate Roads,
   Separate Realities."
M 3262
"Beatles To Do Three-LP Set?"
M 0467
"Beatles To Fight £9.5M ATV Bid."
N 0338
"Beatles To Get $150,000 For Kansas
   City Program."
N 0191
"Beatles Together For Lennon Tribute."
M 0468
"Beatles To Issue Batch Of Records;
   They Are Chiefly Producers,
   Singing Only A Single."
N 0192
"Beatles To Launch A 2d Label, Zapple."
M 0469
A Beatlestol Az Uj Hullamig
B 0270
"Beatles Top English Poll."
M 0470
"Beatles Top Poll!"
C 0045   M 0471
"Beatles To Remember, Beatles To
   Forget."
M 3190
"Beatles Tornado Storms Its Way
   Eastward."
M 0472
"The Beatles' Toronto Take Home Pay:
   100G."
M 0473
"Beatles To Shun U.S. Because Of Tax
   Rift."
N 0193
"The Beatles To Sue Clothing Firm."

N 0194
"Beatles To The Rescue As Fans Take The
   Plunge (Amsterdam)."
M 1756
"Beatles To Unite In Monster Rock Fest
   At Monticello, N.Y."
M 0474
"Beatles Tour?"
M 0864
"Beatles' Tour Ends In Relative Peace."
M 0195
"The Beatles' Touring Days."
M 3272   M 3376
"Beatles 'Tour' No Wow On TV But Disk
   Triumphs In Singles Charts."
M 0475
"Beatles' Tour Spawns The Stripling
   Set; Chi's Newest, Hottest Pop
   Concert Mkt."
M 3114
"Beatles Transmogrified Again: A
   Two-Piano Concerto For Our Time."
M 1296
"Beatles' Tributes, Spoofs & Novelty
   Discs."
M 1435
"Beatles' 'Tripper' Their 10th No. 1
   Hit."
M 0476
"Beatles' Trip Put On TV."
N 0196
"Beatles Triumphant Return Home."
C 0046
The Beatles Trivia Quiz Book
B 0470
"Beatles Tunes Employed Well On 'War'
   Soundtrack."
M 1170
"Beatles Tuning In On Fashion World."
N 0362
"Beatles Tuning Up."
M 0477
"Beatles' TV Film Mystifies British;
   Movie McCartney Directed Brings
   Protests To B.B.C."
N 0197
"Beatles' TV Spec Draws Critical Rap;
   Loses Ratings, But Will Turn
   Profit."
M 0478
The Beatles - 24 Posters
B 0066
"The Beatles:Twenty Years Ago The
   Photogenic Four Arrived In The
   U.S., Where Fans Both Looked And
   Listened."
M 0479
Beatles 2
B 0120
"A Beatle Sues Record Companies."
N 0198
"Beatles' U.K. Books & Magazines."
M 1466
"Beatles' U.K. LPs."
M 0891
"Beatles U.K. Singles Valued."
M 0892
"The Beatles' U.K. T.V. Appearances."
M 1974
"Beatles U.N. Concert? 3 Reportedly Say
   'Let's Go'."
M 1390
"Beatles Under The Microscope."
M 0480
"Beatles Under Wraps In Tokyo
   'Beetorusi' In Tokyo."
M 3155
Beatles Unlimited
F 0048
"Beatles Unlimited First Anniversary."
M 1359
"Beatles Unlimited 2nd Anniversary."
M 0481
"The Beatles Unreleased Recordings."
M 0953
"Beatles Up EMI Fiscal Profit To Peak
   $16,975,000."
M 0482
The Beatles Up To Date

B 0067
"Beatles Up-To-The-Minute Facts."
M 0483   M 0484   M 0485
"Beatles Urge Complete Acceptance."
N 0199
"Beatles USA."
M 0486
Beatles U.S.A. - Collector's Edition
P 0053
Beatles (U.S.A.) Ltd.
P 0054   P 0055   P 0056
"Beatles' U.S. Personals May Be Dented
   By Religioso Rhubarb & DJ
   Blackout."
M 0487
"Beatles Values And Collecting E.P.s."
M 0893
"Beatles Vs. Stones; Rolling Stones As
   Rivals."
M 1835
"Beatles Video."
M 0488
"Beatles Video: 'Interview With A
   Legend' John Lennon With Tom
   Snyder On The Tomorrow Show."
M 3213
Beatles Video Newsletter
F 0049
Beatles Visie
F 0050
"Beatles Visit Widnes."
C 0047
Beatles V Pisnich A V Obrazech
B 0026
"The Beatles Wealth Is A Myth."
M 3710
"The Beatles Welcome Army Petition."
N 0200
"'Beatles Were Not Manhandled'."
N 0201
Beatles Werk Group
F 0051
"The Beatles - What The Merseyside
   Wonders Think Of The Latest Batch
   Of Pop Singles."
M 0489
The Beatles: White Album
S 0077
Beatles Whole True Story
P 0057
The Beatles Who's Who
B 0243   B 0244
Die Beatles - Wie Sie Sich Selbt Sehen
B 0386
"Beatles Will Escape Federal Income Tax
   On Their Earnings In U.S."
N 0202
"'Beatles Will Last, They'll Never
   Die'."
N 0958
"Beatles Will Live Again At
   Philadelphia Festival."
M 0490
"Beatles Will Make $ Million On U.S.
   Tour, Epstein Predicts."
M 0491
"The Beatles Will Make The Scene Here
   Again, But The Scene Has
   Changed."
N 0984
"The Beatles Will Manage Themselves."
N 0203
"Beatles Will Sell Interest In A
   Publishing Company."
N 0204
"The Beatles, Will They Sing Again For
   $50 Million."
M 0492
"Beatles Win Again!"
M 1436
"Beatles Win 5 Awards For Songs They
   Write."
M 0493
"Beatles Win New Fan Club - Top British
   Politicos."
M 0494
"Beatles Winning In East Germany; Group
   Held 'Okay' In Crisis Over
   Cultural Freedom."

N 0978
"Beatles Win Over America."
   M 0495
"Beatles Win Press Award."
   M 0496
"Beatles Woo Shareholders."
   N 0205
The Beatles; Words Without Music
   B 0205
"Beatles Xmas Show."
   M 1011
"The Beatles? Yeah! Yeah! Yeah!"
   M 3158 M 3344
The Beatles Years
   S 0078 S 0079
"The Beatles Years - Ringo Yesterday &
      Today."
   M 1229
The Beatles: Yellow Submarine
   S 0080
The Beatles - Yesterday And Today
   B 0537 B 0538 F 0052 P 0058
Beatles - Yesterday & Today
      Organization
   F 0053
The Beatles: Yesterday ... Today ...
      Tomorrow
   B 0288 B 0289 B 0290 B 0291
"Beatles' Yogi To Tour U.S. With Beach
      Boys."
   M 0497
Les Beatles, Yoko Ono Et Moi
   B 0494
"The Beatles: 'You Never Give Me Your
      Money'."
   M 0498
"Beatles Zap USA, Ltd."
   M 0499
"Beatletalk."
   M 1550
"Beatle Tells Preference For Religions
      Of India."
   N 0206
"Beatle Thinks Group Will Regain
      Harmony."
   N 0207
"Beatle Tunes Become Baroque 'N' Roll."
   N 0410
"Beatle Who Plans For The Future."
   M 0749
"Beatle Who's Changed The Most."
   M 0159
"Beatle Wife Misses The Train."
   N 0208
"A Beatlological Puzzle."
   M 1958
"Die Beat-Musik; Versuch Einer
      Analyse."
   M 1335 M 1336
"Beat: 'Penny Lane' - Modell Einer
      Analyse."
   M 3366
"Beats And Beatles."
   M 0500
"Beat Show."
   M 1536
"Beatsville."
   M 0750
"Beat The Meatles."
   M 2190
"Beattle (Sic) Concert Sold Out."
   N 0209
"Beautiful Boy (Darling Boy)."
   M 1893
"Beauty And The Beatles."
   M 0503
"Bedding In For Peace: John And Yoko In
      Canada."
   C 0347
"Before A Mind Collapses."
   N 0210
"Before History Took Over."
   M 0732
"Beginner's Guide To Imports."
   M 1861
"Be Grateful, Parents!"
   M 1081
Behind The Beatles Songs
   B 0131 B 0132

"Behind The Headlines."
   M 1634
"Behind The Spotlight."
   M 3240
"Behind The $230-Million Offer."
   M 1143
"Being A Short Diversion On The Dubious
      Origins Of Beatles."
   C 0185
"Berryized Beatles, Beatlized Monkees,
      Unmonkeed Dolenz, Jones."
   M 1626
"Bert Kaempfert, 1923-1980."
   M 3531
"Bert Kaempfert: The Man Who Gave Brian
      Epstein The Beatles."
   M 1437
"Best Files $8 Mill Suit."
   M 0533
"Best Of The Beatles."
   M 0534
The Best Of The Beatles
   S 0081
The Best Of The Beatles From Fabulous
   P 0059
Best Of The Beatles - 63 Ways To Meet A
      Beatle
   P 0060
Best Of The Music Makers
   C 0299
"Best Songwriters Since Schubert?"
   M 3305
"The Betrayal Of John Lennon."
   M 3218
"Beware, The Red Beatles."
   M 0536
"Beyond Beatlemania."
   M 2180
"Beziehungen Zwischen Pop Art Und Pop
      Music."
   M 3141
"Bid Briefs; Associated Television."
   N 0215
"Bids And Deals; Hemdale And Triumph In
      £2.3m Package."
   N 0216
"Bids And Deals; Northern Songs Buys
      Lenmac."
   N 0217
"Bids, Deals & Mergers; Associates
      Deals."
   N 0218 N 0219
"Bids, Deals And Mergers; Nems Goes
      Into Music Publishing."
   N 0220
Big Beat And Pop Boys
   M 0539
Big Beatle Fun Kit
   P 0061
"Big 'Beatles' Controvery."
   C 0054
"Big Macca Goes Rhodium."
   M 0540
Big Oltre La Leggenda: John Lennon, Bob
      Marley, Beatles
   B 0074
"Big 7 Gets $6,795 From Lennon."
   M 0541
"Big Time."
   N 0931
"Bill Harry's Detective Column."
   M 1438
"Billy J. Kramer - The 'J' Was For
      Julian."
   M 1439
"Billy Preston Coming."
   M 0543
"Biographie Beatles."
   M 0939
"Biography - George Harrison."
   C 0055 M 0544
"Biography - John Lennon."
   C 0056 M 0545
"Biography - Paul McCartney."
   C 0057 M 0546
"Biography - Ringo Starr."
   C 0058 M 0547
"Biography - Yoko Ono."
   C 0059 M 0548

"Bios."
   M 0549
"Bird On The Wing."
   M 0551
"Birth Of The Beatles."
   M 0189 M 0553 M 0554
"Birth Of The Beatles: A Good Show, But
      Fab Four's Help Was Missed."
   M 0555
"Birth Of The Beatles: Little Insight."
   N 1112
"'Birth Of The Beatles' What It Was
      Like To Be 15 And Greet The 'Fab
      Four' On Their First Day In
      America."
   M 0847
"B Is For Beatles And Baroque;
      Concerning Baroque Beatles Book."
   M 1169
"Bit By The Beatles."
   M 2191
"Bits Of The Beatles."
   M 3050
"Black Flag Flies At Beatles'
      Headquarters."
   M 0560
"Blackpool Pix."
   M 0561
"Blazing Battles Rock Marriage Of
      Ex-Beatle Ringo."
   M 2187
"Blind Date."
   M 0563 M 0564 M 0565 M 0566
   M 0567 M 0568 M 0569 M 0570
   M 0571 M 0572 M 0573
"(Blind Lemon Preston)": Black
      Troubadour; A Credit To His
      Race."
   M 1757
"Blindman."
   M 2513
"Blinkin' Beatles Triumphant Tour."
   M 1557
"Blitz In Britain."
   M 0574
"The Blockbuster Book That Bares The
      Shocking Truth About The
      Sensational Rock Group."
   M 0631
"Blue-Chip Beatles."
   M 0575
"Blue Meanie Beatle."
   M 0576
"Blue Meanies Attack Beatles."
   M 0577
"Blue Meanies No More."
   N 0456
"'Blue Power' Hits Discs; Apple
      Forbidden Fruit?"
   M 3455
"Blueprint For A Beatle: Television
      Cartoons."
   N 0023
"Blues For The Beatles; U.S. Tour;
      Reactions To Lennon Statement."
   M 0578
"BMI Top Writer Awards To McC, Lennon;
      SG-Col, Kirshner As Pubs."
   M 0582
"Bob, George, John, Phil, Ringo, &
      Johnny."
   M 0583
"Bob Wooler."
   M 0505
Body Count
   C 0291
"Boiling Beatles Blast Copy Cats."
   M 0584
"Bomb Fear Over Ex-Beatle Gift."
   N 0226
"Book Facts."
   M 0586
The Book Of Lennon: The Complete Lennon
      Sourcebook
   B 0245 B 0246
The Book Of People
   C 0116 C 0237 C 0271
"Book Reveals Lennon's Wild Side: 'I've
      Always Needed A Drug To

Survive'."
M 0587
"Book Review."
M 0588 M 0589 M 2955
"Book Section."
M 0590
"A Bookshelf Of Beatles Books."
N 0231
"The Book Trade Reacts To Lennon's
Death With Flurry Of Publishing
Activity."
M 1257
"Boosting Peace: John And Yoko In
Canada."
M 3773
"Booting The Beatles."
C 0220
"Bootleg Beatles A Threat."
M 1388
"Bootleg Recording Subject Of Hearing."
N 0227
"Bootleg Releases."
M 0591
"Bootlegs Vs. Capitol Records: The
Continuing Battle Over The Beatle
Vaults."
M 0527
"Born."
M 0592
"Born To Boogie - A Missed
Opportunity."
M 3627
Boss Beatles Fan Club
F 0054
"Boundaries Of Grief."
N 0228
"Bow-Wow Beatle."
M 0595
The Boys From Liverpool; John, Paul,
George, Ringo
B 0482
"The Boys In The BBC Band."
M 1723
The Boy Who Dared To Rock: The
Definitive Elvis
C 0193
"Brace Yourself, They're Back."
M 0598
"The Breakup Of The Beatles...And The
Buildup Of Their Wives."
M 1057
"Brian And The Beatles: Murder Plot Is
Fantasy."
N 0234
"Brian Epstein."
M 0160
"Brian Epstein, Beatles' 29 Yr. Old
Mgr., Turning Impresario And Film
Producer."
M 0604
"Brian Epstein Death Is Ruled
Accidental."
N 0235
"Brian Epstein: Did He Make The
Beatles, Or Did The Beatles Make
Him?"
N 0469
"Brian Epstein In Merger."
N 0236
"Brian Epstein In Vic Lewis Merger."
M 0605
"Brian Epstein Is Found Dead; News
Brings The Beatles Back To
London."
N 0237
"Brian Epstein, Part Three: The
Philippine Affair."
M 0161
"Brian Epstein, Part Two."
M 0162
"Brian Epstein Predicts: I Give The
Beatles Two Or Three Years More
At The Top."
M 0751
"Brian Epstein's Brother Takes Over As
Nems Chief; No Deal With
Beatles."
M 0606
"Brian Epstein, 32, Beatles' Manager;

Singing Group's Discoverer And
Mentor Is Dead."
N 0238
"Brian Epstein, 32, Beatles' Mentor,
Dies In London."
M 0607
"Brian Epstein: Would The Beatles Have
Succeeded Without Him? Part One."
M 0163
"Brian Even Considered The Woolworth's
Label."
M 0894
"Brian Meets George Martin."
M 0895
"Bride For A Beatle."
N 0601
"A Brief Conversation With Mc."
M 0608
"Briefly From The Boardroom;
ATV-Northern Songs."
N 0239
"Briefly From The Boardroom; Northern
Songs."
N 0240 N 0241 N 0242
"Briefs."
N 0243 N 0244
"Bring Back Romance!"
M 0854
"Britain's Beatles' Sales Top
3,000,000."
M 0613
"Britain's Finest Hour."
M 2222
"Britain's Prime Minister Reopens
Birthplace Of Beatles: Yeah!
Yeah! Yeah!"
M 0614
"Britain's Retaliation For Ten Years Of
Imported Rock And Roll."
M 0615
"Britannia Rules Airwaves; Beatles Stir
Home Carbons."
M 3164
British Beat
C 0207
"British Beatles Hottest Capitol
Singles Ever"
M 3453
"British Bookies Now Quoting Odds On
Disk Chart Winners; Rate Beatles
6-1."
M 0616
"The British Boys: High-Brows And
No-Brows."
N 0421
"British Broadcaster Bids For The
Rights To Tunes Of Beatles."
N 0246
"A British Cartoon Film That Should
Please Nearly Everyone."
N 1047
"British Exports Booming; Beatles."
M 0617
"British High Court Winds Beatles' Long
Partnership."
M 0618
The British Invasion
C 0286
"British Invasion."
M 1736
"British Press Cools Toward Beatles."
M 0619
"British Rockers Unite In Concerts For
Kampuchea."
M 1216
"A British Tour."
M 3291
"British View Of Beatle Theology."
M 0620
"Britons Given Chance To Buy Beatle
Stocks."
N 0247
"Britons Resist Closing Of Club."
N 0248
"Britons Succumb To Beatlemania."
N 0689
"Broadcast Ban On Beatles Record."
N 0249
"Buddy Holly's Rare Misses."

M 1743
"Bug Japanese."
N 0255
"Building A Beatles Library."
M 3172
"Building The Beatle Image."
C 0232 M 2385
"BU's Fifth Anniversary Celebration:
Still Crazy After All These
Years."
M 3532
"Business Appointments."
N 0256 N 0257 N 0258
"Business Diary; A Beatle In The City."
N 0259
"Business Diary; BPC's Flourishing
Beatle Book."
N 0260
"Business Diary: Furore Across The
Mersey."
N 0336
"Business Diary; Nemperor Vic."
N 0261
"Business Diary; Pop Go The Rumours."
N 0262
"Business Expert To Aid Beatles."
N 0263
"Business Link For Pop Groups?"
N 0264
"The Business World; Pop Group Pays
More."
N 0265
"But His Teeth Are Regular Pearls."
N 0596
"But Wings Fly High."
M 0701
"Buying The Beatles."
M 0645
"By An Unknown Master - The Baroque
Beatles Book."
M 1623
"By George, A Beatle Is In India."
M 0198
"By The Financial Editor; Northern
Songs Disappoint."
N 0266
"California Teenagers Squeal."
N 0267
"Canada, Peacemaker To The World."
M 1291
"Canada Updated."
M 0126 M 0127
"Canadian Delay For Lennon."
N 0269
"Las Canciones De Los Beatles."
M 0019
"Candy."
M 2514
"Can You Recognise John Lennon?"
C 0070
"Capitol Plots Promo For Rarities Album
Spotting The Beatles."
M 0656
"Capitol Releases $132.98 Beatles Set."
M 2085
"Capitol Says $6.98 Is A Fair Price."
M 0657
"Capitol's Rip Off."
M 3125
"Capitol Wins First Round In Battle
Over Beatles; Disk Orders Top
1-Mil."
M 0658
"Cap Plans To Issue Beatles Rarities
LP."
M 2086
"Captain Returning O.B.E. In Protest."
N 0270
"Cap Throws Block Vs. VeeJay's
Beatles."
M 0659
"Caricature."
M 1511
"Carole King Wins 4 Grammys As Record
Industry Lists 'Bests'."
N 0467
"Carry On, Screamers!"
M 0752
"Cartoon Quiz."

M 0673
"The Case For An LP Of Unreleased
    Material."
M 1862
"A Case Of Jello Venom."
M 1725
"Case Of The Belittled Beatles Tapes."
M 0675
"Caste Changes Or, The Sad Tale Of Four
    Beatles Who Were Not What They
    Supposed."
N 0003
Catalogue Of Autograph Letters,
    Literary Manuscripts And
    Historical Documents (Trinket)
C 0215
Catalogue Of Autograph Letters,
    Literary Manuscripts And
    Historical Documents (Ampersand)
C 0255
Catalogue Of Autograph Letters,
    Literary Manuscripts And
    Historical Documents (Sprint)
C 0256
Catalogue Of Autograph Letters,
    Literary Manuscripts And
    Historical Documents (Iago)
C 0258
Catalogue Of Autograph Letters,
    Literary Manuscripts And
    Historical Documents (Cat)
C 0306
A Catalogue Of Compositions By John
    Lennon & Paul McCartney: Recorded
    By The Beatles And Other World
    Famous Artistes
B 0113
Catalogue Of Rock & Roll Memorabilia,
    1956-1983 (Twistin')
C 0022
"Caught In The Act."
M 0678   M 0679   M 0680   M 0681
M 0682   M 0683   M 0684   M 0685
M 3711
"Cavalier."
M 0686
"'Caveman'."
M 1440
"The Cavern."
M 0164   M 1360   M 2219
"The Cavern: A Revised Map Of The
    Cavern As Described By Allan
    Williams."
M 0687
"A Cavern In Arcadia."
M 1628
Cavern Mecca
F 0055
"Cavern Mecca: Liverpool's Beatle
    Museum And Information Centre."
M 0688
"'Cavern Mecca' Opens In Liverpool."
M 3293
"Cavern Mecca: The Battle Goes On."
M 1205
"CBS Fund Scholarship In Memory Of
    Lennon."
M 0689
"A Cellar Full Of Joys."
M 2467
A Cellarful Of Noise
B 0178   B 0179   B 0180   B 0181
B 0182   B 0183   B 0184   B 0185
"Censored."
M 1485
"Central Park Section To Honor Lennon."
N 0281
Chains
F 0056
"A Chance In A Million."
M 1563
"Changes For The Record."
M 3051
"'Chantez A Bit If You Know Les Mots'."
M 0702
"Chapman Case Judge Refuses To Bar
    Public."
N 0283
"Chapman Gets 20-To-Life Term."

M 0693
"Chapman Getting No Special Guards."
N 0284
"Chapman Given 20 Years In Lennon's
    Slaying."
N 0992
"Chapman, In A Closed Courtroom, Pleads
    Guilty To Killing Of Lennon."
N 0993
"Chapman Is Sentenced."
M 0694
"Chapman: Man Who Stopped The Music."
N 0900
"Chapman Pleads Guilty To Murder."
M 0695
"Chapman Signed As 'John Lennon'."
N 0285
"Chapman's Last Four Days: A Mystery
    Tour Of The City."
N 0318
"Charles Mingus Challenges The
    Beatles!"
M 0753
"Charley HIFI."
M 0710
"Charlotte Moorman."
M 0711
"Chartbeat."
M 1326
"Chartbeat: Beatles Crawl Over Chart."
M 1327
"Chart Crawls With Beatles."
M 2108
Chatterbox - Preiskatalog Fur
    Schallplatten, 1954-81
C 0123
"A Chat With Derek Taylor."
M 1775
"Cheers And Tears As Beatle Marries."
N 1130
"Chevy Chase: We Almost Reunited The
    Beatles."
M 0715
"Chicago '82: We Ain't Going Nowhere
    ... ."
M 3273
"Children Of Paradise - Back To Where
    We Once Belonged."
M 0825
"Children's Records Are Rocking More,
    But The Beat Isn't Affecting Snow
    White."
M 3425
"Child To The Paul McCartneys."
N 0288
"Choice For Northern."
N 0289
"Chris Thomas."
C 0322
"Christmas Time Is Here Again."
M 0719
"Christ, They Know It Ain't Easy."
M 1144
"CHUM Unveils 15-Hour Beatles
    Documentary."
M 3774
Cilla Black Fan Club
F 0057
"Cincinnati Pops Honors Lennon On
    4-City Trek."
M 0720
"Cinema."
N 0944
"City Leaders Urge Strict Gun Control."
N 0291
"City Of Liverpool Beatle Street
    Campaign."
M 2533
"Civil Rights Angles Loom In Beatle
    Ban."
M 0721
"Classified Ads."
C 0186   M 0723
"Classified Ads, Pen Pals, Messages
    etc."
M 0724
"Classified Adverts."
C 0078
"Classifieds."

M 0725
"Clean-Up For Yoko Single."
M 0726
"Cleaver On The Beatles."
N 0295
"Cleffing Beatles Snag 3 Novellos;
    Other U.K. Awards."
M 0728
"Cleveland To Bar Beatles And The Like
    In Public Hall."
N 0296
"Clipping Of McCartney's Wings."
M 1963
"Clipping Paul McCartney's Wings."
M 3682
"The Clive Epstein Interview."
M 2987
"Closed Court In Lennon Case Plea
    Termed Unusual."
N 0994
Club Sandwich
F 0058
"Coast Dejay Paying Beatles $100,000
    Vs. 65% Of Gate For Aug 28 L. A.
    Gig."
M 0731
"Collecting."
M 0661   M 0786   M 1197   M 1198
M 1863   M 2976   M 3175   M 3176
M 3177
"Collecting Beatles' Items: What's
    Available And How Much Should You
    Pay?"
M 0787
"'Collecting The Beatles'."
M 1099
Collecting The Beatles: An Introduction
    & Price Guide To Fab Four
    Collectibles, Records &
    Memorabilia
B 0196   B 0197   C 0028   C 0038
The Collection Of Autograph Letters,
    Historical Documents And ....
    (Rawlins)
C 0257
A Collection Of Beatles Oldies
S 0082
"The Collector."
M 0970
"Collector's Books."
M 1441
Collectors' Carrousel (4907Y)
C 0273
"A Collector's Proposal."
M 1864
"Colonial, Toronto."
M 0790
"Colossal Event."
M 0824
Come Together
F 0059
"Come Together."
M 0792
Come Together: John Lennon In His Time
B 0582
"A Comedy Of Letters."
N 0300
"Comment."
N 0301
"Commentary: His Gift - More Than
    Music."
M 2133
"Commentary: Lennon Helped Pave The
    Way."
M 2010
"Commentary: Lennon Peace Forest."
M 1265
"Commentary: Mourning Becomes
    Celebration."
M 3377
"Comment: How About Long Hair?"
N 0302   N 0303
"Comments: Let Him Be."
M 0793
"Comments On Jesus Spurs A Radio Ban
    Against The Beatles."
N 0304
"Committees, Gleason Aid Lennon's
    Deport Fight."

M 0794
Communism, Hypnotism, And The Beatles
   B 0405
"Company News: Dividends And Profits;
   Northern Songs To Pay 40 Per
   Cent."
   N 0305
"Company News; Extra 2 Points By
   Northern Songs."
   N 0306
"Company News In Brief; Northern
   Songs."
   N 0307
"Company News; Ten Points Extra By
   Northern Songs."
   N 0308
"Compile A Beatles LP And Win A Rare
   Set Of Albums."
   M 0796
"'Compleat Beatles' Push Is On;
   Extensive Cross-Merchandising
   Campaign Launched."
   M 1161
The Compleat Beatles, Volume One
   B 0123
The Compleat Beatles, Volume Two
   B 0124
"The Complete Beatles Bootleg
   Catalogue."
   M 3740
The Complete Beatles Lyrics
   B 0125
The Complete Beatles Quiz Book
   B 0218   B 0219
"Complete Beatles' U.K. LP Discography
   + Values."
   M 0011
The Complete Beatles U.S. Record Price
   Guide - First Edition
   B 0134
"A Complete Catalogue Of The Beatles'
   U.K. Radio Broadcasts."
   M 1975
"A Complete Catalogue Of The Beatles'
   U.K. Radio Broadcasts, Part Two."
   M 1976
"Complete List Of Fan Club
   Secretaries."
   M 0797
"Complete List Of Overseas Fan Clubs."
   M 0798
"The Complete Silver Beatles."
   M 0954
"Concentration Of Squealing Teen-Agers
   Noted At Hotel; Phenomenon Traced
   to English Quartet Called
   Beatles."
   N 0881
"Concentration Of Squealing Teen-Agers
   Noted At Hotel; Later, At The
   Stadium."
   N 0985
"Concepts And Concept Albums."
   C 0283
"Concert."
   M 0799
"The Concert For The People Of
   Kampuchea."
   M 1977
"Concert Reviews."
   M 0800   M 0801   M 0802
"Concert Upset Sees 'Beatles' Draw
   Blasted."
   M 3701
The Concise Beatles Complete
   S 0083
"Confessions Of A Beatle."
   M 3127
"Confessions Of A Beatlefan."
   M 1860
Confessions Of A Cultist: On Cinema,
   1955-69
   C 0281
"Confiscate Nude Beatles Poster In
   Paris; Merely A Montage, Sez
   Creator."
   M 0804
"Congratulations, 'Beatles'!"
   C 0117

"'Constantly Changing Through The
   Years'."
   M 3222
Contemporary Attitudes Towards The
   Music Of The Beatles
   B 0447
"Contractual Boobytrap Holds Up Release
   Of Bangla Desh Benefit LP."
   M 0810
"A Conversation."
   M 0826
"A Conversation With Allan Williams."
   M 1199
"A Conversation With George Harrison."
   M 0629
"A Conversation With May Pang."
   M 1776
"A Conversation With Paul McCartney."
   M 1217
"The Cool Brain Behind The Bonfire."
   M 0650
"Copyright Error Will Cost EMI $$; No
   Royalties Ever Paid On Song In
   1964 Beatles Album."
   M 1479
"Correction."
   N 0310
"Cosmic Gumdrops And Musical Genius."
   N 0595
Couleurs Et Coleres Du Temps:
   L'Integrale Des Poemes Et
   Chansons
   C 0014
"Counting Cost Of Beatles' Visit."
   N 0312
"The Country Awash With Beatles Music."
   N 0313
"A Country House For Paul."
   C 0089
"The Coup That Failed."
   M 2975
"Course On Beatles And Lennon."
   N 0314
"Court Bars Beatles Video."
   M 0833
"Court Gets Wrong Criminal Record In
   Lennon Slaying."
   N 0052
"Court OKs Old German Beatles LP."
   M 0834
"Court Ruling Due On Harrison Disk Suit
   Jurisdiction."
   M 0835
"Court Stops Sales Of Phony Beatles."
   M 0836
"Court Tables Decision On Beatles For
   Week."
   M 0837
"Cover The Beatles - It's Not So Easy
   Now!"
   M 3573
"Cracks Show In Beatles Toronto Teen
   Image Despite Group's SRO
   $150,000."
   M 0842
Crawdaddy
   M 0843
Creem
   M 0844
"Creemedia: Endless Rain Meets Paper
   Cup."
   M 0845
"Critics Scorn Beatle Film But Audience
   Enjoys Itself."
   N 0316
"Crosby's Co. Faces The Naked Truth -
   Bows Nude LP In U.S."
   M 1477
"Crowds Of Lennon Fans Gather Quickly
   At The Dakota And Hospital."
   N 0317
"Cruising With Macca."
   M 1595
"Crusade Against Lennon Memorabilia."
   N 0320
"Cry For A Shadow."
   M 3398
"'Crying At The Chapel' Heads British
   Hit Parade, Topping Beatles For

First Time In Three Years."
   N 0321
"Culture Heroes."
   M 3092
"Culture Shock: The Great White Lie;
   How Broadway Show Evades The
   Press."
   M 1292
"The Curious Case Of The 'Death' Of
   Paul McCartney."
   C 0314   M 3369
Current Biography Yearbook
   C 0055   C 0056   C 0057   C 0058
   C 0059
"Cynthia Lennon Twist Framed."
   M 1463
"Cynthia's Secret - How To Hold Your
   Guy."
   M 0852
"Daddy(?)"
   N 0327
"Daddy Has Gone Away Now: Let It Be."
   M 0832
"The Daily Howl."
   C 0090
Dakota Days: The Untold Story Of John
   Lennon's Final Years
   B 0221   B 0222
"Dali Death-Painting May Provide A
   Clue."
   N 0328
"Dandelions In Still Air: The Withering
   Away Of The Beatles."
   M 0136
"Danger, Beatles At Work."
   M 2387
"The Danger Facing Pop."
   M 3574
Dark Horse
   F 0060   S 0084
"Dark Horse, Pale Rider."
   M 0858
"Dark Horse Record Label Discussed."
   N 0332
"Dark Horse: Transcendental
   Mediocrity."
   M 2194
Date Book
   M 0859   M 0860
Date Book - All About The Beatles
   P 0062
Date Book - All About The Beatles -
   America's Top DJs Interview The
   Boys
   P 0063
Date Book - Exclusive - Paul Talks
   About Jane
   P 0064
"Daughter For Beatle."
   N 0333
"Dave Brubeck Credits Beatles With
   Cracking Music Barriers."
   M 0863
Dave Clark Five Vs. The Beatles, Volume
   1, No. 1
   P 0065
"David Geffen Boycotts 'Billboard'."
   M 2510
"David Platz To Head Northern Songs If
   Beatles Gain Control Of Pub
   Firm."
   M 0865
"Dawn Of The Age Of Venus & Mars:
   McCartneys Wings Take To The
   Stars."
   M 1218
"The Day America Caught Beatle Fever."
   M 0593
"Day At Night."
   M 0884
"A Day In The Life."
   M 0885
A Day In The Life; The Beatles
   Day-By-Day, 1960-1970
   B 0490
"The Day John Lennon Stopped Believing
   In Beatles."
   M 1091
"The Day The King Of Swing Met The

Beatles."
  M 1302
"A Day To Remember."
  M 3307
"A Dead Apple In London; Label's Staff
      Gets Pared."
  M 3677
"'Dead' Beatle Mania Mounts."
  M 0886
"Dealers Gang New Four-Color Beatles
      Posters."
  M 1328
"Dean Backs Lennon Peace Festival."
  N 0340
Dear Beatles
  B 0002   B 0003
"Dear LIFE Reader."
  M 3684
"Dear Paul And Linda."
  M 3501
"The Death And Life Of John Lennon."
  M 1394
"Death At The Dakota."
  M 0914
"A Death In The Family."
  M 0861   M 1175   M 1442   M 3378
"Death Of A Beatle."
  M 2143   M 2579
"Debris Is Hurled At Beatle Concert."
  N 0342
"A Decade Without The Beatles."
  M 0918   M 1784   M 1865   M 2468
  M 3379
Deccas Come And Deccas Go(ne)."
  M 1361
"Decision Near In Lennon Visa Case."
  M 0919
"Decree For Mrs. Lennon."
  N 0343
"Deep Quotes."
  M 0920   M 0921
"Defense Seeks Log Book In Lennon
      Slaying Case."
  N 0344
"Delaney & Bonnie's Super Times."
  M 1519
"Delay Is Expected In Chapman Trial."
  N 0345
"Denmark."
  M 1347
"Deportation Of Lennon Barred By Court
      Of Appeals."
  N 0714
"Depressed In Atlanta."
  N 0347
"Derek Taylor Makes A Radio Teleprinter
      Call From The QE2."
  M 3415
"Derek Taylor's Life With The Beatles."
  M 3416
"Descent Into Madness."
  M 1214
"Desert Island Discs."
  M 0690
"Despite Rumors Of Split, Beatles Cut A
      Big Melon."
  N 0348
"Dick James, Global Publisher."
  M 2261
"Did Allen Klein Take Bangla Desh
      Money?"
  M 1145
"Did Anybody Happen To Hear The Beatles
      In The U.S.?"
  M 0738
"A Different Bag."
  C 0218
"Dig It Plus."
  M 2430
"Dig It; The Beatles Bootleg Book."
  M 0933
Dig It (The Beatles Bootleg Book, Vol.
      One)
  B 0038
Dig - Special Beatles Issue
  P 0066
"Disaster? Well, Not Exactly: There
      Stood The Beatles."
  M 0651

"Discography."
  C 0095   M 0935
"Discography: Lennon's Recording Career
      1961-1980."
  M 0936
"Discord In Manila."
  N 0349
"Discs: Hello Paul - Bye-Bye Beatles."
  N 0350
"Disk Fairy Tale Has Sad Ending As
      Apple's 'Name' Is Mysteriously
      Yanked."
  M 0937
"Disorder In Rush For Beatles Tickets."
  N 0351
"Disques Beatles."
  M 1097
"Disques Du Mas: Imagine."
  M 0938
"Divorced."
  M 0941
"A D.J.'s View Of The Beatles."
  M 0927
"Does Anybody Believe Mahareshi?"
  M 0944
"Don't Condemn John, Pleads An American
      Beatle Person."
  M 0974
"Don't Copy - And Keep It Simple."
  M 0882
"Doomswatch."
  M 3628
"Dossier Pop Music: Les Pop Heureux Ent
      Une Histoire."
  M 0556
"Double Album Alphabet."
  M 2552
"Double Beatle."
  M 3128
"Double Fantasy."
  M 0955
Double Fantasy (songbook)   see   Songs
      From Double Fantasy/Season Of
      Glass
"Do We Still Need The Beatles?"
  M 0978
"Down The Rabbit Hole."
  C 0107
"Down The Up Poll."
  M 0980
"Down Under Pix."
  M 0981
"Do You Want To Know A Secret?"
  M 3397
"Dracula Schmacula."
  M 0990
"Dragonflies, Frogs And The Beatles."
  M 0737
"Drawing A Bead On The Beatles."
  M 0984
"Dream Is Ended."
  C 0096   N 0353
"The Dream Is Not Over."
  M 1200   M 3275
"The Dream Is Over."
  C 0097   M 0557   N 0583
"Drive My Car."
  M 3288
"Drug Rap In Tokyo Brings Down Wings
      And McCartney."
  M 0987
"Drugs Raid On Beatle."
  N 0354
"Druidmania."
  M 2145
"The Dutch Beatles Convention."
  M 0643
"The Dutch Discography."
  M 1881
"The Dutch Discography, Part Two."
  M 1882
"Dylan & The Beatles - I Wanna Hold
      Your Tambourine Man."
  M 3521
"Dylan In The Isle Of Wight."
  M 0992
"Dylan Record Puts Beatles Up A Tree."
  M 0993
"Each Beatle Carrying $5.5 Million

Insurance."
  N 0357
"Early Apple Recordings."
  M 2233
"An Early Interview With The Beatles."
  M 1744
"The Early Years."
  M 2090
"Earth Symphony."
  M 0928
"Eastern Promise."
  M 0979
"East German Commies Surrender To
      Beatles; Battle Was Lost Anyway."
  M 0995
"Ebony And Ivory."
  M 0956
Die Echte Beatles Story
  B 0586
"Editorial."
  C 0099   M 0113   M 0896   M 0996
  M 1814
"Editor's Log."
  M 0795
"Ed Sullivan Devotes Show To Music By
      Beatles."
  N 0440
"Educators Urged To Heed Beatles;
      Music's Relevance To U.S. Life Is
      Tanglewood Topic."
  N 0684
"The Eggman Wears White."
  M 0827
"Eggs Shower The Beatles."
  N 0359
"Eggs Thrown At Beatles."
  N 0360
"The Eggtual Interview About Paul's
      LP."
  M 1001
Eh?
  B 0504
"Eight Days A Week" Beatles Song
      Calendar 1983
  B 0177
8 Days A Week News
  F 0061
"Eight Days In Montreal With John And
      Yoko."
  M 3003
"The Eighteenth Single: How The Beatles
      Recorded Their New Single."
  M 1037
"The 8th New York Beatlefest '81."
  M 1266
"'82 Touring Guide."
  M 0528   M 3480
"'Eleanor Rigby' And All That."
  M 0012
"Eleanor Rigby Comes To Town."
  M 3294
"'Eleanor Rigby': Structure In The
      Arts."
  M 0501
"Elephant's Memory."
  M 0033
"Elephant's Memory Without The
      Plastic."
  M 2083
"Elton John Celebrates His Friend John
      Lennon And Gets A Visit From Yoko
      & Godson Sean."
  M 1008
"Elton - Oh What A Night!"
  M 3595
Elvis: A Biography
  C 0143
"Elvis Presley."
  M 1570
"Elvis Presley And John Lennon: The
      Good Die Young."
  M 1009
Elvis Presley - The Beatles
  B 0029
Elvis: The Final Years
  C 0144
Elvis Vs. The Beatles
  P 0067
"EMI, Beatles To Renew Pact."

M 2239
"EMI May Ration Beatle Album."
N 0363
"EMI Postpones Plans For TV Beatles
    Package."
M 1016
"EMI Spurns Nude Lennon And Yoko On '2
    Virgins' LP."
M 2240
"EMI: The Unreleased Recordings."
M 0108
"EMI - You Know My Game, Look Up The
    Number."
M 3533
"Encyclo(Beatle)pedia!"
M 0870
Encyclopedia Of Pop, Rock And Soul
C 0309
"The End Of An Era."
M 2347
"End Of An Odyssey."
M 0922
"End Of Metaphor."
M 1299
The End Of The Beatles?
B 0112
"The End Of The Performing Beatles."
M 1017
"Endpaper."
M 1018
"End Papers."
N 0429
"End To Beatles' Legal Hassle Due
    Soon."
M 2241
En Flagrant Delire
B 0303   B 0304
"Engaged."
M 1019
"England's Challenge: Beatles Rule!"
C 0145
"England's Wings: Beating The
    Post-Beatle Stigma."
M 1020
English Bound Beatle Fans Club
F 0062
"'Enjoying Beatles'."
N 0893
"Enter Yoko & Exit Battling Beatles."
M 2110
"Epstein."
M 2469
"Epstein Death Accidental; 'Trouble
    From Insomnia'."
N 0364
"Epstein Denies Any Breakup Of
    Beatles."
M 1026
"Epstein Diversifies; Becomes A
    Producer."
M 1027
"Epstein Inquest Opens Today."
N 0365
"The Epstein Interviews."
M 1480
"Epstein Is Buried; Inquest Continues."
N 0366
"Epstein Is Expanding Empire."
M 1028
"Epstein; It's Impossible To Put My
    Feelings Into Words - Cilla."
M 3575
"Epstein Letter."
N 0367
"Epstein: Restless Empire Builder."
M 1567
"Epstein Values 1/4 Beatles Slice At
    $4,000,000."
M 1029
"The Erratic, Tormented Genius Of John
    Ono Lennon."
M 2568
"Etc; Four Beatles, Five Stones."
M 3750
"'Ethel? It's Me, Yeah, Doreen'."
M 1520
"The Eulogies Ended, Yoko Ono Faces The
    Pain Of Life Without John."
M 3214

"Everybody Has A Beatle."
M 3695
Every Little Thing
F 0063
Every Little Thing: The Beatles On
    Record
B 0364
"Every Little Thing: The Story Behind
    'Rarities,' The 'New' Beatles
    LP."
M 3149
"Every Morning Brings A New Day."
M 0114
"Everyone Should Speak Lennon's
    Language."
C 0174   N 0600
"Everyone Wants To Record A Lennon &
    McCartney Song."
M 0165
"Everywhere's Somewhere."
M 1064
"Evidence Of Gaiety."
N 1177
"Ex-Beatle Best Wins Playboy Libel
    Suit."
M 1065
"Ex-Beatle Drummer Files $8 Mil Libel
    Suit Vs. Former Mates, 'Playboy'
    Mag."
M 1066
"Ex-Beatle Harrison's In Town - With A
    Difference: He Arrived On Time
    Without 'An Entrance'."
N 0741
"Ex-Beatle Harrison To Make U.S. Tour."
N 0368
"Ex-Beatle Hit By A & M's Suit."
M 1068
"Ex-Beatle McCartney Forms New Pop
    Group."
N 0369
"Ex-Beatle Paul McCartney Writes To The
    Melody Maker With The Last Word
    On A Well Worn Subject."
M 1069
"Ex-Beatles Aide Ruled Guilty."
N 0370
"Ex-Beatles Keep Trying."
M 0137
"Ex-Beatles McCartney, Harrison."
N 0371
"Ex-Beatles Manager Allen Klein
    Indicted."
M 1131
"The Ex-Beatles - Surmounting The
    Aftermath."
M 0820
"Ex-Beatle Starting Over."
M 1312
"Ex-Beatle Wins Court Fight To Stay In
    U.S."
N 0372
"Ex-Manager Of Beatles And Rolling
    Stones Is Sentenced."
N 0457
"Expert Says He Has Proved - And
    Thousands Believe - Paul
    McCartney Is Dead."
M 1878
"Expert Witness In Two Trials Accused
    Of Lying On Training."
N 0995
"Explicating The Beatles."
C 0178
"The Export Series."
M 0109
"An Expression Of Sorrow; John Lennon
    Shot Dead At 40."
M 0197
Eye
M 1070
"An Eye For The Opportune Moment."
M 1071
"Eye Funds, McCartney Asks Court."
N 0373
"Eyes Of The Beatles."
M 1072
"Fab? Chaos; The TV Film, Magical
    Mystery Tour."

M 1073
"Fab Four."
M 1994
"The Fab Four! Adventures In Hamburg."
M 1560
"Fab Four Facts."
M 2470
"The Fab Four Have Inspired A
    Collecting Coterie."
N 0436
The Fab Four Publication
F 0064
"Fab Four Single!"
M 1074
Fab Goes Filming With The Beatles
P 0068
"Fab Macca: The Truth."
M 1075
"Fab Macca Waives The Rules."
M 1773
Fabulous Goes All Beatles
P 0069
The Face Of Rock & Roll: Images Of A
    Generation
C 0254
"The Faces Of George."
M 3223
"The Faces Of John."
M 1077
"The Faces Of Paul."
M 1078
"The Faces Of Ringo."
M 1079
Facts About A Rock Group, Featuring
    Wings
B 0213
"Facts And Shocks."
M 0166
"Fair Terms For N Songs Investors."
N 0374
"The Family Way, Part II: The Cynthia
    Lennon Interview."
M 1777
"The Family Way: The Cynthia Lennon
    Interview."
M 1778
"The Family Way: The Mike McCartney
    Interview."
M 1779
"Fan Fest Update."
M 1087   M 1201   M 1202   M 1203
M 1786   M 1792   M 1793   M 2369
M 2370   M 2393   M 2471   M 3380
M 3390
"Fans All Over World Honor Lennon."
N 0375
"FanScene."
M 1088   M 1443
"Fans Gather In Liverpool."
M 2472
"Fans Grieve For Lennon At Vigil."
N 0212
"Fans Grieve For Lennon At Vigils."
C 0051
"The Fans Meet The Beatles."
M 0897
"Fans Put On Show To Rival Beatles';
    But TV Rehearsal Goes On Despite
    Shrieks Of Crowd."
N 0971
"Farmer Lennon's Cow."
N 0325
"Father Given Custody Of Yoko Ono's
    Child."
N 0377
Father Lennon's Many Children
F 0065
I Favolosi Beatles
B 0107
"FBI Had Lennon Marked For Bust."
N 0378
"FBI Sought To Arrest Lennon; Feared
    Singer Would Embarrass Nixon."
N 0025
Featuring Paul McCartney And Wings:
    Facts About A Pop Group
B 0214
"Federal Court Upholds Its Jurisdiction
    In Copyright Case Involving

Lennons."
M 1093
"Feedback."
M 1094   M 2259
"Feedback: On The Death Of John
Lennon."
M 0664
"Feeling Of Youth: Beatles."
M 3013
"Ferry Back Across The Mersey."
M 1800
"Festival For Lennon Defended."
N 0382
"15 'New' Beatles Singles."
M 3565
"15 Years Of Beatlemania! Has It Really
Been That Long?"
M 1787
"The Fifth Beatle; 'A Little Help From
A Friend'."
M 2495
"The Fifth Beatle Gets Married."
M 1635
"Fifth Beatles Record."
M 1106
"The 5th International Beatles
Convention."
M 3534
"55,600 - Beatles Play To World's
Largest Audience In New York."
M 3249
"A $50 Million Day's Night."
M 1396
Fifty Years Adrift (In An Open-Necked
Shirt)
B 0546
"Fight For A Nation's Fans."
M 1107
"Fight Stops War Satire Film."
N 0584
Figures Of Light; Film Criticism And
Comment
C 0166
"Filling The World With 'Silly Love
Songs'."
N 0733
"Film Fox."
M 1108   M 1109   M 1110   M 1111
"Filming Pix."
M 1112
"Filming With The Boys In 'A Hard Day's
Night'."
M 3224
"Filming With The Boys In Beatlescope."
M 3225
"Film Music Score By George Harrison."
N 0383
"Films."
M 1113
"Films By Lennons Shown At Cannes;
Beatle Scampers After His
'Apotheosis' Is Screened."
N 0384
"The Films Of The Beatles: A Study In
Star Images."
M 2257
"Film Talk."
M 3226
"Film To Be Shown At Cannes Festival."
N 0385
"Final Bar: John Lennon Obituary."
M 1114
"The Final Interview."
M 1115
Final Placement
C 0094
"Final Speeches In Beatles Case."
N 0386
"Finance, Commerce And Industry;
Beatles As A Market Factor."
N 0387
"Fine John Lennon $360 For Reefers."
M 1116
Fingerpicking Lennon & McCartney
S 0085
"The Fire And The Wheel: John Lennon
And Paul McCartney In
Perspective."
M 1815

"First Aid For 130 At Beatles Show."
N 0388
"First 'Beatles' Disc For Sale?"
M 1118
"First Beatles Xmas."
M 0167
First Book Of Fifty Hit Songs By John
Lennon And Paul McCartney
S 0086
"The First British Beatles Convention."
M 1362
"First Cream For Beatles Film May Net
UA $500,000."
M 1119
"First Full-Length Biography Of The
Beatles."
M 1120
"First Impressions."
M 0898
"First Lennon Single In Five Years
Due."
M 1121
"First Live Performances For Over 2
Years."
M 1122
"The First Polish Beatles Gathering."
M 2175
"The First Time."
M 1123
"A Fitting Memorial For John Lennon."
N 0390
Five Bites Of The Apple
F 0066
"$587,000 Award Against Beatle."
N 0391
"557 Abkco Net May Be Bopped By
Beatles' Breakup."
M 1126
505 Rock 'N' Roll Questions Your
Friends Can't Answer
C 0287
"Fleetwood Mac Wins Rock Prize."
N 0393
"Flock Circling Warwick A Harbinger Of
Beatles."
N 0394
Florida Beatles Fan Club
F 0067
"Fly Away, Paul."
M 3629
"Flying With The Beatles."
M 0923
"Folk And The Beatles."
M 0672
"Folk-Rock: Folk Music, Protest, Or
Commercialism?"
M 0926
"Following The Beatles."
M 1141
"Following The Beatles' Trail."
M 1204
Follow The Merseybeat Road!
B 0293
"Foreword."
C 0247   C 0289   C 0290
"Foreword To The 1983 Edition."
C 0248
"Forget Reunion Of Beatles: McCartney."
M 1158
"Forget The Beatles, Listen To George."
M 3712
"The 4 Gotten 4 Most."
M 3535
"A Forgotten Legacy Of John Lennon."
M 0396
"For Innocence: Sudden Death."
N 0593
"Former Beatle Fails To Get Ban On
Articles."
N 0397
"Former Beatle On Drug Charges."
N 0398
"Former Beatles Manager Klein Back In
Court."
M 2170
"Former Beatles Manager Sues For
Libel."
N 0399
"Former Beatle Sued Over Alleged Loan"

N 0400
"Former Manager Of Beatles Loses High
Court Plea."
N 0401
"Forms Of Adulation."
N 0402
"For Sale: First Beatles Record."
N 0885
"For Service."
N 0403
"For The Love Of Lennon."
N 0331
"For The Record."
M 1132
"For $325, A Chance To Assess The
Legacy Of The Beatles."
N 0946
"A Fortune For A Song."
M 1159
"40 Beatles Fans Arrested."
N 0404
"40,000 Cheer 2 Beatles In Dual Benefit
For Pakistanis."
N 0690
Ein Fotorama Uber Die Beatles
B 0199
Four Aspects Of The Music Of The
Beatles: Instrumentation,
Harmony, Form, And Album Unity
B 0528
"4 Beatles And How They Grew;
Moneywise."
N 0024
"4 Beatles And How They Grew;
Peoplewise."
N 0849
"4 Beatles And How They Grew;
Publicitywise."
N 0882
"Four Cats On A London Roof."
M 1162
"Four Charities Share 250G Take From
John-Yoko's Benefit At Garden,
N.Y."
M 1163
"400 Gather In Vigil For Lennon."
N 0734
"400 Riot As Beatles Arrive In Miami."
N 0405
"4 Individual Beatles Score On Hot 100
For First Time."
M 1164
"Four Little Beatles And How They
Grew."
M 1165
"Four Points Of View: The Magical
Mystery Tour."
M 1764
"4 Singles Make Up First Crop Of
Beatles' Apple Corps Label."
N 0986
"4 Sought By Defense In Slaying Of
Lennon."
N 0406
Fourth Book Of Fifty Hit Songs By John
Lennon And Paul McCartney
S 0087
"4,000 Hail Beatles On Arrival In
Miami."
N 0407
"4,000 Recall Beatles, Yeah, Yeah,
Yeah."
N 0947
"Framing The Beatles."
M 1167
"Frankfurt Combo Puts Sauerkraut On
Revival Of Beatles."
M 1168
Freakshow
C 0121   C 0122
"Freezing Hot Mal."
M 1173
"Freighter Is Delivered Here To 'Peace
Pilot' From Israel."
N 0411
"The French Discography."
M 1883
"French 'Oo-la-la' The Beatles."
M 1481

"Frisco Fans Fierce Devotion Startles
    More Than Beatles' SRO 49G Take."
    M 1183
"From A Boy's Point Of View."
    M 3653
"From Day To Day; Death Threat After
    Beatles Incident."
    N 0412
"From Day To Day; Munich Claims Tax On
    Beatles."
    N 0413
"From Koch To Lennon: A Posthumous
    Cultural Award."
    N 0617
From Me To You
    F 0068
"From Minerva House."
    M 1188
"From Rock To ???"
    M 2431
"From Romance To Romanticism; Analysing
    The Beatles Lyrics."
    C 0069
"From The Crow's Nest: A Bio."
    M 0021
"From The Editor."
    M 1189
"From The Family Album."
    C 0110 C 0111
"From Then To You."
    M 1190
"From The Royal Academy Summer
    Exhibition."
    N 0414
"From The Sketch Pad Of John Lennon's
    First Wife, Cynthia, Come
    Poignant Memories."
    M 3744
"From The 'Top Ten' To Number 17."
    M 3295
"Fuck."
    M 3354 M 3391
"Full Report On Wings World Tour And
    New LP Tracks."
    M 1195
"Fund Lennon Scholarship."
    M 1207
"15 Jahre Beatles."
    M 1208
"Funny Songs, Protest Songs, Song
    Songs."
    M 1209
"Furor Over Beatles."
    N 0415
"Further Reflections On Dec. 8, 1980."
    M 3381
"Gambier Terrace."
    M 1444
"Game Plan."
    M 0713
"'A Garden Of Love'."
    N 0418
"Gary Fawkes."
    M 1233
Gear Box
    F 0069
"Geffen Nets Lennon For Album Package."
    M 1177
"Geffen Records Signs Lennons, Elton
    John."
    M 1799
"Geffen's Coup: Lennon & Yoko Signed."
    M 1237
Geliebter John
    B 0432
A Generation In Motion: Popular Music
    And Culture In The Sixties
    C 0242
"Genitalia Slips Quietly Under The
    Counter."
    M 1538
"George."
    M 1010
George
    P 0070
"George And John."
    M 3728
"George Does A Turn For Ravi."
    M 0103

George Gernal
    F 0070
"George Harrison."
    C 0115 C 0116 M 0754 M 3107
    N 0423
"George Harrison And John Lennon."
    M 3115
"George Harrison And Other Bores."
    M 3265
George Harrison Anthology
    S 0088
"George Harrison Bangla Desh Benefit."
    M 1239
"George Harrison Banned And Fined."
    N 0424
"George Harrison Cranks It Up To 33 And
    1/3."
    M 3782
"George Harrison Discovers The Pleasure
    Of Home, Maui, The Recording
    Studio And Formula One Racing."
    M 3194
"George Harrison: Fall From Grace."
    C 0262
George Harrison Fan Club
    F 0071
"George Harrison Guilty Of
    Plagiarizing, Subconsciously, A
    '62 Tune For A '70 Hit."
    N 0425
"The George Harrison Hamburg
    Deportation."
    M 3296
"George Harrison: His Guitar Isn't
    Weeping Anymore."
    M 0622
"George Harrison In Brazil."
    M 3204
"George Harrison In India."
    M 0988
"The George Harrison Interview."
    M 1261 M 3576 M 3577
"George Harrison: Is There Life After
    Enlightenment?"
    M 3596
"George Harrison: Live In The Material
    World."
    M 1363
"George Harrison Married."
    N 0426
"George Harrison On Abbey Road."
    M 1240
"George Harrison On Beatles; Plays Down
    Reunion Possibilities At Coast
    Party Marking Warner Deal."
    M 3485
"George Harrison On The Record."
    M 1241
"George Harrison: Record Producer!"
    M 2112
"George Harrison: Re-Meet The Beatle."
    M 1178
"George Harrison's George Harrison."
    M 1364
"George Harrison's Guitars."
    M 1365
"George Harrison's Hand Read By Romany
    Clairvoyant, Eva Petulengro."
    M 2373
"George Harrison's Search For
    Anonymity."
    M 1248
"George Harrison's Solo Rarities."
    M 0957
"George Harrison Tells It Like It Is."
    M 3440
"'George Harrison': The Album
    Reviewed."
    M 1978
"George Harrison: The Niceman Cometh."
    M 0105
"George Harrison Writes Film Score."
    M 1242
George Harrison: Yesterday And Today
    B 0381 B 0382
"George Hits At Capitol."
    M 3688
"George In Hippyland."
    M 2566

"George Introduces Hare Krishna."
    M 1243
"George Martin."
    C 0323
"George Martin Looks Back To The
    Beatles And Forward With
    Seatrain."
    M 0851
"George Martin On The Beatle Days."
    M 1244
"George Martin Recalls The Boys In The
    Band."
    M 1518
"George Martin Talks About The
    Beatles."
    M 3731
"George - More To Life Than Being A
    Beatle."
    M 3578
"George, Paul, Ringo, And John; The
    Beatles In The United States."
    M 1891
"George Records 'Krishna'."
    M 1245
"George Speaking."
    M 1636
"George's Solo Career."
    M 1246
"George's Tour Winds Down In New York,
    And Mr. Harrison Goes To
    Washington."
    M 3289
"George's U.S. Visit."
    M 1038
"German Club Where Beatles Began
    Reopens."
    M 1247
"German Police In Summit Conference On
    Strategy To Control Beatle Mobs."
    M 1345
"The German Scene."
    M 3119
"A German Teenager Asks Paul McCartney
    To Send All His Loving - And Lots
    Of Money."
    M 1172
"Germany."
    M 0597
"Germany Updated."
    M 3120
Die Geschichte Der Beatles
    B 0151 B 0152
Get Back
    F 0072 F 0073
"'Get Back' LP In December."
    M 1252
"'Get Back' Postponed."
    M 1253
"Get Back To Northern Songs."
    N 0427
"Getting His Wings."
    M 0147
"Getting Up To Date On John, George &
    Ringo."
    M 1979
"The Ghost Of Ringo Haunts This Group."
    C 0118
"Ghoulish Beatlemania."
    M 2125
"Die Giganten."
    C 0244
"Gimme Some Truth."
    M 1086
"Gimme Some Truth: The Thoughts Of John
    Lennon."
    C 0336
Gimmix Book Of Records
    C 0124
"Girl Gets Back Her Passport."
    N 0431
"Girl On Second Drug Charge."
    N 0432
"Girls In Miami Shriek Welcome To The
    Beatles."
    N 0433
"The Girls They Like."
    M 0168
The Girl Who Sang With The Beatles And
    Other Stories

B 0250   B 0251
"'Give Peace A Chance': An Anthem For
      The Anti-War Movement."
   C 0334
Give Peace A Chance: Music And The
      Struggle For Peace
   B 0455   C 0007   C 0216   C 0229
   C 0259   C 0334
"Glasgow Slaps Ban On Beatles Queues."
   M 1258
"Glass Onion."
   M 0691   M 1260   M 2134   M 3184
The Globe (Volume 27, Number 53.
      December 30, 1980)
   M 1282
"Going For Baroque: Young Swingers Dig
      The Old Style Music."
   N 0966
Going Steady
   C 0165
The Golden Beatles
   S 0089
Golden Beatles, Book 1
   S 0090
Golden Beatles, Book 2
   S 0091
The Golden Beatles - Vocal
   S 0092
The Golden Era Of The Beatles
   S 0093
Gold Key - Beatles Yellow Submarine
   P 0071
"A Gold Mine At The Bottom Of The
      Garden."
   N 0497
"Goodbye Stu!"
   C 0128
"Good-bye To The 'Now Generation'."
   N 0437
"Goodbye To Yesterday."
   M 3630
Good Day Sunshine
   F 0074   F 0075
"Good Egg."
   M 0190
"A Good Guru's Guide To The Beatles
      Sinister Songbook."
   N 0715
The Good Life; Personal Expressions Of
      Happiness By Paul McCartney
   B 0527
"Good Lord, It's The Same Old Song."
   M 1297
"Good Morning America."
   M 2354
Goodnight Vienna
   S 0094
"'Go On,' Said The Beatle, 'Ask Yer
      Mum'."
   M 0784
"The Goon Show Scripts."
   N 0642
"The Gossip Hurts, But Ono Goes On."
   N 0476
"Got To Be Good Lookin'."
   M 1852
"Grammar School Bans Beatle Haircuts."
   N 0443
"Grammy For Yoko Ono Stirs Awards
      Ceremony."
   N 0852
"Grammys: Hard Rock's Soft Underbelly."
   M 1133
"Grand Jury Indicts Allen Klein."
   M 1309
"Grandmother's Comment."
   N 0444
Grapefruit
   B 0418   B 0419   B 0420   B 0421
   B 0422   B 0423   B 0424
"A Graphic History."
   M 2250
The Great Beatle Rip Off
   B 0534
"Great British Achievements: The
      Beatles Conquer The World -
      1960's."
   M 1320
"The Greatest Hits Of 1989."

M 1146
"Great News Of 'The Beatles'."
   C 0131   M 1321
Great Pop Stars
   C 0130
"Great Rock Conspiracy."
   M 2046
Great Songs Of Lennon And McCartney
   S 0095
"Green Apples."
   M 1769
"Greenfield Eyes Effect From The
      Beatles."
   N 0446
"Group After Beatles Fans."
   M 1339
"Group 'No Longer Thought Of As The
      Beatles'."
   N 0450
"Growing Up At 33 1/3: The George
      Harrison Interview."
   M 1262
"Growing Up With Lennon."
   M 1002
Growing Up With The Beatles
   B 0483   B 0484   B 0485
"Growing Up With The Beatles."
   N 0932
"Guest Appearances."
   M 1343
A Guide To Record Collection
   C 0230
"Gun Control."
   N 0452
"Gun Control Hodgepodge."
   M 0655
"Gunfire Kills John Lennon."
   N 0453
"Guns And Logic."
   N 0454
"The Guru: How To Succeed By
      Meditating."
   N 0639
"Haircuts."
   N 0459
"Hair-Dos."
   N 0460
"Half Lennon Fortune Left To Wife."
   N 0461
"Half-Staff Flags Among Tributes To
      John Lennon - World Vigil Set
      Tomorrow - Wife In Seclusion."
   N 0737
"Halt Showings Of Beatles Movie."
   M 3702
"Hamburg."
   C 0196
"Hamburg Souvenirs."
   M 1503
"A Hamburg Survivor."
   M 1392
"The Hamburg Tapes."
   M 1393
"Hamburg: The City Where The Beatles
      Developed Their Original Sound."
   M 1504
"Hands Across The Water; Columbia's
      Singles Sweep."
   M 1329
Hands Across The Water - Wings Tour
      U.S.A.
   B 0234   B 0235
"Hands Off; They're Trying To Bash The
      Beatles."
   M 0755
"A Hard Day's Drive."
   N 0462
"A Hard Day's Knights."
   C 0083   C 0084
A Hard Day's Night
   B 0090   B 0091
"A Hard Day's Night."
   C 0161   C 0281
"'Hard Day's Night': Even Better."
   N 0963
A Hard Day's Night (songbook) see The
      Beatles/A Hard Day's Night
A Hard Day's Night, With The Beatles; A
      Director's Handbook

B 0162
"Harrison, A & M Ties Open New Avenues
      For Beatles."
   M 1171
The Harrison Alliance
   F 0076
"Harrison: All Things Must Pass."
   M 1853
"Harrison & Friends Dish Out Super
      Concert For Pakistan Aid."
   M 1259
"Harrison And The Slow Death Mystery."
   M 1411
"Harrison: An Ex-Beatle Limps Back -
      Vancouver, Can."
   M 1238
"Harrison Benefit For East Pakistanis."
   N 0464
"Harrison Billed $587,000 In 'My Sweet
      Lord' Case; Allen Klein To
      Collect."
   M 1412
"Harrison - Dark Horse In Cannes."
   M 2394
Harrison Herald
   F 0077
"Harrison In Big Bootleg War."
   M 1413
"Harrison Launches Own Label."
   M 1414
"Harrison, On Himself."
   N 0458
"Harrison's Dark Horses."
   M 1596
"Harrison's Extra Texture: Read All
      About It."
   M 1219
"Harrison Song In Dispute."
   M 1416
"Harrison, Starr Plan A U.S. Tour;
      Former Beatles Will Play In At
      Least 12 Cities In Fall."
   N 0948   N 0949
"Harrison's TV Blast Brings Menon
      Reply."
   M 1417
"Harrison Suit Wins 1st Round."
   M 1418
"Harrison Switches Labels."
   M 1419
"Harrison Tour Set: They're All
      Hustling Him."
   M 1420
"Harrison Trial: Is "My Sweet Lord" 'So
      Fine'?"
   M 1249
"Harrison Will Play 50 Dates."
   M 1421
"Harrison Wraps 27-City Tour At Garden,
      N.H.; Ex-Beatle Fizzles."
   M 1422
"Hate Mail Makes The World Go 'Round."
   M 2162
"Hats On To Wolverhampton."
   M 0899
"Haunted By John Lennon's Murder ...
      Frightened Beatle Paul McCartney
      Turns His Home Into A Fortress."
   M 0857
"'Have We All Forgotten What Vibes
      Are?'."
   M 1894
"Hawaii Gun Store Draws Their Fury."
   N 0839
"Hearing Lennon's Secret Messages."
   M 0076
"Hearing On Term In Lennon Slaying."
   N 0466
"Hear That Big Sound."
   M 1467   M 3441
"'Hear The Beatles Tell All'."
   M 0958
"A Heart To Heart Talk With Paul
      McCartney."
   M 1468
"The Heaviest Beatle Of Them All."
   M 1212
"He Blew His Mind Out In A Car; The
      True Story Of Paul McCartney's

Death."
  M 1474
He Dreams What Is Going On Inside His
    Head: Ten Years Of Writing
  C 0085
"Hello, Goodbye."
  M 3749
"Hello, Goodbye, Hello"
  M 1472
Help
  P 0072
"Help, As Interpreted By John Lennon
    And Yoko Ono."
  N 0222
"Help! Four Beatles Surrounded By
    Reunion Rumors."
  M 1473
"The Helpful Beatle."
  M 3227
Help! Red De Beatles!
  B 0254
Help! (songbook) see The Beatles
    Help!
Help! The Beatles
  B 0116
Helter Skelter
  F 0078
Here Are The Beatles
  B 0231
"Here Are The Runners-Up In Our Draw A
    Beatle Competition."
  M 1490
"Here Come Those Beatles."
  M 1323
"Here's Some Things To Tell Your
    Uncle."
  M 3052
"Here's Some Trivia To Test Yourself."
  M 0663
Here, There And Everywhere
  F 0079 F 0080
"Here, There And Everywhere."
  M 2988 M 3382
"Here, There And Everywhere: Part
    Eight."
  M 2995
"Here, There And Everywhere, Part
    Five."
  M 2992
"Here, There And Everywhere: Part
    Four."
  M 2991
"Here, There And Everywhere: Part
    Seven."
  M 2994
"Here, There And Everywhere, Part Six."
  M 2993
"Here, There And Everywhere, Part
    Three."
  M 2990
"Here, There And Everywhere: Part Two."
  M 2989
Here, There & Everywhere: The First
    International Beatles
    Bibliography, 1962-1982
  B 0547
"Here We Go Again!"
  M 0756
"Heroes."
  N 0967
"'Heroes Of Rock 'N' Roll' Airs."
  M 1147
"A Hero's Return To Liverpool."
  N 0472
"He's A Sensitive Soul."
  M 3228
"Heures Et Humeurs D'un Amateur: Un
    Mois A Paris."
  M 2043
"He Was Always Fascinated By The
    Beyond."
  M 1843
"Hiding Justice."
  N 0474
"High Brows Vs. No Brows."
  C 0076 M 0714
"A Highbrow Under All That Hair?"
  M 3747
High Times

  M 1496
"Hightower Heads John, Yoko Anti-Deport
    Drive."
  M 1497
"Hippies To Look Over Island Offered To
    Them By A Beatle."
  N 0480
"Hiram And The Animals."
  M 3345
"Hiram's Report."
  C 0310 M 3346
"Hirsute Trio."
  M 1512
Histoire Du Rock Les Beatles
  P 0073
"A Historical Premiere."
  M 1513
"Historic Beatles-Elvis Meeting."
  M 1514 M 3250
"Historic Cavern Club Given 3-Month
    Reprieve."
  M 1220
"The Historic 1965 U.S. Tour."
  M 1571
Historien Om Beatles
  B 0439
"His Ultimate Contribution."
  M 0862
"The Hit Parader Interview: John
    Lennon."
  M 3045
"Hold Out."
  M 1528
"Holds Press Conference To Kick Off
    Tour."
  N 0483
"Holiday Snaps August 1963."
  M 1529
"Hollywood Bowl."
  M 1535
"Homage From A Fallen Idol."
  N 0761
"Home Is Where The Heart Is ... "
  M 3524
Homenaje A John Lennon
  B 0259
"Home News; Epstein Lawyers Seek Will:
    Funeral To Be In Private."
  N 0484
"Home News; Ringo Starr Sued."
  N 0485
Hommage An John Lennon
  B 0260
L'Hommage De La Bande Dessinee - (A
    Suivre) Special John Lennon
  B 0261
"Honours."
  N 0487 N 0488 N 0489
"Hooliganism 'Will Be Stamped Out';
    Incidents During Visit By
    Beatles."
  N 0490
"Hot As Sun: The Beatles Album No One
    Will Ever Hear."
  M 1404
"Hotel Near Beatles's Home Rejected."
  N 0491
"Hottest McCartneys These Days Don't Go
    For A Song - Linda's Prints Fetch
    $1,000."
  M 1731
"Houston Has Nation's First All-Beatle
    Station."
  N 0492
"How About Long Hair?"
  N 0493
"How Apple Turned Sour."
  N 0851
"How Beatlemania Really Began!"
  M 0169
"How Different From The Cavern Days."
  M 1400
"How Do You Feel About This Undying
    Interest In The Beatles, Ringo?"
  M 1021
"How I Got Publicity For 'Love Me Do'."
  M 0170
"How I Won The War."
  M 1366 M 1637

How I Won The War; Lieutenant Ernest
    Goodbody As Told To Patrick Ryan
  B 0474
"How John Lennon Was Overwhelmed By
    Life And Death."
  N 1038
"How John Was Overwhelmed By Life And
    Death."
  C 0315
"Howling, Not Booing, Says John."
  M 1553
"How Long Can They Last?"
  M 0757
"How Love Me Do Became A Hit."
  M 0900
"How One Man Sold The Beatles To
    America: John Lennon - The Inside
    Story Of His Incredible Life."
  M 1554
"How Paul Beat His Tokyo Blues."
  N 0542
"How Subversive Are The Beatles?"
  M 1565
"How The Beatles Sold 'Sgt. Pepper'."
  M 1745
"How The Electric Guitar Became A Way
    Of Music."
  N 0950
"How The Magical E.P.s Were Made."
  M 1049
"How Tin Pan Alley Beat The Beatles."
  N 0496
"How To Write A Hit! Interview With
    John Lennon And Paul McCartney."
  M 3039
"How TV Reported The John Lennon
    Tragedy."
  M 2509
"How Was The New Album Cover Taken?"
  M 1556
"Hundreds Ignore Cold To Keep Vigil For
    John."
  N 0213
"Hungry Beatles Form Apple In Bid For
    Slice Of Trades' Pie."
  M 1564
"I Am A Beatle Person."
  M 1401
"I Am The (Boston) Walrus."
  M 3308
"I Am Your Singer."
  M 1367
"I Can't Tell You How I Feel."
  M 0115
"Iconic Modes: The Beatles."
  C 0065 C 0066
Icons Of America
  C 0065
"I'd Love ... To Tur .. r .. r .. n You
    On."
  C 0308
"I Don't Believe In Beatles."
  M 1577
"'I Don't Like Anything Different Or
    Unusual' Says John."
  M 1578
"'I Do Play The Drums': Claims Ex-Fab
    Four Ex-Mop Top Ringo Starr."
  M 0846
"I'd Rather Be An Ex-Beatle Than An
    Ex-Nazi!"
  M 0758
"I Feel Like Letting Go."
  M 1368
"'I Felt The Split Was Coming'."
  M 2172
"If I Ever Get Out Of Here."
  M 1369
"If There's Mercy, 'I'd Like It,
    Please'."
  N 0691
"If We Ever Did Anything Together ...
    ."
  M 3046
"I Introduced The Beatles, Says David
    Hamilton."
  M 0171
"I'll Be Waiting For You Baby."
  M 1370

The Illustrated Encyclopedia Of Rock
  C 0027
The Illustrated Rock Almanac
  C 0202
"I Made A Glass Hammer."
  M 3558
Imagine
  F 0081   S 0096
"Imagine."
  M 0637   M 2155
"Imagine All The People Mourning In The
  Rain."
  N 0909
"Imagine: John Lennon Legal."
  M 1134
Imagine John Lennon 1
  B 0083
"Imagine ... Lennon Was A Monster, It's
  Easy (And Profitable) If You
  Try!"
  M 2473
Imagine (songbook) see also John
  Lennon: Imagine
"I'm A Loser - And I've Lost Someone
  Who's Near To Me."
  M 1580
"'I'm A Walrus' With Just A Little
  Lear."
  M 1581
I Me Mine
  B 0238   B 0239   B 0240
"I'm Looking Through You."
  M 3636
"Impassioned Chief Of A Generation's
  Idols."
  M 3090
"Impending Fatherhood Stays Lennon
  Ouster."
  N 0602
"I'm Touring Soon, Says Harrison."
  M 1838
"In And Out Of Books; The Writing
  Beatle."
  N 0800
"In Beatles' Wake: Novel Sounds, Looks
  Pay Off For Singers."
  N 1009
"In Brief; Beatle Baby."
  N 0499
"In Brief; Beatles' Story On Radio."
  N 0500
"In Brief; Climb To See Lennon."
  N 0501
"In Brief; Drugs Class Offer."
  N 0502
"In Brief; £18m Lennon Lawsuit."
  N 0503
"In Brief; Film On Hanratty."
  N 0504
"In Brief; Former Beatle Hurt."
  N 0505
"In Brief; Hindu Festival Ban Over
  Beatles."
  N 0506
"In Brief; Japan Bars Ex-Beatle."
  N 0507
"In Brief; Jet Waits For Pop Star."
  N 0508
"In Brief; Lennon's Warning."
  N 0509
"In Brief; Lennon Tree Destroyed."
  N 0510
"In Brief; McCartney Farm Search."
  N 0511
"In Brief; McCartney Tour."
  N 0512
"In Brief; Mystic Forgives The
  Beatles."
  N 0513
"In Brief; Pop Record Seized."
  N 0514
"In Brief; Ringo Crusade."
  N 0515
"In Brief; Ringo Starr In Crash."
  N 0516
"In Brief; Son For The Lennons."
  N 0517
"In Brief; The Prejudicial Nude."
  N 0518

"In Brief; £300 Beatle Fund."
  N 0519
"In Brief; £2.9m Settlement By Beatles'
  Firm."
  N 0520
"Income Of The Beatles For 19 Months
  Under Klein Management Said To Be
  Over £9M."
  N 0521
"In Defence Of The Beatles' Honour;
  Motion Tabled By Liverpool
  M.P.s."
  N 0522
"In Defense Of Paul McCartney."
  M 1405
Independent Free Apple
  F 0082
Indiana OBFC
  F 0083
"Indian Influence On The Beatles."
  C 0168
"Indian Old Rope Trick."
  M 3556
"Indian Rope Trick."
  M 0931
"India Police Visit Beatles' Retreat."
  N 0523
"Industry Reacts To A & M - Harrison
  Suit."
  M 1406
"In Gratitude."
  M 2359   N 0524   N 0525
"In His Own Words Pete Best Tells Of -
  My Beatle Days."
  M 0532
In His Own Write; And, A Spaniard In
  The Works
  B 0305   B 0306
"Injured In Auto Accident."
  N 0526
"In Memoriam ... "
  M 1582
"In Memoriam: Jimmy McCulloch."
  M 1371
"In Memoriam: Mal Evans."
  M 1583
"In Memoriam: Pete Ham Of Badfinger."
  M 0850
"In Memory Of John Lennon."
  M 1030
"In Memory Of The Cavern."
  M 1584
"In My Life ... A Personal File."
  C 0147
The Inner Light
  F 0084
"In Perspective."
  N 0527
"In Praise Of John Lennon."
  M 0518
"In Praise Of John Lennon: The
  Liverpool Lad As Musician,
  Husband, Father, And Man."
  M 1585   M 3215
"Inquest Is Ordered In Death Of Manager
  Of The Beatles."
  N 0528
"Inscrutable Orientals Flip Lids Over
  Beatles During Tokyo Stand."
  M 1586
In Seiner Eigenen Schreibe
  B 0307   B 0308
In Seiner Eigenen Schreibe/Ein Spanier
  Macht Noch Keinen Sommer
  B 0309
"Inside Beatles."
  M 3793
"Inside John Lennon's FBI File."
  M 2971
"Inside-Out: Electronic Rock."
  M 0942
The Inside Story Of The Yellow
  Submarine
  P 0074
"Inside The Dakota."
  M 1762
"Inside Wings: An Interview With
  Ex-Drummer Joe English."
  M 1587

Instant Karma
  F 0085
"'Instant Memories' Flooding Market."
  M 1788
"Intellectual Lennon: Social
  Revolutionary."
  C 0012   N 0047
"Interesting Facts."
  M 2515
"Intermedia: Tune In, Turn On - And
  Walk Out?"
  N 0686
"International Beatles Marathon."
  M 0880
"Interview: Laurence Juber."
  M 2996
"Interview With Paul."
  M 1310
"In The Bag: Yoko Ono."
  M 1839
"In The Beatles Song Writing Factory."
  M 1588
"In The Beginning/The Early Years."
  M 3297
In The Core Of The Apple
  F 0086
"In The Echo Chamber."
  M 3562
In The Footsteps Of The Beatles
  B 0188
"In The Pop Bag."
  M 1469
"In The Studio."
  M 1638
"In The Studio With Lennon And
  Spector."
  M 3713
"'In Town Where I Was Born'."
  M 1445
"An Introduction To The John Lennon
  Fantasy Story: Yellow Submarine
  Revisited."
  M 3482
"In U.S. Financial Mop Up."
  N 0529
"The Invasion Of A Stately Home."
  M 2142
"In Who's Who In America."
  N 0530
"Irate AFM Flips Lid Over Invasion Of
  'Rocking Redcoats' Sans Culture."
  M 1590
"Irate Beatles To Fight ATV's Move To
  Win Control Of Northern Songs."
  M 1591
"I Read The News Today - Eller Da John
  Lennon Igen Blev Godt Stof!"
  M 0542
"I Read The News Today, Oh Boy."
  C 0137   M 1592   M 1593
"Irish Song By McCartney Banned By
  BBC."
  N 0531
"Irked By Award To Beatles Canadian
  Returns Medal."
  N 0532
"Is Beatlemania Dead? North American
  Tour."
  M 1598
"Is Klaatu Band The Beatles?"
  M 1599
"Is Klaatu Spelled Backwards Really Mop
  Top Four?"
  M 1600
"Israel Bars Beatles."
  N 0533
"Israel Gets First Single In Five
  Years."
  M 1601
"Israel Updated."
  M 3519
"Is Sgt. Pepper Too Advanced For The
  Average Pop Fan To Appreciate?"
  M 1639
"Issue/On John Lennon."
  M 3264
"Is That You In There, Ringo?"
  M 1495
"Is The Beatles Frenzy Cooling Down?"

M 0875   M 2048
"I Sat Belonely Down A Tree."
   M 1895
"I Saw Pinetop Spit Blood."
   M 1597
"The Italian Discography."
   M 1076
"Italy Loves Them."
   N 0534
"It Had To Happen: Promoter Offers Tax
   Break For Book On John Lennon."
   N 0536
"It Happened In 1970."
   M 1610   M 1611   M 1612   M 1613
"It Happened In 1968."
   M 1603   M 1604   M 1605   M 1606
"It Happened In 1969."
   M 1607   M 1608   M 1609
"It Happened In 1967."
   M 1602
"'It's A Hard Night,' Says
   Springsteen."
   N 0535
"'It's All A Fantasy, Putting The
   Beatles Back Together'."
   M 1614
"It's All Music."
   M 0520
"It's Alright."
   M 2015
"It's Easy If You Try."
   M 1615
It's Easy To Play Beatles
   S 0097
"It's Getting Better."
   M 1836
"It's Like Winning The Pools."
   M 0759
"It's Never Too Late."
   M 2556
"It's The Quiet Ones You Have To
   Watch."
   M 3673
...It Was Twenty Years Ago Today...Die
   Beatles Und Die 60ziger Jahre
   B 0486
"I've Come To Terms With My Nose."
   M 0760
"Ives And Beatles."
   M 1000
"'I've Thrown Away 30 Songs' Says
   George."
   M 1616
"I Visited The Beatles On The Set."
   M 3130
"I Wanna Hold Your Hand ... Again."
   M 1618
"'I Wanna Hold Your Hand' Reviewed."
   M 1980
"I Wanna Hold Your Head: John Lennon
   After The Fall."
   M 1824
"I Wanna Hold Your Stock."
   M 1619
"I Want To Live In Peace."
   M 0098
"I Want To Write Songs For Revolution."
   M 1620
"I Was A Very Nervous Character: An
   Interview With George Martin
   About Producing The Beatles And
   Other Things."
   M 1871
"I Was Never Lovable, I Was Just
   Lennon."
   N 0809
"'I Was Shivering Inside ...'"
   M 2474
"Jaded Miami Beach Takes Beatles In
   Stride Despite Shrieking
   Teenagers."
   M 3316
"Jakarta To Burn Beatle Music."
   N 0537
"James Taylor On Apple: 'The Same Old
   Craperoo'."
   M 1539
"January 1 - March 31, 1964 - 90 Days
   That Shook The Industry."

M 0976
"Japanese Deport McCartney For Having
   Marijuana."
   N 0538
"Jean's Rival."
   N 0539
"Jerry Baby's."
   M 1522
"A Jersey Prosecutor Bans Sale Of A
   Beatles' Album."
   N 0540
"Jesus Freaks Silence Lennon."
   N 0541
"Jimmy McCulloch."
   M 1672
"Jimmy McCulloch, Was Guitarist In Paul
   McCartney's Wings Band."
   N 0543
"Joe Jones."
   M 1676
John
   P 0075
"John."
   M 3620
"John Acquires Stuart's Painting."
   C 0152
"John And George Get Their U.S. Visas."
   M 1677
"John & Jerry & David & John & Leni &
   Yoko."
   M 3645
"John And Ono Pitching Pacifism In
   Times Sq."
   M 1678
"John And Yoko."
   M 0562   M 2969   M 3292   M 3714
   M 3715   M 3716   M 3791
"John And Yoko Arrival In Toronto To
   Push Peace Stirs Unpeaceful
   Aura."
   M 1679
"John And Yoko: Busted And Naked."
   C 0153
"John And Yoko Coming Unmoored."
   M 0646
"John And Yoko Disavow Toronto."
   M 1681
"John And Yoko Disgusted."
   M 1682
"John & Yoko Fight Deportation
   Decision; Hardhats Join Appeal."
   M 1683
"John And Yoko In Newark, New Jersey."
   M 1684
"John And Yoko On A Peace Cruise."
   M 1685
"John And Yoko On Marriage, Children
   And Their Generation."
   M 3247
"John And Yoko Ono Lennon: Give Peace A
   Chance."
   M 3135
"John And Yoko On The Town."
   M 1686
"John And Yoko Quit Toronto Festival."
   M 1688
"John And Yoko's Christmas Gifts."
   M 1689
"John And Yoko Sex Seen."
   N 0545
"John And Yoko's First Song."
   M 1690
"John And Yoko Slapped Hard."
   M 1691
"John & Yoko's New Idea: Pop Combo With
   Chimps."
   M 1692
"John And Yoko's Toronto Concert."
   M 0901
"John And Yoko's Wedding Album Issued."
   M 3717
"John And Yoko Talk About Art And
   Vibrations."
   M 1640
John & Yoko: Their Love Book
   P 0076
"John And Yoko: The Long & Winding
   Road."
   M 3117

"John At Home."
   M 1693
"John At Home, Part Two."
   M 1694
"John Brower Wants Your Shit."
   M 0668
"John Comes Together - And How!"
   M 1531
"John: Getting Back To The Roots (Maybe
   Not His, But Nevertheless
   Roots)."
   M 2422
"John Goes One Way, Toronto The Other."
   M 0670
"John In His Own Quotes."
   M 1746
John Lennon
   B 0129   B 0191   B 0273   B 0372
   B 0511
"John Lennon."
   C 0086   C 0094   C 0154   C 0155
   C 0156   C 0208   C 0245   C 0246
   M 0088   M 1231   M 1695   M 1696
   M 1697   M 1841   M 2118   M 2159
   M 3040   M 3337   M 3638   M 3639
   N 0379   N 0546   N 0547   N 0548
"John Lennon: A Celebration."
   M 1698
John Lennon: A Family Album
   B 0274   B 0475
John Lennon: All You Need Is Love.
   vlnl-
   P 0080
"John Lennon: A Man Who Cared: The
   Fabulous Story Of John Lennon And
   The Beatles
   B 0275
"John Lennon: A Memoir."
   M 0727   N 0293
John Lennon: A Memorial Album
   P 0077
John Lennon & The Beatles: A Special
   Tribute
   P 0081
John Lennon And The Beatles Forever
   B 0396
"John Lennon And The FBI."
   C 0007
"John Lennon And Yoko Ono."
   C 0296   M 0959   M 3216
"John Lennon And Yoko Ono - Double
   Fantasy (Geffen)."
   M 1089
"John Lennon And Yoko Ono: Our Films."
   M 1699
John Lennon: An Illustrated Biography
   B 0598
John Lennon: A Personal Pictorial Diary
   B 0540   P 0078
"John Lennon - A Portrait Of The
   Artist."
   M 3536
"John Lennon Appeals."
   N 0549
"John Lennon: A Real Live Fairytale
   B 0268
"John Lennon - A 16 Page Tribute To A
   Man In The Life Of Us All."
   N 0550
John Lennon: A Tribute. No. 1-
   P 0079
"John Lennon/Bag One."
   M 1700
John Lennon (Beatle, Kunstler,
   Provokateur)
   B 0192
"John Lennon: Beatle On His Own."
   M 1337
"John Lennon/Beatles Discography."
   M 1701
John Lennon/Beatles Memory Book
   P 0082
John Lennon Canonization Coalition
   F 0087
"John Lennon Can Stay In U.S."
   N 0551
John Lennon Canzonie Musica
   B 0276
The John Lennon Collection

S 0098
John Lennon - Das War Sein Leben
  P 0083
John Lennon: Death Of A Dream
  B 0096
"John Lennon Describes Own Death: A
    Seance With Beatle's Spirit."
  M 1879
The John Lennon Diary 1969
  B 0310
"John Lennon Disc 'Plastic Ono Band'."
  N 0552
"John Lennon Divorced."
  N 0553
"John Lennon; Dominant Role In A Pop
    Music Revolution."
  N 0554
"John Lennon Drive Forever."
  N 0754
John Lennon: El Genio Beatle
  B 0512
John Lennon En Su Tinta
  B 0311
John Lennon Erinnert Sich
  B 0571
John Lennon Erinnert Sich ("Der Traum
    Ist Aus, Baby!")
  B 0572
John Lennon Fan Club
  F 0088 F 0089 F 0090
"John Lennon Finds Worm In Beatles'
    Apple."
  M 1702
"John Lennon Fined £150 On Drug
    Charge."
  N 0555
"John Lennon Flies 2,000 Miles To Marry
    Quietly."
  N 0556
John Lennon 4 Ever
  B 0515
John Lennon: For The Record
  B 0343
"John Lennon - Genius Or Just A Bore?"
  M 3718
"John Lennon Get Cheesed Off."
  M 1703
"John Lennon: Good Words."
  N 0557
John Lennon Goroku
  B 0387
"John Lennon: Guiding Force In Music
    And Culture Of The 60's."
  M 2388
"John Lennon Had Life After Death Pact
    With Yoko."
  M 1704
John Lennon Hat Mir Das Rauchen
    Verboten (John Lennon Forbade Me
    To Smoke)
  B 0283
"John Lennon: Hello, Goodbye!"
  M 3116
"John Lennon: His Final Words On Beatle
    Music."
  M 1705
"The John Lennon Horoscope."
  M 1706
"The John Lennon I Knew."
  M 0172
John Lennon: Imagine
  S 0099
John Lennon: Im Spiegel Der Weltpresse
  B 0277
"John Lennon In Demonstration."
  N 0558
"John Lennon: Ineligible Alien."
  M 1707
John Lennon In His Own Words
  B 0388 B 0389 B 0390
John Lennon In His Own Write
  B 0312 B 0313 B 0314 B 0315
"John Lennon - In His Own Write."
  C 0157
"John Lennon In 'How I Won The War'."
  M 3640
John Lennon - In Memoriam
  B 0334
John Lennon: In My Life

B 0509
John Lennon In Seiner Eigenen Schreibe
  B 0316
"John Lennon Is Alive And A Voidoid: A
    Rock & Roll Fantasy."
  M 0138
"John Lennon Is A Very Practical Man."
  M 1284
"John Lennon Is Dead, A Man Who Touched
    Truth."
  N 0559
"John Lennon Is Slain In New York."
  N 0560
"John Lennon - Kaerlighed Og Energi."
  M 1342
"John Lennon Key To Beatles' Future As
    Group Loses Their Togetherness."
  M 1708
John Lennon Last Message
  B 0278
John Lennon: La Storia Di Un Mito Che
    Non Muore
  B 0118
John Lennon La Ultima Conversacion
  B 0449
John Lennon - Le Beatle Assassine
  B 0078
"John Lennon Marries Yoko Ono In
    Gibraltar."
  N 0561
"The John Lennon Memorial Peace
    Contest."
  M 1621
"John Lennon: Must An Artist
    Self-Destruct?"
  M 2389 N 0562
John Lennon 1940-1980
  B 0206 B 0398 B 0564
"John Lennon, 1940-1980."
  M 0716
"John Lennon (1940-1980)."
  M 1709
John Lennon 1940-1980, A Biography
  B 0127
John Lennon 1940-1980: Front Page News
    Book
  B 0491
John Lennon 1940-1980: L'Homme, Sa
    Musique, La Tragedie
  B 0397
"John Lennon (1940-1980). Mutmassungen
    Uber Einen Egomaniac."
  C 0158
"John Lennon 1940-1980; Nothing To Do
    To Save His Life."
  M 1825
John Lennon No Reply
  B 0097
"John Lennon: No Secret Interior, Just
    Integrity."
  C 0139 N 0477
"John Lennon (October 9th,
    1940-December 8th, 1980)."
  M 0196
"John Lennon Of Beatles Is Killed;
    Suspect Held In Shooting At
    Dakota."
  N 0632
John Lennon: One Day At A Time; A
    Personal Biography Of The
    Seventies
  B 0193 B 0194
John Lennon: One Day At A Time (Revised
    edition.)
  B 0195
John Lennon Pa Eget Satt
  B 0317 B 0318
John Lennon Par Liu-Meme
  B 0391
"The John Lennon Peace Forest."
  M 1267 M 1268
John Lennon - Plastic Ono Band
  S 0100
John Lennon/Plastic Ono Band: Shaved
    Fish
  S 0101
John Lennon Playboy Interview
  B 0495
"John Lennon Play, 'In His Own Write,'

Is Staged In London."
  N 1127
"John Lennon Remembered."
  N 0563
"John Lennon Remembered, Oct. 9, 1940 -
    Dec. 8, 1980."
  M 1710
"John Lennon Reviews This Week's New
    Pop Records."
  M 1711
"John Lennon, R.I.P."
  M 0623 M 1712
John Lennon: Rock 'N' Roll
  S 0102
"John Lennon's Almanac."
  M 0636
"John Lennon's Bag."
  M 1713
"The John Lennons Buy Land Upstate And
    Will Raise Cattle."
  N 0564
"John Lennons Convey Greetings Via
    Billboard."
  N 0565
"John Lennon's Death."
  C 0159 N 0567
"John Lennon's Death - An Astrological
    View."
  M 1822
"John Lennon's Deportation From U.S.
    Delayed."
  N 0568
"John Lennon's Dream Is Over."
  C 0160 N 0569
"John Lennon Seeks A Visa To Visit U.S.
    This Month."
  N 0570
"John Lennon Seen A Winner But Must Pay
    7G To Big 7."
  M 1714
"John Lennon Sends Back His MBE."
  N 0571
John Lennonsense
  B 0319
"John Lennon's Future."
  M 0761
"John Lennon's Guitars."
  M 1372
"John Lennon's Homosexual Secret."
  N 0232
"John Lennon Shot To Death."
  N 0626
"John Lennon's Journey: Of Triumph And
    Tragedy."
  N 0572
"John Lennon's Killer: The Nowhere
    Man."
  M 3503
"John Lennon's Last."
  M 0739
"John Lennon's Live Recordings."
  M 0960
"John Lennon's Mourners."
  M 2577
"John Lennon's Murderer Gets 20 Years
    To Life."
  N 0358
"John Lennon's Music Will Never Die."
  C 0214 N 0783
"John Lennon Speaking."
  M 1254
"John Lennon's Schooldays."
  M 3751
John Lennon's Secret
  B 0473
"John Lennon's Shocking Secret Life."
  M 2396
"John Lennon's Solo Rarities."
  M 0961
The John Lennon Story
  B 0539 B 0550
"John Lennon's TV Documentary Vs.
    Capital Punishment."
  M 1715
John Lennon: Summer Of 1980
  B 0425 B 0426
"John Lennon's Video Legacy."
  M 1350
"John Lennon's Zippie Legacy."

N 1139
"John Lennon Talks."
    M 0828
"John Lennon: The Great Swan Of
    Liverpool."
    C 0263
John Lennon: The Legend. vln1-
    P 0084
John Lennon: The Life And Legend
    C 0091   C 0097   C 0114   C 0147
    C 0192   C 0329   C 0336   P 0085
"John Lennon: The Untold Story."
    M 1716
"John Lennon: The Very Last Interview."
    M 2475
"John Lennon: The Whole Boat Was
    Moving."
    M 3193
John Lennon Tribute
    P 0086
"John Lennon Tribute Records."
    M 2977
"John Lennon Versus The F.B.I."
    M 3693
John Lennon: Walls And Bridges
    S 0103
John Lennon: Walls And Bridges - Listen
    To This Song Book
    S 0104
"John Lennon, Where Are You?"
    M 3208
John Lennon Wie Er Sich Selbst Sah
    B 0392
"John Lennon Wins 4 Year Battle With
    U.S. Immigration."
    N 0573
"John Lennon Wins His Residency In
    U.S."
    N 0743
"John Lennon: Written In The Stars."
    M 1717
"John Lennon/Yoko Ono."
    M 3266
"John Lennon: Zum Verlust Einer
    Symbolfigur."
    M 1766
"Johnny Be Good."
    M 2188
Johnny Tonight!
    C 0320
"John Ono-Lennon."
    M 1718
John Ono Lennon 1940-1980
    B 0279
"John Ono Lennon: 1940-1980."
    C 0001   N 0001
John Ono Lennon (1967-1980)
    B 0122
"John, Paul, George And Pete ...."
    C 0343
"John, Paul, George, & Ringo . . . And
    Bert."
    M 1719
"John, Paul, George, Ringo ... And
    Linda."
    N 0763
"John, Paul, Ringo And George, M.B.E.;
    Beatles Honored By Queen At Her
    'Keen Pad' As Band Plays
    'Humoresque'."
    N 0968
"John Rennon's Excrusive Gloupie."
    M 2054
"John's Gospel."
    C 0112   M 1191
"John's Last Testament."
    M 1720
"John's Legal Case: Few Options Left."
    M 1721
"John's Letter To Paul."
    M 1896
"John's ... Lithographs."
    M 3775
"John's No. 1 Dream."
    M 0703
"Johnsons Use Beatles' Suite."
    N 0574
"John Speaking."
    M 1641

"John's Psychic Secret."
    M 1174
John Winston Lennon, 1940-1980
    P 0087
John Winston Lennon (1940-1966)
    B 0121
"John, Yoko And Eric Clapton Kick Up
    Their Blue Suede Shoes."
    C 0348
"John, Yoko, & Year One."
    M 3776
"Johnyoko Drive."
    M 1727
"John, Yoko, Kyoko Get Trimmed."
    M 3777
"John/Yoko Lie Low Until The Baby
    Comes."
    M 1728
"The Joyful Noise."
    M 3402
"Judge Denies Motion For New 'Sweet
    Lord' Trial."
    M 1751
"Judge Refuses 'Freeze' On Beatles'
    £1M."
    N 0586
"Judgment To Be Given Later In Beatles
    Case."
    N 0587
"Julian Lennon Visits Yoko."
    M 1752
"Jurgen Vollmer Interview, Part II."
    M 1780
"Jury Choice To Be Difficult For Lennon
    Trial Defense."
    N 0996
"Jury In Tate Trial Listen To Beatles
    Records."
    N 0588
"Just A Little Light Rocca From Macca."
    M 3336
"Just An Ordinary Superstar."
    M 3631
"Just Before The End."
    M 1755
"Just Call It 'Winter Music'."
    M 2516
"Justice For A Beatle: The Illegal Plot
    To Prosecute And Oust John
    Lennon."
    M 3469
"Just Imagine."
    M 1532
"Just The Usual Din As Beatles Open
    Tour In Chicago."
    N 0589
Kaiketsu Beatles No Densetsu
    B 0541
"Karma Submits Plan On Toronto
    Peacefest."
    M 1761
"Keeper Of The Beatles."
    N 0051
"Keeping The Beatles Legend Alive."
    M 3044
"A Kicker Of A Flicker Laid Way Down
    South Where The West Begins,
    Starring Ringo, The Fastest Shot
    In Liddypool, And The Three Other
    Ornery Blokes."
    M 1770
"Kid's New Macabre Game: Is Paul
    McCartney Dead?"
    M 1771
Kid's TV: The First 25 Years
    C 0106
"Kids 'Won't Speak To Me' So Grandmas
    Get Up $50 For Beatles CP
    Benefit."
    M 1772
"Killer Stalked Lennon For Days, Got
    Autograph."
    N 0594
"King And The Beatles Make A Cartoon
    Movie."
    M 1794
Kingdom Beat
    F 0091
"Kirshner Entertainment Links With

Britain's ATV To Form Major Pub."
    M 1802
"Klaatu Update."
    M 0128
"Klein, Beatles' Business Agreement Is
    Spelled Out."
    M 1804
"Klein Claim Act Against Beatles Gets
    Dismissed."
    M 1805
Eine Kleine Beatlemusik: Piano Solo
    S 0105
Eine Kleine Beatlemusik: String
    Quartet, With Optional Double
    Bass
    S 0106
"Klein Explains Apple's Stand."
    M 1806
"Klein: It's John's Peace Festival."
    M 3407
"Klein Refutes McCartney On Beatles'
    State Of $$ Union."
    M 1808
"Klein's Abkco Industries To Take Over
    Beatles' Apple Corps."
    M 1809
"Klein Swings First Deal For Beatles In
    Settling Assets Row With
    Triumph."
    M 1810
"Klein, Three Beatles In Split."
    M 1811
"Klein Vs. Lennon Suit Stays In NY."
    M 1812
"Komm Gib Mir Deine Money."
    M 1884   M 1885   M 1886   M 2997
"Komm Gib Mir Deine Money: Hot
    (Coloured) Record News."
    M 0916
"Komplet Engelsk Diskografi."
    M 1348
"Komponisten Paul McCartney."
    M 2308
"Kremlin Is Going Dada Over Beatles."
    M 1834
Kyojitsu No Setten
    B 0226
"'Kyoko, If You're Listening'."
    M 1840
"L.A. 'Beatlemania' Top Entertainment."
    M 1407
"Label Products Rake In Millions."
    N 0620
"Lack Of Communication, Could That Be
    The Trouble?"
    M 3579
"The Lads From Liverpool."
    C 0175
"Lady Madonna."
    M 1848
"Lady Of Pain."
    M 3597
"Landlords Seek Ban On Beatle."
    N 0622
"The Land Of The Lunapots."
    C 0187
"L.A. 6th Annual Official Beatles Fan
    Convention."
    M 2999
"The Last Ballad Of John & Yoko."
    M 1313
"Last Beatles Show."
    C 0177
"The Last Day In The Life."
    C 0079   M 0733
"Last Estate."
    M 0201
The Last Lennon Tapes: John Lennon And
    Yoko Ono Talk To Andy Peebles,
    December 6, 1980
    B 0450
Last Message
    B 0451
"Last Minute Flashes."
    M 1868
"The Last Session."
    M 2016
"Late News."
    M 1869

The Latest Beatlebook Of Recorded Hits
  - For Guitar
  S 0107
"Latest Dispatch From Liverpool."
  M 2476
"Latest News On Records With Paul,
  John, George & Ringo."
  M 0522
"The Latest Teen Talk From Coast To
  Coast."
  M 1870
"Latest Wills; John Lennon Leaves
  £2.5m."
  N 0625
"Laurence Juber: Winging It With Hope."
  M 0514
"Law And Disorder."
  M 1763
"Lawsuit Spells Breakup For Beatles."
  N 0687
"Lawyer Argues Against Deporting The
  Lennons."
  N 1027
"Lawyers Say Klein Made Beatles' $
  Soar."
  M 1874
"LBJ Ignored As NY Crowds Chase
  Beatles."
  M 1876
"Leader Of A Rock Group That Helped
  Define A Generation."
  N 0951
"Learning From The Beatles."
  C 0249   C 0250   C 0251   C 0252
  M 2507
"Led Zeppelin Supplants Beatles In
  British Poll."
  N 0634
The Left-Handers' Handbook
  C 0061
"Legacy Of John Lennon."
  N 0592
The Legacy Of John Lennon: Charming Or
  Harming A Generation
  B 0406   B 0407
"Legacy Of Lennon."
  C 0183   M 2377   N 0637
"Legalmania Over Beatlemania."
  M 1890
"Legions Of Lennon Admirers To Join In
  Tributes Today."
  N 0738
"Lennon."
  M 0173   M 2216   M 3047   M 3241
  M 3276   M 3383   M 3598
"Lennon Alter Ego."
  M 2141
"Lennon: Always Up Front."
  C 0173   N 0599
Lennon: A Memory
  P 0088
Lennon: An Appreciation
  B 0331
"Lennon & Fonda Sue U.S. & Nixon."
  M 1903
"Lennon And Friend Charged In
  Possession Of Marijuana."
  N 0645
"Lennon And Gun Laws."
  M 1617
Lennon And McCartney
  B 0170   B 0171   B 0172
"Lennon And McCartney."
  M 2245
Lennon & McCartney/Bacharach & David —
  The 60s
  S 0108
Lennon & McCartney 50 Great Songs: All
  Organ
  S 0109
Lennon & McCartney 50 Great Songs:
  Chord Organ
  S 0110
Lennon & McCartney 50 Great Songs: Easy
  Big Note Guitar
  S 0111
Lennon & McCartney 50 Great Songs: Easy
  Big Note Piano
  S 0112

Lennon & McCartney For Clarinet
  S 0113   S 0114
Lennon & McCartney For Flute
  S 0115   S 0116
Lennon & McCartney For Recorder
  S 0117
Lennon & McCartney For Trumpet
  S 0118   S 0119
"Lennon And McCartney Grab Three
  Songwriting Awards In Britain."
  M 1904
"Lennon & McCartney (Songwriters) Ltd."
  M 1642
"Lennon And Ono Spread Peace In
  Surprise Gig At Toronto R & R
  Bash."
  M 1905
"Lennon And Picasso Works Compared."
  N 1131
"Lennon And Primal Scream."
  M 1668
"Lennon And Primal Scream: Janov."
  M 1624
"Lennon And The Gun Controllers."
  M 1033
"Lennon & The No. 9 Connection."
  M 3343
"Lennon And Yoko Ono Remanded."
  N 0646
"Lennon - A Night In The Life."
  M 0762
"Lennon Anniversary; Thousands Gather
  To Honour Dead Beatle."
  N 0286
"Lennon Asked To Play Christ."
  N 0647
"Lennon As Lenin, Or ... Communistic
  Cacophony Comments On And By The
  Christian Crusade's Chief
  Chronicler: Rev. David A.
  Noebel."
  M 0199
"Lennon At Large, Part I: The Wild Ways
  Of Joker John."
  N 0998
"Lennon .... At 40."
  N 1080
"Lennon: Back In The U.S.S.A."
  M 3260
"Lennon: Beatles Could Get Together
  Again."
  M 3096
"Lennon Book Acquired."
  N 0648
"Lennon Buys Irish Isle As A Hippie
  Haven But Natives Wave
  Shillelaghs."
  M 1906
"Lennon Can Stay! Deportation Order
  Overturned."
  M 3470
"The Lennon Case."
  N 0649
"Lennon Case Accused Alters Plea To
  Guilty."
  N 0650
"Lennon Case - A Lemon."
  M 1907
"Lennon Case Lawyer's Life Is
  Threatened."
  N 0627
The Lennon Collection
  S 0120
"Lennon Concert Slated Aug. 30 In
  All-Day Fete To Aid Retarded."
  N 0468
"The Lennon-Cosell Tapes."
  M 0823
"Lennon Cuts Single During 'Bed-in'."
  M 1908
"Lennon Death Puts Cloud Over Youth."
  C 0013   N 0053
"Lennon Death Spurs L.A. Handgun Move."
  M 3393
"'Lennon Energized High Art With Pop'."
  N 0685
"Lennon: Enhver Kvindes Drøm."
  M 2122
"Lennon Exhibitor Draws Picasso Into

His Defense."
  N 0651
The Lennon Factor
  B 0600
"Lennon Fights To Stay."
  N 0652
"Lennon Fight To Stay In U.S. Raises
  Legal Points."
  N 1178
"Lennon Flies A Banner."
  N 0653
"Lennon Gave An Interview On Final
  Day."
  N 0654
"Lennon Gets His Ticket To Ride."
  M 0704
"Lennon Gets Lost In His Rock & Roll."
  M 1854
"Lennon Had Mystical Visions Of His
  Shooting Death."
  M 1909
"Lennon Has A Legacy."
  M 1910
"Lennon Heads Charity Concert For
  Retarded."
  M 1911
"Lennon Health Centre."
  N 0655
"Lennon Helps Gypsies."
  N 0656
"Lennon: I Apologize."
  M 0084
"Lennon Ignored Seer's Warning."
  M 1912
"Lennon In A Sack In Sacher's."
  N 0736
"Lennon In Court Again: $42 Million Of
  Old Gold."
  M 1135
"Lennon In 4-Letter Word Row."
  M 1913
"Lennon Interview On Radio Today."
  N 0657
"Lennon Interview: The Acid Dream Is
  Over."
  M 1914
"Lennon Invitation."
  N 0658
"Lennon Is Given 60 Days To Leave."
  N 0603
"Lennon Is Guilty In Narcotic Case;
  Lawyer Terms Marijuana Part Of
  Past - Fine Is $360."
  N 0659
"The Lennon Issue & Its Cover."
  M 1915
"Lennon Known Both As Author And
  Composer."
  N 0853
"Lennon Lament By Parcel Post:
  Calgary's Mail Art Show Weeps
  Weirdly For John."
  M 1235
"Lennon Larfs."
  M 1897
Lennon League
  F 0092
"The Lennon Legacy."
  M 1255
Lennon Listener
  F 0093
"Lennon Loses A Court Round."
  M 1916
Lennon Lucubration
  F 0094
Lennon Lyrics
  F 0095
Lennon/McCartney
  B 0173   B 0295
"Lennon-McCartney Songalog: Who Wrote
  What."
  M 1917
"The Lennon-McCartney Songs."
  M 0818   M 0819
"Lennon, McCartney Win Five Novello
  Awards As Composers."
  M 1918
"Lennon Makes Plea At Close Of
  Hearing."

N 0660
"A Lennon Memorial."
  N 0661
"Lennon Murder Charge."
  N 0662
"Lennon Murder Suspect Preparing
    Insanity Defense."
  N 0771
Lennon 1981 Color Calendar
  B 0332
"Lennon Not To Play Christ."
  N 0663
"Lennon - Now It's Legs For Peace."
  M 0066
"Lennon Of Beatles Sorry For Making
    Remark On Jesus."
  N 0664
"Lennon Offers An Island."
  N 0665
"Lennon On Drug Charge."
  N 0666
"Lennon, Ono 45 Controversial."
  M 0991
"Lennon, Ono Suit Denied."
  M 1919
"Lennon On Record: Two Decades Of Pop
    Genius."
  C 0009   N 0028
"Lennon On Toronto: 'Bloody
    Marvelins'."
  M 3778
Lennon Photo Special
  P 0089
"Lennon Pictures On Show."
  N 0668
The Lennon Play: In His Own Write
  B 0320   B 0321
"Lennon, Psychedelic Drugs And Acid
    Rock."
  M 3691
"Lennon Pushing The Pop Song To Its
    Limit."
  M 0763
"Lennon Recording At New York Studio."
  M 1920
Lennon Recuerda
  B 0573
"Lennon Remembered."
  M 1782   M 1921
"Lennon Remembered For More Than His
    Music."
  N 0290
"Lennon Remembered For More Than
    Music."
  C 0077
Lennon Remembers
  B 0574   B 0575   B 0576
Lennon Remembers. New ed.
  B 0577
"Lennon Remembers."
  M 1922
Lennon Remembers: The Frankest Beatle
    Reveals All
  B 0578
Lennon Remembers: The Rolling Stone
    Interviews
  B 0579   B 0580
"Lennon Return Prompts Questions."
  M 3384
"Lennon Returns M.B.E."
  M 1923
"Lennon Rocked An Era."
  N 1042
"Lennon Royalties For Peace."
  N 0669
"Lennon's Accused Slayer Ends 2-Day
    Hunger Strike At Riker's Island."
  N 0739
"Lennon's Appeal."
  M 1924
"The Lennons Applaud The Married
    State."
  N 0670
"Lennon's Christmas: TV, Movie, No
    Records."
  M 1925
"Lennons' Deportation Hearing Is
    Delayed."
  N 0604

"Lennons Discuss Deportation, Allen
    Klein, Beatles' Reunion."
  M 3646
"Lennon's Dream Girl."
  N 1029
"Lennon's Eye View."
  M 0883
"Lennons' Final Plea For Residence In
    U.S."
  N 0671
"Lennons Hurt In Crash."
  N 0672
"Lennons In 'Beautiful' Talk With
    Trudeau."
  N 0245
"Lennons In Greece."
  M 1926
Lennon '69: Search For Liberation
  B 0335
"Lennon's Lawsuit: Memo From Thurmond."
  M 1136
"Lennon's Leaping Whimsy."
  M 1304
"Lennon's Life."
  N 1135
"Lennon's Lithographs Picture His Love
    Life."
  N 0673
"Lennons Love U.S."
  N 0674
"Lennon's Memory Is Not For Sale, His
    U.S. Fans Say."
  N 0223
"Lennon's Music: A Range Of Genius."
  M 1523
"Lennon's Next Album."
  M 3599
"Lennon's Nude 'Virgins' Too
    'Controversial' For A Big Mpls.
    Disc Distributor."
  M 1927
"The Lennons On Record."
  N 0322
"Lennons: On TV & Vibing McCartneys."
  M 1928
"The Lennon Sound."
  C 0349
"Lennon Speaks - But Only Just!"
  M 3600
"Lennons Quit In Toronto Fest Tiff."
  M 1929
"Lennons Quit Toronto Peace Festival,
    Claim Producers Balked At Free
    Admission."
  M 1930
"Lennon's Song: The Man Can't F--k Our
    Music."
  M 1148
"Lennon Staff Clue In Hampshire Murder
    Inquiry."
  N 0675
"Lennon Stands In The Way Of Reunion."
  N 0704
"Lennon Started Singing Again - For His
    Wife, His Son, His New Life."
  N 0478
"Lennon Stay Extended."
  N 0676
"Lennon Stays In The Shadows."
  M 3616
"Lennons To Smile For Charity."
  N 0494
"Lennon Stops Levy In Second Round."
  M 1931   M 3783
"Lennon Sues Government, Alleging
    Illegal Wiretaps."
  N 0677
"Lennon Sues Mitchell; Sez Move To Oust
    Him Was A Nixon Conspiracy."
  M 1932
"Lennon Suspect: A Suicide Watch."
  N 0678
"Lennons Win A Skirmish In Battle To
    Remain In U.S."
  N 0679
"Lennons Win Court Point."
  N 0680
"The Lennon Syndrome."
  M 1859

"The Lennon Tapes."
  M 2425
"The Lennon Tapes: 'I Can Go Right Out
    Of This Door Now And Go In A
    Restaurant'."
  M 2426
The Lennon Tapes; John Lennon And Yoko
    Ono In Conversation With Andy
    Peebles, 6 December 1980
  B 0452
"The Lennon Tapes: John Lennon, Yoko
    Ono, Andy Peebles."
  M 1933   M 1934   M 1935
"The Lennon Tapes: 'The Rock Stars Were
    Commenting On What I Was Not
    Doing'."
  M 2427
"Lennon: The Artist, The Beatle."
  M 1673
"Lennon: The Beatle Who Lived - And
    Died - Outrageously."
  M 1844
"Lennon The Chameleon."
  N 0323
"Lennon: The Final Interview II."
  M 1936
"Lennon: The Final Interview III."
  M 1937
"Lennon: The Final Interview IV."
  M 1938
"Lennon: The Final Interview V."
  M 1939
"Lennon: The Final Interview VI."
  M 1940
"Lennon The Outrageous Beatle."
  M 0174
"Lennon: The Working-Class Hero Turns
    Red."
  M 0558
"Lennon Today."
  M 0705
"Lennon: Together Again."
  M 1250
"Lennon To Make Hanratty Film."
  N 0681
"Lennon To Pay."
  N 0682
"Lennon Top Draw At Garden, N.Y.,
    Benefit & News Media Helped Too."
  M 3550
"Lennon To Sing To Peace."
  N 0683
"Lennon To Star In 90-Minute Smile
    Pic."
  M 1941
"Lennon Tribute Planned For Dec. At
    N.Y. Music Hall."
  M 1942
"Lennon Tributes On Record."
  M 2978
Lennon Uber Lennon - Abschied Von Den
    Beatles
  B 0581
Lennon Uber Lennon - Leben In Amerika
  B 0453   B 0454
Lennon Up Close & Personal
  B 0069
"Lennon Update."
  M 2017
"Lennon Vs. McCartney V. Harrison V.
    Starr."
  M 1943
"Lennon Vs. The Fools On The Hill."
  M 3173
"Lennon Visits Pepper."
  M 3601
"Lennon Was Always The Leader."
  N 1030
Lennon: What Happened!
  B 0070
"Lennon Wins Right To Quiz Justice
    Dept."
  M 3471
"Lennon Wins U.S. Stay."
  M 1944
"Lennon Without Tears."
  C 0172   N 0598
"Lennon-Yoko Protest Deportation
    Order."

M 1945
"Less Damage."
N 0618
"Less Screaming And Oh For A Proper
    Meal!"
M 1060
"Less Than A Month Old, The Beatles'
    Apple Label Harvests Big Sales
    Crop."
M 1946
"Lester Since 'A Hard Day's Night'."
M 1540
"Let Him Go Nameless."
M 1783
Let It Be
    F 0096
"Let It Be."
    C 0088   C 0300   M 1303   M 1948
    M 1949   M 2376
"Let It Be: Fans Mourn A Legend Of
    Rock."
N 0590
Let It Be (songbook) see also The
    Beatles: Let It Be
Let It Be - The Only Complete Song
    Album From The Motion Picture,
    "Let It Be."
S 0121
Let's Go Down The Cavern
    B 0296
Let's Go Down The Cavern: The Story Of
    Liverpool's Merseybeat
    B 0297
"Letter From Liverpool, Almost."
M 0791
"Letter From New York."
M 2262
"A Letter From The Publisher ... "
M 1789   M 1790
"Letter To George."
M 0580
"Letter To John Lennon."
N 0233
"Letter To The Editor."
M 1561   M 1956
"Letters."
M 1950 M 1951 M 1952 M 1953
Letters Abroad
    F 0097
"Letters From Beatles People."
M 1954
"Letters; John And Yoko."
M 1955
"Letters To The Editor."
M 1957
"Letters To The Recordings Editor."
M 0649   M 1813
"Letting George Do It."
M 0509
"Die Letzte Interview (The Last
    Interview)."
M 3248
"Levy Loses Lennon Suit."
M 1961
Il Libro Delle Canzoni Dei Beatles
    B 0027
"Life And Life Only."
M 2119
Life At The Dakota: New York's Most
    Unusual Address
    C 0060
"A Life In The Day Of Linda McCartney."
N 0417
Life. Volume 7, Number 2. February
    1984
M 1995
"Life With And Without Lennon: An
    Intimate Interview With Yoko
    Ono."
M 1314
"Life Without Lennon."
N 0693   N 0810
"Life With The Lennons."
M 0764
"Lift Ban On Beatles Video."
M 1996
"The Lighter Side."
M 1997
"The Lighter Side Of John Lennon."

C 0297   N 0999
"Like A Rolling Stone."
    C 0119   C 0120   M 1273   M 1274
Lillian Roxon's Rock Encyclopedia. 2d
    ed.
    C 0279
"Linda Eastman (The Mrs.) In
    McCartney's Group."
M 1998
"Linda McCartney Animated Short At
    Fest; Firm Eyes Full-Lengther."
M 2454
"Linda McCartney's Camera Solo."
N 1140
"Linda McCartney's New Flair For
    Songwriting Awes British Pub
    Exec."
M 1999
Linda's Calendar 1982
    B 0344
"Linda's Other Love Life."
N 0694
"Linda's Paul."
M 2000
Linda's Pictures
    B 0345   B 0346
Linda's Pix For '76
    B 0347
Linda's Plates For '78
    B 0348
Linda's Signs For '79
    B 0349
"Linda's View From The Inside Of The
    Polaroid."
N 0449
"Linda: Wife On The Run."
M 2001
"Lindsay Deplores Action To Deport
    Lennons As A 'Grave Injustice'."
N 0221
"Lion In The Pop Jungle."
N 0696
"Liquidate Beatles' Apple Corps Firm."
M 2003
"Listen, John, Why Don't We Do It In
    The Road?"
M 3719
"List Of Area Secretaries In The U.K."
M 2004
"Liszt, Chopin, Wordsworth And The
    Beatles."
M 2231
The Literary Lennon: A Comedy Of
    Letters
    B 0478   C 0290
The Literature Of Rock, 1954-1968
    C 0141
"A Little Bare."
    C 0197
"Little Richard Collects."
M 2005
Live
    F 0098
"Live Appearances."
M 2006
"Live Beatles On Tape."
M 1391
"Live Beatles Tape From Dec., 1962 To
    Be Made Available Worldwide."
M 2144
"Liverpool Beat Has Its Alger Story:
    Brian Epstein Who Found The
    Beatles."
M 2007
"Liverpool Beatles Convention '81."
M 2998
"Liverpool Cellar Clubs Rock To Beat
    Groups; Long-Haired Youths With
    Guitars Take Charge As Cult."
N 0697
"Liverpool Council To Honor Beatles."
N 0698
"The Liverpool Fan Club."
M 1012
"The Liverpool Fan Club, Part 2."
M 1013
"The Liverpool Fan Club, Part 3."
M 1014
"The Liverpool Fan Club, Part 4."

M 1015
"Liverpool's Best Group."
M 0644
"Liverpool's Magical Mystery Store."
M 2008
"Liverpool Solons Reject Bid For
    Beatles Statues."
M 2009
"Liverpool Sound And The London Roar:
    The Beatles At The Royal Variety
    Performance."
N 0699
"Liverpool's Own."
N 0337
"Liverpool Vigil Today To Mark Lennon
    Death."
N 0700
"Livet Er Det Der Sker."
M 1182
Living In The Material World
    S 0122
"Local Group."
N 0703
"Local Psychic Presents Fascinating
    Transcript Of Her Experience - A
    Message From John Lennon."
M 2014
"Log Of The Yellow Submarine."
M 3698
"London Beat."
    C 0303
"London: Beatle Magic, UFO (R.I.P.),
    And Nice Nice."
M 1734
"London 'Beatlemania' Set, But Suit
    Looms."
M 2019
"London: Beatles Clip Banned."
M 1665
"London Beatles Museum Update."
M 1446
"London Court Ends Beatles Partnership;
    Apple Continues."
M 2020
"London Day By Day; Shining On."
N 0705
"London In Brief."
N 0706
"London Notes."
    M 2021   M 2022   M 2023   M 2024
    M 2025   M 2026   M 2027   M 2028
    M 2029   M 2030   M 2031   M 2032
    M 2033   M 2034   M 2035
"London's Beatles."
N 0707
London Town (songbook) see Wings:
    London Town
"London Town: So What's Wrong With
    Silly Love Songs?"
M 1295
"'London Town': The Fax Behind The
    Trax!"
M 1981
"'London Town': The Story Behind Paul's
    Latest Album."
M 1544
"London: Traffic Moves, Cream In Gear."
M 1666
"London: Yoko Ono's Film 'Number
    Four'."
M 2383
"Lonely Hearts Club Band."
    M 2036   M 3602
"The Long And Winding Road."
M 1447
The Long & Winding Road: A History Of
    The Beatles On Record
    B 0523   B 0525
The Long & Winding Road: A History Of
    The Beatles On Record. Revised
    ed.
    B 0524
The Longest Cocktail Party: An
    Insider's Diary Of The Beatles,
    Their Million-Dollar Apple
    Empire, And Its Wild Rise And
    Fall
    B 0163   B 0164   B 0165   B 0166
    C 0248

"Long Hair Discussion."
  N 0708
"Long Hair For Boys."
  N 0709
"Long Night's Journey Into Day: A
    Conversation With John Lennon."
  M 1395
"Look Back With Longing."
  M 1524
The Look Book
  C 0277
"Looking A Dark Horse In The Mouth:
    George Harrison."
  M 1410
"Looking Backwards: Reflections On
    Nostalgia In The Musical
    Avant-Garde."
  M 3146
"Looking Past The Beatles."
  M 1213
"Looks As If Those Wedding Bells Have
    Broken Up That Beatles Gang."
  M 2037
"Looneytunes: Preserving The Beatles
    Fantasy."
  M 2038
"Lord Atlee Leaves £6,700."
  N 0710
"The Lord Must Want The Beatles To Fly
    Again: He Gave The McCartneys
    Wings."
  M 1671
"Lost: Another Great Spirit."
  C 0146 N 0498
"'Lost' Beatles Songs Uncovered."
  N 0926
"'Lost' Beatles Songs Unearthed By
    BBC."
  M 2041
"Lost Troubadour."
  M 2042
"Lo, The Beatles Descend From Sky For
    Apotheosis In Frisco."
  M 3730
"A Lot Of People Were Crying."
  C 0071 N 0279
Lots Of Liverpool
  B 0566
"Loud Music."
  M 1063
"'Love Beatles'."
  N 0711
"Love From The Beatles."
  M 1482
"Love It And Leave It."
  N 0712
"A Love Letter From John And Yoko To
    People Who Ask Us What, When, And
    Why."
  M 1902 N 0644
Love Letters To The Beatles
  B 0004 B 0005 B 0006
"'Love Me Do'."
  M 1448 M 2477 M 2502 M 3150
  M 3178 M 3385 N 1051
"'Love Me Do' Due From Capitol."
  M 2044
"'Love Me Do': Peter Jones Tells The
    Full Story Behind The Beatles'
    First Hit."
  M 2045
Love Me Do; The Beatles' Progress
  B 0080 B 0081 B 0082
Love Songs (songbook) see The Beatles
  Love Songs
"The Love They Take And Make."
  N 0481
"'The Love You Make'."
  M 0175
The Love You Make: An Insider's Story
  Of The Beatles
  B 0085 B 0086 B 0087
Loving John
  B 0433
Loving John: The Untold Story
  B 0434
A Loving Tribute To John Lennon
  B 0287
"L 7 Gets Beatle Brush."

  N 0713
"A Lucky Liverpool Lady."
  M 2053
"Lucky Luxy & Lovely Linda."
  M 1385
"Lumbering In The Material World."
  M 1149
Luv 'N' Stuff
  F 0099
"The Lyrical Expression Of Adolescent
    Conflict In The Beatles Songs."
  M 3143
Macca
  F 0100
McCartney
  F 0101 F 0102
"McCartney."
  M 0706
"McCartney And Friends."
  M 2429
"McCartney And Jackson Record With
    Quincy Jones."
  N 0716
"McCartney And Wife Sued On 'Another
    Day' Recording."
  N 0717
"McCartney & Wings At Sea."
  M 1221
"McCartney And Wings Give Venice
    Benefit."
  N 1002
"McCartney & Wings To Tour G. Britain."
  M 2056
"McCartney Arrested In Japan On
    Marijuana Charge."
  N 0326
"McCartney Asked To Waive 'On,
    Wisconsin,' Royalties."
  N 0718
McCartney: Beatle On Wings
  P 0090
"McCartney Breaks Off With Beatles."
  N 1003
"McCartney Breaks The Vinyl Curtain."
  M 2057
"McCartney Calls A Rumor On Marriage
    Plans 'A Joke'."
  N 0719
"McCartney Coast Dates Sell Out
    Unannounced."
  N 0720
"McCartney Comes Back."
  M 2058
"McCartney Conglomerate."
  M 2973
"McCartney 'Death' Gets 'Disc Coverage'
    Dearth."
  M 2059
"McCartney Denies Beatles' Reunion."
  M 2060
"McCartney Denies Guv's Bid To Give
    State 'On Wisconsin' Rights As
    Memorial To John Lennon."
  M 0531
"McCartney Disk Bid Is Rejected By
    'Quarryman'."
  M 2061
"The McCartney Empire."
  M 2062
McCartney Family Fan Club
  F 0103
"McCartney Forms New Group."
  N 0721
"McCartney Gets Political."
  M 2063
"McCartney: He Coulda Been A
    Contender."
  M 1293
"M'Cartney In Scotland."
  N 0722
"The McCartney Interview."
  M 0962 M 2064 M 2065 M 2066
"McCartney Is Home From Visit To
    Tokyo."
  M 2067
"McCartney Is Most Honored."
  M 2068
"McCartney Keeping Rights To
    Wisconsin's State Song."

  N 0723
"McCartney: Life After Death."
  M 0624
McCartney Ltd.
  F 0104
"McCartney: Make A Daft Noise For
    Christmas?"
  M 3539
McCartney Maniacs Unlimited
  F 0105
"McCartney Marries, Teen-Age Fans
    Weep."
  N 0724
"McCartney, Martin Tie."
  M 2069
McCartney - Matching Music Book
  S 0123
"McCartney Memory."
  N 0725
The McCartney Observer
  F 0106
"McCartney On His Own."
  M 2070 M 3136
"McCartney On Top."
  N 0581
"McCartney, On Visa, Sees 'Loose'
    Beatles' Reunion."
  N 0633
"McCartney: Packing Pot Was Stupid."
  N 0726
"McCartney Pens Tune For 007."
  M 2071
"McCartney Plays South Of France."
  M 2072
"McCartney Postpones Concert Tour Of
    U.S."
  N 0727
"McCartney: Pressure Cooking."
  M 3632
"McCartney Raps Stigwood 'Pepper' As
    'Unauthorized'."
  M 2073
"McCartney: Rock & Roll On A Wing & A
    Prayer."
  M 2126
"McCartney Says He 'Doesn't Trust
    Klein'; Rebuttal."
  M 2074
"McCartneys Back With A Whole Pack Of
    Geeks."
  M 2075
"McCartneys Buy E. H. Morris Music; To
    Be MPL Subsid."
  M 2184
McCartney's Gazette
  F 0107
"McCartneys Meet Press: Starting All
    Over Again."
  M 1222
"McCartney, Solo, Clearing Up A Few
    Things."
  C 0199
McCartney (songbook) see Paul
    McCartney: McCartney
"McCartney Split With Beatles Denied."
  N 0728
"McCartney Stays In Detention For
    Questioning."
  N 0729
"McCartney Sues Beatles & Co."
  M 2076
"McCartney Sues To Annul Beatles' Apple
    Corps Tie."
  M 2077
"McCartney's Wings Bring National Tour
    To Garden."
  N 0854
"McCartney Takes A Stand."
  M 1855
"McCartney Tells Why He Left."
  N 0730
"McCartney: The Band On The Road."
  M 0740
"McCartney - The Beatle With The Charm
    Is Back."
  N 0952
"McCartney The Family Favourite."
  M 2078
"McCartney To Change Labels."

M 2079
"McCartney: Tour And LP News."
M 2080
"McCartney Tour Off And He Goes Back To
    Jail."
N 0731
"McCartney Tour Of US Bowing In Ft.
    Worth May 3."
M 2081
McCartney II
S 0124
"McCartney II."
M 1982
"McCartney, Wings Plan U.S. Flight."
M 1223
"McCartney, Wings To Benefit Venice."
N 0732
"McCartney Writing Movie."
M 2082
"McGear: Brother On The Run."
M 2089
"McGraw-Hill Wins Book On Beatles; Pays
    $125,000 To Publish Authorized
    Biography."
N 0917
Maclen
F 0108
The Macs: Mike McCartney's Family Album
B 0356
"Mad For John Lennon's Face: Chi Fest
    Shows Solid 52-Minute 'Closeup'."
M 2095
"Madison Square Ovation For Two
    Beatles."
N 0742
Mad. Volume 1, No. 121
M 2096
"Magical History Tour."
C 0179   M 1875
"Magical McCartney Mystery."
M 2260
"Magical Mystery Non-Benefit."
M 2097
Magical Mystery Tour
B 0365   F 0109
"Magical Mystery Tour."
M 1050
"A Magical Mystery Tour: Collecting
    Beatles Telecasts, Part 1."
M 1516
"Magical Mystery Tour Group."
M 2099
"Magical Mystery Tour '76."
M 2981
Magical Mystery Tour (songbook)   see
    The Beatles: Magical Mystery Tour
"Magical Mystery Tour: The Beatles
    Story On Israeli Radio."
M 0506
"The Magic Christian."
M 2517
Magill's Survey Of Cinema, Volume 2
C 0161
"Mag Review: Beatles Appreciation
    Society Bulletin."
M 2100
"Mag Review: Harrison Alliance."
M 1373
"Mag Review: Our Starr Monthly."
M 2101
"Mag Review: The Fab Four Publication."
M 2102
"Mag Review: The Write Thing."
M 2103
"Mag Review: With A Little Help From My
    Friends."
M 2104
"The Maharishi Meets The Press."
C 0171
"The Maharishi Wants Everybody To
    Levitate For Peace, But Some
    Iowans Are Hopping Mad."
M 1399
"Maharishi: Who Ishi? Part One."
M 3537
"Maharishi: Who Ishi? Part Two."
M 3538
"Makes Queen's List."
N 0744

"Making 'I Wanna Hold Your Hand'."
M 2204
Making Music
C 0205
"The Making Of 'A Hard Day's Night':
    Part 1."
M 1475
"The Making Of 'A Hard Day's Night':
    Part 2."
M 1476
"Making Up: McCartney Says In A Song
    What He Wishes He Had Told
    Lennon."
N 0479
"Mal And Neil Tell You How 'All You
    Need Is Love' Was Recorded."
M 1051
"Mal Evans: The Beatles Equipment Road
    Manager."
M 2109
"Mal's Diary."
M 1039   M 1040
"Mal's Page."
M 1041
"Mama's Little Girl."
C 0198
"Man Accused Of Lennon Killing To Plead
    Insanity."
N 0745
"Manitoba Premier To Lennon & Yoko:
    'Bring Your Peace Movement'."
M 2111
"Mannerist Phase; New Album Of
    Recordings."
M 2113
"Man Of The Year."
M 3641
"Man On Death Charge 'Obsessed By
    Lennon'."
N 0628
"Manson Wants To Call Beatle."
N 0751
"The Man Who Discovered The Beatles."
C 0201
The Man Who Gave The Beatles Away
B 0587   B 0588   B 0589   B 0590
B 0591
"The Man Who Really Discovered The
    Beatles."
M 3624
"Mark Chapman's Family."
M 1767
"Market Lessons For Northern Songs."
N 0339   N 1151
"Mary Baker Asks Account Of Beatles'
    Promotional Funds."
M 2136
"Masque Los Beatles."
M 2139
"Matched Pair Of Gunmen."
M 2140
Material World Times
F 0110
Matey For Eighty
B 0350
Maxwell's Silver Hammer
F 0111
"May Pang Looks Back At 'Loving John'
    Days."
M 1827
"M.B.E."
M 2146
"The M.B.E. Controversy."
M 2147
"Meaning OBE & MBE."
N 0760
"Media Masters Meet The Carnal Saints,
    Or Frankenstein Meets The
    Wolfman."
M 1305
"Meditation ... "
M 2148
"A Meditation On John Lennon."
M 1005
"Meeting The Beatles."
M 0640   M 1007   M 1058   M 1290
M 1308   M 1872   M 2149   M 2208
M 2355   M 3043   M 3112   M 3400
M 3551

Meet The Beatles Again
F 0112
Meet The Beatles - Photos From Their
    Personal Album - A Message To You
    From The Beatles Themselves
P 0091
Meet The Beatles - Star Special, Number
    Twelve
P 0092
"Meet The Maniacs."
M 3108
"Meet The Rutles."
M 0508
"Meet The Staff."
M 2150
"Melancholy Masterpiece."
M 2195
"Memorabilia Auction."
M 2164
"Memories Of An Apple Girl."
M 3186
"Memories That Stop Cynthia From
    Finding New Love."
M 2165
"The Menace Of Beatlism."
M 1724
Men's Wear
M 2167
"Merchandiser Calmly Awaits Beatles
    Return; Mrs. Baker Revamps Old
    Lines, Readies New."
M 2168
"A Mercy Plea By John Lennon At U.S.
    Hearing."
N 0762
Mersey Beat: The Beginnings Of The
    Beatles
B 0247   B 0248   C 0011   C 0016
C 0017   C 0018   C 0019   C 0020
C 0021   C 0023   C 0024   C 0029
C 0030   C 0031   C 0032   C 0033
C 0034   C 0035   C 0037   C 0040
C 0041   C 0043   C 0044   C 0045
C 0046   C 0047   C 0053   C 0054
C 0070   C 0073   C 0078   C 0089
C 0090   C 0099   C 0100   C 0101
C 0102   C 0103   C 0110   C 0111
C 0115   C 0117   C 0118   C 0128
C 0131   C 0132   C 0133   C 0135
C 0136   C 0152   C 0155   C 0157
C 0162   C 0175   C 0177   C 0184
C 0185   C 0187   C 0188   C 0189
C 0190   C 0191   C 0195   C 0196
C 0197   C 0201   C 0209   C 0211
C 0213   C 0219   C 0221   C 0222
C 0223   C 0224   C 0231   C 0236
C 0239   C 0240   C 0261   C 0268
C 0269   C 0270   C 0292   C 0301
C 0302   C 0303   C 0311   C 0312
C 0326   C 0327   C 0330   C 0340
C 0341   C 0343   C 0344   C 0345
"Mersey Beaucoup."
N 0667
"Mersey Moptop Faverave Fabgearbeat."
M 0004
"Mersey Roundabout."
C 0327
"Merseyside Mourns Working-Class Hero."
N 0287
"The Mersey Sound."
C 0209   M 2171
The Mess
F 0113
"Message From The Eggman."
M 1127
"A Message To Merseyside."
C 0188
"The Messengers."
M 2174
"Metamorphosis Of The Beatles."
C 0165
"Middle East's Music Playing Hot Chart
    Role."
M 1166
"Mighty Goods: The Beatles."
C 0233   C 0234
"The Mike McCartney Interview."
M 1781
"Mike McCartney Interviewed."

M 2956
Mike McGear Fan Club
F 0114
"Mike McGear: 'Not Just A Brother
....'."
M 1887
"Mike McGear's Wedding."
M 2189
"Mik, The Singing Dancing
Greenlanders."
M 1552
"Millionaire Who Feared Loneliness."
M 2198
"Million Dollar Offer For Beatles."
M 2199
"A Million Heard The Tragedy
Predicted."
M 2242
"Minstrel Extraordinaire."
C 0134   N 0463
"A Miraculous Simplicity."
M 1499
"Miss Eleanor Bron In Beatles Film."
N 0765
"Mr. Alun Owen's Film Script For
Beatles."
N 0766
"Mr. Klein Breaks With The Beatles."
N 0767
"Mr. Lennon Ordered Out Of U.S. In 60
Days."
N 1028
"Mr. Lindsay Denounces Attempt To
Deport Lennons."
N 0629
"Mr. Reagan's Way To Deter Death."
N 0768
"Mrs. Baker Will Hol' Beatles' Han',
Merchandising-wise."
M 2202
"Mrs. Lennon's Apple Farm."
F 0115
"Mrs. Lennon Sues For Divorce."
N 0769
"Mrs. Paul McCartney."
M 2203
"Mix-Master To The Beatles."
M 2207
"M.J.Q. Dig The Beatles."
C 0211
"Mm Hmm."
M 2160
"Monarchs Of The Beatle Empire."
M 2221
"Money And Music."
M 2209
"Money Don't Buy Everything, It's
True."
M 2518
"Money Don't Buy Everything, It's True:
Part Two."
M 2519
"Money Don't Buy Everything, It's True:
Part Three."
M 2520
"Monkees Versus Beatles; Melody Maker
Opinion Poll."
M 2210
"Monogamy And Music: Life Around The
Hearth For Paul And Linda."
M 2211
"Moog."
M 2213
"Moon To Attend Peace Festival?"
M 0669
"Mopheads, M.B.E."
M 2215
"Mop Top Mania Lives ..."
M 2979
"More Adventures In Penny Lane."
N 0776
More Beatles Illustrated Lyrics
B 0028
"More Lennon In Offing."
N 0855
"More Mothers."
M 3557
"More On Beatles Textual Problems."
M 2049

"More Protests Over The Beatles."
N 0777
"More Recent Letters From Beatle
People."
M 2217
"Most Difficult Film The Beatles Never
Made."
M 2225
"The Most Fantastic Game Of Billiard's
Ever."
M 2226
"Motion Pictures: Coming Attractions."
M 2227   M 2228
"Mourners Come And Go To Sad Tones Of
Beatles' Music."
N 0376
Movies Into Film; Film Criticism,
1967-1970
C 0300
"Moving On."
C 0213
"MP Suggested Cricket Pitch
Demonstrations."
N 0780
"Much Travelled Mary."
M 2230
"Mug Of Kintyre."
M 1185
"Multiplying Business Woes Bug The
Beatles."
N 0635
"Munich Court Says Music."
N 0781
"Murray Kaufman, Radio's '5th Beatle'."
N 0784
"'Murray The K' Dies Of Cancer."
N 0785
Murray The K Tells It Like It Is, Baby
C 0167
"Music."
M 2002
"Musical Landscape Of The Beatles."
M 2493
"Musical Revue Salutes Lennon."
M 2247
"Musical Satire From Vanguard And
Electra."
M 2248
"Music And Entertainment."
C 0215
"Music Appreciation: A Crash Course."
M 2129
"Music As Child's Play."
M 1300
Music Business
M 2249
"Musicians On Peace."
C 0216
"Music? It's Just Part Of The Peace
Campaign."
M 3564
"Musicke: Olde Mersey; 'Baroque Beatles
Book' Opened In Concert."
N 0786
The Music Makers
C 0156
The Music Of Lennon & McCartney; 2d
Omnibus Of Popular Songs
S 0125
"The Music Of Sound Or, The Beatles And
The Beatless."
C 0241
The Music Of The Beatles
B 0262
"The Music Of The Beatles."
C 0275   M 3105   M 3106
The Music Of The Beatles From 1962 To
"Sergeant Pepper's Lonely Hearts
Club Band"
B 0417
"Music Of The Beatles From 1962 To Sgt.
Pepper's Lonely Hearts Club
Band."
M 2341
The Music Of The Beatles: Twilight Of
The Gods
B 0376
Music Of The People - From Beowulf To
The Beatles

C 0182
"Musicologically . . . ."
N 1033
"'Music 152,' Yeah, Yeah, Yeah."
N 0013
"Music's Gold Bugs: The Beatles."
C 0008
"The Music The Beatles Recorded."
N 0787
"Music: Words And Music By Yoko Ono."
M 1959
"Musik Im Maxilook: Nostalgie In Der
Rockmusik."
M 3142
"Mutton Dresses As Ram?"
M 0707
"My Beatle Days."
C 0053
My Beatles
B 0395
"My Beatles Collection."
M 1983
"My Carnival."
M 2039
"My Death - By John Lennon."
M 1572
"My Experiment With Truth, Or - The
Search For The Perfect Guru."
N 0764
"My Fat Budgie."
M 1898
"'My First Encounter With The
Beatles'."
M 3192
"My Idea Of A Meeting Of The Beatles
Haters Brigade."
M 0581
"My Meetles With The Beatles."
M 2013
My Music, My Life
C 0293
"My Point Of View."
M 1322
"Mystery Develops Over Beatles Live
Concert."
M 2251
"Mystery Of The Missing Beatles Song."
M 2503
"The Mystery Partly Explained."
M 1643
"Mystery Tour."
M 2252
"Mystery Tour Making Local Stops Soon."
M 2253
"Mystery Tour Shot Down."
C 0087
Mystery Train: Images Of America In
Rock 'N' Roll Music
C 0204
My Sweet Lady Jane
F 0116
"My Turn: The Right To Bear Arms."
M 0519
"Nab Lennon, Yoko On London Drug
Charge."
M 2255
Nantatte Beatles
B 0133
Nashville Diary
B 0351
National Lampoon
P 0093
"National Rifle Association."
M 1819
"National's Triple Bill: In His Own
Write."
N 0789
"Nay, Nay, Nay."
M 2258
"The Nearness Of You."
C 0219
"Near-Riot Scenes Fail To Bug Beatles'
Aussie Tour, But Hong Kong Biz
Slow."
M 3348
"Neil's Column."
M 0079
"The Netherlands."
M 3540

"New Acts."
    M 2266
"New Album In August."
    M 2267
"New Album Out This Month."
    M 2268
"New Albums From Paul & Wings And
    George Harrison."
    M 2269
"New Audience For Beatles Via Movie."
    M 0149
"New Bearings: The Beatles."
    M 0994
"'New Beatle' Klaus Goes Into Hiding."
    M 2270
"The New Beatles Book."
    C 0221   M 2271
"New Beatles Bootlegs."
    M 2272
"New Beatles Double Album Due On
    November 16."
    M 2273
New Beatles Fan Club
    F 0117
"New Beatles Film."
    C 0222   N 0790
"New Beatles Film: 'Let It Be'."
    M 2274
"New Beatles: Happiness Is A Warm Gun."
    M 2275
"New Book News."
    M 2277
"New Books About The Beatles."
    M 0963
"New Culture."
    M 1294
"New Directions For Beatle Business."
    M 2278
"The New Far-Out Beatles."
    M 3442
"The New Harrison Album."
    M 3603
"New Lennons LP."
    M 2279
"New Madness; Rhythm-And-Blues Quartet
    Called The Beatles."
    M 2280
New Patterns Of Musical Behavior In The
    Young Generation In Industrial
    Societies
    C 0062
"New Plastic Ono Single."
    M 2282
"New Recruits To The Beatles Empire."
    M 0176
"New Releases."
    M 0523
"News."
    M 2283
News Collection Japan 1980
    B 0401
"News From Germany."
    C 0223
"News From The U.K."
    M 2087
"News In Brief; American Tour For
    Beatles."
    N 0791
"News In Brief; Awards To Beatles."
    N 0792
"News In Brief; Beatle Leaves
    Hospital."
    N 0793
"News In Brief; Beatles Beat."
    N 0794
"News In Brief; Ready For Australia."
    N 0795
"New Single Sessions."
    M 1052
"A New Slant On Disco And Reggae."
    N 0796
"Newsmakers."
    M 0838   M 0839   M 0840   M 1315
    M 2284   M 2285   M 2286   M 2287
    M 2288   M 2289   M 3093   M 3094
    M 3095
The New Songs Of George, Paul & Ringo
    S 0126   S 0127
The New Songs Of Paul McCartney

    S 0128   S 0129
"A New Sound From A New Team: Paul And
    Linda McCartney."
    M 1286
The New Sound - Yes!"
    C 0008
"Newspaper Sued."
    N 0797
"New Strawberry Fields."
    N 0619
"New Thing For Beatles: Magical Mystery
    Tour."
    M 2290
"New Things For Beatles: Magical
    Mystery Tour."
    C 0194
"New View Of Northern Songs."
    N 0798
"New West Intelligence."
    M 2292
"New Words For A New Age."
    C 0150
"New Year's Day: A Date To Remember
    Each Year For The Beatles."
    M 1644
"New York."
    M 2293
"New York Notebook."
    N 0048
New York Times Magazine
    M 2297
"Next Beatles Trip August 18."
    M 2298
"Next Phase For Northern Songs."
    N 0799
"The Night A Mouse Took The Mickey Out
    Of The Beatles."
    M 3041
"1980 Took Its Toll Of Superstars."
    M 1845
"1983 Beatles Song Poll."
    M 0964
The 1975 John Lennon Interview
    B 0561
"1977 Rolling Stone Critics' Awards."
    M 2301
The 1976 George Harrison Interview
    B 0560
"1964; Gerry And The Pacemakers."
    M 2302
"1964; The Year Of The Beatles."
    M 0765
"1964: Year Of The Beatles."
    M 3593
"1962 - The Beatles Year Of
    Achievement."
    M 2303
"Nine Ways Of Looking At The Beatles,
    1963-73."
    M 3133
"Ninth Beatles Book Competition
    Results."
    M 2304
"No Beatles Appeal - McCartney
    Leaving."
    M 2305
"No Beatle Wigs In The Dining Room."
    N 0801
"Nobody Loves A Beatle Hoaxer."
    M 1104
"Nobody Loves The Beatles 'Cept Mother,
    Capitol, Etc."
    M 2107
"No Book For John This Year."
    C 0224
"No Decision On New Single."
    M 2306
"No Freezing On Beatles' Royalties."
    M 2307
"No Guard For The Beatles."
    N 0802
"No Injunction To Stop Alleged
    Offence."
    N 0803
"No, No, No, Paul McCartney Is Not
    Dead."
    N 0752
"No Opening, But Beatles Show Big."
    M 1828

"No Private Life - But We Love It!"
    M 1408
"No Reply From The Club Where The Beat
    Boom And The Beatles All Began."
    M 3580
"Norman Smith Continues Talking About
    Balancing The Beatles."
    M 1301
"Norman Smith Talks About Balancing The
    Beatles."
    M 2311
"Northern Songs: ATV Near Victory."
    N 0812
"Northern Songs Battle Over But Malady
    Lingers."
    M 2316
"Northern Songs Buying 2 Beatles'
    Lenmac Firm In $1,022,000 Cash
    Deal."
    M 2317
"Northern Songs Director Resigns."
    N 0813
"Northern Songs Gets Another Beatle."
    N 0814
"Northern Songs Ltd. For Beatle Songs
    Unlimited."
    M 1747
"Northern Songs Reports Rise In Fiscal
    '67 Earnings."
    N 0815
"Northern Songs' 'Takeover' Fight Now
    3-Way Battle."
    M 2318
"Northern Songs Talks Continue."
    N 0816
"Northern Songs 3 1/2 Times Covered."
    N 0817
"Northern Songs Widening Videotape
    C'right Defense."
    M 1990
Norwegian Wood
    F 0118
"Norwegian Wood."
    M 0032
Norwegian Wood - Beatles Fanklubb
    F 0119
"Norwich Revisited."
    M 1374
"No Soul In Beatlesville."
    M 3035
Nota Beatles
    F 0120
"Noted Musicians To Aid Venice."
    N 0818
"Not Enough Help From My Friends."
    M 1298
"Notes And Comment."
    M 2319
"Notes And Comment: More Popular, Or
    More Famous, Than Jesus."
    M 2320
"Notes On People."
    N 0273   N 0575   N 0576   N 0577
    N 0578   N 0579   N 0580   N 0605
    N 0606   N 0607   N 0608   N 0609
    N 0610   N 0611   N 0612   N 0613
    N 0614   N 0615   N 0616   N 0819
    N 0820   N 0821   N 0822   N 0823
    N 0824   N 0825   N 0826   N 0827
    N 1118   N 1119
"A Note To E.M.I."
    M 0902
Not Fade Away
    C 0262   C 0263   C 0264   C 0265
"Not For Sale."
    M 3566   M 3567   M 3568
"Not Getting Together Despite $50
    Million Offer."
    N 0828
Nothing To Get Hung About: A Short
    History Of The Beatles
    B 0187
"Nothing To Kill Or Die For."
    N 0297
"'Not Just A Brother ....'."
    M 1888
"Not Marx But Lennon."
    M 2131
"Now Acker Says It, Yeah! Yeah! Yeah!"

M 0766
"Now In United States."
N 0829
"Now It's John Ono Lennon."
N 0830
"Now Its 25 Million Pounds For
    Beatles."
M 2322
"Now Let Boring Controversy Begin!"
M 3633
"Now - 'Live Peace From Toronto'."
M 2323
"No Wonder The Girls Cry."
N 0831
"Now They're A Lot Richer, Some Are
    Sadder, All Wiser."
M 1084   M 2324
"Now We Know How Many Holes It Takes To
    Fill The Albert Hall."
M 2325
"N Songs Hearing Postponed."
N 0832
"NY Benefit Nets A Quarter Million."
M 1105
"NY Hotels Duck Housing Beatles."
M 2294
"N.Y. Judge Rules N.Y. A Fine Place For
    Beatles Suits."
M 1675
"N.Y. Promoter Just About Breaks Even
    On The Beatles' $295,000
    One-Nighter."
M 3165
"NY Times Ad Used For Bernstein Beatles
    Appeal."
M 2296
"The OBE: Lennon's Soul Redeemed."
M 0037
"Obituary."
M 2330 M 2331 M 2332 M 2333
"Obituary; Mr. Brian Epstein: Record
    Request Led Him To Fame With The
    Beatles."
N 0833
Ob La Di Ob La Da
F 0121
"Ob La Di, Ob La Da, Life Goes On."
M 0129
"La Obra Artistica De John Lennon."
M 0015
"Obscurity At Northern Songs."
N 0834
The Ocean View: Paintings And Drawings
    Of Wings American Tour April To
    June 1976
B 0413
Octopus Garden Chapter
F 0122
"Odd Info!"
M 2336
"Oddities."
M 1449
"Odeon, Kensington: Candy."
N 1048
"Off-Beat Film On Beatles; London
    Pavilon: A Hard Day's Night."
N 0837
Official Beatles Fan Club
F 0123
"The Official Beatles Fan Club."
M 0177
Official Beatles' Fan Club "Book, 1970"
B 0414
Official Beatles Fan Club "Book", 1971
B 0415
"The Official Beatles Fan Club
    Newsletter."
M 0788
"Official Overseas Beatles Fan Clubs."
M 2337
The Official Rock And Roll Trivia Quiz
    Book
C 0282
"Official Says Soviet Is Ready To
    Discuss Visit By The Beatles."
N 0211
The Official Sgt. Pepper's Lonely
    Hearts Club Band Scrapbook: The
    Making Of The Hit Movie Musical

B 0529
"Official Up-To-Date List Of Fan Club
    Secretaries."
M 2338
The Official Yellow Submarine Magazine
P 0094
"Off The Road."
M 0036
"Of Many Things; Beatle John Lennon's
    Statement."
M 0874
"Of Rumor, Myth, And A Beatle."
M 2339
"Oh, Grow Up."
M 3356
"Ohio Girls Rush Beatles And Police
    Interrupt Show."
N 0838
"OK 1st Beatles Cut On Non-EMI Label."
M 2344
"Old Beatles - A Study In Paradox."
N 0294
"Old Bowl Concerts By Beatles Due."
M 2345
"The Old Team Again."
M 2346
"Om Og Af Lennon."
M 0517
"On Bass Guitar: Paul McCartney."
M 2348
"On Drums: Ringo Starr."
M 2349
"One And One And One Is Three."
M 2350
"One Beatles Pic His, Second Later;
    Shenson's Unique Reversion Of
    'Durable Legend' Features."
M 2351
"One Guy Standing There, Shouting 'I'm
    Leaving'."
C 0332 M 3642
"100 Casualities In Beatles Queue."
N 0841
"$150m Beatles Blitz All Set To Blast
    U.S. Again."
C 0602
"$150,000 For Book On Beatles."
N 0842
"100% Attendance Is 'In' At George
    Washington."
N 0439
"100,000 Welcome Beatles Home."
N 0843
"$1 M. Lawsuit In Beatles Firm."
N 0844
"1 Million Pounds For Beatles New LP."
M 2356
"One Pair Of Eyes."
M 2051 M 3483
1000 Beatle Facts (And A Little Bit Of
    Hearsay)
B 0402
"$1,000 Lennon Award Established At
    U.C.L.A."
N 0845
The One Who Writes The Words For Elton
    John
C 0317 C 0318
"On John Lennon."
N 1141
"On Lead Guitar: George Harrison."
M 2357
"Only One Beatle Manages To Crack Iron
    Curtain."
M 2358
"Ono Band On Film."
M 3689
"Ono Band Shelve Plans To Issue Old
    Beatles Disc."
M 2362
O'No Foundation
F 0124
"Ono, Geffen, WB Sued For Copyright
    Violation."
M 2363
"Ono John."
M 3358
"Ono LP Broadens Base; Apple Massive
    Promotion."

M 3394
"Ono: More Beatles Than Plastic."
M 0038
Ono Odyssey
F 0125
"On Rhythm Guitar: John Lennon."
M 2364
"On Safairy With Whide Hunter, By
    Beatcomber."
C 0189
"On Stage."
M 1548
"On Stage Pix."
M 2365
On Stage: The Beatles
B 0281
On Stage With The Beatles
B 0282
"On The Death Of John Lennon; Why We
    Kill Our Heroes."
M 0785
"On The Road With Paul McCartney."
M 3331
On The Scene At The Cavern
B 0223 B 0224
On The Scene - Exclusive - The Beatles
    At Carnegie Hall
P 0095
"On The Scene With The Beatles."
M 2192
"On The Wings Of Silly Love Songs."
M 1525
"On Tour With The Beatles."
M 2366 M 3403
"On With The Show, Good Health To You."
C 0092
"Oooops!"
M 1450
"Open-Air Film Show Rejected."
N 0846
"An Open Letter To Beatlefans."
M 3386
"An Open Letter To Beatlefans II."
M 3387
"An Open Letter To John Lennon."
M 2127
"An Open Letter To The Beatles."
M 0930
Orange Apple Jam Chapter
F 0126
"Orchideen Aus Hawai (Die Beatles)."
C 0235
"Order Ex-Beatle To Exit U.S."
M 2367
"The Order Of The British Empire; The
    Prime Minister's List."
N 0847
The Original Beatles Book: Delicious
    Insanity, Where Will It End?
B 0294
The Original Beatles Book - Two
P 0097
"Original Master Beatle Recordings."
M 3179
"Orton And The Beatles: Doomed
    Romance."
M 3604
"The Other Beatle."
C 0231
"The Other Cheek To The Beatles."
N 0319
"Other Noises, Other Notes."
M 2375
"Our American Scrapbook."
M 2378
"Our Back Pages: Apple And The
    Beatles."
M 2379
"Our Back Pages: Mystery Tour."
M 2380
Our Starr
F 0127
Our Starr Monthly
F 0128
Out Of His Head; The Sound Of Phil
    Spector
C 0337
Out Of The Mouths Of Beatles
B 0077

"Outspoken But Charming: A Personal
     Look At The Beatles."
     M 3549
"Over The Water."
     M 1451
"Palace Search For BEM."
     N 0850
"Panel Discusses ATV's New Move."
     N 0863
"The Pantheon."
     M 3137
"Paperback Preview."
     N 0864
"Paperback Talk; Beatlemania."
     N 1123
Paperback Writer International Beatles
     Fan Club
     F 0129
Paperback Writers: An Illustrated
     Bibliography
     B 0249
"The Paperback Writer Session."
     M 2392
Paperback Writer; The Life And Times Of
     The Beatles
     B 0505   B 0506   B 0507
"Park 'Festival' Lends Hand To The
     Retarded."
     N 0311
"Parliament; Beatle Arrest."
     N 0866
"Partners."
     M 0654
"Partnerships."
     C 0264
"Part 1: Rock Beginnings."
     C 0284
"Paterson Submarine Painted Beatle
     Yellow By Pranksters."
     N 0867
"Pattern Of Training For Automation;
     Social Effects Of Less Work."
     N 0868
Paul
     P 0098
"Paul."
     M 1251   M 2397
"Paul!"
     M 3118
"Paul About 'London Town'."
     M 3000
"Paul And Carly: Family Affairs."
     M 2137
"Paul And Linda: 'Alright Tonight'."
     M 0139
"Paul And Linda At Corfu."
     M 2398
"Paul And Linda McCartney: Bionic
     Couple Serves It Your Way."
     M 0140
"Paul & Linda McCartney: The Price They
     Paid For Happiness."
     M 0925
"Paul And Linda On The Run In New
     York."
     M 1877
"Paul And Ringo On Film."
     M 2399
"Paul Asks High Court: Break Up The
     Beatles."
     N 0582
"Paul, Beatles' Battles Behind Him, In
     Control As Biz, Band Blossom."
     M 2400
"Paul Carries That Weight."
     M 3263
"Paul Goes Solo And Shows Talent."
     N 0747
"Paul Joins Battle With ACC For All His
     Yesterdays."
     N 0428
"Paul: Live And Flying."
     M 2205
"The Paul LP You'll Never See."
     M 2401
Paul McCartney
     B 0207   B 0232   B 0269
"Paul McCartney."
     C 0236   C 0237   M 0585   M 1224

     M 2402   M 3643   N 1152
Paul McCartney: A Biography In Words &
     Pictures
     B 0379
"Paul McCartney: Acting His Age."
     M 3561
"Paul McCartney And How He Created
     Wings."
     M 2403
Paul McCartney And Wings
     B 0271   B 0272
Paul McCartney & Wings
     B 0284   B 0366   B 0440   B 0441
     B 0442
Paul McCartney And Wings Fan Club
     F 0130
"Paul McCartney & Wings: Keeping Us
     Guessing."
     M 3555
"Paul McCartney And Wings Talk."
     M 2498
"Paul McCartney: An Exclusive Interview
     With The Prince Of Pop."
     M 0074
"Paul McCartney Arrested In Tokyo."
     N 0869
"Paul McCartney, A Strange And Special
     Meeting."
     M 3351
"Paul McCartney At 40."
     M 2404
Paul McCartney - Beatle With Wings
     B 0227
"Paul McCartney Busted In Tokyo."
     M 2405
Paul McCartney: Canzonie Musica
     B 0095
Paul McCartney Composer/Artist
     B 0354   B 0355   S 0130
"'Paul McCartney: Composer/Artist'."
     M 1452
"Paul McCartney: Confessions Of An
     Unemployed Beatle."
     N 0335
Paul McCartney Dead - The Great Hoax
     P 0099   P 0100
"Paul McCartney Fined For Growing
     Cannabis."
     N 0870
"Paul McCartney Forms A Band."
     M 2406
"Paul McCartney: From The Beginning."
     M 2407
"Paul McCartney: Growing Up, Up, And
     Away From The Beatles."
     M 1215
"Paul McCartney In CBS Deal For
     U.S.-Can., EMI For Overseas."
     M 2185
Paul McCartney In His Own Words
     B 0208   B 0209   B 0210
"Paul McCartney: Is This Man Guilty Of
     Power Pop?"
     M 0665
"Paul McCartney: Keeper Of The Flame."
     C 0265
"Paul McCartney - Lifting The Veil On
     The Beatles."
     M 1230
"Paul McCartney Looks Back."
     M 2196
Paul McCartney: McCartney
     S 0131
"Paul McCartney: New Recording."
     N 0871
"Paul McCartney On Paul McCartney."
     M 2408
"Paul McCartney Paces Fund Drive
     (UNESCO Week For Venice)."
     M 2409
"Paul McCartney Predicts Breakup Of
     Beatles Soon."
     N 0872
"Paul McCartney Punished Enough,
     Japanese Say."
     N 0873
Paul McCartney: Ram

     S 0132
"Paul McCartney Reflects On The Loss Of
     A Friend: What I Should Have
     Said."
     M 1150
"Paul McCartney Reviews The New Pop
     Records."
     M 2410
"Paul McCartney's Guest Appearances."
     M 0965
"Paul McCartney's Guitars."
     M 2411
"Paul McCartney Signs With Columbia
     Records."
     M 3199
"Paul McCartney's Latest Is Exquisite
     But Flawed."
     N 0856
"Paul McCartney's LSD Tell-All Stirs
     Brouhaha."
     M 2412
"Paul McCartney - So Entstand Die Neue
     LP."
     M 2413
"Paul McCartney's One-Man Band."
     M 1225
"Paul McCartney: Songs, Success, And A
     Solo Career."
     M 0521
"Paul McCartney's Solo Rarities."
     M 0966
"Paul McCartney Stages American
     Wingding."
     M 1022
The Paul McCartney Story
     B 0551   B 0552
The Paul McCartney Story, New ed.
     B 0553
"Paul McCartney Takes Court Action To
     Leave Beatles."
     N 1124
"Paul McCartney: Ten Days In The Life;
     Japan Deports Ex-Beatle After Pot
     Bust."
     M 0853
Paul McCartney: The Best Of McCartney
     For Easy Guitar
     S 0133
Paul McCartney: The Best Of McCartney
     For Easy Piano
     S 0134
"Paul McCartney; The Truth And That
     Album."
     M 3720
"Paul McCartney Throws 2 Curves."
     M 2415
"Paul McCartney Throws Swank Party."
     M 2414
"Paul McCartney: Tour By Ex-Beatle."
     N 0874
"Paul McCartney Tour: Optimism
     Bubbles."
     N 1024
Paul McCartney: Tug Of War
     S 0135
Paul McCartney Und The Wings
     B 0156
"Paul McCartney: 'We're Coming To
     Rock'."
     M 3048
"Paul Mauls Debut Rivals; Stevie Sets
     Career Record."
     M 1330
"Paul: Money Can't Buy Him Love."
     M 2416
"Paul Murphy On: The Beatles Live At
     The Star Club."
     M 3012
"Paul On Tour; No Wingsmania Yet."
     M 0104
"Paul Perplex: A British Commentary."
     M 3721
"Paul Plunges Into Work, George Stays
     Cloistered And Yoko Reaches Out
     With Two New Songs."
     M 0072
"Paul: Reunion Ruled Out."
     N 0875
"Paul's At Work."

M 2417
"Paul's Brother: 'I'm Adequate'."
M 1130
"Paul's Brother, M. McCartney."
M 2418
"Paul's Kid Brother Mike."
M 2419
"Paul Soars."
M 2371
"Paul's Party."
M 1947
"Paul Speaking."
M 1645
"Paul's Protest."
M 3605
"Paul's Shout Up At Shipley."
M 2424
"'Paul Started It All'."
M 0871
"Paul's TV Statement."
M 2420
"Paul Talks About Letters, Reporters,
    Films, Songs, People And Things."
M 0903
"Paul - The Cute Beatle Boy."
M 0178
"Paul: With Half Of Wings In A Sling
    He's Still Flying."
M 3424
"Paul Won't Rest His Wings."
M 1226
"Peace And Love."
N 0876
"Peace Anthem."
M 2421
"A Peace Forest In Israel?"
M 0507
"Peer To Question Beatles' M.B.E.s."
N 0877
The Penguin John Lennon
B 0322 B 0323 B 0324
"Pennsylvania Move To Ban Beatles."
N 0878
"Penny Lane For A Song."
N 0879 N 0880
"Pen Pals."
M 2432
"People."
M 2433   M 2434   M 2435   M 2436
M 2437   M 2438   M 2439   M 2440
M 2441   M 2442   M 2443   M 2444
M 2445   M 2446   M 2447
"People And Things That Went Before."
C 0305   M 3310
"People Are Talking About The Beatles,
    Four Parody Singers, Now The
    Passion Of British Young."
M 2448
"The People Behind The Beatles."
M 1748
People For Peace
F 0131
"People Put You On A Pedestal And
    Really Believe You're Different."
M 1733
"People's Album."
M 1533
People Weekly - The Beatles: Will They
    Sing Again For $50 Million
M 2449
Pepperland
F 0132
"Peregrine Worsthorne Discusses The
    Beatles & Mysticism."
M 2450
"Performance."
M 2451   M 2452   M 2453
"Performance: Wings In London."
M 0630
The Performing Self
C 0252
"Personal Ads."
M 2455   M 2456
"Personal Requests."
M 2458
"Perspectives."
M 1275
"Perspectives: Are We Lost In A New
    Dark Age."

M 1276
"Perspectives: 'Bangla Desh' - A Unique
    Film."
M 1277
"Perspectives: Changing With Money
    Changers."
M 1278
"Perspectives: Dealing With Watergate
    And The Lennon Case."
M 1279
"Perspectives: Fair Play For John And
    Yoko."
M 1280
"Perspectives: The British Group
    Syndrome."
M 1281
"Pete Best - A Beatle Talks."
M 3411
"Pete Best At The Star Club."
M 2459
"Pete Best On The 'New' Beatles LP."
M 2460
"Pete Best With All-Stars."
C 0239
"Pete Drake & The Steel Beatle."
M 2314
"Pete In States."
C 0240
"Peter Jones Tells The Truth About The
    Beatles' First Ever Interview By
    A National Pop Paper In August
    1962."
M 2461
"Peter Sellers."
M 3541
Das Phanomen Beatles
B 0464
"Phil Spector."
C 0324   M 2521
Photo Gallery - Rock Fun - Wings
B 0456
"Photographic Impressions Of Beatle
    Songs."
M 1758
Photographs
B 0352
(Photo Of Yoko Ono.)
M 2486
(Photos Of John Lennon.)
M 2571
"The Pick Of The Year."
N 0884
(Picture Calendar For 1977)
B 0353
"Pieces And Comment."
M 2487
The Pierian Press 'Day In The Life' Fab
    Four Twenty-Year Calendar For
    1983
B 0457
The Pierian Press Day In The Life Fab
    Four Twenty-Year Calendar For
    1984
B 0458
The Pierian Press Day In The Life Fab
    Four Twenty-Year Calendar For
    1985
B 0459
"A Pile Of Money On Paul's 'Death'."
M 0638
"Pinning Them Down - If You Can."
N 0886
Pipes Of Peace - Paul McCartney
S 0136
"A Place In The Sun Was His Very
    Favorite Spot On Earth."
M 2492
"Planet News"
M 3794
Plastic Ono Band (songbook) see John
    Lennon - Plastic Ono Band
"Plastic: Wailing With Mrs. Lennon."
M 0039
The Playboy Interview
C 0296
"Playboy Interview: The Beatles."
M 2494
The Playboy Interviews With John Lennon
    & Yoko Ono

B 0496 B 0497 B 0498
"Playing For Paul."
M 3690
"Playing Wrong Notes Seriously."
M 0722
"A Play On The Life Of ...."
M 3484
"Plea By Beatles To Stop Records."
N 0887
"Plea By Music Company Fails."
N 0888
"'Please - No More Jelly Babies!'"
M 0767
"Please Please Me Press Release."
M 2497
"'Please Please Me': The Single That
    Almost Wasn't Made"
M 1749
Pocket Beatles
S 0137
Pocket Beatles Complete
S 0138 S 0139
Pocket Beatles For Guitar
S 0140
"The Poetics Of The Beatles."
C 0181
Poetry Of Rock
C 0127
"Poland."
M 2176
"Poland Updated."
M 2177
"Police Halt Beatles' Show To Avoid
    Riot In Australia."
N 0889
"Police Protection For The Beatles."
N 0890
"Police Seize Lennon Prints In Raid."
N 0891
"Police To Study Pills Found In Home Of
    Beatles' Mentor."
N 0892
"Police Trace Tangled Path Leading To
    Lennon's Slaying At The Dakota."
N 0772
"'Political Censorship'; Now - New BBC
    Irish Ban."
M 2508
"'Political Motive' In Move To Deport
    John Lennon."
N 0544
"Polydor Beatles LP Win Release In
    London Court."
M 3676
"Polyphony And A New Vocal Quartet."
M 1340
Pomelo; Un Libro de Instructiones de
    Yoko Ono
B 0427
"The Pop Artist And His Product: Mixed
    Up Confusion."
M 1962
"Pop In Perspective: A Profile."
M 3138
Poplach Kolem Beatles, Liverpoolskych
    Zpevaku, Notovych Analfabetu,
    Hudbeniku & Autoru ...
B 0117
"The Pop Life."
N 0352
The Pop Makers
C 0298
"Pop Memorabilia Under The Hammer!"
M 2957
"Pop: Miss Flack At Tribute To Lennon."
N 0482
Pop Music And The Blues: A Study Of The
    Relationship And Its Signifcance
C 0210
"Pop Music: Elton John At The Gardens;
    John Lennon Appears, Singing 3
    Pieces."
N 0953
"Pop Music: What's Been Happening."
M 0822
"Pop-Muzyka V Deystivii."
M 3246
"Pop Phenomena."
M 2181

"Popping Off."
  M 3618
"Pop Report."
  M 2526
"Pop, Ritual, & Commitment."
  M 2156   M 2157   M 2158
"Pop Rotogravure."
  M 2206
"Pop Scene."
  N 0894
"Pop Star Blasts The Beatles, Stones,
    Spoonful And More."
  N 0641
"Pop Stars."
  M 0940
Pop Teen, Vol.1, No.1 -
  P 0101
"Pop Think In."
  M 2527   M 2528   M 2529   M 2530
  M 2531   M 2532
"Popular Entertainment."
  C 0255   C 0256
"Popular Entertainment And Ballet."
  C 0257
"Popular Entertainment And Cinema."
  C 0258
"Popular Music, 1965-1969."
  C 0295
"Popular Music, 1960-1964."
  C 0294
Popular Music, Vol 6: 1965-1969
  C 0295
Popular Music, Vol 3: 1969-1964
  C 0294
"A Portfolio."
  M 2535
"Portrait."
  M 2536   M 2537   M 2538   M 2539
  M 2540   M 2541   M 2542   M 2543
  M 2544   M 2545   M 2546   M 2547
  M 2548   M 2549
"Potential $4 Million Box Office For
    Beatles On Closed Circuit TV."
  M 2550
"'Pot Smoked By Beatles At Palace'."
  N 0895
Pottie Bird Beatle Chapter
  F 0133
Pour John Lennon
  B 0001
"Powerhouse Of Pop."
  M 3634
"Pre-fab Product Is Filling The
    Recession-Racked Rock Bin ... "
  M 0856
"Presenting A Concert Of Recently
    Discovered Works By P.D.Q. Bach
    And 'The Baroque Beatles Book'."
  M 2553
"Preserving The Beatles Fantasy."
  M 2554
"Presley Tops Hit Parade On Beatles'
    Home Grounds."
  N 0897
"The Press Conference: John Lennon And
    Yoko Ono Talk About Peace."
  C 0259
"Pretty Penny Lane."
  M 2555
"Priests Burn Beatles Disks In Mexico;
    See Sharp Slump In Sales."
  M 2557
"The Private Life Of Paul And Linda
    McCartney."
  M 2200
"A Private Talk With John."
  M 3779
"The Private Years."
  M 1137
"Probe Into Mystery Death Of City
    Student."
  N 0899
La Prodigieuse Carriere Des Beatles:
    Leur Jeunesse, Leur Popularite,
    Leur Vie Amoureuse
  B 0084
"Produced By George Martin."
  M 3722   M 3723   M 3724
"Producer George."

  M 2558
"Profit From Beatles."
  N 0901
"The Program."
  M 2559
"Programmer's Artist Popularity Poll."
  M 2560
"Program Sellers For Beatles Held; 2
    Seized By U.S. On Charge Of Being
    Bookies Here."
  N 0916
"The Promise Is Gone."
  C 0129   N 0438
"Promoter Fears About Economics Of The
    Beatles."
  M 2561
"Promoter Offers Beatles $30 Million
    For Closed-Circuit TV Concert."
  M 2562
"Prophets."
  M 2563
"Protest By Councilman Blocks Lennon
    Tribute."
  N 0902
"Protest Palls - Says Paul."
  M 1575
"The Provocative Lennon-Ono Marriage."
  M 0999
"Proxymania."
  M 0579
P.S. We Love You: The Beatles Story
    1962/3
  B 0043
"Psychological Characteristics Of
    Beatle Mania."
  M 0867
"A Psychologist Admits Perjury On His
    Degree."
  N 0416
"Publisher-Agent Dispute Ends Lennon
    Book Deal."
  N 0735
"Publisher In Action Over Videotapes."
  M 1991
"Publishers Notes."
  M 2564
"Publishers Sue Lennons For £400,000
    Damages."
  N 0903
"Publishers Sue Mr. McCartney."
  N 0904
"Publishers Sue Spinoff Of
    'Beatlemania' For Infringement
    ('Beatlefever')."
  M 2565
"Punks In Leathers From Liverpool."
  M 2428
"QC Fears Beatles Cash May Not Meet
    Tax."
  N 0905
"Quebec's Subculture: Gilding The
    Beatles."
  M 2218
"Queen Confers Medals."
  N 0906
"Queen Elizabeth 2nd Awards Medals To
    Beatles."
  M 2569
"Queen's Award To Beatles Causing Bit
    Of Ruckus."
  M 2570
"Queen's Decoration."
  N 0907
"Queen's Honors List Includes The
    Beatles."
  N 0688
"'Que Pasa, New York?' Indeed, What Do
    You Say About Suicide?'"
  M 1526
"A Question Of Style."
  M 3657
"Question Time."
  M 1453
"Quiet Crowd Greets Beatles In Canada."
  N 0908
"Quiz."
  M 1454
"Quotes Quiz."
  M 2574

"Radio Fans Mourn John."
  N 0224
"Radio - Featured Programming."
  M 2578
"Radio Stations Ignore Ban On Beatle
    Records."
  M 1333
"Radio: Tribal Drum."
  M 1138
"Raising The Gaity Of Nations."
  N 0934
"Rally For John Lennon On Lenin Hills
    Upsets Police."
  N 0913
Ram
  S 0141
Ram On
  F 0134
Ramparts, Volume 6, No. 3
  M 2581
Ram (songbook)   see also   Paul
    McCartney: Ram
"A Random Note."
  C 0260
"Random Notes."
  M 2582   M 2584   M 2585   M 2586
  M 2587   M 2588   M 2589   M 2590
  M 2591   M 2592   M 2593   M 2594
  M 2595   M 2596   M 2597   M 2598
  M 2599   M 2600   M 2601   M 2602
  M 2603   M 2604   M 2605   M 2606
  M 2607   M 2608   M 2609   M 2610
  M 2611   M 2612   M 2613   M 2614
  M 2615   M 2616   M 2617   M 2618
  M 2619   M 2620   M 2621   M 2622
  M 2623   M 2624   M 2625   M 2626
  M 2627   M 2628   M 2629   M 2630
  M 2631   M 2632   M 2633   M 2634
  M 2635   M 2636   M 2637   M 2638
  M 2639   M 2640   M 2641   M 2642
  M 2643   M 2644   M 2645   M 2646
  M 2647   M 2648   M 2649   M 2650
  M 2651   M 2652   M 2653   M 2654
  M 2655   M 2656   M 2657   M 2658
  M 2659   M 2660   M 2661   M 2662
  M 2663   M 2664   M 2665   M 2666
  M 2667   M 2668   M 2669   M 2670
  M 2671   M 2672   M 2673   M 2674
  M 2675   M 2676   M 2677   M 2678
  M 2679   M 2680   M 2681   M 2682
  M 2683   M 2684   M 2685   M 2686
  M 2687   M 2688   M 2689   M 2690
  M 2691   M 2692   M 2693   M 2694
  M 2695   M 2696   M 2697   M 2698
  M 2699   M 2700   M 2701   M 2702
  M 2703   M 2704   M 2705   M 2706
  M 2707   M 2708   M 2709   M 2710
  M 2711   M 2712   M 2713   M 2714
  M 2715   M 2716   M 2717   M 2718
  M 2719   M 2720   M 2721   M 2722
  M 2723   M 2724   M 2725   M 2726
  M 2727   M 2728   M 2729   M 2730
  M 2731   M 2732   M 2733   M 2734
  M 2735   M 2736   M 2737   M 2738
  M 2739   M 2740   M 2741   M 2742
  M 2743   M 2744   M 2745   M 2746
  M 2747   M 2748   M 2749   M 2750
  M 2751   M 2752   M 2753   M 2754
  M 2755   M 2756   M 2757   M 2758
  M 2759   M 2760   M 2761   M 2762
  M 2763   M 2764   M 2765   M 2766
  M 2767   M 2768   M 2769   M 2770
  M 2771   M 2772   M 2774   M 2775
  M 2776   M 2777   M 2778   M 2779
  M 2780   M 2781   M 2782   M 2783
  M 2784   M 2785   M 2786   M 2787
  M 2788   M 2789   M 2790   M 2791
  M 2792   M 2793   M 2794   M 2795
  M 2796   M 2797   M 2798   M 2799
  M 2800   M 2801   M 2802   M 2804
  M 2805   M 2806   M 2807   M 2808
  M 2809   M 2810   M 2811   M 2812
  M 2813   M 2814   M 2815   M 2816
  M 2817   M 2818   M 2819   M 2820
  M 2821   M 2822   M 2823   M 2824
  M 2825   M 2826   M 2827   M 2828
  M 2829   M 2830   M 2831   M 2832
  M 2833   M 2834   M 2835   M 2836
  M 2837   M 2838   M 2839   M 2840

M 2841   M 2842   M 2843   M 2844
M 2845   M 2846   M 2847   M 2848
M 2849   M 2850   M 2851   M 2852
M 2853   M 2854   M 2855   M 2856
M 2858   M 2859   M 2860   M 2861
M 2862   M 2863   M 2864   M 2865
M 2866   M 2867   M 2868   M 2869
M 2870   M 2871   M 2872   M 2873
M 2874   M 2875   M 2876   M 2877
M 2878   M 2879   M 2880   M 2881
M 2882   M 2883   M 2884   M 2885
M 2886   M 2887   M 2888   M 2889
M 2890   M 2891   M 2892   M 2893
M 2894   M 2895   M 2896   M 2897
M 2898   M 2899   M 2901   M 2902
M 2903   M 2904   M 2905   M 2906
M 2907   M 2908   M 2909   M 2910
M 2911   M 2912   M 2913   M 2914
M 2915   M 2916   M 2917   M 2918
M 2919   M 2920   M 2921   M 2922
M 2923   M 2924   M 2925   M 2926
M 2927   M 2928   M 2929   M 2930
M 2931   M 2932   M 2933   M 2934
M 2935   M 2936   M 2937   M 2938
M 2939   M 2940   M 2941   M 2942
"Random Notes: Beatles Plus Disco
     Equals 'Stars On'."
   M 2943
"Random Notes; Clapton: One Of Those
     Years."
   M 0805
"Random Notes From All Over: 'Golden
     Beatles'."
   N 0915
"Random Notes; Little Richard: The
     Peace Of The Rock."
   M 0806
"Random Notes: McCartney Gets
     Political."
   M 2944
"Random Notes 1979."
   M 2945
"Random Notes; Paul McCartney Gets By -
     With A Little Help."
   M 0807
"Random Notes: Ringo Ailing, Julian
     Hunting."
   M 2946   M 2947   M 2948
"Random Notes: Ringo's Heir."
   M 2949
"Random Notes: 'Why Yoko Made Label
     Switch'."
   M 2950
"Random Notes: Yoko: Tributes And
     Trials."
   M 0808
"R & R Steel The Show."
   N 0911
"Raps Of Wacky Macca."
   M 2243
"Rare Recordings Of Beatle Songs."
   M 0967
"Rarest Rock Show Of All."
   M 1090   M 2951
"'Rarities': Another Look."
   M 2478
"Rattle Of A Simple Girl."
   M 1498
Rave
   M 2952
"Ravi Shankar And George Beatles."
   N 0924
"Ravi Shankar At Home & Abroad."
   M 2580
"Ravi Shankar Gives West A New Sound
     That's Old In East."
   N 0640
"Readables, Listenables, Disables And
     Other Ables."
   M 2958
"Readers And Critics Poll - 1981."
   M 2959
"Readers' Letters."
   C 0261
"Readers' Poll Results."
   M 2960
"Reading For Pleasure: A Slice Of
     Lennon."
   N 0701

"Ready For Les Beatles."
   M 2169
"Reagan, Visiting New York, Talks With
     The Cardinal And Top Blacks."
   N 0278
"The Real American TV Debut Of The
     Beatles."
   M 0538
"Real John Lennon."
   M 1316
The Real True Beatles - By Michael
     Braun, The Writer Who Knows Them
     Best. No. 1
   P 0102
"The Real Truth About The Beatles."
   M 3111
"The Real Way To Remember Lennon."
   N 0857
"Receiver Appointed For The Beatles."
   N 1125
"Receiver For Beatles Would Be
     Disaster, QC Says."
   N 0919
"Receiver Named For The Beatles;
     McCartney Victor In First Episode
     In Legal Contest."
   N 0636
"Recollections Of An Amnesiac."
   M 2120
"Reconstruct Old Beatles Tape; Hamburg
     Songs Will Be Issued By Double H
     Co."
   M 3468
"Record Album Covers."
   N 0921
"Record Company Signs Contract To Issue
     Album By Former Beatle In
     Russia."
   N 1053
"Recording In India: A Special Report
     On George's Recent Visit To
     Bombay."
   M 1042
"Recording Pix."
   M 2962
"Recording Their First Album."
   M 0904
"Recording With The Beatles Then And
     Now."
   M 1053
Recordings Of John, Paul, George &
     Ringo
   B 0230
"Record Notes."
   M 2963   M 2964   M 2965
The Record Producers
   C 0322   C 0323   C 0324
"Record Releases."
   C 0100   C 0101
"Record Reviews."
   M 2966
"Record Reviews (Bootlegs)."
   M 2967
"Records For Christmas."
   N 0922
"Records: Rock, Etc. The Big Ones."
   M 3729
"Record: Yoko Ono, Solo."
   N 0858
"Redefining Beatlemania: A Compulsion
     To Sound Off On All Sensitive
     Issues."
   M 2968
"Rediscovered Historical Beatlefacts."
   M 3267
"Red Nose Folk Of Showbiz."
   M 1334
"Red Rap Beatles."
   N 0923
Red Rose Speedway
   F 0135
Red Rose Speedway (songbook) see
     Wings: Red Rose Speedway
"Reflections On The Death Of The
     Walrus."
   M 2522
"Refried Beatles."
   M 2121
"Reissued Beatle Hits Dominate UK

Chart."
   M 3679
"Reissues Can Never Replace Originals."
   M 0905
"Religioso Slants In Beatles
     Rebellion?"
   M 2982
"Religious Rock: What Is It Saying."
   M 1471
"Remember ... "
   M 1873   M 3151
"Remember Back In 1963 When Tommy
     Topped The Bill Over The
     Beatles?"
   M 1003
"Remember Beatlemania?"
   M 2983
"Remembering .... "
   M 2984
"Remembering 'Sgt. Pepper'."
   M 2985
"Remember Those Cartoons?"
   M 2986
"Remembrance Of Lennon Past."
   M 2504
"A Reminiscence."
   M 1236
"Reporter At Large: Poetic Larks Bid
     Bald Eagle Welcome Swan Of
     Liverpool."
   M 1493
"Report From Granada's Manchester TV
     Studios Where The Stars Gathered
     To Honour The Song Writing Of
     John And Paul."
   M 3005
"A Report From Hiram."
   M 3347
"Report On Lennon."
   N 0927
"Report On The Beatlefest '76, Los
     Angeles."
   M 2040
"Report On The State Of The Beatles."
   M 2094
"Requiem For A Beatle."
   M 0121
"Der Rest Ist Singsang-Ein Ex-Beatle
     Auf Tournee."
   M 1521
"'Restless Spirits Depart, Still We're
     Deep In Each Other's Heart'."
   M 2281
"Results Of The June Song Poll
     Competition."
   M 3006
"Resurrecting The Beatles: Star-Club To
     Stereo; Phonograph Record Made
     From Tape Of 1962 Hamburg
     Performance."
   M 3004
"The Return Of The Beatles."
   M 0067
"A Return Visit."
   M 1646
"Reviews."
   M 3007
"Revised 'Heaven's Gate' Collapses At
     Box Office."
   N 0788
Revolution
   F 0136
"Revolution."
   N 0643   N 0929
"Revolutionary Force 9 Recalls Beatles'
     Song."
   N 0930
"Revolutionary Number 9."
   M 3008
"Revolution Finds Andy Hardy."
   N 1049
"Revolution Is Not All Blood."
   M 3732
Revolution Press
   F 0137
"Revolution Report: How The Beatles
     Recorded Their New Single."
   M 1647
"Revolution! That's What The Beatles

Are Planning With This Apple."
M 3581
"Revolution: The Dear John Letters."
M 3009
Revolver
F 0138
Revolver (songbook) see The Beatles:
Revolver
"Rhythm & Blues Revival - No White
Gloved, Black Hits."
M 3211
Rhythm And Harmony In The Music Of The
Beatles
B 0462
"Rhythm & Harmony In The Music Of The
Beatles."
M 2534
"RIAA Gold Disk Awards Point Up
Beatles' Boff Biz."
M 3010
"Rich Man's Plaything."
N 1050
"Richard Di Lello, Or: A House Hippie
On Tour."
M 3546
"Richard Lester's War Movie To End All
War Movies - Maybe."
M 1137
"The Richard Starkey Story."
M 2313
"Ride On My Fast City-Line."
M 0116
"Riffs: Paul McCartney Is Afraid Of The
Dark."
M 0671
"Riffs: Rutles Give Us Back Our Birth
Right (Kinda)."
M 2163
"Riffs: Yoko Ono's Grief."
M 0529
"The Right Beat?"
C 0068
Ringo
F 0139   P 0103
"Ringo."
C 0226   C 0227   C 0328   M 1129
M 3322   M 3606   M 3607   M 3608
"Ringo!?!"
M 3015
"Ringo Acts Naturally For TV Special."
M 3016
"Ringo & Friends In Country Country."
M 2315
"Ringo And George In California."
M 1043
"Ringo And Harry - Harry And Ringo."
M 2138
"Ringo & £$."
M 3017
"Ringo & Steptoe."
C 0268
"Ringo And The Nashville Cat."
M 3726
"Ringo: A Space Odyssey."
M 3018
"Ringo A Star."
M 3019
"Ringo Caught On Pool Table."
M 3020
"Ringo Cuts Country Album In Nashville,
Harrison Next."
M 3699
"Ringocyclistics."
M 3021
"Ringo: Drums."
M 1375
"Ringo For 'Juke Box Jury'."
C 0269
"Ringo Gets It Off His Chest."
M 3609
"Ringo Goes Single."
M 1397
"Ringo, His Tax Exile, His New Fiancee,
His Rap On A Beatle Reunion."
M 3022
"Ringo In Rome: Candy: Filming Report
From Italy."
M 1044
"Ringo In Rome: Candy: Filming Report

From Italy, Part 2."
M 1045
"Ringo In The Afternoon."
M 2182
"Ringo Loves Her - Yeah! Yeah! Yeah!"
M 3023
Ringo Magazine
F 0140
"Ringo: Mr. Nice Guy Comes Into His
Own."
M 2093
"Ringo 1964."
M 1376
"Ringo On Drums, Drugs, And The
Maharishi."
M 3024
"Ringo On TV Commercial Showing How
Simple Life Is."
M 1579
"Ringo Parodies Twain In Uniquely
Visual Video Bow."
M 1488
"Ringo Produces Book Of Photographs."
C 0270
"Ring O' Records."
M 1377
"Ring O' Records, Ring O' Records."
M 0524
"Ring O' Records Special."
M 0525
"Ringo Remembers ... ."
M 1227
"Ringo, Ringo, Let Down Your Hair!"
M 0020
"Ringo's Agenda: Movie, Music, But No
Beatles."
M 0034
"Ringo's Back."
M 2372
"Ringo's Beatle Bingo."
M 3200
"Ringo Sets Up Shop: Ring-O Records."
M 3245
"Ringo's Latest Discs."
M 3025
"Ringo Smells The Roses."
M 3517
"Ringo's New Album: A Track By Track
Review."
M 3026
"Ringo Speaking."
M 1648
Ringo's Photo-Album
P 0104
"Ringo Stands Up The Queen."
M 3027
"Ringo Starr."
M 2201
"Ringo Starr And Barbara Bach Marry In
London."
N 0935
"Ringo Starr Decree."
N 0936
"Ringo Starr Discusses TV Debut On NBC
Special 'Ringo'."
N 0937
"Ringo Starr: Domesticated Beatle."
M 0913
Ringo Starr Fan Club
F 0141
"Ringo Starr In Hospital."
N 0938
"Ringo Starr Of Beatles Survives
Tonsilectomy."
N 0939
"Ringo Starr Plays Tennis In South
Africa."
N 0940
"Ringo Starr (Richard Starkey)."
C 0271
"Ringo Starrs Again."
M 3028
"Ringo Starr Sets Out To Become A
Legend Of The Silver Screen."
N 0392
"Ringo Starr's TV Special Truly Special
Event."
M 1489
"Ringo Starr Talks Naturally."

M 3029   M 3195
"Ringo Starr, The Former Beatle, With
Barbara Bach, ... "
N 0941
"Ringo Starr Was In The Crowd; John And
Yoko Stayed In Bed."
M 1151
"Ringo Stars In New Rock Film."
M 3030
"Ringo Starts Label."
M 3031
"Ringo Starts Label; No Reunion
Possible."
M 1737
"Ringo's Three Chord Trick."
M 1851
"Ringo's Wedding."
M 3032
"Ringo Taps The Press."
M 3033
"'Ringo' TV Special Has 2 Starrs."
N 0254
"Ringo: What Will He Do Next?"
M 3034
"The Rise And Fall Of The Rock Film."
M 3694
"Rising Filipino Terrorism Is Led By
'Monkees' And Huk 'Beatles'."
N 0979
"R. Meltzer Interviewed."
M 2575
The Road Goes On Forever
C 0225
"Roberta Flack Wins Two Grammies For
Her Records."
N 0942
"Rock Age Hero."
N 0945
"Rock And Fine Art."
C 0048
Rock & Folk (No.118, November 1976)
M 3053
"Rock And Roll Circus."
M 0855
"Rock And Roll Memorabilia."
C 0273
"Rock & Roll Memorabilia Goes Boom."
M 1541
Rock & Roll Memorabilia (Jive)
C 0026
"Rock And Roll Music."
C 0333
"Rock And Roll Revival."
M 2299
"Rock And Roll Revival Surprise: John &
Yoko."
M 2084
"Rock-A-Rama: John Lennon - Rock 'N'
Roll."
M 3054
Rock Art: Fifty-Two Record Album Covers
C 0280
"Rock, Beat, Pop Avantgarde."
M 3329
The Rock Book
C 0226
Rock Dreams
C 0238
Rock Dreams (Rock 'N' Roll For Your
Ears!)
C 0081
Rock E No Shiten (The Story Of Rock)
C 0049
"Rockers Roll In Auction Bucks."
M 3055
Rock Family Trees
C 0339
Rock From Elvis Presley To The Rolling
Stones
C 0148
Rock; From The Beginning
C 0080
"Rock Giants From A-Z: John Lennon:
Pain For Art's Sake."
M 3610
"Rock Giants From A-Z: Paul McCartney:
Putting On The Style."
M 3611
"The Rock Heard 'Round The World."

M 3399
"Rocking Redcoats Are Coming; Beatles
    Lead Massive Drive."
M 3594
Rock Lexikon
C 0288
Rock Music
C 0283   C 0284   C 0285
"Rockmusik Und Kunstmusik Der
    Vergangenheit-Ein Analytischer
    Versuch."
M 3169
Rock 'N' Roll And Advertising Art
    (Boogie)
C 0025
"Rock 'N Roll Auction 1981."
M 0117
"Rock 'N' Rolling: Apple Corp. Losing
    Lennon As Partner."
M 1829
"Rock 'N' Rolling: McCartney's Arrest
    Cancels Japan Tour."
M 1830
"Rock 'N' Rolling: McCartney's Jailing
    Concludes In Japan."
M 1831
"Rock 'N' Rolling: Year One Band Pays
    Tribute To Lennon."
M 1832
"Rock 'N' Roll Is Hell As Beatlemania
    Cuts Swath Thru Germany."
M 1346
Rock 'N' Roll Is Here To Pay
C 0075
"Rock 'N' Roll Music."
M 1856
Rock 'N Roll Music As Recorded By The
    Beatles
S 0142
"Rock 'N' Roll News."
    M 3056   M 3057   M 3058   M 3059
    M 3060   M 3061   M 3062   M 3063
    M 3064   M 3065   M 3066   M 3067
    M 3068   M 3069   M 3070   M 3071
    M 3072   M 3073   M 3074   M 3075
    M 3076   M 3077   M 3078   M 3079
    M 3080   M 3081   M 3082   M 3083
    M 3084   M 3085   M 3086   M 3087
    M 3088   M 3089
Rock 'N' Roll (songbook)   see   John
    Lennon - Rock 'N' Roll
Rock 'N' Roll (songbook)   see   The
    Beatles: Rock 'N' Roll
Rock 'N' Roll: The First 25 Years
C 0321
Rock 'N' Roll Times
B 0567
Rock 'N' Roll Times: The Style And
    Spirit Of The Early Beatles And
    Their First Fans
B 0568
"Rock On!"
M 0708
"Rock: Paul Plus Linda."
M 1857
"Rock Reviews."
M 3644
Rock Session 5
C 0158
"'Rockshow': A Review."
M 1464
The 'Rockshow' Premiere."
M 1984
"Rock's Own Rock On."
M 2183
Rock Stars In Their Underpants
C 0346
The Rock Story
C 0145
"Rod McKuen Says Beatles Saved Folk
    Music Folk."
M 3091
Rolling Stone
P 0105
The Rolling Stone Illustrated History
    Of Rock & Roll
C 0203
"Rolling Stone Interview: George
    Harrison."

M 1667
"Rolling Stone Interview: John Lennon."
M 3098
"Rolling Stone Interview: Paul
    McCartney."
M 1228
"Rolling Stone Interview: Ringo Starr
    And George Harrison."
M 1576
The Rolling Stone Interviews
C 0086
"Rolling Stone Music Awards For 1975."
M 3099
"Rolling Stone 1979 Readers' Poll."
M 3100
"The Rolling Stone Red Suspenders
    Awards; Critics Choice."
M 3101   M 3102
"Rolling Stone Red Suspenders Awards;
    Readers' Poll."
M 3103
The Rolling Stone Rock 'N' Roll Reader
    C 0005   C 0006   C 0036   C 0039
    C 0042   C 0087   C 0088   C 0153
    C 0171   C 0194   C 0199   C 0260
    C 0331   C 0332   C 0333   C 0347
    C 0348
"Rolling Stones; Beggars' Triumph."
M 3139
Rolling Stone; Special Beatles
    Anniversary Issue
P 0106
"Rolling Stones, Their Satanic
    Majesties Request."
M 1816
"Roll Over Australia!"
M 1558
"Roundup."
N 0912
"Routine British Day: Mail, Phone, Bank
    Strikes."
N 1004
"'Rubber Soul' And The Social Dance
    Tradition."
C 0228   M 2342
Rubber Soul (songbook) see The
    Beatles: Rock 'N' Roll
"Rubinstein's Fortissimo, Beats, 'Yeah,
    Yeah, Yeah'."
N 0959
"Ruling On Song Theft Hints More
    Suits."
N 0960
"Rumination And Ruination."
M 0734
"Rumor Mill."
M 3121
"Rumors Of McCartney's Death Put
    Beaucoup Life Into 'Abbey Road'
    Sales."
M 3122
"Rumour-Bustin' Report."
M 1649
"Rumour-Bustin' Report No. 2."
M 1650
"Rundgren Faces The Beatles."
M 3518
"Rush For New Issues; Northern Songs
    Response."
N 0961
"Rutlemania."
M 0917
"Rutlemania Hits TV: 'All You Need Is
    Cash'."
M 3123
"The Rutles."
M 1545
"The Rutles: All You Need Is Cash."
M 3036
"Rutles Forever"
M 3124
"Sales Boost For Lennon Prints."
N 0964
"Salute to Beatles Changes Knott's
    Berry Farm Image."
M 3454
"Salvation: From Billy Sunday To The
    Beatles."
M 3652

Saturday Evening Post. No. 11
M 3144
Saturday Evening Post. No. 28
M 3145
"Saucer Lands In Virginia."
M 2423
"Save Our Lennons Campaign."
M 1534
"Say Blah-Blah Spaniel."
M 3156
"Scenarios For The Revolution In
    Pepperland."
C 0063   M 0594
"The Scene."
M 1817
"Scene & Heard."
C 0132   C 0133
"Scenes: All You Need Is Cash."
M 3301
"Scenes: Lennon Envisioned."
M 3302
"Scenes: New Hash On 'Cash' Flack."
M 3303
"School Programs Revised In Greece;
    Athletics Made Compulsory -
    History Is Rewritten."
N 0970
"Schueler Des 5. Und 6. Schulijahrs
    Analysieren Beatlessongs."
M 1818
"Science Looks At Beatlemania."
M 2374
"Scoop."
M 3187   M 3188
"Scot Teens Who Queued 60 Hrs. For The
    Beatles Were Show Themselves."
M 3191
"A Scouser's View Of The 'Pool."
M 2479
"Screaming Money."
M 0775
"Screen: 'Caveman' With Ringo Starr."
N 0757
"The Screen: Films By John And Yoko At
    Whitney Museum."
N 0448
"'Screwball' Had No Record."
N 0974
The Screw Reader
C 0125
"Sean Lennon: The Wit And Soul Of A
    Beatle In The Body Of An 8 Year
    Old."
M 1317
"Search & Protest In Popular Songs."
M 1285
"Seaside Rock - The Beatles."
C 0292
Season Of Glass (songbook) see Songs
    From Double Fantasy/Season Of
    Glass
Second Book Of Fifty Hit Songs By John
    Lennon And Paul McCartney
S 0143
"The Second Coming Of The Beatles."
M 1765
"The Second Golden Age Of Pop."
C 0142   M 1537
The Second Golden Beatles Album
S 0144
"Second Great Mersey Beatle
    Extravaganza."
M 0110
"Secondhand Beatles."
M 3268
"Secondhand Fans."
M 0603
"Second Liverpool Beatles Convention."
M 3542
"Secret Goodies In 'You're Sixteen'."
M 1338
"Secular Music."
M 0717
"See Hot Bidding From Labels In Future
    For Paul McCartney's Wings."
M 3196
"See McCartney Being Bought Out By
    Other Beatles."
M 3197

"Seen But Hardly Heard."
  N 0975
"See Way Clear For 'New' Beatles LPs."
  M 3680
"Sgt. Pepper."
  M 1054
"'Sgt. Pepper' - A Look Back."
  M 2505 M 3180 M 3388
"'Sgt. Pepper' As Noise."
  M 3704
"'Sgt. Pepper' Gets Busted."
  M 2263
"Sgt. Pepper Hits The Road."
  M 3209
"Sgt. Pepper; Latest Album."
  M 3202
"'Sgt. Pepper' On Broadway."
  M 1139
Sgt. Pepper Posten
  F 0142
"'Sgt. Pepper' Returns."
  M 1152
"'Sgt. Pepper's' Beatle Music May 'Pied
    Piper' Rock Fans To Legit."
  M 3203
Sgt. Pepper's Lonely Hearts Club Band
  B 0174 B 0175
Sgt. Pepper's Lonely Hearts Club Band
    (songbook) see also The
    Beatles: Sgt. Pepper's Lonely
    Hearts Club Band
Sgt. Pepper's Lonely Hearts Club Band:
    The Rock Spectacle
  S 0145
"Sgt. Pepper's Lonely Hearts Club
    Fans!"
  M 2980
"Sgt. Pepper's Odyssey: A Preview Of
    The Movie 'Yellow Submarine'."
  M 2152
"Series Of Concerts To Benefit Victims
    Of African Famine."
  N 0977
"Settling Down."
  M 3277
"Shaggy Englishman Story; British
    Long-Hairs Rolling Stones And The
    Beatles."
  N 0280
"Shake."
  M 3206
"Shares On The Exchange."
  N 0981
"Sharing The Grief."
  M 3210
Shaved Fish (songbook) see John
    Lennon/Plastic Ono Band: Shaved
    Fish
"'She Loves You'."
  M 0814
"Shea Reunion."
  M 3212
"Shell Found At Lennon House."
  N 0983
"Shindig - An On-The-Spot Report."
  M 3229
"Shindig Pix."
  M 3243
"Shindig T.V. Show."
  M 3244
"Shooting Of Reagan Is Leading Notables
    To Increase Security Against
    Assassins."
  N 0695
"Shooting The Beatles."
  M 0634
"Short Ads."
  M 3252
"Short Takes."
  N 1000
"Should The Beatles Come Together?"
  M 3253
Shout!
  B 0408
"Shout."
  M 2309
"'Shout': An Interview With Author
    Philip Norman."
  M 3254 M 3255

Shout! Die Wahre Geschichte Der Beatles
  B 0409
"Shout! My Quest For The True Story Of
    The Beatles."
  N 0811
Shout! The Beatles In Their Generation
  B 0410 B 0411
Shout! The True Story Of The Beatles
  B 0412
"Shout! The True Story Of The Beatles."
  M 0910 M 1455
"Showbiz Has Lost A Nemperor."
  M 1965
"Show Out Of Town."
  M 3256
Show, The Magazine Of Film And The Arts
  M 3257
"Shrieks Drown Beatles At Tribunal
    Recording."
  N 1001
"Shrieks Of 55,000 Accompany Beatles."
  N 0972
Sick - Monster Issue
  M 3258
"Sic Transit Eleanor Rigby."
  M 0046
"Sidelights; Yeah, Yeah, Yeah."
  N 1005
"Silent Tribute To Lennon's Memory Is
    Observed Throughout The World."
  N 0455
"Silly Charlie And The Not-So Red-Hot
    'Pepper'."
  M 2244
"The Silver Beatles."
  C 0073
"Sinclair Freedom Rally Stars Lennon
    And Ono."
  M 3279
"Sing A British Tune."
  N 1006
"Singalong A Beatles - Ugh!"
  M 3280
"Singer Tony Sheridan Sues Over Beatles
    LPs."
  M 3281
"Singing Beatles Need New Deal On
    Finance."
  M 3282
"Singing Beatles Prepare For U.S.;
    British Performers Leaving
    Tomorrow For Tour."
  N 0381
Sisters Under The Skin
  C 0198
"Sitting In The Stand Of The Sports
    Arena."
  M 1378
16 Magazine - Beatles - 100 Pix Never
    Before Seen (Volume 6, No. 9)
  P 0107
16 Magazine Presents: John Lennon And
    The Beatles - A Loving Tribute
  P 0108
Sixteen Magazine Volume 6, No. 2
  M 3286
"'6th Beatle' Mal Evans Killed In Los
    Angeles."
  M 3313
"6,000 Beatle Buffs Flip Their Wigs In
    2-Show Carnegie Hall Blowout."
  M 3166
60s!
  C 0151
The Sixties
  C 0052 C 0105
The Sixties; As Reported By The New
    York Times
  C 0170
"'62 Beatles Album Due."
  M 3287
"The Sizzling New Tell-All Book About
    The Beatles Secret Lives."
  M 0632
"Slaying Stuns Concertgoers."
  N 0965
"Small Sam, By Beatcomber."
  C 0190
"Social History, Entertainment, Sport,

Etc."
  C 0306
"Social News; Beatle Marriage."
  N 1011
"Social Notes."
  M 3314 M 3315
"'So In The End, The Beatles Have
    Proved False Prophets'."
  N 0740
"Un Soiree En Marge."
  M 2050
Solid Gold: The Popular Record Industry
  C 0093
"Solo Beatles."
  N 1153 N 1154
"The Solo Lennon."
  M 3317
"Solo Single From Ringo?"
  M 3318
The Solo Years
  S 0146 S 0147
"So Many Are McCartney's Ideas"
  M 1651
"Some Beatles Fans Undergo A Bit Of A
    Setback."
  N 0324
"Some Beatle Singles Are No Longer
    Obtainable."
  M 1652
"Some Days In The Life."
  C 0192
"Some Interesting Dates From August In
    Past Years."
  M 3319
"Some Outtakes From Beatles History."
  M 3152
"Some Straight Talking By Yoko."
  M 3612
"Something To Be."
  M 3320
"'Something' To Be Released As Single
    In U.K."
  M 3321
"Sometime In L.A.; Lennon Plays It As
    It Lays."
  M 3311
Some Time In New York City - John &
    Yoko
  S 0148
"Some Time In New York City: Lennon
    After The Beatles."
  C 0329
"Sometimes, I Wonder How The Hell We
    Keep It Up."
  M 0768
"Somewhere In Australia."
  M 2229
"'Somewhere In England'."
  M 2132
"Song Company Of Beatles Resists A
    Take-Over Bid."
  N 1012
"A Song For Dreaming."
  M 0829
"Song Is Ended. But Beatles Linger On
    As Advertisers Utilize Tie-In
    Rights."
  M 3323
"Song Of The Month."
  M 3324
"Songs And Sounds Of The Sixties."
  M 0639
"Songs: ATV New Bid."
  N 1013
Songs By George Harrison & Richard
    Starkey
  S 0149
Songs Der Beatles. Texte Und
    Interpretationen. 2d ed.
  B 0217
Songs From Double Fantasy/Season Of
    Glass
  S 0150
"Songs From India On New Beatle LP."
  M 3325
Songs Of John Lennon
  S 0151 S 0152
"The Songs Of Lennon-McCartney Kept
    Beatles Atop Music World."

N 0268
"Songs: The Beatles Sell."
N 1014
"Songs They Never Sang."
M 1157
"Songwriters John And Paul Earned $4
    Mil."
M 3326
"Son Of A ... "
M 1795
"Sons Of 'Great White Wonder'."
M 3327
"Sorrow, Tributes Around The World."
N 1015
"Sotheby's Memorabilia Auction."
M 0146
Il Sottomarino Gallo
B 0517
Sound Effects: Youth, Leisure, And The
    Politics Of Rock 'N' Roll
C 0109
Sound Of Our Time
C 0176
"The Sound Of The Sixties."
N 0778   N 1016
"S. African Broadcastmen Lift 4-Year
    Record Ban On Beatles."
M 1096
"S. African Radio Ban On Beatles'
    Records."
N 1017
Souvenirs Des Beatles
B 0565
Souvenir Song Album
S 0153
"Soviet Critic Asserts The Beatles Are
    Out Of Tune With The Times."
N 1018
"Soviet Newspapers Comment On Lennon -
    Death Attributed To 'Pathological
    Violence' In U.S. - Praise Is
    Lavished On The Beatles."
N 0038
"So What Else Is New? The Beatles Spark
    Coast Riots, Take Home 150G."
M 3330
A Spaniard In The Works
B 0325   B 0326
A Spaniard In The Works: His Second
    Book
B 0327
Ein Spanier Macht Noch Keinen Sommer
B 0328
"A Spawning Run Of Ecological Ideas."
M 3745
"A Speakeasy Party."
M 3332
Speciaal Album
B 0518
"Special 'Mersey Beat' Visit To The
    Beatles Film Set."
C 0162
A Special Tribute To John Lennon
B 0519
"Spector Of The Beatles."
M 3333
"Spector Wows 'Em At Harrison Date."
M 3334
"Split Of Beatles Clips Capitol
    Industries Stock."
M 3338
"Spongers Harassed Beatles Before Klein
    Moved In, Lennon Tells Court."
M 3339
Spotlight Heroes: Two Decades Of Rock
    And Roll Superstars As Seen
    Through The Camera Of John
    Rowlands
C 0278
"Spot The Beatle Contest Photo."
M 3340
"Spreading His Wings."
M 0971
"Springsteen, Audience Remember John
    Lennon."
N 1022
"Sssssssh ... Beatles Recording."
M 3230
"Stage: 'Lennon, A Biography,' Opens."

N 0933
"Standing In The Hall."
M 1379
Star Club
B 0071
"Star Drummer!"
C 0311
"A Starr For Ringo."
M 3140
"Starr! Starr!"
M 2114
"Starr Stir."
N 1020
"Starr Trek."
M 0769
"The Stars Are Shocked After Murder Of
    Lennon."
N 1021
"'Stars' Story: Inspired By Pirate
    Album."
M 1483
Star Time Presents The Beatles
P 0109
"Starting Over."
M 2390
"Starting Over: Life Without John
    Lennon."
C 0164   N 0585
"Starting The Beatles Book."
M 0906
"States Go Beatle Crazy."
M 3350
"The Steady Stream Of Beatles Songs -
    On The Pop Scene."
N 0976
"Steele's Own Tribute To The Beatles."
N 1023
"Stigwood, Shaw Exit Nems Enterprises;
    Beatles Taking Expanded Mgt.
    Role."
M 3360
"Stockholder-Fans Snag Beatles' Music
    Co. Sale."
M 3361
"Stock In Beatle Songs Is Cheaper In
    London."
N 1025
"Stokowski Talks Of Something Called
    Beatles; Conductor And Teen-Agers
    Hold Dialogue At Carnegie On
    British Phenomenon."
N 0865
"Stones' Man For Beatles."
M 3364
"Stones Set Pear A-Rolling."
M 3365
"'Stop And Smell The Roses'."
M 0968
"Stop The World."
C 0102
La Storia Dei Beatles
B 0443   B 0476
"The Story Behind The Hamburg Tapes."
M 1505
The Story Of Rock
C 0050
Story Of Rock - The Beatles
B 0444
"The Strange Case Of John Lennon."
M 2264
"A Strange Day's Night."
M 0782
Strawberry Fields Forever
F 0143
"Strawberry Fields Forever."
C 0313   M 1837   M 2154   M 2395
N 1031   N 1032
Strawberry Fields Forever; John Lennon
    Remembered
B 0211   B 0212
"The Street Signs Go Up."
M 3367
"Strong As Ever; Let It Be."
N 0748
Stuart Sutcliffe
B 0535
"Stuart Sutcliff: Tragic Fifth Man."
N 0298
"Student Editors Vote Beatles Tops."

M 3368
"Student Speaks; Knights Of A Hard
    Day."
M 2232
"Stunned Fans Hold Sidewalk Wake."
N 1034
"Stu Sutcliffe: Would He Have Changed
    The Beatles Had He Lived?"
M 1456
"Sue Harrison Again To Prove Plagiarism
    Had Been International."
M 3370
"Sue Me, Sue You Blues: Harrison's Not
    'So Fine'."
M 3371
"Sue You, Sue Me Blues."
M 2128
Sugao No John Lennon
B 0298
"Sugarwater McCartney."
M 1549
"Suit By Former Beatles."
N 1035
"Suit Says Paul Can't Write Songs With
    Linda Unless We Publish 'Em."
M 3373
Summer Love (Volume 2, No. 47)
P 0110
"Summons Over Lennon Prints."
N 1036
"Super Star Comin' Home."
M 1899
"Superstar Show Makes 'Superb' Bangla
    Set."
M 2382
"Support Growing For UCS 'Strike Pay'
    Proposal."
N 0980
"Surprise U.S. Hit For Paul."
M 3374
"The Surreal Genius Of Rock."
C 0082   N 0309
"Surrender To Peace."
C 0229
"'Surrey Sound' Has Thin B.O. Fringe As
    Beatles Top Minets In Hub
    'Contest'."
M 2012
"Survey Results."
M 3181
"Survey Results II."
M 3182
"Survey Results III."
M 3183
"The Surviving Beatle - And Others."
M 3269
"Suspect Had Told A Devotee To Try To
    Get Autograph Soon."
N 1039
"Suspect In Lennon's Slaying Is Put
    Under Suicide Watch."
N 0773
"Suspect's Dad In Shock - 'He Loved The
    Beatles'."
N 0840
"Suspect, 25, Indicted In Murder Of
    Lennon."
N 1037
"Sustained Performances: Sgt. Pepper's
    Lonely Hearts Club Band."
C 0243
"Suzy And The Red Stripes."
M 3002
"Swan Songs."
M 2220
"Sweden."
M 0526
"Sweden Updated."
M 0648
"Swede Teenagers Brush The Beatles."
M 3395
"Swedish Narks Flack For Wings."
M 3396
"Swinging With The Beatles."
M 3401
"Symbolic Comrades."
M 0718
"Synpunkter Paa Pop."
M 2576

"Take A Good Look At These Album
    Covers."
    M 3404
"Take It Away."
    M 1985
"Take These Broken Wings And Learn To
    Fly; McCartney's Band On The
    Run."
    M 0712
"Taking Popular Culture Seriously: The
    Beatles."
    M 3110
"Taking The Beatles Seriously."
    M 2496
"Taking The Beatles Seriously: Problems
    Of Text."
    M 2130
A Talent For Loving
    B 0126
"Talent In Action."
    M 0977   M 3405   M 3406   M 3407
    M 3408
"A Tale Of Four Beatles, Part I."
    M 3231
"A Tale Of Four Beatles, Part II."
    M 3232
"A Tale Of Four Beatles, Part III."
    M 3233
"A Tale Of Four Beatles, Part IV."
    M 3234
"A Tale Of Four Beatles, Part V."
    M 3235
"A Tale Of Four Beatles, Part VI."
    M 3236
"A Tale Of Four Beatles, Part VII."
    M 3237
"A Tale Of Two Cities' Conventions."
    M 1269
"A Tale Of Two Conventions."
    M 1986
"Tales Of Hearsay And Undisputed Truth
    For Beatle Watchers."
    M 2506
"The Tales Of Hermit Fred."
    C 0191
Talking Pictures. Volume 1, No. 1 -
    Special Beatles Issue
    P 0111
"Talking Through Their Heads."
    M 2343
"Talking To The Beatles."
    M 0179
"Talking With Ringo Starr."
    M 1760   M 3409
"The Talk Of The Town."
    C 0316
"Talk With Yoko."
    M 2310
"Tampa, Florida."
    N 1044
"Tape By Hinckley Is Said To Reveal
    Obsession With Slaying Of
    Lennon."
    N 1045
"Tax Offences By Manager Of Beatles."
    N 1046
"Teen-Age Craze Inspires Ballet."
    N 0049
"A Teenage Hampden Roar Proves They're
    Still The Guvnors!"
    M 3582
"Teen-Agers (Mostly Female) And Police
    Greet Beatles; British Long-Hairs
    In City To Begin 3d Tour Of U.S."
    N 0973
"Teen-Age Siege Of Delmonico's,
    Beatles' Fortress, Ends 2d Day."
    N 0774
Teen Bag's Tribute To John Lennon, No.
    P 0112
Teen Life
    M 3417
"Teens Are Listening To ...."
    M 3418
Teen Scoop
    M 3419
Teen Screen
    M 3420
Teen Screen - Have The Beatles Had It?

Hardly, Luv!
    M 3421
Teen Screen Life Story: Ringo
    P 0113
Teenset Yellow Submarine Special
    P 0114
Teen Talk - Valuable Collector's
    Edition On The Beatles
    P 0115
Teen World - The Beatles - Our
    "Naughty" Nights
    M 3422
"Telegrams In Brief."
    N 1052
The Television Years
    M 3423
Tendenzen Der Pop-Musik: Dargestellt Am
    Beispiel Der Beatles
    B 0157   B 0158
"10 Million Pounds Worth Of Beatles
    Songs."
    M 1486
10th Anniversary Collectors Treasure -
    The Beatles - From Beatle Mania
    To Bangladesh, 1963-1973
    P 0116
"A Terrible Example For Youth."
    M 1153
"Test Ties - Yeah."
    N 1054
"Texas Radio Outlets Don't Accept
    Lennon's Apology As Sincere; Ban
    Still On."
    M 3426
"Thank God For The Beatles."
    C 0180
"Thanks For The Memory."
    M 0770
"Thank U Very Much By Mike McCartney:
    Launch Party."
    M 0180
Thank U Very Much: Mike McCartney's
    Family Album
    B 0357   B 0358   B 0359
"Thank You Beatles, Says Jerry Lee
    Lewis."
    M 3427
"Thank You Very Much And I Hope I've
    Passed The Audition: A John
    Lennon Top 20."
    C 0114
"That I Would Be Around To See It All
    Come True."
    M 1380
"That's The Way He Planned It."
    M 1154
"Theater: Irreverence On London Stage
    Work By John Lennon In 'Triple
    Bill'."
    N 0050
"Theft At The Courthouse."
    N 0471
"Their Fan Club Secretaries: Anne
    Collingham & Bettina Rose."
    M 1653
"Their First Major Booking."
    M 3428
"Their First Movie."
    M 0181
"Their First Visit To Hamburg, Final
    Part."
    M 1508
"Their First Visit To Hamburg, Part
    One."
    M 1506
"Their First Visit To Hamburg, Part
    Two."
    M 1507
"Their Green Street Flat."
    M 0907
"Their Manager: Brian Epstein."
    M 0182
"Their Recording Manager: George
    Martin."
    M 0183
"Their Road Manager: Neil Aspinall."
    M 1654
"Them."
    M 3429

"Theology Of George Harrison."
    M 1232
"There Beneath The Blue Suburban Skies:
    Penny Lane Revisited."
    M 3298
"There Was A Life After The Beatles,
    But Not What His Fans Expected."
    N 0702
"There Will Always Be The Beatles."
    M 0596
"These Catalogues Don't Stand On
    Shelves."
    M 2115
"They Are Loved."
    M 3431
"They Call It Apple Corps."
    N 1055
"They Changed Rock, Which Changed The
    Culture, Which Changed Us."
    N 0447
"They Didn't Have To Be So Nice."
    M 0666
"They Had To Change."
    M 3238
"'They'll Still Call Me An Ex-Beatle
    When I'm 95.' Ringo Tries His
    First TV Special - All By
    Himself."
    M 0866
"They Loved Him, Yeah, Yeah, Yeah."
    C 0319
"They Love Em - Ja! Ja! Ja!"
    M 3583
"They're Bringing Back The Night."
    N 0045
"They're Gonna Make A Big Star Out Of
    WWII."
    M 3312
"They Rose From The Cellar To Conquer
    The World."
    M 1846   M 3432
"They Sought Without Finding."
    M 1850
"They Were Right To Use A Standin Says
    Paul."
    M 0929
"'They Won't Let Us Join The Golf Club'
    Says Ringo."
    M 3433
"Things We Said Today."
    M 0653
Things We Said Today; The Complete
    Lyrics And A Concordance To The
    Beatles' Songs, 1962-1970
    B 0094   C 0069
Things We Tell Today
    F 0144
"Thingumybob."
    M 0815   M 0816   M 1866   M 2480
    M 2481   M 3389   M 3434
"Thingumybob: Dream Of The 13th
    Beatle."
    M 1117
"Thinking About John Lennon."
    M 1325
"The 'Thinking Man's Beatle'."
    N 1056
Third Book Of Fifty Hit Songs By John
    Lennon And Paul McCartney
    S 0154
The Third Golden Beatles Album
    S 0155
"$30 Million For Beatles Reunion Up In
    Air."
    M 3435
"Thirty New Beatle Grooves On Double
    Disc Album."
    M 1046
"Thirty Years After."
    M 2256
"This Column Is For People Who Think
    They Know The Answers .... "
    M 3436
"This Is All About The John Lennon I
    Lost."
    C 0064   N 0230
"This Is Mr. Beat!"
    M 0771
This Is Not Here

B 0428
"This Is Not Here."
    M 3437
"This Month's Beatle Song."
    M 3438
"This Month's Big Six."
    M 3270
"This Morning, Do Something Nice. Try
    To Stop World War III."
    N 1057
"This Week's List Of Birthdays."
    N 1058
"Those Beatles Again."
    M 3789
"Those Inventive Beatles."
    N 0749
"Those Were The Days."
    M 0080 M 0627 M 0674 M 0803
    M 2483 M 3357 M 3443
"Those Were The Days: The Concert For
    Bangla Desh Remembered."
    M 2092
"Threat Of Filmed 'Beatlemania' Too
    Much; Beatles Now Suing."
    M 3444
"Three Beatles Abandon Their Appeal."
    N 1059
"Three Beatles - Allen Klein Split;
    Yoko Ono A Spaniard In Works?"
    M 3445
"Three Beatles To Appeal."
    N 1060
"Three Beatles Wax Christmas Solo LPs."
    M 3446
"Three Cos. Settle Beatles' Pub Suit."
    M 3447
"Three Ex-Beatles File Suit Vs. Klein,
    ABKCO."
    M 3448
"3 Guinness Honors For Paul McCartney."
    M 3449
"Three Likely Reunions And Three We'd
    Like To See."
    M 0772
"Three New Beatles Albums By
    Christmas."
    M 3450
"Three Screaming, Raving Years With The
    Beatles."
    M 3472
"Through A Phone Darkly Or Ringo
    Agonistes."
    M 3198
"Through Lennon's Eyes Darkly."
    M 3451
"Tickets For Beatles Go Fast."
    N 1061
"Ticket To Ride."
    N 1062
"Ticket To Ride: The Beatles Are
    Through."
    M 3780
"Til John Lennon."
    M 0008
"Time Bandits All Handmade In Britain."
    N 0422
"A Time For Fasting For Biafra
    Protestors."
    N 0755
"The Times Diary; Apple First."
    N 1063
"The Times Diary; Beatles' 'Official'
    Biographer."
    N 1064
"The Times Diary; Beatle's Scream."
    N 1065
"The Times Diary; Beatle Style."
    N 1066
"The Times Diary; Cloudy Skies Over
    Beatleside."
    N 1067
"The Times Diary; Moving Up."
    N 1068
"The Times Diary; One Note Rave."
    N 1069
"The Times Diary; Shake Up."
    N 1070
"The Times Diary; The Beatles Buying A
    Novel."

N 1071
"The Times Diary; The Ono Show."
    N 1072
"The Times Diary; Unedited."
    N 1073
"The Times Diary; Using The Run-Out
    Grooves."
    N 1074
"The Times Diary; Yeuch!"
    N 1075
"Title Teasers."
    M 0817
"To Balk At Bias Bookings."
    N 1076
"To Be As Good."
    M 0932
"Der Tod Des Beatle (Die Beatles
    Story)."
    M 1754
"Together Again: John, George, &
    Ringo."
    M 0085
"Tokyo Is Girding For The Beatles;
    Arrival June 30 - 30,000 Tickets
    Drawn By Lot."
    N 1090
"To Look For The Beatles, Try 'B' In
    Who's Who."
    N 1077
"Tom & Dick & Harry & John."
    M 0662
"Tommy, Lennon, Mao, And The Road To
    Revolution."
    M 3352
"Tom O'Neil Remembers Lennon."
    M 2352
"Tomorrow."
    M 2334 M 2335
Tomorrow Never Knows
    F 0145
"Tony Barrow Leaves."
    M 3457
"The Tony Problem."
    M 3458
"Tony Sheridan Remembers Hamburg."
    M 3459
"Too Biased Against Paul"
    M 1128
"To Our Readers."
    M 3461 M 3462 M 3463
"Top Name Shortage Closing Epstein's
    Pop Concert Promotions In West
    End."
    M 3464
"Top Of The Class - Beatle George."
    N 0914
"Top Pay Merger: Lennon Ono Inc."
    M 3097
"Top Twenty: 'The Times, They Are
    A-Middlin'."
    M 1858
"Toronto Finale."
    N 0274
"Toronto Peace Festival."
    M 3465 N 0275
"Toronto Without Lennon."
    M 3466
"Toshiba-EMI Sets Beatles Promo."
    M 1192
"Tour By Former Beatle's Group."
    N 1078
"Touring In The Material World."
    M 1023
"Touring The Beatles' Liverpool."
    N 1079
"Town That Gave The Beatles Away."
    M 3153
"Toy Boy."
    M 1900
"Tracking The Hits: Billboard Hot 100."
    M 3543
"Tracking The Hits: Melody Maker."
    M 3544
"Tracking The Hits: Rozglosnia
    Harcerska, Poland."
    M 2178
"Tracking The Hits: Veronica Top 40."
    M 3467
"Tracks You've Never Heard."

M 1655
"Trade Winds; Phenomenal Success."
    M 1194
"Tragic Childhood Turned Lennon Into
    Young Punk And Shoplifter."
    M 0872
"Trail Of Death - Where It Started."
    M 1847
Trails Of George And John
    F 0146
"Transatlantic Call."
    C 0135
"Transition For ATV."
    N 1081
"Trashing The Lennon Legend."
    N 1082
"'Trials Of Oz': An Open And Shut
    Case."
    M 3647
"Trial Starts Today In Lennon Murder."
    N 1084
"Trial To Start June 1 In Slaying Of
    Lennon."
    N 1085
"Tribal Gods."
    M 1193
"A Tribute To Beatle John."
    M 0003
"Tribute To John Lennon."
    M 1270
A Tribute To John Lennon & The Beatles
    P 0117
A Tribute To John Lennon 1940-1980
    B 0554 C 0001 C 0003 C 0009
    C 0012 C 0013 C 0051 C 0064
    C 0071 C 0072 C 0077 C 0079
    C 0082 C 0096 C 0098 C 0129
    C 0134 C 0138 C 0139 C 0146
    C 0154 C 0159 C 0160 C 0163
    C 0164 C 0172 C 0173 C 0174
    C 0183 C 0208 C 0214 C 0272
    C 0274 C 0297 C 0313 C 0315
    C 0316 C 0319 C 0335 C 0338
    C 0349
"A Tribute To John Lennon On
    Anniversary Of His Death."
    N 1086
"A Tribute To Lennon."
    N 1087
"Tributes To Brian Epstein."
    M 3473
"Trip."
    M 3547
"Triumphant Return!"
    M 3474
"Triumph Investment Trust Buys 70
    Percent Of Nemperor Holdings For
    $1,632,000."
    M 3475
"Triumph's Pact With Beatles."
    N 1088
"Trivia Quiz Winners."
    M 3476
"Trivia Quiz Winners & Answers."
    M 3477
"Trivia Test Winners And Answers"
    M 3478
"Trouble At The Troubadour - Lennon's
    Hard Day's Night."
    M 3479
"Trouble Seemed So Far Away."
    N 1089
"The Trouble With The Beatles."
    M 1542
The True Story Of The Beatles
    B 0500 B 0501
"The Truth About The Beatles' First
    Single."
    M 0908
"The Truth About The Decca Audition."
    M 1461
"The Truth About Those Early Beatles
    Recordings."
    M 1509
"Trying To Make A Sad Song Better."
    M 0642
"Try-Out."
    M 3481
"Tug Of War."

M 0969
Tug Of War (songbook) see Paul
    McCartney: Tug Of War
"Tunes Bear Basic Beaton Discs."
    N 1091
Turn Me On Dead Man
    B 0603
"TV: It's The Beatles (Yeah, Yeah,
    Yeah)."
    N 0441
"TV: McCartney And His Group On A.B.C.
    Tonight; Direct Approach Fits
    Former Beatle Best."
    N 0836
"TV Special & Album: Beatles First Live
    Concert In Two Years."
    M 3486
"TV: The Beatles And Their Audience;
    Quartet Continues to Agitate The
    Faithful."
    N 0442
"12-Medal Man Reacts Sharply To The
    Beatles."
    N 1092
"20th's 'War' Package Dishes Up All
    That & The Beatles, Too."
    M 3487
"20 Fans Greet Beatles."
    N 1093
25 Years Of Rock & Roll
    C 0325
20 Greatest Hits – The Beatles
    S 0156
"2,900–Voice Chorus Joins The Beatles."
    N 1156
26 Days That Rocked The World!
    B 0555
Twilight Of The Gods: The Beatles In
    Retrospect
    B 0377
Twilight Of The Gods: The Music Of The
    Beatles
    B 0378
"Twist And Shout: The Early Days And
    The Beatles Years."
    C 0091
"A Twist Of Fate That Cost His Life."
    M 3488
A Twist Of Lennon
    B 0299   B 0300
"Two Beatle Fans Paroled."
    N 1094
"2 Beatles' Benefits For Pakistanis Are
    Sold Out."
    N 1095
"2 Beatles Cop Novello Award For '64
    Top Song."
    M 3489
"2 Beatles' Copyright Suit Is
    'Confusing'."
    M 3490
"Two Beatles Disagree On Shows For
    Public."
    N 1096
"Two Beatles Earned $18 Million In
    Cleffer Fees."
    M 3491
"Two Beatles Get More Awards."
    N 1097
"2 Beatles' Home Burglarized."
    N 1098
"2 Beatles Lose On Visas."
    N 1099
"2 Beatles Raise 250G For Refugees Of
    E. Pakistan In Historic N.Y.
    Benefit."
    M 1589
"Two Beatles Reunite For Recording
    Session."
    N 1100
"Two Beatles Win Song Awards."
    N 1101
"Two Biographies Of The Beatles Rushed
    Yo Stores; Authorized Version
    From McGraw-Hill Challenged By
    Putnam 'Real Story'."
    N 0430
"Two British Heroes Protest Award Of
    Honors To Beatles."

N 1102
"2 Films Are Inspired By Beatles'
    Music."
    N 0962
"250 Calls To Channel 13 Protest Nudity
    In Movies."
    N 1103
"250,000 Australians Jam Beatles'
    Route."
    N 1105
"212 Police For Beatles."
    N 1104
"235M Estate, & Yoko Gets The Credit."
    N 0758
"Two Icons Of Rock Music."
    N 0859
"2 John Lennon Memorials Draw 4,000 In
    Liverpool."
    N 1106
"Two Of Beatles Rock London With An
    Issue In Their Music Firm; Shares
    Valued At $1.3 Million Are Said
    To Be All Sold Out."
    N 1107
"Two Portraits Of George."
    M 1656
"Two Portraits Of John."
    M 1657
"Two Portraits Of Ringo."
    M 1658
"Two Questions About Lennon."
    M 0068
"Two Rookies Make Their Beatles Movie."
    M 3160
"2,000 Beatle Fans Storm Box Office
    Here; It's An Early Augury Of
    Show In August At Shea Stadium."
    N 0292
"Two To One Against Beatles."
    N 1108
"2 U.S. Students Held In Spain."
    N 1109
"Two U.S. Unions To Boycott British
    Exports."
    N 0630
"The Two Women Who Broke Up The
    Beatles."
    M 1289
"UA, EMI To Handle Beatles' New LP;
    Clarify Act's Status."
    M 3495
"Uden Forbehold."
    M 3559
"UK Colleagues Generous With Their
    Tributes."
    C 0163   M 1750
"U.K. High Court OKs Polydor's Rights
    To Beatle Talk Tapes."
    M 3496
"U.K. Service Honors Lennon."
    M 3497
"UK Teeners' $36 Beatle Vacation With
    Bop & Board."
    M 3498
"U.K. T.V. Bids for Beatle Song Co."
    M 3499
"The Ultimate Supergroup."
    M 0773
"Unbarbershopped Quartet."
    M 3500
Understanding Pop
    C 0149   C 0150
"Undertaking By Beatle."
    N 1110
"Undertakings On Money Owed To
    Beatles."
    N 1111
"An Uneggspected Television Programme."
    M 3502   M 3570
"Unfinished Paintings And Objects At
    The Indica Gallery."
    M 2384
"The Unique Humour Of The Beatles."
    M 1457
"A Unique Reception."
    C 0326
"United Artists Schedules Preview Of
    Beatles Movie."
    N 1113

"United Kingdom."
    M 2523
"Unknown Plays For New Directors;
    National Theatre Triple Bill."
    N 1128
"Unrecognised."
    M 3504
"The Unreleased Albums Of John, Paul,
    George, And Ringo."
    M 3505
"Unreleased Beatles B'cast Tapes To Be
    Aired On U.S. Radio."
    M 3506
(Untitled.)
    C 0072   M 1206   M 2055
Up Against It: A Screenplay For The
    Beatles
    B 0430   B 0431
Up Against The Wall, America
    C 0200
"Up From Liverpool."
    M 1307
Up The Beatles' Family Tree
    B 0267
"Up To Date List Of Fan Club
    Secretaries."
    M 3508
"Up-To-Date List Of Area Secretaries."
    M 3507
"Urgent Checks On New Drug STP."
    N 1114
"U.S.A. (East Coast)."
    M 1271
"U.S. And British Taxers Vie To Shear
    Beatles."
    N 1115
"U.S.A. News From Our Correspondent."
    M 3509
"U.S.A. Updated."
    M 0191   M 0192
"U.S.A. (West Coast)."
    M 0193
"U.S. Ban On Beatles Over Religion."
    N 1116
"U.S. Beatles Memorabilia: A Dealer's
    Eye View Of The Stateside Scene."
    M 1100
"Use Beatles' Disk As Educational Tool
    In Germany."
    M 3510
"US Immigration Now Major Barrier To
    Beatle Reunion."
    M 3511
"U.S. Notes."
    M 3512
"U.S. Orders Lennon Out, But Yoko May
    Remain."
    N 0692
"U.S. Rocks & Reels From Beatles'
    Invasion."
    M 3513
"U.S. Teenagers Welcome The Beatles:
    Capitol Single A Smash, Rush LP."
    M 3514
"U.S. Tour."
    C 0103
"U.S. Tour Of McCartney And Wings Is
    Off To Triumphal Start In Fort
    Worth."
    N 0954
"Usual Sound And Fury Confront The
    Beatles At London Airport."
    N 1117
"The Utrecht Beatles Convention."
    M 3515
"Vatican Accepts Lennon's Apology."
    N 1121
"Vegetarianism: Growing Way Of Life,
    Especially Among The Young."
    N 0597
"Venetian Blinder."
    M 0625
Venus And Mars – Piano/Vocal/Guitar
    Album
    S 0157
"'Venus And Mars': Wings' Non-Stellar
    Flight."
    M 2265
"Verwelktes Kleeblatt; Die Beatles

Retrospektive Und Ausblick."
M 3147
"Very Much A Doer"
M 3239
"Via BBC, Rare Beatles Tunes."
N 0299
Il Viaggio Dei Cuori Solitari: Un Libro
Sui Beatles
B 0031
"'Victory Thru Hair Power'."
M 3167
"Video Settlement To Beatles
Publisher."
M 1992
"The Violent Giants."
M 2186
"Visit From The Beetorusu Gives Tokyo
Police Hard Day's Night."
N 0282
"Visiting George."
M 3552
"Visiting Paul."
M 3553
"Visiting Ringo."
M 3554
"A Visit To The Record Plant And The
Hit Factory."
M 1987
"Visuals: The New Album Art."
M 0018
"Vive Les Beat-tles!"
M 0774
Vivendo Cantando
B 0329
"Voiding Of Lennon Plea Asked."
N 0997
Die Wahre Geschichte Der Beatles
B 0502
Waiting For The Beatles: An Apple
Scruff's Story
B 0072
Walls And Bridges (songbook) see John
Lennon: Walls And Bridges
"Walrus Is Greek For Corpse: Rumor And
The Death Of Paul McCartney."
M 0550
"The Walrus Remembered."
M 3569
"The Walrus Was John."
C 0003 N 0006
"The Walrus Was Ringo."
M 1186
"Walter Shenson: A Hard Day's Night."
M 3587
"Wanna Quick Disc Hit? Cover A Tune
Cleffed By Beatles' Lennon,
McCartney."
M 3588
"Wanted!"
M 3589
"War Is Over! If You Want It."
N 1129
"'War Is Over' If You Want It; Happy
Christmas From John & Yoko."
M 2300
"War Is Over - If You Want It John
Lennon."
M 1402
Das War John Lennon - Alles Uber Ihn
Und Die Beatles
B 0522
"Warner Bros. Subsidiary Mulls Buying
Interest That Beatles Are After."
N 1132
"Warner Joins N Songs Bid."
N 1133
"Warner May Bid For Beatles Ties; Talks
Expected On Deal For 15% Of
Northern Songs."
N 1007
Watching TV: Four Decades Of American
Television
C 0074
Waterfalls
F 0147
"A Wave From Paul."
C 0330
"Wave Of Grief Over John Lennon's
Murder; Violent End Of 1960s Hero

Evokes Parallel With The Killing
Of Kennedy."
N 0631
"WBCN-FM In Lennon Drive."
M 3131
"We All Live In A Yellow Submarine."
C 0285
"Wealth Out Of A Texas Oil Barrel."
N 1138
"'We Can't Please Everyone' Says Paul."
M 3621
"Wedded Bliss: The Erotic Lithographs
Of John Lennon."
M 3622
"Wednesday 22nd Sept. 1982."
M 0017
"We Have A Handful Of Songs And A Band
Called The Beatles."
M 3584
"Weingarten Looks At The Bangla Desh
Album."
M 3623
"The Weird World Of Beatle Novelties."
M 0148
"Welcome Back."
M 3635
Welcome Back Beatles
P 0118   P 0119   P 0120   P 0121
"Welcome For Beatles."
N 1142
"Well, Could A Beatle Go Solo?"
M 0775
"Well Now - Dig This!"
C 0344
The Well-Tempered Lennon-McCartney:
Seven Polyphonic Arrangements For
Piano
S 0158
"We Loved To Turn Them On: A Complete
Beatles U.S. TV Chronology."
M 1791
We Love You Beatles
B 0536
"We Love You - John And God!"
M 1061 M 3545
"Wembley 1976."
M 0504
"We Polish Old Silver - Eastman."
M 1993
"We're Just People."
M 1409
"We're Just Us."
N 1144
"We're Tops Again."
M 3649
"We Said It - And They Did It!"
M 3651
"West Meets East - George Harrison
Talks About Indian Music."
M 3654
"Wet And Wonderful!"
M 1559
"'We Thought People Would Understand'."
M 0830
"We've Lost Part Of Ourselves."
C 0338
"We Wanna Rip You Off."
M 3655
"'We Were Giving It All Away'."
M 3656
"Whales Benefit Beached."
M 3792
"What A Bastard The World Is."
M 2524
"What A Party!"
M 0184
"What Are The Beatles Really Like?"
M 2193
"What Difference Will This Piece Of
Paper Make To The Beatles?"
M 0776
"What Do They Do?"
M 3658
"Whatever Happened To .... ?"
M 3659
"What Every Woman Should Know About The
Beatles."
M 1960
What Goes On

F 0148
"What Goes On?"
M 3705 M 3706
"What Happened In America."
M 3660
"What He Meant Was ... ."
N 1145
"What Makes The Beatles B-E-A-T."
M 0783
"What Next For The Beatles?"
M 3042
"What Next In '66 For Beatles And
Stones?"
M 3661
"What Now For The Beatles?"
M 0876
"What's Beatle."
M 3662
"What's Next For The Fonz? A Guide To
Survival For Henry Winkler From
Yesterday's Teen Idols."
M 3663
"What Songs The Beatles Sang."
N 0848 N 1146
"What The Beatles Didn't Mean To Say."
M 1458
"What The Beatles Have Done To Hair:
Teenaged British Boys."
M 3664
"What The Beatles Prove About
Teenagers."
M 3014
"What The Bloody Hell Is It?"
M 3665
"What The Critics Said."
M 3666
"What They Play - The Beatles."
M 3667
"What They're Saying."
M 3261
"What They Think Of You."
M 3668
"What You Would Like The Boys To Do In
'69."
M 1659
"When Death Is Sudden."
N 0355
"When Did You Switch On?"
M 3669 M 3670
"When I Get On Stage, I Think: Good
God, They're 16, I'm 24."
M 0777
"When I'm 64."
M 0692
When Rock Was Young: A Nostalgic Review
Of The Top 40 Era
C 0253
"When The Beatles Came Marching Home."
M 0778
"When The Screaming Has To Stop."
M 0779
"When Toussaint Goes Marching In;
Riding On The City Of New
Orleans."
M 3681
"When Two Great Saints Meet."
M 3001
"When We Stop Selling Records, We'll
Probably Pack It In."
M 0780 M 3671
"Where Are All The Beatle Fans."
M 3672
"Where Has All The Beatlemania Gone?"
M 2525
"Where They Lived And Played."
M 1459
"Where To Look For Beatles
Memorabilia."
M 1101
"Whisperings."
M 1319
White Album (songbook) see The
Beatles: White Album
"Who Killed The Toronto Peace
Festival."
M 0123
"Wholesome Nonsense?"
N 1147
"Whoop-Up For Wigs."

M 3685
"Who's Not Who - Beatles."
  N 1148
"Who's That Coming Round The Corner."
  M 1381
"Who's 'Used'?"
  N 0277
Who Will Beat The Beatles - The Mersey
    Sound Hits America
  P 0122
"Who Will Get His Wings?"
  M 1382
"Why All The Mystery Over The Magical
    Mystery Tour?"
  M 0877
"Why Are The Beatles So Popular?"
  M 3752
"Why Did They Grow Moustaches?"
  M 1660
"Why Does Nobody Love The Beatles?"
  M 3585
"Why Haven't The Beatles Fixed Another
    Concert Tour?"
  M 1661
"Why I Dig The Beatles."
  M 0878
"Why Is George In New York?"
  M 0069
"Why, It Was Fun!"
  M 3456
"Why Japan Fears Paul McCartney."
  M 1798
"Why Kids Love Lennon."
  M 2212
"Why Not The Real Thing."
  M 1867
"Why Some Wept For John Lennon."
  C 0274   N 0955
"Why The Beatles?"
  M 1662
"Why The Beatles Are Good."
  C 0276
"Why The Beatles (Remember Them?) Have
    So Many Friends In Canada."
  M 3355
"Why The Girls Scream, Weep, Flip."
  N 0346
"Why They Rock."
  N 1149
"Why We Loved The Beatles."
  M 3430
"Why Won't Yoko Release Ten For Two."
  M 1102   M 1103   N 0380
"Why Yoko Will Never Forgive The
    Surviving Beatles."
  M 3686
"Wicker Basket."
  M 3687
Wie Eine Pop-Gruppe Arbeitet
  B 0215
"Wie Eine Pop-Gruppe Arbeitet."
  M 3692
"Wife Was Planning To Divorce John
    Lennon When He Was Shot."
  M 1566
Wij Zijn De Beatles
  B 0503
"Wildcat 'Beatles' Strike."
  M 3696
"Wild-Eyed Mobs Pursue Beatles."
  N 0009
"Wild Fans Of The Beatles A Shocker
    Even To Long-Memory
    Sophisticates."
  M 3697
Wild Life (songbook) see Wings: Wild
    Life
"Will Real Beatles Sing Out."
  N 1155
"Will The Beatles Re-Form?"
  M 1546
"Will The Real ... Acts Imitating
    Beatles, Elvis Are
    Proliferating."
  M 1389
"Will The Real Richard Starkey Please
    Stand Up?"
  M 3586
"Will You Still Love 'Em When They're

64?"
  N 0910
"Wilson Reopens The Cellar Club Where
    Beatles Got Their Start."
  N 0641
"Wimp Rock Will Never Die."
  M 1726
"Win Cynthia's Own Portrait Of John -
    Plus Rare Sets Of Beatles
    Albums."
  M 3733
"Windfalls At Apple."
  N 1157
Wings
  B 0216   B 0592   B 0593
"Wings."
  M 0626   M 3734
"Wings Album Preview; Return Of The
    McCartney Magic."
  M 0709
Wings At The Speed Of Sound
  S 0159
Wings: Band On The Run
  S 0160
Wings Complete
  S 0161
Wings Complete: The Songs Of McCartney
    And Wings
  S 0162
Wings Fan Club
  F 0149
"Wings Fly High."
  M 3412
Wings Fun Club Lyric Book
  B 0594
Wings Greatest
  S 0163
"Wings Hammersmith Odeon Concert."
  M 3522
"Wings In Australia."
  M 1125
Wings Info Center
  F 0150
"Wings In Munich."
  M 0118
"Wings In Sweden '72."
  M 1234
Wings Japan Tour 1980
  B 0595
"Wings Keep It In The Family."
  M 1085
Wings: London Town
  S 0164
"Wings: Melody Maker Band Breakdown."
  M 2499
"Wings: Music For Yesterday - Or
    Today?"
  M 3735
Wings Over America
  S 0165   S 0166
"Wings Over America: Big Bird Touches
    Down; The Most Popular Ex-Beatle
    Talks To You."
  M 0601
"Wings Over California."
  M 0194
"Wings Over Manchester."
  M 3299
"Wings Over The World."
  M 0195   M 3736
Wings Pin-Up & Story Poster
  P 0123
"Wings: Pop Star Of The Month."
  M 3737
Wings: Red Rose Speedway
  S 0167
"Wings Stage Equipment."
  M 1383
"Wings' Story."
  C 0339
"Wings: Taking Off At Last?"
  M 3703
"Wings Talk."
  M 3274
"Wings Tickets Selling Quickly."
  N 1158
"Wings Tour Ends: Up, Up And Away."
  M 1155
"Wings Tour Report; Paul McCartney

Group Lays NY Out Cold With
    Blazing Performance."
  M 1124
"Wings UK Tour 1975."
  M 3738
Wings: Wild Life
  S 0168   S 0169
"Wino Junko Can't Say No."
  M 1384
"Wisdom Of Their Years."
  M 0070
"Wish Elvis All The Best In 'Aladdin'."
  M 0781
"With A Little Help ... "
  M 1460
With A Little Help From My Friends
  F 0151
"With A Little Help From My Friend:
    Social Loafing And The
    Lennon-McCartney Songs."
  M 1622
"With A Little Help From Some Friends,
    Kevin Howlett Finds A Treasure Of
    Lost Beatles Music."
  M 3306
"With A Little Help From Their
    Friends."
  M 0185
"With A Little Help From Their Friends,
    Part Two."
  M 0186
"With George."
  C 0136
"Within His Music."
  C 0098   N 0356
"Within Living Memory."
  N 0756
"With Mike And Bern."
  C 0340
"Without Paul, No Beatles."
  N 0750
"Without The Beatles."
  M 3742
"With Paul In Hollywood."
  M 0599
With The Beatles
  S 0170
"With The Beatles Again!"
  M 0187
"With The Beatles At The Bowl."
  M 3201
"With The Beatles In Bournemouth."
  M 0909
"With The Beatles In India."
  M 3251
"With The Beatles, No. 1: Recording -
    Why It Takes So Long Now."
  M 1055
"With The Beatles, No. 2: The First
    Official Mal Evans Story."
  M 0081
"With The Beatles, No. 3: Paul And Mal
    In The States."
  M 1047
"With The Beatles, No. 4: Our Visit To
    Greece."
  M 1056
"With The Beatles, No. 5: George's
    California Trip."
  M 0082
With The Beatles: The Historic
    Photographs Of Dezo Hoffman
  B 0367   B 0368   B 0369
"Witty John."
  C 0341
"The Wives (And Ladies) That Late They
    Loved."
  M 3674
"WMCA Bans New Single, 'Ballad,' By
    Beatle Lennon."
  N 1159
Women Who Make Movies
  C 0304
"A Wonderful Christmastime For Wings
    Fans."
  M 3748
"Words For A Beatles Album That Will
    Never Be."
  N 1160

"Working Class Hero."
    M 1901   M 3753   M 0559
The Working Class Hero Club
    F 0152
Working Class Heroes: The History Of
    The Beatles' Solo Recordings
    B 0526
Working Class Hero, Vol. I
    F 0153
"World A-Z Discography."
    M 1349
World Of ... John Lennon And The
    Beatles
    P 0124
"World's First In-Depth Preview Of The
    Beatles' 'Get Back' LP
    Recordings."
    M 1663
"World War II Brought To You By The
    Beatles."
    M 0143
"Worldwide Mourning Continues For
    Lennon."
    N 1161
"World-Wide They Sing Slain Beatle's
    Praises."
    N 1019
"Worm In The Apple."
    M 3754
"Worst Beatle Book Yet?"
    C 0345
"Would You Want Your Sister To Marry A
    Beatle?"
    M 2047
"Wrack My Brain: To Be A Paperback
    Writer."
    M 2482
"Writ Against The Beatles."
    N 1162
"Writer Presents Different Picture Of
    Dakota Days."
    N 1163
The Write Thing
    F 0154
"Writing A Book About The Beatles."
    M 3154
"Writing Beatles Cop Top Novellos;
    Other Awards."
    M 3755
"The Writing On The Wall."
    M 1664
The Writings Of John Lennon (In His Own
    Write & A Spaniard In The Works)
    B 0330
"Writing Songs With A Little Help From
    His Friends, Ex-Beatle Gets
    Plagiarism Rap."
    M 3756
"Writing The Score For A Generation."
    C 0138   N 0473
"Writing With Paul."
    M 3757
"Writ Issued On Northern Songs."
    N 1164
"Wrong-handed."
    N 1165
"WWII Brought To You By The Beatles."
    M 3758
"Il Y Avait Kennedy, De Gaulle, Les
    Beatles."
    M 1753
"Y'all Come Hear Ringo."
    M 0510   M 3759
"Yeah, Yeah, Yeah."
    M 2052   M 3760
"Yeah-Yeah-Yeah! Beatlemania Becomes A
    Part Of U.S. History."
    M 0652
"Yeah! Yeah! Yeah! Music's Gold Bugs:
    The Beatles."
    M 0071
"Yeah! Yeah! Yeah! The History Of The
    Beatles."
    M 3761
Yeah, Yeah, Yeah, Zo Zijn De Beatles!
    B 0559
A Year In The Dark; Journal Of A Film
    Critic
    C 0002

"Yellow Matter Custard: Collecting
    Beatles Broadcasts."
    M 1517
"Yellow Perils Of Paulie."
    M 3613
Yellow Submarine
    F 0155
"Yellow Submarine."
    C 0166   M 1470
"'The Yellow Submarine': A Fable For
    Our Time."
    M 3242
"Yellow Submarine Art Is The Thing
    Today."
    N 1008
Yellow Submarine Gift Book
    B 0599
"Yellow Submarine Is Symbol Of Youth
    Churches."
    N 0389
"'Yellow Submarine' Premiere."
    M 3762
Yellow Submarine (songbook) see The
    Beatles: Yellow Submarine
Yellow Submarine; This Voyage Chartered
    By Max Wilk
    B 0584   B 0585
"Yes, I'm Lonely ... "
    M 3763
"Yes, I Remember It Well."
    M 3764
"Yes It Is."
    M 3205
Yesterday
    F 0156
"Yesterday: A '60s Hit Is The World's
    Most Frequently Recorded Song."
    M 3765
Yesterday ... Came Suddenly: The
    Definitive History Of The Beatles
    B 0115
Yesterday Fan Club
    F 0157
"Yesterday, Fifteen Years On."
    M 0881
Yesterday - Les Beatles: Voyage Intime
    Dans Une Legende
    B 0088
"'Yesterday' Mourning Before Sunrise."
    C 0272   N 0943
Yesterday: Photographs Of The Beatles
    B 0200
Yesterday - The Beatles 1963-1965
    B 0201
"Yesterday, Today, & Paul."
    M 1156
"Yet More Beatles."
    N 0272
"Yoko."
    M 3766
"Yoko & John."
    M 0633
"Yoko And Sean: Starting Over."
    M 3217
"Yoko & Son."
    N 1120
"Yoko: An Intimate Conversation."
    M 1318
"Yoko Asks Fans To 'Pray For His
    Soul'."
    N 1143
Yoko At Indica: Unfinished Paintings
    And Objects By Yoko Ono, November
    1966
    B 0429
"Yoko Donation."
    N 1166
"Yoko: How I Rescued John From
    Chauvinism."
    M 0035
"Yoko-John Shave Heads For Peace."
    N 0276
"Yoko Leaves Geffen; New Album Due."
    M 0809
"Yoko: 1981 In Budapest."
    M 2179
"Yoko Notes."
    M 0511
Yoko Only

    F 0158
"Yoko Ono."
    M 0530   M 1256
"Yoko Ono And Her Sixteen-Track Voice."
    M 0831
"Yoko Ono Asks Mourners To Give To A
    Foundation Lennon Favored."
    N 1167
"Yoko Ono Asks, 'Was I Supposed To
    Avoid The Subject?'"
    N 0860
"Yoko Ono At Syracuse: 'This Is Not
    Here'."
    M 3590
"Yoko Ono: In Her Own Write."
    M 1527
"Yoko Ono Inks Worldwide Polydor Deal."
    M 3767
"Yoko Ono, Kunstler Parlay Rock & Law
    For Indian Benefit."
    M 3768
"Yoko Ono Loses Baby."
    N 1168
"Yoko Ono On Her Own 'Walking On Thin
    Ice'."
    N 0861
"Yoko Ono On Yoko Ono."
    M 2360
"Yoko Ono Releases Single."
    M 3769
"Yoko Ono Seeks Daughter In U.S."
    N 1169
"Yoko Ono's Endless Faces."
    M 3770
"Yoko Ono's Film Tribute To Lennon On
    Cable TV."
    N 1170
"Yoko Ono's Former Husband Is Jailed."
    N 1171
"Yoko Ono: 'Still In A State Of
    Shock'."
    M 2018
"Yoko Promos Real 'Top 40' Solo Album."
    M 1801
"Yoko Reaches For That Pain."
    M 3648
"Yoko's Thanks."
    N 1172
"Yoko Sued Over Copyright Claim."
    M 1179
"Yoko Talks About It."
    M 2361
"Yoko: The Lady's A Winner."
    M 3614
"Yoko - The Loneliness Of The Naked
    Artist."
    M 3615
"Yoko To Sue Lord Grade."
    N 1173
"Yoko Visits Elton's Garden."
    M 3771
"You Can Bank On Beatles."
    N 1174
You Can't Do That! Beatles Bootlegs &
    Novelty Records (Includes John
    Lennon Tribute Records)
    B 0466
You Can't Do That! Beatles Bootlegs &
    Novelty Records, 1963-80
    B 0467   C 0247
You Don't Have To Say You Love Me
    C 0217
"You Know What I'd Love To Do? Produce
    An Album For Elvis?"
    M 0879
"You, Me And Handguns."
    N 1150
The Young American Writers
    C 0083
"'Young George': The Second Article On
    The Beatles' Childhood Days."
    M 3784
"'Young John': The First Of A New
    Series On The Beatles' Childhood
    Days."
    M 3785
"Young Lennon Living It Up In London."
    N 1175
"'Young Paul': The Third Article On The

Beatles' Childhood Days."
M 3786

"'Young Ringo': The Fourth And Last
   Article On The Beatles' Childhood
   Days."
M 3787

"Your Album Queries Answered."
M 1048

"Your Letters Answered."
M 3788

"Youths Counsel Troubled Peers; Private
   Group In New Haven Reaches

Counter Culture."
N 1083

"Youth Shot Near Vigil; Crowd Subdues
   Suspect."
N 1176

"LOVE ME DO" THE BEATLES' PROGRESS
Michael Braun

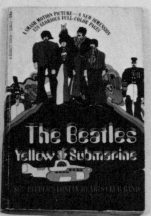

A SMASH MOTION PICTURE—A NEW DIMENSION
128 GLORIOUS FULL-COLOR PAGES

The Beatles
Yellow Submarine

SGT. PEPPER'S LONELY HEARTS CLUB BAND

LATEST PIX & STORIES 1st PHOTOS THE BEATLE MOVIE

LANCER SPECIAL 72-746   50¢

NEW THE BEATLES UP TO DATE

THE DAVE CLARK FIVE

GERRY and the PACEMAKERS

THE SEARCHERS and the MERSEY SOUND

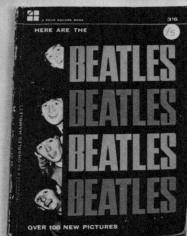

A FOUR SQUARE BOOK   3'6

HERE ARE THE

BEATLES
BEATLES
BEATLES
BEATLES

OVER 100 NEW PICTURES

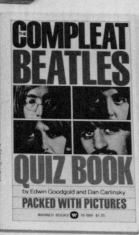

THE COMPLEAT BEATLES

QUIZ BOOK

by Edwin Goodgold and Dan Carlinsky

PACKED WITH PICTURES

WARNER BOOKS   76-589 $1.25

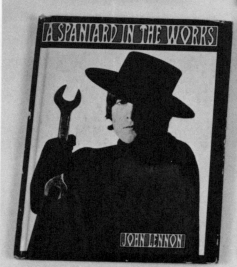

A SPANIARD IN THE WORKS

JOHN LENNON

DIRECT FROM ENGLAND! THE ORIGINAL BOOK ABOUT THE BEATLES!

THE TRUE STORY OF THE Beatles

AS PERSONALLY TOLD TO BILLY SHEPHERD ■ WITH 32 PAGES OF PHOTOGRAPHS PUBLISHED FOR THE FIRST TIME IN THIS COUNTRY

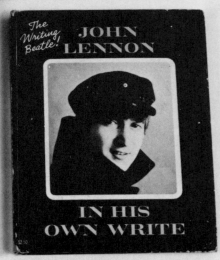

The Writing Beatle!   JOHN LENNON

IN HIS OWN WRITE

A & M Records
    M 0001   M 0227   M 0229   M 1068
    M 1171   M 1406   M 1419   M 2654
    M 2847   M 3283
ABBEY ROAD (book)
    RB0001
Abbey Road Chapter - Apple Tree
    F 0001
ABBEY ROAD (LP)
    C 0121   M 0263   M 1240   M 1638
    M 1669   M 2223   M 2224   M 2268
    M 2346   M 2602   M 2723   M 3122
    N 0749   RR0001   RR0002   RR0003
    RR0004   RR0005   RR0006   RR0007
    RR0008   RR0009   RR0010   RR0011
    RR0012   RR0013   RR0014   RR0015
Abbey Road (recording studio)
    C 0307   M 0002   M 0017   M 0305
    M 0329   M 0946   M 2941   M 3084
    M 3230
Abbey Road: street signs
    M 2863
ABC Theatre, Blackpool, England
    C 0340
ABKCO Industries, Inc.
    M 0005   M 0006   M 0007   M 0375
    M 1126   M 1675   M 1809   M 1826
    M 1988   M 2712   M 2855   M 3448
ABKCO: vs. Apple Corps, Ltd.
    M 1826
Accordian songbook (Beatles)
    S 0033   S 0040
A.C. Gilbert & Co.: sponsors cartoon
        show
    N 0271
ACROSS THE UNIVERSE (book)
    RB0002
Adelaide, Australia: concert
    N 0889
Advertisement
    M 0310   N 0085
Advertisement (Beatles)
    C 0078   M 0014   M 0277   M 0439
    M 0452   M 1328   N 0271
Advertisement (call for Beatle concert)
    M 2296   N 0004
Advertisement (Lennon)
    M 1698   M 1700
Advertisement (Starr)
    M 1579
Advertising: tie-ins to Beatles
    M 3323
Africa: benefit concert
    N 0977
Africa: Wings
    M 2760   M 2761   M 3064   M 3070
Agnew, Spiro T.
    N 0088
AIR TIME (JOHNNY AND THE MOONDOGS
        SILVER DAYS) (LP)
    RR0016
AIRWAVES (LP)
    RR0017
Album cover
    C 0140   M 0516   M 0993   M 1538
    M 1556   M 1609   M 3404
Album cover (Beatles)
    C 0280   M 0018   M 0516   M 0844
    M 0915   M 3133
Album cover (Harrison)
    M 2655
Album cover (Lennon)
    M 1609   M 3080
DAS ALBUM DER BEATLES (book)
    RB0003
Album price
    M 0232   M 0657   N 0165
Album review   see   individual album
        titles
Album values
    B 0049   B 0134   B 0196   B 0197
    C 0230   M 0011   M 0905
Ali, Muhammad
    N 0106
ALL THINGS MUST PASS (book)
    RB0004   RB0005
ALL THINGS MUST PASS (LP)
    M 0509   M 1853   M 3446   M 3450
    M 3712   N 1154   RR0018   RR0019

    RR0020   RR0021   RR0022   RR0023
    RR0024   RR0025   RR0026
"All This and World War II" (film)
    M 0143   M 1170   RF0001   RF0002
    RF0003   RF0004   RF0005   RF0006
    RF0007   RF0008   RF0009   RF0010
    RF0011   RF0012
ALL THIS AND WORLD WAR II (LP)
    M 3312   M 3487   M 3758   RR0027
    RR0028   RR0029
"All Those Years Ago" (song)
    M 0468   M 2567
"All Those Years Ago" (video)
    RF0013
ALL TOGETHER NOW (book)
    M 1796   M 2005   RB0006   RB0007
    RB0008   RB0009   RB0010   RB0011
    RB0012   RB0013   RB0014   RB0015
    RB0016   RB0017   RB0018   RB0019
    RB0020   RB0021   RB0023   RB0024
    RB0025   RB0222
ALL YOU NEEDED WAS LOVE (book)
    M 0963   RB0026   RB0027   RB0028
    RB0029   RB0030   RB0031   RB0032
    RB0033   RB0034   RB0035
ALL YOU NEEDED WAS LOVE (book): excerpt
    M 0562
"All You Need Is Cash" (film)
    M 3123   M 3268   M 3301   M 3303
    M 3404   M 3746
ALL YOU NEED IS EARS (book)
    M 2902   RB0036   RB0037   RB0038
    RB0039   RB0040   RB0041   RB0042
    RB0043   RB0044   RB0045   RB0046
    RB0047
'All You Need Is Love' (ballet)
    M 0207
"All You Need Is Love" (song)
    M 1051   M 2344
Alpert, Herb: Lennon's death
    M 3700
American Federation of Musicians: asks
        for "balance of trade" enforced
        with Britain
    M 1590
Amplifers
    M 1357
Amsterdam, Holland: Beatles
    M 1756   M 1823
Andrews, Nancy
    M 1019   M 3022
"Angel Baby/Be My Baby" (45)
    RR0030
The Animals
    M 3345
"Another Day" (song)
    N 0717
"Apotheosis" (film)
    M 2153   N 0384   RF0014
"Apotheosis" (film): filming
    M 3558
Apple Boutique
    C 0006   C 0039   M 0054   M 0056
    M 0111   M 0730   M 2379   N 0362
    N 0898
Apple Boutique: closes
    N 0124   N 1157
Apple Boutique: opens
    M 0059   N 0019   N 0707
Apple Chapter - OBFC
    F 0008
Apple Corps., Ltd.
    B 0163   B 0164   B 0165   B 0166
    M 0053   M 0054   M 0055   M 0058
    M 0061   M 0111   M 0285   M 0335
    M 0416   M 0438   M 0543   M 1080
    M 1352   M 1353   M 1354   M 1355
    M 1768   M 1806   M 1809   M 2226
    M 2278   M 2379   M 3162   M 3677
    M 3754   N 0263   N 0635   N 0851
    N 0862   N 0887   N 0988   N 1055
    N 1071
Apple Corps., Ltd.: Allen Klein ousted
    N 0636
Apple Corps., Ltd.: Apple Records label
        first releases
    N 0986
Apple Corps., Ltd.: Beatles break-up
    C 0105   M 0560   M 2020   M 2076

    M 2077   M 2241   M 2633   N 1046
Apple Corps., Ltd.: begun
    M 1564   N 0122
Apple Corps., Ltd.: case involving
        unauthorized use of Harrison
        material
    M 0835   M 1418
Apple Corps., Ltd.: company network
    M 0052
Apple Corps., Ltd.: Concert for
        Bangladesh
    M 0060
Apple Corps., Ltd.: dissolution
    M 1943   M 2003   N 0098   N 0107
    N 0110   N 0134   N 0140   N 0142
    N 0159   N 0170   N 0171
Apple Corps., Ltd.: early recordings
        listed
    M 2233
Apple Corps., Ltd.: financial situation
    N 0177
Apple Corps., Ltd.: Lennon shares sold
    M 1829
Apple Corps., Ltd.: recording of
        cantata at Islington church
    N 1063
Apple Corps., Ltd.: release of early
        recordings not banned
    N 0803
Apple Corps., Ltd.: staff "no leaks"
        agreement
    M 2616
Apple Corps., Ltd.: vs. ABKCO
    M 1826
Apple Corps., Ltd.: vs. Allen Klein
    N 0520
Apple Corps., Ltd.: vs. "Beatlemania"
        (play)
    M 2901
Apple Corps., Ltd.: vs. Capitol Records
    M 3234
Apple Films
    M 0335   RF0193   RF0194   RF0195
    RF0196   RF0197   RF0198   RF0199
    RF0200
Apple Peel Players
    N 0018   N 0020
Apple Records
    M 0057   M 0058   M 0367   M 0440
    M 0450   M 0466   M 0469   M 0937
    M 0945   M 1539   M 1946   M 2235
    M 3455   M 3581   N 0192
Apple Records: discography
    B 0375   M 0945
Apple Records: discography of obscure
        recordings
    M 0057
Apple Records: first singles
    N 0986
Apple Records: new singles, 1968
    M 2582
Apple Records: record prices
    N 0165
APPLE TO THE CORE (book)
    RB0048   RB0049   RB0050   RB0051
    RB0052   RB0053   RB0054   RB0055
    RB0056   RB0057
Apple Tree
    F 0001   F 0125
APPROXIMATELY INFINITE UNIVERSE (LP)
    M 2279   RR0031   RR0032   RR0033
    RR0034   RR0035
Archbishop of Canterbury
    N 0021
Argentina Beatles Fan Club
    F 0007
Argentina: fan club
    F 0007
Arias, Olivia Trinidad   see   Trinidad
        Arias, Olivia
"Around The Beatles" (tv film)
    M 1563
Art: Beatles
    B 0032
Art exhibit (Powell)
    M 1463
Art gallery obscenity charge
    N 0026
Art work on the Beatles

M 0273
AS DREAMERS DO (LP)
   M 2460
Asher, Jane
   P 0064
Asher, Jane: rumored marriage plans to
      McCartney
   N 0719
Asher, Jane: photograph with McCartney
   M 1468
Asher, Peter
   M 3548
AS I WRITE THIS LETTER (book)
   RB0058   RB0059   RB0060   RB0061
   RB0062   RB0063   RB0064
AS I WRITE THIS LETTER (book): excerpt
   M 0676   M 0677
Aspinall, Neil
   M 1049   M 1050   M 1051   M 1052
   M 1053   M 1054   M 1055   M 1056
   M 1635   M 1654
Associated Television   see   ATV
AS TIME GOES BY (book)
   RB0065   RB0066   RB0067   RB0068
   RB0069
Atlanta, Georgia: concert
   M 3376   N 0160
Atlantic Records
   N 1132
ATV
   M 0089   M 0090   M 0091   M 0092
   M 0264   M 0279   M 0420   M 1591
   M 1802   M 1989   M 2236   M 2623
   M 3499   M 3702   M 3754   N 0029
   N 0030   N 0031   N 0032   N 0033
   N 0034   N 0035   N 0036   N 0087
   N 0161   N 0173   N 0189   N 0190
   N 0204   N 0215   N 0250   N 0338
   N 0753   N 0812   N 0835   N 0863
   N 1013   N 1081   N 1164
ATV: boardroom statement
   N 0239
ATV: buys Northern Songs, Ltd.
   M 2518   M 2519   M 2520   N 0218
   N 1014
Australia: Adelaide concert
   N 0889
Australia: Beatles
   B 0037   B 0233
Australia: Beatles in Melbourne
   N 0959   N 1105
Australia: Beatles on the charts
   M 1774
Australia: Beatles tour
   M 1557   M 1558   M 1559   M 3348
Australia: boxed singles set
   M 1398
Australia: broadcast ban on Beatle
      songs
   N 0249
Australia: fan club
   F 0028   F 0031
Australia: Harrison
   M 2229
Australia: Melbourne fans
   N 0959   N 1105
Australia: tour
   M 0981   N 0795   N 0889   N 0959
   N 1105
Australia: Wings tour
   M 1127
Austria: Beatles in Alps
   M 1551
Austria: fan club
   F 0147   F 0156
Autoharp songbook (Beatles)
   S 0039
Avedon, Richard: Beatle photos
   C 0277
"The Awakening" (film)
   M 2661
"Away With Words" (multimedia show)
   N 0151
Bach, Barbara
   M 2902   M 2913   M 2953   M 3409
Bach, Barbara: wedding photograph
   N 0941
Bach, Barbara: weds Ringo Starr
   M 0144   M 3023   M 3032   N 0601

N 0935
BACK TO THE EGG (LP)
   M 0096   M 0190   M 1001   M 1127
   M 1543   M 2080   M 3502   M 3682
   RR0036   RR0037   RR0038   RR0039
   RR0040   RR0041   RR0042   RR0043
   RR0044   RR0045   RR0046
BACK TO THE EGG (LP): publicity films
   M 3502
"Back to the Egg" (video)
   M 3570   RF0015
BAD BOY (LP)
   M 1489   RR0047   RR0048   RR0049
   RR0050
Badfinger
   M 0100   M 2963   RR0140
Badfinger: interview
   M 0099
"Bag One"   see   Lennon, John:
      lithographs
Balcon group investment
   N 0175
Baldwin (piano maker)
   N 0044
Balearica Islands, Majorca, Spain:
      Lennon and Ono detained
   N 0061
THE BALLAD OF JOHN AND YOKO (book)
   RB0070   RB0071   RB0072   RB0073
   RB0074
THE BALLAD OF JOHN AND YOKO (book):
      excerpt
   M 1137
"The Ballad Of John And Yoko" (song)
   M 0122
"The Ballad Of John And Yoko" (song):
      banned
   M 0319   M 0444   N 1159
"The Ballad Of Paul and Tokyo" (song):
      parody
   M 2254
Ballet: 'All You Need Is Love'
   M 0207
The Band
   M 2116
BAND ON THE RUN (LP)
   M 1855   M 1858   M 2770   RR0051
   RR0052   RR0053   RR0054   RR0055
   RR0056   RR0057   RR0058   RR0059
BAND ON THE RUN (LP): goes platinum
   M 2780
BAND ON THE RUN (LP): released in
      U.S.S.R.
   M 2057   M 2358   M 2842   N 1053
"Band On The Run" (video)
   M 2227
Bangladesh (benefit concert)   see
      Concert for Bangladesh
Barcelona, Spain: concert
   N 1109
"Baroque Beatles Book" (concert)
   N 0786
THE BAROQUE BEATLES BOOK (LP)
   M 1169   M 1623   M 2248   M 2553
   N 0410   RR0060   RR0061   RR0062
Barrow, Tony
   M 1748   M 3457
Barrow, Tony: interviews the Beatles
   M 0166
Barrow, Tony: letter on SHOUT! (book)
   N 0234
Barrow, Tony: 1963 visit with Brian
      Epstein
   M 0151
"Basketball Jones" (song)
   M 2745
Bassey, Shirley
   M 2024
BBC: bans McCartney song
   M 2729   N 0531
BBC: Beatles broadcasts
   B 0265   B 0266
BBC: Beatles radio special
   M 2031   M 3506   M 3742   N 0299
BBC: 88 Beatle radio broadcasts not on
      record
   M 3306
BBC: "lost" Beatle BBC songs
   M 2041   N 0272

BBC: 1960's LP popularity poll
   M 2034
BBC: radio special
   M 2171
BBC: tapes
   M 1176
BBC: U.S. radio premiere of "lost"
      Beatle songs
   N 1041
Beach Boys
   M 0497
Beatcomber (Lennon)
   C 0189   C 0190
Beatle books
   M 1424   M 2277   M 2980   M 3170
   M 3172   N 0231   N 0430   N 0778
   N 1051
Beatle books: bibliography
   M 3170   M 3172
Beatle college course
   N 0013
"Beatlefan" (magazine): reader's poll
   M 3181   M 3182   M 3183   M 3506
Beatle fans   see also   Beatlemania
Beatle fans   see also   names of
      individual Beatles
Beatle fans
   M 0208   M 0911   M 0922   M 0982
   C 0212   N 0009   N 0072   N 0324
   N 0947
Beatle fans: two teenage girls threaten
      to leap off hotel
   N 1094
Beatlefest
   M 0223   M 0224   M 0241   M 0490
   M 0537   M 0643   M 0647   M 1098
   M 1263   M 1266   M 1269   M 1386
   M 1792   M 1793   M 1833   M 1860
   M 2040   M 2370   M 2393   M 2471
   M 3259   M 3380   M 3390   N 0072
   N 0109   N 0947
"Beatlefever" (play)
   M 0420   2565
Beatle Film Society of America
   F 0018
Beatle image
   C 0232
THE BEATLE INTERVIEWS (LP)
   RR0063
BEATLE MADNESS (book)
   RB0075
Beatlemania   see also   Beatle fans
Beatlemania
   M 0169   M 0225   M 0232   M 0233
   M 0234   M 0235   M 0236   M 0237
   M 0238   M 0239   M 0240   M 0241
   M 0242   M 0243   M 0244   M 0245
   M 0246   M 0247   M 0424   M 0652
   M 0867   M 0875   M 0975   M 0976
   M 1140   M 1141   M 1323   M 1331
   M 1345   M 1346   M 1387   M 1557
   M 1558   M 1559   M 1574   M 1756
   M 1787   M 1876   M 1890   M 1891
   M 2012   M 2150   M 2214   M 2221
   M 2280   M 2374   M 2525   M 2551
   M 2968   M 2979   M 2983   M 2984
   M 3014   M 3114   M 3148   M 3159
   M 3161   M 3166   M 3191   M 3316
   M 3348   M 3350   M 3399   M 3498
   M 3513   M 3514   M 3582   M 3591
   M 3594   M 3695   M 3697   N 0079
   N 0083   N 0092   N 0113   N 0119
   N 0120   N 0128   N 0132   N 0149
   N 0150   N 0155   N 0157   N 0292
   N 0346   N 0351   N 0388   N 0394
   N 0404   N 0405   N 0407   N 0409
   N 0420   N 0433   N 0490   N 0589
   N 0689   N 0697   N 0770   N 0774
   N 0831   N 0838   N 0841   N 0843
   N 0881   N 0883   N 0889   N 0896
   N 0901   N 0971   N 0972   N 0973
   N 0975   N 0982   N 0985   N 1001
   N 1090   N 1093   N 1094   N 1104
   N 1105   N 1117
Beatlemania: beginnings
   M 0169
Beatlemania: Canada
   M 0124   M 0239
"Beatlemania" (play)

M 0235   M 0419   M 0420   M 0443
M 0579   M 1196   M 1264   M 1292
M 1407   M 1487   M 1586   M 1618
M 1627   M 1724   M 1828   M 2019
M 2166   M 2326   M 2327   M 2512
M 2954   M 3256   M 3268   M 3484
M 3702   N 0080   N 0267
"Beatlemania" (play): program
   M 2559
"Beatlemania" (play): sued by Beatles
   M 2901   M 3444   N 0184
"Beatlemania – The Movie" (film)
   RF0016
Beatles: ABC Theatre, Blackpool,
      England
   C 0340
THE BEATLES: A COLLECTION (book)
   RB0096   RB0097   RB0098
Beatles: activities before a concert
   M 3658
Beatles: aerial view of stage during
      concert
   M 2221
THE BEATLES AGAIN (book)
   RB0099   RB0100   RB0101   RB0102
   RB0103   RB0104   RB0105   RB0106
   RB0107   RB0108
THE BEATLES AGAIN (LP)   see also   'HEY
      JUDE' (LP)
THE BEATLES AGAIN (LP)
   M 0268   M 0364   M 3709   RR0076
   RR0077
THE BEATLES - A HARD DAY'S NIGHT (book)
   RB0109
Beatles: album boycott over price
   M 0232
THE BEATLES ALBUM FILE AND COMPLETE
      DISCOGRAPHY (book)
   RB0110   RB0111
Beatles: album of the year, 1968
   M 1603
Beatles: album press release
   M 2497
Beatles: Allen Klein named as manager
   M 0287   M 1804   N 0696
THE BEATLES: A MUSICAL EVOLUTION (book)
   RB0112
Beatles: analysis
   M 0943
THE BEATLES: AN ILLUSTRATED RECORD
      (book)
   RB0113   RB0114   RB0115   RB0116
   RB0117   RB0118   RB0119   RB0120
   RB0121   RB0122   RB0123   RB0124
   RB0125   RB0126   RB0127
Beatles: anti-Beatles club in Bismarck,
      North Dakota grade school
   M 0050   M 3777
Beatles: anti-Beatles movement in
      Detroit, Michigan
   M 3777   N 0243
THE BEATLES APART (book)
   M 0963   RB0128   RB0129   RB0130
Beatles: apartment in London, England
   M 0907
Beatles Appreciation Fan Club
   F 0027
Beatles Appreciation Society
   F 0029
"Beatles Appreciation Society Bulletin"
      (magazine)
   M 2100
"Beatles Around The World" (film)
   M 3702
Beatles: as a business
   M 0054   M 0055   M 0274   M 0296
   M 0304   M 0323   M 0335   M 0345
   M 0346   M 0356   M 0368   M 0405
   M 0418   M 0473   M 0575   M 1808
   M 2136   M 2236   M 2278   M 3162
   N 0804
Beatles: as a musical group
   B 0514
Beatles: as artists
   M 3739
Beatles: as children
   M 3784   M 3785   M 3786   M 3787
Beatles: as folk heroes in East Germany
   N 0978

Beatles: asking concert price
   M 2561
Beatles: as part of British Invasion
   C 0286
Beatles: as producers
   N 0192
Beatles: as subject of dissertation
   B 0128   B 0157   B 0158   B 0336
   B 0447   B 0462   B 0514   B 0528
   M 2257   M 2341   M 2534   M 3304
THE BEATLES: A STUDY IN DRUGS, SEX AND
      REVOLUTION (book)
   RB0131   RB0132
THE BEATLES A TO Z (book)
   M 1180   RB0133   RB0134   RB0135
   RB0136   RB0137
"Beatles At the Beeb" (radio show)
   M 0660   M 0732   M 1723   M 3506
   N 0299
THE BEATLES AT THE HOLLYWOOD BOWL (LP)
   M 0372   M 1535   M 2345   M 2666
   M 2859   M 3201   M 3267   M 3392
   M 3399   M 3525   M 3678   RR0078
   RR0079   RR0080   RR0081   RR0082
   RR0083   RR0084   RR0085   RR0086
   RR0087
THE BEATLES AT THE HOLLYWOOD BOWL (LP):
      bootlegs
   M 3201
Beatles: Australian broadcast ban on
      songs
   N 0249
Beatles: availability of recordings
   M 2524
Beatles: Avedon photos
   C 0277
Beatles: "Ballad of John and Yoko"
      (song) banned
   M 0319   M 0444   N 1159
Beatles: barred by Israel
   N 0533
Beatles: barred in Cleveland, Ohio
   M 3272   M 3503   N 0101   N 0296
Beatles: BBC radio broadcasts
      discovered
   M 3306
Beatles: "Beatlemania" (play) suit
   N 0184
Beatles: biography   see also   Beatles:
      brief biography
Beatles: biography   see also   Beatles:
      early biography
Beatles: biography
   B 0136   B 0137   B 0138   B 0139
   B 0140   B 0141   B 0142   B 0143
   B 0144   B 0145   B 0146   B 0147
   B 0148   B 0149   B 0150   B 0151
   B 0152   B 0163   B 0164   B 0165
   B 0166   B 0189   B 0190   B 0338
   B 0339   B 0340   B 0341   B 0342
   B 0408   B 0409   B 0410   B 0411
   B 0412   B 0480   B 0481   B 0482
   B 0483   B 0484   B 0485   B 0530
   B 0531   B 0532   B 0533   C 0149
   C 0196   C 0197   C 0203   C 0233
   C 0234   M 0073   M 0075   M 0549
   M 0889   M 0939   M 1741   M 1754
   M 1849   M 2221   M 2584   M 3231
   M 3232   M 3233   M 3234   M 3235
   M 3236   M 3237   M 3238   M 3761
   N 0430
BEATLES BIOGRAPHY (book)
   M 1120
Beatles: biography - odd facts
   M 3152
Beatles: boat people benefit concert
      invitation
   N 0214
Beatles: boat people rumored concert
   N 0143
THE BEATLES (book)
   M 0868   M 0869   M 0870   M 0871
THE BEATLES BOOK (Davis) (book)
   RB0138   RB0139   RB0140   RB0141
   RB0142   RB0143
"The Beatles Book" (fan magazine)
   M 0888   M 0906   N 0260
"The Beatles Book" (fan magazine): poll
      for favorite songs

M 0294   M 0295
Beatles: bookies making odds on Beatles
      success
   M 0616
Beatles: boxed record set
   M 2883   M 2885
THE BEATLES BOX (LP)
   RR0088   RR0089
Beatles: break-up   see also   Beatles:
      legal partnership dissolved
Beatles: break-up
   C 0105   C 0122   M 0010   M 0301
   M 0321   M 0331   M 0373   M 0462
   M 0560   M 1057   M 1062   M 1126
   M 1213   M 1288   M 1289   M 1311
   M 1472   M 1674   M 1943   M 2003
   M 2020   M 2076   M 2077   M 2172
   M 2241   M 2305   M 2376   M 2491
   M 3126   M 3189   M 3190   M 3338
   M 3339   M 3445   M 3708   M 3709
   M 3720   M 3780   N 0097   N 0098
   N 0110   N 0350   N 0730   N 0740
   N 0750   N 1003
Beatles: break-up denied
   M 1026   N 0728
Beatles: break-up predicted by
      McCartney
   N 0872
Beatles: break-up rumors
   M 0300   M 0416   M 0449
Beatles: break with Allen Klein
   N 0767
Beatles: Brian Kelly - promoter
   C 0201
Beatles: brief biography   see also
      Beatles: biography
Beatles: brief biography
   C 0006   C 0027   C 0036   C 0080
   C 0087   C 0088   C 0207   C 0279
   C 0288   C 0298   C 0299   C 0309
   C 0325   C 0331   C 0332   M 3708
Beatles: brief biography for disc
      jockeys
   M 0073
Beatles: broadcast rights to songs
   N 0246
Beatles: Buckingham Palace
   N 0895
Beatles: business worries
   N 0635
Beatles: caricature
   M 1511   M 0673
Beatles: cartoon series
   C 0106   M 0215   M 0811   M 0812
   N 0023
Beatles: cartoon series - episode
      synopses
   M 0813
Beatles: cartoon series - list of
      episodes
   M 2986
Beatles: catalogue of U.K. radio
      broadcasts
   M 1975   M 1976
Beatles: celebrities remember first
      time hearing or seeing them
   M 3764
Beatles: chauffeur fined
   N 0114
Beatles: Christmas, 1963
   M 0155
Beatles: Christmas records   see   Fan
      club (Beatles): Christmas record
Beatles: Christmas show
   C 0024   M 0402   M 1011   M 1630
   M 1739   N 0975
Beatles: chronology
   M 1341
Beatles Cine Club
   F 0024
Beatles City Ltd.
   F 0034
Beatles: Clive Epstein writ
   N 0002
Beatles: closed circuit tv
   M 2550
Beatles: closed circuit videotape
      concert - first such event
   M 0311

Beatles: collecting memorabilia see
    Memorabilia (Beatles)
THE BEATLES COLLECTION (EPs)
    RR0090
THE BEATLES COLLECTION (LPs)
    M 2883 M 2885 M 3533 RR0091
Beatles: collection of articles and
    essays
    B 0400
Beatles: comic book
    P 0110
Beatles: command performance
    B 0050
Beatles: concert
    C 0177
Beatles: concert dates
    M 3726 M 3728
THE BEATLES - CONCERT-ED EFFORTS (book)
    RB0144
Beatles: concert film
    M 0241
THE BEATLES CONCERTO (LP)
    M 1296 RR0092
Beatles: concert on tape
    M 0311
Beatles: concert schedules
    B 0558
Beatles: concerts without Starr
    N 0115
Beatles: contest
    M 3340
Beatles: copyright problems after
    break-up
    M 0301
Beatles: copyrights
    M 0312
Beatles: criticized by Red China
    N 0923
Beatles: crossword puzzle
    M 1958 M 3439
BEATLES DAGBOOK (book)
    RB0145 RB0146
Beatles: David Wigg interview LP
    M 3676
"The Beatles: Days In Their Lives"
    (documentary)
    M 0322
Beatles: disc jockies opinions
    M 0460 M 0927 M 0945
THE BEATLES DISCOGRAPHY (book)
    RB0147 RB0148
Beatles: discovered by Brian Epstein
    M 0150 M 3670
Beatles: documentary
    M 0322
THE BEATLES DOWN UNDER (book)
    RB0149 RB0150 RB0151 RB0152
    RB0153
Beatles: early American press
    M 0073 M 0240 M 0248 M 0265
    M 0284 M 0286 M 0288 M 0296
    M 0304 M 0311 M 0314 M 0324
    M 0351 M 0362 M 0365 M 0379
    M 0381 M 0411 M 0422 M 0424
    M 0431 M 0457 M 0458 M 0464
    M 0493 M 0494 M 0495 M 0549
    M 0552 M 0619 M 0652 M 0658
    M 0659 M 1323 M 1568 M 1590
    M 1803 M 1876 M 1890 M 1891
    M 1892 M 2007 M 2105 M 2106
    M 2107 M 2108 M 2246 M 2280
    M 2291 M 2298 M 2385 M 2448
    M 2982 M 3013 M 3164 M 3166
    M 3316 M 3346 M 3429 M 3453
    M 3498 M 3500 M 3513 M 3591
    M 3594 M 3685 M 3696 M 3760
Beatles: early biography see also
    Beatles: biography
Beatles: early biography
    B 0178 B 0179 B 0180 B 0181
    B 0182 B 0183 B 0184 B 0185
Beatles: early career
    B 0073 C 0015 C 0073 C 0091
    C 0343 M 0278 M 0627 M 1437
    M 1439 M 1448 M 1740 M 1742
    M 2090 M 2291 M 2477 M 3295
    M 3296 M 3297 M 3453 M 3493
Beatles: early interview
    M 1744

Beatles: early music
    C 0227 M 3790
Beatles: early 1960s
    C 0008 M 1290 M 1529
Beatles: early photographs
    B 0293 B 0367 B 0368 B 0369
    C 0032 C 0175 M 0278 M 0561
Beatles: early popularity
    C 0099 C 0117 C 0344 M 3453
THE BEATLES: EARLY YEARS (LP)
    M 1968
Beatles: earnings
    M 0323 M 0325 M 0327 M 0335
    M 0345 M 0365 M 0379 M 0380
    M 0412 M 0413 M 0453 M 0454
    M 0491 M 0498 M 0731 M 0743
    M 0842 M 1029 M 1183 M 1738
    M 2012 M 2356 M 2550 M 2561
    M 3161 M 3163 M 3165 M 3282
    M 3326 M 3330 M 3475 M 3491
    M 3710 N 0148 N 0915
Beatles: Eastern Europe
    M 0995
Beatles: editorial
    M 0046 M 0113 M 1814 M 3461
    M 3462 M 3463 N 1016 N 1144
Beatles: editorial letter
    N 0084 N 0090 N 0277 N 0711
Beatles: educational use of record
    M 3510
Beatles: effect on British economy
    M 0265 M 0274 M 0296 M 0297
    M 0347 M 0615 M 0617 M 1320
Beatles: effect on culture
    M 1273 M 2106 M 3110 N 0447
Beatles: effect on radio
    M 1083
Beatles: effect on record market
    M 0271 M 0347 M 0426 M 0482
    M 0976 M 1344 M 1803 M 2107
    M 3592 N 0387
Beatles: E.M.I. contract
    M 0433 M 1321
Beatles: E.M.I. finds 20 unreleased
    studio tracks
    N 0926
Beatles: end of concert touring
    M 1017
THE BEATLES' ENGLAND (book)
    M 3480 RB0154 RB0155 RB0156
THE BEATLES' ENGLAND (book): excerpt
    M 0097
Beatles: EP values
    M 0893
Beatles: exhibit at Abbey Road
    M 0329
Beatles: family trees
    B 0267 M 2250
Beatles: fan club see Fan club
    (Beatles)
Beatles Fan Club of Austria
    F 0156
Beatles: fan letters
    C 0040 C 0054 C 0261
Beatles: fan mail to Col. Wagg
    [M.B.E.s]
    N 0118
Beatles: fans
    M 1659
Beatles: fans at hotel
    N 0394 N 0985
Beatles: fans at London Airport
    N 1117
Beatles: fans besiege Delmonico's (New
    York City)
    N 0774
Beatles: fans in Japan
    N 1093
Beatles: fans reaction
    N 0346
Beatles: fans siege hotel
    N 0881
Beatles: fans welcome in Liverpool,
    England
    N 0843
Beatles: fanzine see also Fan club
    (Beatles)
Beatles: fanzines
    M 3300

Beatles: fiction
    M 1449
Beatles: fictional singles
    M 1865
Beatles: fight release of "Star Club
    Tapes"
    M 0332 M 0628
Beatles: film cancelled
    N 0054
Beatles: film made at the Cavern, 1962
    M 0181
Beatles: film premiere
    M 0247 M 1513 M 2631 M 3129
    M 3347 M 3656 M 3762 N 0136
    N 0486
Beatles: film preview
    N 1113
Beatles: film rejected
    N 0034
Beatles: film release in Communist
    Europe
    M 0333
Beatles: film retrospective in Paris,
    France
    M 0023 M 0600
Beatles: films see Individual film
    titles
Beatles: film work
    B 0167 B 0168 B 0169 B 0241
    B 0373 C 0222 M 0149 M 0219
    M 0334 M 0683 M 1427 M 2257
    M 3372 P 0038 P 0068
Beatles: financial situation after
    break-up
    M 0302 M 0303 M 0455
Beatles: first all-Beatle-music radio
    station
    N 0492
Beatles: first Liverpool, England
    Beatles Convention
    M 0770
Beatles: first non-EMI label recording
    M 2344
Beatles: first record
    M 0357
Beatles: first record at auction
    N 0885
BEATLES FOR CLASSICAL GUITAR (book)
    RB0157
"The Beatles 4 Ever" (film)
    M 2865
THE BEATLES FOREVER (Schaffner) (book)
    M 3154 RB0158 RB0159 RB0160
    RB0161 RB0162 RB0163 RB0164
    RB0165 RB0166 RB0167 RB0168
    RB0169 RB0170 RB0171
THE BEATLES FOREVER (Spence) (book)
    RB0172
Beatles: forgiven by the Maharishi
    N 0513
Beatles For Sale
    F 0039
BEATLES FOR SALE (LP)
    M 1479
THE BEATLES FOR THE RECORD (book)
    RB0173
THE BEATLES (Friedman) (book)
    RB0076
Beatles: future albums, 1989
    M 1146
Beatles: girlfriends
    M 0168
Beatles: girlfriends and wives
    M 3674
Beatles: gold record award
    M 0350
Beatles: gold records
    M 1590
Beatles: gold record winners
    M 0267 M 0284 M 0411
Beatles: Grammy Award
    M 1856 N 0467
Beatles: greatest hits package
    M 3062
THE BEATLES (Hardy) (book)
    RB0077 RB0078 RB0079
Beatles: heavy demand causes rationing
    of THE BEATLES (LP)
    N 0363

Beatles: history of group name
C 0185
Beatles: hit parade
M 2635
Beatles: honored by Knotts Berry Farm
M 3454
Beatles: honored by Liverpool council
N 0698
THE BEATLES ILLUSTRATED LYRICS (book)
RB0174 RB0175 RB0176 RB0177
RB0178 RB0179 RB0180 RB0181
RB0182 RB0183 RB0184 RB0185
RB0186
THE BEATLES ILLUSTRATED LYRICS - I
(book)
RB0187
THE BEATLES ILLUSTRATED LYRICS 2 (book)
RB0189 RB0190 RB0191
THE BEATLES ILLUSTRATED LYRICS -II
(book)
RB0188
Beatles: imitation group
M 0423 M 1389
Beatles: income tax on U.S. earnings
N 0202
Beatles: income with Klein management
N 0521
"The Beatles In Concert - No. 1" (Super
8MM film)
RF0017
"The Beatles In Concert - No. 2" (Super
8MM film)
RF0018
Beatles: Indian influence
C 0168 N 0206
Beatles: influence feared in Saudi
Arabia
N 1070
Beatles: influence of
M 0045 M 0046 M 0452 M 0596
M 1081 M 1153 M 1160 M 1273
M 1306 M 1358 M 1565 M 1724
M 1850 M 2106 M 2186 M 2388
M 3014 M 3133 M 3219 M 3242
M 3328 M 3342 M 3460 M 3483
M 3764 N 0092 N 0865 N 1009
Beatles: influence on art
M 0735 N 0686 N 1008
Beatles: influence on fashion
N 0445
Beatles: influence on hair styles
M 0020 M 1512 M 3167 M 3664
N 0302 N 0303 N 0443 N 0459
N 0460 N 0493 N 0708 N 0709
N 0970 P 0003
Beatles: influence on Liverpool youth
N 0083
Beatles: influence on popular music
M 0271 M 0299 M 0369 M 0556
M 0639 M 0863 M 1273 M 1797
M 2051 M 2174 M 2484 M 3035
M 3133 M 3329 N 0447 N 0746
The Beatles Information Center
F 0043
Beatles Information Center - West
Germany
F 0045 F 0144
"Beatles Information Centre",
Liverpool, England
M 2476
THE BEATLES IN ITALY (book)
RB0192
Beatles: injunction to prevent old
recordings release
N 0174
Beatles: injuries at concert ticket
sales
N 0841
THE BEATLES IN RICHARD LESTER'S "A HARD
DAY'S NIGHT" (book)
RB0193 RB0194 RB0195 RB0196
RB0197
Beatles: in rock literature
C 0141
Beatles: install 16-track recorder at
Apple
M 0305
Beatles: insurance for U.S. tour
N 0357

Beatles: interview
M 0166 M 0179 M 0737 M 0882
M 1744 M 1960 M 2461 M 2494
N 0051
THE BEATLES INTERVIEWS (LP)
M 0951
"The Beatles Interviews" (16MM film)
RF0019
THE BEATLES IN THEIR OWN WORDS (book)
RB0198 RB0199 RB0200
THE BEATLES INTRODUCE NEW SONGS (LP)
RR0093
"The Beatles Introduce New Songs/Shout"
(45)
RR0094
Beatles: investment in Balcon group
N 0175
Beatles: invitation to Venice, Italy
festival
N 0137
Beatles: invitation to visit British
troops in Berlin, Germany
N 0200 N 1052
Beatles: invited to discuss visit to
U.S.S.R.
N 0211
Beatles: Ireland concerts
C 0312
Beatles: Israeli visitation permit
M 0213
Beatles: issue records
N 0192
'Beatle slang' glossary
M 3662
Beatles: leaving for England
N 0113
Beatles: legal battle over U.S. label
M 0552
Beatles: legal partnership dissolved
see also Beatles: break-up
Beatles: legal partnership dissolved
M 0618 N 0107 N 0134 N 0140
N 0142 N 0159 N 0170 N 0171
N 0373 N 0386 N 0450 N 0582
N 0587 N 0608 N 0687 N 0919
N 1046 N 1059 N 1060 N 1111
N 1124 N 1125
Beatles: Lennon and Starr disagree on
shows for public
N 1096
Beatles: Lennon remark on popularity of
Beatles and Jesus
M 0009 M 0413 M 0487 M 0578
M 0721 M 0815 M 0874 M 1061
M 2320 M 2557 M 3545 N 0141
N 0304 N 0664 N 0878 N 1017
Beatles: Lennon remark on popularity of
Beatles and Jesus - debris thrown
at concert
N 0342
Beatles: Lennon remark on popularity of
Beatles and Jesus - drop in
Beatles stock
N 1025
Beatles: Lennon remark on popularity of
Beatles and Jesus - editorial
N 1145
Beatles: Lennon remark on popularity of
Beatles and Jesus - radio ban
M 3426 N 0304 N 0326
Beatles: Lennon remark on popularity of
Beatles and Jesus - U.S. ban
N 1116
Beatles: Lennon remark on popularity of
Beatles and Jesus - Vatican
accepts apology
N 1121
Beatles: letter
M 0930 M 3636 N 0084 N 0090
N 0277 N 0711 N 0848 N 0893
N 0928 N 1149
Beatles: letter (reply to N 0879)
N 0880
Beatles: letters
B 0002 B 0003 B 0004 B 0005
B 0006 B 0114 C 0040 C 0054
C 0261 M 0217 M 0414 M 0649
M 1561 M 1813 M 1950 M 1953
M 1954 M 2217 M 2984 M 3788

N 0496 N 0756
Beatles: libel action over photographs
N 0183
Beatles: listed in Britain's WHO'S WHO
(book)
N 1148
Beatles: listed in WHO'S WHO IN AMERICA
(book)
N 0530 N 1077
THE BEATLES LIVE - AT THE CAVERN (LP)
M 0371
THE BEATLES LIVE AT THE STAR CLUB (LP)
see also "Hamburg Tapes"
THE BEATLES LIVE AT THE STAR CLUB (LP)
M 3004 M 3012 M 3392 M 3399
RR0096 RR0097 RR0098 RR0099
RR0100 RR0101 RR0102 RR0103
RR0104 M 3267 M 3427
THE BEATLES LIVE AT THE STAR CLUB (LP):
mixing the album from the Hamburg
tapes
M 3004
Beatles: live concert planned in
London, England
M 0450 M 2251
Beatles: live concert recordings
M 1391
THE BEATLES 'LIVE' (LP)
RR0095
Beatles: live performance planned, 1968
M 0465
Beatles: "lost" BBC Beatles songs
M 2041 N 0272
Beatles: "lost" BBC Beatles songs -
U.S. radio premiere
N 1041
THE BEATLES (LP)
M 0425 M 0848 M 0849 M 1046
M 1211 M 2113 M 2273 M 3134
M 3642 N 0186 N 0588 RR0064
RR0065 RR0066 RR0067 RR0068
RR0069 RR0070 RR0071 RR0072
RR0073 RR0074 RR0075
THE BEATLES (LP): heavy demand
N 0363
THE BEATLES (LP): poem
M 2552
Beatles: lyrics
B 0007 B 0008 B 0009 B 0010
B 0011 B 0012 B 0013 B 0014
B 0015 B 0016 B 0017 B 0018
B 0019 B 0020 B 0021 B 0022
B 0023 B 0024 B 0025 B 0026
B 0027 B 0028 B 0094 B 0125
B 0205 C 0069 C 0127 C 0181
M 1458 M 1670 M 2049 M 2130
M 2507 M 3324 M 3438 M 3460
Beatles: lyrics analyzed
C 0150 M 2507 N 0782
Beatles: lyrics concordance
B 0094
Beatles: McCartney leaves group
N 0730
Beatles: Mal Evans hired
M 0081
Beatles: marriages
M 2037
Beatles: master recordings
M 3179
Beatles: M.B.E. investiture
N 0119 N 0968
Beatles: meet Benny Goodman
M 1302
Beatles: meet Elvis Presley
M 1514 M 1570 M 2483 M 3250
Beatles: meet the Monkees
M 3332
Beatles: "Melody Maker" (magazine) poll
N 0634
Beatles: merchandise
M 2168 M 2202
Beatles: moustaches
M 1660
Beatles: move to ban them in
Pennsylvania
N 0878
THE BEATLES MOVIE CATALOG (book)
RB0201
"Beatles Movie Medley/Fab Four On Film"

Beatles

(45)
  RR0105 RR0106
"The Beatles Movie Medley" (12-inch
    single)
  M 3567
"The Beatles Movie Medley" (video)
  RF0020
Beatles: museum in Liverpool
  M 3293
Beatles: museum plans
  M 1205 M 1446
Beatles: museum rumors
  M 2938
Beatles: music
  C 0062 C 0182 M 0501 M 0520
  M 1997 M 2051 M 2129 M 2231
  M 2232 M 2463 M 2493 M 2496
  M 2534 M 2646 M 3077 M 3105
  M 3106 M 3305 M 3667 N 0268
  N 0787
Beatles: music analysis
  B 0217 B 0262 B 0376 B 0377
  B 0378 B 0416 B 0417 B 0462
  B 0528 C 0275 M 1335 M 1336
  M 1537 M 1818 M 2340 M 2341
  M 2342 M 3366 N 0409 N 1033
Beatles: musicological research contest
  M 3341
Beatles: music performed in Baroque
    style
  N 0786 N 0966
Beatles: music recorded by others
  B 0113
Beatles: myths
  M 1962
Beatles: namesake streets in Liverpool
  N 0754
Beatles: °new' singles, 1983
  M 3563
Beatles: 1960s
  B 0486 B 0542 B 0543 B 0544
  B 0545 C 0151 C 0170 M 2052
Beatles: 1960's LP popularity poll
  M 2034
Beatles: 1960-1970 daily calendar
  B 0487 B 0488 B 0489 B 0490
Beatles: 1961
  M 1964
Beatles: 1962
  M 0181 M 0251 M 0317 M 0385
  M 0386 M 0387 M 1451 M 2302
  M 2303 M 2461 M 3178
THE BEATLES, 1962-1966 (LP)
  RR0107 RR0108 RR0109 RR0110
  RR0111
Beatles: 1963
  B 0457 M 0156 M 0225 M 0248
  M 0260 M 0318 M 0352 M 0388
  M 0389 M 0390 M 0391 M 0392
  M 0393 M 0394 M 0395 M 0396
  M 0397 M 0398 M 0399 M 0744
  M 0750 M 0766 M 0767 M 0771
  M 0783 M 0882 M 1003 M 1408
  M 1742 M 1744 M 2053 M 3192
  M 3335 M 3349
Beatles: 1963 autumn tour schedule
  M 0280
Beatles: 1963 concert
  C 0171
Beatles: 1963 tour
  M 1742
Beatles: 1963 U.K. tour
  M 0280 M 3428
Beatles: 1964
  B 0067 B 0458 B 0555 M 0976
  M 1997 M 2011 M 3221 M 3307
  M 3350 M 3401 M 3500 M 3593
Beatles: 1964 arrival at Kennedy
    airport
  M 3366 N 0420
Beatles: 1964 U.S. tour
  M 0286 M 0325 M 0340 M 0362
  M 0365 M 0412 M 0472 M 0598
  M 0738 M 0976 M 1082 M 1183
  M 1574 M 2294 M 2298 M 2366
  M 3114 M 3452 N 0012 N 0381
  N 1044 P 0054
Beatles: 1964 U.S. visit
  B 0257 B 0258 M 0067 M 0355

M 0362 M 0422 M 0431 M 0495
  M 1891 M 2246 M 2378 M 2385
  M 2392 M 3316 M 3346 M 3660
  M 3684 M 3760 N 0421 N 0801
Beatles: 1964 world tour
  M 1141
Beatles: 1964-1966
  B 0058
Beatles: 1965
  B 0459 M 2192
Beatles: 1965 Christmas television
    special
  M 0036
Beatles: 1965 U.K. tour
  M 3291
Beatles: 1965 U.S. tour
  M 0327 M 0380 M 0491 M 1571
  M 1629 M 3330 M 3376 M 3781
  N 0094 N 0984 P 0055
Beatles: 1965 U.S. tour begun
  N 0973
Beatles: 1966
  M 3271 M 3413 M 3433 M 3661
Beatles: 1966 U.K. tour
  M 1634
Beatles: 1966 U.S. tour
  M 0413 M 0578 M 1598 M 3512
  P 0056
Beatles: 1967
  C 0249 M 1602 M 1836 M 2094
  M 3403
THE BEATLES, 1967-1970 (LP)
  RR0112 RR0113 RR0114 RR0115
Beatles: 1968
  M 1603 M 1604 M 1605 M 1606
  M 1817
Beatles: 1969
  M 0483 M 0484 M 0485 M 1607
  M 1608 M 1609 M 1659
Beatles: 1970
  M 1610 M 1611 M 1612 M 1613
'THE BEATLES 1971-1976' (LP):
    nominations for fictional Beatles
    album
  M 0083
Beatles: 1974
  M 2803 M 3073
Beatles: 1975
  M 2810 M 3262
Beatles: 1979
  M 1969 M 2945
Beatles: 1980
  M 0326 M 1970
Beatles: 1981
  M 1971
Beatles: 1982
  M 0316 M 1972 M 3410
Beatles: 1983
  M 1973
Beatles: nominations for fictional LP
    'The Beatles 1971-1976'
  M 0083
Beatles: Northern Songs, Ltd. sold to
    ATV
  N 1014
Beatles: nude poster montage
  M 0804
BEATLESONGS! (LP)
  RR0116
Beatles: on handling success
  M 3663
Beatles: on holiday, 1963
  M 0156 M 1529 M 3221
Beatles: on holiday, 1964
  M 3221
THE BEATLES ON RECORD (Russell) (book)
  RB0202
THE BEATLES ON RECORD (Wallgren) (book)
  RB0203 RB0204
Beatles: on set of "A Hard Day's Night"
    (film)
  C 0162
Beatles: on the charts
  C 0029 C 0037 M 0288 M 0289
  M 0353 M 0370 M 0431 M 0475
  M 0476 M 1327 M 1462 M 1774
  M 2034 M 2108 M 2178 M 3543
  M 3544 M 3679 N 0321
Beatles: on the charts after break-up

M 1164
Beatles: on the charts (Holland)
  M 3467
Beatles: on their fans
  M 3668
Beatles: on their future
  C 0303
Beatles: on tv
  N 0971
Beatles: on world tv
  N 0158
Beatles: oppose Vietnam war in New York
    City press conference
  N 0329
Beatles: origin
  C 0185
Beatles: oust Allen Klein
  M 0062
Beatles: Paramount Theatre Benefit show
  N 1043
Beatles: parody
  M 0508 M 1545 M 1560 M 2163
  M 2190 M 3258 M 3301 M 3404
  M 3405 M 3746
Beatles: percent ownership of Northern
    Songs stock
  M 0382
Beatles: photographer's experiences
    shooting the Beatles
  M 0634
Beatles: photograph from "Vogue"
    (magazine)
  M 3657
Beatles: photographic impressions of
    songs
  M 1758
Beatles: photographs
  B 0367 B 0368 B 0369
Beatles: photographs as children
  P 0021
Beatles: photographs of 1964 visit
  M 2378
Beatles: photographs on stage
  M 2365
Beatles: photography contest,
    "Beatlefan" (magazine)
  M 0218
Beatles: picture discs
  M 2368 M 3185
Beatles: pictured on Dylan LP
  M 0993
THE BEATLES (Pirmantgen) (book)
  RB0080
Beatles: plans for live shows
  M 1122
Beatles: police protection in London,
    England
  N 0890
Beatles: police visit retreat in India
  N 0523
Beatles: popularity
  C 0126 M 0013 M 0043 M 0071
  M 0225 M 0239 M 0240 M 0265
  M 0288 M 0289 M 0291 M 0320
  M 0424 M 0458 M 0470 M 0471
  M 0494 M 0603 M 0744 M 1194
  M 1436 M 1568 M 1772 M 1814
  M 2012 M 2107 M 2108 M 2191
  M 2210 M 2221 M 2385 M 2448
  M 2468 M 2507 M 2525 M 2560
  M 2628 M 2982 M 3014 M 3092
  M 3350 M 3429 M 3591 M 3592
  M 3653 M 3662 M 3669 M 3695
  M 3697 M 3752 M 3764 N 0044
  N 0102
Beatles: popularity in Italy
  N 0534
Beatles: popularity in U.S.A., 1964
  M 0457 M 0495
Beatles: popularity in U.S.S.R.
  N 1066
Beatles: portrait in regency dress
  M 3793
Beatles: possible break-up
  C 0042
Beatles: possible business projects
    with the Rolling Stones (group)
  N 0264
Beatles: post-1965

C 0285
Beatles: press award
    M 0496
Beatles: press conference
    M 0417   M 3013
Beatles: pretend reunion concert -
    radio program
    M 0430
Beatles: price guide to recordings
    B 0049   B 0184
Beatles: produce concept album SGT.
    PEPPER
    C 0283
Beatles: produce steady stream of songs
    N 0976
Beatles: program sellers arrested
    N 0916
Beatles: psychedelic music
    M 2463
Beatles: psychological effects
    N 0092
Beatles: published errors
    M 1450
Beatles: publishing activity after
    Lennon's death
    N 0078   N 1123
Beatles: puzzle
    M 0983   M 0985   M 0986
Beatles: quiz
    M 1181
Beatles: quotations
    B 0383   B 0384   B 0385   B 0386
Beatles: radio ban
    M 1333
Beatles: radio ban in South Africa
    N 1017
Beatles: radio broadcasts
    B 0265   B 0266
Beatles: radio broadcasts catalogue
    (U.K.)
    M 1975   M 1976
Beatles: radio documentary
    M 3742   M 3774   N 0500
Beatles: radio programs
    M 0660   M 0732   M 1723   M 3506
    M 3523   N 0299
Beatles: radio special
    M 0660
Beatles: rare recordings
    M 2180
Beatles: rarest singles
    M 0729
Beatles: rate pop singles
    M 0489
Beatles: record industry
    C 0093
Beatles: recording activity
    M 2304   M 2387   N 0116
Beatles: recording at E.M.I.
    C 0195
Beatles: recording console bought
    M 2088
Beatles: recording contract, E.M.I.
    C 0131
Beatles: recording contract, German
    C 0041
Beatles: recording engineer
    M 1301   M 2311
Beatles: recording first LP
    M 0904
Beatles: recordings
    B 0569
Beatles: recordings available in
    different mixes
    M 2489
Beatles: recording session
    C 0301   M 0952   M 1037   M 1039
    M 1049   M 1051   M 1052   M 1054
    M 1055   M 1638   M 1647   M 2392
    M 2962   M 3230   M 3290   M 3442
Beatles: record re-issues
    M 0856   M 0916
Beatles: record sales
    M 0214   M 0288   M 0289   M 0290
    M 0293   M 0296   M 0297   M 0319
    M 0320   M 0336   M 0347   M 0353
    M 0379   M 0411   M 0413   M 0422
    M 0425   M 0426   M 0432   M 0434
    M 0447   M 0448   M 0450   M 0464

    M 0476   M 0482   M 0516   M 0613
    M 0617   M 0657   M 0658   M 0856
    M 0916   M 1166   M 1344   M 1462
    M 1568   M 1590   M 1803   M 1946
    M 2237   M 2238   M 2557   M 2982
    M 3122   M 3387   M 3453   M 3514
Beatles: record sales, 1980
    M 1829
Beatles: records and songs   see
    individual album and song titles
Beatles: records burned in Indonesia
    N 0537
Beatles: record seized in Singapore
    N 0514
Beatles: records set
    C 0124   M 2085   M 2731   M 3533
Beatles: regiment refuses to protect
    them
    N 0802
Beatles: rehearsal
    N 0253
Beatles: reissued LPs hurting sales of
    new recordings
    M 0426
Beatles: reissued recordings
    M 0423   M 1168   M 1462   M 1864
    M 1866   M 2044   M 2980   M 3431
Beatles: reissued recordings - colored
    vinyl
    M 0916
Beatles: reissued recordings dominate
    charts
    M 3679
Beatles: relationship with Epstein
    N 0469
Beatles: release of early recordings
    not banned
    N 0803
Beatles: release single on German label
    "My Bonnie/The Saints" (45)
    N 0703
Beatles: relevance of music to U.S.
    life
    N 0684
Beatles: reply to film critics on
    "Magical Mystery Tour"
    N 0167
Beatles: return to England
    N 0139   N 0901
Beatles: return to Liverpool, England
    M 2391
Beatles: return to London, England
    N 0168   N 1142   M 0494
Beatles: return to London, England on
    Epstein's death
    N 0237
Beatles: reunion concert - fictional
    M 0430
Beatles: reunion for U.N. concert
    M 0272
Beatles: reunion fund appeal
    M 1339
Beatles: reunion impossible due to U.S.
    immigration
    M 3511
Beatles: reunion offer
    M 0403   M 0408   M 0427   M 0492
    M 0920   M 1143   M 1339   M 1396
    M 2296   M 2322   M 2449   M 2562
    M 2897   M 3309   M 3435   N 0154
    N 0828
Beatles: reunion ruled out by McCartney
    N 0875
Beatles: reunion rumor
    M 0282   M 0283   M 0428   M 0429
    M 0715   M 0772   M 0864   M 1142
    M 1158   M 1216   M 1390   M 1473
    M 1546   M 1737   M 1784   M 2060
    M 2124   M 2449   M 2736   M 2741
    M 2742   M 2750   M 2768   M 2779
    M 2781   M 2833   M 2898   M 3011
    M 3096   M 3253   M 3278   M 3309
    M 3435   M 3485   M 3511   M 3632
    M 3646   M 3701
Beatles: review of first 15 years
    N 0910
Beatles: rise to stardom
    C 0206
Beatles: rooftop concert

    N 1004
Beatles: royalties
    M 2005   M 2307
Beatles: royalties claim
    M 0453
Beatles: Royal Variety Performance
    N 0699
Beatles: rumored project with the
    Rolling Stones
    M 0456
Beatles: rumored return to concerts
    M 0378   M 0415   M 0474
Beatles: rumored three LP set
    M 0467
Beatles: rumored U.S. concert, 1968
    M 0377
THE BEATLES (Scaduto) (book)
    RB0081
Beatles: sculpture
    M 3294   N 1023
Beatles: sculpture by Tommy Steele
    M 3294
THE BEATLES SECOND ALBUM (LP)
    M 1590
Beatles: seek ban on release of early
    recordings
    N 0887
Beatles: sell Northern Songs, Ltd. to
    ATV
    N 0218
Beatles: "Shindig" (tv show) appearance
    M 3229   M 3243   M 3244
Beatles: signed by United Artists
    N 0176
Beatles: sign E.M.I. contract to expire
    in 1975
    M 2239
Beatles: singles values
    M 0892
BEATLES '65 (LP)
    M 0748
Beatles: solo careers
    M 0410
Beatles: solo record sales
    M 0290
Beatles songbook   see also   Harrison,
    George: songbook
Beatles songbook   see also   Individual
    musical instruments
Beatles songbook   see also   Lennon,
    John: songbook
Beatles songbook   see also   McCartney,
    Paul: songbook
Beatles songbook   see also   Starr,
    Ringo: songbook
Beatles songbook
    B 0123   B 0124   B 0365   N 0715
    S 0003   S 0004   S 0005   S 0006
    S 0007   S 0008   S 0009   S 0010
    S 0011   S 0012   S 0013   S 0014
    S 0015   S 0016   S 0017   S 0018
    S 0019   S 0020   S 0021   S 0022
    S 0023   S 0024   S 0025   S 0026
    S 0027   S 0028   S 0029   S 0030
    S 0031   S 0032   S 0033   S 0034
    S 0035   S 0036   S 0037   S 0038
    S 0039   S 0040   S 0041   S 0042
    S 0043   S 0044   S 0045   S 0046
    S 0047   S 0048   S 0049   S 0050
    S 0051   S 0052   S 0053   S 0054
    S 0055   S 0056   S 0057   S 0058
    S 0059   S 0060   S 0061   S 0062
    S 0063   S 0064   S 0065   S 0066
    S 0067   S 0068   S 0069   S 0070
    S 0071   S 0072   S 0073   S 0074
    S 0075   S 0076   S 0077   S 0078
    S 0079   S 0080   S 0081   S 0082
    S 0083   S 0085   S 0086   S 0087
    S 0089   S 0090   S 0091   S 0092
    S 0093   S 0095   S 0097   S 0105
    S 0106   S 0107   S 0108   S 0109
    S 0110   S 0111   S 0112   S 0113
    S 0114   S 0115   S 0116   S 0117
    S 0118   S 0119   S 0121   S 0125
    S 0137   S 0138   S 0139   S 0140
    S 0142   S 0143   S 0144   S 0145
    S 0153   S 0154   S 0155   S 0156
    S 0158   S 0170
Beatles: song of the year, 1968

M 1603
Beatles: song parodies
    N 1160
Beatles: songs
    M 2375   M 2926   M 2943   M 3143
    M 3305   M 3588   N 1146
Beatles: songs - different versions
    M 2988   M 2989   M 2990   M 2991
    M 2992   M 2993   M 2994   M 2995
Beatles: songs played at Lennon's death
    N 0313
Beatles: songs played in tribute to
        Lennon
    N 0181
Beatles: songs popularity
    M 3006
Beatles: songs - singers and composers
    M 1868
Beatles: songs to be released on
        upcoming LP
    M 2588
Beatles: songs to dream by
    M 0829
Beatles: songs written for others
    M 0967
Beatles: songwriting award
    M 0381   M 0493   M 1918   M 3489
    M 3755   N 0147   N 0792
Beatles: Soviet criticism
    N 1018
Beatles: Soviet press
    N 0038
Beatles: spark interest in the British
    N 0315
THE BEATLES (Spence) (book)
    RB0082
Beatles: Starr on possible reunion
    N 0825
Beatles: statue fund
    M 0452   M 3741
Beatles: statues in Liverpool, England
    M 2870   N 0336   N 0519
Beatles: statues proposed in Liverpool,
        England
    M 1445   M 2009   M 2870   N 0336
    N 0519   N 1067
Beatles: stock shares
    N 0981
THE BEATLES (Stokes) (book)
    RB0083   RB0084   RB0085   RB0086
    RB0087   RB0088   RB0089   RB0090
    RB0091   RB0092   RB0093   RB0094
Beatles: street names in Liverpool,
        England
    M 2533   M 3367   N 0324   N 0754
Beatles: studying meditation
    N 0464
Beatles: sue clothing firm
    N 0194
Beatles: sue for slander and libel
    N 0185
THE BEATLES TALK DOWNUNDER (LP)
    RR0117
THE BEATLES TAPES FROM THE DAVID WIGG
        INTERVIEW (LP)
    RR0018
THE BEATLES TAPES (LP)
    M 3676
Beatles: teenage fans, 1980s
    M 0603
Beatles: television appearance
    M 3229   M 3243   M 3244
Beatles: television chronology
    M 1791
Beatles: television special
    M 1147   M 1536   M 2751   M 2975
    M 3123   M 3124   N 0451
Beatles: tenth anniversary
    M 0459   M 3053   N 0352   P 0116
THE BEATLES: THE AUTHORIZED BIOGRAPHY
        (book)
    M 3793   RB0205   RB0206   RB0207
    RB0208   RB0209   RB0210   RB0211
    RB0212   RB0213   RB0214   RB0215
    RB0216   RB0217   RB0218   RB0219
    RB0220   RB0221   RB0222   RB0223
    RB0224   RB0225   RB0226   RB0227
    RB0228   RB0229   RB0230   RB0231
    RB0232   RB0233   RB0234   RB0235

RB0236
THE BEATLES: THE AUTHORIZED BIOGRAPHY
        (book - second ed.)
    RB0237
THE BEATLES: THE REAL STORY (book)
    M 3793   RB0238   RB0239   RB0240
    RB0241   RB0242   RB0243   RB0244
    RB0245   RB0246   RB0247   RB0248
    RB0249   RB0250
Beatles: ticker tape welcome
    M 0345
Beatles: to manage themselves after
        Epstein's death
    N 0203
Beatles: to record songs composed in
        India
    M 3325
Beatles: to sing advertisement
    N 0271
Beatles: tour end
    N 0195
Beatles: touring
    M 1060
Beatles: tribute
    M 3518
Beatles: trivia questions
    B 0044   B 0198   B 0218   B 0219
    B 0263   B 0264   C 0282   C 0287
    M 0220   M 0221   M 0663   M 0817
    M 1453   M 1454   M 2574   M 3476
THE BEATLES TRIVIA QUIZ BOOK (book)
    RB0251
Beatles: twentieth anniversary (U.S.)
    M 0479   M 1192   M 1849   M 1995
    M 3430   M 3431   M 3476   M 3477
    M 3478   M 3684   P 0014   P 0040
THE BEATLES - 24 POSTERS (book)
    RB0252
Beatles: two fans threaten leap off
        hotel
    N 1094
Beatles: U.K. Embassy party in
        Washington, D.C.
    N 0201
Beatles: unauthorized use of songs
    M 0420
Beatles: United Cerebral Palsy
        Association benefit concert
    M 1772
Beatles: University of Delaware course
    N 0314
Beatles Unlimited
    F 0048
Beatles: unreleased recordings
    M 1862
Beatles: unreleased single
    M 1074
Beatles USA Ltd.
    F 0092   F 0093   F 0133   F 0146
Beatles: U.S. financial situation
    N 0529
Beatles: U.S. reception
    C 0145   C 0213
Beatles: U.S. tax
    N 0193   N 1115
Beatles: U.S. tour
    N 0155   N 0791   N 0829
Beatles: U.S. tour - 1965
    M 0327
Beatles: vs. Allen Klein
    M 0005   M 0006   M 0007   M 0024
    M 0025   M 0026   M 0302   M 0303
    M 0366   M 1674   M 1675   M 1805
    M 1809   M 1811   M 1826   M 1874
    M 2855   M 3447   M 3448   N 0138
    N 0399   N 0401   N 0520   N 0636
    N 1035   N 1046
Beatles: vs. "Beatlemania" (play)
    M 2901   M 3444
Beatles: vs. Clive Epstein
    N 1162
Beatles: vs. Lord Grade
    M 0374
Beatles: vs. Paul McCartney
    M 2076   M 2077   M 3339   N 0373
    N 0687
Beatles: vs. Pete Best
    M 0533   M 1065
Beatles: voice imitations on STARS ON

LONG PLAY (LP)
    M 1483
Beatles: voice patterns in color
        registers
    M 0310
Beatles: voted tops by poll
    M 3368
Beatles Werk Group
    F 0051
THE BEATLES WHO'S WHO (book)
    RB0253   RB0254   RB0255
Beatles: win awards
    M 0728   N 1097   N 1101
THE BEATLES YEARS (book)
    RB0256   RB0257   RB0258
THE BEATLES: YESTERDAY AND TODAY (book)
    RB0259
Beatles Yesterday & Today Organization
    F 0053
THE BEATLES (Zanderbergen) (book)
    RB0095
BEATLE TALK (LP)
    RR0119
"THE BEATLE THAT TIME FORGOT" (LP)
    RR0347
Beatle wallpaper
    N 0244
Beatle wigs
    M 3685
Beat Publications
    F 0032   N 0260
Beattle §sict concert (Philadelphia,
        Pennsylvania)
    N 0209
BEAUCOUPS OF BLUES (LP)
    M 0510   M 3759   RR0120
BEAUTIFUL DREAMER (LP)
    RR0121   RR0122   RR0123   RR0124
    RR0125
Bed-in
    C 0347   M 0972   M 2596   M 3003
    N 0501   N 0658
Bed-in: recordings
    M 1908
"Beetles" apparel
    N 0017
BEHIND CLOSED DOORS (LP)
    RR0126
BEHIND THE BEATLES SONGS (book)
    RB0260   RB0261
Belgium: Ono art exhibit
    M 2050
Belushi, John: Lennon's death
    M 3700
Berlin, Germany: invitation to Beatles
        to visit British troops
    N 0200   N 1052
Bermuda: Lennons
    M 3085
Bernstein, Sid
    M 2897   N 0004
Berry, Chuck
    M 2622
THE BEST OF GEORGE HARRISON (LP)
    RR0127
THE BEST OF THE BEATLES (LP)
    M 2731
Best, Pete
    B 0073   C 0031   C 0053   C 0219
    C 0231   C 0239   C 0240   M 0972
    M 1604   M 1735   M 2460   M 3184
Best, Pete: interview
    M 3411
Best, Pete: libel suit against Beatles
    M 0533   M 1065   M 1066
Best, Pete: photograph at Star Club
    M 2459
Best, Pete: records and songs
    RR0283   RR0284
Best, Peter   see   Best, Pete
Bibliography (Beatles)
    B 0249   B 0336   B 0447
Bibliography (Beatles): French
    B 0167   B 0168   B 0169
Bibliography (Beatles): international
    B 0547
Big Seven Music Corporation
    M 0541   N 0503   N 0580
"Billboard" (magazine): special issue -

Lennon
  M 3700
Billy J. Kramer and the Dakotas
  M 3529
"The Birth of the Beatles" (film)
  M 0188   M 0189   M 0553   M 0554
  M 0555   M 0847   M 1109   RF0021
  RF0022   RF0023   RF0024   RF0025
  RF0026   RF0027
Bismarck, North Dakota: anti-Beatles
    club
  M 0050
Black, Cilla
  M 2730   M 3530   M 3575
Blackpool, England: ABC Theatre
  C 0340
BLAST FROM YOUR PAST (LP)
  RR0128   RR0129   RR0131   RR0130
"Blindman" (film)
  M 2513   M 2658   M 2669   M 2692
  RF0028   RF0029   RF0030   RF0031
  RF0032   RF0033   RF0034   RF0035
  RF0036
Blood, Sweat & Tears
  M 2670
"Blue Jay Way" (song)
  M 2380
Blues (music)
  C 0210
Boat people: Beatles invited to benefit
    concert
  N 0214
Boat people: rumored benefit concert
  N 0143   N 0704
Bolan, Marc: film documentary
  M 2711
Bombay, India: Harrison interview
  N 0206
Bombay, India: Harrison recording visit
  M 1042
Book review   see   individual book
    titles
Bootlegs (Beatles)
  B 0038   B 0466   C 0220
  M 0040   M 2573   M 0112   M 0298
  M 0343   M 0527   M 0697   M 0931
  M 0933   M 1361   M 1388   M 1418
  M 1434   M 1884   M 1885   M 1886
  M 2180   M 2272   M 2430   M 2465
  M 2997   M 3201   M 3278   M 3327
  M 3740   M 3759   N 0227
Bootlegs (Harrison)
  M 1413   M 1418   M 2735
Bootlegs (Lennon)
  M 2964
BORN TO ADD (LP)
  M 1989
"Born to Boogie" (film)
  N 0027   RF0037   RF0038   RF0039
  RF0040   RF0041
Boston, Massachusetts: Beatlefest
  M 0241
Boston, Massachusetts: Beatles
  M 2012
Boston, Massachusetts: fan convention
  M 1202   M 1203   M 2792   M 2981
  M 3759   N 0109
Boston, Massachusetts: Harrison
  M 2807   M 3308
Boston, Massachusetts: Harrison concert
  M 2807
Boston Pops: Carnegie Hall Lennon
    tribute concert
  N 1087
Bournemouth, England: concert
  M 0887   M 0909
Bowie, David
  M 2814   M 2834
Boyd, Jenny: drug charge
  M 2275   M 3052   N 0432
Boyd, Jenny: passport and drug problems
  N 0431
Boyd, Jenny: photograph with Pattie
    Boyd, Cynthia Powell, and Maureen
    Cox
  M 2379
Boyd, Patricia Anne   see   Boyd, Pattie
Boyd, Pattie
  M 2748   M 2952

Boyd, Pattie: divorces George Harrison
  N 0423   N 0615
Boyd, Pattie: drug charge
  N 0058   N 0059   N 0062   N 0724
Boyd, Pattie: drug raid
  N 0354
Boyd, Pattie: injured in car accident
  M 2707
Boyd, Pattie: photograph with Cynthia
    Powell, Maureen Cox, and Jenny
    Boyd
  M 2379
Boyd, Pattie: portrait with Harrison
  M 1467
Boyd, Pattie: press reception with
    George Harrison
  M 0086
Boyd, Pattie: weds Eric Clapton
  M 2892   M 2894
Boyd, Pattie: weds George Harrison
  M 0086   M 0859   N 0074   N 0426
Boyd, Pattie: with Ron Wood
  M 2769
THE BOYS FROM LIVERPOOL (book)
  RB0262   RB0263   RB0264   RB0265
  RB0266   RB0267   RB0268   RB0269
  RB0270
Brambell, Wilfred
  C 0268
Bramlett, Bonnie
  M 1519
Bramlett, Delaney
  M 1519
Bramwell, Tony
  M 3659
Bratby, John
  N 0414
"Braverman's Condensed Cream of
    Beatles" (film)
  RF0042   RF0043   RF0044   RF0045
  RF0046   RF0047   RF0048   RF0049
  RF0050
Brazil: Beatles discography
  M 0661
Brazil: fan club
  F 0033   F 0098   F 0136
Brazil: Harrison
  M 3204
Brisbane, New Zealand: mob
  N 0360   N 0403
British Broadcasting Corporation   see
    BBC
British Invasion
  C 0286   M 0457   M 1281   M 1736
  M 1797   M 2011   M 2556   M 3164
  M 3594   P 0122
THE BRITISH INVASION (book)
  RB0271
BROADCASTS (LP)
  RR0132   RR0133
"Broadstreet"   see   "Give My Regards To
    Broadstreet" (film)
Broadway
  P 0041   P 0042
Bromley, England: Lennon memorial tree
    vandalized
  N 0510
Bron, Eleanor
  N 0765
Bronstein, Stan
  M 0033
Brubeck, Dave
  M 0863
Buckingham Palace: Beatles
  N 0895
Budapest, Hungary: Ono visit
  M 2179
BUK Records
  M 3680
Butcher cover
  M 0844   M 0915
BY GEORGE! (LP)
  RR0134
BY ROYAL COMMAND (EP)
  RR0135
Calendar (Beatles)
  B 0177   B 0457   B 0458   B 0459
  B 0487   B 0488   B 0489   B 0490
Calendar (Eastman)

B 0344   B 0352
California: Beatles in Los Angeles
  M 3043
California: Beatles, 1964
  M 3452   M 3730
California: Beatles, 1965
  M 3330
California: handgun control
  M 3393
California: Harrison
  M 0082   M 1043
California: Harrison at Long Beach
    Grand Prix
  M 2861
California: Lennon in Los Angeles
  M 0502   M 0662   M 2767   M 3311
  M 3479   N 0609   N 0610
California: Lennons in Los Angeles
  M 2630
California: Lennons possible move to
    San Francisco
  M 3056
California: Los Angeles convention
  M 1833   M 2040   M 2369   M 2370
California: Los Angeles fan convention
  M 2999
California: Los Angeles Harrison visit
  M 0228
California: Los Angeles Lennon statue
  M 3182   N 0945
California: Los Angeles Wings concert
  M 0194   M 3183   N 0720
California: McCartneys plan tour
  M 2832
California: Mal Evans
  M 3313
California: San Diego Wings concert
  M 0194
California: San Francisco airport crowd
  N 0155
California: San Francisco concert
  M 0327   M 1183   N 0108
California: Starr
  M 1043
California, University of   see
    U.C.L.A.
Canada: Beatlemania
  M 0124   M 0239
Canada: Beatles
  M 0124   M 0125   M 0126   M 0127
  M 0128   M 3355
Canada: Beatles discography
  M 0129
Canada: Beatles 1964 visit
  M 1160
Canada: fan club
  F 0021   F 0026   F 0061   F 0107
Canada: Lennon
  M 1291
Canada: Lennon detained by immigration
  N 0269
Canada: Lennon in Toronto
  M 0901   M 1553   N 0274
Canada: Lennon invited to Manitoba
    peace concert
  M 2111
Canada: McCartney concert tickets
  M 2837
Canada: Montreal Lennons bed-in
  M 2596   M 3003
Canada: Toronto concert
  M 0473   M 0842
Canada: Toronto Labor Day concert
    ticket sales
  N 1061
Canada: Toronto Peace Festival
  M 0123   M 0202   M 0668   M 0670
  M 1679   M 1681   M 1688   M 1761
  M 1807   M 1894   M 1905   M 1929
  M 1930   M 2323   M 3465   M 3466
  M 3773   M 3778   N 0274   N 0275
Canada: Vancouver concert
  N 0908
"Candy" (film)
  M 1045   M 2514   M 3020   N 1048
  RF0051   RF0052   RF0053
Cannes Film Festival: Harrison film
    shown
  M 2394   N 0385

Cannes Film Festival: Lennons' film
    shown
    N 0384
"Can't Buy Me Love" (song)
    M 3489
Canterbury, Archbishop of
    N 0021
Capitol Records, Inc.
    M 0058   M 0336   M 0422   M 0438
    M 0527   M 0656   M 0657   M 0658
    M 0659   M 1166   M 1417   M 1806
    M 2011   M 2029   M 2044   M 2085
    M 2086   M 2731   M 2851   M 2881
    M 2883   M 2885   M 2939   M 3062
    M 3125   M 3338   M 3453   M 3514
    M 3688
Capitol Records, Inc.: case involving
    unauthorized use of Harrison
    material
    M 0835   M 1418
Capitol Records, Inc.: McCartney deal
    M 3285
Capitol Records, Inc.: 1982 promo
    flexi-discs
    M 3568
Capitol Records, Inc.: vs. Apple
    Corps., Ltd.
    M 3284
Caricature (Beatles)
    M 1511
Carnegie Hall, New York City
    P 0020   P 0095
Carnegie Hall, New York City: Boston
    Pops Lennon tribute concert
    N 1087
Carnegie Hall, New York City: concert
    M 3166   N 1156
Cartoons (Beatles)
    C 0106   N 0023   N 0271
Cartoons (Beatles): list of episodes
    M 2986
Cassidy, David
    M 3067
CASUALTIES (LP)
    RR0136   RR0137
"Caveman" (film)
    M 1111   M 1440   M 2905   N 0757
    N 0788   N 0944   RF0054   RF0055
    RF0056   RF0057   RF0058   RF0059
    RF0060   RF0061   RF0062   RF0063
    RF0064   RF0065   RF0066   RF0067
    RF0068   RF0069   RF0070   RF0071
    RF0072   RF0073   RF0074
Cavern Club, Liverpool, England
    F 0033   N 0164   M 0278   M 0371
    M 0687   M 0688   M 1220   M 1360
    M 1584   M 1800   M 2219   M 2466
    M 3580   M 0697
Cavern Club, Liverpool, England: fans
    fight to save
    N 0121
Cavern Club, Liverpool, England: fans
    resist club closing
    N 0248
Cavern Club, Liverpool, England: film
    made there, 1962
    M 0181
Cavern Club, Liverpool, England: museum
    M 3293
Cavern Club, Liverpool, England:
    re-opened
    M 0614   N 0641
"Cavern Club": U.S. disco renamed
    M 2336
Cavett, Dick
    M 1417   M 2691   N 0820
CBS Records
    M 2887   M 3199
CBS: scholarship at Julliard as Lennon
    memorial
    M 0689
A CELLARFUL OF NOISE (book)
    RB0272   RB0273   RB0274   RB0275
    RB0276   RB0277   RB0278   RB0279
    RB0280   RB0281   RB0282   RB0283
    RB0284
Central Park, New York City: Lennon
    tribute section "Strawberry
    Fields"

N 0281   N 0418   N 0619   N 1032
N 1172
Central Park, New York City: Lennon
    vigil tribute
    N 0909
Chapman, Mark David
    M 0695   M 1767   M 1783   M 3503
    N 0284   N 0285   N 0318   N 0344
    N 0345   N 0347   N 0358   N 0406
    N 0416   N 0466   N 0474   N 0594
    N 0627   N 0628   N 0650   N 0662
    N 0678   N 0739   N 0745   N 0771
    N 0773   N 0840   N 0900   N 0974
    N 0992   N 0993   N 0995   N 0997
    N 1037   N 1039
Chapman, Mark David: effects of actions
    on Ronald Reagan's attempted
    murderer
    N 1045
Chapman, Mark David: sentenced
    M 0693   M 0694
Chase, Chevy: on reuniting the Beatles
    M 0715
Cheech & Chong
    M 2745   M 3060
Chestnutt, David: drawing of the
    Beatles
    M 0046
Chicago, Illinois: Beatles
    M 0291
Chicago, Illinois: concert
    M 3503   N 0589
Chicago, Illinois: concert opens tour
    N 0589
Chicago, Illinois: convention
    M 1786   M 1792   M 3273
China: criticism of the Beatles
    N 0923
Chong, Tommy
    M 2745   M 3060
Christchurch, New Zealand: mob
    N 0359
Christmas billboards
    N 0566
Christmas record (McCartney)
    M 2800   M 3539   RR0546
Christmas record, 1963 [includes text]
    M 0308
Christmas record, 1964 [includes text]
    M 0049
Christmas record, 1965 [includes text]
    M 0463
Christmas record, 1966 [includes text]
    M 0339
Christmas record, 1967 [includes text]
    M 0719
Christmas record, 1968 [includes text]
    M 0401
Christmas record, 1969 [includes text]
    M 0441
Christmas record (Phil Spector)
    M 2516
Christmas records
    M 0154   M 0155   M 0307   M 1190
    M 1967
Christmas show
    M 0402   M 1011
Christmas show, 1963
    M 1630   M 1739
Christmas television special
    M 0036
Chronology (Beatles)
    B 0487   B 0488   B 0489   B 0490
    B 0562   B 0563   B 0565
Chronology (Beatles, 1962-1965)
    M 3573
Chronology (Beatles, pre-1964)
    M 3493
Chronology (Beatles, pre-1965)
    M 3472
Chronology (Beatles, pre-1967)
    M 3319
Chronology (Lennon)
    B 0564
Chronology (Wings)
    B 0593
Cincinatti Pops Orchestra: Lennon
    tribute
    M 1270

Clapton, Eric
    C 0348   M 0805   M 2382   M 2594
    M 2840   M 2892   M 2894   M 2928
Clapton, Pattie see Boyd, Pattie
Clarinet songbook (Beatles)
    S 0071   S 0113   S 0114
Clarinet songbook (Lennon/McCartney)
    S 0113   S 0114
Clark, Dick
    M 0188   M 0189   M 0554   M 0555
Clark, Dick: "Birth of the Beatles"
    (film)
    M 1109
Clay, Cassius see Ali, Muhammed
Cleave, Maureen: remembers Lennon
    M 0727
Cleveland, Ohio: bars Beatles
    M 3272   M 3503   N 0101   N 0296
Cleveland, Ohio: concert
    M 3272   M 3503   N 0102   N 0296
    N 0838
Closed circuit Beatles concert - first
    such event
    M 0311
Closed circuit tv (Beatles)
    M 2550
Les Club des 4 de Liverpool
    F 0064
Cocker, Joe
    M 2597
Cockrill, Maurice (artist)
    M 1320
COLD TURKEY FOR KAMPUCHEA (LP)
    RR0138   RR0139
Collecting Beatles memorabilia   see
    Memorabilia
COLLECTING THE BEATLES (book)
    RB0285   RB0286   RB0287   RB0288
    RB0289   RB0290   RB0291   RB0292
    RB0293   RB0294   RB0295
COLLECTING THE BEATLES (book): excerpt
    M 1099
Col. Lectiu Beatleman
    F 0121
Colored vinyl repressings
    M 0916
Coloring book (Beatles)
    B 0062
Columbia Records
    M 2887   M 3199
Columbia Records: signs McCartney
    M 2185
COME AND GET IT (LP)
    RR0140
COME BACK JOHNNY (LP)
    RR0141
"Come Together" (song)
    M 2128   M 2622
Comic book: Beatles
    P 0110
Coming Up and Lunch Box - "Odd
    Sox/Coming Up" (45)
    RR0142
"Coming Up And Lunch Box" (video)
    M 2912
Command performance, 1963
    B 0050
COMMUNISM, HYPNOTISM, AND THE BEATLES
    (book)
    RB0296
COMPLAINT TO THE QUEEN (WINGS OVER
    HOLLAND '72) (LP)
    RR0143
THE COMPLEAT BEATLES (book)
    RB0297   RB0298   RB0299   RB0300
"The Compleat Beatles" (video)
    M 0833   M 1161   RF0075
THE COMPLETE BEATLES U.S. RECORD PRICE
    GUIDE (book)
    RB0301
THE COMPLETE SILVER BEATLES (LP)
    M 0954   RR0144   RR0145
Concert for Bangladesh see also
    Bangladesh
Concert for Bangladesh (benefit
    concert)
    M 0060   M 0087   M 0134   M 0135
    M 0773   M 0824   M 1090   M 1145
    M 1239   M 1259   M 1589   M 1806

M 2028   M 2092   M 2319   M 2382
M 2662   M 2671   M 2693   M 2695
M 2703   M 2951   M 3516   N 0464
N 0690   N 0742   N 0819
Concert for Bangladesh (benefit
    concert): review
    M 0799
"The Concert for Bangla Desh" (film)
    M 0135   M 1277   RF0076   RF0077
    RF0078   RF0079   RF0080   RF0081
    RF0082   RF0083   RF0084   RF0085
    RF0086   RF0087   RF0088   RF0089
    RF0090   RF0091   RF0092   RF0093
    RF0094   RF0095   RF0096
"The Concert for Bangla Desh" (film):
    premiere
    M 2709
THE CONCERT FOR BANGLADESH (LP)
    M 0134   M 0810   M 1417   M 1806
    M 2667   M 2671   M 2676   M 2678
    M 2693   M 2695   M 3516   M 3623
    RR0146   RR0147   RR0148   RR0149
    RR0150   RR0151
CONCERTS FOR THE PEOPLE OF KAMPUCHEA
    (LP)
    RR0152   RR0153   RR0154   RR0155
"Condensed Cream of Beatles" (film)
    see "Braverman's Condensed Cream
    of Beatles" (film)
Congress, U.S.: Beatle banner
    N 0046
Connolly, Ray
    N 0864
"The Cooler" (film)
    M 2399   M 2447
Cooper, Paul: Lennon's death
    M 3700
Copenhagen, Denmark: Wings concert
    M 3408
Cosell, Howard
    M 2799
"Count Down" (film)
    M 3058
Cox, Kyoko
    M 1727   M 1840   M 3777   N 0377
    N 0822   N 1169
Cox, Maureen: divorces Ringo Starr
    N 0273   N 0936
Cox, Maureen: expecting third child
    M 2640
Cox, Maureen: photograph with Pattie
    Boyd, Jenny Boyd and Cynthia
    Powell
    M 2379
Cox, Maureen: photograph with Starr
    M 1467
Cox, Maureen: returns from India with
    Starr
    N 0182
Cox, Maureen: weds Ringo Starr
    M 0776   N 0169
Cox, Tony
    N 0377   N 1171
Cracow, Poland: fans convention
    M 2175
Cream
    M 2595
"Creem Magazine": readers poll
    M 2960   M 2961
The Crickets
    M 2867
Crossword puzzle (Beatles)
    M 1958   M 3439
Croyden, England: Beatles concert
    M 1498
"Crying in the Chapel" (song)
    N 0321   N 0897
Czechoslovakia: release of "A Hard
    Day's Night" (film)
    M 0333
The Dakota
    C 0060   M 1762
The Dakota: Lennons move into New York
    City apartment house
    N 1068
DARK HORSE (LP)
    M 0137   M 2194   M 2808   RR0156
    RR0157   RR0158   RR0159   RR0160
    RR0161   RR0162   RR0163   RR0164

RR0165   RR0166
Dark Horse Records
    M 0001   M 1414   M 2782   M 2850
    N 0332
"Dark Horse" (song)
    M 1164
Dave Clark Five
    P 0052   P 0065
"David Frost" (tv show)
    N 0103
Davies, Hunter
    N 0430   N 0842   N 0917   N 1064
    N 1126
Davis, Jesse
    M 2672
DAWN OF THE SILVER BEATLES (LP)
    M 3287
A DAY IN THE LIFE (book)
    M 2506   RB0302   RB0303   RB0304
    RB0305   RB0306   RB0307   RB0308
    RB0309   RB0310   RB0311   RB0312
    RB0313   RB0314   RB0315   RB0316
    RB0317   RB0318   RB0319   RB0320
    RB0321
"A Day In The Life" (song)
    M 0350
"Days In Their Lives" (documentary)
    N 0322
"Day Tripper" (song)
    M 0476
Decca audition
    M 0908   M 1461   M 1644   M 2134
Decca audition recording
    M 2460
THE DECCA TAPES (LP)
    M 0947   M 1361   M 2500   RR0167
    RR0168
DEFACE THE MUSIC (LP)
    M 3518
Delaney & Bonnie
    M 1519   M 2606
Delaware, University of: course on
    Beatles and Lennon
    N 0314
Delmonico's, New York City: siege of
    Beatle fans
    N 0774
Delphi, Greece: Beatle fans
    N 0149
Denmark: Lennon's death
    M 1347
Denmark: Wings Copenhagen concert
    M 3408
DeShannon, Jackie
    M 3764
Detroit, Michigan: anti-Beatle movement
    M 3777   N 0243
Detroit, Michigan: Lennon lithographs
    N 0668
"Dick Cavett" (tv show)
    N 0820
DiLello, Richard
    M 3546
Discography (Apple Records)
    B 0375   M 0057   M 0945
Discography (Beatles)
    B 0049   B 0108   B 0109   B 0110
    B 0111   B 0112   B 0228   B 0229
    B 0230   B 0333   B 0360   B 0361
    B 0362   B 0363   B 0375   B 0446
    B 0447   B 0471   C 0014   C 0095
    C 0284   M 0011   M 0129   M 0621
    M 0661   M 0891   M 0892   M 0949
    M 0950   M 1157   M 1349   M 1701
    M 1820   M 1821   M 3138   M 3205
    M 3494
Discography (Beatles): Australian
    M 1880
Discography (Beatles): bootlegs
    M 2573   M 3740
Discography (Beatles): Brazilian
    M 0661
Discography (Beatles): Canadian
    M 0129
Discography (Beatles): cover versions
    of Beatle songs
    M 1428
Discography (Beatles): Danish
    B 0228   B 0229

Discography (Beatles): Dutch
    B 0559   M 1881   M 1882
Discography (Beatles): EPs
    M 0949
Discography (Beatles): French
    B 0167   B 0168   B 0169   M 1097
    M 1883
Discography (Beatles): German
    B 0055   B 0280
Discography (Beatles): Hamburg
    recordings
    M 0950
Discography (Beatles): Hungarian
    B 0556   B 0557
Discography (Beatles): international
    B 0596
Discography (Beatles): Italian
    B 0031   B 0220   M 1076   M 1097
    M 3205
Discography (Beatles): Japanese
    B 0541
Discography: Beatles-like LPs
    M 3382
Discography (Beatles): live concert
    recordigs
    M 1391
Discography (Beatles): novelty records
    B 0465
Discography (Beatles): Spanish
    B 0337   B 0510
Discography (Harrison)
    M 0957
Discography (Lennon)
    M 0935   M 0936   M 0959   M 0960
    M 0961   M 1348   M 1701   M 3117
Discography (Lennon): French
    B 0564
Discography (McCartney)
    B 0156   B 0593   M 0965   M 0966
Discography (Ono)
    M 0959
Discography (Spector)
    M 2521
Discography (Starr - Ring O' Records)
    M 0524   M 0525
Discography (Wings)
    B 0156   B 0593   M 3555
Dissertation see Beatles: as subject
    of dissertation
District of Columbia see Washington,
    D.C.
Dr. John
    M 2739   M 2767   M 2826
Dolenz, Micky
    M 1626
Dorinish, Ireland: Lennon gift
    N 0480
Double bass songbook (Beatles)
    S 0106
DOUBLE FANTASY (LP)
    M 0718   M 0739   M 0955   M 1089
    M 2893   M 2903   M 2915   M 2916
    M 2930   M 3087   M 3266   M 3398
    N 0322   N 0478   N 0852   N 0884
    RR0169   RR0170   RR0171   RR0172
    RR0173   RR0174   RR0175   RR0176
    RR0177   RR0178   RR0179   RR0180
DOWN AND OUT? (LP)
    RR0181   RR0182
Drugs
    N 0085
Drugs: Beatles
    N 0895
Drugs: Boyd, Jenny
    M 2275   M 3052   N 0431   N 0432
Drugs: Boyd, Pattie
    N 0058   N 0059   N 0062   N 0724
Drugs: Eastman
    M 2818   N 0502   N 0575   N 0579
Drugs: Epstein
    N 0892
Drugs: Harrison
    N 0058   N 0059   N 0062   N 0354
    N 0724
Drugs: Lennon
    M 2255   N 0509   N 0555   N 0645
    N 0646   N 0659   N 0666   N 0714
    N 0866
Drugs: McCartney

M 0252   M 0853   M 0987   M 1798
M 1830   M 1831   M 2405   M 2412
M 2420   M 2908   M 3396   M 3589
N 0129   N 0326   N 0398   N 0511
N 0538   N 0542   N 0575   N 0726
N 0729   N 0731   N 0824   N 0869
N 0870   N 0873   N 1114
Drugs: Ono
   M 2255   N 0645   N 0646
Drugs: Starr
   N 0515
Drums: Starr
   M 1375
Dubrow, Kevin
   M 3764
Dylan, Bob
   M 0252   M 0992   M 0993   M 2644
   M 2682   M 2703   M 2845   M 2927
   M 2928   M 3521
Dylan, Bob: records with Harrison and
      Starr
   M 0583
EARLY YEARS (LP)
   RR0183
East Germany: Beatles
   M 0995
East Germany: Beatles as heroes
   N 0978
East Germany: fan club
   F 0020
Eastman, Linda
   B 0344   B 0345   B 0346   B 0347
   B 0348   B 0349   B 0350   B 0351
   B 0352   B 0353   B 0139   B 0140
   M 0925   M 1057   M 1286   M 1289
   M 1494   M 1773   M 1857   M 1877
   M 1998   M 2000   M 2037   M 2200
   M 2203   M 2211   M 2260   M 2441
   M 2445   M 2592   M 2657   M 2811
   M 2815   M 2816   M 2832   M 2941
   M 3023   M 3084   M 3501   N 0417
   N 0577   N 0763
Eastman, Linda: as composer
   M 1999
Eastman, Linda: as McCartney
      songwriting collaborator
   M 3373
Eastman, Linda: as photographer
   M 2055   N 1140
Eastman, Linda: birth of daughter Mary
   N 0288   N 0333
Eastman, Linda: birth of daughter
      Stella
   M 2677
Eastman, Linda: birth of son James
      Louis
   M 2868
Eastman, Linda: calendar
   B 0344   B 0352
Eastman, Linda: drug arrest
   M 2818   N 0575
Eastman, Linda: drug charge
   N 0502
Eastman, Linda: drug charge dismissed
   N 0579
Eastman, Linda: expecting a baby
   N 0499
Eastman, Linda: expecting birth of
      fourth McCartney child
   N 0614
Eastman, Linda: film short
   M 2454
Eastman, Linda: incognito at Harrison
      concert
   M 3289
Eastman, Linda: interview
   M 1385   M 3626   N 0694   N 1140
Eastman, Linda: marriage plans to Paul
      McCartney
   M 2592   N 0145
Eastman, Linda: on Carly Simon LP
   M 2725
Eastman, Linda: on holiday in Greece
   M 2398
Eastman, Linda: party for new LP
   M 2030
Eastman, Linda: photography
   M 1071   M 1731   N 0449
Eastman, Linda: search for country home

M 2230
Eastman, Linda: solo activity
   M 2942   M 3002
Eastman, Linda: sued on "Another Day"
      recording
   N 0717
Eastman, Linda: U.S.A.
   N 0060
Eastman, Linda: weds Paul McCartney
   N 0082   N 0724   N 1130
"Ebony and Ivory/Rainclouds" (45)
   M 0956   RR0184   RR0185   RR0186
"Ebony and Ivory/Rainclouds" (song)
   M 1329   M 1330
Edelmann, Heinz
   M 1167
Edinburgh, Scotland: Beatles
   N 0794   M 0314   M 3191
Edinburgh, Scotland: concert
   M 0314
"Ed Sullivan Show" (tv show)
   M 3764   N 0433   N 0440   N 0441
E.H. Morris Music: bought by McCartney
   M 2184
"Eleanor Rigby" (sculpture by Tommy
      Steele)
   M 3294   N 1023
"Eleanor Rigby" (song)
   M 0012   M 0501
Electrical and Mechanical Industries
      see E.M.I.
ELECTRONIC SOUNDS (LP)
   RR0187
Elephant's Memory
   M 0033   M 0977   M 2083   M 2715
   M 2724
E.M.I.
   C 0131   C 0195   M 0902   M 3678
E.M.I.: Beatles contract
   M 0433   M 1321
E.M.I.: Beatles sign contract to expire
      in 1975
   M 2239
E.M.I.: Beatles 20th anniversary
   M 1192
E.M.I.: effect of Beatle record sales
   M 0296   M 0297   M 0482   M 1166
   N 0387
E.M.I.: export recordings
   M 0109
E.M.I.: finds 20 unreleased studio
      tracks of Beatles
   M 0926
E.M.I.: has to ration supply of THE
      BEATLES (LP)
   N 0363
E.M.I.: Lennon "ROOTS" LP
   M 1961
E.M.I.: pays royalty for "Kansas
      City/Hey, Hey" (song medley)
   M 1479
E.M.I.: plans greatest hits package and
      tv promotion
   M 1016
E.M.I.: re-issues records for twentieth
      anniversary
   M 3431
E.M.I.: unreleased recordings
   M 0108   M 0953   M 2488   M 2656
England: ABC Theatre, Blackpool
   C 0340
England: Beatles in Hampden
   M 3582
England: Beatles in Leeds
   N 1001
England: Beatles in Liverpool
   M 2391   M 3295   M 3335
England: Beatles in London
   M 0376   M 0494
England: Beatles in Wolverhampton
   N 0312
England: Beatles-related landmarks
   B 0033   B 0034   B 0035   B 0036
   B 0188   B 0566
England: Beatles return
   C 0326   N 0113   N 0139   N 0150
   N 0168   N 0901   N 1117   N 1142
England: Bournemouth concert
   M 0887   M 0909

England: Croyden concert
   M 1498
England: fan club
   F 0014   F 0027   F 0029   F 0032
   F 0034   F 0042   F 0055   F 0057
   F 0058   F 0059   F 0063   F 0071
   F 0078   F 0089   F 0123   F 0130
   F 0138   F 0139   F 0141   F 0145
England: fans at London Airport
   N 0079
England: Leicester concert
   N 1104
England: Liverpool
   M 1430   M 1431   M 2479   M 3153
England: Liverpool Beatles-related
      landmarks
   M 0528   M 1204   M 1429   M 1459
England: Liverpool Beatle street names
   M 2533   M 3367   N 0324   N 0754
England: Liverpool Cavern Club
   M 3580
England: Liverpool concert
   M 1451
England: Liverpool fan convention
   O 0110   M 2472   M 2998   M 3524
   M 3542
England: Liverpool Lennon tribute
   M 3497
England: Liverpool museum
   M 1561   M 2476   M 3293
England: Liverpool's "Beatles
      Information Centre"
   M 2476
England: Liverpool school McCartney
      concert
   M 2904
England: Liverpool's Magical Mystery
      Store
   M 2467
England: Liverpool statue
   M 1445   M 2009   M 2870
England: London Beatles apartment
   M 0907
England: London Beatles concerts
   M 0376
England: London Beatles-related
      landmarks
   M 1006   M 1432   M 1433
England: London concert planned
   M 0450
England: London concerts
   M 0376
England: London memorabilia store
   M 2008
England: London mob
   N 0079   N 0890
England: London Wings concert
   M 0630
England: McCartney in Liverpool
   M 1773
England: McCartney in London
   M 3112
England: Manchester Wings concert
   M 3299
England: Newcastle-upon-Tyne concert
      ticket sales
   N 0351
England: 1963 tour
   M 0280   M 3428
England: 1964 tour map
   M 1107
England: 1965 tour
   M 3291
England: 1966 tour
   M 1634
England: 1975 Wings tour
   M 3738
England: Norwich fan convention
   M 1362   M 1374
England: Official Fan Club
   M 0177
England: return of Starr and wife
   N 0182
England: Sheffield fan convention
   M 2471
England: top LPs
   M 2034
England: twentieth anniversary re-issue
      of records

M 3431
England: Wimbledon fan convention
    M 0897
England: Wings tour announced
    M 3748
England: Wolverhampton concert
    M 0899 N 0312
English, Joe: interview
    M 1587
Epstein, Brian
    B 0178 B 0179 B 0180 B 0181
    B 0182 B 0183 B 0184 B 0185
    C 0100 C 0101 C 0102 M 0125
    M 0160 M 0161 M 0162 M 0163
    M 0182 M 0248 M 0491 M 0563
    M 0568 M 0604 M 0605 M 0606
    M 0650 M 0771 M 0894 M 0895
    M 1024 M 1026 M 1027 M 1028
    M 1029 M 1059 M 1567 M 1748
    M 2007 M 2198 M 2469 M 2527
    M 2987 M 3575 M 3754 N 0178
    N 0635
Epstein, Brian: as concert promoter
    M 3464
Epstein, Brian: Beatles not to replace
    him as manager
    N 0203
Epstein, Brian: burial
    N 0366
Epstein, Brian: death
    M 0607 M 1965 N 0237 N 0238
Epstein, Brian: death called accidental
    N 0235 N 0364
Epstein, Brian: discovers the Beatles
    M 0150 M 3670
Epstein, Brian: estate
    M 0328 N 0710
Epstein, Brian: eulogy
    M 3473
Epstein, Brian: funeral
    N 0484
Epstein, Brian: inquest at death
    N 0365 N 0366 N 0367 N 0528
Epstein, Brian: interview
    M 0160 M 1480 M 1482
Epstein, Brian: lawyers seek will
    N 0484
Epstein, Brian: Lennon remark on
    popularity of Beatles and Jesus
    N 0141
Epstein, Brian: letter from Tony Barrow
    on SHOUT! (book)
    N 0234
Epstein, Brian: NEMS Enterprises, Ltd.
    merger
    N 0236
Epstein, Brian: 1963 visit with Tony
    Barrow
    M 0151
Epstein, Brian: obituary
    N 0833
Epstein, Brian: police study pills
    N 0892
Epstein, Brian: prediction of Beatles'
    future
    M 0751
Epstein, Brian: relationship with
    Beatles
    N 0469
Epstein, Brian: relationship with
    Lennon
    C 0217
Epstein, Brian: sexual rumors of Lennon
    N 0232
Epstein, Clive
    M 0606
Epstein, Clive: interview
    M 2987
Epstein, Clive: resigns as NEMS
    Enterprises, Ltd. director
    N 0256
Epstein, Clive: vs. Beatles
    N 1162
Epstein, Clive: writ against Beatles
    N 0002
Europe: Beatles
    M 1478
Evans, Mal
    M 0081 M 0901 M 1034 M 1035

M 1036 M 1037 M 1038 M 1039
M 1040 M 1041 M 1042 M 1043
M 1044 M 1045 M 1046 M 1047
M 1048 M 1049 M 1050 M 1051
M 1052 M 1053 M 1054 M 1055
M 1056 M 1173 M 1233 M 1583
M 2109 M 2772
Evans, Mal: killed in Los Angeles
    M 3313
Evans, Tom
    M 0099 M 0100
Every Little Thing
    F 0063
EVERY LITTLE THING (book)
    RB0322 RB0323
EXTRA TEXTURE (LP)
    M 1219 M 2827 RR0188 RR0189
    RR0190 RR0191 RR0192 RR0193
    RR0194
"The Fab Four Publication" (magazine)
    M 2102
THE FACTS ABOUT A POP GROUP - FEATURING
    WINGS (book)
    RB0324 RB0325
Fairfield, Iowa: Maharishi Makesh Yogi
    M 1399
Family trees
    M 2250
Family trees (Beatles)
    B 0267
Fan club (Beatles)
    B 0142 F 0001 F 0002 F 0003
    F 0004 F 0005 F 0006 F 0007
    F 0008 F 0009 F 0010 F 0011
    F 0012 F 0013 F 0014 F 0015
    F 0016 F 0017 F 0018 F 0019
    F 0020 F 0021 F 0022 F 0023
    F 0024 F 0025 F 0026 F 0027
    F 0028 F 0029 F 0030 F 0031
    F 0032 F 0033 F 0034 F 0035
    F 0036 F 0037 F 0038 F 0039
    F 0040 F 0041 F 0042 F 0043
    F 0044 F 0045 F 0046 F 0047
    F 0048 F 0049 F 0050 F 0051
    F 0052 F 0053 F 0054 F 0055
    F 0056 F 0057 F 0059 F 0060
    F 0061 F 0062 F 0063 F 0064
    F 0065 F 0066 F 0067 F 0068
    F 0072 F 0073 F 0074 F 0075
    F 0078 F 0079 F 0080 F 0081
    F 0082 F 0083 F 0084 F 0085
    F 0086 F 0091 F 0096 F 0097
    F 0098 F 0108 F 0109 F 0110
    F 0111 F 0112 F 0113 F 0116
    F 0117 F 0119 F 0120 F 0121
    F 0122 F 0123 F 0126 F 0129
    F 0131 F 0132 F 0133 F 0136
    F 0137 F 0138 F 0143 F 0144
    F 0145 F 0147 F 0148 F 0151
    F 0152 F 0153 F 0154 F 0155
    F 0156 F 0157 M 1664 M 2004
    M 2033 M 2338
Fan club (Beatles): Christmas record
    M 0307
Fan club (Beatles): Christmas record,
    1963 [includes text]
    M 0308
Fan club (Beatles): Christmas record,
    1964 [includes text]
    M 0049
Fan club (Beatles): Christmas record,
    1965 [includes text]
    M 0463
Fan club (Beatles): Christmas record,
    1966 [includes text]
    M 0339
Fan club (Beatles): Christmas record,
    1967 [includes text]
    M 0719
Fan club (Beatles): Christmas record,
    1968 [includes text]
    M 0401
Fan club (Beatles): Christmas record,
    1969 [includes text]
    M 0441
Fan club (Beatles): Christmas record,
    1977
    M 1190
Fan club (Beatles): Liverpool, England

C 0327 M 1012 M 1646
Fan club (Beatles): official U.K.
    M 0177
Fan club "book"
    B 0414 B 0415
Fan club (Harrison)
    F 0004 F 0060 F 0070 F 0071
    F 0076 F 0077 F 0084 F 0110
    F 0126 F 0146
Fan club (Lennon)
    F 0059 F 0065 F 0081 F 0085
    F 0087 F 0088 F 0089 F 0090
    F 0092 F 0093 F 0094 F 0095
    F 0108 F 0118 F 0131 F 0146
    F 0152 F 0153
Fan club (McCartney) see also Fan
    club (Wings)
Fan club (McCartney)
    F 0025 F 0026 F 0058 F 0067
    F 0099 F 0100 F 0101 F 0102
    F 0103 F 0104 F 0105 F 0106
    F 0107 F 0108 F 0134 F 0135
Fan club (McCartney, Mike)
    B 0114 F 0069
Fan club magazine see Fan club
Fan club (Ono)
    F 0115 F 0124 F 0125 F 0131
    F 0158
Fan club secretaries
    M 1653 M 2004 M 2338 M 3507
    M 3508
Fan club (Starr)
    F 0122 F 0139 F 0140 F 0141
Fan club (Wings) see also Fan club
    (McCartney)
Fan club (Wings)
    F 0025 F 0026 F 0058 F 0149
    F 0150
Fan convention see also Beatlefest
Fan convention
    M 0880 M 0897 M 1202 M 1203
    M 1263 M 1266 M 1386 M 1786
    M 1792 M 1798 M 1823 M 1833
    M 1860 M 1986 M 2040 M 2175
    M 2369 M 2393 M 2471 M 2472
    M 2792 M 2981 M 2998 M 2999
    M 3259 M 3273 M 3380 M 3390
    M 3515 M 3524 M 3534 M 3542
    M 3759 N 0109
Fan convention: first British
    M 1362 M 1374
Fans see Beatle fans
Fanzine see Fan club (Beatles)
Fashion: influence of Beatles
    N 0445
Fast, Julius
    N 0430
F.B.I.
    B 0582 M 0244 M 2971 M 3693
    N 0025 N 0378
FEELING THE SPACE (LP)
    M 1801 M 2759 RR0195 RR0196
    RR0197 RR0198 RR0199
"Fenian's Ram"
    N 0867
"Film No. 4" (film)
    M 2360 M 2383 RF0097
"Film No. 5" (film)
    M 1941 M 2360
Filmography (Beatles)
    B 0167 B 0168 B 0169 B 0241
Filmography (Beatles): French
    B 0167 B 0168 B 0169
Film review see individual film
    titles
Film(s) see individual film title(s)
FIRST LIVE RECORDINGS, VOL. I (LP)
    RR0200
FIRST LIVE RECORDINGS, VOL. II (LP)
    RR0201
FIVE NIGHTS IN A JUDO ARENA (LP)
    RR0202
Flack, Roberta: Lennon tribute
    performance
    N 0482
Florida: Beatles in Miami
    M 3316 N 0407
Florida: Lennons buy home
    M 2910

Florida: Miami arrival for "Ed Sullivan
    Show"
    N 0433
Florida: Miami fan riot
    N 0405 N 0433
Flute songbook (Beatles)
    S 0041 S 0072 S 0115 S 0116
Flute songbook (Lennon/McCartney)
    S 0115 S 0116
"Fly" (film)
    RF0098 RF0099
"Fly" (film): filming
    M 3558
FLY (LP)
    M 1676 RR0203 RR0204
FOLLOW THE MERSEYBEAT ROAD (book)
    RB0326
Fonda, Jane
    M 1903
Ford, Gerald
    N 0612
Forest Hills Stadium, New York City:
    concert
    N 0985
Fort Worth, Texas: McCartney tour
    starts
    N 0954
FOUR BY THE BEATLES (EP)
    RR0205
Frampton, Peter
    M 2706
France: Beatles
    M 1481
France: Beatles discography
    M 1097
France: Beatles in Paris
    M 0023 M 0051 M 0464 M 2169
    M 3220 N 0037 P 0034
France: fan club
    F 0064
France: Paris Beatles film
    retrospective
    M 0023 M 0600
France: Paris concert
    M 0774 N 0037 N 0132
France: Wings Paris concert
    M 3405
France: Wings tour
    M 2072 N 1078 N 1122
FRANCOIS GLORIEUX PLAYS THE BEATLES,
    VOL. 2 (LP)
    RR0206
Frank, Rick
    M 0033
Franklin, Aretha
    M 2607
Friar Park (Harrison home)
    N 0067
FROM A WHISPER TO A SHOUT (LP)
    RR0207
FROM US TO YOU (LP)
    RR0208
Frost, David
    M 0620 M 1191 N 0103
Furniture design company (Starr)
    M 2721
Furtseva, Minister: invites Beatles to
    discuss U.S.S.R. visit
    N 0211
Gabriel, Wayne
    M 0033
Gaitskell, Lady
    N 0164
Garbarini, Vic: McCartney interview
    M 2064 M 2065 M 2066
Garcia, Jerry
    M 2701
Gates, Bill: interview
    M 0692
Geffen, David
    M 2510
Geffen Records
    M 2950
Genealogy (Beatles)
    B 0267 M 2250
George Harrison Fan Club - OBFC
    F 0070 F 0077
GEORGE HARRISON (LP)
    M 1364 M 1978 RR0209 RR0210

RR0211 RR0212 RR0213 RR0214
    RR0215 RR0216
GEORGE HARRISON 1974 (LP)
    RR0217
GEORGE HARRISON: YESTERDAY AND TODAY
    (book)
    RB0327 RB0328 RB0329
Georgia: Atlanta concert
    M 3376 N 0160
Germany see also East Germany
Germany
    M 0358
Germany: Beatles
    C 0044 M 0358 M 3510
Germany: Beatles in Hamburg
    C 0023 C 0223 C 0326 M 0674
    M 1500 M 1501 M 1502 M 1503
    M 1504 M 1505 M 1506 M 1507
    M 1508 M 1509 M 3296 M 3297
    M 3459 M 3560 N 0779
Germany: Beatles in Hamburg - parody
    M 1560
Germany: Beatles invited to Berlin by
    British army garrison
    N 1052 N 0200
Germany: Beatles mobs
    M 1345 M 1346
Germany: Beatles, 1966
    M 3474
Germany: Beatles recordings
    C 0041
Germany: Beatles-related events
    M 3119 M 3120
Germany: fan club
    F 0025 F 0040 F 0041 F 0045
    F 0068 F 0072 F 0088 F 0140
    F 0144 F 0149 F 0150
Germany: Hamburg fan riot
    N 0404
Germany: Harrison deported from Hamburg
    M 3296
Germany: Munich entertainment tax
    N 0413
Germany: Munich Wings concert
    M 0118
Germany: record market effected by
    Beatles
    M 1344
Germany: Star Club, Hamburg
    B 0071 C 0223 M 1247 M 1426
    M 2604
Gerry and the Pacemakers
    M 2302
"Get Back" (film): premiere
    M 3656
'GET BACK' (LP) see also LET IT BE
    (LP)
'GET BACK' (LP)
    M 0342 M 0343 M 1034 M 1252
    M 1253 M 1663 M 2267 M 2599
    M 2602 RR0218
'GET BACK' (LP): bootlegs
    M 3327
'Get Back' sessions
    M 0952
Gibraltar, Spain: Lennon wedding
    N 0561
Gibson, Bob: caricatures of the Beatles
    M 0673
Gibson, Mike
    M 0099 M 0100
Gilmore, Voyle
    M 3201
Ginsberg, Allen
    M 3764
"The Girl Is Mine" (45)
    RR0219
"Give Ireland Back To The Irish" (song)
    M 1485 M 2415 M 2508 M 3605
    N 0055 N 0531
"Give My Regards to Broadstreet" (film)
    M 2948
"Give Peace A Chance" (film)
    M 2621
"Give Peace A Chance" (song)
    M 1690 M 1908
Glasgow, Scotland
    N 0490
Glasgow, Scotland: concert

N 0388 N 0389
Glasgow, Scotland: McCartney visit
    N 0722
Glasgow, Scotland: queues
    M 1258
Goldbach, Barbara see Bach, Barbara
GOLDEN GREATEST HITS (LP)
    RR0220
Gold records
    M 1590
GONE TROPPO (LP)
    RR0221 RR0222 RR0223 RR0224
    RR0225 RR0226
"Good Day Sunshine" (song)
    M 0829
Goodman, Benny
    M 1302
"Goodnight Tonight/Daytime Nightime
    Suffering" (45)
    RR0227
"Goodnight Tonight" (song)
    N 0796
GOODNIGHT VIENNA (LP)
    RR0228 RR0229 RR0230 RR0231
    RR0232 RR0233 RR0234
The Goody Press
    F 0016
"Gotta Sing Gotta Dance" (tv special)
    M 3314
Grafton Ballroom, Liverpool, England:
    Beatles
    M 3335
Graham, Bill: Lennon's death
    M 3700
Graham, Billy: on McCartney
    N 0068
Grammy Award: Beatles
    M 1856 N 0467
Grammy Award: DOUBLE FANTASY (LP)
    N 0852
Grammy Award: Harrison
    N 0942
Grammy Award: Lennon
    M 1133 M 2708
Grand Prix, Long Beach, California:
    Harrison
    M 2861
GRAPEFRUIT (book)
    N 1072 RB0330 RB0331 RB0332
    RB0333
Great Britain see England; Scotland;
    Ireland
Greece: Beatle hair styles banned
    N 0970
Greece: Beatles visit
    M 1056
Greece: Delphi crowds
    N 0149
Greece: Delphi fans
    N 0149
Greece: Lennon
    M 1926
Greece: McCartneys on holiday
    M 2398
Greenwich Village, New York: Lennon
    M 3302
GROWING UP WITH THE BEATLES (book)
    RB0334 RB0335 RB0336 RB0337
GUINNESS BOOK OF WORLD RECORDS
    [McCartney award]
    N 0705 M 2068 M 3449
Guitars (Harrison)
    M 1365
Guitars (Lennon)
    M 1372
Guitar songbook NOTE: Guitar chord
    boxes may also be found in many
    piano/vocal songbooks.
Guitar songbook (Beatles)
    S 0016 S 0020 S 0024 S 0025
    S 0Q26 S 0027 S 0028 S 0033
    S 0035 S 0036 S 0037 S 0042
    S 0043 S 0046 S 0075 S 0085
    S 0107 S 0111 S 0137 S 0140
Guitar songbook (Harrison)
    S 0088
Guitar songbook (Lennon)
    S 0146
Guitar songbook (Lennon/McCartney)

S 0085
Guitar songbook (McCartney)
  S 0132   S 0157
Gun control: effect of Lennon's death
  M 0519   M 0655   M 1033   M 1819
  N 0452
Hain, Peter
  N 0780
Hair styles: influence of Beatles
  M 0020   M 1512   M 3167   M 3664
  N 0302   N 0303   N 0443   N 0459
  N 0460   N 0493   N 0708   N 0709
  N 0970   P 0003
Hamburg, Germany
  C 0073   N 0779
Hamburg, Germany: Beatles
  C 0023   C 0044   C 0073   C 0223
  C 0326   M 0125   M 0674   M 1197
  M 1198   M 1426   M 1500   M 1501
  M 1502   M 1503   M 1504   M 1505
  M 1506   M 1507   M 1508   M 1509
  M 3296   M 3297   M 3459   M 3560
  N 0779
Hamburg, Germany: Beatles memorabilia
  M 1503
Hamburg, Germany: Beatles parody
  M 1560
Hamburg, Germany: fans riot
  N 0404
Hamburg, Germany: Harrison deportation
  M 3296
Hamburg, Germany: riot by fans
  N 0404
"Hamburg Tapes"
  M 0125   M 0675   M 0948   M 1031
  M 1393   M 1505   M 1509   M 1968
  M 2144   M 2756   M 3004   M 3012
  M 3468   M 3676   M 3680
"Hamburg Tapes": release dispute
  M 0332   M 0628   M 0834
Ham, Pete
  M 0099   M 0100   M 0850
Handel Medallion
  M 2925
Handmade Films
  N 0422
"HANDS ACROSS THE WATER": WINGS TOUR
    USA (book)
  RB0338   RB0339
Hanratty murder case
  N 0653
Hanratty murder case [film]
  N 0504
"Happy Christmas" (song)
  M 2511   M 2694
"A Hard Day's Night" (film)
  B 0064   B 0089   B 0090   B 0091
  B 0159   B 0160   B 0161   B 0162
  C 0161   C 0162   C 0281   M 0155
  M 0448   M 1119   M 1540   M 2361
  M 2572   M 3226   M 3372   M 3587
  M 3666   M 3694   N 0123   N 0176
  N 0766   N 0837   N 1136   P 0030
  P 0039   P 0048   RF0100   RF0101
  RF0102   RF0103   RF0104   RF0105
  RF0106   RF0107   RF0108   RF0109
  RF0110   RF0111   RF0112   RF0113
  RF0114   RF0115
"A Hard Day's Night" (film): ad
    campaign
  M 0439
"A Hard Day's Night" (film): filming
  M 1475   M 1476   M 2298   M 3130
  M 3224   M 3225
"A Hard Day's Night" (film): music
  M 3418
"A Hard Day's Night" (film): 1981
    re-release
  N 0963
"A Hard Day's Night" (film): parody
  M 3258
"A Hard Day's Night" (film): premiere -
    New York
  M 3347
"A Hard Day's Night" (film): preview
  N 1113
"A Hard Day's Night" (film): re-release
  N 0045
A HARD DAY'S NIGHT (LP)

M 0448   RR0235
A HARD ROAD (LP)
  RR0236
Harmonica songbook (Beatles)
  S 0044
Harrison, Dhani: birth
  M 2877   M 2878   N 0616
Harrison, George
  B 0238   B 0239   B 0240   B 0381
  B 0382   B 0560   C 0018   C 0115
  C 0136   C 0293   C 0159   N 0204
  M 0227   M 0566   M 0570   M 0680
  M 0681   M 0682   M 0734   M 0754
  M 0758   M 0805   M 0858   M 0859
  M 0979   M 1010   M 1142   M 1154
  M 1171   M 1178   M 1212   M 1232
  M 1238   M 1243   M 1248   M 1262
  M 1297   M 1411   M 1611   M 1732
  M 1979   M 2021   M 2024   M 2229
  M 2269   M 2289   M 2314   M 2357
  M 2373   M 2375   M 2416   M 2526
  M 2566   M 2580   M 2590   M 2643
  M 2661   M 2668   M 2674   M 2682
  M 2697   M 2730   M 2733   M 2748
  M 2752   M 2769   M 2797   M 2807
  M 2817   M 2873   M 2891   M 2919
  M 2928   M 2952   M 2963   M 2972
  M 3023   M 3066   M 3073   M 3088
  M 3107   M 3115   M 3133   M 3194
  M 3197   M 3204   M 3223   M 3227
  M 3265   M 3270   M 3308   M 3407
  M 3442   M 3485   M 3504   M 3505
  M 3552   M 3623   M 3673   M 3676
  M 3688   M 3728   N 0371   N 0741
  N 0778   N 0859   N 0914   P 0070
Harrison, George: A & M Records
  M 0001   M 0227   M 0229   M 3283
Harrison, George: A & M Records dispute
  M 2847
Harrison, George: activity after
    Lennon's Death
  N 0072
Harrison, George: Andy Williams
    recording session
  M 2747
Harrison, George: as a child
  M 3784
Harrison, George: as a vegetarian
  N 0597
Harrison, George: as composer
  C 0262   M 1616
Harrison, George: as lead guitarist
  M 2357
Harrison, George: as producer of "Time
    Bandits" (film)
  N 0422
Harrison, George: as record producer
  M 2112
Harrison, George: assaults photographer
  N 0076
Harrison, George: at Jerry Garcia
    concert
  M 2701
Harrison, George: at Starr's wedding
  M 2187
Harrison, George: autobiography
  B 0238   B 0239   B 0240
Harrison, George: back together with
    Lennon and Starr
  M 0085
Harrison, George: barred in India
  N 0506
Harrison, George: biography
  C 0116   C 0544
Harrison, George: birth of son Dhani
  M 2877   M 2878   N 0616
Harrison, George: Bob Marley concert
  M 2824
Harrison, George: Bombay, India
    interview
  N 0206
Harrison, George: Bombay, India
    recording visit
  M 1042
Harrison, George: bootlegs
  M 1363   M 1413
Harrison, George: brief biography
  C 0055   C 0116
Harrison, George: California

M 0082   M 1043
Harrison, George: Cannes film festival
  M 2394
Harrison, George: career after Beatles
  B 0075   B 0076   M 0822   M 3262
  M 3379
Harrison, George: childhood photographs
  C 0110
Harrison, George: concert for
    Bangladesh   see also   Concert for
    Bangladesh
Harrison, George: concert for
    Bangladesh
  M 0060   M 0087   M 0134   M 0135
  M 0773   M 0824   M 1090   M 1145
  M 1239   M 1259   M 1589   M 1806
  M 2028   M 2092   M 2319   M 2382
  M 2662   M 2671   M 2693   M 2695
  M 2703   M 2951   M 3516   N 0464
  N 0690   N 0742   N 0819
Harrison, George: concert for
    Bangladesh - film premiere
  M 2709
Harrison, George: concert for
    Bangladesh - fund investigation
  M 2712
Harrison, George: concert for
    Bangladesh - recording
  M 0810   M 1417   M 2671   M 2693
  M 2695
Harrison, George: concert for
    Bangladesh - ticket sales
  N 1095
Harrison, George: concert review
  N 0799   M 0801   M 0802
Harrison, George: consults on Lennon LP
  M 2665
Harrison, George: contributions to
    charity
  M 2798
Harrison, George: Dark Horse Records
  M 1414   M 1419   M 2850   M 3485
  N 0332
Harrison, George: Dave Mason recording
    session
  M 2747
Harrison, George: Delaney & Bonnie
  M 1519
Harrison, George: Delaney & Bonnie tour
  M 2606
Harrison, George: deported from
    Hamburg, Germany
  M 3296
Harrison, George: discography
  M 0957
Harrison, George: divorces Pattie Boyd
  N 0423   N 0615
Harrison, George: driving charge
  M 2025   N 0056   N 0424
Harrison, George: drug charge
  N 0058   N 0059   N 0062   N 0724
Harrison, George: drug raid
  N 0354
Harrison, George: editorial letter
  N 0084
Harrison, George: Eric Clapton's
    wedding
  M 2894
Harrison, George: fan club   see   Fan
    club (Harrison)
Harrison, George: fan letter
  M 0580
Harrison, George: films   see also
    individual film titles
Harrison, George: films
  M 0135   M 1242   M 1277   M 2228
  M 2394   M 2709   M 2878   M 2880
  M 2886   M 3325   N 0383   N 0385
  N 0422   RF0013   RF0076   RF0077
  RF0078   RF0079   RF0080   RF0081
  RF0082   RF0083   RF0084   RF0085
  RF0086   RF0087   RF0088   RF0089
  RF0090   RF0091   RF0092   RF0093
  RF0094   RF0095   RF0096   RF0251
  RF0252   RF0253   RF0254   RF0255
  RF0256   RF0257   RF0258   RF0259
  RF0260   RF0261   RF0262   RF0263
  RF0264   RF0265   RF0266   RF0267
  RF0268   RF0269   RF0270   RF0271

RF0272 RF0273 RF0274 RF0275
RF0276 RF0277 RF0278 RF0279
RF0280 RF0281 RF0282 RF0283
RF0284 RF0285 RF0286 RF0288
RF0289 RF0290 RF0291 RF0292
RF0293 RF0294
Harrison, George: film shown at Cannes
    N 0385
Harrison, George: finances "Life of
    Brian" (film)
    M 2228
Harrison, George: finances Monty Python
    film
    M 2878 M 2880
Harrison, George: fined for careless
    driving
    N 1119
Harrison, George: Friar Park
    N 0067
Harrison, George: Frank Sinatra LP
    M 3078
Harrison, George: Grand Prix, Long
    Beach, California
    M 2861
Harrison, George: guitars - photo
    survey
    M 1365
Harrison, George: Hawaii
    M 2873 M 3194
Harrison, George: hurt in car accident
    M 2707 N 0505 N 0526
Harrison, George: India
    M 0198 M 0988 M 3654 N 0111
    N 0135 N 0206 N 0506 N 1042
Harrison, George: influence of
    M 2319
Harrison, George: influence on
    guitarists
    N 0950
Harrison, George: interview
    B 0560 C 0132 C 0222 M 0622
    M 0629 M 1261 M 1262 M 1408
    M 1409 M 1576 M 1614 M 1636
    M 1667 M 1838 M 2354 M 3011
    M 3440 M 3576 M 3577 M 3578
    M 3596 M 3654 M 3782 N 0206
    N 0458
Harrison, George: interview on Beatles
    M 3485 N 0207
Harrison, George: jam session
    M 2739
Harrison, George: Krishna
    M 1243 M 1245
Harrison, George: Led Zeppelin concert
    M 2749
Harrison, George: Lennon concert film
    screening
    M 2702
Harrison, George: Lennon's death
    M 3700
Harrison, George: Lennon tribute
    N 0468
Harrison, George: Leon Russell to
    record songs
    M 2636 M 2643
Harrison, George: London, England
    apartment looted
    N 1098
Harrison, George: Los Angeles,
    California visit
    M 0228
Harrison, George: makes Queen's list
    N 0744
Harrison, George: McCartney at concert
    M 3289
Harrison, George: meets Dick Cavett
    M 2691
Harrison, George: Moog synthesizer
    M 2213
Harrison, George: "My Sweet Lord"
    (song) case
    M 1135 M 1249 M 1412 M 1416
    M 1751 M 1988 M 2846 M 2923
    M 3370 M 3371 M 3756 N 0391
    N 0425 N 0618 N 0960
Harrison, George: New York City, 1970
    M 0069
Harrison, George: 1974 U.S. tour
    M 0105 M 1023 M 1149 M 1420

M 1421 M 1422 M 2787 M 2796
M 3075 M 3289 N 0368 N 0949
Harrison, George: 1974 U.S. tour
    announced
    N 0827
Harrison, George: 1974 U.S. tour press
    conference
    N 0483
Harrison, George: 1974 U.S. tour -
    ticket sales
    M 3076
Harrison, George: on ABBEY ROAD (LP)
    M 1240
Harrison, George: on Alvin Lee LP
    M 2762
Harrison, George: on Beatles
    M 1408 M 1409
Harrison, George: on Beatles reunion
    M 1614 M 3011
Harrison, George: on Beatles reunion
    offer
    M 0920
Harrison, George: on Cheech & Chong LP
    M 2745
Harrison, George: on Cilla Black LP
    M 2730
Harrison, George: on Clapton LP
    M 2594
Harrison, George: on David Frost show
    N 0103
Harrison, George: on Dick Cavett show
    M 1417
Harrison, George: on Indian music
    M 3654
Harrison, George: on "Saturday Night
    Live" show
    M 3782
Harrison, George: on transcendental
    meditation
    M 2148
Harrison, George: portrait
    M 1072 M 1656 M 2538 M 2547
Harrison, George: portrait with Pattie
    Boyd
    M 1467
Harrison, George: press conference
    M 1241 M 1410 M 2802
Harrison, George: press reception with
    Pattie Boyd
    M 0086
Harrison, George: quotations
    B 0383 B 0384 B 0385 B 0386
Harrison, George: recording activity
    M 2558 M 2819 M 3057
Harrison, George: recording of ALL
    THINGS MUST PASS (LP)
    M 3334
Harrison, George: records and songs
    see also individual record and
    song titles
Harrison, George: records and songs
    M 0134 M 0137 M 0468 M 0509
    M 0810 M 0957 M 1135 M 1164
    M 1219 M 1242 M 1249 M 1364
    M 1412 M 1416 M 1417 M 1751
    M 1806 M 1853 M 1978 M 1988
    M 2194 M 2235 M 2380 M 2567
    M 2667 M 2671 M 2676 M 2678
    M 2693 M 2695 M 2746 M 2808
    M 2827 M 2846 M 2923 M 3321
    M 3370 M 3371 M 3446 M 3450
    M 3516 M 3603 M 3623 M 3712
    M 3756 N 0383 N 0391 N 0425
    N 0618 N 0942 N 0960 N 1154
    RR0018 RR0019 RR0020 RR0021
    RR0022 RR0023 RR0024 RR0127
    RR0134 RR0146 RR0147 RR0148
    RR0149 RR0150 RR0151 RR0156
    RR0157 RR0158 RR0159 RR0160
    RR0161 RR0162 RR0163 RR0164
    RR0165 RR0166 RR0187 RR0188
    RR0189 RR0190 RR0191 RR0192
    RR0193 RR0194 RR0209 RR0210
    RR0211 RR0212 RR0213 RR0214
    RR0215 RR0216 RR0217 RR0221
    RR0222 RR0223 RR0224 RR0225
    RR0226 RR0292 RR0293 RR0294
    RR0295 RR0296 RR0297 RR0298
    RR0340

Harrison, George: records with Billy
    Preston
    M 2664
Harrison, George: records with Dylan
    and Starr
    M 0583
Harrison, George: refused U.S. visa
    N 1099
Harrison, George: reviews pop records
    M 0048
Harrison, George: rumored McCartney
    tiff
    M 2639
Harrison, George: Rutles T.V. special
    M 3301
Harrison, George: separates from Pattie
    Boyd
    M 2797
Harrison, George: Shankar film
    M 3325
Harrison, George: solo career
    M 1246
Harrison, George: songbook see also
    Beatles songbook
Harrison, George: songbook
    S 0001 S 0002 S 0084 S 0088
    S 0122 S 0126 S 0127 S 0149
Harrison, George: song recorded by Joe
    Cocker
    M 2597
Harrison, George: song recorded by
    Ronnie Spector
    M 2653
Harrison, George: songs recorded by
    Jesse Davis
    M 2672
Harrison, George: sought by promoters
    for second benefit concert
    M 2028
Harrison, George: stage musical planned
    M 0450
Harrison, George: Starr LP
    M 2626 M 2840 M 3063
Harrison, George: Starr recording
    session
    M 2737 M 3278
Harrison, George: studies sitar
    N 0640
Harrison, George: sues record companies
    N 0198
Harrison, George: suit over bootlegs LP
    M 2732
Harrison, George: to record in
    Nashville, Tennessee
    M 3699
Harrison, George: tour rumored
    M 2839
Harrison, George: U.K. tour
    M 2787
Harrison, George: unauthorized use of
    his material
    M 0835 M 1418
Harrison, George: U.S. visa awarded
    M 1677
Harrison, George: U.S. visit
    M 1038
Harrison, George: vs. A & M Records
    M 1068 M 1406
Harrison, George: visits Monty Python
    film set
    M 2886
Harrison, George: visits the White
    House
    N 0612
Harrison, George: voice imitator
    M 1483
Harrison, George: Warner Brothers
    Records
    M 1419
Harrison, George: weds Olivia Trinidad
    Arias
    N 1011
Harrison, George: weds Pattie Boyd
    N 0074 N 0426 M 0086 M 0859
Harrison, George: wins Grammy award
    N 0942
Harrison, George: wins "Record Mirror"
    poll
    M 2026

Harrison, George: withdraws from
    Northern Songs Ltd.
    N 0070
Harrison, George: with his sick mother
    M 2634
Harrison, George: with Ravi Shankar
    M 0103   M 2691   N 0924
Harrison, George: "Wonderwall" film
    score
    M 1242   N 0383
Harrison, George: writes songs for
    Martha Reeves
    M 2754
Harrison/Lennon Followers - Beatles USA
    Ltd.
    F 0146
Harrison, Louise
    M 2634
Harrison, Louise: interview
    C 0133
Harrison, Olivia   see   Trinidad Arias,
    Olivia
Harrison, Pattie   see   Boyd, Pattie
Hatfield, Bobby
    M 2698
Hawaii [gun store]
    N 0839
Hawaii: Harrison on Maui
    M 2873   M 3194
Hawaii: McCartneys on holiday
    M 2830
HEAR THE BEATLES TELL ALL (LP)
    RR0237
"Hello/Goodbye" (film short): banned
    M 1665
"Help!" (film)
    B 0116   B 0252   M 1112   M 1173
    M 2361   M 3372   M 3694   N 0316
    N 0319   N 0765   P 0072   RF0116
    RF0117   RF0118   RF0119   RF0120
    RF0121   RF0122   RF0123
"Help!" (film): filming
    M 1058   M 1112   M 1551   M 1960
"Help!" (film): premiere
    M 3129   N 0136
"Help!" (song)
    M 1335   M 1336
Helter Skelter
    F 0078
HER MAJESTY (LP)
    RR0238
"Heroes of Rock 'N' Roll" (tv special)
    M 1147
"Hey, Hey, Hey" (song)
    M 2005
'HEY JUDE' (LP)   see also   THE BEATLES
    AGAIN (LP)
'HEY JUDE' (LP)
    RR0239   RR0240
"Hey Jude/Revolution" (45)
    M 1037
"Hey Jude" (song)
    M 0879
"Hey Jude" (song): three hour version
    M 2632
"Hi Hi Hi" (song): banned on BBC
    M 2729
"The History of the Beatles" (film)
    RF0124
Hit Factory (studio)
    M 1987
"Hit Parader" (magazine): Special
    Beatles insert
    M 0261
Hoffman, Dezo
    B 0367   B 0368   B 0369
Holland: Amsterdam convention
    M 1823
Holland: Beatle convention
    M 0643   M 0880
Holland: Beatles in Amsterdam
    M 1756
Holland: Beatles, 1964
    M 3520
Holland: Beatles on the charts
    M 3467
Holland: fan club
    F 0044   F 0048   F 0050   F 0051
    F 0056   F 0120

Holland: Leiden convention
    M 1986
Holland: McCartney visit, 1976
    M 0114   M 0115   M 0116   M 0119
Holland: Utrecht fan convention
    M 3515   M 3534
Holland: Wings
    M 1351   M 1356   M 1367   M 1368
    M 1369   M 1370   M 1378   M 1379
    M 1381   M 1384   M 3288
Holly, Buddy
    M 1743   M 2867
Hollywood Bowl concert: bootleg LPs
    M 3201
"Hollywood Bowl" (LP)   see   THE BEATLES
    AT THE HOLLYWOOD BOWL (LP)
Hopkin, Mary
    M 2603
Hornby, Lesley   see   Twiggy
HOT AS SUN (LP)
    M 1404
"Hound Dog/Long Tall Sally" (45)
    RR0241   RR0242   RR0243
Houston, Texas: first all-Beatle-music
    radio station
    N 0492
Howard & Windham
    N 0252
"How I Won The War" (film)
    B 0474   M 1366   M 1637   M 3640
    N 0014   N 0584   N 1137
Huebers, Bettina: paternity suit
    against McCartney
    N 0327
Hungary: Ono visits Budapest
    M 2179
"I Am The Walrus" (song) [lyrics]
    M 1581
Idle, Eric
    M 3782
Illinois: Chicago concert
    M 3273   M 3503   N 0589
Illinois: Chicago fan convention
    M 3273
"Imagine" (film)
    M 0646   M 1699   RF0125   RF0126
    RF0127   RF0128
IMAGINE (LP)
    M 0938   M 1532   RR0244   RR0245
    RR0246   RR0247   RR0248   RR0249
    RR0250   RR0251   RR0252   RR0253
"Imagine" (play)
    M 2247
I ME MINE (book)
    M 2882   M 2929   M 3086   RB0340
    RB0341   RB0342   RB0343   RB0344
    RB0345   RB0346   RB0347   RB0349
    RB0350   RB0351   RB0352   RB0353
    RB0358
"I'm Not Ready" (song)
    M 2918
Import recordings (to U.S.)
    M 1861
"I'm Your Angel" (song)
    M 1179   M 2363
Independent Apple Enterprises
    F 0010
Independent Free Apple
    F 0082
India: Beatles
    M 1036   M 3251   M 3325   N 0089
    N 0117   N 0126   N 0139   N 0451
    N 0465   N 0523   N 0638
India: Beatles in Rishikesh
    N 0638   M 1035   N 0638
India: Harrison
    M 0198   M 0988   M 1042
India: Harrison interview
    N 0206   M 3654
India: influence on the Beatles
    C 0168
India: Lennon and Harrison
    N 0111   N 0135   N 0506
India: McCartney
    M 1605   M 2585
Indiana Official Beatles Fan Club
    F 0083
INDIAN ROPE TRICK (LP)
    RR0254   RR0255

India: Starr
    N 0064
India: Starr and wife leave
    N 0182
Indonesia: Beatle records burned
    N 0537
IN HIS OWN WRITE (book)
    C 0016   C 0157   C 0224   M 3157
    M 3747   N 0300   N 0429   N 0701
    RB0354   RB0355   RB0356   RB0357
    RB0358   RB0359   RB0360   RB0361
    RB0362   RB0363   RB0364   RB0365
    RB0366   RB0367   RB0368   RB0369
IN HIS OWN WRITE (book): excerpt
    M 1897
"In His Own Write" (play)
    N 0050   N 0063   N 0789   N 1127
    N 1128
"In My Life" (song)
    C 0127
Innes, Neil
    M 3764
"In Spite of All the Danger" (song)
    M 1118   M 2061
"Instant Karma" (45)
    RR0256
Insurance: Beatles U.S. tour
    N 0357
Interview(s)   see   names of individual
    Beatles
"Interview with a Legend" (film)
    RF0129
IN THE FOOTSTEPS OF THE BEATLES (book)
    RB0370   RB0371
Ippolito, Adam
    M 0033
Ireland: Beatle concerts
    C 0312
Ireland: Lennon protests British policy
    N 0630
Ireland: McCartney song banned
    N 0055
Ireland: McCartney song protest
    M 1485   M 2415   M 3605   N 0055
    N 0531
Ireland, Northern: Oz Trial
    N 0558
"I Sat Belonely Down a Tree" (poem)
    M 1895
Israel: bars Beatles
    N 0533
Israel: Beatles
    M 0507   M 3519   M 3563   M 3655
Israel: Lennon
    M 1265
Israel: radio series on the Beatles
    M 0506
Israel: visiting permit for Beatles
    M 0213
Italy: Beatles discography
    B 0031   B 0220   M 1076   M 1097
    M 3205
Italy: Beatles invited to Venice
    N 0137
Italy: Beatles' popularity
    N 0534
Italy: McCartney in Nice
    M 1666
Italy: Venice Wings concert
    M 2409   M 2848   N 0732   N 0818
    N 1002
"It Don't Come Easy" (song)
    M 2626
IT'S ALRIGHT (LP)
    RR0257   RR0258
Ives, Charles
    M 1000
Ivor Novello award
    M 0381   M 1918   M 3489   M 3755
    N 0147   N 0792
"I Wanna Hold Your Hand" (film)
    M 1980   M 3160   M 3563   M 3655
    RF0130   RF0131   RF0132   RF0133
    RF0134   RF0135   RF0136   RF0137
    RF0138   RF0139   RF0140   RF0141
    RF0142   RF0143   RF0144   RF0145
    RF0146   RF0147   RF0149   RF0150
    RF0151   RF0152
"I Wanna Hold Your Hand" (film):

filming
M 2204
"I Wanna Hold Your Hand" (song)
M 0464   M 3453   M 3514
"I Wanna Hold Your Hand" (song): wins
pre-sale gold disk
M 0411
"The Jack Paar Show" (tv show)
M 3764
"The Jack Parr Show" (tv show): Beatles
1964 appearance
M 0538
Jackson, Michael: records with
McCartney
M 1601   N 0716
Jagger, Mick
M 2610   M 2785
Jagger, Mick: wedding
M 2381
"The Jam"
M 0335
James, Dick
M 1747   M 2261
James, Dick: estimates Beatles gross
M 0335
James, Dick: resigns from Northern
Songs, Ltd.
N 0813
Japan: bars McCartney
N 0507
Japan: Beatles
N 0255   N 0282
Japan: Beatles in Tokyo
M 3155   N 0095   N 0282
Japan: Beatles Tokyo concert
M 1586
Japan: concert tour
N 0188   N 0282   N 1093
Japan: donation for crime victims by
Yoko Ono
N 1166
Japan: fan club
F 0024
Japan: fans greet Beatles
N 1093
Japan: Lennons
M 2869
Japan: McCartney
B 0595   M 1798
Japan: McCartney bust
M 0853   M 0987   M 1831   M 1836
M 2405   M 2908   M 3589   N 0542
N 0726   N 0729   N 0731   N 0869
N 0873
Japan: McCartney drug charge
N 0326
Japan: McCartney drug incident song
parody
M 2254
Japan: McCartney leaves Tokyo
M 2067
Japan: McCartney tour news clippings
B 0400
Japan: Ono concerts
M 2793
Japan: Starr in clothing ads
M 1579
Japan: Tokyo concert
N 0282
Japan: Tokyo concert film
M 0241
Japan: Tokyo concert ticket sales
N 0282   N 1090
Japan: Wings banned on radio
M 0141
Jazz music: influence of the Beatles
and the Rolling Stones
M 0271
Jelly babies thrown at Beatles
M 0767
"Je Suis Le Plus Mieux - The Last
Reunion" (12-inch 45)
RR0259   RR0260
"Jet" (song)
M 2774
John, Elton: duo with Lennon
M 2805   M 3595   N 0953
John, Elton: Geffen records
M 1799

John, Elton: Lennon tribute
M 1008
John, Elton: visit with Yoko and Sean
Lennon
M 1008
JOHN LENNON AND THE BEATLES FOREVER
(book)
RB0372
THE JOHN LENNON COLLECTION (LP)
RR0261   RR0262
JOHN LENNON: DEATH OF A DREAM (book)
RB0373   RB0374
John Lennon Fan Club
F 0095   F 0118
JOHN LENNON 4 EVER (book)
RB0375
JOHN LENNON IN HIS OWN WORDS (book)
RB0376   RB0377   RB0378   RB0379
JOHN LENNON: IN MY LIFE (book)
RB0380
JOHN LENNON 1940-1980, A BIOGRAPHY
(book)
RB0382   RB0383   RB0384   RB0385
RB0386   RB0387   RB0388
JOHN LENNON 1940-1980 (Schworck) (book)
RB0381
JOHN LENNON: ONE DAY AT A TIME (book)
M 1091   RB0389   RB0390   RB0391
RB0392   RB0393   RB0394   RB0395
RB0396   RB0397
JOHN LENNON/PLASTIC ONO BAND (LP)
N 0552   RR0263   RR0264   RR0265
RR0266   RR0267   RR0268   RR0269
JOHN LENNON'S SECRET (book)
RB0398
THE JOHN LENNON STORY (book)
RB0399
JOHN LENNON SUMMER OF 1980 (book)
RB0400
"John, Paul, George, Ringo ... and
Bert" (play)
M 1719
Johnson, Lyndon B.: uses Beatles' suite
in Manila, Philippines
N 0574
Jones, Davy
M 1626
Jones, Quincy: records McCartney and
Michael Jackson
N 0716
Juber, Laurence: interview
M 0514   M 2996
"Juke Box Jury" (British show)
C 0269
Julliard: composition scholarship -
Lennon memorial
M 0689   M 1030
"Junior's Farm/Sally G" (song)
M 1164
"(Just Like) Starting Over/Kiss Kiss
Kiss" (45)
M 1121   RR0270
Kaempfert, Bert
M 1437   M 3531
Kampuchea benefit concert
M 1216   M 1977
'Kampuchea' (LP)   see   CONCERTS FOR THE
PEOPLE OF KAMPUCHEA (LP)
"Kansas City/Hey, Hey" (song medley)
M 1479
Kansas City, Missouri: concert
N 0191
"Kansas City" (song)
M 2005
Kaufmann, Murray   see   Murray the K
Kelly, Brian
C 0201
Keltner, Jim
M 2776
Kennedy Airport, New York City: Beatles
arrive on first visit
M 3362   N 0420
Kenya: Nairobi McCartney visit
M 1041
Keyboards songbook (Beatles)
S 0017
Keyes, Bobby
M 2697
King, B.B.

M 2659
King, B.B.: records with Starr
M 2027
Kinski, Nastassia
M 3764
Klaatu
M 0128   M 1599   M 1600   M 2301
M 2859
KLAATU (LP)
M 0128   RR0271
Klein, Allen
M 0027   M 1807   M 2612   M 2641
M 2669   M 2674   M 2712   M 2854
M 3339   M 3364   M 3445   M 3446
M 3754   N 0138   N 0635
Klein, Allen: as Beatles' manager
M 0028   M 0375   M 1484   M 1808
M 1810   M 3339   N 0521
Klein, Allen: concert for Bangladesh
money
M 1145
Klein, Allen: indicted
M 1131   M 1309
Klein, Allen: named as Beatles manager
M 0287   M 1804   N 0696
Klein, Allen: on Beatles' financial
situation
M 0302   N 0177
Klein, Allen: on concert for Bangladesh
M 1806
Klein, Allen: ousted as Beatles'
manager
M 0062
Klein, Allen: split with Beatles
N 0767
Klein, Allen: tax evasion
M 0330   M 2170   N 0010   N 0077
N 0370   N 1046
Klein, Allen: tax evasion sentence
N 0457
Klein, Allen: vs. Beatles
M 0005   M 0006   M 0007   M 0024
M 0025   M 0026   M 0302   M 0303
M 0366   M 1674   M 1675   M 1805
M 1809   M 1811   M 1826   M 1874
M 2855   M 3447   M 3448   N 0399
N 0401   N 0636   N 1035   N 1046
Klein, Allen: vs. Beatles and Apple
Corps., Ltd.
N 0520
Klein, Allen: vs. John Lennon
M 1812
Knott's Berry Farm: Beatles salute
M 3454
Kramer, Billy J.
M 1439   M 3529
Kristofferson, Kris
M 3764
Kuttner, Yoav: interview
M 0506
Kyoko   see   Cox, Kyoko
"Lady Madonna" (film)
N 0034
"Lady Madonna" (song)
M 1052
Lagos, Nigeria: Wings recording
M 2760   M 3064
Laine, Denny
M 2862
"The Land of the Lunapots" (poem by
Lennon)
C 0187
"The Last Waltz" (film)
M 2116
Las Vegas, Nevada: Beatles
N 0127
"Laugh In" (tv show): Starr
M 2617
Lauper, Cyndi
M 3764
Lazards
N 0259
"Leave My Kitten Alone" (song)
M 1074
Led Zepplin: concert
M 2749
Lee, Alvin
M 2762
Lee, Peggy

M 2786
Leeds, England: Beatles
N 1001
Legal action: Allen Klein - indicted
M 1131   M 1309
Legal action: Allen Klein - libel suit
N 0399
Legal action: Allen Klein - tax evasion
N 0077   N 0370   N 0010
Legal action: Allen Klein - tax evasion
  sentence
N 0457
Legal action: Allen Klein - vs. Beatles
M 0005   M 0007   M 0024   M 0026
M 0062   M 1805   M 1874   M 2855
M 3447   M 3448   N 0138   N 0399
N 0401   N 0636   N 1035   N 1046
Legal action: Apple Corps. - vs.
  Capitol Records, Inc.
M 3284
Legal action: Allen Klein - vs. John
  Lennon
M 1812
Legal action: Barbara Bach - weds Ringo
  Starr
N 0601   N 0935
Legal action: "Beatlemania" (play)
  publishers - sue "Beatlefever"
  (play)
M 2565
Legal action: Beatles - chauffeur fined
N 0114
Legal action: Beatles - "Compleat
  Beatles" (video)
M 0833
Legal action: Beatles - court
  injunction on "Beatlemania"
  (play)
M 0419
Legal action: Beatles - dissolution
M 0618   M 2020   N 0098   N 0107
N 0110   N 0134   N 0140   N 0142
N 0159   N 0170   N 0171   N 0373
N 0386   N 0450   N 0582   N 0587
N 0608   N 0687   N 0919   N 1046
N 1059   N 1111   N 1124   N 1125
Legal action: Beatles - dissolved
N 1068
Legal action: Beatles - enjoin clothing
  maker
N 0017
Legal action: Beatles - injunction to
  prevent release of old recordings
N 0174
Legal action: Beatles - Lenmac sold to
  Northern Songs, Ltd.
N 0217
Legal action: Beatles - MacLen Music
  vs. Northern Songs, Ltd.
M 0837
Legal action: Beatles - NEMS
  Enterprises sold
N 0216
Legal action: Beatles - Northern Songs,
  Ltd. sold to ATV
N 0218   N 1014
Legal action: Beatles - receiver
  appointed
M 0062
Legal action: Beatles - sell interest
  in Northern Songs to ATV
N 0204
Legal action: Beatles - Seltaeb
N 0844
Legal action: Beatles - "Star Club
  Tapes"
M 0628   M 0834
Legal action: Beatles - sue
  "Beatlemania" (play)
M 2901   N 0184
Legal action: Beatles - sue clothing
  firm
N 0194
Legal action: Beatles - sue for libel
  over photographs
N 0183
Legal action: Beatles - sue for slander
  and libel
N 0185

Legal action: Beatles - vs. Allen Klein
M 0005   M 0007   M 0024   M 0026
M 0062   M 1805   M 1874   M 2855
M 3447   M 3448   N 0138   N 0399
N 0401   N 0636   N 1035   N 1046
Legal action: Beatles - vs.
  "Beatlemania" (play)
M 2901   M 3444
Legal action: Beatles - vs. Clive
  Epstein
N 0002   N 1162
Legal action: Beatles - vs. Paul
  McCartney
M 2076   M 2077
Legal action: Beatles - vs. Pete Best
M 0533   M 1065   M 1066
Legal action: Brian Epstein - inquest
  at death
N 0365   N 0366   N 0367
Legal action: Brian Epstein - inquest
  ordered
N 0528
Legal action: Brian Epstein - NEMS
  Enterprises, Ltd. merger with Vic
  Lewis Organ., Ltd.
N 0236
Legal action: Brian Epstein - vs. Pete
  Best
M 0533   M 1065   M 1066
Legal action: Capitol Records - vs.
  Apple Corps., Ltd.
M 3284
Legal action: Capitol Records - vs. Vee
  Jay Records
M 0552
Legal action: Clive Epstein - vs. the
  Beatles
N 1162
Legal action: Clive Epstein - writ
  against Beatles
N 0002
Legal action: Cynthia Powell -
  attempted ban on Lennon articles
N 0397
Legal action: Cynthia Powell - divorces
  John Lennon
N 0553   N 0769
Legal action: Cynthia Powell - granted
  "decree nisi"
N 0343
Legal action: George Harrison - buys
  Friar Park
N 0067
Legal action: George Harrison -
  divorces Pattie Boyd
N 0423   N 0615
Legal action: George Harrison - driving
  charge
N 0056   N 0424   N 1119   M 2025
Legal action: George Harrison - drug
  charge
N 0062   N 0354   N 0724
Legal action: George Harrison - drug
  charge fine
N 0058   N 0059
Legal action: George Harrison - fined
  for assault of photographer
N 0076
Legal action: George Harrison - "My
  Sweet Lord" (song) case
M 1249   M 1412   M 1416   M 1751
M 1988   M 2843   M 2923   N 0391
N 0425   N 0618   N 0960
Legal action: George Harrison -
  restraining order on unauthorized
  use...
M 0835   M 1418
Legal action: George Harrison - sues
  record companies
N 0198
Legal action: George Harrison - suit
  over bootleg LPs
M 2735
Legal action: George Harrison - vs. A &
  M Records
M 1068   M 1406
Legal action: George Harrison - weds
  Olivia Trinidad Arias
N 1011

Legal action: George Harrison - weds
  Pattie Boyd
N 0074   N 0426
Legal action: George Harrison -
  withdraws from Northern Songs
N 0070
Legal action: John Lennon - art gallery
  obscenity charge
N 0026
Legal action: John Lennon - attempt to
  ban Cynthia Powell articles
N 0397
Legal action: John Lennon - buys land
N 0564
Legal action: John Lennon - copyright
M 3490
Legal action: John Lennon - copyright
  case
M 1093
Legal action: John Lennon - deportation
M 0704   M 1134   M 1136   M 1944
M 3470   M 3471   N 0025   N 0042
N 0372   N 0544   N 0546   N 0549
N 0551   N 0568   N 0573   N 0603
N 0604   N 0605   N 0606   N 0607
N 0629   N 0649   N 0652   N 0660
N 0671   N 0676   N 0679   N 0692
N 0714   N 0743   N 0762   N 0826
N 1027   N 1028
Legal action: John Lennon - detained in
  Majorca, Balearica Islands, Spain
N 0061
Legal action: John Lennon - divorces
  Cynthia Powell
N 0553   N 0769
Legal action: John Lennon - drug case
N 0659   N 0666
Legal action: John Lennon - drug charge
N 0645   N 0646   N 0866
Legal action: John Lennon - drug charge
  fine
N 0555   M 1116
Legal action: John Lennon - fines of
  rugby team protestors
N 0682
Legal action: John Lennon - lithograph
  exhibit halted
N 0891
Legal action: John Lennon - lithographs
N 1036
Legal action: John Lennon - mistrial in
  publishing case
N 0518
Legal action: John Lennon - murder case
N 0052   N 0406   N 0416   N 0474
N 0627   N 0650   N 0662   N 0695
N 0771   N 0990   N 0991   N 0992
N 0993   N 0994   N 0995   N 0996
N 0997   N 1037   N 1084   N 1085
Legal action: John Lennon - murderer
  sentenced
N 0358   N 0466   M 0693   M 0694
Legal action: John Lennon - sued by Big
  Seven Music Corporation
N 0503   N 0580
Legal action: John Lennon - sued for
  loan
N 0400
Legal action: John Lennon - sues "News
  of the World" (newspaper)
N 0797
Legal action: John Lennon - TWO VIRGINS
  (LP) banned
N 0540
Legal action: John Lennon - TWO VIRGINS
  (LP) seized
N 0008   N 0921
Legal action: John Lennon - vs. Allen
  Klein
M 1812
Legal action: John Lennon - vs. Big
  Seven Music Corporation
M 0541
Legal action: John Lennon - vs.
  government over wiretapping
N 0677
Legal action: John Lennon - vs. Maclen
  Music
M 2732

Legal action: John Lennon – vs. Morris
    Levy
    M 1961   M 2128
Legal action: John Lennon – vs.
    Northern Songs, Ltd.
    M 2732   N 0903
Legal action: John Lennon – vs.
    Roulette Records
    M 3783
Legal action: John Lennon – weds Yoko
    Ono
    N 0556   N 0561
Legal action: John Lennon – will
    N 0461
Legal action: John Lennon – wins U.S.
    Immigration fight
    N 0573
Legal action: Linda Eastman – "Another
    Day" case
    N 0717
Legal action: Linda Eastman – drug
    arrest
    N 0575
Legal action: Linda Eastman – drug
    charge
    N 0502
Legal action: Linda Eastman – drug
    charge dismissed
    N 0579
Legal action: Linda Eastman – weds Paul
    McCartney
    N 0082   N 0724   N 1130
Legal action: Maclen Music – vs. Paul
    McCartney
    M 3373
Legal action: Maureen Cox – divorces
    Ringo Starr
    N 0273   N 0936
Legal action: Maureen Cox – weds Ringo
    Starr
    N 0169
Legal action: Northern Songs, Ltd. –
    vs. Paul McCartney
    M 3373
Legal action: Northern Songs, Ltd. –
    vs. Video Communications
    M 3447
Legal action: Northern Songs, Ltd. –
    videotape copyright dispute
    M 1991   M 1992
Legal action: Olivia Trinidad Arias –
    weds George Harrison
    N 1011
Legal action: Pattie Boyd – divorces
    George Harrison
    N 0423   N 0615
Legal action: Pattie Boyd – drug charge
    N 0062   N 0724
Legal action: Pattie Boyd – drug raid
    N 0354
Legal action: Pattie Boyd – fined in
    drug charge
    N 0058   N 0059
Legal action: Pattie Boyd – weds George
    Harrison
    N 0074   N 0426
Legal action: Paul McCartney – "Another
    Day" case
    N 0717
Legal action: Paul McCartney – breach
    of trust suit vs. Lord Grade
    N 1173
Legal action: Paul McCartney – buys
    Scottish farm
    N 0462
Legal action: Paul McCartney –
    copyright
    M 3490
Legal action: Paul McCartney – driving
    charge
    N 0057
Legal action: Paul McCartney – drug
    charge
    N 0398   N 0824   N 0870
Legal action: Paul McCartney – Japan
    drug arrest
    N 0869
Legal action: Paul McCartney – Japan
    drug charge

N 0873
Legal action: Paul McCartney – Japanese
    deportation
    N 0538
Legal action: Paul McCartney – man
    trespassing on property
    N 0073
Legal action: Paul McCartney –
    paternity suit
    M 1172   N 0327
Legal action: Paul McCartney –
    trespasser on property charged
    N 0706
Legal action: Paul McCartney – vs.
    Beatles
    M 2076   M 2077   M 3339   N 0373
    N 0687
Legal action: Paul McCartney – vs.
    Northern Songs, Ltd.
    N 0904
Legal action: Paul McCartney – vs.
    Northern Songs, Ltd. and Maclen
    Music
    M 3373
Legal action: Paul McCartney – vs.
    Robert Stigwood Organization
    M 2073
Legal action: Paul McCartney – weds
    Linda Eastman
    N 0082   N 0724   N 1130
Legal action: Pete Best – vs. Beatles
    and Brian Epstein
    M 0533   M 1065   M 1066
Legal action: Ringo Starr – divorces
    Maureen Cox
    N 0273   N 0936
Legal action: Ringo Starr – enjoined
    for Lennons' use of his residence
    N 0622
Legal action: Ringo Starr – sued
    N 0485
Legal action: Ringo Starr – weds
    Barbara Bach
    N 0601   N 0935
Legal action: Ringo Starr – weds
    Maureen Cox
    N 0169
Legal action: Seltaeb
    N 0844
Legal action: Tony Sheridan
    M 3282
Legal action: Tony Sheridan – vs.
    Polydor International and others
    M 3281
Legal action: Vee Jay Records – vs.
    Capitol Records
    M 0552
Legal action: 'Yellow Submarine' suit,
    Paris, France
    M 0051
Legal action: Yoko Ono – awarded
    custody of daughter Kyoko
    N 0822
Legal action: Yoko Ono – breach of
    trust suit vs. Lord Grade
    N 1173
Legal action: Yoko Ono – buys land
    N 0564
Legal action: Yoko Ono – copyright case
    M 1180   M 2363
Legal action: Yoko Ono – deportation
    case
    N 0692
Legal action: Yoko Ono – detained in
    Majorca, Balearica Islands, Spain
    N 0061
Legal action: Yoko Ono – drug charge
    N 0645   N 0646
Legal action: Yoko Ono – Lennon's will
    N 0461
Legal action: Yoko Ono – sued by Big
    Seven Music Corp.
    N 0580
Legal action: Yoko Ono – TWO VIRGINS
    (LP) banned
    N 0540
Legal action: Yoko Ono – TWO VIRGINS
    (LP) seized
    N 0008   N 0921

Legal action: Yoko Ono – vs. Maclen
    Music
    M 2732
Legal action: Yoko Ono – vs. Northern
    Songs, Ltd.
    M 2732   N 0903
Legal action: Yoko Ono – weds John
    Lennon
    N 0556   N 0561
"Legs" (film)
    M 0066   M 2153
Leibovitz, Annie: photography
    M 2535
Leicester, England: concert
    N 1104
Leiden, Holland: convention
    M 1986
Lenmac: bought by Northern Songs, Ltd.
    M 2317   N 0217
"Lennon, A Biography" (play)
    N 0933
LENNON AND MCCARTNEY (book)
    RB0401   RB0402
Lennon, Cynthia see Powell, Cynthia
THE LENNON FACTOR (book)
    RB0403
Lennon Health Centre: Liverpool,
    England
    N 0655
Lennon, John
    B 0001   B 0039   B 0040   B 0041
    B 0042   B 0069   B 0070   B 0074
    B 0078   B 0083   B 0096   B 0097
    B 0113   B 0118   B 0121   B 0122
    B 0127   B 0129   B 0170   B 0171
    B 0172   B 0173   B 0191   B 0192
    B 0193   B 0194   B 0195   B 0206
    B 0211   B 0212   B 0221   B 0222
    B 0245   B 0246   B 0259   B 0260
    B 0261   B 0268   B 0273   B 0274
    B 0275   B 0276   B 0277   B 0278
    B 0279   B 0283   B 0287   B 0295
    B 0298   B 0299   B 0300   B 0301
    B 0302   B 0303   B 0304   B 0305
    B 0306   B 0307   B 0308   B 0309
    B 0310   B 0311   B 0312   B 0313
    B 0314   B 0315   B 0316   B 0317
    B 0318   B 0319   B 0320   B 0321
    B 0322   B 0323   B 0324   B 0325
    B 0326   B 0327   B 0328   B 0329
    B 0330   B 0332   B 0334   B 0335
    B 0343   B 0372   B 0387   B 0388
    B 0389   B 0390   B 0391   B 0392
    B 0396   B 0397   B 0398   B 0406
    B 0407   B 0425   B 0426   B 0432
    B 0433   B 0434   B 0448   B 0449
    B 0450   B 0451   B 0452   B 0453
    B 0454   B 0455   B 0473   B 0475
    B 0478   B 0491   B 0495   B 0496
    B 0497   B 0498   B 0508   B 0509
    B 0515   B 0519   B 0522   B 0539
    B 0540   B 0550   B 0554   B 0561
    B 0571   B 0572   B 0573   B 0574
    B 0575   B 0576   B 0577   B 0578
    B 0579   B 0580   B 0581   B 0582
    B 0596   B 0598   B 0600   C 0007
    C 0070   C 0085   C 0091   C 0112
    C 0153   C 0155   C 0158   C 0341
    M 0015   M 0029   M 0035   M 0064
    M 0068   M 0076   M 0078   M 0084
    M 0088   M 0106   M 0138   M 0145
    M 0172   M 0173   M 0174   M 0199
    M 0200   M 0212   M 0216   M 0517
    M 0518   M 0564   M 0569   M 0633
    M 0636   M 0637   M 0642   M 0669
    M 0696   M 0722   M 0761   M 0762
    M 0763   M 0764   M 0793   M 0826
    M 0840   M 0841   M 0854   M 0855
    M 0861   M 0873   M 0874   M 0883
    M 0885   M 0999   M 1002   M 1005
    M 1077   M 1091   M 1132   M 1137
    M 1138   M 1144   M 1191   M 1193
    M 1212   M 1231   M 1254   M 1255
    M 1265   M 1284   M 1291   M 1312
    M 1314   M 1325   M 1337   M 1342
    M 1402   M 1515   M 1523   M 1524
    M 1553   M 1577   M 1578   M 1613
    M 1615   M 1682   M 1693   M 1694
    M 1697   M 1807   M 1815   M 1824

M 1841   M 1842   M 1843   M 1844
M 1845   M 1847   M 1849   M 1872
M 1899   M 1910   M 1924   M 1925
M 1931   M 1979   M 2017   M 2043
M 2084   M 2091   M 2118   M 2119
M 2122   M 2131   M 2140   M 2141
M 2181   M 2188   M 2208   M 2222
M 2245   M 2256   M 2264   M 2284
M 2288   M 2292   M 2334   M 2343
M 2364   M 2389   M 2416   M 2421
M 2433   M 2435   M 2436   M 2437
M 2438   M 2439   M 2440   M 2443
M 2444   M 2446   M 2473   M 2492
M 2526   M 2530   M 2531   M 2532
M 2568   M 2581   M 2618   M 2661
M 2665   M 2668   M 2674   M 2682
M 2734   M 2759   M 2765   M 2772
M 2776   M 2854   M 2856   M 2869
M 2891   M 2907   M 2935   M 3040
M 3046   M 3047   M 3071   M 3073
M 3085   M 3093   M 3094   M 3097
M 3099   M 3109   M 3115   M 3121
M 3127   M 3133   M 3135   M 3173
M 3187   M 3193   M 3197   M 3222
M 3264   M 3276   M 3277   M 3286
M 3293   M 3311   M 3320   M 3337
M 3343   M 3357   M 3358   M 3377
M 3394   M 3400   M 3415   M 3442
M 3446   M 3450   M 3451   M 3457
M 3505   M 3551   M 3558   M 3562
M 3597   M 3598   M 3599   M 3600
M 3601   M 3610   M 3612   M 3614
M 3615   M 3616   M 3641   M 3683
M 3687   M 3691   M 3713   M 3714
M 3715   M 3716   M 3718   M 3728
M 3744   M 3747   M 3751   M 3753
M 3776   M 3794   N 0043   N 0293
N 0297   N 0323   N 0330   N 0331
N 0341   N 0379   N 0380   N 0527
N 0536   N 0541   N 0545   N 0548
N 0557   N 0572   N 0592   N 0611
N 0639   N 0643   N 0735   N 0778
N 0809   N 0821   N 0857   N 0932
N 0967   N 0998   N 1029   N 1030
N 1042   N 1056   N 1065   N 1080
N 1082   N 1135   N 1139   N 1141
N 1163   P 0075   P 0076   P 0079
P 0081   P 0083   P 0089
Lennon, John: acquires painting by
    Stuart Sutcliffe
    C 0152
Lennon, John: advertisement for "Bag
    One" lithographs
    M 1700
Lennon, John: advertisement for radio
    special
    M 1698
Lennon, John: advertisements
    C 0186
Lennon, John: album cover
    M 3080
Lennon, John: appears with Elton John
    N 0953
Lennon, John: arrested
    M 2587
Lennon, John: art work at festival
    N 0987
Lennon, John: as a child
    M 3785
Lennon, John: as artist
    M 3536
Lennon, John: as author
    B 0478   M 1892   M 1897
Lennon, John: as composer
    C 0263   M 1298   M 1523   M 1588
    M 1642   M 3305   M 3326   M 3588
Lennon, John: asked to play Christ in
    pop opera
    N 0647
Lennon, John: as rhythm guitarist
    M 2364
Lennon, John: as writer
    M 3156   M 3157   N 0800
Lennon, John: at school
    C 0342
Lennon, John: auction of piano
    M 3065
Lennon, John: back together with
    Harrison and Starr

M 0085
Lennon, John: "Ballad of John and Yoko"
    (song) banned
    M 0319   M 0444   N 1159
Lennon, John: barred in India
    N 0506
Lennon, John: Beatle songs played at
    death
    N 0313
Lennon, John: Beatle songs played in
    tribute
    N 0181
Lennon, John: bed-in
    C 0347   M 0972   M 1908   M 2596
    M 3003   N 0501   N 0658
Lennon, John: bed-in recordings
    M 1908
Lennon, John: benefit concert
    M 3550
Lennon, John: benefit concert "One To
    One" Festival
    M 1105   M 1163   M 1911   M 2719
    N 0311   N 0468
Lennon, John: "Billboard" (magazine)
    special issue
    M 3700
Lennon, John: biography
    B 0127   B 0191   B 0192   B 0193
    B 0194   B 0195   B 0221   B 0222
    C 0156   M 0021   M 0545   M 1493
    N 0648
Lennon, John: birthday gift from Starr
    M 2849
Lennon, John: birth of son Sean
    M 0592   N 0517   N 0578
Lennon, John: boat people benefit
    concert
    N 0704
Lennon, John: Bob Dylan
    M 2644
Lennon, John: book by Ray Connolly
    N 0864
Lennon, John: books
    M 3218
Lennon, John: brief biography
    C 0056
Lennon, John: buys cattle
    M 2872   M 2889
Lennon, John: buys Florida home
    M 2910
Lennon, John: buys Irish island
    M 1906
Lennon, John: buys Palm Springs mansion
    M 1110
Lennon, John: buys school for gypsy
    children
    N 0656
Lennon, John: buys upstate New York
    land to raise cattle
    N 0564
Lennon, John: calendar
    B 0332
Lennon, John: Canada
    M 1291
Lennon, John: Capitol Records
    M 2851
Lennon, John: car accident in Scotland
    N 0672
Lennon, John: career after Beatles
    B 0075   B 0076   M 3262   M 3317
    M 3379   N 0702
Lennon, John: Central Park, New York
    City, tribute section "Strawberry
    Fields"
    N 0281   N 0418   N 0619   N 1032
    N 1172
Lennon, John: Central Park, New York
    City, vigil tribute
    N 0909
Lennon, John: changes middle name
    N 0830
Lennon, John: charity performance
    M 1689
Lennon, John Charles Julian   see
    Lennon, Julian
Lennon, John: Christmas ad "War Is
    Over"
    N 1129
Lennon, John: Christmas billboards

M 1689   N 0566
Lennon, John: Christmas single
    M 2511   M 2694
Lennon, John: chronology
    B 0564   C 0192   M 1341
Lennon, John: Cincinnati Pops plays
    Lennon in tribute
    M 1270
Lennon, John: copyright case
    M 1093
Lennon, John: copyright suit
    M 3490
Lennon, John: courthouse painting
    stolen
    N 0471
Lennon, John: cremation
    N 0773
Lennon, John: Dakota tribute vigil on
    anniversary of his death
    N 1086
Lennon, John: death
    C 0094   M 0196   M 0557   M 0664
    M 0733   M 0785   M 0915   M 0922
    M 1009   M 1150   M 1312   M 1394
    M 1402   M 1442   M 1592   M 1717
    M 1729   M 1755   M 1822   M 1825
    M 1837   M 2042   M 2124   M 2141
    M 2143   M 2145   M 2262   M 2281
    M 2325   M 2481   M 2579   M 3116
    M 3210   M 3276   M 3356   M 3377
    M 3378   M 3381   M 3482   M 3540
    N 0210   N 0355   N 0535   N 0559
    N 0583   N 0593
Lennon, John: defended by former
    British ambassador
    N 1118
Lennon, John: defends Allen Klein
    M 3339
Lennon, John: Delaney & Bonnie tour
    M 2606
Lennon, John: denies benefit
    involvement
    N 0310
Lennon, John: deportation
    M 0231   M 0703   M 0794   M 1493
    M 1497   M 1534   M 1903   M 1907
    M 1932   M 1945   M 2367   M 2809
    M 2809   M 2828   M 3074   M 3131
    M 3260   M 3646   N 0221   N 0629
    N 0649   N 1178
Lennon, John: deportation case
    M 0919   M 1136   M 1279   M 1279
    M 1280   M 1721   M 1727   M 1916
    M 1944   M 2713   M 2831   M 3469
    M 3470   M 3471   N 0042   N 0372
    N 0544   N 0546   N 0549   N 0551
    N 0568   N 0603   N 0604   N 0605
    N 0606   N 0607   N 0629   N 0649
    N 0652   N 0660   N 0671   N 0674
    N 0676   N 0679   N 0691   N 0692
    N 0712   N 0714   N 0743   N 0762
    N 0826   N 1027   N 1028
Lennon, John: deportation fight, F.B.I.
    N 0025
Lennon, John: deportation fight won
    M 0704   M 1134   M 3470   N 0573
Lennon, John: deportation stalled by
    pregnancy of Ono
    N 0602
Lennon, John: detained by Canadian
    immigration
    N 0269
Lennon, John: diagram of his last
    movements
    N 0772
Lennon, John: disagrees with Starr on
    shows for public
    N 1096
Lennon, John: discography
    M 0935   M 0936   M 0959   M 0960
    M 0961   M 1348   M 1701   M 3117
Lennon, John: discussed in Parliament
    N 0868
Lennon, John: divorces Cynthia Powell
    M 0974   N 0553   N 0769
Lennon, John: donates £100 for UCS
    N 0980
Lennon, John: donation to New York City
    police

N 0456
Lennon, John: drug charge
  M 2255 N 0645 N 0646 N 0659
  N 0666 N 0866
Lennon, John: duet with Elton John
  M 3595
Lennon, John: early writing
  C 0090
Lennon, John: earnings
  M 3491
Lennon, John: editorial
  N 0402
Lennon, John: editorial eulogy
  M 2281 N 0353 N 0463 N 0547
  N 0567 N 0637 N 1031
Lennon, John: editorial letter
  N 0039 N 0084 N 0396
Lennon, John: effect of murder
  M 0072 N 0695
Lennon, John: effect of murder on gun
    control
  M 0519 N 0655 M 1033 M 1617
  M 1819 M 3393 N 0452 N 0768
  N 1150
Lennon, John: effects of death
  M 0072 M 0664 M 0862 M 1117
  M 1200 M 1347 N 0965
Lennon, John: effects of death in
    Germany
  M 0597
Lennon, John: effects of death in
    Sweden
  M 0526
Lennon, John: effects of death on
    celebrities
  N 1021
Lennon, John: effects of death on youth
  N 0053
Lennon, John: Elephant's Memory
  M 0033
Lennon, John: Elephant's memory concert
  M 2724
Lennon, John: Elton John recording
    session
  M 2790
Lennon, John: Elton John tribute
  M 1008
Lennon, John: estate
  M 0201 N 0758
Lennon, John: eulogies by celebrities
  M 3700
Lennon, John: eulogy
  C 0001 C 0003 C 0009 C 0012
  C 0013 C 0051 C 0064 C 0071
  C 0072 C 0077 C 0079 C 0082
  C 0096 C 0097 C 0098 C 0129
  C 0134 C 0138 C 0139 C 0146
  C 0154 C 0159 C 0160 C 0163
  C 0164 C 0172 C 0173 C 0174
  C 0183 C 0208 C 0214 C 0272
  C 0274 C 0297 C 0313 C 0315
  C 0316 C 0319 C 0335 C 0338
  C 0349 M 0623 M 1236 M 1394
  M 1582 M 1585 M 1592 M 1695
  M 1750 M 1782 M 2010 M 2133
  M 2159 M 2352 M 2377 M 2388
  M 2504 M 2522 M 3090 N 0001
  N 0006 N 0028 N 0047 N 0053
  N 0212 N 0230 N 0279 N 0290
  N 0309 N 0356 N 0438 N 0473
  N 0477 N 0498 N 0585 N 0598
  N 0599 N 0600 N 0685 N 0783
  N 0943 N 0955 N 0999 N 1038
Lennon, John: exhibit
  N 0232
Lennon, John: expecting a baby
  M 1728
Lennon, John: fails to ban articles by
    Cynthia Powell
  N 0397
Lennon, John: fails to ban book by
    Cynthia Powell
  M 2875
Lennon, John: fan club see Fan club
    (Lennon)
Lennon, John: fans
  N 0223 N 0320
Lennon, John: fans grieve at death
  M 2577 N 0212 N 0213 N 0224

N 0286 N 0287 N 0317 N 0375
N 0376 N 0455 N 0590 N 1015
N 1019 N 1034 N 1161
Lennon, John: fasts for Biafra
    protestors
  N 0755
Lennon, John: F.B.I.
  B 0582 M 0244 M 2481 M 2971
  M 3693 N 0378
Lennon, John: film roles
  M 1113 M 1941 M 2874
Lennon, John: films see also
    individual film titles
Lennon, John: films
  B 0474 M 0066 M 0646 M 1113
  M 1366 M 1637 M 1941 M 2095
  M 2360 M 2361 M 2383 M 2621
  M 2874 M 3640 N 0014 N 0384
  N 0448 N 0494 N 0584 N 0681
  N 1050 N 1170 N 1137 RF0097
  RF0125 RF0126 RF0127 RF0128
  RF0394 RF0395 RF0396
Lennon, John: films for benefit exhibit
  N 0494
Lennon, John: film shown at Cannes
  N 0384
Lennon, John: films shown at Whitney
    museum
  N 0448
Lennon, John: film tribute "Walking On
    Thin Ice"
  N 1170
Lennon, John: final RKO interview
  M 2475 N 0654 N 0657
Lennon, John: fined in drug charge
  M 1116 N 0555
Lennon, John: first anniversary of
    death
  N 1089
Lennon, John: first meeting with Ono
  M 3001
Lennon, John: Geffen Records
  M 1237 M 1799
Lennon, John: gives Irish island away
  N 0480
Lennon, John: Grammy Award
  M 1133 M 2708
Lennon, John: Grammy Award for DOUBLE
    FANTASY (LP)
  N 0852
Lennon, John: Greece
  M 1926
Lennon, John: Greenwich Village, New
    York days
  M 3302
Lennon, John: guest appearance
    recordings
  M 0959
Lennon, John: guest recording
    appearances
  M 1343
Lennon, John: guitar reproduction
  M 0094
Lennon, John: guitars – photo survey
  M 1372
Lennon, John: gun control urged at
    murder
  M 3393 N 0291
Lennon, John: gunplay at New York's
    Central Park vigil
  N 1176
Lennon, John: Handel Medallion award
  M 2925
Lennon, John: Hanratty murder case
  N 0653
Lennon, John: Hanratty murder film
  N 0504
Lennon, John: Harry Nilsson recording
    session
  M 2778
Lennon, John: has hair cut
  M 2766 M 3777 N 0069
Lennon, John: his staff queried in
    Hampshire murder case
  N 0675
Lennon, John: honored by church choir
  N 0439
Lennon, John: illustration
  N 0563

Lennon, John: implicated in Peter Hain
    case
  N 0780
Lennon, John: in banned film
  N 0846
Lennon, John: incendiary shell found at
    home
  N 0983
Lennon, John: India
  N 0111 N 0135 N 0506
Lennon, John: influence on music
  M 2010
Lennon, John: interview
  B 0335 B 0343 B 0448 B 0449
  B 0450 B 0451 B 0452 B 0453
  B 0454 B 0494 B 0495 B 0496
  B 0497 B 0498 B 0561 B 0571
  B 0572 B 0573 B 0574 B 0575
  B 0576 B 0577 B 0578 B 0579
  B 0580 B 0581 C 0086 C 0125
  C 0296 M 0558 M 0559 M 0705
  M 0708 M 0823 M 0828 M 1064
  M 1115 M 1316 M 1395 M 1640
  M 1641 M 1673 M 1696 M 1914
  M 1922 M 1928 M 1933 M 1934
  M 1935 M 1936 M 1937 M 1938
  M 1939 M 1940 M 2209 M 2390
  M 2425 M 2426 M 2427 M 2434
  M 2487 M 2799 M 2969 M 3039
  M 3045 M 3098 M 3216 M 3247
  M 3248 M 3564 M 3638 M 3639
  M 3646 M 3757 M 3778 M 3779
  M 3791 N 0225 N 0437 N 0562
Lennon, John: interview on Apple
    Corps., Ltd. ventures
  N 0988
Lennon, John: interview on peace
  C 0259
Lennon, John: interview tapes
  M 1933 M 1934 M 1935
Lennon, John: interview video
  M 3213
Lennon, John: interview with McCartney
    after death
  N 0479
Lennon, John: interview with Ono after
    death
  M 3214 N 0693 N 0810 N 0860
Lennon, John: invitation to play Christ
    in pop opera
  N 0663
Lennon, John: invited to Manitoba,
    Canada, for peace concert
  M 2111
Lennon, John: invites Harrison to
    concert film screening
  M 2702
Lennon, John: Irish Island
  M 2660
Lennon, John: jam session
  M 2739
Lennon, John: "(Just Like) Starting
    Over" (song)
  M 1121
Lennon, John: legal problems
  M 3074
Lennon, John: "Legs" (film)
  M 0066
Lennon, John: Lennon/McCartney songs by
    actual composer
  M 1917
Lennon, John: Lennon Peace Festival
  M 0382 N 0340
Lennon, John: letter
  N 0876
Lennon, John: letter to Paul McCartney
  M 1896
Lennon, John: letters
  M 1718 M 1915 M 1921 M 1951
  M 1952 M 1955 M 1957 M 3009
  N 0496
Lennon, John: life post-Beatles
  C 0329
Lennon, John: literary work
  B 0478 C 0224
Lennon, John: lithographs
  B 0301 B 0302 M 0101 M 1700
  M 2620 M 3622 M 3719 M 3775
  N 0026 N 0615 N 0668 N 0673

N 0891   N 0927   N 0964   N 1036
Lennon, John: lithographs -
    advertisement
  M 1700
Lennon, John: lithographs at auction
  N 0925
Lennon, John: live appearances
  M 2006
Lennon, John: live recordings
  M 0960
Lennon, John: Liverpool, England
    apartment
  M 1444
Lennon, John: Liverpool, England
    Cathedral service
  N 0382
Lennon, John: Liverpool, England
    memorials
  N 1106
Lennon, John: Long Island, New York
    estate
  M 3208
Lennon, John: lyrics
  M 1670   M 1901   M 1913   M 2128
Lennon, John: lyrics analyzed
  N 0782
Lennon, John: McCartney and Ono seek
    return of song rights
  N 0428
Lennon, John: McCartney concert tickets
  M 2838
Lennon, John: McCartney on Lennon after
    his death
  N 0725
Lennon, John: Majorca, Balearica
    Islands, Spain
  N 0061
Lennon, John: marital problems
  M 3074
Lennon, John: Maureen Cleave's
    remembrances
  M 0727
Lennon, John: meditation course
  N 0153
Lennon, John: memorabilia
  C 0147   C 0216   N 0223   N 0320
Lennon, John: memorial
  M 0689   M 1235   N 0112
Lennon, John: memorial contest
  M 1621
Lennon, John: memorial tree vandalized
    in Bromley
  N 0510
Lennon, John: "Mersey Beat" column
  C 0184   C 0185   C 0188   C 0189
  C 0190
Lennon, John: "Mersey Beat" poem
  C 0191
Lennon, John: "Mersey Beat" column
  C 0187
Lennon, John: Mid-East peace radio
  N 0411
Lennon, John: Mid-East peace ship
  N 1057
Lennon, John: Mid-East radio broadcast
  N 0683
Lennon, John: mistrial declared in
    publishing case
  N 0518
Lennon, John: montage for song
  C 0317
Lennon, John: moves into the Dakota,
    New York City, apartment house
  N 1068
Lennon, John: murder
  M 0197   M 0519   M 0542   M 1763
  M 3503   N 0285   N 0328   N 0453
  N 0454   N 0560   N 0594   N 0626
  N 0628   N 0632   N 0772   N 0839
  N 0900   N 0974   N 1039
Lennon, John: murder case
  N 0052   N 0283   N 0284   N 0344
  N 0345   N 0406   N 0416   N 0466
  N 0474   N 0627   N 0650   N 0662
  N 0678   N 0739   N 0745   N 0771
  N 0990   N 0991   N 0992   N 0993
  N 0994   N 0995   N 0996   N 0997
  N 1037   N 1084   N 1085
Lennon, John: murder case, sentence

passed
  M 0694   M 0695   N 0358   N 0466
  N 0693
Lennon, John: murderer see Chapman,
    Mark David
Lennon, John: music performed
  N 0470
Lennon, John: musical tribute
  M 2247
Lennon, John: namesake health center
    opened in Liverpool
  N 0655
Lennon, John: Newark, New Jersey
  M 1684
Lennon, John: newspaper clippings
  B 0491
Lennon, John: New York
  C 0060
Lennon, John: New York City's Central
    Park tribute section "Strawberry
    Fields"
  N 0281   N 0418   N 0619   N 1032
  N 1172
Lennon, John: New York "Times" ad
  M 2895
Lennon, John: nominated Artist of the
    Year
  M 2959
Lennon, John: Northern Ireland
  N 0558
Lennon, John: nude
  M 0230   M 0465   M 1189   M 1477
  M 1538   M 1927   M 2240   M 2589
Lennon, John: obituary
  B 0023   C 0245   C 0246   M 0716
  M 1114   M 1182   M 1580   M 1859
  M 2330   M 2331   M 2332   M 2333
  M 2354   N 0554   N 0853   N 0929
  N 0951
Lennon, John: offers island to
    community of hippies
  N 0665
Lennon, John: on Beatles
  C 0042
Lennon, John: on Beatles possible
    break-up
  M 0449
Lennon, John: on Beatles reunion
  M 3646   M 2750   M 2768   M 3096
Lennon, John: on Beatles reunion offer
  M 0920
Lennon, John: on being married to Ono
  N 0670
Lennon, John: on charity
  N 0222
Lennon, John: on David Frost show (tv
    show)
  N 0103
Lennon, John: on Dick Cavett show (tv
    show)
  M 0820
Lennon, John: on Elephant's Memory LP
  M 2714
Lennon, John: on Elton John single
  M 2805
Lennon, John: on Ono book GRAPEFRUIT
  N 1072
Lennon, John: on peace
  C 0334   M 1685   M 2300
Lennon, John: on "Revolution" (song)
  N 0156
Lennon, John: on "Tomorrow Show" (tv
    show)
  M 3213
Lennon, John: on "Tonight" (tv show)
  C 0320
Lennon, John: on transcendental
    meditation
  M 2148
Lennon, John: "One to One" benefit
    concert
  M 1105   M 1163   M 1911   M 2719
  N 0311   N 0468
Lennon, John Ono see Lennon, John
Lennon, John: Ono awarded custody of
    daughter, Kyoko
  N 0822
Lennon, John: Ono miscarries
  M 2608

Lennon, John: open letter
  M 1902   M 2123   M 2127   M 3009
  N 0644
Lennon, John: open letter from Ono
  N 0524   N 0525
Lennon, John: Oz Trial
  M 2663   M 3647   N 0558
Lennon, John: pays fines for S. African
    rugby team protestors
  N 0682
Lennon, John: performing arts high
    school memorial
  N 0390
Lennon, John: photograph
  M 2535   M 2571
Lennon, John: photograph, aerial, of
    Long Island, New York estate
  M 3208
Lennon, John: photograph with Cynthia
    Powell and son Julian
  M 1467
Lennon, John: photographs
  B 0345   B 0346   B 0347   B 0348
  B 0349   B 0350   B 0351   B 0352
  B 0425   B 0426
Lennon, John: photographs of Liverpool,
    England statue
  N 0472
Lennon, John: plagiarism suit
  M 2128
Lennon, John: plans live LP set
  M 2722
Lennon, John: Plastic Ono Band albums
  M 0039   N 1153
Lennon, John: "Playboy" (magazine)
    interview
  N 0595
Lennon, John: poem
  M 0008   M 1895   M 1898   M 1900
Lennon, John: poetry and prose
  M 1892
Lennon, John: popularity
  M 2212
Lennon, John: portrait
  M 1072   M 1657   M 2539   M 2540
  M 2541   M 2544   M 2545
Lennon, John: possible move to San
    Francisco, California
  M 3056
Lennon, John: press reaction to film
    show
  N 1073
Lennon, John: primal scream therapy
  M 1624   M 1668
Lennon, John: pro-IRA film
  M 2696
Lennon, John: protests
  M 3645
Lennon, John: protests Britain's Irish
    policy
  N 0630
Lennon, John: public reaction to death
  N 0228
Lennon, John: publishing activity after
    death
  M 1257   M 1788   M 3218   N 0078
  N 1123
Lennon, John: quotations
  B 0383   B 0384   B 0385   B 0386
  B 0387   B 0388   B 0389   B 0390
  B 0391   B 0392   C 0336   M 1746
  M 1893
Lennon, John: radio appearance
  M 2629
Lennon, John: radio program
  M 1692
Lennon, John: radio special
  M 1698
Lennon, John: reaction to death
  M 1347   M 1873   M 2176   M 2474
  M 2523   M 3151   M 3275   M 3356
  M 3482   M 3540   M 3763   N 0631
Lennon, John: readers' poll
  M 2960
Lennon, John: recording activity
  M 2788   M 2893   M 2903   M 2915
  M 2916   M 3068
Lennon, John: recording activity
    renewed

M 1920 M 2016
Lennon, John: recording in New York
    City
M 1987
Lennon, John: recording of "Happy
    Christmas"
M 2511
Lennon, John: recording on Geffen
    Records
M 1177
Lennon, John: records and songs see
    also individual record and song
    titles
Lennon, John: records and songs
B 0564   M 0039   M 0319   M 0444
M 0516   M 0718   M 0739   M 0837
M 0921   M 0935   M 0936   M 0938
M 0955   M 0959   M 0960   M 0961
M 0991   M 1089   M 1121   M 1133
M 1148   M 1164   M 1250   M 1348
M 1477   M 1526   M 1533   M 1538
M 1690   M 1691   M 1701   M 1854
M 1901   M 1908   M 1913   M 1917
M 1927   M 1961   M 2120   M 2240
M 2422   M 2511   M 2650   M 2694
M 2708   M 2715   M 2763   M 2795
M 2893   M 2903   M 2915   M 2916
M 2930   M 3054   M 3080   M 3087
M 3117   M 3266   M 3398   M 3455
M 3717   M 3783   N 0008   N 0028
N 0322   N 0478   N 0540   N 0552
N 0852   N 0855   N 0884   N 0921
N 1069   N 1153   N 1159   RR0030
RR0169 RR0170 RR0171 RR0172
RR0173 RR0174 RR0175 RR0176
RR0177 RR0178 RR0179 RR0180
RR0244 RR0245 RR0246 RR0247
RR0248 RR0249 RR0250 RR0251
RR0252 RR0253 RR0256 RR0261
RR0262 RR0263 RR0264 RR0265
RR0266 RR0267 RR0268 RR0269
RR0270 RR0285 RR0290 RR0329
RR0330 RR0331 RR0332 RR0333
RR0334 RR0335 RR0336 RR0337
RR0338 RR0339 RR0393 RR0394
RR0395 RR0396 RR0397 RR0398
RR0399 RR0400 RR0401 RR0402
RR0435 RR0436 RR0437 RR0438
RR0439 RR0440 RR0441 RR0443
RR0444 RR0445 RR0446 RR0447
RR0448 RR0449 RR0450 RR0504
RR0505 RR0506 RR0507 RR0517
RR0518 RR0519 RR0520 RR0521
RR0522 RR0524 RR0545 RR0548
RR0549
Lennon, John: records Mick Jagger song
M 2785
Lennon, John: records re-issued
N 0048
Lennon, John: refused U.S. visa
N 1099
Lennon, John: relationship with Epstein
C 0217
Lennon, John: remark on popularity of
    Beatles and Jesus
N 0141   N 0304   N 0664   N 0878
N 1017   M 0009   M 0413   M 0487
M 0578   M 0721   M 0815   M 0874
M 1061   M 2320   M 2557   M 3545
Lennon, John: remark on popularity of
    Beatles and Jesus - debris thrown
    at concert
N 0342
Lennon, John: remark on popularity of
    Beatles and Jesus - drop in
    Beatles stock
N 1025
Lennon, John: remark on popularity of
    Beatles and Jesus - editorial
N 1145
Lennon, John: remark on popularity of
    Beatles and Jesus - radio ban
M 3426   N 0304   N 0326
Lennon, John: remark on popularity of
    Beatles and Jesus - U.S. ban
N 1116
Lennon, John: remark on popularity of
    Beatles and Jesus - Vatican
    accepts apology

N 1121
Lennon, John: remembered by Bruce
    Springsteen and audience
N 1022
Lennon, John: renews recording activity
M 3384
Lennon, John: response to McCartney
    interview
M 2700
Lennon, John: returns his M.B.E. award
M 0037   M 1923   N 0361   N 0571
N 0850
Lennon, John: reunites with Ono
M 2813
Lennon, John: reviews Spike Milligan
    book
N 0642
Lennon, John: RKO interview
M 1115   M 1936   M 1937   M 1938
M 1939   M 1940   M 2475   M 3248
Lennon, John: Rolling Stone postcard
M 2673
Lennon, John: Ronald Reagan comment on
    death
N 0278
Lennon, John: Rowland photos
C 0278
Lennon, John: royalties
N 1030
Lennon, John: royalties to promote
    peace
N 0669
Lennon, John: rumor of McCartney
    reunion
M 2736
Lennon, John: rumor of split with Ono
M 2766
Lennon, John: rumor of involvement in
    African benefit concert
N 0977
Lennon, John: sale of Holstein cow
N 0325
Lennon, John: sale of Surrey home
M 2627
Lennon, John: sale of Tittenhurst Park
    home
M 2758
Lennon, John: scholarship
M 0689   M 1030   M 1207
Lennon, John: scholarship memorial at
    Julliard
M 0689   M 1030
Lennon, John: seeks custody of Kyoko
    Cox
N 1169
Lennon, John: seeks U.S. visa
N 0570
Lennon, John: sells his interests in
    Apple Corps.
M 1829
Lennon, John: separation from Cynthia
    Powell
M 3051
Lennon, John: separation from Yoko Ono
N 0576
Lennon, John: serenades U Thant
M 2699
Lennon, John: sexual rumors of Epstein
N 0232
Lennon, John: shaves head for peace
N 0276
Lennon, John: silent vigil tribute
M 0193   M 1271   N 0661   N 0700
N 0734   N 0737   N 0738   N 0902
N 0909
Lennon, John: Sinclair freedom rally
M 3279
Lennon, John: songbook see also
    Beatles songbook
Lennon, John: songbook see also
    Lennon/McCartney songbook
Lennon, John: songbook see also
    Lennon/Ono songbook
Lennon, John: songbook
S 0096   S 0098   S 0099   S 0100
S 0101   S 0102   S 0103   S 0104
S 0120   S 0146   S 0147   S 0151
S 0152
Lennon, John: song recorded by David

Bowie
M 2814
Lennon, John: song recorded by Starr
M 2789
Lennon, John: songwriting award
M 3489   M 3755   M 0493   M 0582
M 1904   M 1918
Lennon, John: Soviet response to death
N 0038
Lennon, John: Starr recording session
M 2737   M 3063   M 3278
Lennon, John: statue in Los Angeles
N 0945
Lennon, John: sued by Big Seven Music
    Corporation
N 0503
Lennon, John: sued by music corporation
N 0580
Lennon, John: sued by Northern Songs,
    Ltd.
N 0903
Lennon, John: sued for loan
N 0400
Lennon, John: sues government for
    wiretapping
N 0677
Lennon, John: sues newspaper
N 0797
Lennon, John: television special
M 2591
Lennon, John: to make film on Hanratty
    murder
N 0681
Lennon, John: tops poll as singers'
    favorite singer
M 2728
Lennon, John: Top Twenty
C 0114
Lennon, John: Toronto, Canada
M 0901   M 1553   N 0274
Lennon, John: Toronto Peace Festival
M 0123   M 0202   M 0670   M 1679
M 1681   M 1688   M 1894   M 1905
M 1929   M 1930   M 2323   M 3465
M 3466   M 3773   M 3778   N 0275
Lennon, John: tribute
B 0519   M 0003   M 0121   M 0790
M 1008   M 1270   M 1832   M 2918
M 3215   M 3497   N 0550   P 0078
P 0080   P 0082   P 0084   P 0085
P 0086   P 0088   P 0108   P 0112
P 0117
Lennon, John: tribute by Cincinnati
    Pops
M 1270
Lennon, John: tribute concert at
    Carnegie Hall by Boston Pops
N 1087
Lennon, John: tribute issue
P 0087
Lennon, John: tribute performance
N 0482
Lennon, John: tribute records
M 2977   M 2978
Lennon, John: tribute - reviews
M 3569
Lennon, John: Troubador Club
M 2767
Lennon, John: Troubador Club charge
    dismissed
N 0610
Lennon, John: Troubador Club incident
M 0502   M 0662   M 3479   N 0609
Lennon, John: "Two Virgins" (film)
N 1050
Lennon, John: TWO VIRGINS (LP) banned
M 0516   N 0540
Lennon, John: TWO VIRGINS (LP) seized
N 0008   N 0921
Lennon, John: U.C.L.A. graduate
    research award
N 0845
Lennon, John: University of Delaware
    course
N 0314
Lennon, John: U.S. visa awarded
M 1677
Lennon, John: use of Starr residence
N 0622

Lennon, John: U.S.S.R. rally in Moscow
 N 0913
Lennon, John: vs. Allen Klein
 M 1812
Lennon, John: vs. Big Seven Music
  Corporation
 M 0541
Lennon, John: vs. Maclen Music
 M 2732
Lennon, John: vs. Mitchell
 M 1932
Lennon, John: vs. Morris Levy
 M 1961 M 2128
Lennon, John: vs. Northern Songs
 M 2732
Lennon, John: vs. Northern Songs and
  Maclen Music
 M 1919
Lennon, John: vs. U.S. and Nixon
 M 1903
Lennon, John: video
 M 1350
Lennon, John: Vienna press conference
 N 0736
Lennon, John: visits Buckingham Palace
 N 0895
Lennon, John: visit with Prime Minister
  Trudeau (Canada)
 N 0245
Lennon, John: voice imitator
 M 1483
Lennon, John: warns against use of
  drugs
 N 0509
Lennon, John: weds Yoko Ono
 N 0556 N 0561
Lennon, John: will
 M 1720 N 0461 N 0623
Lennon, John: Willowbrook benefit
  concert
 M 0977
Lennon, John: wins New York City
  cultural award
 N 0617
Lennon, John Winston see Lennon, John
Lennon, John: with Eric Clapton
 C 0348
Lennon, John: WNET "happening" with the
  Lennons receives protests
 N 1103
Lennon, John: "Working Class Hero"
  (song)
 M 1148
Lennon, John: works compared to
  Picasso's
 N 1131
Lennon, John: world wide silent tribute
 N 0455
Lennon, John: writes letter on reunion
  rumors
 M 2742
Lennon, John: Yoko Ono and son Sean two
  years after death
 N 1120
Lennon, John: Yoko Ono asks for prayers
  for his soul
 N 1143
Lennon, John: Yoko Ono asks mourners to
  give to Spirit Foundation
 N 1167
Lennon, John: Yoko Ono miscarries
 M 2608 N 1168
Lennon, Julian
 M 1594 M 1720 M 2937 M 2946
 N 1175
Lennon, Julian: interview
 M 1795
Lennon, Julian: photograph with parents
 M 1467
Lennon, Julian: visits Ono in New York
  City
 M 1752
Lennon/McCartney
 B 0113 B 0170 B 0171 B 0173
 B 0295
Lennon/McCartney: as top BMI
  songwriters
 M 0582
Lennon/McCartney music

 N 0782 M 3005 M 3039 M 3305
Lennon/McCartney songbook see also
  Beatles songbook
Lennon/McCartney songbook
 S 0085 S 0086 S 0087 S 0095
 S 0108 S 0109 S 0110 S 0111
 S 0112 S 0113 S 0119 S 0125
 S 0143 S 0154 S 0158
Lennon/McCartney songs
 M 0165 M 0370 M 0582 M 0818
 M 0819 M 1298 M 1622 M 1642
 M 3588 N 0268
Lennon/McCartney songs: by actual
  composer
 M 1917
Lennon/McCartney songs: copyright
  dispute after break-up
 M 0837
Lennon/Ono songbook
 S 0148 S 0149
"Lennon" (play)
 M 0174 M 2216 M 3241 M 3383
LENNON REMEMBERS (book)
 RB0404 RB0405 RB0406 RB0407
 RB0408 RB0409 RB0410 RB0411
 RB0412 RB0413 RB0414 RB0415
 RB0416 RB0417 RB0418 RB0419
 RB0420 RB0421 RB0422
Lennon, Sean Ono
 M 0530 M 1314 M 3208 M 3214
 M 3217 M 3247 N 1120
Lennon, Sean Ono: birth
 M 0592 N 0517 N 0578
Lennon, Sean Ono: visits Elton John
 M 1008
LENNON '69: SEARCH FOR LIBERATION
  (book)
 RB0423
THE LENNON TAPES (book)
 RB0424 RB0425 RB0426 RB0427
 RB0428 RB0429
Lennon, Yoko see Ono, Yoko
Lester, Richard
 M 1540 M 3665 N 1137
"Let It Be" (film)
 M 1303 M 1542 M 2220 M 2274
 M 2376 M 2624 M 3486 M 3495
 N 0748 N 0790 RF0153 RF0154
 RF0155 RF0156 RF0157 RF0158
 RF0159 RF0160 RF0161 RF0162
"Let It Be" (film): critique
 C 0300
"Let It Be" (film): filming
 M 2593 M 2599
"Let It Be" (film): London, England
  premiere
 M 2631
"Let It Be" (film): premiere
 M 0247 M 3656
LET IT BE (LP) see also 'GET BACK'
  (LP)
LET IT BE (LP)
 M 0832 M 0975 M 1252 M 1253
 M 1547 M 1663 M 1856 M 2267
 M 2376 M 2906 M 3486 M 3495
 N 1049 RR0218 RR0272 RR0273
 RR0274 RR0275 RR0276 RR0277
 RR0278 RR0279 RR0280 RR0281
"Let It Be" (song)
 M 2615
LET'S HEAR ONE FOR LORD BUDDAH (LP)
 M 1363 RR0282
Letterman, David
 M 3764
Letters Abroad
 F 0097
Lewis, Jerry Lee
 M 3427
LIFE AT THE DAKOTA (book)
 RB0430
"Life" (magazine): Special Beatles 20th
  anniversary issue
 M 0262 M 1995
"Life Of Brian" (film) see "Monty
  Python's Life Of Brian" (film)
LIFE WITH THE LIONS (LP)
 RR0507
LIKE DREAMERS DO (LP)
 RR0283 RR0284

LINDA'S CALENDAR 1982 (book)
 RB0431
LINDA'S PICTURES (book)
 RB0432 RB0433 RB0434 RB0435
 RB0436 RB0437 RB0438
LINDA'S SIGNS FOR '79 (book)
 RB0439
Lindsay, Mayor (New York City)
 N 0629
Lindsay, Mayor (New York City): on
  Lennon deportation action
 N 0221
LISTEN TO THIS PICTURE RECORD (LP)
 RR0285
"Lisztomania" (film)
 M 2812 RF0163 RF0164 RF0165
 RF0166 RF0167 RF0168 RF0169
 RF0170 RF0171 RF0172 RF0173
 RF0174 RF0175 RF0176 RF0177
 RF0178 RF0179 RF0180 RF0181
 RF0182 RF0183 RF0184 RF0185
 RF0186 RF0187 RF0188 RF0189
 RF0190 RF0191 RF0192
Lithographs (Lennon): obscenity charge
 N 0026
"Little Malcolm and His Struggle
  Against The Eunuchs" (film)
 RF0193 RF0194 RF0195 RF0196
 RF0197 RF0198 RF0199 RF0200
Little Richard
 M 1479 M 2005
"Live and Let Die" (film)
 RF0201 RF0202 RF0203 RF0204
 RF0205 RF0206 RF0207 RF0208
 RF0209 RF0210 RF0211 RF0212
 RF0213 RF0214 RF0215 RF0216
 RF0217 RF0218 RF0219 RF0220
 RF0221 RF0222 RF0223 RF0224
 RF0225 RF0226 RF0227 RF0228
 RF0229 RF0230 RF0231 RF0232
 RF0233 RF0234 RF0235 RF0236
LIVE AND LET DIE (LP)
 M 2069 M 2071 M 2726 RR0286
 RR0287 RR0288
LIVE! AT THE STAR CLUB IN HAMBURG,
  GERMANY, 1962 (LP) see THE
  BEATLES LIVE AT THE STAR CLUB
  (LP)
LIVE IN GERMANY (EP)
 RR0289
LIVE PEACE IN TORONTO (LP)
 RR0290
Liverpool, England see also Cavern
  Club, Liverpool, England
Liverpool, England see also
  Merseyside
Liverpool, England: "Beatle industry"
 N 0337
Liverpool, England: Beatles
 B 0247 B 0248 B 0296 B 0297
 C 0030 C 0046 M 1430 M 1431
 M 1451 M 2391 M 2479 M 3153
 N 0150 N 0522
Liverpool, England: Beatles Information
  Centre
 M 2476
Liverpool, England: Beatles museum
 M 1561 M 2476 M 3293
Liverpool, England: Beatles-related
  landmarks
 B 0566 M 0528 M 1204 M 1429
 M 1459
Liverpool, England: "Beatle" street
  names
 M 2533 M 3367 N 0324 N 0754
Liverpool, England: Cavern Club
 M 3581
Liverpool, England: Cavern Club and
  Beatles' popularity
 N 0697
Liverpool, England: concert
 N 1062 N 1079
Liverpool, England: Council honors
  Beatles
 N 0698
Liverpool, England: fan club
 M 1012 M 1013 M 1014 M 1015
Liverpool, England: fan convention
 M 0110 M 2472 M 2998 M 3542

Liverpool, England: fans grieve at
  Lennon's death
  N 0286
Liverpool, England: fans resist Cavern
  Club closing
  N 0121 N 0248
Liverpool, England: fans welcome home
  N 0843
Liverpool, England: first Beatles
  convention
  M 0770
Liverpool, England: influence of
  Beatles
  N 0083
Liverpool, England: Lennon Festival
  Cathedral service
  N 0340 N 0382
Liverpool, England: Lennon Health
  Centre opened
  N 0655
Liverpool, England: Lennon memorials
  N 1106
Liverpool, England: Lennon Peace
  Festival Cathedral service
  M 0382 N 0340
Liverpool, England: Lennon tribute
  M 3497
Liverpool, England: McCartney
  M 1773
Liverpool, England: McCartney concert
  M 2904
Liverpool, England: Magical Mystery
  Store
  M 2467
Liverpool, England: Merseyside sound
  N 0699
Liverpool, England: music
  C 0209
Liverpool, England: photograph of
  Lennon statue
  N 0472
Liverpool, England: post-Hamburg days
  M 3295
Liverpool, England: proposed Beatles
  statue
  M 1445 M 2009 M 2870 N 0336
  N 0519 N 1067
Liverpool, England: statue fund
  M 3741
Liverpool, England: streets named for
  Beatles
  M 2533 N 0754
LIVERPOOL LIVE (LP)
  RR0291
Liverpool Productions
  F 0075
Liverpudlian slang glossary
  M 3662
LIVING IN THE MATERIAL WORLD (LP)
  M 2746 M 3603 RR0292 RR0293
  RR0294 RR0295 RR0296 RR0297
  RR0298
Livingston, Alan
  M 2011
Lloyd Webber, Andrew see Webber,
  Andrew Lloyd
London Airport: Beatle fans
  N 0079
London Airport: fans greet Beatles
  N 1117
London, England: Beatles
  M 0376 M 0494
London, England: Beatles apartment
  M 0907
London, England: Beatles-related
  landmarks
  M 1006 M 1432 M 1433
London, England: Beatles return
  N 0168
London, England: concerts
  M 0376
London, England: Hammersmith concert
  N 0128
London, England: live concert planned
  M 0450 M 2251
London, England: McCartney
  M 3112
London, England: memorabilia store
  M 2008

London, England: mob
  N 0079 N 0890
London, England: police protection for
  the Beatles
  N 0890
London, England: Wings concert
  M 0630
LONDON TOWN (LP)
  M 1295 M 1544 M 1981 M 3000
  RR0299 RR0300 RR0301
THE LONG AND THE WINDING ROAD (book)
  M 1447 RB0440 RB0441 RB0442
  RB0443
"The Long And Winding Road" (film -
  provisional title)
  M 0560
Long Beach, California: Harrison at
  Grand Prix
  M 2861
THE LONGEST COCKTAIL PARTY (book)
  M 1441 RB0444 RB0445 RB0446
  RB0447 RB0448 RB0449 RB0450
Long Island, New York: Cynthia Powell
  art exhibit
  M 1463
Long Island, New York: Lennon estate
  M 3208
"Long, Long, Long" (song)
  M 0829
Los Angeles, California: Beatle fans
  convention
  M 1833 M 2040 M 2369 M 2370
  M 2999
Los Angeles, California: Beatles
  M 3043
Los Angeles, California: concert
  M 0380 M 0731
Los Angeles, California: hand gun
  control
  M 3393
Los Angeles, California: Harrison visit
  M 0228
Los Angeles, California: Lennon
  M 0502 M 0662 M 2767 M 3311
  M 3479 N 0609 N 0610
Los Angeles, California: Lennons
  M 2630
Los Angeles, California: Lennon statue
  N 0945
Los Angeles, California: Mal Evans
  M 3313
Los Angeles, California: Wings concert
  N 0194 N 0720
Los Angeles, California: Wings concerts
  sell out unannounced
  N 0720
LOTS OF LIVERPOOL (book)
  RB0451
Louisiana: McCartneys in New Orleans
  M 3681 M 2811 M 0131
LOVE LETTERS TO THE BEATLES (book)
  RB0452 RB0453 RB0454 RB0455
"Love Me Do" (song)
  C 0029 C 0033 C 0117 M 0170
  M 0288 M 0890 M 0900 M 0908
  M 1448 M 2044 M 2045 M 3431
LOVE ME DO - THE BEATLES' PROGRESS
  (book)
  RB0456 RB0457
"Love Me Do" (video)
  RF0237
LOVE SONGS (LP)
  RR0302
THE LOVE YOU MAKE (book)
  M 0175 RB0458
THE LOVE YOU MAKE (book): excerpt
  M 0631 M 0632
LOVING JOHN: THE UNTOLD STORY (book)
  RB0459
Loving Spoonful
  M 0641
L.P. see Album
L.S.D. (McCartney)
  M 0252
"Lucy In The Sky With Diamonds" (song)
  M 2805
Lynch, Kenny
  M 0875
Lyrics

B 0007 B 0008 B 0009 B 0010
B 0011 B 0012 B 0013 B 0014
B 0015 B 0016 B 0017 B 0018
B 0019 B 0020 B 0021 B 0022
B 0023 B 0024 B 0025 B 0026
B 0027 B 0028 B 0059 B 0060
B 0094 B 0125 B 0205 C 0069
C 0127 C 0150 C 0181 M 3324
M 3438
Lyrics: analyzed
  N 0782
Lyrics: attacked by Agnew
  N 0088
Lyrics (McCartney): handwritten
  C 0198
THE MCCARTNEY INTERVIEW (LP)
  M 0962 M 2064 M 2065 M 2066
McCartney, James Louis: birth
  M 2868
McCartney, James Paul see McCartney,
  Paul
McCartney, Linda see Eastman, Linda
MCCARTNEY (LP)
  M 0918 M 1472 M 3126 M 3136
  M 3720 RR0303 RR0304 RR0305
  RR0306 RR0307 RR0308
McCartney, Mary: birth
  M 2600 N 0288 N 0333
McCartney, Mike
  B 0356 B 0357 B 0358 B 0359
  B 0180 M 1779 M 1781 M 2089
  M 2189 M 2418 M 2419 M 3298
McCartney, Mike: fan club see Fan
  club (McCartney, Mike)
McCartney, Mike: interview
  M 1887 M 1888 M 2956
McCartney, Paul
  B 0095 B 0113 B 0156 B 0170
  B 0171 B 0172 B 0173 B 0207
  B 0208 B 0209 B 0210 B 0213
  B 0214 B 0215 B 0216 B 0227
  B 0232 B 0234 B 0235 B 0269
  B 0271 B 0272 B 0284 B 0295
  B 0344 B 0345 B 0346 B 0347
  B 0348 B 0349 B 0350 B 0351
  B 0352 B 0353 B 0354 B 0355
  B 0356 B 0357 B 0358 B 0359
  B 0366 B 0379 B 0401 B 0440
  B 0441 B 0442 B 0456 B 0527
  B 0551 B 0552 B 0553 B 0592
  B 0593 B 0603 C 0011 C 0061
  C 0291 C 0330 M 0016 M 0017
  M 0095 M 0104 M 0106 M 0132
  M 0139 M 0140 M 0145 M 0147
  M 0178 M 0504 M 0515 M 0565
  M 0571 M 0573 M 0585 M 0599
  M 0601 M 0624 M 0625 M 0626
  M 0640 M 0654 M 0679 M 0684
  M 0685 M 0701 M 0706 M 0712
  M 0742 M 0806 M 0807 M 0838
  M 0860 M 0871 M 0925 M 0929
  M 0971 M 1007 M 1022 M 1078
  M 1085 M 1123 M 1124 M 1151
  M 1155 M 1185 M 1195 M 1215
  M 1251 M 1286 M 1293 M 1308
  M 1315 M 1319 M 1351 M 1367
  M 1368 M 1369 M 1370 M 1378
  M 1379 M 1381 M 1384 M 1405
  M 1494 M 1521 M 1549 M 1563
  M 1575 M 1595 M 1651 M 1671
  M 1674 M 1726 M 1773 M 1815
  M 1856 M 1857 M 1877 M 1947
  M 1963 M 2056 M 2072 M 2075
  M 2078 M 2081 M 2126 M 2137
  M 2162 M 2183 M 2200 M 2205
  M 2206 M 2211 M 2243 M 2245
  M 2256 M 2259 M 2269 M 2285
  M 2287 M 2293 M 2308 M 2335
  M 2339 M 2348 M 2371 M 2375
  M 2397 M 2401 M 2402 M 2403
  M 2406 M 2413 M 2414 M 2417
  M 2424 M 2429 M 2441 M 2447
  M 2451 M 2452 M 2453 M 2480
  M 2528 M 2642 M 2649 M 2657
  M 2668 M 2811 M 2815 M 2816
  M 2817 M 2820 M 2837 M 2838
  M 2858 M 2862 M 2885 M 2890
  M 2891 M 2931 M 2932 M 2940
  M 2944 M 2956 M 2973 M 2996

M 3023   M 3073   M 3085   M 3089
M 3121   M 3133   M 3196   M 3197
M 3239   M 3263   M 3269   M 3336
M 3351   M 3374   M 3405   M 3408
M 3442   M 3446   M 3450   M 3481
M 3501   M 3505   M 3509   M 3522
M 3553   M 3561   M 3566   M 3611
M 3613   M 3619   M 3621   M 3625
M 3626   M 3629   M 3634   M 3690
M 3692   M 3721   M 3734   M 3735
M 3736   M 3737   M 3738   M 3748
N 0043   N 0073   N 0335   N 0371
N 0497   N 0577   N 0871   N 1000
N 1152   P 0006   P 0098

McCartney, Paul: Abbey Road studio
    party
    M 2941   M 3084
McCartney, Paul: acquires publishing
    interests
    M 1993
McCartney, Paul: activity after
    Lennon's death
    M 0072   M 0857
McCartney, Paul: album released in
    U.S.S.R.
    M 2058
McCartney, Paul: Allen Klein ousted
    N 0636
McCartney, Paul: artist of the year
    M 3102
McCartney, Paul: as a child
    M 3786
McCartney, Paul: as 'Apollo C.
    Vermouth'
    M 0022
McCartney, Paul: as bass guitarist
    M 2348
McCartney, Paul: as best male vocalist
    N 0393
McCartney, Paul: as composer
    C 0265   M 1298   M 1588   M 1642
    M 2586   M 3305   M 3326   M 3588
    M 3757
McCartney, Paul: as director of
    "Magical Mystery Tour" (film)
    N 0197
McCartney, Paul: asked to produce
    Blood, Sweat & Tears LP
    M 2670
McCartney, Paul: asked to waive
    royalties on "On, Wisconsin"
    (song)
    N 0718   N 0723
McCartney, Paul: as most honored music
    composer/performer
    N 0581
McCartney, Paul: at brother's wedding
    M 3298
McCartney, Paul: at Mick Jaeger's
    wedding
    M 2381
McCartney, Paul: at Starr's wedding
    M 2187
McCartney, Paul: awards
    M 3103
McCartney, Paul: barred in Japan
    N 0507
McCartney, Paul: Beatles break-up
    N 0582   N 1124
McCartney, Paul: Beatles break-up
    rumors
    M 0300
McCartney, Paul: Beatles dissolution
    case
    N 0373   N 0687
McCartney, Paul: Beatles songbook
    N 0715
McCartney, Paul: Beatles split denied
    N 0728
McCartney, Paul: bid on first Beatles
    record
    M 2061   N 0885
McCartney, Paul: biography
    B 0232   B 0379   M 0546
McCartney, Paul: birth of daughter Mary
    M 2600   N 0288   N 0333
McCartney, Paul: birth of daughter
    Stella
    M 2677

McCartney, Paul: birth of son James
    Louis
    M 2868
McCartney, Paul: birthday gift feared
    as bomb
    N 0226
McCartney, Paul: brief biography
    C 0057   C 0236   M 2407
McCartney, Paul: Buddy Holly Week
    M 2867
McCartney, Paul: builds mobile
    recording studio
    M 2887
McCartney, Paul: buys E.H. Morris Music
    M 2184
McCartney, Paul: buys Scottish farm
    N 0462
McCartney, Paul: Capitol Records
    M 2881   M 3285
McCartney, Paul: career after Beatles
    B 0075   B 0076   M 0822   M 3262
    M 3379
McCartney, Paul: cartoon
    N 1058
McCartney, Paul: CBS Records
    M 2887   M 3199
McCartney, Paul: Christmas LP
    M 2800
McCartney, Paul: Christmas record
    M 3539   RR0546
McCartney, Paul: Christmas single
    M 3539
McCartney, Paul: Columbia Records
    contract
    M 2185
McCartney, Paul: composes movie theme
    music
    M 2071
McCartney, Paul: concert at Liverpool
    school
    M 2904
McCartney, Paul: concert in London,
    England
    M 0630
McCartney, Paul: concert in Munich,
    Germany
    M 0118
McCartney, Paul: copyright suit
    M 3490
McCartney, Paul: criticized by Billy
    Graham
    N 0068
McCartney, Paul: death rumor
    B 0603   C 0314   M 0550   M 0638
    M 0816   M 0886   M 1276   M 1474
    M 1607   M 1771   M 1878   M 2059
    M 2286   M 2339   M 2350   M 3122
    M 3219   M 3369   N 0163   N 0752
    N 1075   P 0099   P 0100
McCartney, Paul: deported by Japan
    N 0538
McCartney, Paul: discography
    B 0156   B 0593   M 0965   M 0966
McCartney, Paul: drawings for PAUL
    MCCARTNEY, COMPOSER/ARTIST (book)
    N 1134
McCartney, Paul: driving charge
    N 0057
McCartney, Paul: drug charge in Japan
    M 1830   N 0326
McCartney, Paul: drug charge
    M 0398   N 0824   N 0870
McCartney, Paul: drug charge in Japan
    M 0853   M 0987   M 1830   M 1831
    M 2405   M 2908   M 3589   N 0326
    N 0542   N 0726   N 0729   N 0731
    N 0869   N 0873
McCartney, Paul: drug raid
    N 0511
McCartney, Paul: drug views discussed
    in Parliament
    N 1114
McCartney, Paul: drugs in Sweden
    M 3396
McCartney, Paul: earnings
    M 3491
McCartney, Paul: "Ebony & Ivory" (song)
    M 1329   M 1330
McCartney, Paul: Eric Clapton's wedding

M 2894
McCartney, Paul: expecting a baby
    N 0499
McCartney, Paul: expecting birth of
    fourth child
    N 0614
McCartney, Paul: family life
    M 2172
McCartney, Paul: fan club   see   Fan
    club (McCartney)
McCartney, Paul: fanzine
    M 2860
McCartney, Paul: favorite records
    M 0690
McCartney, Paul: film activity
    M 1108   M 2399   M 2912   M 2948
McCartney, Paul: filming promo video
    M 1985
McCartney, Paul: films   see also
    individual film titles
McCartney, Paul: films
    M 1108   M 1464   M 1984   M 1985
    M 2082   M 2227   M 2399   M 2720
    M 2912   M 2948   M 3502   M 3570
    N 0197   RF0015   RF0201   RF0204
    RF0206   RF0207   RF0208   RF0209
    RF0210   RF0211   RF0212   RF0213
    RF0214   RF0215   RF0216   RF0217
    RF0218   RF0219   RF0220   RF0221
    RF0222   RF0223   RF0224   RF0225
    RF0226   RF0227   RF0228   RF0229
    RF0230   RF0231   RF0232   RF0233
    RF0234   RF0235   RF0236   RF0297
    RF0298   RF0299   RF0339
McCartney, Paul: films video
    M 2720
McCartney, Paul: first rock LP in
    U.S.S.R.
    M 2842
McCartney, Paul: forms group Wings
    N 0369   N 0721
McCartney, Paul: full page ad
    M 2647
McCartney, Paul: "Give Ireland Back To
    The Irish" (song)
    M 1485   M 2415   M 2416   M 3605
    N 0055   N 0531
McCartney, Paul: gives song to Peggy
    Lee
    M 2786
McCartney, Paul: Glasgow, Scotland
    visit
    N 0722
McCartney, Paul: "Goodnight Tonight"
    (song)
    N 0796
McCartney, Paul: guest appearance
    recordings
    M 0965
McCartney, Paul: Guinness award
    M 2068   M 3449   N 0705
McCartney, Paul: guitars - photo survey
    M 2411
McCartney, Paul: guitar stolen
    N 0075
McCartney, Paul: handwritten lyrics
    C 0198
McCartney, Paul: Harry Nilsson
    recording session
    M 2778
McCartney, Paul: has lunch at Lazards
    N 0259
McCartney, Paul: Holland, 1976
    M 0114   M 0115   M 0116   M 0119
McCartney, Paul: hotel near home
    N 0491
McCartney, Paul: house
    C 0089
McCartney, Paul: incognito at Harrison
    concert
    M 3289
McCartney, Paul: interest in Buddy
    Holly
    M 1743
McCartney, Paul: interview
    C 0004   C 0205   M 0074   M 0098
    M 0179   M 0601   M 0608   M 0665
    M 0748   M 0749   M 0853   M 0903
    M 0918   M 0962   M 1075   M 1156

M 1209   M 1215   M 1217   M 1221
M 1224   M 1226   M 1228   M 1230
M 1310   M 1468   M 1499   M 1645
M 2064   M 2065   M 2066   M 2172
M 2196   M 2400   M 2408   M 2700
M 3000   M 3039   M 3118   M 3630
M 3631   M 3632   M 3643   M 3671
M 3703   N 0872

McCartney, Paul: interview on Apple
    Corps., Ltd. ventures
    N 0988
McCartney, Paul: interview on Lennon
    N 0479
McCartney, Paul: interview with BBC
    N 0875
McCartney, Paul: interview with Linda
    Eastman
    N 1140
McCartney, Paul: Japan
    B 0401   B 0595   M 1798
McCartney, Paul: Japanese radio ban
    M 0141
McCartney, Paul: jet waits for him
    M 2829   N 0508
McCartney, Paul: lawyer denounces Klein
    N 0138
McCartney, Paul: Lennon/McCartney songs
    by actual composer
    M 1917
McCartney, Paul: Lennon's death
    M 3700
McCartney, Paul: Lennon tribute
    N 0468
McCartney, Paul: Lennon tribute
    recording rumor
    M 2919
McCartney, Paul: letter from John
    Lennon
    M 1896
McCartney, Paul: letter on cartoon
    N 1165
McCartney, Paul: Los Angeles,
    California Wings concert
    M 0194
McCartney, Paul: L.S.D.
    M 0252
McCartney, Paul: lyrics
    B 0594   M 1670
McCartney, Paul: lyrics analyzed
    N 0782
McCartney, Paul: man trespasses on
    property
    N 0706
McCartney, Paul: marriage plans to
    Linda Eastman
    N 0145
McCartney, Paul: "Mersey Beat" column
    C 0196   C 0197
McCartney, Paul: music copyright empire
    M 2896
McCartney, Paul: music publishing
    holdings
    M 2062
McCartney, Paul: Nairobi, Kenya
    M 1041
McCartney, Paul: New Orleans, Louisiana
    visit
    M 0131
McCartney, Paul: Nice, Italy
    M 1666
McCartney, Paul: Northern Songs
    M 2934
McCartney, Paul: obtains Quarrymen
    single
    M 2932
McCartney, Paul: on Abbey Road studios
    C 0307
McCartney, Paul: on Beatle reunion
    N 0633
McCartney, Paul: on Beatles' financial
    situation after break-up
    M 0302   M 0303
McCartney, Paul: on Beatles reunion
    M 1158   M 2060   M 3632   N 0144
McCartney, Paul: on Carly Simon LP
    M 2725
McCartney, Paul: on drug use
    M 2412   M 2420   N 0129
McCartney, Paul: on holiday in Greece

M 2398
McCartney, Paul: on holiday in Hawaii
    M 2830
McCartney, Paul: on India
    M 2585
McCartney, Paul: on Jane Asher
    P 0064
McCartney, Paul: on Lennon after his
    death
    M 1150   N 0725
McCartney, Paul: on possible Beatles
    break-up
    N 0872
McCartney, Paul: on rumored MacDonald's
    ads
    M 2804
McCartney, Paul: on rumored marriage
    plans to Jane Asher
    N 0719
McCartney, Paul: on Starr LP
    M 2744
McCartney, Paul: on The Osmonds
    M 3069
McCartney, Paul: on "Tonight" (tv show)
    C 0320
McCartney, Paul: on tv with Wings
    N 0836
McCartney, Paul: "On Wisconsin" (song)
    M 0531
McCartney, Paul: opposed to "Sgt.
    Pepper" (film)
    M 2757   M 2876
McCartney, Paul: party for new LP
    M 2030
McCartney, Paul: paternity suit
    M 1172   N 0327
McCartney, Paul: photograph by Eastman
    M 2055
McCartney, Paul: photograph in
    underpants
    C 0346
McCartney, Paul: photograph of Bratby
    portrait
    N 0414
McCartney, Paul: photograph with Jane
    Asher
    M 1468
McCartney, Paul: plans to tour England
    N 0512
McCartney, Paul: plans tour in
    California
    M 2832
McCartney, Paul: platinum LP
    M 2780
McCartney, Paul: portrait
    M 1072   M 2536
McCartney, Paul: press party to launch
    BACK TO THE EGG (LP)
    M 0190
McCartney, Paul: problem with dog
    N 0823
McCartney, Paul: produces Mary Hopkin
    M 2603
McCartney, Paul: produces McGear LP
    M 3072
McCartney, Paul: protests government
    policies
    M 2063
McCartney, Paul: publicity film
    M 3502
McCartney, Paul: quits Beatles
    M 0010   M 2305   M 3126   N 0730
    N 0750   N 1003
McCartney, Paul: quotations
    B 0207   B 0208   B 0210
    B 0383   B 0384   B 0385   B 0386
McCartney, Paul: radio ban on song
    M 2508   M 2540   M 2542   M 2545
    M 2546   M 2548   M 2549   M 2729
McCartney, Paul: record label change
    M 2079
McCartney, Paul: recording activity
    M 2884   M 3059
McCartney, Paul: recording solo
    N 0350
McCartney, Paul: records and songs   see
    also   individual record and song
    titles
McCartney, Paul: records and songs

B 0156   B 0593   M 0055   M 0096
M 0190   M 0671   M 0707   M 0709
M 0918   M 0956   M 0962   M 1001
M 1127   M 1164   M 1218   M 1295
M 1310   M 1329   M 1330   M 1472
M 1485   M 1489   M 1525   M 1543
M 1544   M 1855   M 1858   M 1917
M 1981   M 1982   M 2005   M 2032
M 2039   M 2057   M 2064   M 2065
M 2066   M 2069   M 2071   M 2080
M 2265   M 2358   M 2415   M 2416
M 2508   M 2542   M 2545   M 2546
M 2548   M 2549   M 2726   M 2729
M 2743   M 2770   M 2774   M 2780
M 2800   M 2842   M 2911   M 3000
M 3072   M 3126   M 3136   M 3502
M 3539   M 3555   M 3605   M 3682
M 3720   M 0055   N 0531   N 0717
N 0718   N 0723   N 0733   N 0796
N 1053   RR0036   RR0037   RR0038
RR0039   RR0040   RR0041   RR0042
RR0043   RR0044   RR0045   RR0046
RR0047   RR0048   RR0049   RR0050
RR0051   RR0052   RR0053   RR0054
RR0055   RR0056   RR0057   RR0058
RR0059   RR0140   RR0142   RR0143
RR0152   RR0153   RR0154   RR0155
RR0184   RR0185   RR0186   RR0219
RR0286   RR0287   RR0288   RR0299
RR0300   RR0301   RR0303   RR0304
RR0305   RR0306   RR0307   RR0308
RR0309   RR0310   RR0311   RR0312
RR0313   RR0314   RR0315   RR0316
RR0317   RR0345   RR0346   RR0348
RR0349   RR0350   RR0351   RR0352
RR0353   RR0354   RR0355   RR0361
RR0362   RR0363   RR0364   RR0365
RR0366   RR0367   RR0469   RR0470
RR0474   RR0510   RR0511   RR0512
RR0513   RR0514   RR0515   RR0523
RR0525   RR0526   RR0527   RR0528
RR0529   RR0530   RR0531   RR0532
RR0533   RR0534   RR0535   RR0536
RR0537   RR0538   RR0539   RR0540
RR0541   RR0542   RR0543   RR0544
RR0546
McCartney, Paul: records in Africa
    M 2760   M 2761   M 3064   M 3070
McCartney, Paul: records in Nashville,
    Tennessee
    M 2791
McCartney, Paul: records live tour LP
    M 2844
McCartney, Paul: records soundtrack
    M 2726   M 2755
McCartney, Paul: records with Dave
    Mason
    M 2822
McCartney, Paul: records with Michael
    Jackson
    M 1601   N 0716
McCartney, Paul: records with Starr in
    Montserrat, West Indies
    M 1720   M 2919   M 2920   M 2921
    N 1100
McCartney, Paul: records with Stevie
    Wonder
    M 0691   M 0956
McCartney, Paul: relationship with
    Francie Schwartz
    C 0291
McCartney, Paul: returns from Africa
    M 2761
McCartney, Paul: returns from Tokyo,
    Japan
    M 2067
McCartney, Paul: reviews pop records
    M 2410
McCartney, Paul: rhodium record
    M 0540
McCartney, Paul: rules out Beatle
    reunion
    N 0875
McCartney, Paul: rumored Beatles museum
    M 2938
McCartney, Paul: rumored contract with
    A & M Records
    M 2654
McCartney, Paul: rumored Harrison tiff

M 2638
McCartney, Paul: rumor of Lennon
     reunion
  M 2736
McCartney, Paul: San Diego, California
  M 0194
McCartney, Paul: scores tv special
  M 3314
McCartney, Paul: scrap with Grammy
     photographer
  M 2652
McCartney, Paul: search for country
     home
  M 2230
McCartney, Paul: seeks return of song
     rights
  N 0428
McCartney, Paul: self interview
  M 2408
McCartney, Paul: solo
  C 0199 M 0521 M 2070 N 0747
McCartney, Paul: solo tour
  N 1024
McCartney, Paul: song banned
  N 0055
McCartney, Paul: songbook see also
     Beatles songbook
McCartney, Paul: songbook see also
     Lennon/McCartney songbook
McCartney, Paul: songbook
  B 0354 B 0355 S 0123 S 0124
  S 0126 S 0127 S 0128 S 0129
  S 0130 S 0131 S 0132 S 0133
  S 0134 S 0135 S 0136 S 0141
  S 0157 S 0158 S 0159 S 0161
  S 0162 S 0163 S 0164 S 0165
  S 0166 S 0167 S 0168 S 0169
McCartney, Paul: song on Ireland banned
     by BBC
  N 0531
McCartney, Paul: song parody on Japan
     drug incident
  M 2254
McCartney, Paul: song royalties
  N 0130
McCartney, Paul: songwriter of the year
  M 3100
McCartney, Paul: songwriting award
  M 0493 M 0582 M 1904 M 1918
  M 3489 M 3755
McCartney, Paul: sought for "little
     prince" role
  M 2717
McCartney, Paul: sued by Northern
     Songs, Ltd.
  N 0904
McCartney, Paul: sued on "Another Day"
     recording
  N 0717
McCartney, Paul: surprise U.K. concerts
  M 2705
McCartney, Paul: television special
  M 0195 M 2647 M 2738 M 3736
McCartney, Paul: tour
  N 0874
McCartney, Paul: TUG OF WAR (LP)
  M 0969 N 0856
McCartney, Paul: 21st birthday party
  M 0184
McCartney, Paul: UNESCO benefit
  M 2409
McCartney, Paul: U.S.A.
  M 1047 N 0060
McCartney, Paul: U.S.S.R. release of
     BAND ON THE RUN (LP)
  M 2057 M 2358 M 2842 N 1053
McCartney, Paul: U.S. tour
  N 0952
McCartney, Paul: U.S. tour begins in
     Fort Worth, Texas
  N 0954
McCartney, Paul: vs. Allen Klein
  M 0302 M 0303 M 1808 M 2074
McCartney, Paul: vs. Beatles
  M 2076 M 2077 M 3339 N 0373
  N 0687
McCartney, Paul: vs. Lord Grade
  M 0373 N 1173
McCartney, Paul: vs. Northern Songs,

Ltd.
  N 0888 N 0904
McCartney, Paul: vs. Northern Songs,
     Ltd. and Maclen Music
  M 3373
McCartney, Paul: vs. Robert Stigwood
     Organization
  M 2073
McCartney, Paul: voice imitator
  M 1483
McCartney, Paul: wedding plans with
     Linda Eastman
  M 2592 N 0145
McCartney, Paul: weds Linda Eastman
  N 0082 N 0724 N 1130
McCartney, Paul: Wings see Wings
McCartney, Paul: with family in
     Scotland
  M 2260
McCartney, Paul: writes to "Melody
     Maker" (magazine)
  M 1069
McCartney, Paul: writing film short -
     "Rupert the Bear"
  M 2082
McCartney, Paul: writing movie
  M 2082
McCartney, Peter Michael see
     McCartney, Mike
McCartney, Stella: birth
  M 2677
MCCARTNEY II (LP)
  M 0671 M 1310 M 1982 M 2911
  RR0309 RR0310 RR0311 RR0312
  RR0313 RR0314 RR0315 RR0316
  RR0317
McCulloch, Jimmy
  M 1371 M 1672 N 0543 N 0727
McCullough, Henry
  M 2704 M 2836
MCGEAR (LP)
  M 2089 M 3072 RR0318 RR0319
  RR0320
McGear, Mike see McCartney, Mike
McGuane, Tom
  M 3764
McKuen, Rod: on the Beatles
  M 3091
Maclen Music
  M 2732 N 0717
Maclen Music: copyright dispute with
     Northern Songs
  M 0837
Maclen Music: vs. Lennon
  M 1919
Maclen Music: vs. McCartney
  M 3373
Maclen Music: vs. Northern Songs, Ltd.
  M 2386
THE MACS: MIKE MCCARTNEY'S FAMILY ALBUM
     (book)
  RB0460 RB0461 RB0462
THE MACS: MIKE MCCARTNEY'S FAMILY ALBUM
     (book): excerpt
  M 2418
Magazine cover illustration NOTE: Many
     citations may have cover
     illustrations that are not noted
     here.
Magazine cover illustration: Beatles
  M 0046 M 0130 M 0256 M 0260
  M 0262 M 0539 M 0843 M 0844
  M 0939 M 1849 M 1850 M 1995
  M 2167 M 2180 M 2186 M 2249
  M 2297 M 2449 M 3053 M 3098
  M 3133 M 3144 M 3145 M 3149
  M 3257 M 3430 M 3456 M 3764
  M 3765
Magazine cover illustration: Harrison
  M 0135 M 0859 M 1239 M 2952
Magazine cover illustration: Lennon
  M 0015 M 1070 M 1312 M 1313
  M 1394 M 1717 M 1819 M 1915
  M 2084 M 2141 M 2143 M 2222
  M 2581 M 3045 M 3097 M 3208
  M 3210 M 3215 M 3286 M 3292
  M 3337 M 3622 M 3640
Magazine cover illustration: Lennon,
     Sean

M 0530 M 3217
Magazine cover illustration: McCartney
  M 0074 M 0860 M 1228 M 1251
  M 1286 M 2058 M 2260 M 3118
Magazine cover illustration: Ono
  M 0530 M 2222 M 2932 M 2933
  M 3210 M 3214 M 3215 M 3217
  M 3292 M 3337 M 3766
Magazine cover illustration: Starr
  M 1129 M 3022 M 3258
Magical Mystery Store, Liverpool,
     England
  M 2467
"Magical Mystery Tour" (EP)
  M 1049
"Magical Mystery Tour" (film)
  C 0194 M 0475 M 0478 M 0877
  M 1050 M 1073 M 1643 M 2097
  M 2253 M 2290 M 2328 M 2380
  N 0167 N 0196 N 0197 N 0334
  N 0918 RF0238 RF0239 RF0240
  RF0241
"Magical Mystery Tour" (film): cast
     party
  M 1631
"Magical Mystery Tour" (film): filming
  M 1764 M 2252
MAGICAL MYSTERY TOUR (LP)
  M 1340 M 1625 M 3049 RR0321
  RR0322 RR0323 RR0324 RR0325
  RR0326 RR0327
MAGICAL MYSTERY TOUR (LP): songs on
     singles charts
  M 0475
"Magical Mystery Tour" (super 8MM film)
  RF0242
"Magical Mystery Tour" (videotape)
  RF0243
"The Magic Christian" (film)
  M 1495 M 2517 M 2595 M 2598
  M 3019 M 3656 RF0244 RF0245
  RF0246 RF0247 RF0248 RF0249
  RF0250
Maharishi Mahesh Yogi
  C 0067 C 0171 M 0063 M 0354
  M 0409 M 0497 M 0635 M 0944
  M 1399 M 3537 M 3538 N 0133
  N 0513 N 0638 N 0639 N 0764
Maharishi Mahesh Yogi: parody
  M 2096
Majestic Ballroom concert
  C 0043
Majorca, Balearica Islands, Spain:
     Lennon and Ono detained
  N 0061
Manchester, England: Wings
  M 3299
Manila, Phillipines: airport mob
  N 0089
Manila, Phillipines: Beatles
  N 0349
Manila, Philippines: discord
  N 0574
Manitoba, Canada: Lennon invited for
     peace concert
  M 2111
Manson murder case
  M 1597 N 0588 N 0751
THE MAN WHO GAVE THE BEATLES AWAY
     (book)
  RB0463 RB0464 RB0465 RB0466
  RB0467 RB0468 RB0469
Marijuana (legalization)
  N 0085
Marin, Cheech
  M 2745 M 3060
Marley, Bob
  B 0074 M 2824
Martin, George
  B 0370 B 0371 C 0323 M 0183
  M 0464 M 0895 M 1244 M 1518
  M 1748 M 2069 M 2207 M 2346
  M 2681 M 2902 M 2906 M 3201
  M 3722 M 3723 M 3724 M 3731
Martin, George: interview
  M 0851 M 1871 M 2495
"Mary Had A Little Lamb" (film)
  M 2720
"Mary Had A Little Lamb" (song)

M 2032
Mason, Dave
   M 2747 M 2822
Massachusetts: Beatles in Boston
   M 2012
Massachusetts: Boston fan convention
   M 1202 M 1203 M 2792 M 2981
   M 3759 N 0109
Massachusetts: Harrison
   M 2807 M 3308
MATEY FOR EIGHTY (book)
   RB0470
Maui, Hawaii: Harrison
   M 2873 M 3194
Max, Peter
   M 3315
M.B.E. awards
   M 2146 M 2147 M 2215 M 2569
   M 2570 M 2625 M 0415 N 0688
   N 0760 N 0847 N 0877 N 0906
   N 0907
M.B.E. awards: award returned by
      military men
   N 0040 N 0118 N 0270 N 0777
   N 1092 N 1108
M.B.E. awards: British reaction
   N 0099
M.B.E. awards: Canadian returns his
      medal
   N 0532
M.B.E. awards: investiture
   N 0119 N 0968
M.B.E. awards: Lennon
   M 0037 M 1923 N 0361 N 0571
   N 0850
M.B.E. awards: letters
   N 0487 N 0488 N 0489
M.B.E. awards: military men protest
      awards to Beatles
   N 1102
M.B.E. awards: returned by Lennon
   N 0571 N 0850
Meet The Beatles Again
   F 0112
MEET THE BEATLES (LP)
   M 0422 M 0615 M 3514 RR0328
Melbourne, Australia: Beatles
   N 0959 N 1105
Melbourne, Australia: fans
   N 0959 N 1105
"Melody Maker" (magazine): popularity
      poll
   M 0980 M 2252 M 2637 N 0634
Memorabilia (Beatles)
   C 0017 C 0022 C 0025 C 0026
   C 0028 C 0038 C 0215 C 0273
   C 0306 M 0363 M 0786 M 0787
   M 0893 M 0970 M 1098 M 1100
   M 1101 M 1197 M 1198 M 1465
   M 1466 M 1503 M 1516 M 1517
   M 1541 M 1863 M 1875 M 1983
   M 2180 M 2368 M 3175 M 3176
   M 3177 M 3185 N 0081 N 0229
Memorabilia (Beatles): at auction
   M 0107 M 0117 M 0146 M 0338
   M 1159 M 2164 M 2936 M 2957
   M 3055 N 0166
Memorabilia (Beatles): documents
   C 0255 C 0256 C 0257 C 0258
Memorabilia (Lennon)
   C 0147 C 0216 N 0223 N 0320
Memorabilia (Lennon): at auction
   M 3065
Memorabilia: London, England store
   M 2008
Memorabilia: records
   M 0970
Memorabilia (rock & roll)
   M 1141
Memorabilia: values
   B 0196 B 0197
Memphis, Tennessee: concert
   N 0342
Mercy College: Beatle course
   N 0013
Mersey Beatle Extravaganza
   M 3524
"Mersey Beat" (magazine): readers'
      poll, 1962

M 0471
MERSEY BEAT: THE BEGINNINGS OF THE
      BEATLES (book)
   M 1443 RB0471 RB0472 RB0473
   RB0474 RB0475
Merseyside see also Liverpool
Merseyside
   C 0033 C 0045 C 0292 M 0004
   M 0644 N 0336
Merseyside: fans grieve at death
   N 0287
Mersey Sound
   C 0209 M 2982 P 0122
"Mersey Sound" (radio special)
   M 2171
Mexico: Beatle records burned
   M 2557
Miami, Florida: arrival for "Ed
      Sullivan Show" (tv show)
   N 0433
Miami, Florida: Beatles
   M 3316 N 0407
Miami, Florida: riot by fans
   N 0405 N 0433
"Michelle" (song)
   M 1335 M 1336
"Michelle" (song): wins award
   N 0147
Michigan: Detroit anti-Beatles movement
   M 3777 N 0243
Michigan: Lennon lithographs in Detroit
   N 0668
Midler, Bette
   M 3764
Mike McCartney Fan Club
   F 0069
MILK AND HONEY (LP)
   N 0855 N 1040
Milligan, Spike
   N 0642
MIND GAMES (LP)
   M 2763 RR0329 RR0330 RR0331
   RR0332 RR0333 RR0334 RR0335
   RR0336 RR0337 RR0338 RR0339
Missouri: Kansas City concert
   N 0191
Mitchell, John: Lennon deportation case
   M 1136
Modern Jazz Quartet
   C 0211
"Mods & Rockers" (ballet)
   N 0049 N 0066
Molland, Joe
   M 0099 M 0100
Monaco: Starr shaves head
   M 2841
The Monkees
   M 1626 M 2210 M 3332
Monticello, New York: rumored Beatles
      reunion at rock fest
   M 0474
Montreal, Canada
   N 0501
Montreal, Canada: Lennons bed-in
   M 2596 M 3003
Montserrat, West Indies: McCartney and
      Starr recording session
   M 1720 M 2919 M 2920 M 2921
   N 1100
"Monty Python's Life of Brian" (film)
   M 2228 M 2878 M 2880 M 2886
   RF0251 RF0252 RF0253 RF0254
   RF0255 RF0256 RF0257 RF0258
   RF0259 RF0260 RF0261 RF0262
   RF0263 RF0264 RF0265 RF0266
   RF0267 RF0268 RF0269 RF0270
   RF0271 RF0272 RF0273 RF0274
   RF0275 RF0276 RF0277 RF0278
   RF0279 RF0280 RF0281 RF0282
   RF0283 RF0284 RF0285 RF0286
Moon, Keith
   M 2835
Moorman, Charlotte: performs Ono's
      works
   M 0711
Moscow, U.S.S.R.: Lennon rally
   N 0913
MPL Communications: publishing
      interests

M 1993
Multimedia show: "Away With Words"
   N 0151
Munich, Germany: entertainment tax
   N 0413
Munich, Germany: Wings concert
   M 0118
Murray the K
   C 0167
Murray the K: obituary
   N 0784 N 0785
Museum (Beatles) plans
   M 1205 M 1446
Musicological Research Contest
   M 3341
Music score see Beatles songbook
"Music Joker" (magazine): Special issue
   M 1208
"My Bonnie/The Saints" (45): released
   N 0703
"My Carnival" (song)
   M 2039
"My Fat Budgie" (poem)
   M 1898
"My Sweet Lord/Isn't It a Pity" (45)
   RR0340
"My Sweet Lord" (song)
   M 1135 M 1249 M 1412 M 1416
   M 1751 M 1988
"My Sweet Lord" (song) case
   M 2846 M 2923 M 3370 M 3371
   M 3756 N 0391 N 0425 N 0618
   N 0960
Nairobi, Kenya: McCartney visit
   M 1041
NASHVILLE DIARY (EP)
   RR0341
Nashville, Tennessee: McCartney
   M 2791
Nashville, Tennessee: Starr and
      Harrison recording
   M 3699
'National Apple Week'
   M 0315
National Committee for John and Yoko
   M 1727
"National Lampoon" (magazine) [special
      issue]
   P 0093
Nederlandse Beatles Fanclub
   F 0120
Nemperor Holdings see NEMS
      Enterprises, Ltd.
NEMS Enterprises, Ltd.
   M 0185 M 0186 M 0606 N 0178
   N 0257 N 0258 N 0261
NEMS Enterprises, Ltd.: directors
      resigning
   M 3360 N 0146
NEMS Enterprises, Ltd.: expansion, 1963
   M 0176
NEMS Enterprises, Ltd.: merger
   M 0605 N 0236
NEMS Enterprises, Ltd.: music
      publishing begun
   N 0220
NEMS Enterprises, Ltd.: sold
   N 0216
Nevada: Beatles
   N 0127
Newark, New Jersey: Lennon and Ono
   M 1684
Newcastle-upon-Tyne, England: concert
      ticket sales
   N 0351
New Jersey: fan convention
   M 3390
New Jersey: Lennon and Ono in Newark
   M 1684
New London, Connecticut: fan convention
   M 1203
New Orleans, Louisiana: McCartneys
      visit
   M 0131 M 3681 M 2811
"News of the World" (newspaper): sued
      by Lennon
   N 0797
(THE NEW) 21 (LP)
   RR0342

New wave: influence of Beatles
  M 1358
New York: Long Island Powell art
    exhibit
  M 1463
New York, New York see also Central
    Park
New York, New York: Beatlefest
  M 0537
New York, New York: Beatles
  M 1876 M 3346 M 3347 M 3760
  M 3781
New York, New York: Beatles arrival,
    1964
  M 3362 N 0420
New York, New York: Beatles concert
  M 0380 M 1092 M 1387 M 3161
  M 3163 M 3165 M 3166 M 3212
  M 3249 N 0770 N 0972
New York, New York: Beatles concert
    ticket sales
  N 0292
New York, New York: Beatles press
    conference
  N 0329
New York, New York: Carnegie Hall
    concert
  N 1156
New York, New York: cultural award
    Handel Medallion to Lennon
  M 2925 N 0617
New York, New York: fan convention
  M 1263 M 1266 M 1793 M 1986
  M 2393 M 3380
New York, New York: Forest Hills
    Stadium concert
  N 0985
New York, New York: Harrison
  M 3289
New York, New York: Harrison visit,
    1970
  M 0069
New York, New York: hotels avoid
    Beatles
  M 2294
New York, New York: Kennedy Airport
    arrival, 1964
  M 3362 N 0420
New York, New York: Lennon
  M 3400
New York, New York: Lennon in Greenwich
    Village
  M 3302
New York, New York: 1965 tour
  M 1571
New York, New York: Ono concert
  M 3406
New York, New York: Shea Stadium
    concert
  M 1092 M 1387 M 3163 M 3212
  M 3249 N 0770 N 0972
New York, New York: Shea Stadium
    concert ticket sales
  N 0292
New York: Syracuse Ono art show
  M 3590 N 0434
THE NEW YORK TIMES GREAT SONGS OF
    LENNON & MCCARTNEY (book)
  RB0476 RB0477
New Zealand: Brisbane mob
  N 0360 N 0403
New Zealand: Christchurch mob
  N 0359
New Zealand: concert
  M 0981 N 0120
New Zealand: Wellington concert
  N 0120
Nice, Italy: McCartney
  M 1666
Nigeria: Wings records in Lagos
  M 2760 M 3064
Nilsson, Harry
  M 0502 M 0662 M 2138 M 2710
  M 2778
Nixon, Richard M.
  N 0025
Norman, Philip
  M 3254 M 3255 N 0481
North Dakota: Bismarck anti-Beatles

club
  M 0050
North End Music Stores see NEMS
    Enterprises, Ltd.
Northern Ireland: Oz Trial
  M 2663 M 3647 N 0558
Northern Songs, Ltd.
  M 0090 M 0091 M 0092 M 0374
  M 0405 M 0418 M 0420 M 0865
  M 1591 M 1747 M 2023 M 2316
  M 2317 M 2318 M 2934 M 3361
  M 3499 M 3754 N 0029 N 0030
  N 0031 N 0032 N 0033 N 0036
  N 0070 N 0071 N 0087 N 0093
  N 0100 N 0104 N 0152 N 0161
  N 0173 N 0178 N 0179 N 0180
  N 0189 N 0190 N 0199 N 0204
  N 0205 N 0215 N 0219 N 0250
  N 0251 N 0262 N 0289 N 0338
  N 0339 N 0374 N 0427 N 0717
  N 0753 N 0776 N 0798 N 0799
  N 0812 N 0814 N 0816 N 0817
  N 0832 N 0834 N 0835 N 0863
  N 0961 N 1005 N 1007 N 1012
  N 1013 N 1081 N 1107 N 1132
  N 1133 N 1151 N 1164
Northern Songs, Ltd.: boardroom
    statement
  N 0239 N 0240 N 0241 N 0242
Northern Songs, Ltd.: business report
  N 0265 N 0266 N 0305 N 0306
  N 0307 N 0308 N 0815
Northern Songs, Ltd.: buys Lenmac
  N 0217
Northern Songs, Ltd.: copyright dispute
    with Maclen Music
  M 0837
Northern Songs, Ltd.: director resigns
  N 0813
Northern Songs, Ltd.: earnings
  M 3475
Northern Songs, Ltd.: 1965-66 fiscal
    report
  N 0348
Northern Songs, Ltd.: sold to ATV
  M 2518 M 2519 M 2520 N 0218
  N 1014
Northern Songs, Ltd.: stock
  M 2623
Northern Songs, Ltd.: stock offering
  M 0382 M 1619 M 2258 M 3361
  N 0247
Northern Songs, Ltd.: stock sales
  M 0575
Northern Songs, Ltd.: vs. Lennon
  M 1919
Northern Songs, Ltd.: vs. Lennons
  M 2732 N 0903
Northern Songs, Ltd.: vs. McCartney
  M 3373 N 0888 N 0904
Northern Songs, Ltd.: vs. Maclen Music
  M 2386
Northern Songs, Ltd.: vs. Video
    Communications
  M 3447
Northern Songs, Ltd.: videotape
    copyright
  M 1990 M 1991 M 1992
Norway: Beatles events in 1976
  M 0032
Norway: fan club
  F 0119 F 0142
Norwich, England: first British fan
    convention
  M 1362 M 1374
Novello Award see Ivor Novello Award
Novelty records
  B 0465 B 0466 B 0467 M 1434
  M 1435
"NO. 5" (film)
  M 2095
"Number 9 Dream" (song)
  M 1164
"Number Nine" (youth group)
  N 1083
NO. 3 ABBEY ROAD NW8 (LP)
  RR0343 RR0344
OBFC see Official Beatles Fan Club
Octopus Garden Chapter - OBFC

  F 0122
"Odd Sox/Coming Up" (45)
  RR0142
ODD SOX (LP)
  RR0345
O'Dell, Dennis
  M 0335
Official Beatles Fan Club (OBFC)
  F 0008 F 0070 F 0077 F 0083
  F 0099 F 0122 F 0126
Official John Lennon Chapter (Beatles
    USA Ltd.)
  F 0092 F 0093
Official Yoko Lennon Chapter - Apple
    Tree
  F 0125
Ohio: Beatles barred in Cleveland
  M 3272 M 3503 N 0101 N 0296
Ohio: Cleveland concert
  M 3272 M 3503 N 0296 N 0102
  N 0838
"One to One" Festival (benefit concert)
  M 1105 M 1163 M 1911 M 2719
  N 0311 N 0468
"Only You" (song)
  M 1164
Ono, Yoko
  B 0039 B 0040 B 0041 B 0042
  B 0221 B 0222 B 0418 B 0419
  B 0420 B 0421 B 0422 B 0423
  B 0424 B 0425 B 0426 B 0427
  B 0428 B 0429 B 0494 B 0495
  B 0496 B 0497 B 0498 C 0153
  C 0229 M 0035 M 0064 M 0200
  M 0511 M 0530 M 0633 M 0711
  M 0726 M 0808 M 0809 M 0831
  M 0928 M 0999 M 1057 M 1102
  M 1103 M 1256 M 1289 M 1318
  M 1566 M 1612 M 1676 M 1682
  M 1684 M 1686 M 1720 M 1839
  M 1926 M 2015 M 2018 M 2037
  M 2054 M 2084 M 2110 M 2115
  M 2266 M 2359 M 2384 M 2441
  M 2675 M 2734 M 2765 M 2783
  M 2806 M 2854 M 2856 M 2869
  M 2931 M 2932 M 2974 M 3056
  M 3074 M 3085 M 3094 M 3097
  M 3117 M 3135 M 3208 M 3292
  M 3315 M 3337 M 3394 M 3406
  M 3436 M 3445 M 3551 M 3614
  M 3615 M 3648 M 3686 M 3689
  M 3714 M 3715 M 3716 M 3768
  M 3769 M 3770 M 3776 N 0380
  N 0545 N 0821 N 1163 P 0076
Ono, Yoko: accepts cultural award for
    Lennon
  M 2925
Ono, Yoko: appears with Elton John
  M 3771
Ono, Yoko: art show at Syracuse, New
    York museum
  M 3590 N 0434
Ono, Yoko: art show in Belgium
  M 2050
Ono, Yoko: art work at festival
  M 0987
Ono, Yoko: as composer
  M 1959
Ono, Yoko: as filmmaker
  C 0304 M 2360
Ono, Yoko: asks for prayers for Lennon
  N 1143
Ono, Yoko: asks mourners to give to
    Spirit Foundation
  N 1167
Ono, Yoko: attends Elephant's Memory
    concert
  M 2724
Ono, Yoko: awarded custody of daughter,
    Kyoko
  N 0822
Ono, Yoko: "Ballad of John and Yoko"
    (song) banned
  M 0319 M 0444 N 1159
Ono, Yoko: bed-in
  C 0347 M 2596 M 3003 N 0501
  N 0658
Ono, Yoko: biography
  M 0548 M 1493

Ono, Yoko: birth of son Sean
    N 0517 N 0578
Ono, Yoko: brief biography
    C 0059
Ono, Yoko: buys cattle
    M 2872 M 2889
Ono, Yoko: buys upstate New York land
    to raise cattle
    N 0564
Ono, Yoko: changes record label
    M 2950
Ono, Yoko: charity performance
    M 1689
Ono, Yoko: Christmas ad "War Is Over"
    N 1129
Ono, Yoko: Christmas billboards
    M 1689 N 0566
Ono, Yoko: concert review
    M 0800
Ono, Yoko: copyright case
    M 1180 M 2363
Ono, Yoko: courthouse painting stolen
    N 0471
Ono, Yoko: custody of daughter Kyoko
    N 0377
Ono, Yoko: daughter Kyoko
    M 1840 N 1169
Ono, Yoko: deals with Lennon
    gossip-books
    N 0476
Ono, Yoko: deportation case
    M 1493 M 1497 M 1727 N 0604
    N 0605 N 0606 N 0607 N 0692
Ono, Yoko: discography
    M 0959
Ono, Yoko: donation for crime victims
    in Japan
    N 1166
Ono, Yoko: donation to New York City
    police
    N 0456
Ono, Yoko: DOUBLE FANTASY (LP)
    M 0739 M 0955
Ono, Yoko: drug charge
    M 2255 N 0645 N 0646
Ono, Yoko: effects of Lennon's death
    M 0072 M 0355
Ono, Yoko: fan club see Fan club
    (Ono)
Ono, Yoko: fasts for Biafra protestors
    N 0755
Ono, Yoko: film activity
    M 1941
Ono, Yoko: filming
    M 3558
Ono, Yoko: films see also individual
    film titles
Ono, Yoko: films
    C 0304 M 0066 M 0646 M 1699
    M 1941 M 2095 M 2153 M 2360
    M 2383 M 2621 M 2924 M 3558
    N 0384 N 0448 N 0494 N 1050
    N 1170 RF0014 RF0097 RF0098
    RF0099 RF0125 RF0126 RF0127
    RF0128 RF0295 RF0296 RF0396
Ono, Yoko: films for benefit exhibit
    N 0494
Ono, Yoko: film shown at Cannes
    N 0384
Ono, Yoko: films shown at Whitney
    Museum
    N 0448
Ono, Yoko: first meeting with Lennon
    M 3001
Ono, Yoko: former husband (Tony Cox)
    jailed
    N 1171
Ono, Yoko: Geffen Records
    M 1237
Ono, Yoko: Grammy award - DOUBLE
    FANTASY (LP)
    N 0852
Ono, Yoko: hair cut
    M 3777
Ono, Yoko: health
    M 2771
Ono, Yoko: honored by church choir
    N 0439
Ono, Yoko: "Imagine" (film)

    M 0646 M 1699
Ono, Yoko: in car accident
    N 0672
Ono, Yoko: interview
    B 0494 B 0495 B 0496 B 0497
    B 0498 C 0125 C 0296 M 1314
    M 1640 M 2310 M 2360 M 2361
    M 2487 M 2969 M 3216 M 3247
    M 3564 M 3612 M 3766 M 3791
    N 0225
Ono, Yoko: interview after Lennon's
    death
    M 3214 M 3217 N 0693 N 0810
    N 0860
Ono, Yoko: interview on peace
    C 0259
Ono, Yoko: interview tapes
    M 1933 M 1934 M 1935
Ono, Yoko: Japan concerts
    M 2793
Ono, Yoko: "Legs" (film)
    M 0066
Ono, Yoko: Lennon on her book
    GRAPEFRUIT
    N 1072
Ono, Yoko: Lennon records re-issued
    N 0048
Ono, Yoko: Lennon's estate
    N 0758
Ono, Yoko: Lennon's will
    N 0461
Ono, Yoko: letter
    M 1957 N 0876
Ono, Yoko: letter on Central Park
    Lennon tribute section
    "Strawberry Fields"
    N 1032
Ono, Yoko: Majorca, Balearica Islands,
    Spain
    N 0061
Ono, Yoko: Mid-East radio broadcast
    N 0683
Ono, Yoko: miscarries
    M 2608 N 1168
Ono, Yoko: moves into the Dakota, New
    York City, apartment house
    N 1068
Ono, Yoko: music performed
    N 0470
Ono, Yoko: named in Lennon - Powell
    divorce
    N 0553
Ono, Yoko: New York
    C 0060
Ono, Yoko: New York City concert
    M 3406
Ono, Yoko: New York "Times" ad
    M 2895
Ono, Yoko: New York City's Central Park
    Lennon tribute section
    "Strawberry Fields"
    N 1172
Ono, Yoko: Northern Songs
    M 2934
Ono, Yoko: nude
    M 1189 M 1477 M 1538 M 1927
    M 2240
Ono, Yoko: on art
    N 0435
Ono, Yoko: on being married
    N 0670
Ono, Yoko: on charity
    N 0222
Ono, Yoko: on first anniversary of
    Lennon's death
    N 1089
Ono, Yoko: on peace
    M 1678 M 1685 M 2300
Ono, Yoko: "One to One" benefit concert
    M 1105 M 1163
Ono, Yoko: open letter
    M 1018 M 1902 N 0524 N 0525
    N 0644
Ono, Yoko: opens Lennon namesake health
    center in Liverpool, England
    N 0655
Ono, Yoko: photograph
    M 2486
Ono, Yoko: piano solo concert tour

    M 1801
Ono, Yoko: Plastic Ono Band
    M 0038 M 0039
Ono, Yoko: "Playboy" (magazine)
    interview
    N 0595
Ono, Yoko: pregnancy
    M 1728
Ono, Yoko: pregnancy stalls deportation
    N 0602
Ono, Yoko: pro-IRA film
    M 2696
Ono, Yoko: protests
    M 3645
Ono, Yoko: radio appearance
    M 2629
Ono, Yoko: radio program
    M 1692
Ono, Yoko: readers' poll
    M 2960
Ono, Yoko: recording activity
    M 2753
Ono, Yoko: recording contract
    M 3767
Ono, Yoko: records and songs see also
    individual record and song titles
Ono, Yoko: records and songs
    M 0319 M 0444 M 0516 M 0529
    M 0718 M 0739 M 0921 M 0955
    M 0959 M 0991 M 1089 M 1121
    M 1133 M 1477 M 1526 M 1527
    M 1533 M 1538 M 1676 M 1690
    M 1691 M 1801 M 1908 M 1927
    M 1957 M 2240 M 2511 M 2651
    M 2708 M 2715 M 2753 M 2759
    M 2893 M 2903 M 2915 M 2916
    M 2922 M 2930 M 3087 m 3266
    M 3398 M 3455 M 3717 M 3767
    N 0008 N 0322 N 0478 N 0540
    N 0552 N 0852 N 0855 N 0858
    N 0861 N 0884 N 0921 N 1069
    N 1069 N 1159 RR0169 RR0170
    RR0171 RR0172 RR0173 RR0174
    RR0175 RR0176 RR0177 RR0178
    RR0179 RR0180 RR0195 RR0196
    RR0197 RR0198 RR0203 RR0204
    RR0257 RR0258 RR0263 RR0264
    RR0265 RR0266 RR0267 RR0268
    RR0269 RR0270 RR0413 RR0414
    RR0415 RR0416 RR0417 RR0418
    RR0419 RR0420 RR0443 RR0444
    RR0445 RR0446 RR0447 RR0448
    RR0449 RR0450 RR0504 RR0505
    RR0545
Ono, Yoko: reunites with Lennon
    M 2813
Ono, Yoko: rumor of split with Lennon
    M 2766
Ono, Yoko: seeks return of song rights
    N 0428
Ono, Yoko: separation from John Lennon
    N 0576
Ono, Yoko: shaves head for peace
    N 0276
Ono, Yoko: silent vigil Lennon tribute
    N 0737
Ono, Yoko: Sinclair freedom rally
    M 3279
Ono, Yoko: solo LP, SEASON OF GLASS
    M 0529 M 1527 M 2922 N 0858
    N 0861
Ono, Yoko: songbook see Lennon/Ono
    songbook
Ono, Yoko: sued by music corporation
    N 0580
Ono, Yoko: sued by Northern Songs, Ltd.
    N 0903
Ono, Yoko: Toronto Peace Festival
    M 1679 M 1681 M 1688 M 1905
    M 1929 M 1930 M 2323 M 3465
    M 3466 M 3773 N 0275
Ono, Yoko: TWO VIRGINS (LP) banned
    N 0540
Ono, Yoko: TWO VIRGINS (LP) seized
    N 0008 N 0921
Ono, Yoko: two years after Lennon's
    death
    N 1120
Ono, Yoko: vs. Lord Grade

N 1173
Ono, Yoko: vs. Maclen Music
  M 2732
Ono, Yoko: vs. Northern Songs
  M 2732
Ono, Yoko: visits Budapest, Hungary
  M 2179
Ono, Yoko: visit with Elton John
  M 1008
Ono, Yoko: visit with Prime Minister
  Trudeau (Canada)
  N 0245
Ono, Yoko: wealth
  N 1138
Ono, Yoko: WEDDING ALBUM (LP) released
  M 3717 N 1069
Ono, Yoko: weds John Lennon
  N 0556 N 0561
Ono, Yoko: Willowbrook benefit concert
  M 0977
Ono, Yoko: with Lennon and Eric Clapton
  C 0348
Ono, Yoko: WNET "happening" with the
  Lennons receives protests
  N 1103
Ono, Yoko: "Woman Is The Nigger of the
  World" (song)
  M 0991
"On, Wisconsin" (song)
  N 0718 N 0723
"Open Your Box" (song)
  M 2651
Orange Apple Jam Chapter - OBFC
  F 0126
Orbison, Roy
  M 3764
Organ songbook (Beatles)
  S 0019 S 0029 S 0030 S 0075
  S 0081 S 0109 S 0110
Organ songbook (Lennon/McCartney)
  S 0109 S 0110
ORIENTAL NIGHTFISH (LP)
  RR0346
The Osmonds
  M 3069
"Our Starr Monthly" (magazine)
  M 2101
Owen, Alun
  N 0766
Oz Trial
  M 2663 M 3647 N 0558
Pan American: protests Beatle fans
  N 0079
Pang, May
  M 1827
Pang, May: interview
  M 1776
PAPERBACK WRITER (book)
  RB0478 RB0479 RB0480 RB0481
  RB0482 RB0483 RB0484 RB0485
"Paperback Writer" (song): recording
  session
  M 2392
"Paper Shoes" (film)
  RF0287
Paramount Theatre Benefit Show
  N 1043
Paris, France: Beatles
  M 0023 M 0051 M 0464 M 2169
  M 3220 N 0037 P 0034
Paris, France: Beatles film
  retrospective
  M 0023 M 0600
Paris, France: Beatles recording
  activity
  M 0464
Paris, France: concert
  N 0774 N 0037 N 0132
Paris, France: concert riot
  N 0132
Paris, France: Wings concert
  M 3405
Parnes, Larry
  M 3428
Parrish and Garvitch
  M 2681
Parr, Jack
  M 0538 M 3764
PAUL MCCARTNEY: A BIOGRAPHY IN WORDS &

PICTURES (book)
  RB0486
PAUL MCCARTNEY & WINGS (book)
  RB0487
PAUL MCCARTNEY: BEATLE WITH WINGS
  (book)
  RB0488
Paul McCartney Chapter - OBFC
  F 0099
PAUL MCCARTNEY: COMPOSER/ARTIST (book)
  M 1452 N 1134 RB0489 RB0490
  RB0491 RB0492 RB0493
PAUL MCCARTNEY: COMPOSER/ARTIST (book):
  excerpt
  M 0585
Paul McCartney Fan Club of Scotland
  F 0102 F 0134
PAUL MCCARTNEY IN HIS OWN WORDS (book)
  RB0494 RB0495 RB0496 RB0497
PAUL MCCARTNEY (LP)
  M 2408
PaulVinDon Publishing
  F 0148
Peebles, Andy: taped interviews with
  Lennon and Ono
  M 1933 M 1934 M 1935
Peel, David
  N 0018 N 0020
Pendergrass, Teddy
  M 3764
THE PENGUIN JOHN LENNON (book)
  RB0498
Pennsylvania: move to ban Bealtes
  N 0878
Pennsylvania: Philadelphia Beatlefest
  M 0490
Pennsylvania: Philadelphia Beattle
  §sic† concert
  N 0209
Pennsylvania: Philadelphia Wings
  concert
  M 2126
"Penny Lane" (song)
  M 3366 N 0879
Perkins, Carl
  M 2963
PETE BEST: "THE BEATLE THAT TIME
  FORGOT" (LP)
  RR0347
Peter and Gordon
  M 3548
Philadelphia, Pennsylvania: Beatlefest
  M 0490 M 1386
Philadelphia, Pennsylvania: Beattle
  §sic† concert
  N 0209
Philadelphia, Pennsylvania: Wings
  concert
  M 2126
Philippines: Beatles
  M 0161 N 0089 N 0349 N 0574
Philippines: discord
  N 0089 N 0412
Philippines: Manila discord
  N 0574
Philippines: terrorist group uses name
  'Beatles'
  N 0979
Philippines: threat to UK Embassy
  N 0412
Philip, Prince
  N 0091
PHOTOGRAPHS (book)
  RB0499
Piano/Vocal songbook NOTE: These books
  may also contain guitar chord
  boxes.
Piano/Vocal songbook (Beatles)
  S 0003 S 0004 S 0005 S 0006
  S 0007 S 0008 S 0009 S 0010
  S 0011 S 0012 S 0013 S 0014
  S 0015 S 0018 S 0021 S 0022
  S 0023 S 0026 S 0029 S 0030
  S 0031 S 0032 S 0034 S 0038
  S 0047 S 0048 S 0049 S 0050
  S 0051 S 0052 S 0053 S 0054
  S 0055 S 0056 S 0057 S 0058
  S 0059 S 0060 S 0061 S 0062
  S 0063 S 0064 S 0065 S 0066

  S 0067 S 0068 S 0069 S 0074
  S 0077 S 0078 S 0079 S 0080
  S 0082 S 0083 S 0086 S 0087
  S 0088 S 0089 S 0090 S 0091
  S 0092 S 0093 S 0095 S 0097
  S 0105 S 0108 S 0112 S 0121
  S 0125 S 0138 S 0139 S 0142
  S 0143 S 0144 S 0145 S 0153
  S 0154 S 0155 S 0156 S 0158
  S 0170
Piano/Vocal songbook (Harrison)
  S 0001 S 0002 S 0088 S 0122
  S 0126 S 0127 S 0149
Piano/Vocal songbook (Lennon)
  S 0120 S 0147 S 0151 S 0152
Piano/Vocal songbook (Lennon/McCartney)
  S 0054 S 0086 S 0087 S 0095
  S 0108 S 0112 S 0125 S 0143
  S 0154 S 0158
Piano/Vocal songbook (Lennon/Ono)
  S 0148 S 0150
Piano/Vocal songbook (McCartney)
  S 0123 S 0124 S 0126 S 0127
  S 0128 S 0129 S 0130 S 0131
  S 0133 S 0134 S 0135 S 0136
  S 0141 S 0157 S 0159 S 0160
  S 0161 S 0162 S 0163 S 0164
  S 0165 S 0166 S 0167 S 0168
  S 0169
Piano/Vocal songbook (Starr)
  S 0094 S 0126 S 0127 S 0149
Picasso, Pablo
  N 1131
Plastic Ono Band
  M 2282 M 2362 M 2605 M 2619
PLASTIC ONO BAND (LP) see JOHN
  LENNON/PLASTIC ONO BAND (LP)
PLASTIC ONO BAND (LP) see YOKO
  ONO/PLASTIC ONO BAND (LP)
Plastic Ono Band: album cover
  M 1609
Plastic Ono Band: albums
  M 0038 M 0039 N 1153
Platz, David
  M 0865
THE PLAYBOY INTERVIEWS WITH JOHN LENNON
  AND YOKO ONO (book)
  RB0500 RB0501 RB0502 RB0503
  RB0504 RB0505 RB0506 RB0507
  RB0508 RB0509
PLEASE PLEASE ME (LP)
  M 0904
PLEASE PLEASE ME (LP): press release
  M 2497
"Please Please Me" (song)
  C 0037 M 0158 M 1749 M 3290
Poland: Beatles
  M 2177 M 2178
Poland: Cracow convention
  M 2175
Poland: reactions to Lennon's death
  M 2176
Polydor Records
  C 0041 M 3676 M 3767 M 3790
Polygram Records
  M 2950
Pope John Paul I
  M 2879
Popular music
  C 0104 C 0176 C 0210 C 0242
  M 0556 M 0639 M 0822 M 0926
  M 1285 M 1467 M 1530 M 1797
  M 2156 M 2157 M 2158 M 2161
  M 2299 M 3138 M 3141 M 3142
  M 3211 M 3246 M 3329 M 3441
  M 3574 M 3617 N 0746 N 0894
Popular music: 1960-1964
  C 0294
Popular music: 1965-1969
  C 0295
Popular recording industry
  C 0093
Posters
  B 0066 M 1328
Pottie Bird Beatle Chapter - Beatles
  USA Ltd.
  F 0133
Powell, Cynthia
  B 0298 B 0299 B 0300 M 0852

M 2165   M 3733
Powell, Cynthia: art exhibit
    M 1463
Powell, Cynthia: articles on Lennon
    N 0397
Powell, Cynthia: book on Lennon
    M 2875
Powell, Cynthia: divorces Lennon
    M 0974   N 0553   N 0769
Powell, Cynthia: drawings
    M 3744
Powell, Cynthia: granted "decree nisi"
    N 0343
Powell, Cynthia: interview
    M 1777   M 1778
Powell, Cynthia: misses train to see
    Guru
    N 0208
Powell, Cynthia: photograph with Lennon
    and son Julian
    M 1467
Powell, Cynthia: photograph with Pattie
    Boyd, Jenny Boyd, and Maureen Cox
    M 2379
Powell, Cynthia: remarriage
    M 2613
Powell, Cynthia: separation from Lennon
    M 3051
Presley, Elvis
    B 0029   C 0143   C 0144   M 0781
    M 1009   M 1514   M 1570   M 2483
    M 3250   P 0067
Preston, Billy
    M 0543   M 1154   M 1757   M 2664
    M 2706   M 2782
Preston, Billy: Apple recordings
    M 1106
Prince Philip
    N 0091
Promotional records
    M 3566   M 3567   M 3568
P.S. WE LOVE YOU (book)
    RB0510
Puerto Rico: fan club
    F 0074
Puzzle, crossword (Beatles)
    M 1958   M 3439
Quarrymen
    C 0070   M 0627
Quarrymen: recording at auction
    M 1118   M 1159   M 2061
Quasar
    M 2946
Radha Krisna Temple
    M 1243
Radio ban: Australia
    N 0249
Radio ban: "Ballad of John and Yoko"
    (song)
    M 0444
Radio ban: Beatles
    M 0721   M 1333   N 0249
Radio ban: McCartney
    M 2729   N 0531
Radio ban: Texas
    M 3426
Radio: BBC broadcasts
    M 3306   M 3506
Radio: Beatles
    M 1083
Radio broadcasts (Beatles)
    B 0265   B 0266   M 2031   M 2171
    M 3306   M 3506   M 3523   M 3742
    M 3774   N 0299   N 1041
Radio broadcasts (Beatles): collecting
    M 1517
Radio: collecting broadcasts
    M 1517
Radio interview (Lennon)
    M 1936   M 1937   M 1938   M 1939
    M 1940
Radio: Israeli series on Beatles
    M 0506
Radio Plant (studio)
    M 1987
Radio program (Lennon)
    M 1692
Radio: South African ban
    M 1096

Radio special
    M 0660   M 0732
Radio special (Beatles)
    M 0430   M 1698   M 1723   M 2031
    M 2171
Radio special (Lennon)
    M 1692   M 1698   M 2629
Radio special (Starr)
    M 2578
Radio station: first all-Beatle-music
    format
    N 0492
Radio: U.K. broadcast catalogue
    M 1975   M 1976
"Raga" (film)
    RF0288   RF0289   RF0290   RF0291
    RF0292   RF0293   RF0294
"Rain" (song)
    M 0829
RAM (LP)
    M 0707   RR0348   RR0349   RR0350
    RR0351   RR0352   RR0353   RR0354
    RR0355
"Rape" (film)
    M 2153   M 2360   RF0295   RF0296
RARITIES (LP)
    M 0656   M 1785   M 1867   M 2086
    M 2478   M 2501   M 2909   M 3149
    RR0356   RR0357   RR0358   RR0359
"Reader's Digest" (magazine):
    popularity poll
    M 2628
Reagan, Patti Davis
    M 3764
Reagan, Ronald: comments on Lennon's
    murder
    N 0278
Reagan, Ronald, Jr.
    M 3764
Reagan, Ronald: urged to heed Lennon's
    murder
    N 0291
Rebennack, Malcolm "Mac"
    M 2739   M 2767   M 2826
Recorder songbook (Beatles)
    S 0045   S 0070   S 0117
Recorder songbook (Lennon/McCartney)
    S 0117
Recording industry
    C 0093   N 0591
Recordings
    B 0098   B 0099   B 0100   B 0101
    B 0102   B 0103   B 0104   B 0105
    B 0106   B 0107   B 0472   B 0523
    B 0524   B 0525   B 0526
Recordings: boxed singles set
    M 1398
Recordings: price guide
    C 0123   C 0230
Recordings: reissues
    M 0423
Recordings: reviews
    B 0262
Recordings (solo Beatles)
    B 0526
Record labels
    B 0285
"Record Mirror" poll
    M 2026
Record review   see   individual record
    titles
RECOVERED TRACKS (LP)
    RR0360
RED ROSE SPEEDWAY (LP)
    M 2743   RR0361   RR0362   RR0363
    RR0364   RR0365   RR0366   RR0367
REEL MUSIC (LP)
    M 1328   M 2939   N 0272   RR0368
    RR0369   RR0370
Reeves, Martha
    M 2754
"Remember Love" (song)
    M 1908
"Revolution 9" (song): terrorist group
    uses title as name
    N 0930
"Revolution" (song)
    M 1647   N 0156
REVOLVER (LP)

M 0012   M 0383   M 1510   M 3137
    RR0371   RR0372
Rice, Tim
    N 0647   N 0663
Richard, Little
    M 1479   M 2005
Richie, Lionel
    M 3764
Rifkin, Joshua
    N 0410
RINGO (LP)
    M 1338   RR0373   RR0374   RR0375
    RR0376   RR0377   RR0378   RR0379
    RR0380   RR0381   RR0382   RR0383
Ring O' Records
    M 1377   M 3031   M 3245
Ring O' Records: discography
    M 0524   M 0525
"Ringo's Night Out" (film)
    M 2794
RINGO'S ROTOGRAVURE (LP)
    RR0384   RR0385   RR0386   RR0387
    RR0388
The Ringo Starr Fan Club
    F 0139
RINGO THE 4TH (LP)
    M 3026   RR0389   RR0390   RR0391
    RR0392
"Ringo" (tv special)
    M 1489   N 0254   N 0937
Rishikesh, India: Beatles
    M 1035   N 0638   N 0957
Rivera, Geraldo
    M 2751
Rivers, Johnny
    M 2661
RKO General Radio Network: Lennon final
    interview
    M 1115   M 1936   M 1937   M 1938
    M 1939   M 1940   M 2475   N 0654
    N 0657
RKO General Radio Network: Lennon final
    interview (German translation)
    M 3248
Robert Stigwood Organization
    M 2073
Robinson, Smokey: Lennon's death
    M 3700
"Rock And Folk" (magazine): special
    issue - Beatles 10th anniversary
    M 3053
Rock music
    C 0010   C 0048   C 0049   C 0062
    C 0075   C 0081   C 0109   C 0148
    C 0169   C 0178   C 0202   C 0238
    C 0241   C 0249   C 0253   C 0254
    C 0321   C 0333   M 0942   M 3169
    N 0447
Rock music films
    M 3694
"Rock 'N' Roll Times" (film)
    M 2890
ROCK 'N' ROLL (LP)
    M 1854   M 1961   M 2120   M 2422
    M 3054   M 3080   M 3783   RR0393
    RR0394   RR0395   RR0396   RR0397
    RR0398   RR0399   RR0400   RR0401
    RR0402
ROCK 'N' ROLL (LP): album cover
    M 3080
ROCK 'N' ROLL MUSIC (LP)
    M 1626   M 2121   M 3267   RR0403
    RR0404   RR0405   RR0406   RR0407
ROCK 'N' ROLL - THE BEATLES & JOHN
    LENNON (LP)
    RR0408
ROCK 'N' ROLL TIMES (book)
    M 0209   RB0511   RB0512   RB0513
"Rock Peace" (song)
    M 2282
"Rockshow" (film)
    M 1464   RF0297   RF0298   RF0299
"Rockshow" (film): premiere
    M 1984
Roe, Tommy
    M 1003
"Rolling Stone" (magazine): readers
    poll - McCartney
    M 3100

"Rolling Stone" (magazine): special
    issue - Beatles
    P 0106
"Rolling Stone" (magazine): special
    issue - Lennon
    P 0105
Rolling Stones
    B 0380   M 0006   M 0271   M 0456
    M 0516   M 0641   M 0855   M 1211
    M 1484   M 1816   M 1835   M 2591
    M 3139   M 3305   M 3364   M 3661
    M 3729   M 3750   N 0280
Rolling Stones: possible business
    projects with the Beatles
    M 0456   N 0264
ROOTS (LP) [Lennon]
    M 1961   M 3783
ROUGH NOTES (LP)
    RRO409   RRO410
Roulette Records
    M 1931
Roulette Records: vs. Lennon
    M 3783
Rowland - photographer
    C 0278
Royalties
    M 2307   N 0130   N 0131   N 0162
    N 0586
Royalties (Beatles)
    N 0586
Royalties claim
    M 0453   N 0162
Royalties (Lennon)
    N 0669
Royal Variety Performance
    N 0699
ROYAL VARIETY SHOW (EP)
    RRO411
RUBBER SOUL (LP)
    C 0228   M 3137
Rubin, Jerry
    M 3645
Rundgren, Tod: Beatles tribute LP
    M 3518
"Rupert The Bear" (comics): McCartney
    film short
    M 2082
Russell, Graham: Lennon's death
    M 3700
Russia   see   U.S.S.R.
Rutles
    M 0508   M 0917   M 2163
THE RUTLES (LP)
    M 0508   M 0917   M 1545   M 2163
    M 3036   M 3404   RRO412
Rutles: television special
    M 3123   M 3124   M 3268   M 3301
    M 3303   M 3304   M 3746
Saks, Tony
    M 0348
San Diego, California: Wings concert
    M 0194
San Francisco, California: airport
    crowd
    N 0155
San Francisco, California: Beatles
    M 3730   N 0108
San Francisco, California: concert
    M 0327   M 1183   N 0108   N 0638
San Francisco, California: Lennons
    M 3056
Sargeant, Bill
    M 3309
"Saturday Night Live" (tv show):
    Harrison
    M 3782
Saudi Arabia: Beatles' influence feared
    N 1070
Scholarship (Lennon)
    M 1207
Schwartz, Francie: on her relationship
    with McCartney
    C 0291
Scotland: Beatles
    B 0054   M 0360
Scotland: Beatles in Edinburgh
    M 0314   M 3191   N 0794
Scotland: fan club
    F 0102   F 0134

Scotland: Glasgow concert
    N 0388   N 0389
Scotland: Glasgow queues
    M 1258
Scotland: Glasgow visits
    N 0490
Scotland: Lennons in car accident
    N 0672
Scotland: McCartney buys farm
    N 0462
Scotland: McCartney drug charge
    N 0870
Scotland: McCartney recording session
    M 2862
Scotland: McCartneys
    M 2260
Scotland: McCartney visits Glasgow
    N 0722
Scotland: Wings rehearsal
    M 2821
"Seaside Woman" (film)
    M 2454   M 2914
SEASON OF GLASS (LP)
    M 0529   M 1527   M 1957   M 2922
    N 0858   RRO413   RRO414   RRO415
    RRO416   RRO417   RRO418   RRO419
    RRO420
Seatrain
    M 0851
Seattle, Washington: concert
    N 0719
Sellers, Peter
    M 2808   M 3541
Seltaeb: U.S. law suit
    N 0844
SENTIMENTAL JOURNEY (LP)
    M 2626   RRO421   RRO422   RRO423
Sgt. Pepper's (Lonely Hearts) Club
    F 0142
SGT. PEPPER'S LONELY HEARTS CLUB BAND
    (book)
    RBO514
"Sgt. Pepper's Lonely Hearts Club Band"
    (film)
    B 0174   B 0175   B 0529   M 2757
    M 2858   M 2871   M 3675   N 0054
    RFO300   RFO301   RFO302   RFO303
    RFO304   RFO305   RFO306   RFO307
    RFO308   RFO309   RFO310   RFO311
    RFO312   RFO313   RFO314   RFO315
    RFO316   RFO317   RFO318   RFO319
    RFO320   RFO321   RFO322   RFO323
    RFO324   RFO325   RFO326
"Sgt. Pepper's Lonely Hearts Club Band"
    (film): soundtrack
    M 1152   M 2263
SGT. PEPPER'S LONELY HEARTS CLUB BAND
    (LP)
    M 0350   M 0717   M 1054   M 1340
    M 1469   M 1639   M 1745   M 1836
    M 1889   M 2484   M 2505   M 2507
    M 2985   M 3137   M 3180   M 3202
    M 3388   M 3633   M 3704   M 3729
    N 1074   RRO424   RRO425   RRO426
    RRO427   RRO428   RRO429   RRO430
    RRO431   RRO432
SGT. PEPPER'S LONELY HEARTS CLUB BAND
    (LP): as concept albumm
    C 0283
SGT. PEPPER'S LONELY HEARTS CLUB BAND
    (LP): lyrics
    M 2507
SGT. PEPPER'S LONELY HEARTS CLUB BAND
    (LP): making of cover
    M 1556
SGT. PEPPER'S LONELY HEARTS CLUB BAND
    (LP): pre-release party
    M 1059
SGT. PEPPER'S LONELY HEARTS CLUB BAND
    (LP-RSO)
    RRO433   RRO434
"Sgt. Pepper's Lonely Hearts Club Band"
    (play)
    M 0437   M 1139   M 2073   M 2757
"Sgt. Pepper's Lonely Hearts Club On
    The Road" (play)
    M 2982
Sesame Street record
    M 1989

"Sextette" (film)
    RFO327   RFO328   RFO329   RFO330
    RFO331   RFO332   RFO333   RFO334
Shankar, Ravi
    M 0103   M 2580   M 2782   N 0640
    N 0924   RRO288   RRO289   RRO290
    RRO291   RRO292   RRO293   RRO294
Shankar, Ravi: film
    M 3325
Shapiro, Helen: interview
    M 0157
SHAVED FISH (LP)
    RRO435   RRO436   RRO437   RRO438
    RRO439   RRO440   RRO441
Shea Stadium, New York City: concert
    M 1092   M 1387   M 3163   M 3212
    M 3249   N 0770   N 0972
Shea Stadium, New York City: concert
    ticket sales
    N 0292
Sheet music book   see   Beatles songbook
Sheet music-in-folio   see   Beatles
    songbook
Sheffield, England: fan convention
    M 2471
"She Loves You" (song)
    M 0464
Shenson, Walter
    M 2361   M 3587   N 0051
Sheridan, Tony
    M 3281
Sheridan, Tony: interview
    M 1392   M 3459
Sheridan, Tony: vs. Polydor
    International and others
    M 3281
"Shindig" (tv show) [Beatles]
    M 3229   M 3243   M 3244
SHOUT! (book)
    M 0845   M 0910   M 1128   M 1455
    M 3254   M 3255   N 0481   N 0811
    N 0934   RBO515   RBO516   RBO517
    RBO518   RBO519   RBO520   RBO521
    RBO522   RBO523   RBO524   RBO525
    RBO526   RBO527   RBO528   RBO529
    RBO530   RBO531   RBO532   RBO533
    RBO534   RBO535   RBO536   RBO537
    RBO538
SHOUT! (book): excerpt
    M 2309   N 0805   N 0806   N 0807
    N 0808
SHOUT! (book): letter from Tony Barrow
    N 0234
Siddiqi, Tariq
    N 1175
"Silly Love Songs" (song)
    N 0733
Silver Beatles
    C 0073
Silver Jubilee painting
    M 1320
Simon, Carly
    M 2725   M 3764
Sinatra, Frank
    M 2866   M 3078
Sinatra, Frank: Lennon's death
    M 3700
Sinclair, John
    M 3645
Singapore: Beatle record seized
    N 0514
Singers' favorite singer poll
    M 2728
"Six O'Clock" (song)
    M 2744
"Smile" (film)
    M 1941
Smith, George O'Hara
    M 2021
Smith, Norman (Beatles recording
    engineer)
    M 0904   M 1301   M 2311
Smothers Brothers: at Troubadour Club
    M 0502
Snyder, Tom: Lennon interview
    M 3213
Sociologist in interview on the Beatles
    M 3014
SOMETHING NEW (LP)

RR0442   M 3418
"Something" (song)
    M 3321
SOME TIME IN NEW YORK CITY (LP)
    M 1526   M 1533   M 2715   RR0443
    RR0444   RR0445   RR0446   RR0447
    RR0448   RR0449   RR0450
SOMEWHERE IN ENGLAND (LP)
    M 2132   RR0451   RR0452   RR0453
    RR0454   RR0455   RR0456   RR0457
    RR0458   RR0459
SOMEWHERE IN ENGLAND (LP - Bootleg)
    RR0460
Songbook   see   Beatles songbook
SONGS DER BEATLES: TEXTE UND
    INTERPRETATIONEN (book)
    RB0539
THE SONGS LENNON AND MCCARTNEY GAVE
    AWAY (LP)
    RR0461
"The Songwriters" (tv show)
    M 3280
Songwriting awards
    M 0493   M 0582   M 1904   M 1918
    M 3489   M 3755
"Son of Dracula" (film)
    M 2744   RF0335   RF0336   RF0337
    RF0338
Sotheby Parke Bernet (Beatles)
    C 0038   M 0106   M 0117   M 0146
    M 0338   M 1118   M 2164   M 2957
    M 3055
SOUL ON ICE (book)
    N 0295
South Africa: Lennon to pay protetors'
    fines
    N 0682
South Africa: radio ban on Beatles
    M 1096   M 2648   N 1017
South Africa: Starr visit
    N 0940
Spain: Barcelona concert
    N 1109
Spain: Beatles
    N 0150
Spain: fan club
    F 0121
Spain: Lennon and Ono detained on
    Majorca, Balearica Islands
    N 0061
A SPANIARD IN THE WORKS (book)
    M 3156   RB0540   RB0541   RB0542
    RB0543   RB0544   RB0545   RB0546
    RB0547   RB0548   RB0549   RB0550
    RB0551   RB0552   RB0553   RB0554
    RB0555   RB0556   RB0557   RB0558
    RB0559   RB0560   RB0561
A SPANIARD IN THE WORKS (book): excerpt
    M 1897
Spector, Phil
    C 0324   C 0337   M 2516   M 2521
    M 2619   M 3333   M 3334   M 3713
Spector, Ronnie
    M 2653
Spielberg, Steven
    N 0962
Spinetti, Victor: interview
    M 1206
Spirit Foundation
    N 1167
Springsteen, Bruce
    N 1022
Springsteen, Bruce: Lennon's death
    M 3700
"Stamp Out Beatles" (anti-Beatle
    movement in Detroit, Michigan)
    N 0243
Star Club, Hamburg, Germany
    B 0071   C 0223   M 1247   M 1426
    M 2604   M 3468
Star Club, Hamburg, Germany: closes
    M 0349
Star Club, Hamburg, Germany: photograph
    M 2459
"Star Club" (LP)   see   THE BEATLES LIVE
    AT THE STAR CLUB (LP)
"Star Club Tapes"   see   "Hamburg Tapes"
"Stardust" (film)
    M 2764

Starkey, Barbara   see   Bach, Barbara
Starkey, Elsie: interview
    C 0019
Starkey, Maureen   see   Cox, Maureen
Starkey, Richard   see   Starr, Ringo
Starkey, Zak
    M 2949
Starkey, Zak: interview
    M 1795
Starr, Ringo
    C 0031   C 0061   C 0266   C 0267
    C 0268   C 0269   C 0311   C 0328
    M 0020   M 0034   M 0152   M 0567
    M 0572   M 0710   M 0742   M 0760
    M 0777   M 0790   M 0839   M 0913
    M 0940   M 0990   M 1021   M 1079
    M 1129   M 1186   M 1376   M 1397
    M 1423   M 1528   M 1608   M 1610
    M 1674   M 1770   M 1979   M 2069
    M 2093   M 2182   M 2313   M 2315
    M 2349   M 2372   M 2442   M 2447
    M 2482   M 2529   M 2674   M 2697
    M 2772   M 2826   M 2840   M 2843
    M 2853   M 2891   M 2917   M 2919
    M 2953   M 2963   M 2965   M 3015
    M 3018   M 3021   M 3025   M 3027
    M 3028   M 3033   M 3034   M 3060
    M 3073   M 3101   M 3133   M 3197
    M 3198   M 3200   M 3228   M 3318
    M 3322   M 3433   M 3442   M 3505
    M 3554   M 3606   M 3607   M 3608
    M 3609   M 3627   M 3634   M 3676
    M 3726   M 3743   M 3759   N 1110
    P 0007   P 0103   P 0104
Starr, Ringo: acting career
    M 3081   N 0392
Starr, Ringo: appears at The Band's
    last concert
    M 2116
Starr, Ringo: as a child
    M 3787
Starr, Ringo: as actor
    M 1495
Starr, Ringo: as a designer
    N 0911
Starr, Ringo: as drummer
    M 2349
Starr, Ringo: at Mick Jagger's wedding
    M 2381
Starr, Ringo: attends Wings concert
    M 1151
Starr, Ringo: back together with
    Harrison and Lennon
    M 0085
Starr, Ringo: becomes ill on tour
    N 0795
Starr, Ringo: biography
    M 0547
Starr, Ringo: birthday party
    M 2823
Starr, Ringo: Bob Dylan recording
    M 2927
Starr, Ringo: Bob Marley concert
    M 2824
Starr, Ringo: book of his photography
    C 0270
Starr, Ringo: brief biography
    C 0058   C 0271   P 0113
Starr, Ringo: California visit
    M 1043
Starr, Ringo: career after Beatles
    B 0075   B 0076   M 0820   M 3262
    M 3379
Starr, Ringo: childhood photographs
    C 0111
Starr, Ringo: comments on musicians
    M 3061
Starr, Ringo: concert for Bangladesh
    M 1589   M 2382   M 2951   N 0690
    N 0742   N 0819
Starr, Ringo: concert for Bangladesh
    ticket sales
    N 1095
Starr, Ringo: David Bowie party
    M 2834
Starr, Ringo: designs "kinetic
    sculpture"
    N 0912
Starr, Ringo: directs T. Rex film

    M 2711
Starr, Ringo: disagrees with Lennon on
    shows for public
    N 1096
Starr, Ringo: discography
    M 0524   M 0525
Starr, Ringo: divorces Maureen Cox
    M 0941   N 0273   N 0936
Starr, Ringo: drawing for song
    C 0318
Starr, Ringo: driving school
    M 3082
Starr, Ringo: drums - photo survey
    M 1375
Starr, Ringo: early years
    C 0118
Starr, Ringo: Elizabeth Taylor's
    birthday party
    N 0016
Starr, Ringo: engaged to Nancy Andrews
    M 1019
Starr, Ringo: enjoined for Lennon's use
    of his residence
    N 0622
Starr, Ringo: Eric Clapton's wedding
    M 2894
Starr, Ringo: expecting third child
    M 2640
Starr, Ringo: fan club   see   Fan club
    (Starr)
Starr, Ringo: film activity
    M 2399
Starr, Ringo: film role
    M 2513   M 2514   M 2517   M 2595
    M 2598   M 2647   M 2658   M 2692
    M 2718   M 2764   M 2794   M 2812
    M 2905   M 3019   M 3020   M 3030
    M 3058   M 3081
Starr, Ringo: films   see also
    individual film titles
Starr, Ringo: films
    M 1045   M 1111   M 1440   M 1495
    M 2116   M 2399   M 2513   M 2514
    M 2517   M 2595   M 2598   M 2647
    M 2658   M 2669   M 2692   M 2711
    M 2718   M 2744   M 2764   M 2794
    M 2812   M 2905   M 3020   M 3030
    M 3058   M 3081   N 0027   N 0757
    N 0788   N 0944   N 1048   RF0028
    RF0029   RF0030   RF0031   RF0032
    RF0033   RF0034   RF0035   RF0036
    RF0037   RF0038   RF0039   RF0040
    RF0041   RF0051   RF0052   RF0053
    RF0054   RF0055   RF0056   RF0057
    RF0058   RF0059   RF0060   RF0061
    RF0062   RF0063   RF0064   RF0065
    RF0066   RF0067   RF0068   RF0069
    RF0070   RF0071   RF0072   RF0073
    RF0074   RF0163   RF0164   RF0165
    RF0166   RF0167   RF0168   RF0169
    RF0170   RF0171   RF0172   RF0173
    RF0174   RF0175   RF0176   RF0177
    RF0178   RF0179   RF0180   RF0181
    RF0182   RF0183   RF0184   RF0185
    RF0186   RF0187   RF0188   RF0189
    RF0190   RF0191   RF0192   RF0244
    RF0245   RF0246   RF0247   RF0248
    RF0249   RF0250   RF0327   RF0328
    RF0329   RF0330   RF0331   RF0332
    RF0333   RF0334   RF0335   RF0336
    RF0337   RF0338   RF0382   RF0383
    RF0384   RF0385   RF0386   RF0387
    RF0388   RF0389   RF0390   RF0391
    RF0392   RF0393
Starr, Ringo: furniture design company
    M 2721
Starr, Ringo: gifts from fans
    M 3349
Starr, Ringo: has tonsilectomy
    N 0939
Starr, Ringo: hospitalized
    M 2947   M 3083   N 0938
Starr, Ringo: hurt in car accident
    N 0516
Starr, Ringo: illness
    N 0115
Starr, Ringo: India
    N 0064
Starr, Ringo: interview

C 0019   M 0769   M 0846   M 1227
M 1229   M 1576   M 1648   M 1760
M 2035   M 2114   M 2201   M 3024
M 3029   M 3195   M 3409   M 3586
N 0596
Starr, Ringo: jam session
    M 2739
Starr, Ringo: Japanese clothing ads
    M 1579
Starr, Ringo: Keith Moon
    M 2835
Starr, Ringo: "Laugh In" (tv show)
    M 2617
Starr, Ringo: leaves hospital
    N 0793
Starr, Ringo, Lennon's birthday
    M 2849
Starr, Ringo: Lennon tribute
    M 0468
Starr, Ringo: London, England apartment
    looted
    N 1098
Starr, Ringo: London playboy club
    M 2784
Starr, Ringo: on Beatles reunion
    M 2741   M 2768   M 2781   M 3022
    N 0825
Starr, Ringo: on Billy Preston LP
    M 2706
Starr, Ringo: on Bobby Hatfield LP
    M 2698
Starr, Ringo, on David Cassidy LP
    M 3067
Starr, Ringo: on Harrison LP
    M 2746
Starr, Ringo: on Harry Nilsson LP
    M 2710   M 2778
Starr, Ringo: on his acting in "A Hard
    Day's Night" (film)
    M 1495
Starr, Ringo: on Peter Frampton LP
    M 2706
Starr, Ringo: photograph with Maureen
    Cox
    M 1467
Starr, Ringo: plays tennis in South
    Africa
    N 0940
Starr, Ringo: portrait
    M 1072   M 1658   M 2537   M 2543
    M 2545
Starr, Ringo: private life with fiance
    Andrews
    M 3022
Starr, Ringo: punitive U.K. taxes
    N 0613
Starr, Ringo: quotations
    B 0383   B 0384   B 0385   B 0386
Starr, Ringo: radio special
    M 2578
Starr, Ringo: recording BEAUCOUPS OF
    BLUES (LP)
    M 0510
Starr, Ringo: recording contract
    M 3017
Starr, Ringo: recording oldies LP
    M 2611
Starr, Ringo: recording session
    M 2737   M 3278
Starr, Ringo: record label
    M 1737   M 3031
Starr, Ringo: records and songs   see
    also   individual record and song
    titles
Starr, Ringo: records and songs
    M 0510   M 0524   M 0525   M 0968
    M 1164   M 1338   M 2611   M 2626
    M 2737   M 2744   M 2933   M 3026
    M 3278   M 3517   M 3759   RR0120
    RR0128   RR0129   RR0130   RR0131
    RR0181   RR0182   RR0228   RR0229
    RR0230   RR0231   RR0232   RR0233
    RR0234   RR0384   RR0385   RR0386
    RR0387   RR0388   RR0389   RR0390
    RR0391   RR0392   RR0421   RR0422
    RR0423   RR0462   RR0463   RR0464
    RR0465   RR0466   RR0550
Starr, Ringo: records in Nashville,
    Tennessee

M 3699
Starr, Ringo: records Lennon song
    M 2789
Starr, Ringo: records with B.B. King
    M 2027   M 2659
Starr, Ringo: records with Harrison and
    Dylan
    M 0583
Starr, Ringo: records with Harrison and
    Lennon
    M 3063
Starr, Ringo: records with McCartney
    M 2744
Starr, Ringo: records with McCartney in
    Montserrat, West Indies
    M 1720   M 2919   M 2920   M 2921
    N 1100
Starr, Ringo: returns from India
    N 0182
Starr, Ringo: Ring O' Records
    M 1377   M 3245
Starr, Ringo: rumor of involvement in
    African benefit concert
    N 0977
Starr, Ringo: seeks government grant to
    improve home
    N 1020
Starr, Ringo: shaves head
    M 2841
Starr, Ringo: songbook   see also
    Beatles songbook
Starr, Ringo: songbook
    S 0094   S 0126   S 0127   S 0149
Starr, Ringo: sued
    N 0485
Starr, Ringo: tv special
    M 3016   N 0254
Starr, Ringo: tv special "Ringo"
    M 0866   N 0937
Starr, Ringo: U.S. tour with Harrison
    N 0949
Starr, Ringo: warns against use of
    drugs
    N 0515
Starr, Ringo: wedding photograph
    N 0941
Starr, Ringo: weds Barbara Bach
    M 0144   M 2187   M 3023   M 3032
    N 0601   N 0935
Starr, Ringo: weds Maureen Cox
    M 0776   N 0169
Starr, Ringo: with Harry Nilsson
    M 2138
"Stars On 45" (45)
    M 1483
STARS ON LONG PLAY (LP)
    M 1483   M 2926   M 2943
"Starting Over/Kiss Kiss Kiss" (45)
    see   "(Just Like) Starting
    Over/Kiss Kiss Kiss" (45)
Statues (Beatles): Liverpool, England
    M 0452   M 1445   M 2009   M 2870
    M 3741   N 0336   N 0519   N 1067
Steele, Tommy
    M 3294   N 1023
Stewart, Rod
    M 2815
Stigwood, Robert
    M 0437   M 3360   N 0962
Stills, Steven
    M 2965
Sting
    M 3764
Stockholm, Sweden: Wings concert
    M 1234
STOP AND SMELL THE ROSES (LP)
    M 0968   M 2933   M 3517   RR0462
    RR0463   RR0464   RR0465   RR0466
Storm, Rory
    M 2727
Storm, Rory and the Hurricanes
    C 0118
Strawberry Fields Forever
    F 0079
STRAWBERRY FIELDS FOREVER: JOHN LENNON
    REMEMBERED (book)
    M 0845   RB0562   RB0563   RB0564
    RB0565   RB0566   RB0567
STRAWBERRY FIELDS FOREVER (LP)

RR0467   RR0468
"Strawberry Fields" [New York City's
    Central Park Lennon tribute
    section]
    N 0281   N 0418   N 0619   N 1032
    N 1172
"Street Messiah" (film)
    M 2874
String Quartet songbook (Beatles)
    S 0106
Student editors poll
    M 3368
Student Rock Essay Contest
    M 3352
Submarine: painted yellow by pranksters
    N 0867
SUITABLE FOR FRAMING (LP)
    RR0469   RR0470
Sullivan, Ed
    C 0074   M 2975   N 0441   N 0442
Summer, Donna: Lennon's death
    M 3700
Sutcliffe, Stuart
    B 0535   M 1456   N 0298   N 0899
Sutcliffe, Stuart: death
    C 0128
Sutcliffe, Stuart: painting
    C 0152
Suzy and the Red Stripes
    M 3002
Swan Records: legal battle with Capitol
    and Vee Jay
    M 0552
Sweden: Beatles
    M 0648   M 3395   N 0125   P 0036
Sweden: Beatles concert
    M 3395
Sweden: fan club
    F 0043   F 0053
Sweden: McCartney
    M 3396
Sweden: reaction to Lennon's death
    M 0526
Sweden: rock group visits schools
    N 0125
Sweden: Stockholm Wings concert
    M 1234
Sweden: Wings
    M 3396
SWEET APPLE TRAX (LP)
    M 0112   RR0471
SWEET APPLE TRAX VOL. 3 (LP)
    RR0472   RR0473
Syracuse, New York: Ono art show
    M 3590   N 0434
"Take It Away" (film)
    RF0339
"Take It Away" (film): filming
    M 1985
"Take It Away/I'll Give You a Ring"
    (45)
    RR0474
"Talking Pictures" (magazine): special
    issue - Beatles
    P 0111
Tanglewood (music educators conference)
    N 0684
Tax (Beatles)
    N 0905
Tax (Beatles): entertainment tax in
    Germany
    N 0413
Tax (Beatles): U.S. earnings
    N 0202   N 1115
Tax (Klein)
    N 1046
Tax (Klein): evasion charge
    N 0010   N 0077   N 0370
Tax (Klein): evasion on Beatle record
    sales
    N 0457
Tax (McCartney)
    N 0905
Tax (Starr): U.K. punitive tax
    M 3022   N 0613
Tax: U.S.
    N 0193
Taylor, Alistair: interview
    M 0150

Taylor, Alistair: remembers the Beatles
  M 0187
Taylor, Derek
  B 0542 B 0543 B 0544 B 0545
  B 0546 M 1908 M 2645 M 3415
  M 3416
Taylor, Derek: interview
  M 1775
Taylor, Elizabeth
  N 0016
Taylor, James
  M 1539 M 2783
Television appearances (Beatles)
  B 0241
Television broadcasts (Beatles):
    collecting
  M 1516
Television chronology (Beatles)
  M 1791
Television: closed circuit (Beatles)
  M 2550
Television: collecting telecasts
  M 1516
Television program [Lennon/McCartney
    music]
  M 3280
Television special (Beatles)
  M 1536 M 2751 M 2975 M 3005
  M 3123 M 3124
Television special: "Birth Of The
    Beatles" see "The Birth Of The
    Beatles" (film)
Television special: Christmas 1965
  M 0036
Television special: "Heroes of Rock 'N'
    Roll"
  M 1147
Television special (Lennon)
  M 2591
Television special (McCartney)
  M 0195 M 2647 M 2738 M 3736
Television special (Rutles)
  M 3123 M 3124 M 3268 M 3301
  M 3303
Television special (Starr)
  M 0866 M 1489 M 3016
Television special (Wings)
  M 3736
Television special (Wings, 1979)
  M 0195
"Ten for Two" (film)
  M 1720
Tennessee: McCartney records in
    Nashville
  M 2791
Tennessee: Memphis concert
  N 0342
Tennessee: Starr and Harrison in
    Nashville
  M 3699
Tenth anniversary
  P 0116
Tenth anniversary: Beatles recordings
  N 0352
Texas: Houston all-Beatle-music radio
    station
  N 0492
Texas: McCartney in Fort Worth
  N 0954
Texas: radio ban over Lennon remark
  M 3426
THANK U VERY MUCH (book)
  M 2955 RB0568 RB0569
Thant, U
  M 2699
"That'll Be The Day" (film)
  RF0340 RF0341 RF0342 RF0343
  RF0344 RF0345 RF0346 RF0347
  RF0348 RF0349 RF0350 RF0351
  RF0352
"That'll Be The Day" (song)
  M 1118 M 2061
THEIR SATANIC MAJESTIES REQUEST (LP)
  M 3729
THINGS WE SAID TODAY (book)
  RB0570 RB0571 RB0572 RB0573
  RB0574 RB0575 RB0576 RB0577
  RB0578 RB0579 RB0580 RB0581
  RB0582 RB0583 RB0584

THINGS WE SAID TODAY (book): excerpt
  M 0653
33 1/3 (LP)
  M 3270 M 3782 RR0475 RR0476
  RR0477 RR0478 RR0479 RR0480
  RR0481 RR0482
"This Girl Is Mine" (song): released in
    Israel
  M 1601
"This Song" (45)
  M 3270
"This Song" (video)
  M 3782
Thomas, Chris
  C 0322
A THOUSAND DAYS (book): excerpt
  M 0593
Thurmond, Strom: Lennon deportation
    case
  M 1136
"Time Bandits" (film)
  N 0422 RF0353 RF0354 RF0355
  RF0356 RF0357 RF0358 RF0359
  RF0360 RF0361 RF0362 RF0363
  RF0364 RF0365 RF0366 RF0367
  RF0368 RF0369 RF0370 RF0371
  RF0372 RF0373 RF0374 RF0375
  RF0376 RF0377 RF0378 RF0379
  RF0380 RF0381
Tim, Tiny
  M 3764
"To Know Him Is To Love Him/Besame
    Mucho" (45)
  RR0483
Tokyo, Japan: Beatles tour
  M 1586 M 3155 N 0095 N 0282
Tokyo, Japan: concert
  N 0282
Tokyo, Japan: concert film
  M 0241
Tokyo, Japan: concert ticket sales
  N 0282 N 1090
Tokyo, Japan: McCartney leaves
  M 2067
"Tommy" (film): premiere
  M 2816
"Tomorrow Show" (tv show) [Lennon]
  M 3213
"Tonight" (tv show) [Lennon and
    McCartney]
  C 0320
TONY SHERIDAN AND THE BEATLES (LP)
  RR0484
TOP OF THE POPS (EP)
  RR0485
Toronto, Canada: concert
  M 0473 M 0842 N 1061
Toronto, Canada: Labor Day concert
    ticket sales
  N 1061
Toronto, Canada: Lennon
  M 0901 M 1553 N 0274
Toronto Peace Festival
  M 0123 M 0202 M 0668 M 0670
  M 1679 M 1681 M 1688 M 1761
  M 1807 M 1894 M 1905 M 1929
  M 1930 M 2323 M 3465 M 3773
  M 3778 N 0274 N 0275
Toshiba Records
  M 1192
Tower Ballroom concert
  C 0034
THE TOY BOY (LP - Limited Edition)
  RR0486
"The Toy Boy" (poem)
  M 1900
Transcendental Meditation
  M 2148
T. Rex: film documentary
  M 2711
A TRIBUTE TO JOHN LENNON, 1940-1980
    (book)
  RB0585
"A Tribute to the Beatles" (television
    special)
  M 2975
Trinidad Arias, Olivia
  M 2808 M 3023 M 3782
Trinidad Arias, Olivia: birth of son

Dhani
  M 2877 M 2878 N 0616
Trinidad Arias, Olivia: weds George
    Harrison
  N 1011
Triumph Investment Trust
  N 1088
Trivia questions (Beatles)
  B 0044 B 0198 B 0218 B 0219
  B 0263 B 0264 B 0402 B 0470
  C 0282 C 0287 M 1453 M 1454
  M 2574 M 3476 M 3477 M 3478
Troubador Club, Los Angeles, California
  M 0502 M 0662 M 2767 M 3479
  N 0609 N 0610
Trudeau, Prime Minister (Canada): visit
    with Lennon and Ono
  N 0245
Trumpet songbook (Beatles)
  S 0073 S 0118 S 0119
Trumpet songbook (Lennon/McCartney)
  S 0118 S 0119
"Tug of War" (12-inch single)
  M 3566
TUG OF WAR (LP)
  M 0969 M 2195 M 2404 M 2429
  M 2940 M 3263 N 0856 RR0487
  RR0488 RR0489 RR0490 RR0491
  RR0492 RR0493 RR0494 RR0495
  RR0496 RR0497 RR0498
Twentieth anniversary
  P 0014 P 0040
20 GOLDEN HITS (LP)
  RR0499
20 GREATEST HITS (LP)
  M 1016 RR0500 RR0501
21 (LP)
  RR0342
26 DAYS THAT ROCKED THE WORLD! (book)
  RB0586
20 X 4 (LP)
  RR0502 RR0503
Twiggy
  M 3314
TWILIGHT OF THE GODS (book)
  RB0587 RB0588 RB0589 RB0590
  RB0591 RB0592 RB0593 RB0594
  RB0595 RB0596 RB0597 RB0598
  RB0599 RB0600 RB0601 RB0602
  RB0603 RB0604 RB0605 RB0606
  RB0607 RB0608 RB0609 RB0610
  RB0611 RB0612 RB0613 RB0614
  RB0615
A TWIST OF LENNON (book)
  RB0616 RB0617 RB0618 RB0619
  RB0620 RB0621
"Two Hundred Motels" (film)
  M 2647 RF0382 RF0383 RF0384
  RF0385 RF0386 RF0387 RF0388
  RF0389 RF0390 RF0391 RF0392
  RF0393
"Two Virgins" (film)
  M 1941 M 2095 M 2361 N 1050
  RF0394 RF0395
TWO VIRGINS (LP)
  M 0516 M 0921 M 1477 M 1538
  M 1691 M 1927 M 2240 M 3455
  N 0921 RR0504 RR0505 RR0506
TWO VIRGINS (LP): sales banned in New
    Jersey
  N 0540
TWO VIRGINS (LP): seized
  N 0008
Tyrannosaurus Rex: film documentary
  M 2711
U.C.L.A.: Lennon award for graduate
    research
  N 0845
Ulster, Ireland: "Give Ireland Back to
    the Irish" (song)
  N 0055
U.N. Beatles reunion concert
  M 0272
UNESCO benefit concert
  M 1390 M 1689 M 2409 M 2898
  M 2899 N 0732 N 0818 N 1002
UNFINISHED MUSIC NO. 1: TWO VIRGINS
    (LP)
  RR0504 RR0505 RR0506

UNFINISHED MUSIC NO. 2: LIFE WITH THE
    LIONS (LP)
    RR0507
Union of Soviet Socialist Republics
    see U.S.S.R.
United Artists
    M 2361
United Artists: box office hit with
    Beatle film
    M 0448
United Artists: profits from Beatles
    film
    M 1119
United Artists: signs Beatles for film
    N 0176
United Cerebral Palsy Association:
    Beatles benefit concert
    M 1772
United Kingdom see England; Scotland;
    Ireland
United Nations see U.N.
United Nations Educational Scientific
    and Cultural Organization see
    UNESCO
United States of America see U.S.A.
University of California at Los Angeles
    see U.C.L.A.
UP AGAINST IT - A SCREENPLAY FOR THE
    BEATLES (book)
    RB0622
"Up Against It" (film)
    M 3604
"Up Your Legs" (film)
    RF0396
U.S.A. see also names of Cities and
    States
U.S.A.: Beatles
    C 0035 C 0052 C 0103 C 0135
    M 0041 M 0042 M 0043 M 0044
    M 0191 M 0192 M 0486 N 0094
    N 0381 N 0801 N 1044 P 0034
U.S.A.: Beatles debut planned
    M 0464
U.S.A.: fan club
    F 0001 F 0002 F 0003 F 0004
    F 0005 F 0006 F 0008 F 0009
    F 0010 F 0011 F 0012 F 0013
    F 0015 F 0016 F 0018 F 0019
    F 0022 F 0023 F 0030 F 0035
    F 0036 F 0037 F 0038 F 0039
    F 0046 F 0047 F 0049 F 0052
    F 0054 F 0060 F 0061 F 0065
    F 0066 F 0067 F 0069 F 0070
    F 0073 F 0074 F 0075 F 0076
    F 0077 F 0079 F 0080 F 0081
    F 0082 F 0083 F 0084 F 0085
    F 0086 F 0087 F 0090 F 0091
    F 0092 F 0093 F 0094 F 0095
    F 0096 F 0097 F 0099 F 0100
    F 0103 F 0104 F 0105 F 0106
    F 0108 F 0109 F 0110 F 0111
    F 0112 F 0113 F 0114 F 0115
    F 0116 F 0117 F 0118 F 0122
    F 0124 F 0125 F 0126 F 0127
    F 0128 F 0129 F 0131 F 0132
    F 0133 F 0135 F 0137 F 0143
    F 0146 F 0148 F 0151 F 0152
    F 0153 F 0154 F 0155 F 0157
    F 0158
U.S.A.: McCartney tour
    M 1022 N 0952
U.S.A.: McCartney visit
    M 1047 N 0060
U.S.A.: 1964 arrival at Kennedy
    Airport, New York City
    N 0420
U.S.A.: 1964 tour
    M 0067 M 1082 M 1183 M 1574
    M 2298 M 3452 M 3660 M 3730
    N 0012 N 0381 N 1044 P 0054
U.S.A.: 1964 visit
    B 0257 B 0258 C 0310 M 2246
    M 3316 M 3346 M 3362 M 3513
    M 3760 N 0405 N 0407 N 0420
    N 0421 N 0801 N 1044
U.S.A.: 1965 tour
    M 1571 M 1629 M 3330 M 3376
    M 3781 N 0094 N 0973 N 0984
    P 0055

U.S.A.: 1966 tour
    M 1598 M 3512 P 0056
U.S.A.: 1968 Harrison visit
    M 1038
U.S.A.: 1974 Harrison tour
    M 0105 M 1023 M 1420 M 1421
    M 1422 M 2796 M 3075 N 0368
    N 0483 N 0612 N 0827 N 0949
U.S.A.: 1974 Harrison tour - ticket
    sales
    M 3076
U.S.A.: reception of Beatles
    C 0145 C 0213 M 3514
U.S.A.: tax
    M 0422
U.S.A.: tour
    N 0155 N 0791 N 0829
U.S.A.: Wings tour
    B 0234 B 0235 B 0413 M 0104
    M 0194 M 0601 M 0740 M 1022
    M 3274 M 3331 M 3509 M 1158
U.S.A.: Wings tour postponed
    N 0727
U.S.A.: Wings tour ticket sales
    N 1158
U.S. Congress (Beatle banner)
    N 0046
U.S.S.R.: article on Lennon's death and
    the Beatles
    N 0038
U.S.S.R.: BAND ON THE RUN (LP) released
    M 2057 M 2358 M 2842 N 1053
U.S.S.R.: Beatles invited to discuss
    visit
    N 0211
U.S.S.R.: Beatles popularity
    N 1066
U.S.S.R.: criticism of Beatles
    N 1018
U.S.S.R.: McCartney LP released
    M 2057 M 2358
U.S.S.R.: Moscow rally for Lennon
    N 0913
U.S.S.R.: picks up Beatles tracks from
    E.M.I.
    M 1834
U.S.S.R.: Wings visit
    M 2852
Utrecht, Holland: fan convention
    M 3515
Vancouver, Canada: concert
    N 0908
VANCOUVER 1964 (LP)
    RR0508
Van Scyoc, Gary
    M 0033
Varma, Mahesh Prasad see Maharishi
    Mahesh Yogi
Vee Jay Records
    M 0658 M 0659
Vee Jay Records: legal battle vs.
    Capitol Records
    M 0552
VEGEMITE (LP)
    RR0509
Venice, Italy: Beatles invited to
    festival
    N 0137
Venice, Italy: benefit concert
    M 2409 M 2848 N 0732 N 0818
    N 1002
VENUS AND MARS (LP)
    M 1218 M 2265 RR0510 RR0511
    RR0512 RR0513 RR0514 RR0515
Vereiniging Nederlandse Beatles Fanclub
    F 0044 F 0050 P 0056
Vermouth, Apollo C.
    M 0022
VERY TOGETHER (LP)
    M 2614
Vic Lewis Organ., Ltd.: NEMS
    Enterprises, Ltd. merger
    M 0605 N 0236
Video
    M 0488
Video Communications
    M 3447
Video: copyright by Northern Songs
    M 1990 M 1991 M 1992

Video (Lennon)
    M 1350 M 3213
Videos (Beatles)
    B 0241
Videotape copyright (Northern Songs)
    M 1990
Videotaped Beatles concert: first such
    closed circuit event
    M 0311
Vienna, Austria: Lennon press
    conference
    N 0736
Vietnam War
    N 0329
Vocal songbook see Piano/Vocal
    songbook
Voice patterns of the Beatles in color
    registers
    M 0310
Vollmer, Jurgen
    M 3560 N 0779
Vollmer, Jurgen: interview
    M 1780
Voorman, Klaus
    M 2745 M 2270
Wagg, Col.: returns M.B.E. award
    N 0118
WAITING FOR THE BEATLES: AN APPLE
    SCRUFF'S STORY (book)
    RB0623
"Walkabout" (film)
    M 0335
Walker Art Gallery, Liverpool, England
    B 0032
"Walking On Thin Ice" (film)
    M 2924 N 1170
"Walking On Thin Ice/It Happened" (45)
    RR0516
"Walking On Thin Ice" (song)
    N 0861
Waller, Gordon
    M 3548
Wallpaper (Beatles)
    N 0244
WALLS AND BRIDGES (LP)
    M 1250 M 2795 RR0517 RR0518
    RR0519 RR0520 RR0521 RR0522
Warburg, S.G.
    N 0219
"War Is Over" (Christmas ad)
    M 1689 N 1129
Warner Brothers: Harrison contract
    M 1419
Warner Brothers Records
    M 2850 M 3485 N 1132 N 1133
Warner Brothers - Seven Arts
    N 1007
Warwick Hotel, New York City: fans
    gather
    N 0394
Washington, D.C.: Beatles at U.K.
    Embassy party
    N 0201
Washington, D.C.: Beatles press
    conference, 1964
    M 3013
Washington, D.C.: Harrison
    M 3289 M 3782
Washington, D.C.: press conference
    M 3013
Washington: Seattle concert
    N 0719
"Waterfalls/Check My Machine" (45)
    RR0523
Webber, Andrew Lloyd
    N 0647 N 0663
WEDDING ALBUM (LP)
    M 3717 N 1069
"Welcome Back Beatles" (magazines)
    M 3635
Wellington, New Zealand: concert
    N 0120
THE WELL-TEMPERED LENNON-MCCARTNEY
    (book)
    RB0624
WE LOVE YOU BEATLES (book)
    RB0625 RB0626 RB0627
West Germany see Germany
West Indies: McCartney recording in

Montserrat with Starr
  M 1720   M 2919   M 2920   M 2921
  N 1100
West Midland Beatles Fan Club
  F 0014
Whales benefit
  M 3792
"What a Shame Mary Jane Had a Pain At
  the Party" (45)
  RR0524
"White Album" (LP) see also THE
  BEATLES (LP)
"White Album" (THE BEATLES (LP))
  M 0425   M 3642   N 0186   N 0588
"White Album" (THE BEATLES (LP)): heavy
  demand
  N 0363
Whitney Museum: Lennon films
  N 0448
WHO'S WHO (book)
  N 1148
WHO'S WHO IN AMERICA (book) [Beatles
  listed]
  N 0530   N 1077
Widnes, Lancashire, England
  C 0047
WILD LIFE (LP)
  M 0709   RR0525   RR0526   RR0527
  RR0528   RR0529   RR0530   RR0531
  RR0532
Williams, Allan
  B 0586   B 0587   B 0588   B 0589
  B 0590   B 0591
Williams, Allan: describes the cavern
  M 0687
Williams, Allan: interview
  M 0121   M 1199
Williams, Andy
  M 2747
Willowbrook benefit concert
  M 0977
Wilson, Prime Minister: reopens Cavern
  Club, Liverpool, England
  N 0641
Wimbledon, England: fans convention
  M 0897
Wings
  B 0156   B 0213   B 0214   B 0215
  B 0216   B 0227   B 0234   B 0235
  B 0271   B 0272   B 0284   B 0366
  B 0401   B 0440   B 0441   B 0442
  B 0456   B 0592   B 0593   C 0339
  M 0016   M 0095   M 0131   M 0132
  M 0504   M 0515   M 0551   M 0626
  M 0701   M 0712   M 0971   M 1022
  M 1085   M 1185   M 1215   M 1221
  M 1382   M 1383   M 1587   M 1671
  M 1963   M 1998   M 2269   M 2371
  M 2400   M 2403   M 2406   M 2491
  M 2498   M 2499   M 2679   M 2680
  M 2704   M 2733   M 2777   M 2825
  M 2852   M 2919   M 2996   M 3196
  M 3331   M 3412   M 3424   M 3555
  M 3626   M 3629   M 3703   M 3734
  M 3735   M 3736   M 3737   M 3748
  N 0727   N 0854   P 0090   P 0123
Wings: album released in U.S.S.R.
  M 2058
WINGS AT THE SPEED OF SOUND (LP)
  M 1525   N 0733   RR0533   RR0534
  RR0535   RR0536   RR0537   RR0538
Wings: Australian tour
  M 1125
Wings: banned on Japanese radio
  M 0141
Wings: concert
  M 0504   M 1151
Wings: Copenhagen, Denmark concert
  M 3408
Wings: European tour
  M 2716
Wings: family tree
  C 0339
Wings: fan club see Fan club (Wings)
Wings: formed
  M 2406   M 2680   N 0369   N 0721
Wings: Dutch tour
  M 3288
Wings: French tour

M 2072   N 1078   N 1122
Wings Fun Club
  F 0058
WINGS GREATEST (LP)
  RR0539   RR0540
Wings: Holland
  M 1351   M 1356   M 1367   M 1368
  M 1369   M 1370   M 1378   M 1379
  M 1381   M 1384   M 3288
Wings: Holland tour, 1976
  M 0114   M 0115   M 0116
Wings: Japan
  B 0595
Wings: Japan tour cancelled
  M 0987   N 0731
Wings: London, England concert
  M 0630
Wings: Los Angeles, California concerts
  M 0194   N 0720
Wings: Los Angeles concerts sell out
  unannounced
  N 0720
Wings: lyrics
  B 0594
Wings: Manchester, England
  M 3299
Wings: Munich, Germany concert
  M 0118
Wings: New York City concert
  M 1124
Wings: on tv
  N 0836
WINGS OVER AMERICA (LP)
  RR0541   RR0542   RR0543
WINGS OVER ATLANTA (LP)
  RR0544
WINGS OVER HOLLAND '72 (LP)
  RR0143
"Wings Over The World" (tv special)
  M 3736
Wings: Paris, France concert
  M 3405
Wings: Philadelphia, Pennsylvania
  concert
  M 2126
Wings: platinum LP
  M 2780
Wings: records in Africa
  M 2760   M 3064
Wings: "Rockshow" (film)
  M 1464
Wings: San Diego, California concert
  M 0194
Wings: Scotland rehearsal
  M 2821
Wings songbook see McCartney, Paul:
  songbook
Wings: Stockholm, Sweden concert
  M 1234
Wings: surprise U.K. concert
  M 2705
Wings: Swedish tour
  M 3396
Wings: television special, 1979
  M 0195
Wings: tour
  B 0234   B 0235   B 0413   B 0592
  M 0104   M 0601   M 0740   M 1022
  M 1155   M 1195   M 2056   M 2072
  M 3274   M 3288   M 3331   M 3412
  M 3509   M 3522   M 3738   N 0854
  N 0954
Wings: tour delayed
  M 2836
Wings: U.S.S.R. release of BAND ON THE
  RUN (LP)
  N 1053
Wings: U.S. tour
  M 1223   M 1671   M 2058   M 3079
Wings: U.S. tour postponed
  N 0727
Wings: U.S. tour ticket sales
  N 1158
Wings: Venice, Italy concert
  M 2409   M 2848   N 0732   N 0818
Wisconsin: "On Wisconsin" song
  M 0531
"With A Little Help From My Friends"
  (magazine)

M 2104
Wolverhampton, England: Beatles
  M 0899   N 0312
"Woman/Beautiful Boys" (45)
  RR0545
"Woman Is The Nigger of the World"
  (song)
  M 0991
"Wonderful Christmastime/Rudolph The
  Red-nosed Reggae" (45)
  M 3539   RR0546
WONDERFUL MUSIC (LP)
  RR0547
Wonder, Stevie
  M 1329   M 1330
Wonder, Stevie: Lennon's death
  M 3700
Wonder, Stevie: records with McCartney
  M 0691   M 0956
"Wonderwall" (film score)
  M 1242   N 0383
WONDERWALL (LP)
  M 2235
Wood, Ron
  M 2769
Wooler, Bob
  M 0505
Wooler, Bob: remembers the Cavern
  M 0164
WORKING CLASS HEROES (book)
  RB0628
WORKING CLASS HERO (LP)
  RR0548   RR0549
"Working Class Hero" (song)
  M 0837   M 1148   M 1901   M 1913
  M 2650
"Wrack My Brain/Drumming in My Madness" (45)
  RR0550
"The Write Thing" (magazine)
  M 2103
'Yellow Submarine' (art style)
  N 1008
"Yellow Submarine" (film)
  B 0394   B 0517   B 0583   B 0584
  B 0585   B 0599   C 0002   C 0165
  C 0166   M 0594   M 1167   M 1470
  M 1794   M 3242   M 3698   N 1047
  P 0074   P 0094   P 0114   RF0397
  RF0398   RF0399   RF0400   RF0401
  RF0402   RF0403   RF0404   RF0405
  RF0406   RF0407   RF0408   RF0409
  RF0410
"Yellow Submarine" (film): comic book
  P 0071
"Yellow Submarine" (film): premiere
  M 1513   M 3762
"Yellow Submarine" (film): preview
  M 2152
"Yellow Submarine" (radio special)
  M 2578
"Yellow Submarine" (16MM film)
  RF0411
Yellow submarine [used as symbol]
  N 0389
YESTERDAY AND TODAY (LP)
  M 0844   M 0884   M 0915
"Yesterday" (song): as most covered
  song of all time
  M 3765
YESTERDAY - THE BEATLES 1963-1965 (book)
  RB0629
YOKO ONO/PLASTIC ONO BAND (LP)
  RR0551   RR0552
YOU CAN'T DO THAT (book)
  M 2976   RB0630   RB0631   RB0632
  RB0633   RB0634   RB0635   RB0636
  RB0637   RB0638   RB0639
"You Can't Say I Never Told You" (song)
  M 2503
"You Never Give Me Your Money" (song)
  M 0498
YOUNGBLOOD (LP)
  RR0553
Zappa, Frank
  M 2647
Zapple
  M 0440   M 0469
"Zoo Gang" (tv show): theme
  M 2755